S0-CEX-604

1982

Medical and Health Annual

Encyclopædia Britannica, Inc.

CHICAGO • GENEVA • LONDON • MANILA • PARIS • ROME • SEOUL • SYDNEY • TOKYO • TORONTO

1982 Medical and Health Annual

Library of Congress Catalog Card Number: 77-649875
International Standard Book Number: 0-85229-386-0
International Standard Serial Number: 0363-0366

Printed in U.S.A.

Foreword

The Nobel Prize for Physiology or Medicine is awarded each year to one or two or three individuals; consequently, the public tends to equate one advance with one or two or three men or women. But this impression is wrong.

When Jean Dausset of the University of Paris learned he had won the 1980 Nobel Prize for research on the identification and action of histocompatibility antigens, he said, "My reaction is one of joy, but I feel that I am just a symbol." Indeed, Dausset (and Baruj Benacerraf and George Snell, with whom he shared the prize) are representatives (or symbols) of many who have worked toward the same or similar goals.

In this volume we present a symposium on the Nobel Prize for Physiology or Medicine. It is our hope to foster an appreciation of, among other things, how modern advances depend on the lifetime work of thousands of scientists working in many fields over many decades.

Julius H. Comroe, Jr., looks at how Nobel Prize-winning discoveries in medicine have come about. Though Dr. Comroe is not a Nobel laureate, he has received many awards for his research on cardiovascular-pulmonary disease. He has also done extensive "research on research."

We also asked three Nobel laureates—Frances H. C. Crick (1962), Baruch Blumberg (1976), and Rosalyn Yalow (1977)—if they had foreseen the fundamental importance of their research before they cried "Eureka"; if they ever wanted to give up on the work that eventually led to their discoveries; how science and medicine have changed as a result of their discoveries; and how their lives have changed since they became Nobel Prize winners. Their reflections elucidate the rigors of scientific investigation, as well as the uncertainties, the gambles, the serendipity, and the determination involved in the process of discovery.

The other feature articles in this volume offer the latest medical thinking on a variety of subjects:

"Parasitic Diseases of the Tropics" describes the infections—schistosomiasis, malaria, sleeping sickness, onchocerciasis, and others—that affect an estimated one billion people annually. The author, Donald Heyneman, emphasizes the need for vigorous international efforts to control these scourges.

In "Unlocking the Brain" neurologist Donna Bergen explores the range of tests—many of them new—that makes looking into the skull and diagnosing brain disorders possible.

The drawings of mentally disturbed patients can provide clues to how the individual deals with internal conflicts. In "Window on the Unconscious" art therapist Fred Rappaport analyzes the drawings of three patients to illustrate how "projective art" can be used for diagnostic and therapeutic purposes.

Some individuals go to great lengths to make themselves sick or to mimic illnesses in order to be admitted to hospitals or to be treated as patients. In "The Enigma of Factitious Illness" psychiatrist Don R. Lipsitt considers this bizarre behavior known as Münchausen's syndrome.

In the past year this editor visited the Roman Catholic shrine at Lourdes, France, and found that it is not a miracle mill, as so many have claimed. There are, however, real benefits for the sick and handicapped at Lourdes, and these are probably psychological.

In "Cigarettes Are Very Kool" family practitioner Alan Blum takes a sharp look at the tobacco industry's efforts to deny the health hazards of smoking. The author's professional concern is the health of young people; he considers "juvenile onset smoking" one of the most serious threats to children today. Unfortunately, talk of cancer, heart disease, and emphysema does not have much impact on healthy kids, especially on teenagers who are trying to be sexy, sophisticated, and independent. This group, in short, is an advertiser's dream. Dr. Blum believes it is therefore important to expose the devices the tobacco companies are using to exploit potential smokers.

In "A Patient Becomes a Doctor" Young Chang, a third-year medical student who developed severe kidney disease as a child and later had a kidney transplant, describes "what coping is all about." He reflects on the hardships he faced and touches on his triumphs. He also explains why he chose to pursue a career in medicine.

Other regular sections of the *Medical and Health Annual* are *The World of Medicine,* alphabetical entries reviewing important advances that are being made in every branch of medicine—all written by experts for laymen; *Special Reports* on sudden death in athletes, the placebo effect, vegetarianism, and a number of other topical subjects; and 16 *Health Education Units,* providing up-to-date, practical information on such diverse topics as fatigue, genetic counseling, ingredients in cosmetics, and teething.

Finally, a *First Aid Handbook,* prepared in conjunction with the American College of Emergency Physicians, provides easy-to-follow, illustrated instructions for handling most emergencies.

Ellen Bernstein

—Editor

Contents

Features

The World of Medicine

A review of recent developments in health and medicine

Health Education Units

Instructive and practical articles about common health concerns

First Aid Handbook

Index

Parasitic Diseases of the Tropics

by Donald Heyneman, Ph.D.

The Tropical Zone encompasses a huge area, 47 degrees of latitude wide, covering the Earth for more than 2,600 kilometers (1,600 miles) on either side of the Equator. Within these latitudes lie many of those nations designated the third world—much of South America, Africa, Southeast Asia, the Philippines, Malaysia, Indonesia, nearly all of Central America and the Caribbean, and substantial portions of India, the Middle East, and southern China—33% of the world's population.

Tropical medicine has as its object the treatment of the diseases endemic to this vast area. In addition to those caused by bacteria and viruses are the diseases of parasitism, carried by the region's inescapable flies, mosquitoes, lice, ticks, and mites, and caused by the infection of man by protozoans, schistosomes, tapeworms, hookworms, and filariae. These are the perennial plagues of the Tropical Zone, part of the everyday life of the common man, and very stubborn of eradication. Through centuries of evolution the life cycles of these parasites have become interwoven with the habits of wild, then domesticated, animals and with those of man.

The Tropical Medicine Center at Johns Hopkins University in Baltimore, Maryland, estimates that more than one billion people are victims of tropical disease *each year*. Further, it is very common for an individual to have lifelong infection with more than one parasite. In some cases, the disease induced progresses slowly over a period of years until tissue damage becomes massive enough to cause the breakdown of an organ system. In others an acute phase—lethal to some individuals—is followed by a chronic phase in which the host comes to tolerate the presence of the parasite or to control its damage to tissue through the actions of the body's immune system. In many cases, however, disease is the result of this very reaction to the parasite's presence, as in schistosomiasis, the extreme manifestations of filariasis known as elephantiasis, or blindness from another filarial worm, *Onchocera.*

The difficulties in treating parasite-borne disease are many. The disease-causing organisms usually have complicated life cycles requiring two and frequently three hosts, an intermediate host such as a snail or insect in which the parasite passes the early stages of its life, in many cases a second intermediate or transfer host, and a final host in which the parasite matures and reproduces itself. In onchocerciasis, for example, when a blackfly bites

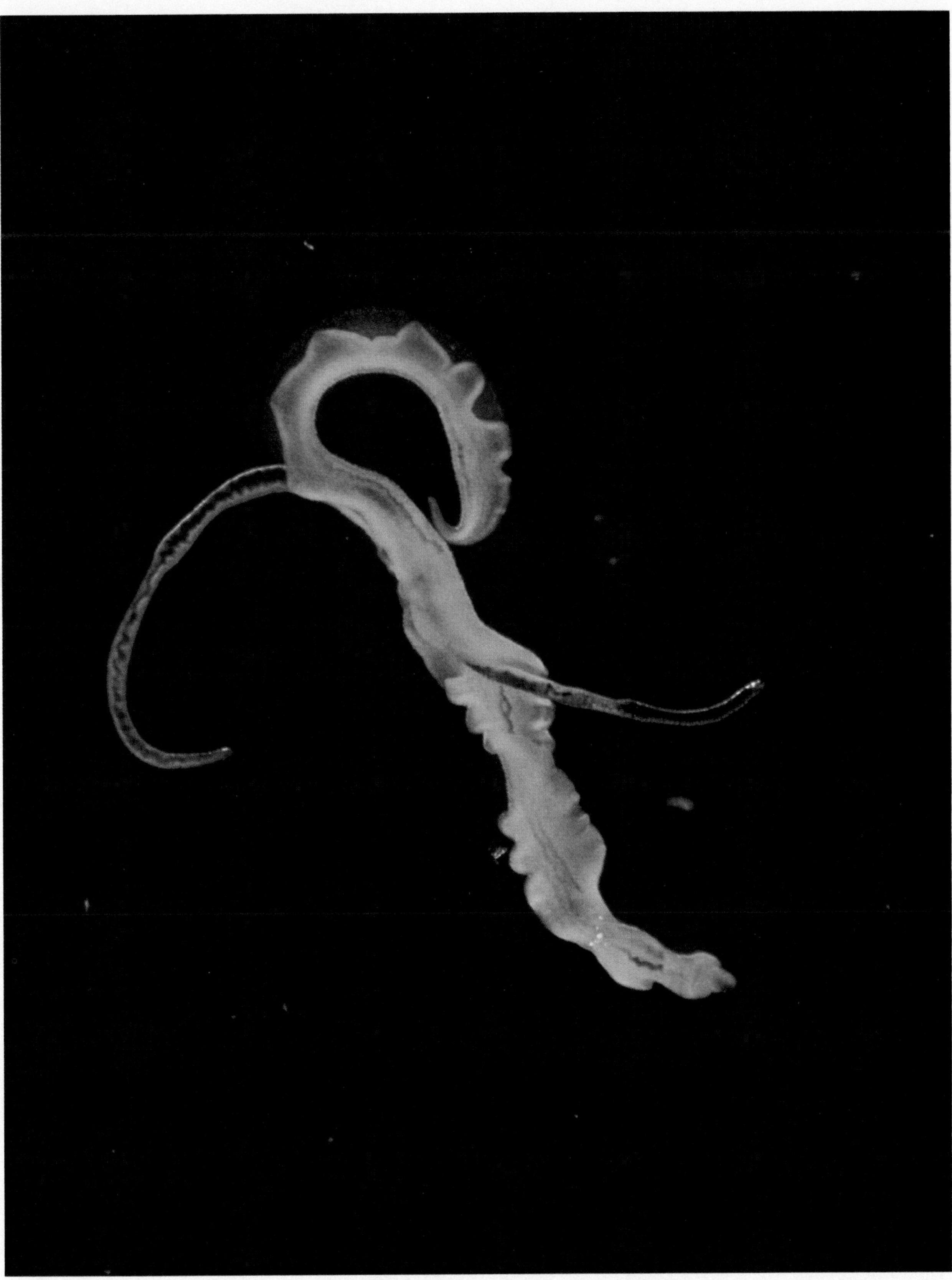

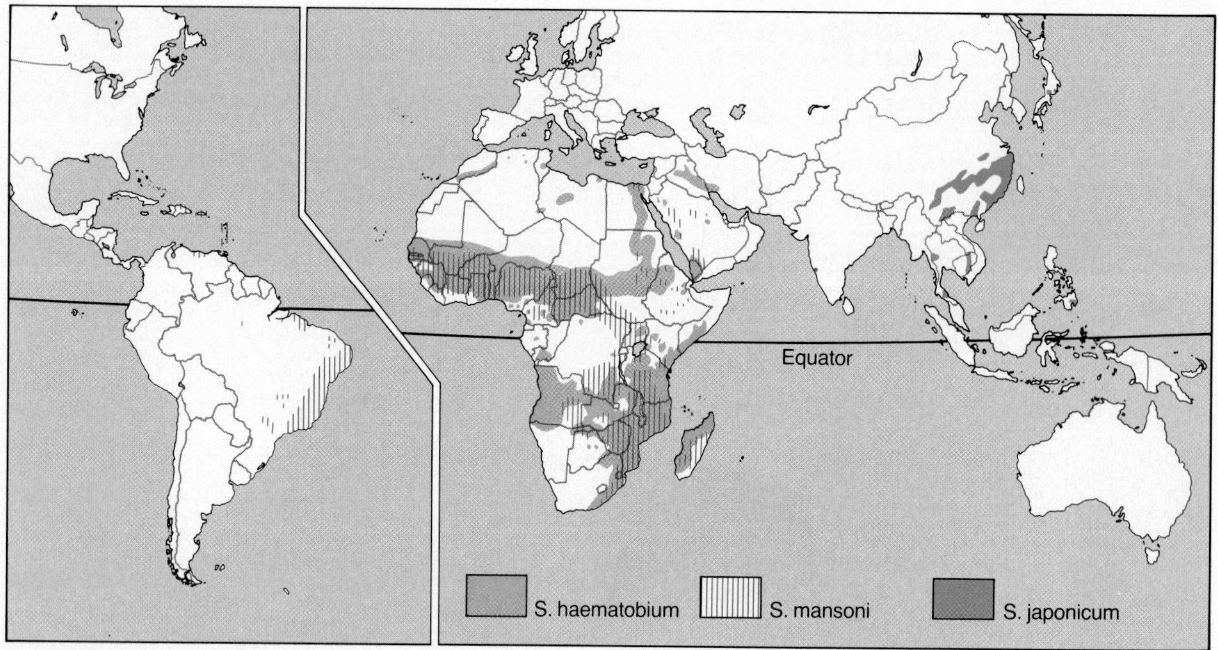

The areas of the Tropics in which the three major types of schistosomiasis are endemic. It is estimated that more than 200 million people in these areas are infected with the disease.

a previously infected human who has literally millions of microscopic filariae in his circulation, the fly sups up the tiny parasites with the drop of blood. The larvae migrate within the body of the fly and develop into an infective phase. When the fly bites another human a few weeks later, these larvae pass from its mouth onto the skin and from there into the blood of the human. A year or so later the adult worms coil up beneath the host's skin to mature in subcutaneous nodules, mate, and produce millions more microfilariae to repeat the cycle.

Breaking this chain at any of its links will stop the disease: kill the microfilariae in the human host, kill or keep off the blackfly vector, kill the adult worms so they cannot reproduce. Each of these tasks presents its own problems. Effective, safe drugs for the treatment of some diseases simply do not exist, or have severe side effects, or require prolonged or costly treatment regimens. In many areas of the world it is impossible to avoid dangerous insect pests, and the wholesale killing of vectors with insecticides damages the environment, even where it may be feasible; in some areas it is not.

Vaccines against tropical disease are not yet available, and for some conditions will never be. Nonetheless, for the large-scale control of parasitic disease they offer the best hope of both curing present cases and also of eliminating the human reservoir of infection. Much current research in tropical medicine is involved with isolating the antigens produced by parasites in the body's tissues so that a vaccine can be developed—a painstaking, elaborate task with success by no means assured.

A survey in the mid-1970s found that 70% of U.S. medical schools devote less than 16 hours to teaching tropical medicine. Because of the climate and good sanitation in the United States, and because the necessary vectors are not present, most doctors see few if any cases of tropical disease. However,

Donald Heyneman, Ph.D., *is Professor of Parasitology in the Department of Epidemiology and International Health at the University of California at San Francisco.*

(Overleaf) Adult male and female worms of Schistosoma mansoni; *the flattened male worm, about one centimeter (0.39 inch) in length, surrounds the more threadlike female. Photomicrograph, Centers for Disease Control, Atlanta, Ga.*

when U.S. soldiers fought in the South Pacific and Southeast Asia in World War II, the Korean War, and the Vietnam war, interest in the cause, treatment, and prevention of these diseases was greatly spurred. International travel and migration have brought the problem home to many large urban centers. London, for example, sees many cases of disease in African and Indian migrants. Thousands of Southeast Asian refugees entered the U.S. in the late 1970s and early 1980s. Many of them possess a legacy of suffering, malnutrition, and exposure to endemic parasites during their years of susceptibility. Danger to their new neighbors and environs is slight, but their need for understanding, treatment, and care is acute.

The great waste of human resources and the toll in human misery through the effects of chronic, debilitating, disfiguring disease are reasons enough for Western medical research to address itself to controlling tropical disease. Moreover, the long-term political benefits of providing this help to less developed nations should not be underestimated. In this instance self-interest and humanitarianism can work together toward a common goal.

Schistosomiasis: a paradigm of tropical disease today

Schistosomiasis is a striking example of the complexity of the parasitic diseases affecting mankind. It has special poignancy and impact among the hundreds of millions of inhabitants of the third world—among these undernourished, impoverished, underemployed, detribalized, translocated, unhappy millions. Refugees—from war, pestilence, hunger, competition, social disruption—are always especially susceptible to infection, but even in a vulnerable people disease does not automatically follow. Illness, as is so well illustrated by schistosomiasis, is a composite effect of parasite on host and host on parasite.

Of all of the tropical and subtropical diseases afflicting mankind, none has a more pervasive, insidious effect on his well-being or potential than does schistosomiasis. In Africa, no sooner is a dam erected, an irrigation canal dug, or an impoundment prepared than this disease appears, to nullify much of the anticipated gain.

Schistosomiasis can be so mild in an individual as to go unnoticed, or it can result in death. Between these two extremes fall the majority of its victims, who suffer painful and debilitating loss of function of the liver, bladder, kidneys, or intestines. In an ill-nourished population with little access to medical care, the burden of the disease may cancel out the overall benefits of any agricultural advance a new water project brings. Controlling the disease and preventing its spread require massive efforts in health education, medicine, sanitation, and agriculture. It is a daunting prospect—more than 200 million people in 70 countries are presently affected, and the disease is spreading.

The same obstacles plague development projects in South America, the Middle East, the Philippines, and Southeast Asia, where the disease closely follows the creation of water projects. Refugees fleeing from drought-stricken areas then carry the worms into other areas—as occurred on a large scale in Brazil following droughts in 1970 and land takeovers in the northeast sector.

T. A. Reyman, Mount Carmel Mercy Hospital, Detroit

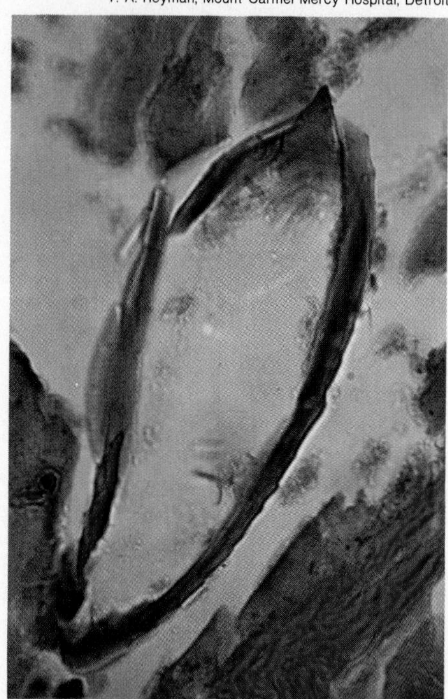

Schistosomiasis has been present in Egypt for at least 4,000 years. The photomicrograph above clearly shows the characteristic egg of Schistosoma *with its pointed spine. It was found in the mummified remains of an Egyptian weaver who died about 3,200 years ago.*

Schistosomiasis, also known as bilharzia or snail fever, is caused by a trematode worm, or fluke, that lives in human blood vessels. For part of the fluke's life cycle, it parasitizes several species of freshwater snails, hence the name snail fever. These blood flukes are all of the genus *Schistosoma* (Greek for split body, as individuals are either male or female, a unique situation among trematode flukes that parasitize humans). Disconcerting though their presence in the blood vessels may be, the half-inch-long worms in the intestinal or bladder veins are not the major cause of concern. It is the innumerable eggs laid by the female worms that do the damage, causing the tissues to respond in a way that results in pathology—inflammation, scar tissue, and loss of organ function.

A disease of antiquity

Many of the early discoveries about the schistosome worms and their cycle of infection in humans were made by European workers in Egypt, where these parasites have been known for at least 40 centuries. The famed Ebers papyrus of about 1550 BC, discovered near Luxor about 1870, mentions diseases regarded as having existed since antiquity—since the 1st dynasty (about 3100 BC). Included are 20 prescriptions for the cure of hematuria (bloody urine), a characteristic symptom of the bladder form of schistosomiasis. The ancient Egyptians believed that blood in the urine produced the worms, rather than the reverse, but the relationship between the two seemed to be clearly recognized. In 1910 Marc Armand Ruffer, a paleopathologist, one who studies the diseases of ancient man, found calcified eggs of *Schistosoma haematobium* in the kidney tubules of two mummies from the 20th dynasty (1200–1085 BC). Shells of the host snail *Bulinus* have also been found in the mud-brick material used in the construction of 4,000- to 6,000-year-old buildings in the ancient city of Babylon. It is assumed that these snails were present in Babylonian irrigation ditches. These findings are strong indicators that human association with schistosomiasis is as old as civilization itself.

The name bilharzia is for Theodor Bilharz, an enterprising German physician who went to Cairo in 1850 to assist the personal physician of the khedive of Egypt and went on to a distinguished medical career there. In a series of letters sent to Germany, he described for the first time three parasites of man, including the blood fluke *Schistosoma,* noted as being of two types based on their distinctive eggs, which he found in both human tissues and human excreta. This new genus was named to honor its discoverer, but the laws of taxonomic priority subsequently set the name *Bilharzia* aside and assigned a name that had been described earlier for the genus: *Schistosoma.*

Both forms of human blood flukes are still abundant in Egypt: *Schistosoma haematobium,* the bladder blood fluke, and *S. mansoni,* the large-intestine blood fluke (named for Sir Patrick Manson, considered by many to be the father of tropical medicine). The investigations that resulted in final clarification of the life cycles of the African schistosomes, including their transmission to humans, were concluded by Robert Thomson Leiper, a British zoologist who became the ultimate authority among helminthologists.

From *Recherches sur la faune parasitaire de l'Egypte*, by Dr. Arthur Looss, 1896

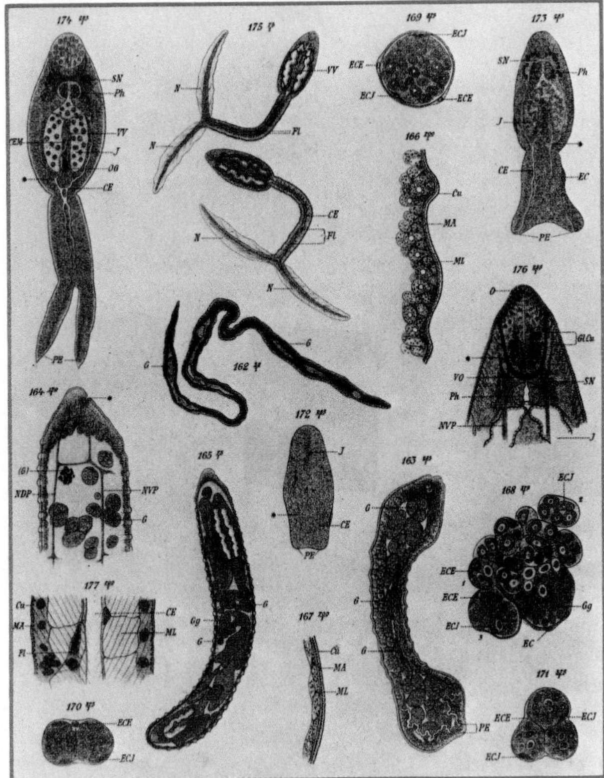

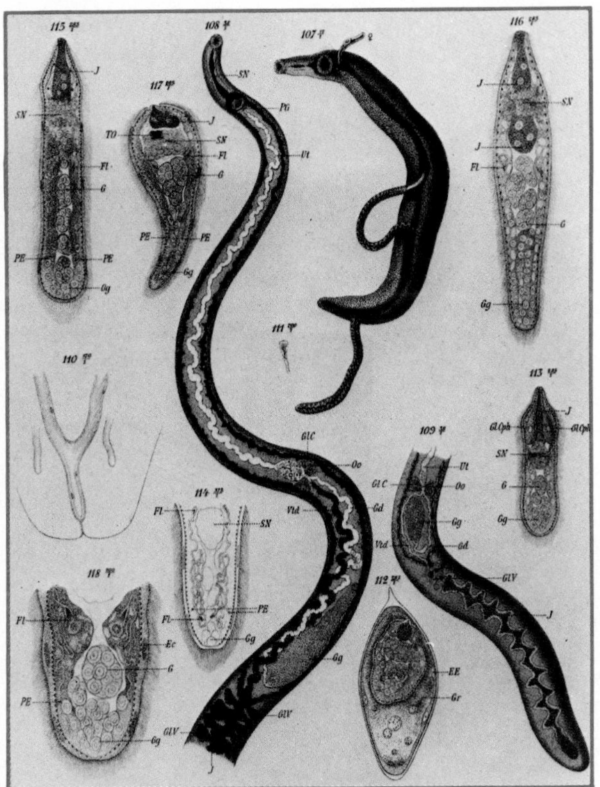

Arthur Looss, a German helminthologist working in Cairo in the 19th century, described the schistosomes in great detail and made superb drawings. The paired male and female worms are shown at the upper right; the cercaria with its forked tail is at the extreme upper left.

It is little wonder that the discovery of the mode of bilharzial transmission was marked by controversy and disbelief. Who could imagine that simply stepping into fresh water might result in one's bloodstream becoming infected with a tropical worm? And that the source of the infective bodies could be near-microscopic thrashing worms that streamed daily out of the body of a snail? But as the details gradually were revealed, the remarkable story of this two-host cycle was repeatedly demonstrated. It was simply too bizarre and elaborate to be accidental. In fact, nearly all of these related worms, the trematode flukes, were shown to have a snail (or other mollusk) as their primary or initial host, from which they pass, usually via a transport intermediate host such as a fish or crayfish, or by pond vegetation, to the final host, a human or other mammal. The remarkable natural history of *Schistosoma* is explained in the photographs and text on pages 12 and 13.

The effects of schistosomiasis

What then is schistosomiasis, the disease? It is not an effect of the presence in the body of the worms, which appear to do little harm. Nor is it the eggs that pass through the body via feces or urine. It is the eggs that are captured within the human tissues that initiate the chain of events leading to varying degrees of debility and, in a small fraction of cases, to death. It is the human body itself, with its remarkable defense systems to combat invaders and protect its internal integrity, that responds so vigorously to these foreign objects, the schistosome eggs.

The natural history of schistosomes is a remarkable instance of biological adaptation and survival. The worms require two hosts, a mammal and a snail, in which they complete their life cycle. (Below left) This scanning electron micrograph shows adult Schistosoma mansoni *worms in great detail as they exist inside the human body. The larger male and the tiny female remain joined for most of their lives. When the worms are fully mature the female leaves the male and migrates to a tiny capillary in the bladder or intestines, a different location for each species. Within these tiny blood vessels the female begins to lay eggs at the rate of hundreds or even thousands per day. (Below center) The eggs are caught and held in place against the capillary wall by a characteristic spine. The embryonic miracidium inside the egg secretes digestive substances that soften the capillary wall and enable the egg to pass into the bowel or bladder. The eggs are then excreted from the body with the urine or feces. (Below right) If the eggs pass from the human host into a freshwater pond or stream, the miracidium hatches from the egg to seek a snail host.*

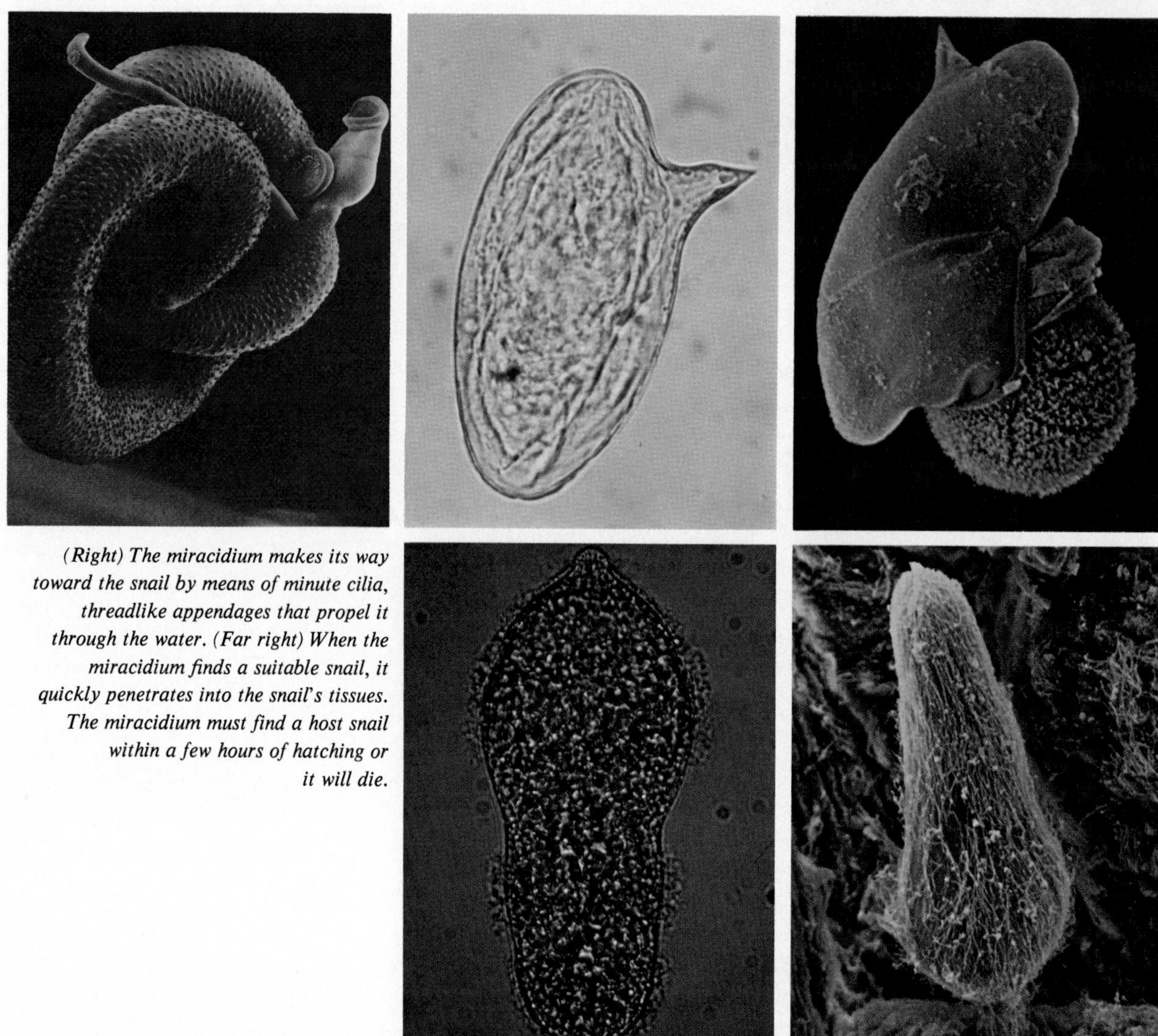

(Right) The miracidium makes its way toward the snail by means of minute cilia, threadlike appendages that propel it through the water. (Far right) When the miracidium finds a suitable snail, it quickly penetrates into the snail's tissues. The miracidium must find a host snail within a few hours of hatching or it will die.

(Top left) M. M. Wong; (top right) John Ford; (others) Harvey Blankespoor, Hope College, Holland, Mich.

(Center) From "A Pictorial Presentation of Parasites"; photograph, Herman Zaiman; (center right) from "A Pictorial Presentation of Parasites"; photograph, P. F. Basch; (others) Harvey Blankespoor, Hope College, Holland, Mich.

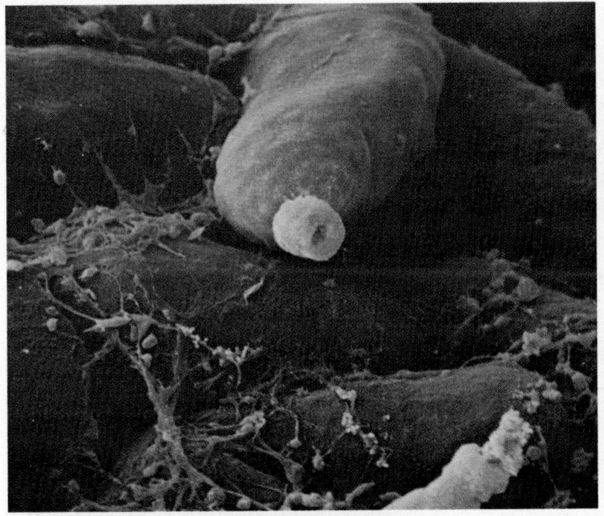

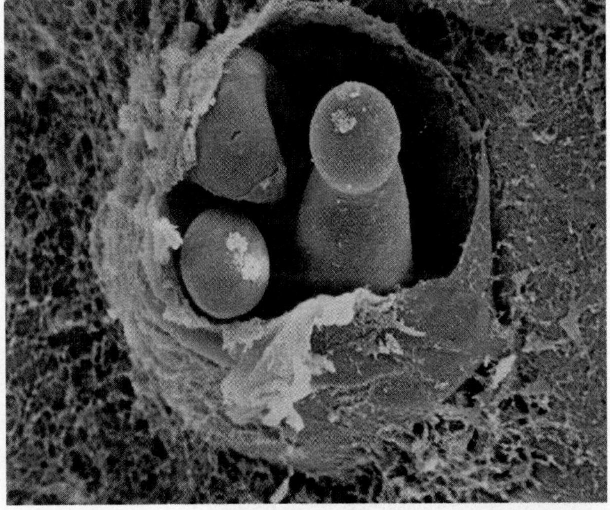

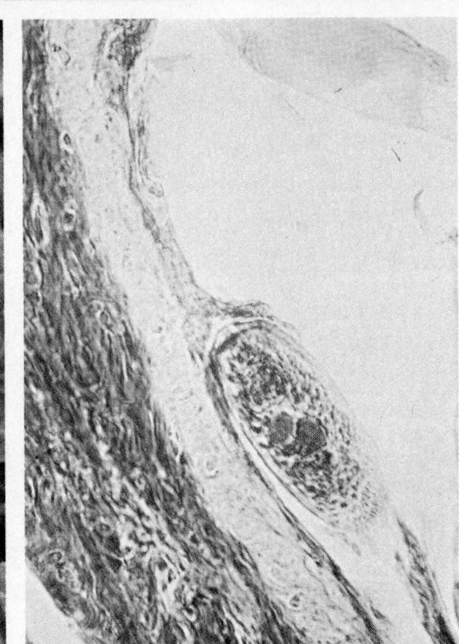

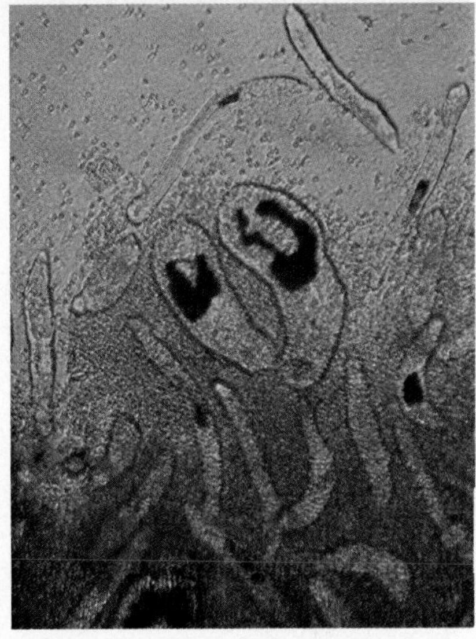

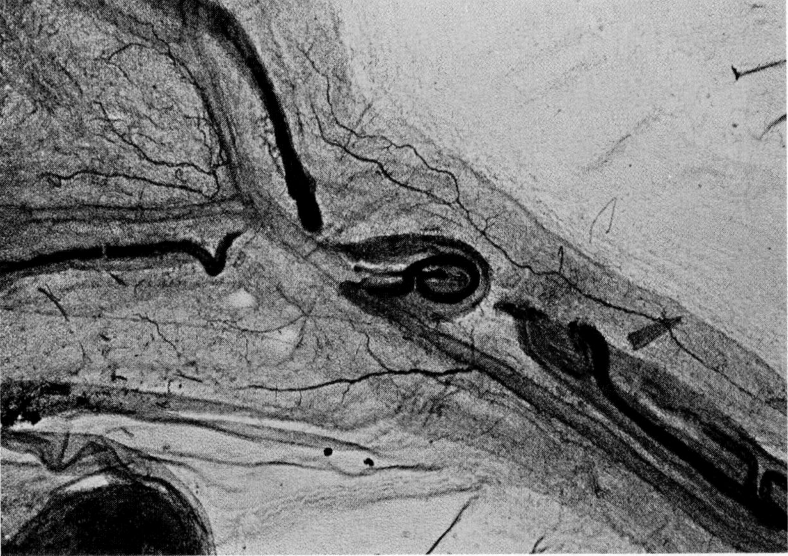

Within the snail's body the miracidium then grows into a sporocyst (top left), which in turn produces daughter sporocysts (top right). The final embryonic form is the cercaria. The cercariae leave the snail host and pass into the water to seek a human host. When the thrashing, fork-tailed cercaria finds a human host, it quickly penetrates into the skin (center left). As it penetrates the tail is lost (center). At this stage the larva is called a schistosomulum (center right). The schistosomulum matures into the adult worm in the human host's blood vessels. The worms can clearly be seen (left) in the mesenteric veins that serve the small intestines.

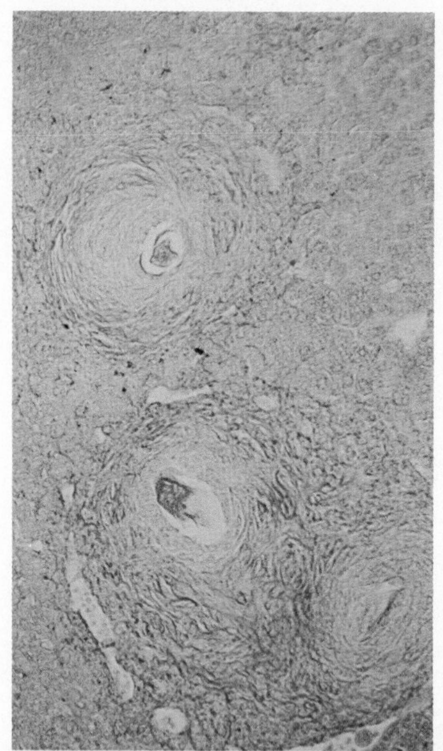

The early stage of the disease is usually mild, marked by some fever, skin eruptions, cough, malaise, and an increased white blood cell (eosinophil) count. As the parasites begin to produce eggs, the host may experience abdominal pain, blood in the urine or stool, or diarrhea, but the symptoms are usually not severe. As the egg production continues, however, a complex series of tissue responses is set in motion that causes the eggs to become centers of inflammatory reactions. The tissues become sensitized and inflamed, and the eggs are trapped and become surrounded by fibrous tissue. Eventually the fibrous masses replace functional tissues and impede the organ's normal activities. The gut wall thickens, loses its muscular tone, and peristalsis suffers; polyps, sources of irritation and hemorrhage, replace functional mucosa in the intestine. The bladder wall thickens when *S. haematobium* is present; elasticity of the wall is diminished; polyps form; and calcium is eventually deposited around the eggs. The ureter may become obstructed at its junction with the bladder. Even a few eggs here can cause fluids to back up toward the kidney, causing hydroureter, a distressing and potentially permanent condition. This pressure may back all the way up into the kidneys, causing an even more severe condition, hydronephrosis. After 20 years of egg deposition—at the rate of 300 per day (for *S. mansoni* or *S. haematobium*) or up to 3,000 per day (for *S. japonicum*) for *each* female worm present—the damage to the host can be severe.

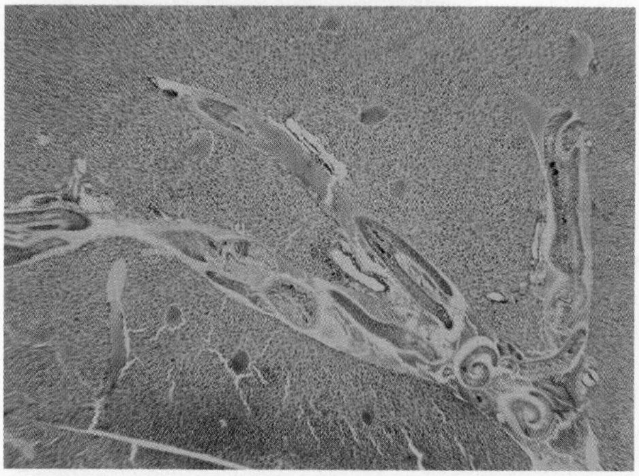

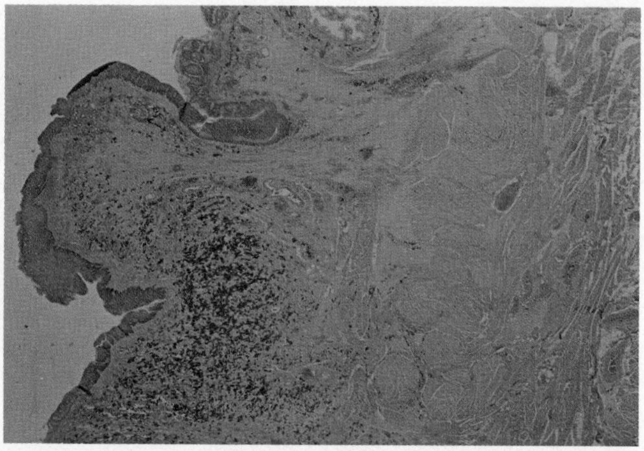

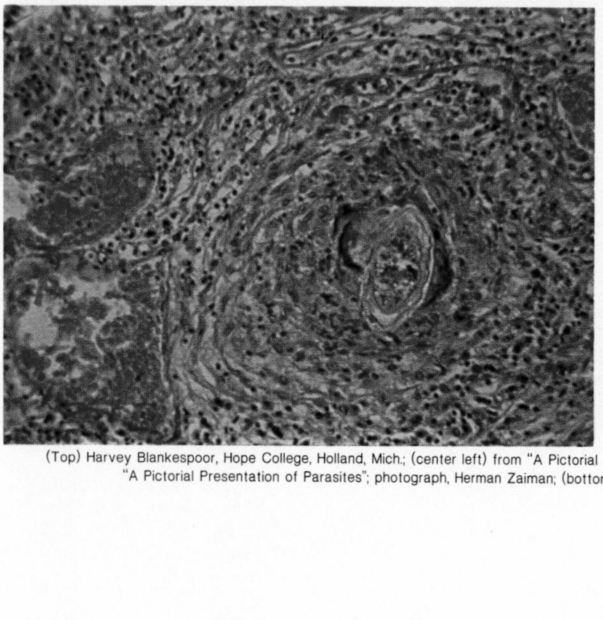

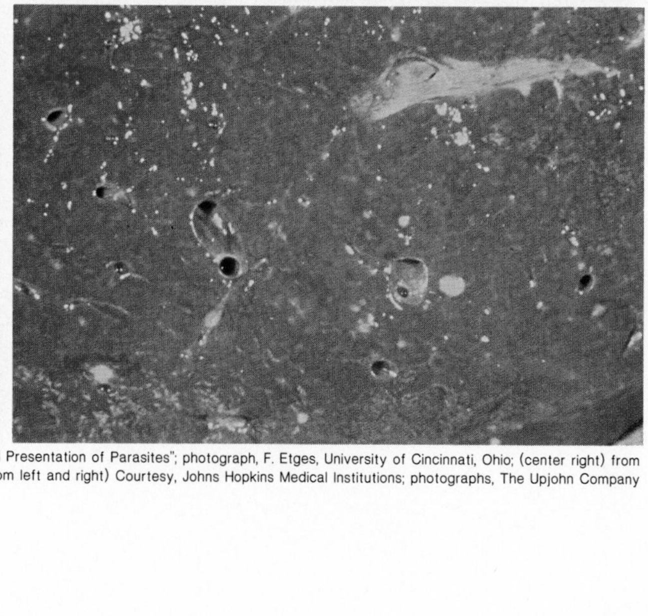

(Top) Harvey Blankespoor, Hope College, Holland, Mich.; (center left) from "A Pictorial Presentation of Parasites"; photograph, F. Etges, University of Cincinnati, Ohio; (center right) from "A Pictorial Presentation of Parasites"; photograph, Herman Zaiman; (bottom left and right) Courtesy, Johns Hopkins Medical Institutions; photographs, The Upjohn Company

As the infection continues over the years, tissues around the blood vessels bearing the worms become so hypersensitized and inflamed that many eggs are prevented from entering them at all, that is, from leaving the circulatory system. Blood flow will then tend to break these eggs loose and carry them back down the mesenteric vessels to the liver, where they lodge in the capillary bed there, the hepatic portals. More inflammation, granuloma, and fibrosis around these eggs follow. A cumulative damage to liver tissues occurs as fibroses collect around the portal walls, greatly thickening the vessels and reducing their normal function as prime centers of food exchange from the intestine to the liver cells and of transport of the many products of the liver's vital metabolic activities back into the body's circulation. This may be a process of years, but it is accompanied by many changes for the worse: increased blood pressure within the liver, distention of the liver and spleen, weakened or distended blood vessels causing varices that may burst and cause hemorrhage, and the collection of fluids within the body cavity (ascites).

The eggs trapped within the body soon begin to do damage. (Opposite page, top) Fibrous granulation tissue forms around the eggs in the liver. (Center left) The worms themselves can be seen in the hepatic veins (of a mouse infected for research in the laboratory). (Center right) The eggs have caused a polyp to form on the surface bladder tissue. (Bottom left) Eggs can also be carried to other parts of the body; here an egg has been caught in lung tissue, where it has caused granulation. (Bottom right) This cross section of human liver shows tubercules caused by the presence of schistosome eggs.

Blood flow may carry the eggs to the lungs, where they become trapped in the arterioles, especially with *S. mansoni.* Fibrosis may result; blood flow may be restricted; and a serious heart disease secondary to the pulmonary blockage, cor pulmonale, often follows. Egg patches have often been reported in the skin (even *adult* worms have escaped in this way) and in the kidneys, spleen, lung, or even the brain.

The damage varies with the host's condition, which is affected by age, nutrition, concomitant infection, and many other factors. Children tend to react less to the eggs, so their tissue damage is less and the eggs are more likely to be excreted than retained. That is why children are the key to control of the parasite. They are the chief egg-passers, and they tend to contaminate suitable waters more readily because they frequently swim and play there, wash, fetch water, and are more commonly exposed to infection. There is also some evidence that adults are relatively resistant to infection. Although an infection may be long-lived, frequent reinfection does not appear to occur readily.

In just a few years' time the damage done to the body is manifest; this boy shows the effects of severe ascites, the collection of fluids within the body cavity.

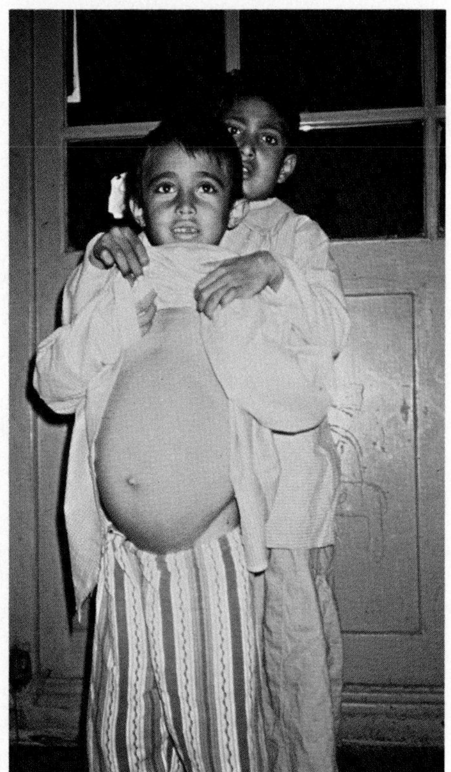

Joseph A. Cook, The Edna McConnell Clark Foundation

Among the 200 million persons now harboring schistosomes throughout the tropical world, severe manifestations of disease are relatively rare. Death from infection is even more so. Most infected persons have reached some sort of a stable host-parasite balance by which the eggs are not adding greatly to the tissue damage. Some of the eggs (perhaps 50%) probably are able to pass out of the body with the excreta. The presence in the body of these parasites simply is another element in the "normal" environment of millions of infected persons. Tests of schoolchildren's learning ability or of the work records and endurance of adults rarely show clear-cut evidence of the worms' negative impact. In part, this is a reflection of the difficulty in finding noninfected persons who have never harbored the worms and of the difficulty in setting up meaningful tests. Yet it is doubtless true that most infected people do adapt and do sustain their lives remarkably well, just as millions do under the handicap of hookworm and malaria and intestinal worms, and many of the same persons also carry on with a schistosome load as well.

The Scope of Tropical Disease

Malaria

Malaria is endemic to 104 countries of Africa, Central and South America, Asia, and Oceania—in areas with over one-fourth of the world's population. The disease is caused by protozoans of the genus *Plasmodium* which are transmitted to man through the bite of an infected female mosquito of the genus *Anopheles* that feeds on humans and is a suitable host for the parasite. Malaria causes recurring fever, mass destruction of red blood cells, enlargement of the spleen, and tissue damage within the liver, bone marrow, kidneys, adrenal glands, and other organs. Despite massive international eradication campaigns, the disease has not been controlled, and is even returning in some areas, such as in India. More than 200 million people have malaria and one million to two million, chiefly infants, die annually of falciparum malaria, the most serious of the forms of this disease, which remains the prime killer of any infectious agent known. In malaria, as in filariasis, the emergence of pesticide-resistant strains of mosquitoes has compounded the difficulties in containing the disease. Even more serious is the drug-resistance the parasites are exhibiting to chloroquine and amodiaquine, two drugs commonly used against the disease. Multiply resistant strains have emerged in Southeast Asia, and new foci of resistance have developed in East Africa, the most ominous threat of all.

French physician and parasitologist Alphonse Laveran received the Nobel Prize for Physiology or Medicine in 1907 for his discovery of the parasite that causes human malaria.

Bibliothèque de l'Ancienne Faculté de Médecine, Paris; photograph, Jean-Loup Charmet, Paris

Sleeping sickness

Sleeping sickness, or African trypanosomiasis, is caused by a protozoan of the genus *Trypanosoma* that is transmitted to man or other mammals by the bite of various species of the tsetse fly, *Glossina*. The disease is present in broad areas of West, Central, and East Africa, with a threatened population of 50 million people. In addition, three million cattle die from the disease each year, a heavy blow in a marginal economy. Some areas are so infested with the flies that they are virtually uninhabitable. The disease in man has a West African or chronic and an East African or acute form, the latter able to kill in weeks or months, the former in one or two years. Both diseases involve inflammation of the lymph nodes, anemia, kidney and liver damage, generalized wasting, encephalitis (inflammation of the brain), and coma—the final or "sleeping" aspect of the disease.

Chagas' disease

Chagas' disease, or American trypanosomiasis, caused by the protozoan *Trypanosoma cruzi*, is common in Central and South America. It is carried by nocturnally feeding cone-nosed or triatomid bugs that live in the cracks of adobe and thatch houses and feed on the occupants—humans and their dogs, cats, rats, and guinea pigs. About 12 million people are affected, and the acute phase of the disease has a 10% mortality. The acute phase, marked by fever, local lymph gland swelling and facial edema, involvement of various organs, and occasional prostration and death, is followed in survivors by a chronic phase that usually lasts the remainder of the victim's shortened lifetime. Many parasites migrate to the heart muscle fibers, where they cause irreversible damage, which eventually may lead to congestive heart failure. Dilation of tubular organs such as the intestine is also common. Improved housing materials can dramatically reduce the incidence of the disease, but a satisfactory drug therapy has not been found.

Brown Brothers

The great bacteriologist Robert Koch (seated center) carried out field research in Africa to seek the cause of sleeping sickness. In this photograph, taken in East Africa in 1906, Koch and his aides are examining blood samples from Africans who have contracted the disease.

Leishmaniasis

Leishmaniasis takes several forms. In Asia, Africa, and the Mediterranean, the protozoan *Leishmania donovani*, carried by certain species of the sandfly *Phlebotomus*, causes kala-azar, which attacks the viscera, especially the spleen and liver. The bone marrow and lymph nodes are also affected. Before the discovery of drug treatments, mortality was thought to be as high as 95%. *Leishmania tropica* causes Oriental sore, ulcerated areas of the skin which can usually be successfully treated. In disease caused by *Leishmania brasiliensis*, however, the mucous membranes are also involved, and often there is extensive destruction of the soft tissues and cartilage of the nose and mouth, resulting in hideous deformities. Most forms of leishmaniasis respond well to drug treatment given in injections over a ten-day period, though several such courses of treatment may be required. But there is no effective, nontoxic oral drug currently available for wide-scale administration.

Onchocerciasis

Onchocerciasis, also known as river blindness, affects 40 million people in Africa and Central and South America. In some parts of Africa 40% of the male population, who work near the rivers and are exposed to blackfly bites, have been blinded by the condition. In Central America a third of the population in some areas may be affected. Infective larvae of the parasitic filaria *Onchocerca volvulus* are transmitted to humans through the bite of blackflies, found in great numbers along fast-flowing streams. The offspring of the filariae, called microfilariae, provoke severe reactions when they migrate to the eye fluids and tissues, ultimately resulting in blindness. Severe skin and lymph node reactions also occur, especially in Africa. The drug that effectively kills the microfilariae can cause severe side effects, including unbearable itching and severe sensitization reactions. Kidney damage as a result of the use of another drug that kills the adult worms limits the use of this therapy.

Filariasis

Filarial parasites affect some 300 million people. In addition to the worm causing river blindness there are two species, carried by mosquitoes, that cause the lymph obstructions which stimulate the host reactions that result in the massive fibrous swellings of elephantiasis. The disease is widely distributed throughout the Tropics, as dozens of species of mosquitoes carry the filariae. Loiasis, endemic in Africa, is caused by the filarial worm *Loa loa*, carried by deer or mango flies of the genus *Chrysops*. More effective, safer drugs are needed to replace the diethylcarbamazine in use since 1947; the repeated doses necessary for cure make full treatment difficult, and allergic and other side effects can be serious. As with other diseases of parasitism, it is difficult to induce patients, who may be in a stage of disease with only mild symptoms, to put up with the hardship of returning for repeated treatments with drugs that cause distress. But until the human reservoir of infection is eliminated, these diseases will remain a major barrier to human fulfillment.

This Liberian man (below) has been blinded by onchocerciasis. (Top right) Researchers are hoping that a diethylcarbamazine lotion that can be applied to the skin will prove effective against the microfilariae that cause onchocerciasis. (Center right) In a Guatemalan clinic, adult Onchocerca volvulus *worms are removed from a skin nodule. Medications given for this condition often cause severe sensitization reactions (bottom right).*

Eric Poggenpohl

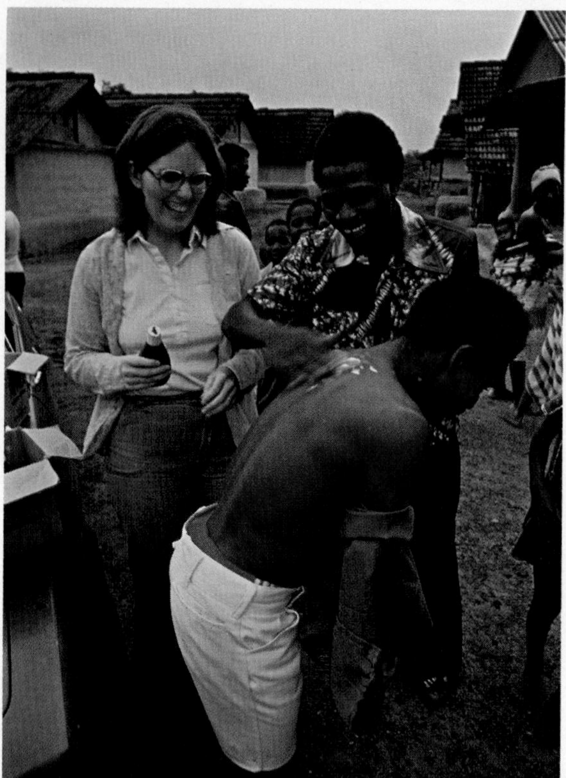

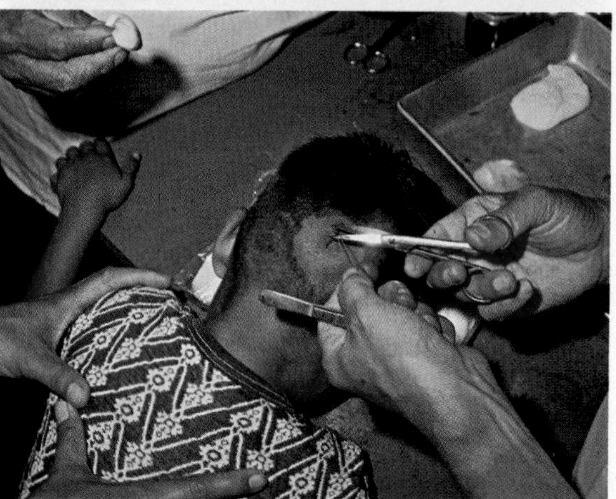

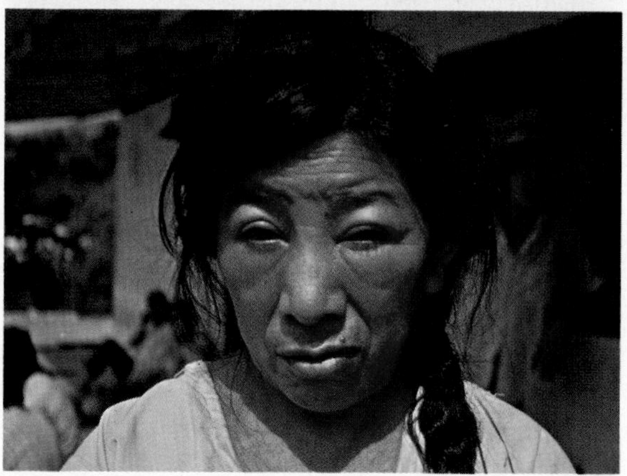

(Top) Eric Poggenpohl; (center and bottom) Everett L. Schiller, Johns Hopkins Medical Institutions

The price of progress

Difficult as is the measurement of the total social and economic cost of schistosomiasis, it is known to be excessive and always directed at those least able to bear up to it—the very young or very old, the poor, the malnourished, the refugees, the rural millions whose exposure is continual and unavoidable. It is especially discouraging to note that the many efforts to upgrade agriculture, extend irrigation canals, bring desert areas into cultivation, and harness the land for more efficient use have provided an improved lot for some but have brought disease to millions more.

Controlling schistosomiasis is a formidable task, far more difficult than fighting a bacterial disease with antibiotics or mass immunizations. Control efforts must consider not only the mass medicine aspects of the infestation but the ecological, agricultural, and social aspects as well. Stopping the spread of the disease can be accomplished by interrupting the human–snail–host cycle. Until recently, drug therapies have been difficult to administer on a large scale. The snails that act as hosts are tiny and easily hidden, and poisons placed in the waters they inhabit have killed beneficial aquatic life. Furthermore, changing the water-use habits of scattered or ill-educated populations presents a nearly insurmountable obstacle. Still, a way to stop the disease must be found. Schistosomiasis is the fastest spreading of all the diseases of parasitic worms affecting mankind today.

Because of the association of irrigation with snails throughout Africa, the snails' remarkable survival, repopulation, and reproductive powers, and the generally inadequate means of human sewage disposal, schistosomiasis has spread to all parts of the continent and to many areas of the Middle East, as well as to areas of South America and the Caribbean. In Yemen, Muslims cleansing themselves before prayer in that desert country must do so in the few available ablution pools, used also by children for play, by others for drinking and washing, and by snails. The result: an infection rate probably in excess of 80%. In Upper Egypt the people flooded off their land by the Aswan High Dam were resettled some 48 kilometers (30 miles) north of the dam in the Kawm Umbu (Kom Ombo) valley. Wherever new villages were located alongside irrigation ditches, the infection rate quickly rose in a year from 5–10% to 60–80%. Villages with piped water located a mile or so from the infected irrigation ditches showed schistosomiasis levels far lower, with infection rates of approximately 20–30%.

Africa. In Ghana, some 80,000 to 90,000 fishermen and tradespeople were resettled along the shores of Lake Volta, a vast manmade lake created in the mid-1960s by damming the Volta River. Infection levels with *S. haematobium* now run over 50% in most lakeside areas. In the Sudan, the economic heart of the country is its agricultural center, the rich Gezira, a cotton-growing region between the two great branches of the Nile, the White Nile from the south and the Rift Valley lakes, the Blue Nile from the highlands of Ethiopia. Former savannah, the Gezira region is now irrigated from two large dams and a carefully managed and extensive system of well-maintained irrigation canals. With the water have come the snails. Settlers in new villages are infected in a matter of months. The Gezira remains a region of economic wealth and of human poverty and disease. Control programs have

(Top) Ralph Muller, Commonwealth Institute of Helminthology; (bottom) Henry van der Schalie

(Top) This Tanzanian child washing in a stream may already be infected with schistosomiasis and may be one of the vehicles through which the disease is perpetuated. (Above) The tiny reddish-brown snails (slightly below center) in the mud at the edge of a rice field in Liberia serve as the intermediate host for schistosomiasis. Because the snails are small it is difficult to find and destroy them. Poisons placed in the water harm useful forms of wildlife and may have unforeseen repercussions in the future.

(Top) Jacques Jangoux—Peter Arnold Inc.; (bottom) Donald Smetzer

The huge water projects created in Africa to advance agriculture have also spread schistosomiasis through vast regions; (top) Akosombo Dam in Ghana on Lake Volta, (bottom) irrigated fields near the Aswan High Dam in Egypt.

demonstrated that it would be possible to poison snails, to treat thousands of the settlers, and to control the disease. But the costly control projects require foreign capital, supplies, and personnel, in addition to continuous dedicated work and surveillance. The localized results are encouraging—but the problem is so immense that the efforts of a few carefully organized projects appear lost in the vastness of the untreated regions. No matter how effective these projects, when the workers leave, the snails return, children play in the water and pass schistosome eggs, the snails become reinfected, and so again do the region's people.

The World Health Organization and allied funding agencies set up an excellent team in Ghana near the Akosombo Dam on Lake Volta to develop means of snail control along the lakeshore and to treat all infected individuals in some 50 communities alongside and near the lake. A 50-kilometer section was studied by a team of biologists, epidemiologists, physicians, and sociologists. Because of their efforts the infection rate dropped from over

50% to under 5% in some areas. In other portions of the test zone, the problems of snail control made the task more difficult, and the reduction was less dramatic though real. After seven years the project was passed to the Ghanian government to continue as a model for West Africa. But in a land of 100% annual inflation, with all of the problems besetting less developed nations, carrying on such a program is a severe strain. At the project's completion, after perhaps ten years and $5,000,000 from the onset, less than 1% of the lake's shoreline will have been controlled. And new lakes are being created all through West Africa, even others in Ghana. Giant dams are under way or planned in Nigeria, Senegal, Upper Volta, and Chad. The tremendous Jonglei drainage project in the southern Sudan to build hundreds of miles of canals will introduce vast and unpredictable social and biological changes as well. Few, if any, of these projects will have high-priority plans to control the snails that will be vastly extended in numbers and range by these projects. So long as the priority to build ditches and dams exceeds the priority to protect the people who will work the new lands, there will be a continued spread of schistosomiasis in Africa.

The Philippines. The size of the problem is most clearly seen in Africa, but it exists elsewhere in different forms. In the Philippines the disease has

(Top) Tor Eigeland—Black Star; (bottom) Yoram Lehmann—Peter Arnold, Inc.

(Above) Fieldworkers in Ghana examine snails collected as part of a World Health Organization schistosomiasis control program. Work done here may aid the millions of people in other infested areas, such as Ghana (top), the newly settled jungle areas of Brazil (top left), and the rice-growing areas of the Philippines (bottom left).

(Top) Toby Molenaar—Woodfin Camp & Associates; (bottom) Ted Spiegel—Black Star spread with the new rice lands of Leyte, Luzon, Mindanao, and other islands. There it is immensely difficult to control. The snail host is amphibious, so it can crawl up on grass stalks and escape poisons (molluscicides) placed in the water. The Oriental blood fluke *S. japonicum* causes an especially severe infection, as the female lays a larger number of eggs than those produced by the other schistosome species. Further, the disease there is a *zoonosis*, a disease of animals that can spread to humans. Hence, control of the infection in humans is not enough; there are water buffalo, horses, goats, cats, dogs, and rodents to worry about, too. And the treatment is complex, requiring a series of shots of a highly toxic drug, tartar emetic (antimony potassium tartrate). However, two new drugs—still being tested—offer the first hope for a mass-treatment, effective, one-dose drug. The drugs are praziquantel and amoscanate, effective against all strains of the schistosomes. But testing must be continued for several more years, not only to study efficacy and dosage but to ensure safety from toxicity and from possible serious side effects.

China. In China a great campaign against schistosomiasis in the Chang Jiang (Yangtze River) Valley was initiated by Chairman Mao early in the regime of the new revolutionary government. Millions were involved in this enormous undertaking, perhaps the largest single public health effort ever mounted. Hundreds of miles of new irrigation canals were dug and old ones covered and replaced. Snails were compressed under dirt, poisoned, collected by hand, exterminated insofar as humanly possible—just as were the other biological enemies of the state: flies, rodents, and sparrows. The program was considered a success. The Chang Jiang was freed of a curse that once was thought to afflict 90,000,000 Chinese. Yet, vast as this program was, it was not as vast as the problem. Infections are still found in the mountains of Sichuan (Szechwan) Province, through which the Chang Jiang flows. The disease is controlled but far from eradicated and may, in fact, be returning to some areas.

Puerto Rico. In the far more circumscribed and controlled island environment of Puerto Rico, mansonian schistosomiasis appears close to final elimination after three decades of work by U.S. Public Health Service and Puerto Rican teams of snail biologists, epidemiologists, and physicians. Yet, even here, small pockets of infection remain, and the near-solution is probably as much attributable to improved standards of sanitation, diet, and general health as to any specific control efforts. Age-old habits of collecting water, eating, washing, and body waste disposal are among the most resistant to change of any human customs. They are so ingrained and such a part of daily life that their modification is strongly resisted. But changes resulting from improved diet, housing, and material goods swiftly bring improved sanitation and reduced contamination of waterways and a large-scale reduction in water contact and waterborne disease transmission.

South America. In South America, only one species, *S. mansoni,* is found, because the particular kinds of snails present can serve as intermediate host of the mansonian form but are unsuitable for *S. haematobium* and *S. japonicum.* Nonetheless, the region is huge and the potential for spread of the disease is great. In Brazil and Venezuela much of the Amazon and

Orinoco regions are considered safe because the rivers are too acidic to allow snails to survive, owing to the high tannin level of many of the forest trees along the waterways. But the rain-forest destruction now under way in large areas has changed these conditions, and some of these streams may soon become suitable for snails. If the snails can survive, schistosomiasis will not be far behind. In addition, new evidence suggests that some snails are changing, losing their natural resistance, and becoming more susceptible to infection by schistosomes. This has occurred in the Paranaíba Valley of southern Brazil—a frightening prospect.

In past years most schistosomiasis infections in Brazil were found among the coastal sugarcane workers and inland marginal farmers and ranchers in the impoverished and malnourished northeast. Major droughts (in 1958 and 1970) and other economic pressures have so worsened social and economic conditions that great numbers of people have left these areas and moved south into newly opened former jungle regions and along the new Transamazônica highway. The migrants brought their schistosomes with them, of course, establishing new foci of infection in the state of Minas Gerais, the cities of Rio de Janeiro and São Paulo, the state of Paraná on the Argentine-Paraguay border, and, more recently, inland to the capital city of Brasília. Anywhere from 8 million to 15 million potential schistosome carriers are involved. In this complex of rapid change, disaffection, migration, and need for cheap migratory work forces, there will be increased pressures on health and new foci of schistosome transmission established. Snail control is probably impossible. Mass therapy is a favored approach, with the new single-dose oral drugs now available. But the ultimate approach is social betterment, improved sanitary facilities, and the availability of piped water. All are sadly lacking, even in the newly constructed villages.

Toward a solution

Schistosomiasis is one of many diseases of the less developed world. But it serves as a striking example of the complexity that encompasses most of them, especially in terms of prevention and control. Perhaps the most important lesson is that man is bound to his environment inescapably. Though he may feel able to fine-tune it to his personal needs and wishes, the interactions are too many, too varied, and too unpredictable to ignore in order to focus on one particular goal, irrespective of the interacting whole. We are one part of the environment, as are our parasites. And we, with them, share a host-parasite interaction in which we are as much a contributor to the cycle as a recipient of its effects.

A solution to the problem of parasite-spread disease, in all of its complexities, requires the best efforts of modern science, which for too long has failed to attack tropical diseases with sufficient vigor. The international partnerships of local government, schools of tropical medicine, and international bodies such as the World Health Organization, the United Nations Development Program, and the World Bank represent a source of hope for that one-third of the world's population laboring under the burden of chronic parasitic disease.

FOR ADDITIONAL READING:

Harwood, R. F., and James, M. T. *Entomology in Human and Animal Health.* 7th ed. New York: Macmillan Publishing Co., 1979.

Heyneman, Donald. "Parasitic Diseases in Relation to Environment, Customs, and Geography." In *Symposium on Parasites: Their World and Ours*, University of Toronto, pp. 1–24. Ottawa: The Royal Society of Canada, 1978.

Hunter, G. W., III; Swartzwelder, J. C.; and Clyde, D. F. *Tropical Medicine.* 5th ed. Philadelphia: W. B. Saunders Co., 1976.

Markell, E. K., and Voge, M. *Medical Parasitology*. 5th ed. Philadelphia: W. B. Saunders Co., 1981.

Nelson, G. S. "Human Behaviour in the Transmission of Parasitic Diseases." *Zoological Journal of the Linnean Society*, Supple. 1, 51 (1972):109–122.

Schultz, Myron G. "Current Concepts in Parasitology." *The New England Journal of Medicine* 297 (1977):1259–61.

Unlocking the Brain

by Donna Bergen, M.D.

The brain within its groove runs evenly and true.

—Emily Dickinson

But what happens when the brain jumps its groove, when a person develops symptoms or signs that his brain is no longer functioning in its proper way? How does a physician make the correct diagnosis of disease in an organ that cannot be seen or touched without life-threatening surgical procedures?

Before the medical advances of the 20th century made "looking into the brain" possible, brain disorder or disease was a mystery, often a terror to be treated by the most desperate of remedies. Until the anatomists of the Renaissance began systematic dissections of brain lesions, any seizures, malfunctions, or erratic behavior could best be explained as being the result of possession by demons. Those exhibiting signs of mental aberration could only be flogged, prayed over, exorcised, or locked away. Understanding the brain and its chemistry is still incomplete, and the concept itself was undreamt of in the centuries in which the brain kept locked its secrets.

Strategies in diagnosis

The major *disadvantage* in trying to diagnose brain pathology is that this very precious organ is sealed snugly inside a hard, close-fitting casing—the skull—which cannot be broached safely outside the operating room. On the other hand, the function of the brain is expressed in a myriad of movements, sensations, reflexes, and even electrical activity, which can be examined and often precisely measured. In addition, such functions relate not just to the brain as a whole, but often to very precisely located parts of the brain, so that it is sometimes possible to predict the site of a brain injury within one to two millimeters, simply by observing the functional effects of disordered brain activity.

In response to this situation two diagnostic strategies have evolved, one to make the sequestered brain more visible, and the other to enable more precise measurements of brain function to be made.

The diagnostic tests described here vary tremendously in their complexity, specificity, cost, risk, and discomfort to the patient. Choosing the most appropriate test for a patient suspected of having a brain disorder must be

Donna Bergen, M.D., *a neurologist, is Director of the Electroencephalography Laboratory at Rush-Presbyterian-St. Luke's Medical Center and Assistant Professor in the Department of Neurological Sciences at Rush Medical College in Chicago.*

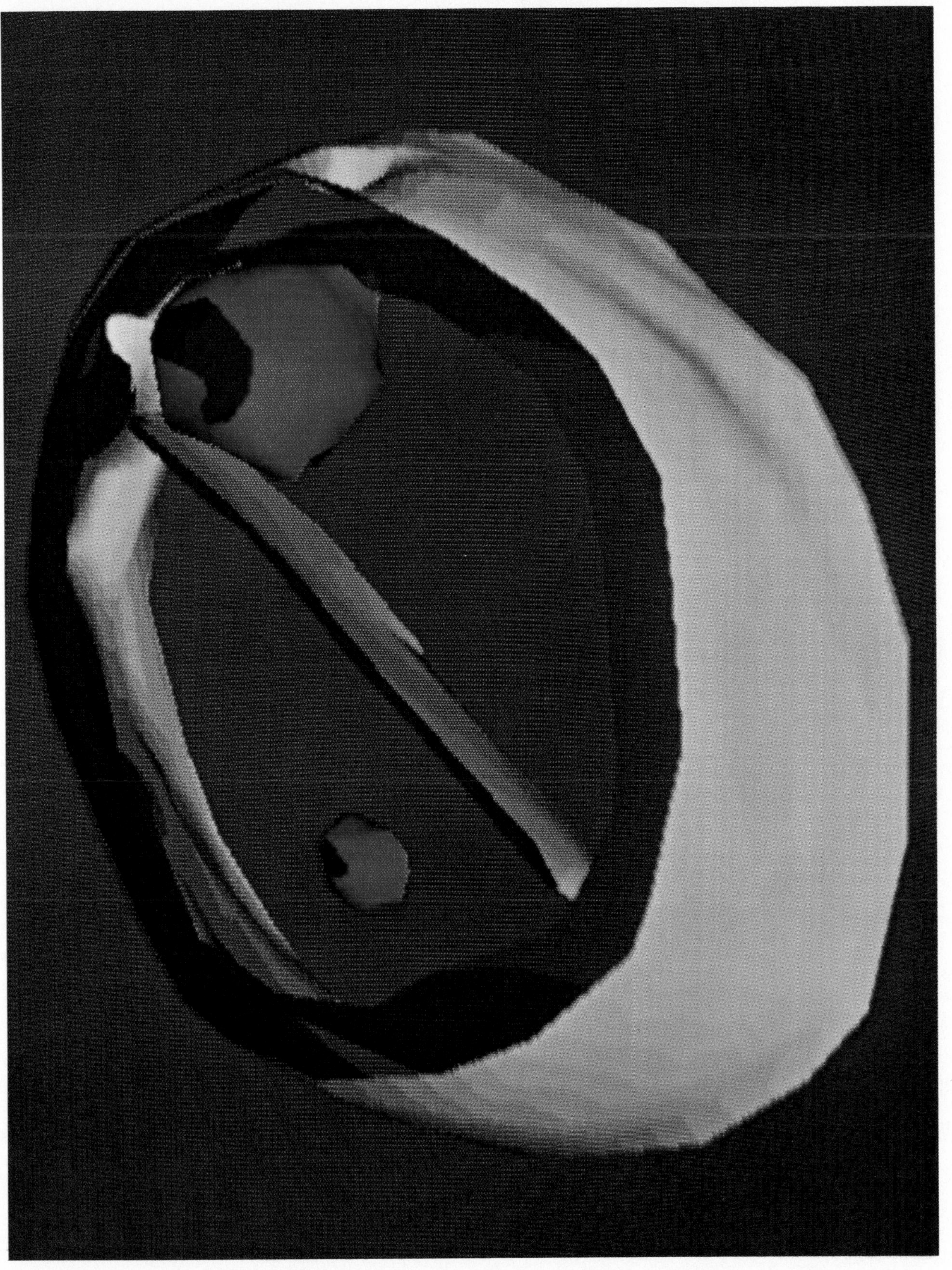

(Top) Prado, Madrid; photograph, Scala/EPA; (bottom left) In the Collection of Her Majesty the Queen, Windsor Castle; photo, National Library of Medicine, Bethesda, Maryland

The secrets of the brain's functions remained locked inside the skull until the technological achievements of the 20th century enabled physicians to both literally and figuratively look inside without threatening the life of the patient. In Hieronymus Bosch's painting "The Cure of Madness" (right) the terror of the patient is set against the concern and determination of his attendants. Great strides were made in understanding the anatomy of the brain by the dissections and descriptions of the physiologists and artists of the Renaissance. Leonardo da Vinci dissected cadavers and made thousands of drawings of bodily structures. His drawings of the brain (below) clearly show the ventricles and other structures.

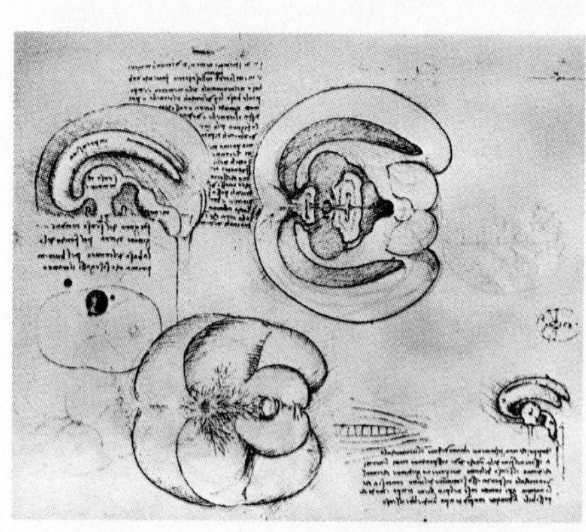

(Overleaf) Using information gathered by CAT scans, the Shelton Stereotactic Technique presents a computer-generated three-dimensional model of a brain tumor. The red areas in the scan show the size and location of the tumors. The green stripe represents the membrane surrounding the brain that folds into the fissure separating the two hemispheres. The encircling yellow-green band represents the skull. Photograph by Dan McCoy—Rainbow

done by weighing these factors carefully. Not all the tests are suitable for any single case, and only rarely would all of them be done on a single patient. Devising the "best" sequence of tests for the individual patient is the challenge that faces the doctor searching for the correct diagnosis.

The first diagnostic test to be applied to the person with symptoms of brain disease historically was and still is the physician's own evaluation of the person's complaints and of the person himself. The brain is organized in such a way that dysfunction in a certain part of it or in a certain type of its cells (neurons) produces symptoms and signs which are very specific to that location or to that neuronal system. The patient's first sentence to the doctor therefore may specify precisely where the disease lies. The middle-aged woman with a small benign tumor growing into the lower part of the brain behind the eyes may tell her physician about a convulsion that was preceded by the sudden experience of smelling a foul odor which no one else could smell. The alert doctor would be able to localize the beginning of the patient's seizure, and thus the part of the brain irritated by the tumor, as the "olfactory gyrus," a small strip of cerebral cortex (the brain's outer layer) whose normal function is the reception and analysis of odors.

In other cases the patient may not be able to tell the doctor enough to localize the disease, but the doctor's examination may reveal some abnormal nervous function or set of functions that betray the exact location of the pathology. For example, a 60-year-old man complains of being "weak all over," a rather nonspecific symptom with a hundred possible causes. A thorough examination, however, reveals changes in some limb reflexes and the presence of a particular type of involuntary muscle twitch in the arms and

Michael Huckman, Rush-Presbyterian-St. Luke's Medical Center

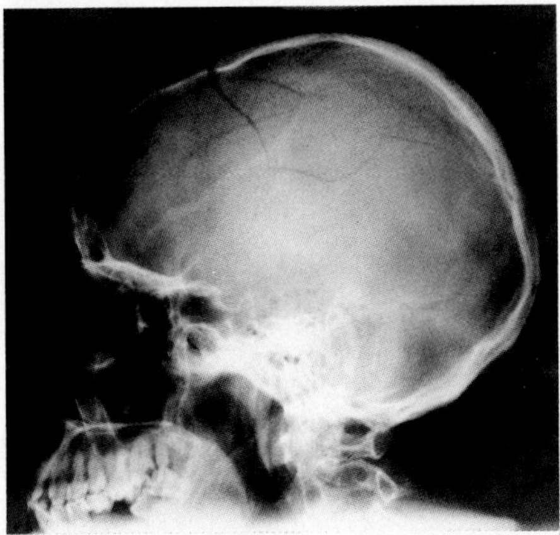

The skull X-ray above reveals a fracture at the top of the head that appears as a dark line moving toward the back of the head. Although the brain itself cannot be seen on an X-ray, in the hands of a skilled interpreter the visualization of the skull can yield a great deal of information.

legs. These findings would allow an immediate diagnosis of amyotrophic lateral sclerosis, a disease causing degeneration of cells in the brain and spinal cord that normally mediate muscle movement.

In both the cases described above, although the knowledgeable physician can make an immediate localization of the problem and feel quite sure of its accuracy, diseases other than tumor or amyotrophic lateral sclerosis can also cause symptoms localized to those areas, and the specific diagnosis must be confirmed by other tests. The medical history and physical examination are tests of function that can tell *where* something is wrong; they can only sometimes say *what* the disease process itself is. For that, doctors may turn to *anatomical* tests to give them literally a picture of what is affecting brain function.

Tests assessing brain anatomy

Skull X-rays. Probably the most commonly used anatomic investigation of the brain is the skull X-ray. Even this test, which has proved its usefulness over the years, does not actually reveal the brain itself, but only its casing, the skull. Often this is enough for the physician to infer the presence of serious brain pathology. A skull fracture that crosses the track of one of the arteries on the surface of the brain, for example, often tears this blood vessel, causing serious bleeding which may fatally compress the brain. Again, certain brain tumors often erode internal parts of the skull in very characteristic ways, so that not only the presence of the growth but even its cell type can occasionally be predicted from a single simple X-ray.

Sometimes internal cerebral structures can actually be seen on an X-ray when calcium accumulates in them as part of normal aging or as a result of disease. Such calcium deposits can provide a convenient marker for the position of normal parts of the brain. The normal location of the pineal gland, for example, is near the center of the brain, exactly halfway between the two sides of the skull. A tumor or blood clot which is displacing and distorting normal brain structures often pushes the pineal gland to one side, and if the gland is calcified this displacement can be identified on a plain skull X-ray.

Ultrasound imaging. In young people and in many older people, however, there is not enough pineal calcification to allow it to be seen on such an X-ray. In these cases the location of midline brain structures can be determined by ultrasound. This device works on a principle similar to radar, sending out waves of sound too high in frequency for the human ear to hear, and detecting them again when they are bounced back. Again the brain provides a convenient marker for its midpoint: the sound waves can be well reflected off the wall of the third ventricle, a fluid-filled, slitlike cavity which lies along the vertical plane halfway between the sides of the brain. Again, any distortion of this structure, either by some space-taking lesion or by brain damage which causes shrinkage of one side or hemisphere, will be detected using ultrasound.

CSF tap. The third ventricle is only one of a system of four ventricles in the normal brain. They contain cerebrospinal fluid (CSF) and communicate with the CSF-filled sac surrounding and cushioning the brain and spinal cord (the subarachnoid space). Blockage of the circulation of this watery fluid is

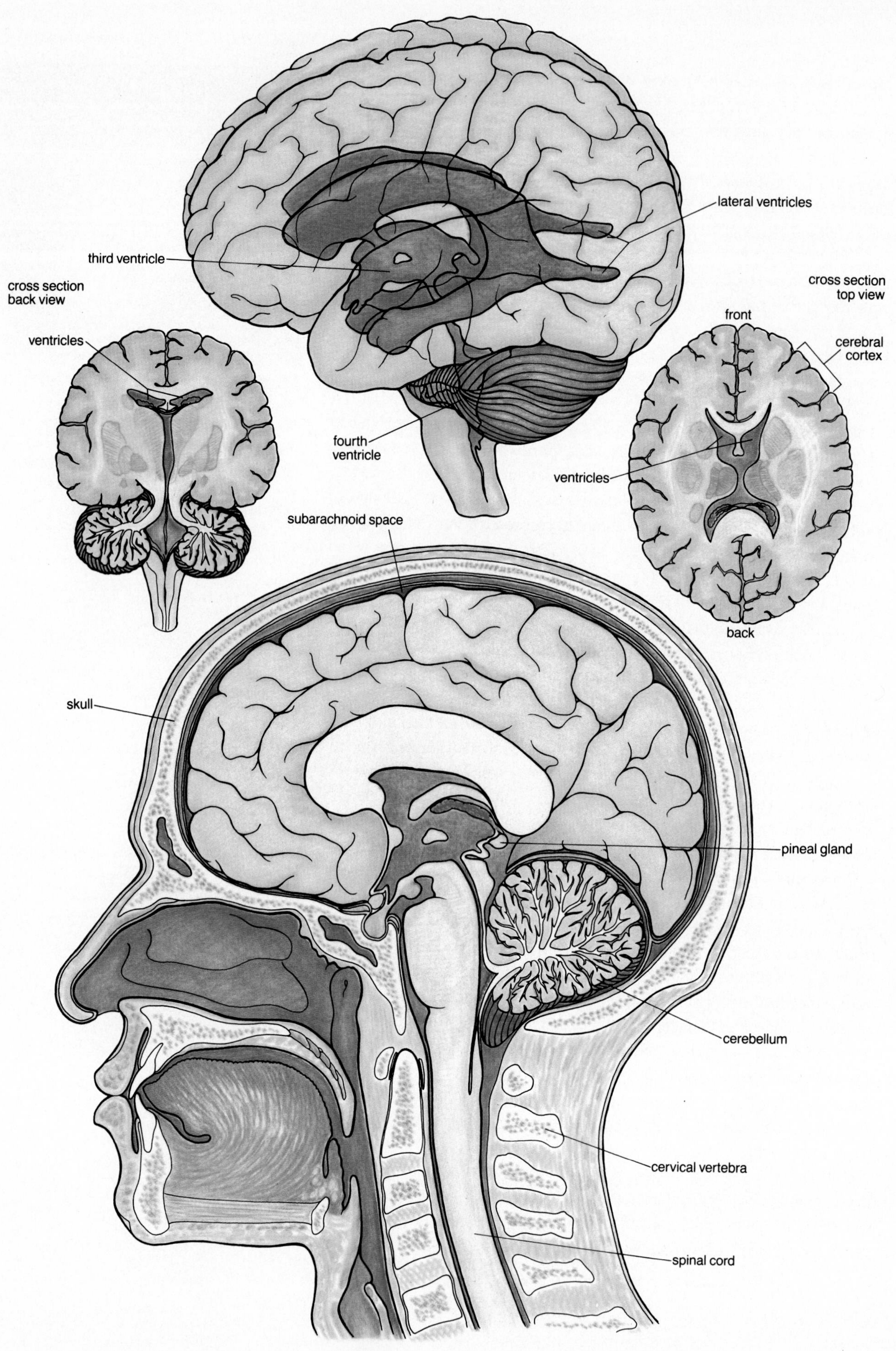

lateral ventricles
third ventricle
cross section
back view
cross section
top view
front
cerebral
cortex
ventricles
fourth
ventricle
ventricles
subarachnoid space
back
skull
pineal gland
cerebellum
cervical vertebra
spinal cord

one cause of hydrocephalus, a condition in which the ventricles become very large, compressing brain tissue and even increasing the size of the head, when hydrocephalus occurs in early childhood. About 1891 a technique for ameliorating hydrocephalus by drainage of this fluid was introduced: the CSF sac extending down around the spinal cord was tapped by passing a needle between the bones of the spine. Other surgical treatments for hydrocephalus soon supplanted this one, but it was quickly noted that infections of the brain or of its membranous sheaths (encephalitis and meningitis, respectively) could readily be detected by examining cerebrospinal fluid obtained by this technique. Spreading a few drops of the fluid onto a culture plate and waiting, for only a few hours in some cases, produces bacterial colonies which can be precisely identified so that the most suitable antibiotics can be chosen for patients with these often fatal infections.

Bleeding into the CSF sac, called subarachnoid hemorrhage, is a serious occurrence which can also be diagnosed unequivocally within just a few minutes by tapping the CSF sac. Brain tumors, multiple sclerosis (a disease causing degeneration of certain brain and spinal cord cells) and other disorders may also cause changes in the chemistry of CSF that may provide helpful diagnostic clues. Best of all for the doctor searching for a diagnosis, the spinal tap or lumbar puncture is safe, quick, inexpensive, and not too unpleasant for the patient.

Pneumoencephalography. Except for the cases of infection and hemorrhage, however, the results of a lumbar puncture can only suggest the presence of certain disorders but rarely can provide enough information for a specific diagnosis. In many brain disorders such as tumor or bleeding into the brain itself, a direct *look* at brain structures and brain pathology is desirable. The CSF-filled ventricles do not appear on a routine X-ray of the head. This is because the X-ray works on the general principle of detecting and picturing differences in tissue densities. The usual clinical X-ray can detect only large differences in tissue density, for example, that between bone and air or between bone and brain tissue; brain tissue and CSF are simply too near in density to be discriminated. If the ventricles were full of air instead of CSF, their density would be sufficiently different from that of the enveloping brain substance for them to show up on X-ray. This is the principle of the pneumoencephalogram (the "air-brain-picture").

For this test a spinal tap is done and some CSF is removed. Air is then injected directly into the subarachnoid space, where if the patient is upright it bubbles upwards into the head and through the ventricles. At this point an ordinary X-ray will reveal the air-filled ventricular system, along with any distortions or displacements of that system. Hydrocephalus, of course, is instantly recognizable using this technique. Brain atrophy, which accompanies the most common forms of senility or "dementia," can also be readily diagnosed. With the aid of specialized X-ray methods, the pneumoencephalogram can demonstrate the effects of tumors only a few millimeters in diameter, especially near the base of the brain.

But pneumoencephalography is quite unpleasant and can be dangerous. In addition, however ingenious and accurate the techniques, ultrasound and pneumoencephalography enable a glimpse at only some of the important

These drawings, from a French text of the mid-1800s, show the effects of hydrocephalus; the fluid-filled ventricles have become greatly enlarged, pressing against the brain tissue. Effective treatment of this condition was not discovered until 1891.

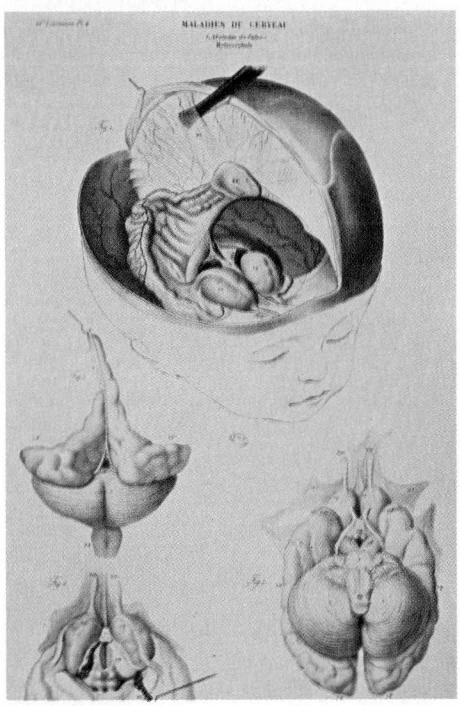
Jean-Loup Charmet

Peter Southwick—Stock, Boston

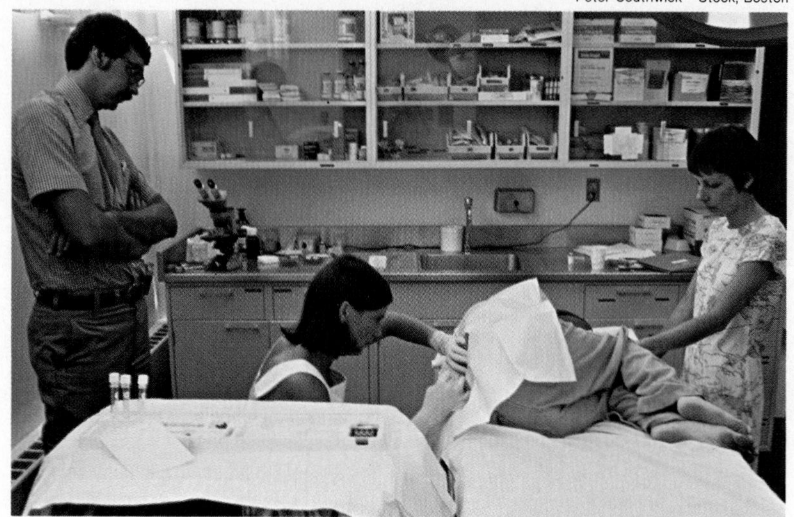

The "spinal tap" takes a sample of the cerebrospinal fluid that circulates around the brain and spinal cord. The technique is useful in diagnosing infections, multiple sclerosis, and some brain tumors.

With the aid of a computer outline of a normal artery, the findings from the arteriogram can assess the state of the cerebral blood vessels. The white area indicates the actual shape of the artery; the computer-generated outline of the normal artery shows both a general narrowing of the artery and the presence of an atherosclerotic plaque obstructing blood flow at the center left.

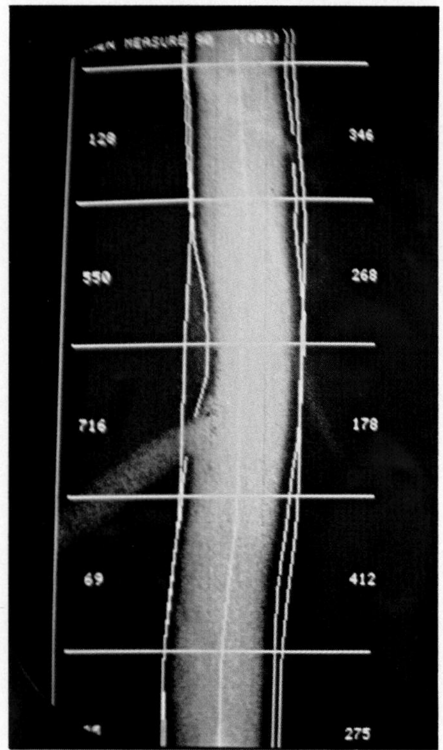

Dan McCoy—Rainbow

structures inside the skull. The brain itself cannot be visualized, for example, nor can the causes or effects of cerebral vascular disease, which ranks only behind cancer and heart disease as a killer of Americans.

A stroke, or cerebral infarction, is the effect of the sudden plugging of one of the arterial blood vessels carrying blood to part of the brain. Sometimes other blood vessels in the vicinity can take over supplying vital oxygen and sugar to the brain, but often the artery which becomes plugged by a blood clot or narrowed by atherosclerotic plaques (hardening of the arteries) is the only one which supplies the area. In that case the brain area whose blood supply has been cut off dies, and the functions served by that area are lost. The result for the victim is usually sudden paralysis, loss of speech, unconsciousness, or a combination of these and many other possible symptoms. Sudden rupture of atherosclerotic arteries can also occur, causing a destructive hemorrhage into the brain that results in similar symptoms. Cerebral infarctions or hemorrhages may also be instantly fatal.

Arteriography. The state of the cerebral blood vessels, and that of the arteries in the neck which lead into the brain, can be evaluated using a procedure that is applied to the blood vessels in many other parts of the body: arteriography or angiography. ("Angio-" refers to blood vessels, while "arterio-" specifies one type of vessel, the artery.) Blood-filled arteries have a density similar to that of tissue surrounding them, and cannot be seen on an ordinary X-ray. Arteriography is the bold act of quickly filling the blood vessels with a very dense liquid dye which is opaque to X-rays and which enables the vessels to be seen on an ordinary X-ray picture. The dye is usually injected directly into an artery in the neck, and as it is carried off by the blood flowing into the head a very rapid series of X-ray pictures is taken. The result is a detailed view of the treelike arterial system, showing the cerebral arteries dividing into a lacework of finer and finer branches. An artery plugged by a blood clot is easily identified as the flow of dye is abruptly cut off in that channel.

For people with cerebrovascular disease, the value of arteriography lies not so much in diagnosing the completed stroke, but in identifying arterial lesions that might presage the occurrence of stroke, so that appropriate prophylactic surgical or medical treatment may be undertaken. The presence of tumors and hemorrhages both inside and outside the brain substance can often be inferred by the distorting effects that they have on the blood vessels pictured by an arteriogram. Congenital malformations of cerebral blood vessels called aneurysms and arteriovenous malformations are also vividly outlined by this method.

Radionuclide brain scan. All X-ray techniques operate on the principle of shooting X-ray beams through the head and detecting what comes out on the other side. It is also possible to put an energy source *inside* the cranium and to detect meaningful patterns in what radiates to the outside. This is the principle of the radionuclide brain scan.

To do such a scan, a radioactive tracer such as technetium is chemically bonded to a carrier molecule and injected into the patient's body, usually into a superficial vein in the forearm or hand. The scanner, which detects the tiny emission of radioactivity from the injected technetium, first takes an immediate, rapid series of pictures which show the isotope being carried along the bloodstream into the brain, giving a rough idea of the patency (unobstructedness) of the largest arteries in the neck and head and showing any large abnormal vascular structures such as arteriovenous malformations. The patient then waits 30 minutes to several hours while the radioactive isotope continues through the body's circulation. Structural damage within the brain will allow the isotope to leak out of the tiniest blood vessels and collect within the nearby brain substance. This collection of radioactive isotope shows up on later scans as an abnormal "hot spot"; a fairly confident diagnosis of tumor, stroke, or hemorrhage can often be made by the shape of the abnormality on the scan. The radioactivity dies out fairly quickly, and the amount emitted during a single radionuclide brain scan is well within the usually defined limits of safety.

Once more, however, the diagnostician finds that many small lesions are missed with nuclide brain scanning. Going on to angiography often helps. But while the angiogram may be the procedure of choice for confirming the presence of an aneurysm or an occluded artery, an intracerebral hemorrhage or tumor that is too small to distort some of the vascular tree will not be detected by an angiogram. Even if distortion does take place, it is often impossible to determine whether the lesion responsible is a hemorrhage or brain tumor, a distinction of obvious importance for proper treatment of the patient. Finally, cerebral angiography is a test which carries significant risk to the patient. A more direct, realistic, and safe picture of the cranium's contents would be valuable.

CAT scan. In 1973 the science of radiology made a dramatic leap forward with the introduction of computerized axial tomography (CAT), a technique which makes use of complex computer techniques to give a realistic, never-before-seen view of inner body structures. Although many groups were investigating the possibilities of computed tomography, credit for the development of the first practical CAT scanner is usually given by name to Godfrey Hounsfield, a British computer engineer. Hounsfield was awarded the 1979 Nobel Prize for Physiology or Medicine, along with Allan Cormack,

Dan McCoy—Rainbow

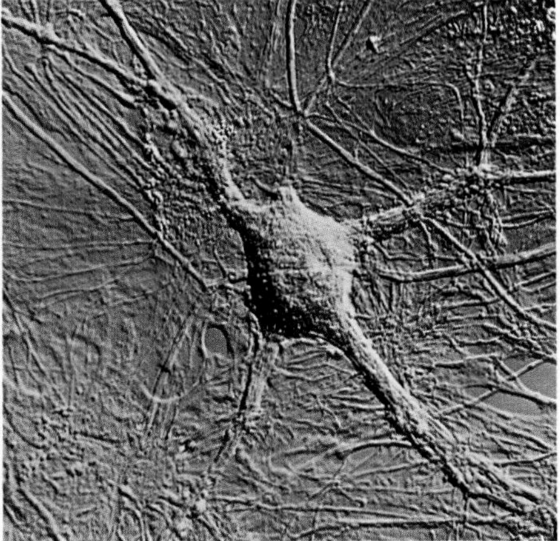

The neuron is the basic unit of brain function. The human brain may contain as many as 10 billion neurons in the brain cortex at birth. As neurons deteriorate they are not replaced; at age 50 about 10% of the original number have ceased to function.

Photographs, Dan McCoy—Rainbow

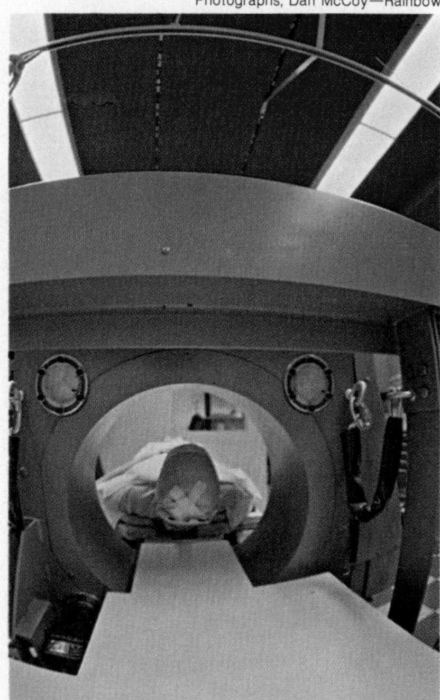

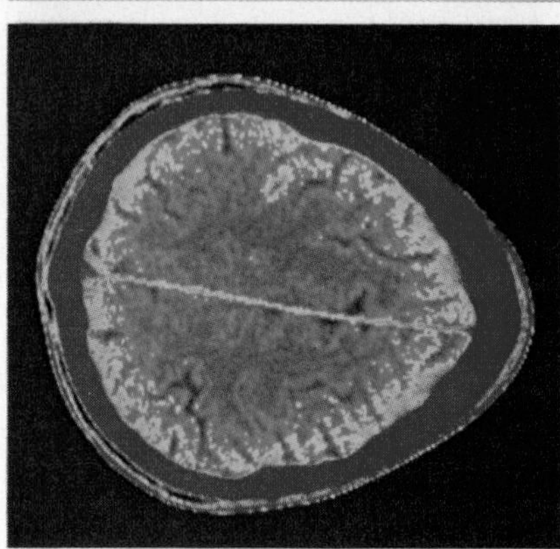

The CAT scan can give the physician a wealth of information about the interior structures of the brain. Unlike conventional X-ray pictures of the brain, which do not differentiate well among various types of soft tissue, the CAT scan can detect and precisely map the varying densities of brain structures. In the scan above the shape and location of the tumor in the upper portion of the picture are clearly discernible.

a physicist at Tufts University, in Medford, Mass., for this achievement.

A brief description of the principles of computed tomography will explain why its invention awaited the development of high-speed computers which were small and relatively cheap enough for practical use. The CAT scan surrounds the head, abdomen, or other body part to be photographed by an array of X-ray detectors. During the test, which takes from a few minutes to an hour, the scanner moves around the body as well as up or down the segment to be scanned, "slicing" through the body with its beams. At each "slice" the data from all the detectors are mathematically analyzed by the computer, and the resulting numbers are translated into tiny patches of gray, black, and white in order to give a picture of the "slice" just photographed. Each cross section comprises over 25,000 such individual areas and patches. The number and speed of the computations needed to provide such figures are quite literally superhuman, but they are just the type of straightforward, routine mathematical manipulations at which computers excel. The result of a CAT scan of the head is a series of pictures which appear as though the head had been sliced across (or vertically, if preferred) like a hard-boiled egg.

The most remarkable thing about these computerized X-rays is their sensitivity. Unlike conventional X-rays, the CAT scan pictures the brain tissue itself. The ventricles show, of course, so that hydrocephalus can be seen, and calcium deposits even smaller than those seen on routine X-ray stand out boldly. In addition, however, most brain tumors larger than the tip of the little finger are detectable with a CAT scanning, as are hemorrhages. And the best part is that CAT scanning is painless and safe, having none of the potentially serious complications of angiography or pneumoencephalography. The simple intravenous injection of a mild, rather dilute radiographic dye during the scan even duplicates many of the remaining advantages of arteriography, such as the ability to show arteriovenous malformations or vascular tumors. It is no exaggeration to say that the CAT scan has revolutionized the diagnostic process, improving upon and in very many cases replacing more dangerous and painful procedures. There is every reason to expect that over the coming years the principles of computed tomography will be applied with more and more technical sophistication, so that CAT scans will give a picture of brain structures that is more and more detailed.

Brain biopsy. The ultimate look at the brain's own anatomy, of course, comes when the doctor can hold a piece of the brain in his hand and look at it under a microscope. This is actually possible, in part at least, with the brain biopsy. Needless to say, the cutting out of a piece of cerebral tissue to obtain a diagnosis is not done with the same ease or readiness as biopsying a bit of muscle or even a lesion within the abdomen or chest. In some cases it is done by a neurosurgeon who must obtain the tissue by drilling a hole in the skull. A brain biopsy can be taken only from an area which is not likely to serve a specific vital function such as speech or movement, and like any brain surgery it carries a well-defined risk of brain injury or even death.

What diagnoses would be worth this risk? Only a few, including some types of serious viral encephalitis in which an early, accurate diagnosis would prompt the physician to use extremely potent antiviral drugs, warn against the transmissibility of the disease, or save the desperately ill patient from other repeated, painful, futile diagnostic procedures.

These tests assessing brain anatomy give only a partial picture as long as brain *function* is ignored. (After all, the CAT scan of a dead man is perfectly normal, at least for a time.) After the doctor finishes the neurological examination, how else can brain function be assessed?

Photographs, Dan McCoy—Rainbow

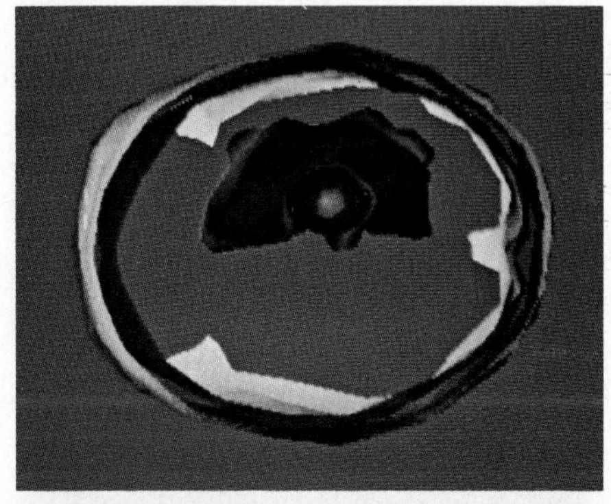

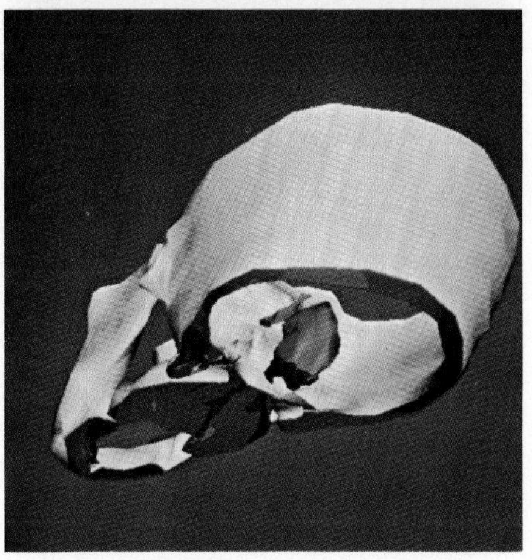

In the past, when the presence of a brain tumor was suspected, surgery on the brain was the only way to get an accurate assessment of the extent of the tumor. These three-dimensional computer-generated models can be viewed from any angle. The red areas on these models are tumors of precisely defined shape. The blue area around the tumor in the upper picture represents swelling of the brain tissues around the tumor.

Tests assessing brain function

Electroencephalography. One of the methods developed in this century is the recording of the electrical activity generated by the brain itself, or rather, by its cells. The brain, like other parts of the nervous system, carries out its functions through the unique ability of its cells to store and discharge electrical energy, just like tiny batteries. Electrical activity can be carried from one cell to another over relatively vast distances along long nerve cell processes (for example, along a sensory nerve process from the big toe all the way up to the neck). At the other end of the scale, tightly packed groups of thousands of neurons may exchange complex patterns of information within a tiny speck of cerebral cortex. Although electrical activity is carried along nerve cell processes and probably exchanged directly between some types of nerve cells, most neurons pass along their electrical "information" to their neighboring cells by elaborating chemicals onto their neighbor's surfaces which then set up fresh electrical activity in those cells.

Such activity at a single-cell level represents only a minute electrical discharge, undetectable except by means of microscopic electrodes maneuvered directly into or very near a discharging cell. Brain functions, however, are mediated not by single cells but by populations of cells working together in synchrony. When such populations of neurons are electrically active, the electrical field which they generate may be strong enough to be detected by sensors or electrodes attached to the scalp. These "strong" electrical fields are still minuscule when compared to the electrical activity generated by the cells in the heart, which is recorded on an EKG, or electrocardiogram; in fact it is about one one-hundredth the strength of the EKG activity.

This sort of brain electrical activity was first recorded in 1929 by Hans Berger and soon afterward was conclusively demonstrated to the skeptical scientific community by Edgar Adrian, a British electrophysiologist, who won the Nobel Prize for Physiology or Medicine in 1932. The test is called the electroencephalogram (EEG), literally the "electric-brain-picture," and it soon proved to be more than a picturesque production of squiggly lines. Grey Walter, for instance, quickly demonstrated that brain tumors distort the EEG recorded on the scalp near them, while activity over the rest of the brain remains normal. Most importantly, the EEG of a person in the throes of an epileptic seizure was found to show patterns seen at no other time. Of equal practical value was the discovery that many people with various types of epilepsy showed abnormal and often specifically characteristic EEG patterns even between seizures when they appeared perfectly well.

The routine clinical EEG today is taken using 20 or more recording electrodes pasted onto the scalp in a predetermined array. The test is painless

Adapted from "Disorders of the Human Brain," Seymour S. Key, © September, 1979 by SCIENTIFIC AMERICAN.
 Tracings provided by Robert R. Young, Harvard Medical School

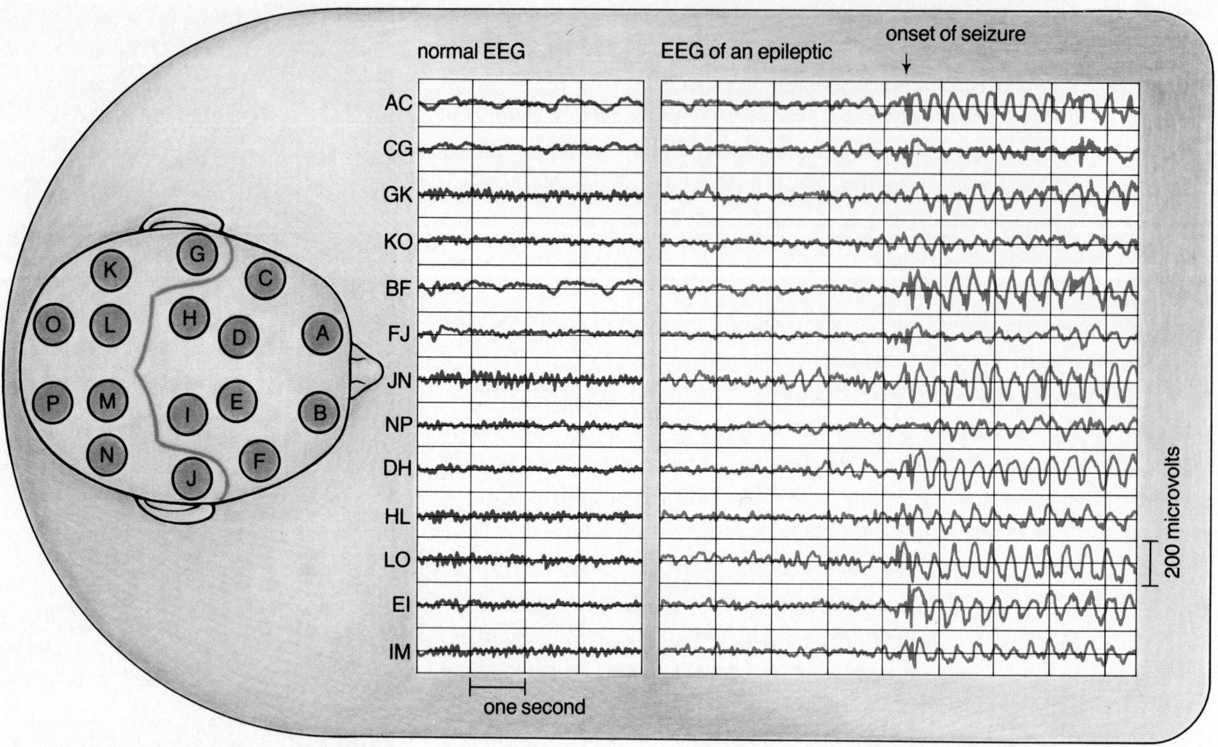

The electroencephalogram (EEG) records the minute amounts of electrical activity in the brain. Electrodes placed on the scalp pick up the variations in activity between two areas, here indicated by letters on the diagram of the head. The tracing at the left are those of normal activity. At the right is an EEG of a person with epilepsy showing the onset of a seizure halfway through the tracing.

and carries no risks. As might be expected, many conditions causing localized or widespread abnormalities of brain function are found to produce an abnormal EEG. Thus encephalitis, most cerebral infarctions, and illnesses causing delirium produce EEG disturbances. Today most structural brain disease (*e.g.,* tumors, abscesses, and hemorrhages) can be detected more reliably with the CAT scan than with the EEG, but the EEG is the only way to "see" and define various types of epileptic discharges and to document and quantitate other functional disturbances of the brain.

Today the principles of electroencephalography are the foundation of many other explorations into the electrical activity of the brain, some of them just recently finding clinical application. One of the most promising techniques is the evoked potential examination. In this type of test the brain's electrical activity is also recorded by electrodes on the skin, but this time neuronal activity is deliberately elicited by giving the person being tested some sort of sensory stimulation—a flash of light, a clicking noise, a brief electrical pulse, or tap on the skin. The sensations caused by such stimuli are mediated by the cellular discharges in the nervous system and thus can be recorded just as spontaneous EEG activity can. Neuronal activity induced in this way is of very low amplitude, however, so that repeated stimuli must be given and the electrical responses summed by a computer in order for them to be detected. The evoked potential curves that result reflect the acquisition and processing of sensory information by the nervous system.

The great clinical value of the evoked potential examination is that the test often shows abnormalities of function of a sensory system when the physician cannot detect any dysfunction by even the most careful physical examination. The evoked potential test thus can serve as an extension of the clinical neurological examination itself.

For example, multiple sclerosis is a disease of the central nervous system that is often difficult to diagnose, since it can mimic the symptoms and signs of many other diseases. The doctor usually must rely on certain typical combinations of clinical findings to make an accurate, firm diagnosis of multiple sclerosis. The evoked potential test has been found capable of providing such typical findings even when the most meticulous physical examination fails to do so. If a confident diagnosis of multiple sclerosis can be made, the patient may be spared further unpleasant or even potentially dangerous diagnostic tests.

Besides being used for the acquisition of evoked potential curves, computers are also being set to various other analytical tasks using ordinary EEG data as the raw material. In fact, once routine EEG waves have been recorded onto magnetic tape, the information may be manipulated in many ways, the number and type of which are limited only by the sophistication of the available equipment and the ingenuity of its users. For example, precise, quantifiable comparisons between the frequency and even the phase of EEG waves generated in two or more brain areas may be made. Such correlations (or the lack of them) between homologous areas on each side of the brain may reflect clinically important cerebral functions. Similar analyses of specific brain areas or comparisons between brain areas are thought by some researchers to offer an objective method of confirming or detecting the presence of brain dysfunction such as dyslexia (inability to learn reading skills) or other learning problems. A complex battery of computer-analyzed EEG and evoked potential tests have recently been assembled and are being tested under the name of "neurometrics"—a sort of electrical profile of cerebral activity. Its usefulness and validity must still be investigated.

PET scan. The newest breakthrough in diagnostic procedures for the brain looks at cerebral function in a completely new way. Put simply, positron-emission tomography (PET) combines the techniques of computerized tomography and radioactive brain scanning. Carbon, nitrogen, or another suitable material is bombarded with subatomic particles, transforming it into an unstable form which breaks down relatively quickly. This breakdown includes the annihilation of a positron-electron pair, a high energy reaction that results in the emission of a pair of gamma rays which shoot away at exactly a 180° angle. A circular array of sensitive scanners are programmed by computer to detect and count each "hit," each time that a pair of scanners at 180° angles sense the arrival of a pair of positrons. The areas emitting these positrons can thus be easily pinpointed. The array of scanners are moved up or down the head, and the computer turns the scanners' complex sums of "counts" at each level into a black and white (or even a colored) picture of a well-defined brain "slice."

The area in which the positron-emitting element is found depends upon what type of compound it is incorporated into before injection. For instance, carbon-11 can be used to form carbon-11-carbon monoxide, which can be inhaled. It reaches the red blood cells, and once in the bloodstream stays

Dan McCoy—Rainbow

There are still vast gaps in our knowledge of the normal brain's function. To provide a baseline for judging an individual's function, the Brain Research Laboratories of the New York University Medical School use a computer to record, measure, and collate information obtained by testing a group of volunteers. Electrodes attached to the volunteer's scalp record the brain activity evoked by hearing a sound from an amplifier behind the chair. Information about the normal brain obtained by this technique is helping neurologists understand what happens when the brain malfunctions due to disorders such as senility, learning disabilities, and hyperactivity.

(Top) Dan McCoy—Rainbow; (bottom) photographs, Michel M. Ter-Pogossian, Washington University School of Medicine

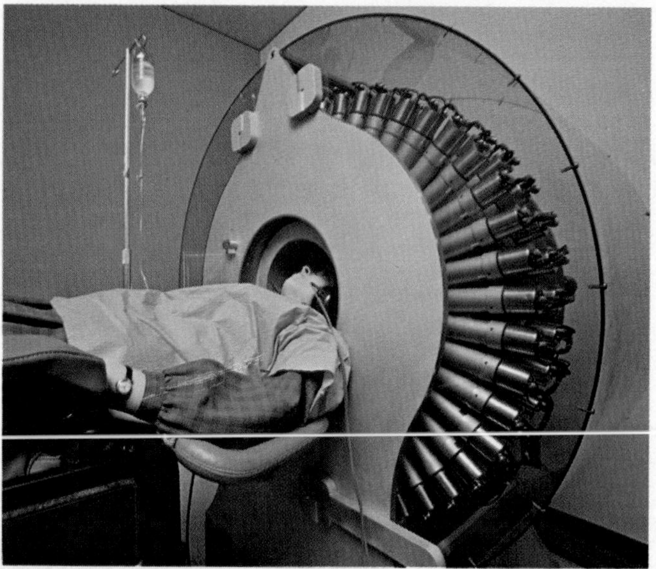

Positron-emission tomography (PET scan) is an exciting new tool for assessing brain function. The first row of photographs below compares the images obtained from a PET scan, at center and left, with that of a CAT scan at right. In this case the patient has had a stroke that has cut off the oxygen supply to the upper left quadrant of the brain. The center row of scans shows (left to right) the blood volume, blood flow, and oxygen consumption in the brain of a patient with epilepsy. The red dot at the center top of the first photo is the site of a focal seizure, indicated by an increase in blood volume. The third row of scans also shows blood flow, blood volume, and oxygen consumption, here in a brain in which there is a meningioma, a tumor originating in the brain's covering membrane. The tumor is located at the exact center of the brain where there is an increase in blood flow and volume but a decrease in oxygen.

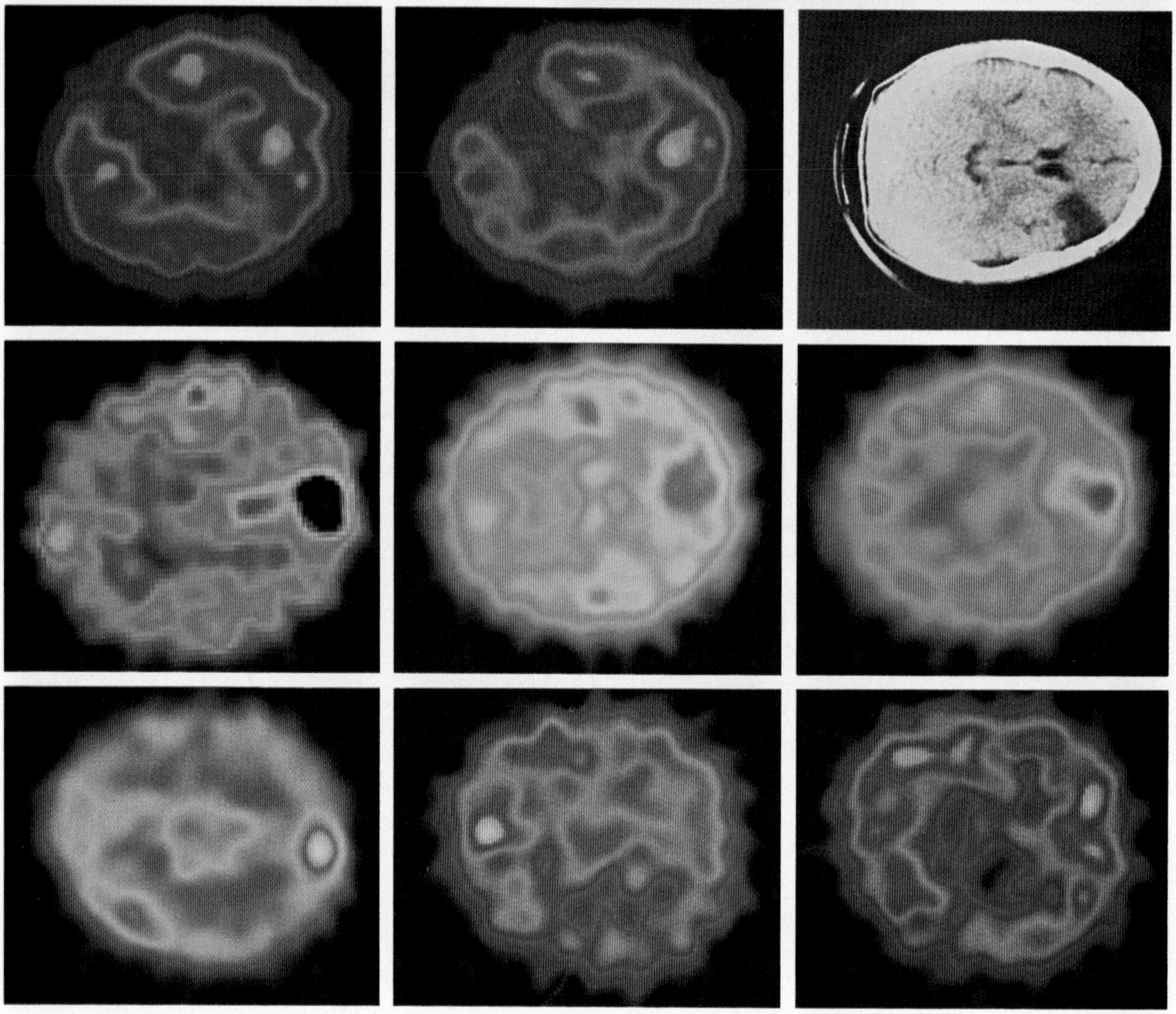

within the blood vessels. The PET scan using carbon-11-carbon monoxide would thus project a picture of normal (or abnormal) blood flow patterns within all the various parts of the brain. The scanning of ^{18}F-2-deoxy-D-glucose, a substance that is readily included in part of the normal cellular metabolic pathway for glucose, can produce a picture of the metabolic activity of various brain regions. This ability to map the level of ongoing regional cellular metabolism, and thus its level of cellular activity, is a unique property of the PET technique that is already being used to answer fundamental questions about brain function near foci of epileptic activity and areas of reduced blood supply.

The future of PET scanning looks exciting indeed. Damaged areas of brain which give rise to epileptic seizures, for example, can be "mapped" using this method. Because of the tomographic technique these areas might include those deep within the brain, too far away for the scalp electrodes of the conventional EEG to detect them. Drugs that are active in the brain can also be labeled, and their distribution may offer clues not only about how the drugs work, but also about the mechanisms of the diseases they are used to treat. Phenothiazines, drugs used in the treatment of schizophrenia, have already undergone preliminary studies with this technique, and schizophrenics themselves have been found by the PET scan to have abnormal regional metabolic "maps." Finally, naturally occurring brain substances can also be labeled for the PET scan, so that many aspects of normal or abnormal regional brain function can be explored harmlessly.

The inevitable rub: PET scanning requires the use of very short-lived isotopes (*e.g.*, 2 to 110 minutes), which must therefore be produced on the spot by a cyclotron—a very expensive device whose use demands the skills and services of physicists and nuclear engineers. At least for the forseeable future, then, PET scanning will be reserved for the largest, best-endowed medical and research centers.

It is clear that there is no single, ideal diagnostic procedure that is precise, reliable, safe, and practical. The clinician will always have to apply his or her own diagnostic skills to select the most appropriate test or combination of tests for each patient suspected of having brain disease. In the end, the diagnosis is made not by the test, but by the physician.

FOR ADDITIONAL READING:

Klass, Donald W., and Daly, David D., eds. *Current Practice of Clinical Electroencephalography.* New York: Raven Press, 1979.

Oldendorf, William H. *The Quest for an Image of the Brain.* New York: Raven Press, 1980.

Patten, John. *Neurological Differential Diagnosis.* London: Harold Starke, 1977.

Peterson, Harold O., and Kieffer, Stephen A. *Introduction to Neuroradiology.* Hagerstown, Md.: Harper & Row, 1972.

Taveras, Juan M., and Wood, Ernest H. *Diagnostic Neuroradiology.* 2nd ed. Baltimore: Williams & Wilkins, 1976.

Ter-Pogossian, Michel M.; Raichle, Marcus E.; and Sobel, Burton E. "Positron-Emission Tomography," *Scientific American.* 243: 171–181, 1980.

Window on the Unconscious: Drawings of Patients

by Fred Rappaport

Although the value of expressing and interpreting emotion through art has long been observed, projective art, as an adjunct to psychiatry in the diagnosis and treatment of mental disorders, has only been recognized as a bona fide field of study in about the last 40 years. So-called projective art represents the visual expression of a person's most fundamental thoughts and feelings, which are derived from the unconscious. Projective drawings have assumed a position of importance in the battery of projective diagnostic tests—which includes the Rorschach and the Thematic Apperception tests—used by psychologists to evaluate patients' emotions, attitudes, and personalities. Increasingly hospitals are incorporating projective art therapy into their treatment programs for psychiatric and psychosomatic illnesses. And art therapy for children has now been joined with drama, dance, music, and even puppetry to form the core of expressive activity programs in what is generally called child life therapy. Such programs now exist in a number of major hospitals, among them Johns Hopkins Hospital in Baltimore, Maryland, Children's Memorial Hospital in Chicago, Grady Memorial Hospital in Atlanta, Georgia, and Children's Hospital Medical Center in Boston.

It was only in the late 19th century that the spontaneous art of the mentally ill began to interest the medical profession. French psychiatrist Max Simon and his Italian colleague Cesare Lombroso were the first to publish their observations about the spontaneous art of mental patients and the significance of the artistic endeavor in relation to the patient's particular illness. It was not the art as such that captured their interest but the visual symbolism used by the patients which became their focus of investigation. Simon and Lombroso recognized that the seemingly senseless images that their patients produced were indeed related to their specific conflicts.

J. Brown

In *A General Introduction to Psycho-analysis* (1920), Sigmund Freud succinctly pointed out the invaluable potential of art as a therapeutic tool, noting that "there is, in fact, a path from fantasy back again to reality, and that is—art." What Freud meant was that art is a function of the brain's coordinated mental, or psychodynamic, processes. Through this projective mechanism the patient communicates with the therapist in a language of visual symbols, conveying both conscious and unconscious information. Projective art thus reflects the configuration of the patient's personality and conflicts, and provides important clues about how the individual deals with anxieties, desires, and needs. There is also something inherently therapeutic in creating.

Because the visual symbols that appear in projective art express individual reaction to conflict, these symbols vary infinitely, and their interpretation must necessarily be made in context. Nonetheless, these symbols are char-

"La Schizophrénie Par L'Image" by Agrégé Robert Volmat, Roche Laboratories, Paris, 1958

Fred Rappaport *is an optometrist and art therapist who lives in Chicago.*

(Overleaf) Painting by 80-year-old female psychiatric patient c. 1960, courtesy of the author

"La Schizophrénie Par L'Image" by Agrégé Robert Volmat, Roche Laboratories, Paris, 1958

The art of schizophrenics vividly depicts the deranged thinking, emotions, and drives characteristic of this mental disorder. Autism is a condition marked by a tendency for complete withdrawal from the world and constituting the basic framework for schizophrenia. (Left) A patient portrays herself encased in a protective capsule (uterus?) which is further protected from the world by a bower of leaves. The four self-portraits by another schizophrenic (opposite page) suggest the progressive deterioration and ultimate fragmentation of his personality.

acteristically closely associated with the patient's body image and general self-image. The case of Mr. A, a Korean War veteran who had had his left arm amputated, offers a vivid example of the extent to which the body image is involved in projective art. In art therapy Mr. A proved an avid artist, drawing tree after tree—each with the lower left branches cut off.

Although projective art often expresses an individual's many conflicting concerns, there are occasional examples of projective drawing that represent "classic" visualizations of a given emotional conflict or personality disorder. Ambivalence, for example, might be represented by two monsters living amicably side by side. The delirium state of advanced alcoholism often is reflected by the depiction of insects and demons. The drawings of patients with anorexia nervosa, a severe eating disorder of teenage girls characterized by self-starvation, tend to be colorless, often an expression of life's emptiness. As the anorexic begins to respond to therapy, she will begin to use color in her drawings.

Many works in modern art show great similarity to the projective art of schizophrenics. In their surrealistic paintings Joan Miró, Yves Tanguy, and Salvador Dalí have explored their fantasies through the liberation of unconscious associations. Pablo Picasso, Juan Gris, Georges Braque, and other cubists have interpreted or exaggerated reality with geometric forms. Marc Chagall and Paul Klee have created dreamlike images and used symbols to emphasize meaning. Whereas the works of these artists are examples of the unrestrained creative imagination asserting itself, schizophrenics directly project their hallucinations, delusions, and obsessions into their drawings; the images they use *are* their reality.

As with any psychoanalytic interpretation, great care and restraint must be exercised in analyzing the art of patients. It is not always possible nor is it always necessary to arrive at a definitive interpretation of every visual symbol. However, several psychoanalytic mechanisms provide the point of departure for understanding the symbolic language of the unconscious in projective art. Some of the most important mechanisms are displacement, sublimation, compensation, and conversion.

Displacement is the transfer of an emotional affect (anger, for example) from the object to which it was originally attached to another associated object. Sadness over the death of a loved one, for example, might be triggered anew when seeing or smelling flowers. Sublimation is a defense mechanism by which socially unacceptable feelings are given expression in a socially acceptable manner. For instance, working out with a punching bag is considered an acceptable means of dispelling hostility. Compensation is another defense mechanism in which one behaves in a manner designed to compensate for real or imagined defects. Some historians have suggested that Napoleon, Julius Caesar, and Alexander the Great all compensated for their small physical statures with brilliant military careers. Conversion is a process by which repressed ideas and emotions are transformed into physical manifestation. The case of Karen, whose art is presented in the following pages, aptly illustrates the mechanism of conversion. When she moved to the city far away from her father, she physically responded to the emotional stress by beginning to cross her eyes.

While projective drawing is an adjunctive tool that serves many purposes—sometimes diagnostic, sometimes therapeutic—its major role, as will be seen with the following cases, is to reflect change. Drawings may show a patient is getting better and resolving conflicts, or they may suggest a progression to a more deranged state. In either case, they can be a useful aid to a therapist in assessing the patient's progress.

The drawings of Karen

Karen is a nine-year-old girl who had been living with her divorced father in a small town in Ohio. However, because her father felt that, alone, he could not offer his daughter the proper family environment, Karen was sent to live with her aunt and uncle in Chicago. After six months in her new home, she was brought into the optometrist's office by her aunt, who had noticed Karen's developing eye problems: her right eye periodically turned outward, and she bent too close to the page when reading.

To understand Karen's eye problems, it is useful to review some of the basic mechanisms of sight. Since we have two eyes, there are two images which must be fused in the brain in order to see a single image. Thus, we actually see with our brain. When we think of a distant object above the horizon, our eyes place themselves in relative divergence; when we think of a nearby object below the horizon, our eyes converge. These inward and outward movements of the eyes must work synergically in order for the individual images to be fused by the brain. This fusion, however, can be interrupted by a psychological trauma, usually resulting in an inability to focus properly, with the weaker eye moving independently of the other, a condition referred to as strabismus, or crossed eyes.

Patients' artwork courtesy of Fred Rappaport

In Karen's case visual examination revealed divergent strabismus, with a weakened right eye tending to turn outward (exophoria) and resultant double vision (diplopia), most likely caused by emotional trauma. Corrective lenses were prescribed, and orthoptic training—professionally supervised exercises of the eye muscles utilizing ophthalmic lenses and prisms—was begun in combination with projective drawing in order to unearth the probable cause of her disorder. Of the many pictures that Karen drew in therapy, the five that follow represent a chronological selection and eloquently express her basic conflict.

Drawing 1.

Therapist: Why is the picture so dark?
Patient: Because it's night, and the moon is shining.
T: Are you afraid of the night? Some kids are, you know.
P: I'm not; I like it at night. I used to be though, but not any more....
T: You used to be afraid of the night?
P: Yes, a little bit.
T: What were you afraid of?
P: Oh, I wasn't really afraid of anything. I just wanted to be with Daddy.
T: (pointing at the drawing) Where is that scenery? Is it any particular place you remember?
P: Well, no special place; it's in the country.
T: Near where you were living in Ohio?
P: Well, it could be anyplace in the country with trees and a river.

The dark colors used in this picture convey a general feeling of loneliness and depression. The trees might be interpreted, as they are in many cultures and by many analysts, as symbols of life-giving power and of growth. Karen herself identified the round object in the sky as the moon, a body which Swiss psychoanalyst Carl Jung interpreted, among various possibilities, as a symbol of totality. The moon becomes even more significant in the drawing since it is connected by a sheaf of light rays with its reflection in the water. If the moon is identified with Karen's father, then the image of the moon's reflection might symbolize Karen herself; and the water might be an image for the fundamental change in Karen's life.

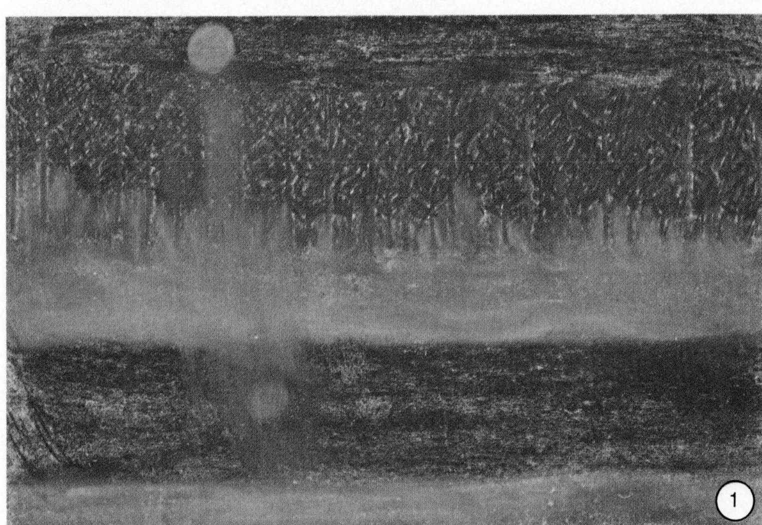

Drawing 2. Drawn several days later, this picture is strikingly similar to the first. The emptiness of the scene and the dark colors reiterate the depressive mood of the preceding drawing; yet there are also significant changes. The moon is no longer reflected in the water; rather its image is replaced by a rowboat stranded on the riverbank. The trees are smaller, spaced farther apart, and now flanked by flowers.

The transformation of the moon's reflection into a rowboat is interesting. The reflection (Karen) "belongs" to the moon (her father); without the moon, there can be no reflection, and likewise without her father, Karen cannot exist. The boat, on the other hand, is an "independent" entity, a vessel of sorts (perhaps signifying the female), and now has supplanted the reflection as a symbol of Karen. However, the stranded boat suggests Karen's "paralysis" in her current environment. The trees that were so tightly crowded in the first picture are now planted farther apart and may offer a more accessible and brighter view of what lies beyond (the future?).

Drawing 3. This drawing represents a transition in Karen's conflict. The night sky has yielded to a refreshing daylight sky. Yet Karen's depression has not entirely vanished; dark blue clouds remain overhead. The sun/moon is shining, and its image is reflected in the water. Here we find dual symbols of Karen—the moon's reflection and the boat—juxtaposed. The boat is now in the water but meanders without purpose. In contrast to the gloomy stillness of the water in the first two pictures, the wavy outlines of the water indicate movement and possibly change and growth.

Drawing 4. The dreary landscape and repetitive theme of the previous pictures have suddenly been transformed into a cityscape. The tall buildings, which look rather like prisons, are separated by canyonlike streets, and the scene suggests Karen's feelings of oppression and isolation within the city. The river still "flows" through the bottom of the drawing, and the sun/moon still haunts the sky. Yet the sun/moon (her father) seems even farther away than before. Nevertheless, Karen has finally decided to abandon rural imagery and move her thoughts to the city. Not insignificantly, however, a small car in the center seems to head out of town.

3

4

Drawing 5. In this drawing Karen depicts her hometown in Ohio with its church steeple (possibly a father symbol). Although the sinuous route in the foreground suggests that the road home may be long and difficult, the light and cheerful colors and the airiness of the scene convey Karen's optimism about her return home.

Also noteworthy is the sun/moon's position on the right in this drawing. In the first three drawings the moon occupied the left-hand side of the page; in the fourth drawing it moved to the center; and here the sun/moon has completed its rightward "transit." According to psychologist John N. Buck, the position of objects in projective drawing is important. The farther the object is to the left of the page, the more likely the subject is to seek immediate gratification of his needs; and as the object moves to the right of the page, the more likely the subject is to control his behavior.

Here the symbolism of the self is not as covert as before. The seven birds flying towards the town are probably symbolic of Karen and her ardent wish to return home to her father.

In the end the series of projective drawings was therapeutic in that it helped confirm the suspicion that Karen's divergent strabismus was psychological in origin. She soon was taken home to live with her father again, where she was happier and more secure, and her crossed eyes straightened out completely after a few months at home. Many youngsters who have a physical manifestation of an emotional problem, as Karen did, are aided by art therapy, in part because they are able to express themselves more freely with colors and figures than they are able to with words. The pictures also help children work through conflicts that they seem unable to confront in other ways.

The drawings of Pat

Pat is 17. Her father died when she was two, and she had no siblings. Her mother remarried but eventually divorced her second husband. Shortly after her mother married a third time, Pat began to show symptoms of mental disorder, aggravated by witnessing frequent fights between mother and stepfather. At age 15, Pat was hospitalized. She was diagnosed as suffering from hebephrenic schizophrenia, which characteristically appears at the onset of puberty and is marked by rapid deterioration of thought processes, hallucinations, absurd delusions, silly mannerisms, and senseless laughter. For several months Pat was too disoriented to participate in the hospital's school program. At that time she was only able to take walks accompanied by an aide, and her oral communication was generally a chaos of disconnected sentences.

The nurse who brought Pat to the art therapy department announced that Pat had made a nuisance of herself on the ward by taking reams of paper and pencils from the office to draw pictures all day and by tearing up each as soon as it was completed. She never showed anyone what she had drawn. In art therapy she was left to adjust at her own pace; she soon stopped destroying her drawings and proved eager to discuss the symbols in them. In her art work Pat expressed a number of repressed fantasies and conflicts. At first she drew with pencil alone, and only later, when she became more assertive, did she begin to use color in her drawings.

Drawing 1.

Therapist: What are those objects you painted white?
Patient: That's a mermaid, a duck with a fishtail; and this is the pumpkin I made. It fits on the body standing in the water. There are fishes with long tails swimming around.

In this rich and complex drawing the female torso with its detached head floating in the air and the mermaid—part maiden and part fish—reveal the patient's fragmented personality. Emphasizing her identification with the torso, Pat inscribed her name above it. Neither of these figures is able to move with complete freedom, perhaps conveying the patient's frustration with the maze of her own conflicts. This feeling is reiterated by the white labyrinth form beside the torso and by the blue grid at bottom left entrapping the yellow fish.

In discussing the drawing the patient insisted upon differentiating between the duck with a fishtail (the mermaid, or Pat) and the duck with feathers, who "always wants to fight" (presumably her mother), facing the donkeylike animal in the center. The donkey was identified by Pat as "an ass who is scared of the duck" and apparently symbolizes her stepfather retreating from the aggressive advances of her mother.

The jolly, red-faced figure also seems to represent her stepfather. When asked about this figure, Pat replies that he "has a silly laugh . . . but always wants to fight with the duck" and that his arms are outstretched "because he is naughty . . . like a devil." The patient seems to like her stepfather and by drawing him with outstretched arms implies that she wants to be embraced by him.

The red object, which Pat called a "mushroom with flowers around it," might be interpreted by its color and shape as the phallus of the red-faced man. The fact that it is detached from the rest of the figure again expresses Pat's fragmented perspective of the world. The phallic symbol is not only surrounded by flowers—symbols of her sexual fantasies—but is also intently

watched by "a lady-deer, a fairy-tale reindeer with long horns and an ear," with whom Pat apparently identifies. Through the intent eye of the deer, Pat is able to satisfy her sexual curiosity and at the same time carefully survey the interaction between the red-faced man and the duck.

When it was suggested to Pat that she sign the drawing, she eagerly obliged both with a bold, florid black crayon signature and with vaginalike shapes and other female symbols drawn everywhere that space permitted. The florid style of the signature expresses aspects of her obsessive-compulsive personality, a certain lack of self-confidence, and a great need for support.

Drawing 2.

Therapist: Did you have a nice time over the weekend?
Patient: Yes.
T: What is that you are drawing?
P: A banana split with cherries; seven cherries for J.C.
T: Who is J.C.?
P: J.C. is the holy man.
T: Did your mother take you to an ice-cream parlor yesterday?
P: Yes, I went alone. There was nobody but the married man. She said it was all right to go.

Drawing a banana split was Pat's way of saying that she had been out over the weekend and had had a good time. The rendering of the banana and cherries is clearly sexual, and the number of cherries may indicate that Pat is focused on the seven days that she must now wait for another home visit. J.C., to whom she referred in her comments, might, of course, be interpreted as Jesus Christ, "the holy man," who probably represents *her* savior, her stepfather. Although Pat enjoyed her outing, she feels guilty for going out alone with "the married man," despite her mother's permission. These guilt feelings crop up repeatedly in the following drawings.

Drawing 3. In order to accommodate this giant cherry, Pat used an oversized sheet and worked so fervently on the drawing that she tore the paper

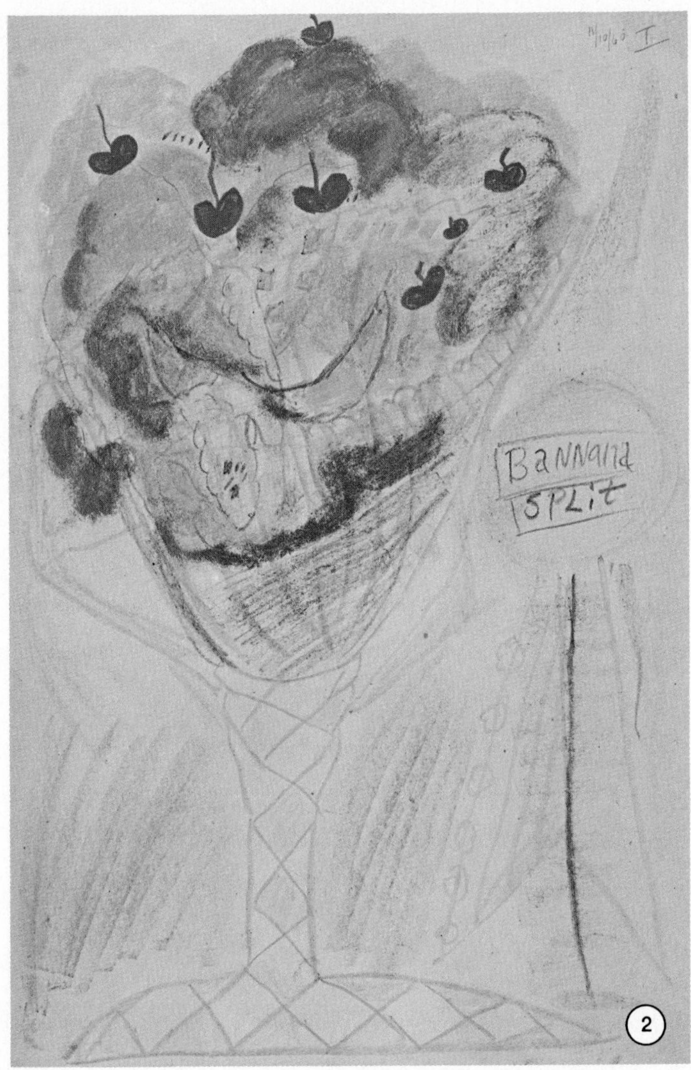

several times. In this drawing she evidently identifies with a woman of great sexual appetite, but her sexual fantasies cause her anxiety. Her signature is now very difficult to read and may suggest an effort to mask her identity as the artist, lest someone think her promiscuous.

Drawing 4. The concerns in this drawing, entitled "Possible Seeds in Wemon [*sic*]," are obvious. Pat expresses her worry about what may happen to her if she continues to be "bad," that is, sexually curious, by filling the orange uterine contour with a number of spermatozoalike shapes.

Drawing 5. According to psychologist Emanuel Hammer, who studied color symbolism in projective drawing, the color orange usually signifies the female gender. Pat has called this drawing "Orange Melon Fruit"; the appropriately orange-colored melon suggests the belly of a pregnant woman, with pubic hair represented by the broad black outline on the right and the vagina by the black and white triangles. The "fruit" is symbolized by the three egg-shaped objects floating in the uterine fluid, the latter suggested by the wavy black lines.

Possible.
Giant

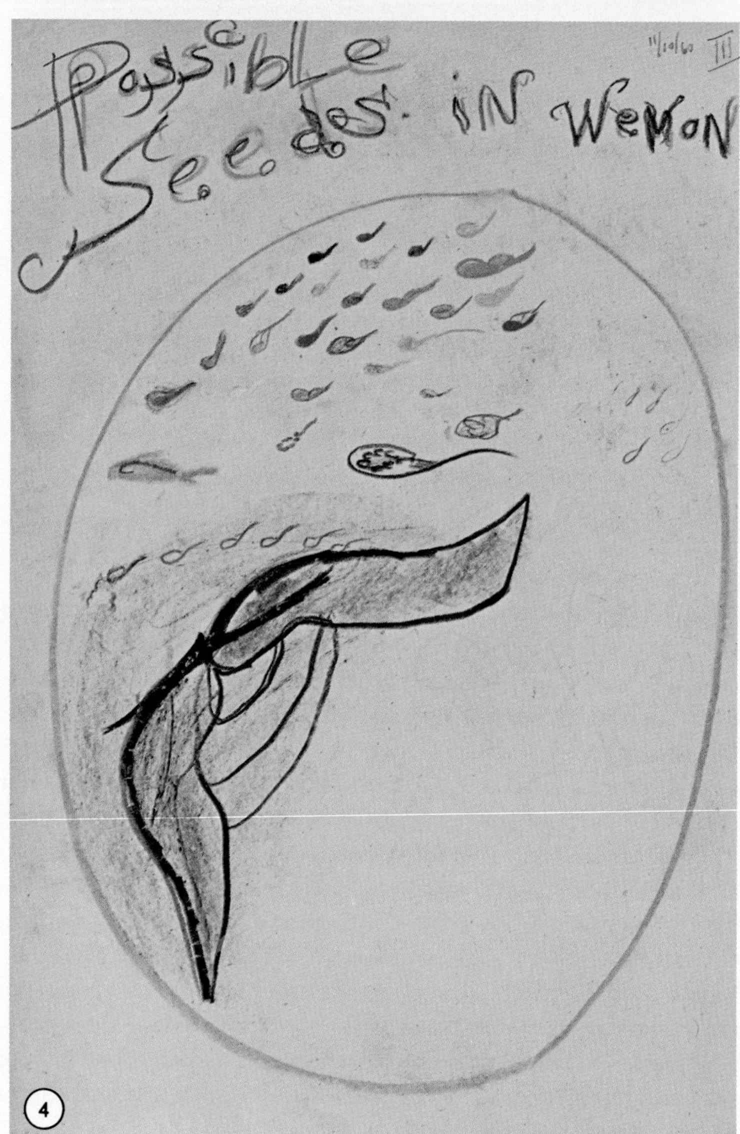
11/10/60
Possible Seedes in Wemon

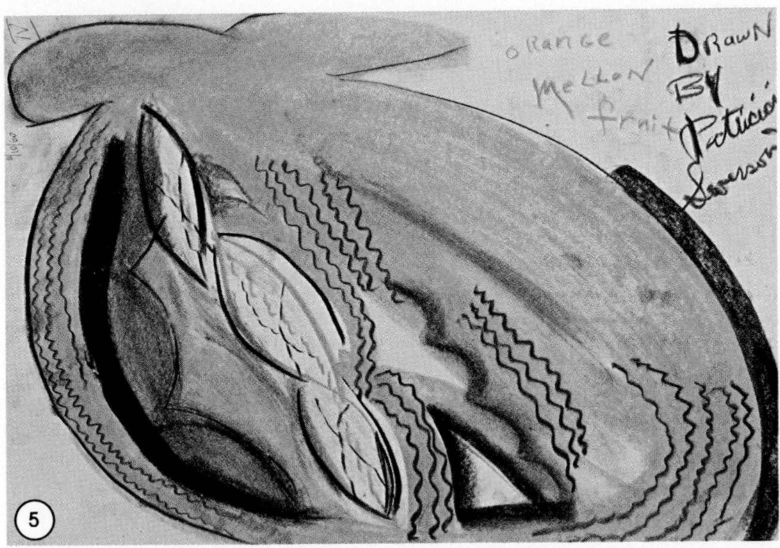

Drawing 6. Pat's anger with herself for her sexual preoccupation is here expressed by the pig, the mole/anus, and the phallic corn on the cob, all of which she identifies with. She makes explicit her unbridled self-fury with various inscriptions, and the picture as a whole represents the other side of her split personality.

The next and final drawing in this series, done in pencil on dark blue construction paper, was not included because it was too faint to be reproduced. Nonetheless, it warrants description. In this drawing Pat again communicates enormous guilt over her sexual feelings, penciling row after row of pigs with breasts, all presumably symbolic of her. Her choice of dark blue paper and pencil, which produced a drawing that was difficult to see, suggests that the anger of the preceding drawing has been replaced by depression and a forbidding "stillness," possibly indicating suicidal tendencies.

Drawing 7. This picture was drawn the day of a dance on the ward, and Pat was very excited. In the center Pat drew herself, using white for her face but omitting the rest of her body. By making her body "transparent," she conveys guilt for her sexual feelings.

To the left of the virginally white face is a black object, resembling the tip of a phallus, which Pat identified as "the black head of the queen's fool coming out from behind the window bars." The queen's fool recalls the red-faced figure in the first drawing and may again represent her stepfather. Her sexual fantasies about him have now become more direct and her guilt feelings correspondingly more pronounced, here suggested by the black window bars. The dancing couple in the drawing announces Pat's hopes for the evening.

Drawing 8. This is one of her many self-portraits, and here she renders a striking likeness of herself. As in most of her self-portraits, the female figure is much oversized. Here the body shape and facial expression convey her narcissism and sexual preoccupation. The hands held behind her back and the not altogether successful effort to erase "Lovely Girl" from the skirt communicate her guilt.

hoEG Pigs.
mole
CORN

6

Wednesday Nite
Dance
Samba Session
Samba
Dress in Gay clothes

7

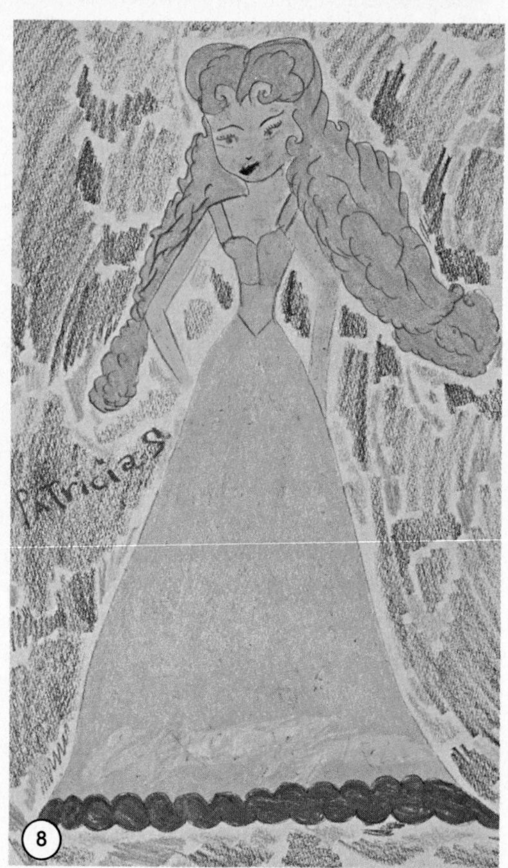
Patricia S

8

miss.
Tiny
9

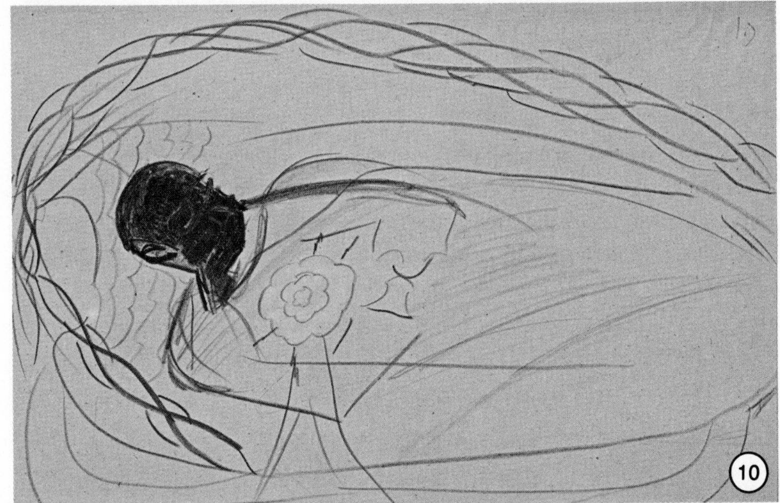
10

11

Drawing 9. The two portraits represent the dual sides of Pat's split personality. The girl on the left, whom Pat named Miss Tiny, wears what she called a "party dress," and her white hair suggests a bridal veil. Miss Tiny depicts the good girl Pat would like to be: desirable to men but still innocent. With fiery red hair, painted nails, and a black negligee, the girl on the right conveys Pat's other side and the accompanying anxiety her sexual feelings inspire. Several details of the drawing—the flamelike rendering of her hair, the black of her costume, the broken high heels, and the clawlike fingernails—suggest tendencies for self-mutilation and even suicide.

Drawing 10. The final drawings were completed after Pat had accompanied her mother to a funeral parlor to pay respects to a woman that Pat did not know. The heavy black pastel used in this drawing conveys her depression around the weekend experience. She blacks out the head of the deceased woman, perhaps identifying with her and not wishing to see herself in the coffin. This pictorial defense mechanism recalls the seventh drawing in which Pat dispensed with her conflicting sexual feelings by making the body in the portrait transparent, or nonexistent.

A second picture (not shown) was done in light pencil, suggesting that Pat's depression had begun to subside. The deceased woman's face was fully drawn since Pat was apparently then able to distinguish between herself and the woman. However, the title given the drawing, "Virgin Parlor-room," may indicate otherwise.

Drawing 11. These funeral parlor pictures show significant improvement in Pat's general mental condition. The depression evident in the previous two drawings was in fact an appropriate response to the experience. Here the depression has appropriately receded; as Pat integrates the experience in her mind, the corpse is diminished in size in the drawing and a great many other objects fill the page. The organization of the many symbols on a single sheet indicates that Pat has begun to introduce order into the realm of her conflicts.

The drawings of Harry

Harry is a 36-year-old veteran of the Korean War. The youngest of three brothers and two sisters, he experienced a difficult childhood and, feeling neglected amid his many siblings, constantly craved attention. The situation was further aggravated by the religious and personality differences of his alcoholic, Jewish father and domineering, Christian mother. At age 20, Harry was inducted into the Army, where his peers generally regarded him as a nuisance. In time, his bizarre behavior, frequent hallucinations, and ultimately his detachment from reality made hospitalization necessary.

Because of his musical talent, he was chosen drummer of the veterans hospital band. Later he met a bandleader of some note and was promised a position in the band after his discharge from the hospital. Subsequently he was rehospitalized several times but was always able in the interim to find work with a band. However, this working environment brought him in contact with drugs, and he eventually became a frequent user of marijuana. The following selection of projective drawings yields clear evidence of Harry's emotional conflicts.

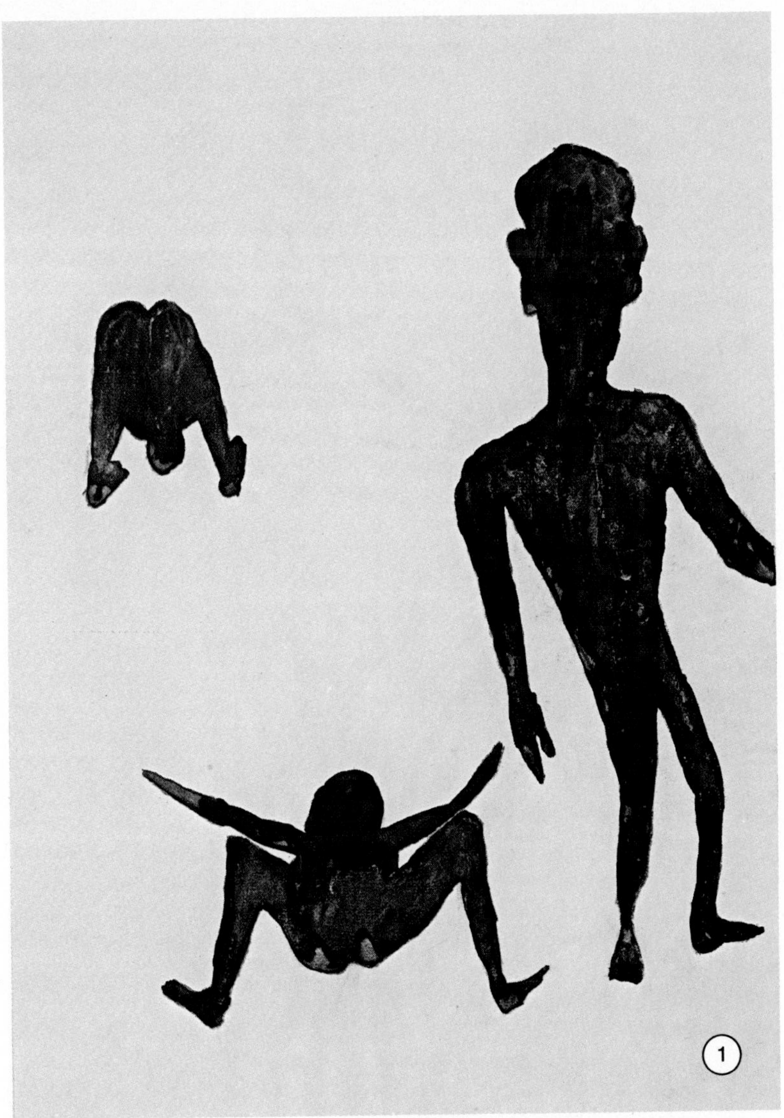

Drawing 1. The three figures in the drawing are doubtless all Harry and together reveal his conflicted self-image. The enlarged head of the figure on the right suggests his notions of grandeur and his intellectual aspirations, while the positions of the two other figures convey deep-seated self-contempt. The blacking out of the entire body in all three figures reiterates his low self-esteem.

Drawing 2. In a group meeting in the hospital ward Harry sees himself as the jester. He again depicts himself as a blackened silhouette in contrast to his vibrantly colored peers.

Drawing 3. In this drawing Harry seems to identify with the menacing figures of Hitler and Trotsky and with a two-faced jesting fool. In the lower left- and upper right-hand corners lurk Harry's angry mother and father (the latter wearing his usual bow tie). He himself bends over (behind the clock) as if to receive his just punishment, whether for generally being bad or for the

2

3

4

5

homosexual tendencies suggested by the crouching and bending positions he frequently adopts in the drawings. The parachutelike open umbrella and the balloon may signal his fervent wish to be saved from disaster, but the clock, reading half past twelve, indicates that time is running out.

Drawing 4. While Harry bends down in the lower left corner, various punishments appear to be meted out around him, further conveying his homosexual and now sadomasochistic tendencies. The book in the left corner may suggest Harry's intellectual aspirations.

Drawing 5. Harry now imagines himself in heaven, where he encounters his father. Having already been punished for his sins, Harry wears a halo; yet his body is blacked out, suggesting nagging doubt about whether he has been entirely cleansed of his misdeeds. With arms hanging by his sides and hands open-fingered and exaggerated in size, Harry communicates his feelings of complete incompetence.

Drawing 6. Here the patient introduces us to his large family. Mother and father stand before thronelike chairs, with Harry in between reduced to diminutive size. Harry's father is portrayed as weak and ineffective, his mother as robust and domineering.

Drawing 7. This second "family portrait" is even more revealing than the first. Harry's mother, essentially lacking female contours, is depicted as very masculine. Her skirt has the appearance of trousers; her hands clasped

near the genital region resemble a penis; and the elongated nose emphasizes her "masculinity." His father is now drawn with a dark brown face, recalling Harry's earlier blackened self-portraits and suggesting that he identifies with his father and likewise considers him weak and ineffective. The father's left hand held behind his back suggests his (or more directly, Harry's) feelings of guilt. Between mother and father lies a submissive dog, presumably Harry. This portrait of his parents together with the crouching positions of the children playing at left offer further evidence of Harry's homosexual tendency.

The preceding seven drawings were executed during Harry's initial hospitalization. He produced the following drawings while working at night as a drummer and visiting the treatment center during the day. These pictures express both his enthusiasm for his work as a musician and his anxiety about the dangers accompanying this kind of life—namely, that drinking, drugs, and bad company will inevitably lead to insanity or death.

Drawing 8. Apparently blaming his mother for his unhappiness, Harry draws his mother literally pushing him down. He also pictures himself crouching on all fours and being stabbed in the back, again suggesting his homosexuality. The clock, embraced by the crouching figure, reminds us that time is running out.

8

10

9

Drawing 9. Here the patient creates his own Holy Trinity: the good heart, the jester, and the bad boy. This trinity is juxtaposed with a Star-of-David-like form, perhaps signaling Harry's confusion about whether to identify with his Jewish father or Christian mother. The homosexual motif reappears with the dagger in his back, and this time he spills or reaches for a bottle of alcohol. The blood and the figure in black with back turned and a halo indicate suicidal tendencies.

Drawing 10. Harry's father now dominates the drawing, and his furrowed brow suggests worry about his son. The head in the lower right corner resembles a dagger with a red bow tie (a less forgiving representation of his father?).

Drawing 11. Harry's self-portrait conveys his continuing conflict and low self-esteem. He is unshaven, sloppily dressed, and surrounded by the devils of alcohol, drugs, and deprivation. He announces his split personality by dividing his several faces with two different colors; the figure with two knives for a head reiterates this message.

Drawing 12. In this drawing Harry summarizes his conflicts. He depicts his love for drumming in nightclubs and for the vices connected with this life, and at the same time conveys his anxiety that these vices may prove his undoing. He is tortured by feelings of guilt and shows us that while he smokes a reefer a Star of David disintegrates behind him.

Therapist: Who is the person with the light face here in the center?
Patient: That's me when I was little, and the red one on the side is me too, and the little black devil smoking. The ass in the middle is me too. Don't you see, I'm making fun of myself.
T: And the bent-over person; is that you too?
P: Sure, that's me too. You should recognize me by now.

Drawing 13. This drawing serves as a sort of epilogue. Harry seems to conclude that only death will offer peace to his soul, which emerges from behind his tombstone to ascend heavenward, leaving the devil behind. Another interpretation is that the year of death on the tombstone coincides with the year that Harry began therapy and might suggest that, whether consciously or unconsciously, Harry also views therapy as a means of salvation, since in therapy he may "put to rest" the dark, tormenting sides of himself.

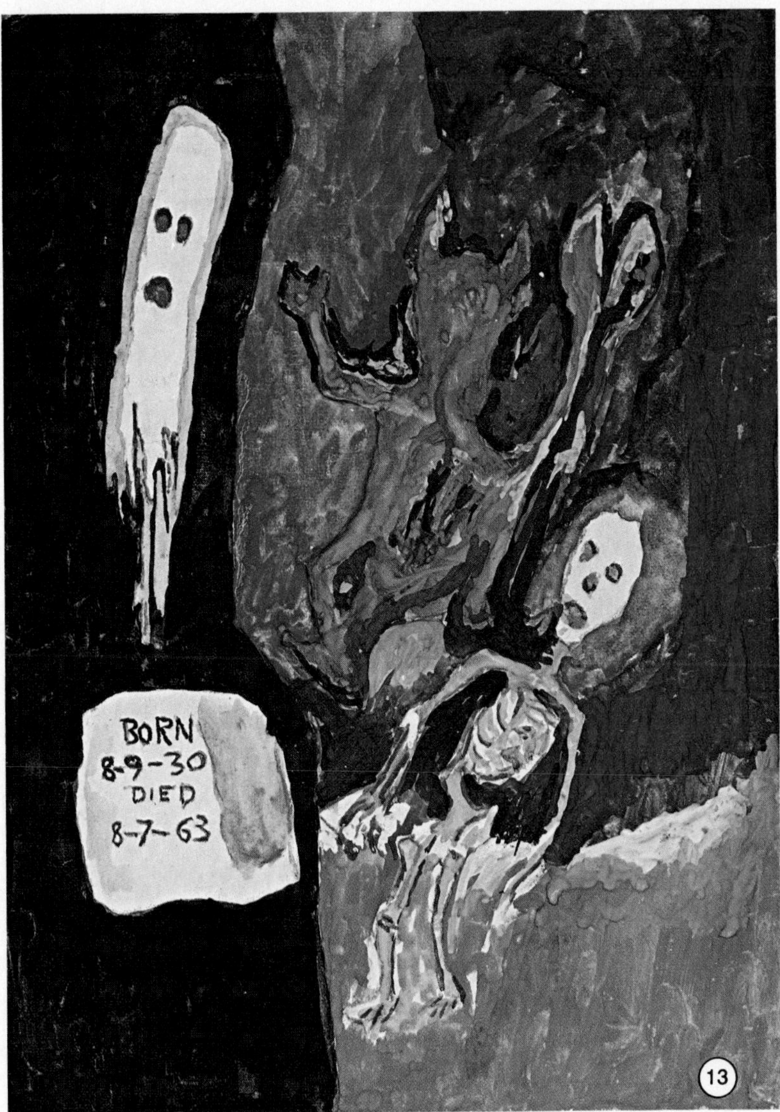

A Symposium:

The Nobel Prize for Physiology or Medicine

Alfred B. Nobel, who established the most prestigious scientific prize in the world, believed the main pathway to health was through science. Since 1901 Nobel Prizes have been awarded to individuals who have made important contributions in the broad area of biomedical sciences encompassed by the terms "physiology or medicine." How have these advances come about? This question is examined in detail in the first part of the symposium that appears on the following pages. Three Nobel laureates then describe the discovery process as it was for each of them and how medical science has changed as a result of their prizewinning work.

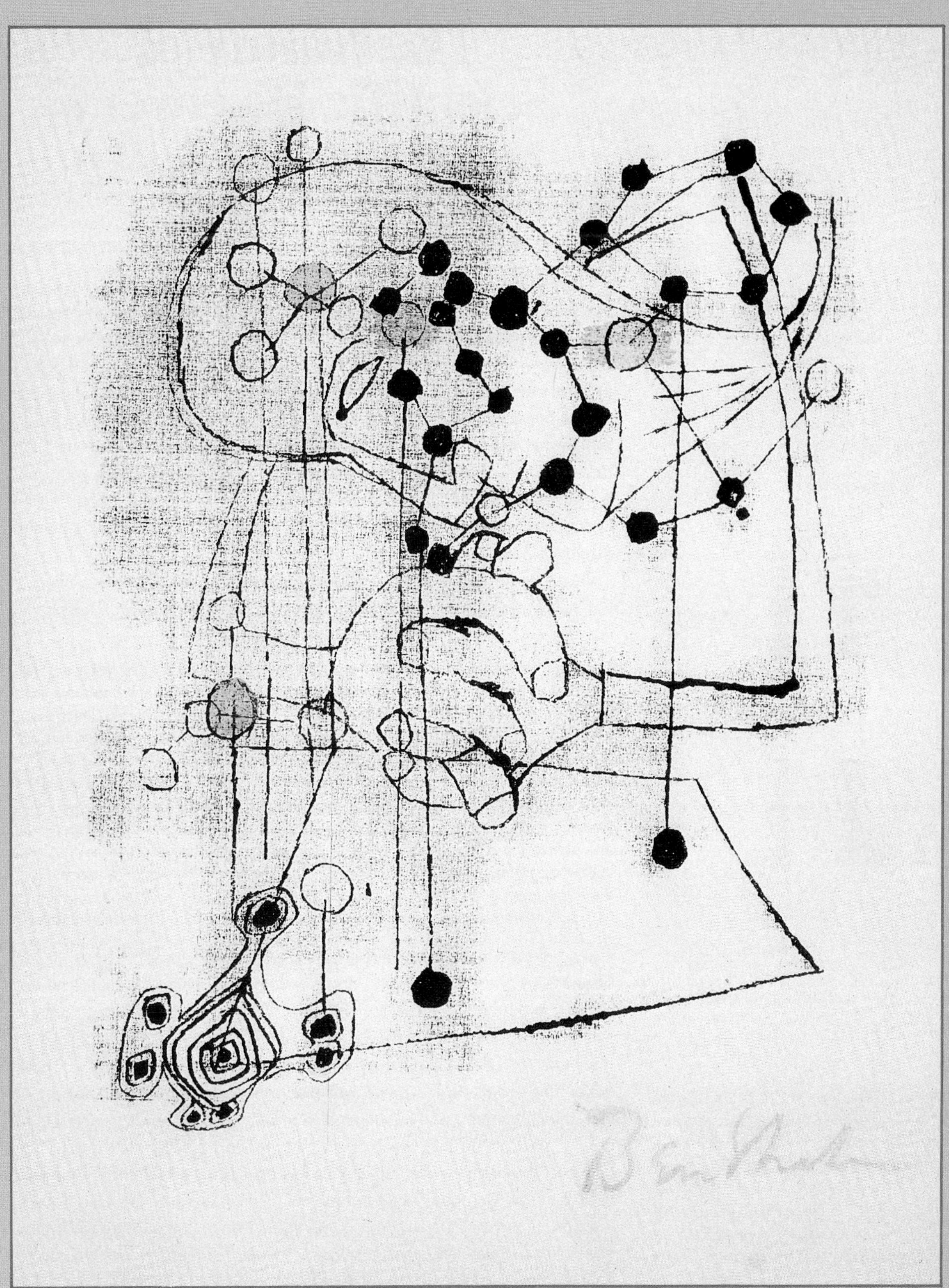

The Nature of Scientific Discovery

by Julius H. Comroe, Jr., M.D.

It seems contradictory that Alfred Bernhard Nobel, Swedish inventor of dynamite, was a pacifist who was later to endow the Nobel Prize for Peace. But the explanation is simple: although the public thought of dynamite as a destructive force manufactured for wartime purposes, Nobel thought of it as an explosive essential for peacetime projects such as mining, tunneling, and excavating; for constructing highways, railroads, and canals; and as a deterrent to war. On refusing an invitation to attend a peace conference he once remarked: "My factories may make an end of war sooner than your congresses. The day when two army corps can annihilate each other in one second, all civilized nations, it is to be hoped, will recoil from war and discharge their troops."

On his death, Nobel left his estate of approximately $9.2 million for international prizes for those who had "conferred the greatest benefit on mankind." His will, establishing the Nobel prizes, says, in part:

> The whole of my remaining realizable estate shall be dealt with in the following way: The capital shall be invested by my executors in safe securities and shall constitute a fund, the interest on which shall be annually distributed in the form of prizes to those who, during the preceding year, shall have conferred the greatest benefit on mankind. . . . one part to the person who shall have made the most important discovery or invention within the field of physics; one part to the person who shall have made the most important chemical discovery or improvement; one part to the person who shall have made the most important discovery within the domain of physiology or medicine; one part to the person who shall have produced in the field of literature the most outstanding work of an idealistic tendency; and one part to the person who shall have done the most or the best work for fraternity among nations, for the abolition or reduction of standing armies and for the holding and promotion of peace congresses.

Why did a pacifist give one prize for peace and three for work in the sciences of chemistry, physics, and physiology-medicine? Because he believed that the main pathway to health was through science, above all natural science, and, according to his belief, it was the conquests of natural science that were to create happiness for coming generations. "To spread knowledge," he wrote, "is to spread well-being. I mean general well-being, not individual prosperity, and with the arrival of such well-being will disappear the greater part of the evil which is an inheritance from the dark ages. The advance in scientific research and its ever-widening sphere stirs the hope in us that the microbes, those of the soul as well as the body, will gradually disappear, and that the only war humanity will wage in the future will be the one against these microbes." In brief, Alfred Bernhard Nobel wanted to abolish diseases of both the body and the soul.

Julius H. Comroe, Jr., M.D., *is Emeritus Director of the Cardiovascular Research Institute at the University of California at San Francisco.*

(Overleaf) "The Scientist" (1957), by Ben Shahn, Collection New Jersey State Museum, Trenton

Alfred Bernhard Nobel, inventor of explosives and ardent pacifist who left most of his fortune in trust to establish international awards, hoped that the only war humanity would wage in the future would be the war against diseases of the body and the soul. The gold medal for physiology or medicine, along with a diploma and a cash award, was first given in 1901. Portrait of Nobel by Emil Österman (1915).

Each Nobel Prize consists of a gold medal, a diploma, and a cash award. The first cash awards in 1901 were $42,000 each; over the years, as income from investments varied, the honorarium has varied from a low of $30,000 to a peak of $212,000 in 1980. It was not Nobel's wish to honor a distinguished older scientist at the end of a brilliant career. Instead he wanted to provide economic independence and stability for some younger scientists whose recent research promised equally important future achievements if they could devote themselves entirely to research. (This was an early form of the Career Investigator awards initiated several decades ago by the American Heart Association and American Cancer Society.) However, it turned out that between 1901 and 1972, although the mean age of all future Nobel laureates in physics, chemistry, and physiology-medicine was about 39 years at the time of their prizewinning research, their mean age at the time they *received* the award was about 52 years, *i.e.,* toward the end of an active career. Thus, in the last few decades, the honorarium in many cases no longer served Nobel's original purpose.

There were other awards for research before Nobel's, and a very large number of prizes established since then. But despite the abundance of annual prizes, medals, and other awards, the Nobel Prize remains the most prestigious scientific prize in the world. What has it done for science? What has it done for scientists? What has it done for public appreciation and understanding of science and scientists?

The aura of the Nobel Prize

Because the monetary award today is only a fraction of what it costs to support the work of a Nobel laureate for six months, we must look elsewhere for long-term benefits. Certainly one of these is stimulating the interest of high school and college students in science, although it is doubtful any student has deliberately elected to enter into a career in science with an all-or-nothing goal of winning the prize. However, it is quite likely that the wide publicity given to the prize once a year has impressed on students the

(Top, left and right) The Bettmann Archive, Inc.; (bottom) National Library of Medicine, Bethesda, Maryland

(Top left) The first winner of the Nobel Prize for Physiology or Medicine was Emil von Behring (in the dark coat) for his work on serum therapy and diphtheria. (Above) The first winner from the United States was Alexis Carrel (in 1912); Carrel, a Frenchman, conducted experiments at the Rockefeller Institute for Medical Research in New York on vascular sutures and the transplantation of blood vessels and organs. (Top right) The first woman to receive the Prize for Physiology or Medicine was Gerty Theresa Cori with her husband, Carl Ferdinand Cori; their 1947 award was for work on the catalytic conversion of glycogen.

respectability and prestige that can be associated with a scientific career whether one becomes a Nobel laureate or not.

Another benefit for science, at least in the United States, is the sense of achievement that Congress must have when the lion's share of the Nobel awards for physiology or medicine go to Americans; between 1950 and 1980, at least one American has been a laureate in 25 of these 31 years, and 44 of the 73 laureates (one, two, or three scientists may be honored in any one year) have been Americans. Congress must believe that its appropriations for science are supporting a very good program indeed.

Harriet Zuckerman has made a searching sociological study of living American Nobel laureates. Some have been able and helped, as Nobel intended, to continue research in their laboratories after the award, without interruption. For each of these, the award has eased the task of obtaining stable financial support and better facilities for his own work and those in his immediate group, and it has attracted outstanding pre- and post-doctoral fellows and visiting professors to work with him.

For some, the prize has given the laureate the courage or confidence to change fields of research, *e.g.,* from high energy physics to the biggest puzzle of all, the mechanisms by which the brain functions. However, most laureates have not been able to maintain their previous research schedules. The Nobel laureate, now indisputably an outstanding authority in his field of science, is usually swamped with requests to serve on high-level committees, task forces, advisory and editorial boards, with innumerable offers to write books, to appear on television programs, or to go on the lecture circuit. Even worse from Nobel's point of view, he may be offered and may accept a full-time high administrative position. One Nobel laureate, André Lwoff, who shared the Prize for Physiology or Medicine in 1965, speaking for himself and his associates, said: "We have gone from zero to the condition of movie stars. We have been submitted to what may be called an ordeal. We are not used to this sort of public life which has made it impossible for us to go on with our work. . . . Our lives are completely upset."

Even as early as 1903, Marie Curie wrote, just after the announcement of her first Nobel Prize for Physics: "We are inundated with letters and with visits from photographers and journalists. One would like to dig into the ground somewhere to find a little peace. . . . With much effort we have avoided the banquets people wanted to organize in our honor. We refuse with the energy of despair." Several months later, the impact of her award still had not diminished: "Our life has been altogether spoiled by honors and fame. . . . I hardly reply to these letters, but I lose time by reading them." Her husband, Pierre Curie, who shared the prize, was equally unhappy and wrote of longing for "a quiet place where lectures will be forbidden and newspapers persecuted."

At least one laureate found a simple way of finding a little peace. Francis Crick devised the following checklist to respond to a myriad of potential overtures:

Dr. Crick thanks you for your letter but regrets that he is unable to accept your kind invitation to:

send an autograph	help you in your project
provide a photograph	read your manuscript
cure your disease	deliver a lecture
be interviewed	attend a conference
talk on the radio	act as chairman
appear on TV	become an editor
speak after dinner	write a book
give a testimonial	accept an honorary degree

Jean-Loup Charmet, Paris

Along with the honor of the Nobel Prize comes the inevitable—and often unwelcome—fame. The Nobel laureate usually must forsake peace, quiet, and privacy. Here, Paul Ehrlich, who won the prize in 1908, is caricatured making his way through a mountain of unsolicited mail. The drawing by Jean Lefort is titled "Le Professeur Ehrlich, Conseiller intime du Kaiser et de pas mal d'autres" (intimate adviser to the kaiser and a great many others).

The temptations dangled before a laureate go far beyond performing in his own specialized field of competence. Some Nobel laureates, singly or as a group, argue for the development (or abandonment) of nuclear weapons, petition for the release of scientists imprisoned in foreign countries, plead for human rights in general, and lobby against mandatory teaching of divine creation in California science texts.

In a few cases, the award of the Nobel Prize has led the laureate to believe that he is now endowed with special talents in fields in which he has had no background or training—a special example of the Peter principle that "every employee tends to rise to his level of incompetence." Thus Linus Pauling, long a recognized genius in chemistry and a 1954 laureate in that field, has become (for the lay public) a shining knight using megadoses of vitamin C to attack the common cold, to slow or stop the advance of malignant tumors, and to solve complex problems of mental disorders. And William Shockley, one of the inventors of the transistor (for which he won the 1956 Nobel Prize for Physics), has become a highly vocal authority on inborn human intelligence and its allotment to various racial groups.

Knowledge of the Nobel awards each year reaches the reading public through front-page stories in every newspaper and in longer accounts of the scientific work involved in major publications such as *Time, Newsweek,* and the *New York Times.* This is significant because, although some Nobel Prizes for Physiology or Medicine have been awarded for discoveries immediately applicable to the prevention or cure of disease, over an 80-year period 85 of the prizes (including both entire and divided awards) were for work that led to better understanding of basic mechanisms by which the body, its organs, tissues, cells, and subcellular particles function, and only

Dan McCoy—Rainbow/TIRR

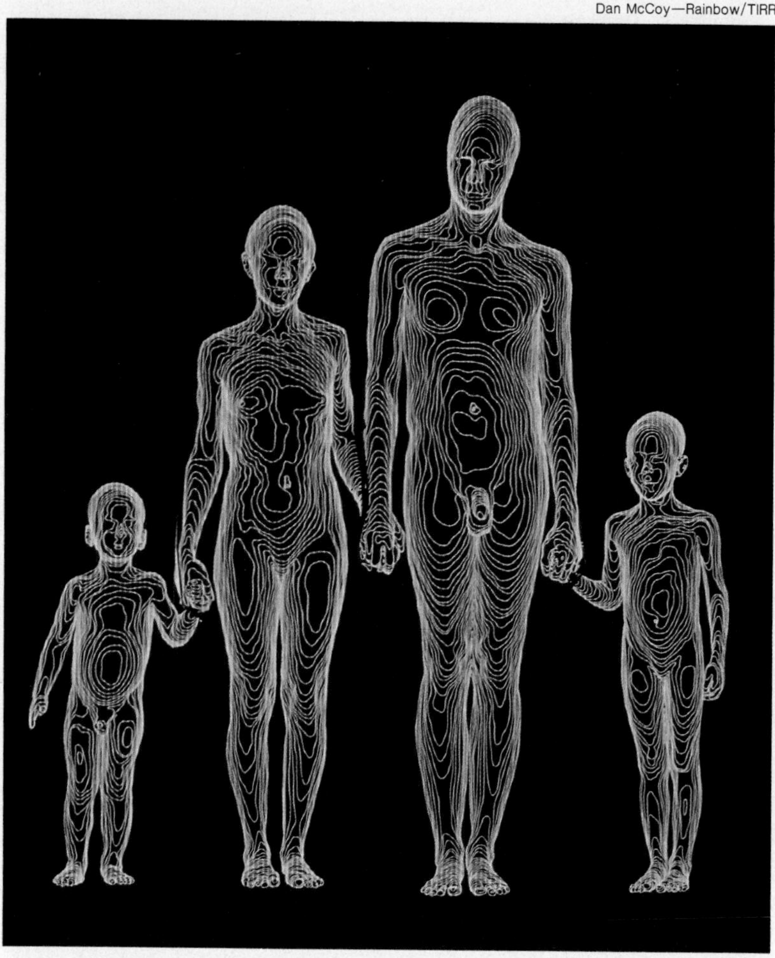

A vast majority of the Nobel Prizes for Physiology or Medicine have been for work that led to better understanding of basic mechanisms by which the body functions. Significantly few have been for discoveries immediately relevant to the diagnosis, prevention, or cure of disease.

27 awards were given for specific advances of immediate relevance to the prevention, diagnosis, or treatment of diseases (*e.g.,* the cause and treatment of diabetes or of pernicious anemia or the discovery of the bacterial causes of disease and use of chemotherapeutic drugs and antibiotics to cure them). And since 1953, 50 awards have been given for work dealing with basic mechanisms and only 6 have been given for specific treatment or diagnosis of disease. In a sense then, the Nobel Prize has become the *basic-science award* for medicine. As Lord Ritchie-Calder has said, it is for "those that made it *possible* rather than for those that made it happen." So the public, through its news media, learns once a year to respect scientific achievements that have not yet made their way to the neighborhood drugstore and seem to have no direct immediate relevance to public health.

And yet, the Nobel Prize, although it has emphasized the importance of basic discoveries underlying modern advances, has given the public an incomplete picture of how scientific advance usually occurs. The Prize for Physiology or Medicine has presented to the public one or two or three heroes each year—superstars—and the public has come to equate one great advance with one or two individuals. Actually, the lifetime work of hundreds of other scientists working in many fields (some unrelated to physiology or medicine) over decades or centuries has been essential to provide the underpinning for work that won the prize some years later.

Philip Siekevitz, professor of biochemistry at Rockefeller University, in a letter to *Science* magazine in 1978, expressed himself forcefully on the incomplete story that accounts of the prizes, especially recently created ones, give to the public: "What is implied is that gains in scientific knowledge are primarily achieved by very exceptional individuals, without any input from the tens whose work in the same field has led to a temporarily final formulation. . . . Thus, the General Motors prizes are to be given for recent published work, as if all that has gone before can be ignored, and only the final step is to be recognized by the huge monetary award."

Research on research

In the early 1970s, my colleague, Robert Dripps, vice-president for health affairs at the University of Pennsylvania, then on sabbatical leave in San Francisco, and I decided it was time for both the public and scientists themselves to learn how great discoveries in medicine and surgery have actually come about. (Dripps died in 1973 and I completed the project over the next four years.) Our interest in this matter was not generated by a debate over the benefits to mankind that flowed from the Nobel Prize or other prizes. It was initiated by Pres. Lyndon Johnson's 1966 remarks: "Presidents," he said, "need to show more interest in what the specific results of research are—in their lifetime, and in their administration. A great deal of *basic* research has been done . . . but I think the time has come to zero in on the targets—by trying to get our knowledge fully applied . . . *We must make sure that no lifesaving discovery is locked up in the laboratory.*" (Italics added.)

The president's words popularized a whole new set of terms in biomedical research: research in the service of man; relevant research; strategy for the cure of disease; targeted research; mission-oriented research; disease-oriented research; programmatic research; commission-initiated research; contract-supported research; and payoff research. These phrases had a great impact on Congress and led to a sharp upsurge in commission-initiated research (as opposed to research initiated by individual scientists), and to encouragement of applied research and development, supported by contracts from the National Institutes of Health (NIH).

Because these important decisions on national biomedical science policy were based mainly on anecdotes, we decided that scientists ought to apply scientific methods to the issue of how best to promote discoveries in medicine. This meant doing serious "research on research." This required intensive study of a broad field and not the reciting of a few "for instances" that we could choose to support any preconceived ideas. We selected the broad field of advances in cardiovascular-pulmonary diseases because collectively these conditions were (and still are) responsible for more than half the deaths in the United States each year. To avoid personal bias, physicians and surgeons in no way connected with our study had to select for us the most important advances in this field that were responsible for early diagnosis, better treatment, or complete cure or prevention of human cardiovascular-pulmonary disease. They did; their "top ten" were:

(Left) The Bettmann Archive, Inc.; (right) Dan McCoy—Rainbow

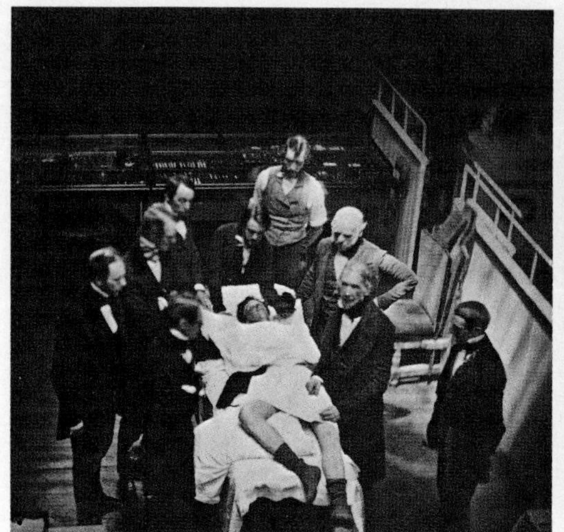

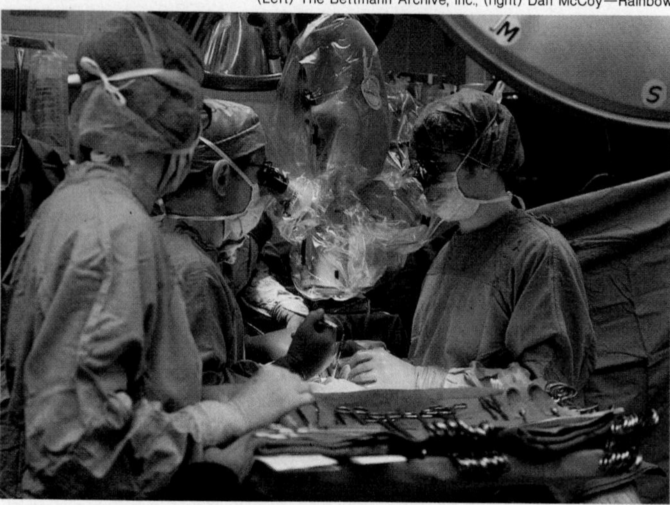

General anesthesia was first employed in 1846. The picture above is a reenactment of the initial ether anesthesia demonstration at Massachusetts General Hospital in Boston. But it was not until the early 1950s that the first successful open-heart operation was performed. Precise visualization of cardiac chambers, a heart-lung machine, and a nontoxic anticoagulant (to prevent clotting of blood) are just a few of the developments that had to occur before complex heart procedures could be routinely performed.

1. cardiac surgery (including open-heart repair of congenital defects and replacements of diseased valves);
2. vascular surgery (including repair or bypass of obstructions or other diseases of the aorta and coronary, cerebral, renal, and limb arteries);
3. drug treatment of high blood pressure;
4. medical treatment of coronary insufficiency (myocardial ischemia; heart attack);
5. cardiac resuscitation (manual and electrical) and implanting cardiac pacemakers in patients with cardiac arrest, slow hearts, or serious abnormal rhythms;
6. oral diuretics (in treatment of patients with congestive heart failure or high blood pressure);
7. intensive cardiovascular and respiratory care units (including those for postoperative care, coronary care, respiratory failure, and disorders of newborns);
8. chemotherapy and antibiotics (including prevention of acute rheumatic fever and treatment of tuberculosis, pneumonias, and cardiovascular syphilis);
9. new diagnostic methods (for earlier and more accurate diagnosis of disease of cardiovascular and pulmonary-respiratory systems); and
10. prevention of poliomyelitis (especially of respiratory paralysis due to polio).

With these advances as our starting point, we then worked backward (again with the help of hundreds of consultants) to identify what had to be learned to make each of the top ten a reality. For each of these we first selected essential "bodies of knowledge" that had to be developed before the clinical advance could reach its present state of achievement. Let us consider, as an example, the first of the ten, cardiac surgery.

When general anesthesia was first put to use in 1846, the practice of surgery expanded in many directions, except for operations on the heart and lungs. Cardiac surgery did not take off until almost 100 years later, and surgeon John Gibbon did not perform the first successful open-heart operation that required complete cardiopulmonary bypass apparatus until 107 years after the first use of ether anesthesia. What held back cardiac surgery? What had to be known before a surgeon could predictably and successfully repair cardiac defects? First of all, the surgeon required precise preoperative diagnosis in every patient whose heart needed repair. That required selective visualization of the cardiac chambers by X-rays after injection of a radiopaque liquid into the circulation. This, in turn, required the earlier discovery of cardiac catheterization and the still earlier discovery of X-rays. But the surgeon also needed an artificial, outside-the-body heart-lung apparatus (pump-oxygenator) to take over the function of the patient's heart and lungs while he stopped the patient's heart in order to open and repair it. A pump required material and a design that would not damage blood; an oxygenator required basic knowledge of the exchange of oxygen and carbon dioxide between gas and blood. However, even a perfect pump-oxygenator would be useless if the blood in it clotted. Thus, the cardiac surgeon had to await the discovery and purification of a potent, nontoxic anticoagulant—heparin, which became commercially available in 1934.

These are just a few examples; obviously, the cardiac surgeon needed many more essential bodies of knowledge. Table I lists 24 such that we believed he needed before he could perform open-heart surgery with confidence that the results would be reproducibly satisfactory. Some, such as antibiotics, are so commonplace today that we forget that even they once had to be discovered. For all ten advances, we identified 137 essential bodies of knowledge.

The roots of great discoveries

It soon became apparent to us that the knowledge essential for these advances had come over decades or centuries from the lifetime work of many thousands of scientists. It was clearly impossible for us to read tens of thousands of their publications, published in many languages, to determine why and how the research of each was done. To narrow the field, we examined about 6,000 published articles and of these identified about 3,400 specific scientific reports that were particularly important to the development of the 137 essential bodies of knowledge. We arranged these chronologically in tables. Table II, which shows the development of electrocardiography, is one example. It lists 47 reports from scientists in 14 countries, whose work spanned three centuries. Ten of these reports are "key articles" and one of the ten won the Nobel Prize for Willem Einthoven of Holland. Without the whole list, however, some might consider that Einthoven invented the electrocardiograph in 1903 in its present form without help from those who preceded or followed him. If there is a serious defect in our story, it is that we did not list hundreds of scientists who contributed something that hastened the discovery of electricity and "animal electricity," that helped to move us from complete ignorance toward full knowledge in that field.

Another example is catheterization of the heart and arteries of man, now an everyday routine test. Physicians and patients think of it only in terms of a patient lying on a hard table with a long plastic tube in his heart. What a cardiac catheterization laboratory actually needs and uses besides a patient, a catheter, a cardiologist, and a nurse is shown in Figure 1. The public forgets or was not told that cardiac catheterization is not a procedure that stands alone; its use depends on many advances in the basic sciences, in clinical investigation, in engineering, and in industrial development.

The first conclusion from our study was that for each of our 137 bodies of knowledge, whether it dealt with poliomyelitis or penicillin, scientists earlier and later than *the* discoverer have always been essential to his discovery and its full development. This is, of course, contrary to the notion perpetuat-

Table I: **Essential bodies of knowledge required for successful open-heart surgery**

preoperative diagnosis of cardiac defects
electrocardiography, echocardiography, and other noninvasive tests
cardiac catheterization
selective angiocardiography (X-ray pictures of the heart and arteries)

preoperative care and preparation
transfusions, blood groups, and typing; blood preservation; separation of blood into numerous components
intravenous infusions; intravenous nutrition
management of infection
assessment of function of the heart, lungs, brain, kidneys, and liver

intraoperative management
asepsis and antisepsis
monitoring EKG; blood pressure; heart rate; blood O_2, CO_2, and acidity; and electroencephalogram
anesthesia and drugs that relax body muscles
survival of bloodless organs at normal and low temperatures
ventilation of open thorax
anticoagulants
pump-oxygenator (outside-the-body heart-lung machine)
elective cardiac arrest; conversion of abnormal rhythms to normal
transfusions; intravenous fluid and salts; acid-base balance
surgical instruments and materials
surgical techniques and operations

postoperative care
relief of pain
general principles of intensive care
chemotherapy and antibiotics
management of postoperative complications
management of congestive heart failure
wound healing

Table II: **Chronological events in the development of electrocardiography**

year	scientist	country	discovery
BC	ancients	—	early manifestations of electricity: electric fish, rubbed amber, lodestone, terrestrial lightning
1660	von Guericke	Holland	first electricity machine (friction of glass and hand)
1745	von Kleist	Pomerania	charge from electricity machine stored in glass bottle and delivered as static electric shock
1745–1750	van Musschenbroek	Holland	electricity stored in Leyden jar; shocks killed small animals
1752	*Franklin	American colonies	kite and key used to charge Leyden jar from lightning; identity of lightning and electricity proved
1756–1757	Caldani	Italy	muscle contracts when it receives discharge from Leyden jar
1780–1786	*Galvani	Italy	stimulation of nerve by Leyden jar and by "electricity machine" caused identical muscle contraction; concept of animal electricity related to contact of dissimilar metal
1791–1794	*Galvani	Italy	contraction of heart muscle produced by discharge from electric eel; contraction of muscle caused by injury to outer membrane
1800	Volta	Italy	electricity generated by dissimilar metals; voltaic pile or battery
1839	Purkinje	Prussia	Purkinje's fibers exist in the cardiac ventricles
1842	*Matteucci	Italy	muscle contracts if its nerve is laid across another contracting muscle
1843	DuBois-Reymond	Germany	described "action current" in nerve as well as muscle
1852	Stannius	Germany	tied ligatures at different points in heart muscle to demonstrate specific conduction paths of impulse
1856	Kölliker & Müller	Germany	frog muscle contraction used as indicator of cardiac currents
1875	Lippmann	France	devised capillary electrometer, forerunner of EKG
1876	Marey	France	described refractory period in early cardiac systole
1878	Engelmann	Holland	studied electrical excitation of isolated frog heart
1879–1880	*Burdon-Sanderson & Page	England	first EKG in intact animals (frogs)
1883	Gaskell	England	sequence of contraction from sinus venosus to atria to ventricles (in frogs)
1887	*Waller	France & England	first human EKG using Lippmann's capillary electrometer
1887	McWilliam	Scotland	noted fibrillary contractions of the heart
1893	*His	Germany	described bundle of fibers that transmit impulses to ventricular muscle
1893	Kent	England	described atrioventricular bundle
1897	Ader	France	used thread or string galvanometer
1903	*Einthoven	Holland	devised sensitive string galvanometer and camera for measuring human EKG and equipment for transmitting EKG signals to a distant galvanometer
1906	Tawara	Japan & Germany	described atrioventricular node

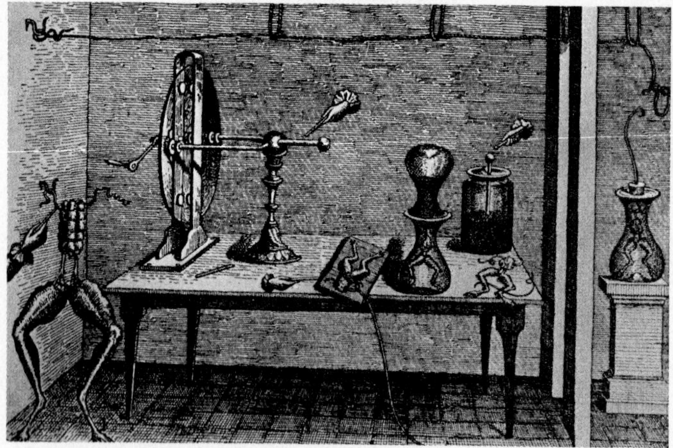

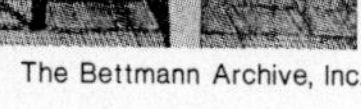

The Bettmann Archive, Inc.

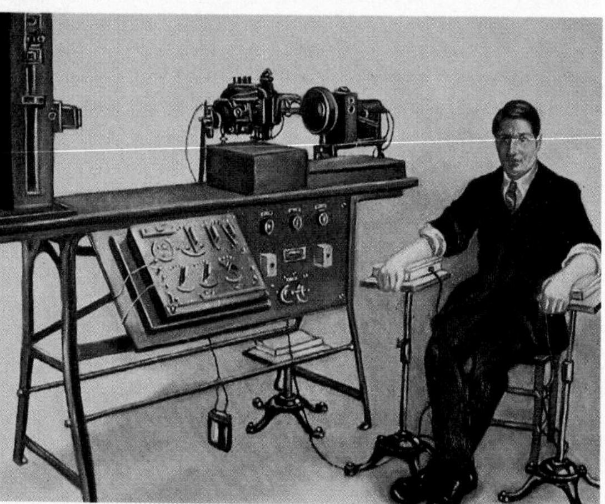

The Bettmann Archive, Inc.

year	scientist	country	discovery
1907	Keith & Flack	England	described cardiac pacemaker (sinoatrial node) in mammals
1908	Mackenzie	Scotland	used polygraph to record venous pulse and cardiac rhythm
1909–1920	*Lewis	England	EKG and arrhythmias in man
1913	Einthoven, Fahr & deWaart	Holland	equilateral triangle theory of EKG
1914	Garrey	USA	mechanisms of cardiac flutter and fibrillation
1915	Lewis & Rothschild	England	excitation wave in dog heart
1918	Smith	USA	EKG changes occurring after ligating branch of a coronary artery (in dogs)
1926	Rothberger	Germany	studied arrhythmias in man
1927	*Craib	England	basis for modern EKG theory
1927	Wenckebach & Winterberg	Germany	studied arrhythmias in man
1930	Craib	England	study of electrical field surrounding heart muscle
1930	*Wilson	USA	laws of distribution of potential differences in solid conductors; modern theory of EKG
1939	*Hodgkin & Huxley	England	electric potential differences recorded across membrane of giant nerve of squid
1946	*Graham & Gerard	USA	first measurement of potential difference between inside and outside of muscle fibers using fine intracellular microelectrodes
1949	Ling & Gerard		
1949	Coraboeuf & Weidmann	Switzerland	intracellular electrode to record mammalian cardiac potentials
1951	*Draper & Weidmann	Australia & Switzerland	intracellular electrode used to measure transmembrane potentials of heart muscle cells
1958	Alanís, González & López	Mexico	electrical activity of bundle of His
1960	Giraud, Puech, & Latour	France	electrical activity of bundle of His in man
1967–1968	*Scherlag, Kosowsky & Damato *Scherlag, Helfant & Damato	USA	recording from bundle of His by cardiac catheter in man
1967	Watson, Emslie-Smith & Lowe	Scotland	recording from bundle of His in patient undergoing cardiac catheterization
1972	Scherlag, Samet & Helfant	USA	critical evaluation of the usefulness and limitations of the His bundle EKG in man

*indicates "key discovery"

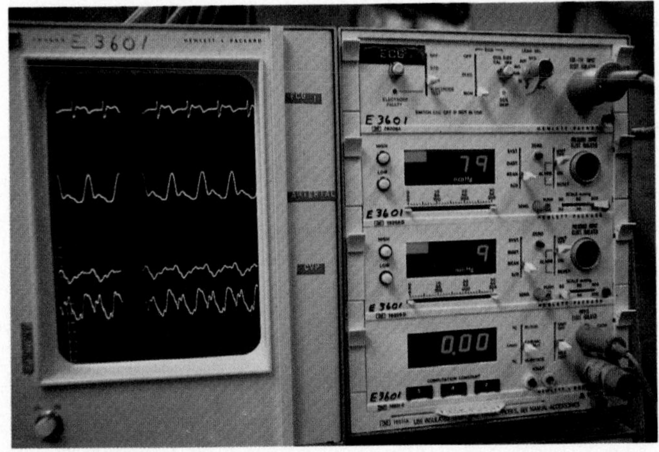

Dan McCoy—Rainbow

The computerized EKG machine (right) is widely used in medicine today as a diagnostic instrument, as a monitor during heart surgery, and in the intensive treatment of coronary patients. It would not have been possible if in the late 1700s Luigi Galvani had not experimented with Leyden jars (devices that stored static electricity) and an electrostatic machine to stimulate the muscles of frogs (left), or if Willem Einthoven (center) had not developed a sensitive string galvanometer and camera device in 1903 for measuring electric properties of the human heart.

Figure 1

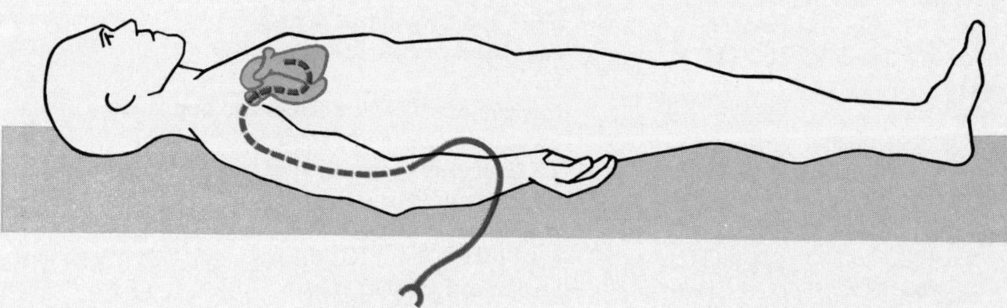

catheters

1. Dacron and nylon weave
2. radiopaque cloth woven
3. opaque synthetic extruded tubes for catheters
4. double lumen, balloon tipped
5. Dotter-Lucas, Rashkind, Swan-Ganz
6. spring-wire guides
7. Cournand-type needle for percutaneous insertion
8. platinum tip catheters for H_2 or ascorbate curves
9. pacing catheters
10. phonocardiographic catheters
11. catheter tip pressure transducer
12. fiber optic catheter

drugs and chemicals

1. sedatives
2. local and general anesthetics
3. oxygen (with tubing, masks, valves, tanks)
4. antiarrhythmic drugs
5. indocyanine green for dye dilution curves
6. radiopaque contrast media
7. sterile solutions
8. antibiotics
9. heparin
10. acetylcholine
11. isoproterenol

X-ray

1. X-ray tube
2. electronics for pulsing
3. image intensifier
4. television camera and monitor
5. video tape recorder
6. disc-type video storage
7. biplane cine camera
8. high contrast cine film
9. projector for still and motion pictures
10. timing of X-ray pulses and cine exposure
11. lead sheets and aprons for protection

biochemistry laboratory

1. macro and micro blood-gas analyzers
2. apparatus for measuring blood pH, P_{CO_2}, P_{O_2} at body temperature
3. gas analyzer
4. spectrophotometer for measuring abnormal Hb
5. densitometer

sterile equipment

1. steam sterilizer
2. ethylene oxide gas sterilization
3. benzalkonium and cyanide solutions
4. sterile brushes, tapes, etc.
5. scrub and preparation solutions

electronic instruments

1. multichannel recorder
2. transducers and amplifiers for EKG, blood pressure, phonocardiograph, polarograph, and heart rate
3. CRO for monitoring
4. FM tape recorder and tape
5. thermistor probe
6. oximeter
7. densitometer
8. defibrillator
9. external and internal pacemaker

calculators

1. slide rule
2. calculator
3. computer

special items

1. microsyringes
2. pressure injector for angiography, timed to match cardiac cycle
3. respiratory valves and spirometers
4. Douglas bags for collecting gas
5. gas sample collectors
6. disposable syringes, stopcocks, and plastic tubes
7. surgical instruments for macro and micro dissection
8. constant withdrawal-infusion syringe

ed by U.S. media—the "one man = one discovery" concept, the superstar concept (*e.g.*, Jonas Salk = polio vaccine). Actually, the Swedes awarded the Nobel Prize to those who made polio vaccine *possible* (John Enders, Thomas Weller, and Frederick Robbins) rather than to those who made it *happen* (Salk and Albert Sabin). In 1969 Robert Berliner, now dean of Yale University School of Medicine, commented:

> Above all we have an enormous job of education to do. We need far more general understanding of how science progresses, of the tortuous paths from distant, unrelated points of departure that converge to bring us where we are. When the press conference is held to announce the current achievement, we need less emphasis on wild speculation about unforeseeable applications and far more on the roots in the

past. We need emphasis not only on the giants on whose shoulders we have stood, but on the contributions of unsung investigators too numerous to mention. We should have the equivalent of a brief 'commercial' before each therapeutic measure, each dose of vaccine, each effective drug: 'This is made possible by the research of Whozis and So and So; we trust you will find it effective and remember what research has done for you.'

Basic versus applied research

The next step for Dripps and me was to determine the relative importance of basic research and of applied research and development in advancing medical science. First we had to consider the question: What is basic research? (sometimes called pure research, fundamental research, or knowledge acquired for its own sake). Because we knew in 1973 that definitions varied, we defined our meaning precisely to be sure that our readers knew what we meant. We classified research as *basic* when the investigator, in addition to observing, describing, and measuring, attempted to determine the *mechanisms* responsible for the observed effects. Our definition means that basic research can be on healthy or sick men, on animals, tissues, cells, or subcellular components. Our definition differs from the concept of some laymen and scientists that research is more and more basic when the unit investigated is smaller and smaller. Further, our definition says that work on small units, such as cells, is *not* "basic" if it is purely descriptive and does

Table III: **Types of research—663 key articles**

clinical advance	basic research not clinically oriented	basic research clinically oriented	other clinically oriented studies	development or engineering for research use	development or engineering for clinical use or other use	review and synthesis	total
cardiac surgery	38	29	24	4	15	0	110
vascular surgery	9	9	14	1	21	3	57
treatment of high blood pressure	53	19	21	0	0	3	96
coronary insufficiency	24	21	22	1	4	1	73
cardiac resuscitation, etc.	18	11	9	0	6	0	44
oral diuretics	25	13	6	0	0	1	45
intensive care	5	9	11	3	10	4	42
antibiotics	26	22	24	0	2	1	75
new diagnostic tests	67	25	8	22	28	2	152
poliomyelitis	4	13	4	1	0	0	22
total	269	171	143	32	86	15	716
% of total	37.6	23.9	20.0	4.5	12.0	2.1	
	← 61.5 →						

Note: The total number of entries in the six categories (716) exceeds the total in Table IV by 53 entries. This is because some key articles fit into more than one category, particularly when articles reporting development of new apparatus also reported research using it.

not lead to better understanding of mechanisms. Our definition of basic research steers clear of whether the research was "investigator-initiated" or "commission-initiated," whether "undirected" or "directed," whether disease-oriented or not, whether supported by grant or by contract, because in our opinion, who *initiated, directed,* or *supported* the research has nothing to do with whether it is *basic*.

Having settled on this definition, we analyzed each of 663 key articles to determine how each investigator carried out his research. We classified these in six categories. (*See* Table III.) The finding that 61.5% of our key articles reported basic work dealing with mechanisms and that other types of research and applications combined accounted for 38.5% of the key articles strongly supports the Nobel policy of recognizing the basic discoveries that preceded and led to clinical applications.

The next step in our "research on research" was to determine whether the key research was clinically oriented. Studies were labeled clinically oriented if the author anywhere in his paper (excluding speculation at the end of his article) mentioned even briefly an interest in diagnosis, treatment, or prevention of a clinical disorder or in explaining the basic mechanisms of a sign or symptom of the disease itself. We classified such work as clinically oriented even if this research was performed entirely on animals, tissues, cells, or subcellular particles.

Research is *not* clinically oriented if the authors in their key article never stated or suggested that their research might have any direct or indirect bearing on a clinical disorder of man, though their work later helped to clarify some aspect of it and even though man was the subject of their research.

The results of classifying the 663 key articles into these two categories are shown in Table IV. Two points deserve emphasis. The first is that our data provide justification for our basic decision to reject the use of conclusions drawn from single case studies (no matter how carefully the studies were done and how persuasively the conclusions were presented) and for our conviction that national biomedical science policy must be based on analysis of a very large segment of biomedical science. Someone looking for evidence to justify *any* position on the support of research can get it by

Table IV: **Orientation of key articles**

clinical advance	clinically oriented	*not* clinically oriented	total	% of total *not* clinically oriented
cardiac surgery	67	40	107	37.4
vascular surgery	42	8	50	16.0
treatment of high blood pressure	39	55	94	58.5
coronary insufficiency	46	24	70	34.3
cardiac resuscitation, etc.	24	18	42	42.9
oral diuretics	19	26	45	57.8
intensive care	32	7	39	17.9
antibiotics	47	27	74	36.5
new diagnostic tests	53	67	120	55.8
poliomyelitis	18	4	22	18.2
total	387	276	663	41.6

(Top) From Eadweard Muybridge, *Animal Locomotion,* 1887, plate 596; photograph, International Museum of Photography at George Eastman House, Rochester, New York; (bottom) The New York Academy of Medicine

quoting only the "right" clinical advance in Table IV as his "for instance." If one picks vascular surgery, intensive care, or poliomyelitis, one can "prove" that clinically oriented research deserves major support; if one selects hypertension or oral diuretics or new diagnostic tests, one can "prove" that research *not* clinically oriented deserves major support.

The second point is that our study of *all* 663 key articles in *all* of the top ten advances showed that 41.6% of them were *not* clinically oriented; at the time of the research, the investigators expressed no interest in solving a clinical problem, although later their work proved to be essential for a clinical advance. This is a very high percentage considering that we were studying discovery in medicine and surgery. It is high in part because of scientific discoveries made by medical scientists solely for the sake of knowledge and in part because of the later application to medicine of research in chemistry, physics, radioactivity, agriculture, biology, botany, zoology, and marine biology. Some examples of key research done with no thought of use in medicine are as follows:

One of the most powerful and versatile analytic methods used in clinical medicine is chromatography. But its first use was in pure science. Mikhail S. Tswett (Tsvet), a Russian botanist, devised it as a way to separate and identify the constituents of green leaves; he extracted them with petrol ether and poured the mixture over a vertical column of calcium carbonate. The main constituents, in this case pigments (green chlorophyll and yellow carotenoids), moved at different rates and so separated as distinct color bands; hence the term chromatogram. Tswett had no thought of using his method for clinical diagnosis.

When André Cournand and Dickinson Richards passed a catheter into the heart of man, it was not to develop a new method of diagnosing congenital or acquired heart disease. They were primarily pulmonary physiologists who wanted to learn more about a basic physiologic problem of how blood and air are distributed to air sacs of lungs. To do that, they first needed to

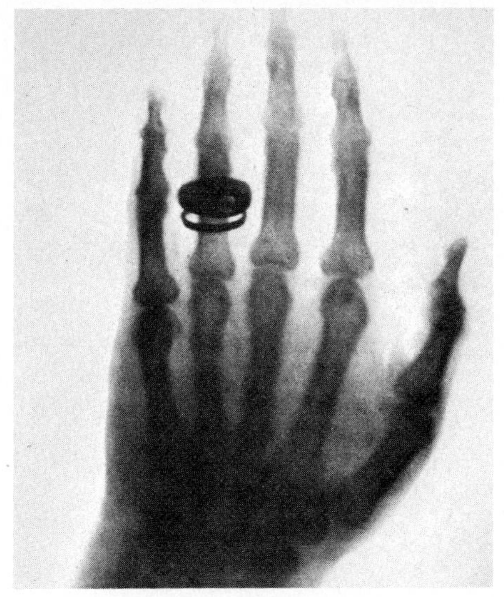

Many advances in diagnosing disease came about as a result of research done with no thought of application to medicine. Eadweard Muybridge had no thought of inventing a device to take motion pictures of X-rays of the heart; all he wanted to do was to discover if, when a horse trotted at full speed, all four of its hoofs were ever off the ground at the same time?—and for that, he needed motion pictures. Wilhelm Röntgen had no thought whatever of diagnosing disease when he discovered X-rays. The picture of his wife's hand was one of his first radiographic images. He also irradiated paper, wood, and aluminum.

measure the oxygen content of mixed venous blood in the right atrium of the heart. A few years later, Richard Bing in Baltimore, Lewis Dexter in Boston, and James Warren in Atlanta began to use the cardiac catheter to diagnose specific defects in patients with congenital cardiac disease.

Naval researchers had no thought of devising echocardiograms to diagnose cardiac deformities when they used sonar to detect submarines under water. Donald Griffin had no thought of measuring the size of a patient's heart when he studied echolocation in bats, the process that allows them, flying at top speed in pitch-black caves, to catch tiny insects also flying at top speed.

When Karl Landsteiner discovered blood groups, it was not part of a program to make blood transfusions safe; he was investigating basic problems in immunology.

When L. F. Shackell in 1909 developed the technique of freeze-drying, it was not to preserve penicillin without loss of potency (there *was* no penicillin) or to preserve plasma and its fractions (there *were* none in 1909). He was working in a school of agriculture, studying a basic problem of the water content of liver and muscle of steers and needed a better method to prevent loss of water during his measurements.

When Jay McLean, a medical student working in the physiologic laboratory at Johns Hopkins Medical School, discovered heparin, he was working on a basic problem (assigned to him by his professor, William Howell) on the biochemistry of factors favoring coagulation of blood; neither he nor Howell had an anticoagulant in mind. Several decades later, heparin was produced commercially and proved to be essential for use of the pump-oxygenator during cardiac surgery.

One of the early blood pumps was the roller pump that Michael De Bakey used in 1934 for transfusing blood—obviously a clinically oriented effort. However, six years earlier two English physiologists, William Bayliss and E. A. Müller, described the same roller pump, which they turned over to C. F. Palmer, Ltd., for manufacture. Bayliss was a cardiovascular physiologist who

©William E. Ferguson

When Cyril A. Clarke, a collector and amateur breeder of butterflies, studied variations in the color of butterfly wings, he had no idea it would lead to the prevention of Rh blood disease in the human fetus.

used his pump for laboratory experiments and not for transfusions in man. The first patented "roller pump" (devised by Rufus Porter and J. D. Bradley in 1855) was in part clinically oriented becase the inventors suggested it might be useful in pumping patients' stomachs and in giving injections.

The fallibility of wise men

Many who are closely concerned with national science policy rather than actively engaged in research believe that research can be greatly accelerated by the generous use and financing of task forces and commissions who "look 5 to 10 years ahead and recommend where research money will do the most good." There has been no systematic, rigorous study of the track record of these task forces, but we can look back at earlier use of task forces and commissions. Some of these have worked extremely well when all the basic information was at hand, when the goal was clear cut, when the time was ripe to wrap up a problem. Several such examples are the mass production of penicillin during World War II and some very successful cooperative clinical trials, such as that on the use of streptomycin in treating tuberculosis.

How effective have they been when the basic information is not at hand and one needs whole new ideas and concepts and methods for scientific advance? Some decisions of this type that involved large sums of money and changed the course of research for many scientists have been wise ones. The decision of the National Foundation for Infantile Paralysis to put much of its resources into basic studies in virology rather than into specific applied programs is credited with speeding the work of Enders and his associates and the development of a successful and safe polio vaccine.

However, when relying entirely on the wisdom of the few wise men on a panel or task force, it must be asked: Can the very wisest of men, even a committee of Nobel laureates, ever be wrong? Here we are compelled to rely on examples or anecdotes. Indeed, in the past, some highly respected men have undoubtedly held back medical progress. Aristotle effectively banned for centuries even the thought of operating on the heart by saying, "The heart alone, of all viscera, cannot withstand injury." His view continued into the 19th century, when C. A. Theodor Billroth, one of Europe's great surgeons, reinforced it by saying in 1883, "A surgeon who tries to suture a heart wound deserves to lose the esteem of his colleagues." In the early 1900s Sir James Mackenzie, the great British cardiologist, believed that it would be useless to operate on heart valves, because it was the muscle of the heart that was at fault and not the valves. A presidential commission consisting of Aristotle, Billroth, and Mackenzie appointed to advise the NIH on the feasibility of open-heart surgery would have concluded: "Impossible, unethical, and useless."

Sir Macfarlane Burnet, a 1960 Nobel laureate, once stated that there was no polio vaccine remotely in sight, and that was in 1949, just several months before the publication of Enders' classic work on the growth of polio virus in nonneural tissue. The eminent British pathologist Sir Almroth Wright did his very best to discourage Sir Alexander Fleming in his work on penicillin, because of Wright's conviction that substances that were toxic to bacteria must also be toxic to man.

Zig Leszczynski—ANIMALS ANIMALS

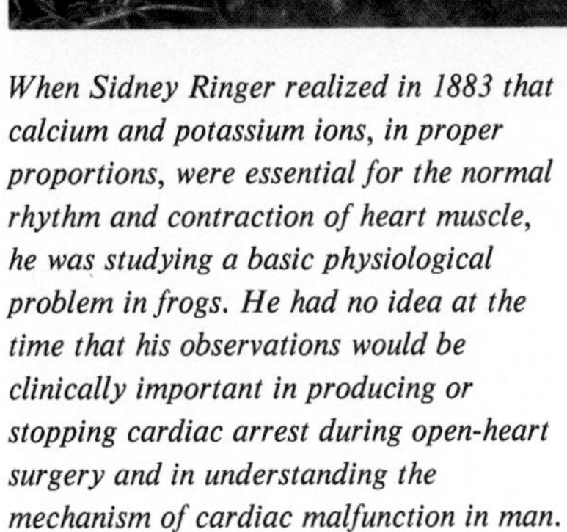

When Sidney Ringer realized in 1883 that calcium and potassium ions, in proper proportions, were essential for the normal rhythm and contraction of heart muscle, he was studying a basic physiological problem in frogs. He had no idea at the time that his observations would be clinically important in producing or stopping cardiac arrest during open-heart surgery and in understanding the mechanism of cardiac malfunction in man.

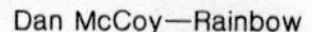

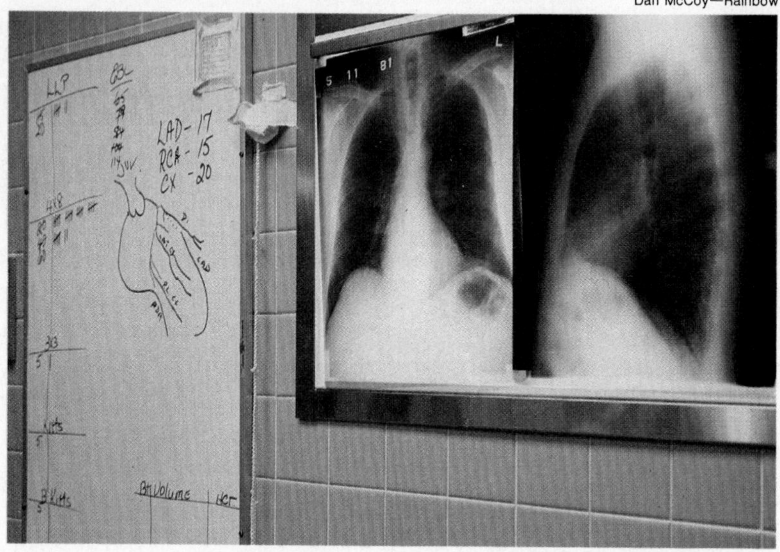

Until about a century ago it was widely believed that successful surgery of the heart would be impossible. Today heart operations offer definitive therapy for all but the rarest forms of cardiac disease.

In 1938 the Medical Research Council of England turned down Sir Ernst Chain's request for very modest support of his research project on the chemical and biochemical properties of antibacterial substances produced by microorganisms (now known as antibiotics)—research which, a few years later (with support from the Rockefeller Foundation), led to the purification of penicillin and a Nobel Prize. Peter Medawar recalls Howard Florey's telling him that wise old gray heads in England shook (or wobbled) regretfully from side to side, pronouncing that the future of antibacterial therapy lay not with extracts of fungi and other medieval-sounding concoctions but with synthetic organic chemicals of which sulfanilamide was the paradigm.

Sir Stephen Paget, author of an authoritative text, *The Surgery of the Chest*, predicted in 1896: "Surgery of the heart has probably reached the limits set by Nature to all surgery: no new method and no new discovery can overcome the natural difficulties that attend a wound of the heart. It is true that heart suture has been vaguely proposed as a possible procedure, and that it has been done on animals, but I cannot find that it has ever been attempted in practice." It was on September 9 of that same year, 1896, that Ludwig Rehn of Frankfurt am Main performed the first successful suture of a human heart wound.

In mid-1964, one of the United States' most eminent scientists, Joshua Lederberg, wrote to the director of the National Heart Institute:

> For some time I have been puzzling why an artificial heart has not yet been made available as a fruit of our technological developments. . . . I believe the problem is technically difficult but easily manageable within the framework of our present scientific knowledge and technical proficiency. We have however permitted it to remain a subject of fragmentary scientific studies rather than of a unified engineering program. We do ourselves a great disservice to neglect the opportunity of a systems response to what is now a well-defined technical problem, which is so much a matter of engineering design, material development and empiric testing and should not be confused with the basic research that was needed at its foundation.

The National Heart Institute (NHI) had indeed been supporting research and development on the artificial heart, but following this letter from a Nobel laureate, the institute drew up a master plan for a systems approach to the artificial heart that called for the signing of contracts by July 1, 1965, and implantation of artificial hearts in patients by February 14, 1970. By 1981, a clinical practical device was still not on the horizon, and the NHI (now the National Heart, Lung, and Blood Institute) had long since decided to emphasize support of short-term ventricular-assist devices rather than the more dramatic implanted plutonium-powered mechanical heart.

Lack of clairvoyance is not limited to biomedical scientists. One example will suffice: Simon Newcomb, a famous U.S. astronomer, professor of mathematics and astronomy at Johns Hopkins University, and editor of the *American Journal of Mathematics,* said in 1903: "Human flight is not only impossible but illogical. A new metal or a new force in nature would have to be discovered before man could fly. Even if by some miracle a man should invent a power machine that could get off the ground, it would inevitably crash and kill its pilot. Once he slackened his speed, down he begins to fall. Once he stops, he falls a dead mass." On December 17 of that year, Orville and Wilbur Wright made their first flight in a heavier-than-air plane near Kitty Hawk, North Carolina.

Because a look backward shows that we cannot guarantee the infallibility of wise men, scientists such as Irvine Page and Harry Eagle favor an alternative—to depend upon the collective wisdom of thousands of scientists instead of (or in addition to) the chancy wisdom of a selected few. This approach appears to have served us well in the past, and no one has yet demonstrated (by objective studies) that it is less effective than commission-directed research.

Approaches to research

No objective analysis has ever been done to determine how the best work of hundreds or thousands of scientists has come about. And we have not attempted to do "research on successful methods of research" because to do so would be extraordinarily difficult. One can try to do such research by (1) careful reading of published articles of each scientist, (2) searching the day-by-day working notebooks of successful scientists, (3) seeking latter-day accounts of eminent scientists on "why and how I did my work," or (4) interviewing scientists after their work has become famous. There are problems with each of these approaches: (1) Today, scientists write in a standard compressed format using as few words as possible (and often avoiding use of plain English language). If a scientist should break these unwritten rules, the editor might well delete anything except a very brief introduction, full details of methods used, full display of data, pertinent discussion, and a reasonable number of references; the cost of print and paper today requires such economies. (2) Few scientists, at the outset of their work, believe that their research will be historically important and do not include in their notebooks a full account of what impelled them to do their pilot experiments. (3) Latter-day accounts by a scientist—let us say, one who has been awarded a Nobel Prize—are as accurate as he can make them (depending on his memory) or as he *wants* to make them (depending upon his current philoso-

Hand-colored wood engraving from Harper's Weekly, 1882

Scientists approach their work in a variety of ways. French chemist and microbiologist Louis Pasteur, who revolutionized medicine by proving bacteria come from bacteria, was a skillful experimenter who devoted himself to careful observation in the laboratory.

phy of scientific research, or the current state of his ego). (4) Interviews are accurate or inaccurate for the same reasons as latter-day accounts.

So our only contribution to answering the question of how successful scientists did their research is anecdotal. Certainly, in our study Dripps and I found that very few followed Francis Bacon's 16th-century method of inductive reasoning, in which one first collects fact after fact and only then thinks of drawing conclusions, concepts, laws, or even hypotheses. Most scientists today start with an idea, a concept, a hypothesis that they (1) want to prove right, (2) want to prove wrong (if it originated with someone else), or (3) simply want to find out, completely and without prejudice, whether it is right or wrong.

Scientists get their ideas in a wide variety of ways: de novo (pure curiosity); from reading the reports of others and seeing a way of carrying their work further, or of amending it or disproving it; from questions put to them by undergraduate or graduate students, postdoctoral fellows, or colleagues; from standing by, helplessly, and watching a patient, a friend, or an animal die because of gaps in our scientific knowledge; by being asked, perhaps by industry, to solve a problem (*e.g.*, how to resuscitate electrocuted linemen); by listening to keen observations of a patient on his own disease; by wanting to test his own capability—to see whether he can solve a problem in biology or medicine—*any* problem; or by serendipity.

The serendipity in discovery

Chance played little role in the discoveries we studied; *serendipity* played an important role. Chance is pure luck—a stumbling and fumbling matter with full-blown discoveries falling into one's lap. If most discoveries occurred by chance, science would have no need for highly intelligent men and women who proceed carefully and doggedly toward a logical goal; all science would need would be a large corps of amateurs bouncing from project to project (as do molecules from other molecules in random motion) and so increasing the number of fortuitous observations and the likelihood of a great discovery.

Serendipity is a word coined in 1754 by Horace Walpole; his definition: "making discoveries, by accidents and sagacity, of things which they were not in quest of." *Webster's New World Dictionary* has changed Walpole's definition to "an apparent aptitude for making fortunate discoveries accidentally"; *Random House Dictionary* defines serendipity as "the faculty for making desirable discoveries by accident." The key word, omitted in modern definitions, is *sagacity*.

Louis Pasteur wrote in the mid-1800s: "Dans les champs de l'observation, le hasard ne favorise que les esprits preparés," which, translated freely, means "Chance favors only the prepared mind." Joseph Henry, a great U.S. physicist, said virtually the same thing some years before Pasteur: "The seeds of great discoveries are constantly floating around us, but they only take root in minds well prepared to receive them." And, said Winston Churchill: "Men occasionally stumble over the truth, but most of them pick themselves up and hurry off as if nothing had happened."

It seems that many discoveries, either clinical or nonclinical, are made—and then developed in different directions—by individuals who not only have prepared minds but are willing to change the direction of their effort, not daily or weekly, but when a new observation, possibly a chance observation, appears to be far more important than the problem before them. This requires three additional qualities besides the ability to observe what chance has put before them: judgment of what is very important, less important, or trivial; a prepared mind; and a flexible mind.

In a number of important instances, authorities or geheimrats have held back the progress of medical science for long periods. It was 14 centuries before a William Harvey challenged the accepted dogma put forth by Galen on the circulation of the blood and so revolutionized medicine. Louis Pasteur changed the whole direction of medicine by proving that bacteria come from other bacteria and not by spontaneous generation, as had been generally believed. Paul Ehrlich opened the door for chemotherapy of infectious diseases with his "magic bullet"—going against existing dogma that a chemical substance that could kill bacteria within a patient would also kill the patient. In general, good scientists not only have a prepared mind but also have a questioning and skeptical mind. It is of interest that Zuckerman's analysis of the religion of U.S. Nobel laureates showed that those whose religious beliefs required absolute acceptance of the printed word (*e.g.*, the Bible) rarely reached the top rung in scientific achievement.

John R. Freeman & Co., London

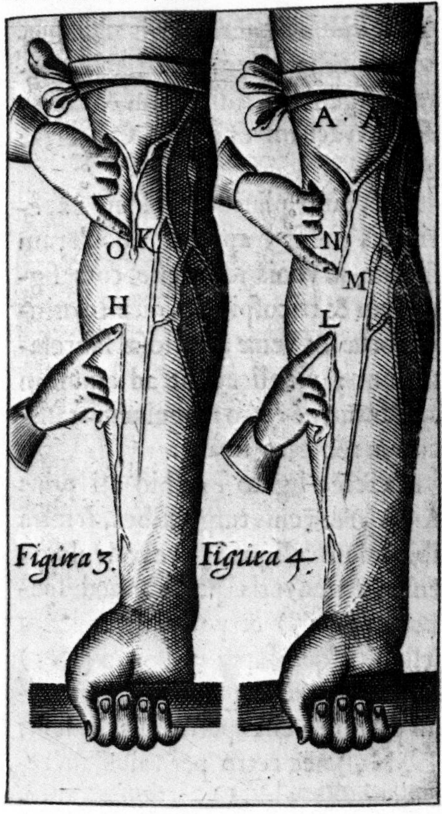

Galen's pronouncements in the 2nd century AD that blood in the human body flowed back and forth like a tide were generally accepted until the 17th century when William Harvey proved that blood can only run in one direction: toward the heart. He demonstrated this by pressing blood upward from a vein section in the forearm. If he released the lower finger, blood flowed into the vein section. But if he released the upper finger, blood would not run backward.

The importance of curiosity

The study that Dripps and I did provided no quantitative data on how one might select, from among millions of boys and girls, those hundreds who will become scientific giants in the future. We *believed*, however, that two matters are important: The first is to identify young people who are curious about the world they live in, who have an inquiring mind, and who persist in asking questions even when there are no easy answers. Probably these youngsters should also possess patience, doggedness, or even stubbornness, for new knowledge rarely comes easily or quickly. They should also display the qualities of flexibility (the ability to accept new ideas and to abandon the old, even though this conflicts with stubbornness) and of judging what is important and what is inconsequential.

(Opposite page) Of course, there is no way to predict who will be the great scientists of the future. But it is almost a certainty that they will be individuals who are intensely curious about the world around them and that they will have a unique ability to see what others before have looked at but have not really seen.

The second is to see to it that these young men and women have an opportunity to get involved in science and research so that they can determine whether they are excited by discovery and can weather the disappointments of initial failures to solve a problem. It matters not what the initial exposure is—whether, as in the case of Charles Best, it is the discovery of insulin, or whether it is something long forgotten, as in the case of John Gibbon who later developed the outside-the-body heart-lung machine essential for open-heart surgery. A number of first publications of those who later became members of the National Academy of Sciences are quite illuminating. Two examples are presented below—the first in full, and the other, with only introduction and conclusions.

A Twelve-Year-Old Blue Jay Recaptured (1934)

On the 17th of November, 1933, a Blue Jay (*Cyanocitta c. cristata*) bearing band number 9612, was taken in a flat trap. This bird had been banded on January 2, 1922, by Mr. Aldred S. Warthin, Jr., at a station located about three hundred yards from the site of recapture. While the numbers were entirely legible, the band had worn thin and was therefore replaced by C333993. The bird has not been retaken since.

This indicates that Blue Jay 9612 was at least twelve and a half years old when it was retaken, more than two years older than the Wren-tit recently reported by E. L. Sumner, Sr. (*Condor*, 36, 1934, p. 170) as the oldest recorded wild passerine bird.

Asteriasterol—A New Sterol from the Starfish and the Sterols of Certain Other Marine Echinoderms (1923)

The present study was undertaken with the view to obtaining information of a chemical nature that might help to explain some of the curious differences that exist between the eggs of the starfish (*Asterias forbesi*) and other echinoderms; more especially those of the sea urchin (*Arbacia punctulata*) and sand dollar. . . .

"*Eureka! Pass it on!*"

Jonathan Rawle—Stock, Boston

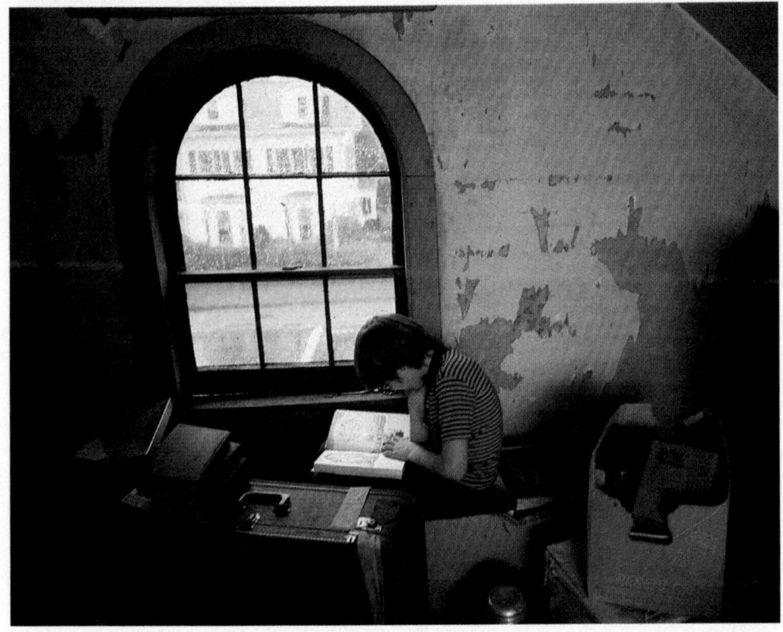

Summary

1. The sterol of the starfish (*Asterias forbesi*) has been isolated, identified, and named.

2. The sterols of the sand dollar (*Echinarachnius parma*) and the sea urchin (*Arbacia punctulata*) have been found to be identical with true cholesterol.

3. The sterols of *Cumingia tellinoides, Choetopterus pergamentaceous,* and *Arenicola cristata* very probably are identical with true cholesterol.

4. The use of $AsCl_3$ as a means of identifying sterols has been extended to oxycholesterol. The reaction is very striking.

The content of these writings cannot, even 40 to 50 years later, be logically connected with any step-by-step progression toward the diagnosis, treatment, or prevention of any human ailment. But in each case, the "first research" must have so fascinated each young scientist that he could not conceive of any career except for one in science. In each of the examples, it was *medicine* that benefited by the subsequent career of the young man; medicine was lucky—it could have been botany or chemistry or physics or anatomy. The first was written by Thomas Weller, later to receive a Nobel Prize for his work (with Enders and Robbins) on poliomyelitis; the second was written by Irvine Page, later to make monumental and lasting contributions to our knowledge of the diagnosis, course, and treatment of one of the major killers in the United States, high blood pressure.

These two had the right combination of qualities that favor making startling new discoveries, such as intense curiosity about the secrets of nature; an imaginative, creative mind; the ability to see what others before have looked at but have not really seen; persistence and perseverance (even stubbornness) and a willingness or even compulsion to be thorough, complete, and rigorous. An important lesson from these examples is that we should not be looking primarily for men and women who can turn something good into something a little better, but rather for men and women who might uncover something unheard of or even undreamed of.

FOR ADDITIONAL READING:

Beveridge, W. I. B. *The Art of Scientific Investigation.* New York: W. W. Norton, 1950.

Comroe, J. H., Jr., and Dripps, R. D. *The Top Ten Clinical Advances in Cardio-pulmonary Medicine and Surgery Between 1945 and 1975: How They Came About.* Washington, D.C.: U.S. Government Printing Office, 1977.

——."Scientific Basis for the Support of Biomedical Science." *Science* 192:105–111, 1976.

Comroe, J. H., Jr. *Retrospectroscope: Insights Into Medical Discovery.* Menlo Park, California: Von Gehr Press, 1977.

Conant, J. B., ed. *Harvard Case Histories in Experimental Science.* Cambridge, Massachusetts: Harvard University Press, 1957.

Liljestrand, G. *Nobel: The Man and His Prizes.* Amsterdam: Elsevier, 1962.

Report of the President's Biomedical Research Panel. Submitted to the President and Congress of the United States, April 30, 1976. Washington, D.C.: Department of Health, Education, and Welfare, 1976.

Zuckerman, H. *Scientific Elite: Nobel Laureates in the United States.* New York: Free Press, 1977.

——."The Sociology of the Nobel Prize: Further Notes and Queries." *American Scientist* 66:420–425, 1978.

Solving the DNA Puzzle

by Francis H. C. Crick, Ph.D.

In April 1953, James D. Watson and I suggested that deoxyribonucleic acid (DNA) had the shape of a very long double helix, consisting of two chains twined round one another and fitting neatly together so that the shape of each was the precise complement of the other. A month later we spelled out just how cells might replicate such a structure. These ideas made it highly plausible that a gene was made of DNA and that the genetic information was carried by the precise sequence of DNA's four bases, or building blocks (simple compounds known as adenine, guanine, cytosine, and thymine).

How did I, a physicist by training, come to be involved in such a discovery? During World War II, I worked as a scientist for the British Admiralty, spending most of my time designing and testing new circuits for magnetic and acoustic mines. When peace finally came I was uncertain what to do. I could have stayed on at the Admiralty but felt no urge to spend the rest of my life designing weapons. As there was little else I knew about, I had a rather wide array of choices open to me, an unusual situation for someone already 30 years old. I realized this was a unique opportunity, which might never come again—to start afresh—and I would be wise to select something that interested me deeply. But how to find out one's real interests? I decided to use what I call the gossip test (gossip being talking about something with relish, even if one is not in full possession of the facts). Using this method to analyze my conversation, I narrowed my choices to two broad areas of science: one involving the borderline between the living and the nonliving (what today we call molecular biology) and the other, the nature of consciousness (how our brains work).

With financial support from the British Medical Research Council (MRC) and with some help from my family, I went to the University of Cambridge, arriving there in September 1947. At first I worked in a tissue culture laboratory and tried to teach myself biology and chemistry in my spare time. A little under two years later I transferred to the physics department, the renowned Cavendish Laboratory, where a small group (also financed by the MRC) headed by Max Perutz, under the guidance of Sir Lawrence Bragg, was trying to solve the three-dimensional structure of a protein by diffracting X-rays from certain protein crystals. With a little help I taught myself X-ray crystallography and resumed the attempt, abandoned because of the war, to get a Ph.D.

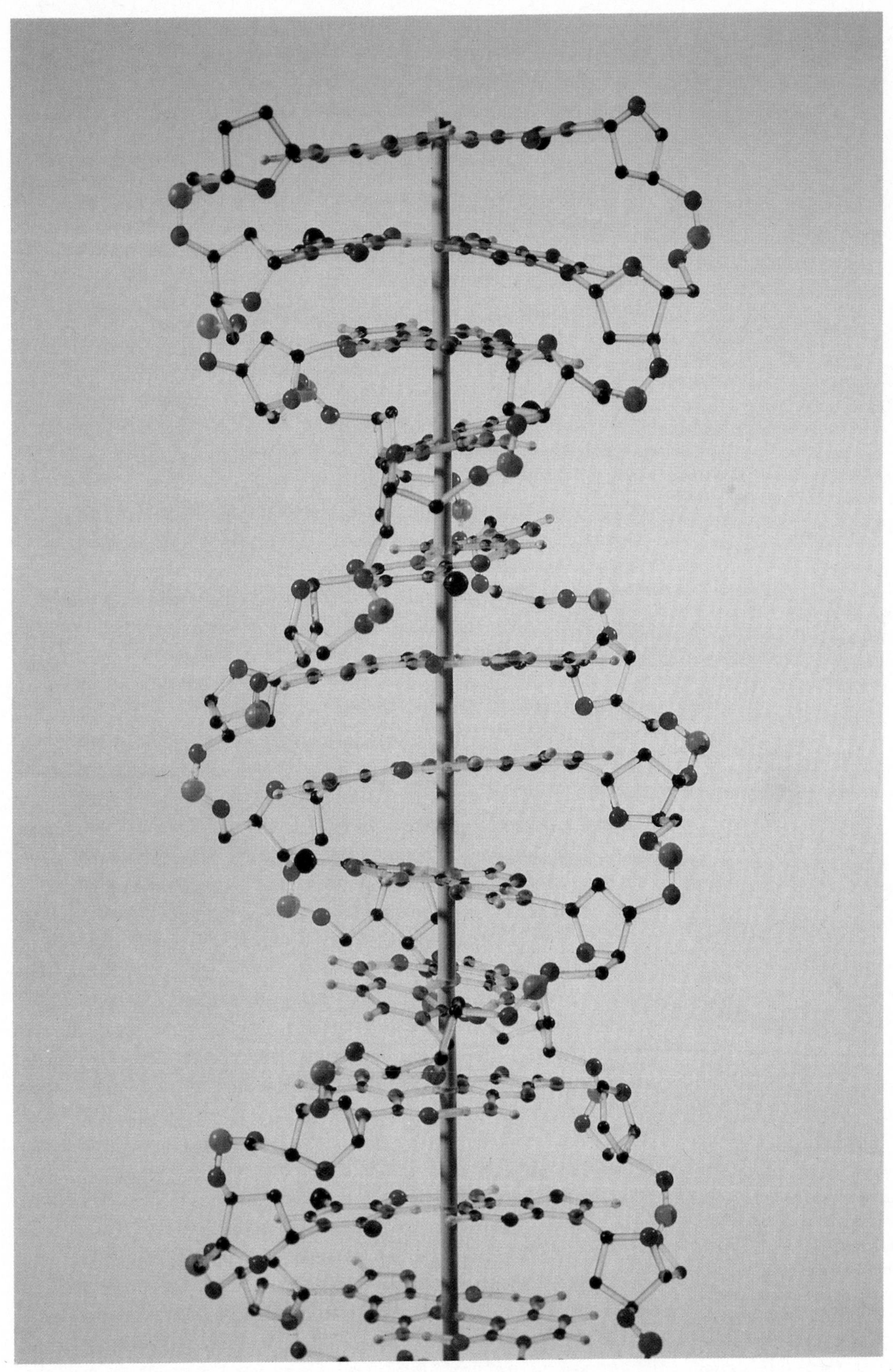

Robert Burroughs—Discover Magazine

By that time I had decided that the most important problem in biology, at this level, was the physics and chemistry of genes—what they were made of, how they were replicated, how they influenced the cell. I had formed the opinion, not entirely novel, that what a gene did was to carry instructions for producing the amino acid sequence of a protein, but what genes were made of, I was less sure. Earlier, scientists had believed that genes were themselves made of protein, but certain experiments hinted that perhaps DNA was also important. My friend Maurice Wilkins (also trained as a physicist and supported by the MRC) at King's College, London, was trying to solve the structure of fibers of DNA. Rosalind Franklin, a trained crystallographer, had been taken on to work on the problem.

A little later, in the fall of 1951, Jim Watson arrived in Cambridge, a young man of 23, already with one year's postdoctoral experience in Copenhagen. He, too, had decided that the physical structure of genes was the key problem in molecular biology and had come to help our colleague John Kendrew. For the better part of two years Jim and I thought and talked about the problem (while I was also working to produce a Ph.D. thesis on protein structure) and from time to time visited King's College where X-ray diffraction experiments were being done. The story of the *personal* interactions among the four of us, Maurice, Rosalind, Jim and myself, and our rivalry with Linus Pauling at the California Institute of Technology in Pasadena (whose son Peter came to share our office), has already been told, originally by Watson himself, more recently by Robert Olby and also by Horace Freeland Judson. Here I want to concentrate on the nature of the *scientific* problem we all faced.

DNA is a polymer, a long molecule made by joining together, head to tail, four similar but distinct subunits called nucleotides. In the early 1950s the *general* chemical formula for DNA was already established, though the exact base sequence of any bit of DNA was still quite unknown. An organic chemical can, for some purposes, be thought of as made up of a set of round balls (the atoms) joined together by stiff pieces of wire (the chemical bonds). At that time the distances between each type of atom—the length of each particular chemical bond—and the angle between each pair of adjacent bonds were known fairly accurately from studies on many other compounds similar to DNA but much smaller. This being so, why was the three-dimensional structure a problem? Surely all this available information would give the shape of the molecule. But that was not the case because within molecules there is fairly free rotation about all the *single* chemical bonds, while the double and triple bonds, when present, are by contrast relatively fixed. Thus DNA could in theory take up many shapes since it had several single bonds in every crystallographic repeat. How could one decide which configuration the molecule, influenced by the weaker and less well-defined bonds between more distant atoms, would take up in practice?

The obvious way would be to take some sort of picture of it. Visible light was hopeless, since its wavelengths are hundreds of times longer than the diameter of the DNA, which makes it far too coarse a probe to resolve the internal details of the structure. The electron microscope was not suitable. To this day, no electron microscope picture has been able to show the

Francis H. C. Crick, Ph.D., *won the Nobel Prize for Physiology or Medicine in 1962, along with James D. Watson and Maurice Wilkins, for the discovery of the molecular structure of DNA. He is currently Kieckhefer Research Professor at the Salk Institute for Biological Studies in San Diego, California.*

(Overleaf) Alfred Owczarzak—Taurus

Photographs, courtesy, Professor Struther Arnott, Purdue University

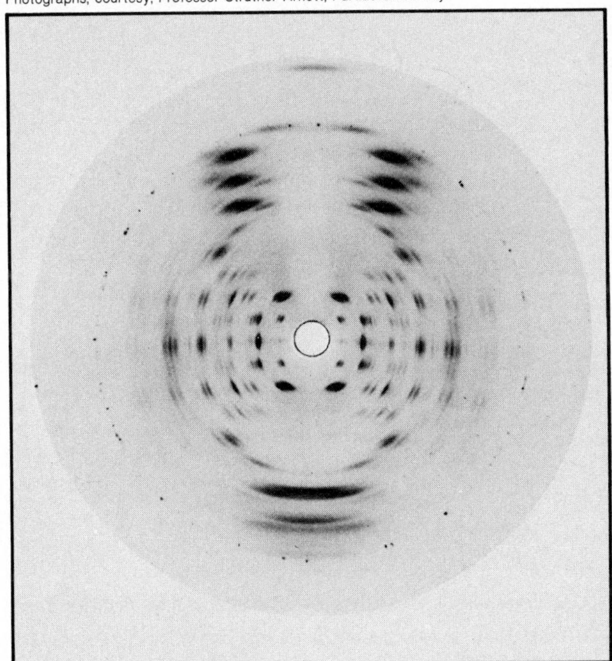

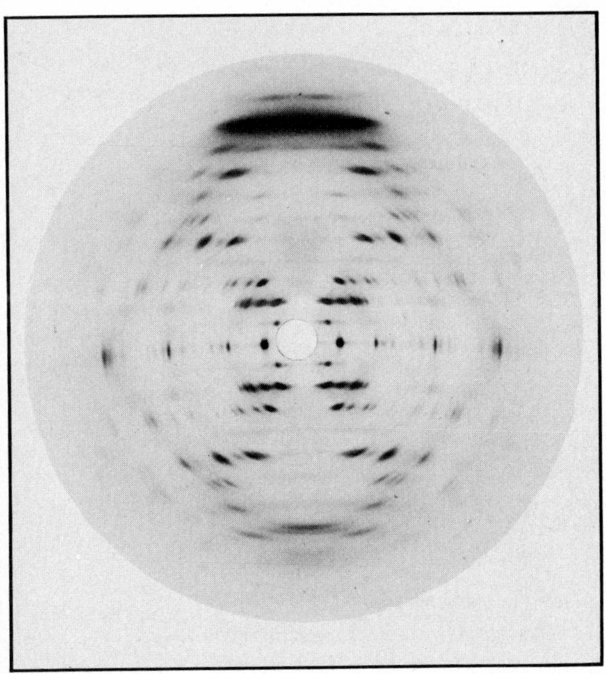

atomic positions in the DNA. There remained X-rays. Their wavelengths are short enough, being about the same length as the typical distance between adjacent atoms, but, unlike light, they are difficult to focus satisfactorily, so instead of a true picture one merely gets a diffraction pattern of the structure. Even to obtain the diffraction, it is necessary to have many molecules together in an ordered array, such as a crystal or a paracrystal, to get a big enough ratio of signal to noise.

What actually diffracts the X-rays is the cloud of electrons surrounding each atom. The X-ray diffraction pattern caught on a series of photographic films (or by Geiger counters) is a 3-D "wave analysis" of the 3-D pattern of electron density. Given the position of all the atoms, it is a straightforward but tedious process to calculate the magnitude of all the spots on the X-ray pictures. Unfortunately the reverse is not true. If we had *all* the parameters of the diffracted pattern then, again, a mathematical synthesis would yield the required 3-D electron density; alas, the darkness of each X-ray spot on the film gives only the *amplitude* of each "wave," not its phase. Thus the picture contains just half the information needed to solve the structure automatically without further assumptions—a maddening restriction.

Small structures can be solved because one can assume that what is diffracting is a set of compact atoms, but DNA is too large a structure for such a method to apply. There is a further snag: the crystalline, or semicrystalline, arrangements of DNA are irregular, so that the information is smudged; the X-ray spots, which would correspond to the higher resolutions, are missing. Thus even if the missing phases were provided in some way, one could not hope to resolve individual atoms, only groups of atoms. One way to obtain the phases is to add a heavy atom to the structure in definite places and then compare the resulting diffraction patterns, with and without these reference points. But this method could not be used on DNA.

X-ray diffraction photographs, which reveal details of the arrangement in space of the atoms inside the DNA molecule, were an important tool in solving DNA's precise three-dimensional structure. Pictures taken by X-ray crystallographers in England in the early 1950s gave some surprising information: that DNA from different species gave identical X-ray patterns and that the structure of DNA could take two forms. (Above left) The diffraction pattern from crystalline DNA in the A form; (right) diffraction pattern from a paracrystalline fiber of DNA in the B form—the form on which Crick and Watson's DNA model was based.

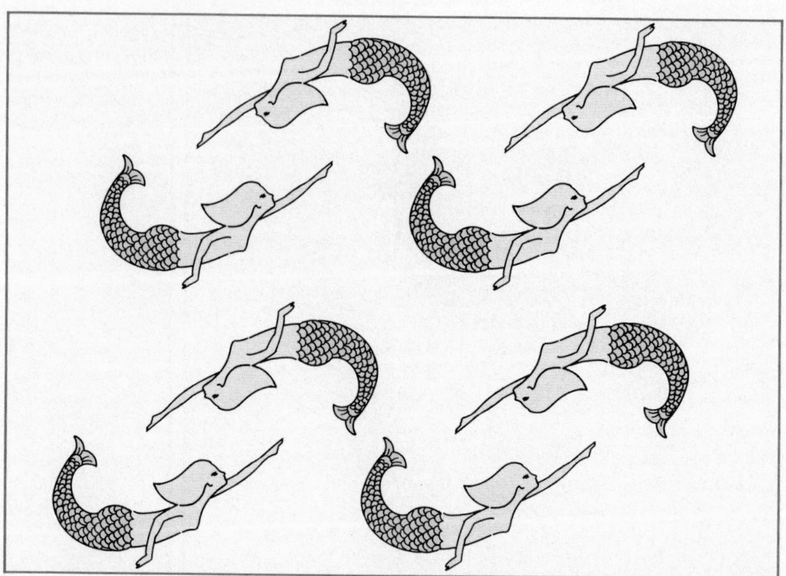

DNA is composed of paired asymmetric units (nucleotides), which together form a symmetric unit cell. The mermaids illustrate this principle. A single mermaid in the scheme is an asymmetric unit; when two mermaids are considered together they form a symmetric unit. The pattern is the same if viewed upside down.

In brief, no method was available to solve the structure in a straightforward way. The information actually available was of two main kinds: first, the chemical formulas plus the parameters for bond lengths and angles, not by themselves enough to define DNA's structure, and second, a limited number of X-ray spots, also insufficient to give the structure without further assumptions. The obvious approach—following the example of Linus Pauling, who had in 1951 discovered the α-helix of proteins—was to see if the *combination* of these two very different sets of data could provide a plausible answer. This meant building an accurate scale model and playing with it until a structure was found that fitted the X-ray data satisfactorily.

Fortunately, some bits of information could be obtained directly from the data. The *positions* of the X-ray spots give unambiguously the size of the repeat unit (known as a unit cell) in space. In favorable cases, the pattern shows the *symmetry* of the unit cell. Given this information, it is possible to deduce the size of the asymmetric unit—the minimum bit of structure which, operated on by all the symmetry elements, will give the entire DNA crystal. From the density of the material—which was not always easy to measure because of the variable water content of DNA fibers—it was then possible to calculate how many atoms there are in the smallest crystallographic repeat.

When the above approach was taken at King's College in the early 1950s it was found that the unit cell was always very large and the apparent asymmetric unit was only a half or a quarter the size. Though researchers could infer that the structure had either two or three chains in it (probably the former), it was far too big to obtain the atomic positions by any orthodox method. But there was a ray of hope. The backbone of the molecule was chemically very regular. Was it possible that, in spite of the variety of base sequences, the backbone formed a regular helix? If so, the true asymmetric unit might be just one nucleotide (or, as we would say now, just half a nucleotide pair). Could the structure then be solved with *this* additional assumption?

Photograph, A. C. Barrington Brown. From J. D. Watson, *The Double Helix,* Atheneum, New York, p.221.

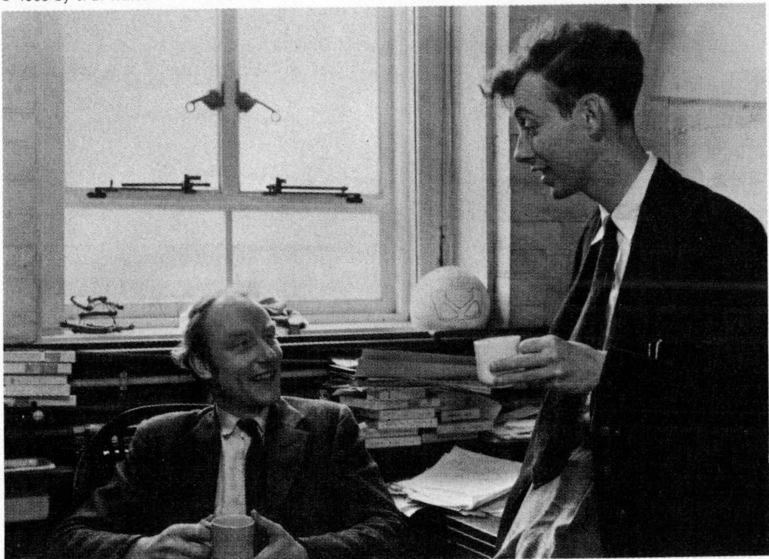

Francis Crick and James Watson in the spring of 1953 at their office in the Cavendish Laboratory in Cambridge. The picture was taken after the publication in the journal Nature *of their letter announcing their discovery of the double helix. The letter began: "We wish to suggest a structure for the salt of deoxyribose nucleic acid (DNA). This structure has novel features which are of considerable biological interest."*

The answer turned out to be yes. By paying attention to the strong features of the X-ray data, it was possible to deduce certain general features of the structure—the way the bases were stacked, for example. Moreover, in 1952 several of us had worked out the mathematical theory for the diffraction pattern of a regular helix. The theory predicts that for a helix, no matter what the exact arrangement of the atoms, there will be a large vacant region of the X-ray photograph—the helix's "signature." From this information one can deduce the parameters of the helical screw axis, which carries one nucleotide pair into the next one. The detailed symmetry of one of the unit cells also suggested that the backbones of the two chains, although helically intertwined, ran in opposite directions.

Only one further concept needed to be resolved. How did an irregular base sequence form such a regular structure? Once we realized, in March 1953, that the bases, though differing in size, could be matched up to give base pairs of identical size and shape, the structure of DNA simply fell out. The two strands of the double helix are held together by chemical bonds between

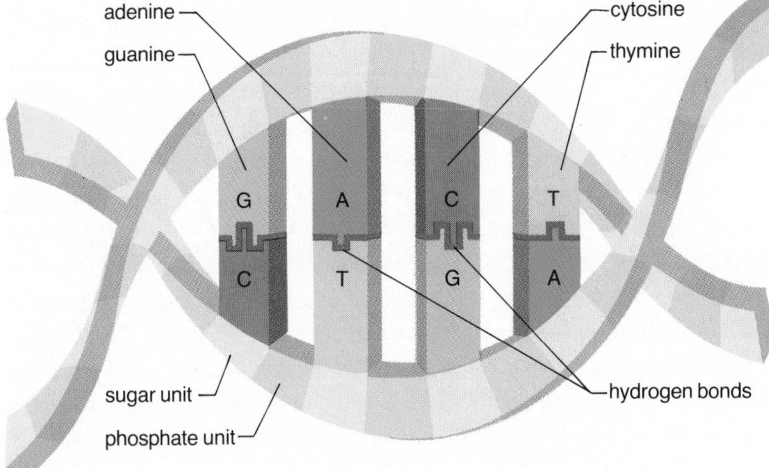

Adapted from "Understanding Biology," by Philip Applewhite and Sam Wilson, New York, Holt, Rinehart and Wilson, 1978

The four DNA bases—adenine (A), guanine (G), thymine (T), and cytosine (C)—that bond single strands of nucleotides. A nucleotide is a three-part unit consisting of a phosphate, a sugar, and a base. A and G, which are similar structurally, are purines; T and C are pyrimidines. C bonds only with G; A bonds only with T.

Photographs, Robert Langridge, Ph.D., Computer Graphics Laboratory, University of California, San Francisco

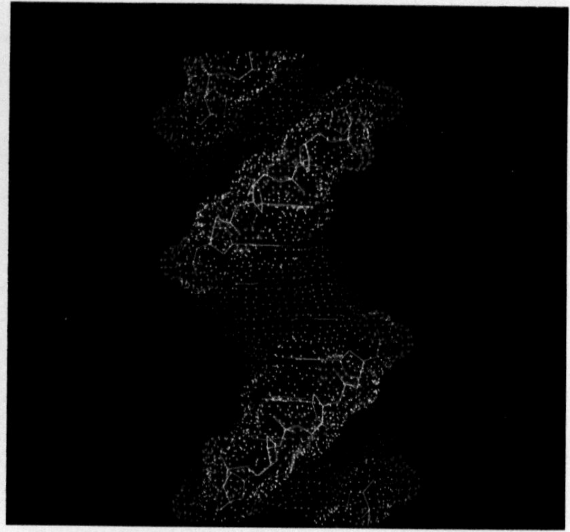

When Crick and Watson constructed their famous model of DNA in 1953 they were not certain they were right. But time has shown the right-handed double-helix structure they proposed to be correct. The computer-rendered image (right), a side view of DNA, shows its spiral structure; the picture at left is another computer image—a cross section of a DNA molecule.

complementary base pairs (adenine always pairing with thymine, cytosine always pairing with guanine). It only took a day or so to build a rough model and a few more days to produce a more refined one. Moreover, the model of DNA explained, in a natural way, the one-to-one base ratios discovered a few years earlier by Erwin Chargaff.

It now sounds all too easy. In fact, the path to the double helix was a twisted one, involving many detailed technical considerations and quite complicated chains of argument. It is hardly surprising that there were many false starts and trails, which have described numerous times already. In 1952 we built a totally incorrect model because of a misunderstanding about the water content of DNA fibers. For quite some time Franklin thought she had evidence that one form of DNA was *not* helical (she was, of course, wrong). We were misled at one point about the exact chemical formulas (the correct "tautomeric form") of the bases and had to be corrected by Jerry Donohue, a crystallographer who shared our office. Early in 1953, Pauling produced a three-chain model, which we knew was incorrect and which prompted us to try again. These were all customary vicissitudes of research, particularly for the kind of research done at the frontiers of knowledge. The accounts have sometimes been distorted by an undue emphasis on the personal factors involved, which has often disguised the real though guarded collaboration of almost all the people concerned. Scientific research is a cooperative venture, even if competition will keep breaking through.

I am often asked what I felt at the time of our discovery. Before we had the vital idea of exactly how to pair the DNA bases we were constantly baffled, since the various bits of data never seemed to fit together properly. After Jim figured out the base-pairing, everything suddenly fell into place. During the actual model building, which took only a few days, I was mostly in a state of constant enthusiasm (Jim had occasional spasms of doubt). Any enthusiasm, though, had to be tempered by the knowledge that our idea was only a hypothesis and might well be misguided or even wrong. But most of this time I was so busy trying to avoid awkward atomic contacts and measuring the coordinates of the atoms that I hardly noticed how I felt. As we were

Photographs, Dan McCoy—Rainbow

DNA can now be cut and spliced and recombined in the laboratory. Genes from higher organisms can be induced to function in bacteria. The potential benefits are many. The test tubes contain replicating plasmid DNA, which can be extracted from the bacterial cell, and bacterial DNA. They form separate bands after being spun on a centrifuge owing to differences in density. The multi-valved machine pictured above is a large fermenter—a biochemical cauldron for growing gene-spliced bacteria.

constructing our model we had only a rough idea of the experimental data that had been obtained at King's College, so shortly thereafter, when we saw the drafts of the papers produced there, we were greatly encouraged to learn how well their data fitted the double helix pattern.

We did realize that, if we were correct, our "discovery" would be very important for biology. The idea that we might get a prize for it (let alone a Nobel Prize) never entered my mind until several years later. In addition to my work on solving DNA's structure I was also spending a good part of my time that summer finishing my Ph.D. thesis (which focused on other work, dealing with proteins and polypeptides). Our papers on the double helix were not part of the body of my thesis. I was also preparing to go to work in Brooklyn for a year.

What has happened since the discovery for which Watson, Wilkins, and I received the Nobel Prize for Physiology or Medicine in 1962? The structure of DNA is now well established: time has shown that our model was correct, that the DNA molecule really is a right-handed double helix. Within the last year or so crystallographers have actually been able to see the atoms in crystals of short lengths of DNA. They have found that in a very salty solution certain special base sequences can form a peculiar left-handed helix. DNA really is the universal hereditary material carrying genetic instructions from one generation to the next. (For certain small viruses, it has been discovered that the genetic messages are carried by DNA's close relative ribonucleic acid, RNA, which in some cases may even be single-stranded.) Also it is now known that the DNA of genes dictates the formation of proteins; three consecutive bases spell out instructions for placing one or another of 20 amino acids into a molecular chain.

Adapted from "Cancer: Science and Society," by John Cairns, San Francisco, W. H. Freeman and Company, 1978

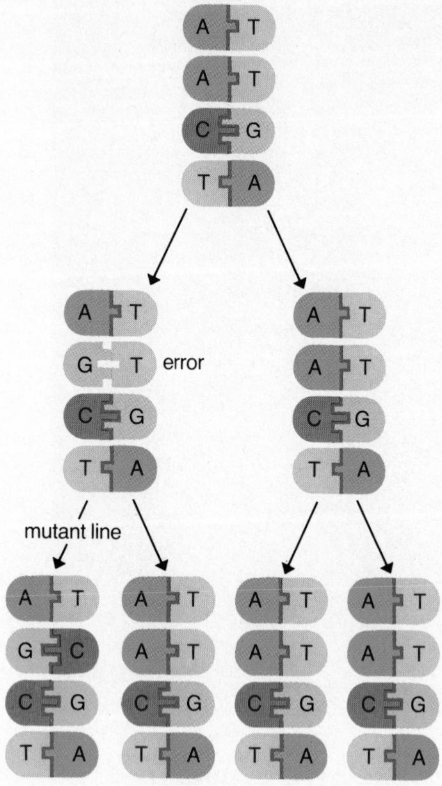

It is hoped that many medical problems, including cancer, will be solved with greater understanding of how genes function. The diagram depicts a mutation due to an error in DNA replication, which has given rise to a permanently mutated line. Such a pattern may explain the basic mechanisms in some forms of cancer. Cancer is a transformation of normal body cells, probably due to an alteration in the DNA. Cancer cells create expanding populations, passing on inappropriate information. In this example, at the time of DNA replication a wrong base (G) is paired with a T. When this stretch of DNA is replicated again, a C will replace the T and a mutant line, in which there is a G-C base pair instead of an A-T pair, will have been created.

The last few years have brought further breakthroughs. The double helix model only displayed the general character of DNA and not the vital sequence of the bases in a particular stretch of DNA. But this specific information can now be obtained rapidly by improved chemical and biochemical methods. In 1980 Fred Sanger, Walter Gilbert, and Paul Berg shared the Nobel Prize for Chemistry for DNA research. Sanger's and Gilbert's work enables sequences thousands of bases long to be worked out, or "read," in a matter of only a few weeks. In addition, with special enzymes as tools, very long lengths of DNA can now be cut into precise pieces and joined onto other bits, generating the technique of gene splicing, or recombinant DNA, which Berg helped pioneer. These new methods are already allowing the sequencing of many different genes, including those that, in certain viruses, produce cancer in animals. For example, with the advances in technology, today if one should want to know the sequence of his two genes (one from his father, one from his mother) for, say, the β-globin chain of hemoglobin, a few weeks' work would give it, provided one supplied a small sample of blood as a source of DNA.

These methods have already allowed the complete sequencing of the DNA of several small viruses, each about 5,000 base-pairs long, and of human mitochondria (energy-producing organelles outside the nucleus of the cells), about three times bigger. A bacterium such as *Escherichia coli* is some 200 times greater than that; in the near future it, too, may well be sequenced completely. How long it will take to sequence the DNA of the entire human genome, perhaps 1,000 times longer than that of *E. coli,* remains to be seen, but in years to come substantial parts of the more important stretches will be sequenced by scientists for one reason or another. There are also efforts to identify *all* the human proteins, perhaps 50,000 different types, using computers and new rapid sequencing techniques.

We can now hope to tackle the major unsolved problem in the molecular biology of higher organisms—how their genes are turned on and off. The solution to this puzzle would help to place embryology on a firm experimental foundation, though we shall need to know just how cells move and interact before we can fully understand how a fertilized egg grows to an adult organism and why this process is not always perfect, as shown by various birth defects. Already we are obtaining new insights into the detailed mechanisms of evolution. And from all this we hope to solve many outstanding medical problems, the majority of which—and this is especially true of cancer—could not be rationally approached without a knowledge of their molecular foundation. A substantial part of these foundations has sprung from the structure of DNA—a wonderful flowering of the small seed that grew in our lab at Cambridge, nourished many years ago by the Medical Research Council.

It is difficult to predict exactly which health problems will be solved and especially when they will be solved. In the short run we expect to see many useful proteins, such as human insulin and human interferon produced in laboratories and made available in useful quantities. Genetic engineering might lead to a general method for curing most viral diseases, which are not touched by our present antibiotics. By typing DNA, we shall be able to diagnose many genetic defects in the very early fetal stages.

In time we may hope for better methods of dealing with cancer. We already know that a small oncogenic virus, having only about 5,000 base pairs of DNA, can produce cancer in animals. We know which of the genes of the virus are responsible as well as their base sequence, which means it is possible to work out the amino acid sequence of the proteins for which they code. Before long we hope to find out exactly how such genes act, so that we can discover what kinds of change lead to cancer's uncontrolled growth and invasiveness.

When the structure of DNA was first suggested many people either ignored it or disbelieved it. Then it was said that although it might be correct it was of little use to anyone. Within the past decade, the revolution in molecular biology enabling scientists to cut, splice, and redesign the hereditary material led some to believe DNA was too dangerous to play with, though these fears were greatly exaggerated. Now, suddenly, Wall Street has decided that, by God, you can make money out of it. (Exactly how much, and by whom, remains to be seen.) Some might say there could be no better testimony to its usefulness.

And what am I doing now? I'm following that other path uncovered by my gossip test over three decades ago: I'm trying to find out how the brain works.

The Bettmann Archive

A scene from Goethe's Faust *depicts the alchemist in search of a substance that will create human life. When recombinant DNA methods were first developed in the 1970s there was widespread public anxiety about the creation of new forms of life in the laboratory and the unleashing of disease-causing microbes. Today most of those fears have been allayed and indeed genetic engineering, which would never have been possible without a basic understanding of the structure of DNA, is viewed as one of the most important scientific advances of the 20th century.*

FOR ADDITIONAL READING:

Crick, F. H. C. "The Explosion of Biological Information," *The Great Ideas Today 1980.* Chicago: Encyclopaedia Britannica, Inc., 1980.

Judson, Horace F. *The Eighth Day of Creation.* New York: Simon and Schuster, 1979.

Olby, Robert. *The Path to the Double Helix.* London: Macmillan, 1974.

Portugal, Franklin H., and Cohen, Jack S. *A Century of DNA.* Cambridge, Mass.: MIT Press, 1977.

Schmeck, Harold M., Jr. "The New Genetics," *1981 Medical and Health Annual.* Chicago: Encyclopaedia Britannica, Inc., 1980.

Watson, James D. *The Double Helix.* New York: Atheneum, 1968.

Watson, James D. *The Double Helix: A Norton Critical Edition,* edited by Gunther S. Stent. New York and London: W. W. Norton & Co., 1981.

"To recombinant DNA!"

Australia Antigen: Key to Hepatitis

by Baruch S. Blumberg, M.D., Ph.D.

One of the most remarkable features of medicine is that some individuals become sick and others remain well even if all are exposed to the same risks, and of those who succumb to illness some recover rapidly and others do not. A part of this difference is due to luck, bad and good, but much of it is a consequence of the remarkable inherited variation within the human species. In 1950, during my third year at Columbia University's medical school, I worked at a hospital in a mining community in the swamp and high bush country of inland Suriname, South America. The great difference in the response of different populations to infectious diseases (in particular the filariad *Wuchereria bancrofti,* the causative agent of elephantiasis) was very impressive. The residents of African origin were much more likely to become chronically infected with the parasite than those who originated in Java, China, or Europe. These people with different origins, cultures, and diets had been brought to the country over the centuries as agricultural laborers and differed greatly in their response to the infectious agents in their new homeland.

Another approach to the study of human variation developed while I was working at the department of biochemistry at the University of Oxford in 1956 and 1957. Serum proteins, biochemicals dissolved in the blood, could be separated under the influence of an electrical field in a sievelike gelatin prepared from potato starch. The patterns obtained with this technique were complex, and several genetically controlled variants of blood proteins were identified. These variants could be used to describe populations genetically by estimating the frequencies of the genes which determined their presence. Over the years we studied populations living under very different environmental conditions to see the pattern of distribution of the genes and from this to make some inferences on function and relation to health and disease. This research resulted in field trips to interesting and exotic locations to study populations practicing their traditional cultures. We observed Basques from Spain; Indians in Alaska, in the southwest United States, in Mexico, in Peru, and elsewhere; Africans from Nigeria; Greeks; Filipinos; and many other populations.

Baruch S. Blumberg

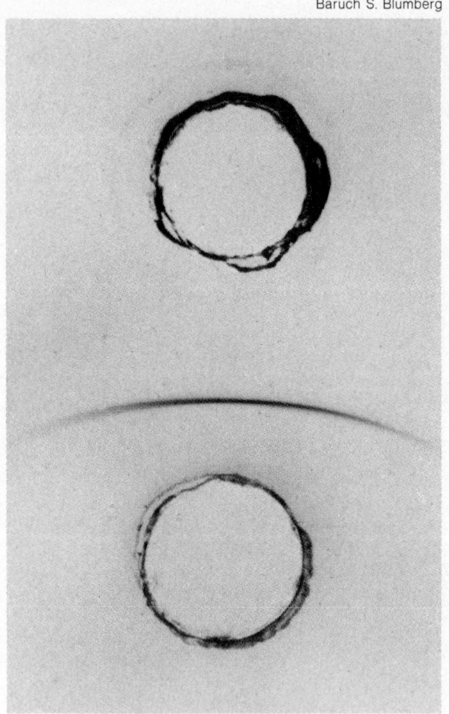

The finding that the serum of a transfused hemophilia patient from New York City contained an antibody that reacted with an antigen present in the serum of an Australian aborigine was crucial to unraveling the mechanism of infection in hepatitis. The simple technique of immunodiffusion was the first method used to detect Australia antigen. In the above immunodiffusion assay, a reaction is indicated by the formation of a precipitin line between the serum from a patient with hepatitis B virus (in the bottom well) and serum containing antibody against the virus (in the top well).

Baruch S. Blumberg, M.D., Ph.D., *won the Nobel Prize for Physiology or Medicine in 1976 for his research on the hepatitis B virus. He is presently Associate Director for Clinical Research at the Institute for Cancer Research in Philadelphia.*

(Overleaf) David Moore—Black Star

It soon became clear that there was a complex pattern of distribution of inherited proteins not only between the populations but also within the populations. We reasoned that some of these differences might be antigenic; that is, they might be different enough so that a person exposed to a variant which he or she had not inherited or acquired, for example by blood transfusion, might develop antibodies against the foreign proteins. Based on this hypothesis, we tested the sera of people who had received a large number of transfusions and therefore would presumably have been exposed to a large number of blood variants to see if they had developed antibodies against antigens present in the blood of other people. We used the technique of immunodiffusion in agar gel to detect the presence of antigen, antibody, or both. Small amounts of serum from a transfused patient were put into a central well cut from a thin layer of gel. Sera selected from a panel which might contain antigen were placed in peripheral wells surrounding the central well. If the serum had an antigen with the same specificity as the antibody in the transfused person's serum, then a visible precipitin band would form in the gel between the two wells. We found, in the serum of one particular patient, an antibody that reacted with a specific antigen, one known to be inherited in some people and found on the low-density lipoproteins of human serum. (Lipoproteins are the proteins which become abnormal in heart disease, diabetes, arteriosclerosis, and other conditions.) Hence this serum from a transfused person determined a previously unknown inherited blood protein system.

We continued to search for additional antibodies in transfused patients which could make apparent other inherited serum systems. One morning we found a precipitin line that had formed between the serum of a transfused hemophilia patient from New York City and the serum from an Australian aborigine which had been included in the test panel. The aborigine serum had been included in our search panel because we knew that there is considerable variation in gene frequencies for serum proteins in different populations; our strategy for increasing the probability of finding a new antiserum included the screening of populations of different origins, for example, from Africa, Asia, Europe, and, in this case, Australia.

Our task now consisted of trying to understand this phenomenon, this observation in "nature." Why did the serum of a transfused hemophilia patient from New York City contain an antibody which reacted with an antigen present in the serum of an Australian aborigine living in a sparsely populated region on the other side of the world? Understanding in science derives from a systematic questioning (that is, the statement of hypothesis) and answering (that is, designing experiments and observations in an attempt to support or reject the hypothesis). To generate hypotheses one needs data. To obtain our data we used the antiserum (antibody-containing serum) from the transfused hemophilia patient to test thousands of sera which had been stored in our blood collection. We found that "Australia antigen" (as it was called) was rare in the United States but common in the Tropics and Asia (Africa, Philippines, Japan, Vietnam, etc.). We included sera from patients with leukemia in the panel tested against the hemophilia antiserum; Australia antigen (abbreviated Au) was common in this group of

Milt and Joan Mann—Cameramann International

patients. Based on these observations we made the hypothesis that Au was inherited and rare in the general population, but people who had Au were more likely to develop leukemia. These and related hypotheses prompted several interesting lines of inquiry. We went to Cebu in the central Philippines to study family distribution of Au and to test the hypothesis that the antigen segregated as if controlled by a simple autosomal recessive gene. Our work in Cebu was conducted under the auspices of a foundation dedicated to the study of leprosy. An unexpected result was the finding that there was a much higher frequency of Au in the lepromatous than the tuberculous form of leprosy. Both of these manifestations of the disease are caused by the same organism, *Mycobacterium leprae,* but the former is associated with unusual immune responses. This led to additional studies on the immunology of Au and leprosy. We spent several summers in leprosy communities and hospitals (in India, Singapore, Philippines, Japan, Australia) obtaining additional information on this fascinating and sometimes tragic disease.

However, the most important consequence of this series of studies was the data that resulted from testing a hypothesis inferred from the original statement. If leukemia and the presence of Australia antigen were related to the same factor, then we predicted that those more likely to develop leukemia would also be more likely to have a high frequency of Au. There are several groups with a high risk for leukemia. Patients with Down's syn-

The discovery of Australia antigen in 1963 made it possible to identify the hepatitis B virus; by the early 1970s researchers were beginning to find that persistent infection with hepatitis is necessary for the development of primary liver cancer. Australia antigen and liver cancer are very common in some tropical regions of the world—particularly in parts of Africa and Asia—where sanitation is poor and where there is easy spread of infection by the fecal-oral route or by insect vectors. It is hoped that further understanding of how the virus is transmitted within families will lead to improved hygiene and prevention of infection.

Philip Jones Griffiths—Magnum

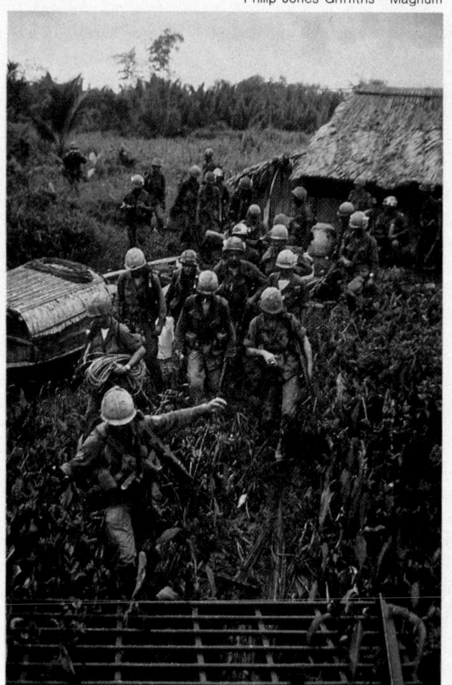

Many U.S. troops in Vietnam were exposed to the hepatitis B virus, which is common in the Vietnamese population. Hepatitis was one of the most frequent causes of illness in U.S. military men during the war, and now many veterans are hepatitis carriers.

drome, a form of mental retardation with an abnormality of chromosome 21 (there are three rather than two of them) have a much higher likelihood of developing leukemia than normal children or children with most other forms of mental retardation. I and my colleagues on this project, W. T. London, A. I. Sutnick, and Irving Millman, tested patients with and without Down's syndrome who were residents of large institutions, and the predictions were fulfilled. The frequency of Au was very much higher than in the controls. This was a very exciting result; it not only gave us confidence in the predictive powers of the hypothesis but also allowed us to observe in great detail individuals who had Australia antigen. In general, an individual who was "positive" for Au when first studied was always positive on subsequent testing, and those found "negative" were consistently so. An important exception to this generalization was subsequently seen. One of our young patients, James Bair, who had been negative when first tested changed to a positive scoring on a later testing. He was admitted to the unit, and the reason for the change soon became apparent. Many proteins are manufactured in the liver, and because James had appeared to have developed a "new" protein we tested his liver function. Between the time that his Au had been negative and the time it became positive he had developed a form of chronic hepatitis. This observation led to a formal hypothesis—that Au was associated with the virus that had caused the hepatitis in James—and accelerated our efforts to test this idea.

A series of studies to test the hypothesis was started, initially in our laboratory and soon in others. The antigen was common in patients with acute hepatitis, particularly those with the form known as hepatitis B, to distinguish it from other forms with different transmission and clinical characteristics. A particle corresponding to the virus was found in the peripheral blood, and soon the whole virus particle (virion) was identified in the blood and livers of people with hepatitis by British workers. We were able to inoculate African green monkeys with serum containing the virus and to demonstrate its infectivity. It lacked many of the characteristics which would have allowed its identification by "classical" virological methods. It did not grow in the usual human or animal tissue cultures, and ordinary laboratory animals did not become infected when inoculated. Au was, at that time, found only in humans and certain nonhuman primate species (chimpanzees, orangutans, gorillas, vervets, etc.). In fact, it appeared that knowledge of virology might have been an actual detriment to discovery if only the usual virological tools were used for identification. In that sense, we were well prepared for the study since none of the scientists in our group were virologists, and the discovery was made using the immunodiffusion technique, which is a relatively insensitive method not usually used to detect viruses.

Confirmation of the identification of the virus followed quickly from many places. The immunodiffusion studies are very simple and do not require expensive equipment; in fact, they hardly require any equipment at all. Reagents were sent to scientists who requested it, and it was possible to duplicate and extend our work on a worldwide scale very rapidly.

One of the most dramatic demonstrations of both the association of Au with hepatitis B virus (HBV) and of its practical applications was in the prevention of post-transfusion hepatitis. A major complication of modern surgery had been the hepatitis that all too often followed the multiple transfusions used in the extensive and long surgical procedures developed in the past decades. Prior to the discovery of Au, it was known that some blood donors were occult carriers of the hepatitis virus. From our studies we predicted that the "Au test" could detect the presence of the virus in the carriers. If that were so, then the serum of all potential blood donors could be tested, and the infected units removed. In due course (primarily as a result of studies in Japan), it was established that most of the carrier units could be identified and removed. Testing for hepatitis B virus in potential blood donors became universal in the United States and many other countries. It has been estimated that about a half billion dollars per year has been saved in medical costs and time lost from work in the United States alone. This exceeds by many times the cost of all research in this area.

The New York Blood Center

Until a little more than a decade ago post-transfusion hepatitis was a major complication of surgery. It has now been virtually eliminated in many countries as a result of a simple test that can detect the presence of hepatitis B virus in potential blood donors.

Another application of our findings became apparent soon after we were able to show that Au was a part of the hepatitis B virus. There was growing evidence that antibody against Australia antigen (the surface antigen of HBV) was protective against further infection with the virus. For example, in early studies Japanese researchers had shown that persons who had antibody against the surface antigen did not develop hepatitis when transfused with blood containing Au. Our studies on patients having multiple transfusions, such as those with thalessemia, and on patients receiving renal dialysis were also consistent with a protective effect of natural antibody against infection with hepatitis virus. By 1968 it had occurred to us that the large amount of antigen present in the serum of carriers might be the basis for the manufacture of a unique vaccine. Providentially, at this time Irving Millman, who had been working at Merck Institute for Therapeutic Research in West Point, Pennsylvania, came to our laboratory at the Institute for Cancer Research in Philadelphia, bringing with him experience in the invention and development of vaccines directed against mycobacteria and pertussis. In due course we learned that the Australia antigen we were detecting was mostly in the form of 22-nanometer particles (a nanometer is one billionth of a meter) and only a small portion was on the outer coat of the whole virus.

In 1968, at the end of the Johnson administration, the U.S. federal government let it be known that it wanted to encourage the practical application of the basic scientific studies it had supported for many years. Furthermore, investigators would be expected to find sources other than the government to fund their work. Urged on by this new imperative, we prepared a patent application which was submitted in October 1969. It described Australia antigen and its relation to the hepatitis virus, the unique nature of the vaccine, and a method for separating surface antigen particles from the (at that time, presumed) infectious virus particle. The method of separation was based on physical and chemical techniques, including centrifugation, column separation, the application of enzymes for the removal of any remaining serum proteins, and additional treatment with formalin and other agents to remove any live virus which may have been retained.

The details of the vaccine and process were published and discussed in papers, lectures, and informal conversations with our colleagues, but we did

(Left) Adapted from "New Vaccine Promises Hepatitis B Protection," Don McLearn, *FDA Consumer*, pp. 22–26, May 1981; (right) Baruch S. Blumberg

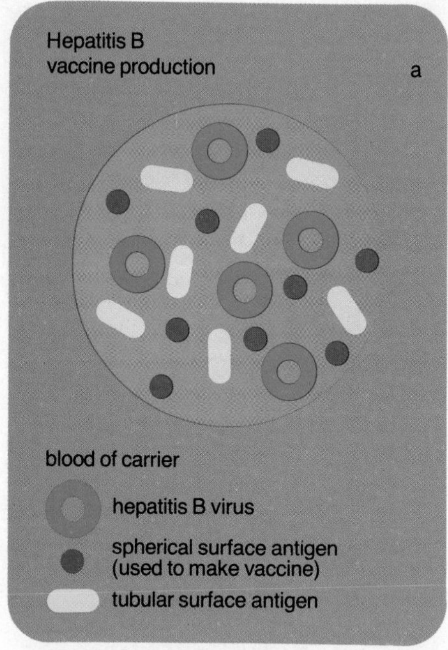

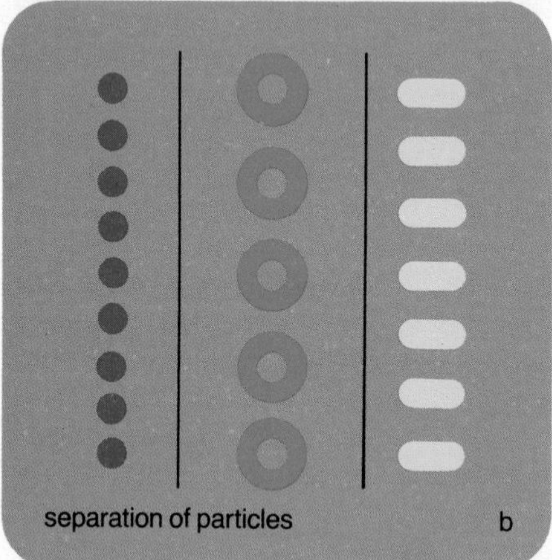

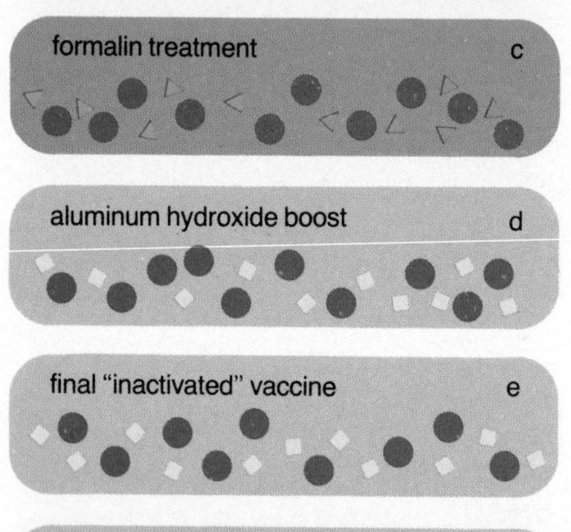

safety, purity, and potency testing f

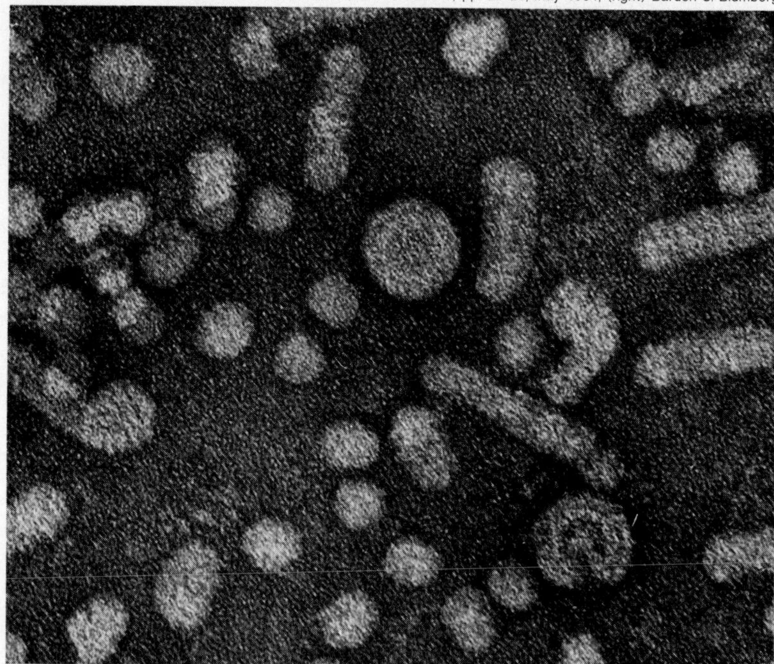

not attempt to actively promote the manufacture of the vaccine at that time. The scientific and medical community was only beginning to know about and accept the concepts and data about HBV and the vaccine, and it did not appear that there would be sufficient interest to stimulate the arduous process of field testing and acceptance by the federal authorities.

During the mid-1970s there were various studies with this vaccine and materials similar to it. In 1981 Wolf Szmuness and his colleagues in New York City did an extensive field trial which demonstrated the vaccine was safe and effective. The vaccine is now being evaluated by the U.S. Food and Drug Administration (FDA), and it is hoped that it will be available for general use in 1982. Similar vaccines against hepatitis B are being prepared in other countries.

Primary cancer of the liver (that is, a cancer which originates in the liver cell rather than originating in another organ and spreading to the liver) is one of the most common cancers in man. In parts of Asia and Africa the frequency may be as high as 30 to 50 per 100,000 of the population, and a frequency of about 150 per 100,000 has been reported from Mozambique. Pathologists have shown that primary hepatocellular carcinoma (PHC) is, in many cases, accompanied and preceded by scarring of the liver (cirrhosis). In the 1950s workers in East and West Africa suggested that the cirrhosis was produced by hepatitis, but they could not test the notion at that time. The discovery of the Australia antigen made it possible to identify HBV, and by the early 1970s studies on the relation between hepatitis and primary cancer of the liver had begun to appear.

In 1972 a meeting on PHC was convened in Kampala, Uganda, and studies on the HBV-PHC relation were described. Although there were some contradictory and ambiguous data, the results were sufficiently impressive to urge a number of researchers, including myself, to test the hypothesis that persistent infection with hepatitis virus is necessary for the development of PHC. During the next few years, evidence in support of this view began to build up until it is now substantial. In presenting the several bodies of data that support the HBV-PHC hypothesis the method of independent evidence has been used. The basic reasoning of this approach is that although any single piece of evidence may have an alternative explanation, the total body of information is best explained by the stated hypothesis. The first observation was that PHC occurs commonly in regions where chronic carriers of HBV are also common and less frequently in areas where they are not. In these regions (and also in regions where neither PHC nor carriers are common) there is a higher frequency of HBV infection among patients with PHC than in controls. PHC is usually preceded and accompanied by several forms of chronic liver disease including post-hepatitis cirrhosis; in areas of high PHC frequency, these diseases are also associated with HBV. The liver cells of patients with PHC contain virus antigens, and there have now been several reports that the DNA of the HBV is integrated into the DNA of the liver cancer cells. Viral DNA integration has been postulated as an essential part of the traditional theory of how viruses cause cancer; the DNA of the virus affects the gene expression of the cell into which it is integrated in a manner to cause malignant transformation. In liver tissue containing PHC there also appears to be integration into the noncancer cells, which will require additional explanation.

A very rigorous test of the hypothesis that persistent HBV infection is necessary for the development of PHC was provided by R. P. Beasley and his colleagues working in Taiwan. They tested a large group of government workers who received their medical care under the same health plan. About 3,500 males between the ages of 40 and 59 who were carriers of HBV were identified. A group of about 19,000 men from the same population who were not carriers were selected for controls. The infected and noninfected individuals were followed for up to about five years to determine who developed PHC. From the hypothesis it would be predicted that the carriers would be more likely to develop PHC. In the Taiwan study 62 men developed PHC, and most of them died during the follow-up period. All but one of these unfortunate people were recruited from the group who had originally been HBV carriers. (The remaining person had antibody against the core of the virus, indicating that he also had been infected with HBV some time in the past.) From this it was estimated that a carrier had a risk of developing PHC that was about 340 times greater than a person from the same environment who was not a carrier of the virus! This is one of the highest risk categories known for human cancer; by comparison the risk of heavy cigarette smokers for cancer of the lung is about 30 times.

In other studies, a family clustering of hepatitis B carriers, chronic liver disease, and PHC was found, and from both direct and indirect evidence it appears that individuals who are infected at an early age, say within the first year or two of life, are much more likely to become chronic carriers than those infected when they are older. Mothers who are chronic carriers appear to be an important source of infection for their young children. These observations led to a series of studies in areas of the world where hepatitis B is

The large amount of antigen present in the blood of hepatitis carriers became the basis for the development of a vaccine. In the first large-scale human trial, completed in 1980, hepatitis vaccine was found to be highly effective. In the future the vaccine will have a profound impact on curbing a major public health problem—hepatitis—and on preventing primary liver cancer—one of the most common cancers in man. On the opposite page the electron micrograph shows blood infected with the hepatitis B virus. The large round patches are the virus; the small spheres and elongated shapes are surface antigen particles. The schematic diagram depicts the basic steps in the production of hepatitis vaccine. First, plasma from chronic hepatitis carriers is collected (a). Surface antigen particles are then separated out and purified by chemical and physical methods (b). The chemical formalin is used to treat and destroy any active virus (c). Aluminum hydroxide is added to the preparation to boost antibody response (d). The production cycle, including final purification (e and f) and safety testing in chimpanzees, takes approximately 65 weeks.

common and traditional family patterns are retained (for example, Senegal, West Africa, and New Hebrides in the South Pacific) to determine which interactions between newborn children, their mothers, and other members of the household could result in early infection. A final objective of these studies is an understanding of how the virus is transmitted as a consequence of intrafamily behavior and how this could be prevented by changes in personal hygiene. It is hoped that such studies done within the context of the culture could lead to public health programs that are acceptable to indigenous populations.

A further piece of evidence on the hepatitis-PHC hypothesis came from a curious set of events and observations. R. Snyder, the director of the Penrose Research Laboratory of the Philadelphia Zoological Garden, has maintained a colony of Pennsylvania woodchucks (*Marmota monax*). Woodchucks kept in the protected zoo environment live much longer than animals in the wild. Postmortem examinations were conducted on about 100 animals that have died over the past 20 years. About 25% died with primary carcinoma of the liver. A virus (woodchuck hepatitis virus, WHV) has been isolated from the blood and liver of these animals. At the time it was discovered, WHV was the only virus similar to HBV. They both have the same diameter (42 micrometers) and appearance. Both have double and single stranded DNA, and both carry their own DNA polymerase. These are characteristics unique to these viruses, and in nearly all other respects the relation between WHV and PHC in the woodchucks is analogous to the HBV-PHC relation in humans.

Since the discovery of the woodchuck virus, similar viruses have been found in Beechey ground squirrels (*Spermophilus beecheyi*) and in certain breeds of Chinese and domestic ducks. In the ducks there may also be an association with a cancer of the liver. Hence, the association between hepatitis B virus and primary cancer of the liver in humans is mirrored by the association of a similar liver cancer with a virus similar to the HBV. This represents a kind of "model" (although it is difficult to decide which is the model for which) and provides not only a further piece of evidence to support the hypothesis, but also an animal system in which further observations and experiments can be done.

In 1971, based on the unusual characteristics of HBV, we had postulated that there was a new class of viruses of which HBV was the first example. We called them Icrons, an acronym on the Institute for Cancer Research in Philadelphia where the work had been done. Molecular biological studies later in the 1970s confirmed its unusual characteristics, and the association with cancer made this class of virus especially interesting. HBV and the newly discovered viruses in the woodchuck, ground squirrel, and other animals are the first members of the Icron group.

How have science and medicine changed since the discovery of Australia antigen and the hepatitis B virus for which I was awarded the Nobel Prize in 1976? The most important consequence may be the possibility of investigating the mechanism by which a virus interacts with a human to result in a deadly cancer. It is now possible to study the virus and its host at many levels: DNA, RNA, cell, tissue, whole organism, and populations, in humans and in woodchucks, ducks, and other animals. We can also study the broader implications of the interactions of HBV and humans, organisms which have been involved with each other for ages. We have found, for example, that parents' response to infection with HBV is related to the sex of their children. HBV carriers are relatively more likely to have boys, and parents with antibody to the surface antigen are more likely to have girls. In addition, fertility appears to be less in the carrier families than the antibody families. Sex ratio and fertility have a profound effect on population size and dynamics. If these findings on HBV are confirmed, it could have an important effect on population planning if the vaccine is widely used in areas of the world where HBV is common, and this coincides with the regions of densest populations.

Post-transfusion hepatitis due to hepatitis B has been nearly eliminated as a consequence of the universal use (in the United States and many other countries) of sensitive tests of donor blood. Hepatitis has been decreased in renal dialysis units by epidemiologic and environmental control. It is expected that the vaccine against the hepatitis B virus will soon be available, and strategies are being planned for its use, along with other public health measures, to control and conceivably eliminate the transmission of the virus. If the vaccine is as safe and effective as the extensive trials that have been completed indicate it to be, then in due course we can predict (and hope) that there will be a major decrease in chronic liver disease due to HBV and in primary cancer of the liver, one of the most common and deadly cancers. If this is so then it will encourage a search for other virus-cancer relations that might also be preventable. The discovery of the Icrons is a first step in this direction.

In some respects the Nobel Prize awards its recipients certain powers and responsibilities. As such, it is important to acknowledge the debt that comes with this "gift." For example, I felt it was crucial to make known as soon as possible the information on the relation between hepatitis B virus and primary cancer of the liver, particularly in regions of the world where hepatitis and PHC are common. If in fact PHC can be prevented by the prevention of hepatitis infection, then it is essential that scientific and public health interest should be activated as soon as possible. It appears that scientists and public officials around the world have been more inclined to listen to the evidence I and my colleagues have presented than they would have had I not been awarded the Nobel Prize; in particular, I found this to be true during a visit to the People's Republic of China in 1977.

The citizens of Philadelphia gave me a reception that seemed comparable to the one given the Phillies baseball team after they won the World Series in 1980. I have since become quite involved in the affairs of the city on a number of levels. At a personal level there have also been changes since I won the prize in 1976. I find that I have been more open to new challenges. One such personal challenge is that after many years of enjoying solitary running, I now participate in long-distance road races and continue to do so despite my record as one of the slowest runners in regular competition in the Delaware Valley.

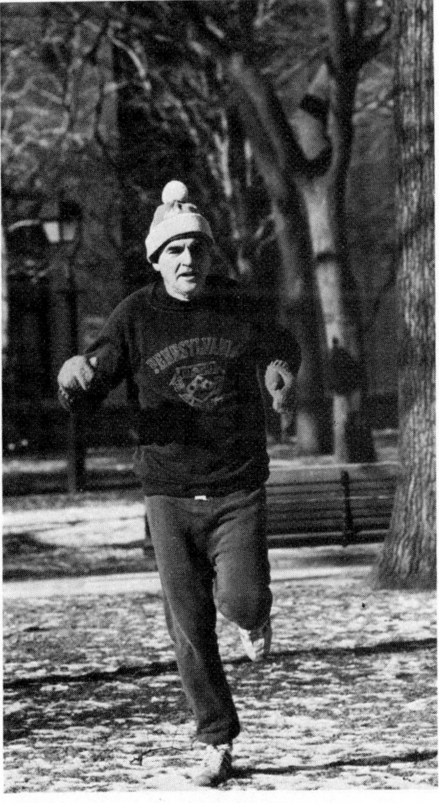

Since he won the Nobel Prize in 1976 Baruch Blumberg has been open to many personal challenges. Once a solitary runner in his home city of Philadelphia, he now competes in races. Thus far he has not won any prizes for his athletic endeavors.

Radioactivity in the Service of Man

by Rosalyn S. Yalow, Ph.D.

Since becoming a Nobel laureate I have been asked on numerous occasions, "How did you feel when you discovered radioimmunoassay?" People are generally disappointed to learn that the development of radioimmunoassay (RIA)—a procedure that can detect and measure minute amounts of biologically reactive substances in the body—was a process, not an event. What was the process?

After completing a Ph.D. in nuclear physics in 1945 at the University of Illinois and working for a short period as an electrical engineer at the Federal Telecommunications Laboratory in New York City, I returned to my alma mater, Hunter College (now Herbert H. Lehman College), in the Bronx, to teach undergraduate physics. The college had no research facilities, and full-time teaching alone was not sufficiently stimulating. I was, therefore, looking for an opportunity to do research. In 1946 the Manhattan Project, which had developed the atom bombs, was supplanted by the Atomic Energy Commission. As a result, radioactive forms of elements (radioisotopes) were made readily and inexpensively available to civilian investigators and industry from a nuclear reactor in Oak Ridge, Tennessee. This marked the practical beginning of the revolutionary applications of radioactivity to the service of man, particularly in medicine.

In December 1947 I was offered a position as part-time consultant to initiate a radioisotope unit in the radiotherapy department of the Bronx Veterans Administration (VA) Hospital, just a short distance from Hunter. The VA had made a commitment to set up such units in several of its hospitals across the United States because of its appreciation that research had to proceed pari passu with the application of radioisotopes in clinical medicine. At that time many expected that the primary role for radioisotopes in the new subspecialty, nuclear medicine, would be a therapeutic one, as replacement for radium, which had been used with moderate success in implants to deliver radiation to malignant tumors. There had already been several reports of the usefulness of radioactive iodine in treating thyroid cancer. Previously, radioiodine had been produced by a cyclotron (a high-energy accelerator). It is of interest that the cost of therapy was reduced from about $1,000 to about $50 when reactor-produced radioiodine from Oak Ridge became available.

Rosalyn S. Yalow, Ph.D., *won the Nobel Prize for Physiology or Medicine in 1977 for the development of the radioimmunoassay technique. She is presently Senior Medical Investigator at the Veterans Administration Medical Center in the Bronx, New York.*

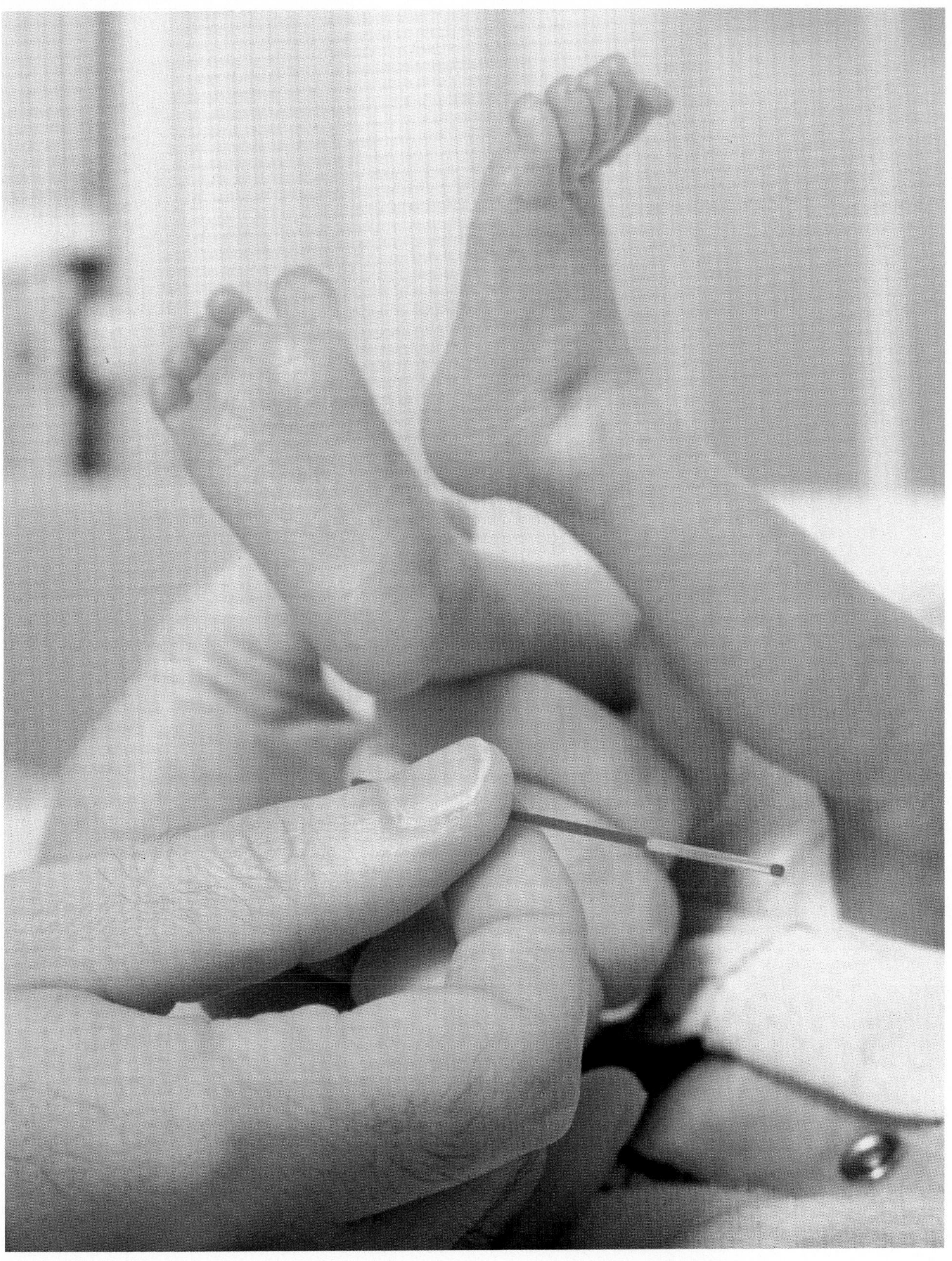

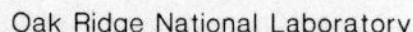
Oak Ridge National Laboratory

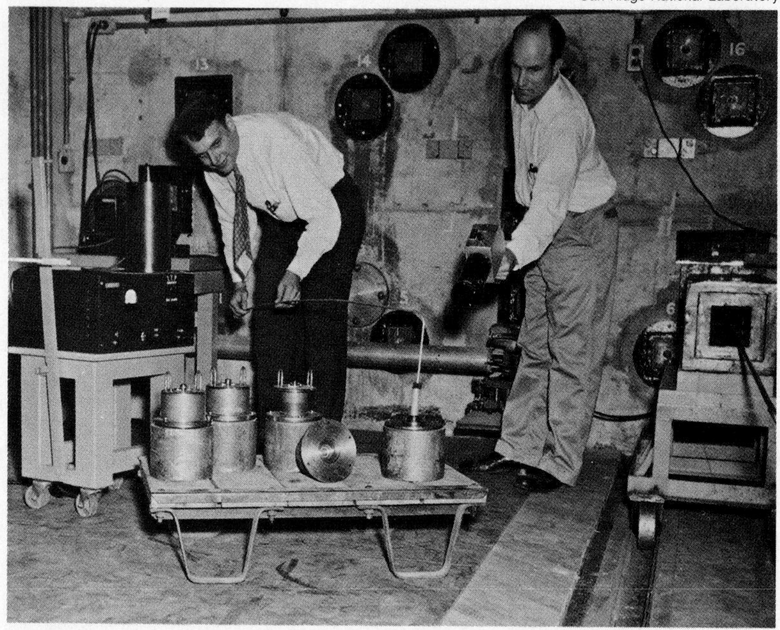

In the mid-1940s radioisotopes produced at Oak Ridge National Laboratory in Tennessee were made available to medical investigators. Here isotopes are being prepared for shipping.

I soon appreciated, however, that the most important use of radioisotopes would be in understanding human physiology and in clinical diagnosis, particularly after the appearance of George de Hevesy's book, *Radioactive Indicators,* which described hundreds of applications of radioisotopic methodology in animal physiology. (De Hevesy received the Nobel Prize for Chemistry in 1943 for his use of radioisotopes as tracers in the study of physiological processes.) It was evident to me that the use of radioisotopes had broad implications for diverse problems in medicine, beyond those recognized at the time. In 1950, when I chose to leave teaching and join the VA full time, I had the good fortune to attract to our unit Solomon Berson, who was completing his residency in internal medicine. In 1954, our unit separated from the radiotherapy department and became an independent radioisotope service. It is worth noting that neither Berson nor I had the advantage of specialized postdoctoral training in biomedical investigation. We learned from and disciplined each other and probably were each other's severest critics. I learned a great deal from his expertise in the fields of physiology, anatomy, and clinical medicine. Together we fashioned a quantitative approach to biomedical investigation using radioisotopic methodology as our tool. In 1968, Berson assumed the chairmanship of the department of medicine at Mount Sinai School of Medicine, but he maintained his affiliation with our laboratory at the VA. Our partnership was to last until his untimely death in 1972, which marked a great loss to clinical and investigative medicine.

(Overleaf) A tiny sample of blood taken from an infant at birth can indicate whether congenital hypothyroidism is present. Immediate treatment can then prevent mental retardation. This kind of screening was impossible before the development of the radioimmunoassay. Photograph, Dan McCoy—Rainbow

In the early 1950s our studies were primarily concerned with the use of radioactive iodine (^{131}I) in the study of thyroid physiology and diagnosis as well as in blood volume determinations. We developed methods to determine the distribution and turnover of serum proteins; using ^{131}I-labeled proteins as tracers we were able to evaluate the behavior of unlabeled materials. It seemed to us that similar methodology could be applied to studies with radioiodine-labeled peptide hormones. (A peptide is a protein of low molecular weight. A hormone is a substance produced in one part of the body and transmitted to another part where it has a specific action.)

Thirty years ago insulin was the hormone most readily available in a highly purified form suitable for radioisotopic labeling. I. Arthur Mirsky had hypothesized that diabetes in the adult might be due to a deficiency of insulin in the circulating blood resulting from its abnormally rapid degradation by an enzyme, insulinase, which is found in the liver, kidney, and elsewhere in the body. This hypothesis was quite reasonable; while it was generally assumed that all diabetes was associated with an absolute deficiency of insulin, it had also been shown that the pancreases of diabetics contained about normal amounts of the hormone. However, when we administered radioiodine-labeled insulin intravenously to diabetic and nondiabetic persons, we observed that, contrary to Mirsky's hypothesis, the labeled insulin disappeared more slowly, not more rapidly, from the plasma of diabetics.

In the 1950s, before the era of oral medications that are now widely used to reduce blood sugar, most diabetic subjects were treated with insulin. We had also noted that labeled insulin disappeared slowly from the plasma of schizophrenics who had received insulin-shock therapy and that newly discovered diabetics could be converted from "rapid disappearers" to "slow disappearers" after several months of insulin treatment. We considered that the slow disappearance of the labeled insulin following intravenous administration might be due to its binding to an antibody, a neutralizing substance that had developed in response to treatment with a foreign protein, beef and/or pork insulin—the types of insulin used in treating diabetes. We reasoned that the failure of previous studies to demonstrate the ubiquitous presence of insulin-binding antibodies might be due to the insensitivity of classic immunologic methods used for their detection. We therefore developed a method with enhanced sensitivity to prove that insulin circulates freely in the plasma of untreated subjects but binds to an antibody in the plasma of insulin-treated subjects, in whom the insulin is not human but "foreign."

We also confirmed that the classic immunologic methods (*e.g.*, immunoprecipitation, red-cell hemagglutination, and complement fixation) failed to reveal the presence of antibodies. These latter types of studies had generated the accepted dogma that insulin was so small a peptide that it was, at most, only on occasion weakly antigenic (stimulating the production of antibodies). To determine the binding capacity of the antibodies we added increasing amounts of stable (unlabeled) insulin to a fixed dilution of antiserum (serum containing antibodies) combined with radioactively labeled insulin. We were able to observe that the fraction of labeled insulin bound to a given amount of antibody decreased as the concentration of unlabeled insulin increased. This observation provided the basis for measuring very small amounts of hormones, now known as radioimmunoassay, or RIA.

Attempts to publish these results met with failure for almost a year. In 1955 our paper was rejected once by *Science* and twice by the *Journal of Clinical Investigation* (*JCI*) since reviewers for both journals were unwilling to accept our heretical conclusion of the ubiquitous presence of insulin-

Courtesy, Rosalyn S. Yalow

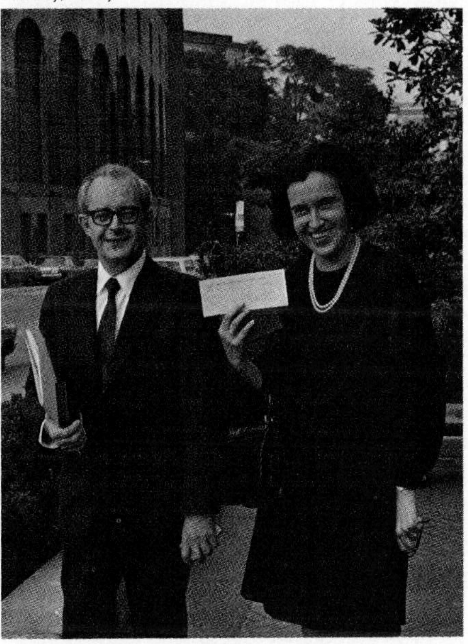

Rosalyn Yalow and Solomon Berson worked in tandem and were jointly honored for their discoveries from 1954 until Berson's death in 1972. In 1971 they received the Dickson Prize for medicine, an award of $10,000 given annually by the University of Pittsburgh School of Medicine.

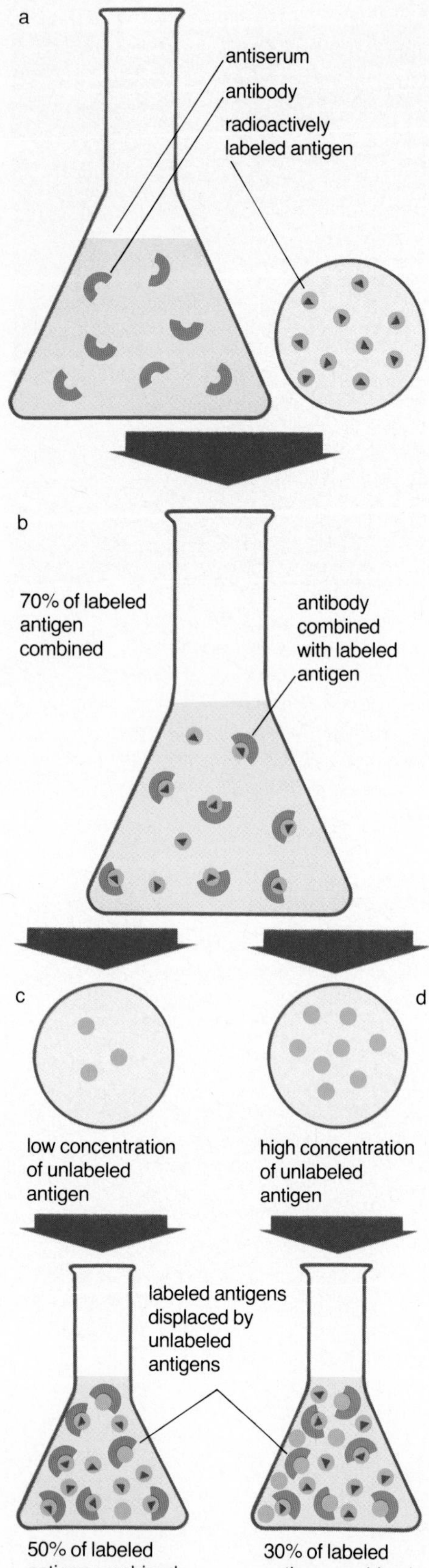

binding *antibodies* in the plasma of insulin-treated subjects. Finally in 1956 the paper was published in the *JCI* after we agreed to substitute "insulin-binding *globulin*" for "antibody" in the title. However, in our discussion we explained that we believed the insulin-binding globulin met the requirements for an antibody. Therefore, we were suggesting that insulin resistance in diabetics could be due to an immune response against insulin, which acted as an antigen. Our faith in the importance of this discovery is evidenced by my having saved the letters of rejection. One of them was published as part of my Nobel lecture. Suffice it to say that many original discoveries are first deemed heresy, as Galileo learned almost 400 years ago.

Three years were to pass from the time we appreciated the RIA principle until we reported in 1959 that we were able to measure circulating levels of plasma insulin in man. What accounted for the delay? Our studies on the distribution and turnover of labeled insulin and the knowledge that patients whose pancreases had been surgically removed required about 30 to 50 units of insulin per day suggested that, in response to a glucose feeding, peak insulin concentrations might be as minute as 0.1 milliunits (a ten-thousandth of a unit) of insulin per milliliter of plasma. However, the available antisera were only sensitive enough to detect about one milliunit of beef or pork insulin per milliliter. At that time human insulin was not available. However, we believed that if we could obtain human insulin it might react even more poorly with these antisera. The dilemma for us, then, was whether to develop methods for extraction and concentration of insulin from human plasma or instead to find a way to improve the sensitivity of a test for the detection of human insulin. We chose the latter approach.

To appreciate better how to select the most sensitve antisera, we studied the kinetics and thermodynamics of the reaction of insulin with antibody, using as tracers the various animal insulins available in sufficiently pure forms. We immunized rabbits, the classic laboratory animal for antibody production, and tested their antisera and those obtained from insulin-treated diabetic humans. Mathematical analysis had indicated that antigen-antibody bindings of higher energies would permit more sensitive radioimmunoassays. Thus we spent three years on related work, but it was not until the spring of 1959 that the day came when we could say "Eureka." Antisera produced in guinea pigs in response to beef or pork insulin provided sufficient sensitivity for the detection of insulin in human blood.

In retrospect, it seems that we initially failed to appreciate the full potential of RIA. However, there were extenuating circumstances. Suitable purified peptide hormones were few in number. Although we successfully demonstrated that insulin *was* antigenic, we were not fully convinced of the ability to produce satisfactory antisera to other peptide hormones, many of which are even smaller than insulin. Methods for labeling peptide hormones were far from ideal. Additionally we were diverted to study problems of radiation damage due to absorption of beta particles from ^{131}I in solutions containing radiolabeled peptides. More generally, precise understanding of the nature of the reaction of antigen with antibody was lacking. Nevertheless, it is now evident that we should have tried earlier to immunize other laboratory animals.

Substances measured by radioimmunoassay

Peptidal hormones

- pituitary hormones
  - growth hormone
  - adrenocorticotropic hormone (ACTH)
  - melanocyte stimulating hormone (MSH)
    - α-MSH, β-MSH
  - glycoproteins
    - thyroid stimulating hormone (TSH)
    - follicle stimulating hormone (FSH)
    - luteinizing hormone (LH)
  - prolactin
  - lipotropin
  - vasopressin
  - oxytocin
- chorionic hormones
  - human chorionic gonadotropin (HCG)
  - human chorionic somatomammotropin (HCS)
- pancreatic hormones
  - insulin
  - glucagon
  - pancreatic polypeptide
- calcitropic hormones
  - parathyroid hormone (PTH)
  - calcitonin (CT)
- gastrointestinal hormones
  - gastrin
  - secretin
  - cholecystokinin (CCK)
  - vasoactive intestinal polypeptide (VIP)
  - gastric inhibitory polypeptide (GIP)
- vasoactive tissue hormones
  - angiotensins
  - bradykinins
- releasing and release inhibiting factors
  - thyrotropin releasing factor (TRF)
  - luteinizing hormone releasing factor (LHRF)
  - somatostatin
- other peptides
  - substance P
  - endorphins
  - enkephalins

Nonpeptidal hormones

- thyroidal hormones
  - thyroxine (T_4)
  - triiodothyronine (T_3)
  - reverse T_3
- steroids
  - aldosterone
  - corticosteroids
  - estrogens
  - androgens
  - progesterones
- prostaglandins
- biologic amines
  - serotonin
  - melatonin

Nonhormonal substances

- drugs and vitamins
  - cardiac glycosides
  - drugs of abuse
  - psychoactive drugs
  - antibiotics
  - CNS depressants
  - vitamin A
  - folic acid
- cyclic nucleotides
- enzymes
  - C_1 esterase
  - fructose 1, 6 diphosphatase
  - plasminogen, plasmin
  - chymotrypsin, trypsin
  - carbonic anhydrase isoenzymes
  - aldose reductase
  - carboxypeptidase B
  - pancreatic elastase
- viruses
  - hepatitis associated antigen
  - murine leukemia viruses (Gross, Rauscher, Moloney)
  - Mason-Pfizer monkey virus
- tumor antigens
  - carcinoembryonic antigen
  - α-fetoprotein
- serum proteins
  - thyroxine binding globulin
  - IgG, IgE, IgA, IgM
  - properdin
  - fibrinogen
  - apolipoprotein B
  - myoglobin
  - myelin basic protein
- other
  - intrinsic factor
  - rheumatoid factor
  - Hageman factor
  - neurophysins
  - staphylococcal β-enterotoxin

It was not until we made the first determination of insulin in human plasma and were surprised to discover that many adult diabetics responded to a glucose load with even greater insulin release than nondiabetic subjects that we realized that RIA would prove to be a powerful tool for dynamic studies of the regulation of the secretion of many peptide hormones. However, traditional bioassay procedures were widely used at that time, and the biomedical community was slow to accept the value of RIA. In the early 1960s we conducted a series of courses to train other investigators in our methodology. Nonetheless, between 1959 and 1965 research papers from our laboratory constituted the major portion of RIA studies reported in the U.S. literature.

However, the growth in the next decade was virtually exponential, and it was estimated in 1975 that in the United States alone over 4,000 hospital and nonhospital clinical and nuclear medicine laboratories performed radioimmunoassays of all kinds, almost double the number a year or two earlier. The technical simplicity of RIA and the ease with which reagents can be obtained in kit form have enabled its extensive use even in nations scientifically less sophisticated than the U.S. Since virtually any organic

Schematic of radioimmunoassay is shown on the facing page. The substance to be analyzed is used as an antigen to raise antiserum in laboratory animals. Extracted antiserum is then mixed with a radioactively labeled quantity of the same antigen (a) such that about 70% of the labeled antigen combines with antibody in the antiserum (b). After portions of this mixture are added to various known concentrations of unlabeled antigen (c and d), the amounts of labeled antigen still bound to antibody—i.e., *that have not been displaced—are isolated and measured. Because the fraction of combined labeled antigen decreases as the concentration of unlabeled antigen increases, many such measurements at various concentrations of unlabeled antigen yield a curve on which can be found unknown amounts of antigen.*

Albany Medical Center, Albany, New York; photographs, Dan McCoy—Rainbow

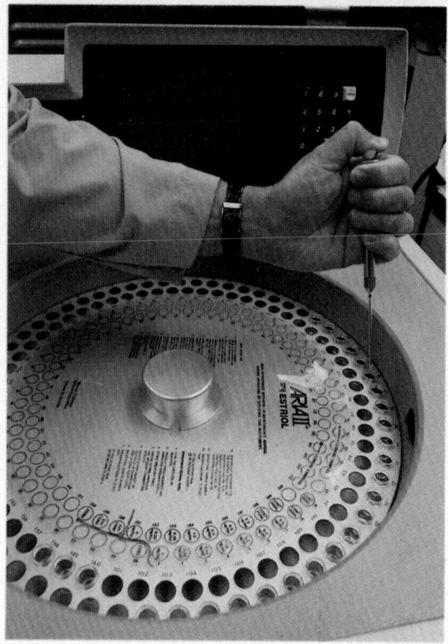

RIA provides quantitative data about substances in the body. In the top photograph a technician is loading specimen tubes into a counting tray of a gamma counter, which can measure precise levels of drugs and hormones in a blood sample. The bottom picture shows an automated RIA system. In this case estriol (one of the estrogen hormones) is being measured.

substance of biologic interest is immunogenic or can be rendered so by coupling it to an appropriate protein, RIA has been applied to the measurement of hundreds of such materials.

RIA was first applied to the measurement of peptide hormones in plasma. These are found in concentrations as low as a millionth of a millionth of a gram in the presence of a billionfold higher concentrations of plasma proteins. Chemical methods were useless to detect these peptides, and bioassay methods were so insensitive that a cup of blood was necessary to perform with far less accuracy and far greater tedium the same determination that could be made on a drop of blood using RIA. Therefore, virtually all the information now available about the regulation of hormonal secretion and the interrelation among hormones has been gleaned with RIA. Furthermore, it has been extensively used for the clinical diagnosis of pathologic states associated with hormonal excess or deficiency. For example, it has been used to determine whether the small stature of some children is due to undersecretion of growth hormone or to other factors. It has been used to determine whether severe ulcer disease is due to a gastrin-secreting malignant tumor or to benign hyperactivity of the patient's gastrin-secreting cells of the gastrointestinal tract. (Gastrin is a hormone that promotes stomach acid release.)

Although chemical methods for the determination of hormones secreted by the thyroid gland or the adrenals, which circulate in much higher concentrations than the peptide hormones, were well known 30 years ago, RIA is now generally the method of choice for measuring these hormones as well.

The remarkable sensitivity of RIA has had a particularly profound effect on public health by enabling the early detection of hypothyroidism. Underactivity of the thyroid occurs in about 1 in 4,000 newborns in the United States. Previously it could not be detected clinically until the baby was several months old, but by that time it was too late since adequate amounts of thyroid hormone are crucial for normal brain development during the first few months of life. However, just a few drops of the neonate's blood can now be sent to a state or regional laboratory in most parts of the country at a cost of about a dollar or two per sample; diagnosis can be made using RIA methodology within a week or two. Necessary treatment with a small pill crushed in the infant's milk or water can be begun promptly. It is now known that children so treated have intellectual development equal to that of their siblings rather than being the victims of irreversible mental retardation. What a bonus for the children, their families, and society.

RIA has also been applied in clinical medicine for the measurement of the circulating levels of drugs such as digoxin used for the treatment of heart conditions and antibiotics used for the treatment of infections. It provides quantitative data about the levels of a drug in the bloodstream—whether they are in the range for effective therapy or perhaps so high as to be toxic. These checks on levels of important drugs with dangerous side effects (such as deafness or kidney failure) are enormously increasing the safety of many therapies. RIA has also been used by pharmaceutical companies in investigations of the distribution and turnover of new drugs in animals before considering the use of these substances in human trials.

The first application of RIA to infectious diseases was in the determination of hepatitis B antigen in blood. A decade ago contamination of blood with this virus accounted for most cases of liver inflammation (hepatitis) occurring in patients several months after receiving a transfusion. Now routine RIA testing of bank blood has resulted in a striking decrease in this cause for a disabling and sometimes fatal disease.

It is evident from this brief review that RIA has been broadly applied in many fields of clinical medicine and biomedical investigation. Recently, I have been predicting that the impact of RIA on the study of infectious diseases in the coming decade may prove as revolutionary as its impact on endocrinology has already been. Infection remains a major public health problem throughout the world and simple inexpensive methods of identifying those infected with diseases such as tuberculosis or leprosy, which are endemic in much of the world, would facilitate eradication of these diseases.

My background as a physicist and, in particular, as a nuclear physicist, has been central to the development of the radioisotopic methodology. I have never had a formal course in biology or biochemistry. In contacts with students I continue to emphasize that formal instruction in graduate schools, though not unimportant, provides a small fraction of the foundation of knowledge gained during professional life. As previously mentioned, my on-the-job training was made easier by my 22-year partnership with Solomon Berson. Undoubtedly our work together had a synergistic effect on both our careers. I deeply regret that he did not survive to share the Nobel Prize with me.

How has the honor of receiving a Nobel Prize affected me? In certain ways, not at all. My laboratory work remains a source of enormous delight. The excitement of planning experiments that will reveal a previously unsuspected secret of nature remains undiminished. However, there have been some changes. I now have a second lab at Montefiore Hospital, also in the Bronx, and the assistance of eight physicians-in-training as associate investigators, compared to only one or two in earlier years. At a time of declining interest in clinical investigation, I am particularly concerned with encouraging young physicians who will make the important discoveries of the future.

There is one disturbing feature about being a Nobel laureate. The public recognition associated with this honor tempts some of us to become instant experts in philosophy and public affairs. I have tried to restrict my activities in the public arena to areas of my special expertise. A major field of interest relates to my training in nuclear physics and my experience in medical physics. In recent years I have often been called upon to voice my opinion on the subject of radiation hazards. I have tried to communicate to the public that many of its fears are unrealistic concerning the dangers of nuclear-power reactors, radioactive waste materials, cosmic rays, and natural radioactivity. These fears, often generated by uninformed pressure groups and the sensationalism of the media, must be countered with facts. Scientists must discuss with the public, in terms it can understand, how scientific progress that serves the common good can be impeded by needless regulation. I feel it is the responsibility of scientists to be willing to invest the time and effort to generate the data required for informed decision making. The aura of the Nobel Prize offers some advantage in fulfilling this responsibility.

Svenskt Pressfoto, Stockholm

Rosalyn Yalow at the Nobel ceremony in December 1977.

FOR ADDITIONAL READING:

Bauman, W. A., and Yalow, R. S. "Immunologic Potency of Recombined A and B Chains of Synthetic Human and Pancreatic Pork Insulins." *Diabetes,* March 1981.

Berson, S. A., Yalow, R. S., *et al.* "Insulin-I^{131} Metabolism in Human Subjects: Demonstration of Insulin Binding Globulin in the Circulation of Insulin Treated Subjects." *The Journal of Clinical Investigation,* Vol. XXXV, No. 2: 170–190, February 1956.

Rasmussen, A. F., Jr. "Hormone Discoveries of the 1977 Nobelists." *1979 Medical and Health Annual,* pp. 224–226. Chicago: Encyclopaedia Britannica, Inc., 1978.

Yalow, Rosalyn S. "Radioimmunoassay: A Probe for the Fine Structure of Biologic Systems." *Nobel Lectures.* Amsterdam and New York: Elsevier Publishing Company, 1978.

The Enigma of Factitious Illness

by Don R. Lipsitt, M.D.

In the average medical encounter physicians assume patients seek help for bona fide problems and patients assume physicians will be eager to alleviate those problems. At least once or twice a year in virtually every hospital in the United States, these basic assumptions are violated in a seismic but not immediately obvious way. Consider the following scenario:

On a busy Friday afternoon in a hospital emergency room, a 34-year-old woman, Anna H., was seen, complaining of severe chest pain on the right side. The pain came on suddenly during a day off from her work as a nurse in another hospital. The pain was very localized and worsened when she took a deep breath or coughed. She had with her a small bottle containing some bloody mucus that she coughed up during one particularly painful episode. For the most part, she had been in good health, although just a few days before she had a transient pain in her leg. She had called a physician friend who suggested that she might have a pulmonary embolism and that she should report to the emergency room right away.

The woman looked anxious but gave an intelligent and clear account of her condition. After preliminary blood tests and X-rays of the chest, she was quickly admitted to the hospital, where there were strict orders for bed rest and anticoagulants were given. It was not unusual that her chest films did not reveal a source of pain, for radiologic evidence of pulmonary embolism is not always present. The results of laboratory analysis of the coughed-up blood sample she had brought to the emergency room were not available until Monday, since the weekend laboratory staff did only the most urgent studies and the findings would not have altered the nature of immediate treatment.

On Monday, the laboratory reported that the bloody mucus had characteristics of menstrual blood, suggesting that the patient had falsified her story. An enraged, overworked intern confronted the patient with the laboratory report, eliciting an equally hostile response from the patient, who accused the physician of ineptness, characterized the hospital as disorganized, and threatened to leave the hospital if more trusting, empathic care were not forthcoming. As the staff became more convinced of the patient's confabulation, the patient became more vocal and intimidating. Finally, after several days, a psychiatrist was asked for a consultation, whereupon the patient indignantly signed herself out of the hospital, accusing its staff of gross incompetence.

The diagnosis: Münchausen's syndrome.

Cases such as that of Anna H. pose a vexing dilemma for the medical profession. How should this baffling behavior be interpreted? Most people find the prospect of sickness and hospitalization objectionable if not frankly frightening; why then do some individuals expend time, energy, and ingenuity seeking just those ends? Explanations that suggest this is a way to find room and board or to receive attention seem feeble alongside the sizable risks that may be involved in such pursuit.

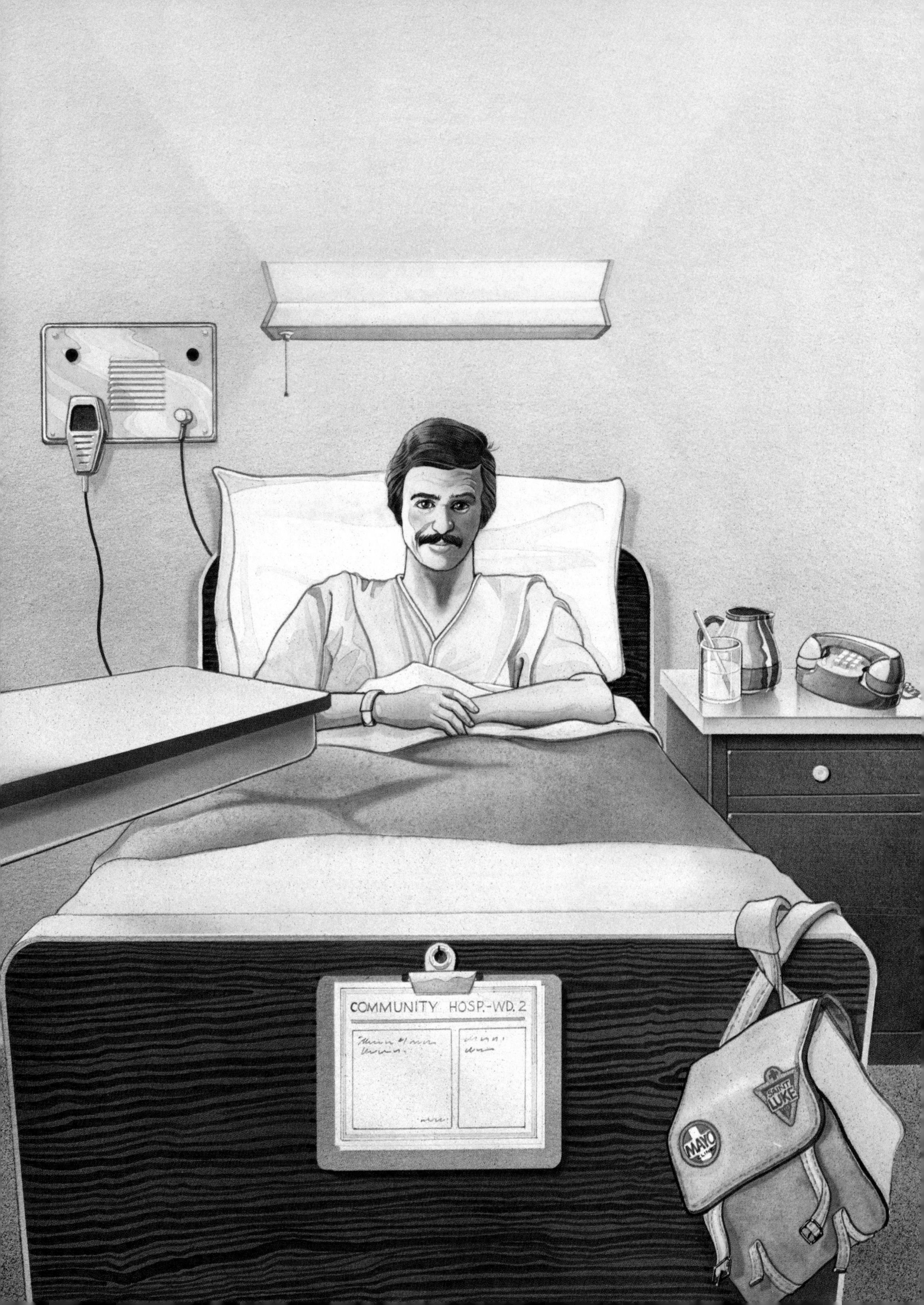
COMMUNITY HOSP.-WD. 2
SAINT LUKE
MAYO

Münchausen's syndrome

The feigning of disease has been recorded for more than a century. Rare cases of outright "malingering"—the voluntary production of symptoms in pursuit of a recognizable goal (*e.g.,* avoiding prosecution)—had been described in the medical literature. But no name was affixed to the feigning of illness that had no obvious goals until 1951. In that year the British medical journal *The Lancet* carried an article by British physician Richard Asher who described "a common syndrome which most doctors have seen, but about which little has been written. Like the famous Baron von Münchausen, the persons affected have always traveled widely; and their stories, like those attributed to him, are both dramatic and untruthful. Accordingly the syndrome is respectfully dedicated to the baron, and named after him."

Curiously, there was little about the baron or his stories that resembled the patients who ultimately carried his name. A soldier who in 1760 retired from fighting with the Russian forces against the Turks, Karl Friedrich Hieronymus, Freiherr von Münchhausen (the extra "h" was later dropped) retreated to live the life of a country gentleman on his estate in Hanover, Germany, where he entertained others with extraordinary tales of his adventures as hunter, soldier, and sportsman. The baron told fanciful tales, which—unlike those of Münchausen patients—were quite intentionally outrageous. The baron's tales had nothing to do with illness, doctors, or hospitals. In fact, many of the "Münchausen" tales were either plagiarized or totally fabricated by Rudolph Erich Raspe, a dilettantish scholar and historian. The real Münchhausen would probably have disapproved of Asher's eponymous dedication, as the patients he described were more like the roguish Raspe, who was known to have deceived and bilked people in prominent positions, which forced him to keep on the move for a good part of his life.

Asher's classic paper described three cases of individuals who had feigned illness, and speculated about the possible motives for the seemingly senseless but intense desire to deceive in this curious way. Asher concluded only that "these patients waste an enormous amount of time and trouble in hospitals." He hoped that exposing their practices would be useful. "If an explanation for the condition could be found," he believed that it just might lead to a "cure" for "the psychological kink which produces the disease."

Seven years later Asher broadened his view of imposturing patients. In an effort to understand "the advantages of illness," he devised the following classification, which he called the "borderlands of malingering":

A. illness as a comfort
   1. hysteria
   2. the proud lonely person

B. illness as a hobby
   1. the grand tour type (rich hypochondriac)
   2. the chronic outpatient (poor hypochondriac)
   3. the eccentric hypochondriac (faddist)
   4. the chronic convalescent (daren't recover)

C. illness as a profession
   1. anorexia nervosa
   2. the chronic artefactualists
   3. Münchausen's syndrome

Don R. Lipsitt, M.D., *is Associate Professor of Psychiatry at Harvard Medical School and Chief of Psychiatry at Mount Auburn Hospital, Cambridge, Massachusetts.*

Illustrations by John Youssi

Asher regarded true malingering as "illness as a purpose" and distinguished it from the "borderlands." He considered those who engaged in "illness as a profession" to be psychopaths—extremely egocentric and antisocial individuals. Asher further differentiated his last category, the Münchausen subset, according to the nature of the chief presenting complaint: (a) laparotomophilia migrans (mainly abdominal symptoms), (b) hemorrhagica histrionica (largely specializing in hemorrhage), and (c) neurologica diabolica (specializing in faints, fits, stupor, etc.).

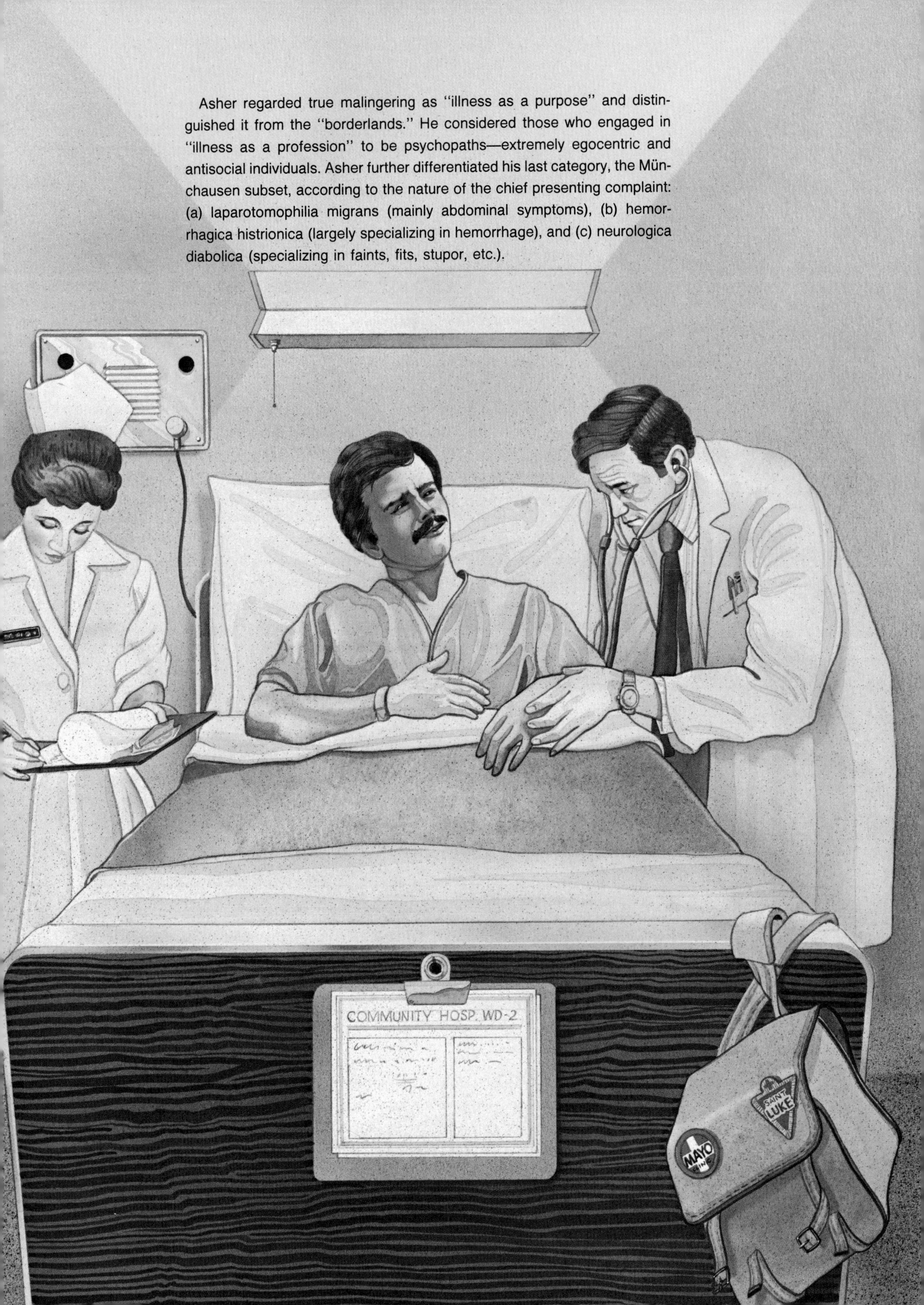

The Münchausen label won wide acceptance. Asher was astounded by the effects of his naming the condition—the amount of international correspondence generated by it and the proliferation in medical journals of related articles, many of which proposed new explanations, but most of which only added to the confusion. Lecturing on "sense and sensibility" before the Medical Society of London in 1959, Asher was prompted to offer a humble apology for having introduced the term Münchausen's syndrome. "I discovered nothing about it [the syndrome]," he said. "Its origin is still shrouded in mystery. I only described something that most doctors knew already and gave it a name, a name which was far from satisfactory, though I have never been able to think of a better one." Asher was disdainful of a psychiatrist-psychologist team who had placed themselves and a flying squad in 24-hour readiness to go anywhere in Great Britain to study suspected cases. These researchers, he noted, keep their subjects in the hospital for months "(to the great benefit of the community) and they ask them what different shaped ink splodges remind them of (with less definite benefit to the community)."

Asher cautioned his colleagues in the medical profession by reminding them that "the words used in clinical medicine have a tremendous influence on the subject they describe. . . . They perpetuate illnesses . . . whose existence is doubtful, they deny recognition to others whose existence is beyond question and they distort textbook descriptions to conform to the chosen word." Prophetic words, indeed, as confusion about the syndrome called Münchausen's has abounded in practice and literature since Asher's day. The pejorative use and misapplication of the term have far exceeded efforts to understand, clarify, and study the condition. Hysteria, malingering, hypochondriasis, psychopathy, pathomimes, and numerous other terms have been inaccurately applied to patients—usually in an effort by physicians to overcome the frustration engendered by those who feign illness. The compendium of labels has enlarged over the years to include: professional patients, hospital addicts, hospital hoboes, hospital vagrants, peregrinating problem patients, crocks, turkeys, gomers, and so forth.

The confusion, however, is not entirely attributable to careless diagnosis. Accurate diagnosis depends upon good history taking, rarely possible with a patient who is feigning illness. Histories obtained from patients with feigned, or factitious, illness are often confabulatory, contradictory, and incomplete. Furthermore, these patients customarily take flight when their ruse is discovered or when psychiatric consultation is mentioned. If these patients remain in care after they are suspected or discovered, the rage and distrust aroused in medical staff may effectively abolish further interest in history gathering and diagnosis.

Despite the significant obstacles, some believable data about so-called Münchausen's syndrome, or factitious illness—terms used more or less interchangeably—have been acquired. The more supportable evidence to date suggests there are commonalities in patients who feign illness for reasons other than malingering. These include the following: (1) illness, institutionalization (usually hospitals), and physicians have played an important role in their lives; (2) impostors of disease have no other overt purpose than to be cast in the role of "patient"; (3) early life experience is marked by severe deprivation, loss, or physical brutality; (4) employment in some health-related field is a frequent finding; (5) a thwarted wish to be a physician is not uncommon; (6) severe difficulty in establishing lasting, meaningful relationships is virtually a hallmark; (7) associated social and legal problems are often discovered; and (8) intelligence level is generally, though not always, high, revealed by knowledge of and capacity to mimic disease and by ability to weave ingenious yet plausible stories of sickness.

One of the most famous Münchausen cases, known as the "Indiana Cyclone," was reported by John Chapman in 1957. A 39-year-old man who claimed to be variously a professional wrestler, a claims collector, and a much-traveled merchant sailor presented himself in general hospital emergency rooms on at least 16 separate occasions, in at least a dozen states and two countries. Usually appearing with blood-spattered clothes and a plausible history of coughing up blood, hospital admission was customarily guaranteed and prompt. Within hours or days, the patient typically became violent, often trashing the premises. Transfer to a locked ward of a mental hospital on several occasions was quickly followed by the "Cyclone's" escape and often by his reappearance at the same emergency room with a story similar to his previous one (and sometimes readmission!). Unfortunately this much-reported case offered little enlightenment about the personality behind or the motivation for such behavior. Nor were any constructive approaches to treatment described in the abundant literature on the impostor from Indiana.

These patients are deceitful, masochistic, manipulative, and alternately ingratiating and openly contemptuous. All succeed in antagonizing their medical attendants. Psychiatrist H. R. Spiro reviewed the entire literature on Münchausen's syndrome through 1968. Of 38 reported cases, ages 23 to 62, there were about twice as many men as women. Common findings included "gridiron" stomachs (from old surgical scars); burr holes in the skull (from needless neurosurgery); vagrancy; seemingly uncontrollable lying, which is often captivating, believable, and "accurate" in medical detail; and a certain consistency in method of operating. The documentation of cases, however, offered not a single detailed life history.

A recent observation of bizarre factitious illness is "Münchausen syndrome by proxy." In several instances mothers have feigned or induced illness in their young children, for which they then seek emergency room care. In the process, the mother is enjoined as an "ally" of the physicians in caring for the child. In this troubling drama, the mother uses her child so that she can gain sympathy in the sheltered hospital environment.

A spectrum of manufactured maladies

Though the term Münchausen's syndrome should be reserved for the most dramatic cases, which are the ones that are most frequently reported, the spectrum of factitious illnesses is broad. At one end is the almost universal "fibbing" to avoid some undesirable activity. The recognized legitimacy of the "sick role" and its rights and privileges alleviate the need to offer complex and sometimes embarrassing excuses when "simple sickness" might accomplish the purpose.

But the spectrum extends beyond the child who wants a day away from school or the spouse's occasional disinterest in sexual activity. Humans have devised a wide array of methods—from the pedestrian to the ingenious—in order to initiate and maintain the role of patient. Methods of deception have included milder forms, such as manipulation of thermometers to create false readings, to much more serious reports of self-injection of foreign bacterial substances or swallowing of potent drugs such as thyroid extract or anticoagulants to create "real disease." While some patients have been known to mix feces with urine to create the illusion of a urinary bladder infection, others have actually produced infection by injecting fecal material into the urethra and bladder. In one case the infection progressed to kidney disease and was fatal.

Other deceptions that have sent zealous physicians on wild goose chases have included surreptitious dropping of collected kidney stones into a bedpan after complaining of severe cramping flank pain as well as simple complaining of vague pains, which the dedicated doctor cannot ignore; in either case pursuit of the problem most often leads to frustration, with the exhausted doctor ultimately rejecting the patient.

Individuals with residual signs of previously treated (and cured) diseases may withhold information about a known "spot" on the lung or a missing organ in order to promote and prolong medical investigation. Neurologists have seen patients with known congenital abnormalities of the nervous system (such as unequal pupil size or atypical nerve distribution to a part of the body) who plead ignorance or surprise at the "finding" in order to embellish it and ensure further workup.

An increasingly common factitious disorder is self-induced hypoglycemia. Because hypoglycemia (lowered blood sugar) can be a side effect of treatment for existing diabetes, deception by self-injection of excess insulin, fasting, or unusual physical exertion often is not immediately suspected. Moreover, since hypoglycemia can occur in a variety of other conditions, the finding of low blood sugar in nondiabetics almost always guarantees concern and extensive medical evaluation by the physician.

In recent years complex technology has introduced new opportunities for deception. Pacemakers, hemodialysis shunts, and other devices have enhanced the virtuosity of individuals inclined to hoodwink medical personnel.

Illness not found but not feigned

Because the physician's response to feeling duped is usually outrage and sometimes even a wish for revenge, he may view all patients whose complaints lead to a dead end as feigners. Provocative complaints that accompany harmless or nonexistent symptoms may spur the wary physician into a promiscuous use of labels, which are more reflective of his own anger than of the patient's problem. Believing that the difficult patient is hell-bent on consciously bedeviling him, the overworked physician may shun his role as diagnostician.

Frequently confused with Münchausen patients are persons with hysterical symptoms. Hysterical symptoms can mimic virtually any medical condition. Conflicting unconscious impulses are "resolved" by the presence of symbolic symptoms that have the appearance of disease or physical change. *Pseudocyesis,* or hysterical pregnancy, for example, can produce amenorrhea, abdominal distention, breast changes, and weight gain in women who have a pathological wish for or fear of pregnancy.

Patients with chronic intractable pain frequently rouse the doctor's wrath when all attempts to diagnose and treat meet with defeat. Symptoms which "refuse" to respond to standard medical therapies, especially in the absence of explanatory disease, can readily suggest fakery. The reality of

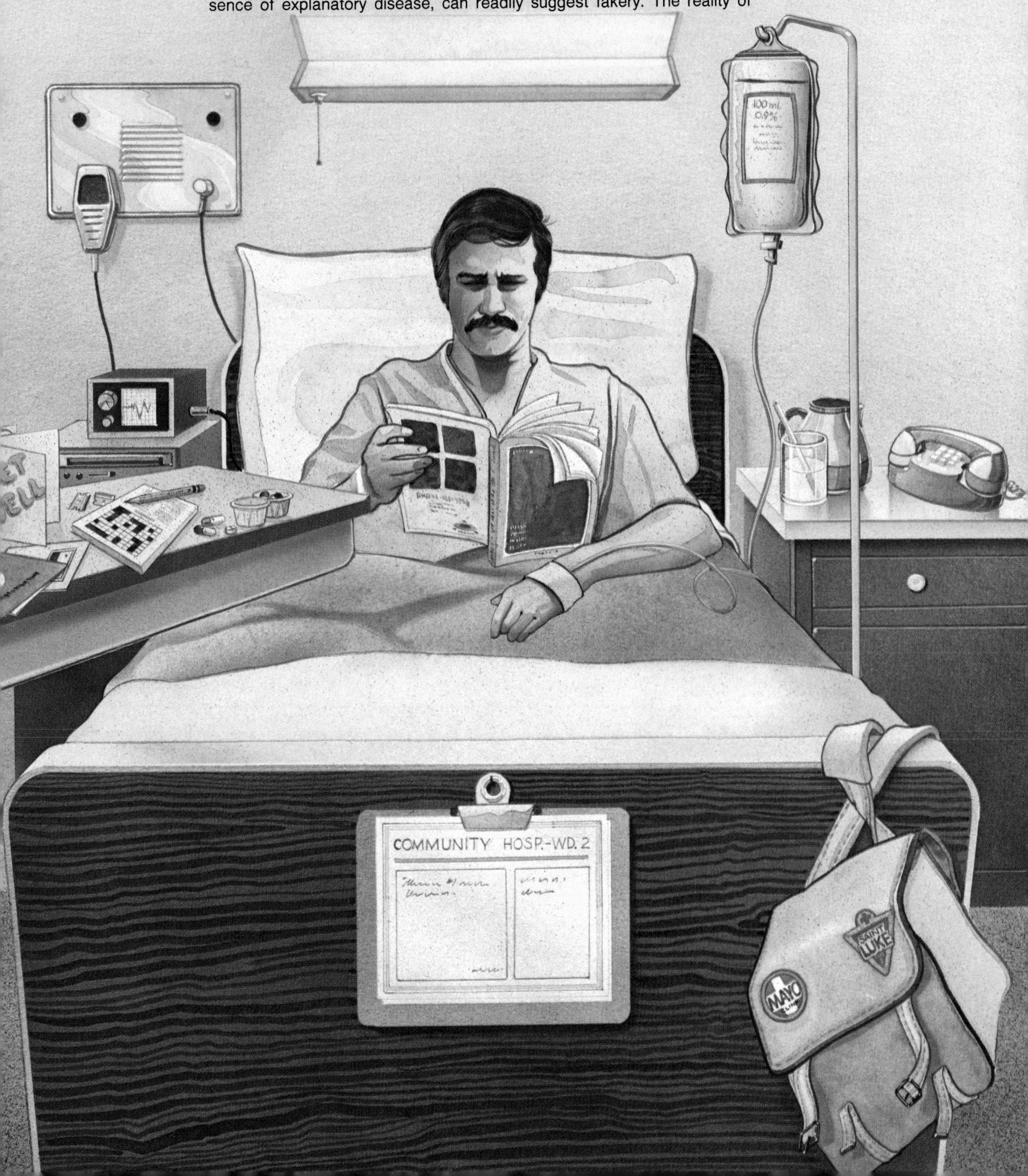

somatic symptoms without obvious stressful life circumstances or emotional turmoil also may cause the physician to assume illness is feigned, but in so doing he runs the risk of overlooking a significant emotional disorder.

Nor must hypochondriacs be considered feigners; patients obsessively preoccupied with disease are not faking their symptoms. Unlike the fraudulent patient they believe they are sick and usually are baffled to hear they are well. Usually their belief in the reality of their illness is so strong they are convinced doctors are tricking them or lying to them. The unconscious element in any of the above illnesses that are not found but not feigned differentiates them from Münchausen's syndrome or factitious illness, with its *conscious* deception.

Münchausen's syndrome versus malingering

All patients who attempt to dupe the medical profession are not true malingerers. Malingerers simulate illness to promote litigation, to win insurance settlements, to avoid prosecution, to obtain drugs, to escape jury duty, and so forth; they always have a concrete and comprehensible goal. The Münchausen patient consciously deceives, but his *motivation* is not concrete. True malingering, contrary to public view, is thought to be very rare and not attributable to a mental disorder.

It is very important for the medical profession to distinguish factitious illness from malingering. The malingerer is usually cooperative but will try to avoid surgery or other painful situations; Münchausen patients, on the other hand, may be abusive and hostile although accepting of surgical and medical interventions (interventions they have sought).

The malingerer's methods may be as imaginative—and dangerous—as those of the Münchausen patient. To obtain transfer to hospitals from jails, prisoners have been known to swallow razor blades, glass, and other objects. Inmates of a French prison were said to have mimicked an epidemic of diphtheria by cauterizing their tonsils and throats with burning straws. So common has malingering been in the armed services that most military surgeons readily detect the less inventive schemes. Some determined individuals have resorted to self-mutilation, creating wounds which they claim to have obtained in battle, or the imitation of some disease native to the region in which they are serving. Owing to the large numbers of malingerers in certain settings, such as the army, physicians may begin to suspect every complaint. But it is the distrusting physician who may fail to make a correct diagnosis by prematurely resorting to pejorative labeling of patients as malingerers—a graver failing.

The American Psychiatric Association has recently reclassified all these maladies in its new *Diagnostic and Statistical Manual of Mental Disorders* (*DSM-III*). "Malingering" is differentiated from "factitious" and "somatoform" disorders. The factitious category includes the *voluntary* production of a wide array of psychological and physical symptoms and self-inflicted wounds and the compulsive Münchausen's syndrome. These differ from somatoform disorders, which are *involuntary,* recurrent bodily complaints, conversion disorders (hysteria), psychogenic pain, and hypochondriasis. These new definitions are meant to enable the physician to make relevant distinctions. Of course, in diagnosing a patient's condition doctors must consider both the *means* employed by the patient to achieve his objectives as well as the *meaning* of the behavior and the symptoms.

The wish to be a patient

"Everyone who is born holds dual citizenship, in the kingdom of the well and in the kingdom of the sick. Although we all prefer to use only the good passport, sooner or later each of us is obliged, at least for a spell, to identify ourselves as citizens of that other place." In *Illness as Metaphor* Susan Sontag articulated the generally accepted notion that most people prefer health to sickness. It is part of the fascination of feigned illness that the reverse is true—some people, it would appear, prefer "that other place."

What could possibly motivate people to want to be sick? Most accounts of Münchausen's syndrome have offered explanations which range from the desire to be the center of attention to the wish to vent negative feelings toward doctors and nurses. However, considering the hazards of hospitalization, diagnostic procedures, and surgical intervention, it would seem that these ends could be attained in a more risk-free manner. To better understand the nuances and complexities of what motivates the Münchausen patient to prefer the "bad passport," it is essential to probe more deeply. A number of psychoanalytic explanations have been offered, which add some illumination to a far-from-well-understood syndrome. Nevertheless, all of them are unsatisfactory.

Both Sigmund Freud and Ernst Simmel, a German pioneer in psychosomatic medicine and a contemporary of Freud, observed and wrote about how children derive pleasure at playing doctor and patient. It is conceivable that in the Münchausen patient there is a resurrection and repeated reenactment of the "doctor-patient game" of childhood. For the illness game to be "legitimate" in adulthood, however, it is important that feigned symptoms be believable. Tales which are too fantastic could prematurely terminate the patienthood experience, *i.e.,* could mean the "game is over."

The peculiar need of Münchausen patients to suffer has challenged some of the keenest observers of human behavior. Most theories hold that it is not pure pain that the sufferer seeks but rather some pleasurable accompaniment of it. It is conceivable that to the affection-deprived individual even the risk of surgery is justified by the chance to be the recipient of total sympathy and care. It has even been suggested that Münchausen patients who are gainfully employed in health-related fields often choose to switch roles from care-giver to care-receiver, much as the youngsters trade off in the doctor-patient game.

One explanation of Münchausen's syndrome holds that manufactured illness may in some perverse way be a reassurance to one who doubts the existence of any feelings. In the face of overwhelming emptiness, for some patients the experience of a needle stick or surgeon's scalpel may seem like the measure of life itself. Psychiatric literature bears accounts of individuals making superficial razor blade slashes on their arms—not to take their lives but to register sensation as confirmation of their existence. The Yiddish writer Sholem Aleichem has expressed this dynamic in one of his characters, who said: "As long as my teeth are chattering, I know I'm alive." The Münchausen patient's escapades, which are often a step short of suicide, may then be life-affirming gestures. But since Münchausen patients live on the edge of disaster—exposing themselves to the risks of self-mutilation, surgery, injections, and potent medications—overstepping the line can mean the end, which was the case for the previously mentioned patient who died of kidney failure.

The illness in a sense *is* the patient's identity, and to disavow it by admitting to trickery would be to experience nonexistence. A Münchausen patient's sense of identity may in fact be sharpened by his perception of being "in control" as he manipulates health care providers—*e.g.,* getting the surgeon to operate in the absence of disease. The rage provoked in the duped physician is also "regulated" by the patient's deliberate ruse. This apparent desire to be in control has prompted many authors to postulate that the Münchausen character needs to lock horns with authority—especially with the physician-father figure—to win redress for deprivations, disappointments, and punishments of early childhood. Credence is lent to this speculation by the frequent encounters Münchausen patients have with police and other authorities, although the fulfillment of their complex psychological needs is gained chiefly in the medical arena.

Not all cases of feigned illness involve high drama. In fact, those who alter their physiology and biochemistry by ingesting anticoagulants, thyroid extract, potassium-lowering diuretics, insulin, and so forth take a more low-key approach, producing only minor symptoms discovered primarily through laboratory tests. But whether the measures are dramatic or subtle, the actions are usually characterized by compulsive repetition (*not* addiction, as has been erroneously suggested by some writers).

The extensive dissembling of Münchausen patients reflects a need for human affection and closeness. In addition to feigning illness, they may pretend to be people in high positions who generally command respect—a diplomat, a war hero, a physician, or a lawyer. Taking on such roles may transiently serve to inflate their egos and make them feel as if they are on equal footing with their doctors, but ultimately Münchausen patients are more likely to alienate care-givers than elicit their respect.

The challenge of treatment

The behavior of perpetrators of factitious symptoms calls out for understanding and help. In some instances, perhaps the most that can be expected is detection, while in others psychotherapeutic approaches aimed at changing character structure and behavior are the hoped-for goal. But the outlook for successful treatment of Münchausen patients, unfortunately, has been very poor; emphasis in recent years has been largely on helping nurses, doctors, and other members of the hospital staff to cope with their own feelings toward these frustrating patients.

Feelings evoked in the would-be helpers often deter them from developing and trying creative ways to work with patients who feign illness. Frustration, anger, futility, helplessness, vulnerability, rage, and contempt effectively stifle the usual wish of health professionals to help. This very attitude of rejection by care-givers, who are also parent-surrogates, may be unconsciously sought by the patient to justify his deep-seated "need" to feel victimized by important people in his life. In this context, an attitude of tolerance and understanding among staff is difficult to foster since the staff's wish to be confrontative and retaliatory is profound. Psychiatric consultants usually spend more time with staff than with the identified patient in attempts to reduce feelings of personal failure, to minimize the impulse to "get even," and to get them to realize that cure is unlikely and that a certain amount of recidivism is common with any chronic illness.

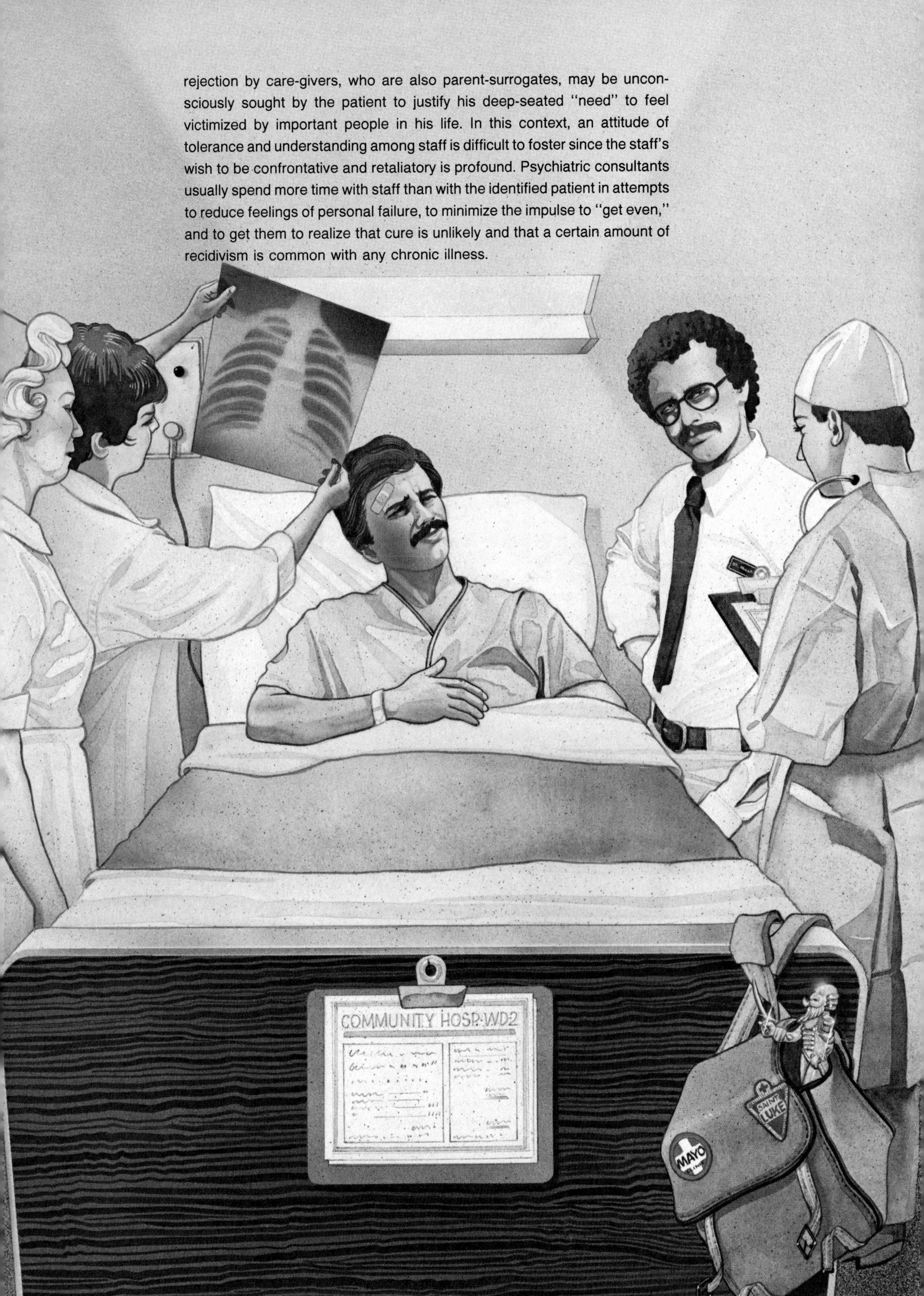

In the past many attempts to deal with these individuals have been less than humane, without any effort to study or understand the behavior. Many have suggested that "treatment" be punitive, including permanent commitment to institutions, legal proceedings, fingerprinting, tatooing, "blacklisting," and so forth. Nurses and emergency room physicians have concocted countermeasures intended to frighten identified impostors away—not unlike Till Eulenspiegel, a peasant jester of the 14th century, who was said to have emptied a hospital of all recidivist patients by proposing a "cure" of cremat-

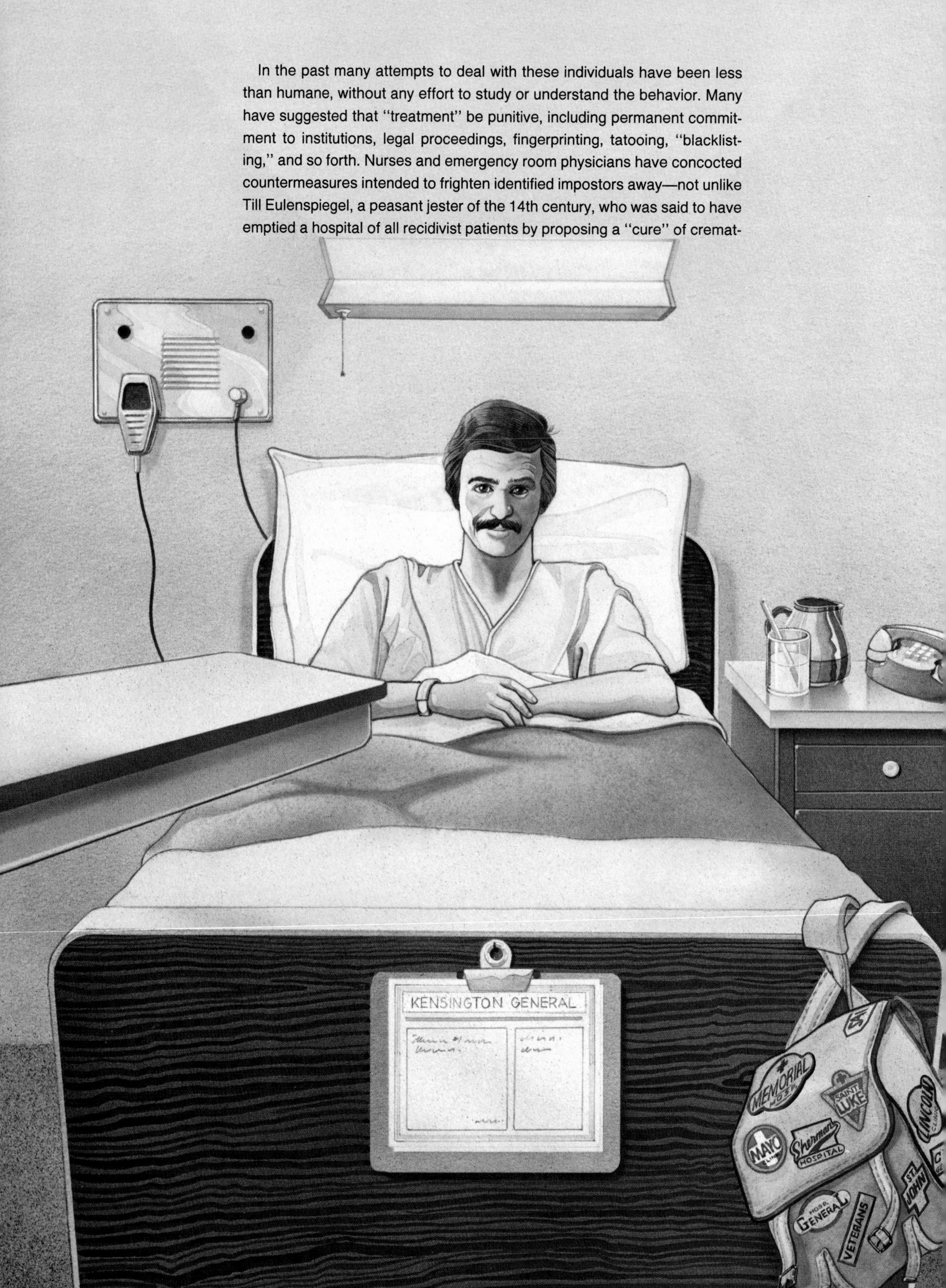

ing the sickest man and feeding the ashes to the remaining patients. Factitious illness should be considered a psychiatric problem rather than the mere chicanery of tricksters, liars, and swindlers.

Unfortunately, the tendency to flee once discovery has been made makes treatment impossible by even the most dedicated and sympathetic professionals. In only about 50% of cases is psychiatric consultation requested, and a much lower percentage of patients are actually seen by psychiatrists before they take flight. In the few instances in which patients have cooperated, their discomfort with "real" interpersonal relations has jeopardized any meaningful alliance between the patient and the therapist.

Electroconvulsive therapy, hypnosis, leukotomy (cutting into the front matter of the brain), and insulin coma therapy have all been tried but, predictably, without success. Newer approaches such as behavior modification or group therapy are scarcely better.

Psychiatrist Theodore Nadelson has proposed a gloomy but realistic "treatment" approach: "There are some patients we cannot repair; we are too late. We can help to limit the damage they do to themselves and others only by first accepting the fact ourselves and by helping other physicians to do the same." Of course, with the occasional patient who has bona fide illness with feigned embellishments, it is essential that staff provide the patient proper *medical* treatment, though little may be achieved in ameliorating *behavior* patterns.

Numerous ethical issues are raised by medical artifactualists. Are they entitled to the same right of confidentiality accorded most patients or have they effectively forfeited their rights through their own breach of trust? Are they entitled to treatment of any kind? Do they deprive others of needed care by bilking the health care system of resources and dollars? Should they be regarded as criminals or as patients? North Carolina has passed a criminal law which makes it a misdemeanor to fraudulently obtain credit at a hospital through false pretense.

These and other questions have yet to be answered. Regrettably there are no solutions on the horizon to the problems posed by the so-called Münchausen's syndrome, which is an exceedingly complex disorder, usually occurring in people who are intelligent, resourceful, and often quite successful at fabricating a huge array of conditions.

FOR ADDITIONAL READING:

Asher, Richard. "Munchausen's Syndrome." *The Lancet,* (1)260:339–341, 1951.

Meadow, Roy. "Munchausen Syndrome by Proxy: The Hinterland of Child Abuse." *The Lancet,* 2:343–345, 1977.

Raspe, R. E., *et al. Singular Travels, Campaigns and Adventures of Baron Munchausen.* London: Cresset Press, 1948.

Sontag, Susan. *Illness as Metaphor.* New York: Farrar, Straus, and Giroux, 1977.

Spiro, H. R. "Chronic Factitious Illness." *Archives of General Psychiatry,* 18:569–580, 1968.

Lourdes

by Ellen Bernstein

In 1970 Serge Perrin, a 41-year-old Roman Catholic accountant from Le Lion d'Anger in northwest France, went to Lourdes. He was unable to walk without crutches; he was blind in the left eye; he had been having increasingly frequent "cerebral attacks" characterized by partial losses of hearing, speech, and consciousness; and his morale was very low. Perrin, who had enjoyed good health up until the age of 35, made the pilgrimage mainly to please his wife and "to learn how to die well," as he was convinced his condition, which had not responded to various drug treatments, was fatal.

Perrin stayed at Lourdes for several days. On his last day he joined hundreds of other invalids, many on stretchers and in wheelchairs, for the communal anointing of the sick in the shrine's underground basilica. Not long after a priest put oil on Perrin's forehead and hands, he felt a strange warmth in his toes. The warmth quickly spread through his feet, then to his legs, and he started to stir in his wheelchair. His wife, thinking he needed to urinate, begged him to be patient. He announced: "I do not know what has happened to me, but I have the impression that I will not need my sticks much longer, and that I could walk."

That day Perrin was able to walk unassisted, and when he took off his spectacles he found he could read signs from a great distance with his left eye. Two years later, after Perrin made several return trips for examination, the Lourdes medical bureau observed "a total absence of any sequelae" to his previous debilitation. His "cure" was confirmed by an international group of doctors in Paris in 1976. Then in 1978 the Roman Catholic Church pronounced Perrin's sudden recovery "humanly inexplicable" and officially recognized its "miraculous character."

The "cure" of Serge Perrin is the most recent officially declared "miracle" —the 64th—in Lourdes history. This is a relatively small number, considering the religious shrine has been attracting throngs of ailing pilgrims from all corners of the Earth for over a century.

Jean-Loup Charmet

In 1858 a 14-year-old girl named Bernadette Soubirous had 18 visions of a beautiful lady at the grotto of Massabielle in Lourdes, France. On her 16th appearance the Lady announced in the local dialect, "I am the Immaculate Conception." At first the townspeople thought Bernadette was mad. But after a rigorous inquiry her visions of the Virgin Mary were declared authentic by the Roman Catholic Church.

Birth of a pilgrimage center

On a cold day in February 1858 a 14-year-old, uneducated girl named Bernadette Soubirous was collecting wood on the riverbank near the grotto of Massabielle in the small Pyrenean town of Lourdes, France, when a noise like a gust of wind caused her to look up. Suddenly there was a light in the hollow of the rock, where a beautiful lady stood and seemed to beckon Bernadette to come closer. The Lady wore a white dress with a blue sash; on each bare foot was a yellow rose, the same color as the chain of the rosary she held. Over a period of several months Bernadette saw this Lady 18 times. During the course of the appearances the Lady, who spoke in the local patois, told Bernadette to pray for sinners and to tell the priests to have a chapel built. The Lady also expressed her desire for people to come to the grotto in procession.

During one apparition a spring of water miraculously issued forth when young Bernadette scratched the muddy ground with her fingers. During another, the "candle miracle" occurred: Bernadette knelt before the Lady, her hands cupped around the flame of a long candle. The candle slipped out of place causing the flames to dance between her fingers for a good ten minutes. But Bernadette never flinched and the fire did not burn her. On the occasion of her sixteenth appearance the Lady said to Bernadette, "I am the Immaculate Conception."

The apparitions caused a great uproar in the town of Lourdes: ardent followers flocked to the grotto to witness Bernadette transfixed by her visions, while angry skeptics denounced the adolescent as an imbecile and a fraud. Only after a four-year, meticulous inquiry did the Roman Catholic Church declare Bernadette's visions of the Virgin Mary authentic.

Pilgrimages began almost immediately—the first pilgrims coming from the surrounding region in southwest France. In 1866 the basilica of the Immaculate Conception was built, fulfilling the request of Our Lady of Lourdes, as the Virgin came to be called. The chancel is situated exactly above the spot where she had appeared. That same year Lourdes got a railway, setting the stage for the first national pilgrimage in 1872. By 1947 more than a million visitors were coming from all of France; from 1948 to the present, Lourdes has received ever increasing numbers of pilgrims from all over the world. The centennial year of Bernadette's death, 1979, brought a record number: 4,582,000—two-thirds of them from outside France. Today an observer is struck by the size of the crowds, the diversity of the countries represented, and the variety of social, economic, and religious backgrounds of those who flock to this small town between the months of April and September. (The town, with a resident population of only 18,000, has over 400 hotels, which makes it the third largest tourist center in France, with only Paris and Nice accommodating more visitors.)

The Virgin never said to Bernadette that sick people would be cured at Lourdes, but during the course of the apparitions a stone mason, who was blind in one eye, came to the grotto of Massabielle. He scooped up a lump of moist earth at the base of the spring and pressed it against his blind eye; when he removed the mudpack, his sight was supposedly restored. A few days later a desperate mother brought her two-year-old paralytic son to the

Ellen Bernstein *is Editor of the* Medical and Health Annual.

(Overleaf) Sipa Press/Black Star

Jean-Loup Charmet

During the course of Bernadette's visions a blind man and a sick baby are said to have been instantly cured at the grotto. Hearing of these "miracles," people from the surrounding regions—many of them ailing—began to flock to Lourdes. Ever since, the shrine has been receiving increasing numbers of pilgrims from all over the world.

spring. She dipped the wailing child into the icy water, and, legend has it, he was instantly cured.

Though today the sick are outnumbered by other visitors and tourists, they are and always have been the center of it all. Indeed Lourdes would not be Lourdes without the presence of the sick. In 1980 some 65,000 unwell people from 110 countries visited the Marian shrine.

Bernadette, who was never cured of her lifelong asthma, and who later developed tuberculosis, entered a convent after the apparitions. For several years she worked in an infirmary, serving invalids. From 1875 until her death in 1879 she was too ill to attend others. But she never complained about her situation, and she openly accepted "the job of sickness." It is not surprising then that the sick and the bedridden have found in the suffering Bernadette a powerful ally. Bernadette was canonized by Pope Pius XI in 1933.

Investigation of miraculous cures

Since the time of Bernadette, the message of Lourdes has been poverty, penance, and prayer; its reputation, however, has come to be associated with sudden and inexplicable recoveries from illness. Lourdes is unique among Catholic shrines where alleged miracles have occurred in having a structure for investigating and recognizing these events.

The medical bureau was established in 1882 because so many sick pilgrims seemed to be getting well while visiting the shrine. The archives of the office record thousands of sudden recoveries from dire illnesses. If, during a visit to Lourdes, a pilgrim discovers that his state of health has dramatically altered he may present himself to the bureau. Lourdes has one full-time resident physician; he is joined in an investigation by all the physicians who happen to be visiting Lourdes at the time—doctors of many nationalities, races, and creeds—many of whom accompany the sick on pilgrimages. Every doctor present can examine, interrogate, and give his opinion.

For a dossier to be started, a pilgrim must have "complete" medical records, confirming the nature and dates of any recent treatments. Many

Sipa Press/Black Star

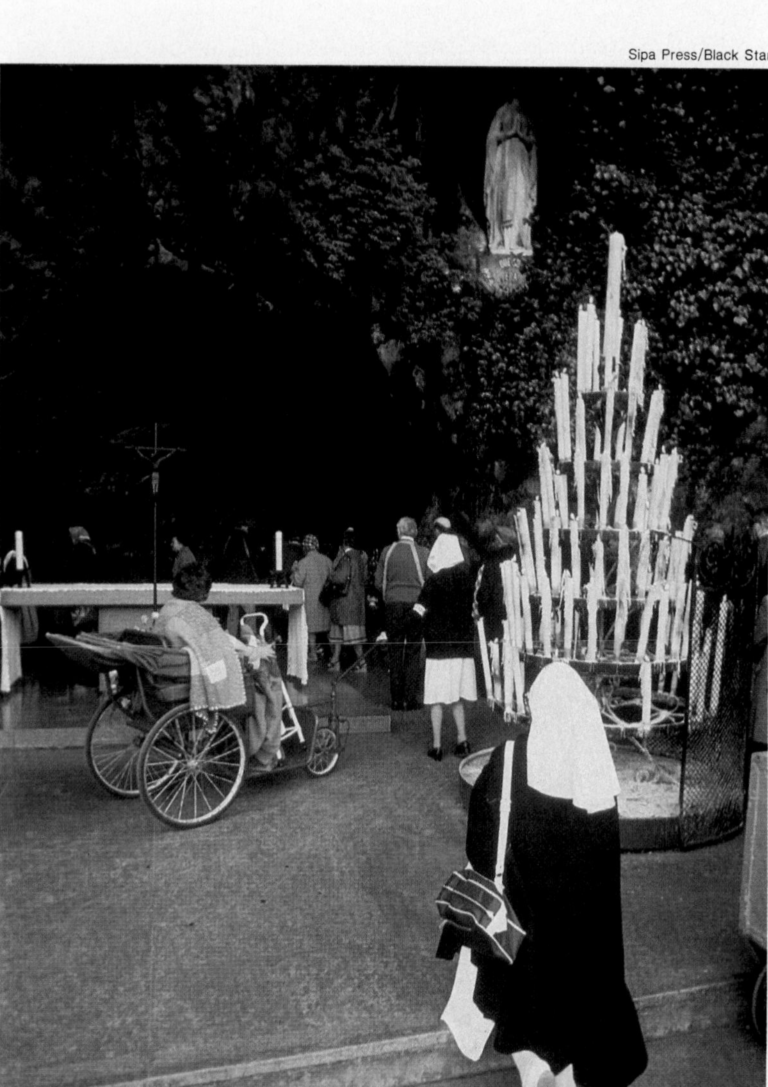

Candles burn day and night at the grotto, where visitors come to pray and to view the spot (marked by a statue) where Bernadette saw the Virgin Mary. At the back of the grotto is the miraculous spring which issued forth under Bernadette's touch during her ninth vision.

sudden recoveries turn out to be the delayed effects of treatments, such as radiation therapy for a tumor. Therefore, the *ineffectiveness* of any therapy must be documented.

In order for the doctors to proceed with an investigation specific criteria must be met. The recovery must be "sudden" and "unforeseen." It must occur "without convalescence." The disease itself must be "serious" or "life-threatening." There must have been a distinct "organic" disorder, not just random symptoms. (Loss of speech in itself is not admissible; loss of speech due to a defined and delineated cerebral lesion is admissible.) There must be "objective evidence" of the previous existence of the disease or disorder, confirmed by tests—X-rays, biopsies, and so forth. No disease for which there are effective modes of treatment is considered. Sudden recoveries from tuberculosis were once commonly investigated by the medical bureau; today tuberculosis is no longer a candidate for investigation owing to the availability of drug therapy. A cure that has satisfied all of the

Bruno Barbey—Magnum

An awesome collection of abandoned crutches hangs above the grotto. Some attribute sudden recoveries, as in those who are suddenly able to walk again, to the religious fervor and the charged atmosphere of Lourdes.

above criteria must also withstand the test of time. Pilgrims are required to return several times over a period of several years fo, reexamination.

Cures that appear to be complete are then submitted to the international medical committee, which currently consists of 30 members from about a dozen Western European countries who meet annually in Paris. The members, representing a wide range of specialties, are appointed by the bishop who serves the adjacent towns of Tarbes and Lourdes. Essentially this jury of physicians votes on a single question: Is this cure medically explicable? If a majority recognizes the *inexplicable* nature of the event, the patient's dossier is passed on to a canonical commission headed by the bishop of the diocese in which the "cured" person lives.

Only the church can make the final decision—*i.e.*, whether or not God has intervened. Before proclaiming a miracle, the church claims to demand substantial evidence of the "truly supernatural character" of the cure.

Of course, there are probably many who leave Lourdes certain they have been "cured" or at least with their conditions made appreciably better who never report to the medical bureau. Many come back with such reports years later, but, obviously, there is no way to verify these cases. Alphonse Olivieri, who was president of the bureau from 1959 to 1971, wrote in *Y a-t-il encore des miracles à Lourdes?* ("Are There Still Miracles at Lourdes?") that he witnessed a great many extraordinary recoveries every year but often it was impossible or impractical to investigate them.

A spectacular sight at the shrine is a collection of dozens of crutches and walking sticks dangling from the rock above the grotto. Supposedly, pilgrims who were dependent on these to get to the grotto to pray were able to walk away without them. Those who are suddenly able to use their legs again may be content to abandon their crutches; they view these personal miracles as a religious experience and, understandably, they may not wish to submit themselves to the rigors of medical investigation.

The dubious cure of Serge Perrin

Serge Perrin miraculously recovered from "a case of recurring organic hemiplegia [paralysis of one side of the body] with ocular lesions, due to cerebral circulatory defects." So said the doctors on the international committee who compiled their findings in a 39-page document. To the lay viewer this report, with its morass of details, might have a convincing flavor. It includes a medical history of the patient and his family, comments from the doctors who treated Perrin, a review of the events from the onset of the illness through the recovery, a discussion of the neurologic and ophthalmologic signs and symptoms, and supporting evidence—before and after visual field diagrams and X-ray pictures.

However, a small sample of specialists in the United States who independently reviewed the document found the case for Perrin's cure highly suspect and the data presented mired in technical verbiage and contradictions. Louis R. Caplan, chairman of the department of neurology at Michael Reese Hospital and Medical Center in Chicago, remarked that the document was "vague" and "obtuse" and that "it is hard to understand the recovery." Donald H. Harter, professor and chairman of the department of neurology at Northwestern University Medical School in Chicago, found an "absence of *objective* neurological abnormalities." Robert A. Levine, assistant clinical professor of ophthalmology at the University of Illinois, pointed out that the visual field diagrams are mislabeled and inconsistent with the text; he found all the conclusions relating to the visual problem "extremely puzzling." The descriptions as a whole he called "a lot of mumbo jumbo." Drummond Rennie, associate professor of medicine at Harvard Medical School, felt that the document produced as a result of the investigation was "unscientific and totally unconvincing."

Because so many pilgrims seemed to be getting well while visiting the shrine, in 1882 a medical bureau was established to investigate these "cures." In 1970 Serge Perrin (below) experienced a sudden and inexplicable recovery from a dire condition, which later became the 64th officially declared "miraculous cure" in Lourdes history.

Jean Durand

Among other things, these reviewers found the neurological workup incomplete: essential laboratory tests were never performed—in particular, a lumbar puncture (spinal tap) and a radioactive brain scan (both of which would be standard in most hospitals). Nor did they find the diagnosis of hemiplegia plausible: more than one part of the patient's brain had to be involved because he had *right* leg weakness and *left* visual and motor findings. Further, a number of Perrin's symptoms—generalized constriction of the visual field and various motor and sensory disturbances—were typical of hysteria. The U.S. specialists agreed that if there was an organic illness at all, multiple sclerosis was a more likely possibility; multiple sclerosis is known to have fleeting symptoms—periods of exacerbation followed by complete or partial remissions.

If Serge Perrin's case is representative, there are good reasons to be distrustful of officially declared miraculous cures at Lourdes. There are also reasons to question the allegedly rigorous system for recognizing them. For one thing, it is evident that the scientific standards are not the highest, since the poor diagnostic workup on patient Perrin was accepted by the Lourdes medical bureau and by the international committee. Moreover, the expertise and skills of the doctors who first see recovered patients at Lourdes and who set the wheels of an investigation spinning are at best a matter of chance since being present at the shrine and being a certified physician are the only

(Left) Jean Ribière; (right) Sipa Press/Black Star

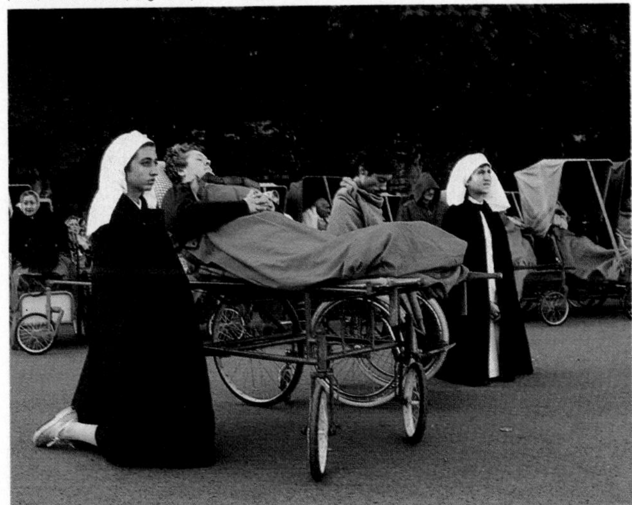

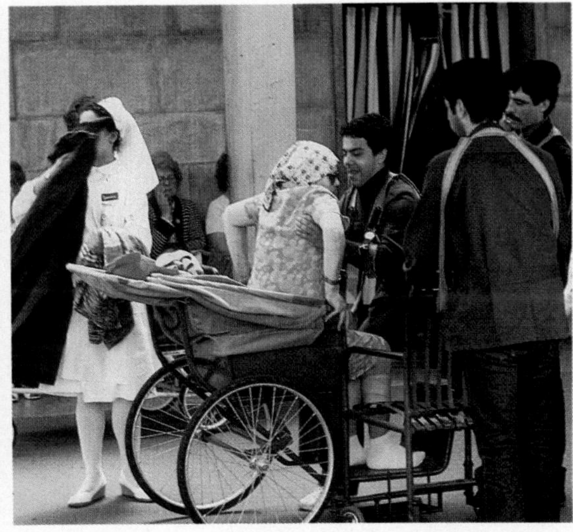

Cures are few and far between and they are not the prime motivating factor for most who journey to Lourdes. Nor is a pilgrimage a substitute for medical care. Rather, pilgrimages represent a renewal of faith, a time of strength, a source of courage, or an opportunity to commune with others.

requirements for joining the medical bureau. Finally, physicians who accompany the sick to Lourdes are likely to be caught up in the awe and excitement of the pilgrimage and therefore they would not be the most objective of judges.

Every doctor would agree there are mysterious and magnificent recoveries—and most have seen remissions in their own patients which they cannot account for. In some cases this is because a disease is self-limiting: it naturally runs its course and then ceases. Other diseases have periods of natural remission and flare-up. Psychosomatic disorders, too, can produce a huge array of baffling symptoms that may disappear as dramatically as they occur. Multiple factors may influence an illness, and multiple factors may influence a cure.

While the medical bureau claims to exclude functional conditions (those not caused by a structural defect) from consideration, this may not be as easy as it sounds. The current president of the medical bureau has been particularly adamant in rejecting the notion that many pilgrims have hysterical illness. But hysterical symptoms can be extremely difficult to diagnose even for the most skilled clinician. At Lourdes the powerful spirit of the place—the charged atmosphere of intense human sympathy—could indeed trigger recoveries from a number of functional ailments, including hysteria. The French writer Émile Zola was one who recognized this possibility.

On visiting Lourdes in 1892 Zola witnessed the cure of an 18-year-old Parisian girl, Marie Lemarchand, who had suffered from pulmonary tuberculosis and ulcers on the face and leg. (Her cure was later authenticated by the church.) In *Les Trois Villes: Lourdes, Rome et Paris* (1894) Zola was sharply scornful of what was often considered the "mystery" of Lourdes. He wrote: "The cures at Lourdes are simply the result of a trauma prepared a long time before, set in motion by the excitement of the journey, the prayers and the hymns, by the ever-increasing emotion generated by the atmosphere of the shrine, and finally brought about by the healing breath produced by the unknown force which emanates from crowds during violent demonstrations of faith."

Jean Ribière

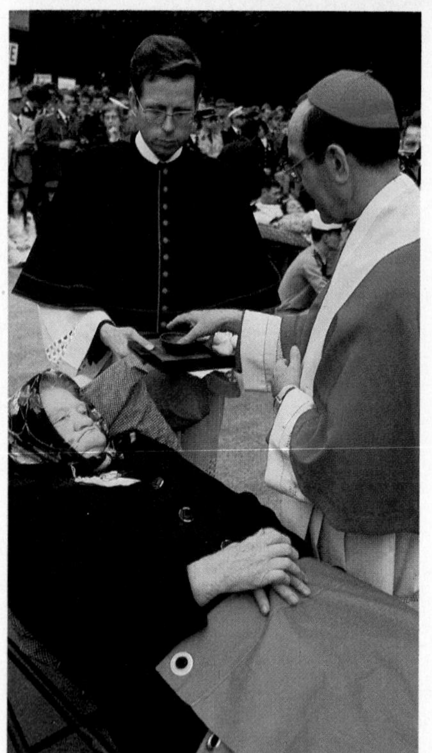

Bruno Barbey—Magnum

Hysterical illnesses (or conversion disorders) have been recognized for centuries as conditions that can mimic all the physical infirmities to which mankind is heir. In *A General Introduction to Psycho-analysis* (1920) Sigmund Freud referred to conversion symptoms as "the mysterious leap" from mind to body, with unconscious anxieties translating into somatic symptoms. A man who wishes to strike another may, for example, develop a paralysis of the arm. Freud was not the first to recognize that hysterical symptoms, particularly paralyses and sensory disturbances, may easily be confused with neurological symptoms.

Hysterical symptoms may also supersede those that first resulted from a physical illness or injury. This overlap of physically and emotionally induced symptoms further complicates diagnosis, as neurologist Louis Caplan and psychiatrist Theodore Nadelson found in their study "Multiple Sclerosis and Hysteria: Lessons Learned From Their Association" (*Journal of the American Medical Association,* June 20, 1980). They showed that the line between organic and functional disease is often blurred. Multiple sclerosis and hysteria coexisted in the patients they studied, and the two conditions shared "prevalence and frequency of equivocal, difficult-to-verify abnormal neurological signs." Significantly, the several U.S. physicians who reviewed the case of Serge Perrin rejected the diagnosis of organic hemiplegia but thought hysteria or just possibly multiple sclerosis might account for the patient's debilitation. Conceivably, he suffered from both.

The waning of miracles

Prayer and participation in religious ceremonies—the lifeblood of the shrine at Lourdes—are generally considered to be powerful factors in recoveries, even in pilgrims who are not devout Catholics. But from the time of Bernadette to the present, skeptics, believers, churchmen, clinicians, and freethinkers have stewed over and argued about "miraculous cures." The scientific-minded have challenged and ridiculed the very notion of modern miracles; many consider it impossible to evaluate matters of faith with any sort of objectivity, since faith, by definition, has no need to justify itself. Zealots who view cures as acts of God see any inquiry into the recovery process as "putting God to the test," *i.e.,* as heresy. Still others have argued that miraculous events *can* be held up to scientific scrutiny.

In 1883 Sir Francis Galton entered the fray with the publication of his elegant and celebrated essay "Objective Efficacy of Prayer." Galton set out to answer the question: "Do sick persons who pray, or are prayed for, recover on the average more rapidly than others?" He undertook a broad survey of how the faithful fare in life. In the world of commerce he noted that when devout men are among the shareholders of a business enterprise—even when the meetings of such enterprises are opened with prayer—its

Though healthy visitors have always outnumbered ailing ones, Lourdes would not be Lourdes without the sick. (Opposite page) Pilgrims are blessed by priests from many lands in one of the most eagerly anticipated ceremonies—the communal anointing of the sick.

Ellen Bernstein

On a cold December day a barefoot pilgrim meditates on the fourteen stations of the cross portraying the final events in the Passion of Christ. The stations are situated on a steep mountainside path reminiscent of the harsh way of Calvary, the site of Jesus' crucifixion. A smaller-scale "way of the cross," on flat ground, is accessible to those in wheelchairs.

commercial dealings are not necessarily more scrupulous or honest. Nor are funds of pious people, charities, or religious bodies, which are deposited in banks, any better protected than those of the profane. For another example Galton turned to architecture. It was once considered an act of faithlessness to put lightning conductors on churches because God, it was believed, would protect the faithful inside. But statistical inquiries showed that churches were no less vulnerable to lightning—nor, for that matter to fires, earthquakes, or avalanches—than other buildings. After this determination, incidentally, all churches were properly protected. When it came to the question of prayer and cures Galton found "hardly any instance in which a medical man of repute has attributed recovery to the influence of prayer." He concluded that prayer does not bring temporal benefits and that only scientific explanations of physiological phenomena are valid.

Jesuit writer Richard F. Clarke, a respected contemporary of Galton, who, unlike Galton, may have had a vested interest in belief in miracles, took a more compromising position on the subject. Clarke acknowledged that talk of miracles tends to "raise a smile on the lips of the educated Protestant," and that all possible objections to miraculous occurrences should be raised, but he sharply criticized skeptics who approached inexplicable cures at Lourdes with an anti-miracle prejudice.

Alexis Carrel, who received the Nobel Prize for Medicine in 1912, aroused the fury of his peers when he insisted the phenomena of Lourdes were worthy of scientific examination. In 1903 Carrel accompanied one of his own patients, Marie Bailly, to Lourdes. He had diagnosed her as having a fatal case of tubercular peritonitis. At Lourdes, before Carrel's eyes, his patient made a sudden and stunning recovery. Carrel wrote later: "Such events are highly significant. They prove the reality of certain links, as yet unknown, between psychological and organic processes. They prove the objective

Like any tourist town catering to millions of visitors each year, Lourdes has its share of commercialism, including tawdry souvenir shops.

(Left) Sipa Press/Black Star; (right) G. Rancinan—Sygma

value of the spiritual activity which has been almost totally ignored by doctors, teachers, and sociologists. They open up a new world for us."

Every position seems to be encumbered by some degree of bias. One could certainly argue that the bishop-appointed European doctors who declared Serge Perrin's cure medically inexplicable approached their evaluation with a *pro-miracle* bias. And one could also say that the U.S. physicians who discredited the "cure" had to bring from their seats in academic medicine decidedly *anti-miracle* leanings.

The subject of miracles at Lourdes is likely to spark debates from now until doomsday. Each side will continue to have its say. In a recent newsletter published by the Lourdes Center in Boston, the Rev. John W. Lynch hurled at contemporary medical men an age-old charge: "What most doctors cannot stand is a miracle. Miracles do not fit in their scientific bag of tricks. If after all their know-how fails and a cure happens, most of them cannot bring themselves to admit a power greater than theirs has taken over."

Alexis Carrel was perspicacious in acknowledging that "as yet unknown" processes would be understood in the future. He was correct in anticipating that mind-body interactions would no longer perplex physicians and that other mysteries of human health and illness would eventually yield their secrets. In the past several decades there has been a virtual explosion of medical knowledge, making "inexplicable" phenomena increasingly rare. From 1883 to 1947 nearly 5,000 cures were accepted as inexplicable by physicians at the Lourdes medical bureau; from 1947 to 1980 there were only 28—less than one per year. Since lack of explanation has more to do with lack of knowledge at the time than with supernatural occurrences, it seems likely that many of the "cures" previously authenticated by the church would not be seen by physicians or clergy as miraculous today.

In the past, for example, doctors could not explain why a cancer melted away because they knew very little about tumors. Only in recent years have medical scientists learned that the human body has malignancies arising all the time and that these cancers may be killed off by the body's own defenses. Today if a cancer disappears it is understood that an attack may have been launched by the body's complex and integrated immune system.

That physicians are unable to provide an explanation for a mysterious recovery from a dire illness does not mean there is no earthly reason for it. Miracles, then, are conditional; they depend on time, place, what is known, and what is not known. As medical sophistication increases, miracles necessarily decrease, which may mean the days of "miraculous cures" at Lourdes are numbered.

Since there have been so few officially recognized miracles and, in fact, these are downplayed by the church, why then does Lourdes continue to attract sick pilgrims? Obviously, many—including the blind, the deaf, the crippled, the maimed, and the dying—still go to Lourdes buoyed up with the expectancy of seeing, hearing, walking, or getting a new lease on life. Even treatable patients may harbor hopes of an instantaneous recovery since many treatments take a long time, are painful, costly, and produce unpleasant side effects; it is a very human desire to be attracted to an alternative that will be quick and painless.

(Left) Sipa Press/Black Star; (right) Oeuvre de la Grotte, Lourdes

Lourdes water is good, clean, drinkable mountain water—nothing more, nothing less. Nonetheless, people display great faith in its powers. They come to drink from the spigots that run along a rock wall; they fill containers to take home; and they are immersed in the icy waters of the baths. In recent years there has been mounting concern that the baths—used by the healthy and the sick—may be polluted.

Inexhaustible waters

The issuing forth of the spring during Bernadette's visions was a surprising if not miraculous event, and indeed two seemingly miraculous cures occurred at the site of the spring just after it began to flow; many subsequent "cures" have also been attributed to use of the water. But Our Lady never promised Bernadette that the water would make anyone better. Moreover, it has been demonstrated repeatedly that the water does *not* have any special properties. Chemical analyses inevitably show that it is neither thermal, radioactive, nor bacteria-destroying; rather it is good mountain water—clear, odorless, colorless, and drinkable.

Nevertheless people from all over the world continue to have great faith in the powers of Lourdes water—and few pilgrims will leave the shrine without some contact with it. They are accommodated.

The spring that issued forth under Bernadette's touch after the Virgin instructed her to "Go, drink at the fountain, and wash yourself there," today supplies 42,000 liters a day. There are a dozen spigots along a rock wall beside the grotto to collect the water. People come to the fountains to wash, to drink, and to fill containers. Every shop in the town sells plastic bottles for this purpose—some in the shape of the Virgin Mary that hold only a few symbolic drops, others that hold four or more liters.

In addition to the fountains the shrine is famous for its baths. But Lourdes is not a health resort in the tradition of Spa, a village in Belgium, or Baden-Baden in West Germany, where people derive beneficial effects from relaxing in naturally warm mineral waters. Every day hundreds of pilgrims bathe in Lourdes's 14 concrete baths housed in a dark, dank, unpleasant smelling building, often waiting several hours in queue, where they pray and prepare themselves for the spiritual act of entering the frigid water.

The sick and the handicapped are carefully immersed in the baths on special stretchers. In the past decade there has been mounting concern that the baths, which are in constant use by both the sick and the healthy, are polluted. In 1979 the medical bureau issued a warning to doctors in charge of pilgrimages: "No pressures should be brought to bear on the sick to take them to the baths if they do no wish to do so or if the doctors treating them have advised against it." The bureau further warned that wounds of the sick should be protected when they are immersed.

Since the waters remain so popular a new facility for performing ablutions was installed in 1980: an open-air trough of running water in close proximity to the bathhouse and thus in an atmosphere of fervor. This innovation helps relieve the load on the baths and serves the handicapped in particular, who can draw up close in their wheelchairs, drink from the taps, and splash themselves.

There is yet another way to "take the waters" at Lourdes. Every shop in town sells *Pastilles à l'eau de Lourdes* (lozenges made from Lourdes water and sugar). The lozenges come with a leaflet that explains, "The inexhaustible waters give pilgrims the refreshment and that cure that suits each one." They are spiritual lozenges, not medicine, "not a substitute for a doctor's prescription."

The Boston-based Lourdes Center imports the water (which is not holy water because it has not received any special blessing) and distributes it in the United States and Canada. In every issue of the center's newsletter, "Echoes of Lourdes," testimonials from users express a profound and often touching degree of faith in curative powers of the water even though it is not promoted as a healing potion: "I use Lourdes water every day on my sore knees." "My mother was delivered from cancer pain." "For the past six years I was handicapped with a sore toe-nail; each Spring I was obliged to have it lanced by the doctors. The same condition would return and cause considerable discomfort and turn black. I applied Lourdes water constantly. A change took place . . . I now have a normal white nail and no infection. I am able to move more freely." "Please send me a bottle of Lourdes Water. I'm 97 years old now, and it is helping me climb to 98."

Psychological cures

Lourdes water is not a magic fluid and despite the blind faith some people display in it, it is not the chief attraction for sick pilgrims. Nor are miracles the primary motivation today. There are other reasons for sufferers to journey to Saint Bernadette's sanctuary.

Most patients are in some ways isolated; many feel abandoned, hopeless, and destined to solitude. Often the sick and handicapped are not seen—they

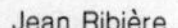
Jean Ribière

are in hospitals, convalescent facilities, or shut up at home. Society discriminates against the sick by excluding them from the mainstream of life. Employers deny them jobs; educational institutions deny them admission; insurance companies deny them coverage. Even family members may unwittingly abandon sick relatives by not including them in family decisions and by not "burdening" them with family problems.

When the sick go to Lourdes they need, above all, to feel counted, accepted, and loved. A 20-year-old woman, handicapped since birth, described herself as a caged bird before her pilgrimage. "I never really left my home on the fourth floor of our old apartment building. My parents protected me and didn't want others to see me . . . Then an able-bodied friend invited me to go to Lourdes. It was the first time I took a train, ate in a restaurant, slept in a hotel. . . ." Going to Lourdes was not only a spiritual pilgrimage for this woman but her first journey into the world, her first real taste of life. She was not cured of her infirmity, but she was cured of her festering isolation.

The real miracles at Lourdes today are the psychological changes that occur in the sick. From the moment they get off the train, where they are greeted by nurses, doctors, nuns, and lay volunteers, the sick find they are the center of attention. Every effort is made to welcome them and make them comfortable. A majority stay free of charge in one of the three *hopîtals* at the shrine. These facilities are not traditional hospitals but infirmaries or reception centers much like medieval Christian hospices where the sick poor assumed a blessed place in the community. The combined capacity of the three centers is 1,552 beds, which serve about 70% of the sick pilgrims; the rest stay in hotels or pensions in town. Two of the *hopîtals* are quite old and austere. The third, Hopîtal Sainte Bernadette, was opened in 1977; its 349 beds and improved medical and sanitary conditions serve the sickest patients, who previously might have hesitated to make a pilgrimage.

G. Rancinan—Sygma

From the moment they arrive at the train station the sick and the handicapped find they are the center of attention. Those who may have felt abandoned and hopeless find at Lourdes a renewed sense of self-importance and the courage to live with their infirmities.

Even the hotels, which are commercially run, have employees who welcome the sick at the train station and transport them to their accommodations. Hotel staff are accustomed to providing special services—filling hot water bottles, refrigerating insulin, and catering to special diets. Many hotels provide one or two free rooms to needy visitors.

Today the emphasis at the shrine is on sick people taking charge of their lives. The volunteer *brancardiers* who escort the disabled in special carriages are instructed to avoid considering these pilgrims as "our dear sick ones." Even the most debilitated pilgrims are encouraged to participate fully in all ceremonies and activities. There are special places reserved for them —always in front—at all gatherings.

Since 1888 the nightly procession of the sick has been a celebrated event attracting thousands of sick and healthy pilgrims. A short religious service at dusk is followed by the magical melting of the crowd, chanting and clutching candles, as it moves from the bank of the river by the grotto toward the grand upper basilica.

The only facility not readily accessible to invalids is the way of the cross, which is laid out on a steep hill covering a distance of 1,530 meters (just short of a mile). But in 1963 a second "way" was constructed on flat ground, about the length of a cafeteria line. It enables those who cannot make the climb as well as those in wheelchairs and on stretchers to partake in the devotional exercise of meditating at each of 14 stations portraying the final events in the passion of Christ.

The contemporary appeal of Lourdes has a lot to do with its *internationalisme*—the unique and rich opportunity for pilgrims to meet others. The sick who come from all corners of the world cannot but find solace when they see they are not alone. Most who come derive a renewed vision of their own lives; pilgrimages are a time of strength and a source of courage. Frequently

Sipa Press/Black Star

The underground basilica of St. Pius X was consecrated in 1958. The concrete structure is a huge elliptical hollow that can hold assemblies of more than 20,000.

patients who are bitter and resentful about their own situations undergo a remarkable change of heart. The transformation is often expressed in prayers such as "I no longer ask a cure for me but for this one next to me, who is sicker and suffering more."

Every year at the basilica of St. Peter's in Rome on the 11th of February, the anniversary of Bernadette's first apparition, there is gathering of pilgrims, many of whom are sick, for the Feast of Our Lady of Lourdes. In 1980 Pope John Paul II delivered a homily in which he described what Lourdes offers the sick:

> Some are sorrowful and suffer illness, grief, misfortunes, hereditary defects, loneliness, physical torture, moral anguish, poor accommodation. Yet each one of these sufferers has a name, a face, a tale to tell. These people, if they are stimulated by the faith, go to Lourdes . . . in quest of relief, comfort, hope. All types of sick people go on pilgrimages to Lourdes, fortified by the hope that, through Mary, the saving power of Christ will be manifested. And, in fact, this power is always revealed, through the gift of serenity, enormous resignation, and sometimes by an improvement in their state of health, or perhaps by the grace of a complete cure. . . . yet a miraculous event remains after all an exceptional event. . . . At Lourdes the sick discover the inestimable value of their own suffering. In the light of faith they come to see and realize the full significance that suffering can have. . . . Lourdes is the epitome of generosity, altruism, and service.

At Lourdes a statue of a blind man kneeling by a cross bears an inscription that sums up what continually happens at the shrine in southern France. It reads, "I came here to regain my sight but I regained something much more important: my faith." For some it is faith in God, for others, faith in humanity, for most, faith in themselves to endure.

Is a pilgrimage a substitute for medical care? An occasional pilgrim may give up on treatment and go to Lourdes as a last resort, hoping for a miracle. But according to the records kept by the press office, the large majority make a pilgrimage in addition to receiving therapy. It is regrettable but widely acknowledged that as medicine has become more scientific, with ever greater capabilities to diagnose and treat disease, it has also tended to become less humane. Patients may see numerous specialists without continuity of care. These people may justifiably feel alienated by their physicians' apparent disregard for their social and psychological needs. At Lourdes they are likely to find the kind of old-fashioned empathy that their doctors may have failed to provide.

A nurse who works in a modern hospital in Paris makes a yearly pilgrimage to Lourdes. Her trips enable her to draw new strength for helping the sick, under conditions that emphasize technology and sometimes make it difficult to comfort people who are suffering.

Pilgrimages for handicapped children

Over the years there have been special pilgrimages of World War veterans, polio patients, accident victims, cardiac patients, even kidney disease sufferers on dialysis. The most heartening (or some might say heartbreaking) gatherings take place every Easter when children suffering from cerebral palsy, spina bifida, epilepsy, muscular dystrophy, congenital heart disease, cystic fibrosis, leukemia, mental retardation, hemophilia, and dozens of other mental and physical "handicaps" convene at Lourdes. Each condition presents its own special problems: cerebral palsy children need to have frequent changes of position during processions; many children have no control over their bowels or bladders; epilepsy attacks may be precipitated by the excitement; dehydration may be a problem in hot weather for children with cystic fibrosis, who may also need to have postural drainage several times a day; and so forth. In order to give special attention to every child's needs the Easter pilgrimages require an extraordinary amount of planning

Are there still miracles at Lourdes? Easter 1981 brought the largest pilgrimage of handicapped children ever. When a journey enables a child to overcome a sense of isolation or feelings of rejection and uselessness, then a kind of miracle has occurred.

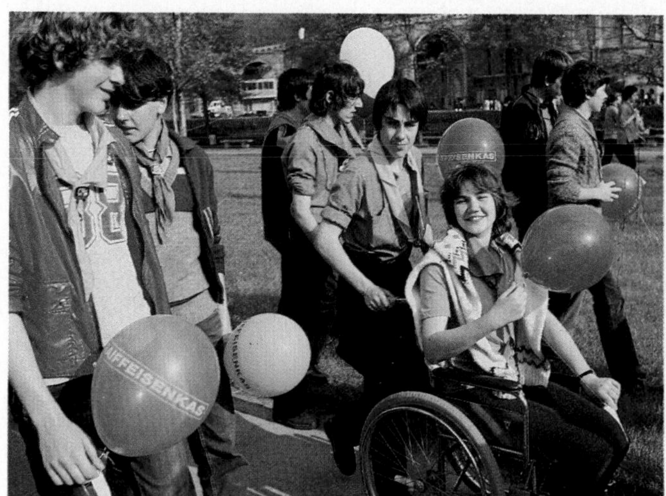

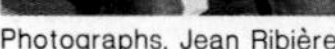
Photographs, Jean Ribière

Jean Ribière

At dusk sick and healthy pilgrims gather for the most celebrated event of all: the candlelight procession. There is electricity in the air as the huge crowd moves from the bank of the river to the grand upper basilica, singing in unison.

and preparation and tremendous dedication and flexibility on the part of staff and volunteers at the shrine.

Some visitors naturally are upset by the sight of so many severely disabled youngsters. Doctors have expressed concern that many of them have been dragged hundreds of miles, away from familiar surroundings, and that they do not understand what is going on. Many doctors have been particularly troubled by the subjection of innocent children to the icy waters of the baths. "I think it's cruelty," said one physician. The consensus is that children should *not* be taken to the baths.

Easter 1981, during the International Year of the Handicapped, brought the largest pilgrimage for mentally and physically handicapped children ever —over 12,000 (including children, their families, and friends, as well as doctors, nurses, aides, and volunteers) from more than 20 countries. The objective of the *Foi et Lumièrè* ("faith and light") celebration was to convey to children at a young age that they have a place in society and in the church and to enable them to overcome feelings of rejection and uselessness. The five-day gathering was for parents, too. Parents need to know they are not alone, that they share with other parents common but often unvented feelings of inadequacy, sadness, and guilt.

The Lourdes Center in Boston raises money to send a group of children on a pilgrimage every year; the children are accompanied by a doctor, nurses, and aides. The cost to send one child is about $1,000. Appeals for funds to send needy youngsters run in the center's newsletter: "Webbed hands, clubbed feet, and a distorted facial appearance are just a few birth defects of this 19 year old. Cranial facial surgery has improved her looks only slightly. Although Joan is retarded and cannot read, she is outgoing and could be employed. . . . A trip to Lourdes would show her people care." Another child, a 16-year-old girl with cerebral palsy, was described as living in excruciating pain. . . . We'd like to cheer her with the promise of Lourdes."

Surely Lourdes is a long way for these children to go for some caring and cheering. But it may be that the excitement and faith generated by the 4,000-mile journey itself to the celebrated sanctuary in the Pyrenees is half the medicine. A reader who sent a check to the Boston center to help a sick child make a pilgrimage wrote that "A visit to Lourdes is a joy and an experience that one carries with them at all times, and with each prayer to Our Lady of Lourdes you find yourself reliving your visit to the Grotto."

The future of Lourdes

The staff responsible for coordinating activities at the grotto and organizing pilgrimages fully expects to receive increasing numbers of healthy and ailing visitors in years to come. As medicine is better able to cure diseases it is anticipated that greater numbers of handicapped persons, accident victims, and the elderly will journey to Lourdes; efforts are being made to meet the special needs of these groups. The shrine also hopes to attract more multilingual volunteers.

In 1971 the grotto press office was established "to communicate with the outside world and to set the record straight." It would be well for that office to concentrate on exploding some of the persistent myths about the Marian sanctuary. Lourdes has never swindled the sick with false promises. Nonetheless, a better effort could be made to convey to the world what the shrine really has to offer: Lourdes is *not* a miracle mill; it is *not* a spa; and the water does *not* have healing powers. Lourdes *is* a unique international meeting place and there is every reason to believe that the sick, the frail, and other sufferers derive innumerable psychological and spiritual benefits from their visits. Wonders *do* occur when pilgrims discover their own strengths and learn the art of living with their maladies.

FOR ADDITIONAL READING:

Buckley, Kevin. "The Miracle of Lourdes," *Geo,* Vol. 3, June 1981.

Carrel, Alexis. *Journey to Lourdes.* New York: Harper and Row, 1950.

Clarke, Richard F. "Modern Miracles," *The Nineteenth Century,* November 1882, pp. 766–780.

Galton, Francis. "Objective Efficacy of Prayer," *Inquiries into Human Faculty and its Development.* London: Macmillan and Co., 1883, pp. 277–294.

Laurentin, René. *Bernadette of Lourdes.* London: Darton, Longman & Todd, 1979.

Neame, Alan. *The Happening at Lourdes: The Sociology of the Grotto.* New York: Simon and Schuster, 1967.

Werfel, Franz. *The Song of Bernadette.* New York: The Viking Press, 1942.

Zola, Émile. *Les Trois Villes: Lourdes, Rome et Paris.* Paris: Charpentier, 1894.

Cigarettes are Very Kool

by Alan Blum, M.D.

When you're a Jet, you're a Jet all the way,
From your first cigarette, 'til your last dying day . . . .

—*West Side Story,* 1957

The picture of a cigarette-smoking street gang member is not quite an anachronism in the 1980s, but compared with the range of hard drugs available to teenagers today, cigarettes seem like little more than leftover forbidden fruit of the halcyon fifties. Hardly a day passes without a news report about angel dust, alcohol, marijuana, cocaine, or Quaaludes. Newspapers print "The Alarming Truth About Marijuana and Your Child"; professional athletes visit schools to denounce drug abuse; politicians rail against dope dealers on school grounds; and parents groups mobilize to rid their community of "head shops" that sell drug paraphernalia.

The seriousness of illicit drug use among young people cannot be denied. Although the media are fearless in their zeal to expose teenage drug and alcohol abuse, they are conspicuously silent about what William Pollin, director of the National Institute on Drug Abuse, has called the nation's number one form of drug dependence: cigarette smoking.

Tobacco, of course, *is* a drug. Although it is not known just how its principal active component, nicotine, acts on the brain, people do become "addicted" to cigarette smoking. As many as 90% of cigarette users say they wish they had not started, and they wish they could stop—but for some reason they cannot succeed. On the other hand, the unpredictability of those who do win the battle—most say they did it on their own (without fancy programs, hypnotism, or other gimmicks), many by going "cold turkey" without experiencing the withdrawal one would expect in a true addiction—suggests that social and psychological factors may play a far greater role in perpetuating cigarette smoking than physiological dependence.

Is there another product as irredeemably harmful that is as extensively promoted? In spite of cigarette smoking's devastating physical and financial toll—350,000 deaths in the United States each year, including more than a quarter of all deaths due to heart disease, and at least one out of every five dollars spent on health care—the manufacturers of cigarettes still receive tax write-offs for advertising expenses.

Alan Blum, M.D., *is a family physician in Chicago. He is also president of DOC (Doctors Ought to Care), a national organization that assists communities in developing new approaches to health education for children and teenagers.*

(Opposite) Courtesy, DOC Archive

Marlboro's Make Your Marlbes Fall Out!

Helen Kernodle

Photographs, Museum of Modern Art

Why do adolescents take up smoking? Identification with role models who symbolize romance and sophistication is one undeniable motivating factor.

Cigarette advertising: creating complacency

Advertising, it would seem, has helped make sure that cigarette smoking is not even considered much of a health issue. By encouraging the public to believe that "everything causes cancer," the cigarette industry helps portray its product as just another victim of Big Brother's trying to tell people how to run their lives. The mass media, which carry the cigarette ads, have done nothing to alter the situation. Public outcry (egged on by banner headlines) over a mere handful of cases of botulism, toxic shock syndrome, or Legionnaires' disease can close businesses. One million cars can be recalled after one death due to a malfunction of a single automobile. Yet newspapers run full-page color advertisements for the product that has been described by the World Health Organization as the single most preventable cause of death and disability.

"Every cigarette ad carries the surgeon general's warning that smoking may be harmful to your health," said one executive of a leading newspaper when asked why his paper could not exert more control over cigarette advertising. "We remain confident that the public, fully informed, ultimately will make those decisions that are in its own best interests." The publisher of *Better Homes & Gardens,* whose magazine aims to be a health-oriented family publication, has stated that in his opinion "those readers who do not smoke will turn past the cigarette advertisements that are of no interest to them."

Just as emphysema, heart disease, and lung cancer have reached epidemic proportions in the United States, the tobacco industry has tried to see to it that cigarette smoking is not viewed as a health issue. The June 1, 1981 issue of *Time,* with a cover story on heart attacks, featured a six-page fold-out ad just inside the cover for Vantage cigarettes. The back cover promoted Winston Lights; Belair, Carlton, Kent III, and Marlboro were advertised within the magazine. Adolescents, looking for role models and at the same time rebelling against authority figures, are a particularly impressionable group. Any adolescent who reads a magazine or a newspaper learns from the advertising that smoking is synonymous with good looks, sexiness, athletic prowess, sophistication, individuality, and even (with "low tar") good health. The purpose of cigarette advertising is not just to sell cigarettes but also to create complacency about the dangers of smoking them.

At least this is the game the tobacco industry has been playing, particularly since 1964, when U.S. Surgeon General Luther Terry and a committee of physicians released the report that irrefutably linked cigarette smoking to emphysema (a generally incurable disease in which the patient slowly suffocates to death—fully aware of what is happening—over months or years) and lung cancer (the literal eating away of the lungs and possibly other organs such as the brain to which the cancer spreads). The Royal College of Physicians in the United Kingdom had released a massive report on these dangers even earlier—in 1962.

(Overleaf) Counteradvertisement is the creation of sixth-grader Helen Kernodle from Des Moines, Iowa.

"Everybody's doing it"

It is a myth that cigarette smoking is thousands of years old and a time-honored tradition, if not an inalienable right. Actually, whereas tobacco has

Photographs, courtesy, DOC Archive

Up until the late 1960s, movie and sports stars were among the heroes and heroines featured in ads for every brand of cigarette. Today's cigarette-promoting models are active, healthy, sexy, fashionable, and tough—but nameless.

been used for centuries, cigarettes—the only tobacco product that requires inhaling—were not mass-produced until a century ago; moreover, while nearly 4,000 cigarettes were smoked for every adult in the United States in 1980, the per capita consumption in 1880 was 25. When the 19th-century German bacteriologist Robert Koch suggested that spitting—such as was practiced by cigar smokers and plug tobacco chewers—spread tuberculosis (the most dreaded disease of the time) and a number of antispitting ordinances were passed, the tobacco industry in the United States shifted gears and began to produce cigarettes. To consummate the switch, it had to use mass media advertising to teach people how to smoke cigarettes: "Do you inhale? Everybody's doing it!" insisted the American Tobacco Company.

Even well into the 20th century, cigarettes still had not caught on—and definitely not among women. But with advertising, the tobacco companies began to appeal to women: "To keep a slender figure, reach for a Lucky instead of a sweet." A well-promoted aura of romance and sophistication made a Camel smoker—man or woman—a "social success." Throughout the '30s, '40s, and '50s on radio and in every leading magazine a plethora of our prettiest people were the models in the ads: Douglas Fairbanks, Jr., Jean Harlow, Fredric March, Joan Crawford, Claudette Colbert, Tyrone Power, Eva Gabor, Frank Sinatra, Maureen O'Hara, Gregory Peck, Linda Darnell, Dean Martin, Jerry Lewis, Bob Hope, the Duchess of Windsor, Mrs. John D. Rockefeller, and Santa Claus. "I'm a singer and my throat comes first. I picked Camels as my steady smoke," said Anne Jeffreys in an advertisement in *Life* in the 1940s. It is sad but poignant that Gary Cooper, Rosalind Russell, John Wayne, Dick Haymes, Robert Taylor, and Nat King Cole all promoted one brand or another of cigarette and subsequently developed lung cancer or other fatal smoking-related diseases.

The cigarette companies also appealed to the all-American boy, who, of course, was likely to be an aspiring athlete. A ten-year-old boy growing up

Photographs, courtesy, DOC Archive

When they saw that smoking had not caught on equally between the sexes, the cigarette companies began to appeal to women. Today it seems astounding, but cigarette ads used to appear in medical journals, and smoking was promoted by doctors.

in the 1930s could pick up the Sunday comic pages and see his favorite athletes—Yankees' stars Joe DiMaggio or Lou Gehrig—saying such things as "Camels don't get my wind" and "Athletes smoke as many as they please." According to sluggers Ted Williams and Stan Musial, Chesterfields were "the baseball man's cigarette." Skater Irving Jaffee, an Olympic gold medalist, said, "It takes healthy nerves to be a champion. That's why I smoke Camels." In the sporting world, track stars, deep-sea divers, sharpshooters, archers, tightrope walkers, jet pilots, water skiers, football players, tennis champions, speedboat racers—even chess, billiards, and bridge players—seemed to attribute their success to smoking cigarettes.

And how did the industry respond to early reports in the 1940s and '50s that associated cigarette smoking with a variety of lethal ailments? "More doctors smoke Camels than any other cigarette," proclaimed R. J. Reynolds. "Not one single case of throat irritation due to smoking Camels." In the *Journal of the American Medical Association* (which accepted cigarette advertising until well into the 1950s), Philip Morris's bellhop, little Johnny, guaranteed that smoking Philip Morris was "safer" according to "many leading nose and throat specialists."

Advertising for American Tobacco's Lucky Strike suggested that some smokers might not realize that they inhale. To be safe, *they* should select a "light" smoke, the one "found less irritating by 20,769 doctors." Lorillard claimed its Old Gold contained "less irritating tars and resins"; it was "fresh as a new spring crocus." For another brand, Lorillard proclaimed, "More scientists and educators smoke Kent." Kent's widely promoted Micronite filter, which was made out of asbestos, was advertised as containing a material "so safe, so pure, it's used to filter the air in many hospitals." By portraying newer cigarettes as "even safer" the tobacco industry effectively eliminated early concerns about the dangers of smoking. Probably the only real advance was in the advertising psychology. Believing that Americans would regard the cigarette filter as analogous to an oil or air-conditioning filter, Liggett & Myers produced a white-coated sage to assert that L & M's cellulose tip was "just what the doctor ordered."

When surveys showed that filter smokers might be looked upon as sissies —since, after all, cigarette smoking was meant to show adult courage, risk-taking, and antiauthoritarianism—Philip Morris led the way with a tattooed cowboy, an inhabitant of "Marlboro Country." Just a few months earlier Marlboro had been advertised as a ladies smoke, "mild as May." A baby was shown in one advertisement saying, "Gee, mommy, you sure like your Marlboros." Throughout the 1950s and '60s, the cigarette companies were the most predominant advertisers on youth-oriented television shows such as "Seventy-Seven Sunset Strip," "The Rebel," and most major televised sports events.

Following the famed surgeon general's report, all cigarettes sold in the U.S. beginning in 1966 had to carry the warning "Caution: Cigarette Smoking May Be Hazardous to Your Health." In 1971 that message was strengthened to: "Warning: The Surgeon General Has Determined That Cigarette Smoking Is Dangerous to Your Health." In 1970 the government banned cigarette advertising from radio and television. But forgotten or misunderstood is the fact that it was the cigarette companies themselves—aghast at the success of counteradvertising that appeared from 1967 to 1970 as the result of a single complaint by the founder of Action on Smoking and Health, John Banzhaf—who removed their own ads to avoid having to be shown up by the clever ads that spoofed cigarette smoking. Kenneth Warner of the University of Michigan pointed out in the *American Journal of Public Health* that the counteradvertisements, featuring some famous personalities but running in off-hours and in low frequency compared to the prime-time jingles for Marlboro, Kent, Salem, and Winston, cut expected cigarette sales growth by upwards of 30% in just three years.

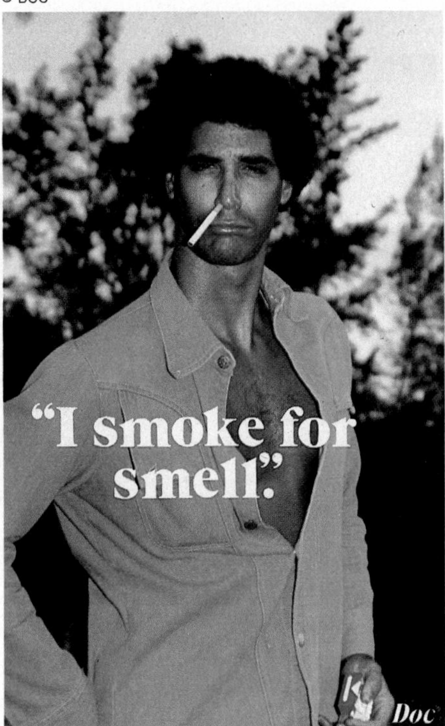

Smoking has long been equated with risk-taking and antiauthoritarianism. This counteradvertisement mimics the macho Winston smoker who boasts "I smoke for taste."

Smoking in the 1980s

The 1980s are marking a new era. Americans are healthier than ever, says the U.S. government. The impression is widespread that people are quitting smoking in droves, and the number of teenagers taking up cigarette smoking is going down. Cigarette advertising no longer appears on television. Cigarette companies are diversifying so rapidly, it is said, that the cigarette income does not even matter. Besides, the cigarettes they are making are safer than ever. The nonsmokers rights movement is winning its battles for clean indoor areas, and the women's health movement is in the vanguard of those discouraging cigarette smoking among teenage girls. Today's athletes do not pose for cigarette ads. Joe DiMaggio is better identified with "Mr. Coffee" than with baseball, and Mickey Mantle and Lou Gehrig are only names in the record book to today's teenagers.

These impressions are, for the most part, wrong. In fact, the problem may be worse than ever before. It is so discouraging to contemplate the problem of cigarette smoking among adolescents that the American Cancer Society, for example, has concentrated the greater part of its antismoking campaign on adults. Although there have been scattered efforts to develop curricular materials concerning the dangers of smoking for grade schools, there is not a single penny's worth of paid advertising aimed at teenagers to counter the cigarette companies' nearly one billion dollars' worth of advertising. While teams of medical researchers are well subsidized to study ways of combating juvenile onset diabetes and juvenile rheumatoid arthritis—serious diseases that affect thousands of children each year—there is not a single physician employed full-time in the United States to counter *juvenile onset cigarette smoking*—a condition afflicting one million teenagers a year.

Overlooked in the much-heralded statements about Americans' supposedly improved health status is that the problem of heart disease among women is on the rise—an increase that closely parallels not only the number of women entering the workplace but also the number who take up cigarette smoking. A California study of 17,000 women published in the *Journal of the American Medical Association* in 1980 found that the risk of heart attack among women who smoke is three times that of nonsmokers; the risk of stroke is fivefold. Although the total number of male smokers is less than it was in 1964, black and Hispanic teenage boys have probably increased their cigarette smoking. Per capita consumption of cigarettes has declined only slightly in the last few years, and total sales are undiminished.

(Left) Vandell Cobb; (right) Richard Younker

In 1970 the U.S. government banned cigarette advertising from radio and television, but the cigarette companies found other ways to convince people to smoke; today their ads are bigger, brighter, more persuasive, and more in evidence than ever.

Even the government's own figures show that there are eight times as many girls aged 12 to 14 who are smoking today as in 1970—the year in which cigarette commercials last appeared on television and radio—and for the first time more females in a major age group (17–18) are smoking than males. An editorial in *Ca—A Cancer Journal for Clinicians* in 1981 expressed alarm that so many girls were starting to smoke before 13, and called smoking "the ticking time-bomb for teenage girls." In Connecticut, where the Department of Health has kept the most accurate records in the United States, the death rate from lung cancer among women has actually surpassed that of men.

Ironically, the publishing business, which had railed against television cigarette advertising for years, grew silent as it became the chief beneficiary of the switch into print advertising. Today the cigarette companies are spending three times what they spent in the last year of televised cigarette advertising.

But the cigarette companies never really went off the air. They shifted instead to the sponsorship of sporting events that are televised—a far less costly, subtler, and possibly more effective selling technique. The showing of Philip Morris's Virginia Slims Tennis Circuit, far from being opposed by women's groups, has been praised for helping to bring women into the big-time, big-money sports era. Even though no major league baseball club would admit to direct sponsorship by a cigarette company, nearly every club receives lucrative income from cigarette advertising in programs and on scoreboards (at the best camera angles). The Marlboro Cup horse race has become one of the top sports events of the year. Its annual telecast includes dozens of mentions of the brand name, pictures of the familiar logo, and even the old Marlboro jingle. The insertion of the Marlboro brand name on race cars is low-cost advertising that is not even perceived as advertising as the cars flash around the track and across the viewers' screens dozens of times during a telecast. Not coincidentally, cigarette companies have become the leading sponsors of events that appeal to risk-taking or rebellious adolescent instincts: racing of dirt bikes, motorcycles, and hot rods, rodeo, and ballooning.

Jean-Claude Lejeune

Emphysema, heart disease, and lung cancer have become epidemic in the United States and other countries. Meanwhile, the tobacco industry is trying to see that smoking is not *viewed as a health issue—in part, by placing cigarette ads alongside articles that discuss these very killers.*

Although one might think that television plays the major role in molding teenage life-styles, the power of the printed medium should not be underestimated. Perhaps *because* the tobacco industry knows that the incidence of lung cancer is likely to surpass that of breast cancer among women by 1983, it has become the number one financier of women's magazines, with the notable exceptions of *Good Housekeeping, Parents Magazine,* and the various brides magazines. The more ostensibly health-oriented women's magazines become, the more cigarette ads crop up alongside the health columns, as if to deny the very notion that smoking is a major health problem. Magazines that appeal expressly to teenage girls, such as *Mademoiselle,* are full of ads that exhort them to "smoke pretty Eve," be "a Thinner with Silva Thins," "come a long way, baby" with Virginia Slims, and "wear a Max—Great looking. Great tasting, too. Long, lean, all-white Max 120's." A girl does not even have to smoke them—she can just wear them. *Mademoiselle*, incidentally, promotes itself to advertisers with the slogan, "Good health, good looks, good living."

When *Rolling Stone,* a magazine widely read by teens, ran a cover photograph of John Lennon in the nude, it received irate mail from parents. One wonders whether parents have expressed any outrage over the Marlboro cowboy on the back cover or the many other ads for different brands of cigarettes—as well as for liquor, rolling papers, and snuff (featuring the Charlie Daniels Band). Similarly, with a day's worth of angry telephone calls, Chicagoans succeeded in removing from all city buses a Bonjour Action Jeans ad campaign that featured a young female's unzipped pants and bare skin beneath. Unopposed, still, are the ads for cigarettes that appear in almost every bus and subway car of the transit system.

One is tempted to suggest that the leading health educator in America—by virtue of its positive, exciting appeal to consumers—is the cigarette industry. The companies even outdo one another to become "lowest in tar" and to proclaim this honor on the sports and fashion pages of daily newspapers. But what does "low tar" mean? Low poison. "Tar" is a composite of over 4,000 separate solid poisons, including at least 35 known carcinogens. Would one go into a supermarket and buy a loaf of bread that contained "only two ounces of poison" or a can of soup that was "lowest in carcinogens"? American Brands says that 17 packs of Carlton are equal in tar (poison) to just one pack of Kent. Does that mean that the consumer can smoke 17 packs a day without an increased risk of disease? The hoax is that certain brands are safer. Safer than what? Than fresh air? Studies show that smokers who switch to a low-tar in the belief that they will be safer are likely to smoke more in order to maintain the level of nicotine. Even on a pack-per-pack basis, low-tar smokers trade off slightly less tar (carcinogen) for more carbon monoxide (heart disease risk factor).

What else will the smoker get besides a strong risk for lung cancer or heart disease? Ammonia, formaldehyde, and hydrogen cyanide are just a few of the noxious gases found in significant concentrations in cigarette smoke. These gases are not just the result of burning tobacco but also a result of chemical additives—more than 1,500 of them, including nitrates as preservatives and propylene glycol, the solvent used as antifreeze—designed to

Courtesy, DOC Archive

WE'RE FIGHTING
FOR YOUR LIFE
American
Heart Association
We offer you more.
More
ACKERLEY
ACKERLEY

keep the cigarette burning smoothly and evenly. Because cigarettes are designed to burn so well, in the United States each year they are the leading cause of home, hospital, and hotel fires, which take the lives of more than 2,000 persons and maim and injure many more.

The failure to reach teenagers

With all that is known about the dangers of cigarette smoking and all the public health hand-wringing, why have we failed to prevent teenagers—girls especially—from taking up cigarettes? How do we explain the reasoning of a 16-year-old girl who chose to keep smoking rather than receive a free trip to Washington, D.C., paid for by former HEW secretary Joseph Califano? "I could have quit for good, but I didn't want to," she said. "It's something to do with my hands."

Ironies abound, as in the scene above. Not only do cigarettes cause cancer and heart disease, but because they are designed to burn so well, they are a leading cause of fires in the United States.

Ken Firestone

Obviously, smoking is initiated by many social influences. Imitation of models—media stereotypes, peers, and significant adults (parents, teachers, doctors)—plays a big role. Unfortunately, most school-based cigarette education programs lack immediacy for students. The programs spell out the dangers and emphasize eventual disabilities. Yet to any adolescent who feels fine and has good health, illness—especially cancer—is an abstract thing. It is difficult to sell health to someone who already believes he has it. Moreover, adolescence is a highly stressful period of development complicated by reactions to puberty. Teens may not be able or willing to see beyond the immediate present. And when looking for role models the disciplinarian parent or teacher or doctor does not hold a candle to the cattle-roping Marlboro man or sleek, clear-skinned gal who gets her Barclay cigarette lit by a dashing gentleman. (Brown & Williamson, incidentally, spent $150,000,000 in less than a year to introduce Barclay, a new brand, an amount that is probably greater than all the money that has ever

Courtesy, DOC Archive

It is hoped that concerned citizens from every age group will join in the crusade to prevent smoking among young people. But teenagers themselves must be in the vanguard of efforts to unsell *cigarettes, as they were in designing this ad bench in Spartanburg, South Carolina.*

gone into research on the effects of smoking and efforts to prevent it.

Schools have also concentrated on the idea that smoking is self-destructive behavior and emphasized "not becoming one of the crowd." But as Daniel Horn, a leader in the field of smoking education, has commented in regard to school-based programs: "There are serious difficulties in attempting to influence young people by teaching them in the classroom to adopt behavior opposed to practices that are encouraged in the larger environment." Cigarette companies can keep up with the latest fads (and in some instances create them) in their depiction of smoking and so remain in vogue far better than the schools. Indeed, the tobacco industry alliance has put together a seemingly unchallengeable multibillion dollar smoking propaganda effort. Camouflaged in all the cigarette ads and often laughed at by teenagers is the health joke of the century: "Warning: The Surgeon General Has Determined That Cigarette Smoking Is Dangerous to Your Health."

As if there were any doubt, the U.S. Federal Trade Commission (FTC) concluded in mid-1981 that the message on cigarette packages had not discouraged smokers. The FTC proposed changes in the size and shape of the printed warning as well as a more direct statement, referring specifically to cancer and heart attacks.

The tobacco industry has been stunningly successful in its opposition to any government-sponsored smoking education programs directed at young people, in its refutation of evidence that smoking is particularly damaging in pregnant women, in its contention—having never admitted that smoking is dangerous in the first place—that it can be made safer, and in its attempt to cover up the crippling toll taken by smoking. Fear arousal has not been sufficient to thwart smoking in adolescents. (It does appear to have some effect in children under ten years of age.) It is the very risk-taking, antisocial tendency of adolescents to which the industry is appealing. Teenagers prob-

Vandell Cobb

Tobacco companies know how to reach teenagers. They sponsor major sporting and musical events such as the Kool Jazz Festivals, which take place in many cities across the United States. This, too, is advertising.

ably do not have an overwhelming desire to breathe in hot carcinogens and poisonous, smelly gases. Rather, they are simply identifying with tough cowboys and sophisticated ladies. It is not just a matter of smoking a cigarette but of picking an image—one buys Marlboros or Virginia Slims, and one selects one's brand carefully.

One report done for the National Institute on Drug Abuse by University of Michigan researchers showed a decline in teenage smoking. Of 17,000 high school seniors 29% smoked in 1977; 21% in 1980. Even though girls were smoking less in 1980 they continued to be heavier smokers than boys (30.1% smoked in 1977, 23.5% in 1980). Among boys, 27.2% smoked in 1977, 18.5% in 1980. The researchers attributed the overall decline in this group, in part, to greater public disapproval of smoking. This survey unfortunately may not accurately reflect the habits of certain populations, where percentages of smokers are probably significantly higher—such as among school dropouts, Hispanics, and inner-city blacks.

Moreover, the problem is by no means gone. And any good news should not lull the public into believing vigilance and counterattack are no longer crucial. Every one of the thousands of unopposed billboards and other advertisements a child grows up seeing represents the cigarette companies' denying the facts and undermining medical science. Educating with the facts *is* important and necessary. But because teens are teens, because the tobacco industry is rich, powerful, and unwilling to acknowledge that its product is a major killer, and because advertising is such a pervasive and effective form of persuasion, some efforts must be made to undo cigarette promotion.

It goes without saying that those who choose to deal with the problem—and it is hoped that they will come from every age group and occupation—must be mindful that cigarette smoking is the number one teenage drug problem. But they need also remember that smoking is as much a serious societal problem as a health problem. The cigarette is a symbol for whatever the tobacco industry wants it to be.

Spreading the antismoking message

How does the United States measure up to other countries in the effort to discourage cigarette smoking among young people? Fair, at best. In spite of activist efforts for clean indoor air by the organization ASH (Action on Smoking and Health) and various chapters of GASP (Group Against Smokers' Pollution) as well as the development of posters and other materials by such groups as the American Cancer Society and the American Lung Association, and repeated public statements on the cigarette problem by surgeons general Luther Terry, Jesse Steinfeld, and Julius Richmond, and by a few outspoken physicians like Alton Ochsner, the United States has largely failed to reach large numbers of children and teenagers. In fact, the United States appears to lag behind numerous other countries—only some of which are mentioned here—in providing incentives for a smoke-free generation.

Canada has fared somewhat better, largely due to the outspoken Canadian Council on Smoking and Health, which is supported by both governmental and charitable groups from every province. The governments of Quebec and Saskatchewan have pioneered in *paid* advertisements on radio and television that discourage smoking (as well as other lethal life-styles such as drunken driving and poor nutrition). Toronto's Non-Smokers' Rights Association, which has widely publicized the hazards to children of second-hand smoke, succeeded in lobbying for one of the most restrictive bans anywhere on smoking in public places as well as a ban on cigarette advertising on the city's transit system. Winnipeg will be the site of the fifth World Conference on Smoking in 1983.

The World Health Organization has declared that in industrialized nations "the control of cigarette smoking could do more to improve health and prolong life than any other single action in the whole field of preventive medicine." But in the vast majority of third world nations, where governments equate tobacco sales with lucrative revenues and where American and British tobacco companies have saturated the media with advertising, there are no government officials or charities charged with tackling the cigarette problem. While there is acrimonious debate over the ethics of promoting infant formula and U.S.-made drugs in developing countries, cigarettes—with no redeeming health value—continue to be far more widely promoted than any other product. To cultivate smoking among the populations of impoverished countries, the tobacco companies give away enormous quantities of cigarettes and—using children as street vendors—sell cigarettes not just by the pack but by the piece. In poorer nations of the world smoking is most popular among the wealthier, better educated, and more "sophisticated." Among male medical students in Nigeria in 1976, 72% were cigarette smokers.

One of the most progressive efforts to combat smoking among children is under way in Nicaragua, where the government has made health and literacy major priorities. In the rest of Central and South America the picture is less sanguine because tobacco is simply too culturally engrained. Although Venezuela has banned cigarette advertising from radio and television and Brazil is beginning to counteradvertise, Mexico is home of the world's largest Marlboro billboards.

Adapted from "Dangers of Smoking, Benefits of Quitting," American Cancer Society

Risks of smoking and benefits of quitting

shortened life expectancy
after 10 to 15 years ex-smoker's risk approaches that of those who never smoked

lung cancer
after 10 to 15 years risk approaches that of those who never smoked

larynx cancer
gradual reduction in risk, reaching normal after 10 years

mouth cancer
reducing or eliminating smoking/drinking lowers risk in first few years; risk drops to level of nonsmokers in 10 to 15 years

cancer of esophagus
since risk is proportional to dose, reducing or eliminating smoking/drinking should lower risk

cancer of bladder
risk decreases gradually to that of nonsmokers over 7 years

cancer of pancreas
since risk seems related to dose, stopping smoking should reduce it

coronary heart disease
risk decreases sharply after one year; after 10 years risk is the same as for those who never smoked

bronchitis and emphysema
cough sputum disappears within few weeks; lung function may improve, deterioration slowed

stillbirth and low birth weight
if smoking is stopped before fourth month of pregnancy, risk to fetus is eliminated

peptic ulcer
ex-smokers get ulcers too, but they heal faster and more completely than in smokers

drug and test effects
most blood factors raised by smoking return to normal; nonsmokers on birth control pill have much lower risk of hazardous clots and heart attacks

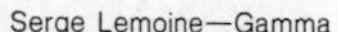
Serge Lemoine—Gamma

Many European countries are far ahead of the United States in efforts to discourage smoking among their youth. Most notable are Norway, Sweden, France, and Great Britain. Prince Charles, an outspoken nonsmoker, has been a persuasive model for British youngsters.

Japan is second only to the U.S. in per capita cigarette consumption. Yet Japan has put more energy into combating cigarette-butt litter than it has in combating the problem of cigarette smoking among young people. China, which ranks high in the production of tobacco, has seen a 15-fold rise in lung cancer in Shanghai and other areas since the mid-1960s and has finally begun warning its citizens of the hazards of smoking. Nonetheless, in 1980 Philip Morris became one of the first U.S. companies permitted to open shop in China. Billboards have made it official: Peking is Marlboro Country.

Although the U.S.S.R. does not have advertising per se, the government still seeks to profit from cigarette sales. Moscow has banned smoking in the city's restaurants, but Sochi, a Black Sea resort that attempted to become the country's first nonsmoking city, was not successful. In many Communist countries, U.S. cigarettes serve as currency.

Partly owing to Muslim religious beliefs, Arab countries have been world leaders in counteracting cigarette smoking and promotion. Saudi Arabia does not permit cigarette advertising. Kuwait fines store owners who post promotional displays for cigarettes. Bahrain bans advertising for cigarettes; in Dubai, advertisers can place billboards for cigarettes in sports stadiums, but only where they cannot be picked up by television cameras. Anwar Sadat's wife, Jihan, is head of the Egyptian Cancer Society and has led the drive to eliminate cigarette advertising from TV, radio, and billboards. In return the cigarette companies have resorted to putting free movie tickets in cigarette packs to boost sales. In Turkey, with one of the world's highest percentage of smokers, the government does not seem as worried about the health of its citizens as it does about Virginia tobacco's overtaking Turkish tobacco as the smoker's choice.

Since 1980 Greece, which has the highest smoking rate on the European continent, has curbed public smoking, banned most cigarette advertising, and started educational counterefforts. Italy has also banned most advertising for cigarettes, but American and British cigarette companies are openly violating the ban, paying small fines in order to continue to advertise.

Some of the most hopeful signs in Europe come from Great Britain, where Action on Smoking and Health is an official arm of the Royal College of

Physicians, and where the *British Medical Journal* and *The Lancet* have mobilized physician attention to the problem. Having pointed out that one in three British smokers started before they were nine years old, the government-supported British Health Education Council has developed several youth-oriented campaigns, including one featuring Superman. Many of the leading athletes in Great Britain have taken out paid advertisements in newspapers calling on the British-American Tobacco Co. to get out of athletics sponsorship. In addition, the British Army is strongly discouraging smoking in its ranks and Prince Charles, publicly stating his distaste for cigarette smoking, has been a superb role model for children and teenagers. Scotland has also gone about its effort with verve, recruiting popular rock stars for its ads. Ireland has begun placing a large warning on all cigarette packs and advertisements: "Smokers Die Younger."

Although Australia wields only a fraction of the power of the tobacco industry, a number of organizations have expressed concern about the health and vulnerability of young people. The Australian Medical Association has taken a leading role in curtailing cigarette smoking. A group called MOP UP (Movement Opposed to the Promotion of Unhealthy Products) succeeded in having a popular children's entertainer removed as a cigarette brand spokesman. Nine of the country's top rugby players starred in a popular 1980 antismoking campaign ("Give yourself a sporting chance. Stop smoking!") that angered league officials concerned about losing tobacco industry sponsorship. Also in 1980 the East Torrens District Cricket Club of South Australia shocked the sports world by rejecting all tobacco sponsorship and by making the international stop-smoking symbol a part of its official uniform. The club was censured by the International Cricket Conference for its "ingratitude" and for turning over some tobacco industry funding to the Anti-Cancer Fund. The most visible actions have been taken by two Australian groups. BUGA UP (Billboard-Utilizing Graffitists Against Unhealthy Promotions), a physician-led organization, defaces billboards advertising cigarettes with spray paint. The Black Lung Liberation Front goes even farther; this group chops down and burns billboards that promote cigarettes. Parodying the slogan for a popular brand, the group's motto is: "Light up a billboard—you'll be glad you did."

American Cancer Society

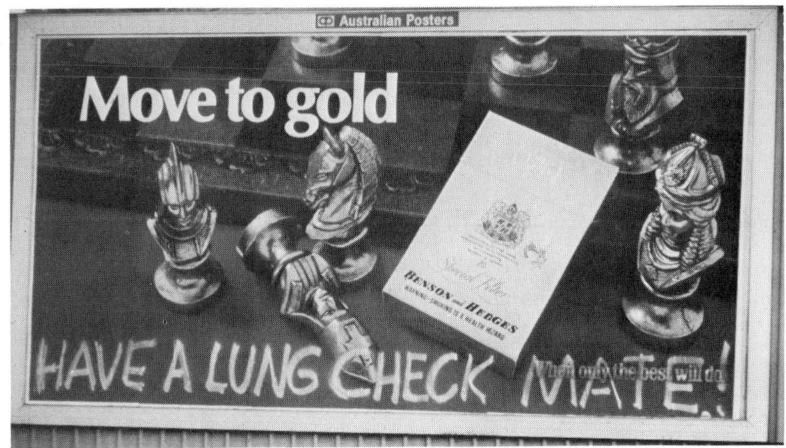

BUGA UP

In terms of widespread public support, Australia is a leader in the fight against cigarette advertising. A group called BUGA UP (Billboard-Utilizing Graffitists Against Unhealthy Promotions) takes to the streets at night with spray paint to deface billboards. The police have been tolerant of this vandalism, which is largely practiced by doctors.

A Patient Becomes a Doctor

by Young J. Chang

As one who is well down the road to an M.D. degree, leaning in the direction of either internal medicine or psychiatry, I have a lot of strong feelings about what it means to be a doctor. I have even stronger feelings about what it means to be a patient, for I am also one who has had a kidney transplant—one who has been in the care of a great many doctors in the past decade. This is my story of how I have coped with disease and, in the course of things, why I chose to pursue a career in medicine.

I wish I could say that I have triumphed totally over my hardships—that I am an exemplar of what is possible when the best of modern medicine is combined with heroic human character—but to do so would be a lie. On the surface, my achievements are many. But to judge how well I have come to terms with my disease on the grounds of these external successes would be a great mistake. There are many quintessential facts of my life that people tend not to see: my anxieties, my insecurities, my gloom. My story may not be as inspirational as that of Helen Keller or Hubert Humphrey, but I believe that acknowledging the grimmer realities of living with disease, pain, handicaps, and so forth—which so many people in this world have—is crucial to understanding what "coping" is all about.

The onset of my illness

First, a word about kidneys and my disease. In the summer of 1971, between the seventh and eighth grades, I was diagnosed as having membranoproliferative glomerulonephritis. The clinical features of the illness are a lot simpler than the name: the normal filtering capacity of both kidneys is slowly destroyed.

The kidneys are two bean-shaped organs, located on either side of the backbone. They lie with their concave side facing inward, approximately between the 11th rib and the highest point of the hip bone; the right kidney lies a little lower owing to the location of the liver. Although each is only about 4 inches long, 2.5 inches wide, and 1.5 inches thick, they normally receive one-fourth of the heart's total output of blood, which is about 1.2 liters per minute. This large flow of blood is an indication of the kidneys' importance, not only as filters of waste products but also as organs crucial to maintaining homeostasis—the constant internal environment necessary for the survival

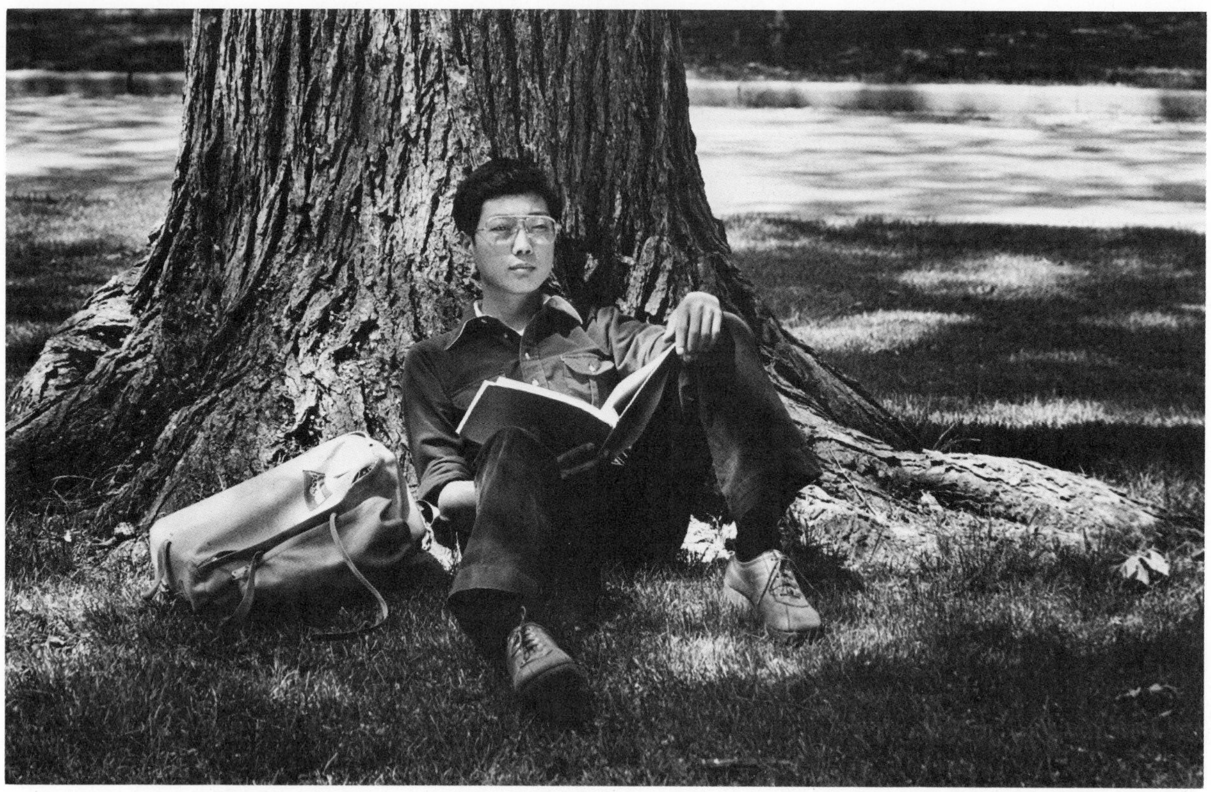

of the billions of cells that make up the human body. They keep constant the acidity and the concentrations of essential chemicals. In addition, they secrete factors that regulate blood pressure (renin) and the numbers of red blood cells in the bloodstream (erythropoietin).

The filtering unit of the kidney is called the nephron. It is composed of a ball of microscopic blood vessels, called capillaries, and a complex system of tubes, called tubules. My disease affected the ball of capillaries, which is called a glomerulus. A pair of normal kidneys have about 2.5 million nephrons. This huge number gives the kidneys enormous reserve capacity, and thus it is rare to see any symptoms in a person with kidney disease until much of the function is lost.

I cannot recall any dramatic changes that first made me aware of my kidney disease. In about the middle of the seventh grade, my parents and I noticed that my face and extremities would be swollen in the mornings when I awoke, but it was certainly nothing to go to the hospital for. At age 12, nothing could be further from my mind than kidney disease. Often I would feel weak and get tired easily, especially after exercise, but I thought it was just because I was out of shape. Besides, I was never known for my athletic abilities. I recall I always came in close to last in the distance runs in seventh grade gym class. The gym teacher told me I didn't have the determination to make it over the initial "pain barrier" of running. He was never too impressed with me—nor I, for that matter, with him.

Young J. Chang, *who had a successful kidney transplant in 1975, is a third-year medical student at the University of Chicago.*

Photographs by Jean-Claude Lejeune

Gradually, my whole body became swollen with fluid that my kidneys were unable to excrete. I looked as if I were pregnant; my usual weight of 125 pounds increased to almost 140 pounds, and standing up, I could not see my toes over my protruding belly. It became clear that I had to go to the hospital. Fortunately, school was out for the summer by then. While in the hospital my abdomen became so large that it hampered my breathing. I felt that I would burst if any more fluid accumulated; my belly was taut as a drum and the only comfortable position was sitting up. I could not deny it any longer—I was seriously ill.

My thoughts then were dominated by fears of the uncertain future. It wasn't yet time for me to worry about dying. But what about my dream of going to the Air Force Academy? Everyone knew they only accepted perfect specimens of health and masculinity. Life was getting complicated and it looked like my dream to be a pilot—not just any pilot, but an Air Force jet pilot, a dashing soldier in uniform, just like my dad once was—would not come true. I remember thinking that it would be five more years before I had to apply to the academy; perhaps I would get better by then.

After one month in the community hospital near our home in Carpentersville, Illinois, about 40 miles from Chicago, it became clear I was not getting any better but worse. They did not have the kind of doctors or the facilities to take care of me. I was referred to a big teaching hospital in Chicago: Rush-Presbyterian-St. Luke's. At this renowned institution things were very different, far from impressive to a 12-year-old to whom "quality" meant new and shiny. Compared to the suburban hospital room, my room at this great medical center was the absolute pits. It was old and dingy; it didn't have a color TV. To add to the frustrations, it seemed like a hundred doctors came in to poke at my distended abdomen and to ask questions I quickly got tired of answering. I remember asking my parents: "Why did you bring me here? What did I do to deserve this illness? Why me?" They didn't answer; they were as frustrated and confused about all this as I was.

"I wish I could say that I have triumphed totally over my hardships. . . . I believe that acknowledging the grimmer realities of living with disease, pain, handicaps . . . is crucial to understanding what 'coping' is all about."

After the preliminary examinations, I was immediately put on a low-sodium (no salt) diet. I had never before had any food that tasted so bland. Being used to heavily spiced and salted dishes of the Korean tradition, it was hard to get adjusted to the blandness. (Later, at home, I cheated often, raiding

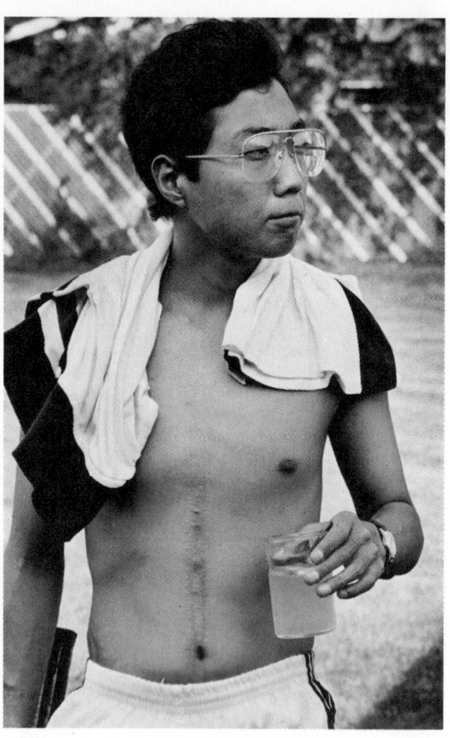

"I worked very hard to deny any emotions I was having about my disease. In moments of solitude, I sometimes felt angry, anxious, self-pitying, and inadequate. One thing was clear: my illness made me feel different from my peers—weaker and somehow less."

the refrigerator at night for some of my mother's cooking.) However, the diet did the trick, with the help of a diuretic, a drug that helps the kidneys excrete more water. My abdomen returned to normal size within a few days, but like "memoirs" of a pregnancy, I had stretch marks on my thighs, abdomen, and lower back. At that time a kidney biopsy was performed; under local anesthetic a small tissue specimen of my kidney was excised with a special needle. The tissue was then sectioned into very thin slices so that it could be viewed under a microscope to assess the kind and extent of the disease. I was released from the hospital on a regimen of diuretics, antihypertensive drugs (to control high blood pressure), and a low-sodium diet—a regimen I was to follow for the next four and a half years. I had spent a total of two months in two hospitals that summer, the end result being a diagnosis of chronic renal (kidney) disease.

The impact of my illness

Changes in me came quickly, and the effects were manifested first at school. The straight-A student of the year before now began to get an occasional B. But now that I was "sick," I didn't have to worry about parental admonishments about doing "bad" in school; I had an excuse. The eighth grade was a disaster. In math I got a C—the first of my academic career; to think that the year before I had received a special honors certificate for my superior performance in math! The only redeeming feature of that year was my performance in music, a subject not considered "academic" by my parents. However, playing my French horn and singing in various choir groups were my only sources of satisfaction and accomplishment, and I hoped they would make my parents proud of me. But my parents had to work on night shifts at a nearby electronics plant, my dad as an electrical engineer and my mother as a technician; they could not come to my concerts. How I had wished they could come and see me play. I wanted them to let me know I was still a "good" son, although I was a sick one. I remember the walks home from the music concerts were long and lonely.

The next year in high school, I got involved in all sorts of clubs and activities. I worked very hard to deny any emotions I was having about my disease. In moments of solitude, I sometimes felt angry, anxious, self-pitying, and inadequate. One thing was clear: my illness made me feel different from my peers—weaker and somehow less. The illusory haven of high school activities offered me temporary sanction from my true turmoil. But eventually my real doubts and fears surfaced. Despite my activities and achievements I saw myself as a failure.

My greatest fear was of being "exposed." Would people still like and accept me if they knew the "true" me? The sick kid? The scared kid who felt that he was inferior and inadequate? The kid who, despite appearances, was totally lacking in self-confidence and self-esteem? In addition, I was a kid with tremendous guilt, for I thought I had brought about my disease. It was a punishment from God for having sinned. It seems absurd now, but from the time I was 12 until I was 16 I sincerely believed that my kidney disease was a punishment for having experimented with masturbation. Everyone knew only bad kids thought about sex and masturbation, but to

actually do it! What a shock that would be for my parents; a son who was not only sickly but also wicked.

Thus I put every effort into being an achiever. After all, how could anyone argue that a kid who was in student government, debate, band, National Honor Society—and still got good grades—was "bad" or "inferior"? I did especially well in biology; in 1973 my science project made it to the state science fair. Gradually, my interest in math and the "hard" sciences such as physics shifted toward the "softer" sciences of biology and chemistry—perhaps the beginning of my interest in medicine as a career.

But for the most part, I engaged only in those things that brought quick results and accolades and quit those that required true work. This approach even showed in my chess game. I would quickly build my position to attack, playing carefully and wisely up to that point. Then if my attack was a success, I would play to the end bent on winning, and usually did; if the attack failed, or if I was down in pieces, I quickly gave up any hopes of winning and played the rest of the game sloppily. I lacked what made the champions great, the determination and courage to endure and fight; when the odds were against me, I was a quitter.

At the start of my junior year in high school, I began to notice that my body was becoming swollen again. I tried my best to deny it. I "forgot" to go to my monthly checkups in Chicago for I was afraid of what the doctors might say: "Your kidneys are getting worse and we may have to put you on an artificial kidney machine." The doctors had discussed the kidney machine with me before, but I was not aware of my fear of it until now. The machine takes your blood, "cleans" it of waste products, and puts it back into you. Usually, you are hooked up to the machine for about four hours, two or three times a week, depending on your needs. The idea of being dependent on a machine would be a painfully direct confirmation of all my inadequacies.

By the time Christmas break came around, I began to get tingling sensations all over my body, and it was difficult to feel certain stimuli in my legs.

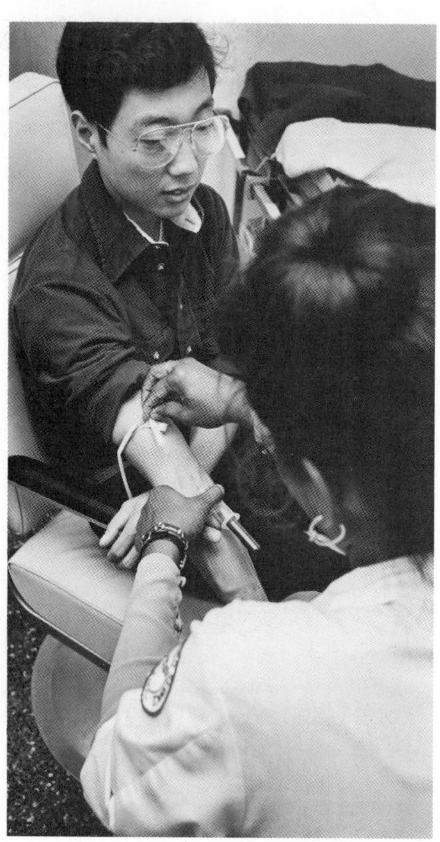

"... the idea of being on dialysis for the rest of my life was unthinkable. ... it is inconvenient and time-consuming for a young and active person, not to mention the psychological trauma of being always dependent on a machine to sustain life."

The severe headaches and painful cramps made life impossible; I tried to ignore the unpleasantness of life by sleeping as much as possible. Finally, it was too much to bear and I asked my parents to take me to the emergency room at Rush in Chicago. The doctors were flabbergasted: how could an intelligent person with any sense wait so long before coming into the hospital? Indeed, by the time I got to my hospital room, my whole body felt as if an electric current was passing through it. My tongue became paralyzed and it was difficult to talk. There was such a buildup of waste products and an imbalance of chemicals in my system, because the kidneys' function had so deteriorated, that even my brain was affected. I was half conscious, half delirious, but still I had enough function to realize how scared I was. I panicked and got angry at the doctors. I wanted to yell out: "Do something!" but my tongue wouldn't move. I thought for sure that this was it, I was going to die at age 16.

At the end of the bed were my parents, my mother crying, my father's face pale with worry. Luckily for me, I don't remember much after this first night. Apparently, I was in a state of delirium for the rest of the week. I just recall waking up one morning feeling well, only to find a tube coming out of my abdomen, my hands and legs tied to the bed; a week had passed without my knowledge. Later, the doctors told me that I was very lucky to be alive.

The dreaded kidney machine

The doctors decided that it was time to put me on hemodialysis, the kidney machine. I had a temporary external shunt put in, a loop of plastic tubing that came out of my right arm. It unhooked at the end so that I could be connected to the machine. I used to joke to my friends who visited me at the hospital that instead of being the bionic man I was the plastic man. I cannot remember how I really felt about that tube in which I could see my blood circulating. Normally, a dialysis patient has an internal shunt that is out of sight, but it takes about two weeks for it to become functional—time I did not have. As soon as possible, however, an internal shunt (connecting an artery to a vein) was placed in my left arm.

I was 16 then, and the idea of being on dialysis for the rest of my life was unthinkable. Moreover, dialysis is far from a perfect "cure." First, it is inconvenient and time-consuming for a young and active person, not to mention the psychological trauma of being always dependent on a machine to sustain life. Second, it does not resolve all the medical problems because it cannot mimic all the functions of the normal kidneys. As a result, people on long-term dialysis generally develop one or more complications, physical as well as psychological. The optimal solution for me was a kidney transplant, not without its own problems, but which could offer a more "normal" and active life than dialysis.

The main problem with transplantation of any kind is rejection by the host's immune system of the donor graft. The same immune system that protects a person from colds and infections can recognize a life-saving graft as foreign tissue and destroy it. To minimize this rejection process, a kidney that resembles the host's tissue as closely as possible must be sought. Thus, transplantation between identical twins will rarely fail, whereas one between two randomly selected people will almost inevitably fail, unless drugs that weaken the immune system of the host are given.

My mother and father were tested to see who had the kidney most compatible with my body in a procedure called tissue typing. I have a sister, but at the time she was only five, too young to be considered. It's funny, but I don't remember anyone asking them how they felt about giving a part of their body to someone else. It seemed they were both willing and eager to give, without questions or doubt—not just a kidney, but anything else I might have required. I guess that is parental love. I am sure the doctors had a long discussion with them on the subject, but I was unaware of it. As it turned out, my mother was to give me a second chance at life, a second birth. The results were disappointing to my father, who wanted to give the kidney as much as, perhaps more than, my mother.

While all the tests were being run for the transplant, I was still in the hospital undergoing hemodialysis. By that time my own kidneys were useless dead weight I carried around, and the machine kept me alive. The wait was relatively short, a little over a month, but it seemed eternal. Time only flies when you're having fun. Three times a week, four hours each time, I sat in a reclining chair in an isolation room. I had to be isolated from other dialysis patients because I had had prior exposure to hepatitis. There was a possibility that hepatitis could be transmitted to the other patients by needles and sharp instruments contaminated with my blood. Although the possibility of this happening was extremely small, they didn't want to take any chances and separated me from the other dialysis patients. The nurses were also extra careful and wore gloves when inserting needles into my arm. The isolation cubicle they called a room had just enough space for the machine and the chair. I was hooked to the machine by two huge needles (the internal shunt in my left arm was now functional), so big that they had to inject local anesthetic to the area before they inserted them. To this day, I have needle scars on my arm, like a heroin addict, to remind me of those awful times. I dreaded those days scheduled for dialysis. Some people read or watched TV while on the machine, but I just slept to pass the time as unaware as possible. The other patients, some of whom were on dialysis for almost ten years, used to tell me that you got used to it; you had no other choice except to die. But I loathed dialysis and vowed to commit suicide if the kidney transplant failed.

My greatest hope: a successful transplant

Almost two months had passed since I first came into the emergency room in that unbecoming state, and the date was set for the transplant: Feb. 27, 1975. Two weeks before the transplant I had my spleen removed; it was enlarged and destroying my platelets. Removing the spleen would help minimize rejection, since it was part of the immune system that would try to destroy the grafted kidney. I was assured that I would be perfectly fine without a spleen; the liver would compensate. The removal of the spleen was the most painful operation I ever had, even more painful than the transplant surgery, although the incision was smaller by about five and a half inches. Thank God for morphine and Demerol.

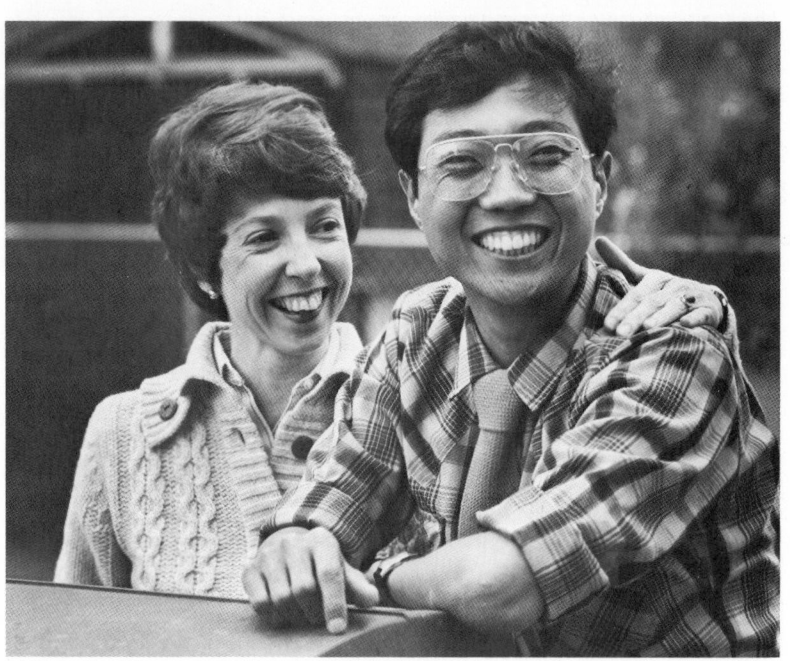

Author with Audrey Fraser, his high school French teacher and enduring friend. She was there to reassure him the morning he had his kidney transplant in February 1975.

The night before the transplant lasted forever. In the evening, I went upstairs to see my mother in her hospital room. She tried to act calm and cheerful, but the fear and anxieties showed through. I don't think she feared what would happen to her, but rather what would happen to me if the kidney rejected. The feelings overcame her, and the tears she tried so hard to hide came pouring forth. I tried to act strong and without fear, but I don't think I convinced her. Throughout the night all sorts of thoughts cluttered my mind. Would the kidney work? It had to! If it didn't, would I really kill myself? How? Suicide had to be painless and clean. I tried very hard to think of all the wonderful things I would do when the kidney started to work: To eat the biggest and saltiest pizza I could order would be a good start. But these dreams of gluttony didn't suppress my anxieties; it seemed morning would never come.

Morning did come and so did the cart that was to take me to the operating room. My mother was already in the operating room having one of her kidneys removed. My dad, my high school French teacher, Miss Fraser, and the nurses all wished me luck. Even in my sedated state, it was amazing how reassuring the warm smiles and kisses were.

When I next woke up, a day had passed and I was in a new room, an intensive care unit. All sorts of tubes were coming out of my body, a couple to drain the surgical site and one to collect the urine. My right arm was hooked to an intravenous bottle, and an oxygen tube connected my nose to the outlet on the wall. Wires were attached to my chest to monitor my heart. I went back to sleep, but when I awoke again, things were still the same. Somehow, this was not what I had expected; I looked like an experiment in a science fiction movie. But I was comforted when I was told that the kidney seemed to be working.

After the initial postoperative period, I began to feel much better. In fact

I became euphoric—I could have bacon and eggs for breakfast; I could have as much salt as I wanted. Even the tubes and wires didn't seem to bother me anymore. I discovered later that much of the euphoria was an effect of one of the drugs that they gave me for immunosuppression.

As the dosage of the drugs was reduced, my euphoria subsided. The drugs that allowed me to keep my kidney were also making me very vulnerable to infections; I had limited defense against the everyday world, which is full of bacteria, fungi, and viruses. In me the common cold could develop into pneumonia and perhaps lead to death. For one month, I was placed in reverse isolation, which meant the medical personnel had to be extra careful not to give me an infection. To top it off, I also found that these drugs, especially the one called prednisone, had several unpleasant side effects. It altered my fat metabolism so that my face became very corpulent; I had a "moonface"—a term familiar to all transplant patients and others who must take cortisonelike drugs for any extended period. It also made my face break out so that I looked like Porky Pig with severe acne. You are probably thinking: "What a superficial kid! He should have been thankful to be alive, but instead he complains about a plump face and a few pimples." I can only say that to a 16-year-old who was insecure to start with, the change in physical appearance had tremendous impact.

I remember how insecure I felt about facing my friends and classmates again the first day back at school. I avoided looking people in the eye, and my gaze was usually directed to the ground. I can recall vividly one girl coming up to me and shouting (so it seemed): "You really got fat!" I tried to rationalize that her comment was meaningless, that she was just insensitive and without the capacity to look beyond appearances. But it still hurt. Of all the things said to me that day, I remember only those four words.

"After the initial postoperative period . . . I became euphoric. . . . Even the tubes and wires didn't seem to bother me. . . . I discovered later that much of the euphoria was an effect of one of the drugs that they gave me. . . ."

"I was . . . admitted to the University of Chicago in September 1975 at age 16. . . . one of my doctors . . . urged me not to shortchange myself, to get the best possible education, and not to be afraid of a tough university with its intense academic and social pressures. He . . . did not permit me to use my illness as an excuse to take the easy road."

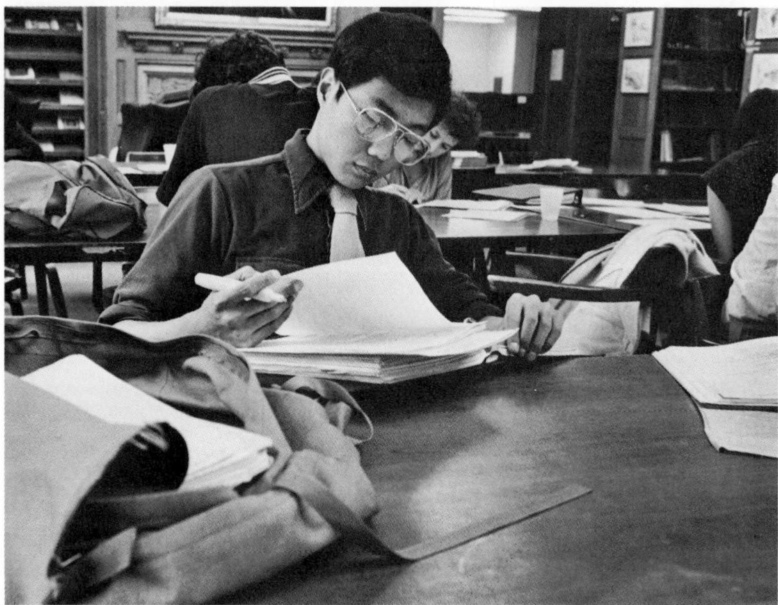

After about two weeks it became clear I could not keep up in school; I got too tired going to classes, so I dropped out and attempted to study at home. About one month after my release from the hospital, blood tests seemed to indicate that my kidney was starting to reject, a so-called acute rejection episode. I went into the hospital again and the dosage of my immunosuppressive medications was raised. Soon the kidney function returned to normal and I was released after about a week. "How many more 'episodes' must I endure?" I wondered. "Will my kidney ever 'take'?" At home, I spent most of my time alone in varying degrees of depression, uncertain about the future. Cold statistics, which told me that 85% of the kidneys survived the first year and that one or two reversible rejection episodes were common, were not very comforting. As it turned out, I only had one more rejection episode that spring—it looked as if the kidney would take.

I was lucky to be admitted to the University of Chicago in September 1975 at age 16 even though I had not completed high school. I considered going to a community college, but one of my doctors, who helped me get into college, urged me not to shortchange myself, to get the best possible education, and not to be afraid of a tough university with its intense academic and social pressures. He had great confidence in my potential and did not permit me to use my illness as an excuse to take the easy road. In a sense, he pushed me to the limit; I am glad he did.

Still looking like Porky Pig with acne, I not only felt self-conscious about my physical appearance, but now I also felt like I was the dumbest kid in college. However, college was new and challenging, and I realized that I really had to work to make the grade. Slowly my confidence rose as I found that I could not only keep up but do well. Unlike high school, the A's really meant something here; I was often tired from studying, but I got satisfaction from what I had accomplished. My achievements finally had value to *me,* even the B's!

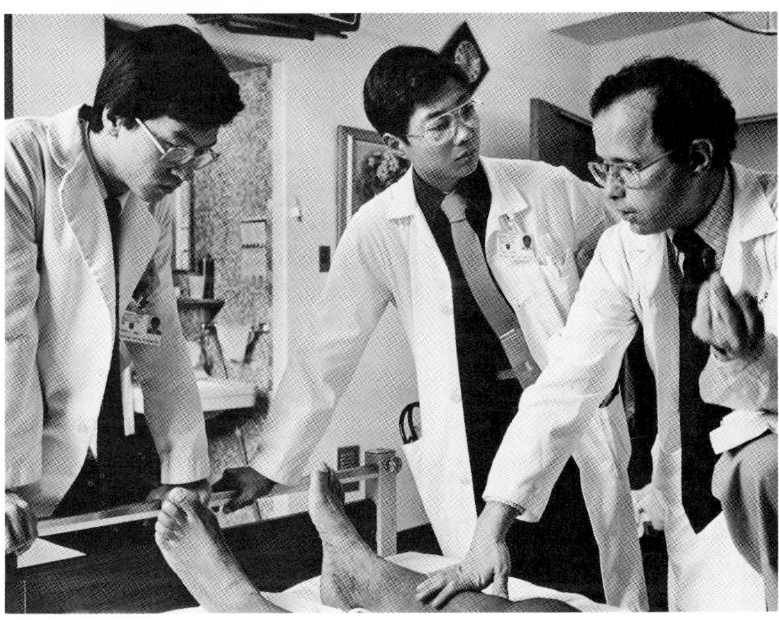

A series of disasters

During the first quarter, I saw the doctors once every two weeks. My kidney was working fine. But before I could finish celebrating the end of the first quarter, disaster struck: I noticed blood in my urine. I was immediately hospitalized and it turned out that I had hepatitis. The cause was linked to one of the drugs for immunosuppression (Imuran), combined with the trauma of an alcohol binge after a final exam.

Back at school I managed to get caught up despite having missed the first weeks of the new quarter. But then disaster struck again. Because of the immunosuppression, I had developed a severe respiratory infection for which I had to be hospitalized once again. This was the last straw. Just when I had pulled myself up, I got knocked down face first in the mud again. I took a leave of absence from college that quarter and went home.

With spring came warm weather and renewed energy to start school again. My health stabilized and school went smoothly until the summer of my second year when I began to notice that my vision was becoming cloudy; it was as if I were looking through a translucent curtain. I was referred to an ophthalmologist who told me I had cataracts in both eyes. Me, 18 years old, with bilateral cataracts! Usually cataracts are associated with old age; rarely do they occur in people my age. Studies have now shown that one of the drugs I was taking, prednisone, can induce the development of cataracts in some transplantation patients. Lucky me!

Soon it became difficult to see without the use of special eyedrops which dilated my pupils. I could only see around the opaque parts of the lenses. I didn't worry too much because the eye doctor had told me the cataracts were completely correctable through surgery. I would wear contact lenses afterwards and my vision would be completely "normal." I trusted her. I had the right eye operated on first. When I came out of the hospital with a patch, I worried about being able to keep up in college with sight in only one eye.

I had decided to take five courses that quarter instead of the normal three or four. Actually, it was part of a plan. By that time, I was sure that I wanted to become a physician, and I knew that the issue of my health could prevent me from getting into medical school. Why should a school invest the time and effort to train a person who might not be able to endure the long and arduous course? If I could take more than the normal load, and do well, despite my health and vision in only one eye, I could make a case for my determination and adaptability; my chances of surviving the rigors of medical training would be just as good as if not better than those of the average applicant. This was also the reasoning behind my decision to graduate from college in three years.

Several months later, during my second eye operation, complications arose and I lost the vision in the left eye completely. For some reason the retina became detached from its supporting tissue. The retina is like the film in a camera, and, needless to say, a camera is useless without the film. Two desperate attempts were made to surgically reattach the retina without success. That summer, which should have been a time of joy and celebration (I had just graduated from college!) was my moment of deepest depression. To make matters worse, I heard of a study done in Boston that showed a 10% chance of a retinal detachment in the single functioning eye in people with my situation. To have kidney failure is one thing, but add to that a possibility of being blind—never to see the world around me again—it seemed so unfair! The college degree that I was so proud of just one and a half months before, the prospect of becoming a physician—all these things seemed so meaningless. For nearly a year I struggled with severe depression and a general sense of hopelessness, then finally mustered the determination to proceed with my plan to go to medical school.

Determination to endure

I am now in my third year of medical school at the University of Chicago. I've had the kidney for almost seven years and it probably will not reject. My eyesight is "stable" and the once obsessive fears of going blind have faded into the backwoods of my mind. Yet there are constant reminders of my illness. Each day I take my assortment of ten pills to prevent rejection of the kidney and to control my high blood pressure. These pills make me feel more tired than the average person, and they lower my tolerance for exercise, which I regret because I would like to be a runner. As it is, I can only jog short distances. In the morning, I go through my daily ritual of inserting an opaque plastic covering, painted with an eye—to hide the shrunken red remnant of my own sightless left eye. And into my precious right eye, I insert my contact lens. As I shower I notice the 22 inches of scars scattered over my abdomen and arms and the numerous stretch marks. But all these things don't affect me emotionally anymore, at least not consciously, and I function for the rest of the day as a "normal" person, not nearly as self-conscious as I once was.

I see now the many ways my illness has heavily determined who and what I am today. More than anything else kidney disease and its consequences have made me feel different from others—somehow weaker and less lov-

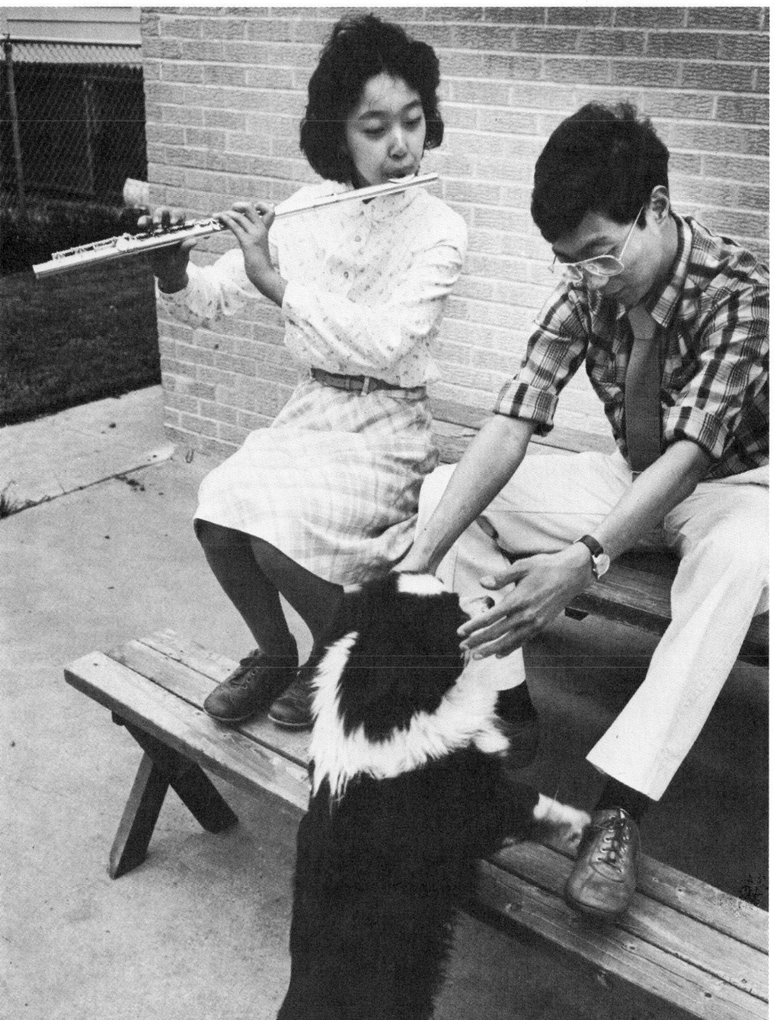

Author with mother; father; sister, Young Hee; and family dog, Bandit.

able. After I was first diagnosed my parents treated me like a fragile glass toy. My mother became very protective and my father less demanding. They didn't allow me to do anything strenuous—mowing the grass, household chores, working in the garden. But I *wanted* to do those chores, to show my parents that I was still the same child—a child they could love and be proud of. Their overprotectiveness had the effect in many ways of depriving me of a normal childhood and reinforcing my feelings of inadequacy. I often felt that I was a burden on them, both emotionally and financially, that they were probably better off without me.

All these feelings of being a burden were compounded by the fact that we were not a very expressive family; we did not hug or kiss each other. It is no one's fault really; rather, it is a reflection of the cultural background of my parents. They were both raised in Korea, where explicit expressions of love are not proper behavior, especially for the male. Yet as a kid growing up in America, watching TV as most youngsters do, I was exposed to the ideals of an American family. Thus my family's stoicism and lack of explicit demonstrations of love were very hard to understand. I often wondered if it was because I was a sickly, unlovable kid. I realize now that my parents do love me and have always been proud of me. Still I regret we are not more outwardly affectionate. Someday perhaps I may be able to say to my dad, to his face, the three words we find impossible to exchange: "I love you."

The relationship with my mother has taken a somewhat different course. Perhaps it is because of the bond that the transplant has created. We have become very close and sometimes it seems she is more a friend than a mother. Yet at times this closeness is supplanted by ambivalent feelings of guilt and resentment. Studies of other transplant patients show that I am not alone. The recipient of a kidney is keenly aware of his obligations to the donor and of the debt that can never be paid. In time this dependency can lead to resentment, which in turn can produce shame and guilt. I am sure I would feel extremely guilty if for some reason my mother died or fell ill because she only had one kidney left; fortunately she is well in all respects. Receiving an organ from the opposite sex also can create fears in the recipient of becoming more like the gender of the donor. In the past I often had worries about being emasculated—an absurdity that I have long since abandoned.

I wonder what would have happened if my father had given me the kidney. Would I be closer to my dad and more distant toward my mother? I will never know, but one thing is clear: the fact that my dad couldn't give me the kidney has made him feel inadequate at times. During the time of crisis, he had been unable to help. My mother has come out of it as the heroine. She got all the public attention—chosen Mother of the Year by the church we attended—the self-sacrificing mother with her unconditional love. All true, but I am sure it didn't make things any easier for my dad.

There is no question that my struggles have made me more sensitive to the people around me. I can empathize with those who suffer, those who feel inadequate or insecure, for in them I see parts of myself. Because of the kidney disease, I have been the recipient of extraordinary compassion and care, especially by the medical personnel I have come in contact with over the years. I feel privileged to have been shown these humane qualities; it has made me optimistic about a human race that too often seems selfish and cruel.

One doctor in particular stands out. He has acted not only as my nephrologist but also as a role model. His advice and encouragement have helped me through many difficult times—medical and emotional. I know I gave him gray hair the time I waited so long to enter the hospital, when I was so close to death; I also know he truly understood what prevented me from acknowledging how ill I was. His faith in my abilities and potential have a lot to do with where I am today. Unfortunately not all the doctors are like him—I remember when it first seemed that I could not wear contact lenses in my right eye, all my ophthalmologist could say was: "You'll get used to wearing cataract glasses." These glasses were more than a quarter-inch thick and they magnified everything by 30%. It was hard to judge distances and I bumped into a lot of people and things. She didn't appreciate the problems the glasses would cause for *me,* a self-conscious, struggling adolescent—not just another "case." After two years of searching on *my own,* I finally found a doctor who made a special contact lens that now gives me far superior vision than the glasses.

I was once an agnostic, but I have become a fervent believer in God, and I have come to believe that all my hardships had a purpose: to make me a better person. I probably will have medical complications in the future, and more occasions to become depressed—in some ways I will always be a patient—but as long as I firmly believe there is a purpose to my life, I feel certain that with the help of God I will have the strength to endure.

So, does this mean I have no regrets about my "deprived" childhood, my months on dialysis, the transplant, the moonface, the eye surgery? Certainly not. I still have my moments of sadness and doubts. However, the once prevalent thoughts of despair have been displaced by my desire to do something worthwhile with my life, to be a competent and caring doctor. Despite the complications, if I had to do it all over again, I would choose transplantation over dialysis without hesitation. My transplant was done in

Author with Drummond Rennie, his doctor and mentor.

1975; since then the kidney transplantation procedure has become safer, with fewer risks for developing complications. I would strongly urge anyone eligible for a kidney transplant to have one.

Finally, as one who is well on his way to becoming a physician, I feel that my capacity to understand others—acquired as a patient—is of utmost value. What makes a doctor necessary and great is not the amount of medical knowledge crammed into his head—a computer could do much better—but his ability to understand and care for the suffering patient. It is this humanitarian aspect of medicine, obvious as that may seem, that makes it an art and not just a technical science.

"I still have my moments of sadness and doubts. However, the once prevalent thoughts of despair have been displaced by my desire to do something worthwhile with my life, to be a competent and caring doctor."

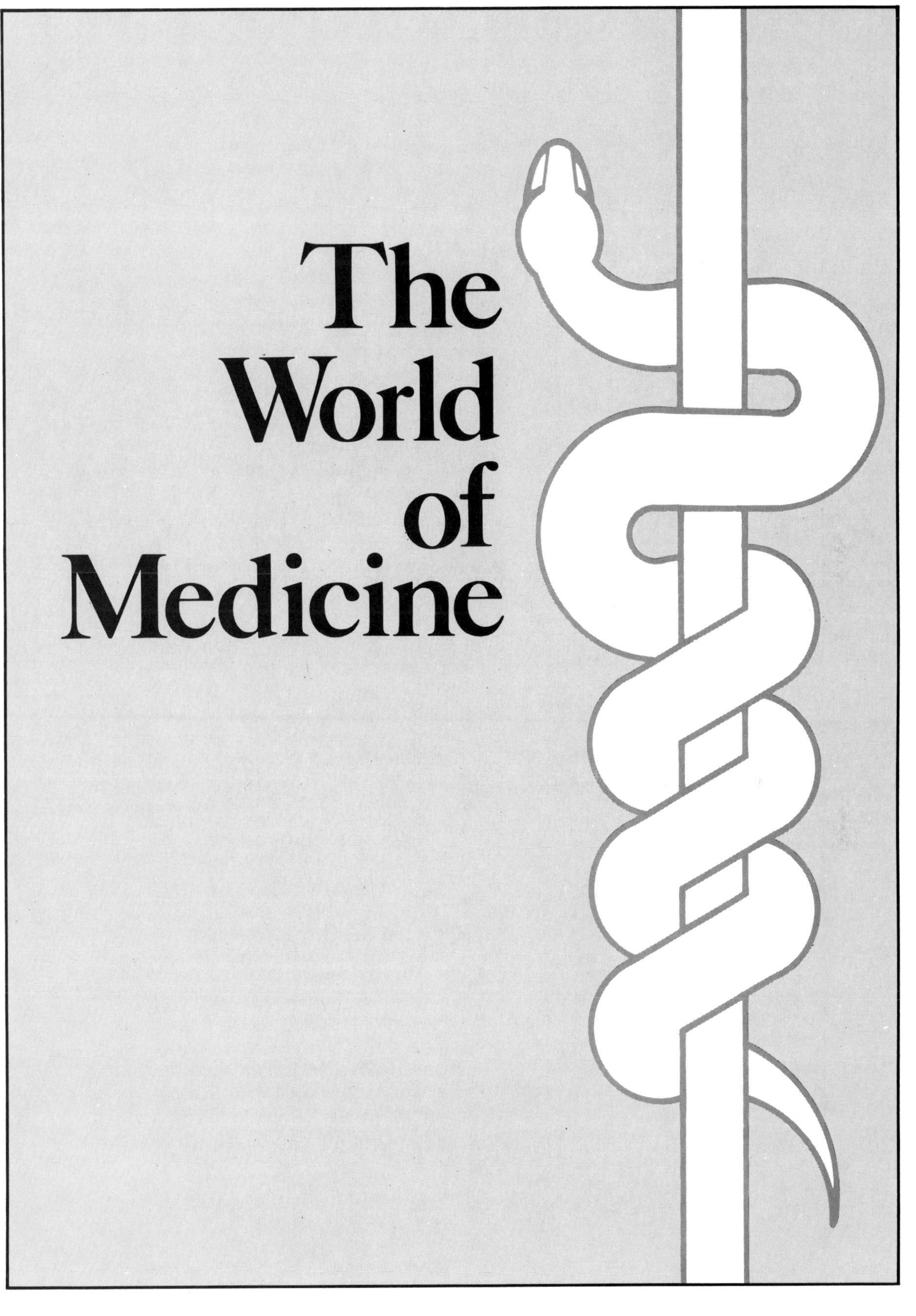
The
World
of
Medicine

Contributors to The World of Medicine

Mark Abramowicz, M.D. *Drugs and Vaccines.* Editor, *The Medical Letter,* New Rochelle, N.Y.

Robert G. Addison, M.D. *Rehabilitation Medicine.* Director, Center for Pain Studies, Rehabilitation Institute of Chicago.

Edward L. Applebaum, M.D. *Ear, Nose, and Throat Disorders.* Professor and Head, Department of Otolaryngology, Abraham Lincoln School of Medicine, University of Illinois, Chicago.

Andrea Ayvazian. *Physical Fitness and Sports Medicine Special Report: Women in Sport: A Changing Sense of Self.* Faculty Associate in Biology, School of Natural Science, and Instructor in the Outdoor Program, Hampshire College, Amherst, Mass.

L. Fred Ayvazian, M.D. *Lung Diseases.* Chief, Pulmonary Section, Veterans Administration Medical Center, East Orange, N.J.; Professor of Medicine, College of Medicine and Dentistry, New Jersey Medical School, Newark; Professor of Clinical Medicine, New York University School of Medicine, New York City.

Donna Bergen, M.D. *Surgery Special Report: Surgery for Epilepsy.* Director, Electroencephalography Laboratory, Rush-Presbyterian-St. Luke's Medical Center; Assistant Professor, Department of Neurological Sciences, Rush Medical College, Chicago.

George L. Blackburn, M.D., Ph.D. *Surgery.* Associate Professor of Surgery, Harvard Medical School; Director, Nutrition Support Service, New England Deaconess Hospital, Boston.

Walter G. Bradley, D.M., F.R.C.P. *Nervous System Disorders.* Professor of Neurology, Tufts University School of Medicine; Associate Neurologist in Chief, New England Medical Center Hospital, Boston.

John P. Bunker, M.D. *Health Care Costs.* Professor of Anesthesia and of Family, Community, and Preventive Medicine, Stanford University, School of Medicine, Stanford, Calif.

Charles M. Cegielski. *World Medical News.* Associate Editor, Britannica Yearbooks, Encyclopædia Britannica, Inc., Chicago.

Robert R. Chilcote, M.D. *Pediatrics.* Assistant Professor of Pediatrics, The University of Chicago, Pritzker School of Medicine.

Marvin I. Clein, Ed.D. *Physical Fitness and Sports Medicine.* Chairman, Department of Physical Education and Sport Sciences, University of Denver, Denver, Colo.

Edward P. Cohen, M.D. *Allergy and Immunity.* Dean, School of Basic Medical Sciences, and Professor of Microbiology and Immunology, University of Illinois Medical Center, Chicago.

Elizabeth B. Connell, M.D. *Gynecology and Obstetrics.* Lecturer, Department of Obstetrics-Gynecology, Northwestern University Medical School, Chicago.

Stephen E. Epstein, M.D. *Heart and Blood Vessels* (in part); *Heart and Blood Vessels Special Report: Sudden Death in Athletes* (in part). Chief of Cardiology, Cardiology Branch, National Heart, Lung, and Blood Institute, National Institutes of Health, Bethesda, Md.

Yehudi M. Felman, M.D. *Sexually Transmitted Diseases.* Clinical Professor of Dermatology and Lecturer in Preventive Medicine and Community Health, Downstate Medical Center, Brooklyn, N.Y.; Director, Bureau of Venereal Disease Control, New York City Health Department.

Estrellita Karsh. *Rehabilitation Medicine Special Report: Children with Handicaps.* Free-lance medical writer, Ottawa.

Warren A. Katz, M.D. *Arthritis and Connective Tissue Diseases.* Clinical Professor of Medicine and Chief, Section of Rheumatology, Division of Medicine, Medical College of Pennsylvania; Attending Physician, Moss Rehabilitation Hospital, Philadelphia.

Hau C. Kwaan, M.D. *Blood and the Lymphatic System.* Professor of Medicine, Northwestern University Medical School; Chief, Hematology Section, Veterans Administration Lakeside Medical Center, Chicago.

Lynne Lamberg. *Skin Disorders* (in part). Free-lance medical writer, Baltimore, Md.

Stanford I. Lamberg, M.D. *Skin Disorders* (in part). Associate Professor of Dermatology, Johns Hopkins University School of Medicine; Chief, Department of Dermatology, Baltimore City Hospitals, Baltimore, Md.

H. Sherwood Lawrence, M.D. *Infectious Diseases; Lung Diseases Special Report: Pneumonia: Evolution of a Killer.* Jeffrey Bergstein Professor of Medicine, Director of Infectious Disease and Immunology Division and Co-Director, NYU-Bellevue Medical Services, Department of Medicine, New York University School of Medicine, New York City.

Bernard Levin, M.D. *Gastrointestinal Disorders.* Associate Professor of Medicine, The University of Chicago, Pritzker School of Medicine; Director, Gastrointestinal Oncology Clinic, The University of Chicago Hospitals and Clinics.

Nathan W. Levin, M.D. *Hypertension.* Head, Division of Nephrology, Henry Ford Hospital, Detroit; Clinical Professor of Medicine, University of Michigan Medical School, Ann Arbor.

Robert A. Levine, M.D. *Eye Diseases and Visual Disorders.* Director, Ultrasonography Laboratory, Department of Ophthalmology, Michael Reese Hospital and Medical Center; Assistant Clinical Professor, University of Illinois Medical Center, Chicago.

Mortimer B. Lipsett, M.D. *Glandular and Metabolic Disorders.* Director, Clinical Center, National Institutes of Health, Bethesda, Md.

Irwin D. Mandel, D.D.S. *Teeth and Gums.* Professor and Chairman, Division of Preventive Dentistry, School of Dental and Oral Surgery, Columbia University, New York City.

Barry J. Maron, M.D. *Heart and Blood Vessels Special Report: Sudden Death in Athletes* (in part). Senior Investigator, National Heart, Lung, and Blood Institute, National Institutes of Health, Bethesda, Md.

Nancy K. Mello, Ph.D. *Alcoholism* (in part). Associate Professor of Psychology, Department of Psychiatry, Harvard Medical School, Boston; Associate Director, Alcohol and Drug Abuse Research Center, McLean Hospital, Belmont, Mass.

Jack H. Mendelson, M.D. *Alcoholism* (in part). Professor of Psychiatry, Harvard Medical School, Boston; Director, Alcohol and Drug Abuse Research Center, McLean Hospital, Belmont, Mass.

Louis A. Morris, Ph.D. *Drugs and Vaccines Special Report: The Placebo Effect.* Psychologist, Food and Drug Administration, Rockville, Md.; part-time faculty, University of Maryland, College Park, and American University, Washington, D.C.

Marcia J. Opp. *Gynecology and Obstetrics Special Report: Is Anything Safe?* Free-lance medical writer, Chicago.

Randolph E. Patterson, M.D. *Heart and Blood Vessels* (in part). Senior Investigator, Cardiology Branch, National Heart, Lung, and Blood Institute, National Institutes of Health, Bethesda, Md.

Edmund D. Pellegrino, M.D. *Medical Education.* President and Professor of Philosophy and of Biology, The Catholic University of America; Professor of Community Medicine and of Clinical Medicine, Georgetown University, Washington, D.C.

Brandy Rommel. *Trends in Medicine and Health Care.* Free-lance writer; former Managing Editor, *The Volunteer Leader,* American Hospital Association, Chicago.

Harold M. Schmeck, Jr. *Allergy and Immunity Special Report: Monoclonal Antibodies.* Science Correspondent, *New York Times.*

Ascher Segall, M.D. *Medical Education Special Report: Learning Medicine in Israel.* Professor of Epidemiology, School of Medicine, and Professor of Education, School of Education, Boston University.

Edith T. Shapiro, M.D. *Psychiatry.* Private practitioner, Englewood, N.J.; Clinical Associate Professor of Psychiatry, College of Medicine and Dentistry, New Jersey Medical School, Newark.

Noel W. Solomons, M.D. *Diet and Nutrition Special Report: Vegetarianism.* Associate Professor of Clinical Nutrition, Department of Nutrition and Food Science, Massachusetts Institute of Technology, Cambridge.

Myron Winick, M.D. *Diet and Nutrition.* Director of the Institute of Human Nutrition and of the Center for Nutrition, Genetics, and Human Development, Professor of Pediatrics, and R.R. Williams Professor of Nutrition, Columbia University College of Physicians and Surgeons, New York City.

Alcoholism

Alcohol abuse has been defined as drinking that harms an individual's health, interpersonal interactions, or both. Although alcohol abuse is a prerequisite for *alcoholism,* the definition of alcoholism also includes tolerance for and physical dependence upon alcohol. *Tolerance* occurs when a person needs increasingly larger amounts of alcohol in order to achieve desired changes in feeling and behavior that originally could be produced by drinking a smaller quantity of alcohol. *Physical dependence* involves the development of withdrawal signs and symptoms after drinking is reduced or stopped. The signs and symptoms range from mild anxiety and shaking to such severe disorders as convulsions, hallucinations, disorientation, confusion, and disturbances of respiration, heart function, and blood pressure.

In addition to physical dependence, both alcohol abusers and alcoholics may experience significant psychological dependence upon alcohol. Such a person may show a great preoccupation with drinking, a strong desire to drink at inappropriate times and places (for example, during the early morning or while working), and difficulty in controlling when drinking starts and stops. The development of alcoholism is often an insidious process that may evolve over years or even decades. Although many persons who abuse alcohol or are alcoholics tend to deny their problem to themselves or others because of fear of stigmatization and rebuke, there is increasing awareness that these people suffer from psychological and medical disorders worthy of compassionate concern and treatment. This humane attitude has been fostered by recent scientific advances in understanding causes and consequences of alcohol abuse.

Causes of alcoholism and alcohol abuse

Alcohol abuse and alcoholism are probably caused by a complex interaction between alcohol, the consumer, and the environmental context in which drinking to intoxication occurs. Although alcohol consumption is necessary for abuse and alcoholism to occur, it is not sufficient in itself.

No single cause of alcoholism has been discovered, but the roles of a number of biological, psychological, and sociological factors have been carefully investigated. It is now well established, for example, that alcoholism tends to run in families. Although many persons who abuse alcohol or develop alcoholism have no family history of alcohol-related problems, recent studies have shown that genetic predisposition may be of importance. In collaborative studies by U.S. and Danish scientists the incidence of alcoholism was determined in men who had been adopted within a few weeks after birth. Adoptees who had a natural parent with alcoholism were compared with those whose natural parents had no history of alcoholism. Men who had an alcoholic natural parent were almost four times more likely to develop alcoholism themselves than were men whose natural parents were not alcoholics. Other studies have confirmed these findings and strongly suggest that alcoholism in natural parents is a better predictor of alcoholism in the offspring than any other single factor or combination of environmental conditions. However, the specific genetic factor that increases the risk of developing alcohol-related problems has not been discovered. Obviously no single gene controls development of such a complex behavioral and biological disorder, but there is little doubt that some combination of heritable factors is of great importance.

Because alcoholism appears to be more prevalent

Alcoholism is an insidious process that evolves over many years. Recent advances in the understanding of the causes and consequences of alcohol consumption have led to better and more humanitarian treatments for alcohol abusers, including the growing numbers of women and teenagers who are drinking to intoxication on a regular basis.

Sybil Shelton—Peter Arnold, Inc.

among persons of certain national or racial groups, it was once believed that differences in the way individuals metabolize or break down alcohol in their bodies might be related to alcoholism. For example, it was hypothesized that the high rate of alcoholism among American Indians might be related to some special way in which these individuals metabolized alcohol. Comparative studies conducted with American Indians, Orientals, and Caucasians have revealed no significant differences in breakdown and elimination of alcohol from the body. It was discovered, however, that regardless of race, sex, or ethnic or national origin persons can increase their rate of alcohol metabolism as a function of past history of drinking. The rate of alcohol breakdown in the bodies of regular heavy drinkers and alcohol abusers is almost double that of social drinkers or abstainers.

Another hypothesis that has not been substantiated by careful scientific inquiry is that problem drinkers possess a unique constellation of personality characteristics. Persons with widely differing personalities may develop alcohol-related problems. In fact alcohol abuse and alcoholism have been observed in a spectrum of individuals ranging from those who have very serious mental and emotional disorders to those who have no such impairments. Alcohol abusers and alcoholics do not consume alcohol to achieve the same salient changes in feeling that are associated with moderate alcohol consumption in normal social settings. Because alcoholics develop significant tolerance, they must consume increasing quantities of alcohol in order to become intoxicated. Large amounts of alcohol produce opposite effects of small or moderate amounts. For example, while moderate social drinking is usually associated with lowered anxiety and depression and increased conviviality and social interaction, heavy drinking increases tension and depression, increases the probability of social isolation, and raises the risk for such inappropriate interpersonal interactions as violent behavior and exaggerated sexuality.

Consequences of alcoholism and alcohol abuse

Some mental disorders that were formerly thought to cause alcoholism or alcohol abuse are now considered as likely to be their consequences. It was once believed that alcohol problems were the result of persons' attempts to "medicate" themselves for recurrent anxiety or depression. A number of studies, however, have shown clearly that both anxiety and depression can either be caused or increased by alcohol abuse. Many persons who are severely depressed and anxious when they abuse alcohol experience great relief when they reduce their drinking or stop completely.

Adverse physical and mental consequences of problem drinking are common. Long-term alcohol abuse may cause diseases of the stomach (gastritis), pancreas (pancreatitis), and the liver (hepatitis and cirrhosis). Alcohol-induced liver disease is a major cause of death and disability among adult males in major urban areas of the U.S. Alcoholics may sustain liver damage even if they have a nutritionally adequate diet. But many problem drinkers tend to eat poorly, a factor that increases the risk of malnutrition and liver disease. Malnutrition and malabsorption (impaired absorption of essential vitamins, minerals, and foodstuffs from the intestinal tract), can lead to serious disease of the nervous system. The deficiency of B vitamins that is often observed in alcoholics may be associated with impairment of visual function, memory, and neuromuscular coordination.

George W. Gardner

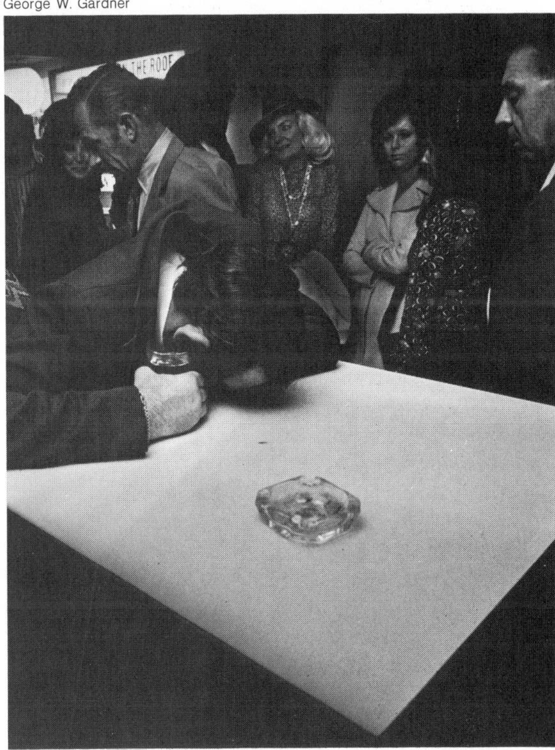

Moderate drinkers are likely to be relaxed and jovial, while heavy drinkers become depressed and socially isolated.

There is also evidence that increased risk for cancer of the mouth, pharynx, and esophagus occurs in alcoholics and alcohol abusers. Both physical and mental disorders have been observed in children of women who are alcoholic or alcohol abusers during pregnancy. It has not been clearly demonstrated, however, that alcohol per se produces deleterious effects on the fetus, because women who drink heavily during pregnancy often smoke heavily, abuse a variety of drugs, eat poorly, and do not receive adequate prenatal health care.

Because heavy drinking tends to increase depression, it is not surprising that risk for suicide may increase in depressed individuals who abuse alcohol.

One of the major adverse consequences of problem drinking in contemporary society is the large number of alcohol-related automobile accidents and fatalities.

New research also has uncovered a possible explanation for the well-known quotation from Macbeth (Act II, scene 3) concerning alcohol's effects on sexuality:

Macduff: What three things does drink especially provoke?
Porter: Marry, sir, nose-painting, sleep, and urine. Lechery, sir, it provokes, and unprovokes; it provokes the desire but it takes away the performance; therefore, much drink may be said to be an equivocator with lechery: it makes him, and it mars him; it sets him on, and it takes him off; it persuades him, and disheartens him; makes him stand to, and not stand to; in conclusion, equivocates him in a sleep, and, giving him the lie, leaves him.

It was found that alcohol directly suppresses production of testosterone, the major male sex hormone, in the gonads. When alcohol enters gonadal tissues such as the testicles it is broken down by biochemical processes that ordinarily would be used to make testosterone. The oft noted paradox in male sexual performance during alcohol intoxication may be associated with decreased levels of testosterone. When testosterone levels are lowered in blood following heavy alcohol intake, this decrease signals the brain to activate the pituitary gland (often called the master gland) to secrete a hormone (luteinizing hormone) that stimulates testosterone production. It is believed that this process may be associated with increased sexual desire during alcohol intoxication.

Treatment

Although a wide variety of treatments currently exists for persons with alcohol problems, no single treatment has been shown to be unquestionably superior. It is now recognized that a combination of programs is often necessary for success. Many communities, municipalities, clinics, and hospital groups have established alcoholism diagnosis, referral, and treatment centers. Individuals who have been drinking heavily for prolonged periods may require hospitalization prior to treatment in order to prevent serious withdrawal signs and symptoms. Inpatient hospital programs often feature combination treatments that may include aversive conditioning therapy, behavior modification, counseling, individual and group psychotherapy, family therapy, drug therapy, and participation in self-help groups.

One of the best known and most important self-help groups for persons with alcohol problems is Alcoholics Anonymous (AA). There are chapters of this organization in most communities in the U.S., and they often provide an important support for alcoholic persons. It should be appreciated, however, that AA is but one component of alcoholism treatment and should not be viewed as the only source of intervention or help.

Persons with drinking problems do not have a hopeless prognosis. Survey studies have shown that about 20% of alcohol abusers will improve without any specific intervention. Individuals who seek combination therapy are highly likely to be free from problem drinking for long periods of time. This is especially true for employed persons with good social resources such as family or other caring persons.

—Jack H. Mendelson, M.D., and Nancy K. Mello, Ph.D.

Allergy and Immunity

Each year thousands of patients needing penicillin for the treatment of a variety of serious illnesses cannot receive the drug because of life-threatening allergic reactions. These people experience wheezing, swellings, a red, itchy skin rash, nausea, and vomiting and may even die. In some people the most minute amount of the drug will cause problems.

In most cases allergic symptoms are not so intense. Many people have hay fever (allergic rhinitis) when they breathe in pollen or other airborne substances to which they are sensitive. Some have asthma attacks when exposed to dust or animal dander; although they recur frequently, the symptoms subside without permanent harm.

Scope of the problem

Patients see doctors for allergic symptoms more frequently than for anything else. Thirty-five million Americans, or one in six individuals, suffer from allergic rhinitis, asthma, eczema (a type of skin rash), hives, sensitivities to food, or other types of allergic illnesses. Costs exceed $1 billion for medication, physicians' services, and hospitalization. This figure does not include the loss to society owing to absences from work or school.

Asthma is a serious problem; each year 2,000–4,000 individuals die from the disease. Approximately nine million Americans suffer from this chronic affliction. In childhood, asthma and other respiratory illnesses are responsible for more than 60% of absences from school. Asthma is not an emotional or psychosomatic illness, nor is it under the patient's control, although emotional problems, understandably, may accompany the disease.

What causes such allergic symptoms? Why does the body react so violently to what apparently are common, harmless substances? Why do some people react to a specific substance but not to others? What new treatments may help victims of allergies?

Some recent insights into these questions have allowed physicians and medical scientists to better understand both resistance to disease and disease of allergic cause. Asthma, allergic rhinitis, and other allergic illnesses are only part of the total picture. Future discoveries in the field of immunology will lead inevitably to the control and manipulation of the antibody response. The prevention of disease, as well as the cure of allergic illness, will be the benefits.

The first descriptions of allergic reactions appear among the earliest writings in history. The Romans and Greeks wrote of patients whose problems, including asthma, clearly were allergic in origin. Early in the 20th century Austrian physician Clemens Freiherr von Pirquet coined "allergy" when referring to any alteration in the immune system, whether helpful or harmful. Currently "immunity" is used to describe helpful reactions; a person is immune to measles, for example, if he had it as a child or to polio if he was vaccinated. "Allergy" refers to a harmful reaction; a person is allergic to ragweed if it causes a stuffy or runny nose and sneezing. "Prophylaxis" (protection) is used to describe the prevention of disease. "Anaphylaxis" is used to describe an extraordinarily severe allergic reaction; it means "without protection."

Allergic reactions and immunity

The human body has the remarkable capacity to recognize and respond immunologically to an extraordinarily diverse variety of disease-causing bacteria and viruses. This is one important way it is protected against disease. Children in primitive societies who grow up under conditions of improper sanitation are exposed daily to the causative agents of typhoid, polio, hepatitis, and many other diseases. Although some become ill, in most instances they grow to adulthood without apparent illness because they rapidly become immune to these life-threatening organisms. Their bodies form antibodies that recognize and inactivate invading germs.

Adults are protected because they successfully resisted an earlier exposure. Antibodies induced by the invasion of one type of organism react with that type only or with closely related strains, but not with others. Exposure to typhoid bacteria, for example, does not lead to immunity to polio; recovery from measles does not protect against mumps. One major characteristic of the immune system is the extraordinarily diverse nature of the response; virtually any substance foreign to one's own body can provoke the formation of specific antibodies. In the research laboratory immunologists often use carefully characterized proteins of known structure as antigens, rather than infectious organisms, to study the antibody response. The body forms antibodies to these nonliving materials just as it does to living organisms such as bacteria.

In some individuals allergic rather than immune responses develop. People commonly suffer allergic rhinitis, asthma, or skin rashes following the ingestion of such foods as lobster, strawberries, or tomatoes. The rash that appears after contact with poison ivy is another example of an allergic reaction; it occurs in the skin. Hives following an allergic reaction to certain medicines is another.

The North American house dust mite pictured here is magnified approximately 400 times. This creature is a component of normal household dust—a source of considerable distress for many allergy sufferers, who experience itching, wheezing, coughing, swelling, and hives.

Battelle's Columbus Laboratories

Types of allergic reactions

Physicians divide allergic reactions into four types, each the result of a different type of "altered immunity": type I, immediate hypersensitivity reactions; type II, cytotoxic allergic reactions; type III, Arthus-type hypersensitivity reactions; and type IV, cell-mediated reactions. Each illustrates a different form of allergy.

Type I are called immediate hypersensitivity reactions because they occur within moments of exposure to the foreign materials or antigens to which the patient is sensitive. An individual with allergy to ragweed experiences symptoms minutes after inhaling ragweed pollen. A patient allergic to bee stings suffers symptoms moments after being stung.

Type I hypersensitivity reactions are mediated by a type or class of antibodies called immunoglobulin E (IgE). IgE antibodies consist of four protein chains, two identical H (heavy) chains and two identical L (light) chains. Heavy chains are approximately twice as large as light chains.

IgE antibodies cover the surface of a unique cell type known as mast cells. As many as 500,000 IgE antibodies may cover the surface of a single cell of this type. Coated mast cells are found throughout the body; for example, in the nose of an individual with ragweed sensitivity or within the linings of the breathing tubes (or bronchi) of a person with asthma. Mast cells store a substance called histamine in tiny granules found in the cytoplasm of the cell. The interaction of IgE on the surface of a cell covered with IgE specific for, say, ragweed pollen leads to degranulation: the release of histamine and other chemical substances from the cell's granules to the surrounding area. It is the released histamine that causes the symptoms of stuffy nose or breathing difficulty. Allergic individuals commonly take antihistamines to relieve their symptoms.

Asthmatic individuals with allergies to pollen have mast cells in the membranes lining their breathing passages. Usually, they are without symptoms until they breathe in the foreign substances to which they are sensitive. As in patients with allergic rhinitis, the mast cells are stimulated to release histamine; the airway narrows, and mucus secretion into the breathing passage leads to the characteristic wheezing and shortness of breath of an acute asthma attack.

Type II allergic reactions result from the action of another class of antibodies, known as immunoglobulin G (IgG). Like IgE, IgG antibodies consist of two light chains and two heavy chains, although the heavy chains of IgG are different in many ways from the heavy chains of IgE. IgG circulates throughout the body in the bloodstream, reaching the innermost regions of each organ and tissue where it is ready to interact with such foreign substances as invading bacteria that might have gained access. IgG, along with other parts of the immune system, helps protect the body from infection by aiding in the destruction of disease-causing organisms.

Antibodies that appear after specific immunization or that are present in the serum after recovery from infectious illnesses are of this type. The destruction of blood cells (hemolysis) occurring after administration of an improperly typed blood transfusion takes place because the body possesses circulating antibodies for foreign red blood cells of a blood type different from its own. One difference between IgE and IgG antibodies is that for the most part IgE remains attached to mast cells; IgG antibodies circulate unattached throughout the system. Differences in the heavy chains between the two classes of antibodies account for this.

Type III hypersensitivity (allergic) reactions result from the deposition of antigen-antibody complexes in the delicate linings of the blood vessels. The Arthus reaction is an example, the phenomenon that follows injections of large quantities of foreign proteins (a method of medical treatment no longer used). Small, soluble antigens appearing in the blood react with specific antibodies, leading to the formation of soluble antigen-antibody complexes. These complexes may become trapped in sensitive blood vessels in the kidney and elsewhere where they trigger large numbers of the body's scavenger cells, the leukocytes and macrophages, to ingest and destroy them. In the process cells in the surrounding tissue are damaged and may be destroyed. Blood may appear in the urine if cells in the kidney are damaged, and painful reactions may occur in the skin. Fever and malaise are common in more generalized reactions.

Type IV reactions are mediated by a class of cells known as lymphocytes; they are small round cells with a prominent nucleus. Certain lymphocytes liberate substances that are toxic to other foreign cell types and invading bacteria. They recognize and destroy the unusual cells. Type IV reactions are delayed; they take as long as 24 hours to develop. Reactions to poison ivy, poison oak, and other sensitizing plants are well-known examples of cell-mediated type IV reactions. The body responds to the oils in such plants in a manner entirely analogous to its reaction to invading microorganisms.

The tuberculin response is another example of a delayed-type hypersensitivity reaction. Doctors often test individuals for tuberculosis by injecting a small quantity of an extract of the tubercle bacillus into the skin of the patient. Prior exposure, but not necessarily active disease (the body's immune system may have destroyed the organisms), is indicated by the appearance of a red, itchy lump at the injection site. It gradually develops over a 24-hour period. The delay in the appearance of type IV reactions is the time it takes for enough lymphocytes to migrate to the site to produce the reaction. Organ transplants that fail and are rejected are another example; a rejected kidney graft is filled with small lymphocytes "protecting" the body against the foreign tissue.

Diagnosing allergies

How does one know if an allergy exists? How does the doctor determine the substance, *i.e.*, the allergen, causing the patient's symptoms?

First the allergist takes a detailed history in an attempt to determine the precise environment in which symptoms occur. Clues may be gained by the patient's occupation, the specific activity that is associated with the reaction, and so on. Some individuals, for example, with allergy to mold spores may experience allergic rhinitis or asthma when entering a dusty, moldy basement. Others may have a skin rash 24 hours following a picnic in the woods. These are the bits of information leading the allergist to suspect the specific causes for the patient's symptoms.

Further valuable information is gained through a series of skin tests. In these tests, the doctor introduces minute amounts of extracts of various substances commonly causing allergic reactions. To pinpoint the allergen, an extract of only one substance, *e.g.*, ragweed pollen, is used for each injection. The positive reactions that may occur are of type I; within 15 minutes they provoke redness and swelling at the site of injection. Patients with asthma resulting from type I reactions to tree pollens react strongly at the site of injection of an extract of such pollen. The patient with ragweed allergy whose symptoms occur in the fall, when ragweed pollen is in highest concentration in the air, may react strongly at the site of injection of an extract of ragweed pollen.

Type IV reactions may be diagnosed by the injection technique. But generally they are detected by applying

Photographs, John Caulfield—The Journal of Cell Biology

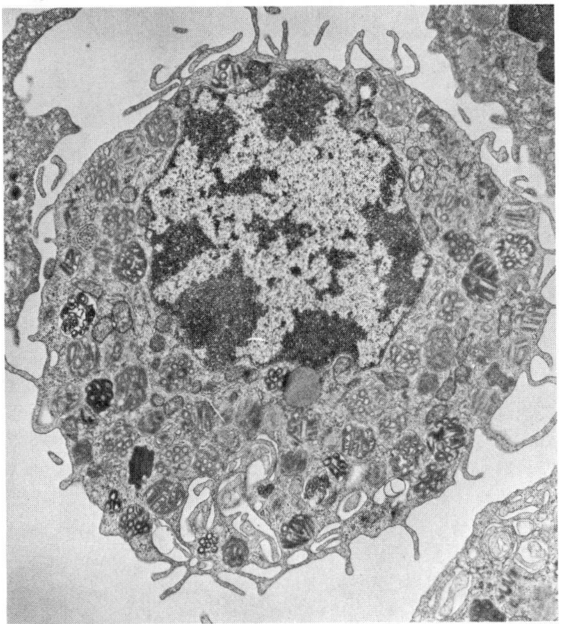

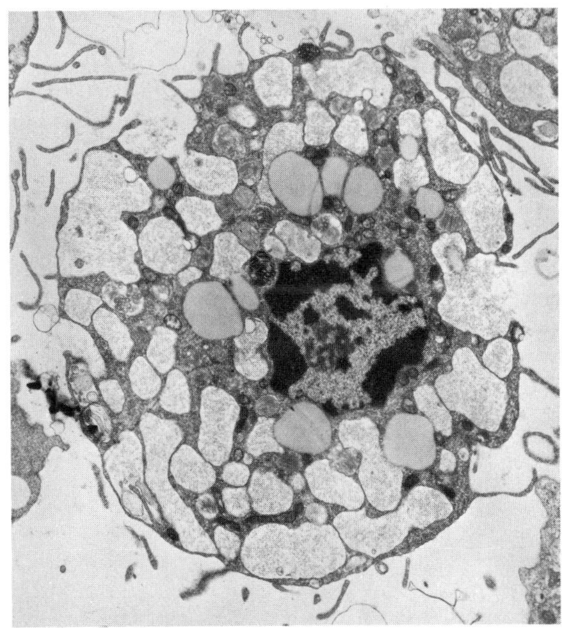

The photomicrograph at left is a mast cell at rest. The photomicrograph at right is a mast cell that has been stimulated by an allergen to release histamine and other chemicals—substances that will trigger the onset of allergic symptoms.

a bit of the suspect material to the skin; a cotton adhesive bandage is used for this purpose. A positive reaction is indicated by a well-localized red rash that develops at the site over a 24-hour period.

The nature of type I reactions in the skin itself lends insight into the allergic mechanism. Histamine released from mast cells in the skin that are coated with IgE specific for ragweed pollen causes swelling and redness at the site of the injection. It leads to increases in the permeability of capillaries and other small blood vessels, allowing serum and blood cells to accumulate at the site. Swelling is seen because excess fluid accumulates.

Blood tests such as the radioallergosorbent test (RAST) are used to detect the presence of IgE antibodies in the serum of allergic individuals. In the RAST, serum is passed through a column of small beads that are coated with suspect allergens. If the serum contains IgE antibodies specific for the allergen, the antibodies bind to the coated beads; they are detected by radioactively labeled antibodies to IgE, which are added subsequently.

In another recently developed test mast cells taken from the blood are stimulated in tissue-culture medium to release histamine by exposing them to different allergens. Higher than normal quantities of histamine found in the medium indicate that an allergy is present.

Treatment

Various treatments are available to sufferers of allergies. The primary objective is to avoid the allergen that causes the problem. The symptoms of asthmatics, for example, may improve substantially if they sleep in bedrooms that are kept free of dust. An air conditioner can prevent pollens and other allergens from gaining access.

For persons with only a few, well-defined allergies a series of hyposensitization shots can be effective in relieving symptoms. During this therapy gradually increasing doses of the specific allergen or allergens are injected repeatedly into the patient over a period of days, months, or even years. These injections have the same effect as an immunization; they stimulate the formation in the blood of IgG antibodies that are specific for the injected substance. Later, when the patient encounters the allergen in the course of daily living, the circulating IgG antibodies bind to the allergen, tying it up chemically so that it cannot react with allergen-sensitive IgE antibodies on the mast cells. Consequently histamine release is prevented.

Medications are very helpful in controlling allergies. One of the most successful new drugs effective for many asthmatics is disodium cromoglycate. It is a powdered aerosol that is inhaled at several intervals during the day and is believed to prevent the release of histamine from mast cells. Disodium cromoglycate functions strictly as a preventive; it is not useful in treating an acute asthma attack.

Other medicines used in treating an acute attack include the catecholamines, such as epinephrine (adrenaline) and isoproterenol. Catecholamines stimulate the enzyme adenylcyclase, which converts adenosine triphosphate (ATP), a nucleotide occurring in all cells, where it represents energy storage, to cyclic adenosine monophosphate (AMP), a key substance in a chain of biochemical reactions that lead to relaxation of bronchial muscle. Both epinephrine and isoproterenol are used effectively to treat type I reactions. Another class used commonly to treat type I allergic responses are the methylxanthines, which include theophylline and caffeine. They inhibit phosphodiesterase, an enzyme that degrades cyclic AMP. Consequently the intracellular level of cyclic AMP rises, leading to dilation of the bronchial passages.

The effects of epinephrine last only an hour or two, and symptoms may return. More recently derivatives of epinephrine that have longer acting desired effects and minimal side effects (epinephrine often causes the heart to beat faster than required) have been used to treat type I reactions. These newer agents include metaproterenol and terbutaline.

Corticosteroids such as cortisone, hydrocortisone, and prednisone are considered to be the most effective agents in treating allergic reactions. Patients with severe asthma, for example, can obtain long-lasting relief using these agents. The problem lies with the serious side effects they provoke. Thinning (demineralization) of the bones and obesity are most troublesome. For certain patients doctors prescribe the use of corticosteroids by inhalation—as a snuff in treating allergic rhinitis and as an aerosol in treating asthma. This "topical" application effectively alleviates symptoms while reducing the more generalized, systemic side effects.

Some patients with asthma inhale catecholamines to stop an acute attack. The effects are useful but potentially dangerous, as the attack often returns in a short time requiring additional, more frequent inhalations of the drug. Eventually the catecholamines lose their effect as the bronchial musculature becomes "exhausted." Patients are advised to use such inhalers cautiously and only under careful medical supervision.

Catecholamines stimulate the breathing passages by reacting with beta-2 receptors on the surface of muscle cells surrounding the bronchi. In this instance muscular relaxation causes the passages to dilate, enhancing air flow.

Altered immunity and cell-surface receptors

Beta-2 receptors for epinephrine are only one example of many types of receptors found throughout the body. They are involved in regulating and coordinating cellular physiology and organ function. Other examples include receptors on muscle cells for such hormones as insulin, receptors on thyroid cells for thyroid-stimulating hormone, and receptors on nerve and muscle cells for neuromuscular stimulation.

Medical researchers now believe that alterations in the immune state may lead to the production of antibodies to receptors themselves; when the function of the receptors is suppressed, a disease state results. Three of the diseases thought to be caused by this process are myasthenia gravis, which diminishes muscular contraction; Graves' disease, associated with an overproduction of thyroid hormone; and insulin-resistant diabetes mellitus, a particularly severe form of diabetes.

Myasthenia gravis is a disease long suspected to be "autoimmune" in origin; *i.e.*, the consequence of antibodies produced by the person toward constituents of his own body. The association of the disease with tumors of the thymus gland, a central organ of immunity, has been noted in many instances.

The transmission of impulses for muscle contraction between nerve cells and muscle fibers involves the release of acetylcholine from the stimulated nerve cells. This simple chemical substance diffuses from the stimulated nerve to adjacent muscle cells, interacting with receptors for acetylcholine that are present on the cell surface membranes. Victims of myasthenia gravis have antibodies in their blood that combine with receptors for acetylcholine on muscle cells. The antibodies bind to the receptors, inactivating and "stripping" them from the surface of the cells. Acetylcholine released from nerve cells cannot bind to muscle cells without free receptors. Consequently persons with myasthenia suffer from diminished muscle contractions.

An excess amount of thyroid hormone is produced by the thyroid glands of persons with Graves' disease. Normally, thyroid-stimulating hormone (TSH) is released from cells at the base of the brain. The hormone travels through the blood to the thyroid gland, interacting with receptor sites that are specific for TSH. The synthesis and release of thyroid hormone occurs as a consequence. Antibodies to the receptor for TSH are found in patients with Graves' disease. These antibodies, it is believed, mimic the effect of TSH, stimulating thyroid cells to form and release an overabundance of thyroid hormone.

Persons with insulin-resistant diabetes respond poorly to the administration of insulin, and their form of diabetes is especially severe. The concentration of glucose in the blood remains abnormally high in spite of the administration of large quantities of the hormone. Cells throughout the body possess receptors for insulin on their surface membranes. Normally insulin produced by the pancreas circulates throughout the body, reacting with specific receptors and thereby affecting cellular metabolism. Patients with insulin-resistant diabetes form antibodies that react with the receptors for insulin. As a result the hormone cannot react with insulin-sensitive cells.

What provokes the body to form antibodies to receptors is still unknown. The phenomenon is yet another example of an "alteration in the immune state."

—Edward P. Cohen, M.D.

Special Report: Monoclonal Antibodies

by Harold M. Schmeck, Jr.

Antibodies have long been a mainstay of biological research, medical diagnosis, and treatment of disease. But within the past five years a way of preparing special antibodies markedly different from those in common use has begun to have profound effects on many areas of medical practice and research. These new antibodies are called monoclonal. The term means that each batch comes from a single clone of cells. Because they are produced by single clones they are much more uniform than conventional antibodies. In fact those from a single clone are all chemically identical. For that reason they permit far more sophisticated uses than even conventional antibodies, which are probably the most sensitive probes and guided missiles known to the world of biology.

Antibodies are special proteins produced by the body's immunological defense system to deal with foreign invasion. They also help preserve the integrity of the body from disruption by anything internal that takes on foreign characteristics. Cancer cells are the most obvious example. Monoclonal antibodies are products of artificially contrived hybrid cells that are made by fusing normal antibody-producing cells with cancer cells of a type called myeloma. The hybrid fused cells are called hybridomas. The means of growing them for antibody production was discovered in 1975; already many uses have been found for them in medical science and practice. A new branch of industry is growing up devoted to the manufacture of these special antibodies. In particular, monoclonal antibodies are already having profound effects on biomedical research. They show promise of having equal impact on diagnostic practices and, in time, on prevention and treatment of disease.

Finely tuned guided missiles

The key studies that gave the world these revolutionary new tools were done in England by Georges Köhler and César Milstein at the Medical Research Council's molecular biology laboratories in Cambridge. The scientists were not thinking at all of the development that came from their work when they began it. Indeed, Milstein said in an article several years afterward that he would hardly have chosen the route they followed if that had been the original intention. Rather, they were studying the manner in which cells may diversify when they are growing in laboratory flasks. These cell growths are known as tissue cultures. An important objective of the original research was to understand the complex genetic arrangements by which antibodies are produced in the body and how mutations can change the outcome. For that work they needed a system for growing, in tissue culture, some cells that would produce easily identifiable antibodies.

Several lines of research converged to give Köhler and Milstein what they wanted. What they actually developed, at least partly by good luck, was something much more important. It was a practical way of making large quantities of extraordinarily pure, uniform, and specific antibodies. Such antibodies could be grown to seek out virtually any target that could elicit an antibody response.

The popularity of antibodies in medical science stems from the fact that they are guided missiles destined to seek specific targets with exquisite precision and sensitivity. To use a familiar example, antibodies produced to protect the body against poliovirus will distinguish easily among the three main types that infect humans. Antibody aimed at type 1 will ignore types 2 and 3. It is for that reason that polio vaccine must contain material from all three types. The function of a vaccine is to alert and stimulate the body's antibody production, but antibodies produced against polio type 1 will not protect against polio type 2 or 3. The extreme selectivity in target—scientists call it specificity—is what makes antibodies so valuable to science. Different types of blood, different kinds of cells and tissues, and seemingly minor family differences in populations of viruses and bacteria can all be distinguished with the help of antibodies.

For many years medical scientists have tried to develop antibodies capable of distinguishing reliably between cancer and normal cells within a person's body. To date they have had little success. Monoclonal antibodies seem likely to make such anticancer guided missiles possible. Ordinary antibodies are not sufficiently fine-tuned for the task, but monoclonal antibodies may have the specificity required. The reasons for the difference show clearly why scientists have such high hopes for the special antibodies the hybridomas can produce.

The antibodies that circulate in a person's blood are made through the action of immunologically active white blood cells called B lymphocytes. Their daughter cells, called plasma cells, actually produce the antibodies, but the B cells have already fixed the targets and identities. Through this system the body can generate many millions of different antibodies each designed to seek and link with its own particular target, called an antigen. By definition an antigen is simply anything against which the body's immunological defense system can direct an antibody response. Even these natural guided missiles of the body are to some degree blunt instruments in comparison with the newly contrived monoclonal antibodies.

The specificity of an antibody molecule is governed by its shape. Each different antibody has a shape which fits in lock-and-key fashion with a corresponding shape on its target. One of the most remarkable features of this defense system is that its inborn repertoire contains virtually all of the shapes any antigen could conceivably take. After choosing the right shape, the immune system produces large quantities of those antibodies that fit the target antigen best. It is not like a locksmith who can fashion a key to fit any lock in the city, but instead like a locksmith who has made keys for all conceivable locks that might exist.

The natural production scheme leads the body to produce a cluster of slightly varied antibodies against the foreign substance that is the target. A complex microorganism such as a virus is likely to have several different antigenic shapes on its surface and a disease-causing bacterium will have many. The body's antibody response will be against more than one of these. This works splendidly for normal defensive needs and for many of the needs of science, but it falls short of the ideal specificity of one missile for any single antigenic target. That almost perfect specificity is just the kind of precise targeting that becomes possible with monoclonal antibodies.

The cell-fusion technique

To appreciate the difference between normal antibodies and monoclonal antibodies it is useful to understand the basic process by which monoclonal antibodies are formed. The key experiment by Köhler and Milstein is a good example. The scientists wanted to grow in tissue culture durable cell lines that would produce known antibodies. For purposes of the research these antibodies had to be easily detected and assayed. It was not difficult to collect antibody-producing cells from an organ such as the spleen of a mouse, but these normal cells would not grow continuously in the laboratory cell cultures. Cancer cells of the kind called myeloma would grow, seemingly forever, in laboratory cultures and they did produce immunoglobulin—the protein substance of antibodies. But these antibodies were almost always random, simply part of the body's immense store of possible types. There was no practical way of identifying them with any specific targets.

But taken together, the two types of cells—normal spleen cells immunized against a known substance and the immunoglobulin-producing cancer cells capable of indefinite growth—did have all the necessary attributes. Why not put them together? That was just what the scientists did.

First they immunized mice against red blood cells of sheep by injecting the animals with small amounts of the blood cells. They chose sheep cells as the target for the antibodies they sought because sheep red blood cells are a much-used standard preparation. Methods for detecting antibodies against them already existed. Next the scientists took immunologically active cells from spleens of these immunized mice and mixed them with mouse myeloma cells that spontaneously produce antibody. Then they added a chemical that tends to make cells fuse when they are growing together in tissue culture. The nutrients in which the cells were grown were carefully selected so that no cells would survive except hybrids resulting from the fusion of a myeloma cell and a normal antibody-producing cell from the mouse spleen. Some of the surviving cells would make the kind of unknown antibodies characteristic of the myeloma. Some would make antibodies against the sheep cells.

There are standard laboratory techniques for segregating growing cells into clones each derived from only a single parent cell. By growing many such individual clones the scientists could single out just what they had wanted at the start—cells that produced large amounts of antibodies that were easy to detect and assay.

But it soon dawned on them that they had much more than that. They had a method for growing individual clones of antibody-producing cells with each clone making only one kind of antibody because every cell in that clone came from the same parent. All the antibody produced by that clone would have exactly the same target.

The production takes ingenuity, skill, and time; it takes about four months to produce a useful hybridoma. But once this is done, a biological tool has been forged that has immense potential. Each clone produces a large crop of antibodies all formed from the same mold, so to speak. These standardized antibodies can be produced in limitless quantity either by large-scale growth in tissue culture or by transplanting cells from a clone into a laboratory animal where the cells will grow, multiply, and produce large amounts of pure antibody, all of the same kind. Furthermore, specimens of the antibody-producing cells from any clone can be frozen and stored indefinitely for future reference and use.

Routine blood typing with monoclonal antibodies is proving more efficient, effective, and reliable than previous conventional methods. The same is true of much related work in the field of serology, which deals with body serums and their reactions. But such uses are only the beginning. "They will have an enormous impact throughout medical practice, from the humdrum diagnostic level to the fashionable frontiers," said an editorial in the medical journal *The Lancet* in 1981.

Monoclonal antibodies and cancer

The *Lancet* editorial specifically addressed monoclonal antibodies and cancer, a subject of great current interest. The promise lies in the ability of these precision-targeted antibodies to recognize subtle differences between cells. The hope is that they will be able

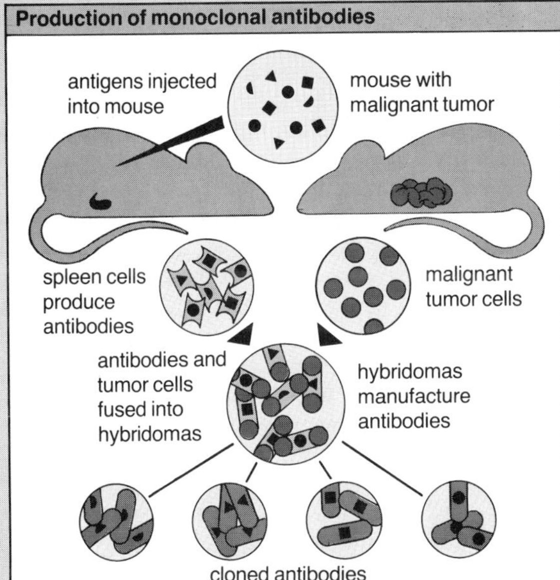

David Scharf—Peter Arnold, Inc.

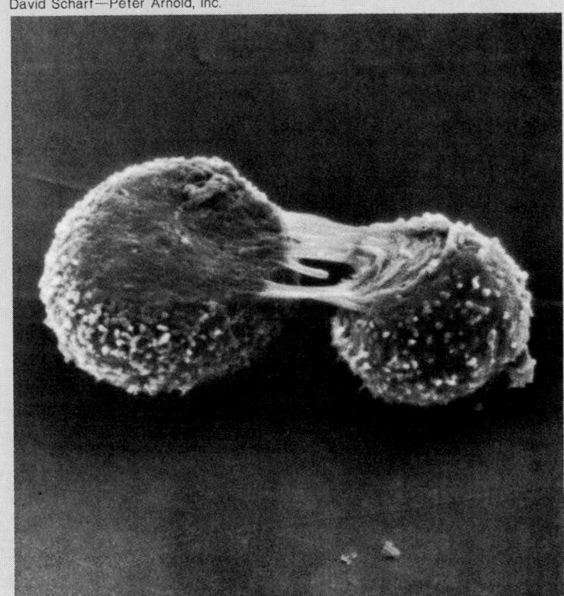

The key studies that produced monoclonal antibodies involved first injecting a mouse with antigen-containing red blood cells from sheep. The mouse's spleen cells each make a particular antibody to a particular antigen. These spleen cells are then fused (photomicrograph at right) with tumor cells from mice to make new "hybridomas," from which antibodies in unlimited quantities can be made.

to distinguish a patient's cancer cells from closely similar normal cells. This achievement would fulfill dreams cancer specialists have had for many decades.

"The preparation of large quantities of antibodies that specifically bind to individual cell types is perhaps the most important benefit of monoclonal antibody technology," said the editorial, "and the most dramatic potential application is in the production of antibodies that home in to the cell surface of tumours in a patient, either to kill the tumours or to carry radiolabels which will permit localisation of tumour deposits."

The potential is obvious in both diagnosis and treatment. By labeling the antibodies with mild doses of radiation, they can be tracked to their final destination in the body by radiation-counting instruments from the outside. If these antibodies do indeed home in selectively on cancer tissue, the radiation emitted from the antibodies can provide a map showing the exact location of cancer cells anywhere in the body. This would be extremely valuable for diagnosis.

The ability to seek out cancer cells could be used just as well to kill them. Some antibodies have killing effects through their own attributes. In addition, the cancer-seeking antibodies could be equipped with a "warhead" of some powerful poison such as diphtheria toxin. Only the target cells would be affected and they would be killed. Probably only one molecule of such a toxin has to be brought to a cell to kill it. This would not require extraordinary marksmanship on the part of the antibodies because there might well be 100,000 copies of the chosen target on a single cell surface.

Paul I. Terasaki and his colleagues at the University of California, Los Angeles, reported in 1981 that they produced monoclonal antibodies against an uncommon type of cancer called leiomyosarcoma. The antibodies were potent enough to kill 3,000 times their weight in cancer cells in test-tube experiments. The scientists said this was an acceptable potency for treatment purposes, but that the antibodies might prove to be either more or less powerful in a patient.

There are potential dangers in attempts to use monoclonal antibodies in cancer treatment. Even with the specificity of the new antibodies, it is possible that indispensable normal cells, such as those of the blood-forming tissues in the bone marrow might exhibit the same antigens as some cancer cells and be hit disastrously by mistake. Many medical research groups are exploring this new field. Just what its final dimensions will be is difficult to predict.

Similarly there has been much activity in using monoclonal antibodies for cancer diagnosis. Scientists at the University of Chicago have produced monoclonal antibodies that bind with receptors in human tissues for the female hormones, the estrogens. Elwood Jensen, a principal investigator in this research, has noted that 25,000 of the breast cancers that develop among women in the U.S. in a year are dependent on these hormones for their maximum growth. For women who have advanced cancers of the hormone-dependent type, the accepted treatment is either removal of the hormone-producing glands or use of drugs that interfere with hormone action. Monoclonal antibodies against the estrogen receptors could be valuable in determining whether a patient's breast cancer is of that hormone-dependent type. This information could be important in ensuring that all breast cancer patients receive the type of treatment best suited to their illness.

Stuart F. Schlossman and his colleagues at Harvard Medical School are using monoclonal antibodies to search for a specific substance in the blood of children suffering from acute leukemia. In a report in *The New England Journal of Medicine,* the doctors said such studies should make it possible to distinguish different types of acute leukemia in what was once thought to be a largely homogeneous disease. Assigning the patients into different subgroups based on the biology of their disease should help give each the best possible diagnosis and treatment.

Recently, Hilary Koprowski's group at the Wistar Institute of Anatomy and Biology in Philadelphia has developed monoclonal antibodies against antigens found in cancer of the large intestine or colon. From these discoveries, too, medical scientists hope for better understanding, better diagnosis, and in the long run better treatment of disease.

Implications for many diseases

The potential usefulness of monoclonal antibodies is by no means limited to cancer. Schlossman's group has discovered that patients suffering from active multiple sclerosis lack a certain kind of immunological defense cell called the supressor T cell. The discovery could be an important clue to the biochemical nature of this disease of the nervous system and might prove valuable in diagnosis and treatment. Key aspects of the research were done with the aid of monoclonal antibodies. "This study emphasizes the important contributions of monoclonal antibodies in the investigation of human disease," said the Harvard group. Schlossman and his co-authors said the antibodies should be similarly useful in studying other diseases of the nervous system and other disorders called autoimmune because they involve derangements in which the patient's own immune defenses turn against some of his or her own tissues.

Because antibodies of this type make it easier to study and manipulate the immunological system, they are expected to help make organ transplantation more successful. The key problem in transplantation is preventing the patient's immune defenses from rejecting the foreign tissue.

The antibodies' sensitivity in detecting minor differences in cells suggested to Edgar Haber of Harvard an ingenious use in diagnosis of heart attacks. When heart cells die during an attack, they become physically disrupted so that some substances normally buried within the cell are exposed and become accessible to antibodies. Monoclonal antibodies against such substances have been used in animal experiments to define the precise location and extent of damage to heart tissue caused by a heart attack. This novel mapping of the precise geography of a heart attack could be extremely valuable in gauging the gravity of a patient's condition quickly and thus helping guide the physician's strategy for helping the patient.

Scientists at several institutions are using monoclonal antibodies to isolate substances from malaria parasites. This work may eventually make possible the first practical vaccine against that huge and currently intractable world health problem.

Other scientists use monoclonal antibodies to detect subtle chemical variations in local populations of the influenza and rabies viruses. The studies are revealing many hitherto unknown aspects of the behavior of these two important viruses.

Because of the great specificity with which monoclonal antibodies choose their particular targets, they are valuable tools for many routine medical tests, particularly those that involve blood. They are also valuable as almost magically efficient means of purifying important substances from a welter of extraneous matter. Monoclonal antibodies have already been used, for example, in speeding the purification of the antivirus substance interferon which is now in great demand.

It is these attributes which have led several commercial firms to produce monoclonal antibodies on a large scale. Several entirely new companies have been set up to make hybridomas and the antibodies they produce. To date almost all of the work in industry and in the medical research laboratory has been with antibodies produced by hybrid mouse cells. For many important applications human antibodies would be preferable. These too are now becoming available. The first two reports of success in producing human hybridomas that make antibodies came recently from Hilary Koprowski's group at the Wistar Institute and Henry Kaplan's laboratory at Stanford University. The availability of human monoclonal antibodies is expected to add another important dimension to this already fast expanding field.

One of the most intriguing talents of monoclonal antibodies is their ability to pull out of a complex, impure mixture one or more extraordinarily pure substances. Each can be captured because it is the sole target of one or another of these extraordinarily precise antibodies. The *Lancet* editorial remarked, "We are in the almost absurd position of being able to raise a pure antibody to an unknown antigen and then prepare the antigen by means of antibody," thus surpassing the feat of finding a needle in a haystack. A scientist can now find the needle without even knowing its identity in advance. It is possibilities of this kind, unpredictable in their impact because of the immense scope and novelty of the field, that make the words monoclonal antibodies two of the most exciting in the whole vocabulary of modern biological science.

Arthritis and Connective Tissue Diseases

What do yucca, blackstrap molasses, the "Magnetron," the New Zealand green-lipped mussel, and horse manure have in common? These and other nostrums, patent medicines, and devices have been and still are used in the treatment of arthritis.

Arthritis is an umbrella term covering numerous rheumatic diseases that manifest themselves as painful inflammation of the joints. Rheumatoid arthritis, probably the most dreaded of these diseases, results in progressive destruction of the joints, sometimes ending in profound disability. Osteoarthritis, bursitis, gout, and systemic lupus erythematosus are other types of common rheumatic diseases. Most rheumatic diseases are chronic, and all tend to interfere with the patient's activities of daily living. The clinical and therapeutic implications of rheumatic diseases may be so complex that the patients and their families suffer severe emotional turmoil.

Arthritis and quackery

These diseases are usually not curable, but "cure" too often is equated with an amelioration of symptoms. Almost all patients can obtain significant relief from a comprehensive management program consisting of drugs, physical and occupational therapy, surgery, and counseling. A variety of medications that have proved beneficial are currently available. These include analgesics, anti-inflammatory agents, and the so-called remission-inducing drugs for rheumatoid arthritis such as gold, penicillamine, and antimalarial compounds. These drugs are approved by the federal Food and Drug Administration (FDA), whose sanction implies that they have been rigidly tested for their efficacy and that any side effects have been identified.

From the patient's point of view, there are many unsatisfactory aspects to treatment. The pharmacologic testing and the FDA approval process of new agents often take years to complete. Moreover, antirheumatic drugs rarely work well in all patients all of the time—a therapeutic response may take months. Physical therapy and other allied modes of treatment may not be accessible to some patients. Many physicians are not adequately trained in the diagnosis and comprehensive, effective management of arthritis. Some patients simply fail to obtain treatments that are readily available. Thus, there are many reasons why patients with arthritis do not obtain optimal care.

Meanwhile, the patient suffers. He continues to have pain, limitation of motion, and decreased ability to function. Out of desperation he seeks the apparently easy way out. He sees an advertisement for an "arthritis cure" in a magazine, or a well-intentioned friend tells him of a special treatment for arthritis rumored to bring "guaranteed" results within weeks. The patient at that point has swallowed the bait. The quack awaits him.

Quackery is big business. Close to $1 billion annually is collected by these merchants to the miserable. More than twice as much money is spent on quackery than on legitimate prescription drugs. For every dollar spent on research to find the cause and cure of arthritis, $25 is given to the quack. Quackery and ineffective, misrepresented, unproved remedies are to be differentiated from those unproved remedies that seem to help and have become a part of standard medical practice even though they have not been fully tested. Quackery and unproved remedies come in all forms: unorthodox drugs and vitamins, local applications, vaccines, venoms, animal products, plants, diets, spas, and devices.

Unorthodox drugs and vitamins

Cortisone, a steroid hormone produced by the adrenal glands, has been advocated for the treatment of certain types of arthritis since 1949. Because of the dramatic improvement that followed the administration of cortisone, it was considered to be a miracle drug. This major accomplishment in exploring the nature and uses of adrenal hormones was accorded the 1950 Nobel Prize for Physiology or Medicine. Afterward, howev-

Cortisone—a potent steroid with serious side effects—is combined with sex hormones in the unproved and illegal arthritis "remedy" Liefcort.

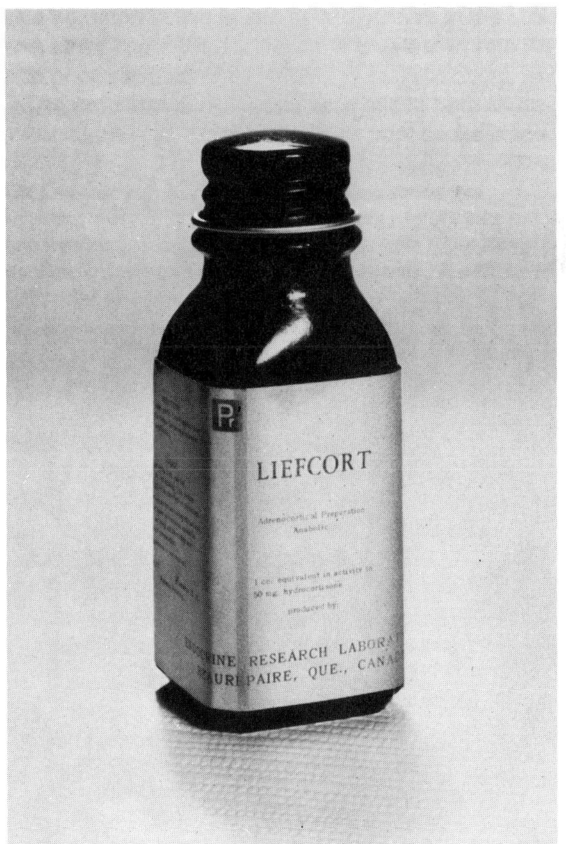

Arthritis Foundation, Atlanta, Ga.

Arthritis Foundation, Atlanta, Ga.; photograph, Jeannine Deubel

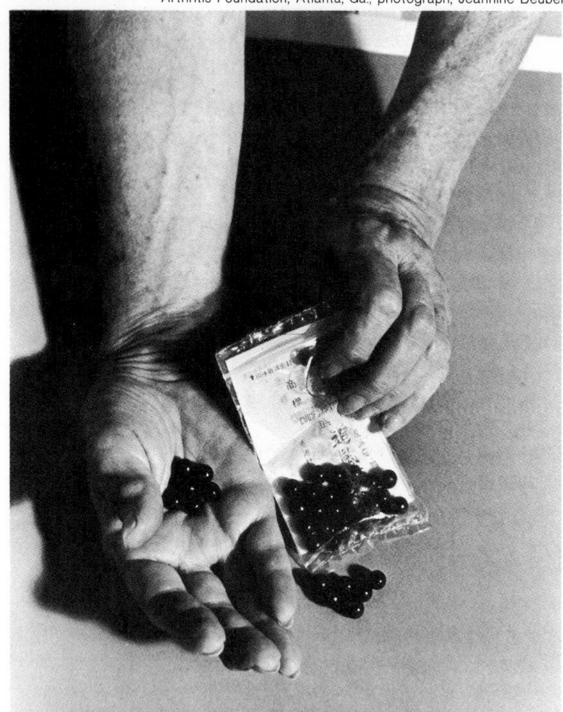

Unscrupulous operators have been peddling Chinese herbal medications for rheumatism. The Arthritis Foundation warns that the side effects of these products could result in death.

er, the side effects of cortisone drugs became known. These include fluid retention, weight gain, cataracts, hypertension, diabetes, brittle bones (osteoporosis), peptic ulcers, and susceptibility to infection. Physicians, still recognizing the value of cortisone, became more moderate in its use and limited it to special cases.

In the 1960s Robert Liefmann promoted cortisone in combination with male and female hormones under the name of Liefcort. Liefcort clinics in Canada flourished as thousands of patients sought relief. To be sure, the formula did relieve pain, at least for a while. The doses that were recommended were quite high, and often patients were not informed of the usual side effects. Reportedly, patients paid in excess of $100 monthly for the medication, which is many times what the component drugs would cost in a pharmacy. Eventually the Canadian Food and Drug Directorate was able to temporarily close the clinics, charging Liefmann with marketing an unproved drug. However, Liefcort subsequently surfaced under other names, such as Holistic Balance Treatment, Balanced Hormone Treatment, and Rheumatril. These drugs were sometimes dispensed from storefront "clinics."

Arthritis sufferers, racked with pain, have sought relief at similar clinics promoting instant cures all over the world, including Piedras Negras and Mexicali, Mexico, near the U.S. border, and Santo Domingo in the Dominican Republic. Rarely do patients realize that they are getting the same drugs that can be obtained legitimately, more cheaply, and more safely in the United States. Most of the tablets contain either cortisone or phenylbutazone (Butazolidin), a potent anti-inflammatory agent, and diazepam (Valium), a widely used tranquilizer.

Some British arthritis sufferers have ordered from Hong Kong a product touted as a Chinese herbal treatment for rheumatism. It is traded under the name Chuei Fong Tou Geu Wan, which translates to "chase the wind through the bones." It contains the cortisone derivative dexamethasone, the anti-inflammatory drug indomethacin, a hydrochlorothiazide diuretic, and diazepam. Chuifong Toukuwan is a similar medication that is shipped by the same Hong Kong manufacturer into the United States. The remedy is sent directly to patients, is available in Oriental food stores, or is even sold by door-to-door salesmen. In addition to anti-inflammatory agents and tranquilizers, it contains acetaminophen and aminopyrine, the latter now banned in the U.S. because it can be fatal when used indiscriminately. The component drugs vary from sample to sample.

The public has long been fascinated with vitamin therapy for arthritis. Even those patients whose disease seems to be well under control sometimes ask their physicians to recommend a vitamin capsule. Whether or not the physician complies, vitamins are widely available either singly or in combination. Magazines such as *Prevention,* which is largely sponsored by vitamin manufacturers, advertise many different types of relatively costly special arthritis formulas. Almost all vitamins have been promoted for arthritis relief at one time or another. Pantothenic acid, a B vitamin, has received the greatest attention in recent years. Yet there is no vitamin that has been proved to be particularly beneficial in treating any type of arthritis. Vitamin therapy for systemic lupus erythematosus has no merit. The use of vitamin C to reduce pain in osteoarthritis needs additional investigation.

Other drugs "pushed" by physician and nonphysician nostrum sellers are the anesthetics cocaine and procaine (Geravital H-3). Proponents of the latter claim it not only relieves arthritis but imparts longevity.

Local medications

Of the long list of balms, lotions, potions, poultices, plasters, liniments, ointments, jellies, and solutions that have been advocated for rheumatism since the beginning of written history, none in recent times has received more attention and has been the subject of more controversy than dimethyl sulfoxide (DMSO). A by-product of paper manufacture first used as an industrial solvent, DMSO is being advocated for a wide variety of musculoskeletal diseases and injuries, inflammations, and infections. Proponents of DMSO are not necessarily involved in intentional quackery, but

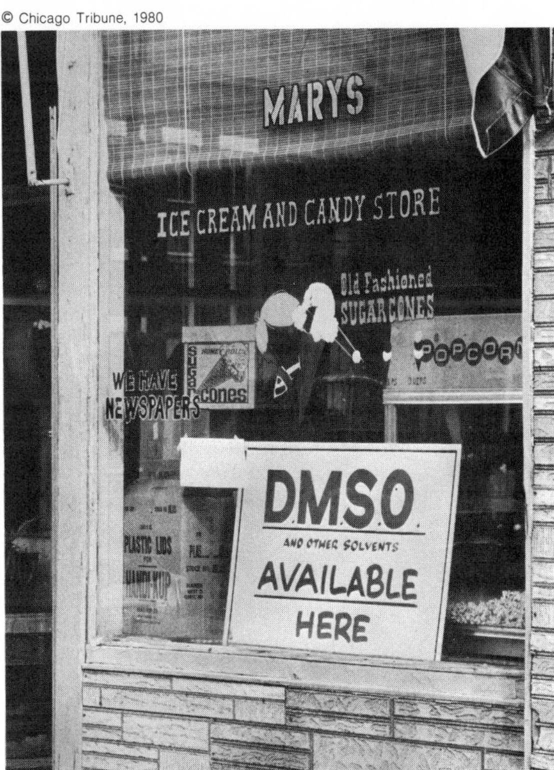

DMSO has been widely touted as a wonder drug for arthritis and other diseases. But this questionable product has yet to be thoroughly and properly studied.

the substance has not been tested completely. The major champion of having the FDA approve the drug as an analgesic and antirheumatic agent is Stanley Jacobs, an Oregon surgeon who has been investigating the compound since the early 1960s.

Currently, DMSO, which is accepted in veterinary medicine, is approved for human use in the United States only for interstitial cystitis, a chronic inflammation of the bladder, and in Canada for cutaneous application in patients with scleroderma, a condition characterized by tightening of the skin.

DMSO is not, as is commonly believed, a harmless compound. Among its side effects, the garliclike taste and odor on the breath and skin, that are noticed within minutes of administration of DMSO, are at worst annoying, but allergic reactions and alterations in eye tissues may be serious. DMSO allows drugs applied to the skin to penetrate easily but can also cause toxins and impurities to be distributed throughout the body. Persons who use industrial or veterinary grades of DMSO are taking this risk.

DMSO shows promise as a local analgesic and possibly an anti-inflammatory agent, but considerably more research is necessary before definitive claims can be made about its actions. The FDA has over 30 applications from pharmaceutical companies and independent investigators to study the potential role of DMSO in medical practice. Organizations such as the Arthritis Foundation are not against studying DMSO; rather, they oppose the sensationalism and "miracle drug" labels that have been attached to it. Even if DMSO proves to be effective for joint injuries, it may have no effect on arthritic conditions.

Vaccines and venoms

The public's preoccupation with vaccines and venoms in the treatment of arthritis is a curiosity. Many inflammatory rheumatic diseases apparently are caused by an altered immune response, but the specific triggering mechanism of this process is not known. It is suspected that some type of bacterial or viral organism may initiate the abnormal response. Vaccines mobilize an antibody response in the human body against such an invading organism, hence the reason for their use in arthritis. But because it is not known what the specific triggering infectious agent is, or even if one exists, it is not now possible to create an effective antiarthritis vaccine. Therefore, vaccines promoted for use in arthritis are of dubious value.

It is theorized by the proponents of bee venom and snake venom (*e.g.,* PROven, a combination of cobra and krait venoms) that these substances are effective because, as foreign proteins, they elicit an immune response that will combat arthritis and, in the case of PROven, multiple sclerosis. Although the rationale is feasible and there is indeed much personal testimony to the effectiveness of venom therapy, the scientific method of investigation has not been applied. A book entitled *Bees Don't Get Arthritis* recommends bee-sting therapy. Symptomatic relief probably ensues because the sting mobilizes an outpouring of cortisone in the body as part of an overall stress reaction rather than as a result of any direct effect of bee venom.

Animal products and plant cures

A recent offbeat arthritis remedy is the New Zealand green-lipped mussel, available as an extract in a foul-smelling capsule most commonly called Seatone. The manufacturer's claim that the substance is effective against rheumatoid arthritis and osteoarthritis has not been accepted by the medical profession because adequate proof is lacking. Cod-liver oil, a staple of arthritis folklore, is supposed to lubricate the joints. Actually, it never reaches them, being broken down into its components in the digestive tract. Burying a rheumatoid patient up to his neck in horse manure is another purported treatment for arthritis. One can formulate one's own opinion of the rationality of this therapy.

Alfalfa, vinegar, and blackstrap molasses are among the plant substances that are still favored by devotees of backwoods medicine. Yucca tablets, derived from the flowering desert plant, are dispensed at a California clinic ostensibly on a research basis but can be found in most health food stores throughout the U.S. The yucca has been used for its medicinal property for years by the Indians of the Southwest. A saponin extract from the yucca is supposed to help arthritis by virtue of its cortisonelike properties, but without adverse effects. "Controlled" studies have been reported by the physicians at the California clinic but have not been substantiated by others.

Arthritis diets

The effect of nutrition on arthritis has been a subject of controversy for more than a century. Each year arthritis diet books are released, many advertised as constituting the "ultimate cure." One such claim is the "nightshades-elimination" diet, promoted by a Rutgers University horticulturist who suggests that tomatoes, white potatoes, peppers, and eggplants—all of the Solanaceae, or nightshade, family—are in essence poison to the joints. Although he has catalogued the testimony of thousands of "cooperators"—people who state that they have success with the diet—proper research methods have not been applied to its testing.

Arthritis sufferers have long been attracted to spas such as Évian-les-Bains in France, where they may derive some psychological benefits from the tonic mineral baths.

Marc Riboud—Magnum

There have been several controlled studies of the effects of other types of diets on arthritis. Weight reduction relieves gout and the arthritis of lower extremities by taking some of the burden off the joints. There is, however, no evidence whatsoever that either elimination or supplementation diets aimed at various foods or substances are otherwise effective.

Spas

The attribution of healing power to mineral waters dates back to antiquity. A spa is a health resort where these minerals are found in springs, lakes, baths, and mud. Spas are located all over the world, but those of Europe are the best known. Mineral waters are categorized as alkaline, acid, saline, or sulfurated. The tonic effect of warm baths, mineralized or not, in a vacation surrounding cannot be denied, yet the pharmacologic and physiologic benefits of spa therapy have not been scientifically documented.

Devices

Magnetic, electrical, and radioactive devices have been touted as panaceas for arthritis for generations. These have included uranium mittens, vryllium tubes, Magnetrons, Parolators, Diapulse Electromagnetic Energy Generators, Perkins Tractors, crushed rock, Detoxacolon (a dangerous pressurized enema), and the biggest hoax of them all, the copper bracelet. Little needs to be said of these gadgets other than that they are ineffective, often are dangerous, and represent the ultimate in arthritis quackery and charlatanism.

The effects of quackery

In most instances the various nostrums and devices promoted for arthritis do not work, but they may *seem* to help because of the intense desire of the suffering patient to get relief, even for a brief time. The hype, promotions, and aura of these deceptions may be so great as to mesmerize the patient. It is common for patients—especially suffering ones—to have high regard for the newest treatment.

The placebo response in medicine is well recognized. Up to 35% of patients with arthritis will have at least a temporary response to whatever is administered them. That is why double-blind controlled studies (neither the investigator nor the subjects know whether a real drug or inert substitute is given) are essential. Only by applying this scientific method can the efficacy of a drug or treatment be proved. Individual testimony is intriguing but is not proof. Furthermore, diseases like rheumatoid arthritis are characterized by frequent exacerbations and remissions. Obviously, if the substance is given just prior to a natural period of improvement, it will seem to work.

Quackery is costly to society and to the patient. The fake pills, diets, and gadgets can cost the unsuspecting patient thousands of dollars. Of greater concern is the toll that quackery takes in human misery. The patient who goes to a quack deprives himself of legitimate medical care that can relieve pain and prevent disability. There are many documented cases of careless administration of unproved treatments that have harmed or caused the deaths of patients. For these reasons the Arthritis Foundation offers some simple clues on how to spot the quack or the promoter of certain misrepresented, unproved remedies. They are as follows:

1. The formula or device is promised as a "cure" for arthritis. (There is no cure for arthritis.)
2. The promoter offers what is called a "special" or "secret" formula.
3. The promoter uses testimonials, rather than scientific documentation, as proof of efficacy.
4. The item is advertised or promoted in sensational news releases.
5. The promoter implies quick and easy relief.
6. The promoter claims to know the cause of arthritis and talks about "cleansing" the body of "poisons."
7. The promoter condemns recognized drug and surgical treatments.
8. No reliable proof or evidence is available.
9. The promoter advocates the use of special diets and nutrients.
10. The promoter accuses the "medical establishment" of deliberately thwarting progress or of persecuting him.

—Warren A. Katz, M.D.

Blood and the Lymphatic System

When a tissue or organ of the body is damaged by disease and cannot repair itself, one method of treatment is to replace it with a transplant. The earliest practical transplant was the cornea of the eye, but replacement of major internal organs was not common until successful kidney transplants were carried out in the mid-1950s. Perhaps the most publicized transplant was performed by South African surgeon Christiaan Barnard, who in 1967 replaced the heart of Louis Washkansky with that of an accident victim and was able to maintain life for 18 days.

To be successful, a transplanted tissue or organ should be accepted by the recipient's immune system, and it should function normally. Organ transplantation entails a number of risks that continue for years after the surgery itself. Consequently it is a procedure commonly used as a last resort when other kinds of treatment have failed.

Bone marrow transplantation

The bone marrow is a tissue that serves as a factory for the manufacture of the body's various blood cells. These cells originate from a common single parent cell type known as the stem cell. When stem cells in the marrow are damaged, leading to bone marrow failure, the body's ability to produce various blood cells is either severely impaired or completely nonexistent. Blood tranfusions can remedy the condition only partially and can provide support for the patient only for a brief time. As a long-term solution to the problem of bone marrow failure, bone marrow transplantation (bone marrow grafting) has recently been advocated.

There are three different types of marrow transplantations: syngeneic (isogeneic), autologous, and allogeneic. A syngeneic, or isogeneic, marrow graft is a transplantation from a donor to a recipient when both of them carry identical tissue antigens, *i.e.*, a graft between identical twins. Tissue antigens are molecular "tags" on the surfaces of cells by which the body's immune system distinguishes foreign tissue from "self." A syngeneic graft will not provoke an immune reaction and consequently is not associated with any immunologic complications. Similar to a syngeneic graft is the autologous marrow transplantation. In this procedure the patient's own bone marrow is first removed and set aside; it is reinfused into the patient at a later time. The autologous transplantation is usually carried out in patients who need treatments that as a side effect destroy bone marrow, such as large doses of radiation therapy or chemotherapy for cancer.

An allogeneic marrow graft is a transplantation between donor and recipient of different genetic origin but within the same species. Because donor and recipient do not share identical tissue antigens, immunologic barriers exist to a successful and uncomplicated transplant. When receiving bone marrow carrying nonidentical tissue antigens, the recipient may develop antibodies against the graft and reject it. In addition, the donor marrow tissue may produce immunologically competent cells belonging to the lymphocyte group that will grow and thrive in the recipient's body. These cells will recognize the foreign nature of the recipient tissue antigens and will produce antibodies against the host. In this situation the transplant actually rejects the host, producing a syndrome known as a graft-versus-host (GVH) disease. These two problems are the main obstacles in the use of bone marrow transplantation as a therapy.

Histocompatibility

In order for a marrow graft to succeed, the tissue antigens of donor and host must be matched as closely as possible. The state of histocompatibility (literally, tissue compatibility) is determined by an identifiable complex of tissue antigens. One method involves detecting and identifying the major histocompatibility, or HL-A, antigens. These are molecules composed of protein and carbohydrate that are found on virtually all human cell surfaces, one exception being the mature red blood cell. More than 50 such antigens have been identified, but only 4 of these are found in any individual. Genetic control of the formation of HL-A antigens is determined

Karl G. Blume, Director, Department of Hematology and Bone Marrow Transplantation, City of Hope National Medical Center, Duarte, Calif.

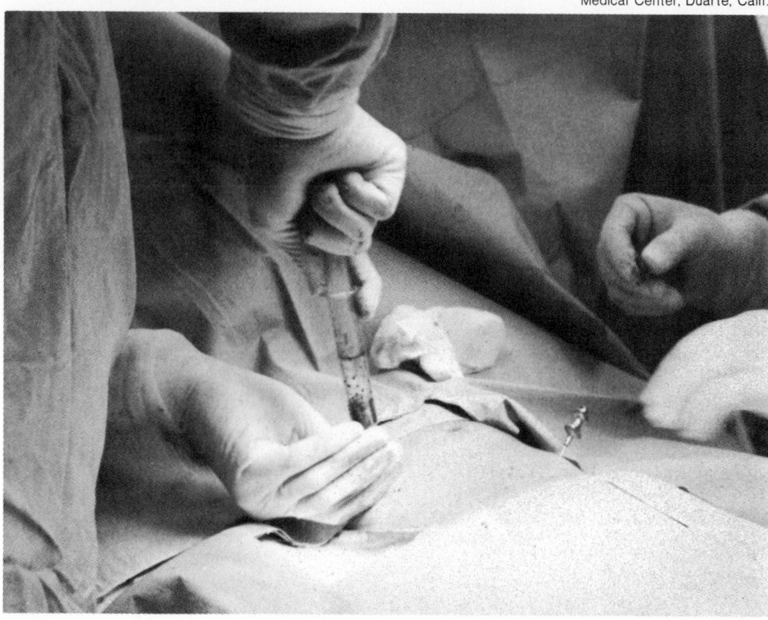

Bone marrow from the pelvic region of a donor is obtained under anesthesia by aspirating it through a hollow needle.

by several closely linked loci (fixed positions of genes) present on a single chromosomal segment on the number 6 chromosome. These loci determine the formation of two specific combinations of HL-A antigens in each given individual. Each of the two combinations is termed a haplotype, and only one haplotype is inherited from each parent. (Paternal haplotypes are often designated A and B, and maternal haplotypes, C and D.) Hence, each child of any marriage can possess one of only four possible haplotype combinations (AC, AD, BC, or BD). It also follows that a 25% chance exists for two siblings to have both of the same haplotypes—*i.e.*, to be HL-A-identical—or to have neither of the same haplotypes; the odds are even that two siblings will share one haplotype. Parents share one haplotype with their children; the other is almost always different.

Predicting the outcome of a tissue or organ transplantation depends in part upon typing the HL-A antigens of the donor and recipient. If donor and recipient are of the same family, HL-A typing can also be used to analyze the inheritance of haplotypes. A two-haplotype match between family members has a chance of success second only to that of syngeneic grafts (from identical twins). Approximately 48% of individuals have at least one sibling with genotypically matched HL-A antigens. With computerized data-collection systems in HL-A-typing centers, it is now possible to maintain a bank of HL-A genotype information so that unrelated individuals can be matched as closely as possible.

Overcoming host resistance to marrow grafting

Resistance of the recipient to transplanted marrow may be inborn owing to histoincompatibility or acquired if the recipient received blood or blood products in a prior transfusion. Sensitization of the recipient to foreign blood cells can occur so that antibodies against donor cells are developed prior to transplantation. To overcome both types of resistance the recipient's defense mechanism and antibody-producing cells must be suppressed prior to grafting. This is achieved by means of irradiation, chemotherapy, or use of an antilymphocyte serum.

The technique of total body radiation has been used successfully since the early days of marrow transplantation. Radiation is delivered to the whole body at a total dose of 1,000 rads (a measure of absorbed radiation) at 3.5 rads per minute, preferably using opposing radioactive-cobalt sources to achieve a more homogeneous radiation. This type of dose eliminates the recipient's bone marrow cells, including all graft-resisting cells. Harmful effects to the rest of the body usually are limited to low-grade fever, nausea, vomiting, diarrhea, and tender swelling of the parotid glands. Such side effects are generally well tolerated and last only one or two days. When used on patients with leukemia, total body radiation has the additional advantage of removing leukemia cells from the body because these cells are relatively sensitive to radiation. Total body radiation can also penetrate to parts of the body such as the central nervous system where conventional chemotherapeutic agents may not reach.

Many chemotherapeutic agents have been used for preparing the recipient, but the most commonly used one is cyclophosphamide (Cytoxan). This powerful immunosuppressive agent has been used for many years against such immunologic disorders as idiopathic thrombocytopenic purpura, systemic lupus erythematosus, and autoimmune hemolytic anemia and as an anticancer agent. The toxicity of this drug is also tolerable; side effects include nausea, vomiting, and, rarely, hemorrhagic cystitis. In daily doses of 50 mg per kilogram of body weight for four days, this drug can prepare the recipient's immune system adequately for the transplant. Other chemotherapeutic agents for this purpose include thioguanine, nitrogen mustard, aminochlorambucil (a chlorambucil derivative), busulfan, and 6-mercaptopurine. Combinations of chemotherapeutic agents have been tried, but results indicate that multidrug regimens are no better than cyclophosphamide alone. A combination of total body radiation and cyclophosphamide, however, definitely has been shown to be better than the use of either alone.

Use of an antilymphocyte serum against the recipient's immune system also has been tried, but results have not been entirely satisfactory. Although it is no longer used as a single mode of treatment, it is sometimes given in combination with total body radiation or chemotherapy. Disadvantages of antilymphocyte serum include its unpredictable potency and its frequent antibody activity against recipient and donor blood platelets (blood components that participate in the clotting mechanism) and sometimes against donor marrow cells.

Technique of marrow transplantation

Marrow tissue from the donor is obtained under anesthesia by aspirating it through a hollow needle from different marrow sites. These sites are various regions in the pelvic bone. Aspirated marrow blood containing marrow tissue is quickly transferred into a tissue culture medium containing the anticoagulant heparin to prevent clotting. The amount that can be aspirated from each bone marrow puncture is only 1 to 3 ml; for a transplant 400–800 ml are needed, requiring many punctures. In spite of this, the procedure is usually well tolerated by the donor. In some transplant centers the donor is given 500 ml of blood during the procedure to replace the volume of blood aspirated from the marrow. This blood is generally the donor's own blood, removed a few days prior to the procedure and stored. This procedure avoids the use of blood from another person with the inherent risks of hepatitis and other immunologic complications of a transfusion.

The pooled aspirated marrow is passed through a stainless steel screen with 0.2-mm openings to produce a suspension of single cells. Clumping of cells or fat in the marrow is avoided to prevent the potentially fatal obstruction of a blood vessel. The marrow is then infused into the recipient through an intravenous drip.

Replication and proliferation of donor marrow requires from 15 to 25 days before it is fully functional. Preparation of the recipient with radiation and chemotherapy will have halted the recipient's own marrow activity completely. Consequently, during this three-week period there is a complete absence of normal marrow function. Supportive measures, including the use of platelet transfusion to maintain an adequate circulating platelet level, must be carried out. Granulocytes, specialized white blood cells that participate in the body's defense mechanisms, may also have to be given. Because of the greater technical difficulty in obtaining large quantities of donor granulocytes for transfusion, they are not given as frequently as platelet transfusions. But whenever there is a clinically apparent infection from bacteria or fungal agents, daily granulocyte transfusions are indicated.

In some centers the recipient is placed in a completely sterile environment with a special filtering system that excludes bacterial contamination. There are no controlled studies that indicate if patients placed in a germfree environment are less likely to develop infections.

Prevention of graft-versus-host rejection

As mentioned above, lymphocytes present in the donor marrow—specifically, immune-competent T-lymphocytes—may start to reject the recipient after entry into the recipient's circulation. Two forms of GVH disease are recognized. The early-onset, acute form is associated with transplantation of large numbers of immune-competent T-lymphocytes into the recipient and with a severe rejection syndrome consisting of diarrhea, wasting, extensive dermatitis, and fever. The illness is severe and is associated with a very high mortality. Fortunately this acute form is very rarely produced in human hosts who receive bone marrow from histocompatible donors.

The more common, chronic form of GVH disease produces less severe symptoms and can develop any time after the bone marrow cells have repopulated the recipient. A characteristic of the chronic reaction is the development of infection due to the rejection of lymphoid tissues in the host. These infections are frequently the cause of death in the chronic form of the disease. Manifestations of rejection in three other organ systems are also seen, namely, skin rash, jaundice due to destruction of liver cells, and diarrhea and abdominal pain due to rejection of cells of the intestinal lining.

Prevention is as important as treatment in GVH disease. Chemotherapeutic agents, particularly cyclophosphamide and methotrexate, have been found very effective in prevention. In addition, both antilymphocyte and antithymocyte serums have been used, although their effectiveness has not yet been determined.

Results for specific disorders

Clinical disorders in which successful marrow transplantations have been carried out include congenital immune deficiency, aplastic anemia, acute leukemia, and accidental exposure to excessive radiation.

In patients with congenital immune deficiency, results are generally good. Because the host's immune function is absent in this disorder, successful "takes," or acceptance of the marrow transplant, are the rule. For aplastic anemia, a disorder in which the bone marrow does not produce sufficient red blood cells, hemoglobin, and other blood components, a recent survey from the International Bone Marrow Transplant Registry indicated that among 116 evaluable patients from 1975 to 1979, 76% showed evidence of graft acceptance. Success was favored in patients who received pretreatment immunosuppression with combined chemotherapy and radiation or chemotherapy and antilymphocyte serum, in comparatively young patients, and in patients with little or no exposure to blood products prior to transplant. Interestingly, the use of donor marrow from males rather than from females produced better results. GVH disease occurred in 52% of the patients, and the one-year survival rate was a disappointing 44%.

The results are similar for acute leukemia patients. The additional problem of management of the leukemia, however, led to a much lower survival rate owing to relapse of the disease. Many of these patients were referred to transplantation centers only when their original disease had failed to respond to chemotherapy. Of scientific importance is the observation that normal donor cells may transform into leukemia cells in the leukemia recipient.

Future prospects

Presently bone marrow transplantation is far from being an answer to the difficult problem of management of a patient with bone marrow failure. Current research is directed toward developing immunologic manipulations that improve the rate of graft acceptance as well as decrease the incidence of GVH reactions.

Another approach under current investigation is the harvesting and storing of a cancer patient's own marrow stem cells, to be returned to the patient following administration of large doses of chemotherapy or radiation therapy. This method permits the patient to receive more intense anticancer therapy than would be tolerated normally.

In spite of the lack of spectacular clinical success, one significant benefit of marrow transplant research has been the development of better support measures for immune-suppressed patients. Another benefit has been an increased understanding of various immune reactions and of immune "tolerance" of tumors.

—Hau C. Kwaan, M.D.

Diet and Nutrition

The three major nutrients required by the body are carbohydrate, protein, and fat. Although all three can be used as fuel, carbohydrate is the most available and the body's preferred source of energy—fats are more complex and do not metabolize efficiently in the absence of carbohydrates, proteins are needed for tissue growth and repair, and the burning of either leaves waste products that increase the work of the kidneys. One gram of carbohydrate can be converted by the body to energy equaling four calories. A small quantity of carbohydrate is stored in the liver in the form of glycogen and is available, when needed, as a rapidly mobilized reserve form of energy. Somewhat more is stored in muscle in a similar form for use during heavier exercise. If more carbohydrate than necessary is eaten, the excess will be converted to fat and stored in the body as a long-term energy reserve. Too much carbohydrate, like too much fat, can lead to obesity.

Simple and complex carbohydrates

A carbohydrate is composed of varying amounts of single sugar molecules called monosaccharides, all of which contain six atoms of carbon, twelve atoms of hydrogen, and six atoms of oxygen. The three most important monosaccharides in the carbohydrates humans consume are glucose, fructose, and galactose. They differ from each other in the arrangement of their carbon, hydrogen, and oxygen atoms, but the body can convert one into another. Very little of our total carbohydrate intake is consumed in the form of monosaccharides. A notable exception is the sugar in many fruits, which is in the form of fructose; recently, fructose from corn sugar has been used as a sweetening agent in certain processed foods.

The "sugar" in the sugar bowl is really sucrose, which is a complex of two monosaccharides, glucose and fructose, and is therefore called a disaccharide. During the process of digestion, the sucrose molecule is split into its constituent monosaccharides, and the glucose and fructose are absorbed into the body separately. Another carbohydrate consumed in the form of a disaccharide is milk sugar, or lactose, the primary carbohydrate in milk, cheese, and other dairy products. Lactose is broken down in the intestines to its constituent monosaccharides, glucose and galactose.

The great bulk of carbohydrate in the natural food supply is in the form of starches (polysaccharides), complex molecules made up of hundreds and sometimes thousands of monosaccharides in long chains, often with numerous branches. Certain of these large branching molecules can be systematically disassembled in the gastrointestinal tract and broken down to their constituent monosaccharides, which are then absorbed. The starches from many grains (*e.g.,* corn, wheat, rice) as well as from certain tubers (*e.g.,* potato, sweet potato, cassava) are digested and utilized in this manner.

Other types of complex carbohydrates cannot be broken down in the human gastrointestinal tract (although they can be in the gastrointestinal tracts of other animals) and hence pass through the human tract in an undigested form. These carbohydrates are

Sidney Harris

called fiber. They come from the bran of certain grains and from certain vegetables that contain cellulose and hemicellulose (*e.g.,* celery, raw leafy vegetables, bean sprouts), and from fruits. Although dietary fiber does not supply any nutrients it is a very important and often overlooked component of the diet.

Refined carbohydrates

By definition any carbohydrate, whether refined or in the natural state, supplies only one nutrient, energy. In fact all are eventually converted into a single molecule, glucose, within the body. It is the glucose circulating in the blood that is utilized by the various tissues as their primary energy source. For the brain, except under special circumstances, it is the only energy source.

The difference between a refined and a natural carbohydrate is the availability of other nutrients, vitamins and minerals and sometimes even protein, that are present in the natural product along with the carbohydrate and that are often removed in the refining process. For example, "brown" rice, the grain with only the husk removed, although mostly carbohydrate in the form of starch, also contains many vitamins and minerals. Polished or refined white rice is devoid of most of these nutrients. The polishing process removes the husk and the bran, wherein most of the nutrients are contained. For people who rely on rice as their staple food, polishing can remove their main source of certain vitamins. The disease beriberi, caused by a deficiency in vitamin B_1 (thiamine), was a major problem in the southern part of the United States at the beginning of this century and has only disappeared as fortification of flour and other foods came into practice. In Southeast Asia, where polished rice is the staple and flour is not fortified, beriberi is still a major health problem.

Today many manufacturers use enriched flour in their products. They have put back some of the nutrients removed in the processing. Proponents of using natural grain products argue, justifiably, that research is still discovering essential nutrients and therefore even if the manufacturer puts back all the *known* nutrients that have been removed, something important may have been left out.

Most experts believe the U.S. diet is too high in calories and yet too low in carbohydrate, particularly complex carbohydrate. Americans consume far too much fat, and fat is the most concentrated form of calories (nine calories per gram) in the food supply. For example, the average U.S. diet is 30–40% fat, 15–20% protein, and 40–50% carbohydrate. The average Chinese diet is 10% fat, 10% protein, and 80% carbohydrate. Both countries have set dietary goals of 20–30% fat, 15% protein, and 55–65% carbohydrate.

Dietary fiber

Not all complex carbohydrate can be converted to energy. The fiber in our diet provides bulk without calories and at the same time, during the passage through the gastrointestinal tract, traps water and certain other substances, such as liver bile. The stool becomes looser and can therefore pass through the gastrointestinal tract more rapidly, relieving constipation, a very common and often extremely debilitating problem, especially in older people.

There is some evidence that, by trapping bile salts, fiber may help lower blood cholesterol levels, since cholesterol is excreted into the gastrointestinal tract attached to bile, whence it can be reabsorbed. Since the looser stool moves more rapidly, the walls of the intestines do not need to contract as forcibly and hence the danger of pockets or outpouchings forming at weak spots is less. Such outpouchings, called diverticula, can be very dangerous, especially if they become inflamed (diverticulitis). Finally, the rapid movement of the stool reduces the amount of time that any potentially toxic substances, particularly carcinogens (agents capable of inducing cancer), are in contact with the bowel wall. There is some evidence that a diet that is high in fiber will give protection from cancer of the colon.

Sucrose and tooth decay

Consuming absorbable carbohydrate in the form of starch rather than sucrose offers several advantages. The monosaccharides are released more slowly and hence a more even supply is available to the body. The bulk is greater than with sucrose and hence it is more filling and less likely to lead to overconsumption. Finally, in one area, dental caries, sucrose per se can cause more difficulties than starch.

Tooth decay caused by dental caries (cavities) is a complex disease involving sugar, bacteria, and the enamel of the teeth. Sugar, primarily sucrose, is fermented by certain common mouth bacteria, releasing acid that can erode the enamel of the tooth. These bacteria also utilize the sucrose to manufacture a gummy material called plaque, which adheres to teeth. The acid released by fermentation under the plaque is trapped against the tooth surface, which it slowly erodes down to the soft pulp. The bacteria can then invade the inner areas of the tooth, causing infection and tissue destruction. Thus, sucrose is just one element in the process of cavity formation, but an important one. Even more important than the amount of sucrose consumed is the form the sucrose is in. Sucrose consumed in a vehicle that sticks to the teeth, such as a gum or a sticky candy, is much more potent in its cavity-producing properties than sucrose consumed in a vehicle that can be easily cleared from the mouth. It is the length of time that the sucrose is in contact with the teeth that is crucial.

Lactose is also capable of inducing cavities. For this reason the practice of putting an infant to sleep with a bottle filled either with sucrose and water or with milk-based infant formula (which contains lactose) is very dangerous. The newly erupting teeth are bathed with a constant drip containing a cariogenic (cavity-producing) agent. Rampant tooth decay has been produced in this manner—the so-called nursing bottle syndrome.

Whereas controlling the amount and form of sugar consumed by children can help in the control of dental caries, two other approaches have been more successful: fluoride added to water and toothpaste makes the enamel more resistant to the acid secretions, and good oral hygiene keeps the number of bacteria to a minimum.

Carbohydrate and obesity

Sugar has been accused of contributing to a number of unhealthy conditions. For example, it has been said that people who consume large amounts of sugar are more prone to develop diabetes later in life or that consumption of too much sugar is associated with coronary artery disease. Neither of these statements is supported by the available data. At present the evidence implicates sugar only in the production of dental caries and in obesity, to the extent that it contributes low-bulk, pleasant-tasting calories. Obesity, of course, is a risk factor in both diabetes and coronary artery disease, and hence it is excess calories and not excess sugar per se that is dangerous.

Just as carbohydrate has been wrongly accused of being a cause of obesity, diets high or low in carbohydrate have been wrongly prescribed for the cure of obesity. In the final analysis it is the total number of calories that is important. To the extent that reducing carbohydrates will reduce calories this dietary approach is useful, but marked reduction in carbohydrate alone leaves a diet that is unbalanced—high in fat, relatively high in protein, and low in the minerals and vitamins often found in foods that are high in carbohydrate. Such diets, especially if followed for a long period, can be dangerous. In addition, this abnormal pattern of eating leaves the dieter to his own devices when the "diet" is over. He has not learned to permanently alter his eating habits.

The lactose deficiency syndrome

The carbohydrate in milk, lactose, can also cause difficulties in a large percentage of the adult population. All infants and young children have an enzyme in their intestines capable of breaking the disaccharide lactose into its two monosaccharides, glucose and galactose.

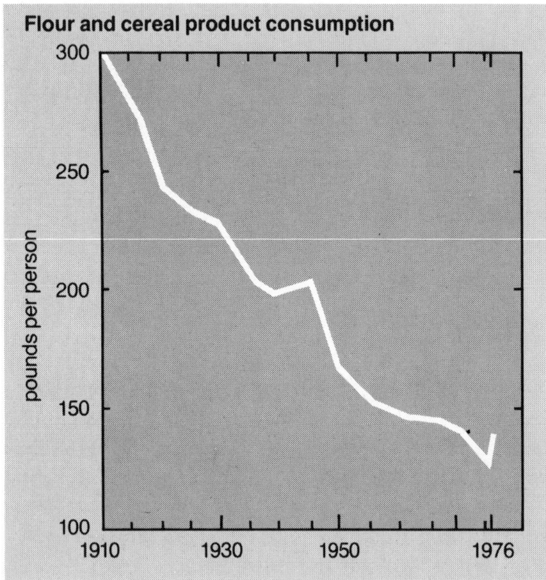

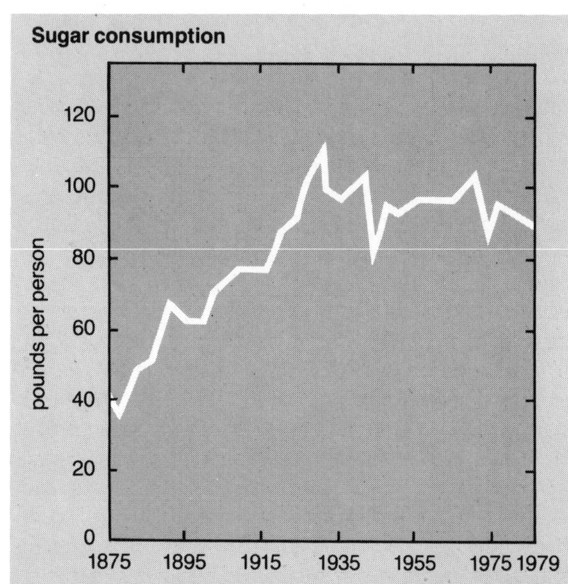

USDA

Richard Younker

Carbohydrate loading is a common practice of marathon runners. Based on the rationale that carbohydrates are the most efficient fuel for muscles during vigorous exercise, the training runner cuts out carbohydrates for several days to deplete the muscles of glycogen. He then eats starchy and sugary foods such as pasta, breads, and ice cream for three days prior to the race to superload muscles with glycogen. This kind of carbohydrate loading is considered to be of only limited usefulness for occasional endurance events.

In most people, with the exception of Western Europeans and their descendants, this enzyme becomes much less active in older children and adults. Thus, many blacks, Asians, and other populations will have trouble tolerating large amounts of milk and certain milk products. In some very sensitive people even one glass of milk can set off a chain of symptoms, including abdominal pain, gas, and diarrhea. Such people usually learn quickly to avoid milk, cream, and other products containing large quantities of lactose.

Carbohydrate loading and athletes

Recently there has been a great emphasis on athletics, particularly the type of athletics that involves long-term stamina, such as marathon running. Some athletes have been using a carbohydrate-loading diet to help them prepare for a competitive event. Such a diet begins in a period of about three days, a week before the event, during which training continues and carbohydrate intake is restricted. This is done to deplete the muscles of all glycogen, the storage form of carbohydrate, and leaves them in a state of readiness to store glycogen rapidly. During the next three days the athlete eats a high-carbohydrate diet—pasta, bread, cakes, and so forth. This is supposed to provide excess carbohydrate, which is taken up rapidly by the glycogen-hungry muscles and stored in the form of readily available glycogen. Thus, at the beginning of the competition the body has available the maximum amount of glycogen for providing rapid and sustained energy.

This approach has a certain amount of merit. There is no doubt that glycogen is the first line of energy defense and can be rapidly mobilized and released when the body's demands are high. The actual carbohydrate load, therefore, is beneficial. The preload restriction is more controversial, based mostly on theoretical considerations and on a few scientific studies. Although previous muscle-glycogen depletion may result in slightly more glycogen storage than simply consuming large quantities of carbohydrate without previously depleting the body's glycogen supply, the restriction phase is unpleasant and may weaken the athlete. Some competitors, therefore, are simply using a two- to three-day precompetition high-carbohydrate diet. Furthermore, carbohydrate stored in muscle is not the only fuel utilized by the body during a sustained effort—half the body's energy needs come from the metabolization of fatty acids.

Following a high-carbohydrate diet on a long-term basis, especially during training, is not recommended. During training one of the most important aims is to build strength in the muscles, particularly those muscles that will bear the major stress of the competitive event. To do this protein is required, because only protein can provide the amino acids necessary to build new muscle tissue and to repair worn muscle tissue. Thus, a long-term training diet, while relatively high in carbohydrate, should also be high in protein. This is not difficult in absolute terms, since the athlete in training must consume large amounts of calories to cover the huge expenditure of energy. Since heavy training cannot be continued during the carbohydrate-loading phase since the glycogen deposited in the liver will be burned up in the training, the carbohydrate-loading diet is useful only when the training can be interrupted before an event. For example, whereas this might work for marathon runners it would not be effective for basketball or soccer players, who compete several times per week. Since most sports do not have extremely long periods between competitions, the carbohydrate-loading diet has at best limited usefulness.

—Myron Winick, M.D.

Special Report: Vegetarianism

by Noel W. Solomons, M.D.

The resurgence of consciousness about nutrition and diet has led to an examination, from a global perspective, of meat consumption in the U.S. and other Western countries. The average per capita consumption of red meat, poultry, and fish in the U.S. in 1979 was nearly 265 lb. Argentina is famous for its consumption of beef, the world's highest per capita; there the grilled steak, *churrasco,* takes on the proportions of a minor religion. In decades past, the Eskimo diet was composed almost exclusively of meat and fish.

It has often been argued on biological grounds that by nature man was meant to be a meat-eater. Prehistoric cave paintings have given us a romantic view of early man as a hunter-trapper, gorging himself with large quantities of game after a successful catch, discarding the well-picked bones by the fire, and fasting until the next hunt. To provide a more factual picture, the fossilized teeth of Paleolithic man have been examined. The stress impressions on the molars suggest that the principal source of calories was not meat, but rather roots, fruits, and nuts. Although the record of the mundane activities of gathering these foods may not have been painted on the walls of his caves, it has been etched in the enamel of the teeth of prehistoric man, and tells us that the caveman was to a large extent a vegetarian.

Still today, the majority of the world's population does not have access to abundant supplies of animal protein, which, in this context, signifies the flesh or organs of meat, fish, or fowl, but not dairy products or eggs. Animal protein is either unavailable or priced beyond the reach of the majority of the people. It constitutes so little of the dietary intake in most less developed countries that much of the world is de facto vegetarian. In Lebanon, the average yearly intake of meat is about 11 lb per capita. In some regions, this vegetarianism has been formalized; the Hindu and Jain religions proscribe the consumption of meat, and this practice is widely adhered to. Thus, in the global and historical perspective, the meat-eaters in the prosperous industrialized countries of today represent a minority of the world's population and constitute an exception in the long history of the human species.

Vegetarianism in Western societies

Since meat is relatively abundant and generally affordable in the West, the exclusion of meat from the diet represents a conscious choice for moral, esthetic, or dietary reasons. Traditionally, vegetarian practices have been observed by some religious or philosophic groups. The Trappist monks, as an expression of humility and discipline, observe an austere dietary regimen which eliminates meats and emphasizes grains and fruits. Most strict adherents of the Seventh-day Adventist Church do not consume the flesh of animals. Members of a movement originating in England, the vegans, abhor the use of any product derived from living, sentient beings. Their diet is exclusively of plant origin. No milk (other than human breast milk) nor eggs are permitted. From similar ethical considerations, clothing articles of leather or fur are also spurned.

In the latter half of the 20th century a new wave of vegetarianism has arisen in the United States and other Western countries. In the early 1970s, the U.S. was confronted by numerous manifestations of dissent in its youth; from this caldron of social and political protest and expressions of alternative life-styles emerged what nutritionist Johanna Dwyer and others were to designate the "new vegetarians." The incentives and motivations for vegetarianism in this new wave were various. Some were derived from philosophical underpinnings in the teaching of yoga or in the Zen macrobiotic movement founded by Georges Ohsawa and popularized in the West in the 1970s.

Many more, however, adopted vegetarian practices from ethical concerns related to gentleness and nonviolence. Explicit health concerns were also important. The notion that meat, because it comes from animals dying in terror in the slaughterhouses, was injurious to health became popular. The new vegetarians also expressed concern about the use of hormones and antibiotics in animal feeds and about excessive concentrations of pesticides, heavy metals, and other toxic substances in animal tissue. For some, the motivation for vegetarianism was political and environmental. Many were impressed by the oft-quoted figure that 16 pounds of grain are required to produce one pound of beef. Frances Moore Lappé's *Diet for a Small Planet,* a vegetarian handbook published in 1971 (revised 1975), deals explicitly with the environmental issues in the commercial production of meat from livestock. Thus, to a greater or lesser degree, a blend of philosophical-religious precepts and health concerns prompted the adoption of vegetarianism.

The classification of vegetarians

Individuals who exclude all forms of foods derived from sentient organisms are called *vegans.* Their diet is composed exclusively of plant foods. A subgroup of vegans whose diet is based primarily on fruits and nuts are called *fruitarians.* Those who include eggs are called *ovovegetarians;* those who include milk or dairy products are called *lactovegetarians;* those who include both nonflesh forms of animal-derived protein foods are called *ovolactovegetarians.* Still other people reject red meat from game or domestic livestock, but accept fish and seafood (*pescovegetarians*) or fowl (*pollovegetarians*). The latter two are often motivated by the health concerns mentioned above, but cannot be considered vegetarians in the strictest sense of the word.

Potential nutritional liabilities

Vegetarians have been concerned about the quality and quantity of essential nutrients in their diets and about the effects of such a diet on children.

Protein-containing foods are essential to provide amino acids, the chemical building blocks for the manufacture of new proteins for the body's tissues. Of the 22 amino acids in mammalian tissues, 9 cannot be synthesized efficiently from scratch in the human body, but must be provided to the body in food. They constitute the so-called essential amino acids. The ability of a food's protein to adequately supply the metabolism of the human body is dependent not only on the amount of protein present, but also on the composition and relative proportion of the essential amino acids in the food. The balance of essential amino acids in milk or eggs is ideal for utilization by the human body. Meat protein is also of excellent quality.

Some foods of plant origin also have a high content of protein. Beans and other legumes have a protein content of up to 23%, whole grains up to 14%. However, the protein from plant foods does not contain the same ideal proportions of essential amino acids that proteins of animal origin do. (*See* diagram, page 207.) Because of this, strict vegans run the risk of a very low intake of utilizable amino acids from the protein in cereal grains, beans, fruits, and vegetables. This is especially true if the diet is based primarily on one source of calories, such as brown rice.

M. A. Crawford, a British neurochemist and nutritionist, has introduced a new note of concern about the vegetarian's nutrients, one regarding the quality of fats. Crawford conducted research on the biochemistry of brain development, and concluded in a report published in 1975 that the preferred structural fats for membranes in the brain must come to humans preformed from other animals. He has speculated that if "synthetic" meats, milks, cheeses, and butter from isolated vegetable protein ever became dominant, the full potential of human brain development would be jeopardized.

The quality of certain minerals is also inferior in foods of plant origin. Iron from red meat, fish, or fowl, for instance, is absorbed much more readily because of its chemical form. The iron in plants is in the form of an inorganic iron salt. Moreover, certain constituents of plants, such as their fibrous strands, gums, and waxes, and phosphated organic molecules, bind iron in the intestine so that it is not well absorbed. Zinc, another mineral important to human health, appears to be more

(Top) John Colwell—Grant Heilman; (others) Grant Heilman

There are political and environmental as well as nutritional motivations for vegetarianism. The average Westerner eats 1 cow, 7 steers, 36 pigs, 36 sheep, and 550 poultry in his lifetime. Nearly five people could be fed for a lifetime on the amount of plant food necessary to raise these animals.

Table I: **Vegetarian dishes with complete protein**
grains with legumes
rice with lentils
rice with black-eyed peas
peanut butter sandwich
bean taco
macaroni enriched with soy flour
bean soup with toast
falafel (chickpea cake) with pita bread
grains with milk
oatmeal with milk
wheat flakes with milk
rice pudding
pancakes and waffles
breads and muffins made with milk
pizza
macaroni and cheese
cheese sandwich
creamed soup with noodles or rice
quiche
meatless lasagna
granola with milk
legumes with seeds
bean curd with sesame seeds
hummus (chickpea and sesame paste)
bean soup with sesame meal
grains with eggs
rice pudding
kasha (buckwheat groats)
fried rice
oatmeal cookies
quiche
egg-salad sandwich
noodle pudding
french toast
vegetables with milk or eggs
potato salad
mashed potatoes with milk
eggplant parmesan
broccoli with cheese sauce
cream of pumpkin soup
cheese and potato soup
vegetable omelet
scalloped potatoes
spinach salad with sliced egg

available to the body if it comes from animal foods than if derived from plants.

The average amount of nutrients essential to adequate human nutrition has been established by a committee of the Food and Nutrition Board of the National Academy of Sciences. These Recommended Dietary Allowances, or RDA's, specify the amount of essential nutrients that are necessary in the diet of persons of various ages to provide for normal metabolism. Some nutrients are in short supply in vegan diets. It is difficult to meet the recommended intakes of calcium and riboflavin (vitamin B_2) in a diet devoid of flesh, eggs, and milk. Vitamin B_{12} is another critical nutrient. In nature, vitamin B_{12} is synthesized by microorganisms. It is abundant in the liver and other animal tissues, and is present in small quantities in eggs and milk. The only plant foods that provide nutritionally relevant amounts of the vitamin are fermented bean curds and pastes such as Japanese *miso* and Indonesian *tempeh;* the vitamin is synthesized by bacterial action during fermentation. Vegetarians generally have much lower intakes of vitamin B_{12} than meat-eaters, and this is reflected in lower circulating levels of this nutrient in the blood. Deficiency of vitamin B_{12} ultimately leads to anemia and neurological abnormalities, but these conditions are nonetheless extremely rare in practicing vegetarians. A much-cited case of presumed nutritional deficiency of vitamin B_{12} in the totally breast-fed infant of a vegan mother was reported by a team of pediatricians in California in 1978 in *The New England Journal of Medicine.* Other physicians, however, have failed to detect this condition in the progeny of vegetarian mothers. It should be noted that vitamin B_{12} is easily available in fortified nutritional yeast or as vitamin supplements.

The vegetarian practices of some individuals rely heavily on one or two foodstuffs to provide the bulk of the dietary calories. In this circumstance, other nutrients can become severely limited as well. Rickets, a bone disease due to vitamin D deficiency, was diagnosed in 1979 in several infants in Boston who were largely breast-fed by mothers following Zen macrobiotic practices. The weaning food used by orthodox adherents of Zen macrobiotics is called *kokoh,* and consists of sesame seeds, brown rice, aduki beans, and oats in water, a bulky preparation. Considering the limited capacity of an infant's stomach, it is difficult to provide the recommended protein and energy intake with this food. Several cases of severe protein-deficiency syndrome have been seen in babies weaned to *kokoh.* An occasional adult vegetarian has also gotten into serious nutritional trouble on a vegetarian regimen. A report in the *Journal of the American Medical Association* in 1967 described the case of a woman in New York, evaluated at the Cornell Medical College, who developed clinical signs of protein deficiency, scurvy (vitamin C deficiency), and folic acid deficiency anemia on a diet based primarily on boiled rice and sesame seeds. Her regimen was based on the most restrictive diet of the Zen macrobiotic program, and she had subsisted on this diet for eight months. She was admitted to the hospital near death, but responded rapidly to nutritional repletion.

Questions have arisen as to whether vegetarian mothers produce an adequate quality and quantity of breast milk. The problems with bulkiness and low density of protein and other nutrients in vegan-weaning foods is a further cause of concern. These issues prompted a group of public health investigators in Boston, headed by Johanna Dwyer, to monitor the growth of the children of vegetarian mothers—most of whom were adherents of Zen macrobiotics—during the first years of life. Their findings, reported in the *Journal of*

Adapted from "Vegetarianism," CONSUMER REPORTS, pp. 357–365, June, 1980

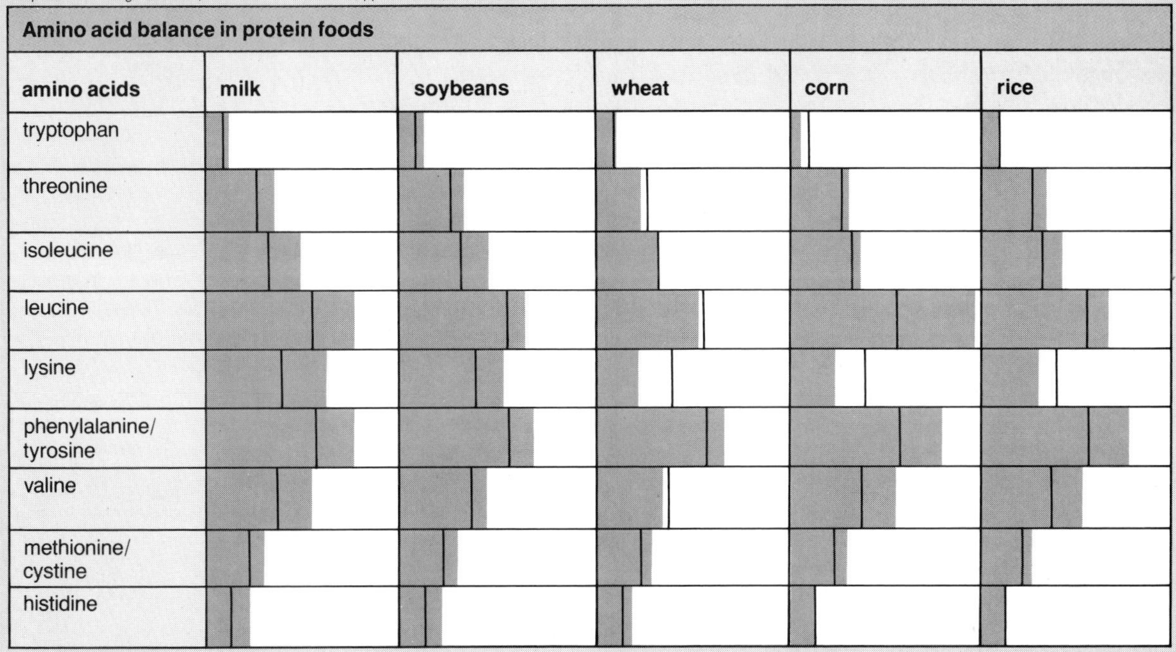

Amino acid balance in protein foods

amino acids	milk	soybeans	wheat	corn	rice
tryptophan					
threonine					
isoleucine					
leucine					
lysine					
phenylalanine/ tyrosine					
valine					
methionine/ cystine					
histidine					

In order to make protein the body requires specific proportions of essential amino acids, which are supplied by foods. Some foods lack certain amino acids. The diagram above superimposes high-quality amino acid levels on the actual levels in five foods. By combining foods, amino acid balance can be adjusted. The lysine missing from rice, for example, can be complemented by the extra lysine in milk.

the American Dietetic Association in 1978, revealed that the infants of vegetarians tended to lag behind the growth curves of their nonvegetarian peers. However, during the third and fourth years of life, vegetarian children actually consumed more calories than a group of nonvegetarian children during the same interval, and caught up with the growth trajectory of their meat-eating peers. Thus, no permanent retardation in growth seemed to be produced in children raised in vegetarian households. Nonetheless, it is known from studies of famine victims that severe protein deficiency in the first few years of life results in deficits in brain development that cannot be reversed by later nutritional supplements.

Potential nutritional assets

The body composition of vegetarians tends toward lean tissue, and their body weights are consistently below the accepted standards of weight-for-age. These standards, it should be noted, are based in the United States on a generally overfed population. Changing from a mixed, meat-containing diet to a vegetarian diet almost invariably results in a weight loss. The risk of obesity, therefore, is reduced by following a vegetarian diet.

Studies in the Boston area revealed a considerably lower average blood pressure in members of vegetarian communes, communes largely organized around the teaching of Zen macrobiotics. Similarly, in these same communities, and among adolescent vegetarians in Great Britain, the circulating concentration of blood cholesterol and triglycerides was reduced below the levels commonly seen in meat-eating populations. It should be pointed out, however, that these groups restricted the consumption of eggs and dairy products as well as meat, and were close to being complete vegans. Moreover, the philosophical and religious components of the Zen macrobiotic life-style may explain part of the protection against hypertension.

A predictable consequence of reducing the animal protein in the diet is the substitution of protein sources of plant origin. Adoption of a vegetarian diet invariably results in an increased intake of dietary fiber, the nondigestible roughage components of plants and fruits. Diets rich in fiber have been credited by some physicians, notably British surgeon Denis Burkitt, with preventing diseases of the colon, hemorrhoids, varicose veins, and cardiovascular disease. Fiber holds water in the colon, increases the bulk of stools, and improves bowel function. In fact, bowel cancer incidence may be lower among people with a high fiber consumption; this association, however, might be due as much to absence of meat and animal fat as to dietary enrichment with fiber.

Can vegetarians have adequate nutrition?

Since the scarcity and cost of meat make most of the world's people de facto vegetarians, as previously noted, it then becomes important, in light of the liabilities discussed above, to ask whether vegetarians can have adequate nutritional health. The answer, according to many nutritionists, is an emphatic *yes.*

Several teams of scientists have compared the nutriture of vegetarians and nonvegetarians. M. G. Hardinge and F. J. Stare in 1954 compared the physical and laboratory findings of nonvegetarians, ovolactovegetarians, and vegans in southern California. The status of the red blood cells and serum proteins was comparable in all three groups. The physical health of all groups was equivalent, although the pure vegans weighed an average 20 lb less than members of the other two groups. Essentially similar findings were reported in 1970 in a comparative study of vegans and meat-eating individuals in London.

There is a caveat, however, to the conclusion that vegetarian diets can provide nutritional adequacy. Vegetarians must pay conscious attention to the inclusion of the necessary quality and quantity of nutrients. Useful guides to developing nutritionally balanced vegetarian menus can be found in Lappé's *Diet for a Small Planet* and Laurel Robertson's *Laurel's Kitchen: A Handbook for Vegetarian Cookery and Nutrition* (1976). Both of these books focus on the central issue of protein quality. As noted earlier, foods of plant origin tend to be deficient in one or another essential amino acid; but, by combining foods in a vegetarian diet in such a way that the relative deficit of a given amino acid in the protein of one item is covered by a relative excess in another, the quality of the protein in a meal is markedly enhanced. This approach to balancing amino acids in vegetarian diets is called *complementation* of proteins. Beans, for instance, have a relative deficiency of the essential amino acid methionine, but an excess of lysine; in corn, the situation is reversed. Thus, if one combines these two foods at a meal—as is common in the bean and tortilla diet of southern Mexico and Central America—an overall protein value approaching that of meat or milk can result. There are three basic rules for the complementation of proteins: combine legumes (dried beans and peas, and peanuts) with grains; combine legumes with nuts and seeds; combine dairy products or eggs with any vegetable protein. Table I on page 206 lists some familiar foods that provide complete protein for vegan or ovolactovegetarian diets.

Milk and dairy products represent an outstanding source of dietary calcium. Thus, sufficient calcium intake is a concern for vegans and ovovegetarians. An Ethiopian grain, teff, and the lime-treated corn used in tortillas are excellent sources of calcium in a vegetarian diet, as are green, leafy vegetables, soybeans, molasses, almonds, and dried fruits.

The absorbability of iron and zinc are reduced by the natural binding substances in plants. Iron absorption can be enhanced by consuming foods high in vitamin C, such as peppers or citrus fruits, and by preparing meals in iron cookware. The zinc content of wheat grains is high. Thus, despite the inhibitory factors, large amounts of whole grains can provide sufficient zinc to the body. Leavening of baked goods made from whole grains tends to free zinc for intestinal absorption. There is evidence that over the long haul the intestinal cells of most vegetarians adjust to extract more zinc from the diet.

In 1973, consultants to the United States Department of Agriculture put together a sample menu for a vegan male that would provide 100% of the RDA's, except for vitamin B_{12}, to an adult. This combination of foods is shown above in Table II. Similarly, for children, considerable attention has been given to the composition of nutritionally sound vegetarian diets. Vegetarian cookbooks such as those mentioned above provide a great deal of information on menu planning and food preparation. Anyone contemplating the adoption of a vegetarian diet for a family should become thoroughly familiar with the nutritional requirements of persons of various ages, and should be aware of possible pitfalls. With careful attention and planning, the vegetarian family can enjoy a diet that is nutritious, varied, tasty, and environmentally sound.

Table II: **Menu for an adult male vegan**

breakfast	
orange	1 medium
bulgur	1 cup
with brewer's yeast	1 tablespoon
toasted wheat-soy bread	1 slice
with honey	1 tablespoon
morning snack	
shelled almonds	¼ cup
lunch	
split pea soup	2 cups
peanut butter sandwich:	
peanut butter	2 tablespoons
whole wheat bread	2 slices
honey	1 tablespoon
fruit-sunflower seed salad:	
apple	½ medium
banana	½ medium
sunflower seeds	¼ cup
lettuce	1 leaf
afternoon snack	
peach	1 medium
dinner	
soybeans	1 cup
brown rice, cooked	1 cup
fried in oil	2 tablespoons
with chestnuts	2 tablespoons
with sesame seeds	2 tablespoons
collards	1 cup
pear	1 medium
evening snack	
raisins	¼ cup

Nutrition Program News, U.S. Department of Agriculture, Washington, D.C., July/August, 1973

Drugs and Vaccines

Every year about a hundred new drugs and vaccines are approved for use by the U.S. Food and Drug Administration. Some are only slightly different from products that were available previously; these may offer some new advantage, such as fewer side effects, a longer duration of action that permits fewer doses each day, or perhaps just a lower cost. Only a few of the year's new drugs offer promise of important gains in the prevention or treatment of disease. The new drugs and vaccines discussed below include some in each category.

A new estrogen

In 1980 Parke, Davis & Co., Detroit, Mich., marketed a new synthetic estrogen tablet for menopausal women that can be taken just once a week. During menopause many women suffer uncomfortable symptoms due to the waning production of estrogens, a group of female reproductive hormones, by the ovaries at this time of life. The most common symptoms, and those most definitely due to a lack of estrogens, are hot flushes of the skin and vaginal discomfort caused by the sudden aging of the lining of the vagina. Many women also become depressed during menopause; it has not been established whether this depression is due as well to a lack of estrogens or is secondary to the abrupt awareness of aging, physical discomfort, and sexual problems that can result from vaginal pain and itching. All of these symptoms can be relieved by taking estrogens. Consequently, prescribing of estrogen replacement at menopause has been very widespread.

Unfortunately estrogen replacement therapy has some serious drawbacks. Estrogens, which are also one of the main ingredients in oral contraceptives, can cause vaginal bleeding, nausea, breast tenderness, and generalized swelling (edema). More importantly, many authorities now believe that estrogen replacement therapy may increase the risk of developing cancer of the uterus, and the risk seems to be greater with longer use of higher doses. The degree of risk has varied in different studies, but one group of scientists estimated that women who take estrogens have 5–14 times greater risk of developing cancer of the uterus, depending on the duration of use. The main advantage of Parke-Davis's new long-acting estrogen, which is called Estrovis, is the convenience of not having to take pills every day. There is no good reason, however, to believe that this estrogen product will be safer than any other. Consequently doctors and their patients need to weigh the benefits against the possible hazards before such drugs are prescribed.

Premature childbirth preventative

Premature birth is the major cause of death in infancy. Prematurity can also cause disabling neurological handicaps such as cerebral palsy and mental retardation. It is still not known exactly what sequence of events makes the normal uterus begin to contract after nine months of pregnancy, nor is it known why in some pregnancies the contractions begin too early. What is known is that the infant has a better chance of surviving if premature labor can be stopped and the delivery postponed.

The traditional treatment for early labor has been bed rest, which is often effective. In the last 15 years physicians have also learned that alcohol can prevent or delay premature labor. Alcohol prevents the brain from releasing a hormone that causes the uterus to contract. Unfortunately one or two martinis are not adequate for this purpose. An alcohol solution given intravenously provides a good chance of stopping labor. This much alcohol leads to an unpleasant degree of inebriation that causes severe nausea and vomiting in the pregnant woman and can seriously affect the infant as well.

Recently a drug for stopping early labor called ritodrine hydrochloride, or by its brand name, Yutopar, was introduced by Merrell-National Laboratories, Cincinnati, Ohio. Like alcohol, ritodrine can be given intravenously, although it is also available in tablets, and so far the new drug appears to be at least as effective as alcohol. In one study labor was postponed for an average of 44 days when women in early labor were treated with ritodrine. But like so many useful drugs ritodrine has some unpleasant side effects. Rapid heartbeat, trembling, headache, nausea, and vomiting occur frequently in patients treated with the drug, and more serious complications can occur in some situations when other drugs must also be used or when the mother has a serious illness.

Marijuana in cancer therapy

Many types of cancer can now be treated with drugs. Some types can be cured by drugs; in others, chemotherapy can produce temporary improvement and prolong life. Many anticancer drugs, however, cause such severe side effects that patients cannot tolerate the doses that are needed for optimal therapeutic effect. Probably the most common of the dose-limiting side effects from cancer chemotherapy is severe nausea and vomiting, which can go on for days without relief. Some patients who have experienced these severe symptoms refuse to go on taking the drugs that cause them, even though they know that the drugs can prolong their lives. Commercially available antiemetic (antivomiting) drugs are often not effective. Recently a number of reports in medical journals have suggested that marijuana can relieve nausea and vomiting in some patients who do not respond to antiemetics.

Although the first indication that marijuana has an antiemetic effect probably came from cancer patients who smoked marijuana, most of the scientific studies

James Nachtwey—Black Star

Lynn Pierson, who died of cancer in 1978, was a strong advocate of making marijuana available to cancer patients to combat the nausea and vomiting caused by chemotherapy.

investigating this effect used capsules containing delta-9-tetrahydrocannabinol (THC), the main active ingredient of marijuana. For these studies marijuana, mainly in the form of THC capsules, was distributed by the U.S. National Cancer Institute to cancer treatment centers as an investigational new drug.

Studies on cancer patients showed that some patients with severe nausea and vomiting that were not helped by other antiemetic drugs (such as Compazine) obtained relief from THC. In some cases a "high" accompanied the antiemetic effect. In older patients, however, particularly those who had no previous experience with marijuana, THC was often no more effective than conventional antiemeticdrugs, and some patients found the side effects of THC more unpleasant.

The most common side effect of THC is drowsiness, which can be marked enough to be disabling. Some patients complain of dry mouth, dizziness, inability to concentrate, and confusion. Less commonly THC causes rapid heartbeat, fearfulness, hallucinations, and irrational behavior.

New rabies vaccine

Rabies is among the most relentlessly fatal of diseases. It is caused by a virus carried in the saliva of infected animals and migrates from the site of a bite along nerve trunks to the central nervous system. Until recently rabies was fatal in every single case ever diagnosed throughout recorded medical history. In the 1970s a child with rabies became the first known survivor, not owing to any particular medical advance but owing partly to the superb physical condition that young school-age children are blessed with and partly to extraordinary nursing care with heroic use of respirators, intravenous fluids, and a galaxy of drugs used to support vital functions in persons on the brink of death. Yet, in spite of this inspiring case, most physicians would consider the earliest symptoms of rabies to be tantamount to a firm sentence of death, and a very unpleasant death at that.

Although rabies cannot be treated, it can be prevented, even after exposure to the bite of an infected animal. One of the most dramatic advances in medical history was Louis Pasteur's discovery that rabies virus was so modified by passage in animals that it could be injected into people without causing symptoms and would protect them against the disease, even after being bitten by a rabid animal. Live-virus vaccines similar to Pasteur's are still used to inoculate animals. Rabies vaccines for human use, however, are made with inactivated (killed) virus prepared in animals or in laboratory cultures of animal cells.

Vaccines prepared from nerve tissue taken from rabies-infected sheep or rabbits, which are still used in some countries, can cause in recipients a high incidence of neurological side effects, including a life-threatening encephalitis (inflammation of the brain). Duck embryo vaccine, the preparation recommended until recently by the U.S. Public Health Service, frequently causes pain, inflammation, and swelling at the site of injection, and sometimes vomiting and fever; severe allergic reactions can also occur in a small percentage of people. In addition, duck embryo vaccine must be given in 23 separate injections, one day at a time—a horrendous procedure for young children, who are often the recipients of bites from animals of undetermined health. Moreover, some people who received all 23 doses, starting shortly after being bitten, nevertheless went on to develop rabies.

The new vaccine, which is called human diploid cell rabies vaccine (HDCV), is prepared from virus grown in laboratory cultures of human cells. Because it is prepared in human cells, it contains much less foreign protein than any previously available vaccine and therefore is much less likely to cause unpleasant or severe reactions in recipients. Consequently much larger amounts of antigen (the part of the virus that confers immunity by provoking the recipient's immune system to produce protective antibody) can be injected at once, and fewer injections are needed. The new vaccine requires a maximum of only six doses. The absence of side effects and the need for fewer doses are important because even though rabies is a rare disease in the U.S., each year 20,000 to 30,000 people are treated with rabies vaccine because of contacts with animals that might have been rabid.

In spite of its safety and convenience, the new vaccine could not be accepted for widespread use until its ability to protect against rabies was proven in the field. Such a test, or clinical trial, could not be done in the U.S. because of the disease's rarity. In 1979 only five people contracted rabies in the U.S., and in 1980, for the first time ever, no human cases were reported at all. Rabies, however, can resemble other diseases, and all cases are not diagnosed. One of the 1979 cases occurred in a patient who received a corneal transplant taken from a donor who had died of undiagnosed rabies. The paucity of cases of human rabies in the U.S. is due mainly to a sharply decreased incidence of the disease in domestic animals, even though the incidence in wild animals has increased. In the U.S. rabies now occurs most often in skunks, raccoons, foxes, coyotes, bobcats, and bats.

Field trials of the new vaccine were conducted in West Germany and Iran, where rabies is still fairly common in rural areas. The vaccine was given, in most cases together with rabies antiserum, to a total of 86 people bitten by dogs or wolves with proven rabies; none of these people developed any sign of rabies. In the U.S., since the new vaccine has been available, no one treated with it after being bitten by a rabid animal has developed the disease. All the evidence to date suggests that this vaccine is an important advance in controlling one of the most feared of all diseases.

A new drug for pain

Zomepirac sodium, which is sold by prescription as Zomax by McNeil Pharmaceutical, Spring House, Pa., is an interesting new pain reliever that became available in the past year. It is one of a relatively new class of drugs called nonsteroidal anti-inflammatory analgesics, which are used particularly for treatment of arthritis but also for other types of pain. Zomepirac has been studied more extensively as a pain reliever than the other drugs in this group, but the others may prove to be similar in their effects.

This new analgesic appears to be more effective than aspirin and free of the addicting properties that limit the use of morphine and other narcotics. The effectiveness of "ordinary" aspirin is commonly underestimated, and much attention is given to drugs popularly considered to be "stronger" pain relievers. Among the better known ones are propoxyphene (Darvon), acetaminophen (Tylenol and other brand names), pentazocine (Talwin), oxycodone (Percodan), codeine, and meperidine (Demerol). Nevertheless, it has not been established that any of these taken in tablet form are more effective than two aspirin tablets. All can cause unpleasant side effects, including addiction, and

"Have you ever noticed that everything in this household is 'extra-strength'?"

some are prominent in the drug culture as drugs of abuse.

The most effective drug available for relief of pain is morphine given by injection. For the most severe types of pain, such as heart attacks or kidney stones, nothing can equal an adequate dose of morphine. For moderate pain, however, orally taken zomepirac appears to be superior to aspirin and comparable to low doses of injected morphine. In patients with fractures and in those who had undergone surgery, zomepirac was equal or superior to aspirin, codeine, pentazocine, and other oral analgesics and as effective as small injections of morphine. If these first results are confirmed when the drug is widely used in the general population (something which often does not happen), zomepirac and possibly the other analgesics of the same type would represent an important medical advance.

Like all drugs, zomepirac has side effects and, like all new drugs, the frequency and severity of these effects are difficult to determine without wide use and at least a few years of observation. The most frequent side effect appears to be gastrointestinal discomfort similar to that occasionally induced by aspirin; generally these symptoms are mild, but sometimes severe bleeding can occur. Like some other analgesic drugs, zomepirac has been implicated as a possible cause of serious kidney damage. Whether the drug is actually the cause of such damage and, if so, how often damage occurs remain to be determined. All studies to date have given no indication that zomepirac has any addicting properties. That claim, however, has been made in the past for many other drugs that subsequently proved to be addicting. Both the safety and effectiveness of zomepirac will be determined by long-term use.

—Mark Abramowicz, M.D.

Special Report: The Placebo Effect

by Louis A. Morris, Ph.D.

Physicians have an amazing array of pharmacologic therapies at their disposal to cure, control, prevent, or alleviate a wide range of diseases and conditions. In part, these drugs work because they directly induce chemical changes inside our bodies; in part, they work because of psychological changes induced by our knowing that we have taken a drug. The psychological effects of drug use are commonly referred to as placebo effects.

Although the term placebo was once used to refer only to an inert substance, such as a sugar pill, research and clinical experience have shown that active drugs also have psychological, or placebo effect, components. For example, the tranquilizer Valium, when used to treat schizophrenia, acts as a placebo because it has no specific pharmacologic effect on this condition. Of course, if the dosage of any active drug is high enough, the pharmacologic effects will dominate the placebo effects, and extremely high dosages of most drugs will produce severe toxicity or even death. To minimize toxic effects, physicians prescribe drugs at the lowest possible therapeutic dose. At this level placebo effects are common and sometimes are essential for drug therapy.

Many treatments of the past, such as bloodletting, were primitive, unscientific, and dangerous. But, owing to the placebo effect, they often worked.

The Bettmann Archive, Inc.

In a common classroom demonstration a group of medical students is given either a placebo or a mood-altering drug. Each student is then asked to guess which drug he or she received. Invariably, the results of their guesses are no more accurate than if they had merely flipped a coin.

Claims about the importance of the placebo effect range from its being a "small treatment for small illnesses" to "the most powerful drug ever produced by the pharmaceutical industry." While many physicians deny that they intentionally make use of placebo treatments, placebo effects have been demonstrated in dentistry, podiatry, ophthalmology, and every branch of medicine including cancer treatment, surgery, and psychotherapy. Placebos have been shown to be addictive, to produce serious side effects, to mimic the effects of active drugs, to reverse the action of potent medicines, and to directly affect brain chemistry, bodily organs, and organic illness.

To appreciate the importance of placebo effects in modern medicine, one need only look back in history. The history of medicine is largely the history of the placebo effect.

By and large, treatments that are actually useful and effective have been available only within the last few decades. In prescientific times, treatments were primitive, largely ineffective, and sometimes dangerous. Patients took almost every known organic and inorganic substance—crocodile dung, teeth of swine, hooves of asses, eunuch fat, fly specks, lozenges of dried vipers, powder of precious stones, bricks, fur, feathers, human perspiration, oil of ants, earthworms, wolves, and spiders. Blood from every known animal was prepared and administered to treat every conceivable symptom. Throughout medical history, patients were purged, puked, poisoned, punctured, cut, cupped, blistered, bled, lesioned, leeched, frightened, frozen, sweated, and shocked.

For thousands of years, physicians prescribed what we now know were useless and sometimes dangerous medications. The survival of medicine as a discipline would have been impossible were it not for the fact that physicians must have helped their patients in some way. Today we know that the efficacy of many prescientific medicines was due to their placebo effect. However, we also wonder how these procedures and substances could have had curative effects. The answer to this question holds great significance for the practice of modern medicine.

The Bettmann Archive, Inc.

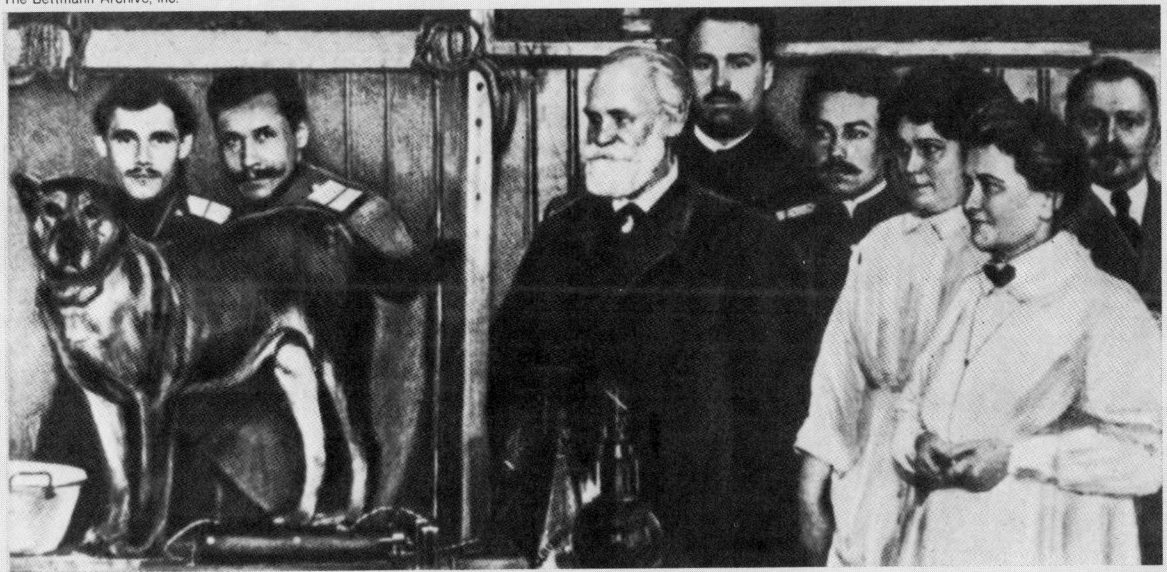

In the late 19th century Russian physiologist Ivan Pavlov demonstrated the placebo effect in dogs. He injected them with morphine, which induced salivation, urination, and vomiting. Soon the dogs began to react before *they were injected when Pavlov merely approached with a syringe.*

Why study placebo effects?

The placebo effect rose to importance during the 1940s, when there was a burgeoning of drug research. Scientists testing to see whether new drugs were effective found that placebo effects created methodological problems. How could a researcher know whether a chemical caused a therapeutic effect if psychological processes caused the same result? Thus, most early investigations of placebo effects were done for the purpose of controlling or eliminating their occurrence. More recently, scientists have studied the placebo phenomena to better understand why, and under what conditions, they occur.

It is important for patients and physicians to recognize the potency of placebo effects for two reasons. First, unless the omnipresence of the placebo effect is acknowledged, patients and physicians may mistakenly attribute a therapeutic benefit to a worthless medicine. This both hinders the development of useful medicines and leads patients and physicians to use placebos (which at best are only partially effective) when active and effective treatments could be administered instead.

For this reason the U.S. government requires that new drugs entering the marketplace first undergo thorough testing. Comparisons are made between two randomly assigned groups; one receives an active test drug, the other a placebo. This procedure ensures that any differences between the groups are due to pharmacologic and not placebo effects.

The second reason for studying the placebo effect is that once the underlying psychological mechanisms are understood, these mechanisms can be applied to treat patients, but only when they are apt to be effective. For example, one of the psychological mechanisms of the placebo effect is operant conditioning, the influencing of behavior by positive or negative reinforcement. This process in now utilized by psychotherapists in the form of behavior modification. It allows certain patients to forgo the risks and side effects of taking potent psychotropic medications.

Who reacts to placebos?

Early investigations found that a fairly constant 30 to 40% of the patients given placebos reacted to them. This consistency led scientists to postulate that certain people were "placebo reactors" and others were "nonreactors." If placebo reactors could be identified, they could then be excluded from drug research studies. This would make the studies more sensitive to actual chemical effects. Additionally, placebo reactors could forgo drug treatment by using less risky placebo therapy.

Subsequent research showed a much broader range of placebo reactions than had been previously recorded. When measured under differing conditions, the number of people reacting to placebos varies from 0 to nearly 100%. Further, people who react to placebos under some conditions do not necessarily react the same way at other times or under other conditions. Most experts now reject the idea that there is a group of individuals who consistently react to placebos solely as a result of some innate factor.

Recently, however, an important experiment dealing with the chemistry of pain perception has caused researchers to revive the theory that certain individuals are indeed placebo reactors, at least when it comes to placebo analgesia.

Because the range of placebo reactions varies so widely, there has been a search for factors that would predict placebo effects. Two types of predispositions to being a placebo reactor have been postulated: general predispositions that exert their influence under a wide variety of conditions, and specific predispositions that become associated with placebo effects only in certain environments.

The search for general predispositions has not been fruitful. Studies have yielded conflicting results on whether age, sex, or intelligence are significant factors. The most extensively studied personality variable is "suggestibility." If it is assumed that reacting to a placebo is merely a manifestation of an individual's general suggestibility, then it would logically follow that suggestibility would correlate positively with placebo reaction. However, this has not been borne out by research. Similarly, other personality traits correlate positively in some studies but not in others.

This lack of success in isolating general factors is probably due to the multitude of ways in which placebo effects are measured, and highlights the complexity of the phenomena. Given such a poor field record, many researchers have turned away from searching for personality characteristics and have focused on specific predispositions and situational factors.

The patient's belief in the ability of his physician to heal him can be powerful medicine in itself.

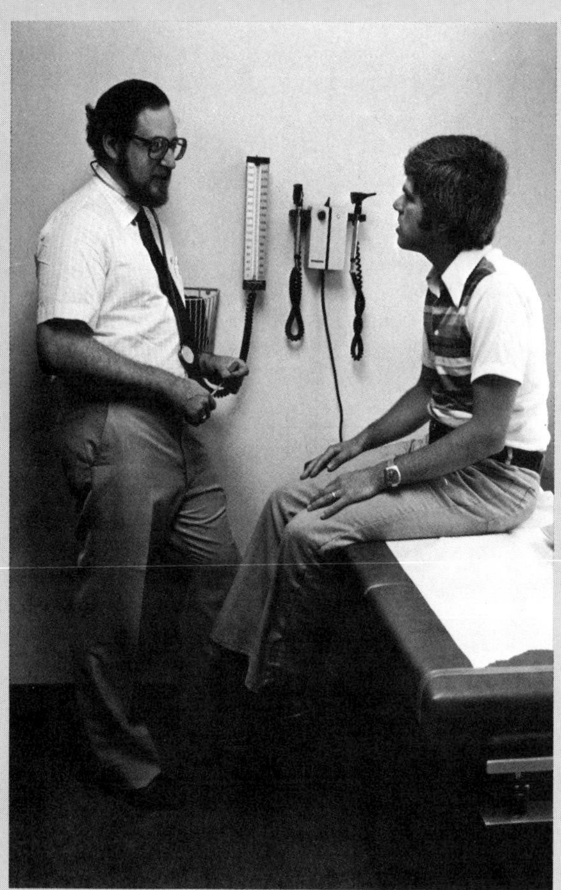

Ken Robert Buck—Stock, Boston

Concepts of placebogenesis

There have been almost as many explanations for the placebo effect as there have been researchers observing it. In general, however, three themes predominate: social influence effects, expectancy effects, and evaluation and interpretation effects.

Social influence effects. The role of physicians in society is unique. They perform and combine functions that have always been important, those of expert, healer, priest, and scientist. Especially to the ill, the physician is among the most powerful individuals in society. In turn, the patient desperately in need of help is severely dependent upon the physician. The special relationship between patient and physician provides the critical elements for "iatroplacebogenesis" (physician-caused placebo effects). Several psychological processes are thought to bear upon socially induced placebo effects.

Although "suggestibility" as a personality trait is not consistently associated with placebo reaction, some theorists view suggestion as a psychological process rather than a personality trait. Studies indicate that there are two separate components of suggestion. Primary suggestion is similar to response under hypnosis, involving direct bodily reaction to the influence of the therapist. Secondary suggestibility depends on the gullibility of the patient. Most studies find placebo effects to be a manifestation of secondary rather than primary suggestibility. According to this view, placebo effects occur when gullible individuals are made to believe that there has been a therapeutic change.

Another significant psychological factor is persuasion. Patients often view physicians as being likable, expert, and trustworthy. These traits are most often associated with the ability to be influential and persuasive. As in the case of suggestion, the social power of the physician is the essential element in this process. Unlike the case of suggestion, however, those reacting to placebos are viewed as rational rather than gullible, because the power of the physician's arguments is stressed, not the yielding of the patient.

The patient is also under pressure to behave in a certain manner. The primary role of the "good patient" is to get well; therefore, the patient who reacts positively to treatment justifies the physician's time, care, and attention.

Physicians communicate role expectations in an overt manner, by simply telling patients what is expected of them. Physicians also communicate covertly, for example, by acting busy or using difficult to understand terms. These cues convey information about appropriate role behavior to the patient. Studies have found that therapeutic benefits are enhanced when the patient and physician hold compatible views of the roles that they are expected to fill.

Experiments conducted by psychologist B. F. Skinner clearly demonstrated that behavior is molded by giving or withholding reinforcement, a process known as operant conditioning. Physicians may deliver rewards by offering encouragement, paying greater attention to the patient's problems, or merely by spending a greater amount of time talking with the patient. The physician may also reinforce certain behavior without intending to do so. A physician who is interested in a rare illness or in completing a study may spend a greater amount of time asking the patient questions about his condition and his response to treatment. The patient may interpret the physician's interest as positive reinforcement.

On the other hand, the physician may withhold rewards from nonresponsive patients or deliver punishments such as inducing fear for failure to follow advice. Operant conditioning effects not only influence the patient's behavior, but they have also been demonstrated to directly affect his physiological responses.

In psychoanalytic theory, transference is an essential ingredient of therapy. The patient forms a special relationship with the therapist and "transfers" unexpressed feelings of love, hate, trust, and mistrust to the therapist. The placebo is viewed as a vehicle that allows the patient to form a dependent relationship with the physician. Positive placebo effects occur when the individual successfully vents internal feelings within the sheltered relationship with an understanding yet powerful physician.

A distinct instance of transference is the process of guilt reduction. Illness appears to propagate guilt reactions in many patients. Some people interpret their illnesses as a sign that they have done something terribly wrong. Impotence, insomnia, and even cancer are examples of conditions that engender these feelings. The physician can reassure patients that their symptoms are signs of illness and not shameful characteristics. Thus, the powerful forces of hope and optimism can be brought to bear. The physician, just like the priest, may serve as confessor and permit patients to shed psychological burdens that foster illness and prevent healing.

Expectancy effects. While establishing special relationships with their patients, physicians communicate their expectations. The uncertainty that patients experience when they are ill causes them to search for any information about their illness, their therapy, and their prognosis. If the physician does not provide adequate information, patients may turn to friends and relatives. Patients may also rely upon their own experiences, ideas, and values to help form clear expectations about what lies ahead for them.

David Austin

GIMME A PLACEBO ON THE ROCKS
Austin

Whereas the learning theory advanced by Skinner stressed the reinforcement of behavior, the theory of classical conditioning, advanced by Russian physiologist Ivan Pavlov, is based upon two events occurring together closely in time. Pavlov himself demonstrated placebo effects in dogs. Initially, when injected with morphine the dogs reacted by salivating, vomiting, and urinating. After repeated injections, the dogs exhibited these reactions when they merely saw Pavlov approach them with a syringe in hand.

Classical conditioning explains the phenomenon of psychogenic vomiting in cancer patients. Some potent cancer drugs induce vomiting as a side effect. After repeated treatments, the side effect occurs once the treatment is taken but before vomiting could possibly be caused by pharmacologic means.

When a person is sick, his belief in the power of his physician or in the therapy he is receiving may be powerfully entrenched. If he does not start to feel better, a state of cognitive dissonance may result. Cognitive dissonance occurs when the individual recognizes the existence of two logically incompatible ideas. Because beliefs such as "the doctor is incompetent" may be unacceptable to the patient's value system, a placebo reaction may be induced to resolve the dissonance.

Anticipation that a drug will produce a physiological effect can lead to the occurrence of that effect. Along with classical conditioning and cognitive dissonance, there are direct methods by which one's beliefs may cause actual bodily state changes. In one classic study, physicians closely monitored the victim of a gunshot wound. Due to the peculiar nature of the wound, the physicians were able to look directly at the stomach lining. They observed that the stomach actually changed color when the patient reacted emotionally.

The most recent evidence for placebo-initiated control of physiological responses is derived from experiments on pain perception. For some people, placebos may trigger the release of endorphins, chemicals produced by the brain that resemble opiate drugs such as heroin. Pain is reduced when our bodies manufacture and release endorphins. In a study of dental patients undergoing molar extraction, a placebo was administered and one hour later patients were treated with a drug (naloxone) that prevents the release of endorphins. For patients who experienced placebo analgesia, the injection of naloxone reversed this analgesic effect, allowing the pain to be felt. Thus, naloxone, which is known to block release of endorphins, also blocked placebo analgesia.

People receiving medical treatment monitor and evaluate their progress by referring to an internally held standard of how the treatment should perform. Some physicians believe that they must emphasize the curative aspects of treatment for placebo effects to function, but overselling a therapy can backfire. In one experiment, insomniacs who were told that a placebo would help them sleep had more trouble than usual in falling asleep. In many cases familiarity with a treatment or a disease leads to more realistic expectations, better internal standards, and less likelihood of a placebo reaction. Thus, placebo effects are more likely to occur when the disease or the treatment is new.

This does not seem to be true, however, of marijuana. Studies of experienced marijuana smokers suggest that they are more likely to experience a "high" when smoking a placebo cigarette than those who have not tried the drug. It appears that some minimal experience is necessary for marijuana placebo effects to occur.

Evaluation and interpretation effects. A third set of conditions that influences placebo effects stem from patients' evaluating their own condition or knowing that they are being evaluated by someone else. Once people know their actions are being measured, they may seek to present themselves in the best possible light, give the most socially desirable answers, or try to please or impress the doctor. Placebo effects induced by response bias are not real therapeutic changes, but are merely artifacts of the evaluation process.

When a person is ill, it may be very difficult for him to interpret his physical reactions. Is a strange sensation in the back of his neck "tension" or is it a "stiff neck"? If he feels that he is under stress he may label the physiological sensation in one way; if he remembers that he slept under an open window he will use the other term. Any potent environmental stimulus will be utilized to help the patient interpret his bodily changes. When the patient has taken a drug, subsequent reactions are likely to be labeled with terms that are consistent with that knowledge.

Positive placebo effects occur when the cause of a change is attributed to therapy when it is actually due to some other factor. For example, people recover spontaneously from numerous illnesses even without therapy. If a drug is taken, the recovery may be attributed to the drug rather than the body's own curative processes.

Negative placebo effects

Placebo effects are often thought of as being entirely positive. However, an early finding of placebo research was that placebos caused negative reactions as well as positive ones.

Various studies have found that 8 to 48% of patients given placebos reported a worsening of symptoms. The violation of internal standards is the most likely explanation for these findings. A physician may hope to induce a placebo effect by exaggerating the efficacy of a treatment. With raised expectations, however, the patient is more apt to observe that the actual benefits of treatment fall far short of what was promised. The patient may conclude that the therapist was mistaken, that the treatment was ineffective, or that the illness being treated was far worse than was originally thought. This latter conclusion can boomerang; the patient may assume his illness is severe, fall prey to worry, and induce a worsening of symptoms.

One tabulation of results from 67 studies indicated that 23% of patients given placebos reported at least one side effect. Since it is often assumed that these side effects occur as a result of suggestion, therapists may be disinclined to forewarn patients about drug side effects for fear that it will increase the incidence of those effects. On the contrary, studies indicate that more fully informing patients does not increase the occurrence of side effects (as predicted by the concept of suggestion). Rather, they indicate that the effect is to increase the likelihood that observed bodily reactions will be interpreted in a manner that is consistent with the knowledge that one has taken a drug (as predicted by the concept of labeling).

Integration

The placebo effect is a complex phenomenon, with a number of potent psychological factors at work simultaneously. For the scientist, the task is not to search for one correct explanation, but to specify the conditions under which the various concepts that explain placebo effects appear to operate. The goal is to maximize the benefits of treatment and to develop more flexible and useful treatments.

Knowledge of placebo effects can help us avoid the problem of the compiler of the *Paris Pharmacologia:* "What pledge can be afforded that the boasted remedies of the present day will not be like their predecessors, fall into disrepute, and in their turn serve only as a humiliating memorial of the credulity and the infatuation of physicians who recommended and prescribed them?"

Ear, Nose, and Throat Disorders

In the past decade otolaryngologists have been prominent pioneers in the clinical application of lasers to disorders of the head and neck area. The term laser is an acronym for light amplification by stimulated emission of radiation. Laser energy is unique because it consists of a single narrow beam of concentrated light of one wavelength. Most visible light is composed of many wavelengths diffused in all directions. To produce high levels of laser energy, large numbers of atoms are stimulated in a gaseous environment to release photons of light as a single pure wavelength. One stimulated atom releases photons of light which stimulate other atoms to release their own energy. A chamber is used to collect the various rays that are produced so that they may be superimposed and produce one high-density beam.

Lasers for surgery

The first lasers were built in the early 1960s; their potential application to surgery was studied in several laboratories during that decade. Experimental work on animals demonstrated the effects of laser energy on living tissue and proved that this destructive force could be controlled with precision greater than that of conventional surgery. The continuous wave carbon dioxide (CO_2) laser was developed in the mid-1960s, and it was soon learned that this type of laser energy produced destruction of living tissues by vaporizing water at the impact site, resulting in disruption of the tissue. The earlier pulsed lasers produced an explosive effect on tissue, but the continuous CO_2 laser's effect was limited to a much more discrete area. Furthermore, examination of tissues adjacent to the area of destruction produced by the laser revealed little damage.

Animal research demonstrated that the laser's effects on living tissue were unique in many respects, and the unique characteristics were desirable in surgery. The laser-induced injuries (lesions) were very discrete, and the amount of tissue destruction could be predicted by controlling the power setting and duration of the laser. Minimal bleeding occurred with the laser because small blood vessels were sealed by the laser beam as the tissue destruction took place. Remarkably little swelling was noted after the production of laser lesions compared to that produced by conventional surgery, and the defects produced by the laser healed rapidly with a minimum of scarring. The laser also provided a means of producing a lesion at some distance from the surgeon without direct physical contact between the surgeon's instrument and the tissue.

Laser treatments for the voice box

Widespread application of the laser to human patients began in the early 1970s and has continued and expanded to the present time. After initially studying the laser's effects on animals and on the larynx (voice box) of cadavers, otolaryngologists used the instrument to treat laryngeal diseases. Although the direct visualization of the larynx (laryngoscopy) via a hollow instrument (laryngoscope) introduced through the mouth had been performed routinely since the turn of the century, the view of the interior of the larynx was much improved by the use of a binocular surgical microscope. Microscopic laryngoscopy was developed during the 1960s at the time that research was being done on the surgical application of the laser.

The coupling of the CO_2 laser to the surgical microscope in 1969 made it possible to employ this new energy source in the treatment of human laryngeal disorders. The surgical microscope provided a magnified, binocular, three-dimensional view of the interior of the larynx, and by superimposing the laser beam onto the visual axis of the microscope, precise aiming of the beam into the larynx was made possible. In actual practice a tiny visible aiming dot can be seen when the surgeon looks through the microscope, and its location within the visualized field can be varied by manipulating a small control stick. When activated, the laser beam then strikes exactly where the surgeon sees the aiming dot in the microscope eyepiece.

Anesthesia techniques had to be adapted to laser surgery of the larynx to make it safe. Noncombustible anesthetic gases are required, since the laser beam could ignite a combustible anesthetic gas. The tubes that are inserted into patients' airways to maintain respiration during general anesthesia also had to be made from noncombustible materials (metal) or covered by a metal foil.

Other precautions are necessary to protect the patient and others in the operating room from the laser beam. Although the laser is damaging only to the tissues that it hits, it can be reflected off metal surfaces such as the laryngoscope or surgical instruments. The misdirected or reflected laser beam is a potential hazard to operating room personnel and to unprotected surfaces of the patient's body. The risks, however, are very slight and simple precautions will prevent any mishaps. The patient's eyes are always kept covered, and the lips are draped with moist gauze, which absorbs laser energy effectively. Operating room personnel are protected by wearing their regular eyeglasses or protective goggles. If the anesthetic breathing tube is in the surgical field—as is usually the case with laryngeal surgery—it is covered and protected from laser impact by moist gauze or cotton.

The larynx is an ideal organ for the surgical application of the laser. It is located so that its interior can be viewed through a hollow tube inserted through the mouth, but this made surgical access via this method of visualization limited by the diameter and length of the tube. Furthermore, the vocal cords are delicate structures, and removal of any tissue other than that

Laura Hofstadter

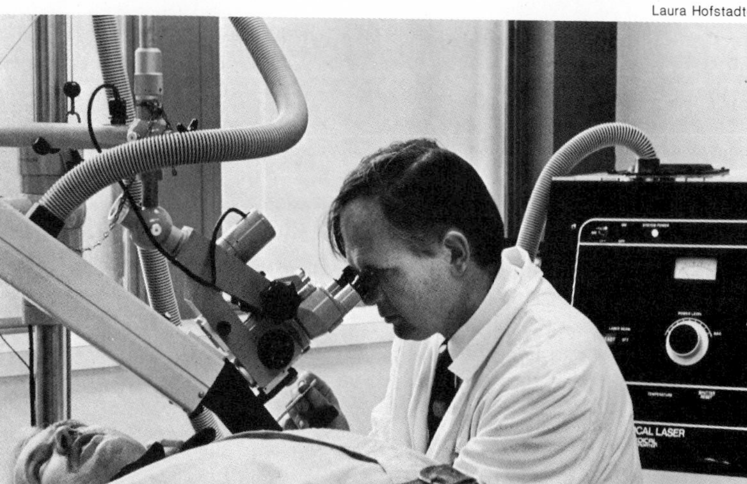

Otolaryngologists are using lasers to treat a wide variety of head and neck disorders. In recent years laser surgery has solved many problems previously encountered in operations on the larynx. Physicians are now testing lasers as a treatment for recurrent ear infections in children. Here a surgeon aims a laser beam at a patient's eardrum with the aid of a microscope.

necessary to eliminate disease is not desirable if voice quality is to be preserved. The laser's ability to remove small amounts of tissue without scarring or damaging surrounding structures and its ability to accomplish this in confined areas at a distance from the surgeon seemed to answer some of the clinical problems posed by laryngeal diseases. During the past decade, laryngeal laser surgery has been used with increasing frequency. It has solved some of the problems posed by the restrictions of operating through a laryngoscope.

Both benign and malignant laryngeal diseases are now treated by laser. Benign growths of the vocal cords often produce hoarseness. Removal of these growths must be complete to insure that they do not recur, but as much undiseased vocal cord tissue as possible must be left undisturbed and scarring kept to a minimum to minimize residual hoarseness from the surgery itself. The laser has been useful for removing many of these benign growths.

Damage to the larynx from scarring due to prior trauma of various types sometimes results in hoarseness or difficulty in breathing because of fusion of the vocal cords or narrowing of the dimensions of the larynx (stenosis). The ability of the laser to remove tissue with little resultant scarring has made it a useful tool in the management of these difficult cases.

Cancers of the vocal cord also produce hoarseness. Treatment of these malignancies requires surgery, radiation therapy, and sometimes a combination of both. The laser has been used successfully to remove certain cancers of the vocal cord, eliminating the need for "open" surgery (through the neck) or radiation therapy. Results of laser surgery for selected cases compare favorably with the results obtained by other treatments.

Laser surgery for vocal cord cancer preserves as much of the normal laryngeal tissues as possible, thus helping to retain a serviceable voice after the tumor has been removed. Although initially used only for very small laryngeal cancers, the laser has been applied increasingly to larger tumors in an attempt to determine its limits in the management of these malignancies. The laser has not, however, completely replaced traditional surgical procedures and radiation therapy.

Expanding applications of lasers

Otolaryngologists have found the laser to be an important addition to their therapeutic options in the management of a number of head and neck disorders. Although the laser has been applied primarily to surgery of the larynx, trachea, and bronchi, it has also found application in the management of diseases of the nose, oral cavity, pharynx, and skin. Other specialists have begun to take advantage of the laser for surgical problems in ophthalmology, gynecology, neurosurgery, and urology, to name a few. The carbon dioxide and argon lasers have been used most frequently, but laser surgery is just in its infancy, and new instruments, techniques, and applications are certain to be developed as the potential of this tool is explored.

—Edward L. Applebaum, M.D.

Eye Diseases and Visual Disorders

In much the same way that a person standing in a doorway with a bright flashlight can scan a darkened room, the ophthalmologist can peer into the cavity of the eye with his ophthalmoscope. With the beam of light from the ophthalmoscope, the eye doctor can examine the retina, a structure the size of a postage stamp that lines the interior of the eye (not unlike wallpaper covering the wall of the darkened room). The retina, which is an outpouching of the brain, together with its connection to the brain—the optic nerve—can often indicate the presence of a problem within the brain or other parts of the nervous system. The retina can also be an indicator of many bodily illnesses such as diabetes mellitus, high blood pressure, hardening of the arteries, and various internal infections.

In examining the retina with the ophthalmoscope, the ophthalmologist looks through the cornea, aqueous humor, lens, and vitreous humor. He is able to see the retina with a beam of light because these structures are normally transparent. However, returning to the darkened room analogy, one will not be able to see the wallpaper pattern very clearly if the room is filled with smoke. Similarly, the ophthalmologist may not be able to see the retina with the light of the ophthalmoscope because one or more of the normally transparent ocular structures have become clouded. For example, the cornea may be opaque because of a scar, the lens may become hazy (a cataract), or the normally transparent humors may be clouded by blood.

To determine if the retina of a patient with a dense cataract will "take a good picture" after surgery or if a diabetic who is considering vitrectomy—removal and replacement of vitreous humor opacified by hemorrhage—will have improved vision, the ophthalmologist must examine the internal structures of the eye. Since the clouding of a normally transparent ocular structure makes it impossible to examine the eye with the ophthalmoscope, in these cases he must use another method—*i.e.,* a sound beam.

The examination of the eye with sound

The technique called ultrasonography, which utilizes an ultrasonoscope, does not have the resolution capability (ability to capture detail) of the ophthalmoscope, nor does it provide the ophthalmoscope's full color spectrum. (Ultrasound pictures reveal only black, white, and shades of grey.) Nevertheless, in recent years ultrasonography has become widely used in ophthalmology because it provides valuable information that cannot be obtained by any other means.

Optics and ultrasonics share many basic principles. Sound beams, like rays of light, may be reflected, bent (refracted), or absorbed. Ultrasonography produces reflected sound, or echoes, and therefore is sometimes called echography. These echoes are produced by the sound beam bouncing off internal structures of tissues, tissue surfaces, and tissue boundaries. These interfaces are usually so small that what is known as "scattering" occurs—*i.e.,* the sound beam is reflected in all directions. Scattered reflections are extremely important because they portray the internal composition of a structure. A finely dispersed hemorrhage, which is a homogeneous structure, produces low reflectivity. A hemorrhage composed of red blood cell aggregates, on the other hand, is a heterogeneous structure and produces high reflectivity. Wide variation in the echoes indicates gross internal movements (swirling of blood clots), whereas a solid tumor would show no wide echo fluctuations. Tiny variations in the echo signal due to spontaneous movements indicate the presence of vascularity and the movement of blood through the structure.

When the surfaces being examined are relatively large and smooth, "specular," or mirrorlike, reflections will take place. Unlike scattered reflections, which exhibit little variation in echo intensity when the direction of the sound beam is changed, specular reflections provide highly varied and specific echo intensities. The sound beam must be directed at an angle perpendicular to the tissue plane to intensify and maximize the reflected echoes. These maximized reflected echoes are largely used to compare and characterize the surfaces of ocular tissues. For example, the echo emanating from the retina is stronger than that from the choroid, but not as strong as that from the sclera. The inner surface of the sclera generates the strongest echoes seen in ophthalmic ultrasonography.

The ultrasound examination is simple to perform, painless, and harmless—features that have contributed to its popularity. The ultrasound frequencies, which range from 5 million to 15 million cycles per second, are not audible. A small hand-held device called a transducer acts as both an emitter and receiver. The sound is emitted in rapidly repeating, brief bursts by electronically induced vibrations of a quartz crystal. Rapid dampening of the resonating crystal limits the duration of each sound pulse to less than 1/1,000 of a second. The crystal, once dampened to a resting state, then begins to vibrate again when struck and stimulated by the returning echoes. Very sophisticated

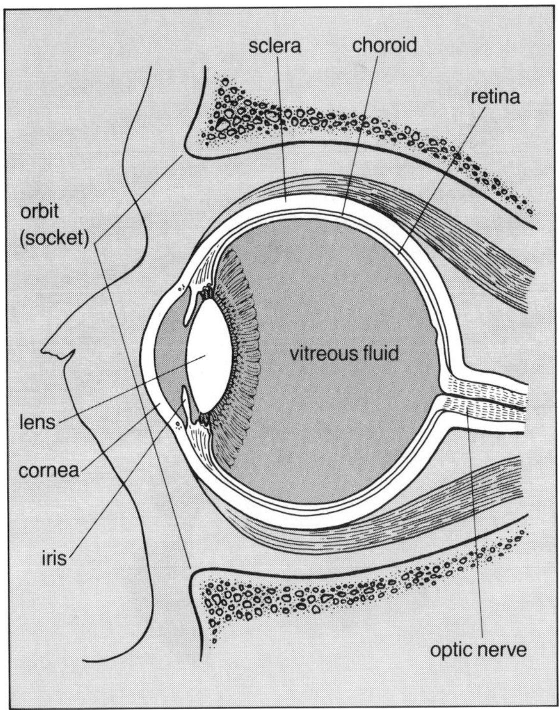

electronics are involved in converting these echo-induced vibrations of the quartz crystal into a visible pattern displayed on a screen. Once displayed, the results can be recorded (*i.e.,* photographed).

The display may show the intensity of returning echoes in two ways: by the amplitude (A-scan) of vertical deflections from a zero base line or by the relative brightness (B-scan) of echo spots. A-scan is preferred to B-scan in measuring echo intensity; analysis of the differences in heights of spikes offers a more accurate picture than the comparisons of dots of varying brightness. A-scan is also the preferred method in the detection of mobility and movement, based on the interrelationship of the A-scan transducer and scattered reflections. On the other hand, sweeping through the ocular tissues with the sound beam of a B-scan transducer permits the synthesis of dots of varying brightness into a two-dimensional, cross-sectional display of the eye. The B-scan display provides topographical information largely based upon specular reflection. It produces an anatomical map, emphasizing location, size, and shape of tissues. Both A- and B-scan techniques provide important information. B-scan is particularly useful in defining the boundaries of ocular structures, while A-scan is more useful in evaluating the inner architecture of tissues. Generally, both are used in ophthalmic ultrasound examinations.

(Below) B-scan transducer aimed at a cross section of the eye. The B-scan ultrasonogram of a normal eye (bottom) shows the relative brightness of echo spots and provides important topographical information about relationships of parts of the eye. From left to right the white areas represent the cornea, lens, and orbit. The dark area in the middle is the acoustically silent vitreal cavity.

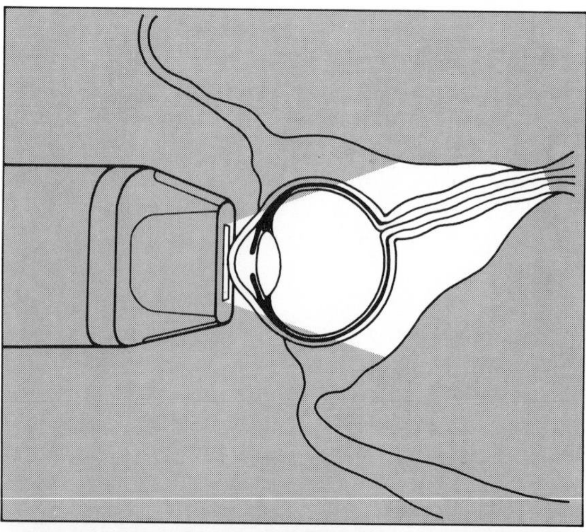

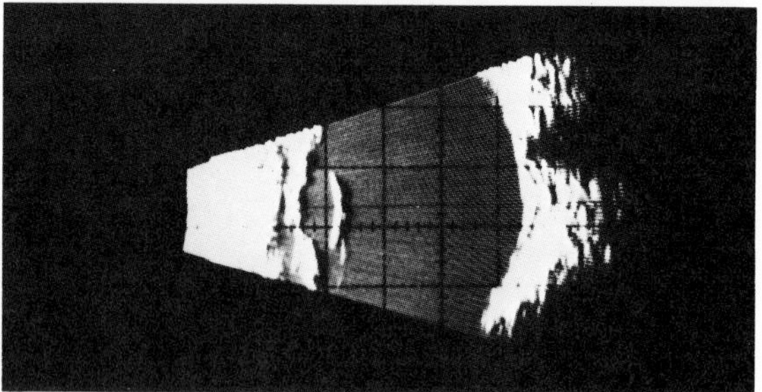

Courtesy, Karl Ossoinig, M.D.

To emphasize the usefulness of ultrasonography and the interrelationship of A- and B-scan techniques, it is helpful to consider two relatively common eye problems: intraocular hemorrhage in a diabetic patient (a serious manifestation of diabetic retinopathy) and intraocular tumors. In both cases important therapeutic decisions are often based upon information that only ultrasonography can provide.

Ultrasound for diabetic retinopathy

In the case of the diabetic with an intraocular hemorrhage, the ophthalmologist often turns to ultrasound because he cannot adequately examine the eye by optical means. The vitreal cavity, normally an acoustically silent, gel-filled transparent space between the lens and the retina, becomes an opalescent to opaque echo-producing chamber when filled with blood. Ultrasonography enables the ophthalmologist to determine the location or position of the retina. The presence of blood in the vitreal cavity will produce echoes of low reflectivity. If, in addition, the retina is detached (*i.e.,* if the sensory retina is separated from the retinal pigment epithelium) a specific high amplitude echo (A-scan) is produced as is a very bright linear band (B-scan). Such findings are very meaningful because an intraocular hemorrhage complicated by a retinal detachment is a very serious matter, requiring a therapeutic approach quite different from an intraocular hemorrhage without detachment. Ultrasound after treatment for either kind of condition will indicate whether the blood is being absorbed and whether therapy has been successful.

Ultrasound for eye tumors

In the case of an intraocular tumor, even if the mass can be seen with the ophthalmoscope, there is often a question whether the tumor is a cancer, a deep hemorrhage, or an inflammatory or degenerative lesion. B-scan pictures help to confirm the shape and outline of the mass. More important, however, echoes emanating from within the tumor can characterize its inner texture and reflectivity, which are best shown with A-scan. Retinoblastoma, the most common eye cancer of childhood, is highly reflective because it contains deposits of calcium, which act like multiple foreign particles, reflecting and absorbing sound, and actually casting an acoustic "shadow" on tissues behind the tumor. Ultrasound findings are very helpful because almost all the other pediatric ocular conditions that mimic a retinoblastoma are of lower reflectivity and do not cast an acoustic shadow. A great number of children have been saved from needless enucleation (re-

Courtesy, Karl Ossoinig, M.D.

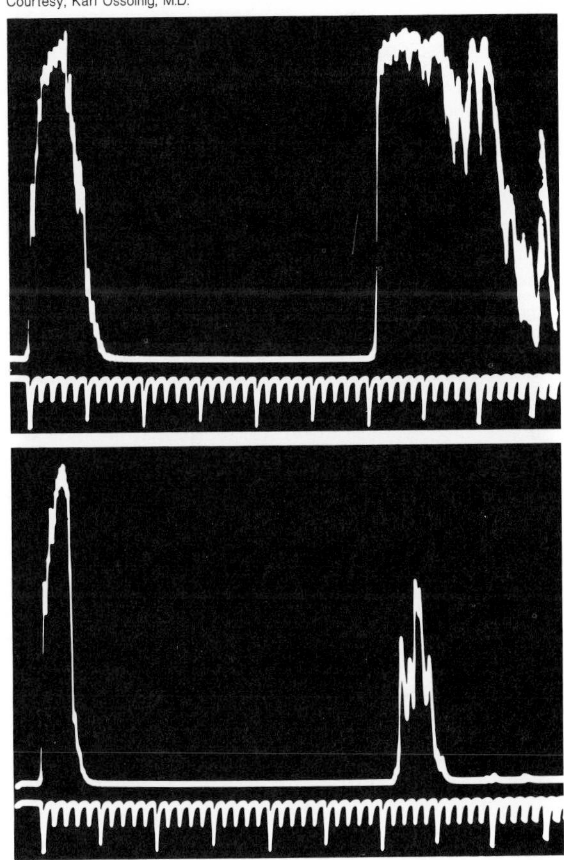

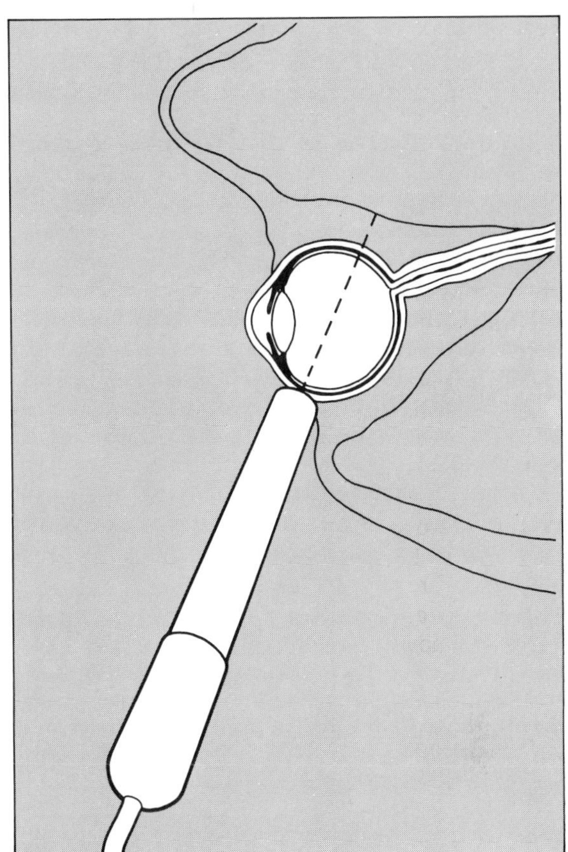

An A-scan transducer is held against the sclera of a normal eye. The top ultrasonogram gives an overview of the inner structures of the eye. The silent zone is the vitreal cavity. The spikes at right represent the wall of the eye and the trailing off of spikes, the orbit. At measuring sensitivity (bottom), the A-scan identifies the eye's delicate layers: the spikes after the vitreal cavity represent the retina (moderately high), the choroid (low), and the sclera (high).

moval of the eyeball) when the ultrasound findings indicated that a retinoblastoma was *not* the cause of the ocular problem.

Malignant melanoma, the most common eye cancer of adulthood, is acoustically of a moderately low reflectivity owing to cellular compactness and uniformity of internal tissue composition of the tumor. Most inflammatory and hemorrhagic conditions that might be mistaken for a melanoma show mobility and are even lower in reflectivity. Other conditions that simulate melanomas, such as benign hemangioma, are of higher reflectivity. Repeated ultrasound examinations are particularly valuable for documenting tumor growth. Many intraocular tumors are currently being treated by irradiation; frequent ultrasound examinations can monitor the shrinkage of the tumor and thus its responsiveness to treatment.

Ultrasound for orbital diseases

Diseases of the orbit—the bony cavity containing the eyeball—create some of the most complex problems in ophthalmology. These diseases of the tissues within the eye socket cause the eye to protrude (proptosis). Because there are over 50 different causes for proptosis, the initial examination of a patient is frequently inconclusive. (Consequently the ophthalmologist may request the consultation of other specialists—in radiology, neurology, otolaryngology, pediatrics, endocrinology, or oncology.) In recent years ultrasonography has provided the ophthalmologist with one of the most rewarding methods of evaluating orbital disease.

The orbit is a very noisy cavity because it contains many highly reflective structures such as large vessels, nerves, and septa (fibrous membranes spanning the orbit and extending into the eyelids) that crisscross through it. Fortunately, almost all orbital diseases are of low reflectivity, producing acoustically quiet areas against the normally noisy background of high reflectivity. For example, the presence of orbital cysts, either originating primarily in the orbit or extending into the orbit from adjacent cavities (sinus or intracranial), can be detected because they have an extremely low reflectivity and are sharply outlined. Rhabdomyosarcoma, a dangerous orbital cancer of childhood, has a very low reflectivity, with borders that are poorly outlined.

Thyroid disease, the most common cause of proptosis in adults, can be detected by the presence of marked enlargement of the extraocular muscles. Extraocular muscles, being homogeneous structures, produce zones of low reflectivity that stand out against the orbital background of high reflectivity. By directing the sound beam perpendicular to the muscle surface, a cross-sectional display can be obtained that permits an accurate measurement of muscle thickness within 0.5 mm. The presence of thyroid-induced proptosis is a virtual certainty if enlarged muscles are found in both orbits.

Another important orbital structure, the optic nerve, like the extraocular muscles, can be displayed and measured owing to its low reflectivity. Careful ultrasonic analysis of the optic nerve can even distinguish the coverings (meninges) of the nerve from the nerve proper. This is of practical importance since the coverings are specifically thickened by a malignant tumor known as meningioma, whereas an optic-nerve glioma, another kind of malignant tumor, specifically enlarges the nerve proper. Even the space between the nerve and its coverings is important because it becomes widened in many conditions associated with increased intracranial pressure. This occurs because the fluid-filled subarachnoid space not only surrounds the brain but extends anteriorly to ensheath the optic nerves. This widening is acoustically detected by ultrasonography.

Even when orbital ultrasonography does not indicate the specific disease, often the ultrasonic findings will suggest the most useful therapeutic approach—*e.g.,* drugs or surgery. The ultrasound examination assists the ophthalmologist by localizing the disease process to a particular area of the orbit, thereby facilitating the surgical exposure of the lesion and permitting its excision or biopsy.

The scans below show a detached retina. A funnel-shaped membrane emanating from the optic nerve characterizes the B-scan (top). The A-scan (bottom) shows a high amplitude echo (spike) in the usually silent vitreal cavity, which signals the detachment. Ultrasonography enables the ophthalmologist to determine the precise position of the detached retina and to formulate an appropriate treatment approach.

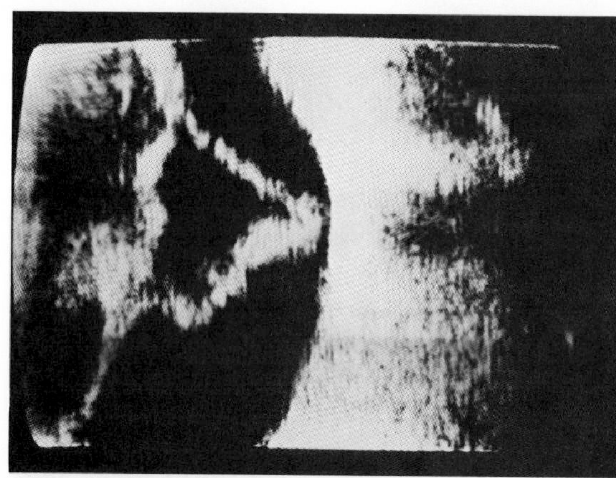

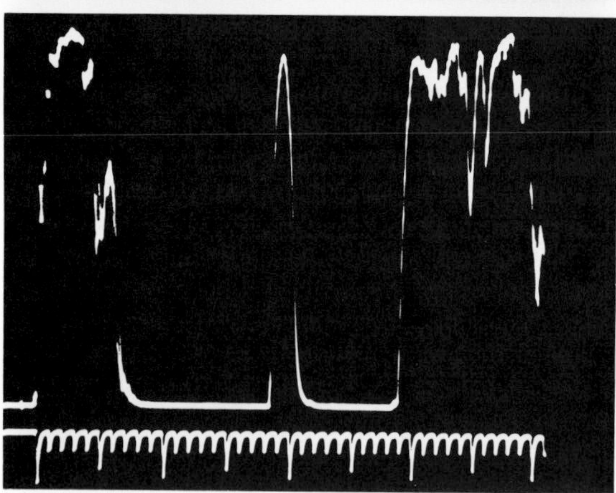

Courtesy, Karl Ossoinig, M.D.

Ultrasound for lens implants

The measurement of size or thickness of a structure by A-scan ultrasonography is called ultrasonic biometry. Thus far we have described the use of ultrasonic biometry in monitoring the size of ocular or orbital tumors and in the detection of abnormal enlargements of the optic nerve or extraocular muscles. Biometry is also used to measure the thickness of normal ocular components and, in particular, to measure the length of the eye in preparation for intraocular lens implantation. The intraocular lens restores vision following cataract removal. Biometry enables the ophthalmologist to determine postoperatively the proper intraocular lens of appropriate strength for the length of the individual patient's eye.

When the transducer is positioned so that the sound beam is perpendicular to the cornea, lens, and retina, maximal echo spikes from these structures are obtained. The distance between the echo spikes produced on the screen, multiplied by the speed of sound in the eye, provides measurements of thickness and size. Not only can the length of the eye be measured accurately within 0.1 mm, but distances between intraocular structures, *i.e.,* distances between the cornea and the lens or between the lens and the retina, can be determined.

Ophthalmic ultrasonography has become an integral part of the problem-solving armamentarium of the ophthalmologist. The current proved usefulness of ultrasound in diagnosis and eye measurements is undoubtedly the greatest stimulus for a number of ongoing research efforts. The application of computer technology is one area of very active research which holds great promise for ultrasonography in the future.

—Robert A. Levine, M.D.

Gastrointestinal Disorders

Acute diarrheal illness continues to be the leading cause of death, especially among children, in many developing countries. It is estimated that more than 15 million infants and children die each year from acute infectious enteritis (intestinal inflammation). Because of increasing recognition during the past decade of rotavirus (especially in children under two) and toxin-producing *Escherichia coli* (in all age-groups) as causes of enteritis, a specific diagnosis can now be made in more than 75% of cases of acute diarrheal illness. On another front, the intestinal parasite *Giardia lamblia,* which was once thought harmless, is now understood to be a common cause of diarrhea, abdominal pain, and other symptoms in several regions of the world, including parts of the U.S.

Major bacterial and viral enteric pathogens
noninvasive bacteria
Vibrio cholerae
Escherichia coli
Clostridium perfringens
Staphylococcus aureus
invasive bacteria
Shigella species
Salmonella species
Vibrio parahaemolyticus
Campylobacter fetus
viruses
rotavirus
parvovirus (*e.g.,* Norwalk agent)
adenovirus
reovirus
calicivirus

Bacterial agents

Bacterial pathogens are responsible for the majority of acute diarrheal illnesses in adults and in children over age two. These microorganisms may be divided into two distinct groups: noninvasive pathogens, which cause no detectable damage to the gut mucosa (the mucus-secreting, nutrient-absorbing lining of the intestines), and invasive pathogens, which penetrate and damage the mucosa of the small and large intestines. Large numbers of noninvasive organisms are necessary for disease to occur because all of their effects stem from an enterotoxin, which is a metabolic by-product. On the other hand, the invasive types require comparatively low numbers to establish their presence and cause bowel inflammation and destruction.

Noninvasive bacteria. Exciting new insights into the sequence of events following ingestion of enterotoxin-producing bacteria have been gained in recent years. Cholera is the prototype of noninvasive bacterial diarrhea in that the causative organism, *Vibrio cholerae,* does not damage the gut mucosa and all effects are mediated by a single enterotoxin that acts only on the mucosal cells of the small intestine. Ingestion of sufficient numbers of the causative organism to ensure survival through the stomach and into the upper part of the small intestine initiates the sequence. The bacteria adhere to the mucosa and multiply in the small intestine, where they produce a powerful enterotoxin. It is a complex protein with a molecular weight of 84,000 daltons and is composed of two major fractions. The binding fraction is composed of five identical 11,000-dalton subunits that bind rapidly to specific glycoproteins in the gut mucosal cell wall. Following cellular binding a lag period of 15–30 minutes occurs before the 29,000-dalton activating fraction of the enterotoxin stimulates the formation of increased intracellular quantities of cyclic adenosine monophosphate (cyclic AMP). Cyclic AMP is responsible for prolonged secretion of isotonic fluid by all segments of the small intestine. This fluid, which is rapidly moved into the intestine from the plasma of the blood, is rich in bicarbonate and potassium. The rate of fluid production is highest for 8 to 10 hours after the mucosa is exposed to the enterotoxin and then gradually decreases over the next 24 hours.

If the antibiotic tetracycline is administered to cholera patients, diarrhea ceases within 24 to 48 hours. The organisms are killed rapidly by the antibiotic, but diarrhea continues for an additional period, albeit at decreasing rates, owing to the enterotoxin that already has been bound at the time of administration of the drug. In cholera patients who do not receive antibiotic, bacteria continue to multiply, and fluid loss will persist for as long as five days. After that time the organisms are usually attacked and destroyed by the body's defense mechanisms.

The major effect of *V. cholerae* is the massive loss of fluid and electrolytes from the body, with resultant dehydration, acidosis (abnormally high acidity of the body fluids), and death. Uniformly effective treatment involves the use of large amounts of simple glucose-electrolyte solutions to maintain continuous restoration of the fluid lost in diarrhea. These can be administered intravenously but also, more importantly, by mouth. Glucose helps the gut absorb sodium; solutions prepared simply by adding 3.5 g sodium chloride, 2.5 g sodium bicarbonate, 1.5 g potassium chloride, and 20 g glucose (1 g = 0.035 oz) to a liter (1.1 qt) of clean drinking water have proved to be extremely effective in the field, even under very trying conditions.

Although cholera is no longer a major cause of death, medical lessons learned from its study have helped further the understanding of the disturbances caused by enterotoxin-producing *E. coli.* These organisms, benign strains of which are common gut inhabitants, have been identified as causative agents in a large proportion of acute diarrheal illness throughout the world. *E. coli* may produce either a heat-labile toxin

World Health Organization; photograph, J. Abcede

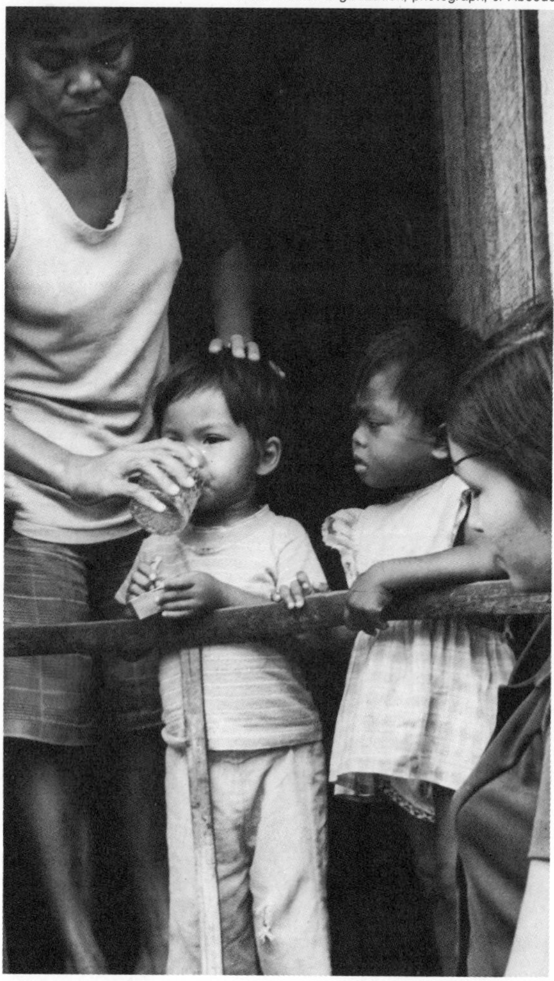

Oral rehydration solutions prepared simply at home are saving the lives of third world children afflicted with acute diarrheal diseases.

(a toxin capable of being broken down by heat), a heat-stable toxin, or both. The heat-labile toxin is similar to the cholera enterotoxin in many respects, whereas the heat-stable toxin is a much smaller molecule. The latter's mechanism of action differs from that of the cholera toxin, although it likewise enhances the outpouring of fluids into the intestine.

The spectrum of illnesses produced by enterotoxin-producing *E. coli* varies from mild travelers' diarrhea to potentially life-threatening illnesses with severe diarrhea quite comparable to that seen in cholera. Again, fluid replacement is important in therapy, but antimicrobial drugs are of little benefit in the treatment of diarrheal disease caused by *E. coli.* Taking doxycycline as a preventative may be an effective means of reducing travelers' diarrhea, although side effects can occur. Similarly, ingestion of large quantities of bismuth subsalicylate (*e.g.,* Pepto-Bismol) may be helpful in reducing the attack rate.

Acute staphylococcal food poisoning results from eating food containing heat-stable enterotoxin B and is not dependent upon bacterial multiplication in the intestines. The mechanism of action of the toxin is not well understood, but both vomiting and hyperperistalsis of the bowel (an abnormal increase in the wavelike contractions that move food through the intestines) are mediated through effects of the toxin on the nervous system. The clinical course is usually short (6 to 12 hours), and in severe cases intravenous fluids may be necessary.

Food poisoning caused by the bacterium *Clostridium perfringens* usually results from eating meat that has not been cooked adequately enough to kill clostridial spores and that has been allowed to remain at room temperature for several hours before ingestion. The sporulating organisms multiply in the small bowel, producing an enterotoxin that causes hyperperistalsis and fluid secretion. (Another clostridial toxin, produced by *Clostridium difficile,* has been incriminated as a major cause of a severe form of colitis called pseudomembranous colitis, which can occur in individuals taking certain antibiotics.)

Invasive bacteria. Invasive bacterial pathogens cause an inflammatory lesion that, if extensive enough, results in the dysentery syndrome: intestinal inflammation, abdominal pain, and severe diarrhea with stools that often contain blood and mucus. An example of such an organism is *Campylobacter fetus* subspecies *jejuni* and *intestinalis.* Mucosal penetration and tissue injury may occur, especially in the colon. This bacterium is thought to be an important cause of diarrhea in children in developing countries, although it also accounts for sporadic cases of diarrhea and colitis in adults in the U.S. and U.K.

Recent research indicates that intestinal illness caused by bacteria of the genus *Shigella* is due to a combination of a noninvasive, possibly enterotoxin-induced diarrhea and an inflammatory invasive bacterial colitis that results in the dysentery syndrome. *Salmonella* species (excluding *S. typhosa,* the agent of typhoid fever) are another example of invasive pathogenic bacteria. Virulent members of this group have the capacity to invade and multiply in the gastrointestinal mucosa, particularly in the ileum (the last section of the small intestine). In addition, certain strains may also produce a toxin that interferes with fluid transport.

As knowledge of the pathways involved in the causation of bacterial diarrheas increases, new and better methods of treatment are being developed. For example, it may be possible to interfere with the action of toxins on the mucosal cells or to inhibit binding of the microorganisms to the intestinal lining.

Antimicrobials should not be used indiscriminately. With the exception of gastroenteritis caused by *Salmonella* species, the drugs to which these bacteria are susceptible may fail to shorten the course of the illness and many prolong the carrier state. Resistance to antibiotics is becoming an increasingly important problem worldwide, and susceptibility of bacterial pathogens to antibiotics needs to be determined for each geographic region.

Viruses

It has become increasingly obvious that bacterial agents account for only about 20% of cases of acute infectious diarrhea in temperate climates. Improved techniques for the identification of viral pathogens have led to the recognition that a number of viruses are responsible for the majority of cases of acute nonspecific gastroenteritis.

Perhaps the best understood viral pathogen is the rotavirus, although several others have been described. In temperate climates this virus is responsible for 40–50% of hospitalized cases of acute enteritis, with incidence rising as high as 80% in the colder months. It is highly contagious and spreads with ease from person to person in homes and institutions. Infection occurs primarily in young children between the ages of six months and three years. The virus is rarely seen in the stools of symptom-free individuals. It invades the mucosa of the small intestine, causing mucosal damage and even significant destruction; levels of enzymes (disaccharidases) produced by the intestinal lining are decreased, resulting in inability to digest such sugars as lactose (milk sugar).

The clinical syndrome of rotavirus infection includes a brief incubation period, early vomiting, and fever and diarrhea that persist for several days. The diarrhea is relieved by fasting. Dehydration is usually mild, but acidosis and death can occur rapidly in some patients.

The Norwalk agent and related viruses (Hawaii and Montgomery County agents) infect all age-groups, and illness most frequently occurs between September and March in the Northern Hemisphere. Pathological changes in the small intestine similar to those seen in rotavirus infection have been described. As a result, transient malabsorption of carbohydrates and fat can occur. The incubation period is 18–48 hours; after a variable syndrome of headache, myalgia (muscular aches), low-grade fever, vomiting, diarrhea, and abdominal cramps, the disease usually passes within 72–96 hours.

A variety of other viruses are currently under study, and use of the electron microscope to examine stool samples from infected children has been an important advance in furthering an understanding of these pathogens. The identification of these organisms, especially human rotavirus, has led to the expectation that a vaccine will be developed to immunize infants against some viruses that cause gastroenteritis.

Giardiasis

The protozoan *Giardia lamblia* was first described in the 17th century by the pioneering Dutch microscopist Antonie van Leeuwenhoek, who discovered the parasite in his own stools. For many years the organism was considered to be harmless but now is recognized as a common cause of intestinal disorders in the U.S. and other countries. Incidence is greatest in regions with poor sanitation.

The organism is highly characteristic in both its trophozoite and cyst stages. During its trophozoite stage,

The Giardia lamblia *parasite (below), long considered harmless, was discovered in the 17th century by Antonie van Leeuwenhoek when he was examining a sample of his own stool under the microscope. Giardiasis has only recently been recognized as a common diarrheal disease.*

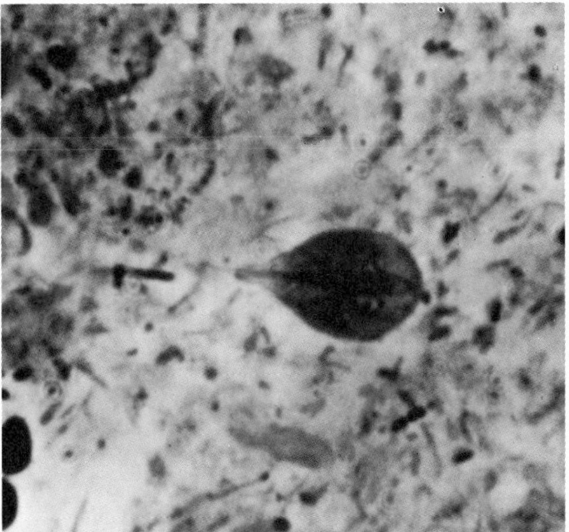

(Left) Rijksmuseum, Amsterdam; (right) J. M. Langham

in which the organism feeds and moves about, it is about 10–20 μm (micrometers, or millionths of a meter) long by 5–15 μm wide and appears bilaterally symmetrical with four pairs of whiplike, propulsive flagella and two nuclei. It is convex on its upper (dorsal) surface, and the front end of its bottom (ventral) surface carries a slight concavity, which is used as a sucking disk. The ovoid cyst, which is a resting, protective stage, is 8–10 μm by 7–10 μm and when mature contains an organism that has four nuclei and a double set of intracellular organelles. These cysts are important in transmission of the disease and can survive more than two weeks in water and raw sewage. The cyst stage ends in the stomach or upper small intestine, each cyst producing two motile trophozoites. These trophozoites usually are found in the duodenum and proximal jejunum (the first two parts of the small intestine), perhaps because of the alkaline environment encountered there. The trophozoites live very close to the mucosa or may be attached to it by the ventral disk.

Several theories have been proposed to explain the mechanism by which the parasite produces its effects. Mechanical blockage of the mucosal brush border (the rough surface covering the epithelial cells that line the mucosa), severe irritation, or associated bacterial overgrowth all have been suggested. In severely infected individuals invasion of the deeper layers of the mucosa may occur. The body's most important defense against the trophozoite is the thymus-derived lymphocyte, which may emerge from the mucosa and attach to trophozoites in the intestinal cavity. Antibodies in the blood also can be found in some individuals, but their importance is unclear. The disease-related changes seen in tissue biopsies of the small intestine in infected individuals are quite variable and range from a normal appearance to an increase in epithelial cell turnover, prominence of lymphoid nodules, and an increase in inflammatory cells.

Giardiasis is endemic in the U.S., and several large water-borne outbreaks have been described both in the U.S. (*e.g.,* Aspen, Colo.) and in the Soviet Union (*e.g.,* Leningrad). Raw sewage may contaminate water supplies, or infection may result from inadequate water-treatment systems. Chlorination may be effective in destroying enteric bacteria yet still not kill *Giardia* cysts. Sedimentation and filtration are used to remove cysts from the surface of water reservoirs. Travelers in Mexico, Southeast Asia, the Middle East, the Far East, southern Asia, and South America also have an increased risk of contracting the disease. Some day-care centers have encountered outbreaks of giardiasis, and the disease has a high incidence in homosexual men.

The incubation period is variable but averages about ten days. Some infected individuals are asymptomatic (not showing symptoms), while others complain of mild abdominal pain, diarrhea, or constipation; yet others (as many as 20%) have more marked debility with intestinal malabsorption, weight loss, and fatigue. Many individuals complain of an excess of intestinal gas, which may give rise to abdominal distension and excessive flatulence. In an occasional victim of an acute severe infection, weakness, chills, and fever occur. The acute infection can last from one to three weeks but may resolve spontaneously, and the organism may disappear from the feces. Others become asymptomatic carriers or have recurrences of clinical symptoms. Individuals with poorly functioning immune systems seem prone to persistent infections. Subacute or chronic infections persist for months and even years. Intermittent episodes of upper abdominal pain, loose bowel movements, flatulence, and belching are common complaints. The cause of these nonspecific symptoms is difficult to diagnose; they are sometimes attributed to peptic ulcer, gallbladder disease, or irritable bowel syndrome.

Diagnosis of a *Giardia* infestation is usually made by examination of a fresh stool specimen. Trophozoites can be found in diarrheic stools, and cysts in solid fecal specimens. At least three stool specimens should be examined because stools may be negative in the early phases or patients may excrete the organisms intermittently. If the degree of clinical suspicion is high and the stools are negative, trophozoites can be demonstrated in the duodenal or jejunal fluid or on biopsy. Special tubes that are swallowed are used to suck the material from the upper intestine. Alternatively, a tiny biopsy capsule on the end of a long tube can be swallowed and one or more tissue samples obtained from the upper small intestine. These samples then can be examined under the microscope after appropriate fixation and staining. As yet there is no blood test that can be used to make the diagnosis.

Several drugs are available for treating giardiasis. These include quinacrine hydrochloride, metronidazole, and furazolidone. Although they are effective remedies, each agent has specific side effects and contraindications (circumstances under which their use is inadvisable). Some controversy exists about the necessity for treating asymptomatic cyst carriers. Because there is a potential for transmission to others, an argument can be made for treating those who have no contraindications such as pregnancy.

There is no medication that can be used to prevent giardiasis. In endemic regions water for drinking or for ice should be boiled or purified using iodine-containing compounds. Unpeeled fruits and vegetables should be avoided or thoroughly cooked.

Because of a continued increase in foreign travel, more individuals will be exposed to the causative agent of giardiasis. Patients and their physicians will need to become more familiar with this disease, and parasitology laboratories must acquire greater expertise in confirming the diagnosis.

—Bernard Levin, M.D.

Glandular and Metabolic Disorders

It is still true that if food intake exceeds energy requirements, weight gain is inevitable. However, scientists have now obtained new insights about the processes of energy expenditure and appetite control. Much of this work has focused on trying to uncover biochemical differences between fat and lean individuals that could have preceded the development of obesity and that, by their nature, would have facilitated weight gain. Although obese persons differ in many ways from thin persons, it has been most difficult to show that these differences preceded the development of obesity since even when obese subjects lose weight they may not correct metabolic abnormalities caused by long-standing obesity. Nevertheless, recent research has led to some new theories about weight gain, which may have practical applications in the future.

Metabolism and obesity

What is the evidence for the hypothesis that obese individuals use less energy than lean individuals and therefore become fat on what would be regarded as a normal diet? It has been known for some 30 years that the basal metabolic rate (energy expenditure at rest) can vary by as much as 30% among normal individuals so that some need more food than others just to maintain their weight. There is another rather prosaic explanation for an apparently abnormal tendency to gain weight; namely, that obese individuals are more placid, have less muscle tension, and tend to move less than their lean counterparts. Of course, some of this could be an effect of obesity rather than its cause. Nevertheless, there are studies of children and adults suggesting that for some people there may be as much as a two-fold increase in caloric intake without weight gain even though their physical activity remains the same. Such studies confirm the common observation that some individuals seemingly "can eat whatever they want and never get fat." If this is really so, then those individuals who consume a higher calorie diet, provided that they have normal rates of gastrointestinal absorption, must also use up more calories if they are to remain in balance.

One possible way to do this other than by increased muscular activity is by producing more heat through a mechanism called nonshivering thermogenesis (NST). The increased heat production in NST is due to some alteration in body metabolism induced by the stimulus of cold. There is now some experimental evidence to support the view that NST may be important in the development of obesity. There is a strain of mice that spontaneously becomes obese; these mice, before the development of obesity, release less heat in response to either shivering or an infusion of noradrenaline, a chemical transmitter of the nervous system closely related to adrenaline. The implication of this study is that the obese mouse becomes obese because it expends fewer of its food calories than its normal counterpart in generating heat; and the excess food that is not burned is stored as fat.

Similar studies have been performed in humans. Three groups of women were tested: obese women with a family history of obesity, lean women who had never had problems with maintaining body weight, and an additional seven women of normal weight who had been obese but who were now able to maintain normal weight by persistent dieting. In the first and last groups of women, the response of the metabolic rate to an infusion of noradrenaline was only half that seen in the lean subjects. This difference in thermogenic response

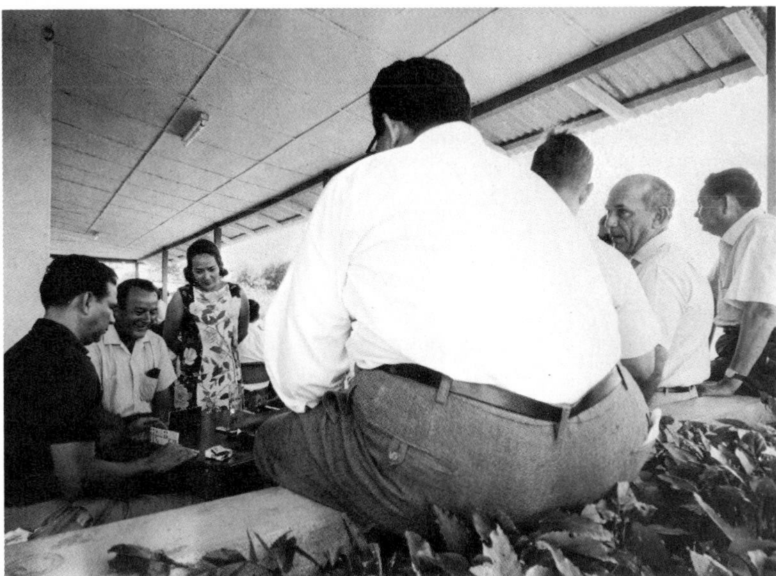

Donald Wright Patterson, Jr.—Stock, Boston

Scientists have recently gained new insights into the complex processes of energy expenditure and appetite control; they are learning that there may be metabolic differences between obese and thin persons.

(heat production, calorie utilization) is the same as that reported for the obese mouse. The interpretation again is that this abnormality favors the development of obesity because fewer calories are dissipated as heat, and further that there is a possibility that the abnormality may be inherited rather than due to obesity itself.

Brown fat. A consequent question facing researchers is that if the obese animal or human burns fewer food calories to generate heat, is this so because all the tissues of the body have this defect or are there specific sites that can be identified? It has been known for some time that when an animal is adapted to cold, it has an increased production of heat that is not due to shivering or other muscular activity. This capacity for NST has been shown to be related to the presence of brown adipose tissue, or brown fat, a specialized type of fat that is abundant in hibernating animals. When a rat becomes adapted to the cold, the amount of brown fat increases and its NST activity also increases. In the genetically obese mouse, the amount of brown fat—tissue that is dark in color and fatty in composition and clustered around the kidneys, adrenal glands, and the heart—is high when the animal is lean, but decreases when it is given enough food to become obese. Since brown fat produces heat and therefore uses more food for calories, the obese mouse uses fewer calories than its lean counterpart.

Some mice become obese because they dissipate fewer food calories as heat than do normal mice. A similar phenomenon has been observed in humans.

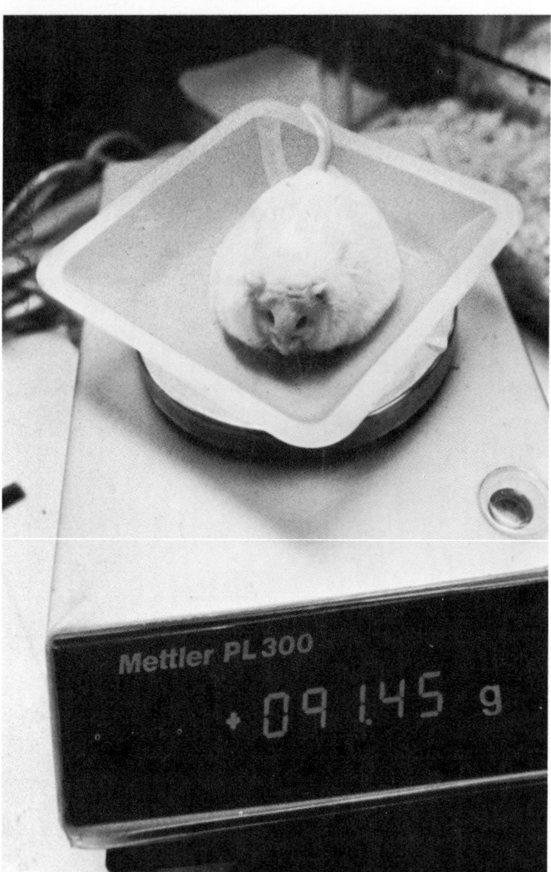

Richard Howard, DISCOVER Magazine © 1981 Time Inc.

These findings were amplified in a recent study that has more direct bearing to humans. Rats were fed a "cafeteria diet"; that is, in addition to their ordinary laboratory diet, new and attractive food items were introduced. Although the laboratory rat that is offered an unlimited amount of its stock diet never becomes obese, the cafeteria diet of highly palatable, high-calorie, high-fat foods resulted in obesity. The experimenters then showed that, as the rats became obese, brown fat increased and that the brown fat prevented the animals from gaining weight as fast as would have been predicted from food intake. The brown fat used up a disproportionately high amount of calories.

What is the significance of these findings for humans? If the increased amount of brown fat is an adaptation to obesity, then those individuals who either did not have enough brown fat or did not develop it would tend to gain weight faster since less of the food would be burned as heat. There is now good evidence that brown fat is present in the infant and persists in the adult. Using a heat sensor, areas of brown fat have been detected in humans by their increased heat production. The next critical steps in this research are to see if there is less brown fat in obese humans—as there is in obese mice and rats—and then to see if the factors regulating the amount of brown fat or its activity are inherited.

Enzymes and weight control. In other studies of the biochemistry of obesity, scientists examined an enzyme (biological catalyst) called lipoprotein lipase (LPL), which has the function of removing fat (triglycerides) from the blood and placing them in fat cells. Obese individuals have slightly higher amounts of this enzyme than do lean individuals. But of greater interest was the finding that although the level of the enzyme dropped markedly during a reducing program, when the weight stabilized, the LPL of the fat cells increased to levels even higher than they had been when they were obese. Thus, in these obese individuals, there was increased activity of the enzyme that facilitated the storage of fat in the fat cell after weight loss. Whether this is a partial explanation of the inability of some obese individuals to maintain weight reduction must be determined by additional studies.

Another new clue to the differences between obesity and leanness was reported in 1981 by a group of Harvard University researchers. All cells in the body must continually and actively move sodium out of the cell and transport potassium in. This is a constant process because cells are bathed in a fluid containing a high concentration of sodium chloride (salt). As much as one-fifth of the total energy expenditure of the body in the resting state is required to carry out this "sodium pump" function. The enzyme that is responsible for sodium transport from the cell is sodium-potassium adenosinetriphosphatase (ATPase). The enzyme ATPase can be measured in the livers of experimentally obese animals or in the red cells of humans. In the obese mouse, the ATPase was considerably decreased, which could mean that less energy was being used to maintain the sodium pump.

When obese patients' red blood cells were similarly studied, the enzyme level was 20% lower than in lean subjects and the amount of salt in the red cells was increased, although not every obese subject showed these changes. If the enzyme levels in the red blood cells are indicative of the enzyme activity throughout the body, then these obese subjects were not using as much energy to maintain their weights as were the lean subjects. Although there was generally an inverse relationship between the enzyme and body weight—*i.e.,* when weight was increased, enzyme was decreased—not all obese subjects showed the reduction, suggesting that obesity per se did not always change the enzyme level. More investigation of the sodium pump and obesity must be done to determine what is cause and what is effect.

What should be restated here is that an excess of food is always necessary to produce obesity, although just what constitutes an excess appears to vary from person to person. It may be that mechanisms for disposing of food calories differ among individuals so that in that sense some people may gain weight more easily than others. However, as yet none of the findings just discussed has been shown to precede the development of obesity, nor has it been possible to find a group of individuals where such findings would predict obesity in later life.

The body's fat cells

Some years ago it was suggested that the number of fat cells in the body is fixed during the first few years of life. Furthermore, it was postulated that those individuals with a large number of fat cells tended to become obese more easily. The mechanism whereby the number of fat cells led to an increase in food intake was not immediately apparent. New research with better methods has now shown that the number of fat cells and the size of the cells *can* increase as weight increases, so the earlier theory now appears to be incorrect.

The brain and appetite

The other large area of research with many new findings involves the central nervous system's control of appetite. It is still unclear why most animals maintain a stable weight even when access to food is unlimited, whereas the human often finds this impossible. Since experimental destruction of certain parts of the brain in animals can produce unrestrained appetite, considerable attention has been focused on the brain control of appetite. Many theories have been proposed and tested, but none so far has received either major support or acceptance.

"Good grief! What have you done to the body the Good Lord gave you?"

In the past five years a new series of chemical messengers has been identified in the central nervous system, and some of them have been found to have direct effects on appetite. One, cholecystokinin (CCK), is a protein hormone that was identified more than 50 years ago. It functions in the gastrointestinal tract to induce the gallbladder to empty its bile when food reaches the small intestine. This seemed to be quite a sufficient function for CCK. But a few years ago it was noted that injection of CCK into fasted mice decreased their appetite. A number of subsequent studies confirmed this; one recent experiment showed that very small amounts of CCK injected into the brains of fasted sheep inhibited their feeding.

The next step in examining this problem was to look at the relation between brain CCK and experimentally produced obesity. It was found that in the genetically obese mouse and in the mouse with obesity produced by localized brain destruction, brain CCK was considerably lower than in normal control animals. These data could be interpreted to mean that the increased appetite of these animals was due to a decreased signal to the brain center that recognizes satiety so that the animals continued eating well past the point of normal fullness. Possibly, the neurologic signal is CCK.

The relevance of these studies in rodents to behavior patterns in humans is difficult to establish. CCK in the brain is present only within nerves; there is no convenient way to measure its level. However, in 1981 the first study showing that administration of CCK decreased appetite in humans was reported. CCK decreased the appetite that was evoked by the smells and sounds of food preparation. The psychologists who carried out this study used both objective and subjective measures of stimulation and gave either CCK or a placebo in random fashion to *normal* volunteers. Their results seemed to confirm the animal studies. Additionally, it was reported that administration of CCK decreased appetite in *obese* subjects. Whether the long-term effects will be the same and whether there will be a measurable effect on weight loss will be determined by future studies.

Another new chemical messenger of the brain has been identified in the past several years, β-endorphin. This is a small protein that has some actions similar to those of morphine and has perhaps as one of its functions the capacity to help the individual withstand pain. When it became possible to measure β-endorphin, it was then shown that it was increased in the blood and in the pituitary glands of mice and rats that were obese on a hereditary basis. Another research group has recently reinforced the idea that β-endorphins were important. This group at the National Institute of Mental Health gave young obese mice small doses of a drug—naltrexone—that antagonizes the actions of β-endorphin and by so doing markedly decreased the rate of weight gain of the mice. Since the drug had little effect on the lean littermates, it seemed likely that the effect on appetite was due to the antagonism to β-endorphin. The endorphins have been related to behavior in many ways so that in the future this approach may have great significance not only for problems of weight control, but for a number of other behavior-related problems as well.

—Mortimer B. Lipsett, M.D.

Gynecology and Obstetrics

Recently two products widely used by women—a drug taken for nausea during pregnancy and tampons, used each month by millions of menstruating women—have received a great deal of attention from the medical profession, the public, and the media, because of questions raised about their safety. Intense investigative efforts have resolved many of the issues surrounding both of these products, but some questions are yet to be answered.

The use of Bendectin in pregnancy

There has been growing anxiety over the past few years about the potential dangers of a number of environmental contaminants and certain drugs that may be teratogenic agents, *i.e.*, substances that cause birth defects. Bendectin, a drug widely used for the treatment of nausea and vomiting associated with pregnancy, has recently come under sharp attack as a possible cause of birth defects. This agent was first marketed in 1956; at that time it contained an antispasmodic (dicyclomine), an antihistamine (doxylamine), and vitamin B_6 (pyridoxine). In 1976 the antispasmodic was removed from the formulation as it was found not to contribute to the effectiveness of the product.

It is estimated that Bendectin has been used by more than 30 million women around the world. Approximately four million prescriptions are written each year for this drug in the United States, representing therapy for somewhere between 10 and 25% of pregnant U.S. women. Its use has been confined almost entirely to the first trimester of pregnancy, when nausea and vomiting are the most common.

Since Bendectin is so widely used, it is not surprising that it has been viewed with concern by both the scientific community and certain consumer groups. Several years ago a study at Harvard School of Public Health linked the drug to congenital heart defects, but the association was considered "weak." A highly publicized trial in the state of Florida attempted to link Bendectin to the birth of a deformed baby. (In a retrial the drug was exonerated.) Some have gone so far as to compare the drug to thalidomide—a sedative taken during pregnancy by European mothers in the 1960s, which caused the births of thousands of babies with serious malformations.

In response to these concerns, the Fertility and Maternal Health Advisory Committee of the U.S. Food and Drug Administration (FDA) met in September 1980 to evaluate the situation. Following a careful analysis of all the available data the committee concluded that no increased risk of human birth defects had been conclusively demonstrated with the use of Bendectin. Therefore, they did not recommend that this drug be removed from the market. In addition, they pointed out that Bendectin has been better studied—with particular attention paid to the risk of birth defects—than other antiemetics and is, therefore, the current drug of choice for the treatment of nausea and vomiting during pregnancy. It was also noted at the meeting that protracted vomiting in and of itself could produce fetal damage.

The committee also observed, however, that there were two studies which left "residual uncertainty" and, therefore, suggested that epidemiologic studies be continued. In addition, the committee recommended that new clinical trials for effectiveness be carried out. It further indicated that there should be a narrower indication for the use of Bendectin, limiting it to patients unresponsive to conservative dietary measures. Finally, the committee recommended the development of a patient package insert (PPI)—information written in easy-to-understand language for the patient—giving the data from the current studies but warning that the scope of the studies was inadequate to rule out a very weak teratogenic effect. The FDA accepted the committee's recommendations in March 1981.

At the present time, surveillance for the safety of the

Mike Keza—Gamma/Liaison

At the Centers for Disease Control, a microbiologist tests blood from toxic shock syndrome patients who have used various brands of tampons.

drug is being continued. Important new information will undoubtedly become available about the use of Bendectin in pregnancy over the next few years as studies gather additional data.

Tampon use and toxic shock syndrome

In June 1980 the use of tampons during menstruation was linked to a rare and poorly understood disease, toxic shock syndrome (TSS). Since then a great deal of information has been gleaned and one brand of tampon has been removed from the market.

History of tampon use. Although the use of vaginal tampons for internal menstrual protection is commonly considered to be a modern innovation, a review of medical history reveals that they have been employed in a variety of forms for centuries. Devices made of rolled lint and of wood covered with an absorbent material were described by Hippocrates. The Egyptians, Babylonians, and Assyrians employed two different types of tampons: soft papyrus was used by affluent women and softened water reeds by the poor. Wealthy Byzantine women utilized high-grade imported wool, specially carded, combed, and rolled. Roman women also used wool tampons, the external surfaces of which were often greased or waxed.

Through the ages the life-styles of women determined whether they used internal or external menstrual protection. In general, those from all levels of society who were physically active or wore a minimum of clothing tended to prefer internal protection (tampons). Those who led sedentary lives or wore more voluminous clothing tended to select some type of external pad. This generalization holds true in many cultures even today; African women engaged in hard labor use tampons of grass or reeds while Turkoman women, who lead more leisurely lives, use sanitary towels.

The morality of the use of vaginal tampons has long been a subject of debate. Allegations have been made that inserting them would destroy the appearance of virginity and that wearing them would cause sexual arousal. Anatomic studies show that the average hymenal orifice measures between 0.75 and 0.875 inches in diameter; tampons measure approximately 0.44 inches. Thus it is unlikely that the hymen—the thin, pliable membrane that surrounds the vaginal opening but only rarely blocks it completely—is injured by tampon insertion. And since the upper portion of the vagina has very few sensory nerves, it is also highly unlikely that the presence of tampons would stimulate an erotic response.

Questions have been repeatedly raised about tampon use and women's health. In the past it was believed that tampons could produce infections, with resultant sterility, by blocking the outflow of menstrual fluid. However, an extensive evaluation of menstruating women whose vaginas were tightly packed with gauze for up to a week failed to show evidence of backing up the flow through the fallopian tubes into the abdomen. Vaginal ulcerations, lacerations caused by inserters, strings breaking off, and rashes have been reported, but in general tampons have been considered safe. In one study, preexisting cervical erosions, often accompanied by vaginal discharge, were noted to *decrease* with tampon usage, and no new lesions were produced.

The marketing of commercially produced tampons in the U.S. began in 1936 after Earle C. Haas, a physician in Denver, Colo., filed the original patent. Tampon manufacturers launched aggressive advertising campaigns and increasing numbers of women switched to this "new" form of menstrual protection. Until the late 1970s, there was a general medical consensus that the use of billions of vaginal tampons had not posed any significant hazard to the health of the women who had chosen this form of menstrual protection. Their use eliminated the chafing and malodor of sanitary napkins and the annoyance of their cumbersome anchoring equipment.

The first reports of TSS. In 1978 an article by a U.S. pediatrician, James Todd, and his associates ap-

Photographs, Bob Fila—Chicago Tribune

A disproportionately high number of TSS cases have been linked to superabsorbent Rely tampons. Above a fully expanded "regular" tampon (left) and a Rely tampon (right), with its unique lateral expansion.

peared in the British medical journal *The Lancet.* They described an acute severe infection in seven children, aged 8 to 17 years. They believed that this disease, called toxic shock syndrome (TSS), was caused by a toxin produced by the bacterium, *Staphylococcus aureus.* The presenting symptoms of this condition included high fever, headache, skin rash, sore throat, nausea, vomiting, diarrhea, and, in severe cases, lowered blood pressure progressing to shock. One of the children died and, during the recovery of the six survivors, it was noted that they all had desquamation, a peeling of the skin, particularly of the palms of the hands and the soles of the feet. It was not reported that three of the patients were menstruating and using tampons, and thus the importance of this link was not recognized until later.

In December 1980 two articles appeared in *The New England Journal of Medicine* on toxic shock syndrome, one by Jeffrey P. Davis and colleagues of the Wisconsin Division of Health, in Madison, and the other by Kathryn N. Shands and colleagues from the Centers for Disease Control (CDC), in Atlanta, Ga. Both papers noted the similarities between the cases on which they were reporting and those described by Todd *et al.* An editorial in the same issue of *The New England Journal of Medicine* noted that a similar disease had been reported as early as 1927. Both the Davis and Shands articles delineated the apparent association of this disease with the use—particularly the continuous use—of tampons by menstruating women. Thus, a new clinical entity had been discovered; multiple epidemiologic and microbiologic studies were promptly set up to try to learn more about the etiology, diagnosis, and treatment of TSS.

Etiology. As investigations into the causes of TSS began, several things became evident. First, although the disease occurred in both sexes, 99% of the reported cases were in women, most of them under the age of 30. Second, 98% of these women were menstruating. Third, in almost all instances, they were wearing vaginal tampons, a disproportionate number using the brand Rely, a so-called superabsorbent tampon. Finally, it was determined by cervical and vaginal cultures that the offending organism was a strain of *Staphylococcus aureus,* and that the syndrome was probably caused by toxins produced by these bacteria.

Inasmuch as the use of tampons, particularly the superabsorbent variety, was clearly implicated as one etiologic factor, the American College of Obstetricians and Gynecologists (ACOG) undertook a study to ascertain the composition and physical characteristics of the superabsorbent tampons on the market. It was found that most of the tampons were made of cotton and rayon; some of them also contained highly absorbent synthetic fibers. To absorb the entire flow of a normal menstrual period only three Rely tampons were required. It is generally believed that a blood-soaked tampon is an excellent culture medium; it can support the proliferation of the bacteria and thus increase the amount of toxin passing into the systemic circulation. Moreover, the growing use of even more highly absorbent tampons could only serve to accentuate the problem.

At the CDC and a number of other laboratories studies were carried out on the *S. aureus* bacterium. Although this organism was found in cultures taken from the cervix, vagina, skin, mouth, nasopharynx, and rectum, it could not be recovered from the blood of women with TSS. Thus some explanation had to be found for the fact that a localized infection was capable of producing a severe fulminant systemic disease. The similarity between TSS and other diseases caused by bacterial toxins such as scarlet fever, Kawasaki disease, and Rocky Mountain spotted fever reinforced the original theory of toxin causation. Further research has established that the infectious agent is a penicillin-resistant strain of *S. aureus.* Two researchers at the University of Washington in Seattle identified two antigenic proteins that distinguish *S. aureus* strains associated with TSS from strains not associated with the disease. In May 1981 Jeffrey Davis and colleagues at the Wisconsin Division of Health reported in *The Lancet* that they had demonstrated that a specific protein (staphylococcal enterotoxin F) of *S. aureus* is strongly implicated as the causative agent of TSS.

Investigators also needed to determine the original source of the bacteria and their route of entry into the vagina. Since staphylococci are frequently present in several areas of the body, particularly the nose, it was at first believed that they could have been transferred from the fingers to the tampons and thus introduced into the vagina. In a recent study, however, the bacteria were found to be present on the vulva in 67% of women even when cervical and vaginal cultures were negative, a totally unexpected observation. In addition, prior studies had shown that tampon usage was sometimes associated with the development of small cervical and vaginal ulcerations, particularly when superabsorbent products were involved. These ulcerations then could provide a major portal of entry for the bacteria. The possibility that the tampons themselves could be the infecting agents was ruled out by microbiologic studies on the tampons, all of which were negative, including unused tampons obtained from TSS victims.

The diagnosis of TSS. In order to collect valid data on the incidence and severity of TSS, the CDC drew up a case definition for the syndrome. The specific symptoms that are necessary for a diagnosis of TSS are as follows: (1) fever of at least 102° F; (2) a sunburnlike rash; (3) extremely low blood pressure (a systolic reading of 90 or less); (4) desquamation one to two weeks after onset of disease; (5) involvement of three or more of the following organ systems: (a) gastrointestinal (vomiting or diarrhea at the onset of illness); (b) muscular (pain or a high level of creatine phosphokinase); (c) mucous membranal (vagina, throat, mouth, or eyes); (d) renal (kidney malfunction); (e) hepatic (liver malfunction); (f) blood (platelet anomalies); (g) central nervous system (disorientation and alterations in consciousness). In addition, negative results on the following laboratory tests contribute to the TSS diagnosis: blood, throat, or cerebrospinal fluid cultures, and serologic tests for Rocky Mountain spotted fever, measles, and leptospirosis.

Treatment. Once it is suspected that a woman has TSS, any retained tampons should be removed, cervical and vaginal cultures taken, and aggressive fluid

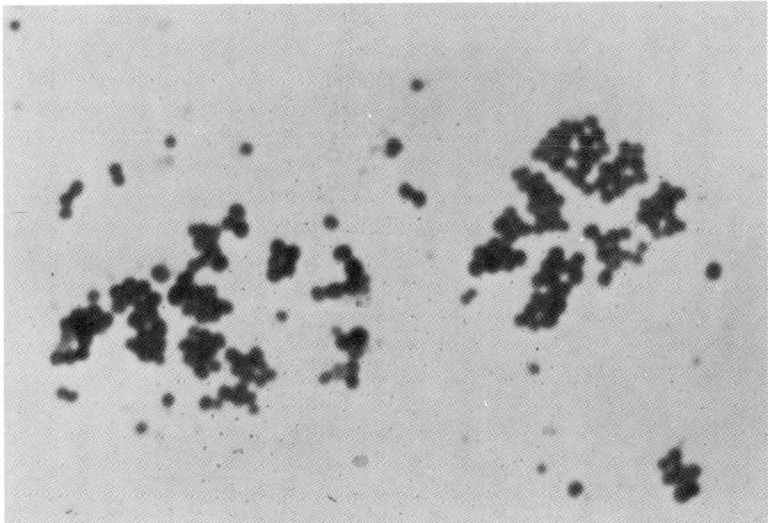

Centers for Disease Control, Atlanta

A penicillin-resistant strain of Staphylococcus aureus *bacterium is believed to produce a toxin that enters the patient's system and causes toxic shock syndrome.*

replacement instituted. There is no evidence to date that antibiotics are effective in the treatment of acute TSS. However, specific antibiotics such as the cephalosporins and certain penicillins seem to be of value in reducing the recurrence rate, which has been estimated to be approximately 30%. Further, it is recommended that women who have developed TSS should not use tampons again, or at least until vaginal cultures for *S. aureus* are negative.

In response to the public anxiety about tampon use the ACOG has made a number of general recommendations. Women need not stop using tampons; however, it would be prudent, at present, to discontinue the use of the newly developed superabsorbent tampons until more conclusive scientific research has been conducted. To reduce the possible risk of tampon use women are advised to alternate tampons with sanitary napkins or "minipads" during a given menstrual cycle. When tampons are used, they should be changed frequently—at least every six to eight hours—to reduce the risk of potential infection. If a woman is using tampons and experiences such symptoms as high fever, vomiting, diarrhea, or a sunburnlike rash, she should discontinue tampon use and consult her physician immediately.

Current status. There appears to be no question that TSS is a distinct clinical syndrome. The true incidence of this syndrome is still being debated. By the end of January 1981, 941 confirmed cases had been reported to the CDC. Cases had also been reported in Canada, Great Britain, The Netherlands, and Sweden. In September 1980, the CDC estimated that the incidence of TSS in the United States was three in 100,000 women of menstrual age per year. For several reasons it now appears, however, that this figure was probably too low. First, it is likely that there was incomplete reporting. Second, the rate was based on only the most severe cases, which met all of the CDC diagnostic criteria; thus, less severe ones were not counted. Third, the original figure assumed incorrectly that all women of menstrual age were actually menstruating.

The true mortality rate is also a matter of continuing debate. There were 73 deaths in the group of 941 patients, giving a case fatality rate of 7.8%. For the above reasons, the accuracy of *this* figure is also being disputed. Most investigators currently believe that the mortality is probably considerably lower. Moreover, it will, in all likelihood, continue to drop as the result of increased public awareness of the disease, leading to earlier diagnosis and treatment.

The precise role played by Rely tampons also remains unclear. The increased incidence of TSS paralleled the increased use of these particular tampons. Even more important, the risk of developing TSS was shown to be statistically higher for Rely tampon users than for users of other brands. Therefore, the manufacturer of this tampon voluntarily withdrew it from the marketplace in September 1980 and launched an advertising campaign, warning about the risk of TSS and asking for the return of any unused tampons. Since that time certain of the other tampon manufacturers have made changes in the formulation of their menstrual products and have also added warnings about TSS to their packages. The TSS problem is clearly not related only to the use of Rely tampons since the syndrome continues to be reported even after their removal from the market and in fact is also seen in areas where they have never been sold.

Another very important consideration is the actual magnitude of the risk to women who wish to use tampons. It is currently believed that the risk for women who have never had TSS is very low, probably somewhere between 3.0 and 6.2 cases per 100,000 menstruating women. But data are not yet available about the true risk for women who have had one or more episodes of TSS (either those who have or have not received antibiotic therapy).

Also unknown is the reason for the apparent protection against TSS offered by any form of contraception. In one study only 31% of TSS patients were using some form of birth control against 70% of a non-TSS group. It has been suggested that the decreased bleeding induced by the use of oral contraceptives (the Pill) may be a factor, but this remains to be proved and does not explain the apparent protection offered by other contraceptive methods.

The CDC reported a decrease in the frequency of TSS cases beginning in September 1980. Possible reasons for a decrease have been explored, from delays in reporting, to seasonal variations, to a decreased interest in reporting; all are unlikely. The most likely explanation for a decrease is a change in the behavior of women. The percentage of tampon users has dropped from 70 to 55%. As women have become more aware of the syndrome, many who continue to use tampons do so only intermittently and they change them more frequently. They also seek medical help earlier, and thus the disease does not progress far enough to satisfy the CDC diagnostic criteria.

Other investigators deny that there has been a drop in the frequency of the occurrence of TSS. They point out that cases have been reported from 48 states, but that there appears to be a direct relationship between the interest of a given medical community in the disease and the number of cases reported. For example, Minnesota, which has only 2% of the U.S. population, has reported 37% of the TSS cases not associated with menstruation. Additionally, in Minnesota and other states involved in the initial reporting of cases, where the level of interest is high, no decrease has been noted. Ongoing investigations will undoubtedly provide the answers to the majority of these unanswered questions over the next several years.

—Elizabeth B. Connell, M.D.

Special Report:
Is Anything Safe?
by Marcia J. Opp

"Since becoming pregnant, I've given up alcohol, coffee, cigarettes, and even diet sodas, because I've read that all of them might harm our unborn baby, and I don't want to take any chances," said a 30-year-old woman. "Now, I've just read that sex might cause an infection and premature labor. What can possibly be next?"

This comment reflects the increasingly prevalent attitude that pregnancy should be a time of abstention and sacrifice if a mother-to-be really places a higher value on her unborn baby's welfare than on her need to indulge herself. The pregnant woman who had envisioned that this time of her life would be joyous and fulfilling may find instead that she is plagued by fatigue, nausea and vomiting, anxiety, and above all, worry.

Although her primary concern is to deliver a healthy baby, the pregnant woman may be confused about how much she must change her daily routine and alter her habits. How seriously is she to take media reports of new laboratory or clinical findings? The public has so often been hit with alarmist reports of the dangers of some common substance—reports that are later discounted or modified—that a great residue of cynicism has resulted. On the other hand, experiences such as the thalidomide tragedy of the 1960s demonstrate that even a substance prescribed by a doctor and thus assumed to be safe can have unsuspected potential for damage. No woman wants to take an action for which she will suffer a lifetime of self-reproach.

The problem for prospective parents is to find some accurate and objective measure of the risks inherent in certain actions or substances and then to decide the degree of risk that they are willing to assume. Lacking the bedrock of definite cause-and-effect relationships, they must base their decisions on the best knowledge available. Common sense and prudence, not obsessive caution, should be the guides when there is doubt. But decisions should be based on fact, not hearsay, old wives' tales, or a friend's personal experiences. There are some areas in which risks are clearly defined.

There is solid consensus among scientists and physicians involved in prenatal research that moderate to heavy alcohol intake, heavy smoking, ingestion of drugs, and poor nutrition during pregnancy seriously endanger an infant's chances of entering the world intact. However, there is less proof that caffeine, sexual activity in the late stages of pregnancy, strenuous exercise, and exposure to pesticides, herbicides, insecticides, and environmental pollution can jeopardize a baby's mental and physical well-being.

Photo Trends

It is still unknown whether environmental pollution can damage an unborn child—this is one of many risk factors that the prospective parent must evaluate.

Once a woman decides to abide by certain restrictions, she has to decide when to begin those preventive measures—before planning to become pregnant, as soon as unprotected intercourse occurs, or after a pregnancy has been confirmed. Waiting the average two months until her pregnancy is confirmed by a physician may be too late. The crucial development stages in the embryo take place in the first 12 weeks after conception, when the bodily structures are formed from the rapidly dividing and differentiating cells. By that time, a woman may have had a half-dozen drinks at a party, had an X-ray for suspected pneumonia, or have taken drugs such as tranquilizers or antibiotics.

Prenatal specialists encourage couples who are trying to conceive to conduct their lives as though the woman is already pregnant. There is great reason for this caution. Each year in the U.S., one in 12 infants is born with a birth defect. In addition, nearly 500,000 pregnancies end in miscarriage or stillbirth, according to estimates by the March of Dimes Birth Defects Foundation. A birth defect may be inherited, caused by environmental factors, or due to a combination of the two. Among the environmental factors are those over which the pregnant woman can exercise total or partial control if she chooses to do so.

Mariette Pathy Allen—Peter Arnold, Inc.

The hope for every pregnancy is the delivery of a healthy, normal baby. Couples planning to have a child must take into consideration the effects of habits such as smoking and the consumption of drugs such as caffeine and alcohol. Any benefit the mother hopes to derive from such habits must be weighed against the possibility of lifelong impairment of the child.

What about alcohol?

It is estimated that 1,500 babies are born every year with physical or mental handicaps because their mothers drank too much wine, beer, or hard liquor while they were pregnant. A minimum safe level of alcohol consumption has not been established—there may even be subtle effects in offspring of occasional social drinkers. Some studies have found a 2½-fold increase in miscarriages among women who had only one drink a day. The alcohol intake in two drinks a day increases the risk of stillbirth and miscarriage and decreases birth weights. Low-birth-weight, undersized babies often fail to thrive and are more susceptible to a host of serious problems both during and after birth.

Epidemiological studies correlating birth defects and amounts of alcohol consumed by pregnant women abound. One of the more provocative findings is that 11% of pregnant women who drank heavily only until they learned that they were pregnant had babies with features of fetal alcohol syndrome. In a Boston study, researchers reported that 32% of pregnant heavy drinkers bore infants with birth defects, compared with 14% in the moderate drinking group, and 9% in the light drinking or abstaining group.

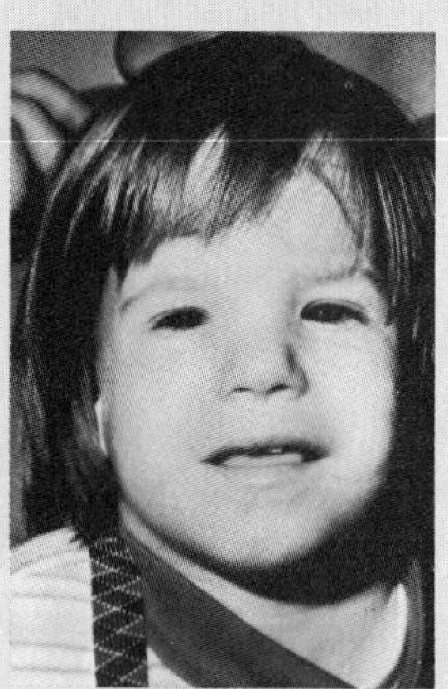

Courtesy, Ann Pytkowicz Streissguth

The fetal alcohol syndrome, manifested by recognizable facial characteristics and a host of mental and physical abnormalities, is caused by excessive alcohol consumption by the pregnant woman. Most experts think it best that women abstain from alcohol completely during their pregnancies.

Children affected by fetal alcohol syndrome (FAS) show a distinct pattern of physical, mental, and behavioral abnormalities, including facial and skeletal irregularities, heart defects, growth deficiency, and in some cases even mental retardation. Particularly distinctive is the combination of distorted facial characteristics—FAS children frequently have a shorter, flatter nose, epicanthic folds at the inner eye, short eye openings, a thin upper lip, a flattened philtrum (the furrow between the nose and upper lip), and a flat mid-face. They are smaller and slower to develop. Subnormal brain size and brain malformations have been documented during autopsies of babies with severe FAS who did not survive.

Central nervous system deficits can be detected at birth by an experienced observer. Long-term studies have documented that a child's hyperactivity or mild learning disabilities in some cases can be traced to the mother's moderate drinking during her pregnancy. (A moderate drinker is classified as one who takes between two and four drinks—one to two ounces of absolute alcohol—daily, and a heavy drinker consumes more than four drinks daily.)

In an evaluation of pregnant women's attitudes about drinking, the Pacific Institute for Research and

Evaluation mailed questionnaires to women who had recently given birth, asking about the woman's knowledge of the effects of alcohol on the unborn child and about the woman's actual drinking practices during her pregnancy. The majority of the new mothers responded that pregnant women should refrain from daily drinking because alcohol during pregnancy could be harmful, but they all did not follow their own advice. The study concluded that "most pregnant women are already aware of the teratogenic effects of alcohol [but their] awareness does not appear to influence risky drinking practices during pregnancy."

At the University of Washington, where pioneering work was done in the early 1970s on the fetal alcohol syndrome, the Pregnancy and Health Program recommends "abstinence from alcohol during pregnancy and for a period of time prior to pregnancy." The National Institute of Alcohol Abuse and Alcoholism in 1980 advised pregnant women to drink no alcohol. There is no doubt that alcohol can have a detrimental effect on the fetus. If a woman decides to take any alcohol when she is pregnant, she must decide whether the risk will be significant at her stage of pregnancy and whether she feels she can assume this risk.

What about drugs?

When the pregnant woman takes medicine, be it cold pills, tranquilizers, sleeping pills, anticonvulsants, or antibiotics, the drugs pass through the placenta, the wall of tissue through which the fetus is nourished. Many drugs—prescription and over-the-counter—pass quickly through the placenta. The drug's effects are intensified in the tiny developing fetus. Some may linger in the fetus because it does not have the capacity to metabolize them efficiently. Testing of individual drugs for adverse effects on the fetus cannot be done for ethical reasons, so data on potential birth defects must be extrapolated from animal studies.

Continuous use of aspirin can reportedly starve the fetus of oxygen and, if used late in pregnancy, it may cause excessive bleeding at delivery. Cleft lip and palate and other congenital malformations have been attributed to use of tranquilizers during pregnancy, while antiepileptic drugs have been linked to congenital defects like those of alcohol consumption. Tetracycline can inhibit bone growth and can cause the child's teeth to be permanently discolored.

The safe use during pregnancy of many commonly prescribed drugs has not been established. The benefit of the drug to the mother must be weighed against possible harm to the fetus. In some cases, for example, when a potent antihypertension medication is being taken, the risk of discontinuing the drug may be as great as or greater than continuing to take it. Any woman contemplating pregnancy or unprotected intercourse should discuss her intake of medication with her physician.

Erika Stone—Peter Arnold, Inc.

Smoking during pregnancy increases the chances of spontaneous abortion, stillbirth, premature birth, and low birth weight.

What about smoking?

Numerous studies, including the United States Collaborative Perinatal Project, confirm the wide range of adverse effects on the babies of mothers who smoked cigarettes during their pregnancies. From an increased immediate risk of spontaneous abortions, stillbirths, premature births, and smaller than normal babies to a long-term risk of decreased rate of learning, smoking is said to cause damage by reducing the amount of oxygen available to the fetus. Any smoker who miscarries or has difficulty becoming pregnant should consider cessation of her habit, experts advise.

In addition to the risk to the fetus, smoking increases the risk of crib death (sudden infant death syndrome) to the newborn by 52%—a statistic that might persuade the fence-sitters to quit. Smoking also contributes to the premature separation of the placenta from the uterine wall—a cause of spontaneous abortion. Such spontaneous abortions are due to smoking in 20–25% of cases.

Fortunately, if the pregnant woman cuts back or stops smoking for even part of her pregnancy these effects can be mitigated.

What about diet?

For years, the medical establishment told women to cut their calories during pregnancy so that they would

Gabor Demjen—Stock, Boston

Proper nutrition during pregnancy is essential to counter the heavy demands of the growing fetus. It is now thought that a woman can gain up to 30 pounds during her pregnancy; too low a gain might result in an undersized infant that has difficulty in thriving during the first crucial weeks of life.

gain only 10 to 15 pounds. This practice resulted in underweight babies that were more susceptible to illness, and some say, to more nervous, high-strung personalities. The pendulum has now swung over to a position that permits a higher weight gain, up to a maximum of 30 pounds and encourages a balanced diet with lots of fresh fruits and vegetables and protein foods.

Some women may decide in addition to cut out all processed foods and drinks containing additives on the theory that if some of the chemicals have been implicated as causing cancer in animals, a cautious course would be to avoid them. The junk-food diets that some young teenaged mothers favor have been blamed in part for their higher incidence of birth defects and complications in pregnancy.

What about sexual relations?

Statistics from numerous human studies support a woman's decision to cut out smoking, drinking, and drugs, and to follow her diet faithfully, but when research is debated, most women believe that a flip of the coin will do as well as careful analysis. For instance, the safety of sex during the last three months of pregnancy has recently come under close scrutiny following publication of a study documenting a higher fetal death rate among pregnant women who have intercourse compared with that of those who abstained. After analyzing nearly 27,000 pregnancies, researchers said they found more infections (156 per 1,000) in the amniotic fluid of fetuses of women who had intercourse at least once a week in the four weeks prior to delivery than among those who abstained (117 per 1,000).

Informal surveys indicate that pregnant women who have not had previous delivery trauma consider that the risks of engaging in sexual relations throughout pregnancy are low enough and the benefits high enough to take the chance.

What about caffeine?

How much is too much caffeine? A number of studies involving rats, rabbits, mice, and chickens have correlated high maternal caffeine intake and embryonic deaths, missing fingers and toes, and retarded skeletal development. Caffeine, a stimulant found in coffee, tea, cocoa, some colas, candies, and medications, has not been officially indicted as toxic to the human fetus. However, the March of Dimes Birth Defects Foundation cautions that preliminary, unpublished studies implicate caffeine in an increased incidence of breech deliveries, poor infant muscle tone, low birth weights, stillbirths, miscarriages, prematurity, and "abnormal-looking" newborns. With a danger level of five cups daily, the majority of women take comfort that their one cup a day coffee habit probably will not result in a birth defect.

The informed choice

Taking a risk in pregnancy is making a choice between a present need or desire—to share a bottle of wine—and the possibility of an unwanted effect at a more remote time—harm to the child. Figuring in the choice are the strength of the present desire, the stage of pregnancy at which the action is taken, knowledge of the severity of the possible effects, and estimation of the likelihood of the occurrence of the effects. In addition, the pregnant woman may feel more than a little resentment over being required to make the needs of her pregnancy the primary factor in her life. A pregnancy should not mean nine months of nervous tension.

Knowledge about the risks in pregnancy may take some of the fun away, but the majority of women say they would rather be apprised of their options so they can make their own decisions. There is no pregnancy that is without risk to the fetus, but some risks can be identified and quantified. When a choice is to be made that may have an important effect on the unborn child, it should be as informed a choice as possible.

Health Care Costs

George Bernard Shaw suggested in his preface to *The Doctor's Dilemma* "[t]hat any sane nation, having observed that you could provide for the supply of bread by giving bakers a pecuniary interest in baking for you, should go on to give a surgeon a pecuniary interest in cutting off your leg, is enough to make one despair of political humanity." When Shaw wrote *The Doctor's Dilemma* in 1913, physicians in Great Britain were paid on the basis of services rendered, so-called fee-for-service. With the introduction of the British National Health Service in 1948, physician specialists, including surgeons, were placed on a salary, and this remains their method of reimbursement in the United Kingdom to this day.

Presumably it was, at least in part, to eliminate the fiscal incentive to provide unnecessary medical services and to avoid the expense of such care that the British (and most national health plans in the world) have abandoned fee-for-service. That they have succeeded in this goal is strongly suggested by the fact that operation rates in the United States, where fee-for-service remains the predominant method of reimbursement, are double those in Great Britain—the average American is twice as likely to undergo surgery in a given year as is the average Englishman or Scot.

Reinforcement to the notion that method of reimbursement and rates for surgical services are causally related is provided by the observation that, within the United States, operation rates for patients cared for under arrangements of prepayment, such as the Kaiser Permanente health plan, are substantially less than for those subscribing to fee-for-service plans. But there is contrary evidence, also. The payment of a fee may not necessarily be the primary determinant of whether such elective operations will be performed, as is demonstrated by the following observations.

A study of unnecessary medical care

Several years ago at Stanford University a survey of physicians and their spouses as surgical patients was conducted. Their surgical histories were compared with those of lawyers, ministers, graduates of Stanford Business School, and of their spouses, with approximately 1,000 in each group. By means of a mail questionnaire, the respondents were asked whether they had ever undergone appendectomy, cholecystectomy (gallbladder removal), thyroidectomy, hemorrhoidectomy, herniorrhaphy (for men), and for women, hysterectomy and mastectomy. The study was carried out in a geographic area of high physician- and bed-to-population rates and high per capita income. The purpose was to predict the impact of consumer education on demands for care in a medical system in which financial barriers are removed. The hypothesis was that physician-patients, as informed consumers, and in the absence of financial incentives for the surgeon, would undergo fewer operations than the other three professional groups. Just the opposite was found. Operation rates for physicians and their spouses were as high or higher than rates for the other groups. Indeed, hysterectomy, an operation often believed to be performed unnecessarily, was performed on physicians' wives at a stunningly high rate—such that half of these women will have lost their uteri by age 65.

From these observations one can conclude that high rates of utilization do not depend on the surgical fee alone. Method of reimbursement was not determined in this study; "professional courtesy" may have resulted in no fee charged in many instances. Many, perhaps most, physicians carry personal medical insurance, and in this circumstance a fee is often charged. It is assumed, however, that where the patient is a physician or a physician's wife, remuneration is unlikely to enter into the surgeon's decision.

From this study, one can also conclude that the

The table compares rates (per 100 respondents) of utilization of surgical services based on a study conducted by Stanford University researchers. The rates are age adjusted, with one-third in each group under 40, one-third in their 40s, and one-third 50 or older.

Operations among four groups of professionals and their wives

	physicians	*ministers*	*lawyers*	*businessmen*	*wives of physicians*	*wives of ministers*	*wives of lawyers*	*wives of businessmen*
appendectomy	23.0	21.7	20.8	20.4	22.3	24.1	16.4	22.0
cholecystectomy	1.8	2.2	1.9	1.2	5.9	4.9	2.9	2.0
herniorrhaphy	10.3	12.4	8.7	11.1				
thyroidectomy	1.4	0.9	0.7	0.6	4.1	2.9	2.3	4.0
hysterectomy					22.6	20.9	20.4	17.3
hemorrhoidectomy	6.9	6.3	7.8	7.7	3.6	4.2	5.4	2.8
mastectomy					3.8	2.3	3.7	2.5
any of the above	36.1	35.8	33.3	34.2	44.9	41.3	38.6	37.0

Adapted from "The Physician-Patient as an Informed Consumer of Surgical Services," John P. Bunker and William Brown, Jr., THE NEW ENGLAND JOURNAL OF MEDICINE, Vol. 290, No.19, pp. 1051–1055, May 9, 1974 physician as patient places a high value on surgical care and that, indeed, physicians believe in the value of the procedures that they provide. This professional self-confidence has been labeled the "technological imperative" by Victor Fuchs, professor of economics at Stanford. Sociologist Eliot Freidson has spoken in terms of the "bias toward illness," reflecting the physician's view that "since he believes that the work he does is all for the good of the client, [he] typically assumes that it is better to impute disease than to deny it and risk overlooking or missing it." Reinforcing this basic professional bias are the considerable added incentives of the threat of malpractice litigation. Suits against physicians for "overlooking" a disease or condition are common. Suits against physicians for performing "unnecessary" procedures are rare.

An absence of data

Method of reimbursement and professional bias both appear to contribute strongly to high rates of medical and surgical utilization. What allows them to play such apparently dominant roles is that the effectiveness of most medical procedures has not been determined. There are reasonably satisfactory data on which to determine whether therapies intended to prevent death or prolong life have succeeded in their objectives. Only a small proportion of medical care is intended to prevent death, however. Most of it is directed toward improvement in the quality of life—in the relief of discomfort, disfigurement, or dysfunction. Clearly, these are highly worthwhile goals.

The figure below shows the cumulative likelihood of hysterectomy in wives of physicians in Santa Clara County, Calif., and in U.S. women. The high rate among physicians' wives suggests that alleged overuse of surgery is not *due to lack of knowledge about medical procedures and their risks.*

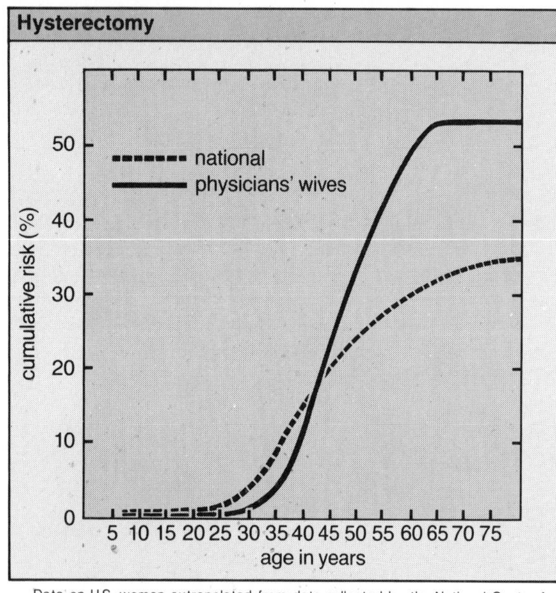

Data on U.S. women extrapolated from data collected by the National Center for Health Statistics

Our methods of measuring the quality of life, however, are crude, and we have carried out relatively few studies of the effects of medical care on the quality of life. Thus, the effectiveness of hysterectomy in the treatment of cancer of the uterus or of a bleeding fibroid tumor are well established. What we do not know are the net benefits of elective hysterectomy and its attendant small but real risks in the treatment of minimally symptomatic dysmenorrhea (painful menstruation). We do not claim that such hysterectomies are not worthwhile; it is simply that we have not carried out sufficient studies to find out. The same is true for large numbers of the procedures that comprise the practice of medicine: diagnostic tests, medications, and hospitalization, as well as operations.

While data on the effectiveness of medical therapies are often inconclusive, physicians (and patients) nevertheless must make decisions. By nature optimistic and self-confident, physicians tend to believe in the effectiveness of the treatments that they use—as was suggested above in discussing the high rates of surgery for physician-patients and their spouses. This combination of poor data and professional optimism strongly encourages the overutilization of diagnostic tests, drugs, operations, and hospitals.

The phenomenon of professional optimism has been convincingly demonstrated by Thomas Chalmers, president of Mount Sinai Medical Center in New York City, and by Frederick Mosteller, professor of statistics at Harvard. Chalmers, Mosteller, and their respective colleagues reviewed published reports of clinical trials and classified them according to the quality of the experimental design: well-designed, randomized, controlled studies on the one hand; poorly designed, nonrandomized studies, on the other. They found that an author's enthusiasm for the procedure he or she was evaluating was inversely related to the quality of the experimental design. Poorly designed studies almost always were interpreted as more favorable to the treatment than were well-controlled studies.

If better data are so important to the appropriate and efficient use of medical therapies, one might reasonably ask why they have not been collected. Indeed, in 1859 Florence Nightingale, after her return from the Crimean War, urged that uniform data on the outcome of medical care in hospitals be made available. Similarly, Ernest A. Codman, an orthopedic surgeon at the Massachusetts General Hospital, in 1913 urged that the medical profession "formulate some method of hospital report showing as nearly as possible what are the results of the treatment obtained at different institutions. This report must be made out and published by each hospital in a uniform manner, so that comparison will be possible. With such a report as a starting-point, those interested can begin to ask questions as to management and efficiency."

That we are only now beginning to collect the data

that Nightingale and Codman requested can be attributed to a variety of factors. Apathy and ignorance have, unfortunately, played a considerable role, and physicians even today are, for the most part, untrained or poorly trained in statistics, probability theory, and epidemiology—skills essential to the evaluation of population-based outcome data. Even more unfortunately, organized medicine has actively opposed the collection and publication of such evaluative data, believing, perhaps, that they may be used by the government as the basis for interfering with or regulating the practice of medicine.

Studying the effectiveness of medical care

Obtaining reliable data on the effectiveness of medical treatments is not a matter only of will and commitment, however. There are formidable technical, ethical, and economic obstacles to the study of the effectiveness of medical care. Observing the use of treatments and recording their outcome may or may not provide reliable data. If a treatment is believed to be effective, it will often appear to be superior in studies with imperfect experimental design, or in studies that are poorly controlled, as Chalmers and Mosteller have so clearly shown. Conclusive data for judging the effectiveness of a specific treatment under most circumstances require a so-called randomized clinical trial. The treatment to be studied is assigned, randomly, to half the group of patients suffering from the condition for which the treatment is designed. The other half of the patients receive the best alternative treatment or, if none is available, a placebo. The randomization process, if properly conducted, offers strong assurance that the two patient groups equally reflect both unknown and known characteristics that might affect the response to treatment.

Randomized clinical trials are carried out for almost all new drugs, but they are less commonly performed for new diagnostic procedures and rarely for new operations. Surgery presents a number of special problems in evaluation. It is often not clear whether the procedure is a new operation or a modification of an old one. Indeed, an operation is apt to be performed in a variety of differing ways, varying, for example, with the surgeon's preference, or perhaps with the special characteristics of the patient. Each variant of the new operation may have to be tested in a separate clinical trial. Furthermore, it may not be clear at the outset just how to do the operation. If possible, the new procedure will have been carried out many times in the animal laboratory, but it is still apt to be necessary to learn how to do it in human beings. The first patients on whom the technique is tested therefore may not do very well; an older, inherently poorer, but familiar alternative treatment might well produce better results initially, although later on the new treatment might prove to be superior. This leads immediately to an ethical problem. If it appears that one treatment is superior to another—as the older procedure would initially be in our hypothetical case—it would be unethical to conduct a clinical trial in which half the patients would receive a treatment believed to be inferior.

There have been very few well-controlled, randomized clinical trials of surgical procedures, largely because of the foregoing difficulties. And for these same reasons it is probably unrealistic to expect to obtain ideal data on future surgical procedures. Nevertheless, it is essential to the rationalization of the organization and delivery of health care to have substantially improved information on the outcomes of treatment than is now available. Physicians must have better data on the basis of which to prescribe rationally. Patients must certainly have better information if they are to choose intelligently in the many circumstances where alternative therapies are valued differently by different patients. And the government and other third-party insur-

Stayskal—Chicago Tribune/New York News Syndicate, Inc.

ers need better information as a basis for decisions whether or not to reimburse the patient.

Is it cost effective to study health care?

What is now needed is a markedly enhanced national capacity to evaluate medical and surgical procedures. It was, indeed, with exactly this goal in mind that the U.S. Congress, in 1978, created the National Center for Health Care Technology (NCHCT). The center was to undertake and support multifaceted assessments of health-care technology, taking into account "the safety, effectiveness, and cost-effectiveness of, and the social, ethical, and economic impact of health-care technologies."

The center's achievement, in its brief three years of existence, has been small, to a large extent because of a low level of funding ($4.1 million, of which $2.8 million is for research, for fiscal year 1981). In late 1981, with the economy hurting on all fronts and widespread agreement that government spending should be reduced, it might seem reasonable that a new agency, not yet performing an essential service, be sacrificed, which has been the recommendation of the Reagan administration. It is also apparently believed by the administration and by many members of the Congress that the NCHCT's evaluative functions can be carried out by another agency, the National Center for Health Services Research (NCHSR). NCHSR is itself, however, seriously underfunded. The president has recommended a budget of $20 million for fiscal 1982, nearly $7 million less than for 1981 and $45 million less than for 1973. It is, therefore, exceedingly unlikely that it will be able to accept these new responsibilities, let alone carry out its current ones.

Two critical questions, at a time of national dollar pinch, are: Will health-services research and technology assessment save money? Are studies of the cost effectiveness of medical care themselves cost effective? The answers are, almost certainly, yes.

Take, as a single example, tonsillectomy. Ten years ago, according to data from the National Center for Health Statistics, more than a million such procedures were carried out annually in the United States. In 1978, this had fallen by half, a fall based in large part on the recognition by physicians of the limited conditions for which this operation is effective. Tonsillectomies cost approximately $1,000 in Palo Alto, Calif., and Medford, Ore., $785 in Waterville, Me., and $745 in Las Cruces, N.M. The saving from not doing a half million tonsillectomies at these prices would pay for all three centers several times over.

Tonsillectomy is not the only procedure whose effectiveness may be unknown or uncertain. The entire controversy over unnecessary treatment is a reflection of the uncertainty of medical outcomes. If better data reduced the number of operations or days of hospitalization by as much as 1%, the saving would be more than a billion dollars. In all likelihood, the effect would be a much greater one.

With the decreasing likelihood of adequate federal funding for studies of the outcomes of medical care, it is now incumbent on the private sector, including the industrial leadership as well as the medical profession, to develop other sources of funding. An obvious potential source of such funding is the medical insurance industry itself, which already suffers an acute need for such data in order to determine which medical and surgical procedures to pay for.

It is, of course, in the enlightened self-interest of the medical profession to have such information available, for it is becoming increasingly clear to physicians, as well as to politicians and to the public, that medical expenditures cannot continue to increase at their extra-ordinary current pace. That the profession may now be willing to join in such an effort is at least possible. Its resistance to governmental fact-finding stems directly from the fear of subsequent regulation of medical practice. If, however, a medical fact-finding capability can be developed within the context of a privately and locally controlled practice of medicine, physicians themselves may respond enthusiastically, rather than reluctantly, in the search for facts that will allow them to take better care of their patients.

—*John P. Bunker, M.D.*

Heart and Blood Vessels

Coronary arteries are the vessels that supply the heart muscle with blood. Blood flow through these arteries is critically regulated to meet the constant demands of the heart muscle, or myocardium, for energy in order for the heart to continue its essential function: pumping blood to all organs and tissues of the body. Compared with other organs the heart, supplied mostly by oxygen carried in the blood, has considerable energy needs even when the body is at rest. However, when the body is under stress, such as during intense exercise, heart rate may increase to 200 beats per minute (from resting values of 60–80), and the heart may pump 20–30 liters of blood each minute (from resting values of about 5 liters). This vastly increased work increases the heart's need for oxygen, and coronary blood flow may increase to a value four to eight times the resting value to meet the demands.

Scientists have long known that atherosclerotic plaques (deposits of lipids and other substances) can form gradually within the coronary artery, causing a narrowing of its interior cavity, or lumen, and thereby decreasing its blood-carrying capacity. Reducing the ability of the coronary arteries to deliver blood to the heart muscle deprives the myocardium of appropriate amounts of oxygen, leading to the typical signs and symptoms of coronary heart disease. The slow, years-long process of plaque development led scientists to

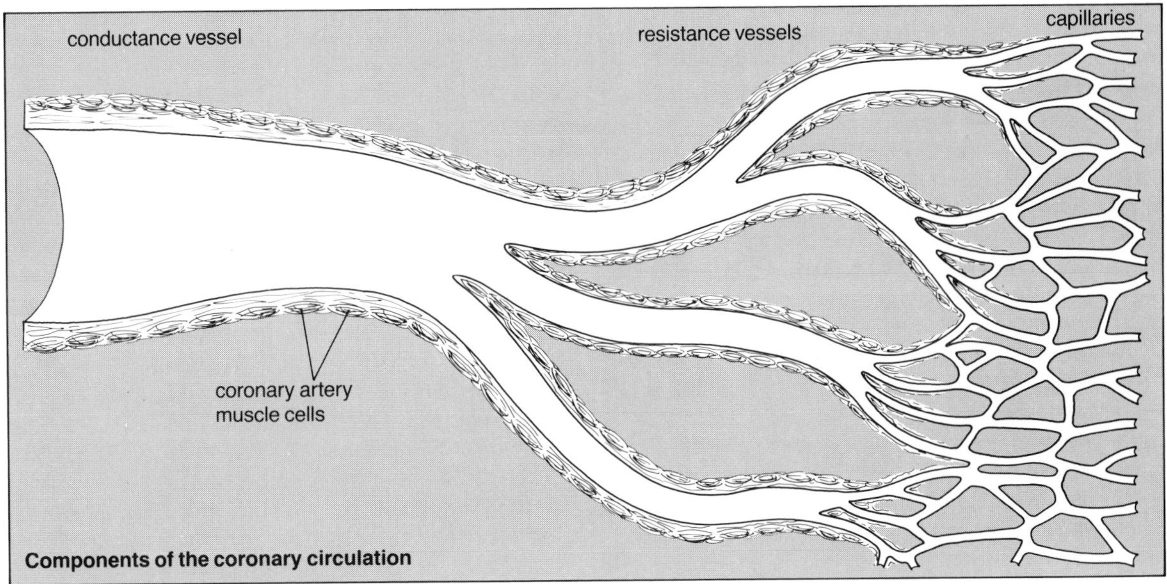

Each coronary artery consists of three portions: a conductance portion on the surface of the heart; resistance vessels called arterioles, which are deeper in the heart muscle, and through which blood flow to the myocardium is regulated by the action of the surrounding muscle cells; and a fine capillary network through which nutrients and gases are diffused.

believe that the signs and symptoms of coronary artery disease could be ascribed to a relatively fixed narrowing, or stenosis, of the coronary arteries. In recent years, however, it has become clear that such stenosis is a much more dynamic lesion. Changes in the degree of stenosis are caused not only by progressive buildup of plaque itself but also by sudden phenomena: deposition of clumps of small blood components called platelets, spasm of the muscle in the wall of the artery, and the formation of blood clots. In fact, recognition of such sudden changes has led to the use of drugs that prevent platelet clumping and relax coronary arterial muscle spasm and to therapeutic approaches that break up blood clots. These new developments are described below.

Consequences of coronary artery occlusion

Basically each of the two coronary arteries can be divided into three segments: a large "conductance" portion, which lies on the surface of the heart; smaller arterioles or "resistance" vessels, which lie within the heart muscle; and extremely fine capillaries, through which nutrients pass from the blood into the myocardium. The arterioles normally are responsible for controlling the amount of blood supplied to the myocardium. When the heart is resting, coronary artery muscle cells constrict the arterioles, thereby reducing flow to the myocardium. As the heart begins to work harder, the arterioles dilate and blood flow increases appropriately. The difference between resting coronary blood flow and the maximum flow that the coronary arteries are able to deliver is called the coronary blood flow reserve.

The above concepts help explain certain clinical features of coronary artery disease. Coronary atherosclerotic plaques develop in the large conductance vessels. Despite their presence, under resting conditions blood flow to the myocardium is not reduced even when the luminal diameter of these vessels is diminished by as much as 50%. This is so because as the plaque increases the resistance to flow offered by the large conductance vessel the arteriole compensates by dilating. Although resting flow is preserved, the increased resistance in the conductance vessels impinges on the coronary reserve and limits the ability of the coronary system to meet the demands of a high cardiac workload. Resting coronary flow decreases only when the narrowing of the vessel becomes so severe that the coronary reserve is completely exhausted and can no longer compensate for further increases in resistance.

When the heart muscle does not receive its needed blood flow, the resulting condition is called ischemia. The clinical consequence of ischemia is chest pain, or angina pectoris. If myocardial ischemia is sufficiently long and severe (usually hours), then heart muscle cells die, a process called infarction (the commonest meaning of the term heart attack).

Ischemia can occur either because the demand for nutrients increases beyond the ability of a moderately narrowed coronary artery to supply blood to the myocardium, as would occur during exercise, or because some process suddenly causes severe narrowing or blockage of the artery so that it cannot deliver sufficient flow even to a resting heart. Thus, when moderate coronary narrowings are present, ischemia is most likely to occur during exercise or other stressful conditions. This fact explains the usual appearance of anginal chest pain during exercise or excitement and also underlies the use of exercise stress tests to detect signs of myocardial ischemia caused by moderate coronary narrowing, when signs and symptoms are absent while the patient is at rest.

Platelets in coronary arterial occlusion

Atherosclerosis, the most common cause of arterial occlusive disease, remains poorly understood. Atherosclerotic plaques of themselves do not necessarily cause complete coronary occlusion, but recent evidence has confirmed that other processes in conjunction with plaque can lead to sudden total occlusion of the artery. One such process currently under suspicion involves the mechanism by which the body is protected against serious bleeding from injuries. When a blood vessel is cut, blood escapes from the vascular system until complex clotting processes are triggered, during which platelets aggregate at the site of injury, an event that mechanically helps stop bleeding.

A group of chemicals called prostaglandins, located in platelets and blood vessel walls, are involved in regulation of platelet aggregation. After platelets clump they release a substance called thromboxane A_2. This substance causes intense spasm of local blood vessels, which further decreases bleeding. The platelet aggregate also releases chemicals that accelerate the clotting system of the blood to form a reinforced clot called a thrombus, thus providing another means by which bleeding is stopped. Finally, platelets may release substances that promote migration of cells from the interior to the surface of blood vessel walls, a process that is believed to lead to the generation of an atherosclerotic plaque. Although these normal protective mechanisms—platelet aggregation, blood vessel constriction, and thrombus formation—are essential to prevent fatal bleeding from minor injuries, it is possible they also contribute to the production of coronary oc-

The progressive buildup of an atherosclerotic plaque and the sudden blockages caused by platelet aggregation, thrombus (blood clot) formation, and spasm of the arterial wall muscles can work separately or together to produce occlusion of a coronary artery and heart attack. Recognition of this complexity has led to the development of a variety of therapeutic approaches, each component of which attacks a specific cause of occlusion.

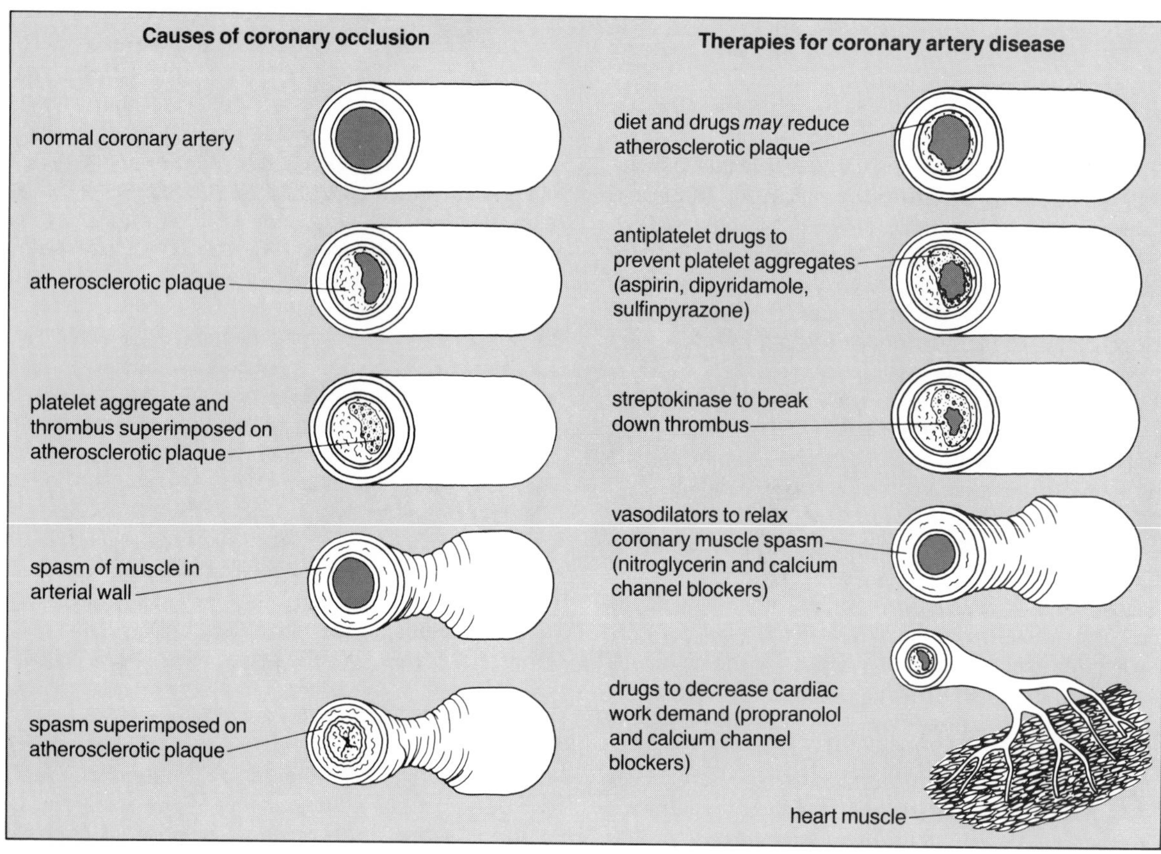

clusions. For example, platelets are found in atherosclerotic plaques and at the site of complete coronary arterial occlusions where a clot has formed on top of partially occluding plaque. Moreover, in animals in which partial coronary occlusions are produced, platelets have been found to clump together to cause complete blockage of the artery, cutting off flow to the myocardium. Thus, the evidence suggests, but does not definitively prove, a role for platelets both in contributing to atherosclerotic plaque and in precipitating sudden coronary occlusion.

Antiplatelet drug treatment

Several drugs such as aspirin, dipyridamole, and sulfinpyrazone inhibit the ability of platelets to clump together by interfering with their prostaglandin regulatory system. Based on evidence that platelets contribute to coronary artery occlusive disease, there have been several clinical trials that have attempted to determine whether such antiplatelet drugs can help patients with coronary artery disease. In one trial patients with atherosclerotic heart disease who had suffered a previous myocardial infarction were selected randomly to receive either the active drug or an identical-looking placebo, so that neither patient nor physician would know whether the drug was administered—a double-blind study design. Patients from 26 hospitals participated, starting 25 to 35 days after myocardial infarction. Sulfinpyrazone therapy was associated with an almost 50% decrease in the death rate from cardiac-related causes. However, some patients treated with sulfinpyrazone, who eventually died, were excluded from analysis of results for what were believed to be valid reasons. Critics of the study have suggested that these patients may have been excluded improperly and that, had they been included, sulfinpyrazone would not have reduced the death rate. The controversy has not yet been resolved.

More recently, randomized double-blind clinical trials of aspirin and dipyridamole in patients after myocardial infarction were completed. The Aspirin Myocardial Infarction Study (AMIS) enrolled 4,524 patients between 30 and 69 years old who had had a myocardial infarction 2 to 60 months previously and followed them for at least three years. Half the patients were assigned randomly to receive three aspirin tablets per day, and the other half received identical-looking placebos. Aspirin did not reduce the number of cardiac deaths that subsequently occurred, although the incidence of recurrent nonfatal myocardial infarction was 22% lower in the aspirin-treated group. This difference, however, was not statistically significant. (For statistical significance the probability that the difference occurred by chance must be less than 5%.)

Another double-blind clinical trial, the Persantine Aspirin Reinfarction Study (PARIS), enrolled 2,026 patients 2 to 60 months after a myocardial infarction. This study randomly assigned 810 patients to aspirin plus dipyridamole (Persantine), 810 patients to aspirin alone, and 406 patients to a placebo. The dose of aspirin was three tablets per day, as in AMIS and several other studies. After an average 41-month follow-up period, death rates from all causes were 12.8% for placebo, 10.7% for dipyridamole plus aspirin, and 10.5% for aspirin alone. Compared with the placebo-treated group, the death rate was 16% lower in the dipyridamole-aspirin treated group and 18% lower in the aspirin group; cardiac-related deaths were 24% lower in the dipyridamole-aspirin group and 21% lower in the aspirin group; and the combined incidence of cardiac death and nonfatal infarction was 25% lower in the dipyridamole-aspirin group and 24% lower in the aspirin group.

Although the 15–25% reductions in myocardial infarctions and cardiac deaths were not statistically significant in these studies, many physicians conclude that there is a group of patients who can benefit from antiplatelet therapy. That statistical significance was not achieved in these studies may be due to several factors. One may be the need to start patients on antiplatelet drugs soon after acute myocardial infarction. Therapy was started late after infarction in many patients in these studies. In particular, more patients started aspirin therapy within six months of their infarct in PARIS than in AMIS, which may explain the slightly more favorable results in PARIS. It also appears that the dosage of antiplatelet drug may be critical to the outcome. For example, ordinary doses of aspirin may inhibit an enzyme in blood vessel walls that actually prevents platelet aggregates from forming on the vessel wall. In platelets the same enzyme promotes platelet aggregation and is inhibited by very low doses of aspirin. Hence, future studies of aspirin will probably employ a dose of only one half tablet per day.

Coronary spasm in coronary occlusion

One of the most exciting recent advances in understanding and treating angina pectoris and myocardial infarction has been the demonstration that coronary arterial muscle can go into spasm and occlude the arterial lumen, reducing or stopping blood flow. Many years ago physicians who placed long, flexible tubes (catheters) into the coronary arteries to inject radiopaque dye for X-rays noted that touching the artery with the catheter often caused the artery to narrow abruptly and stop the flow of blood. Occasionally patients would notice chest discomfort or develop electrocardiographic abnormalities, but the induced spasm was rapidly relieved by removing the catheter and administering nitroglycerin, which relaxes the coronary arterial muscle.

That coronary spasm could be produced by a catheter proved that spasm could occur and cause angina pectoris, but it did not indicate whether or how frequently coronary spasm might occur spontaneously. In recent years several investigators have proven that in many patients with spontaneous anginal chest pain the angina indeed is precipitated by coronary spasm. Spontaneous coronary spasm has been demonstrated most frequently in patients with a pattern of chest pain occurring at rest, instead of during exercise. It is now known that persons with normal coronary arteries and those with arteries narrowed by atherosclerotic plaque can, under certain circumstances, develop acute coronary spasm, resulting in angina and, if prolonged enough, in myocardial infarction.

In addition to this profound spasm at rest, it has been hypothesized that there is a continuous spectrum of severity of coronary spasm. Mild spasm may worsen coronary obstruction in patients who also have atherosclerotic plaques. If the resulting obstruction is severe, angina would appear even with the patient at rest, when the heart is working minimally. If less severe, angina would not occur at rest, but the coronary reserve would decrease. Angina would appear, however, at a lower level of exercise stress than would have been the case if coronary spasm had not occurred.

New drugs for coronary arterial spasm

The most important aspect of the demonstration that coronary spasm occurs and causes heart problems is that coronary spasm is treatable. A long-used drug, nitroglycerin, can relax coronary arterial muscle contraction and is effective for treating most patients with angina caused or worsened by coronary spasm. For many patients, including some who do not respond to nitroglycerin, a new class of drugs called calcium channel blockers causes extremely potent dilation of coronary arteries. These drugs—verapamil, nifedipine, diltiazem, and others—have been very valuable in treating patients with coronary spasm and promise to be among the most important new cardiac drugs available to physicians.

The calcium channel blockers inhibit the passage of calcium into muscle cells via channels in the cell membranes. Since calcium must enter muscle cells for them to contract, blocking the calcium channel causes decreased contraction of arterial muscle, thereby dilating coronary and other arteries. These drugs relieve anginal chest pain occurring at rest due to coronary spasm, but they also have been found to relieve anginal chest pain precipitated by exercise in the absence of any evidence of spasm. The latter effect probably is caused in part by the ability of these drugs to dilate even diseased coronary arteries. In addition, the drugs decrease the work of the heart muscle in various ways. They dilate not only coronary arteries but also other arteries of the body, leading to a fall in blood pressure. The pressure against which the heart must eject blood is thus reduced, leading to a decrease in its workload and therefore its oxygen requirements. Some of the calcium channel blockers also reduce heart rate and the vigor of the heart's contraction, both of which also reduce its oxygen demands. In these ways the drugs correct the imbalance that occurs during exercise between the increased demand of the heart for blood and the limited supply available through a partially blocked coronary artery.

Nonsurgical intervention during heart attack

The traditional therapeutic approach to patients with acute myocardial infarctions has been to relieve pain by bed rest, sedation, and oxygen therapy. Treatment of the precipitating event was not thought possible, and experimental approaches focused on drugs that reduced the amount of heart muscle damaged after coronary occlusion. During the past few years, however, some patients with acute infarctions have had cardiac catheterization studies performed within hours of symptom onset. A catheter is inserted into an artery of the groin or arm and passed to the origin of the coronary arteries, at the base of the aorta. Radiopaque dye is injected, and X-rays of the arteries (coronary arteriograms) are taken. Studies of patients during the acute phase of myocardial infarction indicated that the infarction was caused by total occlusion of a coronary artery, usually by a thrombus clot at the site of a partially occluding plaque.

Previous attempts to restore blood flow through occluded coronary arteries during acute myocardial infarction have involved coronary bypass grafting, a major surgical procedure entailing considerable risk. Also, the time required to prepare the hospital and patient for cardiac surgery undoubtedly allows much blood-deprived heart muscle to die.

Recent studies in Europe and the U.S. have introduced a dramatic new approach to therapy. Investigators performed cardiac catheterization during the acute phase of myocardial infarction in order to infuse drugs directly into the occluded artery. Intracoronary infusion of nitroglycerin reopens the artery in a small number of cases, suggesting that spasm occasionally causes acute infarction. By contrast, infusion of the enzyme streptokinase reopens the great majority of occluded coronary arteries during acute infarction. This enzyme attacks clots directly, breaking the chemical bonds that hold the clots together. Initial studies indicate that the heart muscle can be saved in most patients if the drug is infused within six hours after the beginning of symptoms. Whereas the relative safety, efficacy, and practicality of this experimental procedure remain to be established, preliminary results are encouraging. The information it has provided about the course of acute infarction undoubtedly will lead to more effective treatment in the future.

—Randolph E. Patterson, M.D., and Stephen E. Epstein, M.D.

Special Report: Sudden Death in Athletes

by Barry J. Maron, M.D.
and Stephen E. Epstein, M.D.

Highly conditioned competitive athletes epitomize the most healthy segment of our society. For this reason, the occurrence of sudden death in an athlete is particularly shocking and tragic. The most familiar instance recorded in history of an athlete dying suddenly after extreme physical exertion was described by Herodotus. The privilege of conveying the news of the great military victory at Marathon in 490 BC to the citizens of Athens was bestowed upon a man presumed to be Pheidippides. A trained Greek athlete, he ran from Marathon to Athens (a distance of about 22 miles), delivered his message, and then fell dead.

For years our ignorance of the causes of such catastrophes was clothed in esoteric sounding phrases, such as "sudden death syndrome," which merely masked the fact that the precise causes were unknown. Recently, careful studies performed after death have revealed that a variety of structural malformations of the heart (and the great vessels emanating from the heart) are responsible for the majority of sudden deaths in athletes. These cardiovascular alterations are either congenital (present from birth) or acquired.

Heart disease in young, competitive athletes

Considering the large numbers of participants in competitive and recreational athletic programs, sudden death must be considered a very uncommon event. Nonetheless, an occasional individual, apparently in excellent health, will die suddenly and unexpectedly. Usually this occurs during or just following exertion on the athletic field, and death is thereby attributed to intense physical activity. However, while the intense effort may have been the precipitating cause of death, the underlying cause in the vast majority of young athletes (less than 35 years of age) is some type of severe congenital malformation of the heart. Despite the presence of these abnormalities at birth, individuals so afflicted can compete for many years without either being aware of their life-threatening disease or experiencing significant symptoms.

The most common cause of such deaths appears to be a congenital malformation of the heart known as hypertrophic cardiomyopathy (*hypertrophy* refers to muscular thickening, *cardio* to the heart, and *myopathy* to abnormal muscle). This "new" form of heart

Culver Pictures

"Victory of Marathon," 490 BC. Etching after painting by Cauder.

disease (first described only about 20 years ago) involves primarily the heart muscle (myocardium). It is usually familial—*i.e.,* it is genetically transmitted to offspring.

Hypertrophic cardiomyopathy is characterized structurally by increased mass or weight of the heart and thickening of the wall of the left ventricle. The wall thickening shown by these patients is peculiar in that the portion of the heart separating the right and left pumping chambers (ventricles), called the ventricular septum, is usually much thicker than other portions of the left ventricular wall. In addition, the ventricular septum is characterized by a bizarre cellular architecture in which adjacent myocardial cells are not in their normal parallel arrangement, but rather are arranged at perpendicular and oblique angles to each other. Hypertrophic cardiomyopathy is also a common cause of sudden death in youthful, nonathletic individuals who have not previously experienced cardiac symptoms.

The mechanism by which sudden death occurs is not definitely known at this time. However, it is believed that the abnormalities described above can cause the normal electrical activity of the heart, responsible for initiating each heart contraction, to deteriorate into chaotic electrical activity. This causes ineffective weak contractions, leading to total failure of the heart to pump blood, and thereby to sudden death.

In addition to hypertrophic cardiomyopathy, other congenital malformations of the heart or blood vessels may cause sudden death in young athletes. In one such malformation, the left main coronary artery (the principle artery that supplies oxygenated blood to the heart muscle itself) originates from a position in the root of the aorta that is far removed from its usual location. Because of this positioning, the left main coronary artery follows an unusual course, necessitating it to assume a very acute angle at its origin from the aorta. This acute bend is potentially hazardous. During severe exertion (when the great arteries expand) the left main coronary artery probably becomes severely kinked and narrowed, thereby diminishing the delivery of blood and oxygen to the heart muscle.

Other athletes have a weakening of the wall of the aorta (the large artery that transports oxygenated

(Top left) A normal aortic valve. Several congenital abnormalities of the aortic valve (top right; middle left and right) can cause sudden death in young athletes. If the left main coronary artery does not originate from the normal position in the aorta (bottom left) but instead stems from a position that causes it to follow an abnormal course (bottom right), delivery of blood and oxygen to the heart muscle may be diminished—another potential cause of sudden death.

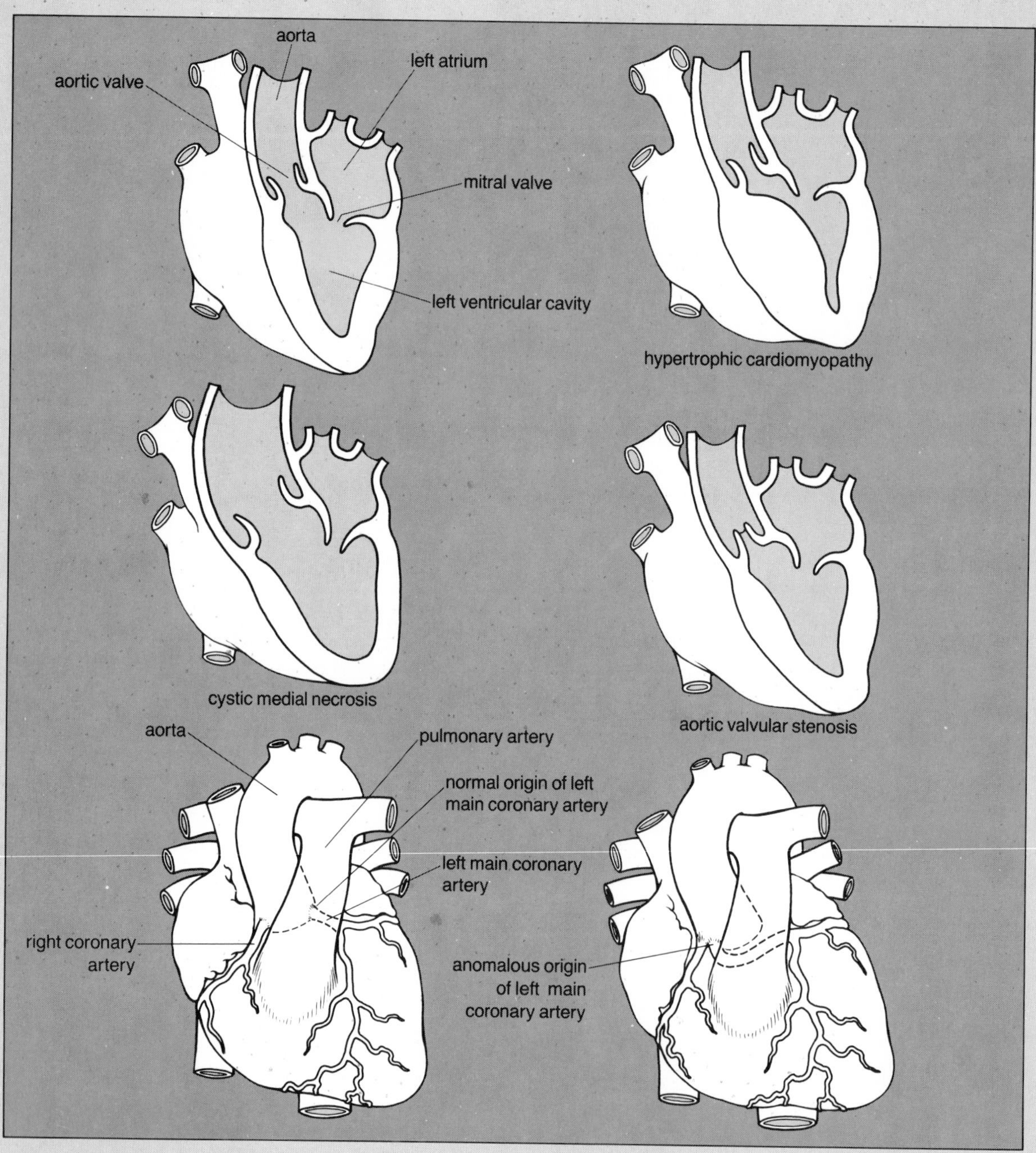

blood from the left ventricle), owing to greatly decreased numbers of elastic fibers. This abnormality is commonly known as cystic medial necrosis. Eventually, such a malformed aorta is unable to maintain even the normal blood pressure to which it is exposed—it ruptures, resulting in death.

Many individuals with cystic medial necrosis of the aorta also have manifestations of a more generalized disease known as Marfan's syndrome. Such patients are tall with long arms and long, slender fingers and often have visual problems due to displacement of the lens of the eye. It is of interest that individuals with Marfan's syndrome and a weakened aortic wall may successfully participate in competitive athletics for many years without experiencing a catastrophic event.

Another potential cause of sudden death in young athletes is narrowing (or stenosis) of the aortic valve. This is a congenital malformation in which the narrowed opening impedes the flow of blood out of the left ventricle when the heart contracts. Because aortic stenosis produces a loud heart murmur, most prospective athletes with this disease are probably identified and disqualified from competition. Therefore, this particular form of heart disease probably does not constitute a major cause of sudden death in athletes.

One type of acquired cardiac disease that is occasionally responsible for sudden death, even in young athletes, is atherosclerosis of the coronary arteries. In this disease fat (lipid) accumulates in the walls of the major coronary arteries and forms plaques. These plaques have the effect of narrowing the arterial lumen, inhibiting the delivery of blood and oxygen to the heart muscle, and resulting in oxygen deprivation (ischemia). Ischemia may precipitate a fatal arrhythmia or, if prolonged enough, could lead to death of a portion of the heart muscle. If a considerable quantity of the myocardium is so affected, normal function cannot be maintained and the individual will die. If less heart muscle is involved, the patient survives and the dead muscle eventually is replaced by scar tissue. This is, of course, a very common disease in men over 50 years, but it may also occur in younger adults and even occasionally in children.

In addition to the diseases just described, there are several other rare but potentially lethal conditions that may occasionally occur in athletes. These include, among others, underdevelopment of the coronary arteries and viral infections involving the heart muscle itself (myocarditis).

Infrequently, sudden death may occur in young athletes who have no demonstrable organic heart disease. Such individuals probably die of abnormalities of cardiac rhythm that arise independently of any structural abnormality of the heart that can be routinely demonstrated at autopsy. Alternatively, death may result from abnormalities unrelated to the heart (such as sudden rupture of an abnormal blood vessel within the brain).

UPI

In 1971 Detroit Lion Chuck Hughes collapsed on the playing field and within an hour died of a heart attack.

Heart disease in older athletes

Increasing numbers of individuals over the age of 35 are now participating in competitive and recreational sports as well as in physical conditioning programs (*e.g.,* jogging). Superior physical fitness at any age, however, does not guarantee protection against exercise-related death. Older athletes may harbor covert cardiovascular disease and die suddenly and unexpectedly while participating in athletic activities. Unlike the more youthful athletes previously discussed, the cause of death in older athletes is not usually a congenital malformation of the heart; in the majority of instances the cause is coronary heart disease.

The condition goes unrecognized during life in many middle-aged individuals who die of underlying coronary artery disease. Symptoms such as chest pain may have been present but were ignored or misdiagnosed. In other individuals symptoms may have been absent or were vague and nonspecific. This "silent" type of coronary artery disease may actually cause small scars in the heart muscle (myocardial infarcts).

Identification of heart disease in athletes

The knowledge that congenital or acquired cardiovascular diseases may be present in apparently healthy athletes, and even cause death in some, naturally raises the following question: How reliably can cardiovascular disease in athletes be identified so that catastrophic events may be averted? The available information indicates that in about three-fourths of those athletes who die suddenly there had been no previous suspicion of cardiovascular disease. This is due largely to the fact that symptoms are either absent or unrecognized. If symptoms are present, they are frequently ascribed to musculoskeletal injury, since physicians usually do not suspect heart disease when evaluating individuals who appear in excellent health.

Even when cardiovascular disease in the athlete is suspected during life, the correct diagnosis is rarely made. The reason for this is that many of the cardiovascular diseases responsible for sudden death in athletes are difficult to identify by the usual routine evaluation, *i.e.,* history and physical examination. Their correct diagnosis often requires sophisticated (and often expensive) laboratory tests for definitive confirmation. For example, patients with hypertrophic cardiomyopathy may have no heart murmur, a normal electrocardiogram and chest X-ray, and no other obvious evidence of heart disease discernible by physical examination. In such instances, confirmation of the diagnosis requires performing a noninvasive diagnostic ultrasound study known as an echocardiogram.

An echocardiogram is a method of viewing and photographing the internal structures of the heart. It utilizes ultrasound, high-frequency sound waves, which are beamed from a hand-held probe (transducer) through the chest wall and which are reflected off the surfaces of cardiac structures. When a photosensitive film is exposed to the reflected signals, a graph and permanent recording is produced. The echocardiogram is a safe and painless test which is performed with the patient lying comfortably on a bed. It permits the physician to calculate the size of the heart chambers, measure wall thickness and motion, view valvular motion, see the spatial relation of different parts of the heart to each other, and detect fluid surrounding the heart. For these reasons the echocardiogram has been used to diagnose a wide variety of heart diseases.

At the present time it appears impractical for communities, schools, or athletic clubs to screen large populations of prospective athletes in an effort to detect those cardiovascular abnormalities that are responsible for the majority of sudden deaths. The major limitation to successful screening is not the lack of tests that can establish the diagnosis of heart disease. Such tests do exist. However, to screen successfully for the most common causes of death in young athletes requires, among other testing procedures, echocardiography, an expensive test requiring considerable technical expertise to be performed well.

Moreover, chronic athletic training produces changes in the heart that, while normal and even beneficial, can mimic abnormalities produced by heart disease. For example, a constellation of clinical findings in athletes has been recognized as the "athlete heart syndrome." These findings include slow heart rate, a soft heart murmur, a variety of alterations on the electrocardiogram, and apparent enlargement of the heart on chest X-ray and echocardiogram. Thus, the electrocardiogram and echocardiogram abnormalities that the normal athlete may show often make it difficult to distinguish between true organic disease of the heart and changes in cardiac structure that normally occur with conditioning over long periods of time.

Nonetheless, limited screening studies that are relatively simple and inexpensive can be performed on *young* athletes, such as listening to the heart with a stethoscope to detect murmurs and obtaining a chest X-ray. Such examinations can identify *some* of those abnormalities that pose risks to young athletes.

In *older* athletes the existence of silent coronary artery disease is not uncommon—far more frequent than in young athletes. Thus, a case can be made for performing exercise electrocardiographic stress tests every few years. This test reveals abnormalities in a portion of individuals with underlying coronary artery disease. The two major problems with routine use of exercise stress testing in middle-aged and older athletes are that it is expensive and a high proportion of the "abnormal" results are falsely abnormal, *i.e.,* the majority of subjects who have no symptoms of heart disease but who have an abnormal electrocardiographic stress test will prove to have normal coronary arteries. Moreover, a high percentage of asymptomatic subjects who die suddenly from coronary artery disease have normal exercise studies and therefore would have gone undetected despite electrocardiographic stress testing.

Is exercise beneficial for the heart?

It is now fashionable to maintain that exercise not only makes people feel better but also decreases the likelihood of heart disease. If heart disease is present, exercise is believed to reduce the risks of premature death. These issues, however, are far from resolved, with some well-known authorities arguing vigorously for, and others against, the merits of exercise as a means of prolonging life.

Most authorities agree it is unlikely that athletic activity exerts beneficial effects on congenital cardiovascular malformations. Thus, young athletes who have one of these forms of heart disease should not participate in intense physical competition. The real disagreement centers mainly on how to manage the individual with atherosclerosis of the coronary arteries. Exercise leads to weight reduction, and may lower elevated levels of blood pressure and of blood cholesterol. Each of these changes is beneficial, and to some extent probably lowers the likelihood of heart disease.

However, exercise does stress the heart, and it is not accidental that many athletes with heart disease who die suddenly do so during an athletic contest or while training or practicing for one. Clearly, each individual athlete with heart disease presents specific problems that must be dealt with on an individual basis. Whether or not a person with heart disease should compete athletically will depend on the type of disease, its severity, and the type of physical activity required. Even when these factors are known, however, there is much that remains to be learned about the relative risks and benefits of chronic athletic conditioning.

Hypertension

High blood pressure, or hypertension, is a disease that anyone may experience from infancy to old age. Fortunately, it can easily be diagnosed by its clinical effects and, most important, it can easily be treated and controlled. Hypertension is nonetheless a major health problem throughout the world. In the U.S. alone, it is estimated that approximately one million people die directly or indirectly as a result of high blood pressure each year.

Hypertension is rightly called the "silent killer" because a person may have high blood pressure with no obvious symptoms whatsoever. Often, it is only when serious complications develop that the patient learns he or she has high blood pressure. At that time, the physician must determine the effects the disease has already had on the patient's heart, brain, kidneys, and blood vessels. Because the effects of high blood pressure can be serious and life threatening, more and more attention is being given to early detection. The sooner a patient with high blood pressure can be treated, the less risk he or she has of suffering a heart attack, stroke, or kidney failure.

High blood pressure may be termed *secondary,* that is, caused by another condition, such as kidney malfunction, hypersecretion of the adrenal gland, or toxemia of pregnancy. Or it may have no known cause, simply appearing on its own, in which case it is termed *essential* hypertension. A survey by the National High Blood Pressure Education Program found that approximately 60 million people in the U.S. have some form of high blood pressure. Over half of these individuals, or 35 million, are estimated to have high blood pressure that should be treated with drugs. Yet only 5 million of these 35 million persons are in fact under a doctor's care for hypertension and learning to control their condition with medication. The remaining 25 million persons with borderline high blood pressure should have regular checkups. Although they need not be treated with drugs, their physician can recommend other measures to help them lower their blood pressure.

Normal versus high blood pressure

The pressure produced by the heart and blood vessels causes the blood to circulate through the body as the heart pumps. A blood pressure measurement consists of an upper reading (the systolic blood pressure) and a lower reading (the diastolic blood pressure). The systolic reading represents the pressure at the time the heart contracts (during systole), while the diastolic reading represents the blood pressure while the heart is not pumping (during diastole). Both pressures are significant.

Blood pressure varies from person to person, and generally increases with age. Life insurance statistics show that even within the normal range the higher the

Jim Anderson—Stock, Boston

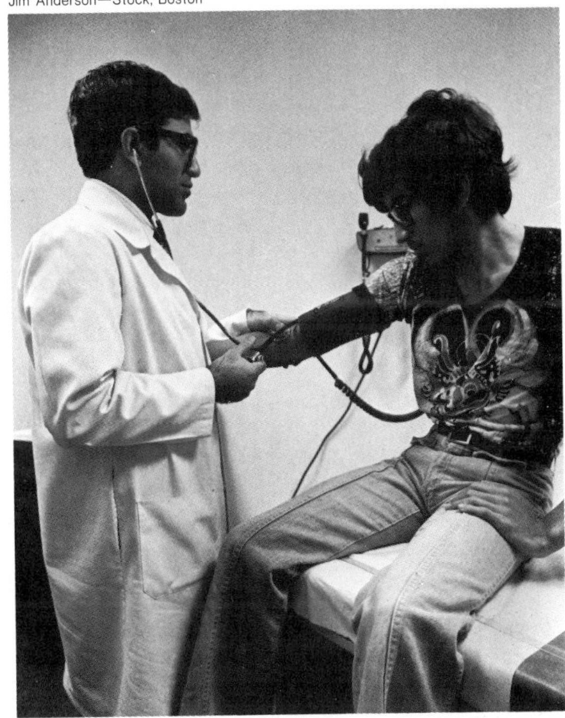

Hypertension, or high blood pressure, is a disease that can be present at any age. It affects approximately 60 million people in the United States.

blood pressure, the greater the likelihood of serious illness and death. The blood pressure level used as a criterion for treatment to reduce the possibility of these consequences has generally been accepted to be 140/90 mm Hg. A slightly higher limit is used for older persons. The measurement 140/90 mm Hg means that, as measured on a sphygmomanometer, the pressure is such that it raises a column of mercury (chemical symbol Hg) similar to that in a fever thermometer 140 millimeters during systole, and 90 mm during diastole.

When the patient's blood pressure is measured, a cuff of suitable size is wrapped snugly around the upper arm and inflated so that it compresses the major artery until no blood can pass through it to the forearm. Listening with a stethoscope, the physician can determine the systolic blood pressure by detecting the first of the Korotkoff sounds, *i.e.,* the sounds made by the blood entering the empty artery as the cuff is deflated. Similarly, the physician determines the diastolic blood pressure by noting the pressure at the point where the sounds either disappear or muffle (according to the convention used).

The blood pressure is approximately the same in both arms and in both legs (with the patient lying down) except in certain pathological conditions. Also, the level of blood pressure in normal individuals varies with activity and with the time of day. Even in patients with high blood pressure it may drop to normal levels during sleep. Because of these wide normal variations, it is often necessary when assessing high blood pressure to take several readings both in the doctor's office and in the patient's home. Moreover, people often confuse high blood pressure or hypertension with tension and think that high blood pressure comes from being tense or nervous. This is not true—many patients who are tense or nervous have normal blood pressure, while many patients who have very high blood pressure are perfectly placid.

Risks of high blood pressure

It has been known for many years from epidemiological and actuarial studies that high blood pressure is a significant risk factor for coronary artery disease, cerebral vascular disease, stroke, and peripheral vascular disease. Damage from high blood pressure begins when the heart must work harder against increased resistance to pump the blood through the circulatory system. To do so, the heart must increase its muscular capacity, but over time the muscle fibers become stretched or dilated so that the heart can no longer pump blood through the body efficiently. Eventually, it may fail altogether. Difficulty in breathing may occur if the blood normally pumped by the heart muscle begins to back up into the lungs.

At the same time, the walls of the arteries that lead to the heart as well as the arteries elsewhere in the body become damaged and build up deposits of fatty material (atheroma) that may lead to thrombosis, or formation of clots. As a result, the arteries become completely blocked (occluded), and the tissues that they supply begin to die from lack of blood. If this process occurs in the heart muscle, a heart attack, or myocardial infarction, may follow. The evidence is convincing that myocardial infarction occurs more frequently in patients with high blood pressure. A stroke can take place if the weakened blood vessels in the brain eventually rupture. When this happens, bleeding in the brain causes the patient to become paralyzed, to lose feeling in the limbs and face, or to lapse into a coma. Peripheral vascular disease occurs when the walls of blood vessels, particularly in the legs, are weakened by high blood pressure and fatty plaques form, obstructing the circulation. When the patient walks he experiences pain, especially in the calves and, in a more severe form, as the blood vessels become completely obstructed, gangrene of the toes occurs.

Loss of kidney function is also a risk for patients with high blood pressure when the blood vessels and tiny filters (glomeruli) in the kidney suffer damage. As the injury becomes extensive, chronic renal failure develops, and hemodialysis treatment with an artificial kidney (at a special dialysis facility or at home) or peritoneal dialysis becomes necessary. A kidney transplant may sometimes be done as an alternative to dialysis in suitable patients. Although a patient may experience these serious complications only after many years of

When the blood pressure is taken, two measurements are made, that during systole, as the heart pumps the blood, and that during diastole, as the heart momentarily rests between beats. If the arteries are narrowed because of fatty buildups, or plaques, within them, the heart must pump harder to drive the blood through the smaller channel.

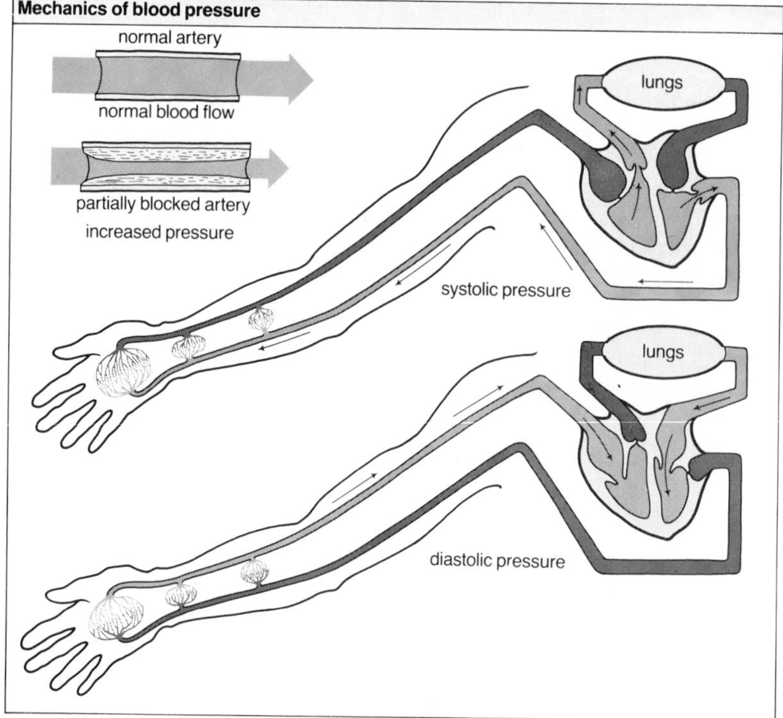

Richard Younker

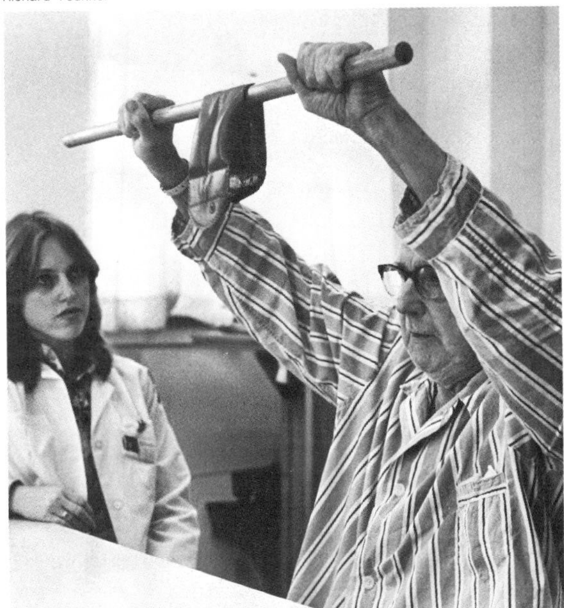

Stroke is one of the most serious consequences of hypertension. Stroke patients must be rehabilitated to regain motion, speech, or other lost functions.

having high blood pressure, the higher the blood pressure, the more likely they are to occur early in the patient's life.

High blood pressure in the black population

Although high blood pressure can occur at any age, its distribution among races differs. Blacks have a greater incidence of hypertension than other population groups, approximately 25% being affected. Not only is the prevalence of high blood pressure among blacks almost twice that among whites, but the mortality rate from hypertensive diseases is three times higher in blacks. Black persons aged 35 to 54 are six to ten times more likely to develop high blood pressure than whites in the same group. While the reasons for this high incidence among blacks are not fully known, some possibilities include genetic factors, the effects of stress, and a high intake of salt. Hypertension in blacks is often present at an earlier age than in whites, and at the time patients first consult a physician they may already have severe damage or serious complications—but this may simply reflect late diagnosis or less adequate treatment. High blood pressure is also one of the commonest causes of renal failure in blacks.

High blood pressure in the elderly

Approximately 40% of whites and more than 50% of blacks over 65 years of age have either isolated systolic hypertension (only the systolic blood pressure is above normal) or systolic-diastolic hypertension. Once the physician decides to treat an elderly person with drug therapy, a minimum drug dosage is prescribed, with dosages increased very gradually over weeks rather than days. In general, the aim is to lower the blood pressure to an acceptable range rather than to normalize it, *i.e.*, to lower the systolic pressure to between 140 and 160 rather than to less than 140.

While many elderly people have other conditions that present special problems, complications such as heart failure or peripheral vascular disease make the need to reduce their blood pressure more rather than less important. Unfortunately, it is often true that many elderly patients have additional psychological, physical, and social factors that make it difficult for them to adhere to therapy. Inadequate diets may make them more susceptible to the potassium loss produced by diuretics; impediments in hearing or eyesight may make it difficult for them to understand and carry out instructions; mental confusion may make them neglect to follow instructions; lack of support from family and friends, fixed incomes, and limitation on health insurance benefits may discourage them from buying their medicines or keeping appointments. For such patients, additional efforts must be made to find remedies for these problems, and when appropriate, to seek aid from social service agencies, community or public health departments, or senior citizens' programs.

Management of high blood pressure

It is important that patients with essential hypertension realize that treatment for their condition will almost invariably last for the rest of their lives. Too often, patients believe that once their blood pressure has returned to normal, further treatment will no longer be needed. Nothing could be further from the truth. In almost every case, when the patient stops treatment the blood pressure again rises, and the patient is again exposed to all of hypertension's risks. Consequently, one of the most important features of management of hypertension is a close relationship between the patient and the person responsible for his or her care. Without the patient's trust, it is very difficult to obtain the degree of compliance essential for managing this disease. In addition, a good patient-physician relationship promotes communication. Thus, in instances in which medicines have unpleasant side effects, the patient can ask the physician to replace the drugs or change the dosages; when there is a poor relationship with the doctor, some patients tend to stop treatment altogether because of the drawbacks of therapy.

Many aspects of the patient's life and habits must be considered before drug therapy can be recommended. In some patients who have very high blood pressure which has been diagnosed for the first time it may be necessary to start drug therapy immediately in order to bring the blood pressure down to a safe level. Most patients will also be given dietary recommendations, since there is considerable evidence that appropriate dietary changes will lower the blood pressure in some patients.

In particular, dietary recommendations emphasize weight reduction and restriction of sodium, chiefly through monitoring the intake of table salt. For some patients with definite hypertension, losing weight has reduced the dosage level of drugs required, and it may occasionally eliminate the need for drug therapy. Sensible advice on weight reduction is a reasonable first step for the physician treating a patient whose blood pressure increase is only borderline. If this approach is not successful, the physician can very soon initiate other measures. The value of reduced sodium intake for hypertensive patients is more conclusive.

There is no doubt that the average salt intake in most Western countries is far higher than necessary for adequate nutrition. Although there are exceptions, a correlation has been found in various communities throughout the world between the amount of salt in the diet and the prevalence of hypertension in the population. In the U.S., the average diet contains about 10–12 grams of salt a day, and a Senate Select Committee on Nutrition and Human Needs has recommended that Americans reduce their salt intake to 5 grams or less a day. Despite the benefits of such a reduction it is difficult to change eating habits in an age where so much food comes from cans or boxes and when accurate information on how much sodium is actually being consumed is hard to obtain. Reducing salt intake may be more acceptable to patients who have significant side effects from their drugs, as they would have a stronger incentive to reduce their drug dosages.

Mild exercise is a valuable supplement to other approaches for some patients. Certain types of isotonic exercise, such as swimming and jogging, increase the systolic blood pressure but decrease the diastolic pressure. As a result, since the average blood pressure rises only slightly, the blood pressure of the hypertensive patient generally remains higher during exercise. Isometric exercise, such as lifting weights or shoveling snow, is accompanied by a much more marked increase in blood pressure since both the systolic and diastolic pressure increase. Consequently, this type of exercise is less beneficial. However, participating in exercise improves cardiovascular function and in some patients may help to reduce the blood pressure. No patient with severe hypertension should engage in heavy exercise without consulting his or her physician.

Drug therapy

In earlier years, the side effects of drugs used to treat high blood pressure were often worse than the disease itself. Today, except in rare instances, high blood pressure can be adequately controlled by drugs with only mild side effects. An extensive range of medicines is available to treat hypertension. Opinions differ among physicians about the order in which these drugs are to

Hypertension Detection and Follow-up Study, 1980

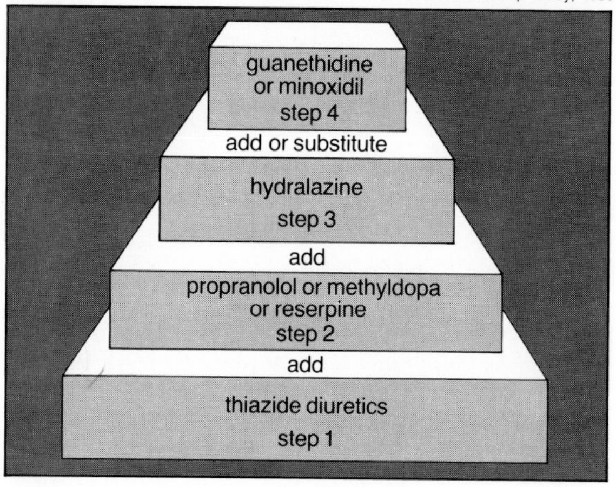

With the stepped-care approach specific types of drugs are used to treat hypertension in a carefully regulated and individualized sequence. First, a diuretic is given to increase the amounts of salt and water excreted in the urine. If that is not adequate, a second type of drug is added to inhibit the activity of the sympathetic nervous system on the heart and blood vessels. Drugs that dilate the blood vessels are the third group added, if necessary. Finally, very powerful adrenergic-inhibiting or vasodilating drugs may be used in very difficult cases.

be given, but according to studies done by the Hypertension Detection and Follow-up Program the stepped-care approach has proven most successful. This approach consists of prescribing a specific kind of drug in a sequence of carefully regulated steps, adding a second drug if the first one does not effectively reduce the patient's blood pressure, then adding a third to the first two if these are ineffective.

The first drug prescribed is usually a diuretic, a substance that acts on the kidney to increase the amount of salt and water excreted in the urine. This drug also reduces the constriction of small blood vessels by its effects on their salt and water content. Diuretics are usually given once or twice a day, sometimes only every other day. One common side effect is a reduction in the blood potassium level. While generally inconsequential, this reduction may be important for patients who are also taking digitalis, since a low serum potassium concentration increases the effect of digitalis on the heart. Other side effects include excessive loss of salt and fluids. In general, the physician will try diuretics alone for two or three weeks.

If diuretics are not adequate, a second group of drugs is added that inhibit the activity of the sympathetic nervous system on the heart and blood vessels. These adrenergic inhibitors include drugs such as clonidine, methyldopa, propranolol, metoprolol, nadolol, and reserpine. If the patient's blood pressure has not been brought under control with the combination of a diuretic and an adrenergic inhibitor, then a third group of drugs is added, vasodilators that reduce the blood pressure by dilating the blood vessels directly. Finally, if these three steps are ineffective, then the powerful adrenergic-inhibiting agent guanethidine or the powerful vasodilator minoxidil may be used. In all but the most difficult cases, this combination of drugs will effectively lower the patient's blood pressure. Also under investigation is a series of new drugs that block the formation of vasoconstrictor substances within the body and reduce the breakdown of substances that dilate blood vessels.

In the very small fraction of patients whose hypertension is resistant to the stepped-care therapy outlined here, if noncompliance and the causes of secondary hypertension mentioned above have been excluded, then it may be necessary to insist that these patients reduce their salt intake. Alternatively, it may be necessary to try to persuade them that they must tolerate some adverse side effects in order to lower their blood pressure to acceptable levels.

Several clinical and community trials have been undertaken in recent years to study the effectiveness of drug therapy and management for patients with both mild and severe hypertension. As a result, the evidence is growing that effective treatment has significant benefit even in mild hypertension. It has also been found that careful, sustained management of patients with high blood pressure can produce clear-cut beneficial results.

Because hypertension can be easily diagnosed and successfully treated, and because its potential ill effects are so severe, a great deal of planning and research has gone into developing screening and treatment programs. Of particular interest are studies that have been conducted to determine which programs are likely to be most effective, cost-efficient, and most readily complied with by the patient.

Work-site programs

Some employees are receiving on-the-job training in how to control their blood pressure. General Motors and other organizations have adopted a work-site hypertension control program developed by the Worker Health Program at the University of Michigan's Institute of Labor and Industrial Relations. The results of these and similar programs indicate that, before the program began, 12–25% of employees were adequately controlling their blood pressures. After the work-site program was implemented, the figure rose to 70–90%.

The program involves screening employees and referring those with high blood pressure for diagnosis and treatment to a physician of their choice in the community. These employees become part of the organization's "caseload" and receive routine blood pressure evaluations and follow-up from the organization's physicians to ensure that they understand and are following the recommended therapy.

Reaching hypertensives by on-the-job screening works well because of the nature of hypertension: it is largely asymptomatic, and since many people are unaware that they have it, they do not seek medical attention for it. Community programs established for mass screening for hypertension may not reach the working population.

In addition to the obvious benefits for the employee, employers benefit as well. Since the employer generally pays at least part of the medical insurance costs, early screening may prevent later and much higher medical expenses. Finally, labor organizations also have an interest in keeping their members healthy and reducing their health care costs.

Clinical trials of treatment programs

Between 1967 and 1972, the Veterans Administration carried out a cooperative study in the U.S. which demonstrated that antihypertensive drugs were effective in reducing morbidity and mortality due to hypertension in middle-aged men with sustained high blood pressure. This trial was a randomized, double-blind study—neither the physician nor the patient knew whether the patient was receiving the prescribed antihypertensive drug or a placebo (that is, a substance with no effect on blood pressure).

The results of this trial showed that patients with diastolic blood pressures between 115 and 129 had a significantly lower incidence of events that resulted in severe medical disability than did the control group, those who did not receive the antihypertensive treatment. Drug treatment also significantly reduced morbid events in men whose baseline diastolic blood pressure was between 105 and 114. However, in the largest group of patients with high blood pressure, those with diastolic readings of 90 to 104, the results were not significantly better when compared with the control group.

To study the effectiveness of various forms of treatment for patients with mild hypertension, the National Heart, Lung, and Blood Institute set up a community-based, randomized control trial. This Hypertension Detection and Follow-up Program screened 158,906 people aged 30 to 69 in 14 communities throughout the U.S., and eventually about 11,000 patients entered the trial. The five-year program was designed to answer the following questions: (1) If special, systematic efforts are made to treat hypertension with the stepped-care approach, would the five-year mortality rate for all hypertensive adults in the community be reduced? (2) Over a long period of time, could a substantial portion of all hypertensive patients be brought under control with drugs aimed at achieving normal blood pressure, and could they be kept under such drug management? (3) Would the benefits of treatment exceed the toxicity of the drugs in patients with mild hypertension as well as in those with severe hypertension? (4) Was any form of hypertensive therapy effective in young adults and in women, and was it equally effective in both blacks and whites? (5) Would antihypertensive therapy lower morbidity and mortality from coronary heart disease, *i.e.*, myocardial infarction?

The patients were divided into two groups, and comparisons were made over the five years of the study. About half were treated with the stepped-care approach, while the other half were referred to their community physicians for treatment. The stepped-care approach involved helping the patient achieve adherence to drug treatment as carefully as possible. Emphasis was placed on seeing that the patient attended the clinic regularly and on using tablet counts to help monitor the patient's adherence to his drug regimen. Economic barriers to compliance were removed wherever possible: drugs, visits to the centers, laboratory tests, and if necessary, transportation were all provided at no cost to the participants. Waiting times were minimized by efficient operation of the clinic and by using various types of health personnel in addition to physicians. Appointments were made at convenient hours, and a physician was always on call to deal with problems related to hypertension.

As might be expected, results showed that blood pressure control was consistently better for the stepped-care group than for the referred-care group. The important part of the study was the evaluation of the beneficial results of careful management of high blood pressure even in patients with mild hypertension. The mortality from all causes was 17% lower in the stepped-care group than in the referred-care group, and 20% lower in the stepped-care subgroup who had diastolic blood pressures of 90 to 104.

When results for blacks and whites were compared, the control of blood pressure was consistently better for the stepped-care group than for the referred-care group.

In general, the difference in the degree of control in the two care modes was less for whites than for blacks of the same sex, and white women in the two groups differed from each other least of all. A likely explanation for these differences is that whites, and particularly white women, may have made greater efforts to obtain successful therapy in the community. The percent reduction in mortality for the stepped-care group compared to the referred-care group was greatest for black women (27.8%), less for black men (18.5%), and even less for white men (14.7%). White women showed no difference in mortality. Since it is too early to be certain of the significance of this last finding, it should *not* be assumed that white women received no benefit from the program and should not be treated. In general, patients over the age of 50 appeared to benefit more from the intense referred care than those who were 30 to 49, but the information is inconclusive. Again, it would be wrong to assume that patients in younger age groups with mild hypertension should not be treated.

Another large trial of a different kind that was carried out in Australia also involved patients with mild hypertension who had complications. It differed from the U.S. study in that a group of patients who received no active treatment (a placebo group) were compared with those patients who were taking antihypertensive drugs. Both groups received the same advice about dietary control and exercise. In the treated group, deaths from cardiovascular disease were reduced by two-thirds and the number of strokes by one-half. The greatest benefit was noted in men over 50.

—*Nathan W. Levin, M.D.*

Infectious Diseases

Immunity to infectious diseases is a state of heightened resistance that blocks the invasion of microbes and viruses and neutralizes their capacity to cause infection. The body's immunity to a particular disease agent is either active or passive in origin. Active immunity arises following direct contact with an infectious agent (such as that causing smallpox or poliomyelitis), usually as a result of recovering from the disease itself. Complete protection from infection can be induced by active immunization or vaccination with attenuated or weakened strains of the agent. Powerfully effective, such immunization has resulted in the recent eradication of smallpox from the globe and has achieved similar success for poliomyelitis in the U.S. and other industrialized nations. In each of the above instances the natural infection or its tamed vaccine substitute causes the body to marshal its own forces of immunity.

Passive immunity, in contrast, is the mere short-term loan of immunity from another individual who has recovered from a specific infection (such as measles or hepatitis). In this instance a concentrated solution of antibody (a protein called immunoglobulin, which neutralizes the virus) is prepared from the blood serum of the recovered individual and injected into the individual who has been exposed to the disease. In the case of measles and hepatitis, as in exposures to most viral agents, the antiserum must be given shortly after exposure and during the incubation period to neutralize the virus before it finds safe refuge within the person's cells. Because it is merely a loan, passive immunity affords only transient protection, about six months in the case of hepatitis. The borrowed antibody becomes used up, leaving the individual susceptible to that infection again.

Recently a new immunizing agent called transfer factor has become available. Transfer factor is unique in that the protection it affords takes effect promptly in the manner of passive immunity, yet it is long-lasting like active immunity. These advantages coupled with its lack of potential for adverse effects make transfer factor an attractive alternative for immunization. Unlike previous biological products adapted for use as immunizing agents, transfer factor is not an attenuated virus, nor is it a product of an immune individual's blood serum but rather of immunologically active white blood cells called lymphocytes.

Origin and effects of transfer factor

Transfer factor, like the serum immunoglobulin products currently used for passive immunization, is prepared from the blood of immune individuals, but from white blood cells rather than serum. The white blood cells are separated from the serum, concentrated, and disrupted by mechanical means to free the cell contents. The cell extract is filtered through a membrane sieve, which retains all the large extraneous molecules of the cells and allows only the small molecules containing transfer factor to pass through in solution. The latter is concentrated by freeze-drying, much like instant coffee, into a powder which can be put into vials and stored indefinitely. When it is to be used, it is dissolved in water and injected like a vaccine.

Transfer factor, a nontoxic natural product of immune lymphocytes, possesses the capacity to transmit most of the immunologic functions of the cells from which it is prepared to the circulating lymphocytes of nonimmune individuals. Although its exact chemical structure is still unknown, it is believed to be composed of building blocks of protein (peptides) coupled to nucleic acid fragments (nucleotides).

Transfer factor has emerged recently as one of the more potent, natural biological regulators of the immune response currently available for human use. Its particular attraction rests in its selective capacity to confer, restore, and augment cellular immune responses. These attributes are ideally suited to redress the particular imbalance in patients brought low by a broad range of diseases that are either caused by or result in depressed cellular immunity.

These properties of transfer factor make it attractive for treating a variety of infectious diseases that are either resistant to antibiotic therapy or for which such therapy is not yet available. The former category includes infections caused by mycobacteria (*e.g.*, tuberculosis and leprosy) or by fungi (*e.g.*, candidiasis, coccidioidomycosis, and histoplasmosis). In the latter category are most viral infections (*e.g.*, herpes zoster, herpes simplex, measles, viral pneumonia, chronic active hepatitis, and cytomegalovirus infection).

Clinical experience following administration of transfer factor as immunotherapy for such infectious diseases, although largely empirical and anecdotal, has repeatedly demonstrated its remarkable potency in restoring cellular immunity and thereby initiating eradication of the infectious agent. This turn of events appears to occur concomitantly with the appearance in the patient's circulation of a new population of lymphocytes that can recognize and engage the microbe or virus as a foreign invader. When confronted with the infecting agent or its products in a test tube, such lymphocytes will promptly exhibit the whole gamut of immune responses that human beings have evolved to eradicate such infections. This repertoire includes lymphocyte proliferation and cell division accompanied by the synthesis and export of distress signals to other scavenger cells (macrophages). Such distress signals include the discharge of such proteins as macrophage chemotactic factor (MCF), which attracts macrophages to the site of confrontation; macrophage inhibition factor (MIF), which impedes their egress; and macrophage activating factor (MAF), which triggers the digestive machinery of the cells for increased killing of

Bill Robinson—ANIMALS, ANIMALS

Transfer factor, a new immunizing agent, is currently being tested using marmosets, which have a high susceptibility to viral infection. It is hoped that transfer factor will become a powerful new weapon for fighting infection.

the ingested microbes. Other secretions by such activated lymphocytes include immune interferon, a substance that blocks the spread of viruses from cell to cell and interferes with their capacity to reproduce more virus. Each of these beneficial materials, which increase the body's resistance to infection, has been detected following the administration of transfer factor.

Transfer factor and disease prevention

Armed with this background delineating the safety and potency of transfer factor as a restorative of cellular immunity in the face of overwhelming infections, scientists reasoned that it might provide even more potent protection to susceptible individuals if administered before infection occurred. To test this hypothesis Russell W. Steele of the University of Arkansas and his colleagues studied the effect of transfer factor on the course of herpesvirus infection in marmoset monkeys. The marmoset was chosen because of its natural defects in cellular immune responses and its uniform susceptibility to devastating illness and death following such viral infection. Attempts to alter this vulnerability would provide an acid test for any beneficial effects of the administration of transfer factor prior to infection. The study also would provide experience with this agent in an animal counterpart of immunodeficient children or patients whose immunity is depressed by such forms of cancer as leukemia and Hodgkin's disease.

For the study, transfer factor was prepared from one human donor with strong immunity to herpes simplex virus and administered to 12 marmosets at various times before the animals were infected with herpes simplex virus. In this classical Pasteurian experiment the two marmosets survived that were inoculated with transfer factor three weeks before being infected with the virus, and only one of the two animals survived that received the same transfer factor three days before viral infection. The remaining eight marmosets, who had received transfer factor at the time of infection or one, three, or seven days after infection, also died. Three control animals who did not receive transfer factor also died. The immunity conferred by herpes simplex immune transfer factor was shown to be specifically protective only against herpes simplex infection when it was administered to three additional marmosets who were then infected with another strain of virus called saimiri; all three died of the leukemic-type disease that the virus produces.

The protective effect of transfer factor demonstrated in marmosets led Steele and his colleagues to evaluate the clinical application of transfer factor to the problem of such viral infections in children who have acute lymphocytic leukemia. This is a form of cancer that, ironically, affects the lymphocytes, the prime movers of the immune response. Although modern cancer chemotherapy can cure the disease in one-third of its victims, these children suffer from the derangement of lymphocytic immune functions caused by the disease itself, which in turn is aggravated by the immunosuppressive effects of the drugs necessary to eradicate the cancerous cells. These effects lead to an immunodeficient state and an increased susceptibility to overwhelming, possibly fatal infections.

Infections with varicella-herpes zoster viruses, which cause chickenpox and shingles, are among the most serious that occur in childhood leukemia. They result in the death of 7% of such leukemic children and pose a life-threatening catastrophe. Zoster immune globulin or plasma has been shown effective if it can be administered within 72 hours after exposure to the disease. Antiviral drugs are being tested, as is a vaccine of live varicella-zoster virus.

As a prelude to a large scale trial, Steele administered one dose of varicella-zoster immune transfer factor to 15 nonimmune children with acute lymphocytic leukemia. Twelve of these children were experiencing drug-induced remission of their leukemic disease, and three were in relapse. Ten of the 12 children in remission responded to transfer factor with acquisition of cellular immunity to varicella-zoster virus, which endured for as long as 1½ years. During this time four of this group became naturally exposed to chickenpox acquired by siblings, and none came down with the disease. The three children in whom the leukemic disease had relapsed did not respond to transfer factor and failed to be converted to an immune state.

Steele's group then embarked on a prospective, double-blind, controlled clinical trial comparing varicella-zoster immune transfer factor to the injection of a placebo consisting of vitamin B_2 and salt solution. Sixty-one patients with leukemia and no immunity to chickenpox were injected either with immune transfer factor (31 patients) or placebo (30 patients) and followed for 1–2½ years thereafter. In the course of the follow-up

Demographic and clinical data on patients with acute lymphocytic leukemia (ALL)

	group	
	transfer factor	placebo
number of patients	31	30
sex (male/female)	20/11	21/9
mean age at diagnosis of ALL	4 yr, 9 mo	4 yr, 5 mo
mean interval since diagnosis	2 yr, 8 mo	2 yr, 4 mo
mean age at enrollment in study	7 yr, 5 mo	6 yr, 9 mo
exposed to chickenpox	16	15
clinical chickenpox	1	13
disseminated disease	0	3
mortality	0	0
received zoster immune globulin	2	3

Courtesy, Russell W. Steele, M.D.

period, 16 patients who had received transfer factor and 15 patients who had received the placebo underwent natural exposure to chickenpox, following contact with infected siblings or playmates. Fifteen of the 16 patients who had received transfer factor and subsequently encountered the varicella-zoster virus did not contract the disease. The sole exception developed a mild case of chickenpox consisting of three vesicles and no systemic symptoms. In contrast, 13 of the 15 patients who had received the placebo developed full-blown chickenpox following natural exposure to the disease. *See* table for a tabulation of these statistics. In the editorial evaluation that accompanied the publication of this report in *The New England Journal of Medicine,* the results of the clinical trial were called impressive.

Future prospects

In addition to the potential benefit to leukemic children of immunization with transfer factor, the study illustrates two broader principles afforded by this new approach to immunity. It suggests that transfer factor may provide an alternative method of immunizing normal individuals to prevent certain infections for which no vaccine is available. It also suggests that immunization with transfer factor may afford protection against certain infections that occur in patients who suffer from diseases that result in immune deficiency. These categories include such patients as organ-transplant recipients, who require treatment with drugs that suppress the immune response in order to control their disease, and patients with disseminated lupus erythematosus. Other categories include patients with a particular cancer of the lymphoid cells such as Hodgkin's disease, lymphosarcoma, or multiple myeloma, as well as cancer patients in general. These people are immune deficient as a result of their underlying disease as well as from the drug therapy necessary to eradicate the cancer cells.

Currently, preparations of transfer factor are available only in research laboratories where the substance is being studied or applied in controlled clinical trials. Research to uncover the biochemical identity of transfer factor and unravel its immunologic mechanism is slow and laborious. Recent findings, however, that it can be separated from contaminating molecules by binding to the related antigen (*e.g.,* diphtheria toxoid transfer factor binds to diphtheria toxoid), give promise of more rapid progress in this line of study.

Such technical advances can provide the knowledge and the means to adapt the production of transfer factor to recombinant DNA technology or cell-fusion techniques, whereby a uniform product can be produced by bacteria or lymphocytes in culture. Such techniques are currently being applied to the production of interferon for clinical use.

Meanwhile, studies also continue on a bovine transfer factor prepared in calves that have been immunized with the desired antigen. Bovine transfer factor has been shown to protect cattle against a parasitic infectious disease called coccidiosis. Bovine transfer factor is also effective in the transfer of cellular immunity when injected into humans. Its chief attraction rests in the large quantities which can be prepared from appropriately immunized calves. In addition there is a vast clinical experience that has established the safety and efficacy of such bovine products as insulin and other hormonal preparations in the treatment of a number of human diseases.

—H. Sherwood Lawrence, M.D.

Lung Diseases

A recent report from the U.S. surgeon general indicates that smoking low-tar, low-nicotine cigarettes is of limited help at best in lowering the risk of lung cancer and other disorders associated with tobacco use. Another report, describing the results of a Japanese study of the nonsmoking wives of heavy smokers, has amassed the best evidence to date of the harmful effects of chronic exposure of nonsmokers to tobacco fumes. Other advances in understanding and treating respiratory problems have been the recognition of a defect in mucosal transport as an underlying cause in several bronchial, nasal, and sinus disorders and continued evaluation of emergency management of choking caused by an obstruction in the airway.

First aid for choking victims

Asphyxiation from inhaled food—appropriately nicknamed the café coronary—each year kills 3,000 persons in the U.S. In terms of total deaths dining is more hazardous than air travel or playing with a loaded gun. Choking on either food or small objects is the leading cause of in-the-home accidental death for children under one year of age and the sixth leading cause of accidental death in the overall population. In 1975 the American Medical Association's Commission on Emergency Medical Services endorsed the so-called Heimlich maneuver for emergency treatment for choking caused by an obstruction in the airway, but proponents of other rescue strategies have since made this controversial as a sole and exclusive recommendation.

Investigations of resuscitative techniques have included pressure measurements in the airways of cadavers, studies of simulated obstructions in silicone-rubber casts of the larynx, and tests on anesthetized baboons whose airways were blocked deliberately with pieces of meat. Heimlich, whose maneuver involves forceful thrusts into the victim's upper abdomen with the rescuer's double-clenched fists, has stigmatized conventional back slaps between the shoulders as potential death blows capable of propelling the foreign body more deeply into rather than out of the central airway. Actual measurements on human volunteers have shown the Heimlich maneuver to create pressures often insufficient to dislodge samples of food from the molded larynx model. Citing evidence that the maneuver can expel from the lungs an air volume of four quarts per second, Heimlich's rebuttal contends that obstructing bodies are better displaced by a large outflow of air rather than by a momentary pressure wave and that elevation of the diaphragm by the impact of a fist in the abdomen, while occasionally fracturing ribs, is the safest and most effective way to deal with choking.

What, then, should be the first-aid rescue procedure for dealing with a choking victim? First, one must appreciate that all who collapse to the floor are not having heart attacks and may indeed have blocked airways that cannot be helped by standard cardiopulmonary resuscitative techniques. Therapy for such blockage must be given within four minutes to prevent death or irreversible brain damage. Cardinal clues for recognizing the problem include (a) distinct features of environment (dining or play areas), (b) abrupt distress, often with a hand to the throat, (c) the inability to speak or utter a sound while retaining, though briefly, all other faculties, and (d) ashen pallor with purple lips, nose, fingers, and toes.

With the help of a specially constructed mannequin, a demonstrator shows the proper position of the hands to perform the Heimlich maneuver to aid a choking victim.

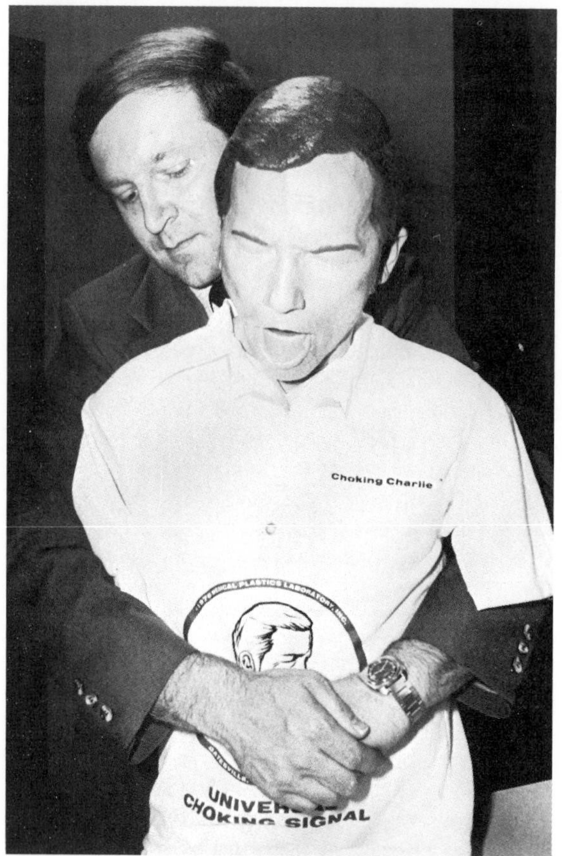

UPI

The blow to the back still carries the vote of most authorities, but the blow should be sharp and hard and reinforced with gravity, *i.e.,* by inverting the patient as effectively as can be done (this works best with children and when the obstruction has bulk and weight). As Heimlich warns, efforts to remove the obstruction with the fingers are potentially dangerous (the lightest touch on an object causing incomplete blockage may make the blockage complete) unless the obstruction is high, visible, and massive. If forceps are at hand they are safer than fingers and may be lifesaving especially if the obstruction is tightly wedged. The Heimlich maneuver is used after these preliminary measures, quickly performed, fail. If the obstruction is successfully eliminated and the victim does not recover promptly, standard cardiopulmonary resuscitation is begun. The person who chokes while alone cannot effectively use back blows or hook food out of the throat. He first should attempt forceful coughing and then modify the Heimlich maneuver by driving his upper abdomen forcefully into a railing, the back of a chair, or other sturdy object.

Acute mountain sickness

Health dangers from high altitudes apply mainly to individuals without prior acclimatization who are rapidly exposed to elevations above 2,450 m (8,000 ft) above sea level. At such heights headache occurs in half of unacclimatized persons and severe, sometimes fatal, illness in about one out of ten, with incidence and severity linked to speed of ascent and altitude attained.

As barometric pressure falls with altitude the partial pressure of oxygen (which depends on the number of oxygen molecules per given ambient volume) diminishes. The body compensates for this decreased availability of oxygen with overly rapid breathing (hyperventilation), which also removes an excessive amount of carbon dioxide, important to the body's acid-base balance. Excess alkalinity of the body fluids (alkalosis) results, which in turn suppresses centers in the brain and elsewhere for respiratory drive and temporarily cancels the adaptive overbreathing, particularly in sleep. Symptoms of acute mountain sickness (AMS) include headache, weakness, shortness of breath, dizziness and general distress with onset within hours to two days. Nausea and vomiting may be severe. During sleep, breathing may be irregular, with repeated episodes of shallow or even absent respiration, and serious tissue underoxygenation can occur. AMS can be prevented by gradual ascents with acclimatization stays of two to four days at intermediate altitudes and by descent to lower elevations for sleep.

Acetazolamide, a sulfonamide drug in common use for glaucoma, is an enzyme inhibitor whose complex actions alter carbon dioxide transport and the body's

Kenneth Gunnar—Photo Researchers

Rapid ascent to or descent from very high altitudes causes a host of physiological reactions that can be severe and even life threatening.

acid-base balance and regulation. Taken for several hours before a necessarily rapid ascent (for example, for a rescue mission), the drug may prevent AMS altogether or alleviate symptoms (nausea, confusion, and headache), and it may benefit persons already at altitude (less insomnia and superior intellectual—but not physical—performance). Taking acetazolamide as a preventive is of less benefit to those who fly rapidly to high altitudes than those who trek or climb, and increased mental alertness is thought to decrease mountaineering accidents. Though it was once thought to act by inducing a state of counteracting acidosis (excess acidity of the body fluids) that stimulates respiration and increases oxygen supply, its effect is now known to be more complex. Although its effect is transient, the body's physiological adjustment to altitude usually takes over before the drug action wears off. It is not recommended that acetazolamide be used for ordinary climbing; a commonsense approach of gradual ascent is by far the safer choice.

Swelling of the face, hands, and feet (more common in women) at high altitudes is not prevented by gradual ascent or acclimatization, and its mechanism is unknown. Acetazolamide can decrease this swelling somewhat, but full recovery may be delayed until descent to sea level and a spontaneous outpouring of large volumes of urine. High-altitude pulmonary edema (fluid in the lungs) resulting in suffocation and frothy expectoration and swelling of the brain with hallucinations, bizzare behavior, and possibly coma are the most serious complications; fatal episodes are reported annually from ski lodges located at altitudes higher than 2,450 m. Sleeping below this altitude appears to be preventive. At altitudes above 4,250 m (14,000 ft) retinal hemorrhages can occur. Usually these disappear completely after several weeks at sea level, but visual field defects persist in rare cases.

Cigarettes and cancer

The U.S. surgeon general's 17th annual review of smoking and health, released in early 1981, held that smokers who switch to low-tar, low-nicotine cigarettes are at only slightly reduced risk of lung cancer and can be given no assurance the frequencies of emphysema, bronchitis, cardiovascular disorders, or birth defects are lessened at all. Reaffirming that "there is no such thing as a safe cigarette," the report found that any safety factor available in low-tar brands is offset by altered "compensatory" behavior: smoking a greater number of cigarettes (one-third of smokers now use low-tar cigarettes, but this third buys half the cigarettes sold in the U.S.), inhaling more deeply, and smoking cigarettes closer to the end.

The report also warned that additional risks might derive from largely undisclosed additives used to replace flavor lost by cutting tar and nicotine content. Under current law, manufacturers are not compelled to release such "trade secret" formulations. The industry has provided a list of 1,500 additives used in cigarettes but no specifications regarding dosage or combinations for given brands. Included in the list are cocoa (banned in England as producing carcinogens when burned), caramel, chalk, shellac, and some suspected or known chemical carcinogens. The government hopes to work out an agreement allowing access to cigarette recipes without violating their confidentiality.

According to a major Japanese study nonsmoking wives of heavy smokers have an increased risk of developing lung cancer, a risk between one-half and one-third that of women who smoke. Among 91,540 nonsmoking women 40 years of age or older who were regularly exposed to their husbands' habit and followed for 14 years, cancer incidence bore a direct relationship to the amount their husbands smoked, and mortality was increased twofold over a control group of nonsmoking wives of nonsmoking husbands. In farm regions, where there were few other environmental contaminants to complicate the results, the risk was more than quadrupled. An increased, but far less significant, risk of developing emphysema and asthma was also apparent among these smoke-exposed wives, but no increase in other kinds of cancer (*e.g.*, of the stomach or cervix) or in heart disease was found. This study, which emphasized that smokers are a menace not just to themselves but to nearby people as well, has been challenged. Other risks of passive smoking, including general discomfort, allergies, reduced lung function, and angina, are well established.

In modifying its recommendations to the public about checkups for the early detection of cancer, the American Cancer Society (ACS) no longer endorses annual chest X-rays and sputum tests in lung-cancer screening—even among heavy smokers and those in high-risk occupations—because so far no long-term studies have proved that finding lung cancer at an earlier stage by these methods has reduced ultimate overall mortality. Such screening programs indeed can detect instances of cancer that are undetectable by other means, the cases detected by screening tend to be in earlier stages, and case-survival rates from the time of detection are improved by screening. Nevertheless, early detection appears to result merely in moving up the time of diagnosis and in increasing the length of time that the patient is aware of the disease, without actually prolonging life. Comparative "survival rates" from such studies can be misleading, measuring mainly a wider interval between a patient's diagnosis and death. The ACS continues to emphasize programs of primary prevention that stress the health advantages of quitting smoking and keeping nonsmokers from starting.

Bronchial mucociliary clearance

The inner lining of the bronchial tree is covered with a delicate carpet of mucus that is continually swept, against gravity, to the throat and then swallowed or expelled in various more-or-less socially acceptable ways. Physical removal of inhaled bacteria along with this sticky film is a key factor in preventing infection of the respiratory tract, and dysfunction of the normal mucus escalator may lead to virulent, recurrent, or chronic forms of bronchitis and pneumonia.

The main propelling force along the airways is generated by the rhythmic wavelike beating of myriads of tiny, hairlike cilia that project from the surface of the lining cells, and the ability of these cilia to whip the mucus in effective synchrony depends upon the integrity of internal linear structures called microtubules that interact by means of "arms" made of the protein dynein. A deficiency of normal ciliary energy results in chaotic, weak, or totally absent mucociliary transport. Dynein-arm abnormalities have been detected by direct electron microscopy in a number of clinical syndromes, heretofore poorly understood, associated with chronic, stubborn, and destructive forms of pulmonary infections, bronchiectasis (dilation of the bronchial tubes), nasal and sinus inflammations, nasal polyps, and otitis media (inflammation of the middle ear). This anatomic predisposition has been demonstrated in biopsy specimens from the nasal lining of siblings as well as by delayed clearance of inhaled radioactive particles from the lungs, and it is believed to be genetic. In male patients the sperm is also examined because its swimming is powered by microtubular contractions structurally and biochemically similar to those responsible for ciliary beating, and individuals with dynein-arm abnormalities are generally infertile since their sperm are immotile.

Replacement therapy involving an energy-source enzyme has corrected the sperm-tail beat frequency and restored sperm motility in an experimental nonhuman sperm model. Investigators have shown parallel compensatory, but not curative, stimulation of ciliary movement in human nasal linings of both normal subjects and patients with the immotile-cilia syndrome. The evidence that activity can be induced in cilia suggests that the primary abnormality is more likely related to a control mechanism than to a basic structural aberration and gives hope both for understanding the cause of and for treating some common pulmonary diseases and a special type of male infertility.

—L. Fred Ayvazian, M.D.

Stayskal—Chicago Tribune/New York News Syndicate, Inc.

Special Report:
Pneumonia: Evolution of a Killer
by H. Sherwood Lawrence, M.D.

"While there has been a remarkable diminution in the prevalence of a large number of all the acute infections, one disease not only holds its own, but seems even to have increased in its virulence. In the mortality bills, pneumonia is an easy second to tuberculosis; indeed, in many cities the death-rate is now higher and it has become, to use the phrase of Bunyan, 'the Captain of the men of death.'" This is how in 1901 Sir William Osler, the renowned clinician who revolutionized bedside teaching in hospitals, characterized the killing disease that struck down huge numbers of both robust and frail citizens each winter and spring.

The infection of the lung caused by the pneumococcus and called lobar pneumonia or just pneumonia did not evoke the stark terror of the plague or the near panic that poliomyelitis epidemics would cause in the 1950s, yet most knew of its dire consequences and recognized that an encounter with the "Captain" was dicey—a fate that was ideally avoided.

In the 19th century pneumococcal pneumonia not only infected children and the elderly—the dramatic illness was so often fatal in older citizens that it was called "old man's friend"—but also indulged in its particular predilection for infecting robust adult wage earners. Consider the emotional, social, and economic havoc wrought when the head of the household was laid low by pneumococcal lobar pneumonia. The family stood by during the stormy course of the illness, hoping and praying that the fever would break and the symptoms would vanish and that the victim would be one of the lucky ones who lived. More often than not, however, he was dead in a week. The grieving wife was forced to find employment, the children were deprived of education and often forced to work themselves. The only treatment available as the disease ran its course was the oxygen tent.

At the beginning of this century physicians would speak of the awesome qualities of the pneumococcus—the fastidiousness of the organism, its devilish capacity to wreak havoc with the lungs of afflicted patients, cutting off their breathing space, spreading to the bloodstream, lodging in the heart valves and eroding them, migrating to the brain to produce coma and meningitis, and spilling over into the joints to tear up the cartilage.

Over the past half century the fears of industrialized populations have shifted from worry about the abrupt death caused by infectious diseases such as pneumonia to a proper concern about more leisurely killers—chronic diseases such as heart disease, stroke, and cancer. This turn of events came primarily as a result of the introduction of antibiotic therapy in the early 1940s. This, with the emergence of higher standards of living, better housing and sanitation, less crowding, and adequate nutrition, combined to give the impression that many infectious diseases no longer posed a threat to human survival.

Recently a research team from the Medical College of Virginia in Richmond studied the tissue of South American mummies and found pneumonia to be a major cause of death in that continent some 3,000 years ago. Evidence for acute pneumonia was found in 44% of 108 mummies studied—a figure remarkably close to the current rate of 37% of hospital deaths. The Virginia researchers concluded that despite a grand arsenal of modern antibiotics, pneumonia is still the most common terminal illness of hospitalized patients.

Pneumococcal pneumonia

Pneumonia, then, is an infectious disease that has not been wiped out. In fact, bacterial pneumonia ranks among the ten leading causes of death in the United States today, and the pneumococcus is responsible for 90% of all pneumonias caused by bacteria. (Viral, rick-

Researchers recently examined South American mummies and found that pneumonia was a major cause of death some 3,000 years ago.

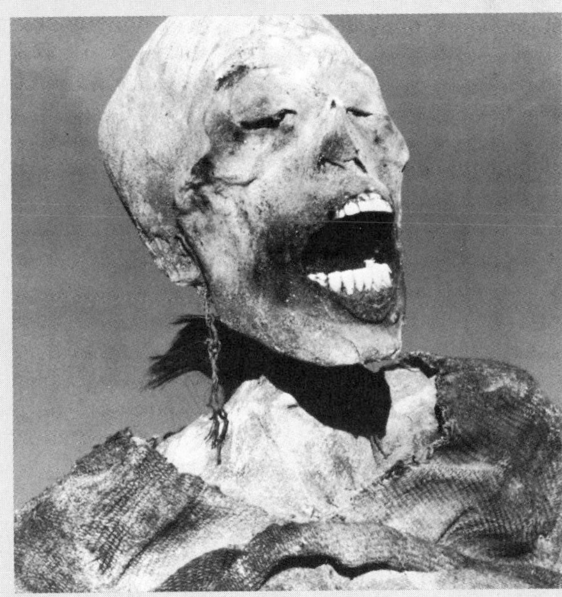

Courtesy, Marvin Allison, M.D., Medical College of Virginia

ettsial, and chlamydial pneumonias are not discussed here.) Many individuals harbor the pneumococcus in their upper respiratory tracts without coming down with the disease. However, a concomitant upper respiratory infection, the common cold, or a bout of influenza can lower natural resistance; the pneumococci descend from the nose and throat to the linings of the air sacs in the lungs, where they reproduce, infect the lung tissue, and cause the disease pneumonia.

It is the nature of its outer sugar capsule, called the type-specific polysaccharide, that gives each group of pneumococci its own individual identification mark and which is responsible for its virulence. There are more than 80 types of pneumococci, yet the three most virulent types (1, 2, and 3) cause about 50% of all the cases of lobar pneumonia in adults, and about 80% of the cases are caused by only eight types. This type of information has a bearing on the design of a pneumococcal vaccine, which is discussed below.

Prodded by the devastation produced by the pneumococcus, Osler made careful bedside observations on all aspects of pneumonia at Johns Hopkins Hospital in Baltimore from 1889 to 1910. It was observed that those patients who recovered from lobar pneumococcal pneumonia did so by crisis, or "lysis," of their fever and symptoms some seven to ten days after the onset of the illness. The onset was marked by the dramatic appearance of shaking chills, fever, knifelike chest pain, cough, and expectoration of bloody or rust-colored sputum. It was discovered that the seven-to-ten-day latent period before spontaneous recovery occurred was the time necessary for the patient to develop specific antibodies.

The infectious cycle in pneumococcal disease begins when the microbe, or germ, grows rapidly in the lungs. Its sugar capsule is a powerful antigen that stimulates the patient to make antibodies which will neutralize it and abrogate its damaging effects on lung function. During the seven to ten days when the patient's immune system is producing antibody, the pneumococci are engulfed by scavenging white blood cells. But in the absence of antibody the attempted rescue mission fails, the scavenger cells are killed by the germ, and the infection mounts. As the infectious cycle continues, pus is formed by clots of dead white blood cells that plug the air sacs and clog the lung, interfering with the body's capacity to get oxygen from inhaled air into the bloodstream.

The real rescue mission can begin when antibody is present and coats the germ, causing its capsule to swell. The swollen, torpid pneumococci are then engulfed and ingested by the white blood cells, which are now in a position to kill the microbe rather than be killed by it. This is the critical role of antibody: to interrupt the cycle of infection and eradicate the germ. However, this process is fraught with chance and dependent upon the delicate balance between the virulence of the particular pneumococcus causing the pneumonia and the inherited ability of the patient to make adequate quantities of antibody before being overwhelmed. This principle laid the cornerstone for the older serum (antibody) therapy of pneumococcal pneumonia, prepared from immune rabbit serum, designed to lend the patient the antipneumococcal antibody.

German bacteriologists Fred Neufeld and Ludwig Händel recognized the need to identify the specific type of pneumococcus causing the disease and devised a method of typing pneumococci on the basis of capsular swelling. Their work led to the treatment of pneumonia with a new antipneumococcal serum in 1910; prepared antibodies caused the sugar capsule of the bacterium to swell and thereby allowed the patient's white blood cells to attack and kill the disease-causing microorganism. This knowledge was extended by Alphonse Dochez and Michael Heidelberger at the Rockefeller Institute in New York City. Also at the Rockefeller starting in 1913, Oswald T. Avery and his colleagues studied the many biochemical and immunological facets of the pneumococcus critical to understanding and treating the disease. The most significant

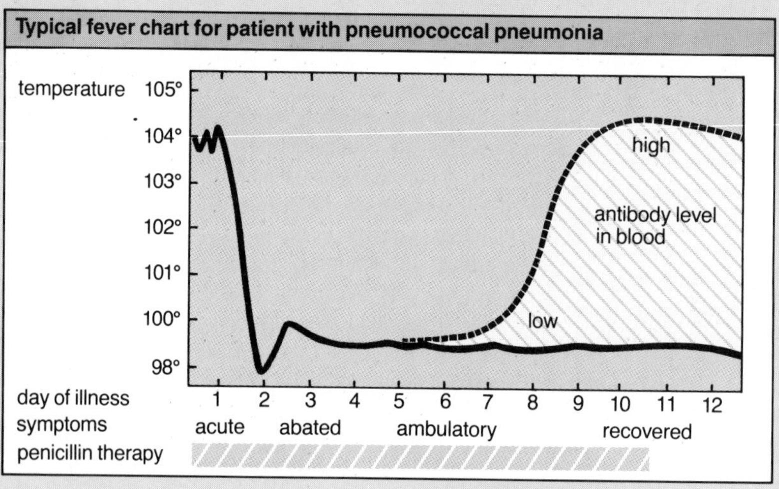

The use of penicillin has had a remarkable effect on the management of pneumonia. Penicillin gives the patient relief of his severe symptoms by fighting the disease during the time his own antibodies are rallying to destroy the infectious agent.

finding which arose from this work was the discovery by Avery, Collin MacLeod, and Maclyn McCarty in 1944 that the DNA of the pneumococcus was the chemical messenger of heredity and caused genetic transformations. They demonstrated that a nonencapsulated, nonvirulent pneumococcus exposed to DNA prepared from an encapsulated virulent pneumococcus was transformed to a virulent strain. This finding marked a watershed in biomedical discovery, the fruits of which are still accruing.

The use of antimicrobial drugs in the treatment of pneumonia began with sulfapyridine by English pathologist Sir Lionel E. H. Whitby in 1938. The use of sulfa drugs greatly improved the outcome in acute pneumonia over serum therapy. Then, in the early 1940s, with the introduction of penicillin in therapeutics the pneumococcus was dealt an even greater blow. Penicillin therapy had a profound impact on taming the pneumococcus since the antibiotic agent interferes with the germ's cell wall synthesis, resulting in a leaky pneumococcus which fails to reproduce itself, absorbs fluid, and bursts like a balloon. Thus penicillin therapy "buys time" by halting the growth of the organism or killing it outright, allowing the patient the interval to make the antibody that will eliminate the pneumococcus finally and terminate the illness.

A stroll through the wards of any large hospital in the winter dramatizes this victory. In most instances a patient is admitted in the evening desperately ill, with high fever and shaking chills, labored breathing, and racking cough. Penicillin therapy is begun, and within 24 to 48 hours, the patient becomes afebrile and strength returns as he begins to recover. By the 14th day he is ready to go home. The penicillin therapy must be continued for eight to ten days from the onset of the illness since cessation of the antibiotic before the patient's antibodies can take over will cause a relapse.

The introduction of antibiotic therapy in the treatment of pneumococcal pneumonias reduced the fatality rate due to this disease tenfold from the level of 20 to 25% in the preantibiotic era to 2.5 to 3% in the postantibiotic era. (*See* graph, this page.) Indeed, in younger patients 10 to 50 years of age who are treated early the fatality rate is as low as 0.5%. The critical role that age exerts in the outcome of pneumococcal pneumonia is also illustrated in the graph.

But even with the antibiotics, the "Captain" has not been brought to bay; there are still some 150,000 to 300,000 cases a year in the United States. The outcome of any infection is still determined by the virulence of the microbe and the capacity of the patient to marshal the forces of immunity and resistance, even in the presence of powerful antibiotics. Over the past decade, there have been reports, mostly outside the United States, of selected strains of the pneumococcus bacterium that are resistant to penicillin and other antibiotics—a cause for concern, which in part led to the newest development in the saga of pneumococcal pneumonia: the general availability of a vaccine composed of the antigens of the most commonly encountered types of pneumococci. The perfection of this preventive measure is a remarkable tribute to the ingenuity and perseverance of a small group of dedicated biomedical scientists.

Although pneumococcal vaccines were administered to populations at risk as early as 1911, the mixed and varied composition of the preparations used and the resulting variations in the degree of immunity produced led to disappointing results. A group of investigators at the Rockefeller Institute isolated and characterized the sugar of the pneumococcal capsule as the critical part of the bacterium required for the immune response. This knowledge was applied to prepare a pneumococcal vaccine composed of the sugars from pneumococci of types 1, 2, 5, and 7. This preparation was given to vaccinate Army troops in the midst of a raging epidemic of pneumococcal pneumonia in 1944; within two weeks the vaccinated group demonstrated immunity. Moreover, the incidence of pneumonia also decreased in the control group, which received no vaccine, owing to the eradication of the contagious pneumococci in the noses and throats of the vaccinated group.

Although the vaccine was licensed and available by 1945, the tremendous impact of this study on the public health of the nation was not fully appreciated at the time, partially because the war had just ended. The unprecedented effectiveness of penicillin and other antibiotics in the treatment and cure of infections on a global scale had generated the belief that pneumococcal infections could be easily treated, therefore immunization was not necessary. Time was to dispel this premature euphoria.

In 1964 Robert Austrian and his colleagues at the

Effects of various treatments in various age-groups on fatality rates for pneumococcal pneumonia

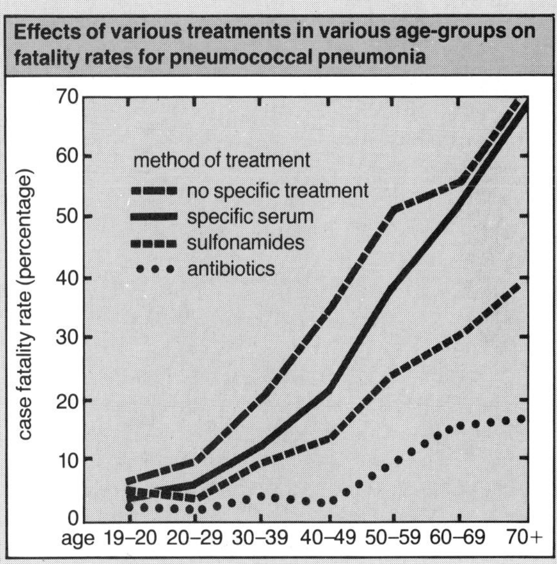

Courtesy, Henry F. Dowling, M.D. Reprinted with permission.

Centers for Disease Control

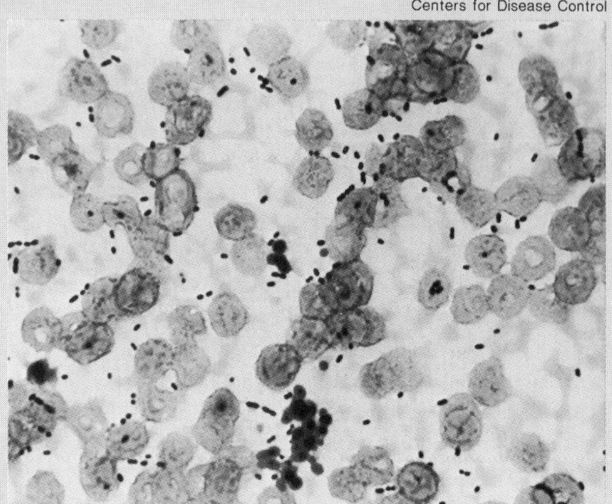

The streptococcus bacterium is one of the infectious agents that can cause pneumonia, usually following a bout of measles, flu, strep throat, or scarlet fever.

University of Pennsylvania demonstrated that as few as six pneumococcal types were responsible for one-half of all the cases of disease in the United States and 12 pneumococcal types for more than three-quarters of the cases. These observations led to the development and testing of a highly effective pneumococcal vaccine that contains the individual sugar molecules from 14 types of pneumococci. Licensed in 1977, the vaccine has been shown to provide protection for three to five years in 80% of vaccinated individuals. There have been only minor reactions to the vaccination, *e.g.*, occasional soreness or redness of the arm at the site of inoculation and rarely a transient and slight elevation of temperature.

It is currently recommended that candidates for pneumococcal vaccination include persons over 50 years of age, patients suffering from chronic diseases of the lungs, heart, liver, or kidneys, patients with diabetes, leukemia and other cancers, and those patients whose immune responses are impaired by disease or loss of a spleen. In the future the anticipated widespread use of the pneumococcal vaccine also promises to further decrease the number of healthy individuals who carry and therefore transmit the microbe.

Gram-negative pneumonia

In the past two decades there has been an increasing incidence of patients with pneumonia caused by gram-negative bacteria. These hardy organisms, when stained with a dye called the gram stain, appear red in color under the microscope ("gram negative"), while the pneumococcus stains blue ("gram positive").

Gram-negative bacilli also differ from pneumococci in that they are normal inhabitants of the bowel. Their sheer quantity along with water constitutes the bulk of fecal material. The bacteria have a number of exotic names such as *Escherichia, Proteus, Pseudomonas, Klebsiella,* and *Serratia.* They do not usually cause disease unless they escape from the bowel and set up housekeeping in the lungs, urinary passages, and kidneys, or on the heart valves. Unlike pneumococcal pneumonia, which is generally contracted outside of the hospital, most gram-negative pneumonias occur *in* the hospital. (Some 10 to 20% of hospital pneumonias are of the gram-negative type.) This arises because patients who are hospitalized for grave illnesses or are undergoing prolonged antibiotic therapy have diminished resistance to infection; in such patients the usual gram-positive bacteria that inhabit the nose and throat are overcome by the gram-negative microbes. The gram-negative bacteria, if aspirated, can result in pneumonia.

Patients can also acquire gram-negative infections as a consequence of certain life-saving measures that are performed in hospitals, such as insertion of an airway tube or attachment to an artificial respirator to sustain breathing in a comatose patient. Even though such equipment is sterilized and sterile precautions are taken by the medical personnel handling it, the risk of infection is constantly present because of the patient's lowered resistance.

Thus gram-negative pneumonia has become a problem of increasing magnitude. However, the awareness of its origins and consequences, coupled with the recent development of a whole new group of extra broad-spectrum synthetic antibiotics, the third-generation cephalosporins, to effectively treat it, have done much to bring it under control.

Staphylococcal pneumonia

Staphylococcal pneumonia is caused by organisms that are carried on our skin or in our nose and throat and that occasionally cause boils and pimples. The staphylococcus can cause pneumonia in healthy individuals but usually requires a predisposing cause that leads to debilitation and lowered resistance such as a bout of influenza.

The incidence of staphylococcal infection of the lungs and heart valves increased precipitously with the burgeoning of the drug culture in the 1960s. Staphylococcal lung infections can occur as the result of the injection of contaminated drugs or the use of contaminated needles and syringes. The staphylococci course through the bloodstream and can settle on the heart valves and then be seeded throughout the lung or can infect the lung (and other organs) directly. Although there are antibiotics effective against staphylococcal pneumonia, it remains a grave threat to life and can result in permanent disability.

Legionnaires' disease: the new pneumonia

Legionnaires' disease made its startling debut as a mysterious epidemic of fatal and near-fatal pneumonias in visitors attending an American Legion convention in Philadelphia in the summer of 1976. The disease causes malaise and headache, high fever and often chills, cough, shortness of breath, and pain in the chest. The publicity which accompanied the appearance of the devastating disease was heightened by the collective inability of microbiologists and epidemiologists investigating the epidemic to determine its cause. All of the known microbial, viral, and chemical causes of pneumonia were exonerated and no cause could be immediately determined. The situation was further confused by the lack of evidence for the usual person-to-person contact in the transmission of the pneumonia. Also, pus, which is common in acute pneumonia, was not present. Laboratory tests failed to show any of the usual pneumonia-causing bacteria.

Five months after the mysterious outbreak the bacterium that caused the disease was finally tracked down in the laboratory and found to be identical or closely related to bacteria, also then unknown, which had caused earlier, puzzling epidemics of pneumonia. The scientific detective work was carried out by persevering and ingenious microbiologists and infectious disease experts from the federal Center for Disease Control in Atlanta, Ga. The isolation of the responsible bacterium enabled medical scientists to determine an effective antibiotic treatment. Erythromycin, which had been used widely to treat cases of Legionnaires' disease, was confirmed as the antibiotic of choice since all strains were susceptible to its killing power. The mysterious invader was named *Legionella pneumophila.* Sporadic outbreaks across the United States that followed the Philadelphia episode were recognized promptly.

Legionnaires' disease presented a baffling epidemiological puzzle when it first appeared in 1976; many of its victims developed fatal pneumonia.

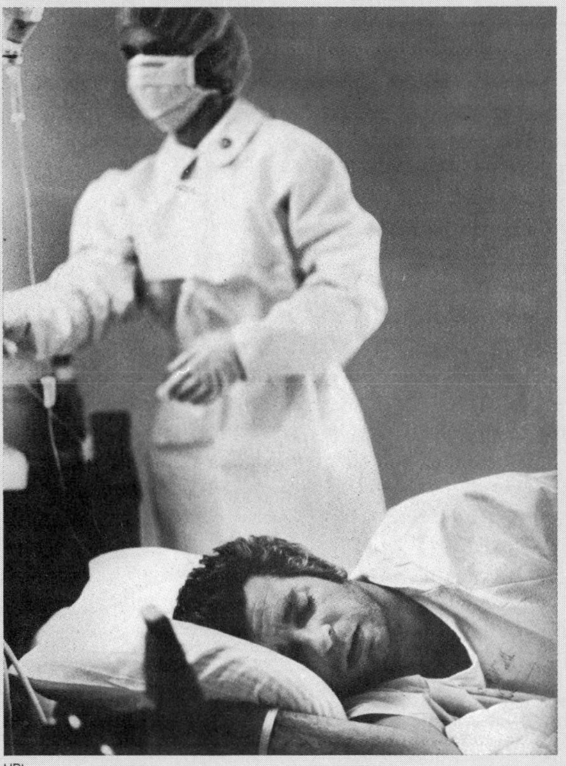

UPI

Although it is fairly well documented that the disease is not spread like pneumococcal pneumonia through person-to-person contact, the exact source of the outbreaks has yet to be determined. Several outbreaks have occurred in individual buildings or their environs. An outbreak in Pontiac, Mich., was traced to a contaminated central air-conditioning unit. The late 1978 outbreak in the vicinity of Macy's department store on 34th Street in New York City was also traced to an air-conditioning unit; the outbreak was suspected to have arisen from aerosolization of contaminated moisture from a central air conditioner into the atmosphere since the disease affected workers and passersby. Still another outbreak has been reported in association with extensive excavation of earth adjacent to a new hospital building in Los Angeles.

Cumulative experience has led to the general suspicion that contaminated water in central air-conditioning units can serve as a focus for disseminating *Legionella pneumophila* in droplets into the surrounding atmosphere.

Recent outbreaks of Legionnaires' disease have occurred in several European countries including the United Kingdom, Portugal, Spain, and Italy. It has also been seen in travelers returning from mainland China. In Europe the locale is usually a resort hotel located on the seacoast. In these instances central air conditioning has been excluded as a cause, but potable water or drainage systems are suspect. Physicians in the U.S. are now alerted to consider the possibility of Legionnaires' disease in returning travelers.

Although healthy individuals can contract Legionnaires' disease, the elderly patient and individuals who are either debilitated or whose immunity is suppressed by drugs or disease are the most common victims. The association of epidemics which occur mainly in the summer and several outbreaks proved or suspected to be related to central air-conditioning units have led to an increasing number of safeguards and monitoring of such units, particularly in hospitals.

For physicians and scientists the discovery of Legionnaires' disease and its causative microbe raised questions of how the bacterium could have been missed for so many years. The answer probably lies partially in the unique requirements for staining tissue samples in the laboratory in order to view the bacterium under the microscope. More to the point, however, the disease may turn out to be a disease of progress—a hazard of civilization which came about with the use of central air conditioning, now so common to life in industrialized society.

Medical Education

How many physicians does a nation need? The answer to this question is important not only to a nation's health but also to the way it allocates its resources. Public policies must effect some equation between the need for physicians and their supply. Yet no method of unquestioned validity is at hand to guide these policies.

In the last decade the United States has moved from having an estimated deficiency of 50,000 physicians to expecting an oversupply of 70,000 in 1990. In the 1960s the U.S. initiated costly measures to encourage the training of physicians. Now, however, there is fear of a glut of physicians and paucity of patients.

A doctor glut

How did such a circumstance arise? What are the implications of the oversupply the U.S. now faces? Can a more reasonable relationship between supply and demand now be effected? These questions, unfortunately, are entangled in a complicated mass of sociopolitical and cultural issues that permits no simple answers.

In the 1960s the U.S. was optimistic about the future. It was thought that the nation could, with proper allocation of resources, eradicate poverty and afford each citizen his portion of the Great Society. In this context, equity of access to quality medical care became a national priority. The projected supply of physicians was judged grossly inadequate to attain this goal and, as a result, federal programs were initiated to increase the number of medical schools, expand their class size, and ease restrictions on entry of foreign-born physicians. Simultaneously, a new category of health worker, the "physician extender" (nurse practitioners and physician's assistants) was created to enhance the physician's productivity.

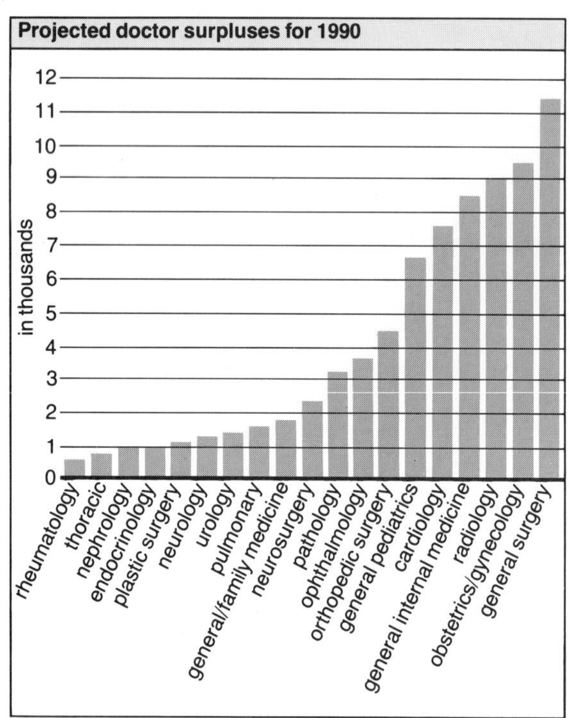

Graduate Medical Education Advisory Committee

These measures were eminently successful. The number of active physicians in 1963 was 260,000. Today it is 428,000. In the same period the number of medical schools, the number of graduates, and the number of foreign medical graduates have all doubled. There are, in addition, approximately 17,000 nurse practitioners and physician's assistants. In 1963 their number was so small that it is not a matter of reliable record.

It is now apparent that the number of physicians is increasing at a greater rate than the population. The latest projections for the year 1990 indicate a supply of 535,750 physicians and a need for 466,000; by the year 2000 the need will be 498,250 and the supply 642,000—an excess of 143,750. Increases are projected for all the major specialties except psychiatry, emergency medicine, and rehabilitation medicine, which will show shortages.

In September 1980 the Graduate Medical Education National Advisory Committee made a series of 40 recommendations to the secretary of the Department of Health and Human Resources for dealing with the impending surpluses. Three major recommendations were aimed at curtailing the very measures introduced in the '60s to expand physician manpower, the committee's advice being to reduce entering-class size in medical schools, limit the entry of foreign medical graduates, and reexamine the use of and need for so-called physician extenders.

These and all other recommendations about the adequacy of the supply of physicians center on the accuracy of estimates of the need for physicians. Supply projections can be made quite accurately, but estimates of need depend on the interaction of complicated sets of factors such as kinds of physicians, their productivity, their geographic distribution, public expectations, the definition of medicine, and even the kind of society desired.

The oversupply projected for 1990 will not affect all kinds of physicians uniformly. Most of the specialties (some 39 were studied) will show large surpluses; the primary care specialties, such as internal medicine, pediatrics, and family medicine, will show only modest surpluses; still others—those mentioned above—will be in short supply.

Assessing the need for physicians

The answer to the question of how many of each kind of doctor will be needed depends very much on the distribution of human disease, on the age and sex distribution of the population, on life-style and personal habits, on occupational and recreational activities, and

U.S. Bureau of the Census

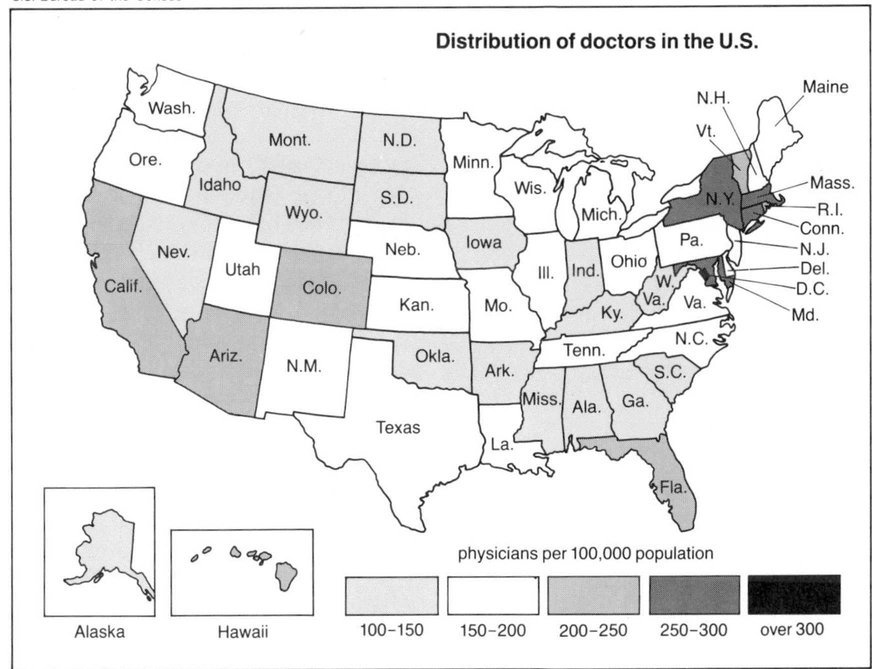

on the priorities the nation sets. Will catastrophic illnesses be deemed most important, or will the focus be on prevention, occupational health and safety, or primary care?

Nature and distribution of disease. Earlier in this century infectious diseases and tuberculosis were the most important concerns of medicine. Today that concern has shifted to heart disease, cancer, accidents, and chronic disease. In the last two decades the need for hospitalization of children has declined, and obstetrical services are less in demand. In the immediate future the demands for care of an ever increasing population of older citizens will be paramount, along with advanced technological treatment of heart disease, cancer, and trauma.

In reporting on the nation's health, the surgeon general of the United States recently emphasized the rising morbidity and mortality ascribable to personal habits such as smoking, use of alcohol, improper diet, and lack of exercise, and to environmental factors such as occupational and highway accidents. Thus, based on these trends, there will be a call for more physicians skilled in the treatment of the chronically ill and for specialists in preventive medicine and rehabilitation medicine. There will also be an increasing need for those skilled in the care of the aged. Though it is difficult to predict exactly which illnesses will predominate in the year 2000, that factor will determine whether there will be too many physicians or too few.

Geographic distribution. Many countries with more physicians per capita than the U.S. have learned that the location of physicians is largely independent of supply. The geographic location of physicians generally does not follow need but follows preferences for educational, social, cultural, and recreational opportunities. In the U.S. many medical schools have for years provided training experiences in rural areas and inner-city clinics to encourage students to settle in underserved areas. These efforts and those of the National Health Service Corps have had a relatively minor impact thus far. The trend of the flight of physicians from rural America and inner cities to suburbia does not seem to be abating.

Physician productivity. Numerical projections cannot tell us how physicians will divide their time between direct patient contact, continuing education, committee and community work, and recreation. The societal trend toward more leisure time has had a significant impact on the work habits and vacation practices of many physicians. Physician productivity, therefore, becomes an important issue in estimating need.

Productivity is also linked closely to the age of physicians, their geographic location, and the degree to which they use physician's assistants and nurse practitioners. There have been some paradoxical responses to oversupply that make prediction particularly difficult. For example, surgeons in some major cities do fewer procedures than previously, while internists venture into fields outside their own—such as minor surgery, dermatology, and office gynecology—to keep up an adequate patient flow. Other physicians, devoting more time to complex technical procedures, have less time for personal contact with patients, thus creating a different kind of need.

Societal aims. Possibly the most significant factor in determining future need has to do with society's ideas and expectations about medicine and physicians. Should medicine be confined to those illnesses curable by technical means? Should the psychosocial aspects of illness be assigned to other health professionals? Is "holistic" medicine, which makes meeting the personal needs of patients an essential part of authentic healing, desirable? Or are preventive medicine and health promotion of greater concern? Each emphasis dictates a unique distribution of the number and kinds of physicians society will require. And each of these distributions differs in turn from a projection based on physicians' geographic preferences.

Equally unpredictable are the social and political values that will characterize tomorrow's society. The political optimism and liberalism of the '60s has been supplanted in the '80s by a more restrained approach to social welfare. The combination of a flagging economy, inflation, and deregulation has dampened the prospect for equitable access to and availability of care for all. Thus, where a nation places health in its political philosophy also determines the number and kinds of physicians it feels it needs.

The availability of physicians bears no constant relationship to the quality of care or the level of patient satisfaction. Standards for both vary widely. In general, the more affluent a country, the less its members are likely to tolerate illness or discomfort of any kind. In some of the wealthiest countries, where the ratio of physicians to population is very favorable, there are complaints about an insufficiency. On the other hand, in less developed countries the tolerance for illness may be so high that the need for care is not even perceived.

Do more physicians mean better care?

Within broad limits there is no close correlation between a nation's health and the supply of physicians. There is no evidence that the comparatively good state of health in the U.S. is directly related to the increased number of physicians. In fact, there is some evidence that the reverse may be true when the oversupply becomes too great. Overmedication, as well as overutilization of surgery, laboratory, and diagnostic procedures, is in evidence today. There are signs, too, that oversupply has injected business-oriented competition into the physician-patient relationship. Clinics and physicians utilize marketing techniques, protect referral channels, and exhibit a proprietary attitude toward medical knowledge and new techniques. Physicians today incorporate, as individuals or groups; corporations and physicians own hospitals and clinics; investors are urged to put money into the health care "industry." Competition of this nature—spurred by a physician oversupply—can erode the moral and ethical obligations a doctor owes his patients.

Where doctors practice has more to do with their social and cultural preferences than where they are needed. Thus inner-city clinics tend to be underserved.

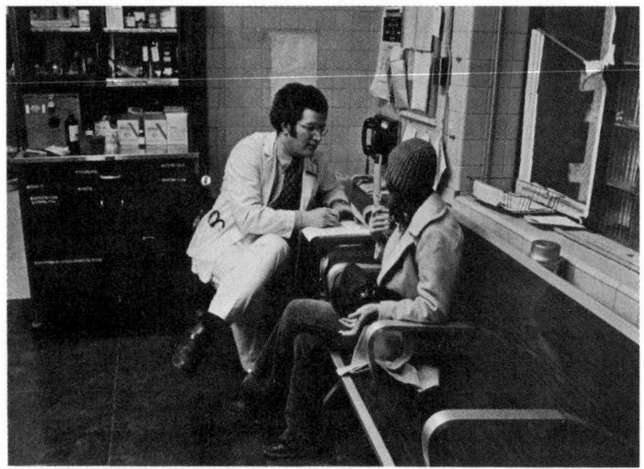

Cary Wolinsky—Stock, Boston

Oversupply can also undermine efforts to achieve equity of access to services, since it favors paying over nonpaying patients. Because the health care market seems impervious to operation of the usual forces of supply and demand, oversupply is unlikely to result in lower prices. The end result may well be a surfeit of physicians competing for a paucity of patients, with prices remaining high and producing a double standard of care for the well-to-do and the not-so-well-to-do.

Challenge for the future

It is clear that rational planning for the future requires a much more sophisticated definition of what is meant by need than is now possible. The intersection of so many factors will make it extremely difficult to arrive at firm figures on how many and what kinds of physicians the U.S. will need in 1990 or 2000.

For medical educators the challenge is especially difficult. The same institutions that effectively responded to the demand in the 1960s to increase the supply of physicians now must deal with the opposite threat of oversupply. Some steps have already been taken. More medical students and medical school graduates are entering the primary care specialties, since most medical schools now have family practice departments and residencies. Most medical schools also offer opportunities for training in rural hospitals and inner-city clinics. It is highly likely that in the next year or two the size of entering medical classes will decrease as the number of openings for training in the most popular specialties decreases. The curtailment of programs for training physician's assistants is already under way in some schools.

The medical schools cannot, and should not, dictate the numbers and kinds of physicians produced. The nation needs a public policy based on a clearer definition of what it expects from medicine before medical schools can plan rationally for the future.

—*Edmund D. Pellegrino, M.D.*

Special Report: Learning Medicine in Israel

by Ascher Segall, M.D.

The provision of medical care in the Negev, Israel's southernmost region, is beset by all the problems that a rapidly industrializing society encounters. The Negev is a semiarid desert constituting approximately two-thirds of Israel's area, about 5,000 square miles of territory. The population of the region in 1980 was close to 400,000, consisting mainly of immigrants from Europe, the Soviet Union, North Africa, and South America, as well as some 45,000 nomadic Bedouin. While the economy is still primarily based on agriculture, the potash, petrochemicals, textile, and glass industries are expanding rapidly. The principal city of the region, Beersheba, has a population of 135,000 and serves a hinterland of ten development towns and 90 agricultural villages.

Health conditions in the Negev have not escaped the impact of the region's social upheavals and industrialization. Infectious diseases are now under control, and chronic conditions such as heart disease and cancer have emerged as the major health problems. The care of patients with chronic diseases demands the attention of a variety of health professionals. Consideration must be given to the quality of life as well as to its prolongation. Although advances in medicine have made methods of prevention and therapy available, at the same time, delivery of medical care has tended to become fragmented, depersonalized, and costly.

These problems are particularly evident insofar as primary care is concerned. Primary care includes making health care services accessible to patients, providing preventive medicine, and assuring integration and continuity of care through the various phases of illness. In the past, there was a sharp demarcation between family practitioners who worked in the community and those physicians based at the central hospital in Beersheba. They worked in relative isolation from each other. The result was a lack of continuity in the medical care that patients received.

A new approach to health care

As part of the effort to rectify this situation, the government of Israel authorized the establishment of a Faculty of Health Sciences at Ben Gurion University of the Negev in Beersheba. A school of medicine, the first component of the faculty, was opened in 1974. It was to have a dual role in the region. First, it was to use academic resources in developing an integrated system for the delivery of comprehensive health care. Second, it was to educate a new type of physician who would have the motivation and competence to function effectively in this system. The new school thus constitutes an experiment in the direct merging of medical education with the provision of health care.

This merging means the medical school will have an important impact on health services in the Negev. Rarely has a medical school participated in the planning and implementation of all levels of an area's health services. In Beersheba this has led to the establishment, under the aegis of the medical school, of a consortium of all Negev health care agencies. Its purpose is to provide a framework for coordination of services and sharing of resources. The dean of the medical school, as director of the consortium, plays a key role in mobilizing the academic resources of the university to aid in designing and evaluating changes in the health care system. Implementing change remains the responsibility of the agencies directly concerned.

Primary care teaching clinics play an important role: they provide community-based academic counterparts to the clinical facilities of the teaching hospitals. They provide opportunities to experiment with new patterns for delivering health care to families. In contrast to their past activities, which were concerned mainly with the treatment of disease, there is today a greater emphasis on prevention and on assuring continuity of care through the various phases of illness. The clinics are developing outreach programs to reach those segments of the population who are less effectively served within the confines of traditional medical care settings.

The staff of the teaching clinics are being augmented, and in the process the responsibilities of physicians, nurses, social workers, and ancillary personnel are being redefined. At the same time, new functional relationships with hospitals and public health facilities are being developed. The effectiveness of the new service is constantly being evaluated. In order to do this the primary care teaching clinics draw upon the full resources of the medical school to identify alternative courses of action and to evaluate the results.

There is a second dimension to the goal of integrating care and education. Within the collaborative framework of the consortium there is a potential to bring about changes in the role of the physician. The linking of the educational program to all facets of health care both stimulates and reflects changes. It is the school's direct involvement in preparing medical students to best meet the needs of the community that characterizes the Beersheba experiment.

Training the new physician

The second mandate given the medical school is to educate physicians whose primary objective will be to provide patient care within a combined hospital-community system. This implies that the primary care dimension of medical practice will receive the emphasis often accorded only to specialty medicine. Two consequences are anticipated. First, a significant proportion of students will be attracted to careers in primary care. Second, all students, whatever their eventual career choices, will have acquired a sensitivity to the primary care dimension of all types of medical practice.

A six-year curriculum is geared to train students who have graduated from high school. Basic sciences, clinical medicine, and public health constitute the three principal areas of teaching. Instruction in each area begins in the first year and continues throughout the six-year program. Both clinical studies and instruction in the basic sciences commence in the first year and continue until graduation. Both proceed in tandem, drawing on whatever fields of knowledge can contribute to solving the problem under consideration.

This spiral approach to medical education stresses the utilization of knowledge from the basic sciences to solve problems similar to those encountered in clinical practice. The complexity of problems and the level at which the students' performance approximates that of practicing physicians increase progressively as the students advance through the phases of the curriculum. Students are expected to assume an increasing degree of responsibility and autonomy as their theoretical knowledge and practical experience grow.

Teaching is integrated both horizontally, among subject areas within a particular phase of the curriculum, and vertically, among subject areas over successive phases. The result is a program for each subject area that spans the full six years of medical studies rather than the traditional, somewhat arbitrary sequence of courses. From the outset, experience in clinical and public health settings is interwoven with classroom instruction in the natural and basic medical sciences.

The sequence in which the courses are taught is generally guided by the principle that the knowledge underlying clinical or public health measures should be acquired prior to experience in their application. At times, however, an approach more akin to the discovery method of learning is used in Beersheba. Students are exposed to situations in which questions arise for which they have not been prepared by theoretical background. They must then use their initiative in seeking answers, taking advantage of all the resources available to them and, in the process, developing patterns of independent study.

Getting students involved with patients as people even before they are able to consider them as medical cases is an important aspect of the program. At the core of the educational process are learning to understand patients in depth, establishing good communication with them, and cooperating with other students and health care providers.

At the end of the first year, for example, students spend time on the maternity ward of the hospital. They follow a mother from her admission through the delivery until she is settled at home with the new baby. They work with the family to make them as comfortable as possible through the delivery and during the early weeks of having a new baby at home. The students are there to learn not the technical aspects of obstetrics but the human needs of families.

Student self-evaluation

Undergraduate medical education is but the first phase of a lifelong process of continuing education for the physician. Study habits and patterns of reasoning play a major role in the future practitioner's ability to adapt to new circumstances and to solve new problems. Concern in Beersheba with these issues has had several significant consequences. Developing the capacity for self-evaluation and self-education has been designated a goal common to all parts of the curriculum. The evaluation system provides continual opportunities for self-assessment, encouraging individual initiative and minimizing the student's reliance on external sources of motivation.

Another related objective is the development of problem-solving skills, shifting emphasis from the cultivation of recall skills to the development of independent and creative thinking. In light of these considerations it is not surprising that the medical student in Beersheba does not passively consume information but plays an active role in all aspects of the educational process—from participation in decision making concerning the overall program of studies to involvement in the planning, implementation, and evaluation of individual courses.

After each course a "debriefing" session is held for teachers, student representatives, and members of the curriculum development unit. The course is reviewed to determine the extent to which its educational objectives have been met, in part measured by the results of examinations. Areas in which difficulties have been encountered are identified by instructors and students, and options for eliminating them are proposed. The interaction provides an opportunity for students and teachers to exchange points of view and to decide together on measures for improving instruction. One or more students may then be assigned to collaborate with the teaching staff in implementing the recommendations. Students assist in revising the course or developing new learning materials, or they may participate in teaching the courses.

Curriculum innovations

A number of curriculum innovations have evolved in the medical school. The "natural history of disease" concept is used as a thematic element in the basic sciences and in clinical teaching. This concept emphasizes identifying the points in time at which intervention may prevent the onset of the disease, reverse the process, or decrease its rate of progress and reduce its burden on both the patient and society. The curriculum planners believe that a balanced study of all phases of the natural history of disease results in a more realistic perception of primary care than does the traditional focus on episodes of hospitalization. This perspective emphasizes the acquisition of skills in preventing disease and in rehabilitation as well as caring for acute conditions. It underscores the physician's responsibility to participate in community health programs. The natural history theme forms part of the mainstream in all branches of study. It is reflected in the content of instruction, methods of teaching, and settings in which learning takes place.

Experience with clinical medicine begins in the first year of study. Students participate in services related to primary and secondary prevention, acute care, and rehabilitation in hospital wards and outpatient clinics, primary care and teaching clinics, occupational health units, rehabilitation facilities, and public health stations. At the same time, they acquire knowledge of the basic sciences related to the provision of medical care. In subsequent clinic training, clinical problems are considered in terms of their natural history, with emphasis on the primary care dimension of each phase.

Instruction in public health is given a major emphasis, beginning in the first year and continuing throughout the program of studies. It comprises identification of community health problems, development and implementation of measures for their solution, and evaluation of results at a community level.

At this stage in its evolution, the educational program in Beersheba has acquired both direction and momentum. The direction has been flexible enough to respond to the health needs of the region, advances in medical knowledge, and changing characteristics of the student body. It should be noted that there is no commitment to novelty as an end in itself. Rather it is the effort to maintain responsiveness that characterizes curriculum development. It is therefore anticipated that both content and methods of teaching will continue to evolve in response to changing conditions. The faculty is kept in step by participating in workshops in educational methods that are offered several times a year.

The future is the test

The first class of students graduated in 1980. Two-thirds of the graduating students made a commitment to return to primary care clinics in the Negev for a period of at least one year after internship. Ultimately, their choice of specialty and selection of geographic area in which to practice will probably be influenced by personal background, economic incentives, and family considerations. It is, however, significant that a high proportion of the first graduates have chosen to begin their practice in primary care in the Negev.

Will these graduates provide a higher quality of health care? It will take some time to assess the impact of the Beersheba curriculum on the quality of the physicians' performance. In the meantime, the case for continuing the educational approach developed over the past seven years rests on the logical premise that competencies and attitudes acquired during medical school do indeed shape the future professional performance of the graduate.

Courtesy, Ben-Gurion University of Negev

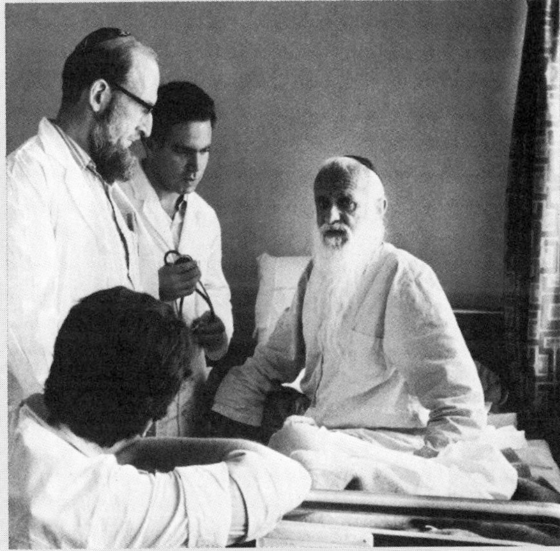

Students become involved with patients as people at the very beginning of their medical education—an important aspect of the Beersheba experiment.

Can the Beersheba approach to medical education be sustained? There are a number of reasons to believe it can. The curriculum appears to have met the expectations of both faculty and students. The program of studies continues to reflect the basic values upon which the medical school was founded in 1974. The curriculum development process facilitates the expression of these values in all aspects of educational policy.

Readiness of the faculty and students to continue in the direction that was charted at the outset is not in doubt. Their ability to do so will be conditioned by constraints in the Beersheba situation. Some are beyond the control of the medical school and will be determined by political, economic, and social developments in the country as a whole.

Others, of a more local nature, include the direction in which the health services in the Negev will evolve. Achievement of the educational goals of the medical school is predicated on simultaneous progress in improving the system for delivering health care in the Negev. As graduates of the school become part of this effort, it is more likely to succeed. In this way what began as the "Beersheba experiment" will acquire a firm basis from which to meet future challenges in health care and the education of physicians.

Nervous System Disorders

The peripheral nervous system consists of motor nerve fibers that run from the spinal cord to the muscles, sensory nerve fibers that run from skin and internal organs to the spinal cord, and fibers of the autonomic (involuntary) nervous system that run to the internal organs and blood vessels. Disorders of the peripheral nerves are called peripheral neuropathies. Although they are among the least well understood of any group of human diseases, recent advances in understanding the structure and function of the peripheral nervous system have allowed a glimmering of insight into the cause and treatment of a number of these disorders.

The peripheral nerves may be thought of as a collection of wires running to or from the spinal cord or the ganglia (dense concentrations of nerve cells) of the autonomic nervous system. Each wire, or axon, is a tubelike extension of a nerve cell body located in the spinal cord or in ganglia close to the spinal cord. The axons range in diameter from 0.1 micrometers (μm; a micrometer is a thousandth of a millimeter) to 20 μm. Axons more than about two micrometers in diameter are surrounded by an insulating sheath of myelin, a complex formed by an enwrapping cell called the Schwann cell. A series of Schwann cells are aligned along the axon. Myelin is a substance rich in lipid (fatty) molecules; it also contains a few specialized proteins.

The peripheral nervous system consists of nerve structures outside the central nervous system. It connects the brain and the spinal cord with the periphery of the body and conducts nerve impulses between them.

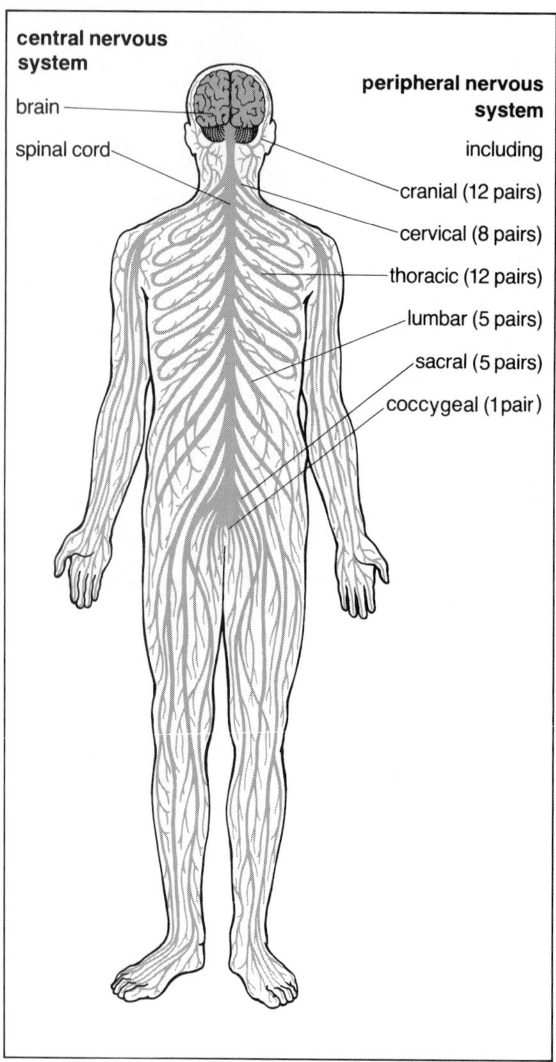

Basic disease processes

Two major types of disease processes occur in the peripheral neuropathies. The axons may degenerate, thereby cutting off the messages running to or from the spinal cord. This type of change is called axonal degeneration. Alternatively, the Schwann cells or myelin sheaths may degenerate, removing the insulation around the axons. This process is called segmental demyelination because only parts of the myelin sheaths are lost whereas others remain intact. Extensive loss of the myelin sheath blocks passage of a nerve impulse and therefore prevents the nerve from carrying the message to or from the spinal cord. Thus, both axonal degeneration and segmental demyelination will produce weakness (loss of motor nerve function) and numbness (loss of sensory nerve function). Recovery from segmental demyelination, however, can be quite rapid because only a small amount of myelin has to be resynthesized to provide enough insulation for the nerve impulse to be conducted. By contrast, recovery from axonal degeneration is slow since the axons regrow at a rate of only two or three millimeters per day.

The reason for axonal degeneration and segmental demyelination in the peripheral neuropathies probably rests in the unusual structure of the nerve cells and the Schwann cells. The nerve cells are extremely long, thin structures that have all their protein-synthesizing machinery stored in the nerve cell body lying in the spinal cord or ganglia. Thus, all of the proteins needed by the axons must be transported from the nerve cell body down the axon in an energy-dependent process termed axonal transport. Interruption of axonal transport, interruption of the synthesis of proteins, or an increase in the demand for energy or proteins will likely cause degeneration of the peripheral parts of the axons. Similarly, the Schwann cells are thin, flat structures with large areas of surface membrane to be maintained. The Schwann cells are unable to produce sufficient myelin if anything causes an increased turnover of proteins or lipids.

The axons play a major role in determining whether the Schwann cells produce myelin and, in fact, supply some of the material for myelin synthesis. Although experimental studies have clearly demonstrated that some diseases are due to abnormalities of the axons and others to diseases of the Schwann cells, there still remains a possibility that some demyelinating diseases are due, in fact, to abnormal signals from the axons. In most human peripheral neuropathies there is a mixture of axonal degeneration and segmental demyelination, although one process may predominate.

Since both the axons and the Schwann cells are so easily damaged, it is not surprising that a very large number of conditions can produce peripheral neuropathies. A doctor faced with a case of peripheral neuropathy therefore must consider a very large number of possible causes and undertake an extensive search for these causes. Some peripheral neuropathies are inherited, some are due to infections, and some are due to the presence of another disease such as diabetes mellitus, cancer, or kidney or liver disease. Some result from poisons or from vitamin deficiencies. Yet others are due to abnormal immunologic responses in the body or to inflammation of the blood vessels interfering with blood supply. Recent developments in the understanding and treatment of a few of these conditions are considered below.

Nerve infections

Leprosy is due to infection of the peripheral nerves by the microorganism *Mycobacterium leprae.* This infection progresses very slowly; to contract leprosy one must be in close contact with an infected person for a prolonged period of time. Nevertheless, leprosy is the commonest cause of peripheral neuropathies in the world today, afflicting an estimated 10 million to 20 million people. In some countries, particularly in Central America, Africa, and India, two of every hundred persons have leprosy.

The condition causes progressive damage of the peripheral nerves and thereby muscle paralysis, atrophy, and loss of sensation. Parts of the body that

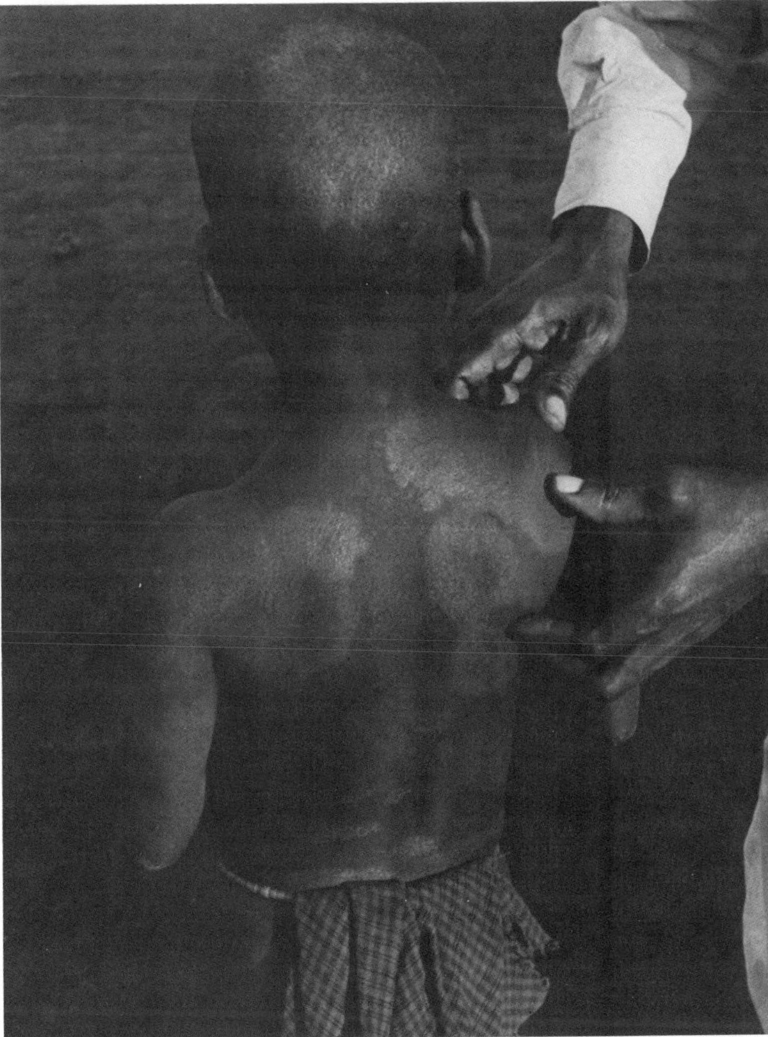

World Health Organization; photograph, P. Pittet

Leprosy is a chronic infectious disease that can cause dramatic skin lesions and damage to the peripheral nerves. For many centuries nothing could be done for lepers except isolate them. But today leprosy can be effectively treated. This young West African boy, whose leprosy has been caught at an early stage, will receive antibiotic therapy. In the future it is expected that a vaccine will protect people in many parts of the world where leprosy is prevalent.

Walter G. Bradley

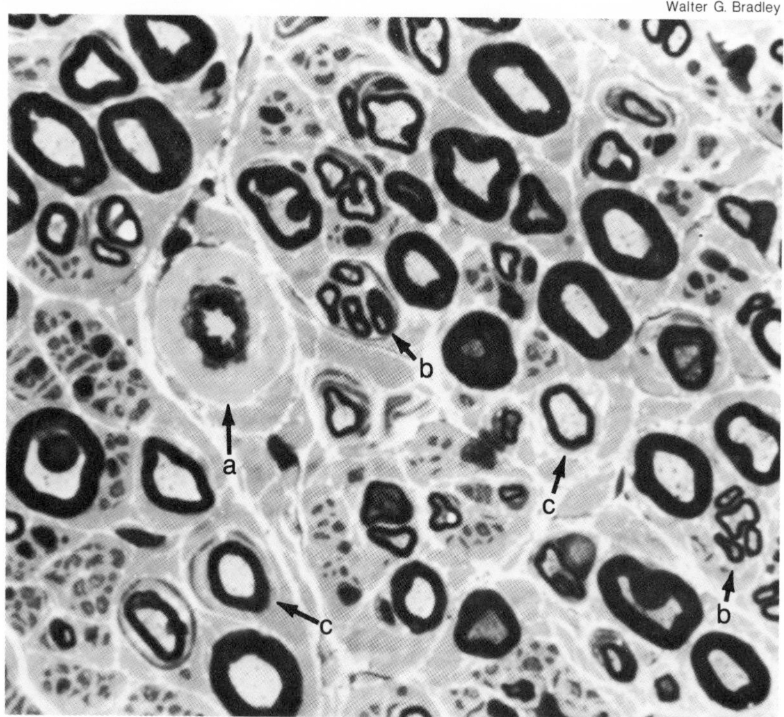

This photomicrograph of a nerve biopsy from a patient with diabetic neuropathy shows the damage to blood vessels, axons, and myelin sheaths characteristic of the disease: (a) a blood vessel with thickened wall; (b) a cluster of nerve fibers regenerating after axonal degeneration; and (c) a nerve fiber with thin myelin sheath indicating partial recovery from segmental demyelination.

lose their sensation are very easily damaged and subject to secondary infections. These secondary infections produce the mutilation that is so characteristic of leprosy.

For many centuries there was no treatment for leprosy, and all that was possible was to isolate lepers in special colonies. In this century attempts to develop drugs to treat leprosy were thwarted because the causative bacterium could not be induced to live outside the human body. Recently, however, it has proved possible to grow the bacterium in the mouse and the armadillo, allowing medical researchers to test for effective drugs and vaccines. Rifampin, an antibiotic, has been shown to kill the leprosy bacillus effectively.

Diphtheria, which was once a frequently encountered cause of peripheral neuropathies, has now virtually disappeared in countries with an effective immunization program. In other countries, however, diphtheric neuropathy continues to be a major problem. The throat infection produced by the causative microorganism releases a toxin into the bloodstream that damages the myelin sheaths and therefore produces paralysis and sensory loss. The paralysis may be so bad that the victim is unable to breathe. If the patient is supported on a respirator for a few weeks, remyelination occurs, often followed by complete recovery.

Interestingly, there is a delay of several weeks between the throat infection and the development of paralysis. It now appears that the diphtheria toxin passes via the bloodstream to the nerves and binds to the Schwann cells. In the Schwann cells the toxin probably inhibits synthesis of a specific myelin protein that has a very slow rate of turnover. Thus, development of demyelination is delayed until a significant deficiency of this protein develops.

Diabetes mellitus

Patients with poorly controlled diabetes are at risk of developing a large number of problems, some of them due to peripheral neuropathies. The most common problem is mild loss of sensation in the feet, sometimes with infections and ulcers of the ball of the foot. This neuropathy may be sufficiently severe that it also affects sensation in the hands and causes muscle weakness of the feet and hands. In other patients there may be involvement of the autonomic nervous system, which may impair control of the bowel, bladder, and sexual function as well as of the heart and blood pressure. Occasionally patients develop acute painful damage to one of the large nerves (such as the femoral nerve) supplying the upper part of the leg.

The cause of peripheral neuropathy in diabetes is still not clearly understood. In most cases there is both segmental demyelination and axonal degeneration. Commonly, nerve damage is first noted or rapidly worsens when the diabetes is out of control and improves when control is improved. Treatment of the diabetes may involve a low-carbohydrate diet, oral drugs to release insulin from the pancreas or to imitate the effect of insulin, or insulin administered by injection.

Insulin is required by most cells to allow rapid uptake of glucose from the bloodstream into the cells for use as an energy source. If there is a deficiency of insulin, the cells are unable to obtain sufficient glucose. A consequent series of metabolic changes includes the accumulation of a number of sugar alcohols such as sorbitol. In addition, in chronic diabetics there is damage to the smaller blood vessels of most tissues, which is sometimes sufficiently severe to reduce the blood supply of those tissues. It is still not clear whether the metabolic derangement or the vascular abnormality is the main factor responsible for the peripheral neuropathies. Currently a number of drugs are being evaluated for their effectiveness in preventing such metabolic derangements. These may prove to be very useful for patients who still develop progressive peripheral nerve disorders despite the best possible control of their blood sugar with insulin.

Chronic liver and kidney diseases

Physicians now treat and maintain patients with chronic diseases of the liver or kidneys for many more years than was possible at the beginning of the century. Thus, patients with kidney failure frequently go onto a chronic renal dialysis program, which intermittently puts their blood through an artificial kidney to remove the waste products that their diseased kidneys are unable to eliminate.

Despite these treatments, however, some patients with chronic kidney or liver disease develop a peripheral neuropathy with weakness and numbness in the feet and hands. Sometimes this indicates that the chronic renal dialysis program is not sufficiently effective; increasing the frequency or length of the dialyses can prevent the neuropathy. Similarly, improving treatment of the liver disease may be effective. Yet in other cases, despite the best therapy, the neuropathy progresses. The exact metabolic cause of peripheral neuropathies associated with liver and kidney diseases is not certain. In chronic kidney failure accompanied by severe peripheral neuropathy, sometimes only kidney transplantation can cure the condition.

Cancer

Patients who have cancer often develop severe loss of weight and muscle wasting (cachexia). This may occur simply because cancer cells demand a large amount of the body's nutriments, producing relative starvation of the rest of the body. Frequently this does not appear to be the case, however, and wasting arises from damage to the peripheral nerves and muscles (carcinomatous neuromyopathy). This damage even may occur in a patient who has only a small tumor. A number of different conditions can occur, including inflammatory disease of muscle (polymyositis), which causes muscle weakness and wasting; a chronic peripheral neuropathy affecting motor and sensory nerves to the feet and hands; or a painful peripheral neuropathy affecting particularly the sensory nerves in the limbs.

It seems likely that these nerve disorders in patients with a small tumor are caused by the release of some substance from the tumor that is toxic to the peripheral nerves. One or two research groups have reported isolation of toxic substances from the bloodstreams of such patients, but these results have not been widely confirmed. If it were possible to characterize such a toxic substance, it might be possible to prevent its effects. Currently all that can be done is to search for the underlying cancer and remove it. This cures the nerve disorder in a number of patients.

Toxic neuropathies

A very large number of industrial chemicals, drugs, and other substances can damage both peripheral and central nervous systems. Some agents appear to damage one or the other system preferentially, but some affect both. Experimentally these neurotoxins are playing an increasing role in advancing scientific understanding of the biochemical processes in peripheral nerves and of the alterations that occur in disease states.

Many of the toxins appear to interfere with the metabolism of such vitamins as thiamine (B_1), pyridoxine (B_6), and nicotinic acid (niacin). These vitamins are essential cofactors required in many of the steps of energy metabolism that are mediated by enzymes in the axons and Schwann cells. Still other toxins recently have been shown to interfere with some of the enzymes themselves. A popular current theory is that many or all of the neurotoxins produce nerve damage by interfering with the production of the energy-rich compounds that are essential for the active processes occurring in axons and Schwann cells. As yet, however, this theory has not led to any active treatment that can prevent the effect of the toxins. Present therapy depends on recognizing that a toxin is causing the peripheral neuropathy and removing the patient from exposure to that toxin.

An increasing number of agents are now being recognized as neurotoxic. Some of these such as lead and mercury have been known for thousands of years. Others are present in foods or drinks that have been prepared since ancient times. An example is alcohol, which when taken in high doses for prolonged periods can give rise to a peripheral neuropathy. Many neurotoxic compounds are the products of the chemical revolution in industry. Increasingly potent chemicals are synthesized for use in a wide range of industrial processes, and many of these can produce peripheral or central nervous degeneration in patients who are exposed to them on either a short-term or a long-term basis. Some examples of neurotoxic compounds are *n*-hexane, which is used as a solvent; carbon disulfide and acrylamide, large quantities of which are used in the paper industry; and tri-ortho-cresyl phosphate, which serves as a high-temperature lubricant.

Still other toxic agents are to be found among drugs used for the treatment of disease. For instance, isoniazid, which is used to treat tuberculosis, and vincristine, an anticancer drug, when taken in high enough doses can damage the peripheral nervous system. The list of potential neurotoxic drugs continues to grow. Damage to the peripheral nervous system also can occur in drug abusers. Alcohol has already been mentioned in this context. "Glue sniffers" risk neurotoxic effects from inhaling the solvents of a number of glues, some of which contain *n*-hexane. Recently peripheral neuropathy has been reported in drug abusers using excessive amounts of nitrous oxide (laughing gas). The mechanism of action of many of these compounds is not yet well known, but the extensive list requires that neurotoxins be considered as a potential cause of a patient's peripheral neuropathy.

—Walter G. Bradley, D.M., F.R.C.P.

Pediatrics

Lymphomas, or cancers of the lymph glands, constitute one of the more common groups of malignancies of children, ranking behind only brain tumors and leukemias in frequency. Recent advances in the therapy of this group of diseases have led to a far more optimistic outlook than was possible ten years ago. This is the result of a more advanced understanding of the biologic behavior of lymphomas and a more sophisticated approach to their treatment that combines surgery, radiotherapy, and chemotherapy.

Current understanding of childhood lymphomas

Each individual lives in an environment inhabited by huge numbers of microorganisms and harbors a variety of microbiologic agents on his skin and on the linings of the gastrointestinal, respiratory, urinary, and genital tracts. In the bowel many of these organisms aid the digestive processes, while any invasive properties they may have are checked by the immune system.

A major component of this system is the class of white blood cells called lymphocytes, which manufacture antibodies and signal other cells to initiate the cooperative process termed inflammation. Lymphocytes are the most numerous of the cells produced by the lymph nodes associated with the bowel. Other lymph nodes are located beneath the skin and stand sentry at the juncture of the limbs to the body, where they can be felt in the underarm and groin areas. Lymphocytes are also found along the coverings of lymphoid nasal and throat tissue, the adenoids and tonsils. In the small bowel the accumulations of lymphoid tissue are termed Peyer's patches. Other specialized immune-system tissues can be found near the surfaces of the eye, ear, vaginal wall, lining of the abdominal cavity, brain, lungs, nose, throat, and in locations throughout the body.

In the normal process of meeting the stress of microbiologic invasion, lymph tissue hypertrophies (increases in cell size and number). This is a controlled growth, however; lymph cells divide in response to a challenge, but when they encounter cells of their own type or other types in the nearby environment, they stop dividing and go into a "resting state."

For reasons not understood, a single cell may lose its growth-control mechanisms and begin to divide inexorably. This unrestricted growth is not necessarily more rapid than normal tissue growth but it crowds out normal cells and accumulates cancer cells in a localized collection termed a tumor of the lymph glands, or lymphoma.

Hodgkin's disease, perhaps the best known of the lymphomas, usually begins in a lymph gland in the region of the neck and spreads downward in a predictable fashion from node to node along a lymphoid chain. That heterogeneous group of lymphomas that are not Hodgkin's disease are collectively termed non-Hodgkin's lymphomas. Though also starting in a lymph gland, they spread in an unpredictable fashion. They may extend first to another lymph node in the region but then enter the bloodstream to spread to other lymph nodes, the coverings of the brain (meninges), or to the marrow of the bone. In bone marrow a single type of multipotential cell, the stem cell, normally gives rise to the large numbers of red cells that carry oxygen, the platelets that help stop bleeding, and the white cells that help stop infections. When lymphoma spreads to the marrow, it may stop normal cell production; this then leads to anemia, bleeding, and serious bacterial infections. The malignant cells may leave the marrow and become visible on stained smears of the peripheral blood, an event termed leukemic transformation.

The cause of lymphomas in the vast majority of children who develop them is unknown. Certain congenital deficiencies of the immune system are associated with a higher rate of lymphoma. There are several types of these conditions, such as Wiskott-Aldrich syndrome, ataxia-telangiectasia, and other immune deficiency states which appear to impair one of the major divisions of the immune system. Very high radiation doses in the range of those used for cancer therapy or that were experienced by those near the epicenter of the atomic bomb explosions in Japan may also predispose an individual to non-Hodgkin's lymphomas; there is no evidence that diagnostic X-rays expose individuals to sufficient doses to increase the incidence of these cancers. In the medical literature certain medications such as Dilantin, an antiseizure drug, have been associated with lymphomas, but this evidence is very controversial and is not currently considered serious enough to withhold the drug from those who would benefit from control of seizures. There is no substantial evidence that lymphomas spread by infection from one individual to another. Though viruses participate in the development of lymphomas in some animals, there is no evidence that this is so with human lymphomas. A possible exception is Burkitt's lymphoma, a type of lymphocytic lymphoma that is more common in certain climates, chiefly in some regions of Africa, and is associated with the Epstein-Barr (EB) virus, a viral particle known to cause infectious mononucleosis. The guilt is strictly by association, however, as there are alternative explanations for this association. For example, it is known that the EB virus infects African children earlier in life than American children, parasitizing B cells, lymphoid tissue associated with antibody production. It is these same B cells that become cancerous in African and American Burkitt's lymphoma, and the EB virus simply may be an innocent bystander while the cancerous transformation is taking place.

Since these diseases may begin in any of the body's lymphoid cells, lymphomas present a diverse group of symptoms. Certain generalizations are warranted, however, in that lymphomas beginning in tissue associated with the bowel and lymphomas presenting as a mass behind the sternum, or breastbone, in the thymus each have distinctive features.

B cell lymphomas

Those tumors that begin in the abdomen most often are found in the lymphoid patches of the small bowel, where the swelling may cause the intestine to "swallow" the mass in the wall, telescoping a portion of the small bowel onto itself, a process termed intussusception. This leads to pain and symptoms not unlike those of appendicitis; when the surgeon explores the abdomen, however, he finds the intussuscepted mass, which can be removed and the adjacent sections of the bowel rejoined. In other instances the tumor cells may spread to other lymphoid tissue of the mesentery (supporting tissue to which the bowel is attached) without intussusception and form a huge mass that can be palpated through the abdominal wall. Since these tumors may surround vital structures as they grow, they are not easily removed.

B cell lymphomas may begin in lymphoid tissue associated with the oral pharynx. As they grow they may loosen a tooth, fill a facial sinus, or appear behind an eye, pushing it forward. Alternatively, they may spread to a neck gland, obliterating the angle of the jaw. This is said to be the most common presentation of African Burkitt's tumor, but these forms also occur in children in other parts of the world. When stained and viewed under the microscope, cells of these tumors have a monotonous blue appearance and contain vacuoles of fat. The nuclei are large and show evidence of being in a continuous state of division. Chromosomal analysis frequently shows an abnormality of number 14, a chromosome thought to be involved in normal B lymphocyte function. When viewed by special techniques that cause cells synthesizing antibodies to fluoresce, these tumors frequently bear a precursor antibody termed immunoglobulin M on their surface. The type of immunoglobulin M found is always of one class, suggesting that the cancer started as a single cell, that it arose through monoclonal proliferation.

Thymic lymphomas

The other major group of lymphomas of children is associated with a mass behind the sternum. The majority of these tumors are thought to arise in the thymus, an organ concerned with resistance to infections such as viral influenza and chickenpox. These tumors grow in the region of the windpipe (trachea) and a major vein that returns blood from the upper part of the body, the superior vena cava. If the tumor is large, it may restrict blood return to the heart or compress the trachea, precipitating a medical emergency with cardiorespiratory collapse. In other instances the patient may have mild difficulty breathing, but the mass may not be apparent until a chest X-ray reveals the abnormal density in the anterior superior mediastinum above the heart and behind the breastbone. Under the microscope cells of thymic lymphomas appear very similar to the cells seen in acute lymphocytic leukemia of children. Indeed, if left untreated these lymphomas will usually spread to the bone marrow and then to the blood, producing a condition indistinguishable from acute lymphocytic leukemia. When this happens, the patient is said to have lymphoma with leukemic transformation. When tested by immunologic methods these cells are often noted to have markers associated with thymic cells known as T markers, in the same way that the gastrointestinal lymphomas often have B markers.

Despite the fact that these tumors take their origin in the immune system, it is quite uncommon for the tumor per se to have any substantial effect on the patient's immunity. In contrast to Hodgkin's disease, patients with non-Hodgkin's lymphomas do not develop serious infections unless they lose white cell production through leukemic transformation or unless they receive powerful chemotherapy that suppresses the immune system.

Progress in treatment

Therapy for these disorders has advanced substantially in the last decade. At first, clinical investigators attempted surgery for localized lymphomas to make the diagnosis and remove the tumor. This was followed by radiotherapy to the residual sites of the disease. This approach substantially prolonged survival, but often the disease would later appear outside of the field of radiotherapy and resist further therapy. Ultimately, the patient would die. For those patients with advanced disease that had spread to other parts of the body, investigators tried to mimic the effects of radiotherapy

American Cancer Society; photograph, Arthur Leipzig

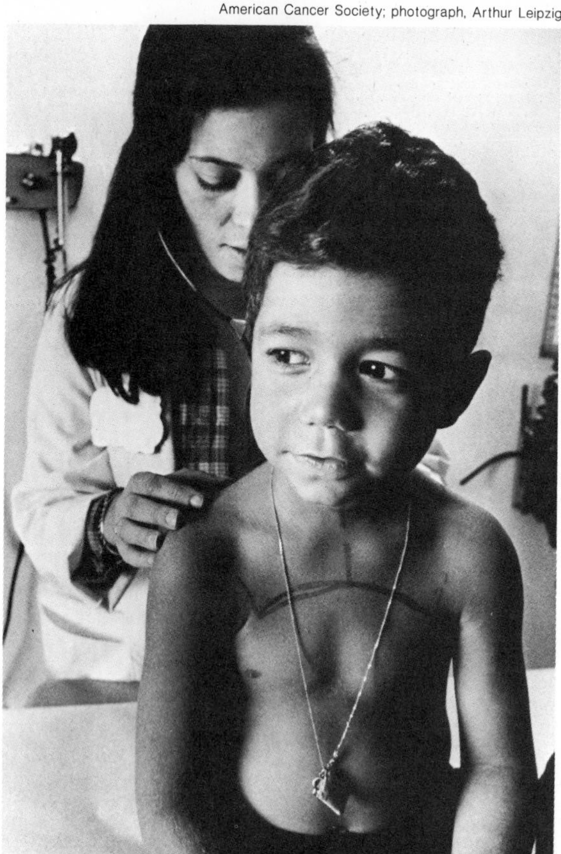

This five-year-old patient with non-Hodgkin's lymphoma is being treated with chemotherapy and has a very good prognosis.

by administering drugs whose mechanism of action was similar to that of X-rays. However, the toxicity of the medication became a problem when doses sufficient to eradicate all cancer cells were administered, and remissions in most cases were short. Then oncologists combined two or more agents that were active against the tumor but toxic to different organ systems. In this way they achieved maximal killing power against the cancer cells while spreading the undesirable side effects over many organs. Working in this fashion, randomized controlled trials by teams of investigators using multiple agents have made steady progress in the treatment of non-Hodgkin's lymphomas.

The randomized trial has been applied to the science of medicine in an extensive way only in the last few decades. It is remarkable that for centuries physicians rarely practiced this highly successful method of ascertaining the most effective of treatment options. The physician is often presented with the dilemma that two or more treatment plans have proved effective for some patients with a particular disease. Usually, only groups of 20 or fewer patients have been studied, however, and it is unclear how effective the therapy may be for subgroups of patients with that disease. Patients differ from one another in many respects, *e.g.,* in age, sex, microscopic variant of disease, extent of disease, and so on. It is now known that many of these variables may affect the prognosis of the disease. Prognostic variables have become extremely important when researchers contrast forms of therapy that appear effective against a disease. If the patients in the two groups are not comparable with respect to these variables, direct comparisons are invalid. Many responsible physicians now ask their patients to enter randomized trials.

If the physician feels that two forms of therapy are effective but cannot tell which is the better, he explains the goals of the study, the nature of the therapy, and side effects for any of the agents proposed and presents alternative therapies possible if the patient should not agree to enter the trial. If the patient accepts the prospects of receiving either therapy and the physician continues to feel that he does not know which particular form would be more advantageous, the patient is randomly assigned to one of the groups, often by a computer that selects one group or the other in a manner analogous to picking names out of a hat.

As this trial continues and the patients begin treatment, the toxicity and results are continuously monitored; when one form of therapy appears superior to another, the less efficacious form is dropped and patients receiving the apparently inferior treatment are placed on the better form. If the results are highly successful, with most patients sustaining long-term remissions, it now may be appropriate to test a form that is similar but has potentially less long- or short-term toxicity than the current form. On the other hand, if most patients fail to sustain long-term remissions, it may be important to try new agents in addition to those already found to be partially effective. In a patient refractory to all conventional therapy, newer and more experimental agents are tried in the hope of prolonging that patient's survival and learning more of that agent's toxicity. If a drug is found active, it is then moved up to trials for newly diagnosed disease where therapy is not yet achieving satisfactory results and added to conventional agents in the hope that the combination will be even more effective.

The physicians conducting these trials have a profound obligation to share and review their data as they go along, to use the most effective technology for treatment and diagnosis available, and to consult with the most knowledgeable specialists in the related areas to ensure that the patient is getting the best treatment. Though it is not necessarily true that physicians who do not practice in this setting cannot deliver excellent care, the patient probably has a better chance of receiving the best care currently available at a center in which pediatric oncologists cooperate with other specialists and meet regularly to evaluate results.

The challenge to the clinical investigator is to plan the best care appropriate for an individual child and his family. Using current plans, it is now likely that the majority of children with lymphoma will remain free of disease even after therapy is discontinued; most will probably be cured.

—Robert R. Chilcote, M.D.

Physical Fitness and Sports Medicine

It is now in the laboratory, not the stadium, that the frontiers of sports are being extended. Athletes are working with scientists using high-speed cameras, automatic gas analyzers, and bicycles that measure energy output. This arena is the province of a new subscience that is interested in the variety of intrinsic and extrinsic variables that influence or limit athletic achievement. Such variables may be characterized as physiological, psychological, sociological, biomechanical, anatomical, mental, and environmental.

Sports science, as this discipline is called, is different from sports medicine. The latter focuses on the health of the athlete and deals with the treatment or prevention of injury. The sports physician and sports scientist work together, but the goal of the sports scientist is not to repair and rehabilitate but to assist the athlete in getting the most from his talent.

Since the early 1950s, Eastern European nations—the U.S.S.R. and East Germany particularly—have used sports technology to effectively dominate international competition in several sports. The emerging interest in the United States in sports science appears to be an attempt to exploit some of the same techniques. In 1977 the United States Olympic Committee established its first Olympic training centers, with sports science given a prominent place.

The work of a sports scientist takes place in a number of specialized laboratories. Sports participants are screened for their capabilities relative to their sports in the areas of kinanthropometry, biochemistry of exercise and energy metabolism, biomechanics, psychomotor and motor abilities, and psychology. Field observations are used to supplement the laboratory observations.

Kinanthropometry

In the kinanthropometry laboratory, data on external and internal aspects of the athlete's bodily makeup are collected. Athlete's move from station to station for an evaluation that provides a basic study of an athlete, focusing on his or her growth, exercise, performance, and nutrition. From a measurement of overall body stature and segment proportions, each athlete is advanced to an elongated darkroom for photogrammetric study. Here, full-length front, side, and rear photographs are taken to provide information about body type, shape, and composition. In another test area the athlete is lowered into a tank capable of underwater weighing, where volumetric displacement is used to calculate the percentage of body fat in his body composition and to predict his ideal body weight.

Knowledge about a young athlete's physical maturity is important for making judgments about his level of skill development. Accordingly, assessments are made of overall bone development, especially through hand and wrist X-rays that show the extent of maturity as the bones change from a more cartilaginous to a more calcified state, and an assessment is made of the stage of puberty that the athlete has reached.

Biochemistry of exercise and energy metabolism

In a temperature- and humidity-controlled laboratory, athletes run on treadmills and pedal bicycle ergometers, which measure the amount of work the muscles do in the pedaling action. An exercise physiologist directs athletes through progressively increasing workloads while recording heart rate, blood pressure, respiratory rate, and EKG's. These data all combine to yield an estimated aerobic capacity, an important measure of present fitness for endurance activity and for determining the effects that training can be expected to have. Aerobic capacity is important to the athlete engaging in prolonged activity. It is a measure of the athlete's ability to efficiently use oxygen. In fact, the better the athlete's aerobic capacity, the more successful he is likely to be in endurance activities.

Anaerobic capacity—the amount of effort an athlete can expend when he is at the threshold of physical exhaustion—is a critical measurement for top-level athletes, particularly in power-related activities such as ice hockey and sprinting. This capacity can be calculated quickly and effectively by measuring body lift as an athlete runs up a staircase past a series of photoelectric beams which record the time. It can be calculated as an athlete works an ergometer by analyzing expired air for CO_2 production. Anaerobic tolerance can also be tested by sampling venous blood, taken at the point of total exhaustion, for lactate concentration. Lactic acid is a by-product of the metabolism of the glycogen that is called up by muscles to fuel extended activity. Its presence brings on fatigue.

Needle-biopsy techniques for studying muscle tissue allow for further analysis of possible levels of athletic performance. For example, research has shown that world-class long-distance runners possess 70–90% "slow-twitch" muscle fibers, which serve well for endurance activity, as opposed to "fast-twitch" fibers, which react quickly for short-term intensive activity. As would be expected, sprinters have a high percentage of fast-twitch fibers. Some sports scientists use such data to predict the suitability of the athlete's physical makeup for a given sport.

Marvin I. Clein

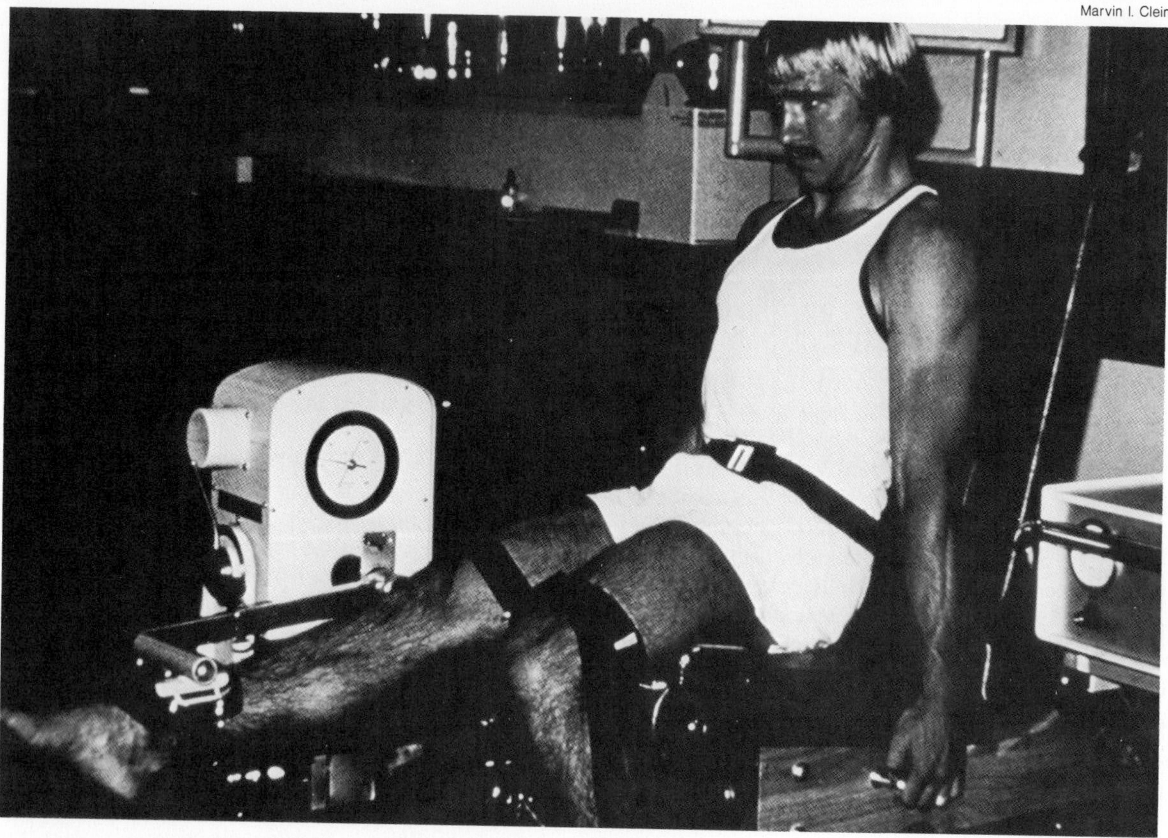

In sports science laboratories researchers are able to observe and study human physical performance. The cybex machine measures the athlete's muscle power, strength, and endurance.

The use of laboratory tests to identify the children that are potential successful athletes has been a subject of continued interest. This practice has been widespread in some Eastern European countries. In theory, the concept has moral and political significance; it is in essence a planned use of human resources for the purpose of sport superiority. In practice, the concept is complicated by the variety of interacting variables that may alter the process of athletic development. Since, for example, the rate of physical maturity differs among individuals, it is unlikely that one can predict how all variables will interact. Thus, statements about future performance are fallible.

Identifying potential future athletes among youngsters appears to center on three interrelated factors. These factors are: (1) determining which youngsters possess a favorable natural endowment for a sport, (2) providing an environment that will ensure optimal development of this endowment, and (3) fostering attitudes deemed necessary for success in a sport.

The incorporation of the these factors into a system to identify and develop top athletes has some obvious difficulties. Other than the complexity of problem solving involved, the system, especially on a large scale, appears to necessitate control of the potential athlete's environment. Such a practice would be more acceptable to nations in which sport is an integral part of the political system.

Biomechanics

The highly sophisticated biomechanics equipment necessary to measure athletic performance is found in only a few laboratories in the U.S. Biomechanics is the study of the mechanisms of human movement, the array of interacting forces at work, for example, when a discus thrower spirals into his delivery or when a diver propels himself off a springboard. Because the bodily proportions of each individual affect his motion in a unique way, electronic analysis is used to correlate masses of data. Motion and power are analyzed through measurements of the electrical activity of muscles, the movement of joints, and the force that motion exerts against a piece of equipment or against a running surface. An athlete in motion, during a tennis serve or a ski turn, is photographed by high-speed cameras; with the assistance of a computer that breaks this motion into a stylized model, the total body motion is available for study, along with quantitative information about body segment velocities, accelerations, forces, and the direction of these forces.

The result of this technological sophistication is the ability to identify and correct such weaknesses as improper timing and muscle action, misdirected applications of force, and inefficient use of equipment. The biomechanist can also study the human interface with equipment and devise, for example, track shoes that take into account the movement characteristics of the runner as well as the composition of the track.

Psychomotor and motor abilities

In the sports science laboratory the athlete is assessed for the physical traits that support performance in a particular sport. Such traits may include muscular strength and power, speed, agility, reaction and response times, balance, flexibility, fine motor dexterity, steadiness, motor accuracy under stress, and a number of visual processing skills—how the athlete responds to cues from the environment during activity.

Overall body strength, the strength of the muscle groups important to a specific sport, and the distribution of strength between the left and right sides of the body are all important measurements. The sports scientist has found the cable tensiometer, developed to measure aircraft control cable, to be extremely adaptable to measuring the major muscle groups in the body. More recent approaches have used electrical strain gauges, which measure the electrical resistance of a wire when stretched, or the cybex machine, which produces scores for muscle power, strength, and endurance.

Dynamic balance is the ability of the athlete to reestablish his gross postural orientation once disturbed. In the sports science laboratory a balanciometer is used to measure adjustment to postural shifts. It should be noted that because balance has proved to be elusive of exact description and appears to be not one ability but rather a group of abilities, a truly satisfactory measurement is yet to be found.

In some activities the range of movement in specific joints is associated with movement efficiency. Electrogoniometry has been used for this measurement on occasion during the actual performance of an activity, but it is impractical for application to large numbers of athletes because of the time needed for placement of the electrodes and the wiring. Other anatomical traits, such as percentage of body fat, segment lengths, and general body type, may influence measures of an athlete's flexibility.

In many, though not all, sports an athlete's ability to respond to external stimuli is essential. Evaluating these measurements varies widely, however, not only with the activity but with different body movements; thus, laboratory and field tests have been designed very specifically. As an example, the response time test for a sprinter would not apply for a figure skater.

In most sports the athlete is required to monitor many visual events simultaneously. A soccer player, for example, must follow the ball with the center of his vision, yet note with his peripheral vision where a teammate has positioned himself. Different visual-processing skills required for different sports may be tested in the laboratory. These include the ability to see objects in space at a given distance, process simple visual information quickly, identify colors and shapes as they move into the visual field, switch attention, and recognize patterns. Recently scientists have also researched the effects of light on body functions, specifically on the endocrine system.

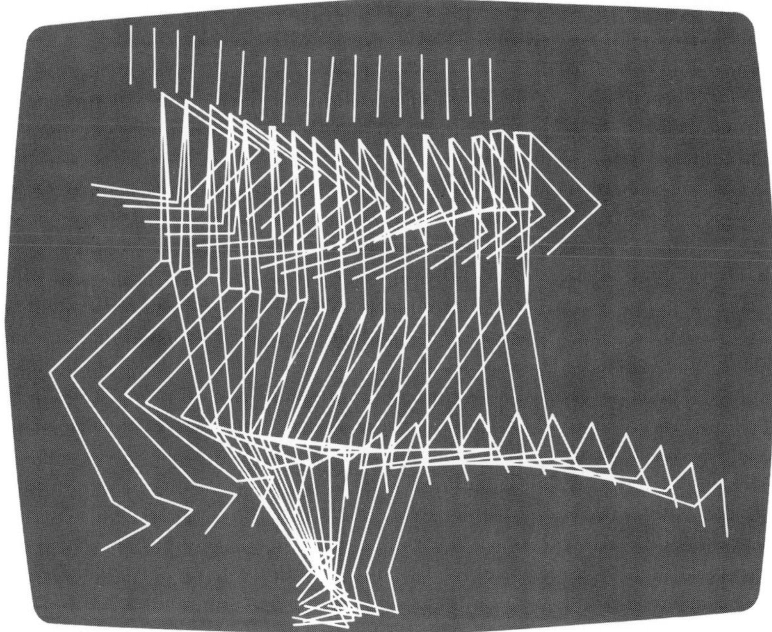

Gideon Ariel, M.D.

Sports scientists are using high-speed films of athletes in action and computers that break down motion into stylized stick figures to study how winning athletes use their bodies. U.S. marathon runner Bill Rodgers is pictured here.

Physiological qualities of basketball players	
quality	effect
ability to use oxygen	repeated efforts over the duration of a game
ability to play without oxygen	jumping, fast break, quick explosive movements
ability to quickly change body positions	maintaining defensive position
ability to move body parts through full range of motion	efficiency of movement
ability to exert an explosive force	jumping, quick moves
ability to reduce muscle tension	skill and accuracy of performance
ability to maintain balance under dynamic conditions	all basketball maneuvers
ability to play with raised body temperature	minimize fatigue
ability to coordinate muscle action	timing, tempo, efficient performance

Psychological factors

The contribution of the clinical psychologist to sports has increased greatly in the last two decades. The effect of psychological theories and methods has been broad, and includes the development of descriptions of common elements in athletes' personalities, the facilitation of communication between athletes and others, the use of behavior modification—including relaxation techniques and motor visual rehearsal, and a focus on the effects of competitive stress. In some laboratories, psychophysiological measures are being used selectively. These include visual measurements such as eye tracking, reaction time, and numerous other tests of perceptual interpretation.

Putting it all together

Because of the variables involved, it is dangerous to try to predict the future success of an athlete based on evaluation results. It is possible, however, to evaluate an individual's present talents and use the information obtained as a reference point from which to help the athlete improve his performance. A useful evaluation incorporates at least three major considerations: the athlete's natural endowments, how these compare to a physiological base that supports success in a given sport, and an identification of the specific muscle groups and anatomical patterns used in the sport in question.

Among those athletes who genuinely excel, there appears to exist a natural endowment in one or more of five factors: (1) a mature oxygen-carrying capacity that enables the athlete to sustain his effort over a period of time; (2) an ability to exert an explosive force, as in a jump or a burst of running acceleration; (3) a body build that provides a mechanical advantage, such as the narrow hips of a sprinter; (4) a well-developed sensory feedback system that allows the individual to direct, adjust, and coordinate movement; and (5) a high level of "fluid intelligence." The latter refers to the athlete's ability to see relationships between parts to a whole, to solve problems, and to interpret situations. Some examples of fluid intelligence are the ability of a ski racer to put together mentally the varying combination of slalom gates on the course, or a basketball player's ability to recognize and adjust to continually changing patterns of play during the rapid action in a game. An additional factor appears to be an ability to function under stress. In competitive events this may be crucial to success.

Each sport requires specialized skills and specific physiological qualities on the part of the players to execute those skills. An example, using basketball, is shown in the table. It is important to note that each of the requirements listed is independent and perhaps unrelated to the others. Furthermore, the muscle endurance necessary for basketball may differ from the muscle endurance for swimming, for example.

Each sport requires the use of specific muscle groups, often in a way unique to the sport. These can be identified through photography and used to evaluate an athlete's performance and to tailor exercises that develop specific sport skills. The evaluation of an athlete that includes these considerations allows for the development of an individualized profile from which can be indentified strengths and weaknesses relative to a sport. From there, a prescribed training program can be developed that is based on measurable data about the athlete.

Within the laboratories of sports scientists, the challenging task of helping athletes develop continues. Successes have been credited to the workouts with treadmills, electronic timers, and so on. Sports science has done nothing, however, to change the nature of sports, it has only deepened our understanding of athletic prowess. The ultimate test is still in the stadium.

—Marvin I. Clein, Ed.D.

Special Report:
Women in Sport: A Changing Sense of Self
by Andrea Ayvazian

In the late 1800s Susan B. Anthony wrote that in the battle for equality women need strong bodies as well as quick minds. In the last century athleticism in women has been gaining momentum with each succeeding decade. The dramatic increase in the numbers and types of sports women are engaging in today reflects their changing vision of themselves.

The scope of women in sports

The number of females in sports has skyrocketed since 1970. According to the National Federation of State High School Associations, female participation in interscholastic sports increased more than seven-fold between 1970 and 1978. Today, 33% of high school athletes are female, according to the Women's Sports Foundation. On the college level, 30% of athletes are female, an increase of 250% since 1970.

Specific examples in various sports events illustrate the change that has occurred in the last decade. Although women were not allowed to enter the Boston Marathon in 1967, one woman who was unaware of the restriction entered and completed the race, even after a judge chased her down the road trying to rip the number off her back. The Amateur Athletic Union (AAU) finally permitted women to run in marathons in 1976; four years later, 449 women ran in the Boston Marathon. The International Olympic Committee has sanctioned a women's marathon for the 1984 games.

According to the U.S. Soccer Federation, one million young women under the age of 19 played soccer in 1980, compared with virtually none in 1970. Six sports federations—tennis, golf, bowling, skiing, racquetball, and basketball—reported in 1980 that financial rewards for female athletes were over $16 million, compared with less than $1 million just ten years prior. There has also been a notable upsurge in the scouting for and recruiting of female athletes for a number of college varsity sports.

In 1908, when this picture was taken, archery was one of the sports that were considered suitable for women; considerable skill must have been necessary to compensate for the cumbersome costume.

The Bettmann Archive, Inc.

George Bellerose—Stock, Boston

Will Waterman—NOLS

Today women's horizons are limited only by their skills and courage. The National Outdoor Leadership School (right) is one of many programs that offer adult women strenuous, challenging wilderness adventures. Women are mastering high altitude mountaineering, and some have made major summit attempts.

Increased participation in sports is not limited to adolescent girls or collegiate women. Women of all ages and in all walks of life are pushing their physical limits and participating in athletic events—engaging in solitary sports as well as joining organized teams. In 1976 an estimated 10,000 women in the U.S. were weight lifting, compared with a few hundred in 1974; and weight training was growing fastest among housewives and office workers. In 1978, when a pantyhose company sponsored a six-mile race through Central Park in New York City, more than 4,000 women entered and completed the run. Participants included teenagers, "born again" athletes who began running at age 30, a few grandmothers, a woman seven months pregnant, and hundreds of novices. Now every major city has races for women runners, and women are running with and against men in races ranging from six miles to 26 miles and longer. Women runners over 30 have been inspired by Ruth Anderson, who at age 46 ran the 1976 Boston Marathon in 3 hours, 5 minutes.

Organized sporting events for females began in the mid-19th century with gymnastics. This was followed by tennis, and then girls' basketball became popular around the turn of the century. Until recently, women who engaged in athletic activities were limited to these sports as well as swimming and diving, archery, bowling, equestrian events, figure skating, field hockey, and golf. Traditionally, females have been barred or discouraged from engaging in competitive team sports, sports that involved bodily contact, lifting heavy weights, or traveling long distances. (In the 1964 Olympics, women were permitted to compete in one team sport—volleyball—the only team game in which there is no possibility of direct body contact between opponents.) Sports for women have emphasized grace and beauty rather than teamwork and strength.

What are the roots of women's growing athleticism? Athletic feminism has evolved, in part, from the modern feminist movement. Women's struggle for equality has involved changing societal norms and expectations and searching for legal solutions. Title IX of the Educational Amendments Act of 1972, the federal directive prohibiting sex discrimination in athletics, has been partially responsible for the progress. Title IX states that "no person in the United States shall, on the basis of sex, be excluded from participation in, be denied the benefits of, or be subjected to discrimination under any education program or activity receiving Federal financial assistance." This is a considerable weapon since 16,000 public school districts and 2,700 colleges and universities receive federal funds. Like the Civil Rights Act of 1964, Title IX is an example of a law resulting from social change and then triggering further change because it is the law.

Of course, Title IX is not without its problems. Since the law provides only a vague outline for action, confusion surrounding its implementation still remains. Title IX does not state that institutions must automatically give women an equal share; equal opportunity (not necessarily equal funding) must be provided commensurate with need. But Title IX has been a catalyst for change: athletic programs have undergone reevaluation; opportunities for women in sports have increased; and discriminatory practices of the past are ceasing.

Women in the outdoors

Concurrent with the increase in the number of women involved in organized sports has been an increase in the number of women involved in rugged outdoor adventures. These women have chosen noncompetitive, nonspectator activities that emphasize individual accomplishment as well as group experiences. Increasingly women are enjoying backpacking, having mastered the skills necessary for extensive backcountry travel; some women have become proficient at high altitude mountaineering, snow and glacial travel, and have made major summit attempts in the Himalayas; there are women competent in technical rock climbing, white water canoeing, kayaking, spelunking (caving), and other outdoor activities requiring interaction with woods, water, and mountains. These wilderness activities do not have competing teams, score boards, or rigid rules of the game. Wilderness travel involves personal challenge, uncertainty, confrontation with natural elements, and good judgment.

During the last ten years, established outdoor programs and schools have experienced a rise in the number of women participants. The National Outdoor Leadership School reports that during the 1979–80 academic year, 36% of the school's 1,400 students were women, a substantial increase over the 6% in 1970–71. Outward Bound, another well-established outdoor program, reports the number of women students increased from 16 to 41% between 1970 and 1979. As a result of women's growing interest in wilderness activities and their desire for special courses, Outward Bound and the National Outdoor Leadership School began offering courses for adult women in 1975 and 1977, respectively. The University of the Wilderness, an adult environmental education institution which organizes wilderness trips and courses all over North America, was incorporated in 1973 and began offering courses especially for women five years later. The university reports that in coeducational activities about 40% of the participants are women.

Many women's outdoors programs and organizations, established within the past decade, have sponsored expeditions and adventures of all sorts, from rafting in the Grand Canyon to trekking in the Himalayas. Although most of the participants in organized outdoor programs that are springing up from coast to coast are 25 to 45 years of age, women in their 50s and 60s are not uncommon, and one participant in a rugged wilderness trip sponsored by a group known as Woodswomen was 76 years old. The Outdoor Woman's School and Women in the Wilderness, both based in the San Francisco Bay area, Women Outdoors, based on the East Coast, and Woodswomen, based in Minneapolis, Minn., are a few of the organizations in which women are challenging their physical limits and demonstrating that they are unafraid of hard work, sweat, and achievement.

Women's physiology

Although women traditionally have been labeled "the weaker sex," research on the physical differences between males and females has revealed that in some respects females are as strong or stronger than males. Women live longer than men (seven years on the average), despite the fact that women bear the stress on their bodies of pregnancy and childbirth (often repeatedly). Women seem to be blessed with rugged constitutions. Historically, women have generally outnumbered men as survivors in shipwrecks and other natural disasters involving exposure to the elements. While men have superior muscle power, women's natural strength appears to be endurance. Women have made outstanding achievements in endurance sports such as swimming and long-distance running. In the 1976 Olympics, for example, two women—Petra Thumer (East Germany) and Shirley Babashoff (U.S.)—swam the 400 meter freestyle event faster than Don Schollander (U.S.) did when he set the World record in the 1964 Olympics.

Male and female physiological development and athletic capability are closely related from birth to puberty. Prior to puberty, if there is a difference in athletic ability, females are probably superior because they mature more rapidly. Generally, prepubescent males and females are approximately equal in strength, aerobic power, and shoulder-width to body-height ratios. With the onset of puberty, however, this situation changes. For females, estrogen levels increase, menstruation begins; and secondary sexual characteristics begin to appear, along with a change in body fat distribution. When the growth period has ended for both sexes, males are generally about 10% larger than females, and have almost double the muscle mass. (Of total body weight, females have about 23% muscle mass, males about 40%.) The larger muscle mass in males is attributed to the effects of androgens (male sex hormones) on muscular development.

The literature in the field of sports physiology frequently reports that although prior to puberty males and females are about equal in the strength-to-weight ratio, the adult woman has about 65% of the strength of the adult man. After accounting for differences in height, the difference is closer to 10%.

Tests conducted at West Point in 1976 on incoming female cadets indicated that the women had one-third the strength of the men in the upper body and two-thirds in the legs. One reason for the smaller difference in leg strength between the two sexes may be that girls in the United States are socialized to engage more in activities that strengthen their legs (walking, running, climbing stairs, bicycle riding) but do not as often engage in activities that increase upper body strength (climbing trees, tossing balls, and lifting weights).

When trained athletes of both sexes are compared, the differences in strength is only about 10%. Jack Wilmore, of the Department of Physical Education, at the University of Arizona, has found that when leg power is expressed relative to body weight, women's strength is only 8% less than men's; and in terms of lean body weight, women are 6% stronger in their legs than men. Wilmore also studied female students in a weight-lifting program and showed that after ten weeks, the women increased their mean strength by as much as 30%. Given greater opportunities to fulfill their physical potential, women may be closing the muscle gap that has existed between the sexes.

Other significant physiological gender differences affect physical performance. Skeletal development in the female stops about one to three years earlier than in the male. The bones of the male grow to be longer, more massive, and of greater density. Longer bones provide better leverage and a greater arc of movement. The broader shoulders on males are an advantage in sports requiring upper body strength. The female has an overall smaller skeletal structure and a proportionally wider pelvis. The wider pelvis combined with shorter extremities give the female a lower center of gravity. Owing to this difference, females excel in sports requiring balance, such as gymnastics.

In the cardiovascular system, the male has a greater oxygen-carrying capacity than the female, a larger heart, and a slower heart rate. In the respiratory system, the female has about a 10% smaller lung capacity. Research has shown that when the sexes are compared on maximum aerobic power or maximal oxygen uptake (the transport of oxygen from the lungs to the tissues during exercise) the average female's capacity is approximately 85% that of the average male. But with optimal conditioning these differences are not significant.

Because males generally grow stronger than females after puberty and develop greater cardiovascular efficiency, they tend to excel in sports requiring power and speed. Females, it has already been noted, tend to excel in endurance sports. This may be a result of the amount of body fat in females (25% of body weight as compared with 15% in males). Even highly trained female athletes have approximately 10% more fat than their male counterparts (15% compared with 5%). Female athletes apparently are able to use these fat reserves for energy in endurance sports such as long-distance swimming and marathon running.

Heat adaptation is an area where a difference between the sexes may have been misunderstood until recently. Because the female has about 10% more adipose (fatty) tissue than the male, her body is better insulated and more effectively prevents excessive heat loss from the internal organs. This insulation causes the skin temperature of the female to be higher in warm weather and lower in cold weather than that of the male. It used to be thought that women could not tolerate the heat generated by extremely vigorous exercise. Also, the female does not begin sweating until the environmental temperature is two or three degrees (Fahrenheit) above the male sweating threshold. However, recent research conducted by a team of physicians in Japan has shown that when women train over a long period of time, they become more adapted to heat than either men or women who have not undergone physical training. Some investigators have suggested that females may actually have a more precisely regulated and economical sweat output than males.

A question that frequently arises in the discussion of the physiology of the female athlete is: are women more prone to injury? Before 1970 women were not allowed to participate in any long-distance running events because they were thought to be physically weak and easily injured. Lack of adequate conditioning, training, and coaching were probably responsible for frequency of injury in female athletes.

Christine Haycock, associate professor of surgery at New Jersey Medical College and an expert in the field of women's athletics, has pointed out that although the number of women participating in sports on the collegiate level has almost tripled since the early 1970s, the number of injuries has not risen proportionately. Haycock has found that the most common injuries of the female athlete are sprains and strains of the ankles and knees. Back injuries, fractures, contusions, and dislocations are somewhat less frequent. In order to separate fact from fiction regarding injury rates of women athletes, Haycock and athletic trainer Joan Gillette Tannenbaum conducted several surveys in the athletic departments of colleges. They found that women athletes sustain the same injuries in relatively the same numbers as their male counterparts (aside from those related to different biological structures). The only injuries that occurred more frequently in women were those in the knee and ankle joints. Because the conditioning, training, and coaching of female athletes continue to improve, it can be expected that the incidence of injury may decrease even more over time.

As more women engage in athletic activities, attention is being directed to the relationship between participation in sports and reproductive function. Among

Today women take part in (clockwise from top left, opposite) powerlifting, ice hockey, softball, distance running, and crewing. As late as 1964 the only Olympic team sport for women was volleyball; the first women's Olympic marathon will be run in the 1984 games. Better knowledge of sports physiology of both sexes is helping break down the barriers to women's competition.

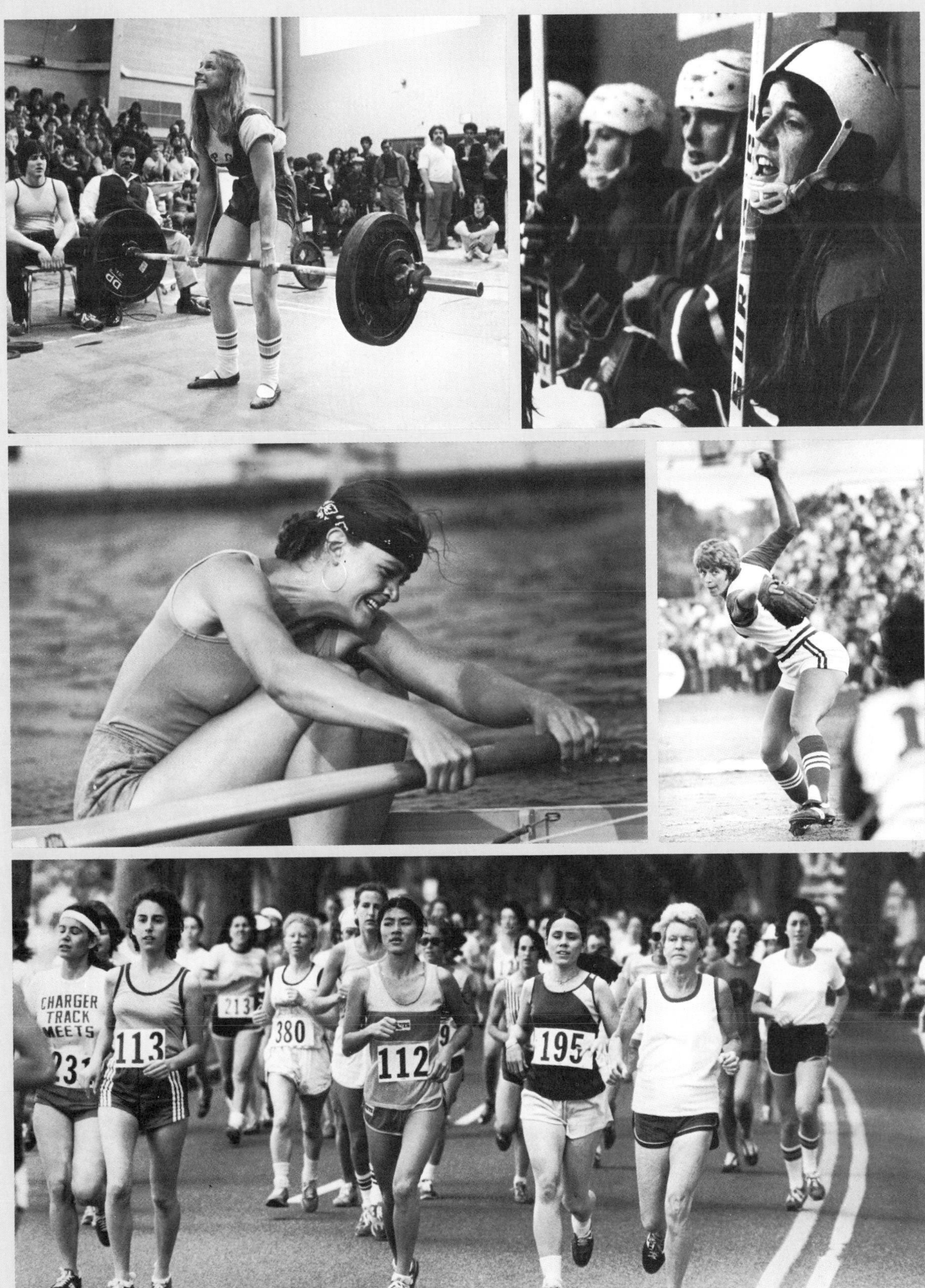

(Top, left) Ken Robert Buck—Stock, Boston; (top and center, right) Pamela R. Schuyler—Stock, Boston; (center, left) Arthur Grace—Stock, Boston; (bottom) Ellis Herwig—Stock, Boston

Tim Carlson—Stock, Boston

Olga Korbut demonstrates a stunning level of strength and flexibility. Because they have a lower center of gravity, women excel at sports such as gymnastics in which balance is a critical factor.

the issues of concern are injuries to the reproductive organs and the effect of exercise on menarche (onset of menstruation) and on menstrual function. Women athletes are now being studied widely to discover to what degree exercise affects the gynecologic, obstetric, and endocrinologic functions.

Research in the early 1960s showed that training and competition did not cause a delay in the onset of menses or affect proper menstrual function. However, there continues to be concern over what appears to be a pattern of delay in the menarche in female athletes. Also, in recent years another menstrual disturbance has appeared in female athletes: amenorrhea (the total cessation of menstruation). These problems may result from excessive weight loss, *i.e.,* the low percentage of body fat in female athletes. Changes in the production and secretion of hormones in the delicate feedback mechanisms of the hypothalamus, the pituitary gland, and the ovaries, are also considered important. It is generally believed, however, that the delay in the onset of menses seen in young female athletes and amenorrhea that occurs in some women athletes do not adversely affect fertility or pregnancy in later life. On the positive side, athletic females with regular menstrual cycles have been found to have less severe menstrual cramps, less premenstrual tension, fewer headaches, and a shorter duration of flow than nonathletes. Moreover, athletic performance during menstruation is not diminished: women have won Olympic gold medals in all phases of the menstrual cycle.

Injuries to the reproductive organs are rare. The bony pelvis provides excellent protection for the internal reproductive organs. Only when the uterus rises from the pelvis in the third month of pregnancy do the reproductive organs become more vulnerable to injury. Although contact sports should be avoided after this time, most physical activities are both appropriate and encouraged. Contrary to the advice given in past decades, physicians now tell their pregnant patients that they need not curtail their exercise or participation in athletic events. A study conducted in Hungary showed that athletic females experienced less difficult labors, shorter labors, and required fewer cesarean sections than their nonathletic counterparts. After delivery, these women achieved greater abdominal tone more quickly and had a more prompt return to prepregnant weight.

Anemia can be a significant problem for athletic females. In sports maximal energy output is dependent on the maximum oxygen-carrying capacity of the blood, making a normal hemoglobin level important to athletic performance. However, many females do not have an adequate intake of iron in their daily diets; also they lose iron with menstruation. This combination of factors can cause iron-deficiency anemia in women—not just in athletic women. Vigorous conditioning workouts also cause a temporary lowering of hemoglobin known as "sports anemia." Female athletes are now being advised to have their hemoglobin levels checked regularly, and many are finding that supplemental iron pills are necessary.

Traditionally women have been socialized into passive roles and have been discouraged from participating in vigorous exercise and competitive sports. Janice Kaplan, who has written about women in sports, has said: "Getting involved in sports is, for most women, far more than a symbolic assertion of female vigor and possibility; once she has done the impossible in sports, why not in everything else?" Indeed the myth of "the weaker sex" is evaporating as women take to the courts, the gymnasium, the track, the woods, the mountains, and the rivers. Women are discovering they can push back what they thought were physical limitations and taste some sweet rewards.

Psychiatry

If a person is suffering from disabling mental illness, it is usually obvious to him or to others. But milder conditions may be difficult to distinguish from a transitory response to the stress of everyday life. The popularity of various "psychotherapies" and of self-help groups contributes to the confusion. Although the best known legitimate (and spurious) therapies are "talking therapies," conventional psychiatric treatment offers additional options including medications, electroshock therapy, and behavior therapy.

A person who needs help may be distressed by the inconclusive nature of the findings about the value of psychotherapy. Evidence is almost totally anecdotal. Psychotherapy has been the subject of considerable attack in recent years, and there has been justifiable skepticism about its effectiveness, largely because *proof* is lacking.

Treatment of neurotic, psychotic, or personality disorders can eliminate or reduce symptoms or effect personality change with improvement in work, love, and play—which are generally considered the three parameters of normal functioning. But therapy is no panacea for a perfect life, and generally, psychiatric treatment is indicated only if there is evidence of diagnosable mental disorder. Normal grief usually is not reason for psychiatric intervention, nor is a life crisis such as divorce necessarily grist for the psychotherapeutic mill. Consider the following examples.

After the sudden deaths of both his parents-in-law (the father-in-law dying in his presence) and the serious illness of a brother, a happily married 40-year-old man became involved in an extramarital affair and left his wife and children. While involved with the other woman he contrived to have sexual liaisons with his wife at motels. He explained this by saying that he had simply met someone he liked better than his wife, but that he continued to feel affection and concern for her and could not abandon her. Meanwhile, he was experiencing insomnia, loss of appetite and weight, and feelings of despair and agitation, alternating with euphoria about his new life. A psychiatrist concluded that this was not normal grief, but an adjustment disorder of adult life with depression, agitation, ambivalence, and other clear-cut psychiatric symptoms, and recommended treatment.

Another man, married for 20 years, had become an international business tycoon. His wife wanted him to live the life of a suburban husband, and wanted him to be at home more. He wished to hire housekeepers and others who could take care of things at home so that his wife could join him in his travels around the globe, but she was unwilling to join him in his new life. He finally decided he was unable to accommodate his wife and had outgrown her. A psychiatrist concluded that differences in potentials, goals, outlook, and opinions had developed until the couple essentially led disparate lives. A divorce seemed to be the solution. Since there was no evidence of psychopathology, psychiatric treatment was not recommended.

Psychiatric treatment modalities

Many people imagine that psychiatric treatment is a mysterious encounter between patient and therapist, where the therapist interprets what the patient says, and the patient improves as he acquires insight. In actuality, there are many kinds of psychiatric treatments used singly or in combination, depending on the patient's problem. The proliferation of hypotheses concerning the causes of and cures for psychiatric symptoms is a reflection of the fact that no single theory explains all or even a single mental or emotional illness. In 1973 Aaron Lazare, a psychiatrist at Harvard Medical School, outlined four "hidden" conceptual models commonly employed in clinical psychiatry, which are useful for understanding what goes on between patient and psychiatrist. These models—medical, psychological, social, and behavioral—are implicitly used by psychiatrists in evaluating and treating patients, but are not always so identified.

Components of all four models were used to evaluate and treat the man previously mentioned whose depression was preceded by illnesses and deaths in the family. It is necessary to know more about the patient in order to see how the models apply. The patient's older brother, an Annapolis graduate, was always more successful than the patient, and the favorite of their father. After the patient failed to receive an appointment to Annapolis he married young, had sev-

"Well, now, how's the old noggin today?"

Drawing by Modell; © 1981 The New Yorker Magazine, Inc.

eral children, and progressed slowly in a modest job. His wife always worked. The wife's parents lived with the couple, babysat, and kept house.

The marriage was basically happy. The parents-in-law encouraged the younger pair to enjoy time away from the children. In turn the patient was an "ideal" son-in-law—loving, considerate, and respectful.

Because the patient was suffering from insomnia, weight loss, and severe depression, the psychiatrist prescribed antidepressant medication (dictated by the *medical* model, which looks at psychiatric illness as a disease, and focuses on causes, signs and symptoms, and prognosis, among other things). The drug helped relieve the depression and anxiety and enabled the patient to get proper rest and to face his problems. The psychiatrist's supportive manner probably produced a placebo effect as well—*i.e.*, a powerful therapeutic response exclusive of the drug's pharmacologic actions.

The patient's unresolved conflicts, which contributed to his present state of depression, are explained by the *psychological* model. The psychiatrist believed that the patient had never resolved his dependency relationships. The patient felt he had disappointed his father; the *unconscious* objective of his life was, then, to please his father. This he accomplished through pleasing the surrogate, the father-in-law, in return for being taken care of. Meantime, the patient continued to have competitive feelings toward his older brother. Both the failure to be able to revive his father-in-law and the illness of his brother precipitated guilt, shame, and despair, because the patient unconsciously connected these misfortunes with the unconscious anger and death wishes he harbored towards his own father and brother. The loss of people to lean on as well as the loss of approving parental figures contributed to the mental and physical symptoms he was experiencing. The flight from home and sexual affair were unsuccessful attempts to ward off a major depression. The patient improved in psychotherapy as he acquired insights about these *unconscious* conflicts. Insight is the illumination of unconscious conflicts through the analysis of defenses, psychological mechanisms that guard against painful self-knowledge.

The patient's flight from sudden, overwhelming responsibilities suggested a *social* disorder, resulting from the disintegration of his social system. The couple was counseled therefore to reorganize their family structure now that the parents-in-law were dead, and to begin to give support to each other and the children in new ways.

The parents-in-law and the patient's wife had always reinforced the patient's dependent, irresponsible behavior by shielding him from the consequences of the hasty marriage and ill-planned parenthood. The wife through her accommodating behavior was reinforcing the current pathological patterns. Treatment in the *behavioral* model was aimed at supporting the patient in his roles of husband and father and discouraging irresponsible actions, such as the affair with the other woman.

While most contemporary psychiatrists are trained in all treatment modalities, they tend to favor the medical and the psychological models; behavior therapy is usually the bailiwick of psychologists and counseling that of social workers. But these divisions are by no means absolute, and there is considerable overlap.

Evaluating treatment for psychotic disorders

Of course, the medical model remains the province of the psychiatrists, who are physicians. In the last 30 years drug treatment has emerged as the optimal therapy for the most serious mental illnesses, schizophrenia and bipolar disorders (manic-depressive psychoses), which are chronic disorders marked by remissions and exacerbations. Electroshock therapy continues to be the optimal treatment for certain severe depressions. But the results are considerably less than 100% successful, and the precise mechanisms of drug actions are not known. Owing to idiosyncracies of individual metabolism and the pharmacologic properties of antidepressant drugs, for example, it has recently been discovered that some patients who fail to respond to usual doses paradoxically respond to low doses. Psychiatry, which has been

Medication can help patients suffering from manic-depressive illness, which tends to manifest itself in recurrent episodes of impaired functioning.

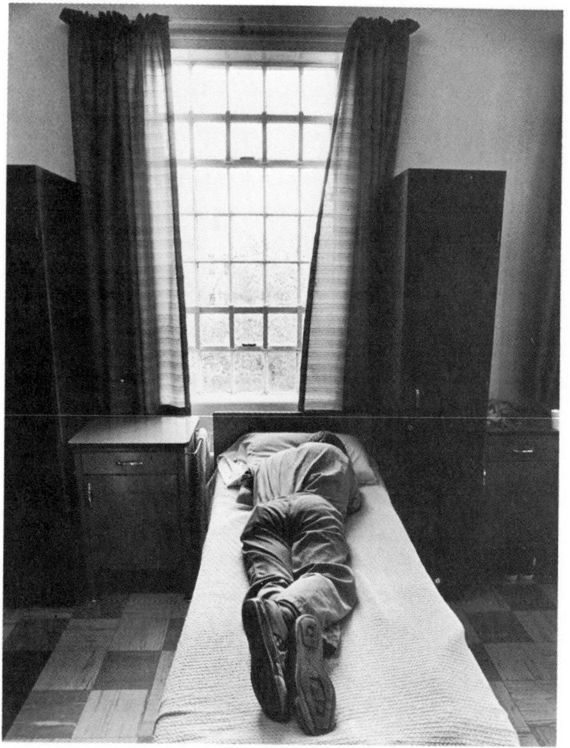

Paul Little © 1981

notoriously poor at prediction, is just beginning to make modest progress towards selecting in advance which patients will or will not benefit from specific drugs. All these drugs have side effects ranging from trivial to potentially or actually lethal. The risk of grave complications always has to be evaluated against the known effects—often catastrophic—of major mental illness on the individual and society.

Patients suffering from manic-depressive illness and other psychotic depressions, generally appear normal between episodes, but symptoms may recur unless the patient remains on medication indefinitely, probably for life. Patients suffering from the different forms of schizophrenia usually show personality deterioration between episodes, even if they remain on medication. The personality difficulties are manifested as bizarre behavior, aloofness, difficulty in interpersonal relationships, and inability to hold jobs, the latter usually due to conflicts with fellow workers and employers as well as impaired concentration.

Many schizophrenic patients receive supportive therapy aimed at maintaining the status quo rather than at effecting dramatic personality change. Such limited goals are frequently disappointing to both patient and family who may initially acquiesce to them but later, out of frustration, may change therapists or treatments as improvement remains modest. The psychiatrist's task in these cases is to promote a form of insight, *i.e.,* the acceptance of the gravity of the patient's condition.

Evaluating treatment for personality and neurotic disorders

Some personality disorders that are manifested as long-standing, maladaptive coping patterns, which are sometimes more disturbing to others than to the patient, can be refractory to treatment. Patients in this diagnostic category may drop out of treatment dissatisfied, or remain in psychoanalysis for decades, often to no avail. In some patients symptoms may persist while personality changes. For example, a patient who habitually overreacted to stress was literally disabled by the pain of his peptic ulcer; in psychotherapy he developed insight into the cause of the ulcer and was then able to resume an active, productive life, even though the ulcer remained.

Unfortunately, acceptable methods of studying most psychotherapeutic techniques for the most part have not been discovered. One often quoted study on psychotherapy showed that group therapy, individual therapy, and simply being placed on the waiting list for therapy were all about equally effective in alleviating neurotic symptoms, which are exaggerated psychological and physiological responses to stress. A major objection to that and similar findings is that such studies deal with averages—that patients afflicted with discrete symptoms and others suffering from more pervasive disorders are evaluated together, allowing the therapeutic failures of the latter group to camouflage the successes of the former.

In 1967 Gordon L. Paul proposed that psychotherapy research should study the "framework of interaction," that it attempt to answer the question "what treatment, by whom, is most effective for this individual with [which] specific problem and under which set of circumstances?" But one of the problems with this approach is that since it includes so many variables it makes comparisons of therapies and therapists extremely difficult.

In 1980 the National Institute of Mental Health began a three-year clinical trial comparing drugs with two forms of psychotherapy in the treatment of depression —the first large-scale study of this kind. Both the patients treated and the psychotherapies have been defined rigorously. This study does not address itself to, and hence will not answer the broad questions, whether psychotherapy can be studied at all in a scientific manner or whether the search for other evaluative techniques will have to be continued.

In the meantime, there is agreement that a common measure of effectiveness of psychotherapy exists even if it is difficult to demonstrate objectively; *i.e.,* the improvement in the patient's condition should be evident to the patient or to others. Owing to their own successes and colleagues' anecdotal successes in treating individuals suffering from anxiety, mild (reactive) depression, phobias, obsessive-compulsive symptoms, and personality disorders, psychiatrists as a group remain largely committed to psychotherapy. Most patients in psychiatric treatment for the above disorders receive some form of therapy modeled on psychoanalysis.

In psychoanalysis, a particularly intense form of psychotherapy, the analysis of the transference is a *sine qua non* of cure, although cure (the disappearance of symptoms) does not, as is sometimes believed, necessarily follow insight. Transference in classical analysis refers to the intense emotional relationship many patients establish with their doctors which mirrors earlier important relationships, usually with parents and siblings. The patient gains a particular kind of insight as he recognizes the distortions in the therapeutic relationship.

Antianxiety agents and sleeping medications may alleviate some neurotic symptoms and insomnia, but generally they are used only for a few weeks at a time, because they are addicting and fail to show long-term benefits.

Success in psychotherapy is determined by the resources of the patient before the illness, by his intellectual potential and social situation, and by the disorder from which he suffers. The therapist contributes training, professionalism, and empathy. Some patients get better because the therapist serves as a role model with whom they can identify. The expectations of both patient and therapist influence outcome. Insight on many levels is a factor in successful treatment, but sometimes there is improvement without insight.

A patient who after years of "unsuccessful" treatment reports a sudden cure because he has fallen in love or joined a self-help group confuses cause and effect. He forgets that intimacy and group involvement were impossible for him before psychotherapy. The psychiatrist often elects not to challenge the patient's defenses provided they improve his functioning. A woman suffering from manic-depressive psychosis was also an alcoholic. After years of drug treatment and supportive psychotherapy she felt strong enough to join Alcoholics Anonymous (AA). She continues to consult her psychiatrist and to take medication, while functioning as an effective leader in AA. But she frequently attacks psychiatrists for their ignorance, and credits AA for her recovery.

The "right" therapeutic milieu

The psychiatrist who treats mental disorders should either be skilled in all treatment modalities or able to make appropriate referrals. Before entering treatment the patient should investigate the therapist through local professional societies and universities.

It has become fashionable to match therapists and patients by race, sex, and so forth. Such congruence can occasionally be useful; it can sometimes entice into therapy otherwise resistant patients. A black woman may feel she can relate only to another black woman, for example. On the other hand, this kind of matching may generate other problems. In one study therapists *perceived* as empathetic, owing to similarities with the patient, were not as effective as others perceived as less empathetic. Excessive identification with the patient's problems may create blind spots for the therapist. Also, a therapeutic setting that is *too* comfortable may impede recovery for the patient since anxiety during psychotherapy is sometimes a catalyst for cure.

In some cases, the "ideal" treatment may have to yield to one less effective if the former is for some reason unacceptable to the patient. For example, although antidepressant drugs are highly effective in psychotic depressions, psychotherapy or even custodial care may have to be substituted if the patient's medical condition or intolerable side effects from drugs preclude their use.

Finally, one study showed that fee is not related to the outcome of therapy. Thus, the most expensive is not necessarily the best.

—*Edith T. Shapiro, M.D.*

Rehabilitation Medicine

Medical practice traditionally operates according to a "disease model," whereby a person with specific physical symptoms goes to a physician, who does something to render that person symptom-free. Ordinarily these stereotyped roles and expectations serve patient and physician fairly well, but certain kinds of disease require a different approach to the healing process. Chronic low back pain presents such a case.

The plague of low back pain

Historically, low back pain has posed an unyielding problem. It is estimated that at some time eight out of ten people will experience low back pain. In the U.S. five million persons are partly disabled and two million unable to work owing to back pain. In Great Britain each year two million adults consult physicians for this affliction. Often it is not possible to define the precise source of the pain.

While various treatments alleviate some cases of low back pain, the consistent success and long-term efficacy of any single form of treatment is not assured. The mixed results of back surgery as well as of more conservative treatments attest to the fact that a complete "cure" has eluded medical practitioners. Two major factors contribute to the limited success of low back treatment in years past. First is the failure to distinguish between acute pain and chronic pain in diagnosis and treatment. Second is the failure to involve the patient actively in his or her own care.

For centuries, various types of physical manipulation have been tried to free patients from the misery of low back pain. This woodcut of 1592 depicts an attempt to straighten the spine.

The Bettmann Archive, Inc.

Ted Thai—Time Magazine

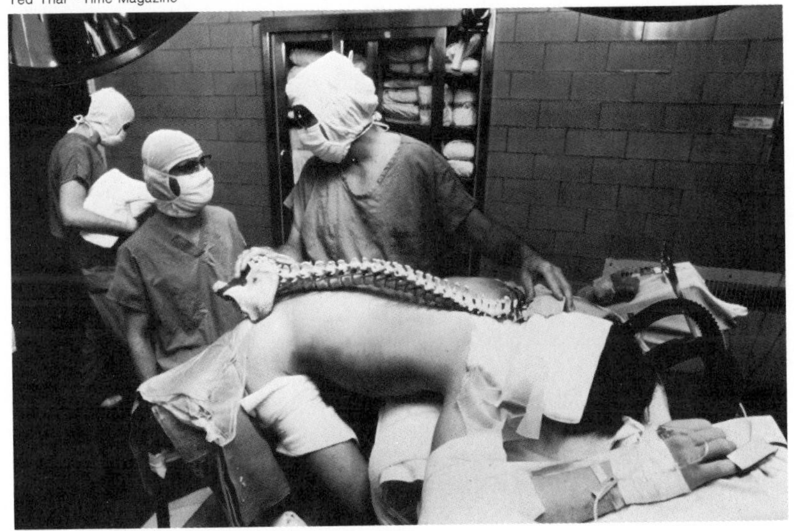

When back pain results from a ruptured intervertebral disc that is placing pressure on a nerve, a laminectomy is sometimes performed to remove the injured disc and relieve the pressure. Unfortunately, the surgery is no guarantee of cessation of pain.

The major objective in treating acute low back pain is to promote healing of injured or painful tissues. Toward that end such measures as bed rest, use of corsets, braces, other supports, and traction may be of value. As a rule, the acute phase lasts about six weeks, the time injured tissue takes to heal. After that time, in the absence of other disease, persistent pain must be considered chronic.

Treatment of chronic pain requires a very different objective: to maximize the patient's physical capabilities so that he or she can resume a normal level of activity. Contrary to expectation, low back pain does not necessarily stop when the tissues have healed, nor does the patient always regain strength and flexiblity comparable to that which was enjoyed prior to injury. Why this is so is not fully understood, but several sequelae to back injury are considered to be contributing factors.

First is the formation of scar tissue, which contracts and must be stretched in order to regain full use of the affected area—a process that can be painful in itself. Second is the loss of muscle strength and muscle tone throughout the body due to inactivity during convalescence. Back pain is enhanced by loss of strength in the abdominal musculature, which normally helps to provide support for the spinal column and helps maintain the spine's proper balance. Third are so-called pain behaviors: ways of sitting, standing, moving, even facial expressions, developed by the patient during the acute phase to avoid strain on the back. Pain behaviors facilitate the concentration of tension in involved muscles and because tension breeds pain, these compensatory postures often foster rather than dispel pain. Fourth, the patient undergoes changes in attitude toward himself. He begins to perceive himself as disabled, becoming more reliant on others (family members, friends, and medical personnel) for his care and less willing to assume responsibility for his own recovery. And, finally, external factors may affect the patient's motivation and progress. Financial disincentives, prolonged litigation in cases of injuries, as well as the attitudes of family members and close friends may reinforce a disability.

In light of the range of problems that beset the victim of chronic low back pain it is not surprising that the so-called medical disease model, which concentrates on isolated symptoms, has obtained only limited success. Moreover, treatment modalities used for acute pain may be not only useless but actually counterproductive in the chronic phase.

Multidisciplinary pain clinics

A relatively new approach to treating persons suffering from chronic low back pain has shown considerable success with inpatients and outpatients. The multidisciplinary pain clinic offers a variety of resources to patients with a wide array of problems. It takes a "holistic" approach to the "total" patient. Especially important, the multidisciplinary approach places primary responsibility for improvement on the patient. Members of the pain team—physicians (orthopedic surgeons, anesthesiologists, neurologists, and other medical specialists), along with physical therapists, occupational therapists, psychologists, social workers, recreation therapists, vocational counselors, nursing staff, and team coordinators—work together to construct and carry out a program of treatment for each individual patient. The team meets frequently to discuss the patient's progress and to adjust the treatment plan according to individual needs. New therapies are easily introduced into the program as they become available.

Even in inpatient settings the individual assumes as much responsibility for his or her own care as possible. This may involve getting to a therapy session on time, rescheduling missed appointments, measuring and recording vital signs each day, doing personal laundry, and so forth. Often the patient has up to nine or ten scheduled hours of activities and appointments a day. Such full scheduling helps him develop stamina for returning to the outside world.

Injection therapy. Some patients benefit from injections of appropriate medication into the pain site. Several types of injection techniques can be used including local blocks, spinal injections, and epidural injections of steroids, the latter involving a local anesthetic followed by the injection of the medication itself. Injections, which are usually administered by an anesthesiologist, may be administered only once or on a weekly basis for up to three weeks.

Physical therapy. Resuming a normal level of activity for most chronic low back pain patients means restoring overall musculature—including those of the extremities and abdominal and back muscles—to their proper strength and tone. It also means learning how to care for the back. A physical therapist is indispensable in these processes as a teacher.

The physical therapist lectures on and demonstrates the principles of body mechanics, posture, pelvic tilt exercises, and muscle function. Body mechanics are ways of moving that apply the least amount of strain to the back. By learning proper body mechanics for such basic activities as sitting, standing, walking, lifting, bending, and so forth, a person can learn to apply these basics to any task. Proper posture prevents muscle strain and tension. Exercises that involve tilting the pelvis forward help flatten the natural S-shaped curve of the spinal column to reduce back strain. Instruction in muscle function teaches patients which muscles are appropriate for certain kinds of exertion.

A therapist demonstrates the proper posture, exercise, and techniques of lifting, carrying, and movement that help relieve the muscle strain that causes much back pain.

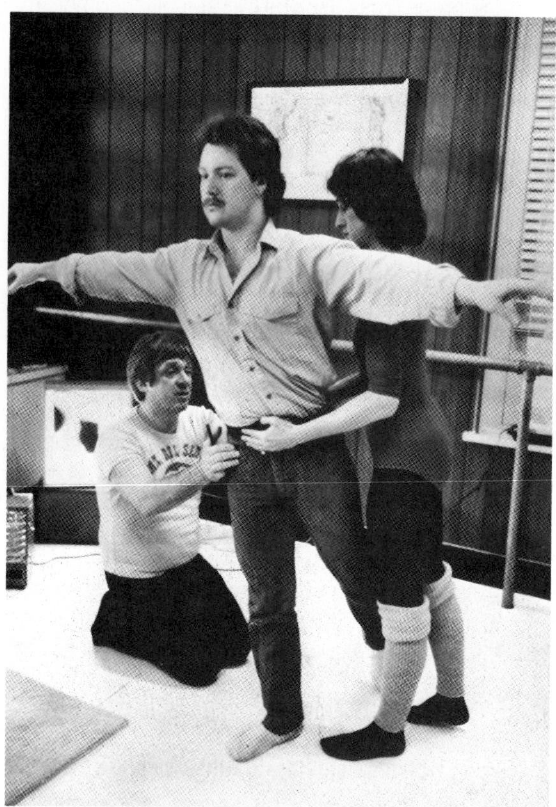

Bill Pierce—Time Magazine

A program of exercises—some conducted in a swimming pool, some on floor mats—helps low back pain patients to improve flexibility, strength, and stamina. Most exercises are conducted in a group, but a special regimen may be prescribed for an individual. Exercise programs help a number of problems common to low back pain sufferers—significant gait abnormalities, impaired sense of balance, and limited range of motion. Other conventional physical therapies such as massage, diathermy, whirlpool, and hot and cold packs may be employed as well.

Occupational therapy. The occupational therapy component in a multidisciplinary pain clinic focuses on problems such as difficulty in dressing, carrying out routine household chores, and other activities of daily living. Occupational therapists teach relaxation and work simplification techniques, which are practiced in conjunction with principles taught in physical therapy and vocational rehabilitation. An especially important component of an occupational therapy program is a regimen of exercises to build strength and flexibility in the extremities.

Videotaping. An extremely useful tool in the multidisciplinary treatment of low back pain is the videotape. At the beginning of a treatment program, the patient is filmed performing a series of ordinary tasks (*e.g.,* walking, bending, reaching, lifting, climbing stairs, and balancing). At the end of the treatment program he or she is filmed again. Such films have proved useful as a diagnostic aid; the videotape gives physicians and therapists an opportunity to observe specific physical limitations as the patient moves. As a research tool the tapes provide records of patient progress.

As a teaching aid for the patient the films are extremely valuable. Patient and therapist can review the initial film together to identify areas which require concentration and improvement. The viewing of these tapes with other low back pain patients in a group is often very enlightening; encouragement, advice, and constructive criticism are frequently more meaningful and acceptable to a patient when coming from other patients who experience back pain. Possibly the greatest benefit of the videotape is that it presents to the patient a true and undeniable picture of himself. Often this picture is an unfavorable one—that of a stiff, poorly coordinated, heavy, grimacing figure—which may be incongruous with his own self-image. But it also has the tendency to generate strong motivation for change and increases the patient's receptiveness to treatment.

Psychology. Psychological services are another indispensable component of the multidisciplinary pain clinic. It is generally agreed that patients with chronic pain develop psychological sequelae that may block recovery if they are unrecognized and untreated. Most chronic pain patients have at some time experienced real psychological difficulty. Most, however, have never had formal psychological counseling. Individual and group therapy sessions give patients an opportunity to voice the problems they have encountered as a result of their pain.

The psychology staff also teach relaxation techniques. The ability to relax voluntarily is important because pain causes muscle tension, which heightens the experience of pain, which in turn leads to greater tension, and so forth in a vicious cycle. In some cases hypnotherapy is a useful method of inducing relaxation. Relaxation training is also facilitated by the use of biofeedback apparatuses. Low back pain patients generally use an electromyograph (EMG) machine which measures muscle tension by means of a sensor electrode attached to the skin of a muscle area and registers the increase or decrease of tension with a scale, a light, or a tone. Practice on a biofeedback machine often enables a patient to learn what he or she can do to control muscle tension.

Psychologists and social workers also offer counseling to the families of patients. The patient who adjusts to his low back pain and learns to take care of himself is not aided by a family that regards him as disabled when he returns home. A number of family problems commonly arise in the wake of chronic pain: the patient's spouse may have to become the wage-earner for the family; recreational activities may be curtailed; the patient, preoccupied with pain, may have become distant from the family; sexual relations may be difficult. Psychological services help all persons concerned to work through such difficulties.

Vocational rehabilitation. Ideally every chronic pain patient interested in returning to work should have some vocational rehabilitation. Vocational rehabilitation specialists provide training that enables the patient to regain old skills. If returning to an old job is impossible, the vocational counselor can identify new job options based on the patient's interests and on job aptitude tests. In some cases different jobs may be available at the previous workplace; in other cases specific modifications worked out by vocational specialist and employer enable the patient to continue working at his old job.

Vogue therapies. "Vogue therapies" refer to a number of "unconventional" treatments which are not successful in all cases, but which show good results in some. One such therapy is transcutaneous electrical nerve stimulation (TENS), in which a mild electrical current is applied to the skin over the pain site, sometimes bringing cessation of pain. Acupuncture may also alleviate pain in some patients. In appropriate cases the pain team may employ hypnosis. Other patients may benefit from biofeedback training, as mentioned above, or from imaging therapies—mind-over-matter techniques of mentally conjuring up pictures of what is happening to the body and causing the pain as well as picturing the desired outcome of treatment: a healthy, pain-free body. All of the so-called vogue therapies may work because the patient believes they will work or for physical reasons of which we are presently unaware.

Christopher Springmann—Black Star

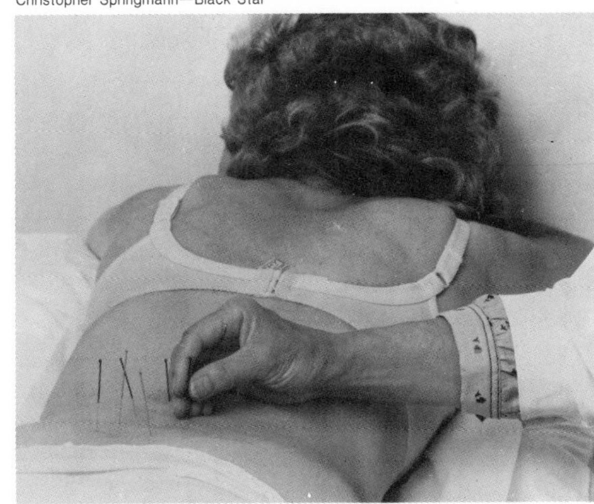

Acupuncture has helped some patients with chronic and intractable pain; biofeedback, drug injections, and even psychotherapy have also proved useful.

Medication. Drugs in the treatment of chronic low back pain usually are a mixed blessing. Narcotics may successfully dull the pain, but the discouragement and loss of self-esteem that chronic pain patients typically suffer are often worsened by the common side effects of these drugs—depression, impaired mental and physical function, and drowsiness. Furthermore, since medications must be taken as frequently as every three or four hours, the patient's attention becomes focused on the pain, preventing him from seeking other solutions.

Since the emphasis of the multidisciplinary approach is to offer a multiplicity of solutions, it is generally recommended that new patients be taken off prescription drugs. Chronic pain sufferers are generally advised to take nonprescription analgesics such as aspirin or acetaminophen only rarely.

These are only some of the treatment components of a multidisciplinary approach to low back pain. Preliminary findings show that this kind of pain management has considerable success in reducing the patient's perception of his pain and increasing his physical capabilities as he conscientiously learns new ways of living.

—Robert G. Addison, M.D.

Special Report: Children with Handicaps

by Estrellita Karsh

The Bettmann Archive, Inc.

Nicholas Andry's 18th-century book on orthopedics recommended techniques for reshaping a child's body. For an elevated shoulder, a child was to carry a ladder or heavy book to depress the raised side.

During World War II, Howard A. Rusk, then a physician for the U.S. Army, began his lifelong mission of restoring, through rehabilitation, not only his patients' invalid bodies but also their dignity and self-worth. His insistence that the "whole person" be treated, and not just the disability, was a spiritual step beyond previous clinical emphasis exclusively on massage and gymnastics. The practical benefits of Rusk's perspicacity were to have wide repercussions in restoring the handicapped to a productive role in society.

This concept was also applied to children, a radical departure from attitudes of the 19th and early 20th centuries that characterized handicapped children, with condescending pity, as "my brave little pets" and categorized "The Blind" and "The Deaf" alongside "The Idiots" (in a 1914 book entitled *Human Derelicts*). Rusk's approach was further still from that of the earliest work on orthopedics, Nicholas Andry's *L'orthopedie,* published in Paris in 1741; like the gardeners of his day who pruned and trained living plants into extraordinary shapes beyond nature, Andry recommended remolding the child's body to conform to an 18th-century standard of beauty.

Every nine seconds a baby is born in the United States. Many of these babies start life with a handicap —whether retardation, learning disability, absence of a limb, a state such as cerebral palsy, a congenital disorder such as a bone or blood disease, or blindness, deafness, or one of a number of syndromes causing both physical and mental handicaps. A National Center for Health Statistics (NCHS) study of 46 states and the District of Columbia for 1973 and 1974 found that 820 of every 100,000 infants were born with a congenital disability that was reported on their birth certificates. The true incidence, the NCHS stated, was much higher, as some disabilities were underreported, while others became apparent later in infancy, and most diseases were not included in the sample. What these figures mean is that thousands of children are born each year who need special help to develop fully. Medicine is responding to these disabled children through pediatric rehabilitation, a relatively new specialty that devotes its efforts to the diagnostic and management techniques that will enable handicapped infants and children to reach their maximal function.

A landmark program

The pediatric rehabilitation program at the Institute of Rehabilitation Medicine, which Rusk founded in 1948 at the New York University Medical Center, has had great influence. Rehabilitation physicians, special education teachers, physiotherapists, speech pathologists, technicians, and other medical personnel from all over the world train at the institute and bring its humanitarian treatment procedures and philosophy back to their own countries. In the United States there are many excellent rehabilitation programs for children

Courtesy, New York University Medical Center Institute of Rehabilitation Medicine; Photos, Lou Manna

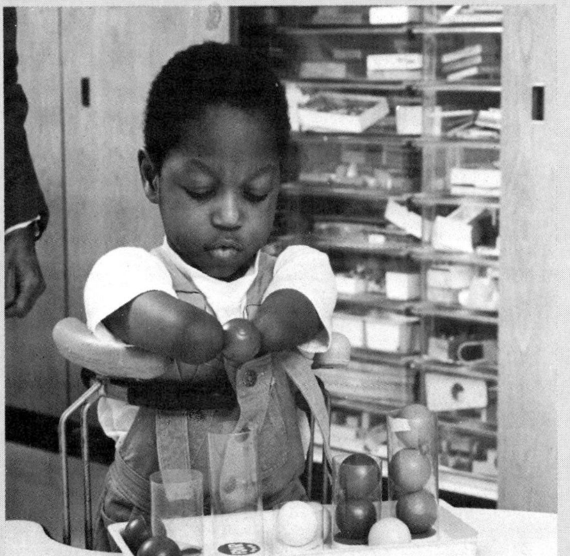

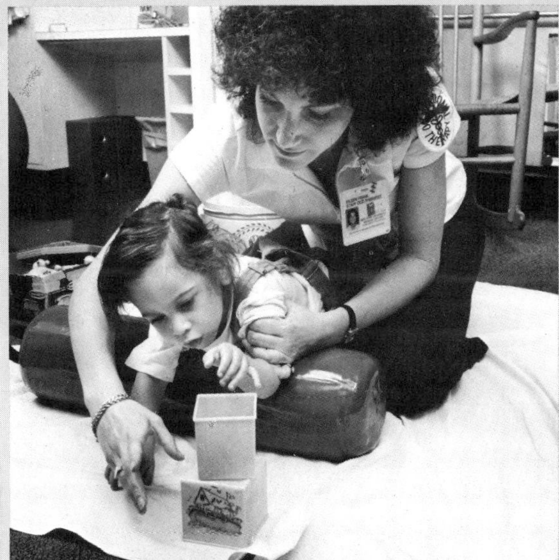

Therapy for children with orthopedic, mental, or sensory handicaps must begin early in life so that the remaining potential is fully exploited. Learning and training at this time helps the child develop to his maximum potential and achieve the fullest measure of independence.

—some in facilities where both adults and children are treated, some that specialize in pediatric rehabilitation alone.

Along the corridors of the pediatric floors of the Institute of Rehabilitation Medicine, the green-dappled wallpaper of trees blooming brings to mind a leafy bower, graphically symbolizing the institute's philosophy of learning and growing. Whatever the handicapping condition—blindness; deafness; cardiac, orthopedic, or neuromuscular disorders; tuberculosis; or mental retardation—each child receives an individually tailored program directed toward helping him to achieve the maximum physical, social, emotional, and educational possibilities within the limits of his disabilities. The child is taught the activities of daily living—dressing, grooming, eating, getting around, going to school—and ways of adjusting to his physical limitations. Emphasis is placed on the child's remaining ability, rather than on his disability.

The 35 young inpatients and 75 outpatients at the institute's three clinics (one for spina bifida, one for limb deformities, and a general clinic) represent a microcosm of children with handicapping conditions. It is estimated that there are more than six million disabled persons in the U.S. under the age of 21. In the school-age population in 1977 there were 860,000 deaf children, 680,000 blind children, 120,000 who suffered some form of paralysis, and 1,230,000 with orthopedic handicaps. In addition, developmental disabilities caused by cerebral palsy, epilepsy, autism, and mental retardation affected nearly 2.5 million children. A substantial minority were multihandicapped; thus their problems were more difficult to cope with.

Merging skill and compassion

It is a formidable task for a child to grow up handicapped, yet at the institute the fragility of the human body is overshadowed by the triumph of the human spirit. For the youngest patient, 18 months old, the hospital is his whole universe and the therapeutic team his surrogate parents. For many young children, vulnerable and temporarily separated from their parents, the hospital is both home and school. For the adolescents, whether handicapped from birth, or learning to adjust to restricted motion, wheelchairs, and physiotherapy, it is the place to confront turbulent emotions and to make realistic vocational decisions about the future.

The average stay at the institute is long, three months, in contrast to the typical five to seven days in acute-care hospitals; the contact with fellow patients and hospital staff is sustained and intense. These patients are not recovering from a temporary illness in seclusion, but rather are learning to move into life.

The institute is a warm and caring place. Loving concern and expertise characterize the therapeutic team. The rehabilitation nurse patiently teaches self-care to those who are in bed and in wheelchairs. A child who can perform necessary toilet activities will never lie helpless and consider himself a burden to his parents. The occupational therapist hands brightly colored sticks to a four-year-old boy; she is preparing him to feed himself with spoons and forks. The physical therapist teaches a seven-year-old girl, an amputee who recently has been given a prosthetic leg, to get up and down curbs, so that she will be able to get along on city streets. And when the patient becomes an adolescent, it will be most important to her that her walking ap-

Courtesy, New York University Medical Center Institute of Rehabilitation Medicine; Photos, Lou Manna

At the Institute of Rehabilitation Medicine therapists work closely with children on a one-to-one basis. For some children, learning to perform the ordinary tasks of daily life is a triumph. The girl above is mastering the use of a knife and fork with her new prosthetic hands.

pears as normal as possible. The speech pathologist repeats words over and over again before a mirror with a three-year-old boy whose speech is slow to return after an automobile accident. Later in the day, she will work with two patients with cerebral palsy and help a child adjust to her hearing aid.

The Institute of Rehabilitation Medicine has a small park which serves as an outdoor developmental playground, an oasis of leaves and wind and movement amidst the hard concrete of New York. Here, children who cannot move easily experience the unrestrained delight and freedom of play which normal children take for granted. To a child who spends his days on a stretcher, it is a joy to feel the wind in his hair or water rushing through his fingers. To a child strapped in a wheelchair, sliding down the protected, specially constructed chute is as exciting as an amusement-park roller coaster. It is more fun to relearn to walk on artificial legs when the goal is to reach a tree house rather than the end of a hospital corridor. When released from the institute, the child probably will have to negotiate subways and apartment stairs or get along on a college campus.

It takes compassion and understanding to work with some patients who may be angry and hostile; a 17-year-old former swimming champion, now paralyzed from his neck down as the result of a spinal cord injury from a diving accident, at first refused help and spoke sharply to the therapists trying to get him involved in rehabilitation. The program's psychiatric counseling and physical guidance yield heartening results: of 130 young patients with spinal cord injuries treated from 1976 through 1979, 83% were either in school or at work. According to Rusk, this has been due to a combination of better surgical techniques, better nutrition and skin care, and electronics. They now have wheelchairs operated manually or by breath, and a voice-controlled computerized wheelchair which responds to 30 commands. Rusk has said that "the implication of countless thousands of severely disabled people, unlocked from their inability to communicate, by sensitive electronic devices which obey even a sigh, is really beyond comprehension."

Over the years, the type of patients treated and the nature of their disabilities have changed. In the past the institute had mainly children with orthopedic disabilities, but now a great many children with birth defects such as spina bifida, limb deformities, and muscular dystrophy, who previously were not given the opportunity to develop, are being treated. The thalidomide disaster of the 1960s may have sparked parents to seek medical help soon after the birth of defective children. With infant stimulation and early-intervention programs, the institute is beginning to treat even children under one year old. Why start so early? Leon Greenspan, director of the children's division at the institute, explains that when a child has a severe birth disability, he cannot relate to people. If he cannot move, he cannot explore; if he cannot explore, he cannot learn; and if he cannot learn, he cannot live in the world. The institute's philosophy is that even if a child is presumed to have only a few years to live he should be treated and helped in every way possible. There may be a cure tomorrow—and life is precious.

Helping parents accept a child's handicap

Becoming a patient at the institute is the first step toward a feeling of self-worth for the child; for the parents, it is the resolution of an emotional cataclysm. The stress on the family of having a disabled child is borne out by a high separation and divorce rate. No matter what the disability, the parents' socioeconomic level, or how conscientious and loving the parents, the diagnosis catapults the entire family into a world for which there is never adequate preparation. The worst moment comes when the pediatrician or obstetrician explains that their little girl perhaps will never walk again or their baby boy may never be able to feed himself. A typical first reaction is denial; parents do not want to hear what the doctor is saying.

Beautiful, healthy children are so much a part of the American dream that learning one has a disabled child is, as one mother described it, "a raw and bleeding emotional wound." Parents inevitably feel guilty. They ask, "What have we done?" "Are we being punished?" "Will he ever be able to live on his own?" "Will he ever be able to hold a job?" "What will become of our child when we die?"

Establishing rapport between physician and parent is the first step in the "habilitation" program. A supportive relationship between parent and pediatrician (or obstetrician) prevents parents from rushing from clinic to clinic in the vain, unrealistic hope that the diagnosis will be reversed. No matter how good a therapeutic program, no matter how up-to-date and sophisticated the therapy and teaching equipment, if a close cooperative relationship with the parents is not established at the first interview, then the program is not likely to be of value.

Child psychiatrists have discovered that, especially from birth to six months of age, when most babies become fascinated with the world around them and the person who cares for them, the positive response of the parents is crucial. A pediatrician at the institute saw a tense, guilt-ridden mother who transmitted these negative feelings to her disabled four-month-old son. This was reflected in the infant's inability to look at his mother, a most abnormal circumstance for a baby his age. Only when the institute's psychiatrist helped the mother talk about her own feelings of isolation and helplessness did the baby begin to respond as well. The mother herself commented, "I cried over his handicap; I cried over my problems. I stopped crying and learned to help him when I understood what was happening to me."

When the decision is made to admit the child to the institute's program, either for infant stimulation or to the primary school, one parent (preferably both) is required to spend an entire day actively involved in the regimen. After the child is released from the hospital, although the institute still offers support and guidance, the prime responsibility for carrying out the program at home rests with the parents.

For the blind or physically handicapped child, participating in outdoors play is an occasion for untempered delight. Exercise sessions in a swimming pool—one part of an individualized rehabilitation program—help a young polio patient strengthen affected limbs.

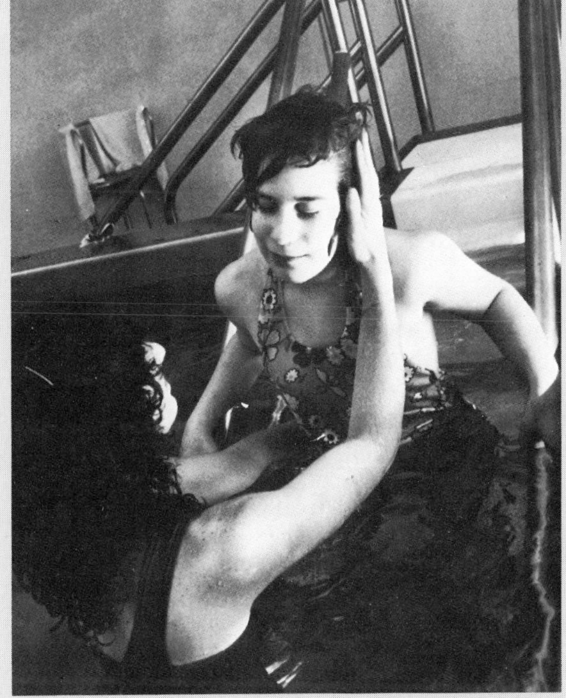

(Left) Courtesy, New York University Medical Center Institute of Rehabilitation Medicine; Photo, Lou Manna (Right) UPI

Individualized programs for growth

In the formation of an individual program for each child, a whole panoply of concerned professionals may be consulted: a psychiatrist, a neurosurgeon for a child with a spinal cord defect, an orthopedist for a child with musculoskeletal deformities, a physiatrist (physician specializing in defects that affect movement and function), and many other professionals, such as speech and language therapists, physical and occupational therapists, and social workers.

For children who have physical and learning disabilities, there is a special education program. The first professional evaluation is recorded on camera and screened before the full staff so that they may see for themselves how well the child uses his eyes and hands and how he manipulates objects. When the testing is over, the program is explained to the parents and they are encouraged to share these experiences first-hand with their children. Throughout the time the child is an inpatient, teacher and parent work together, and the parent can share the child's small, important triumphs. In this learning laboratory all constructional materials have been carefully designed for young handicapped children from six months to six years, to encourage them to explore and interact with their environment and experience the joy of creating and building and playing. But equipment is not as important as the quality of teaching. It is the teacher-to-child relationship that creates the positive learning atmosphere.

At the end of the child's stay as an inpatient, with the supervision of the medical and therapeutic team, the child's abilities and deficits are tested and evaluated by a senior psychologist and a therapeutic program is prescribed, which builds on the child's inpatient experience. If the relationship with the pediatrician has remained supportive, the parents find their trepidation lessening at the prospect of their carrying out a program at home that took seven or eight professionals to maintain in the hospital.

Social aspects of handicaps

Handicapped children are first of all children, with the same needs as their physically independent peers to express anger and frustration. Some cannot run and hide in their rooms, or raise their hands in anger against their brother or sister. Some children must be carried everywhere. It is important they be made to feel emotionally free, even to the extent of being able to express their anger at the person who may be their only source of physical support, as well as coming to grips with what has hurt them. A little boy who was severely burned when a washtub of boiling water overturned required leg and finger amputations; he is now encouraged to play aggressively with water. If he cannot confront his anger, his development as a full human being will be stifled. With the aid of a specially designed adjustable easel, a child without arms can use his feet and still experience the creative thrill of "finger" painting and need not forgo the delicious sensation of smearing paint on paper. In the therapeutic program no activity is insignificant—playing, eating, dressing, expressing emotions.

In 1980 a study about how parents live and cope with childhood disability was conducted by Arlene M. Bregman, who heads parent education for the Muscular Dystrophy Association. She lived as a participating family member with six families of differing social and economic levels, from an opulent apartment on New York City's Park Avenue to a modest one-bedroom house in Shirley, N.Y. Bregman's observations in the children's natural environment, rather than in the structured setting of a hospital or clinic, shed new light on the family's most intimate feelings about having a handicapped youngster. Similar patterns of coping emerged across the six families: all of the parents had altered their perspectives on time, whether their child's disability was stationary or progressive. They emphasized taking each day as it came and making each day fulfilling. All of the parents encouraged the children to be as independent as possible, and all had learned, if they had other children, to set priorities for the whole family and not to make the disabled child the focus of their existence. One family decided against buying the most recently designed wheelchair, which they determined their handicapped child did not really require, in favor of a family vacation in Colorado, from which all would benefit.

After the passage of landmark legislation in 1975 (the federal Education for All Handicapped Children Act, which declared that all children are entitled to free public school education and that handicapped children have an equal right to educational opportunities), the disabled child, previously either kept at home or in a special school, was thrust into the world of able-bodied children. "Mainstreaming"—taking several or all classes in a "regular" school—may produce its share of problems. Greater contact with other children sometimes brings with it thoughtless cruelty from fellow students. Adolescents, especially with their heightened awareness of self-image, react most negatively to their peers who have social disfigurements. The Carnegie Council on Children found that "this social oppression is more harmful to disabled children than their actual physical or mental disability, because it stifles their opportunity to learn new behavior." Obviously it will take more than legislation to change attitudes. But as "normal" children come more and more into contact with the handicapped, they will learn they are not so different. And the handicapped will benefit from socialization with "normal" children. Rusk has said: "Handicapped children are an integral part of society today and do not exist as a group apart with separate lives. Their needs and rights are the same as those of any other person; their problems are the problems of all people."

Sexually Transmitted Diseases

Increased sexual activity among teenagers as well as among adults, the Pill, increasing overt homosexuality, and changing life-styles—each has been cited as the primary factor responsible for the current epidemic of sexually transmitted disease (STD). Whatever the causes, and they are multiple, the rise in the incidence of STD is alarming.

Sexually transmitted diseases are those which are caused by microorganisms transmitted from persons who already have the disease to other persons. Traditionally, some sexually transmitted diseases were called venereal diseases, which usually referred to syphilis and gonorrhea. Unfortunately, most people are unaware that there are many more diseases that can be but are not always spread by sexual contact. In fact, for some of these, the sexual mode of transfer has only recently been discovered. The term sexually transmitted disease is now used to include at least 21 diseases: amebiasis, candidiasis, chancroid, condyloma acuminatum, cytomegalovirus infection, donovanosis, *Gardenerella vaginalis* vaginitis, giardiasis, gonorrhea, granuloma inguinale, hepatitis, herpes progenitalis, lymphogranuloma venereum, molluscum contagiosum, nongonococcal urethritis, pediculosis pubis, salmonellosis, scabies, shigellosis, syphilis, and trichomoniasis.

The sexually transmitted diseases that are of the greatest public health concern are gonorrhea, nongonococcal urethritis, syphilis, herpes, pediculosis, and trichomoniasis.

Gonorrhea

Gonorrhea is by far the most common STD and ranks first among reported communicable diseases in the United States, with over one million cases annually. The causative organism for gonorrhea is the microorganism *Neisseria gonorrhoeae.* In men, gonorrhea infection generally causes dysuria (pain on urination) and sometimes a discharge within the first two weeks of infection. Some men, however, have no symptoms or symptoms so slight that there is no discomfort. In women the disease may be manifested by changed vaginal discharge, mild dysuria, mild pelvic discomfort, or abnormal menstruation, but symptoms may not be sufficient to provoke the patient's suspicion or motivate her to seek care. Laboratory testing, *e.g.,* with a culture or a special smear (Gram's stain; the bacterium is gram-negative) is necessary to confirm the diagnosis.

Complications of gonorrhea are serious and costly. The most common and serious complication of gonorrhea, which affects women, is pelvic inflammatory disease (PID), with more than 273,000 cases occurring annually. Consequences of PID may include sterility, chronic pelvic pain, pelvic abscesses, and ectopic pregnancies. In the United States the economic cost of the consequences of pelvic inflammatory disease is estimated to be more than $1,250,000,000.

Since 1975 the national incidence of reported gonorrhea, although extremely high, has remained stable. This is attributed to massive screening for gonorrhea and educational programs that have resulted in faster treatment of infected sexual partners, who are thus prevented from developing serious complications and are less likely to spread the disease.

Syphilis

Syphilis ranks third among reported communicable diseases in the United States: in 1979 some 67,049 cases of syphilis in all stages were reported. The primary and secondary stages of syphilis usually end six months to one year after the disease has been acquired. During these symptomatic stages, syphilis is highly infectious

The Bettmann Archive, Inc.

"For one pleasure, a thousand pains." A syphilitic sits in a fumigation stove in this 17th-century engraving. Until penicillin was developed in the 20th century, there was no sure cure for venereal disease. Mercury, which is poisonous, was frequently used, leading to another saying, "One evening with Venus, a year with Mercury."

Table I: **Sexually transmitted diseases**	
disease or condition	**annual incidence (est.)**
nongonococcal urethritis	800,000 to 3,000,000
trichomoniasis	600,000 to 3,000,000
genital herpesvirus hominis	250,000 to 300,000
condyloma acuminata (genital warts)	200,000 to 400,000
pediculosis pubis (crab lice)	100,000 to 200,000

and easily spread by sexual contact. After the early stages, during which characteristic lesions appear on the skin, an infected person enters the latent stage, during which there are no outward manifestations and syphilis can be detected only by a serologic (blood) test. Latency may last many years but may still be followed in some patients by the development of late lesions. Congenital syphilis is acquired *in utero* by the developing fetus.

Syphilis control programs have, very effectively, used epidemiologic surveillance and educational strategies to reduce long-range consequences; death and insanity can result from untreated syphilis.

Other sexually transmitted diseases

A number of diseases other than syphilis and gonorrhea can be also sexually transmitted and are frequently seen in venereal disease clinics and by private physicians. These other diseases are causing a significant public health problem and suffering for many people. The true incidence and prevalence of these diseases are difficult to determine since there is no requirement that they be reported on a nationwide basis. However, estimates have been made by the U.S. Centers for Disease Control (CDC) of the more prevalent of these diseases. (*See* Table I.)

Health departments in large cities are beginning to record the incidence of these other sexually transmitted diseases. New York City, for example, has been keeping records on 14 diseases seen in its STD clinics since 1976. More than 74,000 cases were reported during 1979. Almost all, however, were reported from public clinics, as reporting by private physicians is required by law only for syphilis and gonorrhea. (*See* Table II.)

No formal control strategies have as yet been developed for most of the sexually transmitted diseases. However, many of the same preventive measures that are advocated for the control of syphilis and gonorrhea may be useful: using a condom, avoiding sexual intercourse with symptomatic partners, seeking treatment promptly when symptoms are noticed, and referring sexual partners for examination and treatment. Current attempts are relying heavily on patient education, counseling, and public information programs.

The dramatic rise in the incidence of several of these diseases is cause for great concern. Some diseases can have grave complications; others are merely troublesome. Brief descriptions of four of these conditions follow.

Trichomoniasis. A flagellated protozoan, *Trichomonas vaginalis,* produces vaginitis in women and occasionally urethritis in men. Men and women frequently have asymptomatic infections of the genital tract from this organism. Most textbooks describe a classical vaginitis syndrome, consisting of a frothy, yellow-green or white discharge with a red, irritated vaginal wall. Recent studies, however, reveal that these signs are not specific for trichomoniasis, and only a minority of women with this infection will have the classic findings.

Herpesvirus genital infection. At least one STD, genital *Herpesvirus hominis* infection, has been associated with cancer of the cervix and serious morbidity and mortality in infants of infected mothers. Two types of *H. hominis,* type I and type II, commonly infect humans. The common cold sore of the lip is usually caused by type I, and type II usually infects the genital area. Occasionally type II can be found in the oral area and type I in the genital area.

Primary infections of the genital area usually begin three to seven days after infection. The patient may note an area of burning, tingling, or pain on the genitalia; then small, grouped blisters, which ulcerate, ap-

Table II: **Sexually transmitted diseases reported in New York City 1978–1979**		
disease or condition	**1978**	**1979**
candidiasis	665	1,043
chancroid	47	115
condylomata acuminata (genital warts)	438	711
gonococcal pelvic inflammatory disease	307	750
gonorrhea	40,571	41,698
granuloma inguinale	7	5
herpes simplex	623	826
lymphogranuloma venereum	26	34
molluscum contagiosum	79	50
nongonococcal pelvic inflammatory disease	131	321
nongonococcal urethritis	14,886	17,862
pediculosis pubis (crab lice)	1,282	1,526
scabies	214	229
syphilis	5,657	6,702
tinea	486	818
trichomoniasis	1,217	2,115
total	66,636	74,805

Photographs, courtesy, H. A. Blough, R. L. Giuntoli, and JAMA

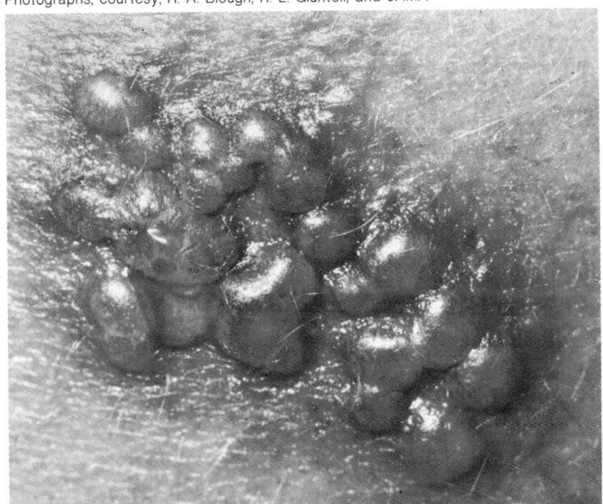

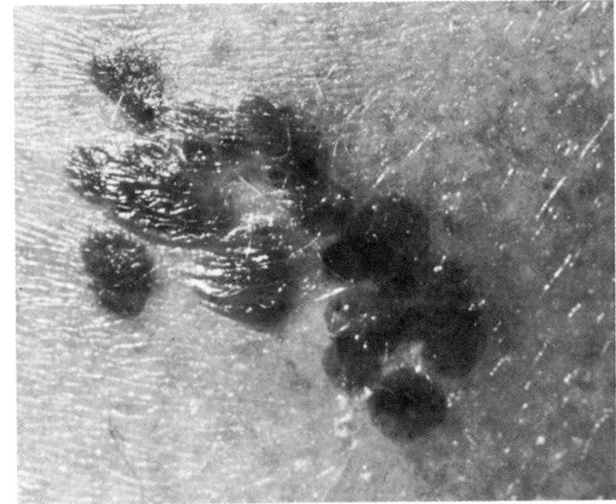

Genital herpesvirus infection causes painful sores (left). Although there is no cure for the infection, treatment with an experimental drug, 2-deoxy-D-glucose, has helped the symptoms (right) in some cases.

pear. Symptoms associated with these lesions are pain, swollen lymph nodes, and constitutional symptoms such as fever. When the lesions occur on the cervix or vaginal wall, women are frequently asymptomatic. The primary infection usually persists for several weeks, heals spontaneously, then may recur. Recurrent infections are usually milder and shorter than primary infection, but can continue intermittently for years. However, some patients have recurrences monthly that are so severe as to be disabling.

Serious consequences are rare in men, but women can transmit the infection to the newborn at the time of delivery if they are having an active flare-up of the infection. Neonatal infection is often fatal or, if the infant survives, may lead to irreversible brain damage.

For pregnant women who have active lesions at the time of delivery, many experts recommend cesarean section to prevent transmission to the newborn. *H. hominis* infections have also been associated with cervical cancer, although a definite cause-and-effect relationship has not been established.

Pediculosis pubis. Phthirus pubis, the crab louse, infests the hair of the pubic region where louse eggs, or nits, are attached to the hairs. After one week the larvae hatch, and in two weeks they develop into mature crab lice. The lice attach themselves to the base of the hair and feed on the blood of the host. Patients become aware of the infection because they see the lice or the eggs, or because intense itching develops after two to three weeks. The diagnosis is confirmed by identifying eggs or lice in the pubic hair.

Nongonococcal urethritis. Urethritis in men that is not caused by gonorrhea is referred to as nongonococcal urethritis (NGU). Postgonococcal urethritis (PGU), a variant of NGU, occurs when urethritis recurs after successful treatment for gonorrhea. PGU probably is due to simultaneous infection with *N. gonorrhoeae* and with some other microorganisms. Microorganisms associated with NGU (and PGU) are *Chlamydia trachomatis* and possibly *Ureaplasma urealyticum.* The incubation period of this disease is longer than that of gonorrhea, lasting from one to three weeks, and the symptoms are often milder. NGU is diagnosed by excluding gonorrhea.

Female contacts of men with NGU are frequently asymptomatic although they are likely to have cervical infection. *Chlamydia* may be transmitted from an infected mother to the newborn and cause eye infections or pneumonia. There is also strong evidence that the causative agents of NGU are associated with miscarriage, pelvic inflammatory disease, and in men epididymitis (inflammation of the epididymis).

Breaking the chain of infection

Diagnostic tests and treatment are not the only keys to the control of STD. Locating everyone who has had sexual contact with an infected person and motivating them to seek treatment is vital to stopping the spread of these diseases.

One of the most significant activities in any STD control program is the work of individuals known as VD (or STD) investigators. These are epidemiologists highly trained in the techniques of interviewing and counseling patients for the prime purpose of identifying and locating their sexual contacts so they can be brought in for diagnosis and treatment. This group of specialists is well established in the public health field. They assist local and state health departments around the U.S. The public health nurse also occupies a pivotal position in the VD control program. She helps in many ways to administer the VD clinic, working with children, teenagers, and pregnant women who are affected by venereal disease at particularly sensitive periods in their lives.

Fred Ward—Black Star

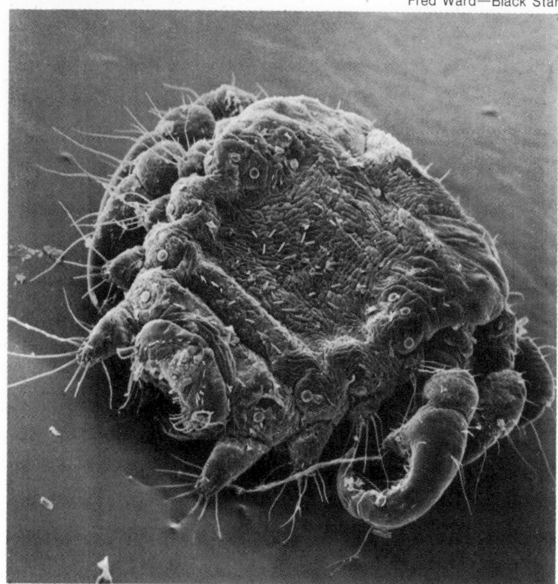

The crab louse, Phthirus pubis, *is usually acquired by sexual contact. Fortunately, safe medications are available to cure an infestation.*

One of the most important duties of the investigator is to interview patients infected with syphilis in order to locate their sex contacts. It is possible for one person with syphilis to infect many other people, and these people can, in turn, pass on their disease without realizing it. All these cases form a chain of infection that can be broken only by locating the people involved and bringing them in for treatment.

The investigator begins by talking with the patient, trying to allay his or her fears, and then describes the function of the health department in the control of VD. He teaches about modes of transmission, the incubation period, asymptomatic and symptomatic VD, and the consequences of an untreated infection. He then asks the patient to provide the names of all recent sexual partners and where they can be reached.

At this time, all the interviewing skills and motivational tools of the investigator come into play. The investigator is careful to assure the patient that his privacy will be respected and that the information will be used only to stop the further spread of the disease and to prevent the patient himself from being reinfected. Most patients are cooperative once they realize the seriousness of the disease and the importance of treating all contacts. There is a small proportion of cases, however, where patients may not be willing to divulge the names of their contacts—sometimes because rapport with the investigator is poor, and sometimes because they simply do not know enough about their sexual partners to locate them.

After the facts have been elicited, the patient is given the option to notify his sex contacts himself. Most patients, however, prefer that the investigator locate their contacts. At no time and under no circumstances will the contacts know who was their informant. The entire process of talking about sexual partners and notifying them of the fact that they have been exposed to the disease is completely confidential. There is no court that can subpoena these health records. If the patient opts to notify his or her own sexual contacts, the investigator continues to work with the patient to see that the contacts are properly diagnosed and treated either by a public health clinic or a private physician.

With the completion of the personal interview, the caseworker proceeds to notify all of the patient's sexual contacts. Here the caseworker attempts to locate these people as quickly as possible and make them aware that they have been exposed to an infectious case of venereal disease. Time is of the essence in controlling the spread of diseases such as syphilis and gonorrhea. All efforts are made to locate contacts within 30 days after the original patients were diagnosed and treated.

The tools of locating contacts and conducting investigations usually consist of extensive use of the telephone and door-to-door fieldwork. In large urban areas where populations are very transient a significant proportion of contacts are never located. Nevertheless, when contacts are located very little resistance is encountered by the investigator. Few people refuse to see a doctor when they learn that they have possibly come into contact with an infectious communicable disease. The danger of working the streets has rarely been a problem for VD investigators because they are usually members of the community and present themselves not as detectives but as public health professionals concerned with the health of the individual and community. The same degree of tactfulness and discretion used in the interview process is used in the caseworker's field follow-up activities. All information about the original interviewed patient is regarded as privileged communication and at no time is the name of the informant brought into the investigation. The caseworker's prime intention is to convince the individual exposed to venereal disease that he should receive a physical examination, a blood test, and if necessary some medical treatment.

There are VD investigators in all parts of the country who cooperate with each other in tracking a case. A person can contract VD in San Francisco and arrive in Boston shortly thereafter and infect another person. To get around this problem, health departments notify each other if the patient reports that he has had sexual contacts in another state.

The importance of treatment

In the past, and even today, people with a sexually transmitted disease, in their fear and desperation, often attempted to treat these diseases with home remedies. All of these treatments are a waste of money and a waste of time.

It was not until 1943 that John F. Mahoney and his co-workers made the discovery that penicillin could cure syphilis and gonorrhea. Before penicillin the treatment was long and expensive and the outcome was uncertain. It was sometimes necessary for an infected person to be admitted to a hospital to be treated.

Penicillin and the development of other antibiotics drastically changed the treatment of STD. These medical advances have made people less apprehensive about sexually transmitted diseases, since the cure is as near as a doctor's office or a public clinic.

The progress made in treating these diseases, however, is not the whole answer to the problem. The problem now is in motivating people with an infection to seek prompt medical attention. Scientific progress has helped foster a careless attitude. "Why worry about VD? A shot of penicillin can cure it." This attitude has prompted control programs to begin to reeducate the public about the possibility of contracting penicillin-resistant strains of gonorrhea and the real likelihood that antibiotics may become ineffective if they are misused in trying to prevent acquiring a sexually transmitted disease.

Controlling sexually transmitted diseases

The control of sexually transmitted diseases is a prime example of the partnership between government and the citizenry. The nature of these diseases and the habits of a highly mobile population demand that all federal, state, and local governments, private physicians, and voluntary organizations share responsibility for control.

The role of state and local health departments. States have the legal obligation for the control of venereal diseases and devote considerable resources toward that end. Most supporting legislation for venereal disease control is promulgated at the state level. Examples of such legislation are the laws and regulations which require case reporting, prenatal serologic screening for syphilis, and examination and treatment services for minors without parental consent being required. The last is a good example of the states' responsiveness to a perceived roadblock to disease control, with most states enacting such legislation during the late 1960s and early '70s.

Local and state health departments are primarily responsible for providing diagnostic and treatment services. There are some 3,000 part-time or full-time public health clinics throughout the U.S. In the past, many clinics provided services for syphilis and gonorrhea only; today more clinics include tests and treatment for other STD's.

The role of the private physician. Since more people with sexually transmitted diseases are being seen by their private physicians than by public clinics or hospitals, the control of STD hinges not only upon the cooperation of doctors in private practice with health departments, but also upon a closer liaison between the public health agencies and the private practitioner. It is necessary, therefore, for the private physician to maintain an adequate level of knowledge of the symptoms and signs, diagnostic procedures, and current treatment regimens if he is to carry out this responsibility. Participating in a continuing medical education (CME) program in sexually transmitted diseases is one way to fulfill this role.

Although the private physician's first responsibility is to his or her patients, physicians do occupy a unique position of respect and influence in their community. Their active support is necessary to see that education about STD is included in the curriculum of schools. Physicians can assist in local support and acceptance of venereal disease control efforts and in encouraging legislation governing STD control. Physicians affiliated with medical schools and hospitals may also be able to set up CME programs and workshops on STD.

The role of the community. The role of the community at large is primarily to support the improvement of local efforts. Throughout the U.S., citizens can organize active groups concerned with the control of the sexually transmitted diseases.

Many of these groups have achieved community-wide support for education programs, hotlines, mass media campaigns, legislation, additional funds for clini-

Education and information are two of the best weapons for fighting the current epidemic of venereal disease. Community groups are making VD control a main goal.

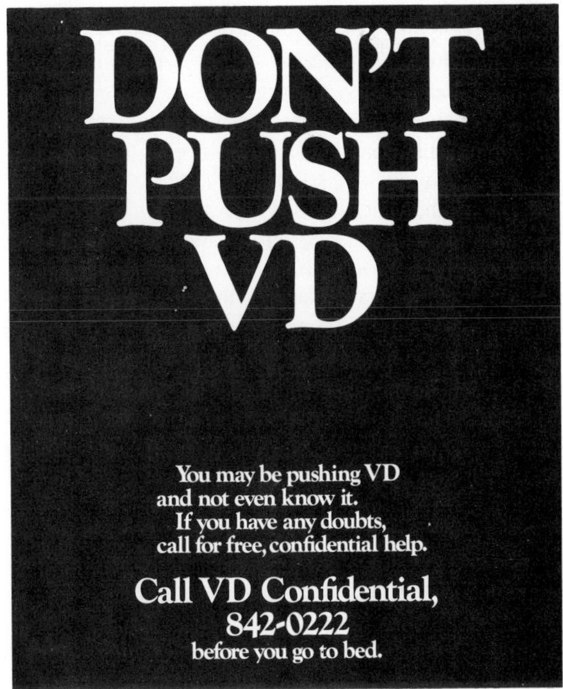

Courtesy, Citizens Alliance for VD Awareness

cal services, and expanded volunteer efforts. Clearly, if local STD control programs are to undertake new initiatives and develop new strategies in controlling sexually transmitted diseases, broad community support must be generated by involved and committed citizens.

—Yehudi M. Felman, M.D.

Skin Disorders

Leisure-time activities, work, environment, illness, and age all are mirrored on the skin. In the past several years, advances in diagnosis and treatment have been made for a number of the more than 1,500 identified skin disorders.

Athletes' skin woes

The wear and tear of vigorous sports activity have added to the medical vocabulary such new entities as the "dunk laceration," for cuts on the hands occurring when players push the ball down through the rim of a basketball net, and "jogger's nipples," for abrasion produced by constant friction from clothing during running. The latter is preventable by wearing a snug-fitting undergarment, covering the nipples with tape, or applying petrolatum to them before running.

Even in persons wearing well-fitting shoes, the fast forward motion of jogging and the rapid starts and stops in tennis have been blamed for "black toe," a discoloration caused by bleeding under the nail that most often affects the big toe. If new, properly fitted shoes do not help the problem, a one-inch incision made in the leather strip of the shoe above the damaged toe or toes will help relieve the pressure.

A similar injury, "black heel," results from forcing the heel against the back of the shoe, particularly during activities played on a floor or on hard ground; most prone to this problem are persons who play basketball, lacrosse, football, and tennis. A piece of felt inserted in the heel to cushion the shock helps minimize the problem. Corns and calluses also are common in the running sports; well-fitting shoes and socks offer the best means of prevention.

Stretch marks, or striae, on the skin are seen in weight lifters, as well as in people who gain or lose weight rapidly. These marks indicate overextension of and damage to the connective tissue below the skin. They are permanent, although they become less noticeable with time. No way of preventing them is known.

Contact dermatitis in athletes may be triggered by allergens and irritants in materials used in the manufacture of athletic shoes, face masks, and other equipment and in adhesive tape. Avoidance is the usual treatment once identification of the culprit has occurred, which can sometimes be an arduous process. For example, it took some sophisticated sleuthing before rashes afflicting a number of National Hockey League players were traced to fiberglass in their hockey sticks.

Excessive exposure to ultraviolet light produces early wrinkling, aging of the skin, and a higher rate of skin cancer. Swimmers and skiers are exposed to light reflected from water or snow, including that striking normally unexposed areas of the skin, such as the underside of the chin. Exposure to ultraviolet light on a cloudy but bright day may be 80% of that on a clear day. The intensity of sunlight increases with altitude; hence, mountain climbers face an increased risk of sunburn as they ascend. It is especially important for people participating in these sports to make use of an effective sunscreen or sun block.

Mountain climbers, skiers, hunters, winter joggers, and other cold-weather-sports enthusiasts are at risk for cold-induced injuries. The most common is superficial frostbite, which first affects exposed parts, such as the tip of the nose and the ears. First becoming red, then waxy or white, the injured skin becomes numb after rewarming. It may turn bluish purple, swell, sting, burn, and even blister. Usually the skin heals completely, but a burning sensation and cold sensitivity may remain for many weeks. Deep frostbite damages underlying tissue; long-lasting results may include pain, itching, and increased perspiration. The recommended treatment for frostbite is rapid rewarming with warm water, 100° to 110° F. Warming over an open fire or on a radiator and rubbing the injured part must be avoided, since the tissues can be further damaged by these actions. Cold injuries can be prevented by dressing in multiple loose-fitting, thin layers of clothing, avoiding touching metal equipment with bare skin, and other commonsense practices.

Sports are also associated with a number of infections. Athlete's foot and jock itch are well known; they result principally from certain fungus infections. These fungi, which find hospitable environments in shoes enclosing constantly perspiring feet and in tight athletic supporters, thrive in damp, hot locker rooms and showers. Warts, due to a virus, also frequently are passed on in such surroundings. The use of good hygiene, of absorbent, antifungal powders, and of protective footwear in showers and dressing rooms can reduce the likelihood of contracting these bothersome infections.

Herpes simplex infections are spread by direct contact. For example, epidemics have been reported among members of wrestling teams, giving rise to the naming of herpes gladiatorum. Research suggests that scrupulous attention to personal hygiene, including showering before and after workouts, along with rules against players in any contact sports playing while blisters or scabs are present, can greatly reduce the frequency of this disease. There is no cure for herpes infections, and painful flare-ups can continue to recur.

Swimmer's ear, acute otitis externa, may result when prolonged exposure to water removes ear wax and

Skin reactions and drugs that can cause them

reaction	generic name of drug	representative trade names	use of drug
acnelike pimples	corticosteroids	Acthar	treat endocrine, rheumatic disorders
	barbiturates	Donnatal, Nembutal	sedative/hypnotics
	bromides	Lanabac Neurosine	sleep aid antispasmodic
	phenytoin	Dilantin	treat epilepsy
	iodides	found in many drug products	nutritional supplements, cough remedies
	isoniazid	INH, Rifamate	treat tuberculosis
	trimethadione	Tridione	treat epilepsy
	dantrolene sodium	Dantrium	treat spasticity
	haloperidol	Haldol	treat psychotic disorders
red-violet, target-shaped sores	barbiturates	Donnatal, Nembutal	sedative/hypnotics
	phenytoin	Dilantin	treat epilepsy
	penicillin	K-Pen, Pentids	treat bacterial infection
	phenylbutazone	Butazolidin, Azolid	treat arthritis, painful shoulder
	sulfonamides	Sulfadiazine, AVC Creme	treat infections
	thiazides	Aldactazide, Diuril	diuretics (water pills)
	griseofulvin	Fulvicin, Grifulvin	treat ringworm infections
painful, red-violet swelling	oral contraceptives	Brevican, Enovid, Ovulen-21	birth control
	bromides	Lanabac Neurosine	sleep aid antispasmodic
	iodides	found in many drug products	nutritional supplements, cough remedies
	penicillin	K-Pen, Pentids	treat bacterial infection
	streptomycin	Streptomycin	treat tuberculosis infections
	sulfonamides	Sulfadiazine, AVC Creme	treat infections
	salicylates	aspirin	treat minor aches, pains
severe rash	allopurinol	Lopurin, Zyloprim	treat gout, uric acid
	aminosalicylic acid	aminosalicylic acid	treat tuberculosis
	gold	Myochrysine	treat arthritis
	thiazides	Aldactazide, Diuril	diuretics (water pills)
	penicillin	K-Pen, Pentids	treat bacterial infection
	meprobamate	Miltown, Equanil	minor tranquilizer
	phenylbutazone	Butazolidin, Azolid	treat arthritis, painful shoulder
rash, hives	salicylates	aspirin	treat minor aches, pains
	penicillin	K-Pen, Pentids	treat bacterial infection
	phenothiazines	Compazine, Phenergan HCl	treat psychotic disorders
	codeine	Actifed-C, Cheracol, Empirin Compound	cough/cold remedies
	coumarin	Dicumarol	anticoagulant
	thiazides	Aldactazide, Diuril	diuretics (water pills)
	isoniazid	INH, Rifamate	treat tuberculosis
measleslike rash	penicillin	K-Pen, Pentids	treat bacterial infection
	allopurinol	Lopurin, Zyloprim	treat gout, uric acid
	mercurials	Phe-Mer-Nite Dicurin Procaine	antiseptic diuretic
	phenothiazines	Compazine, Phenergan HCl	treat psychotic disorders
	thiazides	Aldactazide, Diuril	diuretics (water pills)
	isoniazid	INH, Rifamate	treat tuberculosis
discoloration of skin	oral contraceptives	Brevican, Enovid, Ovulen-21	birth control
	chlorpromazine	Thorazine	treat psychotic disorders
	silver	none	antiseptic
	gold	Myochrysine	treat arthritis
	bismuth	none	treat diarrhea
itchy, brownish rash	barbiturates	Donnatal, Nembutal	sedative/hypnotics
	corticosteroids	Acthar	treat endocrine, rheumatic disorders
	gold	Myochrysine	treat arthritis
	griseofulvin	Fulvicin, Grifulvin	treat ringworm infections
	thiazides	Aldactazide, Diuril	diuretics (water pills)
	penicillin	K-Pen, Pentids	treat bacterial infection
loss of hair	haloperidol	Haldal	treat psychotic disorders
	allopurinol	Lopurin, Zyloprim	treat gout, uric acid
	coumarin	Dicumarol	anticoagulant
	sodium warfarin	Coumadin	anticoagulant
	valproic acid	Depakene	treat epilepsy
	propranolol	Inderide	treat hypertension
abnormal growth of hair	dantrolene sodium	Dantrium	treat spasticity
	phenytoin	Dilantin	treat epilepsy
	thiazides	Aldactazide, Diuril	diuretics (water pills)
	oral contraceptives	Brevican, Enovid, Ovulen-21	birth control

FDA Consumer

other secretions that ordinarily protect the ear. Swimmers can use petrolatum-coated earplugs to help keep ear canals dry. Should the problem develop, it requires medical attention; prescription drugs may help prevent recurrence. Hair, an outgrowth of the skin, can turn green in swimmers who have light-colored hair; the cause of "green hair" is the deposition of copper from chemicals used to combat algae in the pool. The objectionable tinge can be treated cosmetically by use of a mild bleach, or swimmers can wear a protective cap.

Acne can be worsened by irritation produced by the rubbing of sports equipment. Such irritation may occur on the face from football helmets, face guards, or headbands or on the shoulders and back from shoulder pads and straps. Avoiding the irritation is the usual recommendation—advice that may force the patient to choose between clearing the skin and continuing to participate in the sport.

Public health issues

The toxic shock syndrome, a rare but potentially fatal disease that most frequently strikes young menstruating women, often induces severe skin symptoms. The skin turns lobster red, and the tongue also may become bright red. These skin changes are similar to those of scarlet fever. Concurrent symptoms include nausea and vomiting, followed by severe diarrhea and abdominal pain, with fluid loss, fever, and low blood pressure. The illness primarily affects women who use superabsorbent tampons. The cause is believed to be *Staphylococcus aureus* bacteria. As the disorder subsides, massive peeling of the skin on hands and feet commonly develops; some women develop transient hair loss.

The Food and Drug Administration recently revealed that a number of patients had been identified who had chronic skin lesions that did not respond to conventional treatment; the lesions were found to be caused by radioactive gold jewelry. Gold once used for medical purposes in the form of hollow capsules filled with radium gas and implanted in tumors was recycled for use in making or repairing jewelry. Some persons who wore contaminated rings and pins developed persistent skin irritation and skin cancer. More than 100 pieces of radioactive jewelry, all made before 1950, have been located, principally in the western New York state area. The gold will remain radioactive for decades. Public health authorities say it is logical to anticipate that more cases will be identified. Persons who have a long-lasting skin lesion associated with a piece of jewelry—a sore that forms under a ring, for example—should see a physician promptly; health professionals in turn will contact the state radiological health agency or local nuclear medicine laboratory to have the jewelry checked for radioactivity.

To alert physicians to skin reactions which can occur as a side effect of a wide variety of drugs, the American Academy of Dermatology established a reporting system in 1980. Physicians use a toll-free number to phone in reports of adverse reactions. The chart on page 309 lists a number of potential skin problems associated with specific medications.

The National Institute on Aging is supporting investigations into the changes that take place in the skin during aging, both to promote the general well-being of the older population and to use the skin to provide insights into the underlying processes of aging. Now under way are studies of wound healing, the ability of the skin of older persons to react to various stimuli, changes with aging in the capacity to sweat at various sites on the body, the activity of oil glands, and differences in the effects of pathogenic organisms on the skin of younger and older persons. The National Institute for Occupational Safety and Health is supporting research on occupational hazards to the skin and on diseases caused by work-related exposures.

Treatment advances

The outlook for teenagers troubled by acne vulgaris, the common form of acne that begins during adolescence, has improved significantly. Dermatologists feel that preparations now available can control almost all cases. There is hope that 13-*cis*-retinoic acid, a new drug under investigation, will be of benefit against even the most severe, scarring types of acne.

The mainstay of acne treatment continues to be tetracycline, taken by mouth, which has been shown to be both effective and safe even when taken for many years. The past year has seen an increase in the use of effective topical antibiotics, particularly clindamycin and erythromycin. Benzoyl peroxide, a drying antibacterial lotion, is considered effective for many mild cases and is a principal ingredient in many over-the-counter acne preparations. During its testing, 13-*cis*-retinoic acid, taken by mouth, gave dramatic clearing of severe, widespread pustular acne that had failed to respond to other treatment; the improvement was still evident for three years after the therapy was discontinued. The drug has some unpleasant side effects, including dry mouth and dry eyes. Persons taking 13-*cis*-retinoic acid, which is not yet generally available, must be monitored closely.

For patients with kidney insufficiency, itching can be a debilitating problem. The cause for the itching has not been fully identified—in some cases it is due to the overactivity of the parathyroid glands caused by the kidney disease. It also is hypothesized that toxic products that accumulate in the body when the kidneys are not functioning properly tend to act on the skin or the nerves in the skin to produce the discomfort. Even dialysis, the artificial "washing" of the blood to remove waste products, does not reduce this troublesome symptom in all patients. In one study, 85% of patients undergoing dialysis were found to suffer from incapacitating itching, which was so severe as to disturb sleep. Two new techniques seem to reduce or eliminate the itching.

In one small-scale test at Northwestern University Medical School, Chicago, Ill., patients were exposed to increasing amounts of ultraviolet light, which is thought to interfere with the action of the toxins on the skin. After 7 to 20 treatments lasting 3 to 16 minutes in a light booth, eight of ten patients responded with complete relief of itching.

In the other test, patients took charcoal in capsule form; the charcoal may attach to chemical waste products in the intestinal tract, forcing them to be eliminated through the bowel rather than being reabsorbed into the blood. Ten of 11 patients who took the charcoal capsules for eight weeks at the University of Oklahoma and the Oklahoma City Veterans Administration Medical Center gained complete relief. Authors of the study note that the treatment is both safe and economical.

Burn patients will benefit from several recent advances made at the Massachusetts Institute of Technology. Two different approaches have yielded living facsimiles of human skin, described as "skin-equivalent" tissue. Both start with taking a sample of the recipient's own skin, then culturing it in the laboratory. One researcher was able to grow a 100-sq cm graft from a one-square centimeter biopsy; this technique may benefit extensively burned patients who do not have enough healthy skin left from which to take grafts. Although neither skin replacement is presently able to grow oil or sweat glands or hair, trials are in progress to determine if the material can permanently replace skin lost by burns. If successful, the new material not only would promote faster healing but would spare patients the pain of grafts taken repeatedly from other sites on the body. These laboratory-grown grafts are still in the experimental stage, however.

Another advance involves the development of an artificial skin made from constituents of cowhide, shark cartilage, and plastic that lasts longer and works better than biological dressings obtained from pigs and human cadavers. Such dressings, though temporary, sustain the life of massively burned patients until the burned areas can be covered by grafts and the growth of new skin. The new artificial skin does not cause the graft-rejection immune reaction that is a problem with other biological dressings; therefore, the patients need not take immunosuppression drugs that make them vulnerable to life-threatening infections. The artificial skin has been used successfully on ten patients with full-thickness burns over 50 to 90% of their bodies.

For children with one form of epidermolysis bullosa, an inherited skin disorder, the anticonvulsant drug phenytoin seems to offer some relief. Severely affected children with this disorder have skin so sensitive to friction that rubbing an eye, wearing shoes, brushing the teeth, or even swallowing ordinary foods can produce blisters that can cause scarring when they heal. Physicians at Washington University, St. Louis, Mo., and Northwestern University tried phenytoin on these blisters because it had been reported to inactivate collagenase, an enzyme overproduced in this skin disorder. They found it significantly reduced the blistering in 12 of 17 patients.

—Stanford I. Lamberg, M.D., and Lynne Lamberg

Surgery

Microsurgery involves the use of extremely tiny instruments and sutures finer than human hair that can be handled skillfully only under microscopic observation. Such techniques allow the surgeon to dissect and repair small, delicate tissues in such areas as the brain, neck, and fingertips and tiny blood vessels in the limbs.

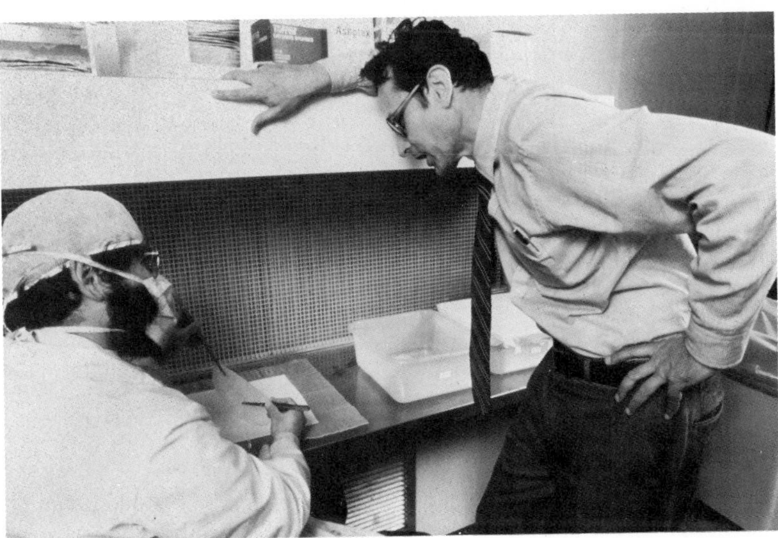

Ira Wyman—Sygma

The development of living replacement tissues that can be used in place of human skin for grafts was recently accomplished by two different groups of researchers. The grafts hold great promise for use with extensively burned patients, sparing them years of painful and debilitating graft procedures.

Microsurgery has undergone its greatest expansion in the past two decades and now makes possible operations to remove brain tumors previously considered inoperable, reattach (replant) severed limbs and fingers in a relatively routine fashion, transfer tissues freely between sites on the body, repair blood vessels and nerves often smaller than one millimeter (about 0.04 in) in diameter, and reestablish blood flow in injured hands and legs that would otherwise have required amputation because of inadequate circulation.

Applications of microsurgery

Each medical specialty makes use of microsurgery in its own way. Ophthalmologists, for example, operate under the microscope to remove cataract-damaged lenses with increased safety and precision, to repair retinal damage or remove scarring, and to secure corneal transplants; ear specialists, to reattach tiny bones in the middle ear; plastic surgeons, to reconstruct parts of the body deformed or damaged by birth defects, accidents, disease, and surgery; and urologists and gynecologists, to repair vasectomies in men who want fertility restored and to open blocked fallopian tubes in infertile women.

Neurosurgeons use microsurgery to excise previously inaccessible tumors deep within the brain, to repair arteries with weakened walls (aneurysms), to remove abnormal connections between arteries and veins, and to increase blood flow to the brain by bypassing blood vessels narrowed by arteriosclerosis. The operating microscope allows neurosurgeons to work in smaller spaces and to place less pressure on the brain while maintaining exposure. This approach minimizes swelling of the brain and thus speeds recovery from these long and delicate operations.

In some cases people who were once told that surgery for their conditions or injuries would be too difficult or imprecise to have much chance of success may now be helped if they seek information about medical centers with microsurgical facilities and surgeons for whom microsurgery is routine practice. It is also important to know that these facilities are available for emergency surgery and can deal successfully with such problems as accidentally severed limbs and fingers even after delays of many hours if the tissue is cleaned, protectively wrapped, and promptly chilled to delay deterioration.

Replantation

One dramatic example of such modern microsurgical virtuosity took place in 1979 when the right hand of a 17-year-old girl was completely severed under the wheels of a New York City subway train. A quick-thinking policeman at the scene retrieved the hand and helped pack it in ice obtained from a nearby restaurant. Taken to Bellevue Hospital, the victim underwent a 16-hour operation that involved cleaning and removing damaged tissues; identifying and matching up exposed blood vessels, nerves, and tendons in the forearm and hand; securing the hand to the arm with a metal rod; microsurgically reconnecting important arteries and veins (in two instances using vein grafts from a foot) and then several tendons and nerves; and finally transferring a skin graft from the girl's thigh to the tip of the thumb. Although deprived of blood supply for several hours, which included more than four hours on the operating table, the hand suffered minimal damage due to cell death.

Indications for replantation depend upon the extent of injury, the condition of the amputated parts, and the ability of the patient to withstand a long operation and an even longer convalescence. For finger, hand, foot, and limb reattachments success is measured not simply by the restoration of blood flow to keep the part alive but also by the return of sensation and of at least some function. Although some loss of strength can be expected in even the most optimistic cases, the successful replant is still far superior in function to an artificial part. At least 500 replantations are performed every year in the U.S. Success rates for replanted thumbs and fingers range from 70 to 90% and for arm and forearm replantations from 30 to 60%. A crucial factor in restoring function in replanted parts is physical therapy; special exercises may be needed for a year or more to produce satisfactory results.

Most often microsurgery exists as an element or phase of an operation, employed by the surgeon for a specific purpose amid more conventional techniques. Occasionally, surgeons trained in microsurgical techniques will join with teams of other surgical specialists to deal with especially complex situations. For example, a 24-hour operation in 1979 at Montefiore

Surgeons peer through microscopes, which magnify tiny nerves and blood vessels, during an operation to reattach a severed hand.

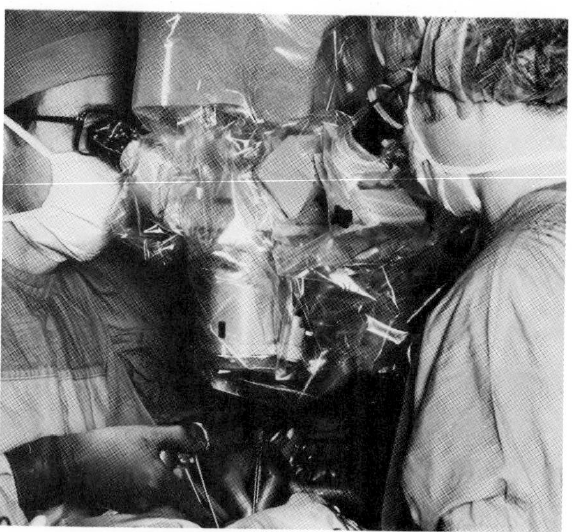

Dan McCoy—Rainbow

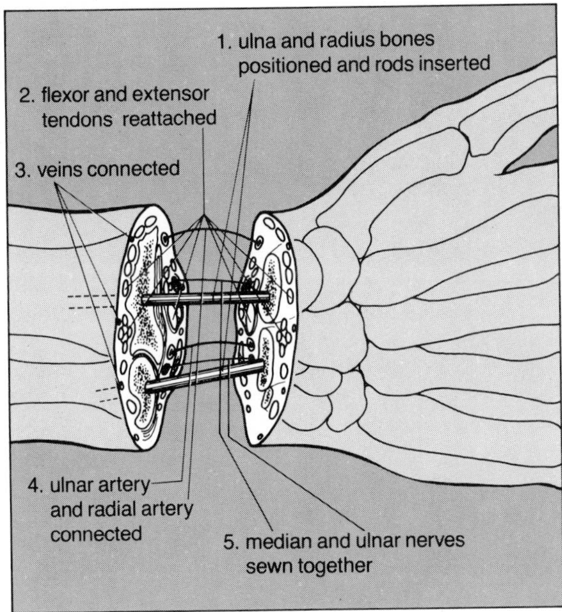
1. ulna and radius bones
positioned and rods inserted
2. flexor and extensor
tendons reattached
3. veins connected
4. ulnar artery
and radial artery
connected
5. median and ulnar nerves
sewn together

John Bartley—The Chicago Tribune

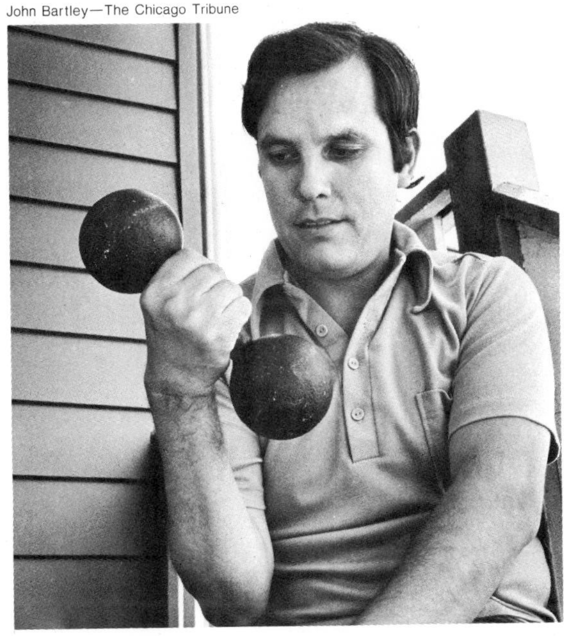

This man lifts weights with hand that was severed at the wrist in an industrial accident in 1977. The operation to reattach his hand involved inserting metal rods between the arm and hand; repositioning the ulna and radius bones; sewing together arteries, nerves, and flexor and extensor tendons; and reconnecting torn veins using veins from the foot. Skin grafts completed the procedure.

Hospital in New York City to restore the crushed and nearly severed left leg of a motorcyclist involved the efforts of plastic surgeons and orthopedic specialists, who alternated in the tasks of microsurgically reconnecting blood vessels, nerves, and tendons, and rebuilding shattered bones.

Tissue transfer

One important innovation brought about by microsurgery is in the use of free tissue transfer in plastic and reconstructive surgery. Previously, in order to move a thick flap of skin and underlying fatty tissue from one site to another, part of the tissue had to be left attached to the original site to maintain blood supply while new vascular connections grew between the tissue and its new site. This necessity required creating a tissue bridge between the two sites for weeks or months or tediously "walking" the tissue one end at a time toward the final site in a series of short intermediate bridges. In recent years, however, the ability of surgeons to match and join millimeter-sized blood vessels using microsurgery has allowed tissue to be shifted between distant sites in a single operation while preserving essential circulation.

Skin, fat, and bone from the groin area have been moved in this manner both to repair nonhealing infected bone after severe lower leg fractures and to reconstruct the jawbone removed because of extensive cancer in the mouth. In patients who have lost a thumb owing to burns or other causes, function of the hand has been improved by transfer of the big toe with its tendons, blood vessels, and nerves to the hand to serve as a thumb. Portions of the intestine have been used to reconstruct the esophagus (swallowing tube) in patients with esophageal cancer in whom other methods have failed. Knowledge of the microscopic blood supply to various muscles has allowed surgeons to use large areas of muscle, fat, and skin to cover pressure sores in bedridden patients or to reconstruct breast defects after mastectomy for breast cancer. Lymph channels have been reconstructed under the microscope to decrease chronic tissue swelling (lymphedema) that may occur after prolonged infection. Also, microsurgery has made it possible to reattach scalp that has been torn away by occupational injuries.

Blood flow improvement

Microsurgery to improve circulation to the brain requires the most careful judgment in order to avoid inappropriate, inadequate, or inadvisable procedures in patients for whom the risk of surgery might outweigh its potential benefits. Many patients with transient ischemic attacks (TIA's) that temporarily obstruct the flow of blood in major arteries to the brain may not withstand the prolonged vessel obstruction required in microsurgery, thus making the risk of complications excessively high. Blood vessel grafts have made possible a variety of bypass procedures between cerebral arteries in the brain and arteries in the scalp.

—George L. Blackburn, M.D., Ph.D.

Special Report: Surgery for Epilepsy

by Donna Bergen, M.D.

Epilepsy is a common condition. About one in every 200 Americans suffers from recurrent seizures. In countries that have a greater number of birth injuries, head traumas, and parasitic infections that involve the brain, the incidence of epilepsy is even higher. Yet seeing someone have a seizure is not a common event, because anticonvulsant drugs now bring complete or nearly complete control of seizures to a majority of epileptics. Like the diabetic taking insulin, most people with epilepsy can live without fear that their illness will intrude into their lives.

Drug-resistant epilepsy

There are still epileptics, however, for whom even high doses of several anticonvulsants cannot bring relief. Some are severely brain-damaged or retarded, even institutionalized. Many, however, are otherwise neurologically intact people whose recurrent seizures disrupt their family lives, their jobs, and their ability to function normally in society.

Seizures are the result of abnormal brain activity. Brain cells, or neurons, function by generating small amounts of electrical activity, similar to a system of tiny batteries and conducting wires. When this activity becomes uncontrolled and its pattern abnormal, seizures may result. Often the abnormal activity appears to start focally in a small group of neurons at or near an injured brain region. If the abnormal activity remains confined to this small site, a "partial" seizure may be the result, manifested perhaps by twitching of a limb, loss of awareness, or an experience of seeing flashing lights. The many possible clinical patterns of partial, or focal, seizures depend on the exact brain regions involved in the abnormal activity. In fact, the clinical characteristics of a patient's attacks often enable the physician to pinpoint the probable site of origin in the brain. If the seizure activity spreads to other regions of the brain, a generalized convulsion may result. Although highly effective anticonvulsant drugs have been discovered, the precise mechanisms of seizure generation and cessation are still unknown, and their elucidation is presently a much pursued goal of medical research.

Only a few medical centers are equipped to perform surgery for epilepsy, which is generally considered a last-resort procedure. First, extensive testing must be done, including monitoring a patient's typical seizures.

Dan McCoy—Rainbow

Why some epilepsies are intractable to medical treatment is an enigma. A clue may lie in the finding that some patients with refractory epilepsy are found to harbor slow-growing brain tumors, small congenital malformations of brain tissue, or traumatic scars. Grossly perceptible, anatomically clear brain injury may predispose a person toward epilepsy that is unusually resistant to drug therapy. For some of these patients, surgery to remove these abnormal brain regions may hold the hope of cure or radical improvement of the seizure disorder.

Deciding for or against surgery

The notion of lopping off a piece of brain tissue that is behaving in a troublesome manner may seem to be an extreme one, and it is. Surgery for epilepsy usually is considered a last resort, only after exhaustive efforts with drug treatment by medical specialists have failed to bring a satisfactory result. Even then, it is not possible to operate on every person with uncontrolled epilepsy. One of the greatest limiting factors is simply the enormous effort, time, and skill that must be expended by a large team of medical specialists on each case even to screen patients for consideration for surgery. This limits the practice to a few large medical centers with specially trained staff and other resources to devote to this work.

How is a decision for or against extirpative surgery (destruction by cutting away) made? The precise question that must be answered in each case is: Can an area of brain be discovered whose removal is likely to reduce or stop the patient's seizures without injury or crippling effects? For example, if there are many sites on both sides of the brain capable of producing various types of seizures, extirpation would be impossible because it would leave the victim cerebrally mutilated and functionally destroyed. Even a single focus of epileptic activity may not be surgically removable if it includes or is near enough to a region of the brain that is vital for

Photographs, Dan McCoy—Rainbow

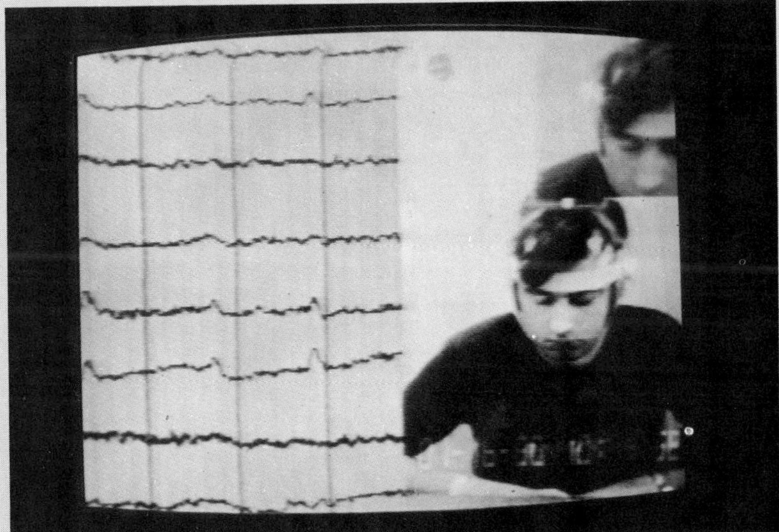

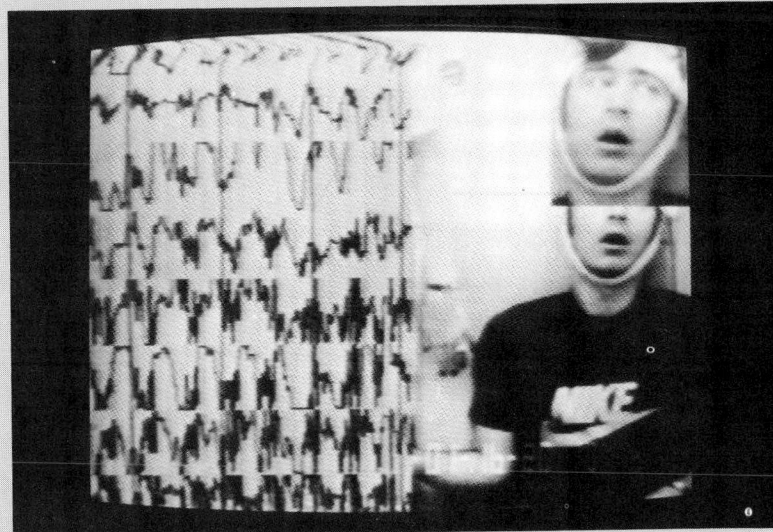

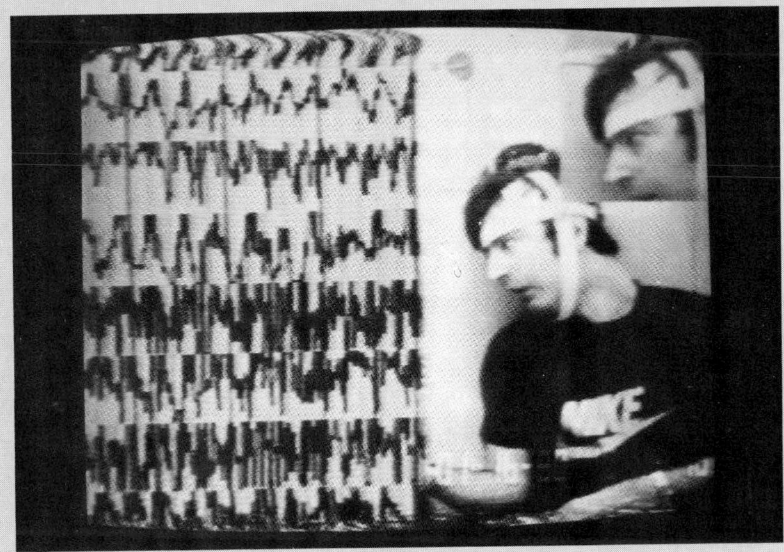

In this series of photographs a severe epileptic seizure is recorded on videotape while an EEG machine charts the patient's brain waves. The seizure peaks in the bottom picture.

the production of speech or limb movement. Determining the precise region responsible for the patient's seizures is thus the main goal of the extensive preoperative tests that must be undergone by patients being considered for surgery.

Presurgical tests

Most of these tests involve electroencephalography, the recording of electrical activity by electrodes placed on the scalp or elsewhere. The first task of the electroencephalographer, usually a neurologist with special training in this field, is to record some of the patient's typical seizures with electrodes glued to the patient's scalp, the technique used routinely for most clinical electroencephalograms (EEG's). To ensure that a series of attacks will occur within a short time, the patient is hospitalized and dosages of some or all of his anticonvulsant drugs are reduced gradually. During this time, continuous EEG recording, often with simultaneous videotaping, monitors the patient day and night so that the fewest possible seizures must be undergone in order to provide the necessary precise characterization of the electrical and clinical aspects of the attacks.

Often the beginnings of the seizures can be seen readily on the EEG. If not, more elaborate measures may be taken to procure this vital information. Recording electrodes may be surgically implanted into those parts of the brain under the highest suspicion of causing the seizures. This is usually done stereotaxically, *i.e.,* by aiming a rigid sheaf of electrodes toward their preselected targets through small holes in the skull, using standard spatial coordinates based on detailed surgical "maps" of brain structures. This procedure may be done under local anesthesia alone. Further monitoring from these depth electrodes then determines the site or sites of origin of the patient's attacks. In some centers such depth monitoring is done in all surgical candidates in order to provide as much information as possible about the electrical patterns reflecting seizure activity.

The immediate effects on the EEG's of injections of seizure-suppressing and seizure-enhancing drugs are usually studied as well. Such tests are used especially in patients who are found to have several potential sites of seizure activity, perhaps on both sides of the brain, in order to pinpoint the one site responsible for their usual, disabling attacks.

In most cases the neurosurgeon must be certain of the location of brain centers responsible for language and speech in each patient, so that damage to them may be avoided at surgery. In most people those centers are located within a fairly well-defined region on the left side, or hemisphere, of the brain. In a minority of healthy people and in many people who suffer brain injury in early childhood (including many with epilepsy), language develops in the right hemisphere. To locate the speech centers, each cerebral hemisphere is briefly and separately anesthetized with an injection of a short-acting barbiturate into each carotid artery, one of which supplies blood to each hemisphere. After an injection into one hemisphere of the brain the patient temporarily loses all the functions of that hemisphere, thus becoming paralyzed and numb on the opposite side of the body; if language is located in that hemisphere, the patient also loses the ability to speak and to understand speech. Because the drug is quickly dissipated and metabolized, these effects vanish within minutes.

Surgical strategies

In most cases the surgery itself demands the skills of a neurosurgeon with experience in this special field. It also requires an electroencephalographer with expertise in the delicate art of recording activity directly from the surface of the brain (electrocorticography), because during the operation a final attempt to localize the electrically abnormal tissue may be made and removal carefully limited to this site. The ultimate aim of all such operations is to remove as much pathologic tissue as possible while sparing the greatest possible amount of normally functioning brain; this includes the meticulous avoidance of disturbing any brain site known to have important motor or language function.

In some cases, especially when multiple sites of epileptic activity are discovered or when the abnormal site is found in a surgically inaccessible or untouchable region, surgical techniques other than outright removal have been used. The surgeon may attempt to destroy central brain areas suspected of being essential to the production or coordination of major convulsions. Based on prior trials in animal models of epilepsy, these assaults on various neuronal groups, or nuclei, include destruction of parts of the thalamus and the fields of Forel. Cutting of neuronal connections where they occur in clearly defined tracts such as the corpus callosum and anterior commissure, both of which allow communication between the two cerebral hemispheres, is another attempt to break up or desynchronize the spreading neuronal activity that causes convulsive seizures. These approaches have met with varying success.

Some neurosurgeons have even tried to harness the brain's own mechanisms for terminating or aborting seizure discharges by implanting electrical stimulators on the surface of the cerebellum, a brain structure with widespread connections affecting both sides of the brain. Initial enthusiasm for this method waned, however, after some carefully designed, objective observations showed limited or negligible benefits from the procedure. Certainly the idea is appealing, however, and ultimately such approaches may offer to many patients the opportunity for permanent relief not only from medically untreatable seizures but also from the fetters and known hazards of long-term drug therapy.

Teeth and Gums

Today the potential to end cavities and tooth loss exists. The destruction caused by dental caries can be virtually eliminated by preventive measures, though the search goes on for better understanding of the decay process and for more precise ways of eradicating decay-causing bacteria. Significant progress is being made toward identifying specific bacteria responsible for gum diseases that cause tooth loss, which may lead to better treatment approaches. Meanwhile, new and better materials and methods for restoring teeth and gums affected by disease are being developed.

Current strategies for preventing decay

Cavities, one of the most common afflictions of modern man, are a relatively late stage in the progressively destructive bacterial disease process known as dental caries. The bacteria involved are concentrated on specific tooth sites in the form of an adherent, gelatinous mat known as bacterial plaque. A decay-producing plaque may contain hundreds of millions of bacteria on a single tooth surface. This teeming community of germs uses sugars as its main source of energy. In the process of generating this vital energy by fermentation, bacteria liberate a variety of organic acids, some of them strong enough to dissolve the tooth substance. Thus, in a sense, teeth become victims of their own environmental pollution. Repeated cycles of acid formation in time can cause decay, manifested in the early stages as a white or brown spot beneath the plaque layer; with continued dissolution of tooth mineral, a clinical cavity develops.

Though individual dentists may advocate certain methods over others, the results of a number of recent investigations tend to support a three-pronged strategy for preventing dental decay: (1) increase the resistance to acid attack by multiple use of fluorides, (2) reduce or modify the intake of sugars, and (3) combat the bacterial plaque by brushing and flossing, by using antiseptic mouthwashes, or by immunochemical means (an anticaries vaccine).

There has been recent evidence that the use of fluorides is even more effective in preventing tooth decay than was previously understood. In areas where optimal levels of fluoride have been introduced into the water supply, reductions of 50–60% in new decay can be consistently seen in the teeth of children who have been exposed to fluoride during the time teeth are forming. Continued contact with fluoride in drinking water, which means fluoride is present in the saliva secretions that are in contact with the teeth, is important to provide maximum reductions in decay. People who have lived their entire lives in communities that have fluoridation have been shown to have a 50% decrease in decay of the roots of the teeth (cementum), an area particularly vulnerable to decay when gums recede due to periodontal disease. The benefits of water fluoridation then are not limited to the younger segment of the population.

National Institute of Dental Research

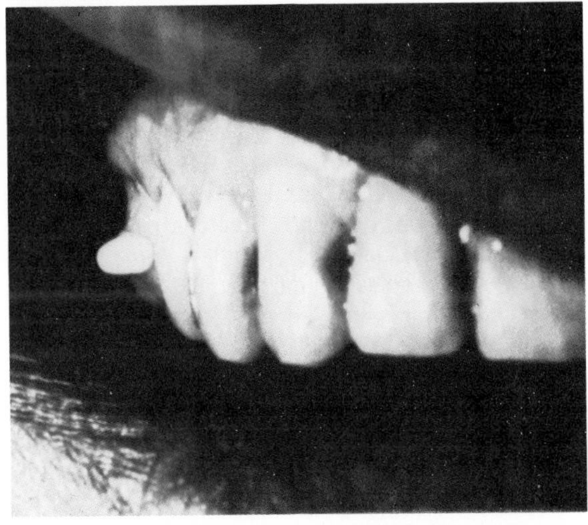

An intraoral system has been developed for the controlled release of fluoride via a small pellet attached to a tooth.

Even in communities that do not have fluoridated water supplies there have been recent reports of 30–50% reduction in decay when comparisons are made with findings 10 and 20 years ago. The wide use of fluoridated dentifrices (toothpastes), the increasing use of fluoridated mouthwashes in school programs, improved oral hygiene practices, and modifications in sugar intake probably have contributed to this major improvement in dental health in the U.S. A number of recent studies attest to the ability of fluoride mouthrinses (0.2% sodium fluoride used weekly or 0.05% sodium fluoride used daily) to reduce new decay significantly even in areas in which fluoride *is* added to the drinking water. This finding of an augmentation effect lends support to the view that decay can be prevented almost completely by multiple use of fluoride.

Other forms of fluoride are also available, such as topical applications given by a dentist or hygienist annually or semiannually. Another way of applying fluoride is with so-called plastic trays (special molds that fit in the mouth and cover the teeth), which can be filled with fluoride gel and applied daily or several times a week at home. Currently under study are "slow release" devices, small plastic capsules that can be cemented onto teeth or orthodontic bands, which deliver optimum levels of fluoride into the mouth over periods of weeks or months. This approach would provide a protective oral environment for patients who are at high risk for decay. This group would include those who have a genetic weakness that makes them prone to decay and those who have a deficit in flow of saliva due to disease or the taking of certain medications which cause dry mouth as a side effect.

Modifying diet to reduce decay unfortunately continues to be difficult to implement because of the widespread use of sugar in most processed foods, the poor eating habits of a large segment of the population—youngsters and adults—including frequent snacking on sugary foods, and the limited availability of sugar substitutes as sweeteners. Xylitol, a nonfermentable sweetener that does not cause bacterial plaque to produce acid, has been widely used in some parts of Europe, but it has been found to produce bladder cancer in some experimental animals. As a result of these findings xylitol is not widely used as a sugar substitute in the U.S. And saccharin, which is used in the U.S., has also been shown to produce cancer in laboratory animals; some studies have found saccharin to be a "weak carcinogen" in humans, but there is a great deal of controversy about the actual risk. Thus, saccharin is not considered an ideal substitute for sugar. Sorbitol and mannitol are low fermentable sweeteners, which are now used in many sodas and confections. Use is limited, however, because of potential digestive upsets when levels above 50 g (about two ounces) a day are consumed by adults and proportionately smaller amounts by children. The search goes on for a safe nonfermentable sugar substitute. In the meantime reducing sugar intake, especially in between-meal snacks, can help reduce decay.

A number of studies have established that thorough brushing and flossing and frequent tooth cleaning in a dental office can have a major impact on decay. The studies indicate, however, that an exquisite level of oral hygiene is required and that there is ongoing need for professional reinforcement of personal oral hygiene techniques. So far there are no safe, effective, chemical agents to use in a dentifrice or mouthwash that can kill or inhibit the decay-causing bacteria in plaque. It is an active area of research but thus far there is no product available.

Perhaps the most dramatic research in the antibacterial area is the attempt to develop an anticaries vaccine. Although there has been steady progress over the last few years it is a very complex area of research and many aspects of the best techniques to use for inoculation remain to be worked out. In addition, since dental decay is not a life-threatening disease, there will have to be proof of complete safety before large-scale vaccinations will be permitted. Effective vaccination techniques have been developed for rats and hamsters. In monkeys, a species with a dental system much closer to that of man, the results of inoculation are not as clear-cut.

Research in humans has been restricted so far to a few volunteers and the results are only preliminary in nature. It appears that the natural immune system in humans can be manipulated by vaccination to give protection against specific bacteria (*Streptococcus mutans*) involved in the initiation of tooth decay. It will be several years, however, before experiments designed to measure the quantitative effect on cavities will be undertaken. In the meantime multiple use of fluorides, a reduction in the amount and frequency of intake of sugar, and daily brushing and flossing to remove bacterial plaque can virtually prevent dental decay.

Periodontal diseases

While dental decay is the major cause of tooth loss below the age of 35, diseases of the gums and supporting tissues of the teeth—the periodontal diseases—result in gradual loosening and loss of teeth in the older segment of the population. The most common periodontal disease is gingivitis, an inflammation of the gums induced by accumulations of bacterial plaque around the teeth. This disease usually first manifests itself at puberty and then tends to exist at a chronic level throughout life with differing degrees of severity.

Gingivitis frequently will progress to periodontitis, an inflammatory disease of the connective tissue (periodontal ligament) and bone that normally support the tooth. As the connective tissue and bone are destroyed by the disease process, a pocket forms between the gum and the tooth. The bacterial plaque grows down along the root and frequently calcifies to form calculus (tartar). The prime irritant in the periodontal diseases is the bacterial plaque. Calcification of this plaque, however, makes self-care more difficult and accentuates the irritation. Plaque removal by proper brushing and flossing and calculus removal and tooth cleaning by the hygienist or dentist are the most effective methods of preventing the progress of periodontal diseases. Gingivitis is completely reversible by proper plaque removal; periodontitis can be effectively arrested. In advanced cases of periodontal disease surgical procedures may be necessary to recontour the tissue and supporting bone to make it possible for patients to maintain their teeth in a healthy state with proper home care.

In a small segment of the teenage and young adult population (1–3%) periodontal disease takes a particularly fulminating form, with marked destruction of the front teeth and first molars. This form of periodontal disease is called localized juvenile periodontitis (LJP), also known as periodontosis.

During the past few years the research emphasis in the periodontal diseases has been bacteriologic; *i.e.,* an attempt to identify the specific bacteria in the periodontal pockets which are responsible for the progression and possibly the initiation of the destructive disease. In chronic periodontitis the most likely candidate appears to be an organism called *Bacteroides asaccharolyticus.* Several groups of researchers have found this bacterium in high numbers in inflamed pockets and have found that its inoculation into germfree rodents resulted in the production of periodontal disease. Other investigators have produced the disease in monkeys and in dogs. Laboratory studies have identified a number of enzymes and noxious products produced by *B. asaccharolyticus* that could account for the destructive periodontal disease.

A second organism seems to be implicated in LJP in young adults. This bacterium, *Actinobacillus actinomycetemcomitans (Y4),* produces a toxic substance, leukotoxin, which can destroy the defensive white blood cells that are mobilized into the gum pocket area to attack the bacteria. Patients with LJP harbor these specific bacteria which can destroy host defensive cells; additionally, the defense cells themselves may be inadequate; *i.e.,* they do not respond fully to the chemical signals responsible for their movement into the zone in the periodontal pocket where the bacteria accumulate. This impairment of the chemical signal is being considered as the basis for a screening test for patients susceptible to periodontal disease.

Identification of specific bacteria in periodontal diseases suggests that prevention and treatment need not be aimed at the total bacterial plaque but can be directed more specifically through the use of appropriate antibacterial agents. Several studies are currently examining the use of antibiotics in the treatment of particularly destructive forms of periodontal disease.

New restorative materials

Although the focus of current dental research is largely preventive in nature, attention is still being given to improvement in materials and techniques for treatment of existing disease. Excellent progress is being made in development of a plastic (composite) filling that blends with tooth color and is strong enough to withstand biting and chewing. Studies over a five-year period have shown that addition of strontium glass filler increases resistance to wear. This type of filling material will be introduced into general use in the near future.

There is ongoing research directed toward improvement in silver amalgam fillings—the major restorative material used by dentists. Modifications of the amalgam formulas, such as addition of small amounts of copper and changes in the techniques for preparing the fillings, have markedly improved clinical performance.

Some patients who require full dentures have lost a considerable portion of the bony support of their jaws to prior disease. Metallic implants are being inserted below the soft tissues in these patients to provide a functional surface to maintain the dentures in place. It is important that the surfaces of these metal implants are microscopically clean so that there is maximum acceptability of these implants by the host tissue. A new process called glow-discharge cleaning sterilizes these devices, which should markedly improve their maintenance in the mouth.

—Irwin D. Mandel, D.D.S.

Trends in Medicine and Health Care

The stereotype of the hospital volunteer is a good-hearted, if shallow-minded, middle-aged lady with time and money to spare who devotes large amounts of both to such innocuous pastimes as pushing a flower cart around otherwise grim wards and throwing elaborate balls to raise funds for the purchase of esoteric laboratory equipment. The image is not altogether wrong—happily for hospitals. Lady Bountiful exists, as does the irrepressible sweet, young candy striper, as do the tireless members of the ladies' auxiliaries who run hospital coffee and gift shops. But these pictures are hopelessly out of date. Today there is an enormous range of volunteer resources and an equally wide array of duties for those who volunteer their time and skills in hospitals.

The changing face of the hospital volunteer

There have been a number of significant developments in U.S. volunteering as a whole, which account for the expansion of the volunteer force and function in hospitals. Among them are the increased numbers of those able and eager to volunteer; a sharp growth in the range of ancillary services offered by health and social welfare organizations, including hospitals; new demands for accountability of institutions to the communities they serve; and the proliferation over the last several decades of self-help movements. Together these phenomena have led to tremendous growth in the number and variety of positions available to prospective volunteers, plus a new sophistication in the motives and abilities of the people willing to fill them.

Of the 37 million people who volunteered in one capacity or another in the U.S. in 1974, the last year for which census figures are available, 15%, or 5.5 million, did so in hospitals. There are approximately 7,000 hospitals in the U.S.; in 1974, 2,907 hospitals reported having a volunteer department to the American Hospital Association (AHA); in 1979 that number rose to 3,424.

More and more, hospitals are finding it necessary and desirable to establish regular volunteer departments—staffed by fully trained, paid personnel who are accountable to hospital administration in the same way as are other department directors. They recruit, train, supervise, and evaluate volunteers. This aspect of professionalism has made it possible to upgrade the number, variety, and responsibility of volunteer positions in hospitals.

Today many volunteers are motivated by more than altruism alone. A volunteer may be looking for a chance to prove his serious career intentions to a professional school. He may want a chance to polish his professional skills or to learn new ones that will

Jean-Claude Lejeune

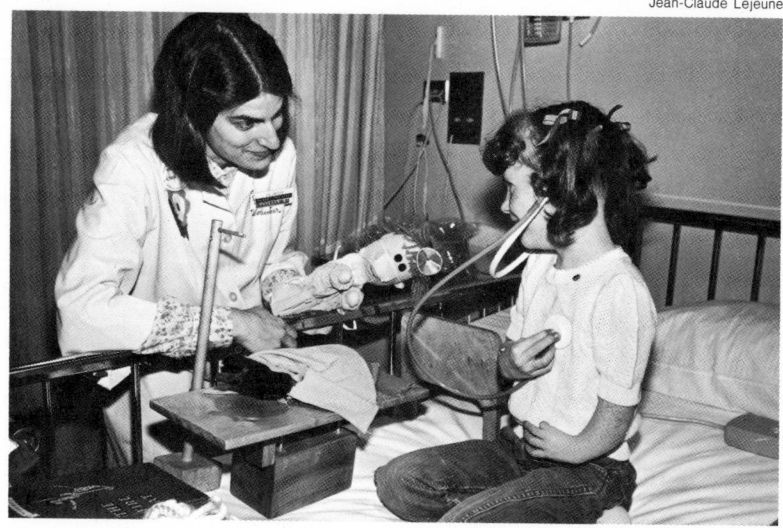

This volunteer puppeteer at Children's Memorial Hospital in Chicago helps ease the fears of a young patient who must have surgery.

translate to the paid work force later; in some cases the right volunteer job can give him the experience he needs on his résumé. (In many states, volunteer experience must, by law, be taken into account on applications for government work.) In Brockton, Mass., Cardinal Cushing General Hospital has a unique preemployment placement program for volunteers who plan to seek full-time employment—not necessarily at the hospital—later. Graduates of this program have found jobs as medical receptionists, sales representatives, office managers, and nursing home workers, after serving "apprenticeships" in the hospital's gift shop, dietary department, and business office.

Volunteers and hospitalized children

Hospitalized children have benefited enormously from the efforts of volunteers. A unique program is that of the Flight Attendant Volunteer Corps. At some 11 hospitals in the U.S., members of this group, made up of about 3,500 stewardesses and stewards from 20 airlines, stage a multimedia program called "Let's Take a Trip" for pediatric patients. Youngsters can vicariously experience journeys to colorful locales all over the world.

A number of hospitals have volunteer puppet therapy programs that prepare youngsters for surgery with the aid of hand puppets. These smallest patients use the puppets to "rehearse" the pre- and postoperative procedures they will be undergoing. Surgeons report that children who have had their questions answered and their fears calmed by the volunteer puppeteers are more at ease, more cooperative, and even more responsive to anesthesia.

Since 1966, patients at the Children's Memorial Hospital in Chicago—often as lonely as they are ill—have been looking forward to Saturday mornings when sailors from Illinois's Naval Training Center at Great Lakes Naval Base—often just as lonely—visit. They come to talk, to play, to help feed, to throw parties—in general to make things a little less lonely.

Youngsters at Children's Specialized Hospital in Mountainside, N.J., depend greatly on volunteers to help them during hydrotherapy treatments for cerebral palsy and various physical handicaps. Housewives, businessmen, retirees—volunteers all—work on a one-to-one basis, under the supervision of a hydrotherapist, to help children learn to move their injured muscles in the water so that later they will move more easily out of it. At The Hospital of the University of Pennsylvania in Philadelphia, volunteers teach handicapped children to ride horses, which increases their confidence and muscular control.

Failure-to-thrive infants at Doernbecher Memorial Hospital for Children in Portland, Ore., are bathed, fed, stimulated, and rocked by volunteers. Without this intensive "mothering," which fosters conditions more favorable for growth, many of the infants would die. At M. D. Anderson Hospital and Tumor Institute in Houston, Texas, volunteers sell holiday greeting cards designed by young cancer patients; the money earned is used to enrich the learning and play environment in the pediatric unit.

Throughout the country, in fact, pediatric wards are becoming more cheerful, stimulating places owing in large part to the number of volunteers who spend time there doing everything from teaching, cooking, reading, singing, drawing, and play therapy to "mothering" and "fathering" in what are most often called "child life" programs. None of these functions is essential to the medical treatment of illness or injury, but few health care professionals would deny that the extra dimension of care offered by volunteers can make an enormous difference in the quality and possibly even the rate of recovery made by hospitalized youngsters.

Children receiving outpatient psychotherapy at Sinai Hospital of Baltimore, Md., frequently have academic deficiencies that either result from or give rise to their emotional problems. A tutorial project offers prolonged, one-to-one tutoring by volunteer teachers to supplement the psychiatric process.

Volunteering by and for the elderly

The elderly have their own sets of problems unique to their age and physical condition. Volunteers have responded by helping older hospitalized patients fill out their complicated Medicare forms (Riverside Hospital, Toledo, Ohio); they inspect and compile reports on nursing homes to aid families who are seeking to place an elderly relative in a good facility (United Hospital Fund of New York); and they deliver hot meals to the homebound (Good Samaritan Medical Center, Zanesville, Ohio). They man Tele-Care phone lines—a system set up for solitary elderly community residents, who call Tele-Care every weekday to "check in." Volunteers (all of whom are themselves over 70) can then take prompt action if someone who is supposed to call does not (Sparks Regional Medical Center, Fort Smith, Ark.).

An experimental project aimed at the innovative utilization of older persons as volunteers was set up by the Hospital Research and Educational Trust and funded by the Edna McConnell Clark Foundation. Six hospitals have developed programs staffed exclusively by older volunteers—the majority of them retired professional persons—who have been trained to handle a broad range of duties. These include screening residents in the community for hypertension, diabetes, and cancer (South Nassau Communities Hospital, Oceanside, N.Y.); conducting educational seminars on preretirement planning and providing counseling for bereaved members of the community (Mount Sinai Hospital, Minneapolis, Minn.); extending the services of the Regional Poison Center at the Cardinal Glennon Memorial Hospital for Children in St. Louis, Mo., through research and educational presentations to the community; and working as cancer research assistants and pararesearchers at M. D. Anderson Hospital and Tumor Institute.

Greater responsibility and acceptance

One of the major differences between the kind of roles volunteers are taking on today and the more traditional roles that volunteers played from the earliest days of hospital care in the U.S. is the degree of specialization. Pushing a flower cart, distributing reading materials, or selling in a gift shop requires little more than a willingness to serve and the ability to interact with people comfortably. But the volunteer department that establishes a victim advocate program to support victims of sexual assault during their hospital stay (as at Denver [Colo.] General Hospital) or the auxiliary that sets up a glaucoma alert program to regularly test community residents for that eye disease (as at Mercy Medical Center in Oshkosh, Wis.) must also be prepared to do highly selective recruiting, arrange for sophisticated training, establish rigorous standards for on-the-job performance, provide for formal means of feedback and evaluation and, if necessary, remove a volunteer from duty.

There has been a parallel move by physicians, long skeptical of any nonprofessional involvement in the medical arena, toward a willingness to trust volunteers and to cooperate actively in their programs. Both trends—professionalism of volunteers and acceptance by physicians—have been spurred by the growing financial burdens hospitals have had to shoulder: there is not enough money to allow for nonessential services in most institutions without the use of volunteers.

Thus, volunteers at University Hospital, Tucson, Ariz., are assisting physicians in the obstetrics-

The Hospital of the University of Pennsylvania

At The Hospital of the University of Pennsylvania, volunteers teach handicapped children to ride horses.

Brokaw Hospital, Normal, Illinois

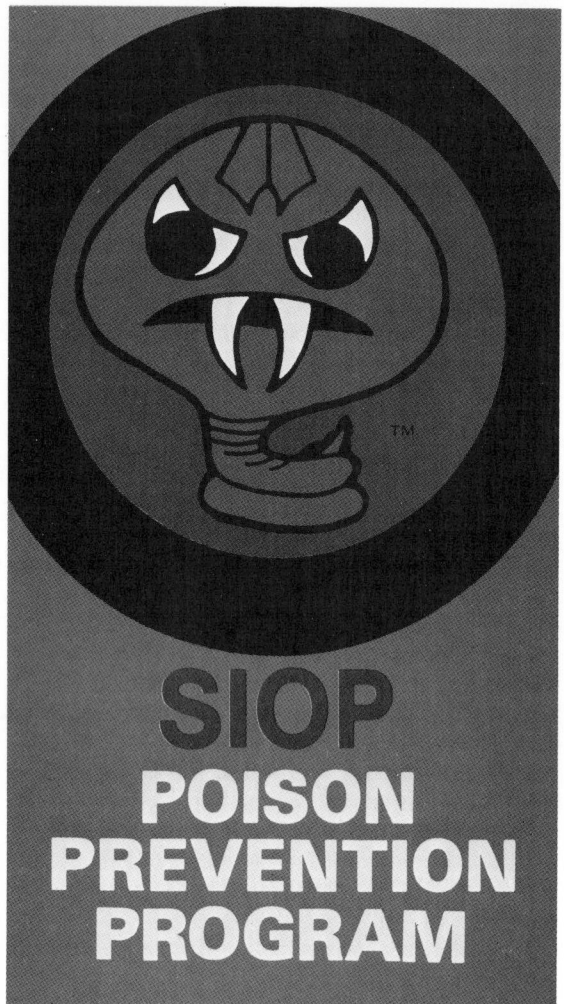

A hospital auxiliary has helped innovate a poison prevention program for Normal, Ill. Snake stickers are put on dangerous substances in the home; when parents say "NO! SIOP!" (poison backwards) children know to stay away.

gynecology service of the outpatient clinic, weighing patients, taking blood pressures, and preparing equipment for Pap smears. The same group of volunteers teaches breast self-examination to women patients. At the Burke Rehabilitation Center in White Plains, N.Y., volunteers provide horticultural therapy for the long-term disabled in a greenhouse paid for by the center's auxiliary. For some patients, this is merely a welcome diversion; for others, it is a prescribed part of their treatment regimen to restore use of their arms and to help regain movement.

At Sinai Hospital of Baltimore, Md., a "Widowed Persons Service" matches up recently bereaved women with trained volunteers who have been widowed at least a year. The purpose, of course, is to provide empathic support during their adjustment to their loss, which usually takes six to eight months. At Worcester Hahnemann Hospital, in Worcester, Mass., counselors, each with a caseload of up to 20 new mothers, offer daily support and assistance to those who choose to breast-feed a first baby. The counselors also hold classes for expectant and nursing mothers.

At Prairie View Mental Health Center in Newton, Kan., volunteers participate in psychodrama—a cathartic component of therapy in which patients act out their conflicts. In Tuscaloosa, Ala., mental patients attend volunteer-run classes on community resources and stress.

As might be expected, volunteer programs in large cities sometimes are plagued by a want of community spirit, compounded by the public's fears of interacting with strangers. But two more examples, drawn from a roster of hundreds, illustrate the imaginative range of volunteer manpower and services currently in force in U.S. hospitals—both set at The Jamaica Hospital in Queens, N.Y.

In the first program, student hairdressers training at the William H. Maxwell Vocational High School in Brooklyn, N.Y., receive class credit for washing, cutting, and setting hair for hospitalized patients. A fresh hairdo is hardly essential, but as anyone who has been hospitalized for more than a few days will attest, this is a very welcome service, and one that does wonders for the morale of patients.

In the second program, first-time juvenile offenders who have committed nonviolent crimes work in Jamaica Hospital's coffee shop, its central supply, building services, and receiving offices, as well as on patient wards. The Queens, N.Y., district attorney offers youths the opportunity to do volunteer work in lieu of serving a sentence. Many of the program participants (whose records are cleared after six months of service without rearrest) have since been employed by the hospital.

Beyond the hospital walls

Hospital auxiliaries are the dues-paying membership organizations that were once the only means of volunteer service to a hospital. In 1979, 4,392 hospitals reported having auxiliaries to the AHA. Today many hospital auxiliaries, whose traditional roles have been taken over by volunteer departments, have increasingly moved beyond the hospital walls in providing voluntary services.

Numerous auxiliaries, working in concert with schools, now offer programs to students to teach them what they, as potential patients, can expect of their hospital. These classes, frequently involving tours of the hospital, slide shows, demonstration of equipment, vocabulary lists, and so forth, are designed to lessen children's fears about hospitalization.

Another example of an innovative child-oriented volunteer service carried out at least in part by a hospital auxiliary is the "No Siop" poison prevention program of Brokaw Hospital in Normal, Ill., which has reduced accidental poisonings of children in the surrounding county by 60%. No Siop (poison spelled backward) uses a special green fanged snake; the symbol is featured on warning labels and educational materials distributed to all 45,000 families in the area as well as to all schools. (This program is based on the finding that the traditional skull-and-crossbones is not sufficiently threatening to small children to serve as a warning.)

The child care centers at Los Angeles County–University of Southern California Medical Center were set up to supervise and entertain the children of adult outpatients who cannot afford babysitters. Thanks to an immunization project developed by the Iroquois Memorial Hospital Auxiliary in Watseka, Ill., every school yard in the surrounding county now boasts a hopscotch grid bearing the names of seven diseases against which all children should be immunized—diphtheria, tetanus, whooping cough, polio, measles, German measles, and mumps.

A program sponsored by the Wisconsin Hospital Association of Auxiliaries advises parents about the need for car safety restraints for infants and makes available lists of models that meet crash-testing standards. (Some 1,000 infants under the age of four die each year in automobile accidents, the leading cause of accidental deaths in childhood; many more are seriously injured, and most are found to have been unrestrained by any sort of car seat.)

Screening communities for various diseases and providing referrals for persons found to be at risk are tasks particularly well-suited to the organizational abilities of auxiliaries, which are able to enlist support from their hospitals as well as from other health care agencies in their communities. A one-day-a-week blood pressure screening clinic is run by the auxiliary of Roseville Community Hospital in California. The auxiliary of North Arundel Hospital in Glen Burnie, Md., spent a year organizing a one-day community health fair, which offered 11 screening tests; films on nutrition, disease detection, and preventive medicine; extensive information about common diseases; and instruction in cardiopulmonary resuscitation and breast self-examination. Over 1,000 residents benefited from the fair, which cost only $274 to stage.

In New Jersey, individual local auxiliaries are cosponsors with the New Jersey Association of Hospital Auxiliaries of a multimedia "careers in health" mobile van, which travels around the state to health fairs, libraries, and schools. Young people can learn about a complete spectrum of possible health-field pursuits: physical and occupational therapies, laboratory and radiological work, medicine and surgery, and hospital business administration.

In many states auxiliaries are moving into legislative action, in support of government policies that benefit health care providers and against those pieces of legislation that would impose further restrictions on hospitals. A quite sophisticated "legislative alert network" was set up by the committee on hospital auxiliaries of the Hospital Association of New York state. The system is able to mobilize 100,000 auxilians to act quickly and in concert on legislative items. The impact of many thousands of postcards, telegrams, and letters about a key issue, received by members of the state legislature, is hardly negligible.

Increasing numbers of auxilians are now being elected to serve on their hospitals' boards of directors. Their special knowledge and viewpoint and their considerable influence within the community are thus being recognized. This kind of leadership role, for which many auxiliaries conscientiously train their members, is no longer an impractical ambition for the prospective volunteer of any age or socioeconomic group.

The field of hospital volunteering has kept pace with the rapid growth of health care in the U.S., managing to expand its own horizons to take in as many kinds of people as are willing and able to serve and as many kinds of programs as are called for by concerned communities. While no volunteer may perform any duty medically essential to patient care, it is no exaggeration to say that if all volunteers were to cease work at hospitals for even one day, their absence would stagger the health care system.

—Brandy Rommel

World Medical News

Among major medical accomplishments recently attained through international cooperation are: a five-year world health checkup, inauguration of a decade-long campaign for clean water and sanitation, recognition for the world's 450 million disabled, and continued progress toward a vaccine for leprosy. Results of a survey described as the largest social service research project ever launched indicate that fertility rates around the world are in sharp decline. Controversy over the use and misuse of infant formula in the third world has gone another round as the World Health Organization approved a code calling on countries to restrict sales and advertising of breast-milk substitutes.

World health: present and future

"Overcast skies, with partial clearing by the year 2000" summarizes the 20-year outlook put forward in the World Health Organization's (WHO's) *Sixth Report on the World Health Situation.* Issued in 1980 and based on a study of the years 1973 to 1977, the two-volume document concludes that poverty and underdevelopment, not the lack of medical technology, continue to lie at the root of most serious health problems. Other than the worldwide eradication of smallpox, the less developed nations, which are home to three of every

WHO Photo/J. Mohr

A World Health Organization immunization team at work administering vaccinations against tuberculosis to children in Uganda, where the disease is widespread.

four persons on the Earth, have experienced "little or no progress" in the reduction of basic infectious, respiratory, and parasitic diseases, although in most instances these afflictions could be "dramatically reduced at relatively modest cost."

A major resurgence of malaria in many Asian, African, and Latin-American countries is partly the result of the growing resistance of parasite-carrying mosquitoes to insecticides (particularly in instances of misuse and overuse) and in some cases of the inability or unwillingness of national governments to pay for these insecticides. Cost again was cited as a factor limiting the implementation of programs that depend on antimalarial drugs. Moreover, an effective vaccine against the disease, which afflicts more than 200 million persons worldwide, may still be ten years away. Other parasitic diseases such as schistosomiasis, filariasis, and onchocerciasis, all of which are caused by infection with worms, continue to kill and debilitate hundreds of millions of victims in the third world.

In the late 1970s less than 10% of children in less developed countries were immunized against six major infectious diseases—tuberculosis, diphtheria, whooping cough, tetanus, measles, and polio—that have been virtually conquered in the developed nations at relatively small expense. It is estimated that each year these diseases kill some five million children under age five and disable a like number. A major project for the 1980s, organized by WHO, is to provide immunization for all the world's children against all six diseases, at a cost of about $3 per child for a set of six vaccinations.

The *Sixth Report* quoted an estimate of at least 400 million for the undernourished of the world, many of whom suffer from specific nutritional deficiencies. Prominent in much of the third world are deficiencies of vitamin A, iodine, and iron and folic acid—all simple to cure in principle. Yet they have remained intractable owing to an approach toward improving medical care that has emphasized big hospitals and high technology rather than more basic prevention programs and mass screening, treatment, and follow-up strategies. Manifested in a condition called xerophthalmia, severe vitamin A deficiency blinds 100,000 young children annually in many countries of Africa, southern Asia, the Middle East, and Latin America. Iodine deficiency can lead to endemic goiter, an often debilitating swelling of the thyroid gland, and to cretinism, a combination of mental retardation, neurological defects, and dwarfism that follows iodine deficiency in the fetus and the newborn. Iodine deficiency is widespread in African, Asian, and Latin-American countries; in some mountainous regions the incidence of goiter in a community approaches 100%. Recent studies in Zaire that followed the children of women receiving long-term iodine supplements uncovered evidence of endemic subclinical thyroid problems that probably affect a much larger share of newborns in a population than detectable cases alone would indicate. Nutritional anemia from deficiencies of iron and the B vitamin folic acid appears in pregnant and nursing women and young children not only in the third world but in the industrialized countries as well.

Another kind of malnutrition, dubbed "malnutrition of affluence" in the report, was also cited as a major problem in the developed countries, particularly the U.S. and Western Europe. Overconsumption of calories and of "junk" and convenience foods takes its toll in obesity, cardiovascular disease, diabetes mellitus, and tooth decay.

Although the first priority for many less developed countries will continue to be the control of infectious and parasitic diseases, the report indicated that "health problems now typical in the developed countries—such as cancer, cardiovascular diseases, mental health and accidents—may well become of major concern to the developing countries as they move along the path of socioeconomic development." Ironically, much of the cardiovascular disease currently experienced in the third world has little to do with development but is instead a complication of rheumatic fever caused by infection with streptococcus bacteria. Because strep infection can be cured with antibiotics before it does damage to the valves of the heart, this serious problem is preventable. Yet in many parts of the world the task of identifying the disease, administering the cure, and following up with prophylactic doses of antibiotic is extremely difficult.

In countries like China where headway is being made against the basic health problems of the poor, cancer is becoming a major cause of illness and death. The WHO report pointed out that cancer prevention will not be simple. One difficulty is that even after a risk factor has been identified, deeply rooted cultural habits may impede its elimination. The report singled out smoking for special attention. In countries where tobacco use is well established, it has been shown to raise the risk of cancer of the lungs, throat, and bladder, as well as the probability of bronchitis, emphysema, and heart disease. "Although the developing countries have not yet had time to experience the grim increase in smoking-related mortality, . . . they must expect it unless they halt and reverse the increase in cigarette consumption. In many less developed countries, the epidemic of smoking-related diseases is already of such magnitude as to rival even infectious diseases or malnutrition as a public health problem."

The good news in the report took the form of long-term projections for the years ahead, contingent on changes in the political climate and socioeconomic setting. Perhaps the most encouraging prediction was of a significant narrowing of the gap in life expectancy at birth between the developed and less developed countries by the end of the 20th century. In 1975 life expectancy at birth for the developed and less developed nations was 72 and 55 years, a difference of 17 years. By the year 2000 these figures will be at least 75 and 65. Nonetheless, among the less developed countries there is still a range of ten years in life expectancy; thus some of these countries will have a longer way to go than others to catch up.

With the rise in life expectancy in the third world will come an increase in the numbers of elderly. It is estimated that by the end of the 20th century seven out of ten citizens of these countries will reach age 65, compared with four or five out of ten in the late 1970s. One of three will reach 80, compared with one out of seven in 1975. For the less developed countries, the message in these figures is that planning for social services for the elderly can no longer be considered a project for the distant future.

Clean water and sanitation for all

It was noted in WHO's *Sixth Report* that fulfillment of its optimistic forecast for improved world health would depend in part on national and international efforts to achieve the goals set forth for the UN International Drinking-Water Supply and Sanitation Decade, 1981–1990. This program, inaugurated in late 1980, came in response to studies in 1975 that showed that more than one billion people in the world lacked adequate sanitation and safe water to drink. In rural areas of the third world only 22% had access to safe water and only 15% possessed disposal facilities for human excrement. According to a WHO estimate 25 million persons die annually from diseases—many of them diarrheal—caused by dirty or insufficient water or poor sanitation. And of a billion cases of diarrhea, more than six million result in death for children of less developed countries.

The program's organizing groups recognized that in order to achieve its stated aim of clean water and sanitation for all by 1990 the program must depend not only on external and internal financial commitments but also on initiatives taken by individual nations. Some observers, however, have expressed doubt that complete success for the program can be achieved even with the best of efforts. Far from the least of formidable hurdles to be overcome is the high cost, which one estimate places at more than $600 billion if each urban home receives its own water tap and sewage connection and each rural home is served by a community hand pump and its own latrine. Strongly affecting cost are the technology chosen and the willingness of sanitary planners to consider appropriate alternatives to high-cost Western technologies like sewer networks and treatment plants, which per household cost more than color television sets. Good, cheap sanitary facilities—for example, improved pit latrines—coupled with health education could be as effective in reducing disease incidence as flush toilets and sewers, and at much less cost. Using such strategies the expense of the UN program might be halved, to $300 billion or less.

One unavoidable problem accompanying installation of water and sanitation systems is their upkeep, an obligation that has not been well met by third world governments in the past. Although it has been suggested that the communities themselves could be trained to maintain their own systems, other than in Communist nations there are few examples of success in organizing and mobilizing community participation.

Yet another problem to be overcome is the difficulty of coupling clean-water and sanitation efforts to primary health care programs. As WHO Director-General Halfdan Mahler admitted, "You can have water supply and sanitation programs without a very striking impact on health." New research on tropical hygiene has indicated that so-called waterborne diarrheal infections like bacterial dysentery are also "water-washed" diseases in that they are spread not only by dirty water but also by contaminated and poorly washed hands, food, and cooking utensils. In such cases simply switching from surface water to cleaner well water will not lower disease incidence significantly. A World Bank survey reported finding a direct relation between diarrheal infections and distance of the water supply from the household, with lowest incidence for households whose water supply is in the house. Unfortunately, the

WHO Photo/P. Almasy

Since one billion people in the world lack adequate sanitation and safe water to drink and millions die annually from waterborne infections, the UN has launched a program to provide clean water for all by 1990. Efforts must be directed at proper use of clean water not just for drinking but also for bathing, cooking, and washing utensils.

need for most governments to choose centralized community water supplies over piped water will mean increasing the risk of contaminating the water during collection, transport, and storage. Studies have also shown that without education in the proper use of clean water individuals may well use it only for drinking and continue to bathe, cook, and wash utensils in water from their traditional contaminated supplies.

Help for the world's disabled

The United Nations declared 1981 the International Year of Disabled Persons (IYDP) in order to call to world attention a problem that affects more than one person in ten. Disabilities can arise from congenital defects; trauma experienced around the time of birth; accidents, wars, and disasters; physical and mental illness; malnutrition; and drug abuse. Their most common forms are physical impairment, sensory impairment, chronic illness, and mental retardation, and they take their greatest toll in the less developed countries, where preventive and rehabilitative programs are in shortest supply. Owing to world population growth, increased life expectancy, industrialization and urbanization, and increased use of the automobile, the ranks of the disabled continue to swell.

It is recognized that no "international year" alone can revolutionize thinking with regard to the disabled. Nevertheless, by raising mass awareness of their plight such a program can trigger the first efforts to counter what Zala N'Kanza, executive secretary of IYDP, described as "social neglect." IYDP's five principal objectives were: to help disabled persons adjust physically and psychologically to society; to encourage governments and international organizations to give the disabled assistance, training, care, and opportunities for work; to encourage study and research aimed at helping disabled persons participate in daily life—for example, by improving their access to public buildings and transportation systems; to educate the public regarding the rights of the disabled to "full participation and equality," the theme of IYDP; and to promote effective measures for disability prevention and for rehabilitation of the disabled.

One step crucial to the success of the program is to supply governments with all available information on recognizing, preventing, and treating disabilities. The *International Classification of Impairments, Disabilities and Handicaps,* published by WHO in 1980, approaches classification of a category of public health issues from a fresh viewpoint in that it takes into account the individual in the context of society. The publication identifies more than 200 types of disabling conditions and distinguishes among three separate but intimately linked problems: impairment, defined as a loss of physical, psychological, or anatomical structure or function; disability, defined as a restriction or lack of ability—caused by an impairment—to perform an activity in a normal manner; and handicap, defined as a disadvantage resulting from an impairment or disability that prevents an individual from filling a normal role. In this light, disabilities and handicaps are seen to be relationships between an individual and his environment and take into account age, sex, marital status, and social and cultural factors. Once the three problems are distinguishable, a kind of hierarchy becomes clear: the physical causes of many impairments need not be disabling provided they are dealt with in time, and disabilities need not be handicaps if help for rehabilitation exists within the community.

To promote community-based rehabilitation WHO, in cooperation with other UN organizations and member nations, has issued *Training the Disabled in the Community,* a manual for use in the less developed countries. The publication comes in response to a great need for suitable instructional materials; it covers the training of disabled persons and their families and includes guides for teachers, community leaders, and planners and policymakers. In late 1980 an experimental version of the manual began field-testing in Africa, Asia, and Latin America. A final version was expected to appear in 1982.

Declining fertility

Results of a massive fertility study begun in 1972, surveying 400,000 women in 20 developed and 41 less developed countries, indicate that the world population explosion is indeed easing and that fertility rates in both the third world and the industrialized nations have fallen significantly. According to Leon Tabah, director of the Population Division of the UN Department of Economic and Social Affairs, "The decline is well established, affects an important part of the world's population and is rapid." Nevertheless, because of the present abundance of young people resulting from comparatively high fertility rates in the recent past, population figures for most countries will continue to climb—to a total of six billion by the year 2000, a 50% increase over the 1978 figure. UN projections show that the world may not achieve "zero growth" until well into the last half of the 21st century, when the total population is expected to have swollen to 11 billion.

The study, titled the World Fertility Survey, was conducted by the International Statistical Institute with the support of the UN and national governments. Given among its reasons for the drop in fertility were a growing desire among Asian and Latin-American families to have fewer children; the spreading use of contraceptives worldwide; a weakening of social and religious restrictions against birth control; and continuing modernization, which is producing a new generation of better educated youth with different attitudes toward work, self-fulfillment, marriage, and children. In addition, in a reversal of previous policies, more third world governments are responding to population pressures and to increasing dissatisfaction of their citizens with large family size by supporting family-planning programs.

For Europe the alarming news from the study is that fertility rates there have plummeted so sharply that they are below replacement levels, the levels needed to maintain present populations. Experts forecast that such a trend could have serious economic and industrial consequences, including labor shortages and higher taxes on the diminished working population to support the retired. Milos Macura, project director of the survey, stated that for Europe, "The whole system which has traditionally worked in favor of fertility has collapsed. The Industrial Revolution, individualism, consumerism —in both Western and Eastern Europe and regardless of the political system of government—are sweeping away traditional pressures that favored the family." In Western Europe, West Germany showed the deepest drop, with a total fertility rate (the number of children each woman would have in her lifetime if current fertility rates remained constant) of 1.4 births per woman, compared with a figure of 2.2 needed to hold the population steady. Other Western European nations whose fertility rates were found to be below replacement levels include Austria, Belgium, Great Britain, Denmark, Finland, France, Italy, The Netherlands, Norway, Sweden, and Switzerland. East Germany also fell below its replacement level with 1.8 births per woman, whereas Czechoslovakia, Hungary, Poland, and Romania were at or near their replacement levels.

In the U.S. the fertility rate fell from its high of 3.5 births per woman in the late 1950s to 1.8 in the 1970s. Despite the decline, the country's previously high rate will ensure a doubling of its 227 million population in less than a century.

Code for infant-formula makers

In May 1981 WHO's member nations voted by an overwhelming majority in favor of a voluntary, international code to outlaw advertising and restrict marketing of infant formula. The vote—118 to 1, with 3 abstentions —came as the latest round in a decade-long controversy that has pitted health professionals and activist groups who view infant formulas as a serious detriment to health in the third world against the baby-food industry, made up largely of Western and Japanese companies. The U.S. stood alone among nations in voting against the code.

Experts on both sides of the debate readily concur with already strong and still growing documentation of the superiority of human milk over artificial substitutes. One reason for its edge over its competitors is that not enough is known about breast milk to duplicate all of its benefits. Another is that the balance of its components continually changes—from the birth of the infant to at least a month later—to meet the infant's changing developmental needs. In addition to fats, milk sugar (lactose), minerals, and an excellent balance of essential amino acids, human milk contains antibodies and living white blood cells from the mother that help protect the infant from infectious disease until its own immune mechanism becomes more fully developed. It also carries substances that enable the body to inhibit bacterial growth, factors that increase intestinal absorption of certain nutrients, and a variety of trace elements that may all prove to have nutritional roles.

Infant-formula critics emphasize the particular importance of these advantages to infants in less developed countries where infectious and respiratory diseases have yet to be brought under control. In addition, some claim that as many as a million third world infants die each year from illnesses associated with the misuse of formulas. Cited are instances in which mothers have mixed powdered formula with contaminated water or reduced the nutritional value of the mix by overdiluting it to cut costs or because they could not read or follow the printed directions. The infant-formula industry has maintained that no convincing evidence exists that the use of formula either discourages breast-feeding or contributes to infant mortality.

Taking as its purpose the "protection and promotion of breast-feeding," the WHO code urges countries to ban advertising of breast-milk substitutes, to shield expectant mothers from salespersons and the distribution of free samples, and to reduce the appeal of product labels. At the same time, the code recognizes a legitimate market for formulas; for example, in cases in which the mother's milk contains health-threatening substances like therapeutic drugs, allergically induced antibodies, or disease organisms. That the code appears to apply to all countries, not just the third world, formed the basis for its rejection by the U.S. government, whose official position has been that approval of the code might make the U.S. morally obligated to pass laws that conflict with existing antitrust legislation and the constitutional guarantee of free speech. The U.S. also expressed concern at the prospect of an agency of the UN becoming involved in the regulation of economic activity and international trade. Some opponents of the U.S. stand considered it simply a cheap concession to the baby-food lobby in that country.

Millions of third world infants allegedly have died from illnesses associated with the misuse of infant formulas. The importance of breast-feeding in less developed nations cannot be overemphasized.

Baldev—Sygma

Vaccine for leprosy

In 1982 controlled trials using human subjects were expected to begin for a new vaccine for leprosy, a serious health problem that affects an estimated 10 million to 15 million people, primarily in tropical and subtropical countries. Although drugs exist that can arrest this potentially blinding and disfiguring bacterial infection, therapy takes years and in some cases is not effective. A vaccine to prevent leprosy has been slow in coming because of the difficulty in finding a suitable medium in which to culture the causative organism, *Mycobacterium leprae,* for vaccine research. In 1971 U.S. investigators discovered that *M. leprae* would grow in the common nine-banded armadillo, producing a disease model that resembled lepromatous leprosy, the more severe form of the disease in humans; in 1974 WHO launched its leprosy vaccine program, which brought research groups into an international network. During the past few years investigators in several countries, both with and without economic support from WHO, have been moving toward a vaccine for humans.

In the course of their work leprosy researchers succeeded in completely separating large numbers of the bacterium from its host tissue, which if included in a vaccine for humans might cause undesirable immune reactions. Injections of the purified, killed bacterium into mice and armadillos demonstrated a much more powerful immunizing effect than was first expected. As of mid-1981, versions of the vaccine had been given to small numbers of humans with promising results, but decisions from WHO on how and where controlled clinical trials would take place were not expected until later in the year. Whereas such trials commonly involve a few thousand subjects, leprosy's low incidence and long incubation time—as much as ten years—eventually may require the use of hundreds of thousands of volunteers, divided into vaccinated and control groups and followed for as long as a decade. If all goes well a leprosy vaccine could be available for general use by the end of the century.

New immunological tests also have been developed to help evaluate the ability of the antileprosy vaccine to induce protective immunity. It is possible that in the future these tests could be adapted for use in screening persons who are suspected to be incubating the disease.

Some observers have wondered if enough armadillos are available or can be bred to protect all persons at risk for the disease—as much as half the world population. According to optimistic calculations the liver and spleen from one armadillo infected for three years yield about 4,000 doses of vaccine. A human population of two billion thus would require a half million animals; an estimated ten million armadillos live in the southern U.S. alone.

—Charles M. Cegielski

Health Education Units

The following articles on important medical topics and health-related concerns are meant to be instructive and practical. It is largely through general health education that individuals can maintain and enhance their physical well-being. While the units emphasize the activation of the layperson's sense of responsibility for his or her own health, their purpose is to inform, not to prescribe.

Contributors

Edward L. Applebaum, M.D.
Sinus Problems
Professor and Head, Department of Otolaryngology, Abraham Lincoln School of Medicine, University of Illinois, Chicago

Ronald Arky, M.D.
Hypoglycemia
Chief of Medicine, Mount Auburn Hospital; Professor of Medicine, Harvard Medical School at Mount Auburn Hospital, Cambridge, Mass.

L. Fred Ayvazian, M.D.
Diagnosing Respiratory Diseases
Chief, Pulmonary Section, Veterans Administration Medical Center, East Orange, N.J.; Professor of Medicine, College of Medicine and Dentistry, New Jersey Medical School, Newark; Professor of Clinical Medicine, New York University School of Medicine, New York City

Charles E. Driscoll, M.D.
Hemorrhoids; Sex Education for Children (in part)
Assistant Professor, Department of Family Practice, College of Medicine, University of Iowa, Iowa City

Jacquelyn S. Driscoll, R.N.
Sex Education for Children (in part)
Iowa City, Iowa

Alvin N. Eden, M.D.
Teething; Reye's Syndrome; Lead Poisoning
Author of child care books and pediatric columnist; Director of Pediatrics, Wyckoff Heights Hospital, Brooklyn, N.Y.; Associate Clinical Professor of Pediatrics, New York University School of Medicine, New York City

Nancy Kennedy, R.D.
Low-Sodium Diets
Therapeutic Dietitian, William Beaumont Hospital, Troy, Mich.; Chairman, Michigan Heart Association Nutrition Committee

Phyllis Klass
Genetic Counseling
Assistant Professor of Genetics in Pediatrics and Obstetrics-Gynecology and Director, Genetic Counseling Program, The New York Hospital-Cornell University Medical Center, New York City

Lynne Lamberg
Ingredients in Cosmetics; Insect Stings; Removing Unwanted Hair
Free-lance medical writer, Baltimore, Md.

Edward R. Leist, Pharm.D.
Photosensitivity Reactions: Drugs and Sunburn; Antianxiety Drugs
Clinical Coordinator, Department of Pharmacy, Norton Children's Hospitals, Louisville, Ky.

Robert E. Rakel, M.D.
Fatigue
Professor and Head, Department of Family Practice, College of Medicine, University of Iowa, Iowa City

Title cartoons by John Everds

Contents

Health Education Unit 1

Photosensitivity Reactions: Drugs and Sunburn

Some drugs and chemicals render the skin abnormally sensitive to certain wavelengths of light, a reaction called photosensitization. Thus, when an individual takes a photosensitizing drug such as tetracycline and is exposed to sufficient sunlight, a sunburnlike photosensitivity reaction frequently results.

Phototoxic reactions usually occur after the first exposure to the drug and sunlight and have the appearance of an exaggerated sunburn. However, the individual does not have to be in the sun for a prolonged period for the reaction to occur, and the response of the skin is different from that seen in a normal sunburn. In a phototoxic reaction, there is a rapid onset of a burning sensation of the exposed skin, followed by redness and swelling. In two to six hours, hives may appear, and at 24 hours, the redness and tenderness associated with sunburn begins. The reaction resolves over the next two to four days, resulting in hyperpigmentation of the skin and peeling. Severe reactions may have a rapid course and result in scarring.

The reaction occurs when the photosensitizing drug absorbs light. Intense heat results, damaging the cells of the skin. The severity of the reaction depends on the concentration of the drug present in the body and the amount of ultraviolet radiation from the sun that is absorbed. Phototoxic reactions rarely occur in dark-skinned or black persons due to the increased ability of their skin to filter out damaging radiation.

Photoallergic reactions affect all races but are less commonly seen than phototoxic reactions. Photoallergy requires prior exposure to the photosensitizing drug for the reaction to take place; this is due to the immunologic basis of the reaction. On first exposure to the drug and sunlight, an individual develops antibodies, and upon repeated exposure the photoallergic reaction occurs. An eczemalike skin eruption is characteristic and even unexposed areas may flare up.

The management of photosensitivity reactions is generally aimed at preventing the reaction from occurring and at ameliorating the effects. When a drug that has the potential for producing a phototoxic reaction has been prescribed, there are certain steps an individual can take to reduce the risk of skin reactions.

First, exposure to ultraviolet radiation should be minimized. The main sources of ultraviolet radiation are direct sunlight, particularly between 10:00 AM and 2:00 PM, and reflected sunlight from white sand beaches, water, snow, or concrete. Fluorescent light sources also emit ultraviolet radiation but cause reactions only in those who are exquisitely sensitive. In addition to the time of the day, the intensity of solar radiation is also influenced by such variables as the season of the year and the amount of cloud cover, spring and summer being times of more intense radiation. Clouds are poor ultraviolet filters and, unless they are very dense, offer inadequate protection from the sun.

Proper clothing minimizes exposure of the skin to ultraviolet radiation. Dark, closely woven fabrics offer the most protection. White clothes when wet will transmit large amounts of ultraviolet radiation to the skin, thus offering little protection. A wide-brimmed hat should be worn to cover the face and neck.

The use of a sunscreen lotion or cream can help prevent a photosensitivity reaction from taking place. Sunscreens are either light-absorbing agents such as para-aminobenzoic acid (PABA) or opaque agents such as zinc oxide that keep radiation from reaching the skin. They should be applied prior to exposure and reapplied during exposure after swimming or sweating. Sunscreens are available without a prescription, but since patients with allergies may react to some of the ingredients in the products, it is best to consult a pharmacist or physician to determine which product is best suited for the individual.

If a phototoxic reaction occurs, a physician should be consulted. Treatment consists of cold-water compresses and cool baths, and antihistamines and anti-inflammatory drugs if indicated. Topical anesthetics should be avoided, since they may also cause skin reactions. For individuals who react persistently, a tan-promoting agent such as Oxsoralen—a drug given by mouth or applied topically—may be given to enhance pigmentation of the skin and increase tolerance to exposure to sunlight.

Drugs that may cause photosensitivity reactions

analgesics and anti-inflammatory agents
- dimethyl sulfoxide (DMSO)
- phenylbutazone (Butazolidin)
- salicylates (aspirin)

anticancer drugs
- dacarbazine (DTIC)
- fluorouracil (Efudex, Fluoroplex)
- methotrexate (Mexate)
- vinblastine (Velban)

anticonvulsants
- carbamazepine (Tegretol)
- phenytoin (Dilantin)
- trimethadione (Tridione)

antidepressants
- amitriptyline (Elavil)
- desipramine (Norpramin, Pertofrane)
- doxepin (Adapin, Sinequan)
- imipramine (Tofranil)
- nortriptyline (Aventyl, Pamelor)
- protriptyline (Vivactil)
- trimipramine (Surmontil)

antifungals
- acrisorcin (Akrinol)
- griseofulvin (Fulvicin-U/F, Grisactin)

antihistamines
- cyproheptadine (Periactin)
- diphenhydramine (Benadryl)
- isothipendyl (Nilergex)

antimicrobials
- chloramphenicol (Chloromycetin)
- chlortetracycline (Aureomycin)
- demeclocycline* (Declomycin)
- doxycycline (Vibramycin)
- minocycline (Minocin)
- nalidixic acid* (NegGram)
- oxytetracycline (Terramycin)
- sulfacytine (Renoquid)
- sulfadiazine (Microsulfon)
- sulfamethazine (Neotrizine)
- sulfamethizole (Thiosulfil)
- sulfamethoxazole (Gantanol)
- sulfamethoxazole-trimethoprim (Bactrim, Septra)
- sulfasalazine (Azulfidine)
- sulfisoxazole (Gantrisin)
- tetracycline (Achromycin, Panmycin, Sumycin)

antipsychotic drugs
- chlorpromazine* (Thorazine)
- fluphenazine (Permitil, Prolixin)
- haloperidol (Haldol)
- perphenazine (Trilafon)
- piperacetazine (Quide)
- prochlorperazine (Compazine)
- promazine* (Sparine)
- thioridazine (Mellaril)
- trifluoperazine (Stelazine)
- triflupromazine (Vesprin)
- trimeprazine (Temaril)

diuretics
- bendroflumethiazide (Naturetin)
- benzthiazide (Exna, Hydrex)
- chlorothiazide* (Diuril)
- cyclothiazide (Anhydron)
- furosemide* (Lasix)
- hydrochlorothiazide* (Esidrix, HydroDIURIL, Oretic)
- hydroflumethiazide (Diucardin)
- methyclothiazide (Aquatensen, Enduron)
- metolazone (Diulo, Zaroxolyn)
- polythiazide (Renese)
- quinethazone* (Hydromox)
- spironolactone (Aldactone)
- trichlormethiazide (Metahydrin)

hypoglycemics
- acetohexamide (Dymelor)
- carbutamide (Nadisan)
- chlorpropamide* (Diabinese, Insulase)
- tolazamide (Tolinase)
- tolbutamide* (Orinase)

sedatives and tranquilizers
- barbiturates
- chlordiazepoxide (Librium)
- methotrimeprazine (Levoprome)

sunscreens
- digalloyl trioleate (Sunswept)
- glyceryl PABA
- para-aminobenzoic acid (PABA, PreSun)

tuberculostatics
- ethionamide (Trecator-SC)
- isoniazid (INH, Nydrazid)

other
- anesthetics (procaine group)
- antimalarials (Chloroquine, Quinine)
- arsenicals
- coal tar* (Zetar)
- dantrolene (Dantrium)
- diethylstilbestrol (DES)
- disopyramide (Norpace)
- estrone (Theelin injection)
- gold salts (Myochrysine, Solganal)
- hexachlorophene (pHisoHex)
- methoxsalen* (Oxsoralen)
- methyldopa (Aldomet)
- oral contraceptives
- pyrvinium (Povan)
- tretinoin (Retin-A)
- trioxsalen* (Trisoralen)

*Reactions occur frequently.

—*Edward R. Leist, Pharm. D.*

Health Education Unit 2

Hypoglycemia

Hypoglycemia, or low blood sugar, has recently received a great deal of attention, due in part to several popular books on the subject aimed at the lay reader. In addition, some physicians have claimed that the condition is at the root of a wide variety of physical and mental symptoms, many of which are generalized and could be attributed to dozens of diseases or abnormal states—headache, dizziness, fatigue, heart palpitations, confusion, anxiety, and inability to concentrate. Reactive hypoglycemia (also known as functional or postprandial hypoglycemia) connotes the lowest level of blood glucose, which occurs two to four hours after a meal. There are those who claim that this normal decline in blood glucose is exaggerated in some individuals and that the low glucose level causes many physical and psychic symptoms. Although reputable clinicians and investigators differ as to the precise criteria that define reactive hypoglycemia, there is unanimous agreement that the entity is not nearly as common as its advocates claim.

The popularization of this entity presents a challenge to the conscientious physician and to the individual who feels he or she suffers from hypoglycemia. It is first necessary to understand the nature of the daily fluctuations in blood glucose and the normal physiologic responses to hypoglycemia.

Physiologic considerations

Certain vital organs, notably the brain and the red blood cells, require glucose as the primary nutrient that fuels their function. Glucose, a simple sugar, is delivered by the blood bathing those organs. Glucose in the blood originates from the foods consumed or from sources within the body. The latter sources include the breakdown of the complex sugar glycogen that the body has stored in the liver and the formation of new glucose in the liver. This latter process, gluconeogenesis, involves the transformation of nutrients such as amino acids to yield the vital sugar. In healthy individuals, circulating glucose levels range from 60 to 120 milligrams per deciliter (mg/dl) of blood during the day. The lowest levels occur in the basal state before breakfast or two to three hours after a meal. Highest levels are noted one-half to one and one-half hours after a meal.

Glucose that originates from foods is absorbed in the jejunum, a portion of the small intestine. Most of the absorbed glucose is taken up by the liver and stored as glycogen; the remainder is available for use by skeletal muscle and adipose tissue, as well as by the brain and red blood cells. The increase in blood glucose that follows a meal causes the release of insulin from the beta cells in the islets of Langerhans of the pancreas. Insulin facilitates the deposition and metabolism of glucose in muscle and fatty tissue. As the levels of blood glucose decline, insulin output from the pancreas slows down. This regulation requires a finely tuned feedback system between glucose and insulin so that there is sufficient glycemia (sugar in the blood) to assure that those organs that have an essential need for glucose will continue to function.

The human brain requires approximately 140 g of glucose every 24 hours. This need does not vary with alterations in physical or mental exercise. If there is insufficient glucose available for the metabolism of cells of the cerebral cortex, the result is a deterioration in higher brain functions, changes in emotional state and personality, and, frequently, aberrant behavior similar to that of alcohol inebriation. Symptoms of confusion, mental dullness, amnesia, seizures, and coma may appear in extreme cases. These are termed *neuroglycopenic symptoms* (*neuro* refers to the nervous system, *glyco* to sugar, and *penic* to a deficiency). Hypoglycemia also affects the control center in the hypothalamus that regulates the autonomic (adrenergic) nervous system, which regulates the functioning of the circulatory system, digestion, respiration, temperature control, and other "nonvoluntary" bodily functions. When the autonomic system is disturbed by hypoglycemia the individual may experience palpitations, sweating, hunger, tremulousness, anxiety, and increased blood pressure and pulse rate. These are termed *adrenergic symptoms.* This alarm reaction warns the individual to seek carbohydrate-containing foods.

In addition, there are a number of internal signals activated by hypoglycemia that work in a coordinated fashion to stimulate the output of glucose from the liver, to divert glucose from non-nervous-tissue organs, and to call on alternative energy sources such as fatty acids as a replacement for glucose. Among these counterregulatory factors are cortisol, epinephrine, and norepinephrine from the adrenal glands; glucagon from the pancreas; and growth hormone from the pituitary gland. Each of these hormones exerts a role in maintaining glucose equilibrium.

Tests to assess glucose metabolism

To assess the body's ability to maintain glucose homeostasis several studies may be employed. Most common is the oral glucose tolerance test, in which the patient drinks a solution containing 75 to 100 g of glucose, and the level of blood glucose is measured at periodic intervals for three to six hours. This test is helpful in the diagnosis of both hyperglycemic (high blood sugar) and hypoglycemic states. The test should never be performed unless the subject has consumed at least 200 to 300 g of carbohydrate for three days prior to testing. An inadequate carbohydrate intake before an oral glucose tolerance test causes an exaggeration of the hypoglycemic phase observed two to five hours after the ingestion of glucose. Failure to acknowledge this rule is a prime factor in the overdiagnosis of hypoglycemia.

There is a wide range of normal blood glucose levels. As many as 42% of healthy individuals exhibit blood glucose levels below 50 mg/dl during the test when sampling is done at hourly intervals. In spite of these low levels, none of the subjects experience symptoms of hypoglycemia. It should be stressed that low glucose levels alone are not a sufficient indicator of reactive hypoglycemia; the subject must also experience symptoms.

As blood glucose levels rise after the ingestion of carbohydrate there is a concomitant rise in circulating insulin. Insulin is readily measured by a standard radioimmunoassay technique; if it is suspected that the body is producing too much insulin, the levels of the hormone should be assessed. Each of the counterregulatory hormones—glucagon, cortisone, and growth hormone—are easily measured in a laboratory.

In instances where hypoglycemia occurs when the individual has been fasting, rather than after a meal, measurement of both basal glucose and insulin is mandatory. As blood glucose values fall during fasting, insulin levels normally fall in tandem. Provided the individual is not taking insulin or an oral hypoglycemic agent, the presence of a low level of glucose and a corresponding elevated level of insulin suggests that the body is overproducing insulin—the usual cause being a tumor of the pancreas. Deficiencies in the hormones that regulate glucose balance may also be at fault. Other rarer causes of nonreactive hypoglycemia are widespread liver damage, the action of certain drugs, and abdominal tumors arising from mesenchymal (connective tissue) cells.

Reactive hypoglycemias

In 1973, when the diagnosis of reactive hypoglycemia was proliferating at an unwarranted pace, three professional bodies—the American Diabetes Association, the Endocrine Society, and the American Medical Association—issued a joint statement to define the criteria required to diagnose reactive hypoglycemia. To establish the diagnosis, a blood glucose level of 50 mg/dl or less must be present when the individual is experiencing symptoms and these symptoms must abate after the ingestion of food or a sugar-containing beverage. The statement cautioned against attributing a wide variety of unrelated diseases to hypoglycemia. While others have modified or extended these criteria, they are sound and have widespread acceptance.

Reactive hypoglycemia can occur in non-insulin-dependent (type II) diabetes mellitus. Some patients who experience adrenergic or neuroglycopenic symptoms three to five hours after a meal are discovered to have non-insulin-dependent diabetes. Usually these individuals are obese and have a strong family background of diabetes. Fasting glucose levels are normal or occasionally slightly elevated. But postprandial glucose levels ascend slowly and reach zeniths of 180 mg/dl or greater and then descend to hypoglycemic levels below 50 mg/dl three to five hours after a meal. Insulin levels rise sluggishly, but after two to three hours are excessively high.

Hypoglycemic patterns disappear in those individuals if the diabetes worsens. But because this form of diabetes is so frequently static, weight reduction and the avoidance of simple carbohydrates are the best therapeutic approaches.

Reactive hypoglycemia also occurs after gastric surgery—this state is called alimentary hypoglycemia. Patients who have part or all of their stomachs removed exhibit an abrupt, abnormally high rise in plasma glucose within 35 to 65 minutes after a meal due to the rapid emptying of the stomach and rapid absorption of the contents by the small intestine. Glucose levels fall precipitously by 90 to 150 minutes after the meal to levels below 50 mg/dl. Only a few of these individuals experience adrenergic and neuroglycopenic symptoms that coincide with the lowest plasma glucose. While almost everyone who has undergone gastric surgery has glucose levels below 50 mg/dl after consuming a glucose-containing solution, the number with neuroglycopenic symptoms ranges from 5 to 10%. The characteristics that predispose an individual to symptoms

E. F. Bernstein—Peter Arnold, Inc.

Hypoglycemia, or low blood sugar, can result in confusion, dullness, anxiety, and a variety of physical symptoms such as hunger, sweating, trembling, and palpitations. It is a grave mistake, however, to assume that these general, vague symptoms are commonly *caused by low blood sugar.*

are poorly defined, but when individuals with alimentary hypoglycemia are screened with the Minnesota Multiphasic Personality Inventory (MMPI), they reveal patterns that indicate prior emotional disturbances. Treatment with low-carbohydrate diets or with drugs that slow the emptying of the stomach should be initiated in symptomatic individuals. Agents that inhibit the adrenergic symptoms are also effective.

Hypoglycemia and emotional states

The largest number of individuals who are diagnosed, or more commonly misdiagnosed, as having reactive hypoglycemia fall into the classification of nonspecific reactive hypoglycemia since no apparent cause is found. Too often the diagnosis is due to a misattribution on the part of the physician or of the patient.

For example: A middle-aged woman complains of "afternoon dwindles"—a feeling of fatigue and anxiety. Her physician orders a six-hour oral glucose tolerance test and a blood glucose of 41 mg/dl is noted at the fourth hour. Both the physician and patient are relieved, for a diagnosis is now "obvious" and thereafter all of the patient's somatic and psychic complaints are attributed to hypoglycemia. In this case the physician has failed to appreciate that many normal subjects have blood glucose levels below 50 mg/dl during a six-hour oral glucose tolerance test.

In other cases, after being informed of the results of a tolerance test, the patient attributes all of his "problems" to the low blood glucose. The patient may not have been informed about the adrenergic and neuroglycopenic symptoms that accompany low glucose levels. Thus, he seeks assistance in the local library or book shop and locates a handful of popular volumes. These books claim that "millions" suffer from some form of hypoglycemia but are unaware of this because hypoglycemia masquerades as a neurosis, as asthma, or even as alcoholism. None of these books offers physiologic data to substantiate such claims.

Many individuals diagnosed or misdiagnosed as having reactive hypoglycemia have emotional disorders. Studies carried out at the Mayo Clinic in Rochester, Minn., and clinics at the University of California's Los Angeles and San Francisco campuses employing the MMPI have revealed that a majority of individuals thought to have reactive hypoglycemia score significantly higher than the general population on the hypochondriasis, depression, and hysteria scales of this inventory, which is frequently used to diagnose psychiatric disorders.

Postprandial hypoglycemia does not cause or aggravate this underlying psychological pattern. Hysterical and obsessive individuals are often concerned with physical complaints. In fact, what has brought the patient to the physician are classical symptoms of depression or anxiety. Reactive hypoglycemia is most often an incidental finding rather than the cause of the patient's symptoms.

While the precise incidence of symptomatic hypoglycemia after a glucose test in emotionally stable, healthy subjects is not known, its occurrence is rare. The mechanisms of bona fide symptomatic reactive hypoglycemia are also unclear. Blood glucose and insulin responses in symptomatic persons are not significantly different from those in asymptomatic individuals. It has been suggested that symptomatic subjects possess a hypersensitive autonomic nervous system that fires impulses to release epinephrine and norepinephrine at glucose levels of 50 mg/dl or slightly less or have an undue sensitivity to normal amounts of these substances.

Treatment

Therapy of symptomatic reactive hypoglycemia requires a restriction in the consumption of foods and beverages that contain high concentrations of sucrose or glucose. Excessive amounts of these simple sugars cause high rises in glucose levels with consequent exaggerated low levels. Some textbooks, as well as the popular literature on hypoglycemia, condemn all carbohydrates, and assume that they all cause extreme fluctuations in blood glucose. But this assumption is unfounded. A growing literature substantiates that legumes, rice, and other foods with a high content of complex carbohydrates cause smaller rises and falls in postprandial glucose than do foods of equal caloric value that are high in simple sugars. Hence, only foods such as pastries, ice cream, or sugary beverages need be restricted.

Diets that are high in protein as well as low in carbohydrates are often prescribed. What is not always considered is that when dietary carbohydrates are severely restricted a portion of the amino acids in dietary protein are transformed by the liver to glucose via the process of gluconeogenesis. Provided that simple carbohydrates are limited, there seems no reason to increase dietary protein.

Unfortunately, the psychiatric disorders uncovered among patients referred for "hypoglycemia" are often quite difficult to manage. Depression may respond to modern psychoactive drugs, but hypochondriasis and hysteria are especially difficult challenges to the therapist. Often individuals with one or the other of these conditions transfer their multiple symptoms to their "hypoglycemia" and seek assurance from their physician that in truth their entire problem is low blood glucose. All too often this illusion is perpetuated since symptoms can be treated in a "harmless" way. However, the true cause of the symptoms is not being treated. A more direct and compassionate approach by the physician helps the patient to correct his misinformation about hypoglycemia and express his real apprehensions and concerns.

—Ronald Arky, M.D.

Health Education Unit 3

Sinus Problems

The paranasal sinuses are cavities within the bones of the face and skull with openings into the nasal cavity. They serve no vital function but are frequently the site of infections and in rare cases give rise to tumors. Contrary to popular belief, problems with the paranasal sinuses account for only a small percentage of patients with the complaint of headache.

The small openings of the sinuses into the nasal cavity should not be abused by chronic overuse of nose drops and sprays, smoking, and chronic exposure to inhaled irritants such as sawdust, chemical fumes, and dry air. Chronic nasal congestion, chronic nasal discharge or bleeding, and persistent pain in or near the sinuses are symptoms that should be evaluated by a physician. Patients with diseases of the paranasal sinuses are often referred to an otolaryngologist, a head and neck physician who specializes in disorders of the ears, nose, and throat.

Anatomy and function

The sinuses associated with the nasal cavity are known as the paranasal sinuses and are eight in number. They consist of hollow cavities in the bones of the skull and are named for the bones in which they are found. The sinuses are paired, four on each side of the nose. The sinus in the forehead (frontal bone) is referred to as the frontal sinus, and the sinus in the cheek (maxillary bone) is the maxillary sinus. Ethmoid sinuses are located in numerous labyrinthine spaces of the ethmoid bone situated between the nose and the eye. The sphenoid bone is deep within the skull behind the nose and contains the paired sphenoid sinuses. All of the sinuses are lined by a mucous membrane continuous with that lining the inside of the nose. There are small openings known as ostia by which the sinuses communicate with the nasal cavity. In the normal state, the sinuses contain air. Although the membrane lining the sinuses secretes mucus, normally the mucus is not retained in the sinus, but passes through the ostia into the nose and from there imperceptibly into the throat, where it is swallowed.

The sinuses add to the resonance of the voice and lighten the head by virtue of the hollowing they produce in the skull. The sinuses may also play a role in allowing the smooth passage of air to and fro through the nose in spite of the rapid surges and sudden stops the inhaled and exhaled air makes during normal breathing. Surgical removal or obliteration of the sinuses, however, results in no appreciable deficit, supporting the probability that they serve no vital function.

Symptoms of sinus disease

Unfortunately, widespread advertising of over-the-counter remedies has misled the public into believing that the paranasal sinuses are at fault for the common nasal and headache symptoms that most people suffer from time to time. Sinus diseases account for only a small fraction of the many patients seen with headaches or nasal congestion. Blockage of a sinus ostium or infection of a sinus can result in headache, but most patients complaining of headaches do not have sinus disease, especially in the absence of nasal symptoms associated with the headaches. Many types of headaches occur in the region of the sinuses and can be mistaken for sinus headache.

Patients commonly refer to their nasal symptoms as "sinus" when discussing them with their physician or friends. This common usage contributes to the misconception of the prevalence of true sinus disease. Although disease of the paranasal sinuses often causes nasal symptoms, most nasal complaints are due to disorders of the nose itself, without accompanying sinus disease.

What then are the symptoms of sinus disease? Pain in the cheek, upper teeth, eyes, forehead, or top of the skull is associated with diseases of the paranasal sinuses. Nasal congestion, purulent (pus-containing) nasal discharge, and thick postnasal drip may also be present. Because of the proximity of the maxillary sinuses to the upper molar teeth and the ethmoid sinuses to the eyes, disorders of these sinuses may masquerade as toothache or an eye infection because of pain felt in these sites. Both benign and malignant tumors can originate in the sinuses. Although they are

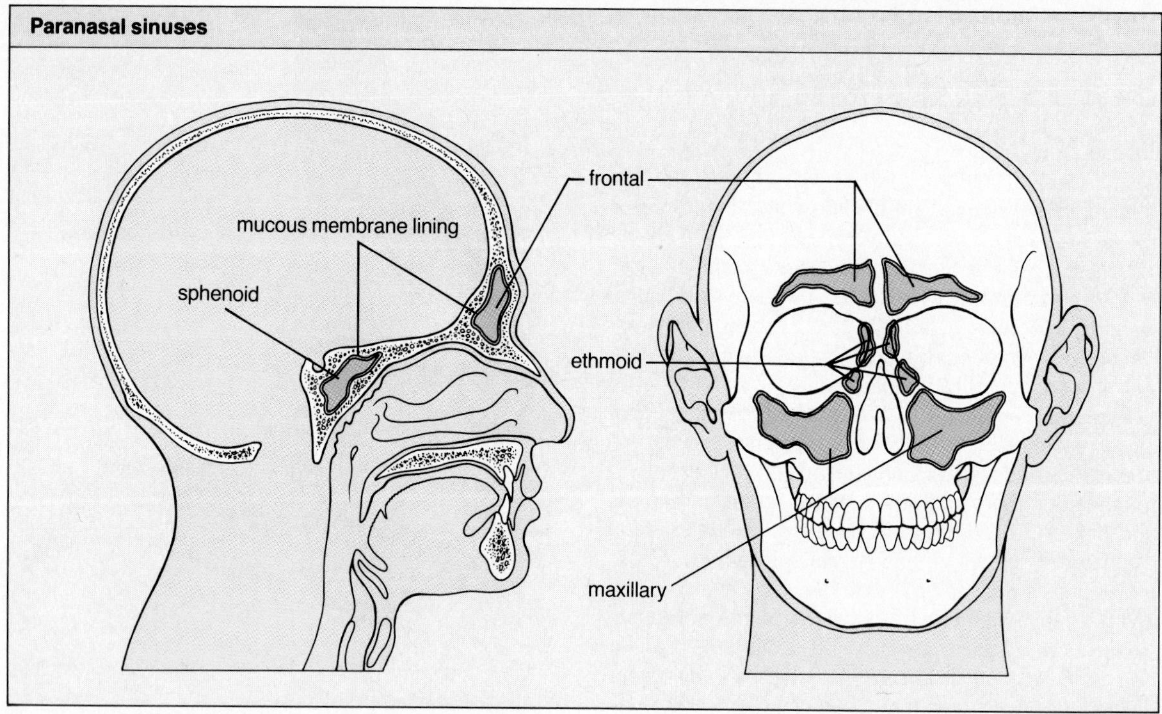

rare, they may result in the above symptoms as well as displacement of the eye, nasal bleeding, and protrusion of the sinus growth into the mouth.

Diagnosis

Because they are located deep within bony cavities, the paranasal sinuses are not easily accessible to physical examination. After listening to the patient's description of his symptoms and examining the nasal cavity, the physician may obtain additional information by observing the amount of light transmitted through the sinuses in the forehead and cheeks when a bright source of illumination is held against them. Failure of a sinus to transilluminate may mean that it is abnormal. However, an X-ray examination is usually necessary for an accurate diagnosis of the type and extent of disease. In addition to simple X-rays obtained in various views, specialized X-ray examinations may be required. Polytomography is a technique that utilizes multiple X-ray exposures with special equipment to produce detailed images. Recently, computerized axial tomographic (CAT) scans have proved to be useful in delineating the nature and extent of sinus disease.

Infections and allergy

Infections and allergic diseases of the sinuses are the most common disorders. Since the symptoms of both types of problems are often similar, it may be difficult to differentiate between the two. In both, patients may have nasal congestion and discharge. Sinus allergy usually accompanies nasal allergy and often produces other symptoms typical of allergic disorders such as sneezing, itching of the nose and eyes, and worsening of the symptoms with change of season or exposure to inhaled allergens (animal dander, dust, pollens, and so forth). A diagnosis of nasal and sinus allergy may be suspected from the history of the patient's symptoms and the typical appearance of an allergic nasal cavity. Examination of the nasal discharge under the microscope often reveals a large number of eosinophils, red-staining white blood cells, characteristic of allergic disorders. The microscopic examination of the smear made from a nasal discharge taken from a patient with an infected nose and sinuses typically will reveal pus cells. Allergic skin testing or examination of the patient's blood serum for changes associated with the allergic state will help confirm a diagnosis of nasal-sinus allergy and identify the type of allergy.

Frequently, relief from the symptoms of allergic nasal-sinus disease can be obtained by the use of antihistamine or decongestant medications taken in the form of capsules or tablets. In very severe cases, steroid (cortisonelike) medications may be necessary. Ideally, the most effective treatment would be to separate the patient from the offending allergy-producing substances or to desensitize the patient so that the nose and sinuses no longer react adversely when exposed to the allergens. This may require removing a pet from the house, adding an electronic filter to the home heating and air-conditioning system, moving to a different geographic location, or "allergy shots"—a series of injections given in the hope of progressively desensitiz-

Courtesy, Edward L. Applebaum, M.D.

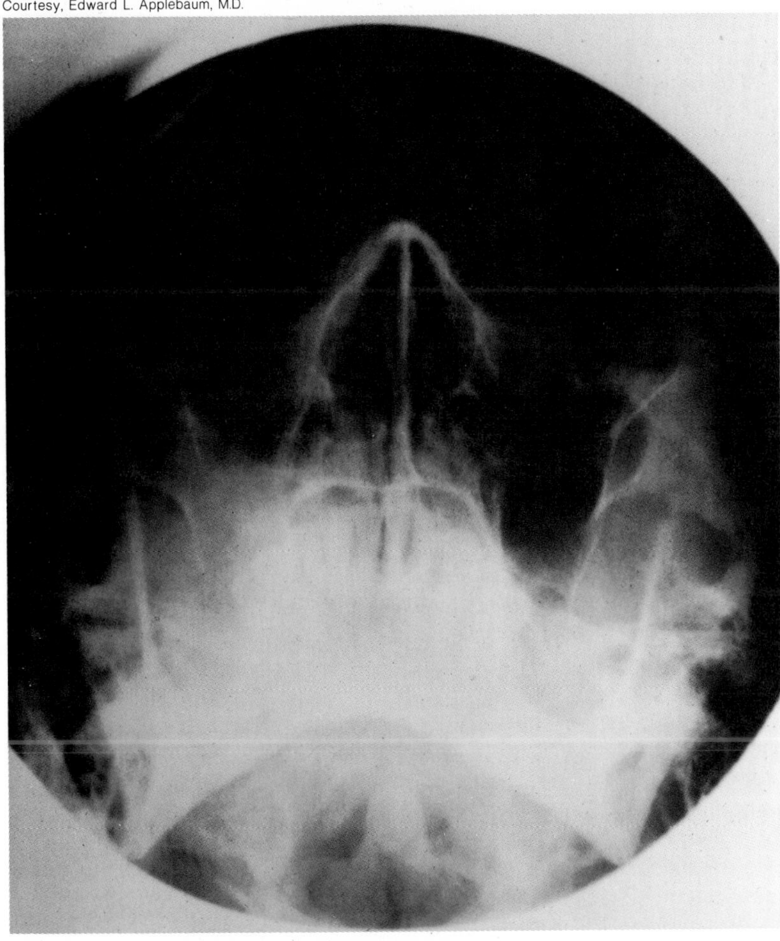

This X-ray clearly reveals the presence of an infected maxillary sinus. The sinus on the right, the dark, roughly semicircular area just below the nose, is a healthy, clear sinus. The corresponding sinus on the left is infected and filled with fluid, making it appear white on the X-ray except for a small area at the upper portion that has remained clear.

ing a patient to the substances implicated as the cause of the allergic symptoms.

Surgery is rarely needed in allergic sinus disease, but may be required to improve nasal ventilation and sinus drainage. Nasal ventilation can be improved by surgically straightening the nasal septum (the partition that divides the nasal cavity into two passages) or by reducing irreversibly swollen nasal tissues. In addition, it may be necessary in some cases to further improve impaired sinus drainage into the nose by creating an enlarged opening into the affected sinus.

Acute sinusitis is an infection of one or more of the sinuses that usually develops as a complication of an upper respiratory infection such as the common cold. The development of acute sinusitis is heralded by pain and tenderness over the affected sinus, nasal congestion, and purulent nasal discharge. If the sinus ostium is swollen closed, there may be no discharge because the infected sinus secretions are trapped in the sinus cavity. Fever and generalized weakness may accompany acute sinusitis. The symptoms of a severe head cold may be similar to those of acute sinusitis, but sinusitis is suspected if the symptoms persist and become accompanied by facial or head pain.

The physician's examination will reveal tenderness of the infected sinus and pus in the nose if the sinus ostium is still open. Sinus X-rays will confirm a suspected diagnosis of acute sinusitis by revealing the involved sinus (or sinuses) filled with abnormal secretion. If there is pus in the nose, a sample may be taken on a cotton swab for bacterial growth analysis to identify the infecting bacteria and give information that is valuable in selecting an appropriate antibiotic.

Treatment of acute sinusitis consists of antibiotic therapy and measures to insure adequate drainage of the sinuses into the nose. Antibiotics are administered for 7 to 10 days, or longer if improvement is slow. Sinus drainage is encouraged by the use of decongestant nose drops, systemic decongestants in the form of tablets or capsules, and inhalation of humidified air provided by a vaporizer or steamy baths and showers. These measures are necessary to prevent the retention of infected secretions in the sinus cavity. Because of the severe pain that results from many cases of acute sinusitis, potent analgesic medications are prescribed for at least the first several days of the infection. Failure of acute sinusitis infection to respond to these measures may indicate the need for changing the antibiotic or irrigation of the sinus. Irrigation is done through the natural sinus opening into the nose or by inserting a needle into the sinus under local anesthesia. Warm salt water is flushed into the sinus cavity to wash out retained infected material. Irrigations may have to be repeated to clear resistant infections.

Nose drops and sprays

A word of caution should be given concerning the use of decongestant nose drops. These are readily available without prescription in the form of short- and long-acting drops and sprays, and are very effective in relieving the nasal congestion and sinus obstruction associated with the common cold and acute sinusitis *when used as directed.* However, use of these products beyond several days becomes counterproductive because of a "rebound" effect that eventually causes nasal congestion rather than alleviates it.

In an attempt to keep the nasal air passages open, the patient uses increasing amounts of the drop or spray more frequently than is recommended. Eventually, the patient finds that he is dependent on the drop or spray for even relatively brief periods of nasal breathing. This vicious circle of increasing use to obtain a diminishing effect must be broken by complete cessation of the use of the medication. After several days or weeks, the nasal lining will return to normal, allowing the patient to breathe through the nose normally. During the often difficult "withdrawal" period, systemic decongestants or steroid medications may be provided to alleviate the patient's symptoms. Systemic decongestants do not cause rebound changes in the nasal lining. Nasal drops and sprays are generally safe and effective medications when used appropriately, but they should not be used for chronic nasal conditions or for a period of more than five to seven days.

Chronic sinusitis

When infection in the sinuses persists for months or even years, it is termed *chronic sinusitis.* Chronic infections often develop as a result of a severe, acute sinusitis that fails to resolve completely, or as a complication of chronic allergic disorders of the nose and sinuses. There is usually impairment of normal sinus drainage, resulting in the retention of infected secretions in sinuses whose mucous membrane linings have become thickened due to the chronic infection.

Chronic nasal congestion and pain in, or near, the affected sinus are symptoms frequently associated with chronic sinusitis. If the sinus ostium is at all open, the patient may complain of a chronic, thick nasal or postnasal discharge. The diagnosis can be made from the patient's history of complaints, physical examination, and characteristic changes noted in sinus X-rays.

Medical therapy similiar to that used in acute sinusitis is sometimes successful, but surgery is often necessary to eliminate the infection and to restore a drainage pathway into the nose. The type of surgery selected varies with the location of the chronically infected sinus. More conservative surgical procedures may be attempted initially: improvement of sinus drainage by surgically repairing a deviated nasal septum or removing obstructing nasal polyps may be all that is required. More often, sinus drainage into the nose must be reestablished by surgically creating a new "window" into the sinus through the nasal wall.

In some cases, the thickened membrane lining the chronically infected sinus must be removed to obtain resolution of the infection, and sometimes surgical obliteration of the infected sinus is necessary. Although this may seem like a radical measure, the surgical loss of a sinus in itself is not harmful since sinuses serve no known important function. Untreated chronic sinus infections are potentially quite dangerous because of the sinuses' proximity to the brain. The spread of infection may cause complications that could result in death. Fortunately, antibiotic therapy and surgery have resulted in a marked decrease in the incidence of serious complications of sinus infections.

Sinus tumors

Benign and malignant growths can develop in the paranasal sinuses, but are uncommon. *Mucous retention cysts* are the most common; they are benign growths usually found in the maxillary sinus on X-ray examination. These cysts rarely cause symptoms and are not often removed.

A potential complication of chronic sinusitis of the frontal sinus is a *mucocele.* This cystlike mass enlarges to fill the frontal sinus and then will actually destroy the sinus's bony walls. As a mucocele continues to enlarge, it will displace the eye. Surgery is necessary to remove mucoceles; to prevent their recurrence, the sinus producing a mucocele often must be surgically obliterated.

The symptoms produced by cancer of the sinuses depend on the sinus involved but may include nasal obstruction, nasal bleeding, cheek swelling, and the appearance of a tumor in the mouth. Surgery is the principal therapy for sinus cancer, but it is often supplemented by radiation therapy and chemotherapy.

—Edward L. Applebaum, M.D.

Health Education Unit 4

Ingredients in Cosmetics

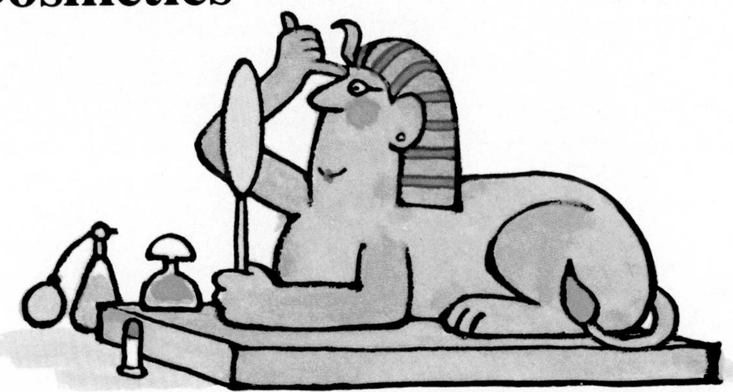

While cosmetics have been used by women and men in all parts of the world throughout history, the sheer volume of cosmetics in use today is unparalleled. Virtually everyone in the United States uses some cosmetic product daily—Americans spend $10 billion every year on some 20,000 separate items. The cosmetic industry is second only to the food industry in number of product units sold annually. But how does the consumer know what he or she is really buying?

Label requirements

Specifically, as required by the Food and Drug Administration (FDA), a cosmetic label must indicate:

(1) what the product is, to avoid confusion about products, for example, of toothpaste and shampoo that are of similar consistency and sold in similar-looking tubes;

(2) the net quantity of contents, a figure such as "1.5 oz.," that may help make meaningful cost comparisons among products with similar ingredients;

(3) the name and address of the manufacturer, packer, or distributor;

(4) a list of ingredients in descending order of predominance, using only recognized chemical names. The labeling requirements permit colors to be listed separately. The words "flavor" and "fragrance" may be used in lieu of actual chemical ingredients, since the composition of these substances may represent trade secrets. Certain other ingredients, if granted trade-secret status by the FDA, also may be omitted; in this instance, the list must end with the words "and other ingredients;"

(5) warnings for certain products, such as aerosols and feminine deodorant sprays, where health hazards may be associated with the product. The one for aerosols containing certain propellants, for example, reads: "Warning: Use only as directed. Intentional misuse by deliberately concentrating and inhaling the contents can be harmful or fatal."

Under federal law, cosmetics are articles that may be "rubbed, poured, sprinkled, or sprayed on, introduced into, or otherwise applied to the human body for cleansing, beautifying, promoting attractiveness, or altering the appearance without affecting the body's structure or functions." Products intended to affect structure and function are classed as drugs.

The flaw in these distinctions is that any substance applied to the human body may affect structure and function. Dyeing, waving, straightening, or conditioning the hair, for instance, can be viewed as altering hair structure. Indeed, the current legal distinction hinges on the claims regarding structure and function made for the product rather than on the ingredients in the product. A preparation to decrease underarm odor is a cosmetic, but the same item marketed to reduce perspiration is a drug. A product that promotes suntanning is a cosmetic; one that prevents burning is a drug. A shampoo that makes the hair smell good is a cosmetic; one that prevents dandruff is a drug. New drugs must be proven safe and effective by their manufacturer before they are marketed, while there are no such requirements for cosmetics. It is up to the FDA to prove that a specific cosmetic is not safe. Most cosmetic manufacturers do test for safety before marketing.

Types of cosmetics

Cosmetics are categorized by the FDA according to their intended use and fall into the following major groups:

(1) baby products (shampoos, lotions, oils, powders, and creams);

(2) bath preparations (oils and bubble baths);

(3) eye makeup preparations (brow pencil, liner, shadow, mascara, and eye makeup remover);

(4) fragrance preparations (colognes, toilet waters, perfumes, dusting and talcum powders, and sachets);

(5) noncoloring hair preparations (conditioners, sprays, straighteners, permanent waves, rinses, sham-

Some common ingredients in cosmetics

ingredient (type)	ingredient (type)	ingredient (type)
acrylate/acrylamide copolymer **(J)**	glycerin **(M)**	petrolatum **(H)**
aluminum chlorohydrate **(D)**	glyceryl stearate **(I)**	phosphoric acid **(O)**
aluminum distearate **(E)**	glycol stearate **(I)**	polysorbate-20 **(I)**
ammonium laureth sulfate **(Q)**	guanine **(F)**	polysorbate-60 **(I)**
ammonium nonoxynol-4 sulfate **(Q)**	gum damar **(S)**	polysorbate-80 **(I)**
amphoteric-2 **(Q)**	hydrated silica **(A)**	PPG-12-buteth-16 **(I)**
animal protein derivative **(M)**	hydrogenated vegetable oil **(H)**	PPG-14 butyl ether **(I)**
beeswax **(H)**	hydrolyzed animal protein **(L)**	PPG-33 butyl ether **(I)**
bentonite **(S)**	hydroxyethyl cellulose **(S)**	propane **(P)**
benzoic acid **(B)**	hydroxypropyl cellulose **(S)**	propylene glycol **(M)**
benzophenone-1 **(T)**	imidazolidinyl urea **(B)**	propylene glycol dicaprylate/dicaprate **(H)**
benzophenone-2 **(T)**	iron oxides **(F)**	propylene glycol stearate **(I)**
benzophenone-4 **(T)**	isobutane **(P)**	propylparaben **(B)**
benzophenone-9 **(T)**	isodecyl oleate **(H)**	quaternium-18 **(L)**
benzophenone-11 **(T)**	isopropyl alcohol **(S)**	quaternium-20 **(L)**
benzophenone-12 **(T)**	isopropyl lanolate **(H)**	quaternium-23 **(L)**
BHA **(C)**	isopropyl myristate **(H)**	SD alcohols **(S)**
BHT **(C)**	isopropyl palmitate **(H)**	sesame oil **(H)**
bismuth oxychloride **(F)**	isopropyl stearate **(H)**	silica **(A)**
borax **(B)**	kaolin **(E,F)**	sodium cocoate **(Q)**
boric acid **(B)**	laneth-10 acetate **(I)**	sodium lactate **(M)**
butane **(P)**	lanolin **(H)**	sodium laureth sulfate **(Q)**
butyl acetate **(S)**	lanolin alcohols **(H)**	sodium lauryl sulfate **(Q)**
butyl alcohol **(S)**	lanolin wax **(H)**	sodium oleate **(Q)**
butylene glycol **(M)**	lauramide DEA **(K)**	sodium PCA **(M)**
calcium carbonate **(A)**	lauric DEA **(K)**	sodium tallowate **(Q)**
candelilla wax **(H)**	lecithin **(I)**	sorbic acid **(B)**
caprylic/capric triglyceride **(H)**	linoleamide DEA **(K)**	sorbitan sesquioleate **(I)**
carbomer-934 **(S)**	magnesium aluminum silicate **(S)**	sorbitan stearate **(I)**
carbomer-940 **(S)**	magnesium carbonate **(A)**	sorbitol **(M)**
carbomer-941 **(S)**	magnesium lauryl sulfate **(Q)**	stearalkonium chloride **(L)**
carnauba **(H)**	magnesium silicate **(S)**	stearamide DIBA stearate **(I)**
castor oil **(H)**	methylcellulose **(S)**	stearamide oxide **(L)**
CD alcohol 19 **(S)**	methylparaben **(B)**	steareth-2 **(I)**
cellulose gum **(S)**	mica **(F)**	stearyl alcohol **(H)**
ceteth-2 **(I)**	microcrystalline wax **(H)**	talc **(F,H)**
cetrimonium bromide **(G)**	mineral oil **(H)**	TEA-lauryl sulfate **(Q)**
cetyl lactate **(H)**	mineral spirits **(S)**	tetrasodium EDTA **(N)**
cetylpyridinium chloride **(G)**	myristyl myristate **(H)**	titanium dioxide **(F)**
cetyltrimethylammonium bromide **(B)**	nitrocellulose **(J)**	toluene **(S)**
chromium hydroxide green **(F)**	nonoxynol-12 **(Q)**	toluenesulfonamide/formaldehyde resin **(J)**
chromium oxide greens **(F)**	octyl dimethyl PABA **(R)**	triclocarban **(G)**
citric acid **(B,O)**	oleth-10 **(I)**	triclosan **(B,G)**
dehydroacetic acid **(B)**	oleyl alcohol **(H)**	triethanolamine **(O)**
dibutyl phthalate **(S)**	ozokerite **(H)**	triethylene glycol **(M)**
diisopropyl adipate **(H)**	paraffin **(H)**	trisodium HEDTA **(N)**
dimethicone **(H)**	pareth-25-12 **(Q)**	ultramarines **(F)**
dioctyl sodium sulfosuccinate **(Q)**	PEG-6 **(I)**	UV absorbers-1, -5 **(T)**
ethyl acetate **(S)**	PEG-15 cocamine **(K)**	water **(S)**
ethylene/vinyl acetate copolymer **(J)**	PEG-32 **(I)**	wool wax alcohols **(H)**
ethylhexyl palmitate **(H)**	PEG-32 stearate **(I)**	zinc oxide **(F)**
ferric ferrocyanide **(F)**	PEG-40 hydrogenated castor oil **(I)**	zinc phenolsulfonate **(G)**
fragrance oils **(U)**	PEG-40 stearate **(I)**	zinc stearate **(F)**
	PEG-75 lanolin **(I)**	
	pentasodium pentetate **(N)**	

Ingredient functions

(A) anticaking agents: keep loose powders free-flowing. **(B) antimicrobials:** preservatives which help destroy and prevent growth of microorganisms such as bacteria. **(C) antioxidants:** preservatives which help prevent deterioration of such ingredients as fragrance oils and emollients which can result in off-odor, off-color, or product separation which can occur if these ingredients react with oxygen in the air. **(D) antiperspirants:** help inhibit the flow of perspiration. **(E) binders:** hold loose powders together when compressed into a solid cake form. **(F) color additives and opacifiers:** impart color or increase coverage. **(G) deodorants:** mask or decrease perspiration odors or help prevent their development. **(H) emollients:** skin conditioners which help prevent or relieve dryness and protect the skin by softening, conditioning, lubricating, and minimizing moisture loss. **(I) emulsifiers:** enable oil and water to mix together to form a smooth lotion or cream. **(J) film formers:** provide a continuous film to decorate (nail enamels) or to control (as in hair sprays). **(K) foamers and foam stabilizers:** create good, long-lasting foaming properties. **(L) hair conditioners:** improve ease of combing, control flyaway hair, and impart sheen. **(M) humectants:** skin conditioners which attract water, thereby further helping to maintain the skin's moisture balance. **(N) mineral suspending agents:** ingredients which bind minerals commonly found in hard water which would otherwise deteriorate the product. **(O) pH adjusters:** control how acid (low pH) or alkaline (high pH) a product is. **(P) propellants:** force a product out of an aerosol container in the form of a spray, mist, or foam. **(Q) soaps and detergents:** cleansing materials which break up and hold oils and soil so that they may be removed easily from skin or hair surface. **(R) sunscreens:** absorb ultraviolet light from the sun's rays to help prevent or lessen sunburn while allowing the skin to tan. **(S) thickeners/solidifiers/liquefiers:** make a product become thicker (less watery), thinner (more watery), or even solid (as in a lipstick). **(T) ultraviolet absorbers:** ingredients which help prevent deterioration of those ingredients which might be affected by the ultraviolet rays found in ordinary daylight. **(U) fragrances:** impart a scent to a product, the skin, or the air.

Published by Consumer Information Center, Avon Products, Inc.

poos, tonics, dressings, and wave sets);

(6) hair coloring preparations (dyes, tints, rinses, coloring shampoos, lighteners with color, and bleaches);

(7) makeup preparations (blushers, face powders, foundations, leg and body paints, lipstick, makeup bases, rouges, and fixatives);

(8) manicuring preparations (basecoats, cuticle softeners, nail creams and lotions, nail extenders, polish and enamel, and polish removers);

(9) oral hygiene products (dentifrices such as toothpaste, mouthwashes, and breath fresheners);

(10) personal cleanliness preparations (bath soaps and detergents, underarm deodorants, douches, and feminine hygiene deodorants);

(11) shaving preparations (after-shave lotions, beard softeners, talcum, preshave lotions, shaving cream and soap);

(12) skin care preparations (cleansing creams, lotions, liquids, and pads; depilatories; face, body, and hand preparations; hormone products; moisturizing preparations; night preparations; paste masks; skin lighteners; skin fresheners; and wrinkle smoothers);

(13) suntan and sunscreen preparations (gels, creams, and liquids including indoor tanning products).

Notably absent from this list is plain soap. So long as no claims are made for a soap, other than that it cleanses, its ingredients may be omitted from the label. A "moisturizing bar" is, however, a cosmetic; its ingredients will be listed.

Ingredient functions

Quite a few of the 3,500 ingredients that go into cosmetics perform the same functions. Many have overlapping functions. A manufacturer's choice of one ingredient over another involves such factors as the cost of raw materials, their look, feel, or smell, and their chemical compatibility with other ingredients.

Antimicrobials, also known as preservatives, keep harmful microorganisms such as bacteria from growing while the product is being stored or used. They also can prevent discoloration or deterioration of the cosmetic. Frequently used preservatives include paraben and benzoic acid.

Colors provide functional colors, as in lipstick or eyeshadow, or enhance the attractiveness of a product, as in a green mint toothpaste or a yellow "egg" shampoo. The law requires that colors be proven safe for their intended use before being added to foods, drugs, or cosmetics; hence, the letters "FD&C" or "D&C" before certified color names or numbers, such as "D&C chromium oxide green" or "D&C red No. 19."

Emollients give the skin a smooth, silky feel. Some, including lanolin and mineral oil, help keep moisture from evaporating from the skin's surface; others, such as glycerin, attract moisture from the air.

Emulsifiers such as glycol stearate make it possible for water and oil to mix together in creams and lotions.

Flavorings are found in such products as toothpastes, mouthwashes, and lip preparations. The specific ingredients are not required to be identified.

Fragrances must be mentioned on the label, but need not be detailed. Some fragrances contain more than 100 specific ingredients and the formulation may be zealously guarded as a trade secret. Even products labeled "unscented" contain a bland fragrance to mask the odor of the chemical ingredients.

Solvents are liquids such as water and alcohol in which solids are dissolved. Water is the most commonly used cosmetic ingredient and makes up more than 90% of some products, where it serves as a carrier or a vehicle for other ingredients; it also provides moisture. This water typically has had minerals removed and has been distilled and purified. Alcohol may be used in cosmetics for its evaporative-cooling effect, as in astringents and after-shave lotions.

Thickeners, solidifiers, and liquifiers contribute to the form of a cosmetic. A foundation, for example, may be a liquid, a cream, or a solid stick.

Adverse reactions

Considering the millions of cosmetic items in daily use, the number of adverse reactions reported is low. Only 343 injury reports were made to the division of cosmetics technology of the FDA in a one-year period ending in September 1980. The largest number of complaints, 30, concerned permanent waves. Most adverse reactions are limited to the skin and are identified as contact dermatitis.

Because consumers typically discard the offending product rather than taking the trouble to complain, the FDA is conducting a nationwide survey of adverse reactions to cosmetics serious enough to be brought to the attention of a dermatologist. Of 180,000 patients seen during a 40-month period, about 500 had a cosmetic-related contact dermatitis. In about half of these patients, neither the doctor nor the patient initially suspected that the dermatologic problem was caused by a cosmetic.

Most reactions are limited to the area of the contact. Skin may itch, develop a rash, or become reddened. Sometimes swelling and burning occur, along with bumps and blisters. Eyelids may swell and eyes may water. Reactions may occur immediately or hours or days later. Irritation also may be caused by accidents, such as getting mascara or shampoo in the eye or leaving a bleach on the hair too long.

Physicians attempt to distinguish irritant from allergic skin reactions. Irritant reactions are more common and may be related to a particular concentration of an ingredient or combination of ingredients; persons with such reactions usually can use similar products at later dates without problems. Allergic reactions, however, indicate specific and chronic sensitivities; once identified, the substance should be avoided.

Ingredients in cosmetics

It is often difficult to identify the offending agent. Irritation on the lips might be a reaction to nail polish in a woman who bites her nails. Nail polish also has been implicated in skin irritation on the legs of women who use it to stop runs in stockings. Dark spots that appear on the skin may be a reaction to sun exposure after use of a photosensitizing fragrance or after-shave lotion.

Cosmetics are not always at fault. A sponge used to apply makeup, rather than the makeup itself, may trigger skin irritation. Nickel in hairpins, eyelash curlers, and earrings may cause a reaction that mimics one from cosmetics.

Using cosmetics safely

Cosmetics are intended for use on intact skin including skin with birthmarks or healed scars. Inappropriate use or misuse of cosmetics frequently is implicated when problems occur. Piling on makeup to cover blemishes may well cause more skin eruptions. An astringent may irritate sunburned skin. Most hair dyes are not intended for dying eyebrows or eyelashes.

"Follow the directions"—this advice is too often neglected. The magnitude of the expected effect—changing hair color, for example—is likely to be related to the length of the directions. Even if you have used the product before, review the directions; new formulations may have prompted changes in procedures or timing. If a patch test is advised, do not forgo it, even if you previously have used the product. Directions for performing the test will be included. Usually what is involved is applying a small amount of the product to an inconspicuous area of the skin—the inside of the arm, for example—and allowing it to remain on the skin for 10 to 15 minutes. After the product is washed off the skin is observed for any changes or irritation. If you are having your hair treated at a professional salon, inquire about patch testing when you make your appointment.

Do not overstock supplies of cosmetics. Many will dry up, discolor, or otherwise deteriorate with age and exposure to the heat and humidity of a bathroom. Cosmetics also are susceptible to bacterial contamination. Discard open products, other than fragrances or aerosols, that you have not used for six months.

Apply cosmetics with clean hands. After using cosmetics, replace lids on jars and boxes. Do not share cosmetics.

Eye products need special cautions. Do not use saliva to moisten shadow or mascara, and do not take a chance on scratching your eye by applying eye makeup while in a moving automobile. Do not use eye cosmetics if you have an eye infection.

Keep your cosmetics out of reach of small children. Creams and fragrances often look or smell good enough to eat.

If you do develop an adverse reaction, do not throw the product away. Return it to the store where it was purchased, or write the manufacturer and send a copy of the letter to the FDA Division of Cosmetics Technology, 200 C Street S.W., Washington, D.C. 20204. If your reaction prompts a visit to the doctor, take the product along. Your doctor can contact the manufacturer to obtain ingredients for patch testing. If a specific ingredient to which you have an allergy can be identified, you can avoid purchasing products containing it.

Current controversies

Hair dye safety. Tests sponsored by the National Cancer Institute, in which mice and rats were fed large doses of chemicals in permanent hair dyes, and tests of the effects of hair dye chemicals on bacteria, suggested that certain of these chemicals may cause cancer. According to the Cosmetic, Toiletry, and Fragrance Association, most manufacturers have reformulated their hair dyes to remove the controversial ingredients. Consumers should be aware that the replacement ingredients are similar chemicals that have not undergone rigorous testing; hence, the question of safety remains open. The industry contends that since hair dyes have been used for 60 years, the risk, if any, must be weighed against the benefits consumers feel that they receive from the use of these products. The Consumers Union, a nonprofit organization that provides information and counsel on consumer goods and services, has argued that chemicals in cosmetics should undergo the same premarket testing and FDA approval process as chemicals in foods and drugs.

Bubble baths. Effective in 1981, the FDA required a label warning on bubble bath products, spelling out directions for use. Following the instructions, it is hoped, will minimize rash, itching, redness, or urogenital irritation associated with the use of these cosmetics. The warning applies to products added to a bath for the purpose of producing foam and containing an active agent that serves as a detergent.

Hypoallergenic cosmetics. While the absolute safety of any ingredient used in cosmetics cannot be assured, the great majority of cosmetics available today are free from ingredients known to cause a significant frequency of adverse reactions. Attempts by the FDA to develop a standard against which products claiming to be hypoallergenic could be measured have been unsuccessful. Hence, the term "hypoallergenic," literally meaning "less likely to cause an allergic reaction," but sometimes interpreted by consumers as meaning "allergy-free," remains a marketing term, not a scientific one. If you have skin problems, it would be best to consult a dermatologist.

—Lynne Lamberg

Health Education Unit 5

Diagnosing Respiratory Diseases

At present there is available to the physician a wide variety of tests to help assess the condition of the lungs and tissues of the respiratory system. These tests vary greatly in availability, specificity, hazard to the patient, and cost.

Some medical tests have low or nonspecific value but are inexpensive and safe, and thus are widely used. Others, of greater diagnostic value, require invasion of the body and may be hazardous, painful, and costly; nevertheless, the physician is justified in calling for them when it is anticipated that the results will disclose the presence of life-threatening conditions for which effective therapies exist. When requiring such tests the physician must explain to the patient the diagnostic need, urgency, risk, and the likelihood of the procedure's yielding the desired information. In these cases the patient must sign an informed consent statement, indicating that he understands the circumstances and agrees to undergo the procedure.

Few tests for respiratory diseases fully satisfy the criteria for an ideal procedure. Some must be conducted only in accordance with strict guidelines to minimize the danger to the patient. On the other hand, there are several innocuous, inexpensive "minor" tests that when skillfully chosen, collated, and interpreted may be as rewarding as a highly specific but hazardous invasive procedure.

Sputum analysis

The color, consistency, odor, and laboratory examination of true expectoration (*ex pectus:* from the chest—as opposed to food, mouth secretions, or postnasal drip aspirated into the lungs and coughed back) provide important information about lung disease. Anyone can develop habits of self-diagnosis by critically examining his own sputum. Changes in usual patterns may be of potential importance for both the normally "dry" nonsmoking noncougher and the smoker who habitually raises unstained mucoid material.

Unavoidable annual seasonal respiratory infections are almost always viral and follow an uncomplicated course. During a bout with colds or flu, cough and sputum production increase, but as long as sputum remains colorless, without odor, and of consistency not thicker than the white of a raw egg there is no justification for antibiotic therapy and, unless breathlessness is alarming, for anything but symptomatic relief of aching and fever.

Simple volume increase in expectorated mucus usually reflects benign hypersecretion from the airways, as in viral tracheitis (infection of the trachea, or windpipe) or chemical bronchitis. When islands of yellow-green material appear or the entire expectoration resembles custard, pus is present and denotes the existence of a bacterial infection (*e.g.,* bronchitis, pneumonia, tuberculosis). Copious and malodorous sputum indicates the destruction of lung tissue, as in lung abscess. Small streaks of blood may reflect trauma to normal mucosal capillaries during violent coughing. If whole blood—fresh or clotted—in small or large volumes is coughed up, the patient must promptly be evaluated by a physician. The causes range from trivial ulceration, irritation by foreign bodies, destructive infections (*e.g.,* abscess or tuberculosis), embolism, or cancer. Despite extensive studies, a percentage of frightening pulmonary hemorrhages remain unexplained and never recur.

Sputum is most commonly used for the identification of pathogenic bacteria and for the detection of cancer cells. The first morning specimen may best represent concentrated lower respiratory tract secretions. That it does can be ascertained by microscopic examination, which will reveal the presence of numerous phagocytes, characteristic white blood cells. Few epithelial cells from the mouth, throat, or larynx will be present. Quick study of stained sputum under a microscope may suggest a tentative bacterial diagnosis; when sputum is spread on nutrient culture media, colonies of disease-causing organisms may grow out within hours, so that the infective bacteria can be definitely identified. The identification of cancer cells from sputum samples can be done only by highly specialized pathologists or technicians.

Transtracheal aspiration

This safe, painless procedure is performed when a sampling of lung secretions is essential for diagnosis and when sputum is by other means unattainable or its authenticity as a lower-tract specimen is in doubt. A special value of such a specimen is that it bypasses the pharynx (throat) and mouth and is free from the bacteria that normally colonize the upper tract.

The patient is given local anesthesia. The physician uses a needle to puncture the skin of the neck and the anterior tracheal wall between its cartilaginous rings just below the level of the larynx. A catheter, a thin plastic tube, is threaded through the needle into the windpipe. Suction is applied and a few drops of mucus are drawn into a sterile syringe. If the trachea is "dry," a small volume of saline solution is injected and some of it retrieved. The catheter is quickly removed, the entire procedure taking less than five minutes.

The chest X-ray

The unique structure of the chest, the bony ribs encaging a blood-filled heart from which delicately outlined vessels branch out into air-filled lungs, produces black-and-white chest X-ray shadows of contrast more vivid than in any other portion of the body. The chest X-ray not only detects and sharply outlines abnormal lung conditions but is important in following the management of a variety of diseases in almost every pathologic category: inflammatory, infectious, and neoplastic. (It does not detect subtle functional or dynamic abnormalities, such as the bronchospasm of asthma or the early stages of heart failure.)

A relatively new technique using both tomography and computerization scans the lungs "slice by slice" and feeds the photographed images into a computer for reassemblage and analysis through a series of cross-section views. With refinement and precision, these computerized axial tomogram scans (CAT scans) separate and minutely define both normal and abnormal thoracic structures, even in hidden recesses and gullies behind the heart and diaphragm and alongside the spine. The CAT scan can find tiny masses not visible or detectable by other means, but it alone cannot determine definitely whether they are malignant or benign; other tests, such as cytology (the examination of cell samples) become important.

Tuberculin skin test

A positive tuberculin skin test is specific evidence that the individual has been or is presently host to the bacteria that cause tuberculosis (tubercle bacilli). While a negative test rules out tuberculosis, a positive test need not mean that the patient has the active disease.

Tuberculin is a purified protein derivative, or extract, of tubercle bacilli, and it serves as the antigen. A small amount is injected into the skin of the forearm; if the individual harbors the tubercle bacilli his natural antibody defense initiates a local inflammatory (antigen-antibody) reaction. In 48 to 72 hours this area of raised, thickened, hardened (never just reddened) skin is measured as positive if it exceeds ten millimeters in any diameter.

An uninfected individual will not react to the skin test because his immune system has no memory (antibody) for the tubercle bacillus. In mass screening and in surveys of schoolchildren, a negative skin test rules out all but very recent infection; when the skin test is positive, the chest X-ray can differentiate those with active tuberculosis from those who have simply been exposed to the bacilli.

Bronchoscopy

The bronchoscope is an illuminated optic tube used for direct visual inspection of the trachea and bronchial airways. The original hollow metal cylinder that was once used required the patient to lie on his back and to extend his neck and straighten the line of his pharynx and windpipe, sword-swallower style. About 20 years ago the Japanese introduced a radically new instrument that utilized the amazing capability of certain fibers to carry illuminated images around corners. Now in almost exclusive use, the fiber-optic bronchoscope is fashioned from many thousands of fine, elongated threads compacted into a plastic tube of under one centimeter in diameter. This flexible and malleable catheterlike structure is introduced through the mouth or nostril under local anesthesia with the patient seated, lying down, or asleep in a relaxed and uncontorted posture. Its reflective light source allows inspection along a twisting and bending path, and the range of visualization is extended to the outer regions of the lungs. By advancing smaller tubes through the bronchoscope, irrigation, suction, delivery of oxygen and medication, and collection of biopsy tissue and other specimens for study can be accomplished under the safety of direct inspection. General anesthesia is rarely required, and most patients tolerate the test well, without undue discomfort.

In skilled hands with proper precautions bronchoscopy is safe, even for the bedridden and ill (oxygen can be supplied during full operation). It is useful and sometimes vital for the evaluation of chest X-ray abnormalities, the investigation of bleeding from the lungs, the aspiration of secretions or brushings for cancer cell analysis or for obscure infections, and the removal of foreign bodies (although general anesthesia and bronchoscopy with a rigid tube may be necessary here, especially in children). The most common use of the bronchoscope is in obtaining biopsy specimens for confirming the presence of cancer.

Open lung biopsy

When the need and urgency for diagnosis is great and less invasive techniques yield no answer, the physician may resort to obtaining lung tissue by open chest surgery through a short incision between two ribs. Although carrying the risks associated with general anesthesia, this procedure is safe, not disfiguring, and often discloses conditions that can then be successfully treated with more extensive resectional surgery (often with an extension of the original "biopsy" incision) or with simple medical regimens. The risks of open lung

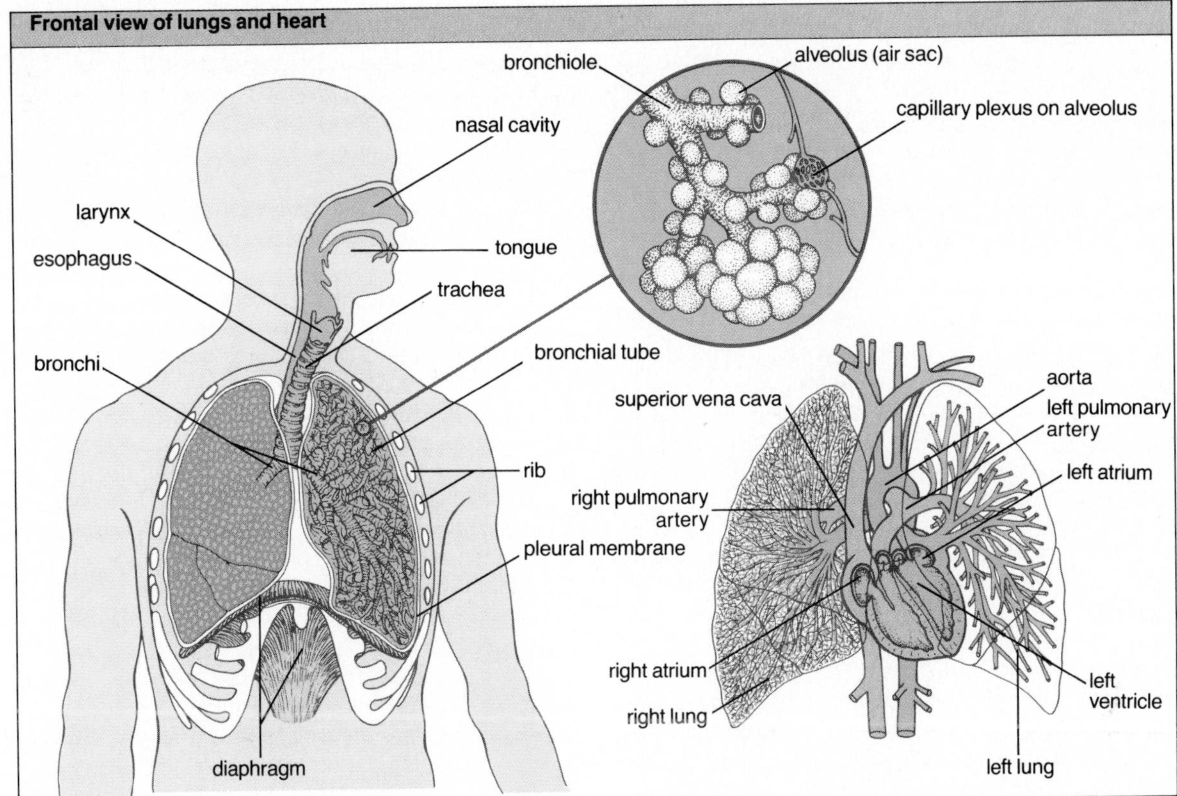

biopsy are higher for those with chronic heart or lung diseases and this must be considered against the advantages of being able to examine directly the tissues and the importance of establishing diagnosis.

Thoracentesis and pleural biopsy

The inner surface of the chest wall and the approximating outer border of the lungs are lined by moist membranes collectively called the pleura. These smooth, lubricated surfaces move against each other painlessly in normal breathing; when inflamed, the movement causes pain (pleurisy). With the excessive secretion from inflammation or disease the membranes separate and a fluid-filled space develops. The reason for accumulating pleural fluid may be obvious (as heart failure) or inapparent.

If required for diagnosis or to relieve symptoms, this fluid can be removed by inserting a needle (under local skin and chest-wall anesthesia) directly into the pleural space; this procedure is known as thoracentesis or chest tap. Special needles can be used to drain the fluid and also to sever a piece of the lining membrane for microscopic examination. Pleural biopsy causes minimal discomfort, has few and minor hazards, and is invaluable in diagnosing tuberculosis and cancer when the first symptom of trouble is pleurisy. The nature of the fluid (*e.g.,* thin, pale amber liquid; blood; or thick pus) and its characteristics (*e.g.,* protein content, cellular composition, bacterial growth) are useful clues for diagnosing infection, trauma, cancer, and sometimes heart, liver, or kidney disease.

Pulmonary function tests

The physiologic capacities and capabilities of the lungs are important for diagnosis, for judging degree of impairment or disability, and in assessing the risk of surgery. Arterial blood gas analysis and spirometry are the main methods of testing these functions.

Arterial blood gas analysis. A rapid estimate of the overall efficiency of lung performance, this test determines the amounts of dissolved gases and acidity in specimens of arterial blood. Until two decades ago considered a radical investigational procedure, the puncture of an artery today is practical, painless, and free of complications, particularly at the wrist or midarm where the pulsations are obvious just below the surface of skin. Taking the blood sample is a skill that is easily mastered, and when properly done, local anesthesia is optional, the artery immediately seals a clean, pinpoint puncture, and bleeding and discomfort are rare. Special electrodes immediately analyze the blood for oxygen (the body's metabolic fuel), carbon dioxide (the waste product), and acid content. These measurements indicate whether the lungs are adequately delivering oxygen, eliminating carbon dioxide, and maintaining acid-base homeostasis.

Spirometry. This test is noninvasive and causes no discomfort but requires coaching and the cooperation of the patient for accurate results. The spirometer is a bellowslike instrument that calibrates the air entering and leaving the lungs over time, and consists of an inverted cylinder loosely fitted into an upright cylinder and balanced by an arrangement of weights and pulleys that make it almost weightless. The lower container is partially water-filled and from above its water level a piece of hollow tubing extends to a disposable mouthpiece for the patient's use. As the patient inspires and expires a stylus attached to the pulley system records airflow as the upper cylinder rises and falls with changes in respiratory volumes.

The test can determine: (1) vital capacity, the volume of gas expressed by complete expiration from fully inflated lungs; (2) residual volume, the amount of gas remaining in the lungs, which can never be forced out after full "emptying" (measured by the dilution factor of a known concentration of inert gas, such as helium, which is inhaled and allowed to diffuse and mix to equilibrium); and (3) total lung volume, the sum of vital capacity and residual volume. Timed spirometry estimates the speed of volume displacement on rapid, forced exhalation. The patterns of these measurements indicate airflow abnormalities (as in asthma), "obstructive" disease (as emphysema), and "restrictive" conditions (as scarring from occupational pulmonary damage).

Identifying pulmonary emboli

Pulmonary embolization is really a complication of another condition: deep-vein thrombosis. The thrombus, or blood clot, forms elsewhere in the body (frequently the legs or pelvis), breaks off, travels with the venous circulation through the right side of the heart. It then lodges in the main pulmonary artery or one of its branches, occluding blood flow to an entire lung or to a segment of a lung. Since such emboli can strike and kill without warning, strategies for early identification and treatment of deep-vein thrombosis in those at risk (patients having recent surgery, trauma, burns, or immobility in the obese or aged) have been devised. There are three procedures for assessing deep-vein thrombosis.

Venography. For years the "gold standard" of diagnostic procedures for detecting the origin of the clot, venography is semi-invasive, time-consuming, and associated with significant X-radiation; it causes discomfort and requires considerable expertise for both execution and interpretation. A "dye" is injected to make the blood vessel and the clot visible on X-ray films and to outline the patterns of blood flow. This material can be irritating and itself can cause further thrombosis.

Radioactive fibrinogen scanning. Fibrinogen (the precursor of fibrin in blood clots), tagged with radioactive iodine, is injected intravenously and during circulation becomes incorporated into any active clot formation. When a radiation detector is passed up the legs, a clot is recognized by an area of increased radioactivity. Less invasive and more accurate than venography, this method is sensitive for veins in the calves but unreliable for clots above the mid-thighs or in the pelvis. Because any inflammatory process may cause local deposition of radioactive fibrin, occasional "false positive" answers result.

Doppler ultrasound and impedance plethysmography. These are two noninvasive methods of measuring the rate of blood flow out of a limb. The blood flow in the limb is first occluded with an inflated blood-pressure cuff, which is then suddenly released. The Doppler method traces the pattern of ultrasound (at frequencies higher than the range of human hearing) as the blood flows, freely or against obstruction, below the sensor. Impedance measures the rate of decrease in the electrical impedance of the limb that occurs when the blood flows out after sudden release, with rapid egress from the normal veins and slower outflow with major obstruction of large veins.

These procedures are safe and noninvasive and good for clot detection in the thighs; consequently, either of these two tests make a satisfactory and safe overall screening combination with radiofibrinogen scanning as an alternative to venography. Besides tracking down the source of blood clots, the physician can also test the lungs for the presence of clots that have become lodged there.

Perfusion lung scan. This technique uses macroaggregates of albumin, a protein, that are slightly larger in size than the diameters of pulmonary capillaries. When a suspension of such particles, radioactively labeled, is injected intravenously, the particles travel to the lungs, are wedged in the small vessels and remain there for several hours. When the body is scanned by a scintillation camera, the radioactivity presents an image of the blood flow, including the detection of areas where blood flow is absent. An entirely normal pattern in a technically well-done perfusion study means that the likelihood of pulmonary embolization is very low, but a positive scan can reflect not only embolization but a number of conditions that alter blood-flow patterns; for example, cysts, emphysema, or pneumonia.

Pulmonary angiogram. A pulmonary angiogram is a venogram of the lung circulation that requires a great concentration of dye at the level of the heart; it is more invasive, carries a small risk, and requires skill in performance and interpretation. It is positive and diagnostic if a filling defect or actual cutoff is demonstrated in a major vessel.

—L. Fred Ayvazian, M.D.

Health Education Unit 6

Genetic Counseling

The recent expansion of knowledge in the science of genetics and its application to genetic disease have made genetic counseling one of the fastest growing medical fields. Also, the widespread use of contraception means that couples now have more control over the number and timing of their offspring. The ability to exercise this type of control brings with it a greater sense of responsibility and a greater emotional investment in the health of each child. Many prospective parents seek guidance from genetic counselors to assure themselves that they have considered everything they should before undertaking a pregnancy.

What is genetic counseling?

Genetic counseling addresses questions about hereditary disease and reproductive risks and is usually conducted at clinics associated with major teaching hospitals. The clinical geneticist is a physician with special training in genetic disease. It is his or her responsibility to confirm a genetic diagnosis and to provide medical information and treatment. While the clinical geneticist may also provide counseling, many clinics have a specially trained counselor on the staff who helps the family understand the facts.

In some instances genetic counseling may require only a single visit, but more often several consultations may be necessary to give the family time to assimilate all the details of their situation so they can plan effectively for the future. If there is a specific disease in the family about which there are questions, medical records and test results will be examined in order to confirm the diagnosis. When the diagnosis of a genetic disease is confirmed the typical course of the disease will be described, along with an explanation of the treatment available. The genetic counselor will explain how the disease is inherited and which family members may be at risk for the disease in themselves or in their children. It should be noted that genetic counseling frequently reassures people that they are *not* at risk when they thought they were.

When there is a reproductive risk the genetic counselor will help the family assess the risk in terms of their beliefs and values. Some parents consider a 5% chance of having an affected child a small, acceptable risk, while others consider this risk too great to take. Another consideration is the seriousness of the inherited condition. There is a wide variation in parents' ability to cope with sickness and handicap in their child. Ideally, the genetic counselor will provide a setting in which the parents can frankly discuss their individual reactions to the situation so they may arrive at a decision that is acceptable to both.

When a couple faces a reproductive risk the genetic counselor will explain the options available. In some diseases, prenatal diagnosis of the fetus is possible. If so, all aspects of the procedure will be discussed as well as the likelihood that the test will be conclusive.

When prenatal diagnosis discloses the fact that a fetus is affected, most couples choose to terminate the pregnancy and hope for better luck in the next pregnancy. Other couples decide to have a prenatal diagnosis even though they would not choose to terminate the pregnancy. There are good reasons for this. In most cases the statistical probability favors a diagnosis of a normal baby. The parents can then relax. If, on the other hand, the result indicates an affected fetus, the couple will have some time to adjust to the eventual outcome and to make plans to accommodate to their situation. In a very few genetic diseases, if the fetus is known to be affected, the physician can plan to begin treatment immediately after birth.

Prenatal diagnosis

Prenatal diagnosis is accomplished by a number of different procedures depending on the particular information the physician is seeking.

Ultrasound (or sonography) is the technique in which sound waves are directed into the pregnant woman's abdomen. As the sound waves meet tissues of different densities they produce reflections which are recorded and translated on a screen into a visual image that can be studied by the physician. Ultrasound can be used to confirm the duration of the pregnancy by measuring the diameter of the fetus's head. The presence of more than one fetus also can be seen. Large malformations of the fetus can be detected. Ultrasound is an important adjunct to the procedure of amniocentesis, which is described below, since it can determine the location of the amniotic fluid as well as the fetal parts and the placenta.

Amniocentesis is accomplished by inserting a hollow needle through the abdomen into the uterus to withdraw a small quantity of the amniotic fluid, the protective liquid surrounding the fetus in the uterus. The procedure causes minimal discomfort; a local anesthetic may be used to numb the skin. The risk of amniocentesis to the pregnancy is small and can be reduced still further by performing it with ultrasound guidance in a hospital by an obstetrician experienced in the procedure. Amniocentesis is usually performed in the 16th to 18th week of pregnancy, as counted from the first day of the last menstrual period.

The amniotic fluid is taken to a laboratory where fetal cells present in the fluid are removed and placed into culture flasks with growth medium for 10 to 14 days. Chemicals are then added to stop the cells from dividing and to cause the chromosomes inside each cell to spread out. The cells are placed on slides, which are studied under the microscope, and photographs are taken of cells in which the chromosomes are best seen. The photograph is printed and enlarged. Each chromosome is then cut out, identified, and arranged for analysis. The information derived from these few cells can be used to predict certain facts about the fetus since the chromosomes of each cell are the same as in every other cell of the body (with rare exceptions).

The most frequent type of abnormality detected is that in which the fetus has an extra chromosome in each cell, as in Down's syndrome and trisomies 18 and 13. Other abnormalities can be predicted when structural abnormalities of the chromosomes are seen. A sidelight of chromosome analysis is that the sex of the fetus will be apparent.

There has been some misunderstanding about the range of problems that can be detected by chromosome analysis. It is important to remember that genes, which are the individual units of heredity, cannot be seen under the microscope, so most genetic diseases are not detectable. Nor can most birth defects be diagnosed by looking at the chromosomes. However, one group of birth defects, called neural tube defects, can be detected with high accuracy by testing the amniotic fluid. A neural tube defect is one in which the fetus has an opening in the cranium or spine that can result in serious handicap or death. The opening permits large amounts of a substance called alpha-fetoprotein (AFP) to escape into the amniotic fluid. Detection of AFP in the amniotic fluid is an indicator of these defects.

Amniocentesis can also be used to detect close to 100 rare genetic biochemical disorders. Tests for these disorders are performed only when a couple is known to be at risk for one of them. They may have already had a child affected with the condition, or the parents may have been determined to be carriers for the disorder in a screening test. Testing the fetal cells for biochemical disorders is technically far more difficult than chromosome analysis—a test for a single biochemical disorder requires a large mass of fetal cells, which may take six or more weeks to grow. Even then the results are not always conclusive.

Fetoscopy is utilized in prenatal diagnosis when blood sampling of the fetus is necessary to make a diagnosis, as in classic hemophilia. Fetoscopy requires the insertion of a viewing instrument having a sampling needle through a small incision in the abdomen. The blood is drawn from one of the fetal blood vessels of the placenta. The risk from this procedure is considerably higher than that from amniocentesis, and the procedure is performed at only a few university-associated hospitals.

Prenatal testing has enabled many high-risk couples to confidently undertake a pregnancy they would otherwise have feared. However, there are ethical issues surrounding prenatal diagnosis that merit consideration. There are dangers in deciding who should or should not be born, especially when distinctions are made between degrees of quality of life. These discussions reach a peak when the question is brought up of using prenatal diagnosis solely to determine the sex of the fetus with the intention of aborting a fetus of the unwanted sex. It is unlikely that any genetic clinic will knowingly utilize its resources for this purpose.

When prenatal diagnosis is either not available or not desired, other options in planning a family may be considered. These include artificial insemination by donor (AID), adoption, or a carefully considered decision not to have children. Clearly these are some of the most important decisions couples will make in their lifetime, and they need all the information and support they can get. Further, once a couple has decided which avenue they wish to follow, the genetic counselor will be able to provide the backup services to help them implement their decision.

Who should have genetic counseling?

Most inquiries at a genetic clinic fall into one of the following groups.

1. *Families in which one or more individuals are affected by a disorder known or suspected to be of genetic causation.* Genetic disorders are caused by one or more of the 100,000 genes that are present on the human chromosomes. Genetic disorders can be loosely divided into two groups, those that result from

the combined action of several genes (polygenic conditions), and those that are caused by a single gene or a single pair of genes. Polygenic conditions impose a relatively small increase in the probability of recurrence of the disorder in family members. Some examples of this group are clubfoot and most congenital heart defects. Single-gene disorders represent a much greater risk of occurrence in the family. A recent catalog lists over 2,800 single-gene disorders; there are genetic disorders known to affect separately each part of the body: *e.g.,* eye, bone, and skin; and others that simultaneously affect multiple parts of the body, such as Usher's syndrome, a disorder that affects both vision and hearing.

Single-gene disorders can be divided into three main groups. The *dominant* disorders are transmitted with a 50-50 probability from one affected parent to each of his or her offspring. The altered gene that causes the disorder is said to be dominant because it produces its effect to some degree regardless of the other genes the person might have. Examples of dominant disorders include achondroplasia (one type of dwarfism) and neurofibromatosis (a tendency to develop tumors on nerve cells).

Recessive disorders are caused by a pair of altered genes, one of the pair having been transmitted by each parent. If both parents are unaffected "carriers," with each pregnancy there is a 25% chance that a baby will receive those genes from both parents and a 75% chance that it will not. If one parent is affected and the

Fetoscopy

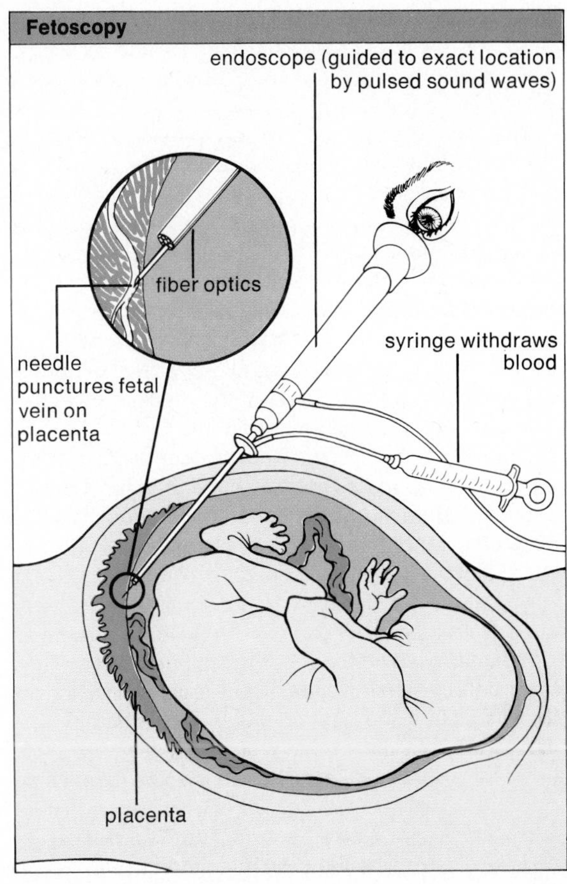

Common inherited disorders

condition	inheritance	carrier test	prenatal test
cystic fibrosis	recessive	no	no
Down's syndrome	chromosomal abnormality	translocation form only	amniocentesis
Duchenne muscular dystrophy	recessive, X-linked	yes (not always conclusive)	sex determination only
galactosemia	recessive	yes	amniocentesis
hemophilia (classic)	recessive, X-linked	yes (better when not pregnant)	sex determination followed by fetoscopy (experimental)
Huntington's disease (Huntington's chorea)	dominant	no	no
neural tube defects	polygenic	no	amniocentesis and maternal serum
phenylketonuria (PKU)	recessive	no	no
retinitis pigmentosa	dominant, recessive, and X-linked forms	X-linked form only	no
sickle-cell anemia	recessive	yes	fetoscopy (experimental), amniocentesis in some cases
Tay-Sachs disease	recessive	yes	amniocentesis
thalassemia (Cooley's anemia)	recessive	yes	fetoscopy (experimental), amniocentesis in some cases

other a carrier, the probability rises to 50% that each baby will be affected. Cystic fibrosis and sickle-cell anemia are the most common recessive disorders in whites and blacks, respectively.

The third main group are the *X-linked recessive* disorders, in which the altered gene is located on the X chromosome, one of two sex-determining chromosomes in humans. Women have two X chromosomes; in carriers, one X transmits the altered gene while the other carries a normal gene. The normal gene dominates the altered gene so that it does not express itself. However, men have only one X chromosome (along with a Y sex chromosome), and the recessive gene is able to express itself. Some of the X-linked recessive disorders are classic hemophilia and Duchenne muscular dystrophy. Women who are carriers for these conditions and whose mate is unaffected have a 50% chance that each of their sons will be affected and a 50% chance that each of their daughters will also be carriers of the gene. Every daughter of an affected man will be at least a carrier since she must have received his X (with its altered gene) in order to be a female.

2. *Families in which a baby has been born with a birth defect.* When a couple sees a genetic counselor because they have just had a baby with a birth defect, they are in a state of shock and disbelief. Typically, they feel guilty because they assume some responsibility for the birth defect. Not infrequently they believe future children will also be defective. The clinical geneticist will examine the child and determine if there is a known genetic component. The couple will learn how the defect came about and what the likelihood is of its happening again. The couple will also learn what treatment is available to help the child overcome the effects of the defect and if there are parent support groups to help them adjust to their new situation.

3. *Women who are 35 or over.* Women in this category are the largest single group seeking genetic counseling. They are appropriate candidates for amniocentesis because they are at increased risk for having a baby with a chromosome disorder such as Down's syndrome. Yet despite the increasing risk, it is reassuring to know that most babies of even the oldest mothers will be normal. Many women are now willing to undertake a pregnancy later in life solely because of the availability of amniocentesis.

4. *Women who have had a child with a chromosome or neural tube disorder.* This is the second largest group referred for amniocentesis. The fact that they have had a child previously with either a chromosome abnormality or a neural tube defect places them at a higher risk for a recurrence. Once again, the actual risk is small but the risk relative to the general population is significantly increased.

5. *Women who have been exposed to radiation or a suspect drug while pregnant.* There has been a great deal of publicity about the harmful effects of radiation and certain drugs in pregnancy. If a woman is concerned about exposure to one of these agents she should ask her doctor, who may have the information or may refer the question to a genetic clinic.

6. *Husbands and wives who are related to each other and are concerned whether their children will be normal.* Marriage between cousins and other relatives is more common in some cultures than in others. Although most of their children are normal, there are some increased risks. To sort out facts from superstitions it is wise for consanguineous couples to seek genetic counseling.

7. *Individuals who are at greater risk to be carriers for a specific genetic disease because they belong to a particular ethnic group.* Some examples of these diseases are sickle-cell anemia in the black population, thalassemia (Cooley's anemia) in the Mediterranean population, and Tay-Sachs disease in the Ashkenazi Jewish population. Each of these disorders is recessive, so both parents must be at least carriers in order to have an affected child. Blood tests can determine if an individual of one of these ethnic groups is a carrier; if both parents are carriers they have one chance in four with each pregnancy that the baby will have the disease. Prenatal diagnosis can now tell if the fetus is affected with Tay-Sachs disease. Fetal blood sampling and new methods of identifying the genes carrying the trait are being developed for the detection of sickle-cell disease and thalassemia.

8. *Women who have had two or more miscarriages.* It has been discovered that of couples who have had repeated miscarriages, a small group will show a chromosome rearrangement (translocation) in one of the partners that may predispose toward the formation of gametes (eggs or sperm) with an unbalanced chromosome complement. In most cases the individual having a translocation will produce normal gametes as well as abnormal ones. A gamete having an unbalanced rearrangement will produce a fetus that will usually abort spontaneously. However, there is the possibility that a few might survive to term, resulting in an abnormal baby. It is important for couples in which one is a balanced translocation carrier to have an amniocentesis to check on the chromosome complement of the fetus.

For further information

A directory of genetic clinics can be obtained from the March of Dimes Birth Defects Foundation, 1275 Mamaroneck Avenue, White Plains, N. Y. 10605; the National Genetics Foundation, 555 West 57th Street, New York, N.Y. 10019; or the National Clearinghouse for Human Genetic Diseases, 805 15th Street, N.W., Suite 500, Washington, D.C. 20005.

—Phyllis Klass

Health Education Unit 7

Fatigue

Fatigue is often a necessary evil, the by-product of hard work required for advancement in life. When it is the result of physical exertion, fatigue is understandable and even pleasant. When it seems excessive and without cause it can give rise to considerable distress. Fatigue is one of the most common symptoms for which people seek help from physicians. Although it can be the early sign of serious disease, fatigue is usually psychogenic—that is, it has a mental cause rather than a physical one.

In one study of 38 patients seen by a cardiologist only one with the primary complaint of fatigue had demonstrable medical reasons for the fatigue. One might reasonably expect to find that fatigue in heart patients would be due to heart failure. Not so. Depression was by far the most common cause. Surprisingly, overwork was rarely involved; in fact, fatigue is the result of depression, boredom, or inactivity far more often than it is the result of overwork alone.

In a study of family physicians' practices, women were found to complain of fatigue twice as frequently as men. Men more often turned to alcohol for relaxation or relief of stress, whereas women were more likely to turn to tranquilizers. Married women were more likely than single women to have a psychological cause for their fatigue, such as anxiety or depression, while single women were more likely to have a physical reason for their tiredness.

Discriminating among causes of fatigue

Regardless of what we know about prevalence or the "usual" causes of fatigue, one should never assume that fatigue is psychogenic without first ruling out physical (organic) disease. Many serious diseases have a gradual or insidious onset, and the first symptom may be quite vague, such as mild tiredness. One of the most difficult tasks in medicine is to diagnose a serious disease in its early, undifferentiated stage. A physician who has known the patient over a period of time will be best equipped to recognize serious problems early. That physician will know how the individual has reacted to stress and disease in the past and will also have previous base-line laboratory studies with which to compare current results.

Continuing fatigue of recent onset warrants medical attention unless there has been tension, frustration, or personal loss that can readily account for the symptoms. If the fatigue is not relieved by rest or pleasant diversion, and especially if it persists more than a few weeks, it should be evaluated by a physician. Underlying physical disease usually presents other evidence that something is wrong, while prolonged fatigue without other signs or symptoms is more likely to be due to work-related stress, marital dissatisfaction, or other emotional problems.

Fatigue due to physical disease is usually not present in the morning, but comes on later in the day and is relieved by rest. Fatigue due to emotional tension or stress is usually present on rising in the morning and wanes to some degree as the day progresses. This kind of emotionally caused fatigue may well occur as a solitary symptom.

Emotional factors

Stress. Fatigue can result from nothing more than the stress of everyday living when the level of frustration exceeds the ability to cope with the day's events. Frustration at work with a supervisor or colleagues is perhaps the most frequent cause of fatigue. The pressure of job dissatisfaction or of never being able to get caught up can lead to tiredness, especially around mid-afternoon or in the evening. A stimulating change of pace, such as midday exercise or a refreshing interlude to look forward to at the end of the day (perhaps a tennis game, a long walk, cooking a meal, taking a class, or going to a movie) may provide a release for built-up tensions and substitute a pleasant tiredness for the fatigue of frustration.

Although stress alone can cause fatigue, it can also precipitate certain more serious medical disorders that have fatigue as one of the primary symptoms. Hyperthyroidism, rheumatoid arthritis, and coronary heart disease are three conditions that can be brought on or made worse by stress.

The compulsive individual. Some people are cursed with a compulsive need to work. The United States is still caught in the Protestant work ethic that gives approval and prestige to those who work hard without complaining. The honest person serves God and "gets ahead" by working hard and complaining little. (Japanese culture has a corresponding maxim that says "To be lazy is to injure one's parents.") Individuals caught up in this work ethic feel guilty when they are not working. They are typical so-called type A personalities, unable to enjoy a day off, even vacations or Sundays. How often have you heard someone complain (actually, boast) that they have not had a vacation in the past five years?

The compulsive perfectionist makes a schedule to fill up every minute of the day, sometimes even to the point of planning when sexual activity would be most convenient. There is no time to be spontaneous since there is already too little time available to complete the day's tasks. Thus does the man work hard in the mines all day to make money with which to buy food so that he can build up his strength in order to work hard in the mines all day.

Fatigue diminishes the ability to concentrate. Hence, many individuals compensate by working longer hours, forcing themselves to complete the task, not realizing that a period of rest or relaxation may have allowed them to concentrate more efficiently and complete the task earlier. Family members and friends can see the wisdom of such periodic rest periods. They want some attention as well and often plead for the companionship these interludes would provide. Unfortunately, the compulsive breadwinner tends not to see the value of rest periods and avoids such guilt-laden relaxation.

Professional people such as physicians, attorneys, and accountants are often very compulsive individuals. Their occupations tend to foster and reward compulsive behavior. On the other hand, housewives and blue-collar workers can also be victims. One study of males suffering heart attacks revealed that 90% of them held down two or more jobs, worked over 60 hours a week, or experienced unusual job-related stress, whereas only 20% of a comparable group not suffering a heart attack worked this hard. Working mothers may have what has been termed "bilateral highway guilt." They feel guilty going to work in the morning as they drop the children at the sitter and feel guilty leaving unfinished work at their desk when they return home in the evening.

People who seem to push themselves hard in an effort to emphasize that they are not to blame if the project—whatever it is—does not work are also compulsive individuals. It is extremely important to them that it be obvious to everyone that they are working hard, even to the point of exhaustion.

Inadequate sleep. Sometimes people complain that no matter how much sleep they get they are still tired when they get up in the morning. This may be because the sleep they do get is not restful. A fretful sleep with much tossing and turning provides insufficient rest. The subconscious may be working overtime, rehashing the day's activities or continuing to wrestle with the day's problems, with the result an inadequate replenishment of the body's energy stores.

Rapid eye movement (REM) sleep is the period when the greatest degree of muscle relaxation occurs. Certain drugs, as well as worry, interfere with REM sleep so that the person awakens feeling tired. Some investigators feel that REM sleep is when "brain repair" occurs and that non-REM sleep is a state of "bodily repair." In any event, poor sleep *quality* means inadequate rest and rehabilitation that can result in daytime fatigue.

The "tired housewife" syndrome. The "tired housewife" syndrome is often the result of overwork, boredom, erratic eating habits, and inadequate exercise. The woman who does not work outside the home suffers primarily from psychogenic fatigue and often feels trapped, frustrated, bored, and ignored. She may feel more tired in the morning than in the evening, but finds that a nap during the day provides no relief. The day-long stress of repetitive household chores and demanding children often goes unrelieved at the end of the day, especially if an unappreciative husband provides no exciting or stimulating outlet to compensate for the day's frustrations.

Such a woman may be an "at-home" counterpart of the compulsive work-oriented male. She is most likely a perfectionist and a fastidious housekeeper. Every minute of her day is occupied, with the little free time that is available devoted to volunteer work or involvement in community services, committee work, the PTA, and so forth. She may feel insufficiently appreciated and may be looking for a more satisfying outlet for her talents, or perhaps simply someone to tell her that she is working too hard and needs a little relaxation.

A normal sleeper's night

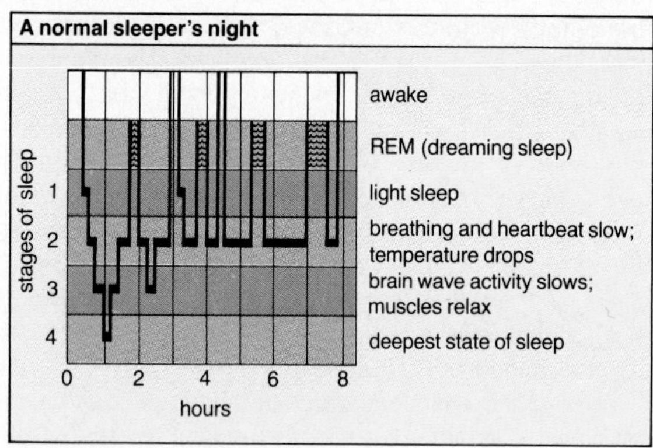

Adapted from *The Sciences*, Dec. 1975, vol. 15, no. 9, p. 25

Depression. Depression is a most common and serious problem. It can usually be treated effectively, but it too often goes unrecognized until it has reached serious proportions. Suicide rates in the United States have risen sharply in recent years, especially among depressed young adults.

The classic signs of depression are: loss of energy, tiredness or easy fatigability, loss of interest in usual activities, decreased sex drive, diminished ability to concentrate (slowed thinking or confused thoughts), feelings of self-reproach or guilt, poor appetite, sleep problems (difficulty falling asleep or remaining asleep, or the opposite problem of an increased amount of sleeping), anxiety, restlessness, or agitation, and recurring thoughts of death or suicide. The earliest signs are usually related to a sleep disturbance and diminished energy, such as "I just can't seem to get going in the morning." Most persons (up to 75%) also have somatic complaints such as headache, low back pain, muscle weakness, dizziness, or stomach problems. A third of the time serious depression takes the form of acute anxiety with palpitations, difficulty in breathing (hyperventilation), and a feeling of fear.

Medical factors

Drugs or medications. There are many drugs that can cause tiredness, and any drug, whether prescription or purchased over the counter, should be suspected as a potential cause of fatigue. Those drugs that are most frequently responsible for fatigue include sedatives, tranquilizers, antihistamines, pain medications, anticonvulsants, some hormones, and some antibiotics. The prolonged use of antihistamines and sedatives can cause fatigue, but so can the chronic use of stimulants such as caffeine (in coffee, tea, cola, and chocolate) or amphetaminelike drugs (in diet pills). Fatigue is most noticeable as a result of the "letdown" that occurs when these stimulants are discontinued. The desire to avoid this letdown and the fatigue associated with it is the stimulus for habitual use and addiction.

Alcohol is another substance that can provide temporary relaxation and can lead to addiction. This can be quite dangerous (even lethal) if excessive amounts of alcohol are taken with tranquilizers. The most commonly prescribed tranquilizers in use today, the benzodiazepines (*e.g.,* Valium, Librium), are relatively safe when used alone but when taken with alcohol can increase in potency to the point where unexpected death occurs. An attempt should be made to develop nonpharmacologic solutions to problems of stress, such as exercise or meditation.

Vitamins are of little help in treating fatigue since the fatigue is rarely due to a nutritional deficiency. They do provide essential chemicals if dietary intake is inadequate, as in the case of an alcoholic who eats poorly. Most of their beneficial effect, however, is a "placebo effect"; the individual is convinced he or she feels better because of the medication, or in this case the vitamins, regardless of any significant supplement to the diet.

Diuretic agents (water pills) may cause fatigue if their use results in the excessive loss of potassium. This loss can be detected by a blood test and the dosage easily adjusted by the physician. Some new medications, called beta-adrenergic blockers (*e.g.,* Inderal), used to treat hypertension and other heart problems, can cause fatigue as an unexpected side effect. Persons taking these drugs may notice weakness of the leg muscles or an inability to climb stairs. Some only notice "perceived exertion"; that is, they feel like they are working harder than usual to accomplish the same task. In any case, they should report this effect to their physician, who may only need to adjust the dosage. Changing from one beta-blocking agent to another oc-

Fatigue can result from boredom and monotony as well as from overwork or mental and physical disease. An effort to work a stimulating but relaxing activity into the day helps relieve this type of fatigue.

casionally provides relief, but there is no good evidence that one beta-blocker is less likely to cause fatigue than another.

Infection. Fatigue can be the only evidence of a hidden infection. Fortunately, most infections that cause fatigue are due to viruses and are usually not serious and of short duration. It is possible, however, to have a potentially serious bacterial infection with an insidious course, the only evidence of which is tiredness and easy fatigability. Tuberculosis is one such infection. Another is an infection of the heart valves called subacute bacterial endocarditis (SBE). Each of these is usually accompanied by other signs or symptoms of infection, although these may also be subtle. If tuberculosis is present, there will usually be a low-grade fever, weight loss, poor appetite, and sweating while asleep (night sweats). SBE is usually accompanied by a low-grade fever, along with a heart murmur and anemia. Persons with abnormalities of the heart valves such as mitral valve prolapse are more susceptible to infections of this type and are given penicillin as a preventive measure whenever they are exposed to the release of bacteria into the blood (for example, during surgery or dental extractions).

Cancer. Although occult, or hidden, malignancy is an uncommon cause of unexplained tiredness, it can cause fatigue and should be considered. Cancers more likely to be associated with fatigue are those occurring in the pancreas, lung, kidney, liver, or bone marrow. In the last type, which affects the blood-forming organs, cancer appears as leukemia or lymphoma and is accompanied by anemia.

Coronary heart disease. It is possible for fatigue to be the only symptom of myocardial infarction or coronary insufficiency. A mild heart attack may occur without causing chest pain, yet it may still slow the circulation of oxygenated blood throughout the body, causing no symptoms other than tiredness.

Anemia. Anemia is commonly one of the first abnormalities considered as a cause of fatigue, yet it is usually not the real cause of the problem. Anemia can be detected easily using a simple blood test. When it does occur, it frequently is due to excessive loss of blood in women who have heavy menstrual periods. In the early stages of iron deficiency anemia there is a decrease in the total amount of iron in the blood. Iron is necessary for the red blood cells to make oxygen-carrying hemoglobin. The red blood cells increase in size in an effort to carry more oxygen per cell, and thus allow many mildly anemic persons to carry on normal activity without fatigue. When the hemoglobin falls to less than 9 to 10 g per 100 ml of blood, an insufficient amount of oxygen is delivered to the tissues. Fatigue then sets in, along with pallor and a rapid pulse.

The treatment of iron deficiency anemia calls for more than merely replacing the lost iron. The source of the bleeding must be identified, and controlled if possible, to ensure that the iron level in the blood will increase. Naturally, when the cause of anemia cannot be found, a more vigorous search for hidden malignancy is warranted.

Pulmonary disease. Fatigue can also result from an insufficient supply of oxygen to the tissues in patients with chronic pulmonary disease, especially when the pulmonary disease is due to prolonged smoking, chronic bronchitis, or emphysema. The excessive work of breathing, combined with a decreased supply of oxygen to the tissues, can result in constant fatigue and a limited capacity for exercise. Treatment is difficult once lung damage has occurred, but stopping smoking is helpful no matter how advanced the disease process.

Thyroid dysfunction. Many people know that an underactive thyroid gland can cause one to be tired and sluggish, but few are aware that fatigue can also occur when the gland is overactive. An underactive thyroid gland (hypothyroidism) results in lassitude, weight gain, and an inability to tolerate cold weather. An overactive gland (hyperthyroidism, or Graves' disease) can also cause fatigue as a result of an increased rate of metabolism. The patient suffering from hyperthyroidism experiences nervousness, anxiety, weight loss, sweating, and an inability to tolerate hot weather. An overactive gland may also cause muscle weakness, particularly in the shoulder or hip muscles, so that the person afflicted will be unable to rise from a squatting position.

A single blood test is normally all the physician needs to identify thyroid dysfunction as the cause of fatigue. When there is decreased function, treatment with thyroid hormone is simple and effective. A variety of methods is available for treating an overactive gland. Treatment can involve surgery, radioactive iodine, or antithyroid drugs, each of which results in a decreased production of thyroid hormone.

Other causes. Some additional disorders that have fatigue as one of the earliest symptoms are diabetes mellitus, rheumatoid arthritis, kidney failure, and adrenal gland insufficiency. These are all relatively uncommon. Another rare but potentially devastating disorder is myasthenia gravis. This is a disease of muscles that results in fatigue of the muscle following repeated use. The first sign of the disease can be drooping of the eyelids at the end of the day. Muscles most frequently affected are of the face, lips, tongue, throat, and neck.

Nutritional deficiency such as that occurring in alcoholism can also result in prolonged fatigue. The problem is not an insufficiency of calories but an inappropriate selection of foods that provide required nutrients. Poor dietary habits, whether in a teenager who eats only junk food or in an alcoholic with poor food intake, also predispose the person to infection through lowered resistance.

—Robert E. Rakel, M.D.

Health Education Unit 8

Hemorrhoids

Over half of the adult population of the Western world has at some time suffered the pain and incapacitating effects of hemorrhoids (also known as "piles" or varicose veins of the anus). A more precise estimate of the prevalence of this disorder is difficult to obtain. A review of three recent textbooks of proctology (the study of diseases of the anus and rectum) found no agreement about prevalence of the disease, with estimates ranging from 50 to 80% of all adults over age 30. Hemorrhoidal disease is not a topic people are likely to discuss openly—indeed it is often a source of great embarrassment—and probably a minority of hemorrhoid sufferers ever visit a physician for relief of this problem. It is known, however, that hemorrhoidal disease is more common in the Western world than elsewhere. Why this is true is only speculation, although diet, exercise, and social customs are thought to be possible causes.

Defining the problem

Hemorrhoids are spongy, blood-containing protrusions at the anal opening or along the first four to five centimeters (1.5–2 in) of the anal canal. These protrusions are actually varicose (dilated) veins. In order to understand more about the condition of hemorrhoids, some explanation of the normal anatomy of the anal region is necessary. The outside and first two to three centimeters (1 in) of the anus, the posterior opening of the intestinal tract, are covered by skin similar to that on the back of the hand. A transition to moist skin (mucous membrane) similar to that inside the mouth occurs at the anorectal line. The anorectal line is important to the classification of hemorrhoids. Above the line is a plexus of veins known as the internal hemorrhoidal vessels; below the line there is another plexus of veins, the external hemorrhoidal vessels. Hemorrhoids (dilated hemorrhoidal veins) arising above the line are referred to as internal hemorrhoids, while those arising below this line are called external hemorrhoids. If both collections of veins are involved the condition is referred to as mixed or combined hemorrhoids.

Above the anorectal line the veins drain to larger internal vessels, which also receive the blood flow from the intestines and liver. The pathway of drainage below the anorectal line is toward the veins of the groin, which receive blood from the legs and muscles. Internal hemorrhoids above the anorectal line are usually painless. The presence of nerve fibers below the anorectal line can cause external hemorrhoid sufferers to experience moderate to severe discomfort.

Internal hemorrhoids are usually classified according to their severity. Stage I hemorrhoids are the mildest form, with bleeding as the only sign. Stage II denotes that the hemorrhoid will protrude out through the anal opening during defecation, but this protrusion spontaneously corrects after the bowel movement. Stage III refers to protruding hemorrhoids that come through the anal opening and can be pushed back up inside, but will not return inside spontaneously. Stage IV hemorrhoids are varicose veins that permanently protrude through the anal opening. Occasionally, protruding internal hemorrhoids become trapped outside the anal opening and are squeezed by inflammation and swelling. A clot forms in these vessels and they are then known as strangulated hemorrhoids. These classifications are important to the various treatments for the disease.

In most patients, internal hemorrhoids occur in three main locations. Two of these locations are on the right side of the body: right anterior (toward the front of the body) and right posterior (toward the back of the body). The third location is in the left lateral area (toward the left side of the body). External hemorrhoids arise anywhere along the verge of the anal opening and are not reducible, which means that the dilated veins cannot be coaxed back into place.

Causes

A number of factors may cause hemorrhoidal disease. The human upright position causes increased pressure within the hemorrhoidal veins, which lack any valves to help reduce the effects of gravity on the blood vessel system. Heredity is also considered to be an important causal factor, since some individuals are predisposed to weakness of the supporting tissues around these veins. Occupations that involve a great deal of heavy lifting and those requiring prolonged sitting or standing

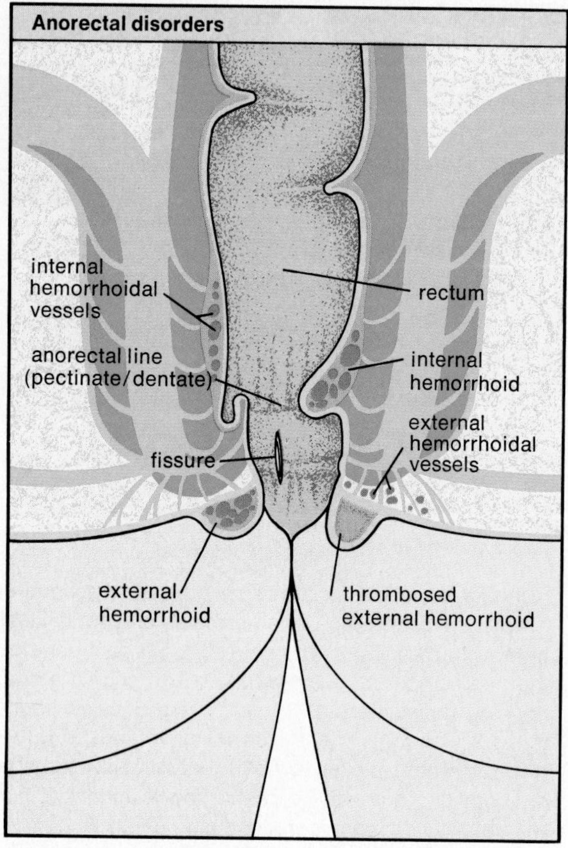

are also responsible for increased pressure on hemorrhoidal veins, which may cause them to protrude. For this reason, truck and taxi drivers and office workers who sit most of the day are believed to be afflicted more than others. Dietary factors may be involved in hemorrhoidal disease. Nutritional habits can affect the stool, sometimes causing constipation, which predisposes to hemorrhoids. A diet low in roughage accompanied by a low intake of liquids contributes to hard stools, which are difficult to pass and cause straining and prolonged sitting on the toilet. Failure to attend to the urge to have a stool or delaying the emptying of the bowel by holding back a movement can also lead to hemorrhoids. Many authorities believe that minor infections of the anal canal can provoke hemorrhoids by creating inflammation and weakening of supporting tissues and of the hemorrhoid veins (phlebitis).

A number of diseases can contribute to the development of hemorrhoids by increasing the pressure on the veins of the anus. These include diarrhea, heart failure, liver disease, chronic coughing associated with lung disease, and cancer of the rectum or pelvic organs.

Probably the most common cause of hemorrhoids in women is pregnancy. As the uterus enlarges, pressure on the hemorrhoidal veins increases. Constipation, a common annoyance of pregnancy, often leads to hemorrhoids. Iron supplements given to prevent anemia during pregnancy can aggravate constipation. Additionally, pushing the baby through the birth canal can produce intense pressure on the hemorrhoidal veins, resulting in a postpartum hemorrhoid problem.

Signs and symptoms

The signs and symptoms of hemorrhoidal disease vary widely. The location of the hemorrhoid and its severity will in large part determine whether a person considers the problem just a nuisance or a matter that requires a doctor's immediate attention.

Internal hemorrhoids are often first recognized when blood appears on the toilet paper or in the toilet bowl after defecation. A few drops of blood coloring the toilet water red can be quite alarming. The loss of blood is due to abrasion or ulceration of the protruding hemorrhoid by passage of stool through the anal canal. Since blood in the stool can be caused by more serious conditions than hemorrhoids, this sign should prompt a visit to the physician for confirmation that the cause is benign. This kind of bleeding is generally not an emergency condition, however. The blood loss is quite small, similar to that from a small cut or scrape.

Pain is rarely associated with internal hemorrhoids unless a coexisting complication is present, such as anal fissure (a small tear in the anal skin), thrombosis (blood clot formation), or strangulation of the hemorrhoids. Only in the case of long-standing hemorrhoidal disease is one likely to discover a lump protruding from the anus. Itching is another unlikely symptom unless chronically protruding vessels are inflamed and produce a mucous discharge.

On the other hand, external hemorrhoids produce varying degrees of pain or rectal pressure, and a palpable lump can be felt on the anal opening. The external hemorrhoid frequently results from a blood clot forming in a protruding vein and has a sudden and noticeable onset, unlike the silent onset characteristic of internal hemorrhoids. Irritation and itching are more common with external hemorrhoids, but bleeding is unusual except where the hemorrhoid is injured or begins to break down by ulceration. When the hemorrhoid is large, clotted, and ulcerated, discomfort can be severe and incapacitating.

Diagnosis

When signs and symptoms of any anorectal disease are first noted, a visit to the physician is warranted mainly if the symptoms are alarming or severe. Many problems are simple, can usually be self-treated, and will come and go entirely within the span of one week.

Self-examination. When symptoms appear to be minor, an individual can usually assess the situation at home. While in the shower or sitting on the toilet, the anal opening and surrounding skin should be felt for protrusions and tenderness. The anus can be inspected while sitting on the toilet and using a hand-held mirror. The presence of a lump at the anal verge, which is tender to touch and appears slightly bluish in color, is most likely an external hemorrhoid. When the lump is moist, mucus covered, red in color, and seems to be coming through the opening rather than appearing on its verge, the problem is most likely an internal hemorrhoid. These conditions are usually mild and temporary and can easily be self-treated. If the problem completely resolves in one week, no further action is necessary.

If the symptoms last more than one week, if they become severe, or if bleeding from the rectum is noted, an examination by a physician is warranted. The primary purpose of this examination should be to rule out cancer as a cause for the symptoms. The physician's next most important job is to make an accurate diagnosis and suggest appropriate treatment. When properly performed, the examination for anorectal disease takes only a few minutes and is relatively free of discomfort or pain for the patient.

Examination by a physician. The doctor's investigation of hemorrhoids will encompass several procedures. He will perform a general inspection of the anal area under good light. He will then feel the skin of the buttocks and that surrounding the anus with a gloved finger. The skin will be checked for growths, inflammation, and perforations, which may be openings of fistulous tracts. He will usually check the groin area to assess the status of the lymph nodes that receive drainage from the anal area. Enlarged lymph nodes may signal infection.

Next, the physician, using a gloved index finger that has been well lubricated, will examine the inside of the anal canal and lower rectum. If there is a very painful spot to be examined, a topical anesthetic lubricant will be used to numb the area. The physician can feel abnormal masses or protrusions, abscesses (pockets of infection), or polyps (small pea-sized growths), and he can ascertain the quality of the stool if any is present in the rectum. When stool is felt in the rectum, a sample is withdrawn on the gloved finger and tested for minute quantities of blood. This check for occult blood that cannot be seen with the naked eye is called a guaiac test. When it is positive for blood on several consecutive office visits, further investigation is indicated, as a colon cancer may be present. About 30% of cancers of the colon can be detected by the physician during a digital exam; these tumors are generally located four to five centimeters inside the anus.

Following the digital exam, the inside of the anal canal and lower rectum are inspected visually. The patient lies on the examining table on one side with knees drawn up, or on hands and knees, depending on patient comfort and physician preference. Instruments used for this visual inspection are tubes approximately 1.75 cm in diameter and made of stainless steel or plastic. They have a powerful light source to illuminate the inside of the bowel. For most hemorrhoidal conditions and other locally occurring problems, such as anal fissure, pruritus ani (itching of the anal skin), and cryptitis (inflammation of the anorectal line), the anoscope is used. This instrument is five centimeters in length and is usually slotted along one side to allow visualization and insertion of probes that can be used for therapeutic purposes along the length of the tube. Other instruments that may be used are the proctoscope (15 cm [6 in] in length) and the sigmoidoscope (25 cm [10 in]). Anyone who has long-standing rectal symptoms or hemorrhoids should have an internal examination in which one of these instruments is used.

Patients may be concerned about the discomfort they will experience during an exam of the anus and rectum. But their fears are largely unwarranted. The examiner should provide a thorough explanation of the procedure beforehand. The instruments can and should be manipulated gently, causing minimal discomfort. Unfortunately, some less-than-considerate physicians may treat patients roughly. Patient preparation for the exam requires only that the lower bowel be emptied just prior to the procedure, either by natural bowel movement or a small enema. The patient may help to eliminate any pain by consciously relaxing and reducing muscle tension during the exam. He should also tell the physician when any discomfort is felt. When the patient is adequately prepared and cooperative the entire procedure takes 15 minutes or less.

Visual examination of the anal canal and lower rectum is crucial because common hemorrhoidal signs and symptoms are shared by a number of other, more serious problems that occur in the anorectal area. Only after an exact diagnosis is made can the patient be reassured of the benign nature of persistent symptoms such as rectal bleeding, itching, and pressure and tenderness in the anal canal. Cancers of the colon, which can produce symptoms similar to hemorrhoidal disease, if detected early, usually can be cured. The importance of a visual exam, therefore, cannot be emphasized enough.

Treatment

Once the diagnosis of hemorrhoids is made and other types of abnormalities have been ruled out, therapy may be started. The general goals for treatment are to relieve pain and reduce swelling. Provided a thorough workup to uncover causative factors has preceded treatment, prognosis for all forms of hemorrhoids is excellent. The type of hemorrhoid (internal or external), the severity of symptoms, and the stage of the disease are the factors that determine the therapy to be used.

Self-diagnosed external hemorrhoids that cause minimal discomfort require only simple treatment. Local application of cold compresses during the first few hours after onset of pain will decrease local blood flow and provide some numbing. The patient should avoid heavy lifting and prolonged standing or sitting. Bed rest may be advisable for a short time. Constipation, with associated straining at the stool, needs to be treated, sometimes by increasing fiber content in the diet, sometimes by drinking extra fluids; in some cases a mild bulk-producing laxative such as psyllium hydrophilic mucilloid (*e.g.,* Metamucil) or a mild fecal softener such as dioctyl sodium sulfosuccinate (available under a number of brand names) may be useful. After 24 hours warm tub baths are helpful in reducing swelling and reducing discomfort. Aspirin taken every four to six hours will help reduce inflammation and provide additional pain relief. Hemorrhoid creams are available without prescription and can be used for their astringent, soothing, and anesthetic properties. The cream should be applied to the surface of the hemorrhoid with a finger and not squirted up inside the anal canal. Caution in the use of these preparations is advised, however, since skin rash can occur if the patient is allergic to any of the ingredients.

Acute thrombosis (blood clotting) may occur in an external hemorrhoid causing such severe pain that removal of the hemorrhoid may be indicated. This can easily be done in the doctor's office. A local anesthetic will be injected and the clotted vein removed in a minor surgical procedure that quickly resolves the problem. No hospitalization is necessary. After two to three days of taking it easy at home the patient is usually able to return to regular activities. Even without treatment, acutely clotted external hemorrhoids will generally heal themselves in two to three weeks.

Stage I or II internal hemorrhoids may be treated conservatively with dietary measures and occasional stool-softening agents. High-fiber foods and increased fluid intake are generally encouraged. Over-the-counter rectal ointments or suppositories have very limited usefulness.

If conservative therapy fails, sclerotherapy or cryotherapy can be used. Sclerotherapy is an office procedure in which the patient is given a hypodermic injection of an irritant sclerosing solution into the tissue beneath the hemorrhoid. Mild aching discomfort may follow this form of therapy, which obliterates the affected tissue. Cryotherapy is another office treatment which involves the application of a freezing probe to the hemorrhoid so that cellular destruction occurs (similar to that caused by frostbite to the skin). This technique is more suitable for larger stage II hemorrhoids and some stage III hemorrhoids. Mild discomfort and discharge of a clear fluid from the rectum usually occur for several days following cryotherapy.

Chronic stage III hemorrhoids are best treated with either rubber band ligation or surgical removal. Rubber band ligation can be done only if the hemorrhoid is completely above the anorectal line and protruding into the anal canal. Special instruments are used to grasp the hemorrhoid and strangle it with a tiny rubber band. The rubber band is left in place so that, after several days of choking off the blood supply to the hemorrhoid, the tissue dies and falls off. Rubber band ligation is painless, easily done in the doctor's office, highly effective, and considerably less costly than surgery. The patient can resume normal activities the day after the procedure.

Hemorrhoidectomy, or the surgical removal of hemorrhoids, is the therapy of last resort. It is indicated when protrusion, pain, bleeding, or very large hemorrhoids are present. Hemorrhoidectomy is a hospital procedure requiring anesthetic and five to seven days' recovery. Symptoms rarely recur after a properly performed hemorrhoidectomy. Surgery is usually feared by most patients, but the only real risk is associated with the anesthetic; the pain experienced after surgery can be controlled with medications. Surgery is usually reserved for stage IV hemorrhoids. But where symptoms of less serious forms are severe enough, an operation may be warranted.

Prevention

Most people are at risk for development of hemorrhoids and therefore should make some effort to prevent their occurrence. Those who work at sedentary jobs should engage in some form of daily exercise. If prolonged car trips are taken, it is wise to stop every 200 miles or so to stretch and get some exercise. Those with minor hemorrhoid problems should avoid lifting weights or other heavy physical exertion.

Diet should include foods that provide bulk and decrease the chances of constipation. Foods high in fiber include bran, celery, whole grain breads, raw vegetables, and fruits. Drinking four or more glasses of water daily is advisable to keep the stools soft and moist. Occasionally, when constipation is a problem, psyllium hydrophilic mucilloid may be taken as a bulk-producing agent in doses of one to two tablespoons daily. Foods such as refined sugars and dairy products may cause constipation and therefore should be limited. Certain medicines may also cause constipation, and should be avoided if possible. Chronic laxative use should always be avoided.

Finally, people who spend prolonged periods on the toilet should alter their habits. Reading on the toilet while waiting for a bowel movement is a common habit that prolongs engorgement of the anorectal veins. The bathroom should not be the "library." People should spend only a few minutes sitting on the toilet. Attention to the urge to defecate and going directly to the bathroom instead of delaying the movement will help to shorten defecation time. These simple measures can go a long way toward preventing the unpleasant problem of hemorrhoids.

—Charles E. Driscoll, M.D.

Teething

There are few subjects more confusing to new parents than teething. Even pediatricians are hard pressed to differentiate teething from other causes of excessive crankiness and crying in a small baby—it is easy to blame teething for all sorts of problems that the baby encounters. Because there are many misconceptions about teething, this discussion should help parents better understand and cope with the process.

The teething process

Teething is the process by which the teeth push through the gums. What is especially puzzling is the great differences in the symptoms and signs associated with teething that are seen from baby to baby. Some babies acquire their entire set of baby teeth with no difficulty at all, while others suffer a great deal of discomfort with the eruption of every single new tooth. There really is no satisfactory explanation for this. The experience of many parents is that one of their children has little or no trouble and another a great deal of trouble. Even twins may have totally different experiences with teething.

When does the teething process begin? Again there is much variation from baby to baby. Rarely, a baby may actually be born with one or two lower central incisors. This event is observed in about one in 2,000 newborns. These teeth usually are loosely attached with very little root formation or bony support. On occasion they may interfere with breast-feeding or may cause pain and discomfort, with the added danger of detachment and possible inhaling of the tooth. In such a case a dentist should be consulted. X-rays may be necessary to assess the situation, and the teeth may need to be extracted.

On the other end of the spectrum, some babies sit down to their first birthday party with no teeth at all. Parents should be assured that in virtually all cases there is absolutely no correlation between the early or late eruption of teeth and the overall physical and mental development of the baby. Very rarely the delayed eruption of all the teeth may indicate a systemic or nutritional disturbance such as hypothyroidism or rickets. If the baby is otherwise developing normally, parents need not be concerned about when the teeth will finally appear. A baby who is thriving and developing normally is guaranteed a full set of 20 baby, or deciduous, teeth. On the average, most babies start to show signs of teething at around three or four months of age, and the first two teeth come in around six to seven months of age.

Mothers often ask the pediatrician to predict when the baby's next tooth will appear. This is not easy—one pediatrician, after carefully examining the gums of a six-month-old, told the baby's mother that there was no sign of any teeth yet. The next morning she called and told him that two teeth had popped through during the night. There is a usual sequence to the appearance of the baby teeth but, again, there is some variation, and if your baby does not follow the usual pattern, there is no need to be concerned. The usual order of events is as follows.

First to appear are the two lower central incisors at 6 to 7 months. These are followed by the four upper incisors at 7 to 12 months. The two central upper teeth often come in widely separated. This is normal. As the rest of the baby teeth come in, this space gradually closes up. So, by one year of age the baby usually has six teeth, two lower and four upper incisors (the front teeth with sharp cutting edges). Then there is usually a pause for a few months followed by the two remaining lower incisors and the four first molars (14–16 months). A space is left between the central teeth and the four molars. Next to come in are the four canines, the pointed back teeth, at 18 to 21 months. By two years of age the baby will probably have 16 baby teeth. Finally, the four second molars, the so-called two-year molars, will appear at 24 to 30 months.

With rare exceptions the child will have a full set of 20 baby teeth before the third birthday. These deciduous teeth start falling out at around 6 years of age and are usually completely shed by 11 years of age.

Care of the new teeth

A discussion of the eruption of teeth would not be complete without including some facts about proper

Erika Stone—Peter Arnold, Inc.

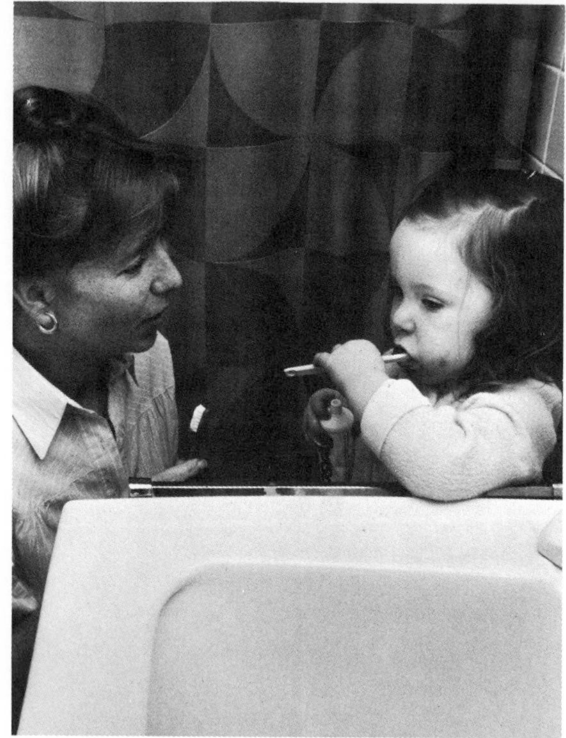

Instruction in proper tooth care should begin as soon as the child is able to manage the toothbrush. Healthy baby teeth help ensure healthy adult teeth.

oral hygiene for the young child and the prevention of dental caries, or tooth decay. Many parents do not realize that specific measures should be taken soon after the baby is born in order to reduce and even prevent tooth decay and gum disease. The pediatrician who routinely brings up this subject with the parents of the newborns will find that parents react to the idea of dental care for infants with surprise. "I don't understand what you are talking about. My baby has no teeth yet, so why worry about it?" Another common response is, "It's just a baby tooth and will fall out soon anyway, so why bother?" The fact is that parents can do a great deal to reduce the incidence of dental disease in their children with some simple, safe procedures, if they are started early enough.

Modern dentistry and pediatrics have one main theme common to both—*prevention.* Deciduous, or milk or baby, teeth can decay just as easily as the permanent teeth and may cause the small child a good deal of pain and suffering. The greatest period of dental caries for the deciduous teeth is between four and eight years of age, but dental decay can develop much earlier than that. A small child whose parents do not take the necessary steps to instill habits of good dental hygiene is more prone to dental caries than the child whose parents act appropriately. The most important point to remember is that a child who is allowed to develop diseased deciduous teeth is more likely to suffer with decayed and damaged permanent teeth later on in life. The reasons for this become clear once the mechanism and causes of dental decay are understood. The three main factors related to dental decay are oral hygiene, diet, and fluoride.

Optimal oral hygiene refers to the proper brushing and flossing of the teeth to rid the teeth of decay-causing bacteria. Both of these procedures should be started as early as possible. Pedodontists (dentists taking care of children) agree that if these simple measures are instituted soon after the eruption of the first tooth they will significantly reduce the incidence of both dental decay and gum disease. A small, soft-bristled toothbrush and a mild toothpaste will help make the experience a pleasant one for the child. The finest grade of dental floss should be used. The early use of a toothbrush and dental floss also sets the proper example and makes it more likely that the child, as he grows, will take over these chores himself and will continue to regularly brush and floss throughout childhood and beyond. There is no question that such a youngster will grow up with healthier teeth and gums. Too many parents wait until the child has a full set of teeth before thinking about oral hygiene care—this is a serious mistake.

Diet plays an equally important role. Eating foods or liquids that contain sugar, especially in forms that stick or cling or promote prolonged contact with the teeth, such as lollipops or lozenges, contribute greatly to the development of dental decay. These foods provide the ideal environment for the production of tooth-destroying acid by the bacteria that are normally found in the mouth and on the teeth. Eating such foods between

"He's teething."

By permission of V. Gene Myers and *Good Housekeeping* © 1979

Erika Stone—Peter Arnold, Inc.

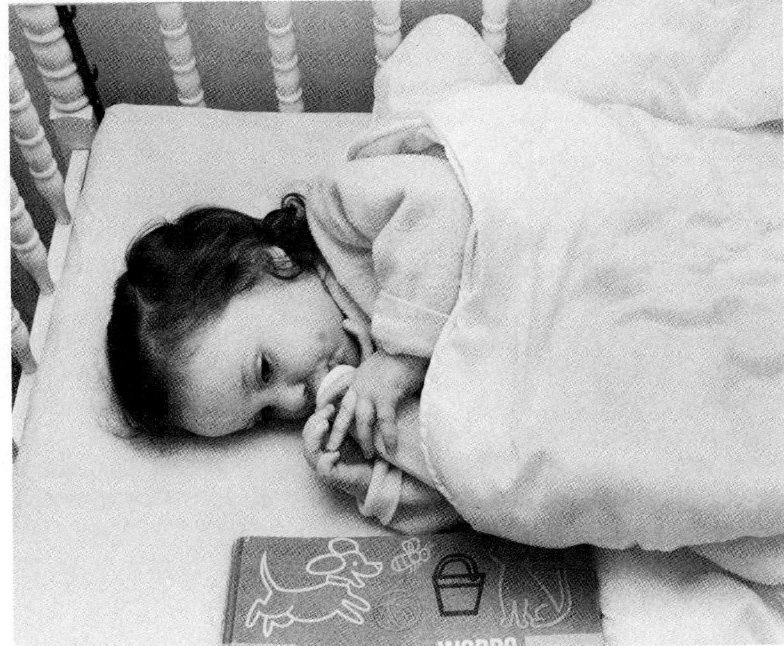

Dentists are frequently called on to treat very young children whose front teeth are decayed because from infancy they have been put to sleep with a bottle of formula or fruit juice, a practice that allows decay-causing sugar to rest against the teeth for hours at a time. The "nursing bottle syndrome" can be prevented by having the child finish drinking before being put to bed or by giving the child plain water in the bedtime bottle.

meals is even more injurious to the teeth than if they are eaten during the meal. It has been clearly demonstrated that if foods containing sugar are eaten at mealtimes they cause less trouble because the saliva and the other foods that are consumed at the same time tend to neutralize the dangerous acid. The lesson to be learned from this is to avoid giving your child junk foods, especially sugary snacks, between meals.

The practice of putting a baby to sleep with a bottle of formula or milk or any sweetened fluid such as juice also should be discouraged. This faulty feeding method frequently leads to so-called nursing bottle caries. It has been shown that babies who suck on a bottle containing milk or juice while lying down for extended periods of time are much more prone to dental decay because of the prolonged contact of the sugar with the teeth. The child may also go to sleep with the liquid in his mouth. Many pediatricians recommend not only that babies not be given a bottle while lying down in the crib, but that fruit juice be fed only by cup. Others do not object to giving a baby juice in a bottle but insist that if this is done the baby should drink it only while in an upright position. If your baby requires a bottle in order to help him fall asleep, make certain that it contains only water. This not only will save your baby's teeth but also will appreciably lower your dental bills.

It has been proven that an extremely effective measure to prevent dental caries is natural or artificial fluoridation of the water supply. The daily use of ingested fluoride dramatically reduces the incidence of tooth decay. Despite some contrary statements in the lay press in recent years, fluoride given in the proper dose is safe and effective and protects both the deciduous and the permanent teeth against dental decay. Fluoride has been used in the United States for over 30 years. Many localities have added fluoride to their water supplies where the natural level of fluoride is too low. It is estimated that 110 million people in the United States drink water containing fluoride. This has resulted in an overall 65% reduction of dental decay.

The committee on nutrition of the American Academy of Pediatrics recently published their new recommendations regarding fluoride supplementation for infants and children. They recommend fluoride supplementation in very early infancy, starting at two weeks and continuing until 16 years of age. The amount of supplemental fluoride is dependent on the fluoride content in the drinking water of the community. The status of a community's water supply with regard to fluoride concentration can be checked by calling the local department of health. If you find out that your water supply does not contain sufficient fluoride, your baby will require extra fluoride by mouth each day. The fluoride can be given in the form of fluoride drops or in combination with a multivitamin preparation. The daily dose of fluoride is determined by the level of fluoride in the water supply. This holds true for both breast-fed and formula-fed babies. Your child's physician should be consulted as to dose and method of administration.

What must clearly be understood is that at birth the deciduous teeth are already 20% calcified (hardened and filled with calcium), and that this calcification process is almost complete by one year of age. In addition, the permanent teeth also are calcified early in life, and by four years of age their calcification is almost complete. Therefore, if fluoride is to be effective in preventing dental decay in both deciduous and permanent teeth it must be started shortly after birth.

How does fluoride work? The mechanism of action is complicated, but the main point is that it is absorbed into the bones and teeth. The fluoride toughens and hardens the developing tooth while it is still hidden in the gum. It is absorbed into the enamel of the teeth and promotes the remineralization of the enamel and therefore helps to harden and strengthen the teeth and so protects against decay. A child who is taught proper oral hygiene early, fed a diet low in sugary foods, and given adequate daily amounts of fluoride will be well protected against the ravages of dental decay.

Caring for the teething baby

How can you decide whether or not your baby is teething? The first clear sign of teething is excessive drooling and dribbling, and this usually begins at about three to four months of age. Some babies become quite irritable and may have a decrease in their appetites. They swallow excessive amounts of saliva during this period and so some babies spit up or vomit more frequently than usual. Also, because of the swallowing of saliva, a number of babies produce slimy, loose bowel movements. Rashes develop around the chin because of the extra drooling and around the anus from the loose stools. Another group of teething babies develops coughs, especially at night. This night cough is caused by saliva dripping back into the throat during sleep. Still other teethers become fretful and cranky and often wake up crying during the night.

Experienced mothers can sometimes predict when a new tooth is starting to erupt by their baby's behavior pattern. Some babies, for example, have signs of a cold or upper respiratory infection before each tooth; others develop diarrhea, get rashes, or start vomiting. During this time it is very easy to blame everything that goes wrong with your baby on the teeth. Since the teething process usually continues for over two years and the signs and symptoms of teething are so variable, almost anything unusual that occurs can be attributed to teething. If you are ever in doubt as to the cause of a symptom, consult your baby's physician.

The old wives' tale that teething causes fever is not true. If your baby has a temperature above 101°, it is *not* due to teething. There must be another explanation for the fever. What is probably true is that the teething process somehow seems to lower the baby's resistance and therefore makes him more susceptible to an infection, such as an ear infection. The loss of sleep combined with decreased fluid and food intake during teething may be the explanation.

When you are faced with a baby who is having difficulty teething, what can you do to relieve the baby's discomfort? First of all, let the baby chew on a rubber teething ring, hard roll, or teething pretzel. A teething baby really appreciates the opportunity to bite and chew. Some babies seem to get added relief when their teething ring is cooled in the refrigerator. Rubbing the baby's gums with your fingers, perhaps with one of the commercial preparations that contain a mild local anesthetic, can also be helpful. If your baby develops a night cough as part of her teething process, elevating her head in the crib can be effective. For the baby who is so cranky that he or she just cannot get to sleep on some evening, try feeding the baby the following mixture: 1 teaspoon whiskey, 2 tablespoons water, and 1/4 teaspoon sugar. This mixture will help the exhausted, miserable infant get some needed sleep, but it should be given very rarely, only when all other means of comfort have proved futile. For the equally exhausted and sleepless parent, this old remedy may do the trick: Pour two ounces of gin into a wide-mouthed glass, dip the tip of your little finger in the glass, shake off the excess and rub baby's gums; then drink the rest of the gin yourself.

The important facts to keep in mind are the following:

1. All babies teethe, and all babies end up with 20 teeth.
2. The age at which the teeth appear is not related to development or intelligence.
3. The signs and symptoms of teething vary from baby to baby.
4. The main signs that a tooth is errupting are drooling and irritability.
5. Teething does *not* cause high fever.
6. The best treatment for teething discomfort is allowing the baby to chew on a firm object and rubbing the inflamed gums.
7. Do not blame all the baby's symptoms on teething.
8. When in doubt, consult your baby's physician.

—*Alvin N. Eden, M.D.*

Health Education Unit 10

Reye's Syndrome

Reye's syndrome is a serious and potentially lethal children's disease causing increased pressure in the brain and liver damage. It is one of the ten major causes of death in children over the age of one. Although this illness is characterized primarily by involvement of the brain and the liver it can strike many other parts of the body as well. The main danger in Reye's syndrome is the acute encephalopathy that results in a marked increase in pressure within the brain. Along with this degenerative disease of the brain there is associated liver disease resulting in a tremendous accumulation of fat, causing a severe loss of liver function. The characteristic fatty changes in the liver have made it possible for this condition to be distinguished from many other childhood degenerative brain diseases of undetermined causes. The association of an acute encephalopathy and a fatty liver adds up to the diagnosis of Reye's syndrome. The cause of Reye's syndrome is unknown and the disease cannot be prevented. There is no specific cure, but in the hands of physicians experienced with Reye's syndrome various methods of treatment can reduce both the morbidity and mortality.

Discovery of the disease

The first description of Reye's syndrome appeared in the medical literature in 1963. Based on his experience over 12 years' time, an Australian pathologist, R. D. K. Reye, and his associates published an article in the British medical journal *The Lancet* entitled "Encephalopathy and Fatty Degeneration of the Viscera: a Disease Entity of Childhood." Between 1951 and 1963 this group had accumulated data on over 20 cases; since 1963, this disease entity has been called Reye's syndrome.

There is some question about whether Reye's syndrome is in fact a new disease. The majority of authorities on the subject believe Reye's syndrome is not new; before 1963 deaths caused by this syndrome may have been misdiagnosed as a number of different diseases or just recorded as deaths from unknown causes. Some investigators find it difficult to accept that it could have been present and misdiagnosed since the golden yellow or white massively fatty livers found at autopsy are so distinctive.

Whether or not Reye's syndrome is a new disease or an old one makes for lively discussion but really is not very important. What is important is that Reye's syndrome is now considered one of the most common causes of childhood viral-associated central nervous system disease in the United States. Reye's syndrome can cause permanent brain damage or can be fatal in a significant percentage of children affected with it. The early diagnosis and immediate hospitalization of infected youngsters in medical centers equipped and staffed to treat Reye's syndrome is the only way to improve the outcome. Any significant delay in the diagnosis and the start of treatment lessens the chances of a full and complete recovery.

Children of all ages are susceptible to Reye's syndrome. A few cases have been reported in infants but the largest number of reported cases are in the 5–15-

year-old group. After the age of 16, the incidence decreases markedly and Reye's syndrome is rarely seen after the age of 18. Boys and girls are affected in equal numbers.

A number of theories have been proposed about the causes of Reye's syndrome but none has been confirmed. We do know that Reye's syndrome is almost always associated with a previous viral infection. At least 16 different viral agents have been identified as causing the prodromal (preliminary) illnesses that preceded the development of Reye's syndrome. In the U.S., influenza type B and chickenpox (varicella) are the two most frequently reported viral diseases seen before the onset of Reye's syndrome.

Reye's syndrome is not contagious. The majority of the cases occur during the winter months, especially in January, February, and March, but the disease has been reported throughout the rest of the year as well.

Although Reye's syndrome has received a great deal of publicity in recent years, it is still a relatively uncommon illness. The number of diagnosed cases has increased during the past few years as awareness has increased and milder forms are now being recognized more frequently. From Dec. 1, 1979, to Nov. 30, 1980, the Centers for Disease Control (CDC) reported 548 cases in the U.S. that met their immunologic definition of Reye's syndrome. As all reporting of cases to the CDC is voluntary, this figure is probably an understatement of actual cases. The CDC estimates that the annual incidence throughout the U.S. is 1 to 2 cases per 100,000 for the population under 18 years of age. The number of cases is greater during years when there are severe outbreaks of influenza B.

Diagnosis, treatment, and prognosis

Since the prognosis of Reye's syndrome is usually determined by how early the diagnosis is made and treatment initiated, it is essential that parents be familiar with its symptoms. As stated previously,these symptoms almost always follow a previous viral infection, usually within one to two weeks. The first sign of Reye's syndrome is the sudden onset of *continuous and persistent vomiting.* At the time of or shortly after the beginning of the vomiting, the child starts to show signs of encephalopathy (involvement of the brain). In mild cases there is weakness, lethargy, unusual quietness, and listless behavior. In more severe cases the child becomes agitated, with increased irritability, aggressive behavior, and other obvious personality changes. Children suffering from the severest form become confused, disoriented, and finally develop convulsions and coma as the pressure within the brain increases.

In infants below six months of age, the diagnosis is more difficult to make, since vomiting is not usually a prominent symptom. The symptoms in infants are rapid breathing, respiratory distress, and periods of apnea (cessation of breathing); these symptoms may progress to convulsions and coma.

Reye's syndrome is a medical emergency. Therefore, if your child shows any of these signs and symptoms it is mandatory that you contact your child's physician immediately. If you are unable to reach your doctor you should immediately take your child to the emergency room of the nearest well-equipped and well-staffed hospital. Every minute counts in a case of Reye's syndrome and any untoward delay may well result in permanent brain damage or even death. The odds are that your child will not have Reye's syndrome, but you cannot take the chance of waiting and hoping that the signs and symptoms will disappear. Any child suspected of having Reye's syndrome should never be kept at home since the disease can progress very rapidly, with serious consequences.

The diagnosis of Reye's syndrome usually is clear-cut. Along with the history and symptoms and the physical examination there are certain laboratory tests that will confirm the diagnosis. The laboratory tests that are most useful are a determination of the blood serum ammonia level and liver enzyme tests measuring SGOT (serum glutamic oxaloacetic transaminase) and SGPT (serum glutamic pyruvic transaminase). In Reye's syndrome these levels will be elevated to at least three times their normal values. A few patients with Reye's syndrome also will have lowered blood sugar levels. With these laboratory-confirmed abnormalities and a cerebrospinal fluid examination that is normal, the case meets the criteria set by the CDC for the definite diagnosis of Reye's syndrome.

After the diagnosis is made, treatment should immediately be started. In the mild forms of the disease the treatment is straightforward. This group of children requires good nursing care with the correction of electrolyte imbalances in the blood by means of appropriate intravenous fluids. In a matter of just a few days children suffering from the mild cases of Reye's syndrome recover completely and with few exceptions are sent home from the hospital within one week. When followed up later, they are found to have no residual brain or liver damage. However, it must always be remembered that a child admitted to the hospital with a mild form of Reye's syndrome can suddenly take a turn for the worse and rapidly deteriorate because of a sudden increase in the pressure in the brain. It therefore is most important that these children be watched very carefully during their stays in the hospital.

The treatment of the severe forms of Reye's syndrome is much more complicated. Since the cause is unknown, there is no specific medication to cure it. There is no clear consensus as to the optimal method of treating the children suffering from the severe forms of the disease. Since the main danger of Reye's syndrome is in the encephalopathy and resulting increased pressure on the brain, treatment must be directed at monitoring and reducing the intracranial pressure.

Since the disease was first described in 1963, many different approaches to treatment have been tried. In Reye's original paper he stated that treatment with corticosteroids, glucose, and insulin did not appear to make any difference in the outcome. In 1972 it was reported that the use of exchange transfusions—replacing a large volume or all of the blood—appeared to improve survival rates. Since that original report a number of other investigators have used exchange transfusions in severe cases of Reye's syndrome. Some of these studies concluded that exchange transfusion indeed was associated with improved survival rates while other studies found no difference in survival between those patients who were treated by exchange transfusion and those who were treated with only intensive supportive measures. Also in 1972 another group of investigators advocated the administration of insulin and glucose as part of the management in order to maintain the body's stores of glycogen. It is difficult to determine how important the use of insulin and glucose is in the treatment of Reye's syndrome since it is usually part of the total therapy the patient receives. In 1975 it was suggested that peritoneal dialysis be used to assist the kidneys in clearing out the excess amount of ammonia and other toxins. Subsequent experience with peritoneal dialysis has shown that this method of cleansing the blood is of little benefit.

Various drugs have been used to help reduce the increased pressure in the brain. Mannitol, a diuretic administered intravenously, appears to be the drug of choice in treating intracranial pressure elevation. In some extreme instances surgical procedures such as craniectomy (opening the skull) have been performed in order to decompress the brain. In the last few years intracranial pressure monitoring has been developed, the most significant addition to the management of Reye's syndrome. Various devices can now be surgically inserted that will continuously record the pressure within the brain. By this method, treatment can be started immediately after there is any rise in intracranial pressure. Before the use of intracranial pressure monitoring, brain deterioration was often so rapid that treatment could not be started in time. Now, even small rises in the pressure within the brain can immediately be detected and appropriate treatment can be given with a drug such as mannitol. By means of this careful monitoring, many more children are being saved and many more now recover without brain damage.

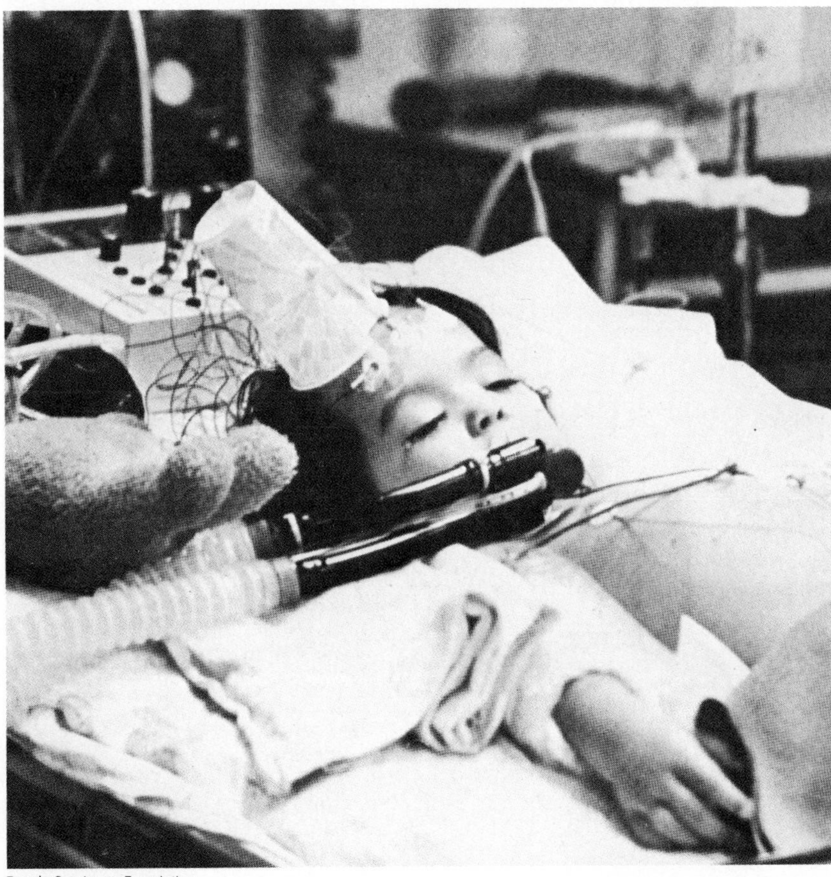

Reye's Syndrome Foundation

The main danger in Reye's syndrome is the marked increase in pressure within the brain. Many more children now survive even the most severe forms of this childhood disease without brain damage, owing to a method of monitoring intracranial pressure.

With early recognition and with the newer methods of treatment the prognosis of Reye's syndrome has gradually been improving. Just a few years ago the nationwide mortality rate was over 50%. Now at least 70% of Reye's syndrome patients survive. According to data from the CDC the mortality rate for the winter of 1976–77 was 38%; the mortality rate for the winter of 1979–80 was 12%.

The survival of a child who develops Reye's syndrome really depends on how early the diagnosis is made and how soon proper treatment is begun. Some children recover completely while others are left with some degree of brain damage that can vary from slight mental retardation to very severe brain dysfunction.

A controversy and a caution

Currently, there is no way to prevent Reye's syndrome. Questions have recently been raised regarding a possible association between Reye's syndrome and the use of aspirin. A high percentage of children with Reye's syndrome were noted to have taken salicylates such as aspirin during their prodromal illness for the fever; some patients with Reye's syndrome have been found to have high levels of salicylate in their blood. On the other hand, Reye's syndrome often occurs in patients who have not previously received any aspirin. It is not known yet whether aspirin makes a child more susceptible to the disease or whether aspirin is a contributing cause of it. Yet because of this possible association, the CDC recommended late in 1980 that "parents should be advised to use caution when administering salicylates to treat children with viral illnesses, particularly chickenpox and influenzalike illnesses." Most clinicians in the field agree that further epidemiologic study of the association between aspirin and Reye's syndrome is necessary.

There is agreement that children should not be given so-called antiemetic medication when they are vomiting. Not only are these drugs ineffective in controlling vomiting but their use may also result in time being lost in establishing the cause of the vomiting as the parents wait for the medicine to work. If the vomiting is the start of Reye's syndrome, this delay can be disastrous.

If the diagnosis of Reye's syndrome is confirmed every effort should be made to transfer the child to a medical facility experienced in handling this disease. You can receive help in finding such a medical center by calling the National Reye's Syndrome Foundation (419/636-2679). Additional information about Reye's syndrome can be obtained by writing the foundation: P.O. Box 829, Bryan, Ohio 43506.

—Alvin N. Eden, M.D.

Health Education Unit 11

Sex Education for Children

Raising children has never been an easy task, and parents rarely feel totally prepared to handle all of the situations that arise. One of the most difficult matters to deal with is sex education. The mere mention of talking about sex to children may send shivers down the backs of parents, causing them to blush, stammer, and head for the nearest exit.

Parents may expect the school or church to provide the necessary details. Usually, when they see their children turning into adults at puberty, parents feel that, if they have not already, they had better sit down and discuss the facts of life before they all have to face an unwanted pregnancy. But sex education should not be a last-minute effort when a child reaches puberty.

Sources of sex information

A young child learns much just by observing his parents' behavior. The parent's male-female interaction instills in the small child a foundation for later behavior as well as for moral values. The child can see how his mother and father treat each other, and the child grows up thinking this is the way things should be in a marriage. Parents are the primary role models for their sons and daughters, and that is a very basic part of sex education.

In addition the parents talk, or do not talk, to the child about sex. This issue comes up very early in life, whether parents realize it or not. Children, in their complete and honest innocence, ask some pretty tough questions even when they are toddlers. Take for instance toilet training, when a little boy may touch his penis and ask, "What's *this* thing? Why doesn't Suzie have one too?" The manner in which a parent answers those questions can communicate a great variety of things. The parent may say, "That's your penis. Boys have one and girls don't. Instead they have a vagina." This has answered the child's question and no more may be asked at this time. However, if the parent moves the boy's hand away and admonishes him not to touch "down there," the child will learn quickly that this body part should not be mentioned. The parent gives the message, "I do not want to talk with you about such things." Parents can give another message when they laugh at sexual jokes and seem to have a secret life behind closed doors, yet tell their child that sex is dirty or a "no-no." A child's curiosity is piqued to know why this is good for parents and bad for him, and confusion about appropriate sexual behavior begins.

Another strong influence on children today is the mass media—newspapers, magazines, TV, radio, and movies. Children are constantly barraged with sexual images, innuendos, and glamorized sex. Unfortunately, this is part of the child's sex education, too. Children are going to learn about sex even if parents do not say one word to them about it.

Fostering an atmosphere of openness and trust

Teaching about sex does not have to be a chore for parents. Sex is a normal function, and sexual feelings and behavior are part of everyday life from infancy to old age; learning about sex should occur just as naturally within the family unit. If parents wait until their children are 13 or 14 to discuss these issues, then they will be far too late. Morals, values, and inaccuracies have already been learned, perhaps taught to the child by uninformed childhood peers or by the mass media.

Sex education is a continuing learning experience that should be shared and nurtured by the entire family. If discussing sex with parents becomes as comfortable as discussing any other important human activity, then the child will have the opportunity to grow and develop into the informed human being that most parents hope their child will be. Truthful and factual information leads to rational and intelligent choices, while myths and secrecy can lead to adjustment problems later in life.

Ideally sex education should follow a life-cycle approach, dealing with increasing amounts of information and centered about events that happen in the family.

Sex education for children

Toddlers and preschoolers are perpetually full of questions. It seems that every sentence starts with "Why?" and the questions never seem to end. When talking about sex, be quite sure you know exactly what the question is before you answer. For instance, if a five-year-old girl asks, "Where did I come from?" be sure she wants to know how she was made as opposed to the city where she was born. Now, if the question *is* about her birth, and not her birthplace, take a deep breath, recall the information from the books you have been saving, and give an honest answer. But only answer in terms the child can handle at her particular stage of maturity, and only answer the questions that are asked. There is no need at this time to go into complex discussions of anatomy and physiology. Save that for later when those concepts can be understood. Providing an honest answer to every question a preschooler asks may only supply part of the information needed, but it establishes permission to ask the other questions that will come later.

Seizing the moment

The impending arrival of a new baby in the family is a wonderful opportunity for sex education. This is a "teachable moment" when information is needed, and the child's natural curiosity at seeing a pregnant woman is a cue for the lessons to begin. The type and amount of information depends on the child's age. As an example, the following explanation could be given by a parent to a five- to nine-year-old child. Parts of the explanation are appropriate for the younger child, too. The parent might say:

You need to know that, just as cats have kittens and dogs have puppies, people have babies. Whether it is dogs, cats, or people, it takes one male and one female to have a baby. Stop and think of all the ways that men look different from women. Men have hair on their face and women do not. Eyes can be different colors and body sizes can be different. Just as all of these things are different, various parts of the body in a man are different from a woman.

Men are flat-chested, but women have two larger areas on their chest called breasts. Breasts are very important when a baby is born because this is where milk is made, and some babies drink the milk that is made in the breast. Sometimes a mother does not want to feed her baby from the breasts, so she uses a bottle. Both do the job nicely.

Further down, between the legs, both men and women have some hair that grows there. This hair grows on every person when they start to become an adult. But there is another difference here. A man has a penis, and a woman doesn't. She has a vagina, and a man doesn't.

The penis and vagina are very important parts of the body when it comes to making a baby. For a man and a women, being alone and spending time together to share affection is not only a very special time, but a private time. They get as close as they can to each other, touching, kissing, and hugging. The man's penis goes into the woman's vagina and releases a sticky juice called sperm. If the man's sperm can meet a woman's egg which comes from the ovary and fertilize it, then a baby has been started. This doesn't always happen. Only sometimes.

Don Casper—Chicago Tribune

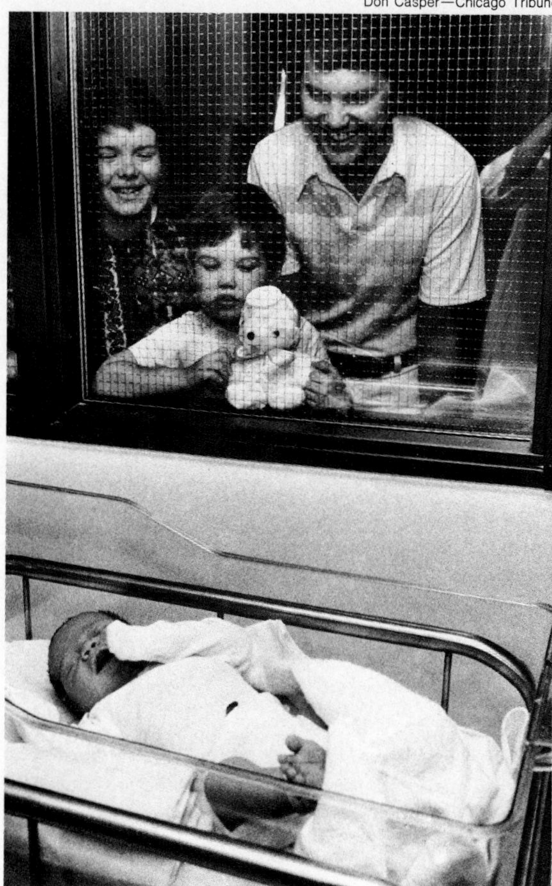

The birth of a baby is an ideal time for sex education. A unique program at a Chicago hospital allows this three-year-old to view his new baby brother.

The woman's uterus is in her abdomen, or belly, where the baby grows. The uterus gets larger and larger over a nine-month time period and so does her belly. Each month the baby grows a little more until it is big enough to be born. You may be able to feel a woman's abdomen and feel the thumping of a baby moving inside. Babies move more and more as they grow bigger.

At the end of nine months, the baby is born. The woman usually goes to the hospital to have a doctor help deliver the baby. Muscles in the mother's body in the uterus where the baby lies squeeze until finally the mother can push the baby out through the vagina. Sometimes it takes many hours for a baby to be born. It is very hard work, so it is called labor.

That is the whole story on how you were made and where you came from. That is how our new baby was made and how it will be born. It is pretty much a miracle and seems to take a very long time, but the love we feel when we see our baby sure makes it worth it.

Other opportunities to give information include bath time, especially when siblings share a tub of water or a parent helps to shower a child while in the shower also. Body similarities or differences are quite obvious at this time, and if the curiosity of a child leads to questions, then this is the right time to answer them. The naturalness and acceptance of nudity without shame can also be taught here, but accompanied by a certain propriety within the family circle. A respect for privacy and the sense of propriety must be balanced with some element of permissive viewing. A child needs to know how to look at the human body without embarrassment, but not to be an exhibitionist. The diaper changing of a sibling can also raise questions that can be handled just as at bath time.

As a child grows old enough to become influenced by a peer group of friends, family education needs to be available to provide alternative information—especially to correct the myths and misinformation given a child by friends. Consider a situation such as this: A family is driving down the highway and a child in the back seat leans forward and says, "Dad, is it true that making love means the man puts his penis inside a woman's vagina?" The father, white-knuckled and tightening his grip on the steering wheel, says, "Yes, that's true." The child then exclaims, "Yuck, I'll never do *that!*"

Here is an example of a child verifying what he has heard from others. That the child felt comfortable asking his father this question indicates that a permissive attitude for discussion was already present and that the child knew he would get a trustworthy answer. The child's reaction of distaste is a natural one and need not arouse alarm or fear in the parent.

It is never quite clear where children get the ideas they do about sex, but it certainly does seem that they have no lack of theories and like to share them. Another example that illustrates the creative imagination of the child talking about sex is the following interaction between a mother working in the kitchen and her son. She is suddenly interrupted by her son who has been at a friend's house. He asks, "Mom, Roger told me that making love is like the way you operate a stick of deodorant. Is that true?" The mother, unclear as to what he is asking, clarifies the question by saying, "What do you mean?" Her son says, "Well, he said that a penis slips in and out of a vagina like the deodorant slides up and down in the container." (Think how you might respond to that question!) The mother replies, "Well, yes, it is sort of like that." She may go on to clarify this further and inquire if the child has other questions to be answered at that time.

Education at puberty

The onset of puberty can be a very difficult time for a child. Interest in the opposite sex has begun, and yet children do not quite know how to handle the multitude of feelings and emotions bombarding them at this time. There seems to be a definite division of "popular" and "unpopular" children. The "popular" group has the attention of the opposite sex. This reveals itself in a variety of ways such as giggling, teasing, tickling, or kicking each other. Meanwhile, the less "popular" child observes this behavior, lamenting the fact that he or she is not part of these activities. A familiar statement made to many parents by such children may be "Popular kids have *all* the fun. If this is what puberty is, then I don't want to go through it!"

"I have a question, and a follow-up question."

Puberty truly is a distressing time for everyone, "popular" and "unpopular" alike, and the sensitive handling of children requires a very patient and understanding parent. The parent can help by clarifying the various emotions that are present and getting the child to verbalize them. It may help to guide a child over these tumultuous years if the parents share recollections of their own childhood, and assure their children that all young people experience some of the same feelings. Basic discussions as to the hormonal changes taking place in both girls and boys keep the child reassured that he or she is normal instead of vastly different from others of the same age.

The menstrual cycle starts about this time, but the lessons should have begun long before. Children have seen the sanitary napkins or tampons a mother purchases. The child may have observed a mother using them. A relaxed attitude helps a child ask questions and get important information. To know that a mother needs to use these articles plays a significant part in helping both boys and girls to understand this basic biologic function—boys should be included in these conversations. Playing down the inconvenience or discomfort of menses and stressing the specialness of the ability to carry a baby will help young girls adopt a functional and healthy approach to menstruation.

Some tips for parents

The use of basic stories gives the parent a starting point from which to work for future questions that will come up. The parent must be able to give a concise, accurate, and simple explanation. As a child grows and matures, the stories can be expanded and elaborated whenever the child is ready to hear more. Remember that a basic rule to follow is never to offer more information than the child wants to have. A relaxed attitude in answering questions will open the door for later discussions. It will also be easier for the parent if the emotionally difficult job of "teaching about sex" is spread out over time.

Talking with a child about sexual questions is best done immediately, as the questions are asked. Delaying discussion serves no useful purpose. It may seem to be far easier to put the child off for a talk later on, but the questions may be forgotten, or never properly answered, and the child may not ask again. Furthermore, if the parent's embarrassment is acknowledged when it occurs, but the questions are dealt with anyway, the child receives the message that his parents can be approached even during times of stress. And this is, after all, a very important additional goal for parents to attain.

The responsibility for sex education should be shared by both parents—one should not expect the spouse to do all the teaching. It is just as acceptable for mothers to teach boys and for fathers to teach girls. The old sayings, "Wait till your father gets home" or "You'd better ask your mother about that" are inappropriate. It is advisable for both parents, before talking to their children, to agree on what values and factual information should be taught and what language should be used. Consistency is extremely important to avoid the child's misunderstanding the information given.

Television shows and movies that may deal with or allude to sexual matters can be useful if the parent watches with the child and attempts to answer questions that arise about situations portrayed on the program.

There are a number of books and pamphlets available at many levels of understanding. At the end of this article is a listing of some of these written materials. Take a look at the suggested resources, and at others that are available at bookstores or in the library. Decide which ones *you* would feel comfortable using with *your* child. You can obtain further assistance with resources through Sex Information and Education Council of the United States (SIECUS), 84 Fifth Avenue, Suite 407, New York, N.Y. 10011, or through the Planned Parenthood Federation of America, 810 Seventh Avenue, New York, N.Y. 10019.

It is a good idea to review all written and illustrated materials before the child gets them, so that you are aware of the content and can be prepared to answer questions. It is also wise to use more than one resource just to help give a different perspective. Keep them available for frequent reference.

Of course, visual aids can be a great help, but they should not be the only source of teaching. Nothing can replace all the benefits a child obtains from personal discussions with parents. Armed with a few basic principles of sex education, parents will find it easier to teach sexual information to their children and prevent many of the problems that can arise in adolescence. A child who is comfortable talking with parents will easily ask more questions later.

Bibliography

For children and parents to use together.

Andry, Andrew C., and Schepp, Steven. *How Babies Are Made.* New York: Time-Life Books Inc., rev. 1979.

Gordon, Sol and Judith. *Did the Sun Shine Before You Were Born?* New York, N.Y.: Third Press, 1974.

Johnson, Corinne Benson, and Johnson, Eric W. *Love and Sex and Growing Up.* Philadelphia: J. B. Lippincott, 1970 and 1977.

Lerrigo, Marion O., and Cassidy, Michael A. *A Doctor Talks to 9–12-Year-Olds.* Chicago: Budlong Press, 1976.

May, Julian. *How We Are Born.* Chicago: Follett Pub. Co., 1969.

Mayle, Peter. *Where Did I Come From?* Secaucus, N.J.: Lyle Stuart, Inc., 1973.

Meilach, Dona Z., and Mandel, Elias. *A Doctor Talks to 5–8-Year-Olds.* Chicago: Budlong Press, rev. 1974.

Nilsson, Lennart. *A Child Is Born.* New York: Delacorte Press, rev. 1977.

Uslander, Arlene; Weiss, Caroline; and Weiss, Lee D. *A Doctor Discusses Talking with Your Child About Sex.* Chicago: Budlong Press, 1978.

Verdoux, Christiane; Cohen, Jean; Kahn-Nathan, Jacqueline; and Tordjman, Gilbert. *The Illustrated Family Guide to Life, Love and Sex for Early Childhood.* New York: Grossett and Dunlap, 1974.

Widerberg, Siv. *The Kids' Own XYZ of Love and Sex.* New York: Stein & Day Pub., 1972.

For parents.

Berenstain, Jan and Stan. *How to Teach Your Children About Sex.* New York: McCall Pub. Co., 1970.

Block, William A. *What Your Child Really Wants to Know About Sex, and Why.* Englewood Cliffs, N.J.: Prentice-Hall, 1972.

Burt, John J., and Meeks, Linda Bower. *Education for Sexuality.* Philadelphia: W. B. Saunders, 1975.

Diamond, Milton, and Karlin, Arno. *Sexual Decisions.* Boston: Little, Brown & Co., 1980.

Otto, Herbert A. *The New Sex Education.* Chicago: Association Press, Follett Pub. Co., 1977.

Pomeroy, Wardell B. *Your Child and Sex.* New York: Delacorte Press, 1974.

Uslander, Arlene; Weiss, Caroline; and Telman, Judith. *Sex Education for Today's Child.* Chicago: Association Press, Follett Pub. Co., 1977.

Uslander, Arlene, and Weiss, Caroline. *Dealing with Questions About Sex.* Palo Alto, Calif.: Education Today Co., Learning Handbooks, 1975.

—Charles E. Driscoll, M.D., and Jacquelyn S. Driscoll, R.N.

Insect Stings

The National Institute of Allergy and Infectious Diseases (NIAID) estimates that one out of every 250 persons, or about one million people in the United States, has an allergy to insect stings. Life threatening, potentially fatal reactions may develop within minutes of a sting, even in persons stung previously without experiencing more than localized pain, redness, and swelling.

In the United States, stings of bees, yellow jackets, hornets, wasps, and ants are known to cause approximately 40 deaths every year. Allergists believe the number is higher, with many sudden deaths at golf courses, tennis courts, swimming pools, and patios mistakenly attributed to heart attacks. A panel convened by NIAID in 1978 to review emergency treatment of insect-sting allergy concluded that everyone is a potential victim.

"Once stung, twice shy" is a familiar motto. In years past persons with known sensitivity to insect stings could only try to avoid future stings. One Baltimore woman had not been outside with her children for eight years, since the summer when she nearly died from a sting. Her problem has been remedied, for today effective immunization is available. An individual's tolerance can be raised by a series of injections of increasingly greater amounts of the specific venom or venoms to which he or she is allergic.

Troublemakers

There are an estimated 100,000 different species of "membrane-winged" insects, or Hymenoptera. Over 16,000 species of stinging Hymenoptera live in the United States. With rare exceptions, those causing problems are wasps (principally yellow jackets and hornets), bees (honeybees and bumblebees), and ants (mainly fire ants).

The stinging mechanism often is likened to a hypodermic syringe. Found only in females, it has small venom-filled sacs at its base. When the stinger's point is thrust into a victim, venom is pumped down a hollow canal in its center. The "needles" of most stinging Hymenoptera are straight and can be withdrawn and used repeatedly. The honeybee, however, has a barbed stinger. While a honeybee can sting another insect and escape with the stinger intact, its barbs become anchored when plunged into the tougher human skin. When it tries to leave, or is brushed away, both stinger and venom sacs are torn from the abdomen. The injured bee quickly dies.

The likelihood of stings is less determined by species than by geography and time of the year. On the southeast and west coasts of the U.S., the most common stings are from honeybees; in the southwest, wasps; in the northeast, yellow jackets. Ants are principally a problem in the southeast. In all areas insects are most active in warm weather.

Eradication of the Hymenoptera population would not only be impossible but undesirable; they are crucial to plant pollination and destroy many harmful insects. Their numbers are enormous. Authorities have estimated that, for example, in suburban and rural Pennsylvania, the number of stinging Hymenoptera nests may be 50,000 to 100,000 per square mile. The population is thought to have increased substantially in the past 20 to 30 years because of the expansion of suburbia and increased availability of attics and insulated walls that prove attractive hibernation sites for overwintering queens.

Types of reactions

Although reactions to insect stings vary, the severity is thought to be related to individual sensitivity, not to the insect species. The toxicity of insect venom is such that virtually everyone develops at least a local reaction to a sting.

Normal reactions may include pain, redness, swelling, itching, and warmth at the site of the sting. These symptoms may be severe and last several hours, but when they remain confined to the area of the sting, they are viewed as normal inflammatory responses. Ordinarily, sting reactions fade within a few hours.

Toxic reactions develop when a large volume of venom pours into the body in a short period of time. A toxic reaction typically is the result of multiple stings received when an insect colony is disturbed. Symptoms include cramps, headache, fever, drowsiness, and occasionally death. A lethal dose is thought to be 100 or more stings; however, a case has been reported of a man who was stung 2,243 times at one time, yet survived.

Allergic reactions can be triggered by a minute amount of venom, although the severity of the reaction is thought to be related to the volume of venom received. Stings may produce swelling in a limb or trigger a whole-body reaction. Reactions vary in intensity: slight reactions may involve hives, itching, fatigue, and feelings of anxiety; indeed, these tremulous feelings often are misread by others as a hysterical overreaction. Moderate reactions also might involve swelling, chest tightness, dizziness, stomach cramps, and occasionally nausea or vomiting.

In severe reactions, any of these symptoms might be present, but there also will be more serious symptoms, including difficulty in swallowing or breathing owing to swelling of the lining of the larynx, weakness, and confusion. The most serious reaction is shock or anaphylaxis. Blood pressure falls, and respiration, heart action, and circulation become impaired; the victim may collapse and, if not properly treated, die within as little as five minutes.

Reactions generally occur at the time of the sting; usually, the sooner the symptoms appear, the more severe the reaction. However, reactions may occur several hours, or even two weeks, later. Delayed reactions often involve painful joints, fever, hives or other skin rashes, and swollen lymph glands.

The natural history of allergic reactions to insect stings is not well charted. While it has yet to be documented that reactions get progressively worse, there also is no evidence to the contrary. A study at the Johns Hopkins Medical Institutions, Baltimore, Md., found that 60% of adults with a previous reaction and positive results on venom skin tests had systemic reactions when challenged with an actual sting. Investigators are trying to develop ways of identifying allergic persons at greatest risk of future reactions.

How insect allergy is diagnosed

In persons with a history of an apparent allergic reaction to an insect sting, skin tests are used to determine the specific insect venoms involved. First, to screen for extreme sensitivity, the skin may be pricked with an amount of venom equivalent to 1/10,000 of a sting. If results are negative, greater amounts (but still very dilute) of the suspect venoms are applied to a lightly scratched area or injected into the top layer of the skin. A welt or inflammation developing within 15 minutes indicates an allergic response. Some persons are sensitive to venoms from several insects. Further laboratory tests may be used to assess hypersensitivity. The radioallergosorbent test, or RAST, measures the concentration of certain venom-specific antibodies, known as IgE antibodies, in the patient's blood. The leukocyte histamine release, or LHR, assays the histamine discharged from certain blood cells when they are exposed to venom; histamine is among the substances causing allergic symptoms.

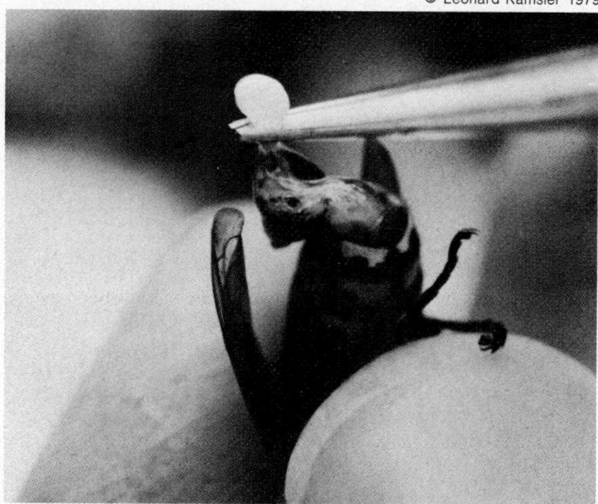

The venom sacs from honeybees, wasps, hornets, and yellow jackets are removed in the laboratory to be used to prepare injections of allergens to desensitize individuals who have severe reactions to insect stings.

Perhaps 15 to 30% of the population would, if tested, have positive skin tests. When stung, these persons have experienced normal reactions. Since allergists are not now able to predict who is at risk of a future allergic reaction, and since preventive immunization is not recommended, diagnostic tests for insect allergy are not used as screening tests.

How insect allergy is treated

Treatment known as desensitization or immunotherapy has been used by physicians for many years to treat various types of allergies, including those to pollens and molds, as well as insect stings. This treatment involves a series of injections of diluted amounts of the allergen to build up the patient's tolerance.

Immunization to venom is accomplished far more rapidly than is usual for allergens such as pollen or mold, for which the dose is increased slowly. A typical regimen would involve three injections of diluted venom at 30-minute intervals the first day. The third injection might contain 100 times the quantity of the first but still would be less than the amount of venom in a single sting. Shots thereafter would be at weekly intervals, for about six weeks, or until a "maintenance dose" is reached; this dose is equivalent to two stings. Intervals between shots gradually are increased to four, six, and sometimes eight weeks, with laboratory tests for antibodies performed to assess the continuing success of the immunization.

When maintenance status is reached, there is a

drama-filled challenge to demonstrate success: a real sting, given in the hospital, with staff and emergency equipment standing by. At the Johns Hopkins Medical Institutions, where the venom therapy was developed, nearly 500 persons have had this test. Over 95% experienced only a normal, local reaction; even the others had far milder reactions than they previously had experienced and, with additional treatment, were successfully immunized.

Until recently, physicians used not the venom alone but extracts of the whole bodies of insects (WBE) to try to desensitize insect-allergic persons. Reports of clinical success, which today's researchers say are explained by the spontaneous cure rate, helped justify continuing use of WBE.

Mary Loveless, an allergist and professor emeritus at Cornell University Medical College, New York City, has argued over the years that venom alone triggers reactions to stings. To resolve the issue, scientists needed sophisticated laboratory tests to identify venom protein antibodies. Even today, the specific allergens in each venom have yet to be isolated.

However, in 1974 two case reports of bee sting allergy successfully treated with bee venom were presented at the annual meeting of the American Academy of Allergy. In 1976 researchers at the Johns Hopkins Medical Institutions reported studies showing venom therapy to be more effective than WBE. Clinical trials of venom therapy were subsequently conducted at several research hospitals.

In 1979 venoms for diagnosis and treatment of insect sting allergy were approved by the Food and Drug Administration (FDA) for use in the United States. The allergenic extracts panel of the FDA, which reviews drugs for their efficacy and safety, has recommended that WBE be discontinued in favor of the venoms.

Presently available venoms include those from wasps, honeybees, two kinds of hornets, yellow jackets, and a "mixed" formula. Bumblebee and fire ant venoms are not yet on the market.

Entomologists say venom from millions of insects is needed to provide vaccines for just one year for the United States and Europe. It takes, for example, roughly 25 separate honeybee or 50 yellow jacket stings to provide the venom needed for maintenance doses for one patient for one year. Honeybee venom is collected by giving bees just enough of an electric shock that they release venom without sacrificing their stingers. Other insects must be collected alive, frozen, and dissected, and the venom extracted. "Raw" venom then is purified and sterilized before use.

An estimated 35,000 persons in the United States currently are receiving venom therapy. The great majority of the country's allergists are using the new treatment. The cost of the first year of venom therapy ranges from several hundred dollars to more than $1,000, depending on the number of venoms involved, times given, and fees for physicians' services and laboratory studies.

Patients currently are told that therapy may need to be continued indefinitely. Long-term exposure to venom is not thought harmful; beekeepers, for example, often receive a great number of stings over a lifetime. Concerns are, of course, magnified in the case of children. Venom desensitization treatment currently is considered appropriate only for persons with a history of a whole-body reaction and positive skin test reactions. In some cases it has been recommended for persons with severe reactions. For those with milder reactions, it is sometimes presented as an option.

A five-to-ten-year study that will involve 400 children who have experienced systemic reactions was

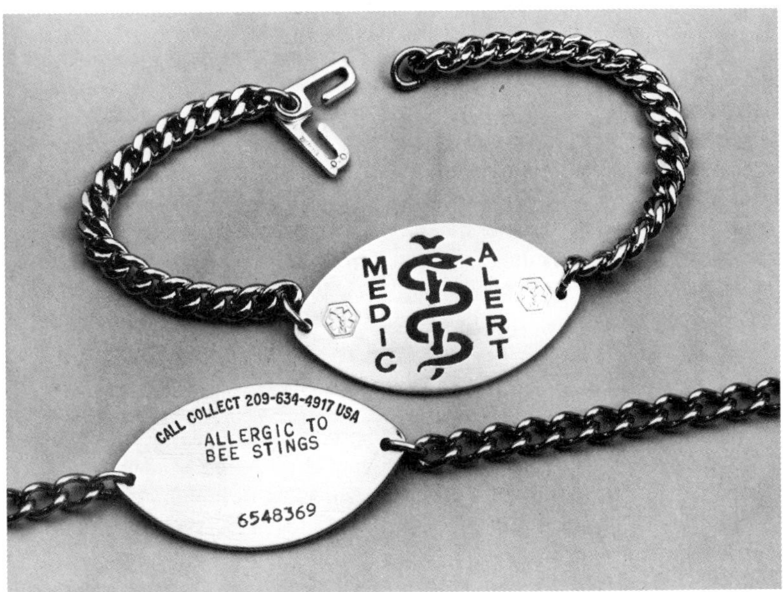

Medic Alert Foundation International, Turlock, California

An individual who is known to be highly sensitive to insect stings should wear a tag or bracelet that carries this information. In case of being stung, if the individual is unable to tell hospital personnel what has happened, the bracelet will alert the emergency team so that the proper therapy can be begun with no time wasted.

launched in 1979 at the Johns Hopkins Medical Institutions. The study aims to delineate the natural history of untreated insect allergy, to determine whether the benefits of venom therapy outweigh its disadvantages, and to improve physicians' ability to predict the true risk of future reactions for individual patients. Children are being studied because they rarely experience death or serious disability after a sting and because the financial and psychological costs of life-long therapy are higher than for adults.

By the end of the first two years of the study, nearly 200 children aged 3 to 16 had been enrolled. More than half had been stung accidentally at least once since enrollment. Even among members of this group who, for purposes of the study, were not given venom therapy, only 10% experienced systemic reactions, almost all more mild than their earlier reactions. Hence, the preliminary results suggest that, as with other types of allergies, insect sting allergy is likely to be outgrown.

Preventing stings

No repellents are effective against stinging insects. Sweet-smelling ones even may attract them. Commonsense measures will help avoid stings. Do not go barefoot outside. Wear close-fitting clothing, including a long-sleeved shirt and long pants, to keep insects from getting caught between the material and your skin. Avoid bright-colored clothing and flowery prints, shiny buckles, and jewelry.

When planning to be outdoors in warm weather, do not use perfumes, hair sprays, after-shave lotions, scented soaps, and other products with strong odors. Remember that fields of clover, flower beds, flowering shrubs and trees, orchards, trash cans, and the like are feeding grounds for insects; be cautious. Keep car windows rolled up when the car is empty and, if possible, when driving. Do not attempt to swat an insect while driving; pull over and let it out of the car. When picnicking, keep food covered until you are ready to eat and clean up promptly. Sweet, sticky foods such as jam, Popsicles, watermelon, cola drinks, and beer attract insects. Take care when cutting grass, moving logs, or working outdoors; you may disturb a nest. Hymenoptera seem particularly attracted to persons who are active and perspiring.

Note that a summer cottage may present a hazard in the winter; wasps nesting in the rafters may become active when the cottage is heated.

Check your house for signs of nesting. Look under eaves, behind shutters, under open steps, in attics. If you detect an underground nest, wait until insects have returned for the night to apply insecticide; repeat the following evening. Do not flood the hole with water; you most likely will make the insects furious. Better still, call a professional exterminator.

Crushing a stinging insect near its hive may release an odor that brings the colony out to attack. For the same reason, if one person is stung, others in the area are more likely to be; move away. If an insect hovers around you, protect your face with your arms or hands. Even if you accidentally disturb a nest, do not wave your arms and run. Activity may excite the insects; try to move away slowly and get into a car or building. If you confront a midair swarm, drop to the ground, with face down.

If you are allergic to insect stings, take extra precautions. Do not eat or drink outside. Stay indoors immediately after a rain. Wear emergency medical identification to help bystanders assist you if you are stung. Identification bracelets and necklaces are available from the Medic Alert Foundation, Box 1009, Turlock, Calif. 95381.

First aid

When a person is stung, remove the stinger and venom sac (if left) by gently scaping or flicking it with a fingernail or knife; do not squeeze it as you may push more venom in. Apply a cold compress or ice to reduce pain, swelling, and itching. Toothpaste, mud, ammonia, meat tenderizer, and other home remedies have not been proven effective. Check to be sure tetanus immunizations are up-to-date; stingers sometimes are contaminated with bacteria and may cause infections.

Any reaction other than a local one demands consultation with a physician. If a person appears to be experiencing a systemic reaction, seek medical help immediately. The immediate application of a cold compress or ice will help delay absorption of venom. If the sting is on an extremity, a constricting band placed above the sting site may be useful. Be prepared to undertake basic lifesaving measures such as mouth-to-mouth resuscitation.

Anyone with a known allergy should carry an emergency insect-sting treatment kit. Kits, available with a doctor's prescription, contain epinephrine for injection, a tourniquet, antihistamine tablets, and alcohol swabs. Examples of such kits are the Ana-Kit (Hollister-Stier, Spokane, Wash.), which contains a pre-loaded syringe that requires the user to unsheath the needle and insert it in the thigh before pushing the plunger, and the Epi-Pen (Center Laboratories, Port Washington, N. Y.), an automatic device requiring only the release of a safety catch and pressure against the skin.

Recognizing that insect sting allergy can occur without warning in anyone, both the American Academy of Allergy and the American Medical Association support the administration of epinephrine by properly trained laypersons in emergencies. They have advocated changes in laws to permit use of the emergency kits by such persons as lifeguards, schoolteachers, coaches, camp counselors, and forest rangers.

—Lynne Lamberg

Health Education Unit 13

Lead Poisoning

Lead poisoning (plumbism) in children is a major health problem in the United States today. One of the negative results of the Industrial Revolution, this totally man-made disease can cause varying degrees of permanent, irreversible brain damage. Although what must be done to eradicate lead poisoning has been known for many years, the necessary steps have not yet been taken, especially by legislators. Society has the knowledge and tools to eliminate the problem once and for all, but each year millions of children continue to be exposed and poisoned by dangerously high levels of lead in the environment.

Lead has no known normal function in the human body. If intake is not excessive, lead can be excreted in the urine, bile, and sweat without causing adverse effects. However, if lead is absorbed in amounts beyond the maximum "daily permissible intake" (DPI) of 93–133 micrograms (μg) it begins to accumulate in the body. Tissue-lead levels increase, resulting in toxic effects to the bone marrow, the kidneys, and especially the brain. Young children are particularly vulnerable to the harmful effects of lead.

The most important result of lead poisoning in children is its effect on the central nervous system. This results in severe, acute degeneration of the brain in the most extreme cases and altered neuropsychological behavior at lower levels of exposure.

The scope of the problem is enormous. When children under the age of six years who live in a hazardous environment are tested, between 3 and 20% are shown to have elevated blood-lead levels. The U.S. Centers for Disease Control in Atlanta, Ga., reported that in the third quarter of 1980, 63 childhood lead poisoning prevention programs had screened 127,341 children and identified 5,482 of these children as having lead toxicity, or levels of lead above the established safe limits. At Kings County Hospital in Brooklyn, N.Y., servicing an inner-city, low socioeconomic area, 15% of all the children screened required treatment for elevated lead levels. Lead poisoning is not just an inner-city problem but also strikes children on farms and in small towns throughout the United States; children with elevated lead levels have been identified throughout the country. The magnitude of the problem of lead poisoning is much greater and the consequences much more severe than was previously believed.

Sources of lead

Lead-based paint is still by far the single most important "high dose" source of lead in the United States. Before 1950 most houses were painted with paint containing large amounts of lead. In 1950 the first law banning the use of lead-based paint inside the house was passed. In 1973 the U.S. federal government forbade the sale via interstate commerce of paint containing more than 0.5% lead. According to the 1970 census, there are about 30 million pre-1950 houses still in use, a high percentage of which are hazardous in terms of the lead on their walls. Many of these homes are now in deteriorated condition, making them particularly dangerous, since the leaded paint becomes more readily available in the form of paint chips and dust. The plaster on the walls is another major source of lead, since through the years the lead in the paint has leached into the plaster behind the paint.

Since the introduction of leaded gasolines in 1923, airborne lead has become another important source—the lead from automobile exhausts is a major contributor to the high lead content of soil and dust. Foragers for edible wild plants have found that plants growing near heavily traveled roads contain high levels of lead. Another source of lead is dust from smelter manufacturing plants. Individuals who work in lead-smelting factories bring lead dust home on their clothing. A reaction can occur between pottery made with lead glazes and high-acid foods such as fruit juices or colas; this results in the lead leaching out into the beverage. Other sources include lead-soldered cans, lead battery, electrodes, and old plumbing that uses lead pipes. Lead pipes are especially dangerous when in contact with soft water. If lead shot, fishing weights, or leaded jewelry are swallowed, they are retained in the stomach, where the lead slowly dissolves over a period of weeks to months. Old furniture, cribs, and toys on which lead-based paint was used are yet another dangerous source of excessive quantities of lead. Finally, persons who have chewed on newspapers have also developed lead poisoning.

Those at risk

The peak incidence of lead poisoning is seen in children between two to three years of age. At this age most young children put everything they can grab into their mouths. They are also much closer to the ground and so are closer to the lead-laden dirt and dust.

Certain groups of children are most susceptible to lead poisoning. These high-risk groups include those toddlers living in deteriorating houses and those living near heavily traveled streets, highways, and thruways. At greatest risk is the child who suffers from pica. Pica is the habit of eating nonfood materials—the word is derived from the Latin word for magpie, a bird that has a voracious and indiscriminate appetite. Pica is a perverted appetite for inedible substances, even such harmful substances as clay, plaster, ashes, or charcoal. It is not merely the random mouthing and tasting that many children do to satisfy their oral curiosities; pica is a persistent and purposeful pursuit of and consumption in quantity of inedible substances. For example, a child with pica who has a craving for plaster will actually pick it out from the walls with great determination and tenacity.

Crumbling plaster and lead-based paint represent an immediate health threat for the toddler, who will taste and may continue to eat the flakes and chips.

Jeff Albertson—Stock, Boston

There is no known single cause, physical or psychological, for most cases of pica, although poor nutrition, lack of supervision, and inadequate intervention by the parents have been implicated in some cases; anemia has been suggested as a cause. It is known that some children with organic brain damage have pica—if the child craves lead-containing substances, the lead may aggravate the pica by increasing the brain damage.

Thirty percent of children who manifest pica develop lead poisoning. Most significant, various studies have shown that 70 to 90% of all children with lead poisoning have pica. But even if your child does not have pica, he or she can still become poisoned with lead.

Male children and female children are equally affected. The incidence of lead poisoning is greater in nonwhites than in whites, due to socioeconomic factors rather than to any genetic predisposition. There is a high recurrence rate. The main reason for this is that most children with lead poisoning have pica and continue to eat material loaded with lead. After being treated they often go right back into the environment that caused the lead poisoning in the first place.

Symptoms of lead poisoning

The signs and symptoms of lead poisoning are variable and depend upon the amount of lead taken into the body. In the case of the child who ingests very high concentrations of lead the result is acute encephalopathy. These children have a sudden onset of persistent and intractible vomiting, ataxia (loss of equilibrium), changes in sensorium (sensory perceptions) or state of consciousness, convulsions, and coma. These signs and symptoms develop because of severe cerebral edema, or swelling. Those children suffering from less dangerous levels of lead poisoning have more subtle manifestations, often making the diagnosis difficult to establish. The child may simply be slightly irritable. He may have a decrease in appetite or decreased play activity or occasional vomiting and constipation. Many of these children have an associated iron deficiency anemia. The hemoglobin is reduced because one of the biochemical systems most sensitive to lead is the heme biosynthetic pathway. Simply stated, lead interferes with the synthesis of heme (a major constituent of hemoglobin) and so leads to iron deficiency anemia.

If the diagnosis is delayed, the child with lead poison-

Adapted from *The Merck Manual of Diagnosis and Therapy*, 13th ed., Rahway, N.J.; Merck Sharp & Dohme Research Laboratories, 1977

Lead levels in blood

lead per 100 g of whole blood	significance
15–40 μg	normal, unexposed children
40–60 μg	abnormal or undue exposure
60–80 μg	mild symptoms
80–100 μg	a medical emergency, with or without symptoms
> 100 μg	risk of encephalopathy, with or without symptoms

The amount of lead in the blood can be precisely measured. Safe treatments are available to cleanse the body of lead before irreversible damage is done.

ing may lose recently acquired developmental skills. Lead intoxication can reduce the intelligence quotient (IQ) and may also lead to minimal brain dysfunction. It can cause aggressive behavior disorders, progressive loss of speech, and poor school performance later on. Unfortunately, the intellectual deficits that the lead poisoning produces are often irreversible.

Treatment and prevention

Because of the nonspecific nature of the clinical signs and symptoms of lead poisoning and the potentially devastating effects on the young child's brain, parents must continually be on the alert. The safest approach to lead poisoning is to prevent it from ever happening. If your young child suffers from pica it is absolutely essential that your physician be told about it. There are very simple, accurate blood and urine tests that can be carried out in most laboratories that measure the lead levels in the body. It is crucial that all children with pica be tested periodically for their lead levels. Further, every effort must be made to eliminate all old paint and plaster, both from the inside and outside of homes. This preventive measure is even more important if a child has pica, but it should be done even if there is no pica. Removing or refinishing old furniture that has been painted with lead-containing paint is also recommended. Further, children should not be present during the burning and scraping of paints containing lead.

It is only by screening large numbers of young children that those suffering from lead levels not yet causing overt symptoms will be identified and treated. Many states and cities have conducted and are continuing to conduct large-scale screening programs for preschool children in an attempt to pick up those asymptomatic youngsters with potentially damaging levels of lead in their blood.

There is some controversy about the actual levels of lead in the blood that are dangerous to the child and therefore about when to treat. As medical scientists have learned more about the subtle effects on the central nervous system from lower levels of lead, the threshold, above which treatment should be instituted, has been reduced. Whereas years ago 70 or 80 μg per dl (deciliter) was considered toxic, most authorities now would treat any child with a blood lead level over 50 μg per dl. In very recent years, some investigators have considered 40 μg per dl dangerous. Many children now being tested in screening programs are found to have blood-lead levels of 30 to 50 μg per dl; one large-scale study of two million children showed that 7% had blood-lead levels greater than 40 μg per dl. A number of these children did not suffer from pica but nevertheless had high blood-lead levels.

There are simple, safe, and effective methods of treating lead poisoning. The specific type of treatment depends on the severity of the disease and the level of the lead found in the blood. The child with signs of acute lead encephalopathy requires emergency management. Treatment is directed at reducing the increased pressure and swelling within the brain as rapidly as possible, along with lowering the blood-lead level. There are a number of chelating agents given orally or by injection that are used to bring down the high level of lead. Chelating refers to the combining of a metal with another substance. The metal ion becomes firmly bound into a ring within the chelating molecule and thus is drawn out of the blood and excreted in the urine. If chelation treatment is started before there are any clinical signs and symptoms of lead poisoning, the risk of the child's developing permanent brain damage is reduced and frequently eliminated. With proper treatment the blood-lead level can be lowered to a safe level in a short period of time. There

The presence of lead in this child's bones can be seen in the dark areas at the ends of the long bones of the arm, where the metal has collected.

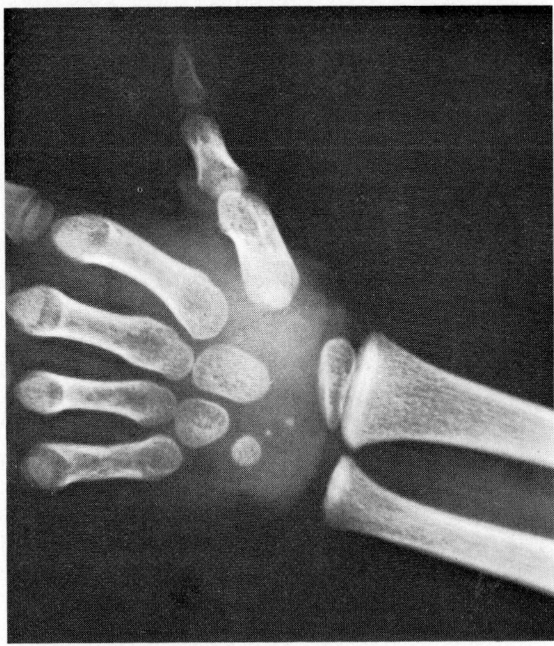

From *Pathologic Basis of Disease*, by Stanley L. Robbins, M.D. and Ramzi S. Cotran, M.D., 2nd ed., Philadelphia; W. B. Saunders Company, 1979

are times when the lead-poisoned child requires two or more separate courses of chelation therapy before the blood lead reaches a safe level.

Crucial to the whole problem of lead poisoning is to maintain a high index of suspicion and to test for lead whenever the diagnosis is even remotely suspected. If you suspect that your child may have ingested lead, insist on a blood-lead level test. Any child who has been treated for lead poisoning must be followed carefully after therapy. Obviously, the possible sources of lead that caused the problem must be eliminated. In some cases, this may actually mean moving to another house or apartment. The treated child also requires periodic screening tests later on. Brothers and sisters of the affected child should all be screened for their lead levels. The correction of any associated iron deficiency anemia often seen in lead poisoning may, in some cases, reduce or stop the child's abnormal cravings for nonfood substances.

The keys to eliminating lead poisoning are education and prevention. The two most important steps that must be taken are: (1) a concentrated effort to remove all the leaded paint and plaster from the environment of our children and (2) the passage of legislation that will make it illegal to burn leaded gasoline in any automobile on any road in the U.S. While lead continues to pollute the environment, more and more screening programs must be set up to identify those children with potentially dangerous levels of lead in their systems. Any child suffering from pica is at extremely high risk for developing lead poisoning and so must be monitored very carefully. Children suffering from iron deficiency anemia should also be screened regularly for lead levels. Those children living in inner cities in substandard housing also require frequent lead-level determinations. Until all the sources of excessive lead are finally eliminated, including paint, plaster, dirt, dust, gasoline, and more, none of us can relax our efforts to prevent our children from being poisoned by lead.

—Alvin N. Eden, M.D.

Health Education Unit 14

Antianxiety Drugs

The widespread use of minor tranquilizers in the United States has given rise to the fear that Americans are becoming a "tranquilized society." Though mankind has always sought relief from anxiety, the only remedies available were herbal preparations and alcohol until the development of barbiturates at the turn of the century. Another dimension was added in 1960 with the beginning of the era of minor tranquilizers, primarily the benzodiazepines, most widely distributed under the brand names Librium and Valium.

In 1977, U.S. physicians wrote over 68 million prescriptions for benzodiazepines, the majority for diazepam (Valium). The estimated retail value of these drugs was over half a billion dollars. In a given year, it has been estimated that 20% of women and 14% of men in the U.S. take Valium.

A better name for the minor tranquilizers is the antianxiety agents. The table lists the drugs found in this category. The antianxiety agents should not be confused with the major tranquilizers (Thorazine, Stelazine, etc.), which are used to treat schizophrenia, paranoid disorders, and other psychotic problems.

Anxiety is defined as "an unpleasant state, characterized by uneasiness and apprehension." The benzodiazepines are often prescribed to treat the symptoms of nervousness, tension, and sleep disorders commonly seen with anxiety. The benzodiazepines are medically indicated in the management of anxiety disorders, in the symptomatic relief of acute agitation and tremor associated with acute alcohol withdrawal, in adjunctive relief of skeletal muscle spasm, and in adjunctive therapy of convulsive disorders. The U.S. Food and Drug Administration (FDA) has stated that the benzodiazepines should not be used to treat anxiety or tension associated with everyday life. Rather, these drugs should be used for the short term when anxiety is symptomatic and produces undue anguish for the patient.

Mechanism of action

The exact mechanism of action of the benzodiazepines is unknown. They produce antianxiety, sedation, hypnosis, skeletal muscle relaxation, and anticonvulsant effects by acting on several areas of the central nervous system (CNS). Their ability to depress the central nervous system ranges in effect from mild sedation to sleep to coma.

In 1977 the discovery of receptors in the brain for benzodiazepines led to a new theory on how they might work. The presence of receptor sites in the brain suggests that the body has its own innate antianxiety agents that it can release under the pressure of daily stress. Some people with anxiety may be deficient in some way in their own antianxiety agents and therefore need minor tranquilizers. Of further interest is the fact that these receptors are not for the barbiturates and other sedatives, but appear to be specific for the benzodiazepines.

Magnitude and appropriateness of use

Statistics show that Valium has been the most widely prescribed drug in the United States for the past 12 years. Third-party-payment statistics indicate that 10,000,000 Americans took a benzodiazepine drug in 1978. Over 500,000,000 persons have taken these drugs since 1960. This widespread use has been due to their high level of safety, compatability with many prescription and nonprescription drugs, and low incidence of fatal overdose. A breakdown of prescriptions written for benzodiazepines shows that 40% are written by family practitioners and osteopaths, 19% by internists, 18% by psychiatrists, 10% by surgeons, and another 13% by other types of physicians.

The question that often arises is whether this widespread use of antianxiety drugs is appropriate. A study performed in the early 1970s in Oakland, Calif., evaluated minor tranquilizer use in 735 noninstitutionalized adults ranging in age from 18 to 64 years. It found that 20% of the study population took a minor tranquilizer at least once during the previous year. In all, 10% took the drugs for fewer than seven days—low-level usage; 4% for more than seven days but less than 60 days—medium-level usage; and 6% for more than 60 days—high-level usage. The study showed that regular use of minor tranquilizers was not as frequent as expected. In addition, it was found that usage increases with an increase in the number of health problems that an individual has.

Drawing by Dunn; © 1976 The New Yorker Magazine, Inc.

"What was the name of that tranquilizer we took?"

Physicians may tend to overprescribe these drugs because of patient pressure and the economics of time. Often the patient will try to pressure a physician into prescribing a drug in order to feel that he is being properly treated. And the physician will give in to avoid taking extra time to talk with the patient or to avoid dealing with the patient's problems with life.

Dangers

There are a few contraindications to the use of benzodiazepines. They should be avoided by patients who are allergic to them, who are psychotic, or who have narrow-angle glaucoma. They may be used in patients with open-angle glaucoma who are being treated with appropriate therapy. Benzodiazepines should not be used during pregnancy, particularly the first trimester, because of an increased risk of birth defects. These drugs also are excreted in breast milk and should be avoided by nursing mothers.

Benzodiazepines may adversely affect some functions of the central nervous system, depending on the level of the dosage. Drowsiness is commonly experienced during the first few days of therapy but is usually mild and transient in nature. Lack of muscular coordination and confusion may be seen in elderly and debilitated patients. These effects can be reversed with a reduction in dosage. On the other hand, some patients may exhibit a paradoxical CNS stimulation that results in an agitated state and insomnia.

Dependence on the benzodiazepines has been reported and appears to be related to the level of dosage and duration of treatment. Abrupt withdrawal of Valium in patients receiving 30 to 45 mg per day for a prolonged period can lead to a withdrawal syndrome similar to that seen with alcohol or the barbiturates. (A usual daily dosage for symptomatic relief of tension and anxiety ranges from 2 mg to 10 mg two to four times a day.) The withdrawal syndrome consists of both behavioral and physiologic changes, the most prominent being an alteration in mood. The withdrawal syndrome usually appears within five to nine days after abrupt discontinuance of the drug.

It is often difficult to distinguish withdrawal from a return of the patient's symptoms of anxiety. It usually takes two weeks for anxiety symptoms to reach their fullest after discontinuance of a benzodiazepine drug, and this helps in distinguishing the two. A gradual tapering of the dose before stopping therapy can minimize the risk of withdrawal syndrome. The dependence risk associated with benzodiazepine use is low and is much less than that seen with barbiturates and other sedatives.

There is little evidence at this time that the long-term use of benzodiazepines has the same physical, psychological, social, and economic effects as seen with many drugs of abuse, such as alcohol or heroin. It will take many more years of clinical use to determine any long-term effects since the benzodiazepines have been marketed only since 1960.

Interactions

There are certain drugs that interact with the benzodiazepines and can cause problems, mainly drowsiness and extreme CNS depression. The most common interactions are with alcohol and other CNS depressants. It should be noted that the combined effect of the interaction is synergistic, *i.e.,* much greater than simply the sum of the effects of the two drugs if taken singly. Anyone taking a benzodiazepine who has also consumed alcohol should avoid driving an automobile or operating dangerous machinery, since he will be less alert and unable to perform certain tasks adequately. The following categories of drugs potentiate (activate synergistically) the CNS depressant effects of the benzodiazepines: phenothiazines, narcotics, barbiturates, monoamine oxidase (MAO) inhibitors, and antidepressants.

Cigarette smoking, on the other hand, seems to reduce sedation and drowsiness associated with the benzodiazepines. Nonsmokers have a 10% incidence of drowsiness, while light smokers have 7% and heavy smokers 3%. The cause of this decrease, if real, is unknown. (One explanation might be that people who smoke heavily are the type who will have less drowsiness independent of smoking.)

Food and antacids decrease the rate of absorption

Peter Southwick—Stock, Boston

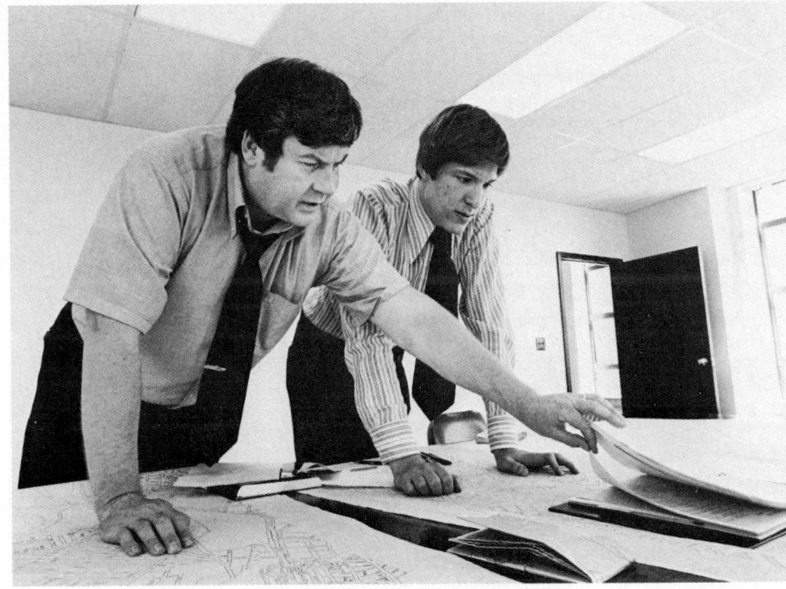

Work-related stress is one reason there is widespread reliance on antianxiety drugs in modern society. But the use of the so-called minor tranquilizers to relieve the tensions and anxieties of everyday life is considered inappropriate.

of the drug but do not affect the amount of the drug absorbed. The result is a delayed onset of action when the benzodiazepines are taken with food or antacids.

Consumer information

As of July 1981, the FDA will require pharmacists to dispense a patient package insert (PPI) with ten different categories of drugs, one of which will be the benzodiazepines. The PPI program is intended to promote informed use of drugs through increased education of the patient. In the past, the lay public has had few appropriate, unbiased sources of drug information. The medical terminology in the *Physician's Desk Reference* (*PDR*) is aimed at doctors, and those books about prescription drugs written for the layman often contain the bias of the author.

The PPI is written in easily understood, nonscientific language. It explains the conditions for which the drug is prescribed and cautions about its use, the possibility of side effects and dependence, and the dangers of overdose or drug interaction. Sample paragraphs from the insert for benzodiazepines such as Valium and Librium state:

"If you miss a dose of this medicine, do not take twice as much the next time. Also, do not change the dosage unless told to do so by your doctor.

"If you have been taking benzodiazepines for a month or more your doctor should reassess your con-

Antianxiety agents

generic name	brand name
benzodiazepines	
chlordiazepoxide hydrochloride	Librium
chlordiazepoxide	Libritabs
chlorazepate dipotassium	Tranxene
clorazepate monopotassium	Azene
diazepam	Valium
oxazepam	Serax
lorazepam	Ativan
prazepam	Centrax
propanediol carbamates	
meprobamate	Equanil; Miltown; others
tybamate	Salacen; Tybatran
antihistamines	
hydroxyzine hydrochloride	Atarax
hydroxyzine pamoate	Vistaril
miscellaneous	
doxepin hydrochloride	Adapin; Sinequan
chlormezanone	Trancopal

Adapted from *The Benzodiazepines: Use, Overuse, Misuse, Abuse*, by John Marks, Lancaster, England; MTP Press Limited © 1978

Substances of potential abuse

substance group	abuse level	illicit traffic	psychological dependence	physical dependence	medical or commercial availability	effects extend beyond taker
benzodiazepines	low	sporadic	+	+	+	?
narcotics	high	+++	+++	+++	+	yes
hallucinogens	high	++	+++	−	+	yes
stimulants	high	+	+++	+	+	yes
barbiturates	moderate	small	++	++	+	?
alcohol	high	++ when banned	+++	++	+++	yes
tobacco	high	open availability	+++	?+	+++	yes

Various drug classes (medical and social) are compared in terms of potential abuse in the above table. The evaluations are based on the World Health Organization's criteria for exerting legal controls on drugs.

dition and your continued use. The effect of these drugs for the relief of anxiety for periods longer than four months has not been studied. If you feel that your medicine is not helping, discuss it with your doctor."

Guidelines for use

Once anxiety has been diagnosed and a benzodiazepine prescribed, there are certain steps a patient can take to optimize therapy.

1. Use the drug only at times of unusual stress. Continuous use for a period greater than four months in duration should be avoided.
2. Avoid excessive dosage.
3. Avoid taking other CNS depressants concurrently, unless specifically instructed to by your physician.
4. Avoid alcohol.
5. Read the information in the patient package insert to increase your knowledge of the drug's proper use.

By following these guidelines, patients can achieve optimal therapeutic benefit from the benzodiazepines while minimizing the risks associated with their use.

—Edward R. Leist, Pharm.D.

Health Education Unit 15

Removing Unwanted Hair

Hair normally grows nearly everywhere on the skin, the palms of the hands, soles of the feet, and lips being the most obvious exceptions. Even though the range of normal hair growth is quite wide, social and cultural factors may cause some individuals to view perfectly normal growth as cosmetically unacceptable—in the United States, women tend to consider removal of underarm and leg hair essential to good grooming. Fashions are a factor, too. Women who ignore hairs on chest or abdomen during the winter may view them with alarm in the swimsuit season.

Factors in hair growth

Abnormal, excessive growth, known as hirsutism, has a variety of causes. Medical concern focuses on hair that is coarser, longer, or more profuse than average for the sex, race, and age of the person involved.

Sex is a prime influence on hair growth; men tend to be hairier than women, although there is considerable overlap in hair growth between the sexes. About 20% of women have hair on the chest and midline of the abdomen, while about 20% of men do not. Even close relatives of the same sex may differ considerably in their amount of hair growth.

Race also influences hair growth. Whites, for example, tend to be hairier than blacks. Among whites, Mediterranean and Semitic peoples are hairier than Nordics or Anglo-Saxons. Among racial groups, the least hairy are Orientals and American Indians. Racial differences in hairiness reflect differing sensitivity of hair follicles to stimulation by hormones, particularly the family of hormones known as androgens.

At puberty, the body's output of growth hormone and androgens causes the fine, light-colored hairs of childhood to become longer, coarser, and darker. While both men and women produce androgens, the greater amount produced in men accounts for their greater hairiness. In men, hair grows to its maximum; excess hormone will not increase hair growth in a healthy man or cause a beard to grow in some Chinese, Indian, or black men. In women, however, hair ordinarily does not grow to its maximum; excess hormone will cause greater growth. During puberty, pregnancy, and menopause, times of hormonal changes, some women notice an increase in facial or body hair.

Indeed, most complaints of "excessive" hair are made by women. Most often the problem is cosmetic, but sometimes it is associated with physical disorders.

In both adults and children, a rapid or dramatic increase in hair growth or the appearance of hair in areas where it has never grown before or where it is usually not seen are conditions that should prompt a visit to a physician. Examples include pubic hair on a child before the expected age for puberty, a beard on a woman, or hair next to the nose or around the eyes in either men or women.

Hirsutism meeting such criteria in women most often is ascribed to excess androgens, produced by the ovaries and the adrenal glands; glucocorticoids, also from the adrenal glands; and growth hormone, from the pituitary gland. The normal range of these hormones, as determined by blood and urine tests, is so wide that a level that is excessive in one woman may be normal in another. A diagnosis of hormone imbalance sometimes is confirmed only by the success of treatment involving hormone manipulation.

Some women with hirsutism manifest other signs of hormone imbalance, such as menstrual irregularities, infertility, virilism, obesity, acne, and oily skin. Rarely, tumors of the ovaries, adrenal glands, or pituitary gland produce excess amounts of hormones, leading to hirsutism; indeed, excess hair may be the earliest sign of the tumor. When tumors are present, results of blood and urine tests typically are markedly outside of the normal range.

Excessive hair growth may be a response to friction or pressure, as from a cast. In these cases it is usually transient. Excessive hair growth also may be an unwanted side effect from certain drugs used for such disorders as epilepsy, asthma, arthritis, gynecologic disorders, and osteoporosis. Injections of testosterone given to suppress milk production after childbirth may cause hirsutism, along with mild acne. Some birth control pills, particularly those with lower dose estrogens, also may trigger excessive hair growth.

Once an underlying disorder is corrected, typically by treatment with drugs or surgery, or when the specific drugs involved are discontinued, production of excessive hair generally no longer increases. However, the hair follicles that previously were stimulated frequently continue to produce hair. There are no drugs that effectively "turn off" excess hair growth in otherwise healthy persons. Other than medical treatment, removal or concealment are the customary approaches to dealing with unwanted hair.

Permanent hair removal

Electrolysis is the only safe way to remove hair permanently. The procedure involves insertion of a fine needle into each individual hair follicle. Electric current passes through the needle to destroy hair germ cells and prevent future growth. There are several methods; the safest uses a galvanic low-voltage current. The newer electrocoagulation, also known as diathermy, is quicker but requires extreme care to avoid scarring; it utilizes high frequency alternating current.

The amount of discomfort a person undergoing electrolysis feels depends on his or her personal sensitivity to pain, the amount of fatty tissue in the area acting as a "cushion" for the shock, and the competence of the electrologist.

Since a site such as the upper lip may have hundreds of hairs, each requiring a skilled operator approximately a minute to locate and treat, the process—typically performed once or twice a week in half-hour or hour-long sessions—may take months or even years to complete. A certain percentage of hairs will be "resting," that is, not in active growth, at any one time; it may be months before all hairs have grown out to the point where they can be treated.

Generally, for a few hours following electrolysis the area around each hair follicle treated will show some reddening; sometimes crusts form. Even with an experienced operator, scarring may occur; an individual's likelihood of developing scarring is unpredictable. Further, regrowth of a variable percentage of treated hairs is inevitable; one reason is a failure to hit the hair root. Some hair roots may have multiple bulbs; even though one is destroyed, the other will produce hair. Sometimes the hair follicle curves in such a way that the root is unreachable.

Hairs growing from a mole can be removed by electrolysis; doing so may even cause the mole to shrink. Before having a mole treated in this fashion, however,

"I had 'em rolling in the aisles until I inadvertently mentioned the Queen's mustache."

One method of temporary hair removal is waxing. The area to be stripped of hair is covered with a layer of sticky wax that pulls out the hair as the wax is removed.

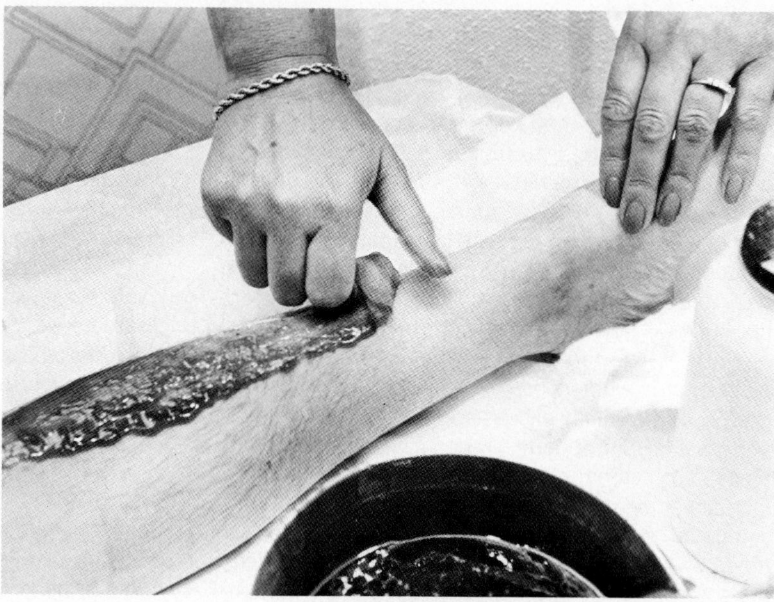

Courtesy, Bonwit Teller, Chicago; photograph, Jean-Claude Lejeune

it is wise to seek a physician's advice; moles occasionally undergo malignant changes. Since flat warts can be spread by electrolysis, treatment of a wart infection should be completed before the procedure is begun.

Charges for electrolysis vary; $20 to $25 for a half-hour session would not be unusual in a metropolitan area in the U.S. Training and certification requirements for electrolysis practitioners vary considerably across the nation. Some states have no requirements at all; in others, electrolysis must be performed under the supervision of a physician. Some states make training and examination mandatory.

Word of mouth probably is the most reliable way to find a competent electrologist. Dermatologists, physicians specializing in the skin, often are able to refer persons to electrologists; some perform the service themselves or have a trained technician in the office.

With regard to do-it-yourself electrolysis devices, the position taken by the Food and Drug Administration (FDA) is that "If done by an expert, electrolysis usually gives good results. But it can be painful, time consuming, costly, and lead to infections. Thus, consumers should be particularly careful about using any of the home electrolysis devices that are on the market. Considerable skill and dexterity are required to perform electrolysis properly, and most people would probably be better off going to an expert instead of trying to do it themselves."

Courtesy, Christine M. Jensen; photograph, Jean-Claude Lejeune

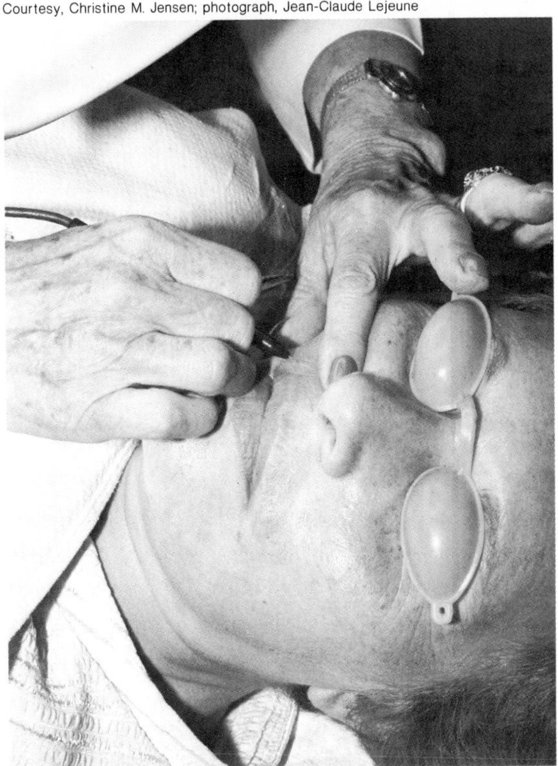

Electrolysis permanently stops hair growth by obliterating the hair follicle. Dermatologists often can recommend skilled electrologists.

Temporary hair removal

Shaving, for both women and men, is the most popular way to get rid of unwanted hair. Hair that grows back after shaving may feel thicker or look more obvious because shorter hairs are less flexible than longer ones and because new hair growth sticks straight out rather than lying flat against the skin. However, shaving does not accelerate hair growth or make hair thicker or darker.

The key element in getting a close, comfortable shave is adequate wetting of the hair. It takes two and one-half to three minutes before hair becomes thoroughly wet and hence soft, pliable, and easier to cut. Hot water helps speed the process. Shaving creams and lathers help keep water from evaporating, make it easier for the razor to glide over the skin, and serve as a guide to areas already shaved. Shaving experts say a person can get a perfectly adequate shave without lather in the shower with warm water flowing over the skin, a method women often use. Incidentally, there is no medical reason for women to avoid shaving unwanted hair on the face but most choose other methods, objecting to the stubble or the masculine association.

Dry shaving is harder on the skin and shortens the life of the blade of the razor. Smoothing the skin while shaving by applying tension to remove small wrinkles and folds helps give a smoother shave, although excessive tension, particularly over bony spots such as chin or knees, may make the skin protrude at hair follicles in a gooseflesh pattern and lead to uneven cutting and skin irritation.

Men have an estimated 15,000 whiskers on the face, with the densest growth generally on the upper lip and center of the chin. Some men require as many as 600 strokes of the razor per shave. While sharp blades, greater pressure against the face, shaving against the grain, and extensive stretching of the skin all give a closer shave, they also increase the amount of skin that is scraped off and increase the risk of ingrown hairs. The sharply angled hair tip—particularly on curly hair—may poke back through the skin and act as a foreign body, producing inflammation. Ingrown hairs often are an acute problem for black men, who may find that growing a beard or using facial depilatories are ways of avoiding such trouble. Other advice includes use of an adjustable razor with a sharp blade set at an angle that is not too close or use of an electric shaver, a method thought to be less irritating.

Men with acne in the beard area also need to exert caution to avoid irritation; standard advice includes shaving less often, not pressing hard, and avoiding tender spots. There is no harm in shaving over moles in the beard area or elsewhere; shaving will not cause moles to get bigger. Warts, however, require a visit to the doctor; because they are caused by a virus, the razor may spread them.

Plucking or *tweezing* is used for scattered hairs and for shaping eyebrows. Tweezing hair from a mole may prove irritating and is not advised. Electronic tweezers have been the subject of FDA action because of what the agency has contended are misleading claims. The manufacturers of these devices, whose trade names include Depilatron, Depillex, and Bioepilator, said their products would destroy hair regenerative cells; the FDA asserts these tweezers are no better than ordinary nonelectrified tweezers.

Depilatories are chemical agents that break down the structure of the hair so that it can be detached easily from the skin. The specific chemical ingredients are targeted at hair and, when the product is used as directed, cause little or no irritation to surrounding skin. Because depilatories remove hair just below the skin surface, new hair growth becomes obvious at a slightly slower rate than after shaving.

Some persons are more likely to develop irritation from depilatories than others; they include persons prone to "detergent hands" or sensitive to ammonia cleansers or strong soaps. Application of a quarter-sized test patch usually gives an indication of whether irritation is likely to develop. Guidelines for appropriate use include observing time limits, not applying the product near the eyes, not using it on irritated skin, and not using it immediately before or after applying antiperspirants to the treated area.

Waxing results in the removal of large numbers of hairs from the skin at one time. "Hot" waxing involves the application of a thin liquid to the skin; when the wax hardens, it is ripped off quickly against the direction of hair growth, pulling out hairs imbedded in it. The sensation often is likened to the removal of adhesive tape from the skin. If the wax is too hot at the time of application, it can cause burns; persons trying waxing at home should not heat the wax on a stove but rather on a warming tray just until it is melted. "Cold" waxing utilizes prepared strips similar to adhesive tape. After a number of years, damage to large numbers of hair follicles by either method of waxing often reduces hair growth.

Abrasives, such as pumice or fine emery paper, may be used to rub off hairs at the skin surface. They are inexpensive and easy to use but take such a long time that they are impractical for large areas. Rubbing too vigorously can cause skin irritation.

Concealing unwanted hair

Bleaching is an effective way to conceal unwanted hair and often is used for face or arms. Bleaching products can be purchased or made at home. A standard formula is one ounce of 6% hydrogen peroxide (known as 20 volume peroxide) plus 20 drops of household ammonia plus enough baking soda or soap flakes to make a paste. Make a small batch first; apply to a test area on an arm for 30 minutes to see if irritation develops. If not, make a new batch and apply it promptly, since the bleaching action starts with mixing. Wash it off after 10 minutes; if hairs are not bleached thoroughly, repeat the next day. If dark hairs turn orange instead of blond, modify the basic formula by cutting down or eliminating the ammonia. Repeated bleaching may damage hair, which, in this instance, is a desirable effect.

—Lynne Lamberg

Health Education Unit 16

Low–Sodium Diets

Over the last decade people in the United States have grown increasingly concerned about the healthfulness of the foods they eat. This concern has been heightened by an increased awareness of the relationship of diet to various diseases such as hypertension (high blood pressure). Sodium in the diet has been implicated in hypertension, and for years physicians have advised hypertensive patients to follow low-sodium diets.

What is sodium?

Sodium is an element needed by the body to regulate fluid balance and preserve the integrity and function of body cells. It is the commonest element in the blood, while potassium is its equivalent as the commonest element inside the cells. Many people are confused about the difference between sodium and table salt. Salt is a compound of two elements, sodium and chlorine—about 40% sodium and 60% chlorine by weight. It is the *sodium* content of table salt, food, and food additives that is of health concern today.

The average American eats about 2 to 2½ teaspoons of salt per day (10–12 grams), equivalent to 4 to 5 grams of sodium. Only about 25–30% of that sodium comes from the saltshaker; another 25–30% occurs in meat, grains, dairy products, fruits, and vegetables; and the remainder comes from processed foods. The National Research Council of the National Academy of Sciences recommends a sodium intake of 1.1 to 3.3 grams (1,100 to 3,300 mg) per day for adults as safe and adequate—far less than the average American intake. So it is not just people with heart disease and high blood pressure who need to cut down on sodium. The amount of sodium one actually needs each day depends on factors such as environmental temperature (some sodium is lost through perspiration), humidity, amount of exercise, and state of health.

Why a low-sodium diet?

In 1977 the Senate Select Committee on Nutrition and Human Needs released a now-famous report entitled *Dietary Goals for the United States.* One of the goals stated: "Limit the intake of sodium by reducing the intake of salt to about five grams a day." These goals were aimed at *all* of the people of the U.S. Then in 1979 the U.S. surgeon general issued a report *Healthy People,* which contained seven U.S. Dietary Guidelines—one of which was "avoid too much sodium." These two reports based their recommendations to reduce dietary sodium on studies that have shown that a reduction of sodium in the diet can reduce, and may even prevent, high blood pressure in susceptible individuals. High blood pressure, or hypertension, is one of the three major risk factors for atherosclerosis, a leading cause of death in the U.S. today.

Low-sodium diets are used for diseases other than hypertension such as congestive heart failure and liver failure. In most instances, the rationale behind the use of a sodium-restricted diet is to prevent, control, or ameliorate fluid retention (edema). When water accumulates in the body, this is a sign that something is wrong. Because the cells and fluids of the body are in equilibrium and the concentration of salts in the water both inside and outside cells is held constant, retention of sodium means retention of water in the majority of cases. People receiving very small amounts of sodium in the diet would therefore tend to retain less water as edema. The situation may be especially dangerous for older persons because of a greater tendency toward heart disease. When the body retains sodium and water together, reducing sodium intake usually not only relieves the discomfort of edema but also decreases the workload of the heart and helps control blood pressure by decreasing fluid volume in the circulation.

Table I: **Comparison of diets for different daily levels of sodium***

	500 mg	1,000 mg	2,000 mg	3,000 mg
milk	2 cups milk; avoid buttermilk and dutch-process cocoa	2 cups milk; avoid buttermilk and dutch-process cocoa	2 cups milk; buttermilk and dutch-process cocoa within limits	2 cups any milk
meat	4 oz fresh meat, fish, or poultry†	5 oz fresh meat, fish, or poultry†	6–8 oz fresh meat, fish, poultry; avoid cured, smoked, or canned meats or fish; regular cheese within limits*	6–8 oz fresh meat, fish, poultry; cured, smoked, or canned within limits*; regular cheese within limits*
fruit	any fresh, frozen, or canned; avoid tomato and vegetable juices	any fresh, frozen, or canned; avoid tomato and vegetable juices	any fresh, frozen, or canned; avoid tomato and vegetable juices	any fresh, frozen, or canned; tomato and vegetable juices limited*
vegetables	fresh, frozen, or low sodium canned; avoid certain ones‡	fresh, frozen, or low sodium canned; avoid certain ones‡	fresh, frozen, or regular canned within limits*	fresh, frozen, or regular canned
bread	low sodium bread, rolls, crackers	2 slices regular bread; low sodium bread, rolls, crackers as desired	4 slices regular bread; low sodium bread, rolls, crackers as desired	any type of bread or rolls, regular crackers within limits*
cereals	only salt free	only salt free	unsalted cooked and certain dry cereals	any cereals
desserts	avoid any with baking powder or baking soda	avoid any with baking powder or baking soda	2 regular desserts; salt-free as desired	any desserts
soup	unsalted homemade or unsalted canned	unsalted homemade or unsalted canned	unsalted homemade or unsalted canned	regular commercial soup is limited*
beverages	coffee, tea, regular cocoa, fruit drinks, lemonade	coffee, tea, regular cocoa, fruit drinks, lemonade	coffee, tea, regular cocoa, carbonated beverages, fruit drinks, lemonade	any
fats	unsalted butter or margarine, salad dressing, oil, or shortening	unsalted butter or margarine, salad dressing, oil, or shortening; salted butter or margarine within limits*	salted butter or margarine, oil, or shortening; unsalted salad dressing	salted butter or margarine, oil, or shortening; regular salad dressings are limited*
misc.	only salt-free condiments and seasonings	only salt-free condiments and seasonings	regular condiments and seasonings are limited*; salt-free as desired	regular condiments and seasonings are limited*; salt-free as desired

*Special measured amounts of certain higher sodium items can be planned into the diet by a dietitian.

†One egg or one ounce of low sodium cheese, tuna, or salmon may be substituted for one ounce of meat.

‡Certain vegetables are naturally high in sodium and should be used only if planned into these diets by a dietitian: artichokes, beets and beet greens, carrots, celery, chard, dandelion greens, kale, lima beans, mustard greens, peas, spinach, and turnips.

In many hypertensive persons and those with congestive heart failure, a high-sodium diet is more difficult to handle because of an increase in the hormone aldosterone. This is produced in the adrenal glands in response to renin, an enzyme produced by the kidneys, whose blood supply has been decreased. In turn aldosterone causes the filtering mechanism of the kidney to reabsorb sodium avidly into the body, preventing its loss in the urine. A high sodium intake will further increase sodium retention and tend to raise the blood pressure even further. In very severe, or malignant, hypertension, sodium accumulates in the arterial wall, interfering with natural regulation of blood pressure.

In severe cirrhosis of the liver, there are several reasons why water and sodium are retained. There is an increased venous pressure in the portal vein so that fluid accumulates in the abdominal cavity (a condition called ascites). The failing liver cannot produce albumin, the principal protein of the blood, so the osmotic pressure of the blood falls. Water in the tissues outside the blood capillaries is no longer drawn back into the blood by osmosis; it stays where it is as edema fluid. As a result, there is less blood circulating; this decreased blood flow also triggers the renin-aldosterone system, and again there is increased sodium retention. Moreover, in cirrhosis there is decreased destruction of aldosterone by the failing liver, so very high levels are found in the body.

In normal people, sodium balance is maintained by the kidneys. If more sodium is ingested, more appears in the urine; and if there is less in the diet, renal excretion can be reduced to almost zero in three or four days. In acute renal failure, when the kidneys stop working suddenly or as an end result of chronic kidney failure, again no urine can be made. The chief regulator of sodium and water balance has shut down, so the physician and patient must meticulously adjust water and sodium intakes. In conditions where urine output is normal but there is heavy loss of blood albumin through damaged kidneys, the situation is equivalent to liver failure. Sodium and water retention follow the reduced blood osmotic pressure and the high levels of aldosterone in the blood. In chronic kidney diseases there is usually a period (lasting weeks or years) in which the kidneys just lose sodium and water. For this reason, both sodium and water must be measured in the daily urine and the loss replaced exactly.

Giving up salt

If a person is going to follow a strict low-sodium diet,

Table II: **Sodium content of prepared foods**

food	serving size
high: over 500 mg sodium per serving	
broth, bouillon, or consomme	1 cup
canned mixed dishes (*e.g.,* chili, spaghetti, macaroni and cheese)	¾ cup
celery, onion, or garlic salt	1 teaspoon
dried or chipped meat	1 ounce
meat tenderizers	—
monosodium glutamate (MSG)	—
olives	4 medium
pickles, most types	1 medium
sauerkraut	⅔ cup
seasoning mixes	1 package
seasoning salts	1 teaspoon
soup—canned, dried, or frozen	1 cup
soy sauce	1 tablespoon
T.V. dinners	one
table salt	1 teaspoon
medium: 200–500 mg sodium per serving	
bacon	4 strips
buttermilk	1 cup
canadian bacon	1 ounce
canned fish (*e.g.,* tuna, salmon)	¼ cup
canned or potted meat (*e.g.,* Spam)	1 ounce
canned vegetables	½ cup
catsup	2 tablespoons
cheese curls (snack food)	1 ounce
cold cuts or luncheon meat	1 ounce
commercial biscuits, muffins, pancakes, or waffles	one
corn chips	1 ounce
corned beef	1 ounce
creamed cottage cheese	½ cup
ham	1 ounce
highly salted natural cheese (feta, Parmesan, blue)	1 ounce
hot dog	one
mustard	2 tablespoons
pickle relish	2 tablespoons
pork rinds (snack food)	1 ounce
potato chips	1 ounce
pretzels	1 ounce
processed cheese	1 ounce
salad dressing	2 tablespoons
200–500 mg continued	
salt pork	1 ounce
salted crackers	4–6
salted nuts	3–4 ounces
salted popcorn	2 cups
sauces:	
barbecue	2 tablespoons
chili	2 tablespoons
steak	2 tablespoons
tomato	2 tablespoons
tartar	2 tablespoons
Worcestershire	2 tablespoons
sausage (breakfast)	2 links
tomato juice	¾ cup
V-8 juice	¾ cup
ready-to-eat cereal, most types*	¾–1 cup
low: less than 200 mg sodium per serving	
bacon-flavored bits	1 tablespoon
bread	1 slice
butter or margarine	1 tablespoon
carbonated beverages	12 ounces
certain cheeses (ricotta, cheddar, swiss, mozzarella)	1 ounce
commercial rolls	one
cookies, plain	3–5
dried beans, peas, lentils	any amount
fresh meat, fish, poultry	3–4 ounces
fruit or fruit juice (except tomato or vegetable)	any amount
mayonnaise	2 tablespoons
milk, yogurt, ice cream	1 cup
pasta or rice	any amount
peanut butter	2 tablespoons
sherbet	1 cup
shortening or cooking oil	any amount
spices and flavorings	any amount
tomato paste	1 cup
unsalted bread	any amount
unsalted cooked cereal	any amount
unsalted nuts, crackers	any amount
vegetables, fresh or frozen, or canned without salt	any amount†
vinegar	any amount

*The following cereals are low in sodium: shredded wheat, puffed wheat or rice, wheat germ, Frosted Mini Wheats, unprocessed bran.

†Limit frozen peas or lima beans to ½ cup.

one of the first things he will have to do is get rid of the saltshaker. One teaspoon of salt contains approximately 2,000 mg (or 2 grams) sodium—that is, two-thirds of the total allowance for the day on a liberal sodium-restricted diet but twice the total allowance for the day on a moderate sodium-restricted diet. The taste for salty foods is acquired and, although it may take some time to get used to, eating without salt need not be especially difficult.

The level of sodium restriction for each individual depends on the disease for which he is being treated and his general physical condition. Table I gives some basic differences between the various levels of sodium-restricted diets. For a healthy person, it would be appropriate to follow the 3,000-mg (or 3-gram) sodium diet recommended by the National Research Council and by the U.S. Dietary Guidelines.

It should be evident from the table that there are many similarities among the different diets. The diets should be individualized for each person by a physician or by a trained dietitian or nutritionist. For instance, if a person does not drink milk, he may have more servings from another food group or have a little cheese instead. In some cases, even table salt may be worked into the diet.

Shopping and reading labels

Unfortunately, purchasing food for a low-sodium diet can be difficult. At present, the sodium content of a food product is not a part of nutrition labeling unless the food carries the designation "low sodium." There is a wide variety of low-sodium foods available today, normally found in the dietary foods section of most grocery stores. These products, which include everything from dill pickles and potato chips to cornflakes and cottage cheese, often cost twice as much as their regular salted counterparts. However, these special dietary products are absolutely necessary for anyone who is on a diet that restricts sodium to less than 1,000 mg, unless he wants to make all of his food from scratch.

Much of the food preparation for anyone watching sodium in his diet will have to be done from scratch in any case. This is because there are so many other sodium-containing ingredients added to processed foods besides salt. One must read labels carefully to make sure the product one is purchasing does not contain sodium benzoate (a preservative), sodium bicarbonate (a leavening agent), sodium nitrite (a curing agent), sodium phosphate (a wetting agent), sodium propionate (a flavor enhancer), or monosodium glutamate (MSG, a flavor enhancer), to name a few. These hidden sources of sodium make many processed foods forbidden on a low-sodium diet. Table II lists the sodium content of various processed foods. Table III lists various nonprescription drugs, which can contain quite high levels of sodium.

Table III: **Sodium content of selected nonprescription drugs**

type of product	trade name	sodium content (mg per dose)
analgesic	(various)	49
antacid analgesic	Bromo-Seltzer	717
	Alka-Seltzer (blue box)	521
antacid laxative	Sal Hepatica	1,000
antacids	Rolaids	53
	Soda Mint	89
	Alka-Seltzer Antacid (gold box)	276
	Brioschi	710
laxatives	Metamucil Instant Mix	250
	Fleet's Enema	250–300 (absorbed)
sleep-aids	Miles Nervine Effervescent	544

Adapting recipes and eating out

Not only is it difficult to purchase food to conform to a low-sodium diet but also one has to be very selective when eating in a restaurant. Generally, choose plain steaks, chops, chicken, or fish, and ask that they be prepared without salt. Raw vegetable salad with oil and vinegar or lemon juice as a dressing is acceptable. Choose a baked potato with or without butter or margarine, depending on the level of sodium restriction (unless unsalted butter is available). A fruit cup for an appetizer and sherbet for dessert could complete the meal. Most bread products and vegetables will contain salt, so again these may be included, depending on the level of sodium restriction. Never eat in fast-food restaurants. Most menu items have more than 500 mg sodium—except perhaps a plain hamburger.

Many cookbooks for low-sodium diets are available. They suggest creative uses of herbs and spices to flavor foods without salt. These would be especially helpful for the strict dieter who finds most of the special dietetic products costly or unacceptable.

Recommended cookbooks

Bagg, Elma W. *Cooking Without a Grain of Salt.* Garden City, N.Y.: Doubleday and Co. Inc., 1964.

Claiborne, Craig, and Franey, Pierre. *Craig Claiborne's Gourmet Diet.* New York: Times Books, 1980.

Conason, Emil G., M.D., and Metz, Ella. *The Salt-Free Diet Cook Book.* New York: Grosset and Dunlap, 1969.

Cooking Without Your Salt Shaker. American Heart Association Northeast Ohio Affiliate, Inc., 1978.

Schell, Merle. *Tasting Good: The International Salt-Free Cookbook.* New York: Bobbs-Merrill, 1981.

—Nancy Kennedy, R.D.

FIRST AID HANDBOOK

Produced in cooperation with the Educational Materials Committee of the American College of Emergency Physicians, G. Richard Braen, M.D., Chairman.

Authors

Roy D. Beebe, M.D., and G. Richard Braen, M.D.

Contents

Illustrations by John Youssi

Emergency Care and First Aid

Properly administered first aid can make the difference between life and death, between temporary and permanent disability, or between rapid recovery and long hospitalization. First aid is most frequently employed to help a family member, a close friend, or an associate, and everyone should be familiar with first aid techniques and should know how best to use the emergency care system.

Public education and public awareness of potential roles in first aid have lagged behind the development of the emergency care system, which includes emergency medicine as a special area of medicine, better equipped and better staffed emergency facilities, paramedical care, communications, and transportation. The concept of first aid as simply the immediate care of the injured person is obsolete. Today a person administering first aid must be able to establish priorities in care and must understand and implement *basic life support* in an attempt to maintain vital functions. Education will reduce the chances of error and the possibly harmful results of well-meant but misdirected efforts.

Accidents are the leading cause of death among persons one to 38 years of age. In addition, over 800,000 Americans die annually of heart attacks, and a great majority of these die before they reach a hospital. The annual cost of medical attention and loss of earning ability amounts to billions of dollars, not to mention the toll in pain, suffering, disability, and personal tragedy. Thus, the delivery of quality emergency care and public education in basic life support and first aid must be accorded a high priority.

Use of This Handbook

The purpose of this handbook is both to educate and to serve as resource material for commonly encountered emergencies. It is arranged in three sections. The first deals with basic life support and the treatment of immediately life-threatening emergencies. One must understand these concepts *before* an emergency arises, since the necessary techniques must be employed immediately, almost by reflex, if the victim is to be saved.

The second section deals with emergencies that are not immediately life-threatening. It covers the common emergencies in alphabetical order.

The final section covers prevention, preparation, and use of the emergency care system. Prevention is still the least expensive medicine, and several of its most important principles will be discussed. Each home should be prepared for an emergency by having a readily accessible first aid kit, appropriate telephone numbers, etc. This section also discusses what to do and what to expect at the emergency department.

Section One:

Basic Life Support—Treatment of Immediately Life-Threatening Emergencies

Cardiopulmonary Arrest (Heart and Respiratory Failure)

Cardiac arrest is the most life-threatening of all emergencies. If circulation and breathing are not reestablished within minutes, the brain will suffer irreparable damage. Cardiopulmonary resuscitation (CPR), or basic life support, if begun early enough, can be lifesaving. This very simple procedure requires no special equipment and can be begun by *any person* who has taken the time to receive appropriate instruction. Before attempting to utilize this procedure, one would be well advised, in addition to reading the description of basic life support that follows, to undertake formal certification in CPR. Such instruction is readily available through the American Heart Association or the Red Cross.

What Is Cardiopulmonary Arrest?

There are two absolutely vital systems in the body that must function if life is to continue: the *respiratory* system (lungs and respiratory tree) and the *circulatory* system (heart and blood vessels). The overall function of these two systems is to get oxygen into the blood and then to all parts of the body.

0-4 MIN.	CLINICAL DEATH	BRAIN DAMAGE not likely
4-6 MIN.		BRAIN DAMAGE probable
6-10 MIN.	BIOLOGICAL DEATH	BRAIN DAMAGE probable
OVER 10 MIN.		BRAIN DAMAGE almost certain

Phases of brain damage and death following cardiac arrest.

If either of these systems fails, or "arrests," death occurs very quickly unless the function is restored by CPR.

Respiratory or breathing failure has two basic causes: 1) obstruction of the intake of air or exchange of oxygen into the blood, and 2) impairment of the part of the brain (respiratory center) that controls the rate and depth of breathing. Obstruction can result from several factors, including the presence of large pieces of foreign material (such as food) in the upper airway, swelling and closure of the airway (as in severe acute allergic reactions), and damage to the oxygen-exchanging membranes in the lung (from drowning and smoke inhalation). By far the most common cause of upper airway obstruction that occurs in the patient who has been rendered unconscious is the flaccid tongue that falls backward against the back of the throat and obstructs the airway. The respiratory center may be suppressed by drugs (narcotics, sedatives, alcohol), and carbon monoxide, electric shock, and an interrupted supply of oxygen to the brain, as when the heart has stopped.

If the heart stops pumping, or arrests, the tissues of the body do not receive the blood and oxygen they need. When this happens to the brain, there is an almost immediate loss of consciousness and breathing stops.

What To Look For

If a cardiopulmonary arrest has occurred, the victim *always:* is unconscious; has no pulse in the neck (carotid pulse); is not breathing. The carotid pulse can be checked by feeling with the thumb and middle finger on either side of the windpipe (trachea). If a pulse is present, it will be felt here.

What To Consider

Any person who suddenly collapses (becomes unconscious), has no detectable pulse in the neck, and is not breathing has suffered a cardiopulmonary arrest. (A person who collapses while eating and is unable to breathe may well have a large piece of food caught in his windpipe. This is not literally a cardiac arrest,

Lifting the jaw forward will help to open the airway. This is the preferred technique if there is suspected neck injury.

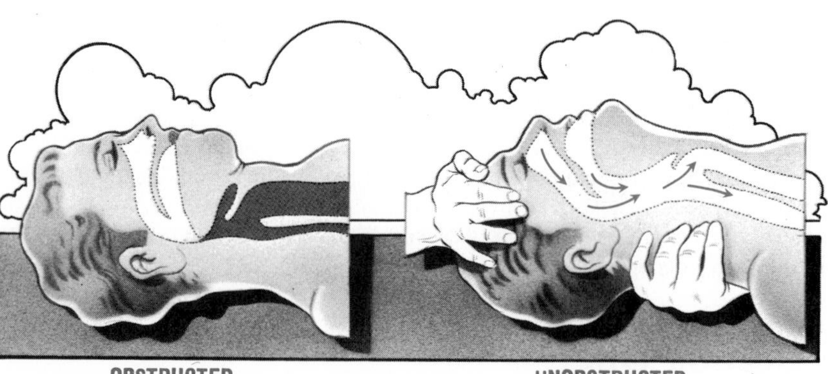

The back of the tongue may obstruct the airway. Lifting the victim's neck and tilting the head backward will open the airway. This method should not be used if there is any suspicion of neck injury.

but has been called a "café coronary" and will be discussed below.)

What To Do: The ABC's of CPR

If a person suddenly collapses and loses consciousness, it must be decided immediately whether a cardiopulmonary arrest has occurred. Any delay can result in permanent brain damage or death. Try to awaken the victim. If he cannot be awakened and if there are no palpable pulses (carotid) in the neck, begin the ABC's of cardiopulmonary resuscitation.

(A) Airway. **The first requirement is to assure a clear, unobstructed airway.**

1. Place the victim on his back.
2. Hyperextend the neck (lift the victim's neck and tilt his head backward as shown in the illustrations) and then lift the victim's chin forward; this lifts the tongue away from the back of the throat and helps to enlarge the airway. (Hyperextending the neck should not be done if there is any suspicion of neck injury.)

3. Listen for breathing by placing your ear near the victim's mouth, and watch the victim's chest for signs of breathing.
4. If there is no evidence of breathing, open the victim's mouth and remove any obvious foreign materials—false teeth, food, vomitus.

(B) Breathing (Mouth-to-Mouth Resuscitation). **If opening and clearing the airway do not produce spontaneous breathing, it will be necessary to breathe for the victim.**

1. With the victim's head in the hyperextended position, pinch his nostrils closed, take a deep breath, and place your mouth tightly over his mouth.
2. Exhale quickly and deeply, four times in rapid succession, each time removing your mouth and letting air escape passively from the victim's mouth.
3. If there is great resistance to your breath, no rise in the victim's chest, and no escape of air from his mouth, the airway may still be obstructed.
   a) Further hyperextend the victim's neck and lift his jaw.
   b) Look again for foreign objects in the mouth and throat.
   c) If none are found, you will have to try a different approach. Roll the victim on his side toward you and deliver four firm slaps between the shoulder blades. With the victim on his back, place your fist just above his navel and forcefully push once. Combined, these may force air out of his lungs and dislodge any foreign body that is trapped deeper in the airway; if so, the material should be removed from the victim's mouth.
4. If the mouth cannot be opened or is severely damaged, mouth-to-nose resuscitation may be used.

(C) Chest Compression. **After assuring an open airway and delivering four breaths, check for carotid pulse in the neck, on either side of the windpipe. If there is no pulse, perform chest compression, or external cardiac massage.**

1. Kneel beside the victim.
2. Place the heel of your hand just below the middle of the victim's breastbone and your other hand on top of the first. Do not let your fingers touch the victim's ribs or you may compress the wrong part of the chest.
3. Leaning directly over the patient, give a firm thrust straight downward. Let the weight of your shoulders do the work.
4. The breastbone should be pushed downward about two inches in the adult, and the compressions should be repeated 60 to 80 times each minute. (Note: Use of this procedure may crack some of the victim's ribs; proceed carefully, but do not stop CPR, since the alternative is death.
5. CHEST COMPRESSION (EXTERNAL CARDIAC MASSAGE) SHOULD ALWAYS BE ACCOMPANIED BY ARTIFICIAL RESPIRATION!
   a) If there are *two rescuers:* one ventilation should be interposed between every five compressions at a compression rate of 60 per minute.
   b) If there is only *one rescuer:* two ventilations should be interposed between every 15 compressions at a compression rate of 80 per minute.

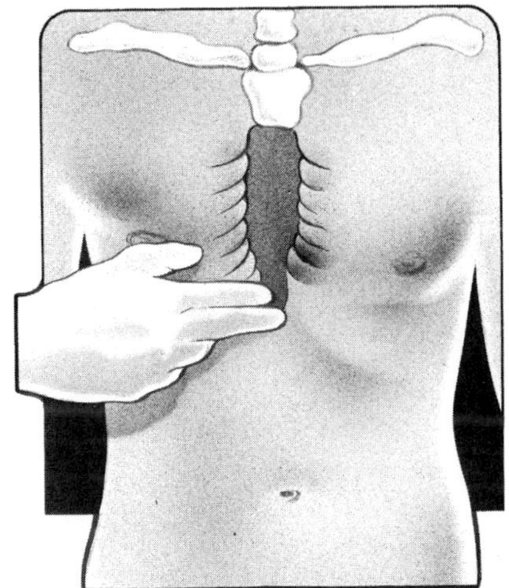

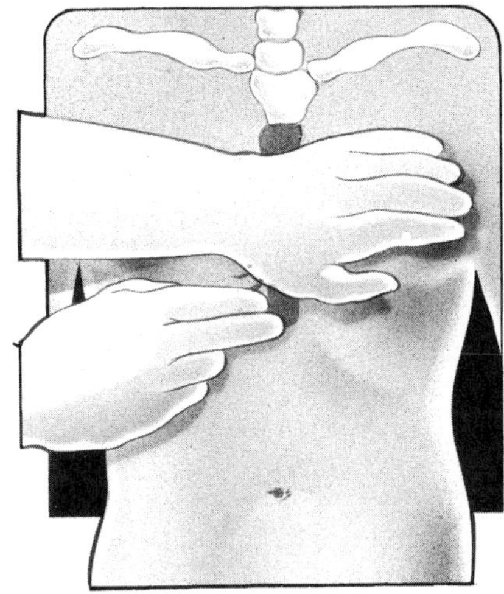

Find the tip of the sternum. The correct hand position for cardiac compression is two finger breadths above the tip of the sternum.

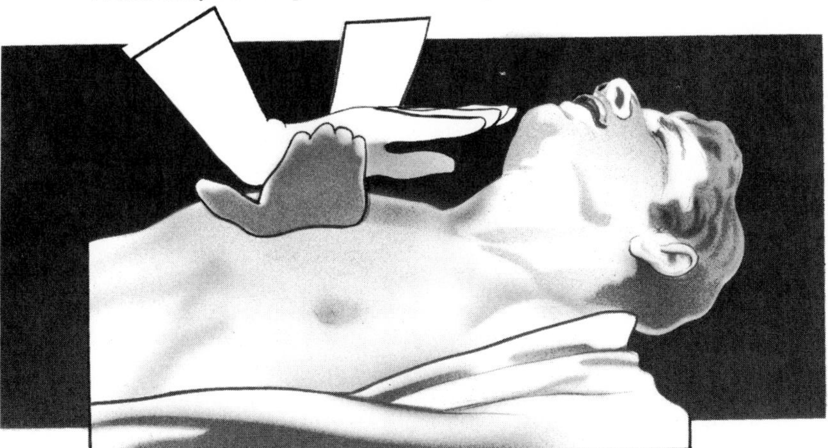

Place the heel of one hand on the sternum, and the heel of the other hand on the back of the first. Compressions of the chest should be done without placing the fingers on the chest wall.

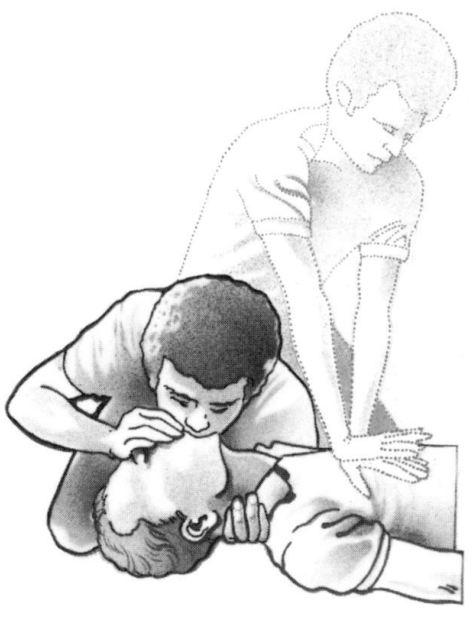

In "one-man" resuscitation, give two breaths between compressions at the rate of two breaths for every fifteen compressions.

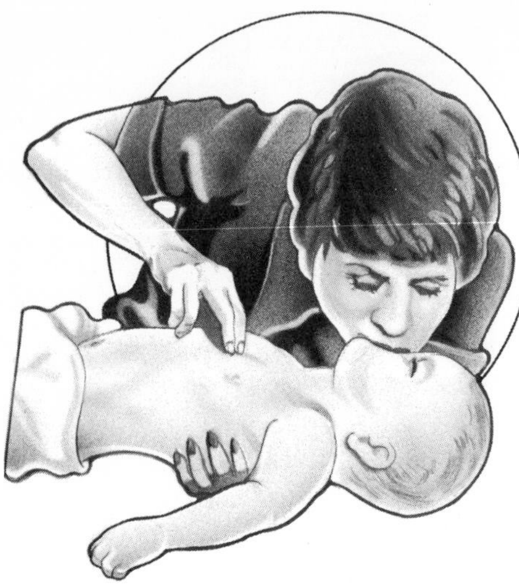

One person can resuscitate an infant by giving quick breaths while compressing the chest with the fingers of one hand.

6. If the victim is a child, the ABC's of CPR are the same except:
   a) Foreign bodies are more common in the airway.
   b) The person administering CPR puts his mouth over both the mouth and the nose of the victim.
   c) If an infant's head is flexed back too much, further obstruction of the airway can occur.
   d) Shallower breaths (puffs) should be used at 25 to 30 per minute.
   e) Exert pressure over the center of the breastbone, as the heart chambers (ventricles) to be compressed are higher in a child's body.
   f) Using only your fingertips, compress the chest ¾ to 1½ inches at a rate of 100 to 125 compressions each minute.

What Not To Do

1. Do not try to use CPR on any person who is alert and awake, or on any person who is unconscious but is breathing and has pulses.
2. Never compress the upper or lower ends of the breastbone; CPR is effective only when the flexible part of the breastbone that lies directly over the heart is compressed.
3. Do not interrupt CPR for more than 15 seconds, even to transport the victim.
4. Unless you are completely exhausted, do not stop CPR either until the victim is breathing adequately on his own and has a pulse, or until the care of the victim is taken over by more experienced medical personnel.
5. If the victim is revived, do not leave him unattended, because he may arrest again and require further CPR.

"Café Coronary" or Severe Choking While Eating

Anyone who collapses while eating may well have had a heart attack, but he may be choking on a large piece of food (usually meat). This most frequently occurs in older people, usually those who have poor teeth or false teeth, and frequently it is associated with some alcohol intake.

What To Look For

1. Before collapsing and losing consciousness, a victim who has been eating, possibly while also talking or laughing, may suddenly stand up and walk from the table, clutch his throat, or exhibit violent motions.
2. *He will not be able to talk.*
3. He may become blue.

What To Consider

The victim may be having a heart attack, but heart attack victims usually are able to talk prior to collapsing; they usually do not display quick violent motions, but collapse suddenly.

What To Do

The person will soon become unconscious and die if the obstructed airway is not cleared.

If the person is still standing:

1. Ask the victim to nod if he has food stuck in his throat.
2. Stand behind him and place one clenched fist in the middle, upper abdomen just below the ribs. Place your other hand on top of the first hand.
3. Give a very forceful pull of the clenched fist directly backward and upward under the rib cage (a bear hug from behind).
4. This will, ideally, act like a plunger and force the diaphragm upward, pushing any air left in the lungs out the windpipe and expelling or loosening the trapped object. The procedure may be repeated several times.
5. Once loosened, the foreign object can be pulled out.

Food obstructing the airway in a "café coronary" may be loosened or expelled by an upper abdominal thrust or hug; using the fist of one hand placed in the abdomen just below the rib cage, give a forceful jerk upward.

If the victim has already collapsed:

1. Place him on his back, open his mouth and look for and remove any visible foreign material.
2. If none is seen, place the heel of your hand on the victim's mid-upper abdomen and give a forceful push.
3. This should dislodge the foreign material into the mouth, from which it can be removed. Repeat the procedure as often as necessary.

4. If, after the object has been cleared, the victim still is not breathing, is unconscious, and is without a pulse, begin CPR.

What Not To Do

Do not stop CPR efforts until the victim revives or more experienced personnel arrive.

What To Expect

If the problem is noted early and foreign material is removed, the chances for the victim's survival are excellent.

Drowning

Fatal drowning and near drowning are common occurrences. Like cardiac arrest and "café coronary," drowning requires immediate action and basic life support.

What Is It?

Near or reversible drowning is much more common than fatal drowning. The near drowning victim may have no symptoms or he may need help because of severe respiratory distress and confusion. The drowned victim will be unconscious, will have no pulse, and will not be breathing.

What To Consider

1. The water may damage the lining of the lungs, resulting in a decreased ability to exchange oxygen from the air into the blood. Following a near

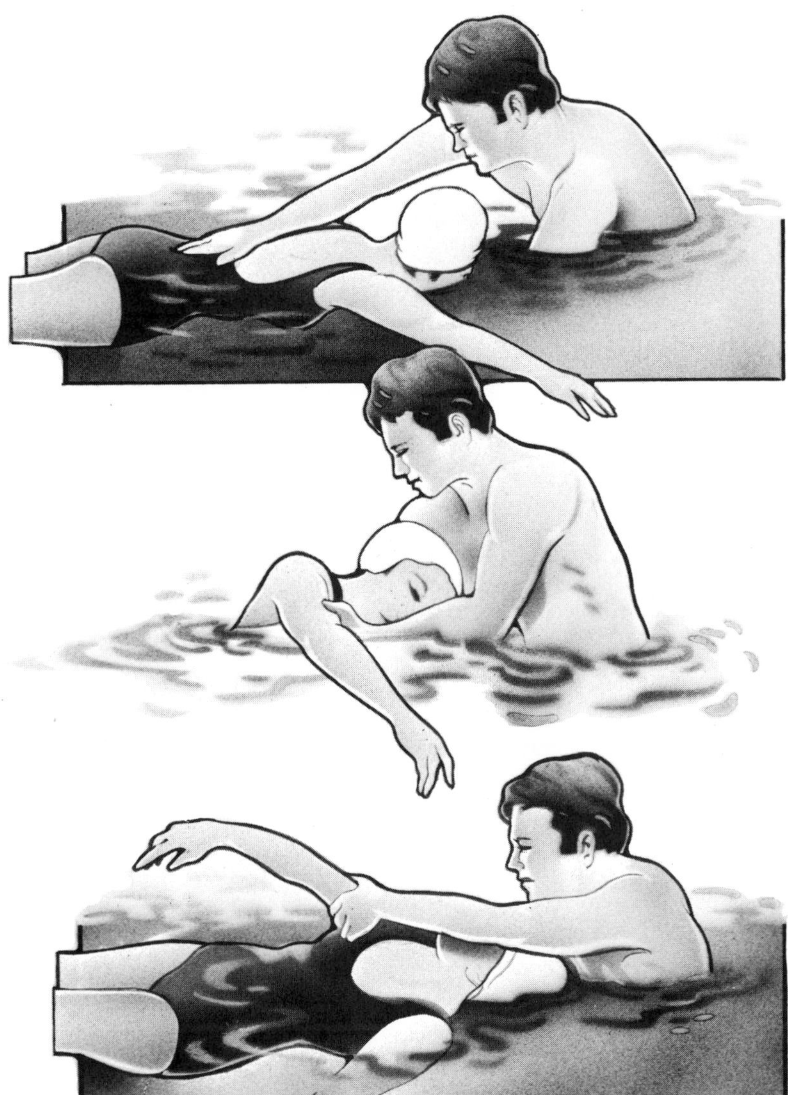

If there is a chance that a drowning victim has also injured his neck, particular care should be taken to protect the neck from further injury. The victim may be floated onto a board for removal from the water (see following page).

drowning the victim may suffer a cardiac arrest.

2. Always consider the possibility of an associated injury—for example, a broken neck, which is likely if the victim has dived into the water.

What To Do

1. Begin mouth-to-mouth resuscitation if the victim is unconscious and is not breathing, even while he is still in the water.
2. Give four quick breaths, followed by one breath every five seconds.
3. Remove the victim from the water without interrupting artificial respiration except for a few seconds (one minute at most). Once he is out of the water begin CPR.
4. If the victim has a suspected spinal injury, he should be placed on his back on a flat board for removal.
5. The victim of near drowning should be taken to the hospital *immediately*. If oxygen is available it should be used, and the victim should be watched closely for the possibility of cardiac arrest.
6. The distressed victim who has difficulty breathing, has blue color, and is semiconscious may require only artificial respiration, but be sure.

What Not To Do

1. Do not use the manual (arm lift) method of artificial respiration; it doesn't work.
2. Do not try to drain water from the victim's lungs.
3. Do not fail to take near drowning victims to the hospital immediately; such victims may quickly develop respiratory difficulty.
4. Do not stop CPR until more experienced medical personnel take over, or until you are completely exhausted.

Electric Shock

What Is It?

Even the relatively low voltages of electrical appliances that are used around the home can cause fatal electrocution. Death results from paralysis of the breathing center in the brain, from paralysis of the heart, or from uncontrolled, extremely rapid twitching (fibrillation) of the heart muscle.

What To Look For

1. The possibility of electrocution should be considered whenever an unconscious victim is found near an electric wire, a socket, or an appliance.
2. Electrical burns may or may not be apparent.

What To Consider

1. There are other possible reasons for unconsciousness, such as a head injury, seizure, or drug or alcohol ingestion.
2. Think of possible associated injuries (head injury, neck injury) before moving the victim.

What To Do

1. Disconnect the victim from the electrical source as quickly and safely as possible. This can be done by disconnecting the plug or appliance or by shutting off the main switch in the fuse box.
2. Alternately, use a dry, nonconductive, nonmetallic stick or pole to move the wire or victim. DO NOT TOUCH THE VICTIM UNTIL HE IS DISCONNECTED OR YOU MAY BECOME ANOTHER VICTIM.
3. If the victim remains unconscious and shows no pulse or respiration, begin CPR immediately. Continue until the victim revives or until more experienced medical personnel take over.
4. If there is an associated head, neck, or back injury, let trained medical personnel transport the victim.
5. Upon awakening, victims of electric shock often are confused and agitated, and, for a short time, they may need protection from falls and additional injuries.

What Not To Do

1. DO NOT TOUCH THE VICTIM UNTIL HE IS DISCONNECTED.
2. DO NOT MOVE THE VICTIM IF THERE IS A HEAD, NECK, OR BACK INJURY, EXCEPT TO REMOVE HIM FROM DANGER.

What To Expect

Even with adequate CPR the victim may need more advanced life support such as electric heart shock. However, he generally can be managed with basic CPR until more advanced life support becomes available.

Drug Overdose and Carbon Monoxide Poisoning

What Is It?

Although deaths from drug overdose and carbon monoxide poisoning may be associated with suicide attempts, such deaths do occur in other settings. An unsuspecting heroin addict may inject an exceptionally pure cut of the narcotic. A child may explore the medicine cabinet and ingest some sleeping pills, pain pills, or even antidiarrheal pills. Carbon monoxide poisoning occurs frequently in automobiles with faulty exhaust systems, in industry, and in burning buildings. These poisons all suppress the breathing center in the brain.

What To Do

1. If the person who has ingested pills is unconscious and without pulse or breathing, begin CPR.
2. If the victim is unconscious and is not breathing, but *has* pulses, perform mouth-to-mouth resuscitation only. Respiratory arrest is common in drug overdoses.
3. When transferring the victim to the hospital, take along any bottles and pills that may be associated with the poisoning.
4. Remove the victim from the carbon monoxide exposure and begin CPR.

What To Expect

Following a large drug overdose, even with adequate CPR the victim may not begin to breathe on his own or may not wake up for many hours, and he may need extended life support at the hospital in an intensive care unit.

Massive Hemorrhage (Bleeding)

Following the control of a victim's cardiorespiratory function, the next most urgent priority for the person giving first aid is to control hemorrhaging.

What Is It?

If major bleeding occurs, a large vessel (artery or vein) may be involved. Lacerated arteries tend to produce a pulsating stream of blood, signifying an injury that needs immediate first aid.

What To Consider

If the victim is bleeding massively, shock or inadequate blood circulation may develop and the victim may become unconscious or may have a cardiopulmonary arrest.

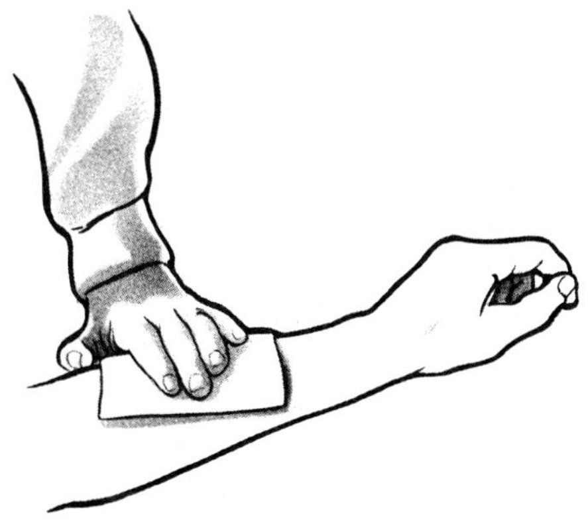

Direct, firm pressure is frequently the best way to stop bleeding.

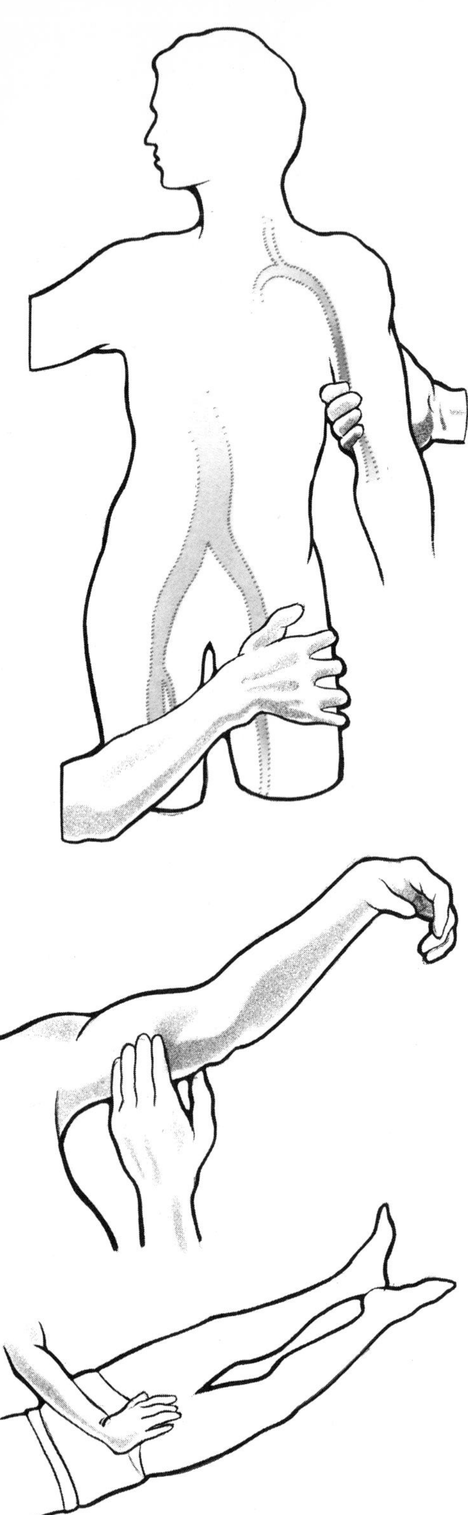

If bleeding is too extensive to stop with direct pressure, locate the brachial or femoral arteries and apply pressure to stop bleeding distal to those points.

What To Do

1. Have the victim lie down to prevent fainting.
2. If he already has fainted, raise his feet higher than his head.
3. If the victim is unconscious, and there are no pulses or breathing, begin CPR.
4. With a clean cloth or sterile dressing, apply *direct pressure* over the wound to halt the bleeding. Most major bleeding (even arterial) will stop in a few minutes if this method is used.
5. Maintain the pressure until better trained medical personnel take over.
6. If severe bleeding of an arm or leg does not stop after several minutes of direct pressure, try to stop the circulation in the artery supplying the blood by pressing firmly against it with your hand or fingers. There are points (shown in the illustrations) on each side of the body where arterial pressure can be used to stop bleeding. (There are also pressure points in the head and neck, but they should *not* be used because of the danger of interrupting the supply of blood to the brain or the intake of air.)
7. When the bleeding stops, tie the dressing firmly in place.

What Not To Do

1. DO NOT TRY TO USE ARTERIAL PRESSURE POINTS IN THE HEAD OR NECK.
2. THE USE OF TOURNIQUETS SHOULD BE DISCOURAGED because they are often ineffective and do more harm than good.
3. If the injury has been caused by a large foreign object that is protruding from the victim's body, do not remove it, or you may further aggravate the injury.

What To Expect

1. Most bleeding can be controlled by direct pressure.
2. Lacerations of the scalp bleed profusely but are rarely associated with massive blood loss.
3. Lacerations of the torso may have penetrated into the chest or abdomen and must be evaluated by a physician.

Section Two:

Common, Not Immediately Life-Threatening Emergencies

Animal Bites

All animal bites (dog, cat, and wild animal, as well as human) are dangerous and need medical attention. In addition to the injury itself, there is a chance of infection, including tetanus and rabies.

Bites from wild animals, particularly skunks, foxes, raccoons, and bats, always should be evaluated by a physician.

What To Do

1. Thoroughly scrub the wound with soap and water to flush out the animal saliva. This should be done for at least ten minutes.
2. Cover the wound with a dry, clean cloth or dressing.
3. Consult a physician immediately for further cleansing, infection control, repair, and possibly for tetanus and rabies prevention.
4. If possible the animal should be caught or identified and reported to the local authorities for observation.

What Not To Do

Do not mutilate the animal, particularly its head. (If it is a wild animal and is killed, tests can be run by the local authorities to determine if it was rabid.)

Automobile Accidents

Even with the slower, safer speeds on U.S. highways, automobile accidents still account for the largest number of the nation's accidental deaths, as well as for numerous fatalities elsewhere. Automobile accidents may cause complex or multiple injuries, and priorities must be considered for the care of the injured.

What To Do

1. Turn the car's engine off if it is still running.
2. Do as much first aid as possible *in* the car.
3. Move the victim only under the following circumstances.
   a) The car is on fire.
   b) Gasoline has spilled and there is a *danger* of fire.
   c) The area is congested, unsafe, and presents the danger of a second accident.
4. Check the patient for breathing and pulses.
5. Control any hemorrhaging.
6. If there is a head and neck injury or fracture of an extremity, wait for medical help before moving the victim, except to insure breathing or to stop significant bleeding.
7. If the victim must be moved to a medical facility, splint any fractures and support his head, neck, and spine on a backboard.
8. As soon as possible the accident should be reported to the appropriate authorities.

What Not To Do

Do not move unnecessarily a victim who is unconscious or who has a head or neck injury. It may be necessary to move a victim who has no pulse and is not breathing, or who is bleeding severely.

Backache, Acute

Most frequently, back pain is of recent onset and follows some type of acute exertion or unusual activity, such as lifting a heavy object. The pain usually results from muscular strain and may not become bothersome until hours after the exertion. Back pain that is associated with acute injury or with pain radiating down the legs may indicate a serious problem and demands immediate medical evaluation. In addition backache accompanied by blood in the urine might indicate injury to the kidney or the presence of a kidney stone, while backache with fever or urinary pain might signify the presence of a urinary tract infection.

What To Do

1. If a backache is nagging, mild, of recent onset, and is associated with recent activity, and if there is no pain radiating into the hip or leg, and if there is no bowel or urinary problem, it may be treated with:
   a) Absolute bed rest for 24–72 hours.
   b) A firm, nonsagging bed—a bed board might be used.
   c) Local heat or warm tub baths.
   d) Aspirin or an aspirin substitute might be helpful.
2. If the back pain is severe, with pain radiating into the hip or legs, or if it is associated with bowel or urinary problems, the victim should see a physician as soon as possible.
3. If the back pain follows an accident, it should be evaluated by a physician.
4. Back pain that does not improve within 48 hours should be evaluated by a physician.

Bleeding from the Rectum

The acute onset of bright red bleeding from the rectum may be caused by bleeding *hemorrhoidal* veins. The usual history includes constipation and straining to defecate, leading to bright red blood dripping into the toilet bowl and onto the toilet paper, frequently with associated rectal pain. The problem is common among pregnant women.

Rectal bleeding requires medical evaluation. If the stools are black and tarry, it is imperative to get a medical evaluation as soon as possible. The possibility that the bleeding originates higher in the intestinal tract must be considered, since bleeding within the rectum may be a sign of an ulcer, tumor, or inflammation.

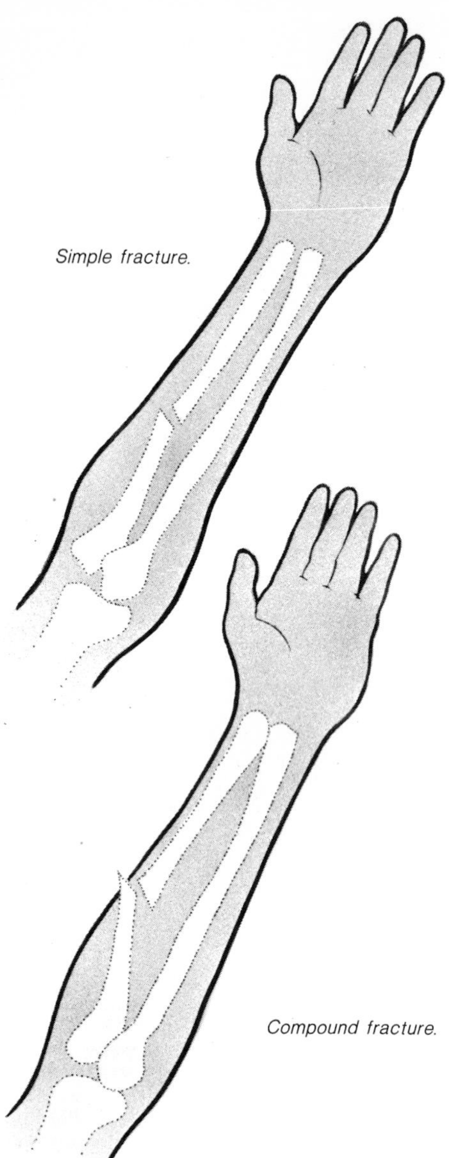
Simple fracture.

Compound fracture.

What To Do

1. If the bleeding is due to hemorrhoids:
   a) Warm tub baths three or four times daily may promote healing.
   b) Lubricating ointment such as petrolatum may decrease irritation to the hemorrhoids during bowel movements.
   c) Drinking plenty of fluids will soften the stool, as will bran cereals or stool softeners available from drug stores.
2. If bleeding persists, see a physician.
3. Get a physician's evaluation for black, tarry stools or for bright red rectal bleeding that is not known to be from hemorrhoids.

Blisters

Blisters are generally caused either by burns or by friction on the skin. Burn-related blisters can result from contact with flame or hot objects or with certain chemicals, and from severe sunburn or scalds. Blisters represent injuries to only a partial thickness of the skin. When a blister breaks, there is a loss of the natural protective insulation of the skin. Open, broken blisters are vulnerable to infection and tend to promote the loss of body fluids by evaporation. If blisters are very large, evaporation may be severe and may result in dehydration.

What To Do

1. Small blisters should not be opened. They should be protected with dry, soft dressings to prevent rupture.
2. Blisters resulting from contact with chemicals should be immediately and copiously washed with tap water to dilute the offending agent.
3. If a blister ruptures, the area should be washed gently but thoroughly with mild soap and water. The skin that covered the blister should be carefully removed, and the wound should be covered with a dry, sterile dressing.
4. Blisters of large areas of the body should be treated by a physician.

What To Expect

1. The pain from blisters usually subsides after one to two days.
2. Almost all blisters break and slough after four or five days, and the wound heals in about two weeks.
3. Ruptured blisters often become infected. Note any increased redness, pain, swelling, or heat about the wound, and be particularly aware of any red streaking up the extremity, pus from the wound, or fever.

Boils, Pimples, and Styes

When sweat glands of the skin become plugged, there may be bacterial growth and an accumulation of infected material (pus) inside the gland. Frequently, the accumulation of pus is absorbed by the body's natural defense processes. Occasionally, the area of infection expands, forming an abscess or boil (called a stye when on the eyelid). These are painful swellings that are red, warm, and can vary from less than a half inch to several inches in size. When these infections have reached this stage, the only way that the body can heal itself is to let the pus out through the skin.

What To Do

1. Apply warm, moist compresses as often as possible throughout the day (for 15 minutes every four hours).
2. When the boil or stye "points" and then ruptures, wipe the pus away gently with a dry, sterile cloth and cover it with a dressing. Continue to use warm, moist compresses.
3. If there are multiple boils or if the infection seems to be large, contact a physician.

What Not To Do

Do not attempt to squeeze or puncture boils, pimples, or styes. If hot compresses are used, early boils and styes may resolve. Most will "point" and rupture in two or three days and will then rapidly heal.

Broken Bones (Fractures)

A broken bone should be suspected whenever a person complains of pain with the loss of the normal use of an extremity. Fractures are seldom in and of themselves life-threatening emergencies, and one must make sure that the victim is safe from further harm and has good respiration and pulses before making any attempt to immobilize or move an injured person. Any victim suspected of having a broken neck or broken back should be handled in a special manner. (*See* Broken Neck or Back, below.)

There are two types of fractures that are important to recognize. Most fractures are "simple" or "closed," and the broken bone does not protrude through the skin. There are times, however, when the broken bone does pierce the skin; such breaks are known as "compound" or "open" fractures.

A word about sprains is in order here. Sprains may be managed at home if they are very mild. Aspirin, rest, elevation of the affected extremity, and local ice packs are the best treatment. If a sprain is severe, however, it should be treated like a fracture, and medical attention should be sought.

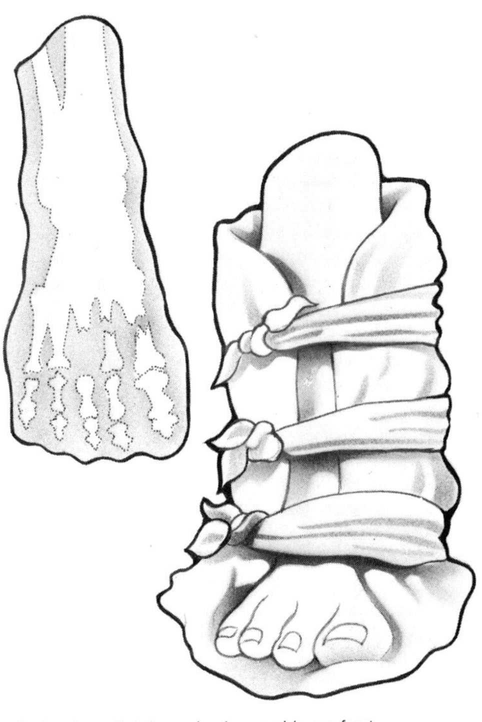

A simple splint for a broken ankle or foot may be made with a pillow or folded blanket or jacket and secured with roller bandages, tape, and so forth.

A broken forearm should be splinted and a sling should be applied. If a splint is not available, the sling itself will reduce the pain.

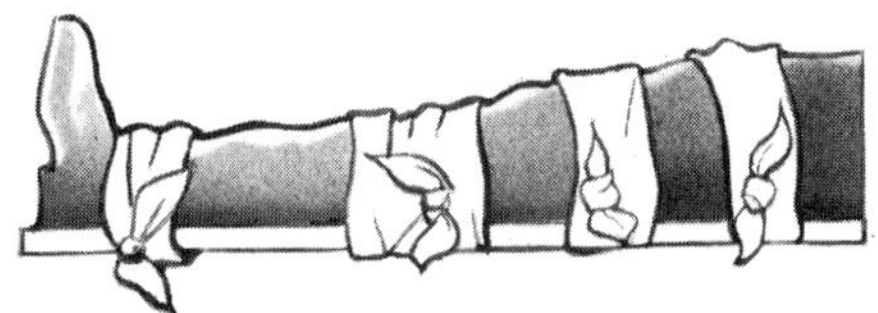

A broken bone in the lower leg should be splinted before transporting the victim.

What To Do

1. Make certain that the victim is breathing adequately and has pulses before even considering first aid for the fracture.
2. When there is reason to suspect multiple broken bones, or when the neck, back, pelvis, or thigh might be broken, it would be best to let trained emergency personnel transport the victim to the hospital.
3. If the broken bone protrudes through the skin, cover it with a dry sterile dressing, but do not try to push it back in. If there is excessive bleeding, use direct pressure to stop it. (*See* Massive Hemorrhage, above.)
4. If the victim must be moved, the fracture should be immobilized with splints to prevent further damage and to make the victim more comfortable (the pain of a fracture is caused by the two ends of the broken bone rubbing together). The basic principle of splinting is to immobilize the broken bone by securing the affected limb to some firm object (a piece of wood, broom handle, ski pole, several newspapers or magazines, or even an injured leg to the uninjured leg). Both ends of the splint must extend beyond the area of suspected fracture; the splint may be secured with bandages, belts, sheets, or neckties. Most injuries of the arm, wrist, or hand can be stabilized simply with a sling.

A broken collarbone can be splinted by first applying a sling to the arm, and then applying a wrap around the arm and chest, to reduce movement of the arm.

What Not To Do

1. Do not try to transport any accident victim who has an obviously unstable

(floppy) extremity without stabilizing or splinting it first. Even though fractures can be disturbingly displaced, deformed, and very painful in themselves, they rarely represent life-threatening emergencies. If fractures are immobilized adequately, there frequently is a marked reduction in pain.
2. Do not attempt to move a victim with a suspected broken neck or back without trained medical personnel, unless it is absolutely necessary to do so.

Broken Neck or Back

The possibility of injury to the spine (neck and back) must be considered whenever a person is:

1. Involved in an accident of any type and subsequently complains of back or neck pain, has any degree of paralysis or weakness of an extremity, or has numbness or tingling of an extremity or part of his body.
2. Injured about the face or head in an accident, or is rendered unconscious.

What To Do

1. Make certain the victim is breathing and has pulses.
2. Unless it is absolutely necessary, do not move the victim, but let trained medical personnel do it.
3. Unless he is unconscious, the victim is safest on his back; avoid attempts to pick up his head or to move his neck.
4. If the victim is unconscious, convulsive, or vomiting, he should be rolled—carefully, and preferably by two people—onto his side, and his head should be supported very carefully on a pillow or coat.
5. If it is absolutely necessary to move the victim, he should be placed on a firm board. This should be done cautiously, with several people supporting the whole spine and the head. The neck or back should not be flexed (chin moved toward the chest or head dropped back).

What Not To Do

1. Do not allow any accident victim who complains of neck or back pain to sit or stand.
2. Do not give the victim anything to eat or drink.

Bruises and Black Eyes

Any direct trauma to the soft tissues (skin, muscles, etc.) of the body may injure the blood vessels as well. The damaged blood vessels then leak blood which, when it accumulates under the skin, at first looks black, in a few days looks yellow-brown, and then is reabsorbed. Also, direct trauma may cause swelling or fluid collection under the skin. The area about the eye, because of the loose tissue present, is particularly prone to this swelling, and when blood collects the result is a "black eye."

Bruises are frequent problems and are usually benign in that they represent minimal injury and get better by themselves. However, if the force is adequate, associated injuries can occur, including fractures, ruptured abdominal organs, collapsed lungs, and injuries to the eyeball. If there is an obvious deformity, severe pain, or impaired motion of an extremity, or if there is impaired vision, blindness, severe pain in the eye itself, or double vision, a physician should evaluate the injury.

What To Do

1. As soon as possible, place a cold compress or an ice bag (a towel soaked in ice water or a towel-covered plastic bag of ice) on the bruise. This will reduce the pain and swelling and should be continued for several hours.
2. Restrict any movement of the injured part, because the less it is used during the first few hours, the less it will swell. Elevation of the bruised part above the level of the heart also decreases swelling.

If the injury is only a bruise, the victim should be able to use the extremity. Most bruises and black eyes will enlarge and worsen in appearance for up to 48 hours after the injury, after which they will gradually shrink. The blue-black color becomes yellow-brown and then disappears in 10–14 days. If multiple bruises that are not associated with trauma appear over the body, a physician should be contacted, because this may indicate a blood clotting disorder.

Burns

The skin can be burned by flames, hot objects, hot liquids (scalds), excessive sun exposure, chemicals, and contact with electricity. There are three degrees or depths of burns:

First degree—reddened, hot, very painful, no blisters. Heals spontaneously.
Second degree—painful, red, blistered. Usually heals spontaneously.
Third degree—deep burns can be white or black and are always painless. These may require skin grafts.

Many burns that appear to be first degree may later develop blisters and may actually be second degree. Second-degree and third-degree burns frequently become infected and need more attention and care than do first-degree burns. Electrical burns frequently look small but may be much deeper than suspected. Burns in children and older people are more serious.

What To Do

1. For sunburn see below.
2. For flash burns, scalds, and small burns, towels or sheets soaked in cool water should be applied immediately for comfort.
3. If it is a chemical burn, the area should be washed copiously and continuously (under a running faucet if possible) for 15–30 minutes.
4. The burn should be dressed with sterile, dry, soft dressings.
5. If burns involve large areas of the hands or face, they should be examined by a physician.
6. Electrical burns should be treated by a physician.
7. Burns, like cuts, require tetanus prevention.

What Not To Do

1. Do not apply ointments, sprays, or greases to large wounds.
2. Never use butter on any burn.
3. Do not break blisters.
4. Do not pull off any clothing that adheres to the burn.

If a small burn becomes encrusted, has pus, or shows red streaking, it may be infected and should be seen by a physician. If large areas of the body have second- or third-degree burns, there may be an excessive water loss from the body with consequent shock. People with extensive burns, especially young children and old people, are very likely to go into shock, and they should be transported to a hospital emergency department as soon as possible. "Shock," in this case, refers to a low level of circulating bodily fluids, not to a psychological state.

Chest Pain

It is well established now that most heart attack deaths result from *treatable* disturbances of the heartbeat. The overall emphasis must be to get the person with a heart attack into an intensive care unit as soon as possible. To accomplish this there must be:

1. Equipped and staffed emergency departments.
2. Better prehospital care and transportation.
3. Public education on the signs and symptoms of a heart attack.
4. Public education on the techniques of basic life support—CPR. (*See* Cardiopulmonary Arrest, above.)

Denial of the pain and its significance, ascribing it to other causes (heartburn, gas, or pulled muscles), and trying different remedies (antacids or antiflatulence medications) often lead to fatal delays in proper medical treatment. Everyone must be aware of the significance of chest pain and heart attack.

Severe chest pain must always be considered a medical emergency. A correct diagnosis can only be made by a *physician*, using an appropriate medical history, an examination, and sometimes several laboratory tests—an electrocardiogram, chest X-ray, and blood tests.

There are several aspects of chest pain that are important. Heart attack pain is often described as a *dull* ache, tightness, squeezing, or as a heavy feeling that is usually diffusely located over the front of the chest. It is often associated with aching in the shoulders, neck, arms, or jaw. Many people become short of breath, sweaty, nauseated, and may vomit. If any of these symptoms occurs in an adult, he must be transported immediately to the nearest physician or emergency department.

What To Do

1. Chest pain, especially with the symptoms listed above, demands *immediate* medical attention. An ambulance should be called immediately.
2. While waiting, make the person comfortable and reassure him.
3. Do not give him anything by mouth except what a physician has prescribed.
4. Do not make him lie down if he is more comfortable sitting.
5. Do not leave him unattended. He may suffer a cardiac arrest and may require basic life support (CPR).

There are many other causes of chest pain that may need medical attention. Chest pain associated with fever and cough could be a symptom of pneumonia. Chest pain associated with coughing up blood or associated with thrombophlebitis (pain in the calf or thigh) might represent a blood clot in the lungs. A collapsed lung might cause chest pain and sudden shortness of breath.

There are numerous causes of chest pain, such as severe heartburn, viral pneumonia, inflammation of the cartilages of the ribs, and pulled muscles, that are not life-threatening, but a physician must make these diagnoses.

Childbirth, Emergency

Childbirth is a natural and normal phenomenon, and it rarely requires advanced medical training to carry out a safe delivery. For a variety of reasons (inadequate transportation, very short labor, etc.) many babies are born unexpectedly, outside of the hospital.

Labor is the cyclical contraction of the uterus (womb) which helps to open up the end of the uterus (cervix) to allow passage of the baby. These contractions usually are painful and occur with increasing frequency and duration until the delivery. The duration of labor is different for every woman. Frequently labor lasts for 12 or more hours for a first baby, but the time may be reduced to a few hours or less for the woman who has borne several children.

Delivery is the passage of the baby through the birth canal and the vagina. The mother will usually experience *rectal* pressure and will know that the child is being born. The reflex action is to push or "bear down." The child's head and hair will be visible at the opening of the vagina. If the woman is "pushing" and the infant is visible, the birth is imminent. If a foot, an arm, the buttocks, or the umbilical cord is first to appear, take the mother to a hospital immediately.

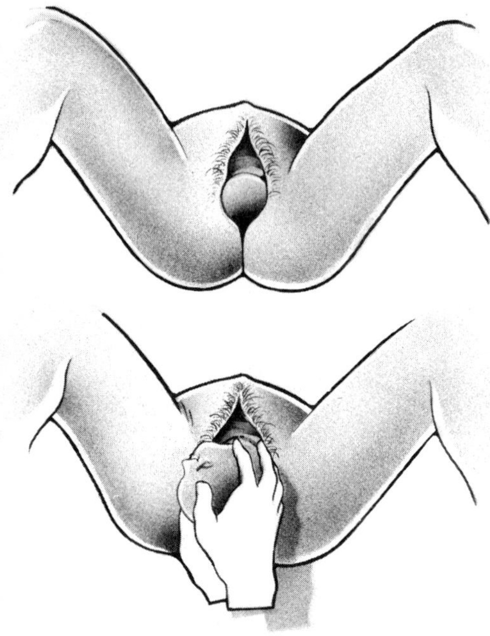

If childbirth is imminent, the top of the baby's head will begin to bulge through the mother's labia. Support the head with one hand on each side (not over the baby's face), and ease the shoulders out. The baby will be quite slippery, so be careful not to drop it.

What To Do

1. Let nature take its course. Do not try to hurry the birth or interfere with it.
2. Wash your hands and keep the surroundings (sheets, etc.) as clean as possible. (Fresh newspaper is often sterile, if sheets or blankets are unavailable.)
3. Support the emerging baby and let it slide out.
4. Once the baby is delivered, support him with both hands, keeping his head lower than the rest of his body to allow the fluid to drain from his mouth.
5. Place the infant on a dry towel or sheet and cover him immediately. Heat loss is a problem for newborn babies.
6. Aluminum foil wrapped around the baby's body will retard heat loss.
7. If the baby is not breathing begin mouth-to-mouth resuscitation, very gently, using puffs of air from your cheeks.
8. It is not necessary to cut the umbilical cord, and one may choose to have this done at the hospital. If medical care will be significantly delayed, however, use the following procedure to cut the cord: using a clean (boiled) ribbon, cord, or string, tie the cord tightly at two points, one that is four inches from the baby and the other at least eight inches from the baby. Cut the cord with clean, boiled scissors between the two ties.
9. Do not wash the white material from the baby (this is protective).
10. Warmly wrap the infant and transport it to the hospital.
11. After the child has been delivered, knead the womb by applying firm pres-

sure to the lower abdomen.

12. The mother should remain lying down until the bleeding stops and the placenta (afterbirth) has been expelled.
13. When the placenta is expelled, minutes after the birth of the child, it should be retained and taken to the hospital for examination.

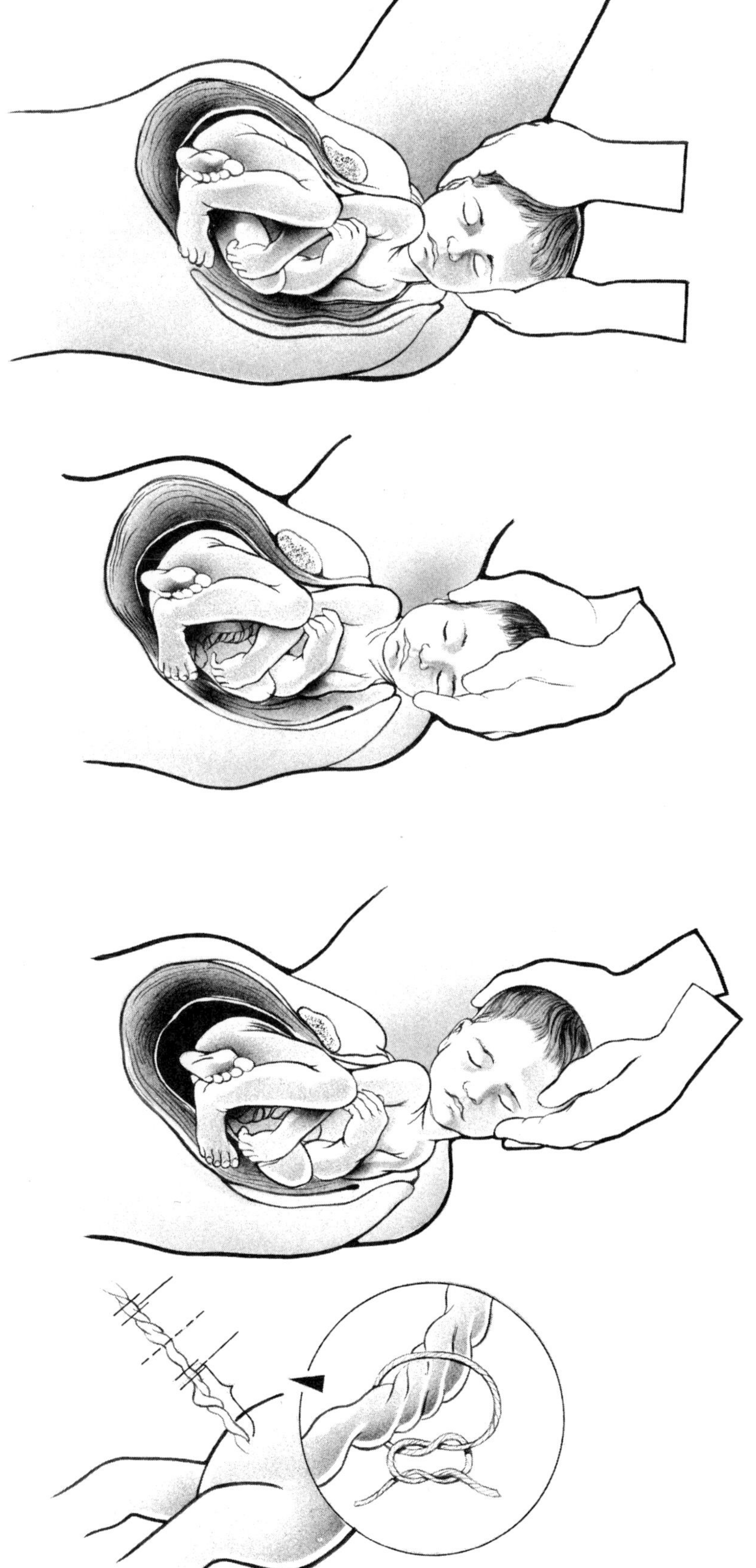

After delivery, the umbilical cord may be tied using a sterilized cord. Tie the cords at four and eight inches from the baby.

CORE TEMPERATURE	SYMPTOMS
94°	CONFUSION
90°	HEARTBEAT BECOMES IRREGULAR
86°	LOSS OF MUSCLE STRENGTH DROWSINESS AND UNCONSCIOUSNESS
77°	CARDIAC ARREST AND DEATH

As the body's core (central) temperature drops, the victim becomes confused and ultimately may die.

Cold, Overexposure, and Frostbite

Overexposure. Each year many people die from cold exposure resulting in *hypothermia*. The people who are particularly at risk include elderly persons with poor circulation, individuals who unpreparedly become exposed to low temperatures and high winds, and people who are intoxicated with alcohol. Poor circulation, poor protection from the elements, and alcohol dilate blood vessels in the skin and allow heat loss that lowers the body core (central) temperature. Malfunction of the brain, heart, and lungs may then occur.

What To Do

1. Remove the person from cold exposure and place him in the warmest place possible.
2. Cover the patient to prevent further loss of body heat.
3. If the victim is awake and able to swallow, give him *warm, nonalcoholic* drinks.
4. Watch for a cardiac arrest and be prepared to carry out CPR.

What Not To Do

1. Do not give alcoholic beverages.
2. Do not leave the person unattended.
3. Do not risk burning the person by the use of hot water bottles.

Frostbite. Frostbite is a common injury in winter weather, particularly when low temperatures are combined with wind. Exposed, small parts of the body are the most susceptible (nose, ears, fingers, toes, and face). Again, the elderly and the intoxicated are the most susceptible. Initially, the involved part begins to tingle and then becomes numb. Frozen tissue usually is dead white in color.

What To Do

1. Remove the person from the cold as soon as possible.
2. Every effort should be made to protect the frozen part. If there is a chance that the part might refreeze before reaching medical care, it may be more harmful to thaw it and let it refreeze than to await arrival at the treatment area for thawing.
3. Rapid rewarming is essential. Use lukewarm (not hot) water between 100° and 110° F (37– 43° C) or use warmed blankets. Within about 30 minutes, sensation may return to the part, which may become red and swollen. At first the rewarmed part will tingle, but it will begin to be painful and tender to the touch.
4. When the part is warm, keep it *dry* and clean. If blisters appear, use sterile dressings.
5. See a physician as soon as possible.

What Not To Do

1. Do not give alcoholic beverages.
2. Take care not to burn the person by using water that is too hot.
3. Do not let the part refreeze.
4. Do not rub the injured part; friction may cause further damage.

Convulsions

Convulsions and epileptic attacks are frightening to watch. The victim's lips may become blue, he may make a crying noise, his eyes may roll back, and his body may be jerked by uncontrollable spasms. Many seizures occur in people with known seizure disorders who have forgotten their medications, in alcohol abusers who have recently stopped drinking, and in children with an acute febrile illness (febrile seizures or seizures associated with fever in children). *Febrile convulsions* are quite common among children aged six months to three years. They result from an abrupt rise in the child's temperature and are generally of short duration (usually ending by the time the victim arrives at the emergency department). The victim usually awakens soon after the seizure.

What To Do

1. Turn the victim onto his side so that saliva is able to drain out without being inhaled into the victim's lungs.

2. If it can be done safely, place a rolled handkerchief in the victim's mouth between his teeth to prevent him from biting his tongue. Do not force a spoon or other object into the victim's mouth.
3. Most people who have had a seizure need prompt medical attention at the nearest emergency department.
4. The child with febrile convulsions is treated by reducing the fever. Cool towels or sponge baths may help to lower the child's temperature.
5. If the victim has fallen or shows evidence of head trauma, he should be assumed to have a broken neck and should be treated accordingly. (*See* Broken Neck or Back, above.)

What Not To Do

1. Do not force objects into the mouth of the convulsing person.
2. Do not get bitten by the convulsing person.
3. Do not try to restrain the convulsive movements. Protect the victim from further injury.

Following the seizure (most last less than ten minutes) the person will usually fall asleep or will be confused.

Do not assume that the seizure is "just a seizure" in either a child or an adult, since seizures may be signs of other problems such as head injury, meningitis, or tumor.

Croup

What Is It?

In the fall and winter months, when houses are dry and warm, young children (usually younger than three years) may develop a "croupy," barking cough. This condition usually is caused by a viral inflammation of the trachea (windpipe) and of the larger airways, and the infection may cause severe respiratory distress.

What To Do

1. For mild cases (most cases), lowering the temperature in the room and using a humidifier will quickly help the croupy breathing. A bathroom filled with steam from a running shower may be helpful.
2. Aspirin and liquids may be used to combat low-grade fever.
3. If there is a high fever, difficulty in swallowing or talking, or respiratory distress, the child should be seen by a physician as soon as possible.

Most cases of croup are mild, and they will usually clear up after two or three days if corrective measures are taken.

Cuts, Scratches, Abrasions

Small cuts, abrasions, and scratches are common occurrences and generally require only thorough cleansing and bandaging for protection. Some cuts are larger and may require stitches for closure to minimize scarring, to reduce the chance of infection, and to restore function. Deeper cuts may involve blood vessels, and they may cause extensive bleeding or may damage muscles, tendons, or nerves.

What To Do

1. All minor wounds and abrasions should be *thoroughly* washed. There should be no dirt, glass, or foreign material left in the wound. Mild soap and water are all that are necessary.
2. Bleeding can be stopped by direct pressure that is applied over the wound with a sterile, dry dressing, and by elevating the injured part.
3. Most wounds should be covered with a dressing to protect them from further harm and contamination.
4. All bites (human or animal) should be treated by a physician because of the likelihood of infection. (*See* Animal Bites, above.)
5. If there is any question about the need for sutures, the wound should be examined by a physician.
6. If the wound is dirty or extensive, or if the victim's tetanus immunization is not up to date, there may be the need for a booster immunization.

7. Watch carefully for signs of infection (usually they do not appear for several days). The signs are:
   a) a reddened, hot, painful area surrounding the wound,
   b) red streaks radiating from the wound,
   c) swelling around the wound, with fever and chills.

If an infection appears, see a doctor at once.

Diabetic Coma and Insulin Reaction

Diabetics have difficulty using the sugar in their blood. *Insulin* lowers the blood sugar level. As would be expected, it may be difficult to adjust the daily insulin requirement to the intake of sugar-containing foods and to the individual's activity level. Because of this, some diabetics occasionally suffer either from *insulin reaction* (which is a blood sugar level that is too low) or from *diabetic coma* (which can be thought of as a blood sugar level that is too high).

Insulin reaction, or acute hypoglycemia, may cause the person to become acutely confused, incoherent, sweaty, or shaky. Eventually, the person may lose consciousness.

What To Do

1. Determine if the victim is a diabetic.
2. If he is *conscious*, give him some form of sugar (a lump of sugar, candy, sweets, or soft drinks that are not artificially sweetened).
3. Even if recovery is prompt, all victims should be evaluated by a physician.

What Not To Do

Do not try to give sugar to someone who is unconscious.

Diabetic coma with hyperglycemia (a high blood sugar level) is quite different. The onset is more gradual, taking several hours or longer. The victim may have warm, flushed skin, with a very dry mouth and tongue. He frequently may be drowsy but rarely is unconscious. His breath may smell fruity (like nail polish remover), and he may be dehydrated.

What To Do

A person in a diabetic coma needs prompt treatment by a physician.

Diarrhea (in a small child)

Diarrhea may be caused by many factors, ranging from simple nondigestion of eaten foods to such conditions as bacterial or viral infections of the intestinal tract. In a small child, acute prolonged diarrhea may rapidly cause dehydration and death. The younger the child and the more prolonged the diarrhea, the more dangerous is the threat to health. Maintenance of adequate hydration is the main goal of therapy.

The signs of dehydration are: lethargy, dryness of the mouth and armpits, sunken eyes, weight loss, and the absence of urination. A child who continues regularly to wet his diapers generally is not dehydrated.

What To Do

1. Small children with acute diarrhea should be given water, liquid Jell-O, or pediatric salt solutions. Milk and whole foods should be withheld for the first 24 – 48 hours of the diarrhea. In acute diarrhea, the bowel is unable to digest and absorb some of the sugars in milk, which worsens the diarrhea.
2. If the diarrhea persists for more than 48 hours, a physician should be contacted.
3. If the diarrhea causes signs of dehydration, or if the child stops taking in fluids, a physician should be contacted immediately.
4. Almost all diarrheal states in children are well on the road to recovery within 48 hours. For the bottle-fed child, half-strength formula can be substituted for regular formula for one or two days before resuming full-strength formula. If the diarrhea persists, a physician should be consulted.

What Not To Do

1. Do not continue milk and whole food during an acute diarrheal state.
2. Do not use adult antidiarrheal medications for children.

Dislocated Joints

It is frequently impossible to tell the difference between dislocated joints and broken bones until X-rays have been taken.

What To Do

1. Probable dislocations in the hand, arm, shoulder, or jaw usually do not require an ambulance for transportation to the hospital. Victims should, however, be transported safely and comfortably.
2. If there is a dislocation of the hip or knee, ambulance transportation will be needed.
3. Slings or splints may be helpful. (*See* Broken Bones, above.)

What Not To Do

Do not attempt to move or manipulate the joint, or to set a dislocation yourself; the bone may be broken if these procedures are done improperly.

Eye Pain (something in the eye)

Even a small speck of dirt in the eye can cause intense pain. The covering of the eye is quite sensitive and, even after the foreign material is removed, there may be a feeling of irritation. Redness and tears are frequently present.

What To Do

1. Examine the eye by pulling the lower lid down while lifting the upper lid off the eyeball. Most specks will be visible.
2. Gently splash water from a faucet to attempt to remove the foreign material.
3. Gently attempt to wipe the speck off with a moistened corner of a clean cloth, handkerchief, or cotton swab.
4. If the speck does not come off *easily*, or if there is persistent discomfort, a physician should be seen as soon as possible.
5. If irritating liquids are splashed into the eye, irrigate the eye with cool tap water for 30 minutes and then seek medical attention.

Fainting—Dizziness

Fainting is a sudden but momentary loss of consciousness. There are a variety of causes for it, including fatigue, hunger, sudden emotional upset, poor ventilation, etc. The person who has fainted looks pale and limp but is breathing and has a normal pulse. Simple fainting is not associated with chest pain or seizures, and the unconsciousness does not last for more than one or two minutes.

If a person faints, place him on his back or side and elevate the legs above the head.

What To Do

1. Place the victim on his back or side, with his legs higher than his head.
2. Check his airway, breathing, and pulses.
3. Apply cold compresses to the victim's forehead, and have him inhale aromatic spirits of ammonia.

4. If fainting is associated with chest pains, seizures, or severe headache, or if it lasts more than one or two minutes, the victim should be transported by ambulance to a physician.
5. If a person reports that he feels faint, have him sit with his face in his lap or stretch out on his back until he feels better.

Fainting is a relatively common problem and almost always quickly resolves in one or two minutes. Nevertheless, other causes should be considered—heart attack, stroke, internal bleeding, and insulin reaction.

Fever

Fever is an elevated oral temperature above 98.6° Fahrenheit or above 37° Celsius. Fever is a manifestation of the body's response to infection (viral or bacterial) or to foreign substances that the body is attempting to reject. People with fever frequently report muscle and bone pains, headaches, chills, and a hot feeling. Viral infections (colds, influenza, and even viral gastroenteritis) almost invariably are associated with low-grade fevers and are the most common causes of such fevers.

In susceptible children younger than three years of age, a *rapidly* rising fever may induce febrile seizures. (*See* Convulsions, above.)

What To Do—Adults

1. Aspirin and acetaminophen (aspirin substitute) are the two most effective antifever medicines available. If used appropriately, they not only effectively lower the temperature but also will provide some relief for the bone and muscle aches.
2. The person with fever should take a lot of fluids, as higher temperatures increase evaporation of water and thus accelerate dehydration.
3. Bed rest helps.
4. If the fever is very high (102° or more) and persistent (most fevers last less than 24 hours), a physician should be consulted.
5. Fever associated with chest pains, shortness of breath, cough, or with the production of sputum, or with confusion, headache, a stiff neck, abdominal pain, or earache should be evaluated by a physician as soon as possible.

What To Do—Children

1. Fever of 100° or more in an infant (less than 30 days old) is always an emergency, and the child should be seen immediately by a physician. Every household should have a thermometer for taking children's temperatures.
2. In addition to fluids and bed rest, children with temperatures over 100° may be given aspirin or acetaminophen (aspirin substitute) every four hours in doses of not more than 60 mg for each year of life.
3. The child *should not be* overly dressed but should be dressed lightly (T-shirt and diapers are enough).
4. If a child develops a temperature of 103° or more, and the fever does not respond to aspirin or acetaminophen, the child should be placed in a tub of lukewarm water (not cold) and should be sponged for at least 30 minutes.
5. If the fever still does not respond, a physician should be contacted.
6. Any child with a febrile seizure, lethargy, signs of dehydration, or excess irritability should be seen by a physician.

What Not To Do

Do not sponge a child with alcohol; it is potentially toxic and is flammable. The sudden cold is often frightening to a child.

Food Poisoning

Food poisoning is a term applied to the combination of nausea, vomiting, or diarrhea that is attributed to contaminated food. The symptoms may be identical to those of viral gastroenteritis (stomach flu), but with the lack of an associated fever. Some other causes of the same symptoms include emotional stress, viral infections, inorganic or organic poisons, or food intolerance. Food poisoning itself is caused by toxins produced by bacteria growing in the food. The most common organism causing food poisoning is the *Staphylococcus*. In

Staphylococcus food poisoning, vomiting and diarrhea generally develop within one to 18 hours following ingestion of the contaminated food.

What To Do

1. Generally, food poisoning resolves spontaneously within a few hours. Clear liquids should be offered as tolerated.
2. If vomiting or diarrhea is prolonged, dehydration may develop. In some cases, medical attention should be sought.

What Not To Do

1. Do not take antibiotics. They are useless in this type of poisoning.
2. Do not force the victim of food poisoning to drink fluids if he has any respiratory difficulty. Victims who develop respiratory difficulty should be seen immediately by a physician.

Foreign Objects in the Nose, Ear, Throat

Nose

1. If the object cannot be withdrawn or teased out easily, consult a physician at once.
2. Do not allow violent nose-blowing.
3. Do not deeply probe the nose yourself. You may push the object deeper into the nostril or you may cause harm to the nasal tissues.

Ear

1. If the object cannot be withdrawn easily, consult a physician.
2. The tissues of the ear are very delicate and can easily be damaged. Pushing the object in further may even rupture the eardrum.

Throat

1. Large objects caught in the throat can cause severe difficulty in breathing (*see* Café Coronary, above). This requires immediate care.
2. Small objects can be swallowed—coins, fishbones, etc. Such smaller objects that get caught or that irritate the throat and that cause no difficulty in swallowing or breathing should be given a chance to pass. Drinks of water followed by eating soft foods—such as bread—may help. If the object remains caught or if irritation persists for more than two or three hours a physician should be notified.
3. Someone who has an irregular object—such as a pull tab from a beverage can, a piece of wire, or glass—caught in his throat needs immediate medical attention.

Head Injury

Injuries to the head may include lacerations and contusions of the scalp, fractures of the skull, or brain injuries. Whenever someone has suffered a serious injury to his head, one must always consider whether there might have been an associated injury to the neck. If there is a possibility of an associated neck injury, the victim should not be moved except by skilled personnel unless there is a chance that he might inhale secretions or vomitus. In that case, the victim may be very carefully rolled onto his side.

What To Do

1. Severe, deep lacerations should not be cleansed or irrigated. Instead, sterile dressings should be placed over the wound and should be secured snugly with a roller bandage. Heavy pressure should not be applied to severe lacerations because there may be an associated fracture of the skull and too much pressure may drive a fragment of bone into the brain.
2. Note any loss of consciousness or altered mental status. An examining physician will need this information.
3. Make sure that the victim's pulse and respiration are normal. If the victim might inhale his secretions or stomach contents, very carefully turn him onto his side. Note the size of the victim's pupils. If the victim is unconscious or confused and one of his pupils becomes larger than the other, this is a medical emergency and he should be seen immediately by a physician.

If there is an open head injury, apply a sterile dressing and secure it with a roller bandage. If there is significant bleeding, apply the roller bandage firmly.

4. Keep the victim lying down, but do not place a pillow under his head since doing so may cause further damage to the neck if it also has been injured.
5. Make sure that the victim's airway remains open. At times, CPR or artificial respiration (see above) may be needed.

Any head injury accompanied by a loss of consciousness should be evaluated by a physician as soon as possible. Even though the victim may regain consciousness, further brain damage may develop.

Heatstroke (sunstroke), Heat Exhaustion (heat prostration), and Heat Cramps

Heatstroke is a failure of the body's ability to keep itself cool and maintain a normal temperature. The first symptom is usually confusion, irrational behavior, passing out, or seizures. The patient has a fever, and the pulse is usually rapid and weak. Heatstroke generally affects the elderly, young infants, persons with heart disease, athletes or others doing hard work under hot conditions, and persons who have been drinking alcohol. This is a very serious condition, and immediate treatment is necessary.

What To Do

1. For heat exhaustion, move the victim to a cool place and elevate his legs. If he can take fluids by mouth, give him small amounts of water.
2. Heat cramps may also be treated with salt solutions taken orally (½ teaspoon of salt in a glass of water).
3. Heatstroke, manifested primarily by a very high temperature, should be treated by placing the patient in a cool place, by removing his clothing, and by applying cool water or ice packs to his body. The victim's extremities should be massaged vigorously to aid circulation, and immediate cooling is crucial.
4. If the victim has suffered from heatstroke, heat exhaustion, or prolonged heat cramps, medical attention should be sought.

What Not To Do

1. Avoid giving water without added salt, because this may further deplete the body's salt concentration.
2. Avoid the immediate reexposure of the victim to the heat, because he may be very sensitive to high temperatures for a time.

Nosebleeds

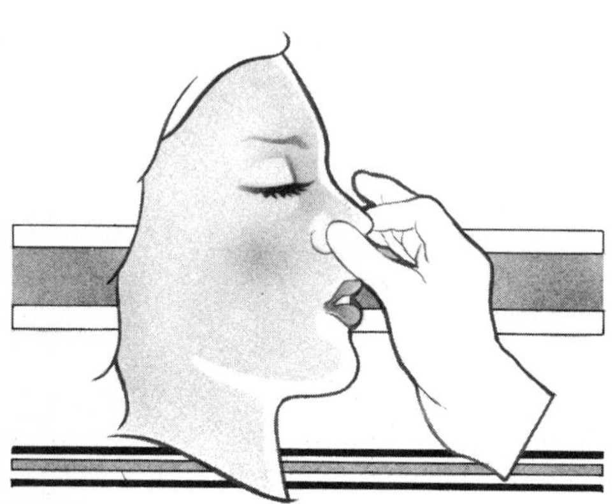

A nosebleed frequently can be stopped by firmly pinching the nose closed.

Nosebleeds are generally caused by trauma to the nose, which can result from nose-picking, from colds when there is hard nose-blowing, or from drying of the nasal mucosa. Most commonly, nosebleeds originate from the area of the nasal septum. Nosebleeds may also be associated with hypertension, bleeding disorders, or nasal tumors.

What To Do

1. To prevent the inhalation or swallowing of blood, have the person sit up and lean forward.
2. Gently squeeze the nose closed for 10 to 15 minutes by the clock.
3. If the bleeding stops have the victim rest quietly for a few hours. During this time there should be no stooping, lifting, or vigorous nose blowing. Seek medical attention if the nosebleed is profuse or prolonged. The blood loss from a nosebleed can be considerable, and some people even go into hemorrhagic shock following a nosebleed.

What Not To Do

Do not allow the victim to resume normal activities for a few hours after the nosebleed has subsided.

Poisoning

Poisoning is a common occurrence, particularly in households in which there are children. For the most part poisoning is accidental, but occasionally someone will ingest a poison during a suicide attempt. Households should be equipped to handle poisoning, and syrup of ipecac should be available.

Generally there are five kinds of poisons that might be ingested: a) pesticides, b) drugs, c) strong alkalies and acids, d) petroleum products, e) poisonous plants.

Two of these, petroleum products and strong alkalies and acids, are worthy of special note, because vomiting should *never* be induced if they have been ingested. Examples of petroleum products include turpentine, paint thinner, furniture polish, gasoline, and liquid shoe polish. Examples of strong alkalies include drain cleaner, lye, and some bleaches. In the case of strong alkalies or other strong substances that may cause chemical burns, the mouth and esophagus are burned when the poison is swallowed. If the person is made to vomit, he will be burned a second time as the chemical is passed up the esophagus and out the mouth again. In the case of petroleum products, vomiting may lead to inhalation of the poison, with a resulting chemical pneumonia.

The best way to handle poisons is to take precautions against their ingestion, particularly when small children are present. Medicines, detergents, and cleaning products should all be placed on a high shelf, not under the sink where children can easily find them. In addition, poisons should be kept in appropriate containers. It is dangerous to keep gasoline or furniture polish in a soft drink bottle because a child may drink from that bottle, thinking that it contains a soft drink.

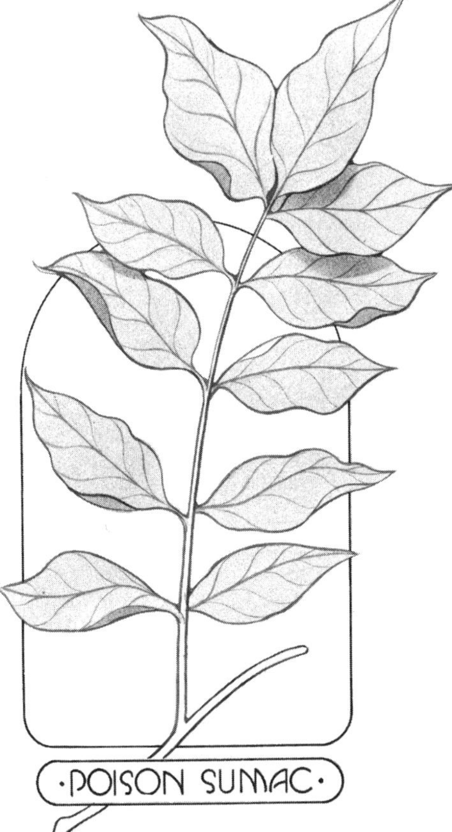

What To Do

1. Initially, give ½ glass of water or milk to anyone who has ingested a poison, unless the victim is *unconscious* or is having convulsions.
2. Decide whether or not to induce vomiting. Look in the victim's mouth for burns that might indicate the ingestion of an acid or alkali. Also, smell the victim's breath to see if it smells like a petroleum product. If either sign is present, do not induce vomiting. If the poisoning has been caused by pesticides, drugs, or poisonous plants, vomiting may be induced by putting one's fingers into the back of the victim's throat to induce gagging and vomiting, or by using syrup of ipecac. Children should be given approximately one teaspoon to one tablespoon of syrup of ipecac, and adults should be given two tablespoons. Vomiting should occur within 20 to 30 minutes.
3. Contact your local physician or emergency department for further instructions. A Poison Control Center may recommend specific antidotes. Antidotes that are listed on the packaging of poisonous products may not be correct or the procedure for their administration may be faulty. It may be better to contact a Poison Control Center for specific instructions.
4. If respiratory difficulty or shock develop, they should be treated appropriately.

What Not To Do

1. Do not allow poisons to be within the reach of children.
2. Do not induce vomiting if alkalies, acids, or petroleum products have been ingested.
3. If the victim is unconscious or is having convulsions, do not give him water, and do not induce vomiting.
4. Do not store poisonous materials in food bottles or jars.

Poison Ivy, Poison Oak, and Poison Sumac

Contact with poisonous plants such as poison ivy, oak, or sumac frequently produces local itching and redness in allergic individuals. In some people the rash that develops is characterized by vesicles (small blisters). More severe reactions include headache, fever, and malaise.

What To Do

1. Contaminated clothing should be removed and all exposed areas of the body should be washed with soap and water.
2. Once the rash has developed, soothing lotions may be applied to the skin. Many of these lotions are available without prescription at a pharmacy. Cool, moist compresses also are valuable for relieving itching.
3. If blisters appear and begin to ooze, they may be treated with wet dressings —sterile gauze pads saturated with a solution of baking soda and water

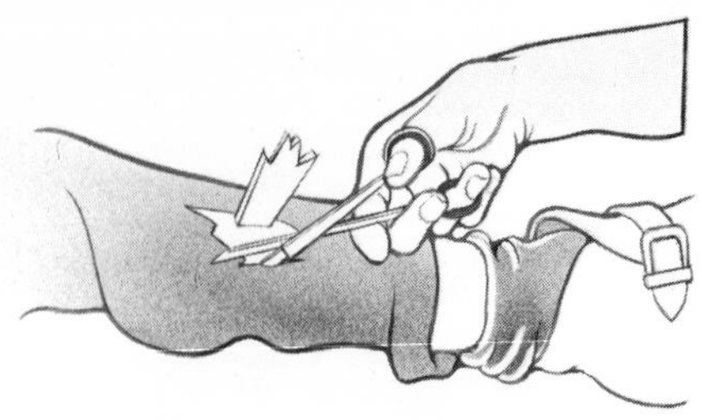

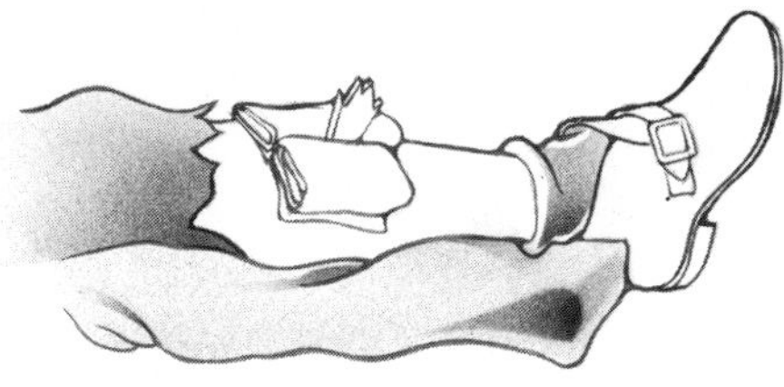

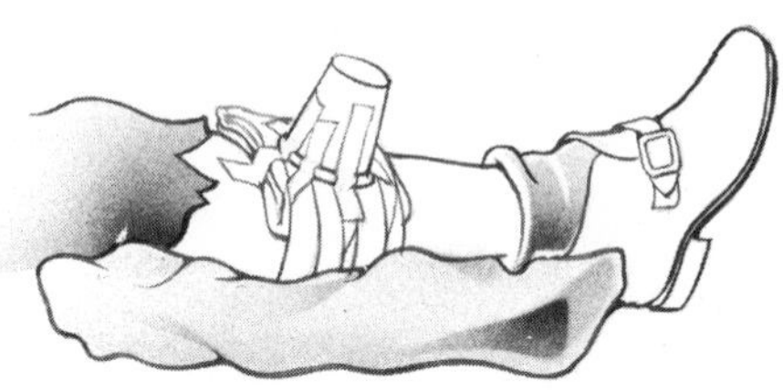

Objects stuck deep through the skin (or into the eye) should not be removed. If the object is too large to be secured in place by simply using a dressing, a paper cup taped over it may reduce further injury.

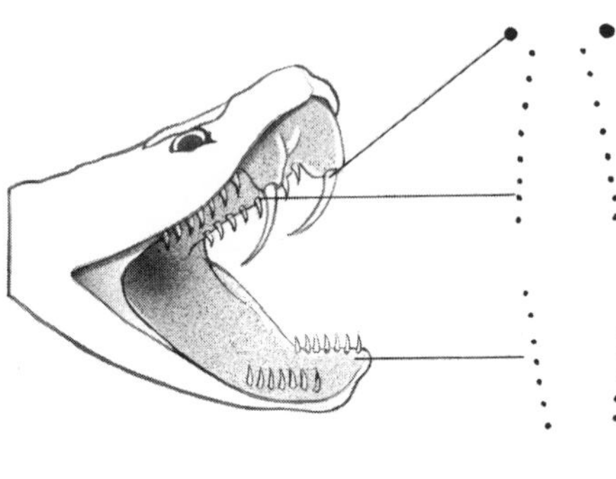

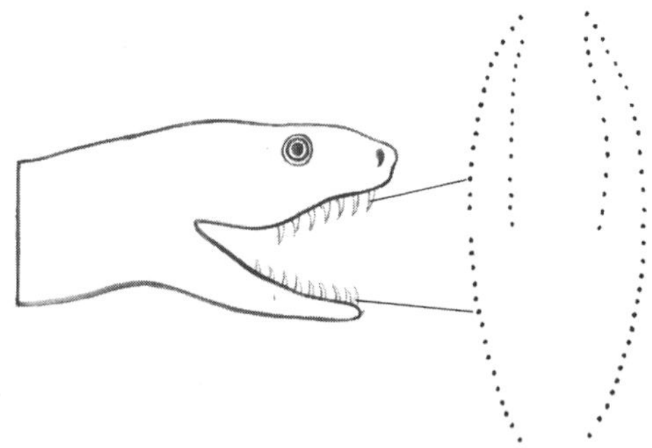

Pit vipers generally produce conspicuous fang marks. Nonpoisonous snakes and coral snakes will not leave fang marks.

(one tablespoon of baking soda to one pint of water).

4. If a severe reaction occurs, if there is a fever, or if a large area of the body is involved, seek medical advice.

Puncture Wounds

Puncture wounds are created by penetrating objects such as nails, knives, sticks, and needles. Puncture wounds do not bleed as readily as lacerations and thus there is less natural cleansing of the wound and a higher rate of infection.

What To Do

1. The site of the puncture wound should be cleansed with soap and water, after which a clean dressing should be applied.
2. For severe puncture wounds, seek medical attention to guard against tetanus infection and for consideration of antibiotic therapy.

What Not To Do

Do not remove any foreign object that is protruding from the wound. As moving the object may cause further damage, the physician should attend to such wounds.

Rape

Rape is the unlawful carnal knowledge of a woman by a man, forcibly and against the woman's will. In the United States, rape is common, and friends or relatives are frequently called on to render assistance to rape victims.

What To Do

1. The rape victim should be protected from further harm and should be assured that she is safe.
2. If she is injured and is bleeding, direct pressure should be applied to the bleeding points. Never, however, apply hard pressure to the rectal or vaginal areas.
3. If she has a broken extremity, it should be treated appropriately.
4. Always remember that a rape victim has an absolute right to refuse medical, legal, or psychological help; however, she should be encouraged to see a physician as soon as possible.

What Not To Do

1. Even though the victim may feel unclean, she should be advised not to bathe, douche, or urinate, because doing so may destroy some evidence needed by the medical examiner.
2. The scene of the crime should not be touched, because this may invalidate existing evidence that would lead to the conviction of the attacker.
3. The victim should be advised not to change her clothing until she has been examined medically, because some evidence may be lost.

The trauma of the rape victim does not end with the rape itself. She may develop psychological problems or have marital difficulties for days or even years following the incident. In many communities, counseling services have been established specifically for the benefit of these victims.

Snakebite

In the United States there are two groups of poisonous snakes: the coral snakes and the pit vipers. The coral snake is found from North Carolina to Florida, through Louisiana to central Texas. The Sonoran coral snake is found in Arizona and southwestern New Mexico. The pit vipers include the copperhead, water moccasin, and rattlesnake. Rattlesnakes and other pit vipers account for the greatest number of the venomous snakebites in the United States, while coral snakes account for a very small number. Coral snakes produce relatively inconspicuous fang marks. Pit vipers produce a more conspicuous injury, with fang marks surrounded by swelling and blood-filled blisters.

The effect of a poisonous snake's bite depends on the size of the victim, the location of the bite, the amount of venom injected, the speed of absorption of the venom into the victim's circulation, and the amount of time between the bite and the application of specific antivenom therapy.

copperhead

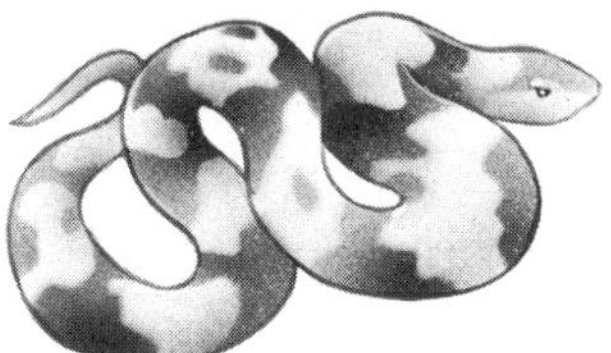

water moccasin

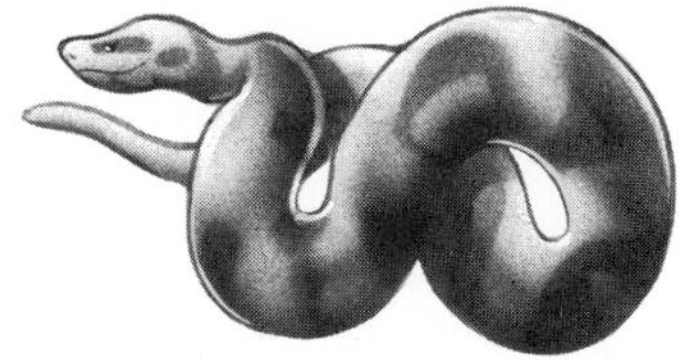

coral snake

diamondback rattler

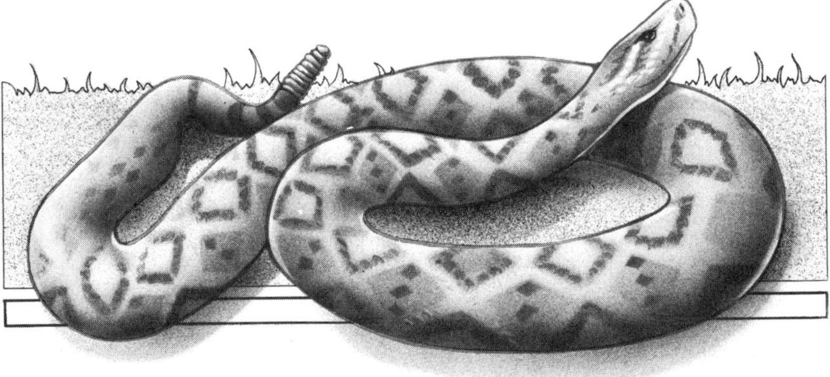

What To Do

1. First aid begins with reassuring and calming the victim.
2. The victim should be transferred to a physician as soon as possible. Even if the bite was inflicted by a nonpoisonous snake, a physician may want to give tetanus prophylaxis and antibiotic therapy.
3. Immobilization of the bitten extremity will help retard absorption of the toxin.
4. A tourniquet applied above the bite may retard systemic absorption of the venom and may be useful when there is a delay in reaching an emergency department. The tourniquet should not be so tight as to cause disappearance of peripheral pulses in the foot or the hand.

What Not To Do

1. Incisions over the fang marks are not recommended.
2. Do not give the victim alcohol in any form because it may increase absorption from the skin.

Spider Bites and Scorpion Stings

The reaction to the toxins of spiders and scorpions varies from mild, with resulting local pain, redness, and swelling, to severe, with convulsion, nausea, vomiting, muscular pain, and even shock. In the United States the two spiders that are generally the most harmful are the black widow spider (*Latrodectus mactans*) and the brown recluse (*Loxosceles reclusa*).

What To Do

1. Wash the wound with soap and water and apply a clean dressing.
2. A medication like aspirin may help relieve the pain.
3. For spider bites, scorpion bites, and any insect bite associated with intense pain, severe swelling, and discoloration, a physician's evaluation should be sought.
4. If the spider or scorpion has been killed, don't discard it. A physician may be able to further identify the species if he sees it.

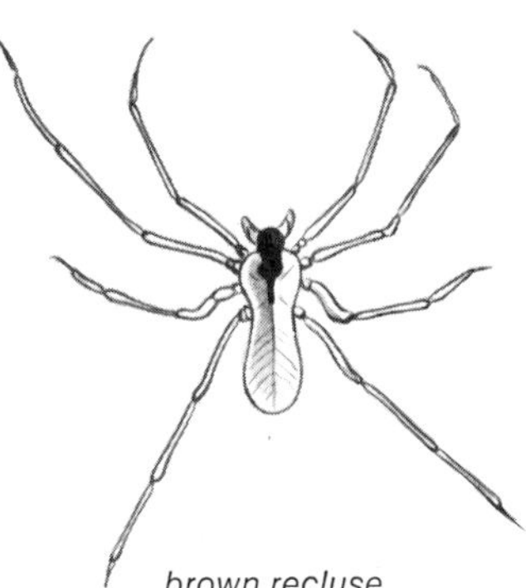

brown recluse

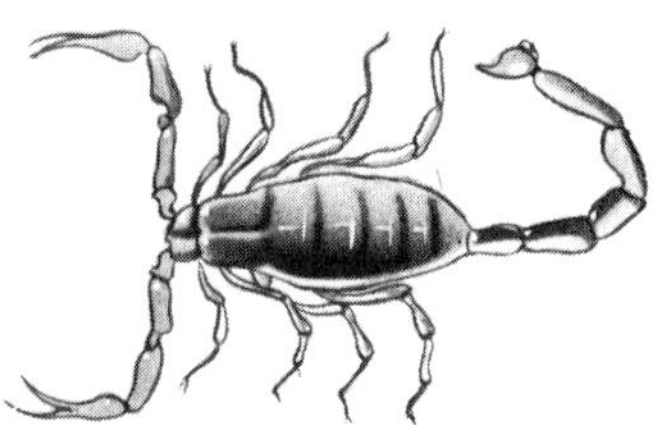

scorpion

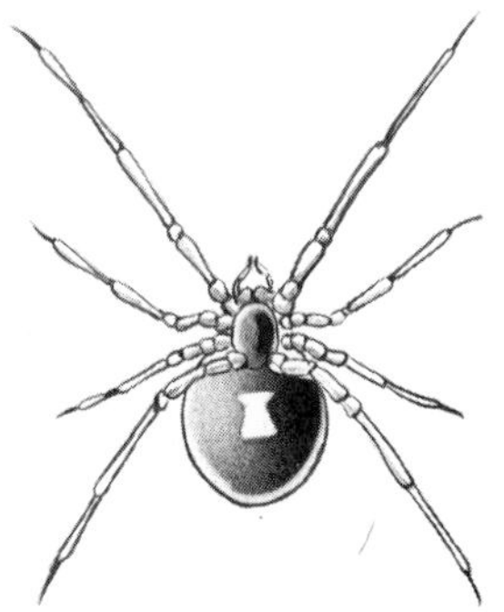

black widow

The brown recluse spider is about one inch in length overall, including the legs; it has a dark, violin-shaped marking on its lighter back. Scorpions range from one-half to seven inches in length. The body of the female black widow spider is about one inch long, and there usually is a reddish, hourglass-shaped marking on the underside of the abdomen.

Stings (Wasp, Bee, Yellow Jacket, and Hornet)

The stings from these insects are relatively common, and they rarely cause death except in highly sensitive individuals. The sting may be painful, but the symptoms are usually mild and are of short duration.

Some people are highly sensitive to insect stings and may develop an allergic reaction, possibly with anaphylaxis (a massive allergic reaction) and subsequent death.

What To Do

1. Most people have no problem from an insect sting, and relief from the local discomfort can be obtained from various home remedies—local cool compresses or a solution of cool water and baking soda.
2. Aspirin or an aspirin substitute sometimes helps.
3. If the person is highly sensitive to insect bites and has developed allergic reactions in the past, seek *immediate* medical attention. If medical attention will be delayed more than a few minutes, attempt to remove and discard the stinger and attached venom sac (in the case of the honeybee) by carefully scooping it out with a fingernail. Ice should be applied to the area of the bite.

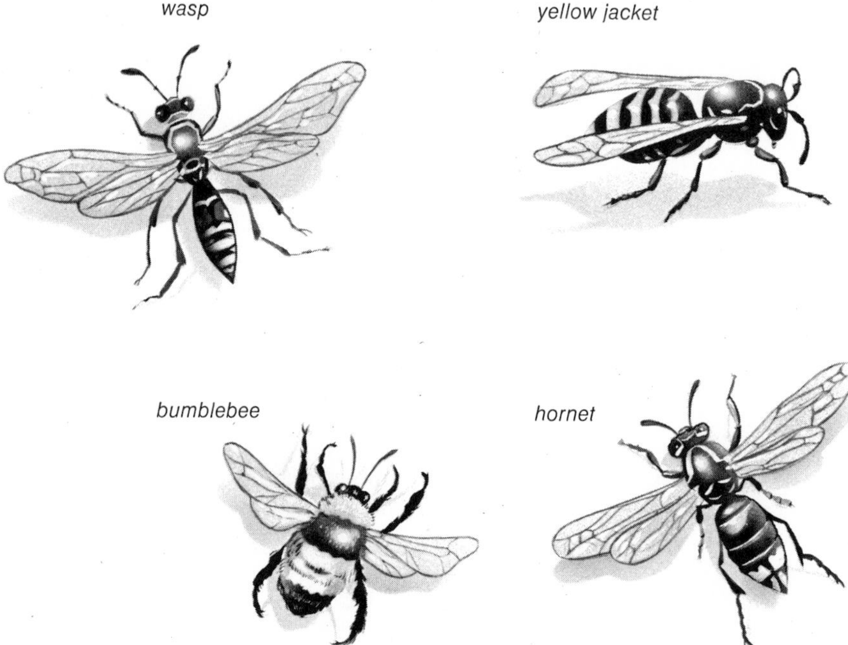

Stroke

Strokes are often referred to as cerebral vascular accidents. "Cerebral vascular" refers to the blood vessels in the brain, which are affected either by a clot or by rupture with subsequent hemorrhage. Major strokes may be accompanied by facial weakness, an inability to talk, the slurring of speech, loss of bladder and bowel control, unconsciousness, paralysis or weakness (particularly on one side of the body), or difficulty in breathing and swallowing. Sometimes strokes are associated with vomiting, convulsions, or headaches.

The most important things to watch are breathing and vomiting. Recovery from strokes is quite variable.

What To Do

1. If the victim is having difficulty breathing, his airway should be opened. (*See* Cardiopulmonary Arrest, above.)
2. The victim should be positioned on his side so that his secretions will drain out of his mouth and not into his airway.

3. If vomiting occurs, the victim should be kept on his side and his mouth should be wiped clean of vomitus.
4. Get prompt medical attention for all stroke victims.

What Not To Do

1. Fluids should never be administered by mouth unless the victim is fully conscious.
2. The victim should not be left alone for any length of time because of the chance of his vomiting and then inhaling the vomitus.

Sunburn

Ordinary sunburn is caused by overexposure to the sun's ultraviolet rays. The initial symptoms may begin as early as one hour after exposure and are manifested in painful redness and swelling of the area, and, in more severe cases, in the formation of blisters over the sun-exposed areas. When very large areas of skin are involved, fever, gastrointestinal upset, and weakness may occur.

Fair-skinned people and people taking certain medications should avoid exposure to the sun. Even dark-skinned people should initially avoid being in the bright midday sun for longer than 30 minutes. For added protection there are many good sun-screening ointments, creams, and lotions available. The most common and most effective ingredient in these is para-aminobenzoic acid (PABA), which screens out the ultraviolet rays that cause sunburn.

What To Do

1. Mild sunburn can be treated at home with cool compresses.
2. If there is an accompanying fever, aspirin may help.
3. Commercially available lotions often have a soothing effect on the skin.
4. For more severe cases, it may be necessary to consult a physician.

What Not To Do

1. Avoid further exposure to the sun until the acute reactions have subsided.
2. Avoid greasy preparations.

Sunburns usually resolve themselves, but occasionally the blisters become infected. If much of the skin has peeled off, the underlying skin will be quite sensitive to reexposure to the sun for several days or weeks.

Unconsciousness

Unconsciousness is a sleeplike state from which one may or may not be arousable. A person in "stupor" may be aroused with stimulation and only then with difficulty, while a person in coma cannot be aroused even by the most powerful stimuli.

The most common causes of unconsciousness are fainting, intoxication with alcohol, head trauma, strokes, poisoning or drug overdoses, seizures, diabetic acidosis, hypoglycemia, various types of shock, and hypoxia. Elderly, poorly nourished, or otherwise debilitated people are more prone to unconsciousness regardless of the nature of their illness.

The cause of unconsciousness is often difficult for even a physician to diagnose, and laymen should be careful not to ascribe a patient's unconscious state to something like intoxication. Alcoholics are of course not immune to other more serious causes of unconsciousness.

What To Do

1. Any unconscious person should be checked for an open airway and for palpable carotid pulses (*see* Cardiopulmonary Arrest, above).
2. If the person is not arousable but is breathing well and has good carotid pulses, he should be placed on his side so that he will not inhale any stomach contents if he vomits.
3. Anyone who is comatose should be evaluated by a physician. If drug ingestion or poison is suspected, the containers from the suspected toxin should be brought to the emergency department. Observations made about the person before his lapse into unconsciousness also will be of great help to the examining physician.

What Not To Do

1. Unconscious persons should not be left alone for any length of time, except for summoning help.
2. Fluids should never be administered by mouth and vomiting should never be induced.
3. Do not unnecessarily move an unconscious person unless you are certain he does not have a neck injury.

If unconsciousness resulted from a fainting attack, the victim may awaken within a few minutes. If unconsciousness recurs or if the person remains unconscious for several minutes, an evaluation by a physician should be sought.

Vomiting

Vomiting is the action by which the stomach rids itself of its contents. Vomiting can be caused by disturbances in either the abdomen or the head.

Causes of vomiting arising in the abdomen include: irritation or mechanical obstruction at any level of the intestinal tract, or irritation of abdominal organs like the gallbladder.

Causes of vomiting that originates in the vomiting centers in the head include: emetics (drugs), various toxins (poisons), increased pressure inside the head, decreased oxygen content of the blood in the head, disturbances of the semicircular canals of the ear (as occurs with seasickness), and, occasionally, psychological factors.

Severe or prolonged vomiting may lead to dehydration. When vomiting is associated with respiratory difficulty it may indicate that some of the vomitus was inhaled, and this is a medical emergency.

Simple acute vomiting may be caused by the effects of alcohol on the stomach lining, by dietary indiscretions, by viral gastroenteritis, or by the morning sickness of pregnancy. Severe or prolonged vomiting may reflect more severe gastrointestinal or systemic disease.

What To Do

1. Care should be taken to turn bedridden people onto their sides, so that they do not inhale any vomited stomach contents.
2. If a comatose person vomits, he should be turned onto his side and the vomitus should be cleared from his mouth.
3. After the initial episode of vomiting, solid food should be withheld temporarily and clear liquids should be given. (A clear liquid is one through which it is possible to read a newspaper.)
4. If the person goes twelve hours without vomiting, solid foods may be resumed, beginning with dry foods such as crackers.
5. If vomiting is prolonged or associated with severe abdominal pain, seek medical attention.

What Not To Do

1. Milk or formula should not be given to infants until the vomiting has subsided.
2. Solid foods should not be given to adults and children until the vomiting has subsided.

Section Three:

The Emergency Care System

To be most effective, emergency care must begin as soon as possible at the scene of an accident. In the home—one of the most common accident sites—there are two important steps that should be taken *before* an accident occurs: prevention and preparation.

The cheapest and most effective medicine is prevention. Every attempt to make the home as safe as possible is mandatory. Accidents in the home may be prevented by keeping stairways well lit and entryways unobstructed, by the careful placement of loose rugs, by proper care and maintenance of electrical appliances and cords, and by the proper shielding and use of power tools.

First Aid Kit for the Home

Every home should have a separate box (not just the medicine cabinet) containing at least the following supplies

First Aid Tools

Thermometer, oral
Thermometer, rectal
Flashlight
Hot water bag
Pair of scissors
Pair of tweezers
Packet of needles
Safety matches
Ice bag

First Aid Material

Aspirin, adult
Aspirin, children's, or aspirin substitute
Bottle of ipecac syrup (2 to 3 oz)
Bottle of aromatic spirits of ammonia
Antiseptic cream for burns
Sunscreen medication (para-aminobenzoic acid)

First Aid Dressings

Sterile 4″ × 4″ dressings
Gauze (2″ wide) for bandaging
Box of assorted adhesive dressings
1″ adhesive tape

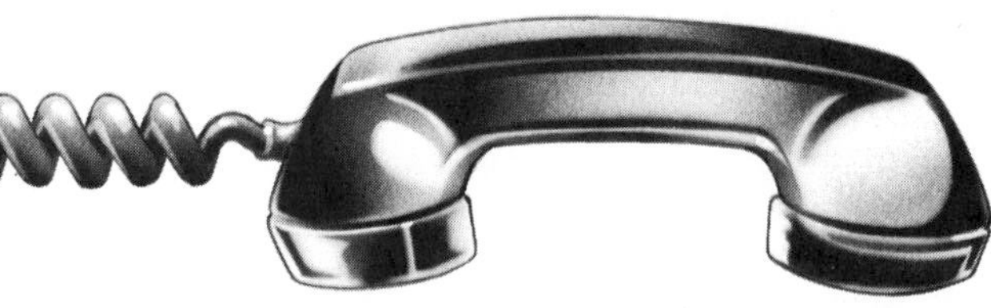

Appropriate List of Telephone Numbers

911 (the universal emergency call number in some communities)
Local hospital emergency department
Ambulance or rescue squad
Police department
Family physician
Poison Control Center (if one is available in the area)
Fire department

Particular care should be taken in the home to prevent poisoning. All prescription and over-the-counter drugs (including aspirin, cold remedies, and vitamins) should be stored in "child-proof" containers. In addition, old medications should be flushed down the toilet. The passage of time may cause drugs either to lose their potency or, through evaporation, to increase in potency. All medicine should be stored out of the sight and reach of children.

All cleaning solutions, drain and oven cleaners, solvents, and petroleum products (kerosene, gasoline, turpentine, charcoal lighter), insect spray, roach tablets and roach powder should be stored on high or locked shelves where children can't get at them. Never put any of these substances in a beverage or food container. Beverage bottles look particularly inviting to toddlers.

Prehospital Care

Whenever there is *anything but* the most simple injury or medical problem, it is best to call an experienced ambulance or rescue squad. It is always better to err on the side of calling EMS people rather than procrastinating at the victim's expense. Many services are upgrading their capabilities with better equipment and training. Most ambulance drivers and attendants are at least basic Emergency Medical Technicians (EMT's). The EMT's have received 81 hours of intensive first aid training, have passed a minimal proficiency test, and are certified by a state health agency. Many communities also have advanced EMT's (paramedics) available for emergency care. These individuals are basic EMT's but have had an additional 500 to 1,000 hours of intensive training in advanced life support (defibrillation, use of intravenous medications, advanced airway management, etc.). They generally function through radiocommunications with a hospital-based physician.

To Summon Emergency Aid

Have the telephone numbers of an ambulance service or, if none is available, the local police or fire department readily accessible. When you call, be as calm as possible. *Do not* hang up until all of the following information has been given: a) your name; b) your location (how to get there); c) your telephone number; d) the type of emergency (number of people involved, etc.).

The Emergency Department

The emergency department of the local hospital is the best facility to evaluate and treat true emergencies. Because many people may be seeking emergency care at the same time for different degrees of emergencies, the emergency department might seem to be a very confusing place. Most emergency departments, however, are organized to quickly establish priorities for care, and to provide appropriate treatment for each individual as soon as possible within the limits of those priorities.

The system starts with the nurse, who usually sees the victim first and, by means of a few basic medical questions or tests (temperature, blood pressure, pulse, etc.), attempts to determine the nature of the victim's problem. This nurse is trained to recognize life-threatening problems and to assure that they are seen and evaluated first. In an emergency department patients are not seen on a first-come, first-served basis. For example, a person with a sprained ankle would have to wait to be seen until a man with severe chest pains had been treated.

Better hospital emergency departments have physicians present around the clock to see and treat emergencies. These physicians are specialists in the treatment of emergency problems. Their availability in the hospital and their special training make them the physicians best suited to initially evaluate and stabilize any true emergency. The emergency physician's practice frequently is confined to the emergency department, and he should not be assumed to be in competition with one's regular physician.

Index

This is a three-year cumulative index. Index entries to *World of Medicine* articles in this and previous editions of the *Medical and Health Annual* are set in boldface type, *e.g.,* **Eye Diseases and Visual Disorders.** Entries to other subjects are set in lightface type, *e.g.,* hemodialysis. Additional information on any of these subjects is identified with a subheading and indented under the entry heading. The numbers following headings and subheadings indicate the year (boldface) of the edition and the page number (lightface) on which the information appears.

Eye Diseases and Visual Disorders
82–218; **81**–216; **80**–219
acute mountain sickness complications **82**–261
Buying Glasses and Contact Lenses **80**–327
cancer **81**–226
diabetes complications **80**–154
first aid **82**–413; **81**–413; **80**–417
headache symptoms and effects **81**–27
infectious diseases and interferon's use **81**–259
microsurgery and treatment use **82**–312
pediatrics
Children and Medicine **80**–22
venereal disease in infants **80**–363

All entry headings, whether consisting of a single word or more, are treated for the purpose of alphabetization as single complete headings and are alphabetized letter by letter up to the punctuation. The abbreviation "il." indicates an illustration.

a

b

d

e

j

k

l

n

O

p

S

t

x

y

z

To extend the tradition of excellence of your Encyclopaedia Britannica educational program, you may also avail yourself of other aids for your home reference center.

Described on the next page is a companion product–the Britannica 3 bookcase–that is designed to help you and your family. It will add attractiveness and value to your home library, as it keeps it well organized.

Should you wish to order it, or to obtain further information, please write to us at

Britannica Home Library Service
Attn: Year Book Department
P. O. Box 4928
Chicago, Illinois 60680

Britannica 3 custom-designed BOOKCASE

- requires less than 1 x 3-ft. floor space
- laminated pecan finish resists burns, stains, scratches
- Early American styling enriches any setting
- case size: 35¾″ wide, 9¾″ deep, 27⅝″ high

This offer available only in the United States

Student Study Guide

to accompany Petrucci's
General Chemistry,

THIRD EDITION

Periodic Table of the Elements

IA	IIA	IIIB	IVB	VB	VIB	VIIB	VIII	VIII	VIII	IB	IIB	IIIA	IVA	VA	VIA	VIIA	0
1 **H** 1.008																	2 **He** 4.003
3 **Li** 6.941	4 **Be** 9.012											5 **B** 10.81	6 **C** 12.011	7 **N** 14.007	8 **O** 15.9994	9 **F** 18.998	10 **Ne** 20.18
11 **Na** 22.990	12 **Mg** 24.305											13 **Al** 26.98	14 **Si** 28.09	15 **P** 30.97	16 **S** 32.06	17 **Cl** 35.453	18 **Ar** 39.95
19 **K** 39.10	20 **Ca** 40.08	21 **Sc** 44.96	22 **Ti** 47.90	23 **V** 50.94	24 **Cr** 52.00	25 **Mn** 54.94	26 **Fe** 55.85	27 **Co** 58.93	28 **Ni** 58.71	29 **Cu** 63.55	30 **Zn** 65.38	31 **Ga** 69.72	32 **Ge** 72.59	33 **As** 74.92	34 **Se** 78.96	35 **Br** 79.90	36 **Kr** 83.80
37 **Rb** 85.47	38 **Sr** 87.62	39 **Y** 88.91	40 **Zr** 91.22	41 **Nb** 92.91	42 **Mo** 95.94	43 **Tc** (99)	44 **Ru** 101.07	45 **Rh** 102.91	46 **Pd** 106.4	47 **Ag** 107.87	48 **Cd** 112.40	49 **In** 114.82	50 **Sn** 118.69	51 **Sb** 121.75	52 **Te** 127.60	53 **I** 126.90	54 **Xe** 131.30
55 **Cs** 132.91	56 **Ba** 137.34	57* **La** 138.91	72 **Hf** 178.49	73 **Ta** 180.95	74 **W** 183.85	75 **Re** 186.2	76 **Os** 190.2	77 **Ir** 192.22	78 **Pt** 195.09	79 **Au** 196.97	80 **Hg** 200.59	81 **Tl** 204.37	82 **Pb** 207.2	83 **Bi** 208.98	84 **Po** (210)	85 **At** (210)	86 **Rn** (222)
87 **Fr** (223)	88 **Ra** 226.03	89† **Ac** (227)	104 **(Ku)**‡ (257)	105 **(Ha)** (260)													

‡ or Rf (in dispute)

*Lanthanide series:	58 **Ce** 140.12	59 **Pr** 140.91	60 **Nd** 144.24	61 **Pm** (145)	62 **Sm** 150.4	63 **Eu** 151.96	64 **Gd** 157.25	65 **Tb** 158.93	66 **Dy** 162.50	67 **Ho** 164.93	68 **Er** 167.26	69 **Tm** 168.93	70 **Yb** 173.04	71 **Lu** 174.97
†Actinide series:	90 **Th** 232.04	91 **Pa** 231.04	92 **U** 238.03	93 **Np** 237.05	94 **Pu** (242)	95 **Am** (243)	96 **Cm** (247)	97 **Bk** (247)	98 **Cf** (251)	99 **Es** (254)	100 **Fm** (253)	101 **Md** (258)	102 **No** (255)	103 **Lr** (256)

Atomic weights are based on carbon-12. More exact values are listed on the inside back cover. Numbers in parentheses are mass numbers of most stable isotopes of radioactive elements.

Student Study Guide

to accompany Petrucci's
General Chemistry,

THIRD EDITION

Robert K. Wismer

Millersville State College
Millersville, Pa.

Macmillan Publishing Co., Inc.
New York
Collier Macmillan Publishers
London

Printed in the United States of America

Macmillan Publishing Co., Inc.
866 Third Avenue, New York, New York 10022

Collier Macmillan Canada, Inc.

ISBN: 0-02-395030-7

Printing: 2 3 4 5 6 7 8 Year: 2 3 4 5 6 7 8 9

ACKNOWLEDGMENTS

Any book is the product of many individuals and this one is no exception. Many improvements are due to their efforts; errors that remain are mine. I owe a special debt of gratitude to Professor Ralph H. Petrucci for his frequent advice during the writing and his comments on the final version.

The students of Introductory Chemistry I and II at Millersville State College class tested this study guide during the spring and summer of 1981. Among them they reworked all of the problems, found innumerable errors, and made many suggestions for improvement.

The Chemistry Department faculty at Millersville State College have been most supportive during the writing process. Special thanks go to Professor Jan Shepherd, who suggested many improvements in Chapters 24 and 25, and to Professor Donald Gauntlett, who reviewed the manuscript and helped with the class testing.

Christine Roda, Linda Sheets, and Jennifer Fisher typed the manuscript. Those at Macmillan Publishing Company–Kate Moran, Greg Payne, Jack Snyder, and especially Elisabeth Belfer–have been encouraging, helpful, and patient throughout the process of writing and production.

But I owe the largest debt of gratitude to my wife Debbie and my son Michael. They have endured a husband and father preoccupied with "the book" for more than a year and have constantly loved, supported, and encouraged him.

Robert K. Wismer

Contents

How to Use This Book

The purpose of this study guide is to help you learn chemistry. Students of chemistry have a wide variety of backgrounds and different reasons for taking chemistry. There is something of value here for all —the good student, the less able student, and even the instructor. Because of this, you may not find all of the material useful to you. However, each suggestion is worth an honest effort on your part. It is the result of several years of experience helping students with what many of them consider a very difficult subject—chemistry.

Chemistry is both an art and a science. Thus, its study requires a different approach than does the the study of many other subjects. It is not sufficient to read the text once, twice, or even several times. In fact, if you follow that approach you will spend a great deal of time on chemistry but probably will not learn it.

Learning chemistry requires that you do three things: write, practice, and test yourself. Writing helps you firm up your ideas and thus makes you aware of what you really know and what you don't know. Francis Bacon stated it best: "Reading maketh a full man, conference a ready man, and writing an exact man."

Practice in study means that you practice solving problems. You certainly would not expect to be able to play a difficult piano composition without first practicing it. Neither can you expect to be able to solve problems without practice.

Finally, you need to test yourself. This has two purposes. First, it helps you find out how well you have learned what you have studied. Second, you should feel more at ease during class examinations, since you have already examined yourself.

This study guide contains material to help you with these three areas of study. Although the study guide can be used with any textbook, it is designed for use with *General Chemistry: Principles and Modern Applications*, Third Edition, by Ralph H. Petrucci (Macmillan Publishing Co., Inc.). This book is referred to throughout the study guide as the *text*. Each chapter in the study guide considers the same material as the *text* chapter of the same number.

The study guide is organized around objectives. Throughout the study guide, each objective is referred to by chapter number and objective number; thus objective 14–5 refers to objective 5 in Chapter 14. Occasionally, a figure or a table in the *text* is referred to in a review. All of these figures and tables are reprinted in Appendix II of this guide.

Organization by objectives divides the material of each chapter into more easily comprehended parts. Each chapter begins with short essays on each objective, grouped under "Review of Objectives." These reviews explain the material, describe how to work problems, and give detailed examples of worked-out problems. The reviews are taken from classroom experience and include many analogies, examples, and illustrations. The analogies often are fanciful, sometimes ridiculous. This is necessary to have them illustrate the intended point and it does make them more memorable. Sometimes topics are explained from a different viewpoint from that of the *text*. There is no contradiction here but mutual reinforcement. If you have trouble with a topic, a different viewpoint may be enough to make it clear. Even if you have no difficulty, the alternate view may highlight aspects which had not occurred to you and thus increase your appreciation of the topic.

For objectives involving memorization, and especially for learning new terms, 3 × 5 cards are very useful. Write the term on one side of the card and your version of the definition on the other side. You can carry the cards with you and study them during spare moments: waiting in line, before class starts, and so on. In addition, you can shuffle the cards to make sure you know the terms in any order, pick out the hard ones and concentrate only on those, and turn the cards over to look at the definition and then recall the term.

Most objectives require learning either a new concept or how to solve a new type of problem. For those involving a new concept, first read the review carefully and then try to summarize the concept in your words. Since a 3 × 5 card probably is too small for most concepts, this summary should be written in your lecture notebook (see "How to Take Good Notes"). Notice that both definitions and new concepts should be stated in your words. Copying from a book will help you very little. Putting the definition or concept in your words ensures that you understand it. This is what you want. After all, you are the one who has to learn it and be able to use it.

The problem-solving objectives include a detailed example of the type of problem being considered. The "tricks of the trade" are included in these examples, and often one type of problem is solved by two or more methods so that you will better understand how the answer is obtained. Sometimes there will be but one example, solved by a method different from that of the *text*. Keep in mind that there are many ways to solve a given problem and choose the one which is easiest for you. When a method of solving a problem is broken down into several steps, each step is explained.

You gain practice in problem solving by doing, so the "Review of Objectives" section is followed by "Drill Problems." These problems are grouped by objective, and their presence is indicated in the review section by a star (★) in the margin beside the objective number.

The drill problems are straightforward questions based on each objective. By working them, you are practicing your mastery of that objective (rather like practicing scales or chords when learning to play the piano). If you drill yourself and become confident in these basic techniques, solving problems in which several are combined will be much easier. There should be enough drill problems for each objective for you to practice until you know how to solve that type of problem. Answers to all drill problems are given in Appendix I. The drill problems all use actual data, not "made-up" numbers. This should give you a better feeling for the "real world" of chemistry.

When you can solve the drill problems, go on to those of the *text*. The drill problems give practice in the technique of solving problems. Those in the *text* require that you be able to use these techniques in solving more involved problems.

For testing you will find in each chapter four "Quizzes" and a "Sample Test." The quizzes are designed to be a quick way to check your knowledge. There are four so that you can check your progress at several points: before you intensively study the chapter, during your study, and just before a class examination. The tests are included to give you some idea of the kinds of questions you might encounter on a class examination. The test questions are different in style within each chapter and between chapters. Different instructors use different style questions and knowing many styles can be of great help on examinations. Answers to the quizzes are in Appendix I, as are detailed solutions to the tests.

All problems have been twice solved by the author. The entire book has been class tested with a 25¢ reward offered for each error that was found. Nonetheless, errors may still be present. The author would very much appreciate notification of such errors and any suggestions for improvement.

How to Take Good Notes

There are several steps involved in producing a good notebook—one which will help you in your study of a subject. Although what follows is written for a chemistry lecture notebook, it can be adapted with small modifications for the lecture notebook of any subject.

The first step is prior preparation. Before going to lecture, skim the material in the text which will be covered. Do not read in detail. You are trying to get an overview of what is to be taught so that you understand how it is organized and how each topic relates to the others. Write a brief outline in your lecture notebook. You also should write out questions about points which seem unclear.

During lecture take notes on only one side of each page. You will need the other side later. Many professors write all important material on the board and of course you will copy this in your notebook. Think about your outline and your questions as you take notes, and answer those questions which you can.

Immediately after lecture, review the notes you have written. Correct the items which are wrong, add material you remember, and emphasize important points. This should take five minutes at most and it is *absolutely essential* that you do it immediately, while the lecture is fresh in your mind. The longer you delay, the less value this process will have.

The evening of lecture, read the portions of the text and the study guide which were covered in lecture. Use the blank sides of the notebook pages to write clarifications and any questions which you may have. Often, just the process of writing down a question will clarify the concept enough that you will understand it.

Now try to work the problems. Start with the drill problems and work some from each objective. If you can't solve a certain type of problem, reread the review of that objective and the appropriate part of the text. If you still can't solve it, write down a specific question in your notebook. Try to identify which part of the problem you can't solve and solve the rest of the problem or detail how you will solve it.

Ask other students in the class for answers to your questions. Sometimes they will understand concepts which you don't and often you will be able to help them. But don't just work problems to get the right answer. Make sure you understand the technique well enough so that you can easily solve the problem yourself.

Finally, ask your instructor for help with your unanswered questions. By working on your own and writing down your questions you know exactly what to ask and you understand the answer much better. Don't wait until the day before the exam to question your instructor. Do it daily as each new question arises. Write the answers to your questions in your notebook. Also write an example of each type of problem which gave you trouble.

Now you have a notebook which really is helpful. It not only contains your lecture notes but also has questions and answers on every point which gave you trouble. Such a notebook is invaluable when you study for class exams and also when, in a later course, you want to refresh your knowledge.

Chapter 1

Matter—Its Properties and Measurement

REVIEW OF OBJECTIVES

0. Define and use the terms listed in "Some New Terms."

This should be your first objective in each chapter. You should write each term and its definition on a 3 × 5 card. Then compose a sentence using the term. A very serious mistake is to copy definitions and sentences from the book. The definitions should be in your words so they make sense to you. Let's consider "heterogeneous mixture." One definition is that such a mixture segregates into physically distinct regions of differing properties. How can this be restated? Perhaps as "A mixture which, by itself, separates into parts which I can easily tell apart." Now think about examples. Fruit cocktail is one. You easily can distinguish the pears from the juice, the pineapple, and the grapes. Another example is Italian salad dressing which has been shaken. On standing, the oil separates from the vinegar and the herbs are clearly seen as separate pieces. Finally, use the term in a sentence and provide at least one example.

1. Classify common materials as element, compound, heterogeneous mixture, or homogeneous mixture.

Pick everyday substances, classify them, and write your choices down on paper. The substances you choose should be simple ones: the graphite in your pencil, wood, a penny, a stone, air, vinegar, water, milk, aluminum foil, and so on.

2. Learn the names and chemical symbols of the more common elements, including the first twenty.

This is a memorization job: to know the symbol which goes with the name and vice versa for the common elements. "Common" means different things to different people, but a reasonable goal would be those elements with atomic number from 1 (H) to 20 (Ca) along with Br and I. The atomic number is the whole number in each box in the periodic table, often given the symbol Z. This is a 3 × 5 card project with the name on one side and the symbol on the other.

3. Distinguish between physical and chemical properties and changes.

Choose some simple substances and write down everything you know about each one. Then decide which property is physical (does not depend on either reacting the substance with another or on producing a new substance) and which is chemical (does so depend). Consider wood. It is brown or tan (physical), breaks more easily with the grain than across it (physical), floats in water (physical), burns in air (chemical), turns black in sulfuric acid (chemical), and is somewhat flexible (physical).

4. Describe the features and limitations of the scientific method.

To start with, write a brief summary of the scientific method, using the terms *hypothesis, law, theory,* and *experiment*. Now contrive a fanciful example of the scientific method. One might be

Law: All Nordic children have fair skin, blond hair, and blue eyes.
Hypotheses: Trolls eat dark-haired, -eyed, or -skinned children (mythological).
The lack of sun prevents young children's skin, eyes, and hair from "tanning" (environmental).
Children inherit these traits from their parents (genetic).
Experiments: The mythological hypothesis can be discarded based on the principle known as "Occam's razor": the explanation which makes the fewest assumptions is the best. After all, trolls are imaginary–they never have been observed.

The environmental hypothesis can be rejected by noting the results of moving Nordic infants to sunnier climates. Their hair, eyes, and skin do not darken.

Just because the mythological and environmental hypotheses are invalid, the genetic one is not necessarily true. Experiments are needed to test it, such as moving Nordic parents to sunnier climates and observing the traits of their children. You also should realize that no amount of testing serves to "prove" a hypothesis. There is always the possibility of the hypothesis failing a future experimental test. Then a new explanation must be devised.

What are the limitations of the scientific method? One criticism is that the method is too rigid. It does not provide for arriving at conclusions from insufficient data–a process that often is a mark of genius. Can you think of others? You will develop a better appreciation for any method or theory if you are aware of both what it can and cannot do.

4a. Review simple units in the English system.

You should know some common English units, the relationships between them, and their common abbreviations. The most important ones follow.

Volume measure:	gallon (gal) = 4 quarts (qt)
	pt (pt) = 16 fluid ounces (fl oz) = 2 cups (c)
	quart = 2 pt = 32 fl oz
	tablespoon (T) = 3 teaspoons (tsp) = 1/2 fl oz
Linear measure:	yard (yd) = 3 feet (ft)
	mile (mi) = 1760 yd = 5280 ft
	foot = 12 inches (in.)
Mass measure:	pound (lb) = 16 ounces (oz)
	ton = short ton = 2000 lb

5. State the basic units of mass, length, and volume in the metric system, and the common prefixes which are used.

There are three units: gram (g), meter (m), and liter (L) for mass, length, and volume, respectively. The following prefixes should be memorized (a 3 X 5 card project).

deci	(d)	1/10	one tenth of
centi	(c)	1/100 or 10^{-2}	one hundreth of
milli	(m)	1/1000 or 10^{-3}	one thousandth of
micro	(μ)	1/1,000,000 or 10^{-6}	one millionth of
kilo	(k)	1000 or 10^3	one thousand
mega	(M)	1,000,000 or 10^6	one million

You should also learn how to put the prefixes and the units together and write the abbreviation of the resulting unit (for example, mg for milligram or 1/1000 gram).

6. Learn the relationships between English and metric units.

There are a great number of relationships. You can reduce them to three if you know the interrelationships in each system. You can choose one to learn from each column below (or you can learn them all).

Mass	*Length*	*Volume*
kg = 2.20 lb	m = 39.37 in.	C.946 L = qt
453.6 g = lb	2.54 cm = in.	L = 1.057 qt
28.35 g = oz	30.48 cm = ft	29.6 ml = fl oz

This can be a 3 X 5 card project.

7. Understand the relationship between SI and metric units.

You only need to be aware at this point that rather than using the gram, centimeter, and liter as basic units, SI uses the kilogram (1000 g), meter (100 cm), and cubic meter (m^3, 1000 L). The liter is being replaced in SI by the cubic decimeter (dm^3).

★ **8. Be able to convert between Fahrenheit and Celsius temperatures.**

You need to memorize two relationships

$$°C = (°F - 32) \times 5/9 \quad \text{and} \quad °F = (°C \times 9/5) + 32$$

and be able to use them. For example, 112°F = ? °C.

$$°C = (112 - 32)(5/9) = 80(5/9) = 44.4°C$$

25°C = ? °F.

$$°F = (25 \times 9/5) + 32 = 45 + 32 = 77°F$$

−30°C = ? °F.

$$°F = (-30 \times 9/5) + 32 = -54 + 32 = -22°F$$

It is useful to have a "feel" for various temperatures. The following may help.

0°C = 32°F	water freezes, winter day
5°C = 41°F	early spring morning
10°C = 50°F	early spring afternoon
15°C = 59°F	mid spring afternoon
20°C = 68°F	heated home in winter
25°C = 77°F	cooled home in summer
30°C = 86°F	summer afternoon
35°C = 95°F	hot summer day
37°C = 98.6°F	normal body temperature

Notice that a 5°C temperature rise corresponds to a 9°F increase.

★ **9. Write a conversion factor from a relationship between two quantities.**

★ **11. Use conversion factors to solve problems.**

The most powerful technique which you can learn in solving problems is the conversion factor method (or the factor units method or dimensional analysis). The method will help you not only in general chemistry but in any problem solving course in the sciences. People use the technique in different manners. One way is

(1) Identify what is wanted and what units it should have and write it down.
(2) Identify what is given (what you start with) and write it down with its given units.
(3) Multiply what is given by one or several conversion factors until you have changed the units into those of the answer.

EXAMPLE 1-1 How many teaspoons are in 5.00 gallons?

(1) ? teaspoons (tsp) (2) 5.00 gallons (gal)

(3) $5.00 \text{ gal} \times \frac{4 \text{ qt}}{\text{gal}} \times \frac{32 \text{ fl oz}}{\text{qt}} \times \frac{3 \text{ tsp}}{0.5 \text{ fl oz}} = 3840 \text{ tsp}$

There is no demand that you work from left to right in a problem. You might well have remembered 3 tsp = 0.5 fl oz first and have started with that.

EXAMPLE 1-2 How many gallons are in 1.00 cubic foot (ft^3)?

There is no simple relationship between gallons and cubic feet in the English system, but there is a relationship between volume and cubic length in the metric system (L = 1000 cm^3). Thus, the steps are

(1) ? gal (2) 1.00 ft^3

$$(3)\ 1.00\ \text{ft}^3 \times \left(\frac{12\ \text{in}}{\text{ft}}\right)^3 \times \left(\frac{2.54\ \text{cm}}{\text{in}}\right)^3 \times \frac{\text{L}}{1000\ \text{cm}^3} \times \frac{\text{qt}}{0.946\ \text{L}} \times \frac{\text{gal}}{4\ \text{qt}} = 7.48\ \text{gal}$$

Notice that in this case we started in the center (L = 1000 cm^3) of the string of conversion factors and worked outward. Notice also that we cubed two relationships (12 in. = ft and 2.54 cm = in.) to get the cubic units of length we wanted. Finally recognize that it is essential that you learn the relationships in the English system and those in the metric system and the relationships between the two systems so that you have a sufficient pool or reserve of relationships to use in constructing conversion factors.

We should mention another technique which can be used–ratios or proportions. To convert 5.00 in. to cm using this technique, one sets up the ratio

1.00 in. is to 2.54 cm as 5.00 in. is to ? cm

or 1.00 in. : 2.54 cm :: 5.00 in. : ? cm

$$or\quad \frac{1.00\ \text{in.}}{2.54\ \text{cm}} = \frac{5.00\ \text{in.}}{?\ \text{cm}}$$

A little algebra gives

$$?\ \text{cm} = 5.00\ \text{in.} \times \frac{2.54\ \text{cm}}{1.00\ \text{in.}} = 12.7\ \text{cm}$$

which is the conversion factor method. Thus, they *are* equivalent. But the ratio technique is cumbersome (you have to set up a new ratio for each change of units), it does not allow you to work forward or backward or from the middle out in solving a problem, and it adapts poorly to squaring and cubing units.

★ **10. Understand density and how it produces conversion factors.**

Density is both a physical property of a substance and the means of converting between the mass and the volume of that substance. There are generally only three kinds of problems involving density.

a. Given mass and volume, determine density: A 732 g object occupying 242 ml has what density?

$$\text{density} = \frac{\text{mass}}{\text{volume}} = \frac{732\ \text{g}}{242\ \text{ml}} = 3.02\ \text{g/ml}$$

b. Given volume and density, determine mass: A 27.4 ml gold (19.3 g/ml) object has what mass? The conversion factor method is applied here.

(1) ? g Au (2) 27.4 ml Au (3) $27.4\ \text{ml} \times \dfrac{19.3\ \text{g Au}}{\text{ml}} = 529\ \text{g Au}$

c. Given mass and density, determine volume: A 75.2 g piece of zirconium (6.49 g/ml) has what volume? Again apply the conversion factor method.

(1) ? ml Zr (2) 75.2 g Zr (3) $75.2\ \text{g Zr} \times \dfrac{\text{ml Zr}}{6.49\ \text{g}} = 11.6\ \text{ml Zr}$

10a. Understand "percent" and how it produces conversion factors.

Recognize that percent means parts per hundred. Thus, 40.0% C in acetic acid means 40.0 g of carbon in 100.0 g of acetic acid. If we wish to know the weight of acetic acid which contains 247 g of C, we proceed via the conversion factor method as follows.

(1) ? g acetic acid (2) 247 g C (3) $247 \text{ g C} \times \frac{100.0 \text{ g acetic acid}}{40.0 \text{ g C}} = 618 \text{ g acetic acid}$

★ **12. & 13. Determine the number of significant figures in a number or in the result of a calculation.**

Here is another 3 X 5 card project. Write down the five rules given in the text for determining significant figures and the rules for addition, subtraction, multiplication, and division one per card in your own words and memorize them. You might want to add the rounding rule: "When rounding a number ending with 5, round up or down so that the digit before the 5 becomes or remains an even number." Practice your understanding of the rules with the drill problems and rewrite the rules if necessary to make them more useful to you.

★ **13a. Express numbers in scientific notation.**

This is almost a part of being able to work with significant figures. A pair of rules might be the following.

a. A number in scientific notation is written as a many-digit number with only one significant figure to the left of the decimal point. This many-digit number is multiplied by 10 to some power.

b. The power of 10 is determined by starting with the original number and counting the number of places which the decimal point must be moved in order to have only one significant digit to the left of the decimal point. For each place left the decimal point is moved, the power of 10 is increased by 1. For each place right the decimal point is moved, the power of 10 is decreased by 1.

EXAMPLE 1-3 $1742 = 1.742 \times 10^3$ Since the decimal point was moved 3 places left to transform 1742 to 1.742, the power of 10 is 3.

$0.0008649 = 8.649 \times 10^{-4}$ Since the decimal point was moved four places right to transform 0.008649 to 8.649, the power of 10 is −4.

$114.692 \times 10^6 = 1.14692 \times 10^8$ Since the decimal point was moved 2 places left to transform 114.692 to 1.14692, the power of 10 is 6 + 2 = 8.

DRILL PROBLEMS

8. A. 32°F = ____ °C B. 100°F = ____ °C C. 98.6°C = ____ °F
D. 25°F = ____ °C E. 100°C = ____ °F F. 4.0°C = ____ °F
G. −14°F = ____ °C H. 500°F = ____ °C I. −60°C = ____ °F
J. −273.15°C = ____ °F

9. & 11. (1) One or two conversion factors per problem.
A. 7.3 ft = ____ in. B. 6.40 qt = ____ fl oz C. 12750 yd = ____ mi
D. 37.54 oz = ____ lb E. 16.54 cm = ____ mm F. 0.0374 m = ____ μm
G. 146 cm³ = ____ L H. 37.54 L = ____ m³ I. 27.2 kg = ____ mg
J. 206 g = ____ lb K. 250 cm³ = ____ fl oz L. 7.30 ft = ____ m
M. 12.0 fl oz = ____ L N. 187 lb = ____ kg O. 8.5 in. = ____ cm
P. 1.00 gal = ____ L Q. 1.00 cup = ____ cm³ R. 0.500 oz = ____ g
S. 127 lb = ____ kg T. 22.4 L = ____ gal U. 28.3 g = ____ oz
V. 100 cm³ = ____ fl oz W. 15.0 m = ____ yd

(2) Using units raised to higher powers.
A. 100 yd³ = ____ m³ B. 1.00 m³ = ____ yd³ C. 1.00 ft³ = ____ in.³
D. 1.00 in.² = ____ cm² E. 1.00 ft² = ____ cm² F. 1.00 yd³ = ____ gal
G. 55.0 gal = ____ ft³ H. 250 in.³ = ____ L

10. Sample densities: water, 1.00 g/cm³; ethanol, 0.789 g/cm³; copper, 8.92 g/cm³; iron, 7.86 g/cm³; lead, 11.34 g/cm³; gold, 19.3 g/cm³; table salt, 2.17 g/cm³.
A. 5.00 cm³ water = ____ g = ____ oz B. 5.00 cm³ gold = ____ g = ____ oz

C. 5.00 cm^3 Pb = _____ g = _____ oz
D. 250 cm^3 ethanol = _____ g
E. 250 cm^3 water = _____ g
F. 50.0 g Pb = _____ cm^3
G. 50.0 g Cu = _____ cm^3
H. 1.00 lb Fe = _____ cm^3
I. 1.00 lb Au = _____ cm^3
J. 4.00 lb salt = _____ cm^3
K. 1.00 qt water = _____ lb
L. 1.00 qt ethanol = _____ g
M. 5.00 lb Fe = _____ in.^{3}
N. 5.00 lb Au = _____ in.^{3}

10a. A. A copper penny weighs 3.015 g and contains 95.0% Cu. What is the weight of copper present?

B. An automobile weighs 1.00 ton and contains about 13% Al and 75% iron (Fe). What is the mass of Al present? What is the volume of Fe in liters if Fe has a density of 7.86 g/cm^3?

C. Air contains 78% N_2 and 21% O_2 by volume. A house 40.0 ft × 30.0 ft × 14.0 ft contains how many liters of nitrogen? How many liters of air must one have in order to have 680 L of oxygen?

D. 50.0 lb of tin is sufficient to produce how many pounds of soft solder which contains 70.0% Sn and 30.0% Pb?

E. Liquid bleach contains 5.0% sodium hypochlorite (NaOCl). How many pounds of bleach can be made from 1.00 lb of NaOCl? How many gallons is this if bleach has a density of 1.04 g/ml?

F. Soft whiskey is about 42.0% ethanol and 58.0% water. It has a density of 0.933 g/ml. How many quarts of soft whiskey contain 1 lb of ethanol?

G. A certain vinegar is 5.00% acetic acid and has a density of 1.007 g/ml. How many liters of vinegar contain 100.0 g of acetic acid?

H. A solution of 36.00% sulfuric acid in water has a density of 1.271 g/ml. How many grams of sulfuric acid are needed to make 5.00 L of this solution?

I. A copper penny weighs 3.015 g and contains 95% Cu. If Cu costs 80¢/lb, what is the value of the copper in 100 pennies? How many pennies contain one dollar's worth of Cu?

J. The compound silver nitrate contains 63.5% Ag. If Ag costs $12.00/oz, what is the value of the silver in 125 g of silver nitrate? How many grams of silver nitrate contain a dollar's worth of Ag?

12. & 13. (1) How many significant figures are in each of the following numbers?

A. 1837	B. 3.14145 × 10^4	C. 6005	D. 0.08206
E. 0.000014	F. 302400	G. 632	H. 8.732
I. 14.163000	J. 14.000	K. 19.7324	L. 302400.0
M. 149356	N. 205.8	O. 0.0019872	P. 8.7300
Q. 1900	R. 20000	S. 426.1	T. 1200.43
U. 1900.00	V. 0.00743	W. 6000	X. 60.0

(2) Round off each of the following numbers to four significant figures.

A. 6.16782	B. 213.25	C. 1200.43	D. 3135.69
E. 6.19648	F. 14.163000	G. 0.0022457	H. 152.00
I. 0.0019872	J. 302400	K. 14.16300	L. 3.14145 × 10^4

(3) Multiplication and division.

A. 1.86/3.14
B. (6.6262 × 10^{-27})(2567)
C. (37.2)(1.5)
D. (200)(87.45)
E. (998)(32.157)/36
F. 4.51545/0.15
G. (5.00 × 10^2)/36.72
H. 374.1/1800
I. 31.11/2.04
J. (1.40 × 10^8)(37.842)/147.3562

(4) Addition and subtraction.

A. 104 + 37.2 − 18.57
B. 87.6 − 0.005
C. 6.23 + 915 − 1012.7
D. 87.9 + 11.3 + 9.6
E. 36.516 + 0.00258 − 32.157
F. 6.47 × 10^2 + 4.2 × 10^1 + 6.8
G. 4.30 + 29.1 + 1000.3452
H. 204.5 − 96.5 − 32.1

(5) Combined operations.

A. (94.3)(12) − 7.62 + 300.0
B. (5.19 × 10^{-2} + 1.83)(2.19 × 10^2)
C. 3.18 × 10^{-1} + 1.6 × 10^{-2} + (6.40/12.1) − 2.19
D. ((3.18)(2.4)/1.92) − 0.17
E. 1.32 + 0.006 + (28/43)

13a. Express each number in scientific notation.

A. 0.00374	B. 1200	C. 4063.89
D. 175.1 × 10^3	E. 6460.4 × 10^7	F. 0.06627 × 10^{-25}

G. 9475×10^{-6}
H. 0.00374×10^{7}
I. 0.0000142×10^{1}
J. 17645
K. 212,000,000
L. 0.00266
M. 843×10^{5}
N. 94.00×10^{6}
O. 0.0004963×10^{-4}
P. 843.214×10^{-3}
Q. 0.000212×10^{12}
R. 0.00839×10^{2}
S. 894.13
T. 0.0000008314
S. 49000.6
V. 9204×10^{5}
W. 87012×10^{23}
X. 0.001413×10^{-4}
Y. 17645×10^{-15}
Z. 0.00266×10^{3}
AA. $0.0000008134 \times 10^{2}$

QUIZZES

Each of the following short quizzes is designed to test your mastery of the objectives of this chapter. Limit yourself to 20 minutes for each one. The questions are multiple-choice; choose the best answer for each question.

Quiz A

1. A 6.0-in. rule is how long in centimeters? (a) 6.0/2.54; (b) 6.0/39.37; (c) (6.0)(36)(39.37); (d) (6.0)(2.54); (e) none of these.
2. What is the mass in pounds of a small child who weighs 23.0 kg? (a) (23.0)(1000/454); (b) (23.0/2.20); (c) (23.0/1000)454; (d) (23.0)(1000)(454); (e) none of these.
3. 742 ml is how many fluid ounces? (a) 742/946; (b) 742/[(946) (32)]; (c) (742/32)(946); (d) (742)(946)(32); (e) none of these.
4. An object weighs 946 g and occupies 241 ml. What is its density? (a) 241/946; (b) 241 + 946; (c) (241)(946); (d) 1/[(241)(946)]; (e) none of these.
5. Italian salad dressing is an example of (a) an element; (b) a compound; (c) a homogeneous mixture; (d) a heterogeneous mixture; (e) none of these.
6. The density of margarine is 0.96 g/ml. What is the mass of 250 ml? (a) 1/[(0.96)(250)]; (b) 0.96/250; (c) 250/0.96; (d) (250)(0.96); (e) none of these.
7. 88 ft/s is how fast in meters/min? (a) (88/12)(2.54/100)(60); (b) (88)(12)(2.54)(60/100); (c) (88)(12)(100/2.54)(60); (d) (88/12)(100/2.54)/60; (e) none of these.
8. Matter which cannot be further separated by physical means but which can be separated by chemical means is called a(n) (a) element; (b) compound; (c) homogeneous mixture; (d) heterogeneous mixture; (e) none of these.
9. A concise summary of many observations is called (a) a law; (b) a theory; (c) an experiment; (d) a hypothesis; (e) none of these.
10. 32°C is equivalent to (a) 0°F; (b) 58°F; (c) 18°F; (d) 50°F; (e) none of these.
11. Phosphorus, sodium, and helium have the symbols (a) Ph, Na, H; (b) P, So, He; (c) P, Na, He; (d) Ps, Na, He; (e) none of these.
12. Which answer has the correct number of significant figures? (a) $(14.7 + 24.312) \times 87.27 = 3402$; (b) $(58 + 18 + 51)/3.000 = 36$; (c) $[97.2/(114 - 37)] = 1.26$; (d) $(1.172 - 0.4963)(4.194) = 2.83$; (e) none of these.

Quiz B

1. The density of gold is 19.3 g/ml. What is the volume of 231 g? (a) 231/19.3; (b) 19.3/231; (c) (19.3)(231); (d) 1/[(19.3)(231)]; (e) none of these.
2. What is the volume in milliliters of one cup? (a) (1/2)(946/2); (b) (1)(2)(946)(2); (c) (1)(2)(946/2); (d) (1/2)(946); (e) none of these.
3. A 6-ft person is how many centimeters tall? (a) (6)(12)(2.54); (b) (6/12)(2.54); (c) (6)(2.54/12); (d) (6)(12/2.54); (e) none of these.
4. One acre equals how many square meters (640 acres = 1 mi^2)? (a) $(1.0)(640)/[(1760)(36)(0.0254)]^2$; (b) $(1.0/640)/[(1760)(36)(0.0254)]$; (c) $(1.0/640)/[(1760)(36)(0.0254)]^2$; (d) $(1.0)[(1760)(36)(0.0254)]^2$; (e) none of these.

5. Matter which cannot be further broken down by chemical means is called a(n) (a) element (b) compound; (c) homogeneous mixture; (d) heterogeneous mixture; (e) none of these.
6. "A less dense solid will float in a more dense liquid" is an example of (a) a hypothesis; (b) a theory; (c) an experiment; (d) a law; (e) none of these.
7. An object weighs 314 g and occupies 432 ml. What is its density? (a) (314)(432); (b) 432/314; (c) 314/432; (d) 1/[(314)(432)]; (e) none of these.
8. 200 lb equals how many kilograms? (a) (200/454)(1000); (b) (200)(2.20); (c) (200)(454/1000); (d) (200)(1000/454); (e) none of these.
9. Sound is an example of (a) an element; (b) a compound; (c) a homogeneous mixture; (d) a heterogeneous mixture; (e) none of these.
10. Carbon, fluorine, and lithium have the symbols (a) C, F, Li; (b) Ca, Fl, Li; (c) C, Fl, Li; (d) Cr, F, Li; (e) none of these.
11. Which answer has the correct number of significant figures? (a) (37 + 54 + 42)/3.000 = 44.3; (b) (726 + 835)/24.0 = 65.04; (c) (202 + 74)/73.1 = 3.8; (d) (1.43 + 7.26 + 9.1)/14.23 = 1.250; (e) none of these.
12. 432°C is equivalent to (a) 720°F; (b) 272°F; (c) 835°F; (d) 810°F; (e) none of these.

Quiz C

1. A procedure designed to test the truth or validity of an explanation about many observations is called (a) a law; (b) a theory; (c) an experiment; (d) a hypothesis; (e) none of these.
2. An object weighs 764 g and occupies 265 ml. What is its density? (a) 265/764; (b) 764/265; (c) (265)(764); (d) 1/[(764)(265)]; (e) none of these.
3. What is the volume in quarts of a 250-ml beaker? (a) (250)(1000)(1.057); (b) (250/1000)(0.946); (c) (250/1000)(1.057); (d) (250)(1000/1.057); (e) none of these.
4. What is the mass in kilograms of an object which weighs 29.0 lb? (a) (29.0/454)(1000); (b) (29.0)(2.2); (c) (29.0)(1000/454); (d) (29.0)(454/1000); (e) none of these.
5. If a room is 10.0 m wide, its width in feet is (a) (10.0)(100/2.54)/12; (b) (10.0/1000)(2.54/12); (c) (10.0)(1200/2.54); (d) (10.0)(100)(2.54)(12); (e) none of these.
6. The density of copper is 8.92 g/cm^3. What is the volume of 651 g? (a) (651)(8.92); (b) 8.92/651; (c) 651/8.92; (d) 651 + 8.92; (e) none of these.
7. 14.7 lb/in.^{2} equals how many kg/cm^2? (a) 14.7(0.454)(2.54)^2; (b) (14.7)(454)(2.54)^2; (c) (14.7/2.20)(2.54); (d) (14.7)(2.20)/(2.54)^2; none of these.
8. Red food coloring is an example of a(n) (a) element; (b) compound; (c) homogeneous mixture; (d) heterogeneous mixture; (e) none of these.
9. Matter which can be separated by physical means but *not* by chemical means is called a(n) (a) element; (b) compound (c) homogeneous mixture; (d) heterogeneous mixture; (e) none of these.
10. Bromine, magnesium, and beryllium have the symbols (a) B, Ma, Be; (b) Br, Mg, B; (c) Br, Mn, Be; (d) Br, M, B; (e) none of these.
11. Which answer has the correct number of significant figures? (a) (107.4 − 17.2)/9.164 = 9.843; (b) 9.843 × (44.7 − 65.2) = 1082; (c) (1.172 + 0.4963)(3.145) = 5.25; (d) (651 + 8.92)/14.174 = 46.558; (e) none of these.
12. 450°F is equivalent to (a) 250°C; (b) 232°C; (c) 218°C; (d) 778°C; (e) none of these.

Quiz D

1. An object weighs 876 g and occupies 923 ml. What is its density? (a) 923/876; (b) 876/923; (c) (923)(876); (d) 923 + 876; (e) none of these.
2. An automobile weighs 2750 pounds. What is its mass in megagrams? (a) (2750/2.20)(1000); (b) (2750)(2.20)(1000); (c) (2750)(2.20)/1000; (d) (2750/2.20)/1000; (e) none of these.
3. 100 yd is how long in meters (36 in. = 1 yd)? (a) (100)(36)(2.54); (b) (100)(36)(2.54/100); (c) (100/36)(100/2.54); (d) (100/36)(2.54/100); (e) none of these.
4. What is the volume in milliliters of 37.5 fl oz (32 fl oz = 1 qt)? (a) (37.5)(32/946); (b) (37.5/32)(946); (c) (37.5)(32)(946); (d) 37.5/[(32)(946)]; (e) none of these.
5. 13.6 g/cm^3 equals how many lb/qt? (a) (13.6/454)(1000/0.946); (b) (13.6)(454/1000)(1.057); (c) (13.6)(454)(1.057/1000); (d) (13.6/454)(1000/1.057); (e) none of these.

6. Gold is a(n) (a) element; (b) compound; (c) homogeneous mixture; (d) heterogeneous mixture; (e) none of these.
7. Matter which can be further separated by physical means but which appears uniform to the eye is called (a) an element; (b) a compound; (c) a homogeneous mixture; (d) a heterogeneous mixture; (e) none of these.
8. An explanation of many observations which has been proven true by many tests is called (a) a law; (b) a theory; (c) an experiment; (d) a hypothesis; (e) none of these.
9. The density of silver (Ag) is 10.5 g/ml. What is the volume of 475 g? (a) 475/10.5; (b) 10.5/475; (c) 1/[(475)(10.5)]; (d) (475)(10.5); (e) none of these.
10. Hydrogen, potassium, and chlorine have the symbols (a) H, Po, Cl; (b) Hy, K, C; (c) H, K, Cl; (d) H, P, Ch; (e) none of these.
11. Which answer has the correct number of significant figures? (a) (10.46 + 1.7394)/12.2 = 1.000; (b) (14.234 + 0.005169)/0.1243 = 115; (c) (0.723 + 9.746)/15.493 = 0.6757; (d) (300.4 + 0.00216)/9.18745 = 32.697; (e) none of these.
12. 98.6°F is equivalent to (a) 54.7°C; (b) 37.0°C; (c) 120°C; (d) 86.8°C; (e) none of these.

SAMPLE TEST

This test is designed to take 30 minutes. Treat it as if it were an in-class examination. Only allow yourself a periodic table for reference and a calculator. Express your answers with the correct number of significant figures and with proper units.

1. A 10-karat gold ring contains 41.7% gold and weighs 10.72 g. If gold sells for $652.50/oz, what is the value of the gold in the ring?
2. In the production of ammonia, the following processes occur.
   a. *Air* is liquefied at low temperature and high *pressure.*
   b. The *temperature* of the *liquid air* is raised gradually until the oxygen boils off. Essentially pure *liquid nitrogen* remains.
   c. *Natural gas* is reacted with *steam* to produce *carbon dioxide* and *hydrogen*. The proportions of the products vary with the composition of the natural gas.
   d. The hydrogen and nitrogen (both as gases) are combined at high pressures and temperatures. They react to form *ammonia gas*. Some unreacted hydrogen and nitrogen remain.
   e. The gases are cooled until the ammonia liquefies, and then the still gaseous hydrogen and nitrogen are recirculated to react again.

   Each of the steps above involves a physical or a chemical change. Indicate which occurs in each step and briefly explain why you chose as you did.
   Each of the *italicized* words above refers to an element, a compound, a mixture, or none of these. Identify each one.
3. Perform the following conversions.
   a. 12.5 lb/in.^{2} = ____ oz/cm^2 = ____ kg/m^2
   b. 77.4°F = ____ °C
   c. 5.2 m^3 = ____ L = ____ qt

Chapter 2

Development of the Atomic Theory

REVIEW OF OBJECTIVES

★ **1. State and apply the laws of conservation of mass, definite composition, and multiple proportions.**

The first goal is to firmly master your versions of these three laws: (a) mass is neither created nor destroyed; (b) a compound has the same composition, no matter what its source; and (c) the ratio of the masses of one element combined with a constant mass of another in different compounds is a small whole number.

Application involves recognizing when the laws are violated and when they are obeyed. For example (for the law of conservation of mass), 4.00 g of methane plus 16.00 g of oxygen produce 11.00 g of carbon dioxide plus how much water? If water and carbon dioxide are the only products, 9.00 g of water must be produced. This is because there are 20.00 g of reactants (methane and oxygen) and there must be the same mass of products.

EXAMPLE 2-1 (The law of constant composition) A sample of methane taken from a mine (mine gas) was found to contain only C and H with 3.00 g C for every 1.00 g H. How much hydrogen should be present in 100.0 g of methane taken from a natural gas well?

Note that 4.00 g of the mine gas methane contains 3.00 g C and 1.00 g H. These proportions should be the same for the natural gas methane. Thus, we can use the conversion factor method.

(1) ? g H (2) 100.0 g methane (3) $100.0 \text{ g methane} \times \frac{1.00 \text{ g H}}{4.00 \text{ g methane}} = 25.0 \text{ g H}$

EXAMPLE 2-2 (The law of multiple proportions) There are four compounds which contain hydrogen, chlorine, and oxygen.

	%H	%Cl	%O
Hypochlorous acid:	%H = 1.91%	%Cl = 67.7%	%O = 30.5%
Chlorous acid:	= 1.46%	= 51.9%	= 46.8%
Chloric acid:	= 1.18%	= 42.0%	= 56.8%
Perchloric acid:	= 0.99%	= 35.3%	= 63.6%

We discuss how to obtain these percentages in the next chapter. Consider a fixed weight, say 10.0 g, of chlorine (any fixed weight will do). The combining weights of oxygen in order are

10.0 g Cl × (30.5 g O/67.7 g Cl) = 4.51 g O 4.51/4.51 = 1.00
10.0 g Cl × (46.8 g O/51.9 g Cl) = 9.03 g O 9.03/4.51 = 2.00
10.0 g Cl × (56.8 g O/42.0 g Cl) = 13.5 g O 13.5/4.51 = 3.00
10.0 g Cl × (63.6 g O/35.3 g Cl) = 18.0 g O 18.0/4.51 = 4.00

If we divide each combining weight by 4.51 g, we see that they are related as 1:2:3:4. In other words, they are related as small whole numbers.

Notice carefully that percents are converted to masses in grams here, as was done in objective 1-10a. These are the masses present in 100.0 g of each compound. There is nothing special about 100.0 g. We can use another mass, but 100.0 g makes the calculation simply a matter of replacing the "%" with "g."

2. State the basic assumptions of Dalton's atomic theory.

You should write down and firmly master your versions. Shortened versions are (a) Elements are composed of indestructible atoms. (b) Atoms of a given element are alike; atoms differ between elements. (c) Atoms unite in small whole number ratios to form compounds.

3. Know the characteristic properties of cathode rays and of canal rays.

A short list of cathode ray properties is (a) straight-line travel; (b) travel from cathode when current is flowing; (c) deflected as if negatively charged; (d) properties are independent of current source, tube material, cathode material, and gas which originally fills the tube; (e) invisible but give off light when they strike glass; and (f) have mass.

Canal rays (positive rays or anode rays) form when electrons (cathode rays) knock electrons out of neutral atoms. Canal rays thus are positive ions or cations (cat'-eye-uns). The properties of canal rays are (a) straight-line travel; (b) travel toward cathode when current flows; (c) deflected as if positively charged; (d) properties depend on the gas which filled the tube but *not* on other factors; (e) the rays have mass but are invisible unless they strike certain other objects. Canal rays do not consist of fundamental particles since the properties of the rays are not the same under all circumstances but depend on the gas which originally filled the tube. These properties lead to the idea that the atom is composed of both positive and negative parts and the negative parts (the electrons) are easily removed. You should memorize your versions of the properties of these two types of rays.

4. Describe the production of x rays, the phenomenon of radioactivity, and the characteristics of α, β, and γ radiation.

X rays are given off when cathode rays (electrons) are stopped by an object. X rays penetrate matter easily and do not have mass or charge. The degree to which they penetrate matter depends on the type of matter, principally its density.

Becquerel discovered radioactivity by chance. He observed that certain materials produce penetrating radiation which is unaffected by attempts to enhance or diminish it. Radioactivity is a characteristic property of certain elements. α (alpha) particles are $^4He^{2+}$ cations. They are massive, have poor penetrating power, but high ionizing power. β (beta) particles are electrons. They have moderate penetrating and ionizing powers. When α or β particles are emitted from an atom, the atom changes to one of a different element (as is described in objective 23–2). γ (gamma) rays are very high energy x rays. They have high penetrating power but low ionizing power. They leave unchanged the atom from which they are emitted except for carrying away energy.

5. Describe Thomson's *e/m* experiment, Millikan's oil drop experiment, and Rutherford's gold foil experiment.

In Thomson's experiment, a beam of electrons of known energy is deflected by a magnetic field which makes the beam curve. The radius of the curve depends on three things: the energy of the electrons, the mass of the electrons, and the strength of the magnetic field. The energy of the electrons, in turn, depends on their charge. Thomson knew the magnetic field strength but neither the mass nor the charge of the electron. To make the experiment clearer, you can imagine an experiment very similar to Thomson's. Attach a weight to a spring and, holding the other end of the spring, whirl the weight about you over your head. The distance between your head and the spring (the radius of the curve) depends on three things as shown in Table 2-1.

TABLE 2-1
Relation between Thompson's experiment and its analog

Depends on	To make radius of curve greater	Analog in magnetic field strength
Mass of weight	increase mass	electron mass
Speed of weight	increase speed	electron energy
Stiffness of spring	use a slacker spring	magnetic field strength

Millikan's experiment is designed to determine the unit of charge. Oil drops are charged using x rays and allowed to fall between two charge plates. The charge on each drop can be determined by varying the voltage between the plates until the electrical force felt by the charged drop just balances the force of gravity, and the drop stands still. The charges on the drops are always found to be an exact multiple of 1.60219×10^{-19} coulomb.

In Rutherford's experiment, α particles were beamed at thin gold foil. Most of the particles passed straight through, but some were deflected, a few by great angles. This experiment is similar to shooting BBs through a hole into a hot air balloon, in the center of which is a metal object. If enough BBs are shot, the size and shape of the metal object can be deduced simply by noting where the BBs strike the inside surface of the balloon. *Your* descriptions of these three experiments should be committed to memory.

6. State the features of Rutherford's nuclear atom and how it differs from Thomson's model of the atom.

The Rutherford atom consists of a very small nucleus (about 10^{-13} cm in diameter) which contains all of the positive charge and more than 99.9% of the mass of the atom, surrounded by a tenuous cloud of electrons. The electrons possess all of the negative charge, less than 0.1% of the mass, and fill most of the space in the atom (which is about 10^{-8} cm in diameter).

Thomson's model lacks the nuclear kernel. The negative electrons are embedded in a uniform sphere of positive charge, rather like plums in a pudding. The model is called "plum pudding" model.

7. Do simple calculations involving the masses and charges of protons, neutrons, and electrons.

The numbers which you should have firmly in mind are those which follow.

	Proton	*Neutron*	*Electron*
Charge	+1	0	−1
Mass, amu	1.0073	1.0087	0.00055

The unit of charge is that of an electron: 1.602×10^{-19} coulomb. The atomic mass unit, amu (also called the dalton, d) equals 1.66×10^{-24} g. Note that the electron mass is about 1/1830 that of the proton. The calculations generally involve determining charge-to-mass ratios.

★ **8. List the numbers of protons, neutrons, and electrons present in atoms and ions, using the symbolism $^{A}_{Z}X$.**

The complete symbol for an atom or an ion consists of the elemental symbol sourrounded by subscripts and superscripts. Two of the four "corners" thus created are used for an atom and the third for an ionic species. (The fourth is used in writing formulas of compounds.)

(1) The leading superscript (upper left) is the mass number. Older books may show the mass number as a trailing superscript (upper right), as this was correct until about 1960. Thus ^{235}U was U^{235} (Often one encounters U-235 instead of ^{235}U, especially in newspapers and magazines.)

(2) The leading subscript (lower left) is the atomic number. It is used for emphasis since the elemental symbol determines the atomic number but it is often included for emphasis.

(3) The trailing superscript (upper right) is the charge or the number of protons (the atomic number) minus the number of electrons. The sign (— or +) is always included. This number will be zero for a neutral atom, but the zero will be written only for emphasis.

For example, $^{19}_{9}F^{-}$ has an atomic number of 9 (9 protons), a mass number of 19 (19 nucleons = 9 protons + x neutrons and thus x = 10 neutrons), and a charge of −1 (9 protons − y electrons = −1 where y = 10 electrons).

★ **9. Describe how atomic mass ratios are determined by mass spectrometry and use these ratios to determine relative atomic masses.**

The mass spectrometer is an elegant version of Thomson's experiment for determining the charge-to-mass ratio of canal rays which was described in objective 2-5. The important addition is a velocity selector (the electric and magnetic fields just after the collimator) to ensure that all ions are of the same velocity. The instrument determines ratios of atomic masses and from these ratios one computes relative atomic masses.

For example, if naturally occurring carbon were analyzed, the ratio of the mass of carbon-13 to that of carbon-12 would be 1.083613. The mass of carbon-13 is then

$$\text{mass of } ^{13}\text{C} = 1.083613 \times 12.00000 = 13.00335$$

★ **10. Calculate the atomic weight of an element from the known masses and relative abundance of its naturally occurring isotopes.**

The atomic weight of an element is the decimal number appearing in the element's block in the periodic table. For example, the atomic weight of carbon is 12.01115. This weight represents an average atomic mass. It can be found using the combining weights of the elements in chemical reactions and in compounds. These combining weights represent the average masses of many atoms of the same element. These atoms have somewhat different masses because all of the various stable isotopes are included.

An example may make the concept and the calculation of atomic weights clearer. Suppose the average weight of an athlete of an 80-member track team is 82 kg (180 lb). The team consists of 52 runners weighing exactly 67 kg (147 lb) each and 28 shot-putters weighing 110 kg (242 lb) each. The coach obtains the total team weight as:

$$\begin{aligned} 52 \text{ runners} \times 67 \text{ kg/runner} &= 3.5 \text{ Mg} \\ 28 \text{ shot-putters} \times 110 \text{ kg/shot-putter} &= \underline{3.1} \text{ Mg} \\ \text{Total} &= 6.6 \text{ Mg} \end{aligned}$$

and the average weight of each athlete as

$$(3.5 \text{ Mg} + 3.1 \text{ Mg})/80 \text{ athletes} = 6.6 \text{ Mg}/80 \text{ athletes} = 82 \text{ kg}$$

(Remember: Mg = 1000 kg.) Any of the following expressions also may be used to calculate the average weight.

$$\frac{[52 \text{ runners} \times (67 \text{ kg/runner})] + [28 \text{ shot-putters} \times (110 \text{ kg/shot-putter})]}{80 \text{ athletes}} = 82 \text{ kg}$$

$$\frac{52 \text{ runners}}{80 \text{ athletes}} \times \frac{67 \text{ kg}}{\text{runner}} + \frac{28 \text{ shot-putters}}{80 \text{ athletes}} \times \frac{110 \text{ kg}}{\text{shot-putter}} = 82 \text{ kg}$$

$$\frac{0.65 \text{ runner}}{\text{athlete}} \times \frac{67 \text{ kg}}{\text{runner}} + \frac{0.35 \text{ shot-putter}}{\text{athlete}} \times \frac{110 \text{ kg}}{\text{shot-putter}} = 82 \text{ kg}$$

The last expression is of the same type as that which is used to determine average atomic weight. We use the fraction of atoms (athletes) of each isotope (runner or shot-putter) times the mass of that isotope to find the average mass of all the atoms (the average mass of an athlete).

DRILL PROBLEMS

1. (1) Conservation of mass.

A. If 3.41 g of hydrogen sulfide is combined with 4.80 g of oxygen, what should the products weigh? If the products are 21.9% water, what is the mass of water produced?

B. 7.95 g of copper(II) oxide is combined with 0.20 g of hydrogen. What is the mass of the products? The products are 77.9% Cu. What mass of Cu is produced? What is the percentage of Cu in copper(II) oxide?

C. Sugar, a carbohydrate, can be decomposed by heating to produce only carbon and water vapor. If 18.0 g of sugar is heated, the carbon which remains has a mass of 7.2 g. What is the mass of water vapor driven off? What was the percentage of water in the sugar before it was heated?

D. Iron(III) oxide, when reacted with carbon at high temperatures, produces solely molten iron and carbon dioxide. 3.192 g of iron(III) oxide and 0.36 g of carbon produce 1.32 g of carbon dioxide. How much molten iron is produced? What is the percentage of iron in iron (III) oxide? How many grams of carbon dioxide are produced when 1.00 g of molten iron is made? How many tons of carbon dioxide are produced when 1.00 ton of molten iron is made?

E. When 9.56 g of copper(II) sulfide is heated in the presence of 4.80 g of oxygen, the products contain 55.4% copper(II) oxide. What is the total mass of the products? What mass of copper(II) oxide is produced?

F. When 18.0 g of wood is burned in oxygen, the products weigh 37.2 g and contain 29.0% water. What mass of water is produced? What mass of oxygen is needed? How much oxygen is needed to burn 4.00 lb wood?

(2) Definite proportions.

A. Sulfur dioxide produced by reacting copper(II) sulfide with oxygen contains 50.1% S. If 57.2 g of sulfur dioxide is made by *burning sulfur in oxygen*, how much sulfur was burned? How much oxygen was used?

B. Carbon dioxide produced by reacting iron(III) oxide with carbon contains 27.3% C. How many grams of carbon must be burned in oxygen to produce 100.0 g of carbon dioxide? How much oxygen is needed?

C. Water produced by reacting hydrogen with oxygen contains 11.1% H. How many grams of hydrogen must be reacted with hot copper(II) oxide to produce 75.0 g of water? How much oxygen is present in 75.0 g of water?

D. When calcium carbonate (limestone) is heated, the calcium oxide (lime) which is produced contains 28.5% O. How much oxygen is needed to produce 74.2 g of lime when Ca is reacted directly with oxygen (lime is the only product)? How much Ca is needed?

E. When pure table salt is obtained from sea water it contains 39.3% Na. 14.0 g of chlorine reacted with an excess of Na also produces table salt as the only product. How much table salt will be produced? How much Na will react?

F. Ammonia produced by reacting magnesium nitride with water contains 17.6% H. The direct reaction of hydrogen and nitrogen produces solely ammonia. How much ammonia can be made from 32.1 g of hydrogen? How much nitrogen is needed?

(3) Multiple proportions

Each problem below gives the percentage of elements in several compounds. Demonstrate that the law of multiple proportions is valid in each case. The oxides of carbon are given as an example.

			g O/ g C	
carbon monoxide	42.9% C	57.1% O	1.33	1.33/0.89 = 1.49 (X 2 = 3)
carbon suboxide	52.9% C	47.1% O	0.89	0.89/0.89 = 1.00 (X 2 = 2)
carbon dioxide	27.3% C	72.7% O	2.66	2.66/0.89 = 2.99 (X 2 = 6)
A. potassium oxide	83.0% K	17.0% O		
potassium peroxide	71.0% K	29.0% O		
potassium trioxide	62.0% K	38.0% O		
B. acetylene	7.7% H	92.3% C		
methane	25.0% H	75.0% C		
ethane	20.0% H	80.0% C		
ethene	14.3% H	85.7% C		
C. chlorine monoxide	18.4% O	81.6% Cl		
chlorine dioxide	31.1% O	68.9% Cl		
chlorine heptoxide	61.2% O	38.8% Cl		
D. sulfur monochloride	52.5% Cl	47.5% S		
sulfur dichloride	68.9% Cl	31.1% S		
sulfur tetrachloride	81.6% Cl	18.4% S		
E. ammonia	82.4% N	17.6% H		
hydrazine	87.5% N	12.5% H		
hydrazoic acid	97.7% N	2.3% H		
diimine	93.3% N	6.7% H		

F.	orthophosphoric acid	3.1% H	31.6% P	65.3% O
	phosphorous acid	3.7% H	37.8% P	58.5% O
	hypophosphorous acid	4.5% H	47.0% P	48.5% O
G.	sulfurous acid	2.4% H	39.1% S	58.5% O
	sulfuric acid	2.0% H	32.7% S	65.2% O
	peroxomonosulfuric acid	1.8% H	28.1% S	70.1% O

8. Fill in the blanks in the table below. Some of the combinations are impossible. If so, write IMPOSSIBLE across the line. The first line is completed as an example.

	Symbol	*Ionic charge*	*Mass number*	*Atomic number*	*No. of electrons*	*No. of neutrons*
	$^{122}Sn^{2+}$	+2	122	50	48	72
A.	____	____	81	35	36	____
B.	____	+3	59	____	____	32
C.	$^{43}Ca^{2+}$	____	____	____	____	____
D.	____	−3	____	7	____	8
E.	____	0	20	10	____	____
F.	____	____	127	53	54	____
G.	____	+1	23	____	____	12
H.	$^{192}Os^{4+}$	____	____	____	____	____
I.	____	+3	26	____	____	30
J.	____	+2	52	24	____	____
K.	____	____	60	27	25	____
L.	____	−1	17	____	____	8
M.	$^{80}Se^{2-}$	____	____	____	____	____
N.	____	−4	14	____	____	8
O.	____	+4	118	50	____	____

9. Fill in the blanks in the table below. The first line is completed as an example.

	Mass of first isotope	*Ratio of masses: 1st to 2nd isotope*	*Mass of second isotope*
	13.00335	1.083613	12.00000
A.	190.9609	0.7745905	____
B.	77.9204	____	69.9243
C.	70.9249	____	14.0067
D.	68.9257	____	18.9984
E.	45.9537	0.283281	____
F.	____	4.80336	52.9407
G.	____	4.98818	49.9461
H.	____	1.50951	105.907
I.	63.9280	____	6.01888
J.	53.9389	1.29638	____
K.	77.9204	1.43613	____
L.	57.9353	____	150.923

10. Fill in the blanks in the table below. Make use of the periodic table to fill in the first two columns.

	Element		*Isotope A*		*Isotope B*	
	Symbol	*Atomic weight*	*Atomic weight*	*% Abundance*	*Atomic weight*	*% Abundance*
A.	____	____	6.015	7.42	7.016	____
B.	B	____	10.013	____	11.009	____
C.	____	12.011	12.000	98.89	____	____

	Element		*Isotope A*		*Isotope B*	
	Symbol	*Atomic weight*	*Atomic weight*	*% Abundance*	*Atomic weight*	*% Abundance*
D.	____	____	19.992	90.4	21.991	____
E.	____	63.54	62.930	____	64.928	____
F.	Cl	____	34.969	75.53	____	____
G.	____	39.102	38.964	93.1	____	____
H.	____	____	68.926	60.4	70.935	____
I.	Br	____	78.918	____	80.916	____
J.	Rb	____	84.912	72.15	____	____

QUIZZES (20 minutes each)

Select the best answer to each question.

Quiz A

1. There are two stable isotopes of chlorine.

   Cl-35 = 34.9689 amu (75.53%)
   Cl-37 = 36.9659 amu (24.47%)

   What is the atomic weight of chlorine? (a) (0.7553)(34.9689) + (0.2447)(36.9659); (b) (34.9689 + 36.9659)/2; (c) (0.7553)(36.9659) + (0.2447)(34.9689); (d) (75.53)(34.9689) + (24.47)(36.9659); (e) none of these.
2. $^{35}Cl^-$, ^{40}Ar, and $^{39}K^+$ all have the same (a) mass number; (b) atomic number; (c) number of electrons; (d) number of neutrons; (e) none of these.
3. When 16.0 g of methane was burned in 64.0 g of oxygen, 44.0 g of carbon dioxide (CO_2) and 36.0 g of water were produced. This is an example of the law of (a) conservation of mass; (b) multiple proportions; (c) definite proportions; (d) relative proportions; (e) none of these.
4. Isotopes always have the same (a) mass number; (b) atomic number; (c) number of electrons; (d) number of neutrons; (e) none of these.
5. A subatomic particle which has very small mass and a negative charge is called (a) a proton; (b) a neutron; (c) an electron; (d) an isotope; (e) none of these.
6. According to experimental evidence, cathode rays do *not* possess which property? (a) negative charge; (b) fundamental particle; (c) radioactivity; (d) mass; (e) they possess all these properties.
7. The combination which led to the charge on the electron was (a) Dalton–oil drop; (b) Rutherford–gold foil; (c) Millikan–oil drop; (d) Thomson–magnetic field; (e) Becquerel–gold foil.
8. Dalton's assumptions included (a) isotopes; (b) the nuclear atom; (c) indestructible atoms; (d) electrons; (e) none of these.

Quiz B

1. There are two stable isotopes of silver.

   Ag-107 = 106.9041 amu (51.82%)
   Ag-109 = 108.9047 amu (48.18%)

   What is the atomic weight of silver? (a) (0.5182)(108.9047) + (0.4818)(106.9041); (b) (108.9047/0.5182) + (106.9041/0.4818); (c) (0.5182)(106.9041) + (0.4818)(108.9047); (d) (106.9041 + 108.9047)/2; (e) none of these.
2. When two carbon oxide samples are analyzed, one is found to contain 36.0 g of C and 32.0 g of oxygen, while the other contains 12.0 g C *in* 28.0 g of the oxide. This is an example of the law of

(a) conservation of mass; (b) multiple proportions; (c) definite proportions; (d) fixed percentages; (e) none of these.

3. $^{19}F^-$, ^{20}Ne, and $^{24}Mg^{2+}$ all have the same (a) mass number; (b) atomic number; (c) number of electrons; (d) neutron number; (e) none of these.
4. A subatomic particle which has the same mass as the hydrogen nucleus and a positive charge is called (a) a proton; (b) a neutron; (c) an electron; (d) an isotope; (e) none of these.
5. Two atoms with the same number of neutrons are called (a) protons; (b) neutrons; (c) electrons; (d) isotopes; (e) none of these.
6. A fundamental particle of the atom is the (a) alpha particle; (b) beta particle; (c) x ray; (d) canal ray; (e) none of these.
7. The combination which led to the proposal that the atom has a nucleus was (a) Rutherford–gold foil; (b) Dalton–plum pudding; (c) Thomson–oil drop; (d) Millikan–oil drop; (e) Becquerel–radioactivity.
8. Canal rays are the same as (a) positive ions; (b) negative ions; (c) electrons; (d) neutrons; (e) none of these.

Quiz C

1. There are two stable isotopes of gallium.

   Ga-69 = 68.9257 amu (60.4%)
   Ga-71 = 70.9249 amu (39.6%)

   What is the atomic weight of gallium? (a) (0.604)(68.9257) + (0.396)(70.9249); (b) (68.9257 + 70.9294)/2; (c) (0.396)(68.9257) + (0.604)(70.9249); (d) (60.4)(68.9257) + (39.6)(70.9249); (e) none of these.
2. Both HCl and HBr are strong acids with similar properties. It is also true that most chlorine compounds are similar chemically to the corresponding bromine compounds. This is an example of the law of (a) conservation of mass; (b) multiple proportions; (c) definite proportions; (d) average reactivity; (e) none of these.
3. The *mass* of an element expressed on a scale where carbon-12 has a weight of 12.00000 is called (a) mass number; (b) atomic weight; (c) natural abundance; (d) isotope mass; (e) none of these.
4. An entity which contains only protons and neutrons is called (a) an atom; (b) a molecule; (c) an ion; (d) a nucleus; (e) none of these.
5. ^{40}Ca, ^{39}K, and ^{41}Sc all have the same (a) number of electrons; (b) mass number; (c) atomic number; (d) neutron number; (e) none of these.
6. All of the following scientists were involved in determining the *structure* of the atom *except* (a) Thomson; (b) Rutherford; (c) Millikan; (d) Dalton; (e) Becquerel.
7. Which of the following is *not* a property of canal rays? (a) straight-line travel; (b) fundamental particle; (c) mass; (d) have positive charge; (e) depend on the gas in the tube.
8. Which of the following is *not* a fundamental particle of the atom? (a) proton; (b) neutron; (c) beta particle; (d) alpha particle; (e) none, all are fundamental particles.

Quiz D

1. There are two stable isotopes of europium.

   Eu-151 = 150.9196 amu (47.82%)
   Eu-153 = 152.9209 amu (52.18%)

   What is the atomic weight of europium? (a) (0.4782)(152.9209) + (0.5218)(150.9196); (b) 150.9196/52.18 + 152.9209/47.82; (c) (47.82)(150.9196) + (52.18)(152.9209); (d) 150.9196 + 152.9209; (e) none of these.
2. When decomposed chemically a 73.0 g sample of HCl produces 71.0 g Cl_2 and 2.0 g H_2, while a 34.0 g sample of H_2S produces 32.0 g S and 2.0 g H_2. This is an example of the law of (a) conservation of

mass; (b) multiple proportions; (c) definite proportions; (d) hydrogen conservation; (e) none of these.

3. A subatomic particle which has about the same mass as the hydrogen nucleus and a negative charge is called (a) a proton; (b) a neutron; (c) an electron; (d) an isotope; (e) none of these.
4. ^{104}Pd, ^{105}Pd, and ^{108}Pd all have the same (a) mass number; (b) atomic number; (c) number of electrons; (d) neutron number; (e) none of these.
5. "Compounds are composed of atoms combined in simple whole number ratios and all atoms of the same element have the same weight" is an example of (a) a law; (b) a theory; (c) an experiment, (d) an observation; (e) none of these.
6. Choose the *incorrect pair.* (a) alpha–radioactivity; (b) Rutherford–nuclear atom; (c) Millikan–electric charge; (d) Dalton–isotope; (e) cathode rays–electrons.
7. Which of the following is a form of radioactivity under a different name? (a) proton; (b) neutron; (c) isotope; (d) hydrogen nucleus; (e) none of these.
8. The mass of an atom is determined by the number of (a) protons; (b) neutrons; (c) electrons; (d) isotopes; (e) nucleons.

SAMPLE TEST (30 minutes)

1. An attempt was made to determine the atomic weight of element X. X forms a compound with oxygen which contains 46.7% X and has the formula XO. Oxygen's atomic weight is 16.00 amu. What is the atomic weight of X?
2. Match the terms in the left-hand column one-for-one with those in the right-hand column by writing the correct letter in each blank.

a. same atomic number	___ Millikan
b. alpha particle	___ Rutherford
c. proton number	___ Thomson
d. atomic theory	___ isotope
e. x ray	___ atomic number
f. electron charge	___ mass number
g. nuclear atom	___ Dalton
h. proton	___ fundamental particle
i. isotope	___ radioactivity
j. nucleon number	___ cathode tube emission

3. A certain element contains one atom of mass 10.013 amu for every four atoms of mass 11.009 amu. Compute the atomic weight of this element.

Stoichiometry I: Elements and Compounds

REVIEW OF OBJECTIVES

★ **1. Obtain and use relationships between the mole, Avogadro's number, and atomic weight.**

The atomic weight is the nonintegral number appearing with each element in the periodic table. In Chapter 2 we thought of the atomic weight as the average weight of an atom of a particular element. It is very inconvenient (some might say impossible) to work with individual atoms. Therefore, chemists have chosen a larger quantity–Avogadro's number–of atoms to work with. If the atomic weight of an element is expressed in grams, that mass will contain Avogadro's number of atoms of the element.

Avogadro's number is truly huge–6.023×10^{23}. If it is written with four significant figures, the last two digits of the number (23) are the same as the exponent. The number is so large that if the fifty United States were covered with Avogadro's number of peas, the country would be covered to a depth of 6.4 km (4.0 mi). Thus, we weigh out an amount of material and, using the weight of Avogadro's number of atoms (the atomic weight), determine how many atoms are present.

Usually chemists are not concerned with how many atoms are present. They simply need to know that there are enough atoms of each element. Hence, they speak of moles of atoms. A mole of an element contains Avogadro's number of atoms. To make the concept clearer, imagine that a packer of machinery must put 500 bolts into each box. For each bolt there must be one nut and two washers for a total of 500 nuts and 1000 washers. Counting these out would take quite a long time. Knowing the weights of 100 pieces of each type (100 bolts = 99.1 g, 100 nuts = 42.7 g, 100 washers = 41.2 g) makes the job much faster and almost as accurate as counting. After some time the instructions to the packer might even be phrased: "Put in five dops of bolts (one dop weighs 99.1 g)." ["Dop" is a made-up nonsense unit. One dop contains 100 pieces.] The packer now is not concerned with how many bolts are in a "dop." In a similar fashion, chemists are not concerned very often with how many atoms are in a mole. A mole is a convenient amount of material to work with–much more so than individual atoms.

The abbreviation for mole is mol. Other symbols such as m, $\overline{m}$, and M are incorrect and should not be used as abbreviations for mole, for they will cause confusion.

One mole of an element (a) contains Avogadro's number of atoms; (b) contains 6.023×10^{23} atoms; and (c) has a mass in grams equal to the atomic weight of the element. Each one of these relations can be used to construct a conversion factor. Sample factors are

$$\frac{6.023 \times 10^{23}\ \text{atoms}}{\text{mole}} \qquad \frac{6.023 \times 10^{23}\ \text{Mg atoms}}{24.312\ \text{g Mg}} \qquad \frac{24.312\ \text{g Mg}}{\text{mol Mg}}$$

EXAMPLE 3-1 87.4 g Mn is equivalent to how many moles of Mn?

(1) ? moles Mn (2) 87.4 g Mn (c) $87.4\ \text{g Mn} \times \dfrac{\text{mol Mn}}{54.9\ \text{g Mn}} = 1.59\ \text{mol Mn}$

EXAMPLE 3-2 47.2 g Cs contains how many atoms?

(1) ? Cs atoms (2) 47.2 g Cs

(3) $47.2\ \text{g Cs} \times \dfrac{6.023 \times 10^{23}\ \text{Cs atoms}}{132.9\ \text{g Cs}} = 2.14 \times 10^{23}\ \text{Cs atoms}$

EXAMPLE 3-3 How many moles are present in 5.00×10^9 atoms? (We do not have to specify which element since there is the same number of atoms–Avogadro's number–in a mole of any element.)

(1) ? moles (2) 5.00×10^9 atoms

(3) $$5.00 \times 10^9 \text{ atoms} \times \frac{\text{mole of atoms}}{6.023 \times 10^{23} \text{ atoms}} = 8.30 \times 10^{-15} \text{ mol}$$

2. Distinguish between a mole of atoms and a mole of molecules.

A molecule is simply a cluster of atoms bound together. In our nut-bolt-washer analogy, a bolt with two washers on it and the nut screwed on is similar to a molecule (Fig. 3-1). If these were preassembled, the packer would simply weigh out "dops" of assemblies (224.2 g/"dop"). Similarly, chemists find it convenient to work with moles of molecules since molecules are "preassembled" groups of atoms.

It is wise at this point to notice that some elements do not exist as individual atoms or as a large solid mass of somewhat attracted atoms but rather as distinct molecules. You should firmly memorize the following forms: H_2, F_2, Cl_2, Br_2, I_2, O_2, S_8, N_2, P_4.

★ **3. Distinguish between formula unit and molecule, empirical formula and molecular formula, and formula weight and molecular weight.**

As we have said, a molecule is a group of atoms bound together. The atoms in a formula unit are not necessarily bound together. In our nut-bolt-washer analogy, a formula unit consists of a nut, a bolt, and two washers, whether or not they are bound together. The grouping of 1 nut + 1 bolt + 2 washers is the smallest collection of pieces which contains the pieces in the same ratio as they are in when packed for shipment. Likewise, the formula unit is a small collection of atoms which contains the atoms in the same ratio as they are in the compound.

A molecular formula counts the actual number of atoms of each element in the molecule. Thus, the molecular formula of hydrogen peroxide is H_2O_2, and each molecule contains four atoms: two O and two H. An empirical formula expresses the *smallest* combining ratio of the atoms in a compound. For hydrogen peroxide the empirical formula is HO. To change a molecular formula into an empirical one, divide the subscripts by the largest whole number which will go evenly into all of them. In the case of H_2O_2 this number is 2. Some examples follow.

Compound name	*Molecular formula*	*Divide by*	*Empirical formula*
hydrazine	N_2H_4	2	NH_2
propene	C_3H_6	3	CH_2
diborane	B_2H_6	2	BH_3
acetic acid	$C_2H_4O_2$	2	CH_2O

Just as the atomic weight in grams is the mass of a mole of atoms, so the formula weight is the mass of a mole of formula units and the molecular weight is the mass of a mole of molecules. It is proper to refer to any one of these three weights as the mole weight (abbreviated mol wt or MW). To determine the mole weight (sometimes called the molar mass), one starts with the chemical formula for the compound. Interpret the subscripts as indicating the number of moles of each element in a mole of the compound. Then remember that a mole of an element has a mass equal to the atomic weight of that element in grams.

EXAMPLE 3-4 Determine the formula weight of CsF.
One mole of CsF contains one mole of Cs and one mole of F. Thus,

$$1 \text{ mol Cs} \times \frac{132.9 \text{ g Cs}}{\text{mol Cs}} = 132.9 \text{ g Cs}$$

$$1 \text{ mol F} \times \frac{19.0 \text{ g F}}{\text{mol F}} = \frac{19.0 \text{ g F}}{151.9 \text{ g/mol CsF}}$$

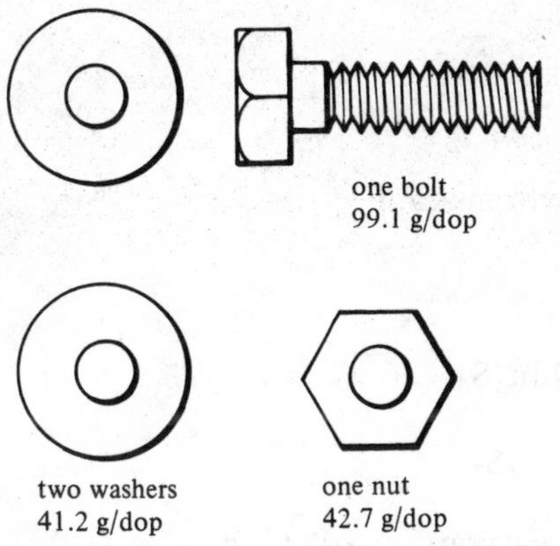

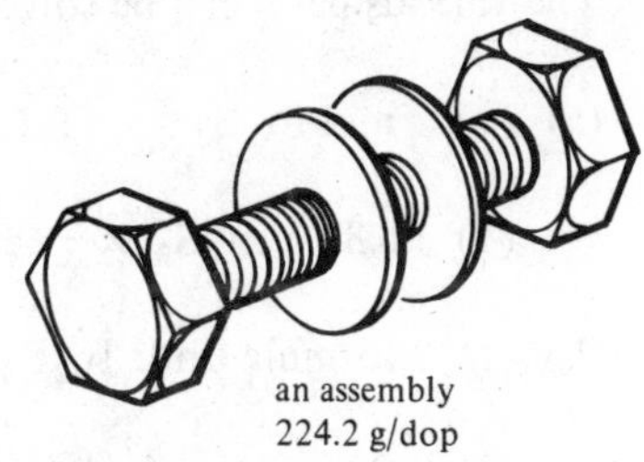

FIGURE 3-1 Two formula units—the dop
In the left formula unit, the pieces are not bound together, while in the right formula unit they are—a "molecule" is formed.

EXAMPLE 3-5 Determine the mole weight of acetic acid, $HC_2H_3O_2$.
Acetic acid contains 4(1 + 3) mol H, 2 mol C, and 2 mol O. Thus, the calculation becomes

$$\begin{aligned} 4 \text{ mol H} \times 1.00 \text{ g H/mol H} &= 4.00 \text{ g H} \\ 2 \text{ mol C} \times 12.0 \text{ g C/mol C} &= 24.0 \text{ g C} \\ 2 \text{ mol O} \times 16.0 \text{ g O/mol O} &= \underline{32.0 \text{ g O}} \\ & 60.0 \text{ g/mol } HC_2H_3O_2 \end{aligned}$$

EXAMPLE 3-6 Determine the formula weight of aluminum sulfate, $Al_2(SO_4)_3$.
A mole of the compound contains two moles of Al and three moles of sulfate ions. Since *each* mole of sulfate ion contains one mole of S and four moles of O, three moles of sulfate ions contains three moles of S and twelve moles of O (3 mol of sulfate ions × 4 mol O/mol sulfate ions). Thus the formula weight can be determined.

$$\begin{aligned} 2 \text{ mol Al} \times 27.0 \text{ g Al/mol Al} &= 54.0 \text{ g Al} \\ 3 \text{ mol S} \times 32.1 \text{ g S/mol S} &= 96.3 \text{ g S} \\ 12 \text{ mol O} \times 16.0 \text{ g O/mol O} &= \underline{192.0 \text{ g O}} \\ & 342.3 \text{ g/mol } Al_2(SO_4)_3 \end{aligned}$$

★ **4. Calculate the numbers of atoms, ions, formula units, or molecules in a substance from a given mass or vice versa.**

Once we can determine mole weights (objective 3-3) we can find the amount of a given mass in moles. We must know something about the substance before we can state whether these are moles of molecules. Only covalent compounds exist as molecules. All binary compounds composed of two nonmetals are covalent. (See objective 3-5a for definitions of metals and nonmetals.) Thus HCl, H_2O, NH_3, and PCl_5 all are covalent compounds and exist as molecules.

All binary compounds composed of a metal and a nonmetal are ionic. Thus NaCl, MgF_2, $FeCl_3$, and Mg_2S all are ionic and do not contain molecules. Ionic compounds are made of ions. When we select a number of ions equal to the number given in the formula, we are selecting a formula unit and not a molecule. The formula unit of NaCl consists of a Na^+ cation and a Cl^- anion. The formula unit of $FeCl_3$ consists of one Fe^{3+} cation and three Cl^- anions.

EXAMPLE 3-7 11.34 g In_2S_3 contains (a) how many moles? (b) how many formula units? (c) how many molecules? (d) how many In^{3+} ions?
The mole weight of In_2S_3 is determined as follows.

$$2 \text{ mol In} \times 114.8 \text{ g In/mol In} = 229.6 \text{ g In}$$
$$3 \text{ mol S} \times 32.1 \text{ g S/mol S} = 96.3 \text{ g S}$$
$$= 325.9 \text{ g/mol } In_2S_3$$

The various parts can be solved using the conversion factor method.

(a) (1) ? mol In_2S_3 (2) 11.34 g In_2S_3

$$(3)\ 11.34 \text{ g } In_2S_3 \times \frac{\text{mol } In_2S_3}{325.9 \text{ g } In_2S_3} = 0.03480 \text{ mol } In_2S_3$$

(b) (1) ? formula units In_2S_3 (2) 0.03480 mol In_2S_3

$$(3)\ 0.03480 \text{ mol } In_2S_3 \times \frac{6.023 \times 10^{23} \text{ f.u. } In_2S_3}{\text{mol } In_2S_3} = 2.096 \times 10^{22}\ In_2S_3 \text{ formula units}$$

(c) No molecules since In_2S_3 is not a covalent compound.
(d) (1) ? In^{3+} ions (2) 11.34 g In_2S_3

$$(3)\ 11.34 \text{ g } In_2S_3 \times \frac{\text{mol } In_2S_3}{325.9 \text{ g } In_2S_3} \times \frac{6.023 \times 10^{23} \text{ f.u. } In_2S_3}{\text{mol } In_2S_3} \times \frac{2\ In^{3+} \text{ ions}}{\text{f.u. } In_2S_3} =$$

$4.192 \times 10^{22}\ In^{3+}$ ions

★ **5. & 6. Know the names, formulas, and charges of the ions in *Tables 3-1 and 3-3 in the text* and be able to write formulas and names of the compounds formed from these ions.**

The first goal is straightforward memorization and a 3 X 5 card project. Write the name of the ion on one side of the card and the symbol or formula of each ion with the correct charge on the other side. Then practice until you can recall one while looking at the other.

It may seem early to learn chemical nomenclature and how to write formulas. But these form the basis of the language of chemistry. Chemists speak to each other using the names of compounds, but chemical formulas are most useful for calculations. Thus, to understand chemists you must have a firm grasp of nomenclature and to work problems you need to be good at writing formulas. Far too many students find chemistry difficult simply because they haven't mastered nomenclature and formula writing.

Naming ionic compounds is surprisingly simple. One writes down the name of the cation (positive ion), follows it with a space, and then the name of the negative ion or the anion. For example consider iron(III) chloride, sodium nitrate, and mercury(I) phosphate.

Writing formulas from names is not quite so simple. The formula contains more than the cation and anion formulas or symbols. In addition the cation and anion symbols must be multiplied so that the total charge from the cations just balances the total charge of the anions. The total cation charge plus the total anion charge equals zero.

Fortunately, there are not very many ways to combine cations and anions. A look at *Tables 3-1 and 3-3 in the text* reveals that cations have charges of +1 (like Li^+), +2 (Ca^{2+}), and +3 (Al^{3+}). Cations also exist with higher charges, but +4 (Ce^{4+}) is the highest positive charge you are likely to encounter. Anions seem to come in only three varieties: −1 (like F^- or MnO_4^-), −2 (CrO_4^{2-} or S^{2-}), and −3 (PO_4^{3-}). Thus there are only twelve (3 X 4) different types of compound formulas.

The easiest type of formula occurs in the compounds in which anion and cation charge are equal but of opposite signs. Sodium chloride is made of Na^+ and Cl^- ions and the total anion and cation charges sum to zero if we take one anion and one cation: NaCl. In like manner, magnesium sulfate is composed of Mg^{2+} and SO_4^{2-} ions and has the formula $MgSO_4$. Finally, aluminum phosphate is $AlPO_4$. These compounds lie along the diagonal [from top line of column (1) to third line of column (3)] in Table 3-1.

The next easiest type of compound has one ion with a charge of +1 or −1. Then we look at the charge on the other ion and see how many of the +1 or −1 ions are needed. For example, sodium phosphate is composed of Na^+ ions (charge = +1) and PO_4^{3-} ions (charge = −3). To balance the −3 charge of the phosphate ion requires a total cation charge of +3, which is supplied by three Na^+ ions. Compounds of this general type lie across the top line and down column (1) of Table 3-1.

TABLE 3-1
Formulas for twelve common types of ionic compounds
Examples are given in brackets, [ ]

		Anions					
		(1)		(2)		(3)	
Cation		X^-	[F^-]	X^{2-}	[$SO_4{}^{2-}$]	X^{3-}	[$PO_4{}^{3-}$]
M^+	[$NH_4{}^+$]	MX	[NH_4F]	M_2X	[$(NH_4)_2SO_4$]	M_3X	[$(NH_4)_3PO_4$]
M^{2+}	[Ca^{2+}]	MX_2	[CaF_2]	MX	[$CaSO_4$]	M_3X_2	[$Ca_3(PO_4)_2$]
M^{3+}	[Al^{3+}]	MX_3	[AlF_3]	M_2X_3	[$Al_2(SO_4)_3$]	MX	[$AlPO_4$]
M^{4+}	[Ce^{4+}]	MX_4	[CeF_4]	MX_2	[$Ce(SO_4)_2$]	M_3X_4	[$Ce_3(PO_4)_4$]

The remaining compounds are like aluminum sulfate, composed of Al^{3+} and $SO_4{}^{2-}$ ions. One method of finding the number of each type of ion is

(1) Use as many anions as the value of the cation charge. In this instance, the cation charge of Al^{3+} is +3, so we use 3 anions.
(2) Use as many cations as the negative of the value of the anion charge. Sulfate's charge is −2, so we use 2 cations.
(3) If the two numbers you have produced (number of cations and number of anions) can both be divided evenly by the same number, do so before you write down the formula.

An example will make the use of step (3) clearer.

EXAMPLE 3-8 What is the formula of cerium(IV) oxalate?
The formula for cerium(IV) is Ce^{4+} and that for oxalate is $C_2O_4{}^{2-}$. (1) Ce^{4+} has charge = +4. Thus, use 4 $C_2O_4{}^{2-}$ anions. (2) $C_2O_4{}^{2-}$ has charge = −2. Thus, use 2 Ce^{4+} cations. (3) But 4 and 2 both can be divided evenly by 2. This yields 2 $C_2O_4{}^{2-}$ anions and 1 Ce^{4+} cation and a formula of $Ce(C_2O_4)_2$.

Remember: *Simply because a compound's name and formula can be written does not mean that the compound exists.*

★ **5a. Be able to write formulas and names of simple binary covalent compounds.**

As the text states, covalent compounds are formed between nonmetallic elements. The easiest way to identify the nonmetals uses the periodic table. The nonmetals are in that area of the table above and to the right of a zigzag line running from between B and Al to between Po and At. All other elements are metals.

Although there are a few exceptions (such as water, H_2O; ammonia, NH_3; and methane, CH_4), the names of binary covalent compounds are obtained from the names of the two elements. The elements are named in the same order as they appear in the formula. The first element name is unchanged; the ending of the second is changed to "-ide." The element names have prefixes depending on the subscript of that element in the formula, except that the prefix mono (meaning one of) is rarely used. The other prefixes are: di = 2, tri = 3, tetra = 4, penta = 5, hexa = 6, hepta = 7, and octa = 8.

★ **7. Use chemical formulas as a source of conversion factors for stoichiometric calculations.**

A chemical formula is not only "a recipe for something you wouldn't want to eat," as a sixth grader said, but also contains many relationships. $CuSO_4 \cdot 5H_2O$ contains 1 Cu atom, 1 S atom, 9 O atoms, and 10 H atoms *or* 1 copper(II) ion, 1 sulfate ion, and 5 water molecules. A mole of $CuSO_4 \cdot 5H_2O$ contains 1 mol Cu atoms, 1 mol S atoms, 9 mol S atoms, and 10 mol H atoms *or* 1 mol of copper(II) ions, 1 mol of sulfate ions, and 5 mol of water molecules. We already have used these relationships in obtaining the mole weight of a compound. The mole weight of $CuSO_4 \cdot 5H_2O$ is 249.6 g/mol. We can use the relationships in other ways, as Example 3-9 illustrates.

EXAMPLE 3-9 How many moles of oxygen atoms are in 29.95 g $CuSO_4 \cdot 5H_2O$?

$$29.95 \text{ g cmpd} \times \frac{\text{mol cmpd}}{249.6 \text{ g cmpd}} \times \frac{9 \text{ mol O atoms}}{\text{mol cmpd}} = 10.8 \text{ mol O atoms}$$

★ **8. Use a compound's formula to determine its percent composition.**

The percent of one element in a compound is given by the relationship

$$\frac{\text{mass of element}}{\text{mass of compound}} \times 100$$

Both masses are determined in the course of computing a compound's mole weight.

EXAMPLE 3-10 What is the percent of oxygen in $CuSO_4 \cdot 5H_2O$?

$$\% \text{ O} = \frac{\text{mass O}}{\text{mass compound}} = \frac{144.0 \text{ g O}}{249.6 \text{ g } CuSO_4 \cdot 5H_2O} \times 100 = 57.69\% \text{ O}$$

Usually the calculation of the percent composition simply starts with the formula of the compound, as in the next example.

EXAMPLE 3-11 What is the percent H in $(NH_4)_3PO_4$?
First compute the mole weight, which gives 149.0 g/mol. Then use the masses computed in the course of computing the mole weight to compute the percent by mass of the desired element.

$$\% \text{ H} = \frac{12.0 \text{ g H}}{149.0 \text{ g } (NH_4)_3PO_4} \times 100 = 8.05\% \text{ H}$$

★ **9. Use the percent composition of a compound to determine its empirical formula.**

The percent composition of a compound gives the combining *masses* of the elements. The empirical formula gives the combining numbers of atoms or *moles* of atoms in the compound. Obtaining the empirical formula involves first determining how many moles of each element are present. Then reduce these numbers of moles to a ratio of integers.

EXAMPLE 3-12 A compound contains 27.3% C and 72.7% O. What is its empirical formula?
First find the amount in moles of each element.

$$27.3 \text{ g C} \times \frac{\text{mol C}}{12.0 \text{ g C}} = 2.28 \text{ mol C}$$

$$72.7 \text{ g O} \times \frac{\text{mol O}}{16.0 \text{ g O}} = 4.54 \text{ mol O}$$

This would give $C_{2.28}O_{4.54}$ as the formula, but we wish to have whole numbers as subscripts. One technique is to divide all mole numbers by the smallest so 2.28 mol C and 4.54 mol O become 1.00 mol C and 1.99 mol O. Thus we obtain a formula of $CO_{1.99}$ or CO_2.

EXAMPLE 3-13 A compound contains 54.5% C, 9.1% H and 36.4% O. What is its empirical formula?
First find the amount of each element in moles contained in 100.0 g of compound.

$$\left.\begin{aligned} 54.5 \text{ g C} \times \frac{\text{mol C}}{12.0 \text{ g}} &= 4.54 \text{ mol C} \\ 9.1 \text{ g H} \times \frac{\text{mol H}}{1.0 \text{ g}} &= 9.1 \text{ mol H} \\ 36.4 \text{ g O} \times \frac{\text{mol O}}{16.0 \text{ g}} &= 2.28 \text{ mol O} \end{aligned}\right\} \textit{then} \left\{\begin{aligned} \frac{4.54}{2.28} &= 1.99 \text{ mol C} \\ \frac{9.1}{2.28} &= 4.0 \text{ mol H} \\ \frac{2.28}{2.28} &= 1.00 \text{ mol O} \end{aligned}\right.$$

The empirical formula is C_2H_4O.

★ **10. Use the masses of CO_2 and H_2O produced from the complete combustion of a compound containing only C, H, and O to determine the percent composition of the compound.**

The combustion analysis of a compound containing only C, H, and O requires the chemist to weigh the compound, burn it in oxygen, and then weigh the two products of combustion: carbon dioxide and water. *All* of the carbon in the compound is in the carbon dioxide, and all of the compound's hydrogen is present in the water. The masses of these two elements now in the products (CO_2 and H_2O), but originally in the compound, are first computed. The mass of oxygen is then computed by subtraction, if necessary. We determine the percentage of oxygen by difference because the oxygen in the products is from two sources: the compound which was burned and the oxygen in which it was burned. This is not the case with the carbon or the hydrogen.

EXAMPLE 3-14 4.27 g of a C–H–O compound produces 10.78 g CO_2 and 1.89 g H_2O when burned in air. What is the compound's percent composition?

The masses of C and H are found by

$$\text{mass C} = 10.78 \text{ g } CO_2 \times \frac{\text{mol } CO_2}{44.01 \text{ g } CO_2} \times \frac{\text{mol C}}{\text{mol } CO_2} \times \frac{12.01 \text{ g C}}{\text{mol C}} = 2.942 \text{ g C}$$

$$\text{mass H} = 1.89 \text{ g } H_2O \times \frac{\text{mol } H_2O}{18.0 \text{ g } H_2O} \times \frac{2 \text{ mol H}}{\text{mol } H_2O} \times \frac{1.01 \text{ g H}}{\text{mol H}} = \underline{0.212 \text{ g H}}$$

$$3.154 \text{ g C \& H}$$

The mass of O is then found by difference

$$\text{mass O} = 4.27 \text{ g compound} - 3.154 \text{ g C \& H} = 1.12 \text{ g O}$$

and the percent composition is

$$\% \text{O} = \frac{1.12 \text{ g O}}{4.27 \text{ g cmpd}} \times 100 = 26.2\% \text{ O}$$

$$\% \text{H} = \frac{0.21 \text{ g H}}{4.27 \text{ g cmpd}} \times 100 = 4.96\% \text{ H}$$

$$\% \text{C} = \frac{2.94 \text{ g O}}{4.27 \text{ g cmpd}} \times 100 = 68.9\% \text{ C}$$

★ **11. Use precipitation analysis results to determine the percent of compounds in a mixture or of elements in a compound.**

A very powerful technique available to chemists is that of isolating one element or compound within a solid which settles to the bottom of a liquid solution. Such a solid is called a precipitate. Precipitates are separated from the solution, dried to a constant composition, and weighed. The following example gives a sample of the type of calculations required.

EXAMPLE 3-15 14.21 g of a silver-containing alloy is dissolved in nitric acid. Sodium chloride solution is added, and a silver chloride precipitate is produced. The solid is washed, dried, and weighed. Its mass is 15.32 g. Determine the percent of silver in the alloy.

All of the silver is present in the 15.32 g of AgCl. We first determine the mass of Ag.

$$15.32 \text{ g AgCl} \times \frac{\text{mol AgCl}}{143.323 \text{ g}} \times \frac{\text{mol Ag}}{\text{mol AgCl}} \times \frac{107.870 \text{ g Ag}}{\text{mol Ag}} = 11.53 \text{ g Ag}$$

$$\% \text{ Ag in alloy} = \frac{\text{mass Ag}}{\text{mass of alloy}} \times 100 = \frac{11.53 \text{ g Ag}}{14.21 \text{ g alloy}} \times 100 = 81.14\% \text{ Ag}$$

12. Apply precipitation analysis to determine atomic weights.

Dalton's most serious handicap in determining atomic weights was that he did not know the formulas of the compounds which he analyzed. But if we know the chemical formula, the determination of atomic weight is straightforward.

EXAMPLE 3-16 The sulfur present in a 11.78-g sample of M_2S is precipitated as 17.27 g $BaSO_4$. What is the atomic weight of element M?

We first compute the mass of S in the $BaSO_4$ (and thus also the mass of S in M_2S).

$$\text{g S} = 17.27 \text{ g } BaSO_4 \times \frac{\text{mol } BaSO_4}{233.40 \text{ g } BaSO_4} \times \frac{\text{mol S}}{\text{mol } BaSO_4} \times \frac{32.06 \text{ g S}}{\text{mol}} = 2.372 \text{ g S}$$

Hence in the 11.78 g of M_2S there are $11.78 - 2.372 = 9.41$ g M. Now we can determine the number of moles of S.

$$\text{mol S} = 2.372 \text{ g S} \times \frac{\text{mol S}}{32.06 \text{ g S}} = 0.07399 \text{ mol S}$$

and since 1 mol S unites with 2 mol M in M_2S, the 11.78 g of M_2S contains

$$0.07399 \text{ mol S} \times \frac{2 \text{ mol M}}{\text{mol S}} = 0.1480 \text{ mol M}$$

Now we compute the atomic weight of M.

$$\text{at wt M} = \frac{\text{mass M}}{\text{mol M}} = \frac{9.41 \text{ g M}}{0.1480 \text{ mol M}} = 63.5 \text{ g/mol M}$$

DRILL PROBLEMS

1. Fill in the blanks in the table below. The first line is done as an example. Use the periodic table when needed.

	Element	*Atomic weight*	*Mass of element, g*	*Amount, mol*	*No. of atoms*
	Cs	132.9	47.2	0.355	2.14×10^{23}
A.	H	____	____	0.412	____
B.	____	32.1	87.4	____	____
C.	O	____	____	1.59	____
D.	C	____	____	____	3.02×10^{23}
E.	____	35.5	____	0.0427	____
F.	____	14.0	2.14	____	____
G.	Mg	____	99.1	____	____

H.	____	31.0	____	____	3.01×10^{24}
I.	Br	____	____	6.12×10^{-5}	____
J.	K	____	____	____	8.69×10^{19}
K.	Be	____	____	5.02×10^{10}	____
L.	____	19.0	3.02×10^{-4}	____	____

3. Determine the mole weight of each compound below.
A. Hg_2Cl_2 B. NaCl C. $SnCl_4$ D. $Ca(HS)_2$ E. $NaHCO_3$
F. $Al(NO_3)_3$ G. $BaCl_2$ H. H_2O_2 I. HCN J. $C_2Cl_6S_2$
K. $(NH_4)_2CrO_4$ L. B_2H_6

3a. Fill in the blanks in the table below.

Molecular formula	*Mole weight*	*Mass of compound*	*Moles of compound*
A. $(NH_4)_2CrO_4$	____	174 g	____
B. Li_2SO_3	____	____ g	2.47
C. NaCl	____	8.21 oz	____
D. AgClO	____	____ g	0.0694
E. $FeCl_3$	____	0.124 lb	____
F. H_2O_2	____	5.00 lb	____
G. NaOH	____	____ g	1.47
H. $Mg(CN)_2$	____	____ g	0.00836
I. $Hg(NO_3)_2$	____	4.12 g	____
J. CuCl	____	____ g	7.97
K. $NaNO_3$	____	1.43 lb	____
L. $HBrO_4$	____	____ g	2.18

5. & 6. A. NaCl B. $Al_2(SO_4)_3$ C. $SrCl_2$ D. $CrHPO_4$ E. $Na_2S_2O_3$
F. CuCl G. $FePO_4$ H. Li_2SO_3 I. $KHSO_4$ J. $(NH_4)_2CrO_4$
K. $Ca(C_2H_3O_2)_2$ L. $Cu(HS)_2$ M. $MgCO_3$ N. $Cr(CN)_3$ O. $BaSO_4$
P. potassium permanganate Q. sodium acetate R. iron(III) chloride
S. strontium nitrate T. silver chlorate U. copper(I) oxide
V. mercury(I) nitrate W. iron(III) nitrite X. strontium bicarbonate
Y. zinc dihydrogen phosphate Z. potassium chromate AA. magnesium cyanide
BB. aluminum oxide CC. sodium hydroxide DD. calcium hypochlorite

5. Give the name or formula, as appropriate, of each compound.
A. H_2O B. H_2S C. CO_2 D. N_2O_3 E. P_2O_5 F. ICl_5
G. NCl_3 H. SCl_4 I. ClO_2 J. SO_3 K. nitrogen oxide
L. diphosphorus pentoxide M. ammonia N. hydrogen fluoride
O. silicon tetrafluoride P. xenon hexafluoride Q. phosphorus tribromide
R. silicon disulfide S. methane T. boron trichloride

7. A. How many C atoms are in 14.7 g $NaHCO_3$?
B. What is the mass of 1.42×10^{20} NH_3 molecules?
C. What is the mass of 64.2 mol $CsIO_3$?
D. How many O atoms are in 74.2 g $Al_2(SO_4)_3$?
E. How many molecules are in 163.7 g HCl?
F. How many atoms are in 82.3 g H_2O_2?
G. What is the mass of 7.42×10^{27} H_2SO_4 molecules?
H. What is the mass of 27.32 mol $(NH_4)_2Cr_2O_7$?
I. How many atoms are in 64.2 g NH_4MnO_4?
J. What mass of $BaCl_2$ contains 23.1×10^{19} ions?
K. How many O atoms are in 2.68 lb $NaClO_3$?
L. In $C_4H_{10}O$ how many moles of C are present with 18.4 mol H?
M. In NH_4CN how many moles of H are present with 0.125 mol C?
N. In $K_4Fe(CN)_6$ how many moles of C are present with 74.2 mol K?
O. In $Al_2(SO_4)_3$ how many moles of Al are present with 16.2 mol O?

8. & 9. Fill in the blanks in the table below. The first line is an example.

	Empirical formula	*"Empirical" weight*	*Elements and percent by weight*					
	NH_4Cl	53.5	N	66.4	H	7.5	Cl	26.2
A.	______	______	H	2.44	S	39.02	O	______
B.	NaOH	______	Na	______	O	______	H	______
C.	______	______	Mg	______	C	14.2	O	56.9
D.	$Al(NO_3)_3$	______	Al		N	______	O	______
E.	______	______	Li	6.5	Cl	______	O	60.2
F.	ZnC_2O_4	______	Zn	______	C	______	O	______
G.	______	______	K	39.6	Mn	27.9	O	______
H.	$Mg(CN)_2$	______	Mg	______	C	______	N	______
I.	______	______	Cu	51.4	C	______	O	38.9
J.	H_3PO_4	______	H	______	P	______	O	______
K.	______	______	Hg	______	Br	35.0	O	21.0

10. Each line below gives the mass of a carbon-hydrogen-oxygen compound which has burned completely in oxygen to give the specified masses of CO_2 and H_2O. Based on these data, determine the empirical formula of each compound.

	Mass of compound, g	*Mass of* CO_2*, g*	*Mass of water, g*
A.	1.320	1.489	0.914
B.	74.6	226.3	115.8
C.	8.14	11.19	9.16
D.	0.0152	0.0514	0.0105
E.	0.943	2.412	0.987
F.	11.7	22.4	13.7
G.	19.4	28.5	11.6
H.	7.32	11.84	5.81
I.	0.0255	0.0244	0.0100
J.	0.556	0.388	0.159
K.	146	222	45
L.	92.4	317.6	52.0

11. Fill in the blanks in the table below. The first line is done as an example.

	Sample mass	*Element being determined*	*Precipitate*		*Percent of element in sample*
			Formula	*Mass, g*	
	14.21	Ag	AgCl	15.32	82.14
A.	13.20	Ba	$BaSO_4$	15.14	______
B.	96.41	Mg	MgO	17.46	______
C.	9.915	Pb	$PbCrO_4$	11.321	______
D.	82.44	Ca	$Ca_3(PO_4)_2$	1.42	______
E.	19.00	Al	Al_2O_3	10.56	______
F.	14.32	Cr	Cr_2O_3	5.17	______
G.	0.847	Li	Li_3PO_4	0.201	______
H.	37.32	F	CaF_2	40.03	______
I.	1.755	S	$BaSO_4$	1.972	______
J.	1.650	C	$CaCO_3$	13.124	______

12. The mass and formula of a compound are given below, in the first two columns. The compound is dissolved in water and the anion of the compound reacts with another cation to form a precipitate of known identity. The formula and mass of the precipitate are given in the second two columns. Use these data to determine the atomic weight of the metallic element present in the original compound. (*Hint:* Recall Example 3-16.)

Original compound		Precipitate		Atomic weight of M
Formula	Mass, g	Formula	Mass, g	
A. MS	44.72	$BaSO_4$	114.99	____
B. MCl_3	13.27	AgCl	35.17	____
C. MCl_2	6.34	AgCl	21.00	____
D. MF	13.62	CaF_2	12.66	____
E. $M(SO_4)_2$	20.10	$PbSO_4$	36.70	____
F. $M_2(SO_4)_3$	59.87	$BaSO_4$	122.53	____
G. M_2CO_3	24.55	$CaCO_3$	17.76	____
H. $M_2(CrO_4)_3$	54.39	$PbCrO_4$	82.87	____

QUIZZES (20 minutes each)

Choose the best answer for each question or fill in the blank.

Quiz A

1. A compound contains 37% N and 63% O. Its empirical formula is (a) NO_2; (b) NO; (c) N_3O_2; (d) N_2O_3; (e) none of these.
2. The mole weight of Cu_2SO_4 (Cu = 63.5, S = 32.1, O = 16.0 g/mol) is (a) 63.5 + 32.1 + 16.0; (b) (2 X 63.5) + 32.1 + 16.0; (c) 63.5 + 32.1 + (16.0 X 4); (d) (2 X 63.5) + 32.1 + (4 X 16.0); (e) none of these.
3. What is the mass fraction of oxygen in $C_6H_{12}O_6$ (C = 12.0, H = 1.00, O = 16.0 g/mol)? (a) 16.0/(12.0 + 1.00 + 16.0); (b) 16.0/[12.0 + (2 X 1.00) + (6 X 16.0)]; (c) 16.0/[(6 X 12.0) + (12 X 1.00) + (6 X 16.0)]; (d) (6 X 16.0)/[12.0 + (2 X 1.00) + 16.0]; (e) none of these.
4. 34.1 is the mole weight of which compound (H = 1.0, S = 32.1, Cl = 35.5, P = 31.0, Si = 28.1 g/mol)? (a) HCl; (b) SiH_4; (c) H_2S; (d) PH_3; (e) none of these.
5. How many molecules are contained in 1.0 g H_2O (H = 1.0, O = 16.0 g/mol; $N = 6.023 \times 10^{23}$)? (a) (1.0/16.0)*N*; (b) (1.0/17.0)*N*; (c) (18.0/1.0)*N*; (d) (17.0/1.0)*N*; (e) none of these.
6. How many moles of atoms are contained in 15.0 g H_2SO_4 (H = 1.0, S =32.1, O = 16.0 g/mol)? (a) 15.0/98.1; (b) 7 X 15.0/98.1; (c) 15.0/49.1; (d) 7 X 15.0/49.1; (e) none of these.
7. An atom or group of atoms which has an excess or deficiency of electrons is called (a) an atom; (b) a molecule; (c) an ion; (d) a nucleus; (e) none of these.
8. The formula of iron(III) phosphate is (a) $Fe_2(PO_4)_3$; $CrHPO_4$; (c) $FePO_3$; (d) $FePO_4$; (e) none of these.
9. The name of $Sr(HCO_3)_2$ is (a) strontium oxalate; (b) strontium carbonate; (c) sodium bicarbonate; (d) strontium bicarbonate; (e) none of these.
10. The name of P_2O_5 is (a) potassium peroxide; (b) diphosphorus pentoxide; (c) phosphorus peroxide; (d) dipotassium pentoxide; (e) none of these.
11. The formula of iodine pentafluoride is ______________________.

Quiz B

1. A compound contains 46.7% N and 53.3% O. What is the empirical formula of the compound? (a) NO; (b) NO_2; (c) N_2O_3; (d) N_2O; (e) none of these.
2. 97 g/mole is the mole weight (H = 1.0, Br = 79.9, S = 32.1, O = 16.0, P = 31.0 g/mol) to *two significant digits* of (a) HBrO; (b) H_3PO_4; (c) H_2SO_4; (d) $H_2S_2O_2$ (e) none of these.
3. The mass fraction of carbon in Na_2C (Na = 23.0, C = 12.0 g/mol) is (a) 12.0/[23.0 + (12.0 X 2)]; (b) 12.0/23.0; (c) 12.0/[(23.0 X 2) + 12.0]; (d) 12.0/(23.0 + 12.0); (e) none of these.
4. The mole weight of $Mg_3(PO_4)_2$ (Mg = 24.3, P = 31.0, O = 16.0 g/mol) is (a) 24.3 + 31.0 + 16.0; (b) 24.3 + 31.0 + (16.0 X 6); (c) (24.3 X 3) + 31.0 + (16.0 X 4); (d) 24.3 + ([31.0 + (16.0 X 4)] X 2); (e) none of these.

5. How many atoms are contained in 95.0 g Fe_2O_3 (Fe = 55.8, O = 16.0 g/mol; $N = 6.023 \times 10^{23}$)? (a) $(2 \times 95.0)/71.8$; (b) $[(5 \times 95.0)/71.8]\,N$ (c) $(95.0/159.6)\,N$; (d) $[(5 \times 95.0)/159.6]N$; (e) none of these.
6. How many moles of formula units are contained in 45.1 g Al_2O_3 (Al = 27.0, O = 16.0 g/mol)? (a) 45.1/43.0; (b) 45.1/102.0; (c) $(5 \times 45.1)/43.0$; (d) $(5 \times 45.1)/102.0$; (e) none of these.
7. Benzene contains 7.7% and 92.3% C. Its mole weight is 78.0 g/mol. From this information and the atomic weights of H and C, one could determine by calculation (a) empirical formula, only; (b) molecular formula; (c) percent composition, only; (d) percent yield; (e) none of these.
8. The formula of mercury(I) cyanide is (a) $Hg(CN)_2$; (b) HgCN; (c) MgCN; (d) $Hg_2(CN)_2$; (e) none of these.
9. The name of $CrSO_3$ is (a) cerium sulfite; (b) chromium(II) sulfite; (c) chromium(III) sulfate; (d) chromium(II) sulfate; (e) none of these.
10. The formula of dinitrogen trioxide is ______________________________.
11. The name of SO_3 is ______________________________.

Quiz C

1. A compound contains 1.8% H, 42.0% O, and 56.0% S. What is the empirical formula of the compound (H = 1.0, O = 16.0, S = 32.1 g/mol)? (a) H_2SO_4; (b) H_2SO_3; (c) HSO; (d) $H_2S_2O_3$; (e) none of these.
2. 51.7 is the mole weight of which compound (Na = 23.0, K = 39.9, Mg = 24.3, Li = 6.9, Cl = 35.5, F = 19.0, S = 32.1, P = 31.0 g/mol)? (a) NaCl; (b) KF; (c) MgS; (d) Li_3P (e) none of these.
3. What is the mass fraction of Mg in $Mg(ClO_3)_2$ (Mg = 24.3, Cl = 35.5, O = 16.0 g/mol)? (a) 24.3/(24.3 + 35.5 + 16.0); (b) $24.3/[24.3 + 35.5 + (3 \times 16.0)]$; (c) $24.3/[24.3 + (2 \times 35.5) + (2 \times 16.0)]$; (d) $24.3/[24.3 + (2 \times 35.5) + 6 \times 16.0]$; (e) none of these.
4. The formula weight of $Al(ClO_4)_3$ (Al = 27.0, Cl = 35.5, O = 16.0 g/mol) is (a) $27.0 + [3 \times (35.5 + 16.0)]$; (b) $27.0 + (3 \times 35.5) + (12 \times 16.0)$; (c) 27.0 + 35.5 + 16.0; (d) $27.0 + [(35.5 + 16.0) \times 3]$; (e) none of these.
5. How many atoms of all kinds are contained in 42.1 g of CaC_2 (Ca = 40.1, C = 12.0 g/mol; $N = 6.023 \times 10^{23}$)? (a) $(42.1/52.1)(2)\,N$; (b) $(42.1/52.1)(2)\,N$; (c) $(42.1/64.1)(3)\,N$; (d) $(42.1/64.1)(2)\,N$; (e) none of these.
6. How many oxygen atoms are contained in 63.5 g of Cl_2O_7 (Cl = 35.5, O = 16.0 g/mol; $N = 6.023 \times 10^{23}$)? (a) $(63.5/183)\,N$; (b) $[(7 \times 63.5)/167]\,N$; (c) $[(7 \times 63.5)/183]\,N$; (d) $[(7 \times 63.5)/167]\,N$; (e) none of these.
7. Ethane is 20% H and 80% C. From this information and the atomic weights of C and H, one could *determine* by calculation (a) empirical formula, only; (b) molecular formula; (c) percent composition, only; (d) percent yield; (e) none of these.
8. The name of $FePO_4$ is (a) fermium phosphate; (b) iron(II) phosphite; (c) iron(III) phosphate; (d) iron(II) phosphate; (e) none of these.
9. The formula of magnesium chlorate is (a) $Mg(ClO_3)_2$; (b) $Mn(ClO_3)_2$; (c) $MnClO_2$; (d) $MgClO_4$; (e) none of these.
10. The name of Cl_2O_7 is ______________________________.
11. The formula of silicon tetrafluoride is ______________________________.

Quiz D

1. What is the mass fraction of carbon in CH_3CN (C = 12.0, H = 1.00, N = 14.0 g/mol)? (a) $(2 \times 12.0)/[(2 \times 12.0) + (3 \times 1.00) + 14.0]$; (b) 12.0/(12.0 + 1.0 + 14.0); (c) $12.0/[12.0 + (3 \times 1.00) + 14.0]$; (d) $12.0/[12.0 + (3 \times 1.00) + 12.0 + 14.0]$; (e) none of these.
2. The mole weight of $Na_2S_2O_3$ (Na = 23.0, S = 32.1, O = 16.0 g/mol) is (a) $[2 \times (23.0 + 32.1 + 16.0)] + 16.0$; (b) 32.1 + 23.0 + 16.0; (c) $2 \times (23.0 + 32.1 + 16.0)$; (d) $(2 \times 23.0) + 32.1 + (3 \times 16.0)$; (e) none of these.

3. A compound contains 46.7% O, 51.8% Cl, and 1.5% H. This compound's empirical formula is (O = 16.0, Cl = 35.5, H = 1.0 g/mol) (a) HClO; (b) $HClO_2$; (c) $HClO_3$; (d) $HClO_4$; (e) none of these.
4. 102.5 is the mole weight of (Na = 23.0, Cl = 35.5, O = 16.0 g/mol) (a) NaCl; (b) NaClO; (c) $NaClO_2$; (d) $NaClO_3$; (e) none of these.
5. How many hydrogen atoms are contained in 14.8 g of C_3H_8 (C = 12.0, H = 1.0 g/mol; N = 6.023 X 10^{23})? (a) (14.8/13)(3) N; (b) (14.8/13)(8) N; (c) (14.8/44)(3) N; (d) (14.8/44)(8) N; (e) none of these.
6. 8.75 g $AlCl_3$ contains how many moles of *ions* (Al = 27.0, Cl = 35.5 g/mol)? (a) 8.75/(27.0 + 35.5); (b) 8.75/[(3 X 27.0) + 35.5]; (c) 8.75 X (27.0 + 35.5); (d) 8.75/[27.0 + (3 X 35.5)]; (e) none of these.
7. A group of atoms, bonded together, with no excess or deficiency of charge is called (a) an atom; (b) a molecule; (c) an ion; (d) a nucleus; (e) none of these.
8. The name of Hg_2SO_3 is (a) mercury(I) sulfite; (b) mercury(II) sulfite; (c) mercury(I) sulfate; (d) mercury(II) sulfate; (e) none of these.
9. The formula of copper(II) nitrite is (a) $CuNO_2$; (b) $Cu(NO_3)_2$; (c) $Co(NO_2)_2$ (d) $Cu(NO_2)_2$; (e) none of these.
10. The formula of diphosphorus trioxide is ______________.
11. The name of SCl_4 is ______________.

SAMPLE TEST (30 minutes)

1. A synthetic food company is attempting to make synthetic alcohol. Before the product is tested on laboratory animals, it is chemically analyzed. In determining the compound's empirical formula, a chemist burns 9.72 g of the compound in oxygen. The products are 16.88 g CO_2 and 9.21 g H_2O. Please determine the empirical formula of the compound, assuming that it contains only the elements C, H, and O.
2. Iron is important in the body primarily because it is present in red blood cells and acts to carry oxygen to the various organs. Without oxygen these organs will die. There are about 2.6 X 10^{13} red blood cells in the blood of an adult human, and the blood contains a total of 2.9 g of iron. How many iron atoms are there in each red blood cell?
3. Supply the name or the formula of each compound as appropriate.

a. ammonium cyanide	b. $Mg_3(PO_4)_2$	c. iron(II) acetate
d. PbS	e. mercury(II) chloride	f. $KBrO_2$

Stoichiometry II: Chemical Reactions

REVIEW OF OBJECTIVES

1. List the observable events which accompany a chemical reaction: appearance of a gas or a precipitate, change of color, production of heat, light, or sound.

When a physical change occurs, the resulting substance has the same identity as it did before the change. Examples are the boiling of water to produce steam and the melting of wax. In addition, physical changes can be reversed by a very simple procedure. For example, liquid water is produced when steam condenses.

A chemical reaction produces a new substance with a different set of properties. For example, heating limestone produces lime and carbon dioxide.

$$CaCO_3(s) \rightarrow CaO(s) + CO_2(g)$$

Reversing a chemical reaction is often a more complex procedure. To produce $CaCO_3$ from CaO, water is added to produce slaked lime.

$$CaO(s) + H_2O(l) \rightarrow Ca(OH)_2(s)$$

The slaked lime then reacts over a long period with carbon dioxide in the air.

$$Ca(OH)_2(s) + CO_2(g) \rightarrow CaCO_3(s) + H_2O(l)$$

Another distinction between physical changes and chemical reactions is that the equation for a physical change involves only one substance on each side of the equation. For example,

Melting ice:	$H_2O(s) \rightarrow H_2O(l)$
Boiling alcohol:	$C_2H_5OH(l) \rightarrow C_2H_5OH(g)$
Making diamonds:	C(graphite) → C(diamond)

A chemical change, on the other hand, involves *at least* three substances in the equation. For example,

Heating limestone:	$CaCO_3(s) \rightarrow CaO(s) + CO_2(g)$
Burning magnesium:	$2\ Mg(s) + O_2(g) \rightarrow 2\ MgO(s)$
Burning methane:	$CH_4(g) + 2\ O_2(g) \rightarrow CO_2(g) + 2\ H_2O(l)$

The new substance produced in a chemical reaction may be a gas or the product may be less soluble than the reactants and precipitate. Also the product color can differ from that of the reactants. The energy involved in destroying the reactants and forming the products often appears as heat, making reaction mixture warmer or cooler. Sometimes the energy is produced as light or sound.

2. Write word equations and symbolic equations for chemical reactions.

Chemical equations are summaries of experimental results. "A solution of lead(II) nitrate is added to a solution of potassium chromate. A bright yellow precipitate forms, which is later identified as lead(II) chromate. Evaporation of the remaining solution produces crystals of potassium nitrate." The word equation is

lead(II) nitrate solution + potassium chromate solution = solid lead(II) chromate + potassium nitrate solution.

Even more compact is the symbolic equation

$$Pb(NO_3)_2(aq) + K_2CrO_4(aq) \rightarrow PbCrO_4(s) + KNO_3(aq)$$

★ **2a. Know the names, formulas, and charges of the ions in Table 4-1 and be able to write the formulas and names of compounds formed from these ions and those in *Tables 3-1 and 3-3 in the text.***

TABLE 4-1
Names, formulas, and charges of some common ions

Monatomic ions				Polyatomic ions			
As^{3+}	arsenic	Mn^{2+}	manganese(II)	BrO^-	hypobromite	IO^-	hypoiodite
Cd^{2+}	cadmium	Tl^+	thallium(I) *or* thallous	BrO_3^-	bromate	IO_3^-	iodate
Co^{2+}	cobalt(II)	Tl^{3+}	thallium(III) *or* thallic	BrO_4^-	perbromate	IO_4^-	periodate
Au^+	gold(I) *or* aurous	Sn^{2+}	tin(II) *or* stannous	$Cr_2O_7^{2-}$	dichromate	MnO_4^{2-}	manganate
Au^{3+}	gold(III) *or* auric	Sn^{4+}	tin(IV) *or* stannic	CNO^-	cyanate	MnO_4^-	permanganate
H^+	hydrogen			CNS^-	thiocyanate	O_2^{2-}	peroxide
Pb^{2+}	lead(II) *or* plumbous			FO^-	hypofluorite	HS^-	bisulfide
Pb^{4+}	lead(IV) *or* plumbic			$C_2O_4^{2-}$	oxalate	HSO_3^-	bisulfite

This is a 3 X 5 card project. Learning the names, formulas, and charges of ions will enable you to write names and formulas of compounds. It also will help you in predicting the products of some chemical reactions (see objective 4–4).

★ **2b. Know the names and formulas of the common acids.**

The common acids you should know are

H_2SO_4	sulfuric acid	H_3PO_4	phosphoric acid
HCl	hydrochloric acid	$HC_2H_3O_2$	acetic acid
HNO_3	nitric acid	H_2SO_3	sulfurous acid

Notice that acid names are formed differently from those of salts. HNO_3 is not "hydrogen nitrate" but nitric acid. There are definite rules for forming the name of each acid, starting with the anion's name. All one does is remove the anion's suffix (the last three letters of the name in each case) and replace it with the acid's suffix as illustrated in Table 4-2. In the case of binary acids (those composed of hydrogen and only one other element) the prefix hydro- also is used.

TABLE 4-2
Nomenclature of acids

		Examples	
Anion suffix	Acid suffix	Anion name and formula	Acid name and formula
-ite	-ous	nitrite, NO_2^-	nitrous acid, HNO_2
-ate	-ic	oxalate, $C_2O_4^{2-}$	oxalic acid, $H_2C_2O_4$
-ide	(hydro-) -ic	iodide, I^-	hydroiodic acid, HI

★ 3. Balance chemical equations by inspection.

An unbalanced equation tells us the identities of the reactants and the products, but does not tell us how much of each is consumed or produced. We need the balanced chemical equation. Balancing by inspection means that you look at the equation and multiply each species by a whole number placed before the chemical formula of that species so that the equation is balanced. The equation is balanced when there are the same number of atoms of each type on both sides of the equation. The whole numbers inserted into the equation are called stoichiometric coefficients. *Do not change the chemical formulas of the reactants or products!*

EXAMPLE 4-1 Balance the equation

$$H_2(g) + O_2(g) \rightarrow H_2O(l)$$

The formula of water shows that hydrogen and oxygen unite in a ratio of 2:1, but the left-hand side of the equation shows one mole of H_2 uniting with one mole of oxygen. The first step in balancing is to multiply $H_2(g)$ by 2—that is, assign $H_2(g)$ the stoichiometric coefficient of 2. This produces

$$2\,H_2(g) + O_2(g) \rightarrow H_2O(l)$$

Counting atoms, we see 4 H and 2 O on the left-hand side and 2 H and 1 O on the right-hand side. So we multiply $H_2O(l)$ by 2—that is, 2 becomes the stoichiometric coefficient of $H_2O(l)$.

$$2\,H_2(g) + O_2(g) \rightarrow 2\,H_2O(l)$$

Alternatively, we could have noticed that in

$$H_2(g) + O_2(g) \rightarrow H_2O(l)$$

there are 2 O atoms on the left-hand side and only 1 O atom on the right-hand side. Thus 2 would be the stoichiometric coefficient of water, producing

$$H_2(g) + O_2(g) \rightarrow 2\,H_2O(l)$$

Then, we would have observed that there are 2 H atoms on the left-hand side and 4 H atoms on the right-hand side which would lead to 2 for the stoichiometric coefficient of $H_2(g)$, as before.

We also could have "balanced" this equation by changing H_2O to H_2O_2. This is incorrect because we changed the formula of the product.

EXAMPLE 4-2 Balance the equation

$$Pb(NO_3)_2(aq) + K_2CrO_4(aq) \rightarrow PbCrO_4(s) + KNO_3(aq)$$

This equation is easy to balance if we recognize that only ionic compounds are involved and total the number of ions on each side. There are the same number of Pb^{2+} and $CrO_4{}^{2-}$ ions on each side, but there are 2 K^+ and 2 $NO_3{}^-$ ions on the left-hand side and only one of each on the right-hand side. To make the number of K^+ and $NO_3{}^-$ ions the same on each side we merely need to assign 2 as the stoichiometric coefficient of $KNO_3(aq)$.

EXAMPLE 4-3 Balance $NH_3(g) + O_2(g) \rightarrow NO(g) + H_2O(l)$

We first notice that N and H are combined in a ratio of 1:3 on the left-hand side and thus they must be produced in that ratio on the right-hand side. A complication arises because of H being present in H_2O where there are 2 H atoms in the compound. This requires an even number of H on the left side of the equation. Thus, the coefficient of NH_3 is 2.

$$2\ NH_3(g) + O_2(g) \rightarrow NO(g) + H_2O(l)$$

We now balance N and H atoms with stoichiometric coefficients for NO(g) and $H_2O(l)$.

$$2\ NH_3(g) + O_2(g) \rightarrow 2\ NO(g) + 3\ H_2O(l)$$

There are now 2 O atoms on the left and 5 O atoms on the right-hand side. We could use 5/2 as the coefficient of $O_2(g)$,

$$2\ NH_3(g) + \frac{5}{2}\ O_2(g) \rightarrow 2\ NO(g) + 3\ H_2O(l)$$

but it is preferable to use whole numbers (integers) as stoichiometric coefficients, so we multiply all coefficients by 2.

$$4\ NH_3(g) + 5\ O_2(g) \rightarrow 4\ NO(g) + 6\ H_2O(l)$$

There are only two rules to be followed when balancing by inspection.

(1) *Never* change the formulas of the compounds.
(2) Make sure there are the same number of atoms of each element on both sides of the equation.

Your ability to balance equations depends on how much you practice.

★ **3a. Balance "ionic equations" by inspection.**

The technique of balancing is the same, but there is one additional rule to follow.

(3) Make sure that the total charge on the left-hand side equals the total charge on the right-hand side.

For example,

$$Al + Cu^{2+} \rightarrow Al^{3+} + Cu$$

has the same number (one) of each atom on each side, but the charge on the left is 2+ while that on the right is 3+. In the balanced equation, the atomic balance is maintained by using the same coefficient for both forms of aluminum (Al and Al^{3+}) and likewise for both forms of copper (Cu^{2+} and Cu).

$$2\ Al + 3\ Cu^{2+} \rightarrow 2\ Al^{3+} + 3\ Cu$$

Note that copper's coefficient (3) and aluminum's charge (+3) are the same.

★ **4. Predict the products of some simple chemical reactions: combination, decomposition, displacement, and metathesis reactions.**

One of the major accomplishments of chemistry is the ability to predict the products of chemical reactions. The type and number of products produced depend on the class of the reaction. There are four simple classes of reactions: combination, decomposition, displacement, and metathesis or double displacement. *Combination:* In a combination reaction, two substances unite to produce a single compound. The two substances may be two elements

$$C(s) + O_2(g) \rightarrow CO_2(g)$$
$$Cu(s) + S(s) \rightarrow CuS(s)$$

or two compounds

$$SO_3(g) + H_2O(l) \rightarrow H_2SO_4(l)$$
$$CaO(s) + H_2O(l) \rightarrow Ca(OH)_2(s)$$
$$Li_2O(s) + CO_2(g) \rightarrow Li_2CO_3(s)$$

or an element and a compound

$2\ FeCl_2(s) + Cl_2(g) \rightarrow 2\ FeCl_3(s)$
$2\ Cu_2O(s) + O_2(g) \rightarrow 4\ CuO(s)$

Notice that the products are all composed of ions which you have already learned (Cu^{2+}, S^{2-}, Ca^{2+}, OH^-, Fe^{3+}, Cl^-, O^{2-}) or are compounds which should be familiar by now (CO_2, NH_3, H_2SO_4).

Decomposition. In decomposition reactions, a single compound produces two or more substances. These substances may be compounds

$CaCO_3(g) \xrightarrow{\Delta} CaO(s) + CO_2(g)$

$NH_4HCO_3(s) \xrightarrow{\Delta} NH_3(g) + H_2O(l) + CO_2(g)$

Or they may be elements

$2\ HgO \xrightarrow{\Delta} 2\ Hg(l) + O_2(g)$

$MgCl_2(l) \xrightarrow[\Delta]{\sim} Mg(l) + Cl_2(g)$

or they may be elements and compounds.

$2\ KClO_3(s) \xrightarrow{\Delta} 2\ KCl(s) + 3\ O_2(g)$

$NaNO_3(s) \xrightarrow{\Delta} 2\ NaNO_2(s) + O_2(g)$

Again, notice that the compound products either are familiar (NH_3, CO_2, and H_2O) or are composed of ions which you have learned (Ca^{2+}, O^{2-}, K^+, Cl^-, Na^+, NO_2^-).

Notice also that heat (Δ) or electricity ($\sim$) is normally required to decompose compounds. Few compounds decompose spontaneously.

Displacement. In a displacement reaction one element reacts with a compound to take the place of one of the elements in that compound. Some examples are

$Zn(s) + CuSO_4(aq) \rightarrow ZnSO_4(aq) + Cu(s)$
$2\ Na(s) + 2\ H_2O(l) \rightarrow 2\ NaOH(aq) + H_2(g)$
$Mg(s) + 2\ HCl(aq) \rightarrow MgCl_2(aq) + H_2(g)$
$3\ H_2(g) + Fe_2O_3(s) \rightarrow 3\ H_2O(l) + 2\ Fe(s)$
$Cl_2(g) + 2\ KI(aq) \rightarrow 2\ KCl(aq) + I_2(s)$

In each equation above, the "displacing element" is written first and the element which is displaced is written last.

Metathesis. Metathesis or double displacement reactions occur when two ionic compounds "change partners" or swap ions.

$BaCl_2(aq) + K_2SO_4(aq) \rightarrow BaSO_4(s) + 2\ KCl(aq)$
$NaCN(aq) + HCl(aq) \rightarrow HCN(g) + NaCl(aq)$
$2\ KOH(aq) + H_2SO_4(aq) \rightarrow 2H_2O(l) + K_2SO_4(aq)$
$MgCO_3(aq) + 2\ HCl(aq) \rightarrow H_2O(l) + CO_2(g) + MgCl_2(aq)$
$Na_2SO_3(aq) + 2\ HI(aq) \rightarrow H_2O(l) + SO_2(g) + 2\ NaI(aq)$

In the first three equations it is clear that the cations have exchanged anions. For example, Ba^{2+} is associated with Cl^- in the reactants of the first equation and with SO_4^{2-} in the products. This fact is not so evident in the last two equations until we recognize that the first two products in each case are the result of decomposition reactions.

$$\text{"}H_2CO_3(aq)\text{"} \rightarrow H_2O(l) + CO_2(g)$$
$$H_2SO_3(aq) \rightarrow H_2O(l) + SO_2(g)$$

"$H_2CO_3(aq)$" is enclosed in quotes because the evidence for the existence of this compound is rather poor. The *driving forces* which cause metathesis reactions to occur are discussed in objective 4-13b.

★ **5. Predict the combustion products of carbon-hydrogen and carbon-hydrogen-oxygen compounds and write a balanced equation.**

Combustion means that the compound burns in oxygen, $O_2(g)$. The only products formed when C—H—O or C—H compounds burn completely in oxygen are $CO_2(g)$ and $H_2O(l)$. The resulting equation is balanced by inspection.

EXAMPLE 4-4 Write the balanced equation for the combustion of $C_3H_7OH(l)$.
First write the unbalanced equation.

$$C_3H_7OH(l) + O_2(g) \rightarrow CO_2(g) + H_2O(l)$$

Then balance by inspection.

$$2\ C_3H_7OH(l) + 9\ O_2(g) \rightarrow 6\ CO_2(g) + 8\ H_2O(l)$$

★ **6. Derive from balanced chemical equations conversion factors for use in stoichiometric calculations.**

It is important to notice that a given chemical equation can be interpreted either in terms of atoms, ions, molecules, and formula units or in terms of moles of these entities. For example, there are two ways of interpreting the equation

$$2\ Na(s) + 2\ H_2O(l) \rightarrow 2\ NaOH(aq) + H_2(g)$$

The first is that 2 sodium atoms react with 2 water molecules to produce 2 formula units of sodium hydroxide (or 2 sodium ions and 2 hydroxide ions) and 1 hydrogen molecule. The second is that 2 moles of Na(s) react with 2 moles of $H_2O(l)$ to produce 2 moles of NaOH(aq) and 1 mole of $H_2(g)$. Consequently, if we are given the number of moles of a reactant or a product and the balanced chemical equation, we can determine the amounts of all other species involved.

EXAMPLE 4-5 3.4 mol $H_2(g)$ is produced by the reaction

$$Mg(s) + 2\ H_2O(l) \rightarrow Mg(OH)_2(aq) + H_2(g)$$

Find the amounts of Mg(s) and $H_2O(l)$ which reacted and the amount of $Mg(OH)_2(ag)$ produced.
The balanced equation informs us that 1 mol $Mg(OH)_2(aq)$ is produced for every mol $H_2(g)$ produced. Thus,

$$3.4\ \text{mol}\ H_2(g) \times \frac{1\ \text{mol}\ Mg(OH)_2(aq)}{1\ \text{mol}\ H_2(g)} = 3.4\ \text{mol}\ Mg(OH)_2(aq)$$

Notice carefully that 1 mol $H_2(g)$ is not *equal* to 1 mol $Mg(OH)_2(aq)$. They are *equivalent* to each other in that they are produced together. In like fashion, we determine the amounts of reactants consumed.

$$3.4\ \text{mol}\ H_2(g) \times \frac{1\ \text{mol}\ Mg(s)}{1\ \text{mol}\ H_2(g)} = 3.4\ \text{mol}\ Mg(s)$$

$$3.4\ \text{mol}\ H_2(g) \times \frac{2\ \text{mol}\ H_2O(l)}{1\ \text{mol}\ H_2(g)} = 6.8\ \text{mol}\ H_2O(l)$$

Notice in each case that the stoichiometric coefficient for each species is used in the conversion factor.

It is essential that you thoroughly master this. All of the material in this chapter either leads up to or depends on this objective.

★ **7. Solve problems based on balanced chemical equations with quantities given or sought in a variety of units.**

This objective combines the previous objective with the techniques of using conversion factors which you mastered in studying Chapters 1 and 3. The conversion factor method, outlined in objectives 1–9 and 1–11, is the technique which you should use. One or more of the conversion factors will be obtained from a balanced chemical equation.

EXAMPLE 4-6 Hydrogen gas has a density, under normal conditions, of 0.0824 g/L. What volume of hydrogen gas in liters is needed to produce 2.50 lb of iron from $Fe_2O_3(s)$? Water is the other product of the reaction.

$$Fe_2O_3(s) + H_2(g) \rightarrow Fe(s) + H_2O(l)$$

Review objective 4–2 if you have trouble with this step. The equation then is balanced (objective 4–3)

$$Fe_2O_3(s) + 3\,H_2(g) \rightarrow 2\,Fe(s) + 3\,H_2O(l)$$

and we can now apply the conversion factor method.

(1) ? L $H_2(g)$ (2) 2.50 lb Fe(s)

(3) $2.50 \text{ lb Fe} \times \frac{454 \text{ g Fe}}{\text{lb}} \times \frac{1 \text{ mol Fe}}{55.8 \text{ g}} \times \frac{3 \text{ mol } H_2(g)}{2 \text{ mol Fe(s)}} \times \frac{2.02 \text{ g } H_2(g)}{\text{mol } H_2(g)} \times \frac{\text{L } H_2(g)}{0.0824 \text{ g } H_2(g)} =$

748 L $H_2(g)$

★ **8 & 9. Learn the terms associated with solutions including molar concentration unts, compute concentrations and solutions volumes, and solve dilution problems.**

The first part of this objective requires that you define in your own words and commit to memory the following terms: solute, solvent, solution, concentration, aqueous solution, and molarity. You also should be familiar with a common symbol for molarity, brackets around the chemical formula of the solute. Thus, [NaCl] means the molar concentration of sodium chloride. The definition of molarity (molarity = moles of solute/liters of solution) suggests three types of problems.

EXAMPLE 4-7 (Determine molarity given moles of solute and liters of solution.) 205 ml of solution contains 4.1 g NaCl. What is the concentration of the solution, in moles per liter?

We divide the *amount* of solute (in moles) by the *volume* of solution (in liters).

$$\text{Molarity} = \frac{4.1 \text{ g NaCl} \times (\text{mol NaCl}/58.5 \text{ g NaCl})}{205 \text{ ml solution} \times \text{L}/1000 \text{ ml}}$$

$$= \frac{0.070 \text{ mol NaCl}}{0.205 \text{ L Soln}} = 0.34\,M$$

EXAMPLE 4-8 (Determine moles of solute given solution volume and molarity.) 327 ml of 1.52 *M* KNO_3 contains what amount of solute in moles? The concentration is a conversion factor.

(1) ? mol KNO_3 (2) 327 ml solution

(3) $327 \text{ ml soln} \times \frac{\text{L}}{1000 \text{ ml}} \times \frac{1.52 \text{ mol } KNO_3}{\text{L soln}} = 0.497 \text{ mol } KNO_3$

EXAMPLE 4-9 (Determine volume of solution given solution concentration and moles of solute.) What volume in ml of 0.628 *M* $AgNO_3$ solution contains 55.1 g $AgNO_3$?

(1) ? ml solution (2) 55.1 g $AgNO_3$

$$(3)\ 55.1\ \text{g AgNO}_3 \times \frac{\text{mol AgNO}_3}{169.9\ \text{g AgNO}_3} \times \frac{\text{L soln}}{0.628\ \text{mol AgNO}_3} \times \frac{1000\ \text{ml}}{\text{L}} = 516\ \text{ml solution}$$

The last type of problem is the dilution of solutions. We first determine the amount of solute in the original solution by the technique of Example 4-8 and then compute the molarity using the new volume and the method of Example 4-7.

EXAMPLE 4-10 54.0 ml of 0.623 *M* KNO_3 solution is mixed with 114 ml of 0.357 *M* $NaNO_3$ solution. What is the final concentration of sodium ions, $[Na^+]$?

$$114\ \text{ml soln} \times \frac{\text{L}}{1000\ \text{ml}} \times \frac{0.357\ \text{mol NaNO}_3}{\text{L soln}} \times \frac{\text{mol Na}^+}{\text{mol NaNO}_3} = 0.0407\ \text{mol Na}^+$$

Total solution volume = 54.0 ml + 114 ml = 168 ml.

$$[\text{Na}^+] = \frac{\text{mol Na}^+}{\text{L solution}} = \frac{0.0407\ \text{mol Na}^+}{168\ \text{ml} \times (\text{L}/1000\ \text{ml})} = 0.242\ M$$

Sometimes advantage is taken of an alternate definition of molarity,

$$\text{molarity} = \frac{\text{millimoles of solute}}{\text{milliliters of solution}}$$

because most solution volumes are expressed in milliliters rather than in liters. The solution of Example 4-11 becomes

$$114\ \text{ml soln} \times \frac{0.357\ \text{mmol NaNO}_3}{\text{ml soln}} \times \frac{\text{mmol Na}^+}{\text{mmol NaNO}_3} = 40.7\ \text{mmol Na}^+$$

$[Na^+] = 40.7\ \text{mmol}\ Na^+/168\ \text{ml} = 0.242\ M$

Notice that if $[NO_3^-]$ had been requested in Example 4-11 we would have determined the amount of NO_3^- present in each solution, added the two amounts, and divided by the solution volume, as follows.

$$\text{mmol NO}_3^- = 114\ \text{ml} \times \frac{0.357\ \text{mmol NaNO}_3}{\text{ml soln}} \times \frac{\text{mmol No}_3^-}{\text{mmol NaNO}_3}$$

$$+\ 54.0\ \text{ml} \times \frac{0.628\ \text{mmol KNO}_3}{\text{ml soln}} \times \frac{\text{mmol NO}_3^-}{\text{mmol KNO}_3} = 40.7 + 33.9\ \text{mmol NO}_3^-$$

$$= 74.6\ \text{mmol NO}_3^-$$

$$[\text{NO}_3^-] = \frac{74.6\ \text{mmol NO}_3^-}{168\ \text{ml soln}} = 0.444\ M$$

This complication only arises when the same component is present in the two solutions being mixed.

★ **10. Solve stoichiometry problems when either the reactants or the products are species in solution and concentration and volume data are given.**

This objective is a combination of objectives 4–7 and 4–9, and therefore only requires using the techniques you have already mastered to solve somewhat more involved problems.

★ **11. Be familiar with the technique of titration—know how the experiment is performed, what data are collected, why an indicator is used, and how to use the data.**

Titrations involve reactions in solution which go to completion (see objective 4–13b). A known volume of solution is measured out and it is titrated with the titrant, a solution of known concentration. Titrant is added until the endpoint of the titration is reached. The titrant is added in such a way that its total volume is known precisely. Often an indicator is used to produce a color change when the endpoint is reached.

The data are (a) the chemical reaction which occurs, called the titration reaction; (b) the volumes of the solution to be titrated and of the titrant; and (c) the concentration of the titrant. One determines the concentration of the titrated solution or the amount of solute present. Consequently, this objective is an application of objective 4–10.

★ **12. Determine the reactants in excess, the limiting reagent, and the amounts of products produced in a chemical reaction.**

Limiting reagent problems, as they are commonly called, are based upon the fact that reactants combine in definite amounts to produce products. Thus, if there is an excess of one reactant that excess will undergo no chemical change. The reactant which determines the final amount of product is the limiting reagent.

Chemical reactions are different in this regard from cookie recipes. Using 12 oz of chocolate chips to make ten dozen cookies when the recipe requires 16 oz only causes the cookies to have a scant number of chocolate chips. We still get cookies.

Chemical reactions are more similar to automobile production. If a manufacturer has only 5000 spark plugs, only 1250 four-cylinder cars can be produced. Likewise 5000 tires limits the manufacturer to 1000 cars. It makes no difference that the manufacturer has 9000 engines and 4000 car bodies on hand.

Limiting reagent problems are most easily solved by determining the amount of product which can be produced from each reactant. The limiting reagent is that one which produces the least amount of product.

$$5000 \text{ spark plugs} \times \frac{1 \text{ car}}{4 \text{ spark plugs}} = 1250 \text{ cars}$$

$$5000 \text{ tires} \times \frac{1 \text{ car}}{5 \text{ tires}} = 1000 \text{ cars}$$

$$4000 \text{ bodies} \times \frac{1 \text{ car}}{1 \text{ body}} = 4000 \text{ cars}$$

$$9000 \text{ engines} \times \frac{1 \text{ car}}{1 \text{ engine}} = 9000 \text{ cars}$$

Hence, only 1000 cars can be produced. Notice that it is *not* the smallest number of parts (4000 bodies) which is limiting but the number of parts which produce the smallest number of cars. Example 4-11 applies this concept to a chemical reaction.

EXAMPLE 4-11 1.50 g of Mg reacts with 342 ml of 0.350 *M* HCl solution to produce what mass in grams of $MgCl_2$? What mass of the excess reactant is left over?

The reaction is a displacement.

$$Mg(s) + 2\,HCl(aq) \rightarrow MgCl_2\,(aq) + H_2\,(g)$$

$$1.50 \text{ g Mg} \times \frac{\text{mol Mg}}{24.3 \text{ g Mg}} \times \frac{\text{mol } MgCl_2}{\text{mol Mg}} = 0.0617 \text{ mol } MgCl_2$$

$$342 \text{ ml soln} \times \frac{\text{L}}{1000 \text{ ml}} \times \frac{0.350 \text{ mol HCl}}{\text{L soln}} \times \frac{\text{mol } MgCl_2}{2 \text{ mol HCl}} = 0.0599 \text{ mol } MgCl_2$$

Thus, the HCl is the limiting reagent and only 0.0599 mol $MgCl_2$ is produced. We convert to grams for a final answer.

$$0.0599 \text{ mol MgCl}_2 \times \frac{95.3 \text{ g MgCl}_2}{\text{mol MgCl}_2} = 5.71 \text{ g MgCl}_2$$

To determine the amount of Mg (the excess reactant) left over, we first compute the amount which reacted.

$$342 \text{ ml soln} \times \frac{\text{L}}{1000 \text{ ml}} \times \frac{0.350 \text{ mol HCl}}{\text{L soln}} \times \frac{\text{mol Mg}}{2 \text{ mol HCl}} \times \frac{24.3 \text{ g Mg}}{\text{mol Mg}} = 1.45 \text{ g Mg}$$

and subtract the amount used from the 1.50 g provided.

$$\text{Amount in excess} = 1.50 \text{ g} - 1.45 \text{ g} = 0.05 \text{ g Mg}$$

★ **13. Compute the amount of product produced or reactant consumed by two or more simultaneous reactions.**

Simultaneous reactions either consume an identical reactant or produce an identical product. One is asked to determine the amount of reactant consumed or the amount of product produced. The techniques of solving stoichiometric problems (objective 4-7) are used for each reaction in turn and the results are added.

EXAMPLE 4-12 What amount of $AgNO_3$ is consumed when 406 ml of a solution which is both 0.100 *M* in KCl and 0.250 *M* in Na_2CrO_4 reacts completely?

The equations are both metatheses.

$$KCl(aq) + AgNO_3(aq) \rightarrow AgCl(s) + KNO_3(aq)$$
$$Na_2CrO_4(aq) + 2\ AgNO_3(aq) \rightarrow Ag_2CrO_4(s) + 2\ NaNO_3(aq)$$

The amount of $AgNO_3$ required to react with KCl is

$$406 \text{ ml} \times \frac{\text{L}}{1000 \text{ ml}} \times \frac{0.100 \text{ mol KCl}}{\text{L soln}} \times \frac{\text{mol AgNO}_3}{\text{mol KCl}} = 0.0406 \text{ mol AgNO}_2$$

The amount of $AgNO_3$ required to react with Na_2CrO_4 is

$$406 \text{ ml} \times \frac{\text{L}}{1000 \text{ ml}} \times \frac{0.250 \text{ mol Na}_2\text{CrO}_4}{\text{L soln}} \times \frac{2 \text{ mol AgNO}_3}{\text{mol Na}_2\text{CrO}_4} = 0.203 \text{ mol AgNO}_3$$

Total $AgNO_3$ required = 0.0406 mol + 0.203 mol = 0.244 mol.

★ **13a. Compute the amount of product produced by two or more consecutive reactions.**

Consecutive reactions produce products from reactants in a series of steps rather than in a single reaction. Thus a stoichiometric problem will not contain just one conversion factor obtained from a chemical reaction, but several—one from each step.

An example of a series of reactions is the Solvay process, used to produce sodium carbonate and consisting of six steps.

$$CaCO_3(s) \xrightarrow{\Delta} CaO(s) + CO_2(g) \quad [1]$$
$$CaO(s) + H_2O(l) \longrightarrow Ca(OH)_2(aq) \quad [2]$$
$$Ca(OH)_2(aq) + 2\ NH_4Cl(aq) \longrightarrow 2\ NH_3(g) + 2\ H_2O(l) + CaCl_2(aq) \quad [3]$$
$$NH_3(g) + CO_2(g) + H_2O(l) \longrightarrow NH_4HCO_3(aq) \quad [4]$$
$$NaCl(aq) + NH_4HCO_3(aq) \longrightarrow NaHCO_3(s) + NH_4Cl(aq) \quad [5]$$
$$2\ NaHCO_3(s) \xrightarrow{\Delta} Na_2CO_3(s) + H_2O(g) + CO_2(g) \quad [6]$$

EXAMPLE 4-13 What mass of sodium carbonate in grams can be produced from 64.0 g of $CaCO_3(s)$ using the Solvay process?

$$64.0\text{ g } CaCO_3 \times \frac{1\text{ mol } CaCO_3}{100.0\text{ g}} \times \frac{1\text{ mol } CO_2}{1\text{ mol } CaCO_3} \times \frac{1\text{ mol } NH_4HCO_3}{1\text{ mol } CO_2} \times \frac{1\text{ mol } NaHCO_3}{1\text{ mol } NH_4HCO_3}$$
$$\times \frac{1\text{ mol } Na_2CO_3}{2\text{ mol } NaHCO_3} \times \frac{106.0\text{ g } Na_2CO_3}{1\text{ mol } Na_2CO_3} = 33.9\text{ g } Na_2CO_3$$

The principal difficulty in solving this type of problem is in tracing a given part of the product (in this instance C was used) through the series of reactions. Often this tracing is more easily done if one works backward from the products.

13b. Distinguish between reactions which go to completion and reversible reactions and know that reactions go to completion when one of the products is a gas, a precipitate, or a covalent compound.

The techniques which we have learned in this chapter can be applied successfully only to reactions which go to completion. Reversible reactions require techniques which are described in later chapters. A reaction goes to completion because of the formation of

(a) A precipitate as in $AgNO_3(aq) + NaCl(aq) \rightarrow AgCl(s) + NaNO_3(aq)$.
(b) A gas which escapes from the reaction mixture as in $NaCN(aq) + HCl(aq) \rightarrow HCN(g) + NaCl(aq)$.
(c) A covalent compound–$H_2O(l)$ in this case–from ionic compounds as in $NaOH(aq) + HCl(aq) \rightarrow H_2O(l) + NaCl(aq)$.

You are not expected at this point to know which compounds are precipitates. You should be able to recognize covalent compounds as being composed of two nonmetals. Additionally you should have a short list of common gases firmly in mind, such as

Gaseous compounds: CO_2, SO_2, H_2S, HCN, NH_3, CH_4
Gaseous elements: H_2, N_2, O_2, F_2, Cl_2

These three kinds of substances (gas, precipitate, covalent compound) are often referred to as driving forces since they drive the reaction to completion.

★ **14. Determine the overall reaction for a process consisting of several steps.**

The easiest way to do this is by combining the chemical reactions as if they were algebraic equations, eliminating those species which appear on both sides. For the Solvay process, equations [1] through [6] in objective 4–13a, we proceed as follows.

[6] + 2 × [5] = [7]

$\cancel{2\,NaHCO_3} + 2\,NaCl + 2\,NH_4HCO_3 \rightarrow Na_2CO_3 + H_2O + CO_2 + \cancel{2\,NaHCO_3} + 2\,NH_4Cl$

$2\,NaCl + 2\,NH_4HCO_3 \rightarrow Na_2CO_3 + H_2O + CO_2 + 2\,NH_4Cl$ [7]

[7] + 2 × [4] = [8]

$2\,NaCl + \cancel{2\,NH_4HCO_3} + 2\,NH_3 + \cancel{2}\,CO_2 + \cancel{2}\,H_2O \rightarrow$
$Na_2CO_3 + \cancel{H_2O} + \cancel{CO_2} + 2\,NH_4Cl + \cancel{2\,NH_4HCO_3}$

$2\,NaCl + 2\,NH_3 + CO_2 + H_2O \rightarrow Na_2CO_3 + 2\,NH_4Cl$ [8]

[8] + [3] = [9]

$2\,NaCl + \cancel{2\,NH_3} + CO_2 + \cancel{H_2O} + Ca(OH)_2 + \cancel{2\,NH_4Cl} \rightarrow$
$Na_2CO_3 + \cancel{2\,NH_4Cl} + \cancel{2\,NH_3} + \cancel{2}\,H_2O + CaCl_2$

$2\,NaCl + CO_2 + Ca(OH)_2 \rightarrow Na_2CO_3 + H_2O + CaCl_2$ [9]

[1] + [2] = 10

$CaCO_3 + \cancel{CaO} + H_2O \rightarrow \cancel{CaO} + CO_2 + Ca(OH)_2$ [10]

[9] + [10] = overall reaction = [11]

$$2\,NaCl + \cancel{CO_2} + \cancel{Ca(OH)_2} + CaCO_3 + \cancel{H_2O} \rightarrow Na_2CO_3 + \cancel{H_2O} + CaCl_2 + \cancel{CO_2} + \cancel{Ca(OH)_2}$$

$$2\,NaCl + CaCO_3 \rightarrow Na_2CO_3 + CaCl_2 \qquad [11]$$

This procedure requires that you manipulate the equations so as many species cancel as possible. It takes practice.

★ **15. Define the terms actual yield, theoretical yield, and percent yield and compute these quantities for a given reaction.**

The theoretical yield of a reaction is the computed amount of product based on the amount of reactants used. Often this is a limiting reagent problem. The actual yield is the amount of product actually produced (often called the experimental yield). The percent yield is derived from their ratio.

$$\text{percent yield} = \frac{\text{actual yield}}{\text{theoretical yield}} \times 100$$

Often problems involving consecutive series of reactions (objective 4–13a) will be complicated by including the percent yield of each reaction.

DRILL PROBLEMS

2. Write a balanced equation for each of the following word equations.

A. aluminum + magnesium oxide → magnesium + aluminum oxide
B. aluminum chloride + ammonium hydroxide → aluminum hydroxide + ammonium chloride
C. silver nitrate + sodium phosphate → silver phosphate + sodium nitrate
D. chlorine + potassium iodide → potassium chloride + iodine
E. ferric sulfate + calcium hydroxide → ferric hydroxide + calcium sulfate
F. barium nitrate + ammonium carbonate → barium carbonate + ammonium nitrate
G. potassium hydroxide + sulfuric acid → potassium sulfate + water
H. ferrous hydroxide + hydrochloric acid → ferrous chloride + water
I. cupric sulfate + hydrogen sulfide → cupric sulfide + sulfuric acid
J. silver nitrate + potassium chromate → silver chromate + potassium nitrate

2a. (1) Name the following compounds.

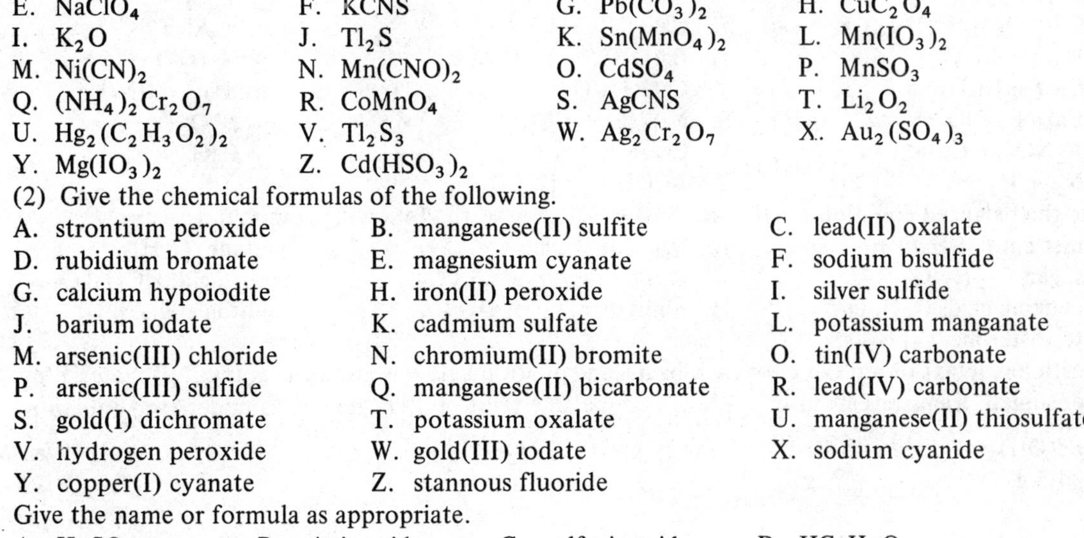

A. $K_2Cr_2O_7$ B. $AgBrO_3$ C. $Mg(HSO_3)_2$ D. KIO
E. $NaClO_4$ F. KCNS G. $Pb(CO_3)_2$ H. CuC_2O_4
I. K_2O J. Tl_2S K. $Sn(MnO_4)_2$ L. $Mn(IO_3)_2$
M. $Ni(CN)_2$ N. $Mn(CNO)_2$ O. $CdSO_4$ P. $MnSO_3$
Q. $(NH_4)_2Cr_2O_7$ R. $CoMnO_4$ S. AgCNS T. Li_2O_2
U. $Hg_2(C_2H_3O_2)_2$ V. Tl_2S_3 W. $Ag_2Cr_2O_7$ X. $Au_2(SO_4)_3$
Y. $Mg(IO_3)_2$ Z. $Cd(HSO_3)_2$

(2) Give the chemical formulas of the following.

A. strontium peroxide B. manganese(II) sulfite C. lead(II) oxalate
D. rubidium bromate E. magnesium cyanate F. sodium bisulfide
G. calcium hypoiodite H. iron(II) peroxide I. silver sulfide
J. barium iodate K. cadmium sulfate L. potassium manganate
M. arsenic(III) chloride N. chromium(II) bromite O. tin(IV) carbonate
P. arsenic(III) sulfide Q. manganese(II) bicarbonate R. lead(IV) carbonate
S. gold(I) dichromate T. potassium oxalate U. manganese(II) thiosulfate
V. hydrogen peroxide W. gold(III) iodate X. sodium cyanide
Y. copper(I) cyanate Z. stannous fluoride

2b. Give the name or formula as appropriate.

A. H_2SO_4 B. nitric acid C. sulfuric acid D. $HC_2H_3O_2$
E. acetic acid F. HCl G. H_3PO_4 H. H_2SO_3

Uncommon acids

I. HIO_3 J. hydrofluoric acid K. nitrous acid
L. HFO M. $H_2C_2O_4$ N. periodic acid
O. H_2MnO_4 P. hypobromous acid Q. hydrocyanic acid
R. HIO S. carbonic acid T. permanganic acid
U. perchloric acid V. $HClO_2$

3. Balance the following equations by writing in the proper stoichiometric coefficients.

A. $P + O_2 \rightarrow P_2O_5$
B. $Na + O_2 \rightarrow Na_2O_2$
C. $Al + HCl \rightarrow AlCl_3 + H_2$
D. $Ca + H_2O \rightarrow Ca(OH)_2 + H_2$
E. $FeCl_3 + Ca(OH)_2 \rightarrow Fe(OH)_3 + CaCl_2$
F. $Al + N_2 \rightarrow AlN$
G. $HCl + Fe_2O_3 \rightarrow H_2O + FeCl_3$
H. $Cl_2 + H_2O \rightarrow HCl + HClO_3$
I. $CaSO_3 + H_2SO_4 \rightarrow CaSO_4 + H_2O + SO_2$
J. $Al(OH)_3 + HCl \rightarrow AlCl_3 + H_2O$
K. $NaCl + H_2SO_4 \rightarrow Na_2SO_4 + HCl$
L. $Pb(NO_3)_2 \rightarrow PbO + NO + O_2$
M. $HNO_2 \rightarrow HNO_3 + NO + H_2O$
N. $Ca(OH)_2 + H_3PO_4 \rightarrow Ca_3(PO_4)_2 + H_2O$
O. $SiF_4 + H_2O \rightarrow HF + SiO_2$

3a. (1) Balance the following ionic equations by writing in the proper stoichiometric coefficients.

A. $Cu + Fe^{3+} \rightarrow Cu^{2+} + Fe^{2+}$
B. $Zn + H^+ \rightarrow Zn^{2+} + H_2$
C. $H^+ + S^{2-} \rightarrow H_2S(g)$
D. $Pb^{2+} + Hg^{2+} \rightarrow Pb^{4+} + Hg_2{}^{2+}$
E. $Fe^{3+} + Sn^{2+} \rightarrow Fe + Sn^{4+}$
F. $H^+ + N^{3-} \rightarrow NH_3(g)$
G. $CN^- + Fe^{2+} \rightarrow Fe(CN)_6{}^{4-}$
H. $Bi^{3+} + S^{2-} \rightarrow Bi_2S_3(s)$

(2) Write the following as ionic equations by eliminating the ion or ions which are unchanged from one side to the other and then balance the result. All substances are in aqueous solution unless otherwise indicated.

Example: $H_3PO_4(aq) + Ca(OH)_2(aq) \rightarrow Ca_3(PO_4)_2(aq) + H_2O(l)$
becomes $H^+(aq) + OH^-(aq) \rightarrow H_2O(l)$

A. $HCl + Pb(NO_3)_2 \rightarrow PbCl_2(s) + HNO_3$
B. $Ca(OH)_2 + Na_3PO_4 \rightarrow Ca_3(PO_4)_2(s) + NaOH$
C. $BaCl_2 + K_2CO_3 \rightarrow BaCO_3(s) + KCl$
D. $KCl + H_3PO_4 \rightarrow K_3PO_4 + HCl(g)$
E. $KOH + H_2SO_4 \rightarrow K_2SO_4 + H_2O(l)$
F. $CaS + HCl \rightarrow CaCl_2 + H_2S(g)$
G. $AgNO_3 + K_2CrO_4 \rightarrow KNO_3 + Ag_2CrO_4(s)$
H. $BaCl_2 + Na_2SO_4 \rightarrow NaCl + BaSO_4(s)$
I. $CdSO_4 + H_2S \rightarrow CdS(s) + H_2SO_4$
J. $FeCl_3 + NaOH \rightarrow Fe(OH)_3(s) + NaCl$

4. Classify each of the following reactions as combination, decomposition, displacement or metathesis; predict the products; and balance the resulting equation.

A. $Al + Br_2 \rightarrow$
B. $Al + Fe_2O_3 \rightarrow$
C. $AlCl_3 + KOH \rightarrow$
D. $BaCl_2 + Na_2CO_3 \rightarrow$
E. $BaCl_2 + AgNO_3 \rightarrow$
F. $BaO + SO_3 \rightarrow$
G. $Ba(OH)_2 +$ "H_2CO_3" ($CO_2(aq)$) $\rightarrow$
H. $Br_2 + H_2 \rightarrow$
I. $Cd(NO_3)_2 + (NH_4)_2S \rightarrow$
J. $Ca + H_2O \rightarrow$
K. $HCl + Al \rightarrow$
L. $H_2O + Li_2O \rightarrow$
M. $Ba(OH)_2 + H_3PO_4 \rightarrow$
N. $BaO + H_2O \rightarrow$
O. $CaO + HCl \rightarrow$
P. $CaO + CO_2 \rightarrow$
Q. $Ca(OH)_2 + HNO_3 \rightarrow$
R. $CaO + HNO_3 \rightarrow$
S. $NH_3(g) + HCl(g) \rightarrow$
T. $SO_2 + O_2 \rightarrow$
U. $AgNO_3 + Cu \rightarrow$
V. $Cl_2 + FeCl_2 \rightarrow$
W. $Cl_2 + KI \rightarrow$
X. $N_2 + H_2 \rightarrow$
Y. $Al(OH)_3 + H_2SO_4 \rightarrow$

5. Write the balanced equation for the combustion of each of the following compounds.

A. methanol, CH_3OH
B. benzene, C_6H_6
C. pentane, C_5H_{12}
D. sugar, $C_{12}H_{22}O_{11}$
E. carbon monoxide, CO
F. acetic acid, $HC_2H_3O_2$
G. benzoic acid, $C_7H_6O_2$
H. ninhydrin, $C_9H_6O_4$
I. naphthalene, $C_{10}H_8$
J. testosterone, $C_{19}H_{28}O_2$

6. & 7. Beneath a reactant or a product of each balanced equation below is given the amount of material produced or consumed. Densities are given in the column at the right. Fill in the blanks under each equation.

	$Fe(OH)_3(s)$	+ $3\ HCl(aq)$	→ $FeCl_3(s)$	+ $3\ H_2O$	*Density*
A.	34.5 g	____ g	____ g	____ cm^3	H_2O 1.00 g/cm^3
B.	____ g		21.2 cm^3	____ g	$FeCl_3$ 2.90 g/cm^3
C.	____ g	18.2 g	____ g		

	$C_5H_{12}(g)$ +	$8\ O_2(g)$ →	$5\ CO_2(g)$ +	$6\ H_2O(l)$	
D.	14.3 g	___ g	___ g	___ cm^3	H_2O 1.00 g/cm^3
E.	___ g		1.26 L	___ g	CO_2 1.96 g/L
F.	___ g	1.46 g	___ L	___ cm^3	

	$N_2(g)$ +	$3\ H_2(g)$ →	$2\ NH_3(g)$	
G.	1.46 g	___ g	___ g	NH_3 0.625 g/L
H.	___ g	___ g	21.4 L	
I.	___ g	19.4 g	___ L	

	$6\ HCl(g)$ +	$2\ HNO_3(aq)$ →	$4\ H_2O(g)$ +	$2\ NO(g)$ +	$3\ Cl_2(g)$	
J.	18.4 g	___ g	___ g	___ L		NO 1.34 g/L
K.	14.2 L	___ g		___ g	___ g	HCl 1.63 g/L
L.	___ L		___ g	___ L	19.4 g	

	$3\ Cu(s)$ +	$8\ HNO_3(aq)$ →	$3\ Cu(NO_3)_2(aq)$ +	$2\ NO(g)$ +	$4\ H_2O(l)$	
M.	3.14 g	___ g		___ g		NO 1.34 g/L
N.	___ g		___ g	2.16 L		Cu 8.96 g/cm^3
O.	19.4 cm^3	___ g	___ g	___ L		
P.	___ cm^3		21.2 g	___ L	___ g	

8. & 9. (1) Each line in the table below represents a different solution. Fill in the blanks based on the numbers given.

Solute			*Solution*	
Identity	*Mass, g*	*Moles*	*Volume, ml*	*Concentration, M*
A. $HC_2H_3O_2$	___	___	250.0	3.414
B. HCl	___	1.270	400.0	___
C. $Pb(NO_3)_2$	___	0.221	___	1.104
D. $BaCl_2$	___	___	275.0	0.888
E. NaCl	14.3	___	___	1.462
F. KNO_3	49.7	___	174.0	___
G. $KHCO_3$	___	___	200.0	1.064
H. KBr	13.75	___	350.0	___
I. HNO_3	___	12.4	___	6.00
J. CsCl	___	0.200	___	1.207
K. H_2SO_4	___	___	400.0	13.026
L. H_3PO_4	21.9	___	300.0	___

(2) In each line in the table below, two solutions (or solvent and a solution) are mixed to produce a new solution. Fill in the blanks based on the numbers given.

Solution A			*Solution B*			*Final Solution*		
Solute	*M*	*Volume, ml*	*Solute*	*M*	*Volume, ml*	*Solute*	*M*	*Volume, ml*
A. KNO_3	0.250	120	water		450	KNO_3	___	___
B. HCl	0.250	___	water		___	HCl	0.100	600
C. $MgSO_4$	1.74	87.5	water		___	$MgSO_4$	1.00	___
D. NaCl	1.40	120	water		500	NaCl	___	___
E. $MgSO_4$	2.40	___	water		___	Mg^+	0.250	300
F. Na_2SO_4	3.00	140	water		___	$SO_4{}^{2-}$	0.50	___
G. K_2SO_4	0.350	120	water		600	K^+	___	___
H. $Al(NO_3)_3$	0.750	___	water		___	$NO_3{}^-$	0.250	400
I. KNO_3	0.642	100	NaCl	0.342	200	Na^+	___	___
J. Na_2SO_4	0.578	50.0	KCl	0.618	___	Na_2SO_4	0.214	___
K. $NaNO_3$	0.745	100	NaCl	0.312	200	Na^+	___	___
L. $MgSO_4$	0.134	___	Na_2SO_4	0.817	___	$SO_4{}^{2-}$	0.400	500
M. KCl	___	___	HCl	1.00	300	Cl^-	1.45	600
N. $NaNO_3$	1.50	200	$Mg(NO_3)_2$	2.00	300	$NO_3{}^-$	___	___

10. Beneath a reactant or a product in each equation below is given either the mass of the species or the volume and concentration of the species in solution. Fill in the blanks using the data provided. To simplify the calculations, assume that any water produced does not dilute the final solution.

	$3\ AgNO_3(aq)$ +	$Na_3PO_4(aq)$ →	$Ag_3PO_4(s)$ +	$3\ NaNO_3(aq)$
A.	25.0 ml, 1.20 *M*		____ g	100 ml, ____ *M*
B.		____ ml, 100 *M*	13.2 g	200 ml, ____ *M*
C.	____ ml, 2.00 *M*		____ g	150 ml, 1.75 *M*
D.		84.0 ml, ____ *M*	6.25 g	____ ml, 1.40 *M*

	$Mg(CN)_2(s)$ +	$H_2SO_4(aq)$ →	$2\ HCN(g)$ +	$MgSO_4(aq)$
E.	13.4 g		____ g	____ ml, 1.00 *M*
F.	____ g	____ ml, 6.00 *M*	9.47 g	
G.	____ g	172 ml, 3.50 *M*	____ g	172 ml, ____ *M*
H.	____ g		____ g	200 ml, 1.75 *M*

	$Al_2O_3(s)$ +	$3\ H_2SO_4(aq)$ →	$Al_2(SO_4)_3(aq)$ +	$3\ H_2O(l)$
I.	2.31g	____ ml, 6.00 *M*		____ g
J.	____ g		174 ml, 3.12 *M*	____ g
K.		196 ml, 1.00 *M*	196 ml, ____ *M*	____ g
L.	____ g	____ ml, 1.00 *M*		7.42 g

	$2\ KOH(aq)$ +	$CO_2(g)$ →	$K_2CO_3(aq)$ +	H_2O
M.	274 ml, ____ *M*	____ g	274 ml, ____ *M*	17.4 g
N.	194 ml, 1.00 *M*	____ g	____ ml, 0.50 *M*	____ g
O.	142 ml, ____ *M*	1.34 g		____ g
P.		____ g	86.5 ml, 1.00 *M*	____ g

	$2\ KOH(aq)$ +	$H_2SO_3(aq)$ →	$K_2SO_3(aq)$ +	$2\ H_2O(l)$
Q.	182 ml, 1.00 *M*	50.0 ml, ____ *M*	____ ml, 0.750 *M*	____ g
R.	____ , 1.32 *M*		143 ml, 1.00 *M*	____ g
S.		____ ml, 4.50 *M*	____ ml, 3.21 *M*	14.3 g

11. Determine the concentration of the substance being titrated in each reaction which follows.

A. $HCl(aq) + NaOH(aq) \rightarrow NaCl(aq) + H_2O(l)$
25.0 ml 18.7 ml
Titrant: 0.100 *M* NaOH [HCl] = ____ *M*

B. $HNO_3(aq) + KOH(aq) \rightarrow KNO_3(aq) + H_2O(l)$
20.00 ml 26.42 ml
Titrant: 0.125 *M* KOH(aq) $[HNO_3]$ = ____ *M*

C. $HCl(aq) + KOH(aq) \rightarrow KCl(aq) + H_2O(l)$
17.42 ml 20.00 ml
Titrant: 1.43 *M* HCl(aq) [KOH] = ____ *M*

D. $HNO_3(aq) + NaOH(aq) \rightarrow NaNO_3(aq) + H_2O(l)$
19.74 ml 25.00 ml
Titrant: 1.50 *M* $HNO_3(aq)$ [NaOH] = ____ *M*

E. $H_2SO_4(aq) + 2\ KOH(aq) \rightarrow K_2SO_4(aq) + 2\ H_2O(l)$
20.00 ml 20.41 ml
Titrant: 0.100 *M* KOH(aq) $[H_2SO_4]$ = ____ *M*

F. $2\ HNO_3(aq) + CaO(s) \rightarrow Ca(NO_3)_2(aq) + H_2O(l)$
20.13 ml 1.75 g
$[HNO_3]$ = ____ *M*

G. $2\ HCl(aq) + Mg(OH)_2(aq) \rightarrow MgCl_2(aq) + 2\ H_2O(l)$
19.40 ml 25.00 ml
Titrant: 0.100 *M* HCl(aq) $[Mg(OH)_2]$ = ____ *M*

H. $CaCO_3(s) + 2\ HCl(aq) \rightarrow CaCl_2(aq) + H_2O(l) + CO_2(g)$
19.41 of 1.00 *M* HCl titrates 5.00 g of solid containing $CaCO_3(s)$. $CaCO_3$ in solid = ____ %

I. $AgNO_3(aq) + NaCl(aq) \rightarrow AgCl(s) + NaNO_3(aq)$
17.42 ml 25.00 ml

Titrant: 0.100 M $AgNO_3(aq)$ $[NaCl]$ = ____ M

J. $2\,AgNO_3(aq) + K_2CrO_4(aq) \rightarrow Ag_2CrO_4(s) + 2\,KNO_3(aq)$
50.00 ml 19.21 ml
Titrant: 0.500 M $K_2CrO_4(aq)$ $[AgNO_3]$ = ____ M

K. $Sr(NO_3)_2(aq) + Na_2SO_4(aq) \rightarrow 2\,NaNO_3(aq) + SrSO_4(s)$
25.00 ml 27.20 ml
Titrant: 0.100 M $Sr(NO_3)_2(aq)$ $[Na_2SO_4]$ = ____ M

L. $Al_2O_3(s) + 6\,HNO_3(aq) \rightarrow 2\,Al(NO_3)_3(aq) + 6\,H_2O(l)$
24.31 ml of 0.100 M $HNO_3(aq)$ titrates 0.100 g Al_2O_3-containing solid. Al_2O_3 in solid = ____ %

M. $Na_2CO_3(s) + 2\,HCl(aq) \rightarrow 2\,NaCl(aq) + H_2O(l) + CO_2(g)$
13.41 ml of 0.25 M HCl titrates 4.00 g Na_2CO_3-containing solid. Na_2CO_3 in solid = ____ %

N. $Mg(CN)_2(s) + H_2SO_4(aq) \rightarrow MgSO_4(aq) + 2\,HCN(g)$
17.21 ml of 0.500 M H_2SO_4 titrates 1.05 g $Mg(CN)_2$-containing solid
$Mg(CN)_2$ in solid = ____ %

O. $KCNS(aq) + AgNO_3(aq) \rightarrow AgCNS(s) + KNO_3(aq)$
20.00 ml 14.23 ml
Titrant: 0.200 M $AgNO_3(aq)$ $[KCNS]$ = ____ M

12. Below each equation is given the mass of each reactant. Determine the mass in grams of the underlined product and the mass of each excess reactant which is left over.

A. $3\,AgNO_3(aq) + Na_3PO_4(aq) \rightarrow \underline{Ag_3PO_4(s)} + 3\,NaNO_3(aq)$
102 g 25.4 g

B. $Ba(OH)_2(aq) + H_2SO_4(aq) \rightarrow BaSO_4(aq) + \underline{2\,H_2O(l)}$
105 g 83.1 g

C. $4\,C(s) + BaSO_4(s) \rightarrow \underline{4\,CO(g)} + BaS(s)$
12.4 g 13.2 g

D. $Zn(s) + 2\,HCl(aq) \rightarrow ZnCl_2(aq) + \underline{H_2(g)}$
7.15 g 14.2 g

E. $Mg(s) + S(s) \rightarrow \underline{MgS(s)}$
21.3 g 19.4 g

F. $Cu_2O + 2\,HCl(s) \rightarrow \underline{2\,CuCl(s)} + H_2O(l)$
49.7 g 32.1 g

G. $4\,NaOH(aq) + SiO_2(s) \rightarrow Na_4SiO_4(s) + \underline{2\,H_2O(l)}$
146 g 84.3 g

H. $2\,Al(OH)_3(s) + 3\,H_2SO_4(aq) \rightarrow Al_2(SO_4)_3(aq) + \underline{6\,H_2O(l)}$
242 g 127 g

I. $SO_3(l) + 2\,HNO_3(aq) \rightarrow \underline{H_2SO_4(aq)} + N_2O_5(g)$
47.2 g 195 g

J. $6\,HCl(aq) + Fe_2O_3(s) \rightarrow \underline{2\,FeCl_3(aq)} + 3\,H_2O(l)$
143 g 204 g

K. $2\,HNO_3(aq) + 3\,H_2S(g) \rightarrow \underline{4\,H_2O(l)} + 2\,NO(g) + 3\,S(s)$
123 g 164 g

L. $Na_2TeO_3(s) + 4\,NaI(s) + 6\,HCl(aq) \rightarrow Te(s) + 2\,I_2(s) + 3\,H_2O(l) + \underline{6\,NaCl(s)}$
174 g 157.1 g 63.2 g

M. $4\,Zn(s) + H_3AsO_4(aq) + 8\,HCl(aq) \rightarrow \underline{4\,ZnCl_2(aq)} + AsH_3(g) + 4\,H_2O(l)$
105 g 194 g 128 g

N. $2\,KNO_3(aq) + 4\,H_2SO_4(aq) + 3\,Hg(l) \rightarrow \underline{K_2SO_4(aq)} + 3\,HgSO_4(aq) + 4\,H_2O(l) + 2\,NO(g)$
48.7 g 102 g 193 g

O. $3\,K_2Cr_2O_7 + 2\,C_2H_3OCl(aq) + 12\,H_2SO_4(aq) \rightarrow 6\,CrSO_4(aq) + 4\,CO_2(g) + \underline{Cl_2(g)} + 15\,H_2O(l)$
247 g 92.1 g 374 g

13. Answer each question based on the reactions which precede it.

$AgNO_3(aq) + NaCl(aq) \rightarrow AgCl(s) + NaNO_3(aq)$
$Pb(NO_3)_2(aq) + 2\,NaCl(aq) \rightarrow PbCl_2(s) + 2\,NaNO_3(aq)$

A. 14.5 g of a $AgNO_3$–$Pb(NO_3)_2$ mixture which is 74.0% $AgNO_3$ consumes how many grams of NaCl? how many ml of 0.500 M $NaCl(aq)$?

$CaCO_3(s) + 2\,HCl(aq) \rightarrow CaCl_2(aq) + H_2O(l) + CO_2(g)$
$NaHCO_3(s) + HCl(aq) \rightarrow NaCl(aq) + H_2O(l) + CO_2(g)$

B. 17.4 g of a $CaCO_3$–$NaHCO_3$ mixture which is 45.0% $CaCO_3$ produces what mass of $CO_2(g)$? consumes how many ml of 0.100 *M* HCl?

$2\,KOH(s) + CO_2(g) \rightarrow K_2CO_3(s) + H_2O(l)$
$2\,LiOH(s) + CO_2(g) \rightarrow Li_2CO_3(s) + H_2O(l)$

C. 74.2 g of a KOH–LiOH mixture which is 17.2% KOH consumes what mass of $CO_2(g)$? produces what total mass of solid?

$H_2SO_4(aq) + 2\,KOH(aq) \rightarrow K_2SO_4(aq) + 2\,H_2O(l)$
$HCl(aq) + KOH(aq) \rightarrow KCl(aq) + H_2O(l)$

D. 347 ml of a solution with $[H_2SO_4] = 0.640\,M$ and $[HCl] = 0.935\,M$ consumes what volume of 0.623 *M* KOH? produces what mass of $H_2O(l)$?

$Mg(s) + 2\,HCl(aq) \rightarrow MgCl_2(aq) + H_2(g)$
$2\,Fe(s) + 6\,HCl(aq) \rightarrow 2\,FeCl_3(aq) + 3\,H_2(g)$

E. 9.52 g of a Mg–Fe mixture containing 17.4% Mg produces what mass of $H_2(g)$? consumes what volume of 0.200 *M* HCl(aq)?

$ZnO(s) + H_2SO_4(aq) \rightarrow ZnSO_4(aq) + H_2O(l)$
$Al_2O_3(s) + 3\,H_2SO_4(aq) \rightarrow Al_2(SO_4)_3(aq) + 3\,H_2O(l)$

F. 84.6 g of a ZnO–Al_2O_3 mixture containing 43.6% ZnO produces what mass of $H_2O(l)$? consumes what volume of 3.47 *M* H_2SO_4?

$3\,AgNO_3(aq) + Na_3PO_4(aq) \rightarrow 3\,NaNO_3(aq) + Ag_3PO_4(s)$
$2\,AgNO_3(aq) + Na_2CrO_4(aq) \rightarrow 2\,NaNO_3(aq) + Ag_2CrO_4(s)$

G. 17.3 g of a Na_3PO_4–Na_2CrO_4 mixture containing 26.1% Na_2CrO_4 produces what mass of $NaNO_3(aq)$? what total mass of solid?

13a. Answer each question based on the reactions which precede it.

$2\,CuS(s) + 3O_2(g) \rightarrow 2\,CuO(s) + 2\,SO_2(g)$
$2\,SO_2(g) + O_2(g) \rightarrow 2\,SO_3(g)$
$SO_3(g) + H_2O(l) \rightarrow H_2SO_4(aq)$

A. 19.4 g of CuS(s) produces what mass of $H_2SO_4(aq)$?
B. 27.5 g of H_2SO_4 requires what mass of $O_2(g)$?

$2\,NaCl(s) + H_2SO_4(aq) \rightarrow Na_2SO_4(aq) + 2\,HCl(g)$
$6\,HCl(aq) + 2\,Fe(s) \rightarrow 2\,FeCl_3(aq) + 3\,H_2(g)$
$CuO(s) + H_2(g) \rightarrow Cu(s) + H_2O(l)$

C. 83.1 g of Cu(s) requires what mass of NaCl(s)?
D. 34.2 g of $H_2O(l)$ requires what volume of 12.5 *M* $H_2SO_4(aq)$?
E. 28.2 g of NaCl produces what mass of Cu(s)?

$N_2(g) + 3\,H_2(g) \rightarrow 2\,NH_3(g)$
$4\,NH_3(g) + 5\,O_2(g) \rightarrow 4\,NO(g) + 6\,H_2O(l)$
$2\,NO(g) + O_2(g) \rightarrow 2\,NO_2(g)$
$3\,NO_2(g) + H_2O(l) \rightarrow 2\,HNO_3(aq) + NO(g)$

F. 85.1 g N_2 produces what mass of $HNO_3(aq)$? Do not recycle by-product NO(g).
G. 14.3 g HNO_3 requires what mass of $H_2(g)$?

$CaCO_3(s) \rightarrow CaO(s) + CO_2(g)$
$CaO(s) + H_2O(l) \rightarrow Ca(OH)_2(aq)$
$Ca(OH)_2(aq) + 2\,NH_4Cl(aq) \rightarrow CaCl_2(aq) + 2\,NH_3(g) + 2\,H_2O(l)$

H. 19.5 g $CaCO_3(s)$ produces what mass of $CaCl_2(aq)$?
I. 73.9 g $CaCO_3(s)$ produces what mass of $NH_3(g)$?
J. 43.1 g $H_2O(l)$ requires what mass of $CaCO_3(s)$?

$2\,P(s) + 3\,Cl_2(g) \rightarrow 2\,PCl_3(g)$
$PCl_3(g) + 3\,H_2O(l) \rightarrow H_3PO_3(aq) + 3\,HCl(g)$
$HCl(aq) + AgNO_3(aq) \rightarrow AgCl(s) + HNO_3(aq)$

K. 21.7 g P(s) produces what mass of AgCl(s)?

L. 34.2 g $Cl_2(g)$ produces what volume of 3.40 *M* $HNO_3(aq)$?
M. 27.4 g AgCl(s) requires what mass of P(s)? of $Cl_2(g)$?

14. Write the overall reaction for each of the five reaction series just given in the drill problems for objective 4–13a.

15. In each line below each reaction, determine the mass of reactant, the mass of product, or the percent yield as requested.

$2\ P(s) + 3\ Cl_2(g) \rightarrow 2\ PCl_3(g)$

	$P(s)$	$PCl_3(g)$	% yield
A.	24.6 g	100.0 g	____ %
B.	19.3 g	____ g	74.2%
C.	____ g	81.2 g	63.0%

$CaCO_3(s) \rightarrow CaO(s) + CO_2(g)$

	$CaCO_3(s)$	$CaO(s)$	% yield
D.	87.6 g	30.7 g	____ %
E.	143 g	____ g	74.1%
F.	____ g	45.3 g	82.4%

$4\ NH_3(g) + 5\ O_2(g) \rightarrow 4\ NO(g) + 6\ H_2O(l)$

	$NH_3(g)$	$O_2(g)$	$NO(g)$	$H_2O(l)$	% yield
G.		48.2 g		30.7 g	____ %
H.		____ g	137 g		73.5%
I.	14.6 g			____ g	89.7%

$Fe_2O_3(s) + 3\ H_2(g) \rightarrow 2\ Fe(s) + 3\ H_2O(l)$

	$Fe_2O_3(s)$	$H_2(g)$	$Fe(s)$	$H_2O(l)$	% yield
J.	64.7 g			14.0 g	____ %
K.		18.9 g	____ g		94.6%
L.		____ g		14.3 g	79.6%

$2\ HNO_3(aq) + 3\ H_2S(g) \rightarrow 4\ H_2O(g) + 2\ NO(g) + 3\ S(s)$

	$HNO_3(aq)$	$H_2S(g)$	$H_2O(g)$	$NO(g)$	$S(s)$	% yield
M.	124 g				85.1 g	____ %
N.		8.43 g	____ g			93.1%
O.		____ g		1.74 g		90.2%

QUIZZES (20 minutes each)

Choose the best answer or fill in the blank for each question.

Quiz A

1. The name of $NaNO_2$ is ______________________________ .
2. The formula of sulfuric acid is ______________________________ .
3. $AlPO_4 + Ca(OH)_2 \rightarrow Ca_3(PO_4)_2 + Al(OH)_3$ When this equation is balanced with integer coefficients, the coefficient for $Al(OH)_3$ is (a) 1; (b) 4; (c) 6; (d) 2; (e) none of these.
4. $Fe_2O_3 + C \rightarrow Fe + CO$ When this equation is balanced with integer coefficients, the sum of all the coefficients is (a) 4; (b) 8; (c) 5; (d) 7; (e) none of these.
5. $PCl_5 + 4\ H_2O \rightarrow H_3PO_4 + 5\ HCl$ 12.0 g PCl_5 (208.5 g/mol) produce how many grams of HCl (36.5 g/mol)? (a) 12.0(36.5 × 5)/208.5; (b) 12.0(36.5/208.5); (c) 12.0 × 36.5/208.5; (d) 12.0/208.5; (e) none of these.
6. $Fe_2O_3 + 3\ H_2 \rightarrow 2\ Fe + 3\ H_2O$ 15.0 g Fe_2O_3 (159.6 g/mol) and 3.1 g H_2 (2.0 g/mol) produce how many grams of H_2O (18.0 g/mol)? (a) 15.0(18.0/159.6); (b) 15.0(18.0/159.6) × 3; (c) 3.1(18.0/2.0) × 3; (d) 3.1(18.0/2.0); (e) none of these.
7. Complete and balance and underline the driving force.
   $Na_2S(s) + HCl(aq) \rightarrow$ ______________________________
8. How many ml of 14.5 *M* HNO_3 must be diluted to produce 5.00 L of 1.00 *M* solution? (a) 5000(14.5/1.00); (b) 5000(1.00/14.5); (c) 5.00(1.00/14.5); (d) 5.00(14.5/1.00); (e) none of these.
9. 56.7 g of sodium bicarbonate (84.0 g/mol) is enough solute for how many ml of 2.77 *M* solution? (a) (56.7/84.0)/2.77; (b) (84.0)(56.7)(2.77); (c) (84.0/56.7)(1000/2.77); (d) (56.7/84.0)(1000/2.77); (e) none of these.

10. $N_2(g) + 3\,H_2(g) \rightarrow 2\,NH_3(g)$ has an 85% yield. How many grams of $NH_3(g)$ are produced from 12.0 g $N_2(g)$? (a) (12.0/28.0)(2)(0.85)(17.0); (b) (12.0/14.0)(2)(17.0/0.85); (c) (12.0/28.0)(2)(17.0/0.85); (d) (12.0/14.0)(2)(0.85)(17.0); (e) none of these.

Quiz B

1. The name of $Mg(ClO_3)_2$ is ______________________.
2. The formula of sodium hypofluorite is ______________________.
3. $NO_2 + H_2 \rightarrow NH_3 + H_2O$ When this equation is balanced with integer coefficients, the coefficient of nitrogen dioxide is (a) 1; (b) 2; (c) 3; (d) 4; (e) none of these.
4. $H_2S + O_2 \rightarrow H_2O + SO_3$ When this equation is balanced with integer coefficients, the sum of the coefficients is (a) 4; (b) 5; (c) 6; (d) 8; (e) none of these.
5. How many moles of SO_2 are produced when 72.0 g H_2O is produced by the process $2\,H_2S + 3\,O_2 \rightarrow 2\,H_2O + 2\,SO_2$ (H = 1.0, S = 32.1, O = 16.0 g/mol)? (a) (72.0/17.0)(3/2); (b) (72.0/18.0); (c) (72.0/17.0)(2/3); (d) (72.8)(18.0); (e) none of these.
6. $2\,Al + Fe_2O_3 \rightarrow Al_2O_3 + 2\,Fe$ 2.5 g Al(27.0 g/mol) and 7.2 g Fe_2O_3 (158.9 g/mol) produce how many grams of Fe (55.9 g/mol)? (a) 2.5(55.9/27.0); (b) 7.2(55.9/158.9); (c) 2.5(55.9 X 2)/(27.0 X 2); (d) 7.2(55.9 X 2)/158.9 (e) none of these.
7. Complete and balance and underline the driving force
   $Al_2O_3(s) + H_2SO_4(aq) \rightarrow$ ______________________.
8. 67.5 ml of a 3.15 *M* solution is diluted to 2.50 L with water. The molarity of the resulting solution is (a) (3.15)(67.5)(2500); (b) (3.15/67.5)/2500; (c) 3.15(67.5/2500); (d) 3.15(2500/67.5); (e) none of these.
9. 151.6 ml of a 0.45 *M* solution of iron(II) chloride contains how many grams of solute? (a) (151.6)(0.45)(126.8); (b) (151.6/1000)(0.45)(146.1); (c) (151.6/0.45)(126.8); (d) (151.6/0.45)(146.1); (e) none of these.
10. $CO(g) + 2\,H_2(g) \rightarrow CH_3OH(l)$ has a 72.1% yield. 14.0 g $CH_3OH(l)$ requires how many grams of hydrogen? (a) (14.0/32.0)(2)(2.0/72.1); (b) (14.0/32.0)(2)(1.0/72.1); (c) (14.0/32.0)(2)(2.0/0.721); (d) (14.0/32.0)(2)(2.0)(0.721); (e) none of these.

Quiz C

1. The name of $RbBrO_4$ is ______________________.
2. The formula of nitric acid is ______________________.
3. $H_3PO_4 + NaOH \rightarrow H_2O + Na_3PO_4$ When this equation is balanced with integer coefficients, the coefficient for H_2O is (a) 1; (b) 2; (c) 3; (d) 4; (e) none of these.
4. $AgNO_3 + CuCl_2 \rightarrow Cu(NO_3)_2 + AgCl$ When this equation is balanced with integer coefficients, the sum of all the coefficients is (a) 8; (b) 5; (c) 6; (d) 4; (e) none of these.
5. $2\,C_3H_7OH + 9\,O_2 \rightarrow 6\,CO_2 + 8\,H_2O$ 47.2 g CO_2 (44 g/mol) requires how many grams of C_3H_7OH (60 g/mol)? (a) 47.2[(6 X 44.0)/(2 X 60.0)]; (b) 47.2[(2 X 60.0)/(6 X 44.0)]; (c) 47.2(60.0/44.0); (d) 47.2(44.0/60.0); (e) none of these.
6. $Mg_3N_2 + 6\,H_2O \rightarrow 3\,Mg(OH)_2 + 2\,NH_3$ 2.5 mol Mg_3N_2 (100.9 g/mol) and 6.0 mol H_2O (18.0 g/mol) produce how many grams of NH_3 (17.0 g/mol)? (a) (6.0/18.0)(2 X 17.0); (b) 2 X 17.0; (c) 2.5(2 X 17.0); (d) (2.5 X 120.9)(2 X 17.0); (e) none of these.
7. Complete and balance and underline the driving force
   $NaOH(aq) + H_2SO_4(aq) \rightarrow$ ______________________.
8. If 85.6 ml of a 6.75 *M* solution is diluted to 6.20 L with water, what is the concentration of the final solution? (a) 6.75(85.6/6.20); (b) 6.75(6.20/85.6); (c) 6.75(6200/85.6); (d) 6.75(85.6/6200); (e) none of these.
9. 433 ml of a 0.675 *M* solution of sodium sulfite contains how many grams of solute? (a) (433/1000)(0.675)(126.1); (b) (433/1000)(0.675)(142.1); (c) (433)(0.675)(103.1); (d) (433)(0.675)(126.1); (e) none of these.
10. $2\,SO_2(g) + O_2(g) \rightarrow 2\,SO_3(g)$ has a 93.7% yield. How many grams of $SO_3(g)$ are produced from 6.75 g $SO_2(g)$? (a) (6.75/64.1)(80.1/93.7); (b) (6.75/64.1)(80.1/0.937); (c) 6.75/0.937; (d) (6.75/64.1)(80.1)(93.7); (e) none of these.

Quiz D

1. The name of H_2SO_4 is ______________________________.
2. The formula of sodium bicarbonate is ______________________________.
3. $PCl_3 + H_2O \rightarrow H_3PO_3 + HCl$ When this equation is balanced with integer coefficients, the coefficient of hydrochloric acid is (a) 6; (b) 2; (c) 3; (d) 4; (e) none of these.
4. $SCl_4 + H_2O \rightarrow H_2SO_3 + HCl$ When this equation is balanced with integer coefficients, the sum of all the coefficients is (a) 4; (b) 6; (c) 8; (d) 10; (e) none of these.
5. How many moles of NH_3 are required to produce 256 g N_2H_4 via the process $4\ NH_3 + Cl_2 \rightarrow N_2H_4 + 2\ NH_4Cl$ (N = 14.0, H = 1.0, Cl = 35.5 g/mol)? (a) (256/16)(4); (b) (256/32)(2); (c) (256/32)(4); (d) 256/(32 × 4); (e) none of these.
6. $2\ Fe_2O_3 + 3\ C \rightarrow 4\ Fe + 3\ CO_2$ 18.0 g Fe_2O_3 (159.8 g/mol) and 2.5 g C (12.0 g/mol) produce how many grams of Fe (55.9 g/mol)? (a) 18.0(55.9/159.8); (b) 18.0(4 × 55.9)/(2 × 159.8); (c) 2.5(55.9/12.0); (d) 2.5(55.9 × 4)/(3 × 12.0); (e) none of these.
7. Complete and balance and underline the driving force
   $CaCO_3(s) + HCl(aq) \rightarrow$ ______________________________.
8. How many ml of a 17.0 *M* HCl solution is necessary to produce 2.0 L of a 3.00 *M* HCl solution? (a) (2000/17.0)/3.00; (b) 2.00(17.0)(3.00); (c) 2000(17.0/3.00); (d) 2000(3.00/17.0); (e) none of these.
9. 81.2 ml of a 14.0 *M* solution of nitric acid contains how many grams of solute? (a) (81.2/1000)(14.0)(81.0); (b) (81.2/1000)(14.0)(63.0); (c) (81.2)(14.0)(47.0); (d) (81.2)(14.0)(65.0); (e) none of these.
10. $2\ P(s) + 5\ Cl_2(g) \rightarrow 2\ PCl_5(g)$ has a 89.0% yield. 19.2 g $PCl_5(g)$ requires how many grams of $Cl_2(g)$? (a) (19.2/208.5)(5/2)(71.0/0.890); (b) (19.2/66.5)(5/2)(71.0/0.890); (c) (19.2/208.5)(71.0)(0.890); (d) (19.2/66.5)(5/2)(71.0)(0.890); (e) none of these.

SAMPLE TEST (30 minutes)

1. Give the name or formula, as appropriate, of each of the following compounds.
   a. $Pb(CNS)_2$ b. lead(IV) thiosulfate c. arsenic sulfide
   d. $Mn(BrO)_2$ e. HNO_2 f. ammonium bicarbonate
   g. periodic acid h. stannous sulfide
2. What volume in ml of 0.160 *M* KNO_3 must be mixed with 200.0 ml of 0.240 *M* K_2SO_4 to produce a solution having $[K^+] = 0.400\ M$?
3. Complete and balance the following equations.
   a. $BaCl_2 + AgNO_3 \rightarrow$ b. $Ca(OH)_2 \xrightarrow{\Delta}$ c. $NH_3 + HCl \rightarrow$
   d. $Zn + CuSO_4 \rightarrow$ e. $C_2H_6O_2 \rightarrow$
4. Consider the reaction $CuO(s) + 2\ HCl(aq) \rightarrow CuCl_2(aq) + H_2O(l)$. If 55.2 g CuO is added to 158 ml of 2.70 *M* HCl, what mass of H_2O is formed?
5. 26.4 g of a NaOH–CaO mixture containing 40.0% CaO reacts with HCl according to the equations

   $$NaOH(s) + HCl(aq) \rightarrow NaCl(aq) + H_2O(l)$$
   $$CaO(s) + 2\ HCl(aq) \rightarrow CaCl_2(aq) + H_2O(l)$$

   All of the mixture reacts, and there is no HCl left over. The resulting solution is evaporated to dryness. What is the weight of solid obtained?

Chapter 5

Gases

REVIEW OF OBJECTIVES

★ **0. Be able to convert between the common units of pressure.**

Your goal is to firmly commit the following expressions to memory.

$$\begin{aligned} 1.00 \text{ atmosphere (atm)} &= 760 \text{ mmHg} = 760 \text{ torr} \\ &= 101{,}325 \text{ N/m}^2 = 101{,}325 \text{ pascal (Pa)} \\ &= 14.7 \text{ lb/in.}^2 \\ 1000 \text{ Pascal} &= 1.000 \text{ kilopascal (kPa)} \end{aligned}$$

Notice that there is no abbreviation for torr; t is incorrect.

1. Explain the operation of a mercury barometer, an open-end manometer, and a closed-end manometer and be able to use the data obtained with these instruments.

All liquid-filled pressure-measuring devices operate on the same principle. A liquid is confined in a U-shaped tube, as shown in Figure 5-1a. If the pressure is different on the two ends of the liquid column–that is if P_1 differs from P_2–the liquid levels in the two arms of the tube will be different. The liquid level is higher on the low pressure end of the tube. In all parts of Figure 5-1, P_1 is a lower pressure than P_2. The difference in pressures, $\Delta P = P_2 - P_1$, is proportional to the vertical distance between the two liquid levels, h.

$$\Delta P = P_2 - P_1 \propto h \quad \textit{or} \quad \Delta P = gdh \qquad [1]$$

In equation [1], g is the gravitational constant, 9.80 m/s^2 or 980 cm/s^2, and d is the density of the liquid. Normally, we know one of the pressures (P_1 or P_2), are given or can measure a value of h, and wish to find the other pressure, knowing the density of the liquid.

There is a simpler method of determining ΔP than equation [1]. This depends on the fact that a denser liquid produces a smaller level difference. In fact, for two liquids, A and B,

$$h_A d_A = h_B d_B \quad \textit{or} \quad h_A = h_B d_B / d_A \qquad [2]$$

We frequently use mercury (d_A = 13.6 g/cm^3) as liquid A because 760 mmHg = 1.000 atm.

EXAMPLE 5-1 An open-end manometer is filled with dibutyl phthalate (DBP, d = 1.047 g/cm^3). If the level difference is 625 mm, what is the pressure difference in atmospheres?

$$\Delta P = h_{Hg} = 625 \text{ mm DBP} \times \frac{1.047 \text{ g/cm}^3}{13.6 \text{ g/cm}^3}$$

$$= 48.1 \text{ mmHg} \times \frac{1 \text{ atm}}{760 \text{ mmHg}} = 0.0633 \text{ atm}$$

In a closed-end manometer and in a barometer the pressure in the low pressure end is almost zero. It equals the vapor pressure of the liquid being used. At 25°C, the vapor pressure of mercury is 6×10^{-6} atm, that of glycerol is 6×10^{-7} atm, and that of dibutyl phthalate is 2×10^{-7} atm. See objectives 11-3 through 11-5 for a discussion of vapor pressure.

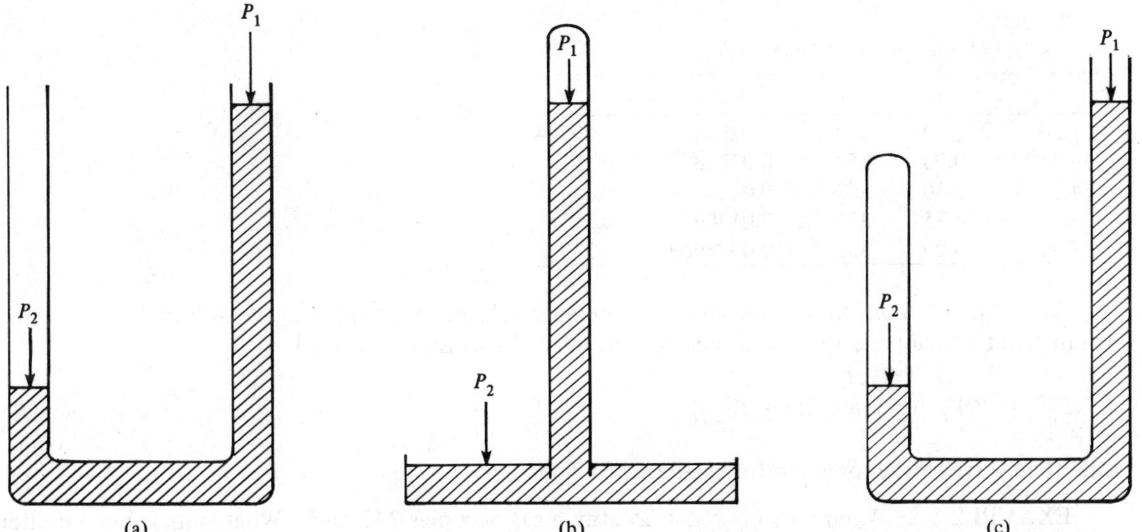

FIGURE 5-1 Liquid-filled pressure-measuring devices
(a) General principle; open-end manometer. (b) Barometer. (c) Closed-end manometer.

★ **2. Learn Boyle's law both mathematically and graphically and be able to use it in calculations.**

Boyle observed that for a fixed amount of gas at a constant temperature the product of volume and pressure is a constant. The condition of fixed amount means that the apparatus must not leak, but it also means that no physical or chemical change which produces or consumes a gas may occur within the container. Notice that nothing is stated about the units which pressure and volume must have. Any units are satisfactory, but they must be consistent: all pressures must be measured in the same units (for example, inches of mercury, in. Hg) as must all volumes (for example, in.^{3}). (These are the units Boyle used.) Graphically, the law is demonstrated when one plots $1/V$ vs. P (Figure 5-2a) or $1/P$ vs. V (Figure 5-2b) and obtains a straight line. Other plots give curved lines. The data for Figure 5-2, given in Table 5-1, are part of Boyle's original data.

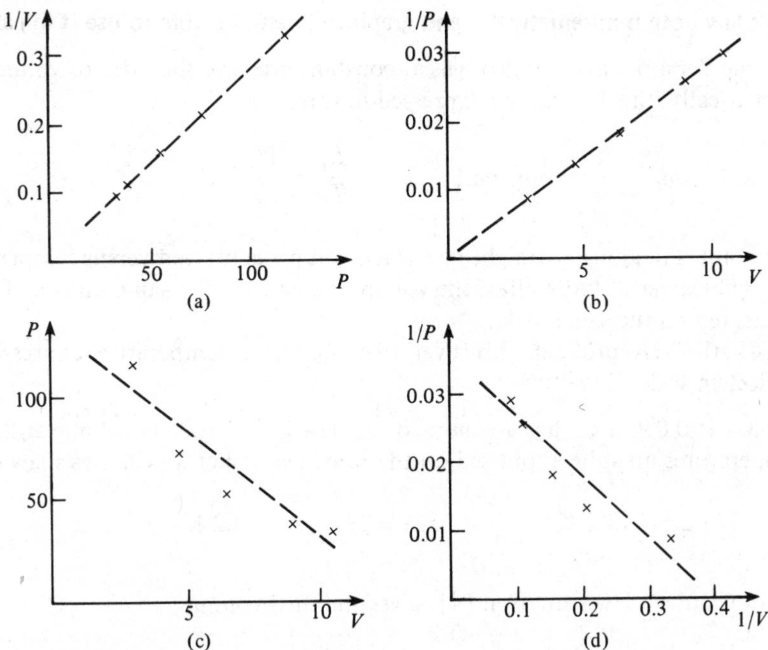

FIGURE 5-2 Graphs of Boyle's pressure–volume data
In each graph, the dashed line is the best straight line (estimated visually) through the data points.
(a) $1/V$ vs. P, (b) $1/P$ vs. V, (c) P vs. V, (d) $1/P$ vs. $1/V$

TABLE 5-1
Boyle's data of pressure and volume

P, in. Hg	V, in.^{3}	$P \times V$	$1/P$	$1/V$
33.50	10.50	352.8	0.02985	0.09524
39.25	9.00	353	0.02548	0.111
54.31	6.50	353	0.01841	0.154
74.13	4.75	352	0.01346	0.211
117.56	3.00	353	0.0085063	0.333

Problems based on this law, often called pressure-volume problems, supply an initial pressure and volume and a final pressure or volume. A convenient expression to use is

$$P_i V_i = P_f V_f \quad (i = \text{initial}; f = \text{final})$$

One then solves this expression for the desired value.

EXAMPLE 5-2 When measured at 1.25 atm, a gas occupies 247 cm^3. What is its volume in liters at a pressure of 76.5 mmHg?

Since the two given pressures are in different units, we convert one of them.

$$1.25 \text{ atm} \times \frac{760 \text{ mmHg}}{\text{atm}} = 950 \text{ mmHg} = P_i$$

Then equation [1] gives the final volume.

$$950 \text{ mmHg} \times 247 \text{ cm}^3 = 76.5 \text{ mmHg} \times V_f$$

$$V_f = 247 \text{ cm}^3 \times \frac{950 \text{ mmHg}}{76.5 \text{ mmHg}} = 3.07 \times 10^3 \text{ cm}^3$$

$$3.07 \times 10^3 \text{ cm}^3 \text{ (L/1000 cm}^3) = 3.07 \text{ L}$$

★ **3. Learn Charles's law both mathematically and graphically and be able to use it in calculations.**

Charles observed that for a fixed amount of gas at constant pressure the ratio of volume to temperature is constant. Mathematically, this law can be expressed in three ways.

$$V = \text{constant} \times T \quad or \quad \frac{V}{T} = \text{constant} \quad or \quad \frac{V_i}{T_i} = \frac{V_f}{T_f} \qquad [4]$$

Graphically, data points fall along a straight line when volume is plotted versus temperature. The only requirement for graphical data is that all of the volumes must have the same units and all of the temperatures must be measured on the same scale.

When solving Charles's law problems, however, one *must* use a temperature expressed on an absolute scale such as the Kelvin scale.

EXAMPLE 5-3 At 0.0°C a gas has a volume of 22.414 L. What is its volume at 25.0°C?

Both temperatures must be expressed on the Kelvin scale before Charles's law can be used.

$$T_i = 0.0 + 273.2 = 273.2 \text{ K} \qquad T_f = 25.0 + 273.2 = 298.2 \text{ K}$$

Then application of Charles's law, equation [4], gives the final volume.

$$\frac{22.414 \text{ L}}{273.2 \text{ K}} = \frac{V_f}{298.2 \text{ K}}$$

$$V_f = 22.414\text{ L} \times \frac{298.2\text{ K}}{273.2\text{ K}} = 24.47\text{ L}$$

4. Understand kelvin temperature and an absolute zero of temperature.

When Charles's law (V = constant $\times$ T) is carefully examined, one concludes that a gas will occupy no volume once its kelvin temperature has been lowered to zero. Charles's law (V/T = constant) in not valid on the Celsius scale; for example,

$$\frac{V_i}{T_i} = \frac{22.414\text{ L}}{0°\text{C}} = \infty \quad but \quad \frac{V_f}{T_f} = \frac{24.47\text{ L}}{25.0°\text{ C}} = 0.979\text{ L/°C}$$

It is valid only on the kelvin scale.

$$\frac{V_i}{T_i} = \frac{22.414\text{ L}}{273.2\text{ K}} = 0.08204\text{ L/K} \quad \text{and} \quad \frac{V_f}{T_f} = \frac{24.47\text{ L}}{298.2\text{ K}} = 0.08206\text{ L/K}$$

4a. Be able to convert between Celsius and kelvin temperatures.

The relationship to be memorized is T (K) = t (°C) + 273.15. Notice that the degree sign (°) is not used in expressing kelvin temperatures, which are represented by a capital T. Celsius temperatures, formerly called centigrade temperatures, are symbolized by a lowercase t. It is very important to know that *all problems involving gas laws must use kelvin temperatures.*

5. Know what is meant by STP and the STP molar volume.

STP is the abbreviation for Standard Temperature and Pressure: T = 273.15 K and P = 1.000 atm. The volume occupied by one mole of an ideal gas at STP is 22.414 L. This is termed the STP molar volume of an ideal gas.

EXAMPLE 5-4 What volume of H_2 (g) measured at STP is needed to reduce 36.1 g WO_3 according to

$$WO_3\text{(s)} + 3\ H_2\text{(g)} \xrightarrow{\Delta} \text{W(s)} + 3\ H_2O\text{(l)}$$

The problem is solved using the conversion factor method.

$$36.1\text{ g }WO_3 \times \frac{\text{mol }WO_3}{231.8\text{ g }WO_3} \times \frac{3\text{ mol }H_2}{\text{mol }WO_3} \times \frac{22.4\text{ L }H_2}{\text{mol }H_2} = 10.5\text{ L }H_2$$

6. Know and be able to use Avogadro's law.

Avogadro's law states that equal volumes of gases at the same temperature and pressure contain equal numbers of molecules (or of moles) of the gases, even if the gases are different. It is crucial to compare gases at the *same pressure and temperature*; otherwise the law is invalid. Avogadro's law is expressed mathematically as

$$V = n \times \text{constant} \quad or \quad \frac{V}{n} = \text{constant} \quad or \quad \frac{V_1}{n_1} = \frac{V_2}{n_2} \qquad [5]$$

6a. Deduce the ideal gas equation from the simple gas laws and R from the STP molar volume.

The three gas laws are

Boyle's: V = constant/P (fixed n and T)
Charles's: V = constant $\times$ T (fixed n and P)
Avogadro's: V = constant $\times$ n (fixed P and T) [6]

If the three gas laws [6] are combined, we obtain

$$V = RnT/P \quad \text{more often written} \quad PV = nRT \tag{7}$$

Since the STP molar volume of a gas is 22.4 L,

$$R = \frac{PV}{nT} = \frac{(1.000 \text{ atm})(22.414 \text{ L})}{(1.000 \text{ mol})(273.15 \text{ K})} = 0.08206 \text{ L atm mol}^{-1} \text{ K}^{-1} \tag{8}$$

The ideal gas constant should be memorized, including its units. Also notice that the gas laws are named after their discoverers and they are *always* referred to this way. Boyle's law in never called "the pressure-volume gas law."

★ **7. Solve for one of *P, V, n,* or *T* when given values of the other three.**

Example 5-5 illustrates the type of problem.

EXAMPLE 5-5 What is the volume of 3.04 moles of gas confined at 741 mmHg and 14.0°F? We first express the pressure in atmospheres and the temperature in kelvins.

$$741 \text{ mmHg} \times \frac{1.00 \text{ atm}}{760 \text{ mmHg}} = 0.975 \text{ atm}$$

$$°\text{C} = (°\text{F} - 32) \times \frac{5}{9} = (14.0 - 32.0)\left(\frac{5}{9}\right) = -10.0°\text{C}$$

$$T = -10.0 + 273.15 = 263.2 \text{ K}$$

We then solve the ideal gas equation for V.

$$V = \frac{nRT}{P} = \frac{(3.04 \text{ mol})(0.0821 \text{ L atm mol}^{-1} \text{ K}^{-1})(263.2 \text{ K})}{0.975 \text{ atm}} = 67.4 \text{ L}$$

Notice that the units of the expression cancel appropriately.

★ **7a. Obtain the value of one final variable, given values of the other final variables and of all the initial variables, excluding those which remain unchanged, in the ideal gas law.**

This is often called an "initial–final" problem. It depends on a rearranged ideal gas law, $R = PV/nT$, which produces equation [9].

$$\frac{P_i V_i}{n_i T_i} = \frac{P_f V_f}{n_f T_f} \quad (i = \text{initial}; f = \text{final}) \tag{9}$$

Any of the simple gas laws can be obtained from this equation. Equation [9] also can be used to solve problems for which there is no "law."

EXAMPLE 5-6 2.40 mol of an ideal gas is confined in a 26.4 L vessel at 250.0 K. If an additional 2.00 mol of gas is added to the vessel and the pressure does not vary, what must be the final temperature?

Notice that this problem does not explicitly state that the volume of the container does not vary. It could be a balloon, for instance. However, the final volume is not given and thus one *assumes* that the volume does not change. You often will have to make such an assumption to solve a problem. Both volume and pressure are fixed and thus $V_i = V_f$ and $P_i = P_f$. Using equation [9],

$$\frac{P_i V_i}{n_i T_i} = \frac{P_i V_i}{n_f T_f} \quad \text{or} \quad n_i T_i = n_f T_f$$

We are given the following data.

$n_i = 2.40$ mol $\qquad T_i = 250.0$ K
$n_f = n_i + 2.00$ mol $= (2.40 + 2.00)$ mol $= 4.40$ mol

which produces

$$(2.40 \text{ mol})(250.0 \text{ K}) = (4.40 \text{ mol})T_f$$

$$T_f = \frac{(2.40 \text{ mol})(250.0 \text{ K})}{4.40 \text{ mol}} = 136.4 \text{ K}$$

Notice that the equation we produced, $n_iT_i = n_fT_f$, is not one of the classical gas laws.

We conclude with a word of caution. Frequently it is stated that this kind of problem can be solved with an equation of the type

$$T_f = T_i \times (\text{mole ratio})$$

in which the "mole ratio" is the quotient of the two numbers of moles. In order to confine more moles in the same volume at the same pressure, the temperature must be reduced. This kind of intuitive or "gut" feeling about how gases should behave comes only with experience, which many general chemistry students lack. Thus, you may get the ratio upside down, especially in the heat of an examination. Starting with equation [9] is safer.

★ **8. Learn the alternative version of the ideal gas law for calculating mole weights of gases and working with gas densities.**

An alternative form of the ideal gas law is given in equation [10].

$$PV = \frac{m}{(\text{MW})} RT \qquad [10]$$

Equation [10] is obtained from the ideal gas law, equation [7], by substituting.

$$n = m/(\text{MW}) \qquad [11]$$

m = the mass of the gas and (MW) = the gas's mole weight. It is convenient but not essential that you know the combined equation [10]. The two parts, equations [7] and [11], work just as well, as Example 5-7 illustrates. You should use whichever technique you find easier.

EXAMPLE 5-7 What is the mole weight of a gas if 11.770 g has a volume 5.00 L at 30°C and 742 mmHg? *Using the combined equation [10]:*

$P = 742$ mmHg $\times$ 1 atm/760 mmHg $= 0.976$ atm
$T = 30°\text{C} + 273° = 303$ K $\qquad m = 11.770$ g $\qquad V = 5.00$ L

$$PV = \frac{m}{(\text{MW})} RT$$

$$(0.976 \text{ atm})(5.00 \text{ L}) = \frac{11.770 \text{ g}}{(\text{MW})} (0.821 \frac{\text{L atm}}{\text{mol K}})(303 \text{ K})$$

$$(\text{MW}) = 60.0 \text{ g/mol}$$

Using the ideal gas equation [7] and equation [11]:

$(0.976 \text{ atm})(5.00 \text{ L}) = n(0.0821 \text{ L atm mol}^{-1} \text{ K}^{-1} (303 \text{ K})$
$n = 0.196 \text{ mol} = m/(\text{MW}) = 11.770 \text{ g}/(\text{MW})$
$(\text{MW}) = 11.770 \text{ g}/0.196 \text{ mol} = 60.0 \text{ g/mol}$

★ **8a. Be able to combine gas mole weights with empirical formulas to determine molecular formulas.**

Percent composition data only enable us to determine the empirical formula of a compound, but several compounds may have the same empirical formula. The mole weight of the compound allows us to determine the compound's molecular formula if we know its empirical formula. Thus, if the gas of Example 5-7 has an empirical formula of CH_2O, its molecular formula will be an integral multiple of the empirical formula: CH_2O, $C_2H_4O_2$, $C_3H_6O_3$, etc. The "empirical weight" is the weight of 1 mol C, 2 mol H, and 1 mol O or 12.0 g + 2 X 1.0 g + 16.0 g = 30.0 g. Since the mole weight (60.0 g/mol) is twice the empirical weight (30.0 g/mol of "empirical units"), the molecular formula must be twice the empirical formula, or $C_2H_4O_2$.

★ **9. Be able to solve stoichiometry problems involving gases.**

A large variety of stoichiometry problems involve using the ideal gas law either to determine the moles of reactant or product or to determine the volume (or occasionally the pressure) of a reactant or product. If you can solve stoichiometry problems and work with the ideal gas equation you should have little trouble with these.

In solving problems involving the law of combining volumes, however, the given data often are insufficient to allow you to compute the number of moles. Remember that equal volumes of gas at the *same temperature and pressure* contain equal numbers of moles. When temperature and pressure are fixed, gas volumes can be used in the same way as numbers of moles.

EXAMPLE 5-8 3.04 L of O_2 (g) and excess SO_2 (g) both at 297 K and 3.51 atm are combined.

$$2\ SO_2(g) + O_2(g) \rightarrow 2\ SO_3(g)$$

What volume of SO_3 (g) is produced?

We assume that the pressure and temperature remain fixed. Thus, we have

$$3.04\ L\ O_2(g) \times \frac{2\ L\ SO_3(g)}{1\ L\ O_2(g)} = 6.08\ L\ SO_3(g)$$

★ **10. Be able to work with mixtures of gases, using (a) the ideal gas equation, (b) Dalton's law of partial pressures, or (c) Amagat's law of partial volumes.**

Because ideal gas molecules do not interact with each other, a mixture of several gases will display properties which are the sums of the individual properties. Each gas in the mixture acts as if the other gases were not present, unless a chemical reaction occurs. Thus the total pressure is the sum of the partial pressures.

A partial pressure is the pressure that one of the gases would exert if it were confined in the same volume at the same temperature. In like fashion, the total gas volume is the sum of the partial volumes. A partial volume is the volume each gas would occupy if it were confined at the same total pressure and temperature as the mixture. This additive feature of pressures and volumes is valid only for ideal gases. For other states of matter only masses and amounts (in moles) can be summed to obtain the total mass and total amount of the mixture.

EXAMPLE 5-8 2.46 L of argon at 0.320 atm and 400 K is combined with 4.12 L of neon at 0.440 atm and 400 K in a rigid 5.00 L container at 400 K. Determine (a) the total final pressure, (b) the partial pressure of argon in the 5.00 L container, and (c) the partial volume of neon in the 5.00 L container.

We first compute the amount of each gas, and the total moles of gas placed in the 5.00 L container.

$$n_{Ar} = \frac{PV}{RT} = \frac{(0.320\ atm)(2.46\ L)}{(0.0821\ L\ atm\ mol^{-1}\ K^{-1})(400\ K)} = 0.0240\ mol$$

$$n_{Ne} = \frac{(0.440\ atm)(4.12\ L)}{(0.0821\ L\ atm\ mol^{-1}\ K^{-1})(400\ K)} = 0.0552\ mol$$

$$n_{total} = n_{Ar} + n_{Ne} = 0.0240\ mol + 0.0552\ mol = 0.0792\ mol$$

(a) To compute the final pressure

$$P_f = \frac{nRT}{V} = \frac{(0.0792 \text{ mol})(0.0821 \text{ L atm mol}^{-1} \text{ K}^{-1})(400 \text{ K})}{5.00 \text{ L}} = 0.520 \text{ atm}$$

(b) The pressure in the 5.00 L container due to argon can be computed in two ways.

$$P_{Ar} = \frac{n_{Ar}RT}{V} = \frac{(0.0240 \text{ mol})(0.0821 \text{ L atm mol}^{-1} \text{ K}^{-1})(400 \text{ K})}{5.00 \text{ L}} = 0.158 \text{ atm}$$

or

$$P_{Ar} = \frac{n_{Ar}}{n_{total}} P_f = \frac{0.0240 \text{ mol}}{0.0792 \text{ mol}} \times 0.520 \text{ atm} = 0.158 \text{ atm}$$

(c) The partial volume of neon is computed using its mole fraction (objective 12–2b).

$$V_{Ne} = \chi_{Ne} V_{total} = \frac{n_{Ne}}{n_{total}} V_{total} = \frac{0.0552 \text{ mol}}{0.0792 \text{ mol}} \times 5.00 \text{ L} = 3.48 \text{ L}$$

11. Be able to compute the pressure of gases collected over water.

When a gas is collected over water, it is mixed with water vapor. Thus, the total pressure of the mixture is the sum of the pressure of the gas collected and the vapor pressure of water.

$$P_{total} = P_{gas} + P_{water} \qquad [12]$$

The vapor pressure of water varies with the temperature and a table of values is given in Table 5-2.

TABLE 5-2
Vapor pressure of water at various temperatures

t, °C	P, mmHg	t, °C	P, mmHg	t, °C	P, mmHg	t, °C	P, mmHg
13.0	11.2	19.0	16.5	25.0	23.8	31.0	33.7
14.0	12.0	20.0	17.5	26.0	25.2	32.0	35.7
15.0	12.8	21.0	18.7	27.0	26.7	33.0	37.7
16.0	13.6	22.0	19.8	28.0	28.3	34.0	39.9
17.0	14.5	23.0	21.1	29.0	30.0	35.0	42.2
18.0	15.5	24.0	22.4	30.0	31.8	36.0	44.6

12. Know the postulates and the basic mathematical relationships of the kinetic molecular theory of gases.

The postulates are a set of assumptions about the molecular structure of gases and how these molecules interact. One form of these assumptions is

1. Gases are composed of molecules.
2. Gas molecules have no volume (they are point masses).
3. Gas molecules neither attract nor repel each other (there are no forces between them).
4. Gas molecules are in constant, random motion.

The kinetic energy of an average ideal gas molecule is given by two equations.

$$\bar{e}_k = \tfrac{1}{2} m\bar{u}^2 \qquad [13]$$

$$\bar{e}_k = \tfrac{3}{2} kT \qquad [14]$$

$$k = R/N = \text{Boltzmann's constant} = 1.38 \times 10^{-23} \text{ J molecule}^{-1} \text{ K}^{-1} \qquad [15]$$

13. Deduce the simple gas laws from the kinetic molecular theory.

Let us consider Boyle's law as an example. One of the consequences of random motion of molecules is that molecules are continually hitting the sides of the container. The average molecular speed, and thus the average force exerted by each collision with the wall, depends on only the temperature. If we now compress the gas into a smaller volume, each collision will still impart the same force, but there will be many more collisions. In fact, if we halve the volume, there will be twice as many collisions, and the pressure will double. That there will be twice as many collisions can be hard to believe, but consider one gas molecule traveling only back and forth between two sides with constant speed. If the distance between the two sides is halved, this molecule should hit each side twice as often.

You should write down the same type of explanation for each of the other simple gas laws: Charles's, Avogadro's, and Dalton's.

★ **14. & 15. Compute molecular velocities and know and apply Graham's law.**

When the two expressions for average kinetic energy, equations [13] and [14] of objective 4–12, are combined and solved for $\sqrt{\bar{u}^2} = u_{rms}$, one obtains

$$u_{rms} = \sqrt{\frac{3kT}{m}} = \sqrt{\frac{3RT}{(MW)}}$$

m = molecular mass (kg/molecule), (MW) = mole weight (kg/mole of molecules), and R = 8.314 J mol^{-1} K^{-1}, giving a velocity in m/s. This expression is true for all ideal gases, specifically for two different gases at the same temperature.

$$u_{rms}(A) = \sqrt{\frac{3RT}{M_A}} \quad and \quad u_{rms}(B) = \sqrt{\frac{3RT}{M_B}} \qquad [16]$$

$$\frac{u_{rms}(A)}{u_{rms}(B)} = \sqrt{\frac{(MW)_B}{(MW)_A}} \qquad [17]$$

This equation, obtained from the theory, is similar to Graham's law, which was experimentally obtained. In fact, Graham's law (1833) came before the kinetic molecular theory of gases (1860–1890). An example of Graham's law is the rate at which a helium-filled toy baloon deflates–far faster than a similar balloon filled with air. This occurs because the lower-mole-weight helium effuses more rapidly through the small pores in the balloon than the higher-mole-weight oxygen and nitrogen of the air.

EXAMPLE 5-9 Determine the average velocity of a xenon molecule at 37°C (310 K).

$$u_{rms} = \sqrt{\frac{3 \times 8.314 \text{ J mol}^{-1}\text{K}^{-1} \times 310 \text{ K}}{0.1313 \text{ kg/mol}}} = 243 \text{ m/s}$$

Note that the unit joule is equal to kg m^2 s^{-2}

EXAMPLE 5-10 How much faster than air does helium effuse through a pinhole? The average mole weight of air is 29.0 g/mol.

$$\frac{\text{rate of He}}{\text{rate of air}} = \frac{u_{He}}{u_{air}} = \sqrt{\frac{(MW)_{air}}{(MW)_{He}}} = \sqrt{\frac{29.0 \text{ g/mol}}{4.00 \text{ g/mol}}} = 2.69$$

Helium effuses 2.69 times as fast as air.

16. Explain why real gases differ from ideal gases and how the differences lead to the van der Waals equation. Know under what conditions gases are most nearly ideal.

Two assumptions of the kinetic molecular theory are clearly incorrect: gas molecules do have volume, and they do attract each other. If these facts were not true, liquids would have no volume since the molecules composing them would have no volume. Furthermore, liquids would spontaneously and completely vaporize as nothing would act to hold the molecules together. The ideal gas equation is modified to account for the volume of molecules and the forces between them.

The volume in the ideal gas equation is a free volume, the space within which molecules are free to move. In a real gas, however, the molecules take up or exclude some of the volume of the container.

free volume = container volume − excluded volume

or $V_{free} = V - nb$ (b = excluded volume per mole of gas) [18]

The ideal gas pressure assumes the molecules do not attract each other. But because there is such an attraction, the molecules slow down as they approach the wall. They are attracted by the other molecules back into the body of the gas. Hence they strike the wall less hard and the measured pressure, P_{meas}, is less than the ideal pressure would be. The corrected pressure, P_{corr}, approximates what the ideal gas pressure would be.

$$P_{corr} = P_{meas} + \frac{an^2}{V^2} \qquad [19]$$

The constant a is multiplied by the square of the concentration of the gas, n/V. The concentration is squared because molecule A attracts molecule B, but molecule B also attracts molecule A.

The final equation [20] is the van der Waals equation.

$$\left(P + \frac{an^2}{V^2}\right)(V - nb) = nRT \qquad [20]$$

The constants a and b principally depend on what gas is being considered. To a small extent, they also depend on pressure and temperature.

The volume correction ($-nb$) will be insignificant if it is small compared to the volume of the container. For a given quantity of the gas, the container volume is large when the pressure is low and the temperature is high. A large container volume also means that the concentration is low and thus the pressure correction ($+an^2/V^2$) will be small. Hence, a gas will behave ideally at low pressure and high temperature.

DRILL PROBLEMS

0. Fill in the blanks in each line below.

A. 30.0 atm = ___ lb/in.^{2} = ___ kPa

B. 142 mmHg = ___ lb/in.^{2} = ___ Pa

C. 242 lb/in.^{2} = ___ atm = ___ kPa

D. 5.00 × 10^2 atm = ___ torr = ___ Pa

E. 5.00 × 10^2 mmHg = ___ atm = ___ Pa

F. 5.00 × 10^2 Pa = ___ atm = ___ torr

G. 5.00 × 10^2 lb/in.^{2} = ___ atm = ___ Pa

H. 3.52 kPa = ___ lb/in.^{2} = ___ mmHg

2. Fill in the blanks in the table below.

	P_i	V_i	P_f	V_f
A.	732 mmHg	6.49 L	1.02 atm	___ L
B.	30.0 mmHg	35.2 L	___ atm	35.2 ml
C.	9.75 Pa	1.46 L	923 mmHg	___ L
D.	104 kPa	22.4 L	___ atm	1.00 L
E.	247 kPa	0.972 L	143 torr	___ L
F.	1.43 atm	0.947 qt	___ atm	4.06 qt
G.	65.0 lb/in.^{2}	342 ft^3	14.7 lb/in.^{2}	___ ft^3
H.	175.5 kPa	12.4 m^3	___ kPa	8.46 m^3
I.	1.11 atm	85.2 L	0.506 atm	___ L
J.	4.11 atm	24.2 m^3	___ mmHg	100.0 m^3

3. Fill in the blanks in the table below.

	V_i	T_i	V_f	T_f
A.	6.49 L	273 K	____ L	94.2°C
B.	0.947 qt	446 K	3.37 qt	____ K
C.	85.2 L	200 K	____ L	400 K
D.	24.2 m³	37.0°C	19.4 m³	____ °C
E.	22.4 L	273 K	____ L	298 K
F.	22.4 L	273 K	100.0 L	____ K
G.	14.7 L	50.6°C	____ L	300 K
H.	342 ft³	300 K	67.4 ft³	____ °C

7. Fill in the blanks in the table below.

	P	V	n	T
A.	1.23 atm	____ L	2.50 mol	298 K
B.	1.00 atm	22.4 L	1.46 mol	____ K
C.	2.64 atm	1.23 L	____ mol	143 K
D.	____ atm	9.61 L	8.41 mol	312 K
E.	746 mmHg	____ qt	1.00 mol	87.6°C
F.	1024 kPa	14.7 L	9.00 mol	____ °C
G.	5.17 atm	94.2 L	____ mol	25.0°C
H.	1726 kPa	____ L	4.40 mol	37.0°C
I.	____ torr	173 qt	1.26 mol	−40.0°C
J.	1.00 atm	____ L	12.4 g CO_2	94.2°C
K.	7.43 lb/in.²	91.6 L	____ g H_2O	293°F
L.	____ lb/in.²	123 gal	9.63 g Ne	31°F
M.	1.46 X 10³ Pa	84.1 m³	143 g He	____ °C
N.	9.47 atm	____ L	22.0 g Xe	14.6°C
O.	522 mmHg	19.2 L	____ g CH_4	83.1°C
P.	____ torr	245 L	19.6 g N_2	250.0 K

7a. (1) Fill in the blank in each line. All numbers have the units given in the column headings unless otherwise specified. All substances are ideal gases and the number of moles does not change within each line.

	P_i, atm	V_i, L	T_i, K	P_f, atm	V_f, L	T_f, K
A.	1.42	7.26	274	3.74	2.16	____
B.	0.926	24.7	80.1°C	1.42	____	481
C.	1.43	7.32 qt	91.7°C	____	3.17	260
D.	476 torr	9.32	____	8.23	0.164	27.2°C
E.	2.72	____	403	0.247	10.3	52.4°F
F.	____	82.1 gal	96.4°C	1.79	47.2	294
G.	829 torr	500 ml	73.1°F	0.725	1.42	____
H.	32.1	16.4	24.7°C	7.15	____	578
I.	466 torr	8.83	98.6°F	____	8.92 qt	78.0°F
J.	1776 torr	68.4	____	1086 torr	54.3	347
K.	5.13	____	671°C	2.62	9.13	403
L.	____	1.34	72.4°C	1.46	8.71	272

(2) Fill in the blank in each line below.

A.	$T_i = 296$ K	$n_i = 14.3$ mol	$T_f = 123$°C	$n_f =$ ____ mol
B.	$P_i = 14.3$ atm	$n_i = 1.23$ mol	$P_f =$ ____ atm	$n_f = 2.16$ mol
C.	$V_i = 22.4$ L	$n_i = 1.00$ mol	$V_f = 14.2$ L	$n_f =$ ____ mol
D.	$T_i = 500$ K	$n_i = 2.74$ mol	$T_f =$ ____ °C	$n_f = 1.43$ mol
E.	$P_i = 21.2$ atm	$n_i = 5.00$ mol	$P_f = 12.3$ atm	$n_f =$ ____ mol
F.	$V_i = 19.4$ L	$n_i = 1.32$ mol	$V_f =$ ____ L	$n_f = 4.61$ mol

8. Fill in the blanks in each line which follows. The numbers have the units given in the column headings unless otherwise specified.

	V, L	*P*, atm	*n*, mol	*M*, g/mol	*T*, K	*Mass*, g	*Density*, g/L
A.	25.0	2.00	____	____	27°C	____	1.25
B.	____	10.4	2.32	____	165	75.0	____
C.	72.1	468 torr	1.76	____	____	34.2	____
D.	34.6	____	0.832	17.4	−14°C	____	____
E.	10.4	1364 kPa	1.54	27.3	____	____	____
F.	134	72.1	____	79.2	279	____	____
G.	____	7.15	5.32	34.1	217	____	____
H.	____	3.12	1.91	____	36.0°C	76.4	____
I.	____	5.27	____	80.9	302	417	____
J.	____	____	2.73	75.2	463	____	2.14
K.	____	____	1.26	____	275	104	0.312
L.	____	____	____	44.0	350	396	4.16
M.	____	34.6	____	____	46.3°C	4.76	54.0
N.	75.2	0.268	____	____	450	____	0.178
O.	3.74	24.2	5.441	____	____	____	145
P.	7.42	1.74	____	8.42	____	____	87.4

8a. The mass and empirical formula of each gas used in part (1) of the drill problems for objective 5-7a are given. Determine the molecular formula of each gas.

A. 19.3 g CH_2 B. 101 g CHF C. 73.3 g CF D. 1.75 g NH_2
E. 9.16 g CH_2 F. 168 g O G. 1.17 g CH H. 991 g NO_2
I. 9.48 g C_2H_2N J. 158 g CHO K. 43.4 g CH_2O L. 17.1 g CH_2O

9. (1) Balance each equation if needed and then fill in the blanks in each line. All gases have the same pressure and temperature.

	C_5H_{12}	+	$O_2(g)$	→	$CO_2(g)$	+	$H_2O(g)$
A.	7.41 L		____ L		____ L		
B.			____ L		87.9 L		____ L
C.	6.75 L		73.1 L		____ L		____ L

	$N_2(g)$	+	$H_2(g)$	→	$NH_3(g)$
D.	27.2 L		____ L		____ L
E.	8.63 L		25.2 L		____ L
F.	____ L		____ L		21.4 L

	$6\ HCl(g)$	+	$2\ HNO_3(g)$	→	$4\ H_2O(g)$	+	$2\ NO(g)$	+	$3\ Cl_2(g)$
G.	9.14 L				____ L		____ L		
H.	____ L				2.17 L		____ L		____ L
I.	1.46 L		0.521 L		____ L		____ L		

	$4\ NH_3(g)$	+	$5\ O_2(g)$	$\xrightarrow{Fe}$	$4\ NO(g)$	+	$6\ H_2O(g)$
J.	4.61 L				____ L		____ L
K.	36.0 L		42.1 L		____ L		____ L
L.			____ L		2.74 L		____ L

	$4\ NH_3(g)$	+	$3\ O_2(g)$	→	$2\ N_2(g)$	+	$6\ H_2O(g)$
M.	____ L		____ L		19.2 L		
N.	24.9 L		18.6 L		____ L		____ L
O.	____ L		____ L		____ L		14.6 L

(2) A given quantity of a C–H–O compound is burned in $O_2(g)$. Both products and reactants are at the pressure and temperature specified. Fill in the blank in each line.

A. 14.2 g $C_2H_6(g)$ → ____ L $CO_2(g)$ 1.94 atm, 50°C
B. 42.1 L $C_3H_8(g)$ + 19.2 g $O_2(g)$ → ____ L $H_2O(g)$ 0.746 atm, 428 K

C. 7.07 g $C_2H_5OH(l)$ + ____ L $O_2(g)$ → ____ L $CO_2(g)$ 0.203 atm, 540 K
D. 1.43 L $C_3H_8(g)$ + ____ L $O_2(g)$ → ____ L $CO_2(g)$ 0.761 atm, 397 K
E. 8.16 L $H_2CO(g)$ + ____ g $O_2(g)$ → ____ g $H_2O(l)$ + ____ L $CO_2(g)$ 0.331 atm, 100°C
F. 1.43 g $C_6H_6(l)$ + 9.14 L $O_2(g)$ → ____ L $H_2O(g)$ 0.621 atm, 150°C
G. 12.3 L $CH_4(g)$ + 123 L $O_2(g)$ → ____ L $CO_2(g)$ 0.714 atm, 200°C
H. 1.13 g $C_2H_6O_2(l)$ + 4.37 L $O_2(g)$ → ____ L $CO_2(g)$ 0.506 atm, 350 K
I. 9.06 g $C_3H_8O(l)$ → ____ L $CO_2(g)$ 1.23 atm, 74°F
J. 8.32 g $C_6H_{14}(l)$ → ____ L $CO_2(g)$ + ____ g $H_2O(l)$ 790 torr, 50°C

10. Fill in the blank in each line below. Gas A is mixed with gas B to produce the mixture of gases. All gases are ideal, and no chemical reactions occur.

	Gas A			*Gas B*			*Mixture*		
	P, atm	*V*, L	*T*, K	*P*, atm	*V*, L	*T*, K	*P*, atm	*V*, L	*T*, K
A.	1.04	27.2	298	0.96	21.2	304	1.00	____	298
B.	2.14	7.86	250	1.32	9.42	273	____	11.6	260
C.	1.21	8.17	308	1.41	16.2	308	1.31	25.0	____
D.	1.73	3.12	298	____	2.14	298	204	6.15	298
E.	1.96	74.2	401	1.96	4.01	____	1.96	80.0	374
F.	1.43	2.13	298	____	2.13	298	7.42	2.13	250
G.	2.17	14.6	294	2.17	16.4	306	4.34	____	300
H.	3.00	17.2	286	3.00	17.2	2.90	____	17.2	294
I.	1.62	9.46	271	2.61	8.46	271	1.23	17.9	____

14. & 15. A. How fast is the average molecule of each of the following gases traveling at 300 K? He, Ne, H_2, N_2, O_2, CO_2, Ar, H_2O, NH_3, CH_4.
B. At what temperature is the average speed of each of the following molecules equal to 300 m/s? He, Ne, H_2, N_2, O_2, CO_2, Ar, CH_4, NH_3, H_2O?
C. How much faster does He effuse than N_2 at 300 K?
D. How much faster does N_2 effuse than O_2 at 1.50 atm?
E. If 1.25 mol He effuses in 8.00 hr, how long is needed for 1.25 mol of Ar to effuse? Both gases are at 74°C.
F. If 0.230 mol N_2 effuses in 12.4 hr, how long is needed for 12.4 mol of H_2O to effuse? Both gases are at 4.71 atm.

QUIZZES (20 minutes each)

Choose the best answer for each question.

Quiz A

1. STP refers to which one of the conditions? (a) 1.00 atm, undefined temperature; (b) 1.00 atm, 0°C; (c) 760 torr, 298 K; (d) 100 torr, 0°C; (e) none of these.
2. The kinetic energy of a gas is directly proportional to its (a) temperature; (b) pressure; (c) volume; (d) composition; (e) none of these.
3. A mathematical statement of Boyle's law is (a) V/T = constant; (b) V/n = constant; (c) P/T = constant; (d) PV = constant; (e) none of these.
4. At 1000°C the pressure of a gas is 5020 kPa. What is its pressure in kPa at 3450°C? (a) 5020(1273/3723); (b) 5020(3723/1273); (c) 5020(3450/1000); (d) 5020(1000/3450); (e) none of these.
5. At 850 kPa and 252 K a gas occupies 17.9 ml. What is its Kelvin temperature at 722 kPa and a volume of 625 ml? (a) 252(722/850)(625/17.9); (b) 252(722/850)(17.9/625); (c) 252(850/722)(17.9/625); (d) 252(850/722)(625/17.9); (e) none of these.
6. 4.0 L of argon at 600 mmHg and 2.0 L of xenon at 300 mmHg are put in a 6.00 L container. The final pressure is (a) 3000 mmHg; (b) 480 mmHg; (c) 500 mmHg; (d) 450 mmHg; (e) none of these.

7. 2.30 mol of gas occupy a volume of 62 ml at 6.14 atm and what kelvin temperature? (a) (6.14)(62)/[(2.30)(0.082)]; (b) (6.14)(2.30)(62)/(0.082); (c) (6.14)(0.062)/[(2.30)(0.082)]; (d) (6.14)(0.062)(0.082)/(62); (e) none of these.
8. 85.1 g of gas occupies 120 L at 0.224 atm and 450°C. Its mole weight is (a) 85.1(0.082/0.224)(450/120); (b) 85.1(0.224/0.082)(120/450); (c) 85.1(0.224/0.082)(120/723); (d) 85.1(0.082/0.224)(120/723); (e) none of these.
9. In the reaction 4 NH_3(g) + Cl_2(g) → N_2H_4(g) + 2 NH_4Cl(s), how many liters of ammonia will combine with 14.0 L of chlorine? (a) (14.0/22.4); (b) (14.0)(22.4)(4); (c) (14.0)(4); (d) (14.0/22.4)(1/4); (e) none of these.
10. A gas has a temperature of 200 K. What is its kelvin temperature if the average kinetic energy of the molecules doubles? (a) ($\sqrt{2}$)(200 K); (b) 200 K; (c) (2)(200 K); (d) (3/2)(200 K); (e) none of these.

Quiz B

1. The postulates of the kinetic molecular theory include all those below *except* (a) no forces exist between molecules; (b) molecules are point masses; (c) molecules are attracted to the walls of the container; (d) molecules are in random motion; (e) none of these.
2. The mutual attraction of gas molecules is an important aspect of (a) Avogadro's law; (b) Dalton's law; (c) Graham's law; (d) van der Waals theory; (e) none of these.
3. Subtracting the vapor pressure of water from the total pressure of a gas collected over water is an example of the application of (a) Avogadro's law; (b) Dalton's law; (c) Graham's law; (d) van der Waals theory; (e) none of these.
4. A gas has a volume of 16.0 L at 37°C. What is its volume in liters at 82°C? (a) 16.0(82/37); (b) 16.0(37/82); (c) 16.0(310/355); (d) 16.0(355/310); (e) none of these.
5. At 1.70 atm and 27°C a gas occupies 14.0 L. What is its volume in liters at 1.05 atm and −3°C? (a) 14.0(1.70/1.05)(270/300); (b) 14.0(1.05/1.70)(270/300); (c) 14.0(1.05/1.70)(300/270); (d) 14.0(1.70/1.05)(300/270); (e) none of these.
6. 1.0 L of hydrogen at 700 kPa and 2.0 L of nitrogen at 1000 kPa are put in 3.0 L container. The final pressure is (a) 900 kPa; (b) 800 kPa; (c) 850 kPa; (d) 750 kPa; (e) none of these.
7. How many moles of gas occupy 3.14 L at 272 K and 0.112 atm? (a) (0.112)(272)/[(0.082)(3.14)]; (b) (0.082)(272)/[(0.112)(3.14)]; (c) (0.112)(3.14)/[(0.082)(272)]; (d) (0.082)(3.14)/[(0.112)(272)]; (e) none of these.
8. 22.4 g of gas occupies 15.2 L at 77°C and 3.21 atm. Its mole weight is (a) 22.4(0.082/3.21)(350/15.2); (b) 22.4(0.082/3.21)(77/15.2); (c) 22.4(0.082/3.21)(15.2/350); (d) 22.4(3.21/0.082)(350/15.2); (e) none of these.
9. In the reaction 2 H_2S(g) + 3 O_2(g) → 2 H_2O(l) + 2 SO_2(g), how many liters of O_2 are needed to produce 16.2 L of SO_2? (a) (16.2)(2/3); (b) (16.2)(3/2); (c) (16.2); (d) (16.2)(22.4)(3/2); (e) none of these.
10. The rate of effusion for a gas (38 g/mol) is 3.14 L/s. What is the rate in L/s for a second gas (28 g/mol)? (a) 3.14(38/28); (b) 3.14(28/28); (c) 3.14 $\sqrt{38/28}$; (d) 3.14 $\sqrt{28/38}$; (e) none of these.

Quiz C

1. If the kelvin temperature of a gas is doubled, then (a) the average molecules moves twice as fast; (b) every molecule moves twice as fast; (c) every molecule has twice the kinetic energy; (d) the average molecule has twice the kinetic energy; (e) none of these.
2. The ideal gas constant has the value of 0.08206. The units of this number are (a) L atm mol^{-1} K^{-1}; (b) L torr mol^{-1} K^{-1}; (c) ml torr mol^{-1} K^{-1}; (d) ml atm mol^{-1} K^{-1}; (e) none of these.
3. $PV = nRT$ is a statement of (a) Avogadro's law; (b) Dalton's law; (c) Graham's law; (d) van der Waals theory; (e) none of these.
4. At 5.12 atm the temperature of a gas is 47°C. What is the Celsius temperature at 7.14 atm? (a) 320(7.14/5.12) − 273; (b) 320(5.12/7.14) − 273; (c) 47(5.12/7.14) + 273; (d) 47(7.14/5.12) + 273; (e) none of these

5. At 250 torr and 150°C, a gas occupies 75.2 L. What is its volume in liters at 520 torr and 275°C? (a) 75.2(250/520)(275/150); (b) 75.2(250/520)(548/423); (c) 75.2(520/250)(548/423); (d) 75.2(520/250)(275/150); (e) none of these.
6. 3.0 L of neon at 640 kPa and 2.0 L of xenon at 250 kPa are put in a 5.0 L container. The final pressure is (a) 445 kPa; (b) 484 kPa; (c) 2420 kPa; (d) 406 kPa; (e) none of these.
7. 2.24 mol of gas exerts what pressure in atm at 25°C and a volume of 72 L? (a) (2.24)(0.082)(25)/(72); (b) (2.24)(0.082)(72)/(298); (c) (2.24)(72)(298)/(0.082); (d) (298)(72)(0.082)/(2.24); (e) none of these.
8. 22.4 g of gas occupies 22.4 L at 273 K and 2.24 atm. Its mole weight is (a) 22.4; (b) 22.4(2.24/0.082)(273/22.4); (c) 22.4(0.082/2.24)(273/22.4); (d) 22.4(0.082/2.24)(546/22.4); (e) none of these.
9. In the reaction $3\ H_2S(g) + 2\ HNO_3 \rightarrow 3\ S + 2\ NO(g) + 4\ H_2O$, how many liters of $H_2S(g)$ are needed to produce 75.1 L of NO(g)? (a) (75.1)(2/3); (b) 75.1(3/2); (c) (75.1/22.4)(3/2); (d) 75.1; (e) none of these.
10. 3.12 mmol of Ne (20.2 g/mol) effuses through a pinhole in 14.2 min. How many minutes are needed for 3.12 mmol of methane (CH_4, 16.0 g/mol) to effuse through the same pinhole? (a) 14.2; (b) 14.2(20.2/16.0); (c) $14.2\sqrt{20.2/16.0}$; (d) $14.2\sqrt{16.0/20.2}$; (e) none of these.

Quiz D

1. Pressure is the result of (a) molecular speed only; (b) molecular speed and size; (c) molecular size only; (d) repulsive forces between molecules; (e) none of these.
2. Gases approach ideal behavior closest under what set of conditions? (a) high temperature, low pressure; (b) low temperature, low pressure; (c) high temperature, high pressure; (d) low temperature, high pressure; (e) none of these.
3. Equal volumes of two gases at the same temperature and pressure have (a) equal weights; (b) Avogadro's number of molecules; (c) identical chemical compositions; (d) the same number of molecules; (e) none of these.
4. At 946 mmHg the volume of gas is 2.54 L. What is its volume in liters at 454 mmHg? (a) 2.54(454/946)(760); (b) 2.54(454/946); (c) 2.54(946/454)(760); (d) 2.54(946/454); (e) none of these.
5. At 8.59 atm and 25°C a gas occupies 16.2 L. What is its pressure in atm at 421 K and a volume of 14.0 L? (a) 8.59(421/25)(16.2/14.0); (b) 8.59(25/421)(14.0/16.2); (c) 8.59(298/421)(14.0/16.2); (d) 8.59(421/298)(16.2/14.0); (e) none of these.
6. 2.0 L of argon at 400 kPa and 3.0 L of neon at 600 kPa are put in a 5.0 L container. The final pressure is (a) 500 kPa; (b) 520 kPa; (c) 580 kPa; (d) 2600 kPa; (e) none of these.
7. 0.82 mol of gas exert what pressure in torr at 23°C and a volume of 72 L? (a) (0.82)(0.082)(296)(760)/(72); (b) (0.82)(0.082)(296)/(72); (c) (0.82)(0.082)(72)/(296); (d) (0.82)(0.082)(296)/[(72)(760)]; (e) none of these.
8. 374 g of gas occupy 82.4 L at 12.4 atm and 750 K. Its mole weight is (a) 374(0.082/12.4)(750/82.4); (b) 374(0.082/12.4)(82.4/750); (c) 374(12.4/0.082)(82.4/750); (d) 374(12.4/0.082)(750/82.4); (e) none of these.
9. How many milliliters of O_2 are needed to form 200 ml of NO?

$$4\ NH_3(g) + 5\ O_2(g) \rightarrow 4\ NO(g) + 6\ H_2O$$

(a) 200(4/5); (b) 200(4/6); (c) 200(5/6); (d) 200(6/4); (e) none of these.
10. 2.45 ml of methane (CH_4, 16.0 g/mol) effuses through a pinhole in 1.25 min. What is the mole weight (in g/mol) of a second gas if 2.45 ml of it (measured at the same *T* and *P*) require 2.61 min to effuse through the same pinhole? (a) $16.0(2.61/1.25)^2$; (b) 16.0(2.61/1.25); (c) $16.0\sqrt{1.25/2.61}$ (d) $16.0\sqrt{2.61/1.25}$; (e) none of these.

SAMPLE TEST (20 minutes)

1. Convert the units of each of the following properties as indicated.
   a. Pressure: 26.4 lb/in.^{2} = ____ atm = ____ kPa
   b. Volume: 2.0 ft^3 = ____ m^3 = ____ L
   c. Temperature: 92.0°F = ____ °C ____ K
2. A gas having the pressure, vilume, and temperature given in the previous problem has a mass of 1.305 lb. What is the mole weight, in g/mol, of this gas?
3. What is the numerical value of the ideal gas constant R when it has the units ml mmHg mmol^{-1} K^{-1}?
4. Two gases are to be mixed into a 5.000 L container at 291.0 K. Gas A originally is confined in 14.20 L at 1.067 atm and 303.1 K. Gas B originally is confined in 1.251 L at 26.42 atm and 327.5 K. Once they are mixed in the 5.000 L container,
   a. What is the total pressure?
   b. What is the partial pressure of Gas A?
   c. What is the partial volume of Gas B?
5. 1 mol of helium and 1 mol of neon are mixed in a container.
   a. Which gas has the larger mass?
   b. Which gas has the greater average molecular speed?
   c. Which type of molecule strikes the wall of the container most frequently?
   d. Which gas exerts the larger pressure?

Chapter 6

Thermochemistry

Chapter 6

REVIEW OF OBJECTIVES

1. Distinguish between heat and work.

Work moves an object through a distance and heat raises its temperature. Although we can transform work completely into heat, we cannot transform heat completely into work. The difference is that work is an organized form of energy and can move large objects. Heat is more random and mainly is able to make small particles—atoms and molecules—move more rapidly.

In addition, heat and work only appear during energy *changes.* We do not speak of absolute energies. We can readily measure energy as it moves between system and surroundings, but we cannot measure it in place.

★ 2. Use specific heat to determine temperature changes and quantities of heat.

Specific heat is the quantity of heat required to raise the temperature of one gram of a substance by one degree Celsius. Specific heat depends on the nature of the substance being heated. The specific heat of water is larger than that of iron. Specific heat has the units of Joules per gram per degree Celsius (J g^{-1} $°C^{-1}$) or calories per gram per degree Celsius (cal g^{-1} $°C^{-1}$). The quantity of heat absorbed by an object whose temperature changes is given by equation [1].

$$\text{heat absorbed} = (\text{mass})\,(\text{specific heat})\,(\text{temperature change})$$
$$q = (m)\,(\text{sp. ht.})\,(\Delta T) \qquad [1]$$

($\overline{C}_p$) is the quantity of heat needed to raise the temperature of one mole of a substance by one degree Celsius. It has the units of J mol^{-1} $°C^{-1}$ or cal mol^{-1} $°C^{-1}$. Thus the heat absorbed by an object is given by equation [2].

$$q = (n)(\overline{C}_p)(\Delta T) \qquad (n = \text{number of moles of substance}) \qquad [2]$$

There is a standard convention for using the symbol Δ (delta). It represents the final value minus the initial value of a property: $\Delta T = T_f - T_i$; $\Delta n = n_f - n_i$; $\Delta V = V_f - V_i$; and so forth.

EXAMPLE 6-1 What quantity of heat is needed to raise the temperature of 500.0 g Cu ($\overline{C}_p$ = 24.5 J mol^{-1} $°C^{-1}$) from 20.0 to 50.0°C?

$$\text{heat} = n\overline{C}_p\Delta T$$
$$= 500.0\text{ g}\left(\frac{\text{mol Cu}}{63.54\text{ g}}\right)\left(24.5\,\frac{\text{J}}{\text{mol °C}}\right)(50.0°\text{C} - 20.0°\text{C})$$
$$= 5.78 \times 10^3\text{ J} = 5.78\text{ kJ}$$

One can combine equation [1] or [2] with the law of conservation of energy to determine specific heats of materials or final temperatures of mixtures.

EXAMPLE 6-2 150.0 g H_2O (sp. ht. = 4.184 J g^{-1} $°C^{-1}$) at 20.0°C is mixed with 100.0 g V (sp. ht. = 0.502 J g^{-1} $°C^{-1}$) at 100.0°C. What is the final temperature of the mixture?

We use the law of conservation of energy first.

$$-\text{heat gained by V} = \text{heat gained by } H_2O$$

$$-(100.0\text{ g})(0.502\frac{\text{J}}{\text{g °C}})(T_f - 100.0\text{°C}) = (150.0\text{ g})(4.184\frac{\text{J}}{\text{g °C}})(T_f - 20.0\text{°C})$$

$$-50.2T_f + 5.02 \times 10^3 = 627.6T_f - 1.26 \times 10^4$$
$$1.76 \times 10^4 = 677.8T_f \quad or \quad T_f = 26.0\text{°C}$$

EXAMPLE 6-3 140.0 g H_2O at 25.0°C is mixed with 100.0 g of metal at 100.0°C. The final temperature of the mixture is 29.6°C. What is the specific heat of the metal?

$$-\text{heat gained by the metal} = \text{heat lost by the water}$$
$$-(100.0\text{ g})(\text{sp. ht.})(29.6\text{°C} - 100.0\text{°C}) = (140.0\text{ g})(4.184\text{ J g}^{-1}\text{ °C}^{-1})(29.6 - 20.5)\text{ °C}$$
$$(7040\text{ g°C})(\text{sp. ht.}) = 2694\text{ J} \quad or \quad \text{sp. ht.} = 0.38\text{ J g}^{-1}\text{ °C}^{-1}$$

3. Realize that heat and work are merely two different ways in which energy appears.

It seems obvious to a casual observer that heat and work are different. Heat always is associated with changes either in temperature or in the state of matter, as from solid to liquid. On the other hand, work is associated with motion. Actually, heat and work are simply two different ways in which energy appears. Nevertheless, both the English and the metric systems have two units for energy—one for heat and the other for work.

calorie: the heat needed to raise the temperature of one gram of water from 14.5 to 15.5°C (Calorie, spelled with a capital C, is a nutritional Calorie, equal to 1000 calories).

Btu (British thermal unit): the heat needed to raise the temperature of one pound of water one degree Fahrenheit at or near 39.1°F.

Joule: the work done when a force of one newton acts through a distance of one meter.

foot-pound: the work done when a force of one pound acts through a distance of one foot.

The calorie presently is defined in terms of the Joule as one calorie = 4.184 Joule (precisely). The Joule is an SI unit. The calorie eventually will be discarded.

★ **4. & 5. State the first law of thermodynamics and the sign conventions for heat and work, and use equation [3], $\Delta E = q - w$.**

The first law of thermodynamics also is called the law of conservation of energy. A convenient statement is that energy is neither created nor destroyed, merely changed from one form into another.

$$\Delta E = q - w \qquad [3]$$

ΔE is the change in the internal energy of the system. q is defined as the heat absorbed by the system. If the system actually gives off heat during a process, then that heat has a negative sign by convention. This is a universal convention. w is defined as the work which the system does on its surroundings. If the surroundings do work on the system, then that work has a negative sign by convention. (Although the convention for heat is universal, that for work is not. Many writers use exactly the opposite convention: positive work is that done *on* the system, and if the system does work on the surroundings, that work is negative. In addition, these authors usually symbolize internal energy by U, rather than by E, so that the change in internal energy becomes $\Delta U = q + w$. This second convention is used in the British Commonwealth.)

When work is done on a system or when heat is absorbed by the system, energy is flowing into the system and ΔE must be positive; the system's internal energy must increase. When the system is emitting heat or doing work, energy is leaving the system and ΔE must be negative; the system's internal energy must decrease. Remember that we only can determine *changes* in internal energy, never its absolute value.

6. Know the meaning of the concept "state function," especially as demonstrated by internal energy.

The concept of a state function is one of the most powerful in all of thermodynamics. A state function, or state property, is one that only depends on where the system starts (its initial state) and where it ends (its final state). A state function does not depend on how the change in the system occurred (the pathway). The distance from New York to Los Angeles is a state function. Yet the actual mileage traveled depends on the route. The mileage traveled is a path function. Both heat and work are path functions, although they may equal state functions if the pathway is defined in a specified manner. Some other state functions are temperature, mass, volume, pressure, and density.

★ **7. Calculate the heat of a reaction at constant volume, q_V, using bomb calorimetry data.**

The heat given off by a reaction occurring in a bomb calorimeter increases the temperature of both the bomb and the water which surrounds it.

$$\begin{aligned} q_V &= -\text{ heat gained by water} - \text{heat gained by bomb} \\ &= -(\text{mass } H_2O)(\text{sp. ht.})(\Delta T) - (C_B)(\Delta T) \end{aligned} \qquad [4]$$

C_B is the heat capacity of the bomb–the quantity of heat required to raise the temperature of the bomb by 1°C. $\Delta E = q_V$ because no work can be done on (or by) the system if its volume does not change. This is because $w = P\Delta V$ (and if the volume does not change, $\Delta V = 0$). Notice that a path function (heat) has been restricted by specifying its pathway (one of constant volume) so that it equals a state function.

EXAMPLE 6-4 0.927 g of benzoic acid is burned completely in a bomb surrounded by 1.000 kg H_2O. The heat of combustion of benzoic acid is 26.42 kJ/g. The temperature increases from 25.12 to 29.36°C. What is C_B?

$$\begin{aligned} q_V &= (-26.42 \times 10^3 \text{ J/g})(0.927 \text{ g}) = -2.45 \times 10^4 \text{ J} \\ &= -(\text{mass } H_2O)(\text{sp. ht.})(\Delta T) - C_B(\Delta T) \\ &= -(1000 \text{ g})(4.18 \frac{\text{J}}{\text{g °C}})(29.36\text{°C} - 25.12\text{°C}) - C_B(29.36\text{°C} - 25.12\text{°C}) \\ &= -1.77 \times 10^4 \text{ J} - C_B(4.24\text{°C}) \\ -C_B &= (-2.45 \times 10^4 \text{ J} + 1.77 \times 10^4 \text{ J})/4.24\text{°C} = -1.6 \times 10^3 \text{ J/°C} \\ C_B &= 1.6 \text{ kJ/°C} \end{aligned}$$

★ **8. Explain the purpose of enthalpy and be able to compute one of ΔH or ΔE given the other for a reaction involving gases.**

The heat given off at constant volume equals the change in internal energy.

$$\Delta E = q_V \qquad [5]$$

Most reactions run at constant pressure. The heat given off at constant pressure equals the change in enthalpy.

$$\Delta H = q_P \qquad [6]$$

Enthalpy is a state function related to internal energy.

$$\Delta H = \Delta E + P\Delta V \qquad [7]$$

$$\Delta \bar{H} = \Delta \bar{E} + \Delta \bar{n}_g RT \qquad [8]$$

Equation [8] is the more convenient to use. $\Delta \bar{n}_g$ is the difference between the stoichiometric coefficients of the gaseous products and those of the gaseous reactants in the balanced equation for the chemical reaction.

Equations [7] and [8] depend strongly on the concept of a state function. Equations [5] and [6] tell us how to *measure* the state functions ΔE and ΔH. We determine the heat given off by the system at constant volume or at constant pressure. But once ΔE and ΔH have been measured, we can combine them, disregarding the different conditions of measurement. We can do this because ΔE and ΔH are state functions.

We take similar advantage of state functions in many common calculations. For example, the difference in your body weight from week to week depends on how much food you eat and how much exercise you get. Food and exercise are converted into common units, nutritional Calories.

The term $\Delta\bar{n}_g$ in equation [8] is often misinterpreted. As *the text* correctly illustrates, $\Delta\bar{n}_g$ is computed by subtracting the sum of the stoichiometric coefficients of the gaseous reactants from the sum of the stoichiometric coefficients of the gaseous products. Values of $\Delta\bar{n}_g$ for five reactions follow.

$$N_2(g) + 3\,H_2(g) \rightarrow 2\,NH_3(g) \qquad \Delta\bar{n}_g = 2 - 4 = -2$$
$$Mg_3N_2(s) + 6\,H_2O(l) \rightarrow 3\,Mg(OH)_2(s) + 2\,NH_3(g) \qquad \Delta\bar{n}_g = 2 - 0 = +2$$

$$C_3H_7OH(l) + \tfrac{9}{2}\,O_2(g) \rightarrow 3\,CO_2(g) + 4\,H_2O(l) \qquad \Delta\bar{n}_g = 3 - 4.5 = -1.5$$

$$4\,P(s) + 5\,O_2(g) \rightarrow 2\,P_2O_5(s) \qquad \Delta\bar{n}_g = 0 - 5 = -5$$
$$4\,NH_3(g) + 3\,O_2(g) \rightarrow 2\,N_2(g) + 6\,H_2O(l) \qquad \Delta\bar{n}_g = 2 - 7 = -5$$

Notice that both $\Delta\bar{H}$ and $\Delta\bar{E}$ in equation [8] have a line over the symbol, an overscore. This overscore means that these are molar quantities. They are expressed in units of energy per mole (J/mol). "Per mole of what?" you may ask. In the first three equations above, the answer is per mole of $N_2(g)$, $Mg_3N_2(s)$, or $C_3H_7OH(l)$, respectively. In the last two equations per mole means: for 4 moles of P(s), 2 moles of $P_2O_5(s)$; for 4 moles of $NH_3(g)$, 6 moles of $H_2O(l)$, and so on.

Thus if we express the energy of a reaction in kJ/mol, as is usually done, we mean that the stoichiometric coefficients in the balanced equation indicate the amount in moles of reactants and products. A concise way of stating these ideas is the enthalpy change *per mole of reaction.* Note that $\Delta\bar{H}$ and $\Delta\bar{E}$ usually are given in kJ/mol whereas $R = 8.314$ J mol^{-1} K^{-1}. Thus $\Delta\bar{n}_g RT$ must be converted to kJ/mol before it is combined with $\Delta\bar{H}$ and $\Delta\bar{E}$.

EXAMPLE 6-5 When 0.1640 g $NH_3(g)$ reacts at 293 K via $4\,NH_3(g) + 3\,O_2(g) \rightarrow 2\,N_2(g) + 6\,H_2O(l)$, $q_V = -3.651$ kJ. Compute $\Delta\bar{H}$ for this reaction (rxn).

$$\Delta\bar{E} = -\left(\frac{3.651\text{ kJ}}{0.1640\text{ g NH}_3}\right)\left(\frac{17.02\text{ g NH}_3}{\text{mol NH}_3}\right)\left(\frac{4\text{ mol NH}_3}{\text{mol rxn}}\right) = -1517\text{ kJ/mol}$$

$$\Delta\bar{H} = \Delta\bar{E} + \Delta\bar{n}_g RT$$
$$= -1517\,\frac{\text{kJ}}{\text{mol}} - \left(\frac{5\text{ mol gas}}{\text{mol rxn}}\right)\left(8.314\,\frac{\text{J}}{\text{mol K}}\right)(293\text{ K})\left(\frac{\text{kJ}}{1000\text{ J}}\right)$$
$$= -1517\text{ kJ/mol} - 12.2\text{ kJ/mol} = -1529\text{ kJ/mol (of reaction)}$$

9. Explain how to use a Styrofoam coffee cup calorimeter and interpret the data obtained.

A nest of Styrofoam coffee cups with a lid is almost a perfectly adiabatic container–very little heat is lost or gained by the system inside the cups. All of the heat produced or absorbed by any process within the cup produces a temperature change in the system.

$$\text{heat absorbed} = (\text{mass})(\text{sp. ht.})(\Delta T) \qquad [1]$$

The heat is produced by a chemical reaction occurring within the system rather than being added from the surroundings. The experiment is conducted at constant pressure and thus we measure q_P.

EXAMPLE 6-6 50.0 ml each of NaOH(aq) and HCl(aq), both at a concentration of 1.00 *M* and a temperature of 20.5°C, are mixed in a Styrofoam cup calorimeter. The final temperature of the system is 27.3°C. The resulting 0.500*M* NaCl(aq) has a density of 1.02 g/ml and a specific heat of 4.02 J g^{-1} °C^{-1}. Compute $\Delta\bar{H}$ for the reaction

$$NaOH(aq) + HCl(aq) \rightarrow NaCl(aq) + H_2O(l)$$
$$q_P = [(1.02\text{ g/ml})(100.0\text{ ml})]\,(4.02\text{ J g}^{-1}\,°\text{C}^{-1})(27.3°\text{C} - 20.5°\text{C}) = 2.79 \times 10^3\text{ J}$$

This is the heat *absorbed by the solution.* The heat produced by the reaction is the negative of this value.

$$q_{p,\,rxn} = -2.79 \times 10^3 \text{ kJ} = \Delta H_{rxn}$$

The amount of NaCl then is computed.

$$\text{no. mol NaCl} = 0.1000 \text{ L soln}\left(\frac{0.500 \text{ mol NaCl}}{\text{L soln}}\right) = 0.0500 \text{ mol NaCl}$$

Finally, we compute $\Delta\bar{H}$.

$$\Delta\bar{H} = \frac{\Delta H_{rxn}}{\text{no. mol NaCl}} = \frac{-2.79 \times 10^3 \text{ J}}{0.0500 \text{ mol NaCl}} = -55.7 \times 10^3 \text{ J/mol} = -55.7 \text{ kJ/mol}$$

10. Apply Hess's law of constant heat summation.

We do not have to actually run a chemical reaction in order to determine how much heat it will produce or consume. We simply combine the heats of a series of consecutive reactions whose overall result is the same as the reaction which we wish to study. On paper we go from the same reactants (initial state) to the same products (final state) but by a different pathway.

EXAMPLE 6-7 What is $\Delta\bar{H}°$ for the reaction C (graphite) + 2 S (rhombic) → CS_2 (l)? Although this reaction has not yet been observed, the following reactions have been.

(*a*) C (graphite) + O_2 (g) → CO_2 (g) $\quad \Delta\bar{H}° = -\ 393.5$ kJ/mol
(*b*) S (rhombic) + O_2 (g) → SO_2 (g) $\quad \Delta\bar{H}° = -\ 296.9$ kJ/mol
(*c*) CS_2 (l) + 3 O_2 (g) → CO_2 (g) + 2 SO_2 (g) $\quad \Delta\bar{H}° = -1075.2$ kJ/mol

We combine the given reactions: (*a*) + 2(*b*) − (*c*). Whatever we do to the reactions (multiply them by a constant or change their sign–reverse them) we also do to the associated $\Delta\bar{H}°$s.

(*a*)	C (graphite) + O_2 (g) → CO_2 (g)	$\Delta\bar{H}° = -\ 393.5$ kJ/mol
2(*b*)	2 S (rhombic) + 2 O_2 (g) → 2 SO_2 (g)	$\Delta\bar{H}° = -\ 593.8$ kJ/mol
−(*c*)	CO_2 (g) + 2 SO_2 (g) → CS_2 (l) + 3 O_2 (g)	$\Delta\bar{H}° = +1075.2$ kJ/mol
	C (graphite) + 2 S (rhombic) → CS_2 (l)	$\Delta\bar{H}° = +\ 87.9$ kJ/mol

10a. Know the definitions of standard state and of standard formation reactions and write the standard formation reaction for any substance.

In order to use Hess's law, all reactants and products must be under the same conditions. Consider the CO_2 (g) produced by reaction (*a*) in objective 6–10 and consumed by reaction −(*c*). If reaction (*a*) produces CO_2 (g) at 298 K and 1.00 atm and reaction −(*c*) requires CO_2 (g) at 323 K and 4.00 atm then energy is needed to heat and compress the gas.

If reactants and products are in a well-defined state at one temperature, then no energy is needed for heating and compression (or produced by cooling and expansion). The standard state is a pressure of one atmosphere or, for a substance in solution, a concentration of one mole per liter of solution. The degree sign (°) on $\Delta\bar{H}°$ indicates that the molar enthalpy change is measured at the standard state. The standard state does not mention the temperature. Temperature should be given in kelvins as a subscript, $\Delta\bar{H}°_{298}$. Often, however, this subscript is omitted and 298 K is assumed.

The standard state also does not mention anything about the form of the substance. We can speak of the standard state of the two allotropes of oxygen, O_2 (g) and O_3 (g) or ozone. We also can refer to the standard state of steam, H_2O(g); of ice, H_2O(s); and of liquid water, H_2O(l). It is helpful to speak of all substances as being formed from one set of reactants. Since all matter is composed of atoms, we pick the most stable or lowest-energy form of each element.

These ideas are contained in the *standard formation reaction:* the reaction which produces one mole of a substance in its standard state from the elements in their standard states and most stable forms. For example,

$$2\,C(\text{graphite}) + 3\,H_2(g) + \tfrac{1}{2}\,O_2(g) \rightarrow C_2H_5OH(l)$$
$$2\,P(\text{white}) + \tfrac{5}{2}\,O_2(g) \rightarrow P_2O_5(s)$$
$$Ca(c) + \tfrac{3}{2}\,O_2(g) + C(\text{graphite}) \rightarrow CaCO_3(s)$$

The stable forms of the elements at 25°C (298.15 K) are given in Table 6-1.

TABLE 6-1
Most Stable Forms of the Elements at 25°C

H_2 – gas	He – gas	C – graphite
N_2 – gas	O_2 – gas	F_2 – gas
Ne – gas	P – white solid	S – rhombic solid
Cl_2 – gas	Ar – gas	Mn – crystalline, α
As – gray solid	Se – gray solid	Br_2 – liquid
Kr – gas	Cd – crystalline, α	Sn – white solid
Sb – crystalline, III	I_2 – solid	Xe – gas
Hg – liquid	U – crystalline, III	
All other elements – crystalline solid, (c) or (s)		

11. Explain how standard molar enthalpies of formation are established.

The standard molar enthalpy of formation is the heat evolved at constant pressure (the enthalpy change) when the standard formation reaction occurs. But what if the reaction does not occur as written? We already have answered this question in Example 6-7. The reaction

$$C(\text{graphite}) + 2\,S(\text{rhombic}) \rightarrow (CS_2(l)$$

does not occur, and it is the formation reaction for CS_2 (l). We determined $\Delta\overline{H}^\circ_f$, the standard enthalpy of formation, for CS_2 (l) by combining the $\Delta\overline{H}^\circ$ values of several reactions which do occur.

★ **12. Apply Hess's law in the special case of standard formation reactions, that is, compute $\Delta\overline{H}^\circ_{rxn}$ from ΔH°_f values.**

Standard formation reactions greatly simplify the application of Hess's law.

EXAMPLE 6-8 What is $\Delta\overline{H}^\circ_{rxn}$ for the oxidation of ammonia in the presence of a platinum catalyst?

$$4\,NH_3(g) + 5\,O_2(g) \xrightarrow{Pt} 4\,NO(g) + 6\,H_2O(l)$$

	$4\,NH_3(g)$	$5\,O_2(g)$	$4\,NO(g)$	$6\,H_2O(l)$
$\Delta\overline{H}^\circ_f$:	−46.19	0.00	90.37	−285.85 kJ/mol

Below each substance is listed its standard molar enthalpy of formation in kJ/mol. The $\Delta\overline{H}^\circ_f$s are equivalent to the following thermochemical equations.

(*d*)	$\tfrac{1}{2}\,N_2(g) + \tfrac{3}{2}\,H_2(g) \rightarrow NH_3(g)$	$\Delta\overline{H}^\circ = -\;46.19$ kJ/mol
(*e*)	$O_2(g) \rightarrow O_2(g)$	$\Delta\overline{H}^\circ = 0.00$ kJ/mol
(*f*)	$\tfrac{1}{2}\,N_2(g) + \tfrac{1}{2}\,O_2(g) \rightarrow NO(g)$	$\Delta\overline{H}^\circ = +\;90.37$ kJ/mol
(*g*)	$\tfrac{1}{2}\,O_2(g) + H_2(g) \rightarrow H_2O(l)$	$\Delta\overline{H}^\circ = -285.85$ kJ/mol

Notice that $\Delta\overline{H}^\circ_f$ for O_2 (g) is 0.00 kJ/mol since the product of the formation reaction *is* an element in its most stable form [In contrast, $\Delta\overline{H}^\circ_f$ = 142.3 kJ/mol for ozone, O_3 (g).] Equations (*d*) through (*g*) can be combined to yield the equation for the catalytic oxidation of ammonia: −4(*d*) −5(*e*) + 4(*f*) + 6(g).

−4 (*d*)	$4\,NH_3(g) \rightarrow 2\,N_2(g) + 6\,H_2(g)$	$\Delta\bar{H}° = +\ 184.8$ kJ/mol
−5 (*e*)	$5\,O_2(g) \rightarrow 5\,O_2(g)$	$\Delta\bar{H}° = \ \ 0.00$ kJ/mol
+4 (*f*)	$2\,N_2(g) + 2\,O_2(g) \rightarrow 4\,NO(g)$	$\Delta\bar{H}° = +\ 361.5$ kJ/mol
+6 (*g*)	$6\,H_2(g) + 3\,O_2(g) \rightarrow 6\,H_2O(l)$	$\Delta\bar{H}° = -1715.1$ kJ/mol
	$4\,NH_3(g) + 5\,O_2(g) \rightarrow 4\,NO(g) + 6\,H_2O(g)$	$\Delta\bar{H}° = -1168.8$ kJ/mol

Notice that the numbers which we used to multiply reactions (*d*) through (*g*) are the stoichiometric coefficients in the original equation! In order to determine $\Delta\bar{H}°_{rxn}$ for a reaction, we first add the $\Delta\bar{H}°_f$ values for the products, each one multiplied by the stoichiometric coefficient which that substance has in the reaction. From this sum of product $\Delta\bar{H}°_f$s we subtract a similarly constructed sum of reactant $\Delta\bar{H}°_f$ values.

$$\Delta\bar{H}°_{rxn} = \sum_{products} \nu_{prod}\,\Delta\bar{H}°_{f,\,prod} - \sum_{reactants} \nu_{reac}\,\Delta\bar{H}°_{f,\,reac} \qquad [9]$$

In equation [9], the νs are the stoichiometric coefficients in the balanced chemical equation. For the calculation of Example 6-8, equation [9] becomes

$$\begin{aligned}\Delta\bar{H}°_{rxn} &= 4\,\Delta\bar{H}°_{f\,NO(g)} + 6\,\Delta\bar{H}°_{f,\,H_2O(l)} - 4\,\Delta\bar{H}°_{f,\,NH_3(g)} - 5\,\Delta\bar{H}°_{f,\,O_2(g)}\\ &= 4(90.37) + 6(-285.85) - 4(-46.19) - 5(0.00)\ \text{kJ/mol}\\ &= -1168.8\ \text{kJ/mol}\end{aligned}$$

DRILL PROBLEMS

2. (1) Fill in the blanks in each line which follows. The numbers have the units given in the column headings unless otherwise specified.

	q, J	m, g	sp. ht., J g^{-1} °C^{-1}	t_i, °C	t_f, °C
A.	640	124	0.931	25.0	____
B.	____	75.2	0.587	20.0	30.0
C.	374	103	____	19.5	25.4
D.	1300	____	0.863	17.2	30.1
E.	194 cal	125	0.750	21.2	____
F.	____	142	1.086	66.1°F	52.3°F
G.	876	4.32 oz	____	22.1	30.4
H.	444	____	0.0953 cal g^{-1} °C^{-1}	19.4	26.5
	q, J	n, mol	$\bar{C}_p$, J mol^{-1} °C^{-1}	t_i, °C	t_f, °C
I.	1962	14.0	72.0	19.3	____
J.	83.5	____	32.1	20.4	22.1
K.	572	1.65	____	21.4	35.7
L.	____	4.32	26.1	19.7	17.3
M.	1043	5.72	56.2	16.8	____

(2) Fill in the blank in each line which follows. Substances A and B are mixed, and the mixture has the temperature given in the right-hand column. The system is adiabatic.

	Substance A			*Substance B*			*Mixture*
	m, g	*Sp. ht.* J g^{-1} °C^{-1}	*t*, °C	*m*, g	*Sp. ht.* J g^{-1} °C^{-1}	*t*, °C	*t*, °C
A.	52.0	4.18	25.0	194	____	35.0	31.2
B.	124	4.60	20.0	10.2	0.412	75.2	____
C.	76.4	4.31	15.0	24.2	1.326	____	27.3

D. 142	3.90	24.7	____	0.435	68.4	37.4
E. 7.51	0.682	94.1	____	3.66	27.2	39.0
F. 9.64	1.293	85.7	274	____	12.8	25.9
G. 7.28	3.06	106.0	15.4	4.18	____	82.0
H. 16.3	1.188	23.1	75.6	3.90	47.5	____
I. 12.8	1.686	64.7	105	3.06	19.4	____

5. Fill in the blanks in each line below. The first line is an example.

	Heat (of system)	*Work done*	q	w	ΔE
	143 J absorbed	96 J by surr.	143 J	−96 J	239 J
A.	196 J evolved	123 J by system	____	____	____
B.	189 J evolved	247 J on system	____	____	____
C.	647 J absorbed	92.4 J on surr.	____	____	____
D.	1362 J absorbed	321 J by system	____	____	____
E.	142 J evolved	254 J by surr.	____	____	____
F.	802 J absorbed	897 J by surr.	____	____	____
G.	−1432 J absorbed	937 J by surr.	____	____	____
H.	972 J evolved	432 J by system	____	____	____

7. Fill in the blank in each line below. m = the mass of substance burned in the calorimeter and q_s is that substance's heat of combustion in kJ/g.

m, g	q_s, kJ/g	m_{H_2O}, g	C_B, kJ/°C	t_f	t_i
A. 0.750	26.45	1043.3	____	24.1°C	20.0°C
B. 0.932	____	1032.1	1.614	26.9°C	20.5°C
C. 0.516	17.29	974.1	1.312	____	19.6°C
D. ____	34.09	836.4	1.435	77.9°F	68.1°F
E. 3.000	14.25	1017.0	____	25.9°C	17.3°C
F. 0.816	____	894.3	1.826	22.1°C	15.1°C
G. ____	40.56	1055.2	1.414	26.4°C	18.8°C
H. 1.024	13.08	1000.0	1.732	____°F	59.1°F

8. Determine $\Delta \bar{H}$ and $\Delta \bar{E}$ for each reaction below. q_P or q_V is given in kJ per gram of the first reactant. Assume $T = 298$ K.

A. $C_4H_9OH(l) + 6\,O_2(g) \rightarrow 4\,CO_2(g) + 5\,H_2O(l)$ $q_P = -36.11$ kJ/g
B. $C_6H_5OH(s) + 7\,O_2(g) \rightarrow 6\,CO_2(g) + 3\,H_2O(l)$ $q_V = -32.56$ kJ/g
C. $PCl_5(g) + H_2O(l) \rightarrow POCl_3(g) + 2\,HCl(g)$ $q_P = -0.4410$ kJ/g
D. $2\,Cl_2(g) + 7\,O_2(g) \rightarrow 2\,Cl_2O_7(g)$ $q_V = -3.864$ kJ/g
E. $H_2(g) + Br_2(g) \rightarrow 2\,HBr(g)$ $q_P = -35.95$ kJ/g
F. $2\,B_5H_9(g) + 12\,O_2(g) \rightarrow 5\,B_2O_3(s) + 9\,H_2O(l)$ $q_V = -71.137$ kJ/g
G. $SOCl_2(l) + H_2O(g) \rightarrow SO_2(g) + 2\,HCl(g)$ $q_P = -2.842$ kJ/g
H. $CCl_4(g) + 2\,H_2O(g) \rightarrow CO_2(g) + 4\,HCl(g)$ $q_V = 1.1526$ kJ/g

9. Fill in the blank in each line below. Assume the solution formed has a specific heat of 4.00 J g^{-1} °C^{-1}.

Solute	*Mass used, g*	m H_2O, g	t_f,°C	t_i, °C	$\Delta \bar{H}°$ *solution,* kJ/mol
A. $KClO_3$	9.04	91.20	22.4	29.7	____
B. $NaNO_3$	8.61	157.98	____	18.6	−21.38
C. NH_4Cl	18.13	____	17.1	22.0	+15.15
D. NH_4NO_3	15.27	473.15	22.7	25.1	____
E. NaOH	11.73	143.06	____	20.0	−42.89
F. NaCl	11.98	104.32	____	20.1	+ 3.88
G. RbI	74.24	569.87	25.0	28.4	____

10. For each lettered part, compute $\Delta \bar{H}°$ for the first reaction by appropriately combining the $\Delta \bar{H}°$s of the remaining reactions.

Reaction	$\Delta \bar{H}°$, kJ/mol
A. $CO_2(g) + H_2(g) \rightarrow H_2O(l) + CO(g)$	
$H_2(g) + \frac{1}{2} O_2(g) \rightarrow H_2O(l)$	-285.9
$CO(g) + \frac{1}{2} O_2(g) \rightarrow CO_2(g)$	-393.5
B. $2\,C_2H_5OH(l) + O_2(g) \rightarrow 2\,C_2H_4O(l) + 2\,H_2O(l)$	
$C_2H_5OH(l) + 3\,O_2(g) \rightarrow 2\,CO_2(g) + 3\,H_2O(l)$	-1370.7
$C_2H_4O(l) + \frac{5}{2} O_2(g) \rightarrow 2\,CO_2(g) + 2\,H_2O(l)$	-1167.3
C. $2\,C(gr) + \frac{5}{2} H_2(g) + \frac{1}{2} Cl_2(g) \rightarrow C_2H_5Cl(g)$	
$H_2(g) + \frac{1}{2} O_2(g) \rightarrow H_2O(l)$	-285.9
$C(gr) + O_2(g) \rightarrow CO_2(g)$	-393.5
$C_2H_4(g) + HCl(g) \rightarrow C_2H_5Cl(g)$	-72.0
$C_2H_4(g) + 3\,O_2(g) \rightarrow 2\,CO_2(g) + 2\,H_2O(l)$	-1410.8
$H_2(g) + Cl_2(g) \rightarrow 2\,HCl(g)$	-184.6
D. $Na(s) + \frac{1}{2} Cl_2(g) \rightarrow NaCl(s)$	
$2\,Na(s) + 2\,HCl(g) \rightarrow 2\,NaCl(s) + H_2(g)$	-637.4
$H_2(g) + Cl_2(g) \rightarrow 2\,HCl(g)$	-184.6
E. $2\,XO_2(s) + CO(g) \rightarrow X_2O_3(s) + CO_2(g)$ (X is a metallic element)	
$XO_2(s) + CO(g) \rightarrow XO(s) + CO_2(g)$	-83.7
$X_3O_4(s) + CO(g) \rightarrow 3\,XO(s) + CO_2(g)$	$+25.1$
$3\,X_2O_3(s) + CO(g) \rightarrow 2\,X_3O_4(s) + CO_2(g)$	-50.2
F. $2\,MnO_2(s) + CO(g) \rightarrow Mn_2O_3(s) + CO_2(g)$	
$MnO_2(s) + CO(g) \rightarrow MnO(s) + CO_2(g)$	-150.6
$Mn_3O_4(s) + CO(g) \rightarrow 3\,MnO(s) + CO_2(g)$	-54.4
$3\,Mn_2O_3(s) + CO(g) \rightarrow 2\,Mn_3O_4(s) + CO_2(g)$	-142.3
G. $3\,V_2O_3(s) \rightarrow V_2O_5(s) + 4\,VO(s)$	
$2\,V(s) + \frac{3}{2} O_2(g) \rightarrow V_2O_3(s)$	-1213
$2\,V(s) + \frac{5}{2} O_2(g) \rightarrow V_2O_5(s)$	-1561
$V(s) + \frac{1}{2} O_2(g) \rightarrow VO(s)$	-418
$V(s) + O_2(g) \rightarrow VO_2(s)$	-720
H. $V_2O_5(s) + 3\,V(s) \rightarrow 5\,VO(s)$	
Data as in G.	
I. $Fe_2O_3(s) + 3\,CO(g) \rightarrow 2\,Fe(s) + 3\,CO_2(g)$	
$Fe_2O_3(s) + CO(g) \rightarrow 2\,FeO(s) + CO_2(g)$	-2.9
$Fe(s) + CO_2(g) \rightarrow FeO(s) + CO(g)$	$+11.3$
J. $2\,C(gr) + H_2(g) \rightarrow C_2H_2(g)$	
$CaO(s) + H_2O(l) \rightarrow Ca(OH)_2(s)$	-65.3
$CaO(s) + 3\,C(gr) \rightarrow CaC_2(s) + CO(g)$	$+462.3$
$CaC_2(s) + 2\,H_2O(l) \rightarrow Ca(OH)_2(s) + C_2H_2(g)$	-125.5
$2\,C(gr) + O_2(g) \rightarrow 2\,CO(g)$	-220.9
$2\,H_2O(l) \rightarrow 2\,H_2(g) + O_2(g)$	$+571.5$
K. $Cu(s) + \frac{1}{2} O_2(g) \rightarrow CuO(s)$	
$Cu_2O(s) + \frac{1}{2} O_2(g) \rightarrow 2\,CuO(s)$	-143.9
$CuO(s) + Cu(s) \rightarrow Cu_2O(s)$	-11.3

10a. Write the standard formation reaction for each substance.

A. $C_2H_5OH(l)$ B. $(NH_4)_2SbCl_5(s)$ C. $Hg_2Cl_2(s)$ D. $H_3PO_4(s)$
E. $NaIO_3(s)$ F. $SnF_2(s)$ G. $XeO_3(s)$ H. $HNO_3(l)$
I. $KBrO_3(s)$ J. $ICl_3(g)$

12. Using the enthalpies of formation (all in kJ/mol) in Table 15-1 (page 199), determine the enthalpy change for each reaction cited.

A. $CaCO_3(s) \rightarrow CaO(s) + CO_2(g)$
B. $NH_3(g) + HCl(g) \rightarrow NH_4Cl(s)$
C. $NH_3(g) + H_2O(l) + CO_2(g) \rightarrow NH_4HCO_3(s)$
D. $CaO(s) + 2\,HCl(g) \rightarrow CaCl_2(s) + H_2O(l)$

E. $Li_2CO_3(s) \rightarrow Li_2O(s) + CO_2(g)$
F. $Li_2O(s) + H_2O(l) \rightarrow 2\ LiOH(s)$
G. $4\ NH_3(g) + 3\ O_2(g) \rightarrow 2\ N_2(g) + 6\ H_2O(l)$
H. $4\ NH_3(g) + 5\ O_2(g) \rightarrow 4\ NO(g) + 6\ H_2O(l)$
I. $2\ NO(g) + O_2(g) \rightarrow 2\ NO_2(g)$
J. $3\ NO_2(g) + H_2O(l) \rightarrow 2\ HNO_3(l) + NO(g)$
K. $2\ HNO_3(l) + Li_2O(s) \rightarrow 2\ LiNO_3(s) + H_2O(l)$
L. $Li_2O(s) + 2\ HCl(g) \rightarrow 2\ LiCl(s) + H_2O(l)$
M. $LiOH(s) + HCl(g) \rightarrow LiCl(s) + H_2O(l)$
N. $4\ LiNO_3(s) \rightarrow 2\ Li_2O(s) + 4\ NO_2(g) + O_2(g)$
O. $CaO(s) + H_2O(l) \rightarrow Ca(OH)_2(s)$

QUIZZES (20 minutes each)

Choose the best answer for each question. For problems with a numerical answer, an answer is correct if it is within 1% of the correctly computed value.

Quiz A

1. The standard state of a substance is the (a) pure form at 1 atm; (b) most stable form at 25°C and 1 atm; (c) most stable form at 0°C; (d) pure gaseous form at 25°C; (e) none of these.
2. 75.0 g of water at 10°C is mixed with 125.0 g of water at 50°C. The final temperature of the mixture is (a) 30°C; (b) 40°C; (c) 35°C; (d) 25°C; (e) none of these.
3. $2\ Mg(s) + O_2(g) \rightarrow 2\ MgO(s)$ $\Delta \bar{H}° = -1203$ kJ/mol The heat given off in kJ/mol when 1.0 g of MgO(s) is formed is (a) 29.9; (b) 1203; (c) 601.7; (d) 14.9; (e) none of these.
4. 10.0 g of H_2O (sp. ht. = 4.184 J g^{-1} °C^{-1}) cools from 60 to 30°C. The amount of heat lost to the surroundings equals how many Joules? (a) 1393; (b) 62.8; (c) 12.6; (d) 1255; (e) none of these.
5. Which is the formation reaction for NO(g)? (a) $\frac{1}{2}\ N_2(g) + \frac{1}{3}\ O_3(g) \rightarrow NO(g)$; (b) $N(g) + O(g) \rightarrow NO(g)$; (c) $NO_2(g) \rightarrow NO(g) + \frac{1}{2}\ O_2(g)$; (d) $N_2O_3(g) \rightarrow NO(g) + NO_2(g)$; (e) none of these.
6. $Sn(s) + 2\ Cl_2(g) \rightarrow SnCl_4(l)$ $\Delta \bar{H}° = -545.2$ kJ/mol
   $SnCl_2(s) + Cl_2(g) \rightarrow SnCl_4(l)$ $= -195.4$
   What is $\Delta \bar{H}°$ in kJ/mol for $Sn(s) + Cl_2(g) \rightarrow SnCl_2(s)$? (a) 349.8; (b) −349.8; (c) 740.6; (d) 195.4; (e) none of these.
7. $C_2H_6(g) + \frac{7}{2}\ O_2(g) \rightarrow 2\ CO_2(g) + 3\ H_2O(l)$ $\Delta \bar{H}° = -1541$ kJ/mol
   $H_2(g) + \frac{1}{2}\ O_2(g) \rightarrow H_2O(l)$ $= -286$
   $C(gr) + O_2(g) \rightarrow CO_2(g)$ $= -393$
   Compute $\Delta \bar{H}°$ for $2\ C(gr) + 3\ H_2(g) \rightarrow C_2H_6(g)$ in kJ/mol. (a) −1541; (b) 862; (c) 469; (d) 103; (e) none of these.
8. $SnO_2(s) + 2\ H_2(g) \rightarrow Sn(s) + 2\ H_2O(l)$
   $\Delta \bar{H}_f°$: −580.7 0.00 0.00 −285.9 kJ/mol
   $\Delta H°$ for this reaction in kJ/mol is (a) 294.8; (b) 8.9; (c) −294.8; (d) −571.8; (e) none of these.

Quiz B

1. Each of the following is a stable form of an element *except* (a) $O_2(g)$; (b) $F_2(g)$; (c) C(diamond); (d) $N_2(g)$; (e) all of these are stable.
2. 15.0 g of water at 100°C is mixed with 85.0 g of water at 20°C. The final temperature of the mixture is (a) 60°C; (b) 32°C; (c) 50°C: (d) 48°C; (e) none of these.
3. The molar heat of combustion of acetylene (26 g/mol) is −1301 kJ/mol. Combustion of 0.130 g of acetylene produces how many kilocalories of heat? (a) 50.05; (b) 384.9; (c) 6.51; (d) 169.1; (e) none of these.
4. 10.00 g HCl solution (sp. ht. = 4.017 J g^{-1} °C^{-1}) is heated from 25.0 to 40.0°C. The solution gains how many Joules of heat? (a) 602.6; (b) 627.6; (c) 654.0; (d) 1004; (e) none of these.

5. Which is the formation reaction for $H_2O(l)$? (a) $H^+(aq) + OH^-(aq) \rightarrow H_2O(l)$; (b) $H_2O(g) \rightarrow H_2O(l)$; (c) $H_2(g) + \frac{1}{2} O_2(g) \rightarrow H_2O(l)$; (d) $H_2(g) + \frac{1}{3} O_3(g) \rightarrow H_2O(l)$; (e) none of these.
6. $MnO_2(s) \rightarrow MnO(s) + \frac{1}{2} O_2(g)$ $\Delta\bar{H}° = +136.0$ kJ/mol
   $MnO_2(s) + Mn(s) \rightarrow 2\ MnO(s)$ $= -248.9$
   Compute $\Delta\bar{H}°$ in kJ/mol for $Mn(s) + O_2(g) \rightarrow MnO_2(s)$. (a) −112.9; (b) −384.9; (c) −520.9; (d) +361.9; (e) none of these.
7. $2\ ClF(g) + O_2(g) \rightarrow Cl_2O(g) + F_2O(g)$ $\Delta\bar{H}° =$ ' 167.4 kJ/mol
   $2\ ClF_3(g) + 2\ O_2(g) \rightarrow Cl_2O(g) + 3\ F_2O(g)$ Δ $=$ 341.4
   $2\ F_2(g) + O_2(g) \rightarrow 2\ F_2O(g)$ $= -43.5$
   Compute $\Delta H°$ in kJ/mol for $ClF(g) + F_2(g) \rightarrow ClF_3(g)$. (a) −217.5; (b) −435.0; (c) +223.6; (d) −130.2; (e) none of these.
8. The standard enthalpy change for the reaction

   $NH_3(g) + \frac{3}{4} O_2(g) \rightarrow \frac{1}{2} N_2(g) + \frac{3}{2} H_2O(g)$

   $\Delta\bar{H}_f°$: −46.0 0.0 0.0 −241.8 kJ/mol

   in kJ/mol is (a) −195.8; (b) +316.7; (c) −408.8; (d) −316.7; (e) none of these.

Quiz C

1. An element involved in a formation reaction as a reactant is *not* (a) pure; (b) at 1.00 *M* concentration; (c) at 1.00 atm pressure; (d) in its most stable form; (e) none of these.
2. 25.0 g of water at 50°C is mixed with 15.0 g of water at 30.0°C. The final temperature of the mixture is (a) 40.0°C; (b) 42.5°C; (c) 37.5°C; (d) 35.0°C; (e) none of these.
3. The absorption of 15 kJ of heat by a system which does 49 kJ of work on its surroundings causes a total change in the internal energy, ΔE, of the system equal to (a) −34 kJ; (b) +64 kJ; (c) +34 kJ; (d) −64 kJ; (e) none of these.
4. 1674 J of heat is absorbed by 25.0 ml of NaOH ($d = 1.10$ g/ml; sp. ht. = 4.10 J g^{-1} °C^{-1}). The temperature of the NaOH goes up how many Celsius degrees? (a) 17.2; (b) 14.2; (c) 14.8; (d) 18.0; (e) none of these.
5. Which is the formation reaction for $CO_2(g)$? (a) $C(dia) + O_2(g) \rightarrow CO_2(g)$; (b) $C(gr) + O_2(g) \rightarrow CO_2(g)$; (c) $CO(g) + \frac{1}{2} O_2(g) \rightarrow CO_2(g)$; (d) $CaCO_3(s) + CaO(g) \rightarrow CO_2(g)$; (e) none of these.
6. $CH_4(g) + 2\ O_2(g) \rightarrow CO_2(g) + 2\ H_2O(g)$ $\Delta\bar{H}° = -890.4$ kJ/mol
   $CH_2O(g) + O_2(g) \rightarrow CO_2(g) + H_2O(g)$ $= -563.5$
   Compute $\Delta\bar{H}°$ in kJ/mol for $CH_4(g) + O_2(g) \rightarrow CH_2O(g) + H_2O(g)$. (a) −236.6; (b) +118.3; (c) −326.9; (d) −1453.9; (e) none of these.
7. $2\ LiOH(s) \rightarrow Li_2O(s) + H_2O(l)$ $\Delta°\bar{H} =$ 379.1 kJ/mol
   $LiH(s) + H_2O(l) \rightarrow LiOH(s) + H_2(g)$ $= -110.9$
   $2\ H_2(g) + O_2(g) \rightarrow 2\ H_2O(l)$ $= -285.9$
   Compute $\Delta H°$ in kJ/mol for $2\ LiH(s) + O_2(g) \rightarrow Li_2O(s) + H_2O(l)$. (a) −128.6; (b) −17.7; (c) 268.2; (d) 551.4; (e) none of these.
8. The standard enthalpy change for the reaction

   $2\ H_2S(g) + 3\ O_2(g) \rightarrow 2\ H_2O(l) + 2\ SO_2(g)$

   $\Delta\bar{H}_f°$ −20.1 0.000 −285.8 −297.1 kJ/mol

   in kJ/mol is (a) −562.8; (b) +562.8; (c) −3.14; (d) −477.4; (e) none of these.

Quiz D

1. A system which exchanges heat with its surroundings and is kept at a fixed temperature is (a) open; (b) closed; (c) adiabatic; (d) isothermal; (e) none of these.

2. 77.0 g of water at 95°C is mixed with 23.0 g of water at 5°C. The final temperature of the mixture is (a) 50.0°C; (b) 63.6°C; (c) 23.6°C; (d) 74.3°C; (e) none of these.
3. A gas absorbs 40 J of heat and then performs 15.2 J of work. The change in internal energy of the gas in Joules is (a) −24.8; (b) 14.8; (c) 55.2; (d) −15.2; (e) none of these.
4. 40.0 g of solution has its temperature raised from 25 to 50°C by the addition of 4067 J of heat. Its specific heat (in $J\ g^{-1}\ °C^{-1}$) is (a) 4.31; (b) 4.07; (c) 4.18; (d) 2.03; (e) none of these.
5. Which is the formation reaction for $SO_3(g)$? (a) $S(mono) + \frac{3}{2} O_2(g) \rightarrow SO_3(g)$; (b) $2\ SO_2(g) \rightarrow SO_3(g) + SO(g)$; (c) $SO_2(g) + \frac{1}{2} O_2(g) \rightarrow SO_3(g)$; (d) $H_2SO_4(l) \rightarrow H_2O(l) + SO_3(g)$; (e) none of these.
6. $CO(g) + \frac{1}{2} O_2(g) \rightarrow CO_2(g)$ $\Delta\bar{H}° = -282.8$ kJ
   $C(gr) + O_2(g) \rightarrow CO_2(g)$ $= -393.3$
   What is $\Delta H°$ for $C(gr) + \frac{1}{2} O_2(g) \rightarrow CO(g)$ in kJ/mol? (a) +282.8; (b) −676.1; (c) +110.5; (d) −110.5; (e) none of these.
7. $H_2S(g) + \frac{3}{2} O_2(g) \rightarrow H_2O(l) + SO_2(g)$ $\Delta\bar{H}° = -562.3$ kJ/mol
   $S(rh) + O_2(g) \rightarrow SO_2(g)$ $= -297.1$
   $H_2(g) + \frac{1}{2} O_2(g) \rightarrow H_2O(l)$ $= -285.8$
   Compute $\Delta\bar{H}°$ for $H_2(g) + S(rh) \rightarrow H_2S(g)$ in kJ/mol. (a) 562.3; (b) 265.3; (c) 276.6; (d) −20.6; (e) none of these.
8. $CH_3OH(l) + \frac{3}{2} O_2(g) \rightarrow CO_2(g) + 2\ H_2O(l)$
   $\Delta\bar{H}_f^\circ$: −238.5 0.0 −393.3 −285.3 kJ/mol
   $\Delta\bar{H}°$ for this reaction in kJ/mol is (a) −140.8; (b) −725.4; (c) +154.8; (d) −154.8; (e) none of these.

SAMPLE TEST (15 minutes)

1. Write the formation reactions for
   a. $SnCl_4(s)$ b. $C_6H_5COOH(s)$ c. $COCl_2(g)$
2. Compute $\Delta\bar{H}_{rxn}^\circ$ for each of the following reactions. The value of $\Delta\bar{H}_f^\circ$ in kJ/mol is given below each species.
   a. $SiO_2(s) + 4\ HF(g) \rightarrow SiF_4(g) + 2\ H_2O(g)$
   −859.4 −269 −1550 −285.9
   b. $2\ CuS(s) + 3\ O_2(g) \rightarrow 2\ CuO(s) + 2\ SO_2(g)$
   −48.5 0.00 −155 −296.9
3. Each mole of LiCl gives off 37.2 kJ of heat when it dissolves in water. What will be the final temperature when 5.00 g LiCl dissolves in 110.0 g of water at 20.00°C? The solution has a specific heat of $4.00\ J\ g^{-1}\ °C^{-1}$.

Electrons in Atoms

REVIEW OF OBJECTIVES

★ **1. Apply the basic expression relating the frequency, wavelength, and velocity of electromagnetic radiation, using appropriate units.**

Equation [1] is the relationship between the frequency of radiation ν (pronounced "nu") and its wavelength λ (lambda).

$$c = \lambda\nu \qquad [1]$$

The constant velocity of light has a value of $c = 2.9979 \times 10^8$ m/s. We shall use the three significant figure value, $c = 3.00 \times 10^8$ m/s.

Fortunately, frequency is consistently expressed in units of hertz (Hz). However, previous usage has resulted in different ways of writing hertz: /sec, /s, s^{-1}, cycles per second, cycles, and cps.

With wavelength the situation is not as simple. First, wavelengths are often not written in scientific notation as are frequencies. For example, red light has a wavelength of 7.60×10^{-7} m or 760 nm. Second, three non-SI units of wavelength are or have been used. They are the micron (μ) = 10^{-6} m = micrometer (μm), the millimicron (mμ) = 10^{-9} m = nanometer (nm), and the Ångstrom (Å) = 10^{-10} m = 10^{-8} cm = 0.1 nm = 100 pm. To use equation [1] we convert wavelengths to meters.

EXAMPLE 7-1 A radio station broadcasts on a frequency of 95 kilocycles. What is the wavelength of this radiation in km?

95 kilocycles is the same as 95×10^3 Hz. Rearrangement of equation [1] produces $\lambda = c/\nu$.

$$\lambda = \frac{3.00 \times 10^8 \text{ m/s}}{95 \times 10^3 \text{ s}^{-1}} = 3.2 \times 10^3 \text{ m} \times \frac{\text{km}}{1000 \text{ m}} = 3.2 \text{ km}$$

EXAMPLE 7-2 Electromagnetic radiation with a wavelength of 3429 Å has what frequency?

$$\nu = \frac{c}{\lambda} = \frac{3.00 \times 10^8 \text{ m/s}}{(3429\text{Å})(\text{m}/10^{10}\text{ Å})} = 8.75 \times 10^{14} \text{ Hz}$$

★ **2. List the various types of radiation and their approximate wavelengths.**

This objective involves learning the relationships shown in *Figure 7-3 in the text*. You should realize that the boundaries between the various regions in the electromagnetic spectrum are not sharp divisions but rather gradual transitions.

It is helpful to associate the various types of radiation with the changes in matter which they produce or which produce them as shown in Table 7-1. These associations are mutual. Thus, infrared radiation may cause changes in the vibrations of molecules when it strikes these molecules, or a change in how a molecule is vibrating may give off infrared radiation.

3. Know how light is dispersed into a spectrum and the difference between continuous and line spectra.

When light passes through a prism, it is refracted or bent as it enters and as it leaves the prism. Different frequencies of light are refracted to different degrees. High-frequency (short wavelength) light is refracted

TABLE 7-1
Change in matter associated with various types of electromagnetic radiation

Type(s) of radiation	Associated change in matter
Cosmic rays and γ rays	Nuclear transformations (changes in structure of the nucleus)
X rays	Inner electron transitions in atoms
Ultraviolet rays and visible light	Outer electron transitions in atoms and electron transitions in molecules
Infrared radiation	Vibration of atoms in molecules
Microwave radiation and radar	Rotation of molecules

most and low-frequency (long wavelength) light is refracted least. Thus, among the colors of visible light, red light is refracted least, next orange, then yellow, green, blue, indigo, and finally violet, which is refracted most (see Figure 7-1). (Note that the initial letters of the colors spell ROY G BIV, which may help you remember them.) It helps in remembering to think of high-frequency light as interacting the most frequently with the matter of the prism as it passes through and thus being bent the most. This is only a memory aid and not what actually occurs; all of the refraction occurs at the surfaces of the prism on entrance and exit.

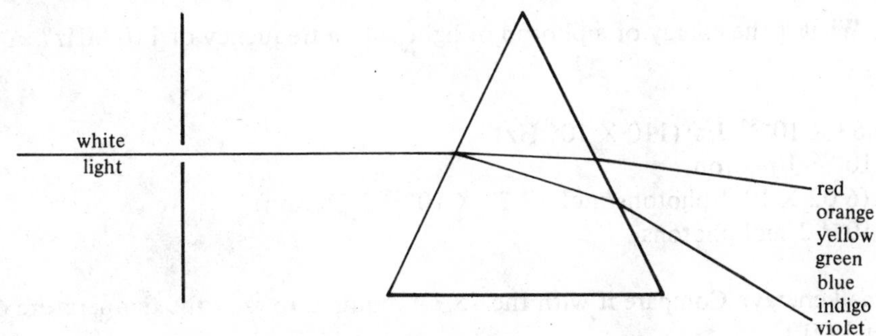

FIGURE 7-1 Dispersion of white light by a prism.

When white light is dispersed by a prism, it produces a continuous spectrum. When an element is heated in a flame and the resulting light is passed through a prism, the spectrum consists of several lines. The pattern of lines is characteristic of the element which was heated. A line spectrum also is an emission spectrum. A neon light is a common example of a heated element giving off light. Elements can be tentatively identified by the colors which they give to a flame. Some of these flame colors are given in Table 7-2.

TABLE 7-2
Flame colors of some of the elements

Element	Color
Lithium	Carmine
Sodium	Orange-yellow
Potassium	Violet
Rubidium	Red
Cesium	Blue
Calcium	Orange-red
Strontium	Brick red
Barium	Yellowish green
Copper	Azure blue
Lead	Light blue

★ **4. Use the Balmer equation to determine the wavelengths of lines in hydrogen's spectrum.**

The Balmer equation is a specific example of the Rydberg equation, [2].

$$\frac{1}{\lambda} = R_H \left(\frac{1}{n^2} - \frac{1}{m^2}\right) \qquad [2]$$

The numbers n and m are whole numbers with m larger than n. R_H = 109,678 cm^{-1}. The Balmer equation results when $n = 2$. The wavelengths then calculated are those of the Balmer series—a set of visible lines emitted by hydrogen. When $n = 1$, the Lyman series is produced in the ultraviolet region. The remaining series are all in the infrared: Paschen ($n = 3$), Brackett ($n = 4$), Pfund ($n = 5$), and Humphreys ($n = 6$). The Rydberg equation describes these lines and is simply a summary of the data. It is not based on a theoretical model.

EXAMPLE 7-3 What is the wavelength of the Lyman ($n = 1$) series line with $m = 2$? Is this visible radiation?

$$\frac{1}{\lambda} = 109{,}678\left(\frac{1}{1^2} - \frac{1}{2^2}\right) = 82258.5 \text{ cm}^{-1}$$

$$\lambda = 1/(82258.5 \text{ cm}^{-1}) = 1.216 \times 10^{-5} \text{ cm} = 121.6 \text{ nm} \quad \text{(ultraviolet)}$$

★ **5. Know and be able to use Planck's equation.**

Planck's equation, $E_p = h\nu$, enables us to relate the energy and the frequency of light.

EXAMPLE 7-4 What is the energy of a photon of light with a frequency of 110 MHz? A mole of such photons?

$$E_p = h\nu = (6.63 \times 10^{-34} \text{ J/s})(110 \times 10^6 \text{ Hz})$$
$$= 7.29 \times 10^{-26} \text{ J/photon}$$
$$\bar{E} = N_A E_p = (6.02 \times 10^{23} \text{ photons/mol})(7.29 \times 10^{-26} \text{ J/photon})$$
$$= 4.39 \times 10^{-2} \text{ J/mol photons}$$

This is a truly small energy. Compare it with the 75.3 J required to raise the temperature of one mole (18.0 g) of water 1.00°C.

Frequently $E_p = h\nu$ and $c = \lambda\nu$ are combined to yield equation [3], whose use is illustrated in Example 7-5.

$$E_p = hc/\lambda \qquad [3]$$

EXAMPLE 7-5 400 kJ is required to break a mole of N—H bonds. What is the wavelength of the radiation with sufficient energy to break one N—H bond?

First we determine the energy needed to break one bond from $\bar{E} = N_A E_p$ or $E_p = \bar{E}/N_A$.

$$E_p = (400 \times 10^3 \text{ J/mol})/(6.02 \times 10^{23} \text{ bonds/mol})$$
$$= 6.64 \times 10^{-19} \text{ J/bond}$$

Then we determine the wavelength from a rearranged version of equation [3].

$$\lambda = hc/E_p = (6.63 \times 10^{-34} \text{ J/s})(3.00 \times 10^8 \text{ m/s})/(6.64 \times 10^{-19} \text{ J})$$
$$= (3.00 \times 10^{-7} \text{ m})(10^9 \text{ nm/m}) = 300 \text{ nm}$$

This light is just beyond the visible in the ultraviolet.

This partly explains why some substances deteriorate when they are exposed to sunlight—the bonds are disrupted.

6. & 7. Be familiar with Bohr's model of the hydrogen atom: the assumptions, the picture of the atom, the energy expression, and the energy-level diagram.

In a successful attempt to explain the Rydberg equation, Bohr proposed a model of the hydrogen atom based on several assumptions.

1. The electron moves around the nucleus in one of several circular orbits. The electron does not spiral into the nucleus as classical physics requires.
2. In each orbit of radius r, the angular momentum of the electron ($m_e vr$, where m_e and v are the electron mass and velocity) is restricted to values of $nh/2\pi$ where n is a whole number.

$$m_e vr = nh/2\pi \qquad [4]$$

3. When the electron moves from one orbit to another, the energy difference (ΔE) between the two orbits appears as light emitted (if the second orbit is of lower energy) or absorbed (if the second orbit has higher energy) by the atom.

$$\Delta E = h\nu \qquad [5]$$

After considerable mathematics, these equations give an expression for the energy of each orbit.

$$E_n = \frac{1}{n^2}\,(2.181 \times 10^{-18}\ \text{J}) \qquad [6]$$

The difference in energy between two orbits is

$$\Delta E = (\frac{1}{n^2} - \frac{1}{m^2})(2.181 \times 10^{-18}\ \text{J}) \qquad [7]$$

The wavelength of light absorbed or emitted is given by the Rydberg equation, [2], which *now* is based on a theoretical model. When the energies given by equation [6] are plotted, an energy-level diagram results (*Figure 7-13 in the text*). This diagram illustrates the various possible values of ΔE. Another aspect of each series of the hydrogen spectrum is the series limit. The energy levels get closer to each other as n, the quantum number, increases. Thus, the spectral lines also are closer in both wavelength and frequency.

8. Appreciate de Broglie's and Heisenberg's ideas.

A serious problem with Bohr's model is *why* his assumption $m_e vr = nh/2\pi$ is true. This was explained in 1924 by Louis de Broglie who stated that a particle has a wavelength given by equation [8] where m is the mass of a particle traveling with velocity v.

$$\lambda = h/mv \qquad [8]$$

A whole number of wavelengths must fit in a circular orbit.

$$n\lambda = 2\pi r = \text{circumference} \qquad [9]$$

$$or\ \ nh/mv = 2\pi r \ \ \text{or} \ \ nh/2\pi = mvr \qquad [10]$$

Equation [10] is Bohr's assumption (equation [4]). De Broglie's equation does much more than support Bohr's theory. It expresses a fundamental fact of nature. Particles moving at high velocities have wave properties. But even this statement is incomplete. Particles *are* waves. It merely depends on how we observe them. In the same way, a woman can be both a mother to her children and a college professor, depending on how we observe her. (Also, think of a coin twirling in the air. Is it heads or tails while in the air?)

Another consequence of the wave-particle duality is the Heisenberg uncertainty principle.

$$\Delta x \Delta p > h/2 \qquad [11]$$

This uncertainty is not due to the crudeness of our measuring devices but rather is a fundamental limitation of nature. This leads to a different picture of the electron in the atom. Bohr's definite orbits have been replaced by orbitals—regions of space within which we have a reasonable chance (for example, better than 90%) of finding the electron.

An orbital is somewhat similar to the boundaries of a city. We believe that there is a good chance or a high probability of finding the population of the city within the city limits. In the same way there is a high probability of finding the electron within the boundaries of the orbital.

9. Know the difference between Bohr's and Schrödinger's models of the atom.

Bohr treated the electron as a classical particle fixed in certain orbits defined by its wavelength. Schrödinger allows the electron to fully express its wave properties. Thus Schrödinger's electron does not plod around an orbit but totally fills the space of the orbital. It does not fill this space as would a fly in a cage but rather as a gas fills a bottle. But it does this not by breaking into fragments or making itself bigger but rather in the same way that a sound wave fills a room. Unfortunately the mathematics describing the Schrodinger atom are more complex than those which describe the Bohr atom.

★ **10. Know the quantum number relationships produced by wave mechanics.**

The *principal quantum number,* designated by n, can only be a whole number larger than zero.

$$n = 1, 2, 3, 4, 5, \ldots \quad [12]$$

Electrons with the same principal quantum number are in the same *shell* or *level.* Often the shells are designated with capital letters.

Value of n:	1	2	3	4	5
Shell:	K	L	M	N	O

Thus all electrons with $n = 1$ are in the K shell. The average distance of the electron from the nucleus depends almost entirely on n. The *azimuthal quantum number,* l (also called the orbital quantum number), is a nonnegative whole number less than n.

$$l = 0, 1, 2, 3, \ldots, n - 1 \quad [13]$$

Electrons with the same values of n and l are in the same *subshell* or *sublevel.* Subshells are designated by lower case letters.

Value of l:	0	1	2	3	4	5	6	7
Subshell:	s	p	d	f	g	h	i	k

(The letters are the initial letters of the words in: "Sober physicists don't find giraffes hiding in kitchens." This fanciful sentence is a convenient memory aid.) The energy of an electron in a many-electron atom depends on the sum $n + l$. l also specifies the general shape of an orbital. The *magnetic quantum number,* m_l (or m, also called the orientation quantum number), ranges from $-l$ to $+l$ by a whole number steps.

$$-l, -l + l, -l + 2, \ldots, -1, 0, +1, \ldots, l - 1, l \quad [14]$$

Electrons with the same values of n, l, and m_l are in the same *orbital;* m_l specifies the general orientation of the orbital (the direction to which it "points").

★ **11. Know what an orbital is and the appearance of *s*, *p*, and *d* orbitals.**

An orbital is a region of space in which there is a good chance or a high probability of finding an electron. All s orbitals are spherical in shape and increase in radius as n increases. p orbitals have a double squashed sphere shape (see Figure 7-2). Each squashed sphere is called a *lobe*, and the region of zero electron probability between the two lobes is a *node.* A p orbital corresponds to $l = 1$ and thus there are three p orbitals since m_l can equal -1, 0, or $+1$. Since $l = 2$ for d orbitals, there are five values of m_l $(= -2, -1, 0, +1, +2)$ and thus five d orbitals. These are shown in Figure 7-3. Except for d_{z^2}, each orbital has four lobes and two nodes and looks rather like a four-leafed clover or four teardrops pointing to a common center.

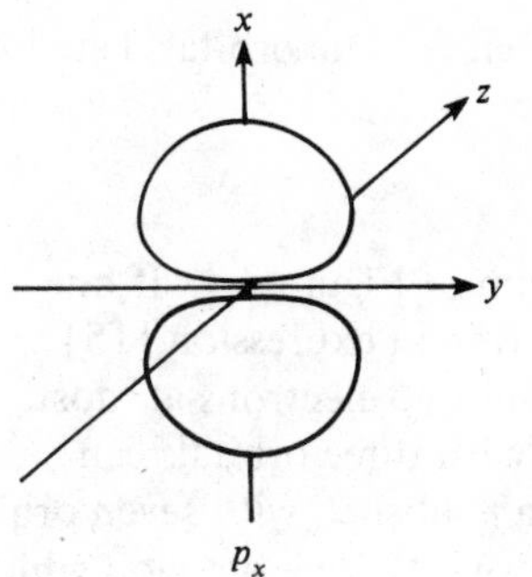

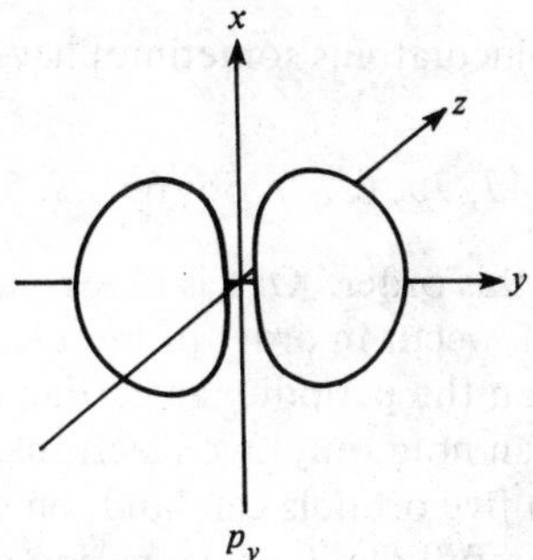

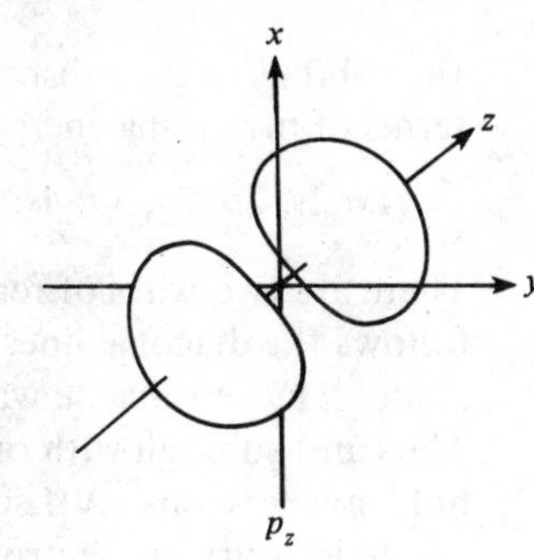

(a) The orbitals as they actually appear

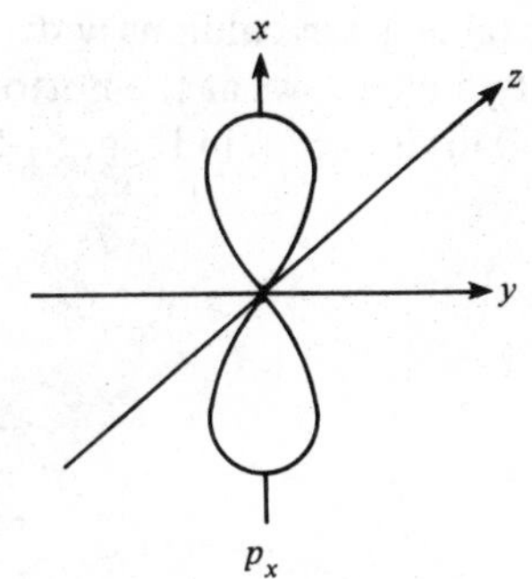

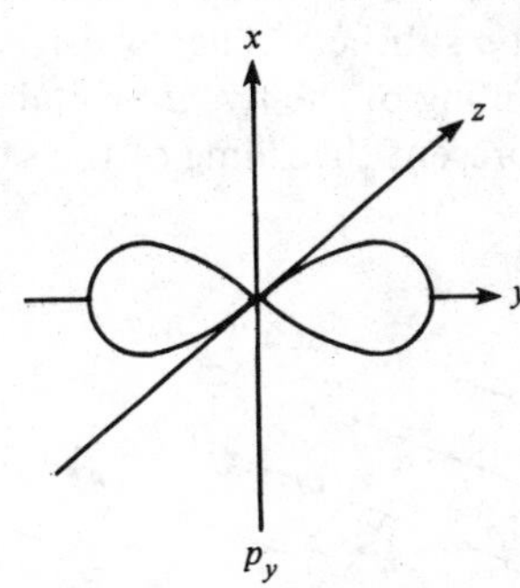

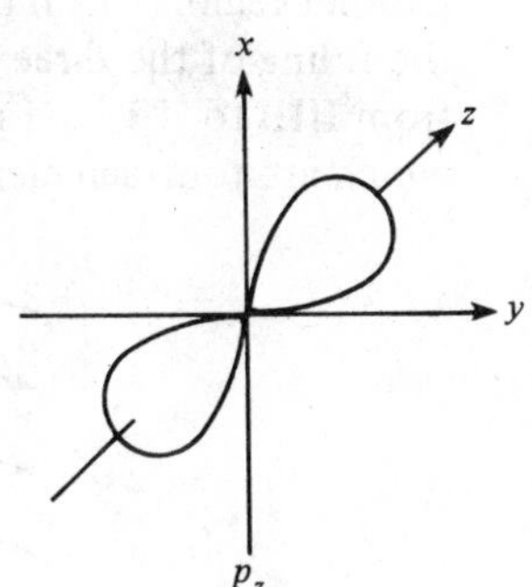

(b) The orbitals as they usually are drawn

FIGURE 7-2 The *p* orbitals.

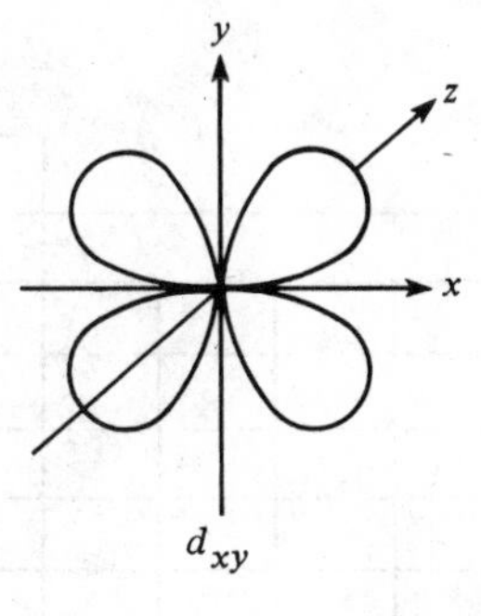

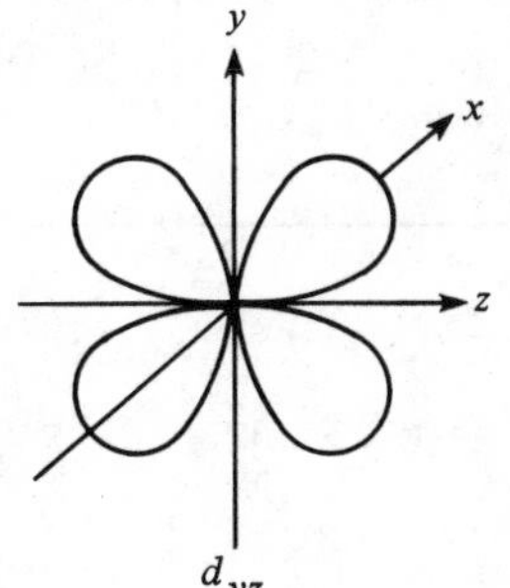

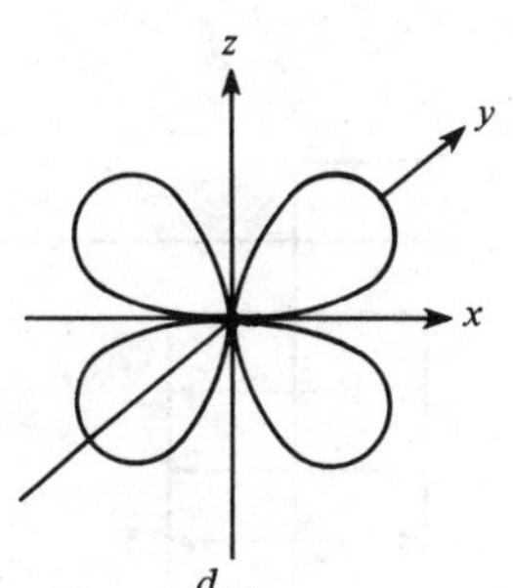

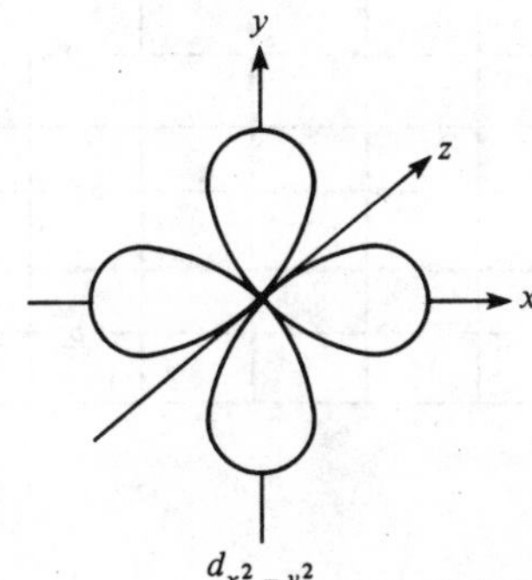

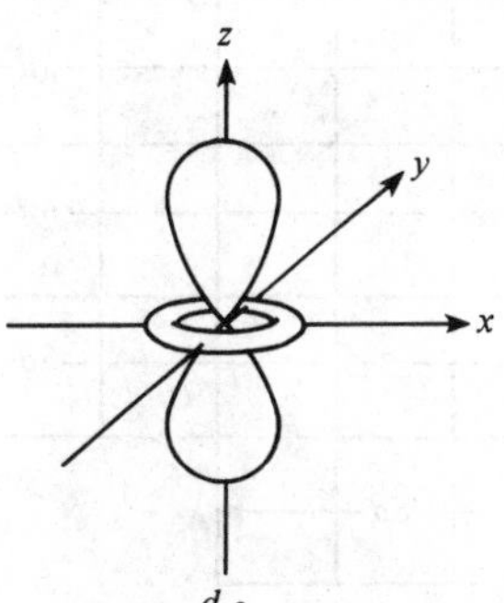

FIGURE 7-3 The five *d* orbitals.

12. Know how orbital energies are modified when more than one electron is present in an atom.

For one-electron atoms and ions (H, He^+, Li^{2+}, and so forth) orbital energies depend on only the principal quantum number *n*. As other electrons are added, the principal shells are split into subshells. All of the orbitals in the same subshell of an isolated atom have the same energy. (As we shall see later in the text, the orbitals in the subshells of combined atoms sometimes have different energies). The orbitals listed in terms of increasing energy are

$$1s, 2s, 2p, 3s, 3p, 4s, 3d, 4p, 5s, 4d, 5p, 6s, 4f, 5d, 6p, 7s, 5f, 6d, 7p \qquad [15]$$

There are two ways of remembering this order. One is based on the line diagram of Figure 7-4. If one follows the diagonal lines, the orbitals occur in order of increasing energy, as given in expression [15]. A much more valuable way is based on the periodic table. Each orbital can hold two electrons at most. Thus an *s* subshell with one orbital can hold only two electrons. A *p* subshell with three orbitals can hold six electrons. A *d* subshell with five orbitals can hold ten electrons, and a *f* subshell with seven orbitals can hold fourteen electrons. Now carefully look at the periodic table. Notice that there is a region which is only two columns wide. These columns, headed IA and IIA, represent the filling of *s* subshells. There is another region which is six columns wide. The columns, headed IIIA, IVA, VA, VIA, VIIA, and 0, represent the filling of the three orbitals in each *p* subshell. The "waist" of the periodic table is ten columns wide—from IIIB to IIB—and represents the filling of the five *d* orbitals. Finally, the two long rows at the bottom, which are fourteen elements wide, represent the filling of the seven *f* orbitals. This is shown in Figure 7-5.

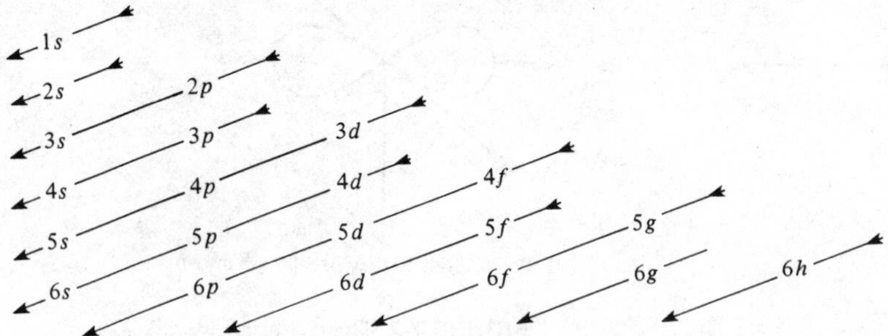

FIGURE 7-4 Order of subshell filling.

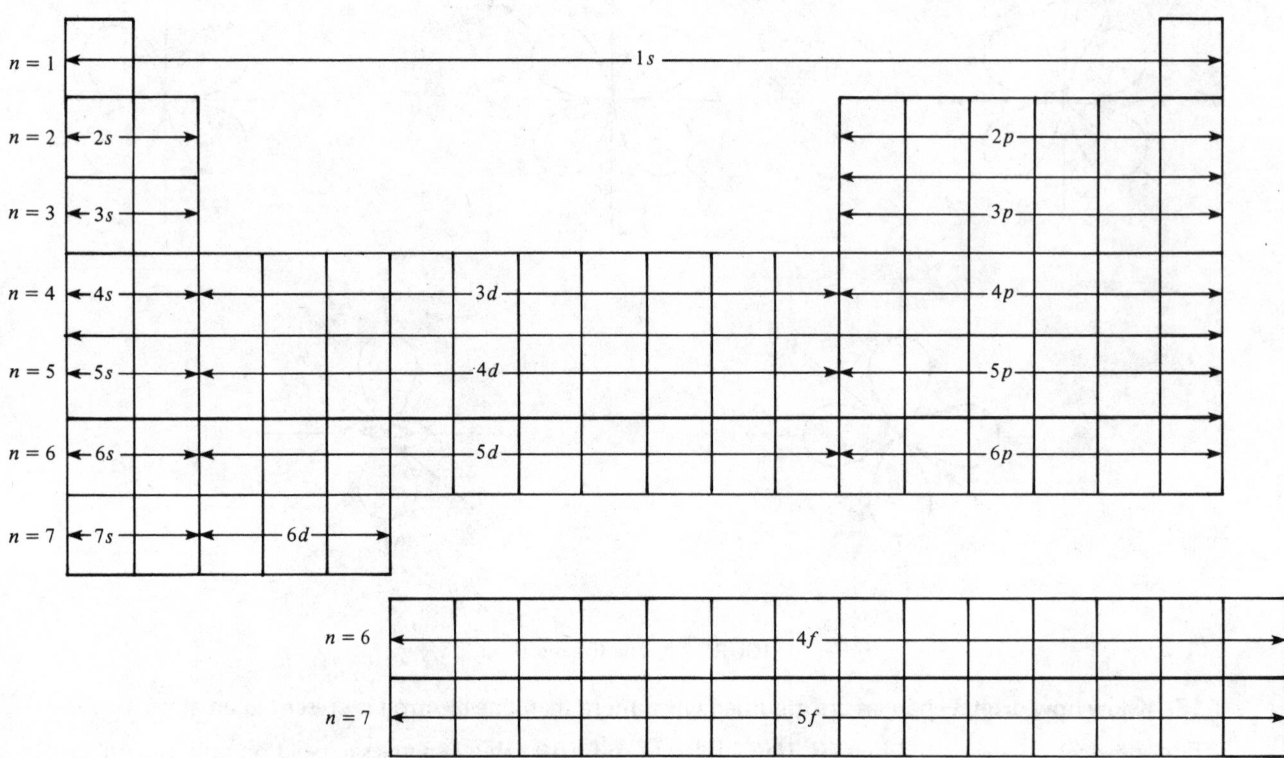

FIGURE 7-5 Order of subshell filling based on periodic table.

★ **13. Learn the three basic principles governing electron configurations.**

1. *The order in which orbitals are filled.* This order is given in expression [15] and two ways of memorizing it are discussed in objective 7-12.
2. *The Pauli exclusion principle and its implications.* The Pauli exclusion principle states that no two electrons in an atom may have the same set of four quantum numbers. An orbital is all electrons with the same values of n, l, and m_l. Hence m_s must be different for the electrons in an orbital. But m_s can have only two values: either $m_s = +\frac{1}{2}$ or $m_s = -\frac{1}{2}$.

$$\text{number of electrons/orbital} = 2 \qquad [16]$$

The number of orbitals in a subshell is governed by the range of m_l: from $m_l = -l$ to $m_l = +l$ by whole number steps. There are only $2l + 1$ values of m_l for a given value of l.

$$\text{number of orbitals/subshell} = 2l + 1 \qquad [17]$$

$$\text{number of electrons/subshell} = 2(2l + 1) \qquad [18]$$

The number of subshells in a shell is determined by the value of n. There are n subshells in each shell, from $l = 0$ to $l = n - 1$.

$$\text{number of subshells/shell} = n \qquad [19]$$

In Table 7-3, the subshells of each shell are listed and the capacity of each subshell is given in parentheses.

TABLE 7-3
Electrons in shells and subshells

Shell	Subshells (electron capacity)	Total electrons in each shell	
1	$1s(2)$	2	$= 2$
2	$2s(2)\ 2p(6)$	$2 + 6$	$= 8$
3	$3s(2)\ 3p(6)\ 3d(10)$	$2 + 6 + 10$	$= 18$
4	$4s(2)\ 4p(6)\ 4d(10)\ 4f(14)$	$2 + 6 + 10 + 14$	$= 32$
5	$5s(2)\ 5p(6)\ 5d(10)\ 5f(14)\ 5g(18)$	$2 + 6 + 10 + 14 + 18$	$= 50$

3. *Hund's rule of maximum multiplicity.* The multiplicity of an atom is related to its total spin or the sum of the m_s quantum numbers. Hund's rule states that when electrons fill orbitals of the same energy they do so in such a way that the total spin is as large as possible. Suppose, for example, we have six electrons to place in five d orbitals. The five d orbitals can be represented by five boxes and the electrons by arrows—pointing up (↑) if $m_s = +\frac{1}{2}$ and down (↓) if $m_s = -\frac{1}{2}$. The three possibilities are summarized in Table 7-4. Hund's rule tells us to choose the last of these three.

TABLE 7-4
Possible electron configurations of six d electrons

Configuration	Number of electrons with $m_s = +\frac{1}{2}$	$m_s = -\frac{1}{2}$	Total spin
[↑↓][↑↓][↑↓][ ][ ]	3	3	0
[↑↓][↑↓][↑][↑][ ]	4	2	1
[↑↓][↑][↑][↑][↑]	5	1	2

★ **14. Apply the Aufbau principle and write electron configurations in many different ways.**

The Aufbau process is one in which the electron configuration of an atom is built upon the configuration of the previous atom. There are many ways to indicate the electron configuration of an atom. One way is to give the four quantum numbers of the last electron. Table 7-5 lists the quantum numbers for the elements with atomic numbers up to $Z = 10$. It is a cumbersome technique and does not account for those cases (of which chromium is an example) in which the quantum numbers of one of the underlying electrons change.

There is no good reason for assigning $m_s = +\frac{1}{2}$ before $m_s = -\frac{1}{2}$. We could have assigned them in the opposite order to make H be: $n = 1, l = 0, m_l = 0, m_s = -\frac{1}{2}$. You should be consistent in assigning either $m_s = +\frac{1}{2}$ or $m_s = -\frac{1}{2}$ first.

TABLE 7-5
Quantum numbers of the last electron added for the first ten elements

Quantum number	H	He	Li	Be	B	C	N	O	F	Ne
n	1	1	2	2	2	2	2	2	2	2
l	0	0	0	0	1	1	1	1	1	1
m_l	0	0	0	0	−1	0	+1	−1	0	+1
m_s	$+\frac{1}{2}$	$-\frac{1}{2}$	$+\frac{1}{2}$	$-\frac{1}{2}$	$+\frac{1}{2}$	$+\frac{1}{2}$	$+\frac{1}{2}$	$-\frac{1}{2}$	$-\frac{1}{2}$	$-\frac{1}{2}$

There also is no preferred order for assigning m_l values. Table 7-5 shows them assigned in increasing order ($m_l = -1, 0, +1$) but they can be assigned in decreasing order ($m_l = +1, 0, -1$). Either order is correct, as long as you are consistent. A more compact way of showing an electron configuration is by an energy-level diagram, so called because the vertical direction indicates approximate orbital energy. The basic diagram to be filled in is shown in Figure 7-6a. Each box represents an orbital to be filled with two electrons indicated by arrows. An upward arrow (↑) indicates $m_s = +\frac{1}{2}$; a downward arrow (↓), $m_s = -\frac{1}{2}$. The electron configurations of C, Ca, and P are shown in Figure 7-6. When energy-level diagrams are written out on one line, as in Figure 7-7, they are called orbital diagrams. In the case of chromium, we have not built upon the electron configuration of vanadium. The usual rule of thumb is that half-filled and filled shells are unusually stable and if they can be obtained by "moving" only one electron between very closely spaced energy sublevels one should do so. The closely spaced sublevels are the following groups: (4*s*, 3*d*), (5*s*, 4*d*), (6*s*, 4*f*, 5*d*), and (7*s*, 5*f*, 6*d*). This is an extension of Hund's rule. It works quite well for elements up to atomic number 60 but not very well after that.

A more compact notation is the *spdf* or spectroscopic notation. One writes the subshells in order of increasing energy, as in expression [15], and then indicates the number of electrons in each subshell with an exponent. Sometimes the orbitals are written in order of increasing *n* value. Both methods are shown in Table 7-6.

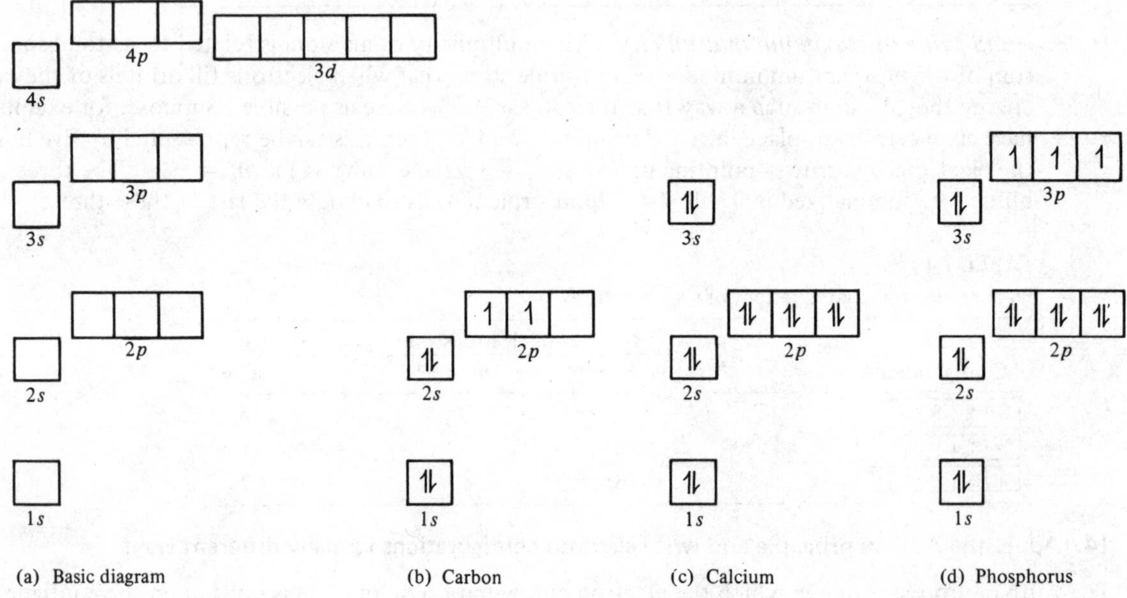

(a) Basic diagram (b) Carbon (c) Calcium (d) Phosphorus

FIGURE 7-6 Energy level diagrams.

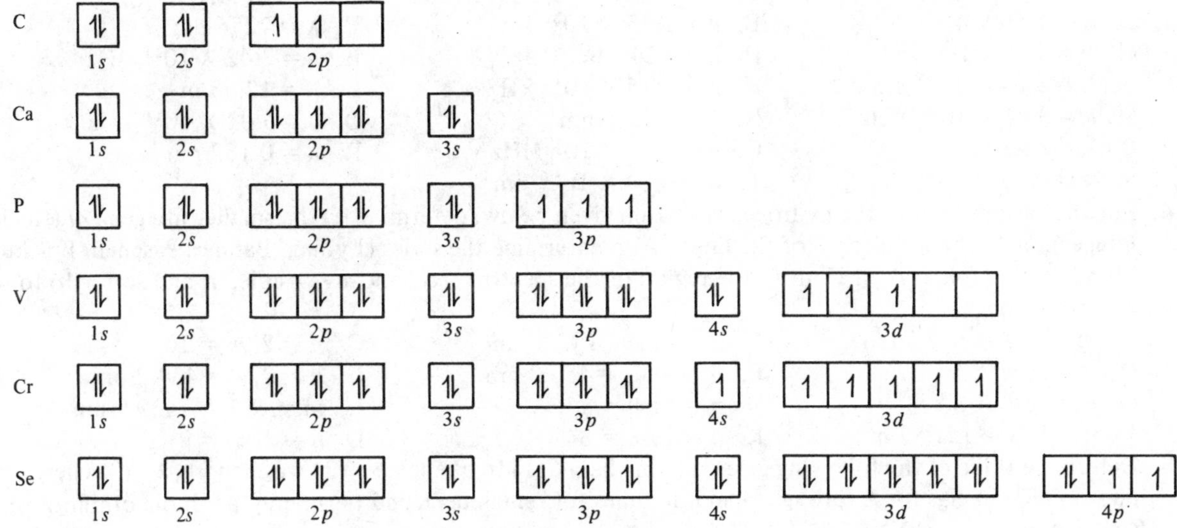

FIGURE 7-7 Orbital diagrams for C, Ca, P, V, Cr, and Se.

TABLE 7-6
spdf notation for C, Ca, P, V, Cr

	Ordered by energy	Abbreviated	Ordered by n
C	$1s^2\ 2s^2\ 2p^2$	$[He]\,2s^2\ 2p^2$	$1s^2\ 2s^2\ 2p^2$
Ca	$1s^2\ 2s^2\ 2p^6\ 3s^2$	$[Ne]\,3s^2$	$1s^2\ 2s^2\ 2p^6\ 3s^2$
P	$1s^2\ 2s^2\ 2p^6\ 3s^2\ 3p^3$	$[Ne]\,3s^2\ 3p^3$	$1s^2\ 2s^2\ 2p^6\ 3s^2\ 3p^3$
V	$1s^2\ 2s^2\ 2p^6\ 3s^2\ 3p^6\ 4s^2\ 3d^3$	$[Ar]\,4s^2\ 3d^3$	$1s^2\ 2s^2\ 2p^6\ 3s^2\ 3p^6\ 3d^3\ 4s^2$
Cr	$1s^2\ 2s^2\ 2p^6\ 3s^2\ 3p^6\ 4s^1\ 3d^5$	$[Ar]\,4s^1\ 3d^5$	$1s^2\ 2s^2\ 2p^6\ 3s^2\ 3p^6\ 3d^5\ 4s^1$
Se	$1s^2\ 2s^2\ 2p^6\ 3s^2\ 3p^6\ 4s^2\ 3d^{10}\ 4p^4$	$[Ar]\,4s^2\ 3d^{10}\ 4p^4$	$1s^2\ 2s^2\ 2p^6\ 3s^2\ 3p^6\ 3d^{10}\ 4s^2\ 4p^4$

One often abbreviates the *spdf* notation by writing the symbol for the last noble gas in brackets to represent its electron configuration. The *spdf* notation does not tell us how the electrons are paired in the unfilled subshells. Often this information is expressed by writing the designation for each orbital in the unfilled subshells, as shown in Table 7-7.

TABLE 7-7
Extended *spdf* notation

C	$[He]\ 2s^2\ 2p_x^1\ 2p_y^1$
Ca	$[Ne]\ 3s^2$
P	$[Ne]\ 3s^2\ 3p_x^1\ 3p_y^1$
V	$[Ar]\ 4s^2\ 3d_{xy}^1\ 3d_{xz}^1\ 3d_{yz}^1$
Cr	$[Ar]\ 4s^1\ 3d_{xy}^1\ 3d_{xz}^1\ 3d_{yz}^1\ 3d_{z^2}^1\ 3d_{x^2-y^2}$
Se	$[Ar]\ 4s^2\ 3d^{10}\ 4p_x^2\ 4p_y^1\ 4p_z^1$

DRILL PROBLEMS

1. & 2. Given the frequency (or wavelength), determine the wavelength (or frequency) of each of the following. Also classify each according to its region: gamma (γ) rays, x rays, ultraviolet (uv) radiation, visible light, infrared (ir) radiation, microwaves, radar waves, television (TV) waves, or radio waves.

A. $\nu = 2.7 \times 10^{14}$ Hz
B. $\lambda = 1.54$ Å
C. $\nu = 25$ MHz
D. $\lambda = 1.50$ km
E. $\nu = 1.75 \times 10^{22}$ Hz
F. $\lambda = 7256\ \mu m$
G. $\nu = 51.5$ kHz
H. $\lambda = 124$ cm
I. $\nu = 7.42 \times 10^{11}$ MHz
J. $\lambda = 5.04 \times 10^{-5}$ cm
K. $\nu = 3.15 \times 10^{12}$ kHz
L. $\lambda = 12.45$ m
M. $\nu = 8.46 \times 10^{16}$ MHz
N. $\lambda = 1.359$ mm
O. $\nu = 5.02 \times 10^{11}$ kHz
P. $\lambda = 82.5$ nm
Q. $\nu = 14.6 \times 10^{3}$ MHz
R. $\lambda = 0.132$ pm
S. $\nu = 8.46 \times 10^{10}$ Hz
T. $\lambda = 4.04 \times 10^{-6}$ pm

4. For the various lines of the hydrogen spectrum given below, determine n (the smaller integer), m (the larger integer), or λ (the wavelength of the line). Also determine the series (Lyman, Balmer, Paschen, Brackett, Pfund, or Humphreys), or identify the region of the spectrum (cosmic, uv, visible, ir, and so forth) to which the line belongs.

A. $m = 3, \lambda = 656.5$ nm
B. $n = 1, \lambda = 102.6$ nm
C. $n = 2, m = 10$
D. $n = 3, m = 4$
E. $m = 4, \lambda = 486.3$ nm
F. $n = 2, \lambda = 434.2$ nm
G. $n = 4, m = 8$
H. $n = 6, m = 7$
I. $m = 6, \lambda = 7459.9$ nm
J. $n = 1, \lambda = 121.57$ nm
K. $n = 2, m = 8$
L. $n = 1, m = 9$

5. Determine three of the following given one of them: (1) frequency, ν; (2) wavelength, λ; (3) energy per photon, E_p (in ergs for A through H and in joules for remainder); and (4) energy per mole of photons, $\overline{E}$ (in kJ/mol).

A. $\lambda = 1.54$ Å
B. $\overline{E} = 418$ kJ/mol
C. $\nu = 105 \times 10^{6}$ Hz
D. $E_p = 1.07 \times 10^{-15}$
E. $\lambda = 527$ nm
F. $\overline{E} = 28.5$ kJ/mol
G. $\nu = 6.12 \times 10^{12}$ Hz
H. $E_p = 8.13 \times 10^{-20}$ erg
I. $\lambda = 1.34$ km
J. $\overline{E} = 0.526$ kJ/mol
K. $\nu = 512 \times 10^{3}$ Hz
L. $E_p = 3.14 \times 10^{-17}$ J
M. $\lambda = 6.15$ cm
N. $\overline{E} = 0.725$ kJ/mol
O. $\nu = 34.2 \times 10^{15}$ Hz
P. $E_p = 1.24 \times 10^{-13}$ J

10. (1) Give the letter designations (such as p_x, p_y, and p_z) and the set of magnetic quantum numbers (−1, 0, +1) for the orbitals in each of the following subshells.

A. $1s$
B. $3p$
C. $4d$
D. $5s$
E. $4f$
F. $4p$
G. $3s$
H. $2p$
I. $5d$
J. $3d$

(2) Give the number and letter designations (such as $2s$ and $2p$), and the total number of electrons in each of the following shells.

A. *K* shell
B. *M* shell
C. 2nd shell
D. $n = 4$
E. 5th level

11. Sketch each of the following sets of orbitals, each set on the same axes and to approximate scale.

A. $1s, 2s, 3s$
B. $2p_x, 2p_y$
C. $3d_{xy}, 3d_{x^2-y^2}$
D. $2p_x, 3p_x$
E. $3p_z, 3d_{z^2}$
F. $3d_{xz}, 3d_{z^2}$
G. $3s, 3p_x$
H. $3d_{xy}, 4d_{xy}$

13. Each symbol is followed by an electron configuration which violates one of the following principles: (1) the order of filling or the Aufbau principle; (2) the Pauli exclusion principle; (3) Hund's rule of maximum multiplicity; (4) Hund's rule extended–stability of full and half full subshells; (5) allowed quantum numbers (objective 7-10).

State which principle is violated by each configuration and give the correct configuration for each atom.

A. N $1s^2\ 2s^2\ 2p_x^2\ 2p_y^1$
B. Al $1s^2\ 2s^2\ 2p^6\ 2d^3$
C. B $1s^2\ 2s^3$
D. P $1s^2\ 2s^2\ 2p^6\ 3p^5$
E. Cu [Ar] $4s^2\ 3d^9$
F. Be $1s^2\ 1p^2$
G. Mg [Ne] $\underline{11}$
H. C $1s^2\ 2s^1\ 2p_x^1\ 2p_y^1\ 2p_z^1$
I. V $1s^2\ 2s^2\ 2p^6\ 3s^2\ 3p^6\ 3d^5$
J. S [Ne] $3s^2\ 3p_x^2\ 3p_y^2$
K. Mn [Ar] $4s^1\ 3d^6$
L. N $1s^2\ 1p^5$
M. Ag [Kr] $5s^2\ 4d^9$
N. Na $1s^2\ 1p^9$

O. Ni [Kr] $5s^2\ 4d^2_{xy}\ 4d^2_{xz}\ 4d^2_{yz}\ 4d^2_{z^2}$
P. Sc [Ne] $3s^2\ 3p^6\ 3d^3$
Q. Cl $1s^2\ 1p^6\ 2s^2\ 2p^6\ 3s^1$
R. C $1s^2\ 2s^2\ 2p^2_x$
S. Cl [Ne] $\underline{11}\ \underline{11}\ \underline{1}$
T. B $1s^1\ 2s^1\ 2p^1_x\ 2p^1_y\ 2p^1_z$

In your own words, state each of the following principles or rules and give two examples illustrating its use.
U. Hund's rule extended;
V. Hund's rule of maximum multiplicity;
W. the aufbau principle;
X. Pauli exclusion principle.

14. (1) Give the symbol of the element of lowest atomic number which has the characteristics listed in each of the following parts. Also give the electron configuration of the element.
A. one electron with $m_l = 2$
B. two unpaired electrons
C. four pairs of electrons
D. two electrons with $n = 3$ and $l = 2$
E. three electrons with $n = 3$
F. eleven p electrons
G. five d electrons
H. three electrons with $m_l = -2$
I. five electrons with $m_l = +1$
J. five electrons with $m_l = 0$
K. five electrons with $m_s = +1/2$

(2) The last few quantum numbers of the electrons or the last part of the electron configurations of a number of elements are given below. Identify each element based on its electron configuration. (For example, B might be: $n = 2, l = 1, m_l = -1, m_s = -1/2; n = 2, l = 0, m_l = 0, m_s = +1/2$.)
A. $3s^2\ 3p^4$
B. $n = 4, l = 0, m_l = 0, m_s = -1/2;\ n = 3, l = 2, m_l = -2, m_s = +1/2$
C. $5s^2\ 4d^2$
D. $n = 5, l = 2, m_l = +2, m_s = -1/2;\ n = 6, l = 1, m_l = -1, m_s = +1/2$
E. $5d^1\ 4f^1$ F. $4d5$ G. $3d^3$ H. $4p^4$
J. $n = 5, l = 0, m_l = 0, m_s = +1/2;\ n = 5, l = 0, m_l = 0, m_s = -1/2$

(3) Give the electron configuration of each of the following elements using both the abbreviated *spdf* notation and also an abbreviated orbital diagram.
A. N B. S C. Cl D. Si E. Cu
F. Na G. Cs H. Ce I. Sc J. O
K. Fe L. Sr

Further Questions. (1) Using the Aufbau principle, the Pauli exclusion principle, and Hund's rule of maximum multiplicity write reasonable electron configurations for atoms of the following elements.
A. K B. C C. Mn D. Sc E. Cr
F. Au G. Si H. Zn I. Mg J. Fe
K. P L. Fe M. U N. Ne O. Pr
P. Ag Q. Al R. Sn S. Ge T. Mo
U. Ga V. Ca W. I X. W Y. B
Z. Cu

(2) Compare these to the known configurations in the text. Which are different and how?

QUIZZES (20 minutes each)

Choose the best answer for each question.

Quiz A

1. The statement that one cannot measure the speed and position of the electron simultaneously is the (a) Heisenberg uncertainty principle; (b) Pauli exclusion principle; (c) rule of maximum multiplicity; (d) periodic law; (e) none of these.

2. An experiment or effect that demonstrates that light is a particle is the (a) sun's spectrum; (b) destructive interference of light; (c) photoelectric effect; (d) electron microscope; (e) none of these.
3. The shape of a *p* orbital is (a) spherical; (b) similar to figure 8; (c) similar to a four-leaf clover; (d) conical; (e) none of these.
4. Which series of subshells is arranged in order of increasing energy? (a) 6*s*, 4*f*, 5*d*, 6*p*; (b) 4*f*, 6*s*, 5*d*, 6*p*; (c) 5*d*, 4*f*, 6*s*, 6*p*; (d) 4*f*, 5*d*, 6*s*, 6*p*; (e) none of these.
5. The light with the highest energy among those given below is (a) television waves; (b) infrared (heat) waves; (c) ultraviolet rays; (d) microwaves; (e) radio waves.
6. The radiation with the highest frequency has a wavelength of (a) 300 cm; (b) 200 nm; (c) 8.2 m; (d) 1.00 nm; (e) 7.31 μm.
7. A certain radiation has a frequency = 6.7×10^{14} s^{-1}. What is its wavelength in nanometers? (a) $(6.62 \times 10^{-34})(6.7 \times 10^{14})$; (b) $(3.0 \times 10^{8})/[(6.7 \times 10^{14})(10^{9})]$; (c) $(3.0 \times 10^{8})(10^{9})/(6.7 \times 10^{14})$; (d) $(6.7 \times 10^{14})(10^{7})/(3.0 \times 10^{8})$; (e) none of these.
8. The energy in joules of a photon of wavelength 1.23×10^{-5} m is (a) $(6.63 \times 10^{-34})(3.00 \times 10^{8})/(1.23 \times 10^{-5})$; (b) $(6.63 \times 10^{-34})/(1.23 \times 10^{-5})$; (c) $(3.00 \times 10^{8})/(1.23 \times 10^{-5})$; (d) $(1.23 \times 10^{-5})/(6.63 \times 10^{-34})$; (e) none of these.
9. The number of unpaired electrons in the outermost subshell of a Mg atom is (a) 0; (b) 1; (c) 2; (d) 3; (e) none of these.
10. $1s^2\ 2s^2\ 2p^6\ 3s^2\ 3p^6\ 4s^2\ 3d^3$ is the ground state electronic configuration of (a) chromium; (b) vanadium; (c) scandium; (d) niobium; (e) none of these.
11. A Na atom must gain or lose how many electrons to achieve an inert gas electronic configuration? (a) gain 2; (b) gain 1; (c) lose 1; (d) lose 2; (e) none of these.
12. [Ar] $4s^2\ 3d^1$ is the ground state electronic configuration for (a) titanium; (b) zirconium; (c) vanadium; (d) calcium; (e) none of these.

Quiz B

1. What is an electron? (a) a wave; (b) a particle; (c) either, depending on how it is observed; (d) neither; (e) no one knows.
2. The principle which is based on electrons attempting to be as far apart as possible is (a) Bohr theory; (b) Heisenberg principle; (c) exclusion principle; (d) Hund's rule; (e) none of these.
3. Which two orbitals are both located between the axes of a coordinate system and not along the axes? (a) d_{xy}, d_{z^2}; (b) d_{yz}, p_x; (c) d_{xz}, p_y; (d) $d_{x^2-y^2}, p_z$; (e) none of these.
4. All of the terms are quantum numbers *except* (a) principal; (b) magnetic; (c) spin; (d) valence; (e) none of these.
5. The light with the longest wavelength among those given is (a) infrared ray; (b) microwave; (c) radiowave; (d) x ray; (e) none of these.
6. The radiation with the highest energy has a frequency of (a) 3.12×10^{1} Hz; (b) 7.13×10^{7} Hz; (c) 4.12×10^{3} Hz; (d) 3.00×10^{10} Hz; (e) 2.96×10^{5} Hz.
7. Radiation having a frequency of 3×10^{15} Hz has a wavelength of (a) 10 nm; (b) 100 nm; (c) 1000 nm; (d) 10,000 nm; (e) none of these.
8. Light having a frequency of 4.5×10^{10} s^{-1} has an energy in joules given by ($h = 6.62 \times 10^{-34}$ J s) (a) $(6.62 \times 10^{-34})(3.0 \times 10^{8})/(0.67)$; (b) $(3.0 \times 10^{8})(6.62 \times 10^{-34})$; (c) $(4.5 \times 10^{8})(6.62 \times 10^{-34})$; (d) $(6.62 \times 10^{-34})/(4.5 \times 10^{10})$; (e) none of these.
9. The number of unpaired electrons in the outermost subshell of a C atom is (a) 0; (b) 1; (c) 2; (d) 3; (e) none of these.
10. The four quantum numbers that could identify the third *p* electron in sulfur are

	n	l	m_l	m_s
(a)	3	0	1	$+\frac{1}{2}$
(b)	2	2	−1	$+\frac{1}{2}$
(c)	3	2	1	$-\frac{1}{2}$
(d)	3	1	−1	$+\frac{1}{2}$
(e)	none of these			

11. [Kr] $5s^2\ 4d^{10}\ 5p^5$ is the electronic configuration of (a) Br; (b) I; (c) At; (d) Te; (e) none of these.
12. Which represent the electronic structure of the element having the atomic number 17? (a) $1s^2\ 2p^8\ 3d^7$; (b) $1s^2\ 2s^8\ 3p^7$; (c) $1s^2\ 2p^2\ \ 2d^6\ 3f^7$; (d) $1s^2\ 2s^2\ 2p^6\ 3s^2\ 3p^5$; (e) none of these.

Quiz C

1. That the electronic configuration of N is $1s^2\ 2s^2\ 2p_x^1\ 2p_y^1\ 2p_z^1$ instead of $1s^2\ 2s^2\ 2p_x^2\ 2p_y^1$ is postulated by (a) the Bohr–Sommerfeld theory; (b) the Pauli exclusion principle; (c) the Heisenberg uncertainty principle; (d) Hund's rule of maximum multiplicity; (e) none of these.
2. In the equation $1/\lambda = R(1/2^2 - 1/n^2)$, R is known as the (a) ideal gas law constant; (b) Boltzmann constant; (c) Rydberg constant; (d) Balmer constant; (e) none of these.
3. The shape of most *d* orbitals is (a) spherical; (b) figure 8; (c) figure 8 with a donut; (d) clover leaf; (e) none of these.
4. An atom in a $4f$ orbital has principal, n, and orbital, l, quantum numbers, respectively, of (a) 3 and 4; (b) 4 and 4; (c) 4 and 3; (d) 4 and 5; (e) none of these.
5. The unit of frequency among those given is (a) cm^{-1}; (b) s^{-1}; (c) Hz^{-1}; (d) pm; (e) none of these.
6. The radiation which has the highest energy is (a) $\lambda = 560$ nm; (b) $\lambda = 56.0$ cm; (c) $\lambda = 5.60\ \mu m$; (d) $\lambda = 300$ nm; (e) $\lambda = 56.0$ nm.
7. The frequency of a microwave with wavelength of 0.750 cm is (a) $0.750/3.00 \times 10^{10}$; (b) $6.63 \times 10^{-27}/0.750$; (c) $3.00 \times 10^{10}/0.750$; (d) $0.750/6.63 \times 10^{-27}$; (e) none of these.
8. Radiation having a frequency of $3.3 \times 10^{15}\ sec^{-1}$ has how much energy in joules? ($h = 6.6 \times 10^{-34}$ J s) (a) 2.0×10^{-49}; (b) 6.0×10^{-19}; (c) 3.0×10^{18}; (d) 2.2×10^{-18}; (e) none of these.
9. The number of unpaired electrons in the outermost subshell of a Cl atom is (a) 0; (b) 1; (c) 2; (d) 3; (e) none of these.
10. The four quantum numbers that could identify the *second* 2*s* electron in the nitrogen atom are

	n	l	m_l	m_s
(a)	1	0	1	$+\frac{1}{2}$
(b)	2	1	0	$-\frac{1}{2}$
(c)	2	0	0	$-\frac{1}{2}$
(d)	3	0	0	$+\frac{1}{2}$

(e) none of these.

11. A Mg atom must gain or lose how many electrons to achieve an inert gas electronic configuration? (a) lose 1; (b) lose 2; (c) lose 3; (d) gain 1; (e) none of these.
12. The electron configuration of iron is (a) [Ar] $4s^2\ 3d^6$; (b) [Xe] $6s^2\ 4f^{14}\ 3d^7$; (c) [Ar] $3d^8$; (d) [Ar] $4s^1\ 3d^7$; (e) none of these.

Quiz D

1. In Bohr's atomic theory, when an electron moves from one energy level to another energy level more distant from the nucleus of the same atom (a) energy is emitted; (b) energy is absorbed; (c) no change in energy occurs; (d) light is emitted; (e) none of these.
2. We employ several rules when determining electronic configurations. Which of the following do we *not* use? (a) Aufbau principle; (b) Heisenberg principle; (c) Pauli principle; (d) Hund's rule; (e) none, we use all of these.
3. Which two orbitals both point along rather than between the axes of a coordinate system; (a) $p_z, d_{x^2-y^2}$; (b) d_{z^2}, d_{xy}; (c) d_{xy}, p_z; (d) d_{yz}, p_x; (e) none of these.
4. When an electron has a principle quantum number of 1 ($n = 1$), the orbital quantum number l must be (a) +1; (b) 0; (c) −1; (d) without restriction; (e) none of these.
5. The symbol λ is used in spectroscopy to represent (a) frequency; (b) energy; (c) speed; (d) wavelength; (e) none of these.

6. The light with the longest wavelength has which of the following frequencies? (a) 3.00×10^{13} Hz; (b) 4.12×10^{5} Hz; (c) 8.50×10^{20} Hz; (d) 9.12×10^{12} Hz; (e) 3.20×10^{9} Hz.
7. A radio wave has a frequency of 5.0 kHz. Its wavelength in *meters* is (a) $(3.0 \times 10^{10})/(5.0)$; (b) $(3.0 \times 10^{10})/(5.0 \times 10^{3})$; (c) $(3.0 \times 10^{8})/(5.0 \times 10^{3})$; (d) $(3.0 \times 10^{8})/(5.0)$; (e) none of these.
8. Radiation having a wavelength of 500 nm has an energy of (in J) (a) $(6.6 \times 10^{-34})(3 \times 10^{8})/(5 \times 10^{-7})$; (b) $(6.6 \times 10^{-34})(5 \times 10^{-5})/(3 \times 10^{8})$; (c) $(6.6 \times 10^{-34})(3 \times 10^{8})/500$; (d) $(3 \times 10^{8})(500)/(6.6 \times 10^{-34})$; (e) none of these.
9. Unpaired electrons are found in the ground-state atoms of (a) Ca; (b) Ne; (c) Mg; (d) P; (e) none of these.
10. The four quantum numbers of the *last* electron to be placed into a Ca atom are

	n	l	m_l	m_s
(a)	4	1	0	$+\frac{1}{2}$
(b)	3	0	1	$-\frac{1}{2}$
(c)	4	1	0	$-\frac{1}{2}$
(d)	4	0	0	$-\frac{1}{2}$
(e)	none of these.			

11. The number of electrons that a P atom must acquire to achieve a noble gas electronic configuration is (a) 1; (b) 2; (c) 3; (d) 4; (e) none of these.
12. The ground-state electron configuration of silicon is (a) $1s^2\ 2s^2\ 2p^6\ 3s^2\ 3p_x^2$; (b) $1s^2\ 2s^2\ 2p^6\ 3s^2\ 3p_x^1\ 3p_y^1$ (c) $1s^2\ 2s^2\ 2p^2$; (d) $1s^2\ 2s^2\ 2p^6\ 3s^2\ 3d^2$; (e) none of these.

SAMPLE TEST (20 minutes)

1. An FM station broadcasts with a 3.28 m wavelength. What is the energy (in kJ) per mole of photons emitted by this radio station?
2. Sketch the outline of each orbital on the axes above the symbol for the orbital.

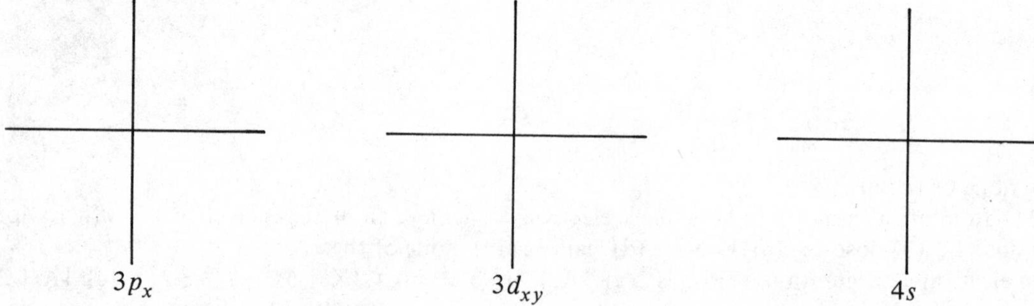

$3p_x$ $3d_{xy}$ $4s$

3. Give the full *spdf* electron configuration of each of the following atoms.
   a. P b. Mn c. Si
4. Give the abbreviated orbital diagram of the electron configuration of each of the following atoms.
   a. Co b. Al c. O

Chapter 8

Atomic Properties and the Periodic Table

REVIEW OF OBJECTIVES

1. Apply the periodic law to selected properties of the elements.

The periodic law states that the physical and chemical properties of the elements vary periodically with atomic number. This is shown in graphs of atomic volume (*Figure 8-1 in the text*), ionization energy (*Figure 8-8 in the text*), and melting point (Figure 8-1) against atomic number. The same general pattern of peaks and valleys occurs in each graph.

2. Describe the various areas of the periodic table by using the terms: periods, groups, families, representative elements, transition elements, and others.

A *period* is a (horizontal) row in the periodic table. There are seven periods. A *group* or a *family* is a (vertical) column in the periodic table. Elements of the same family are called *congeners.* For example, He, Ne, Ar, Kr, Xe, and Rn are congeners. Several families have special names.

Family IA is the *alkali metals.* Family IIA is the *alkaline earth metals.* Family VIIA is the *halogens* (meaning salt formers). Family 0 is the *noble gases*, the rare gases, or the inert gases. Family VIA is the *chalcogens* (meaning chalk formers). Family IB is the *coinage metals.* Fe, Co, and Ni are the *iron triad.* Ru, Rh, Pd, Os, Ir, and Pt are the *noble metals*. The "B" families and family VIII are the *transition metals* or transition elements. Ce through Lu are the *lanthanoids*, the lanthanide metals, or the rare earth metals. Th through Lr are the *actinoids.* The lanthanoids and actinoids taken together are the *inner transition elements.* The "A" families and family 0 are the *representative elements.*

★ **3. Describe the Aufbau process using the periodic table as a guide.**

★ **4. Explain the basic features of the electron configurations of the representative and transition elements, especially the number of valence electrons in each representative group.**

We used the periodic table in learning the order in which orbitals are filled in objective 7–12 (see Figure 7-5). The electron configurations of atoms determine their physical and chemical properties. An atom shows mainly its outer electrons–those in the shell of highest principal quantum number. Therefore, there is a striking difference in chemical and physical properties between representative families, because each family differs by one or more outer shell electrons. There is not quite so large a difference between transition families, because these families differ by inner shell electrons. The number of outer shell (that is, *s* and *p*) electrons of a representative element equals the family number. These outer shell electrons are called *valence electrons.*

5. Describe metals, nonmetals, metalloids, and noble gases in several ways and locate them in the periodic table.

Noble gases are the elements in group 0. Nonmetals are in the triangular block in the upper right corner of the A groups (H, C, N, O, F, P, S, Cl, Se, Br, and I). Metalloids are the two diagonal rows just below and to the left of the nonmetals (B, Si, Ge, As, Sb, To, Po, At). Metals are the remaining elements.

Physically, pure metals generally are malleable and ductile, melt at moderate temperatures, and conduct heat and electricity well. (These properties change drastically when two metals are mixed together or alloyed.) Nonmetals tend to be insulators and form small molecules which condense into solids poorly and hence the solids melt easily (except carbon which has a very high melting point). Chemically, metals lose

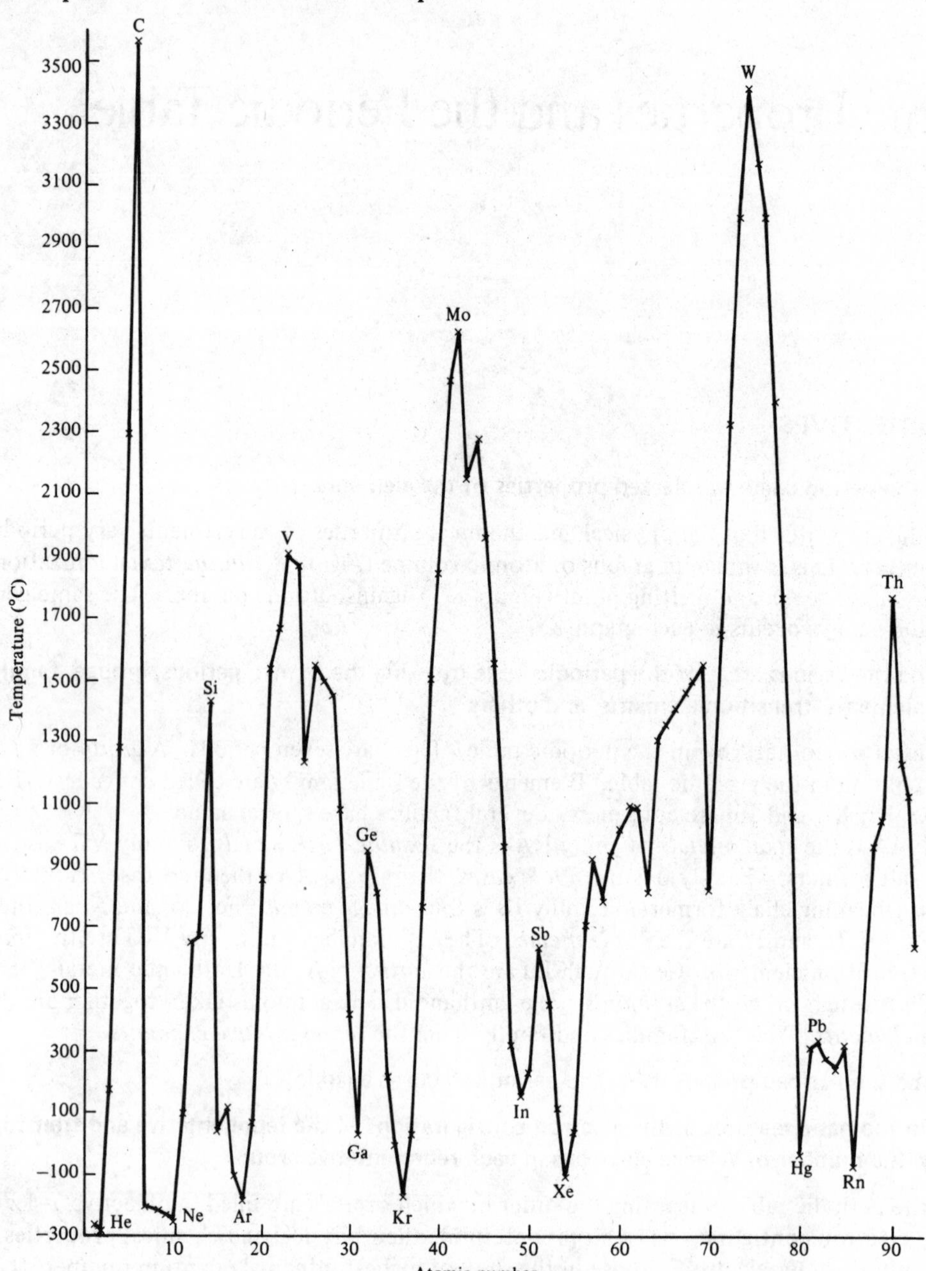

FIGURE 8-1 Melting points of the elements vs. atomic number.

electrons and form cations, whereas nonmetals gain electrons and form anions. Metallic oxides form basic solutions in water. Nonmetallic oxides form acidic solutions.

Metals rarely combine chemically with each other. Nonmetals combine chemically to form definite compounds with nonmetallic properties. When metals combine with nonmetals, ionic compounds are formed. These compounds have high melting points and the melt conducts electricity but the solid does not.

Metalloids are elements with physical and chemical properties between those of metals and those of nonmetals. For example, their oxides form aqueous solutions which are amphoteric, meaning that they can react with either acids or bases.

★ **6. Explain what is meant by atomic size, covalent radius, ionic radius, van der Waals radius, and metallic radius; know the general trends in atomic size which occur within families and groups.**

Atoms are not small hard balls but indefinite spheres. Defining where the electron cloud of an atom ends is like trying to measure the extent of the metropolitan area of a city. But with both cities and atoms we can determine the center. For atoms we measure the distance between two centers, divide this in half, and call the result the atomic size.

All atoms are not normally bound together in the same way. Some are bound by covalent bonds in molecules, some are attracted to each other in ionic crystals by ionic forces, and some are held in metallic crystals by the force of a "sea" of electrons acting as "glue" between cations. Fortunately, it is possible to form molecules of nearly every element (except the noble gases) in which two like atoms are held together by a covalent bond. The covalent radius is often called the atomic radius. There are several family and period trends in atomic size.

1. Atomic size regularly increases from top to bottom in a family (i.e., "down" a family). More electrons with the same outer configuration are present around the nucleus (see Figure 8-2).

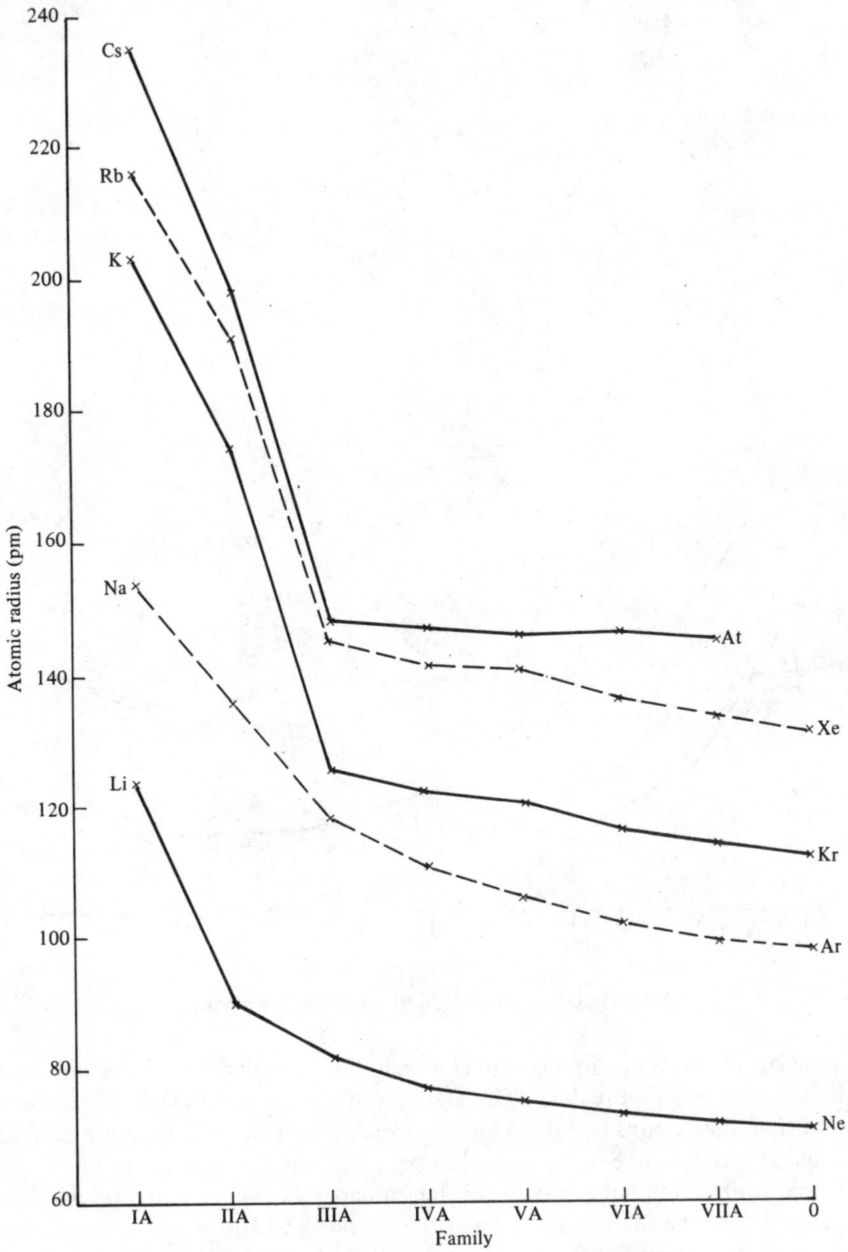

FIGURE 8-2 Atomic radii of the representative elements.

2. Atomic size gradually decreases from left to right in a period of representative elements (i.e., "across" a period), as shown in Figure 8-2. The explanation is that within a family all electrons are being added to the same shell. It is helpful to think of these shells as being similar to the layers of an onion. As each

electron is added, the shell or layer becomes more populated. But at the same time, protons are being added to the nucleus which therefore attracts the electrons more strongly. Hence the shell is pulled closer to the nucleus.

3. Across a transition series atomic size gradually but somewhat irregularly decreases then increases at the end of the series (see Figure 8-3). Within a transition series electrons are added to an inner *d* shell. This inner shell gradually will decrease in size, but since these *d* electrons shield the outer electrons, the outer shell should increase in size. The two trends oppose each other with the shielding effect predominating at the end of the series.

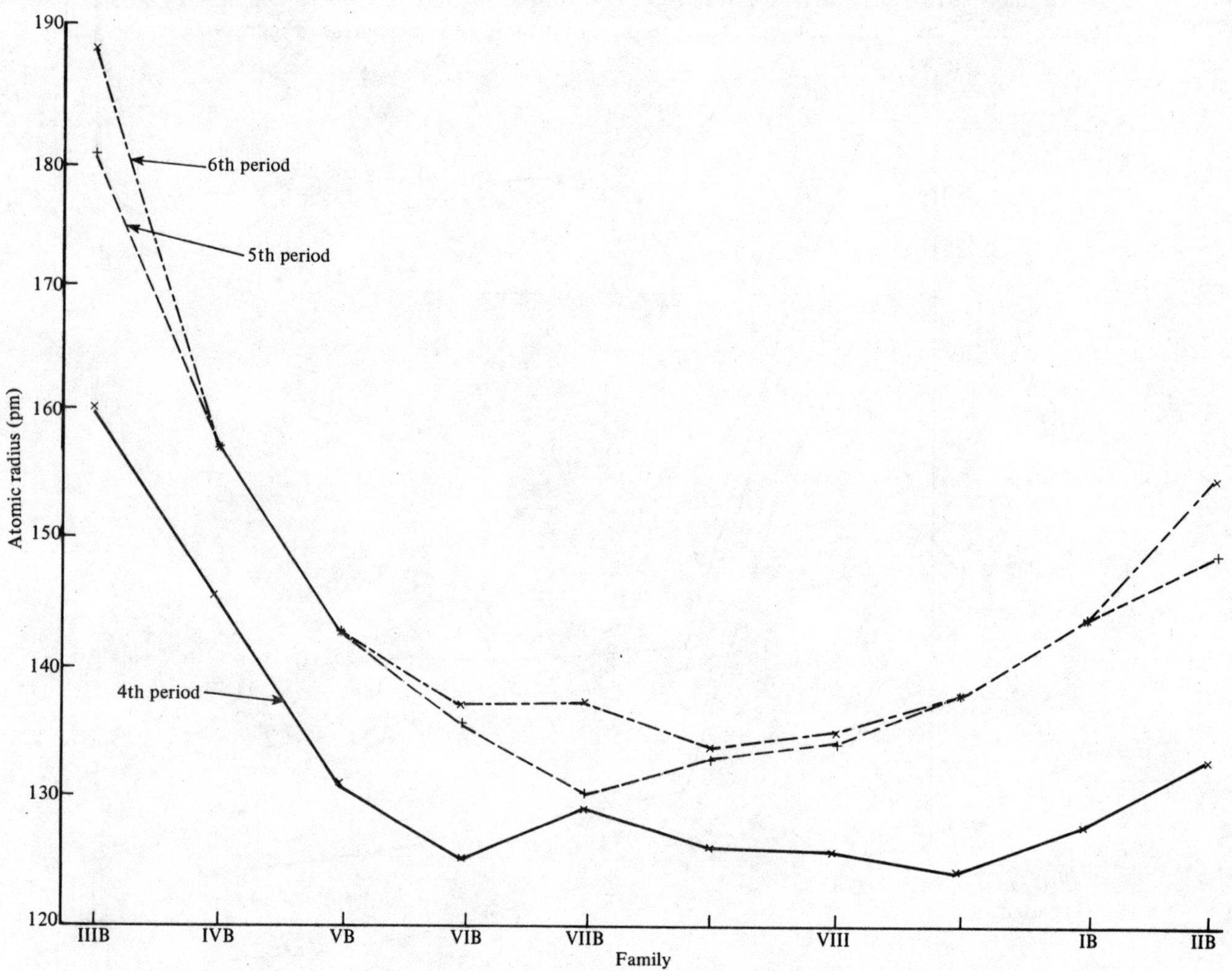

FIGURE 8-3 Atomic radii of the transition elements.

4. Across the lanthanoids the atomic radii gradually but irregularly decrease and the radii of the +3 cations steadily decrease (see Figure 8-4). This steady decrease in size, called the lanthanoid contraction, is due to the addition of electrons to a deep inner subshell (the 4*f* subshell). Note carefully the relative sizes of atoms and ions in Figure 8-4; the ions are very much smaller than the atoms.

The lanthanoid contraction helps to explain the similarity in chemical and physical properties between the transition elements of the fifth (Y to Cd) and the sixth (La to Hg) periods. Because of the lanthanoid contraction, atomic sizes are almost the same in the fifth and sixth transition periods. Since the outer electron configurations are the same, the properties are very similar.

5. The size of an isoelectronic ion decreases as the positive charge on the ion increases (see Figure 8-5). The explanation is that the larger nuclear charge exerts more pull on each electron and thus pulls these electrons in closer.

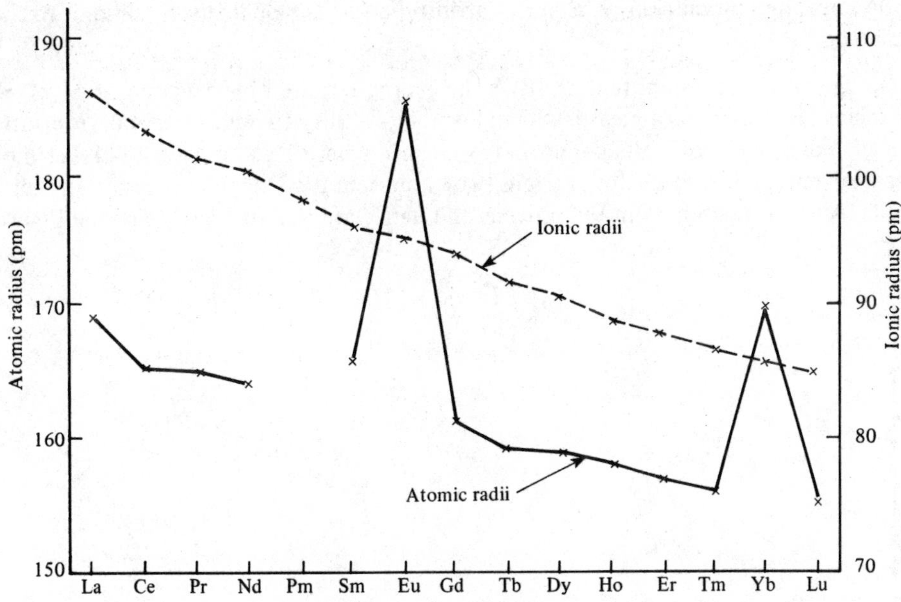

FIGURE 8-4 Atomic and ionic radii of the lanthanides.

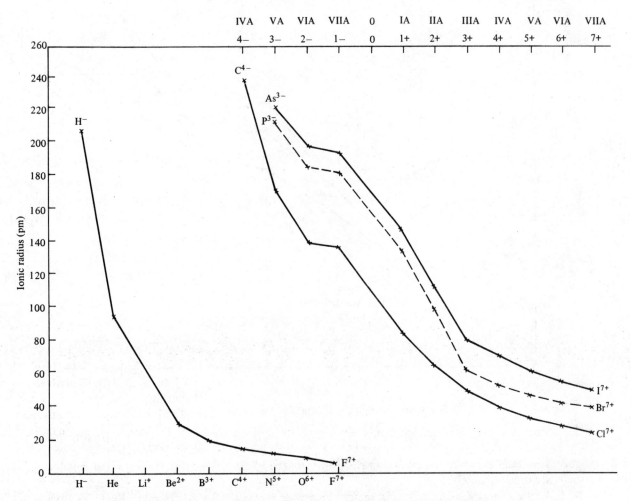

FIGURE 8-5 Ionic radii of the representative elements (isoelectronic series).

★ **7. Define the terms ionization energy, electron affinity, and electronegativity; predict the periodic trends in these properties.**

Ionization energy (or ionization potential, IP) is the energy required by the process $M(g) \rightarrow M^+(g) + e^-(g)$. The ease of losing an electron is a measure of an element's ability to act as a metal. Ionization energies are measured in kJ/mol or electron volts per atom (eV/atom), where 1 eV/atom = 96.49 kJ/mol.

1. Ionization energy decreases down a family of representative elements. As atoms get larger, the outermost electrons are further from the nucleus and hence are less strongly held (see Figure 8-6).

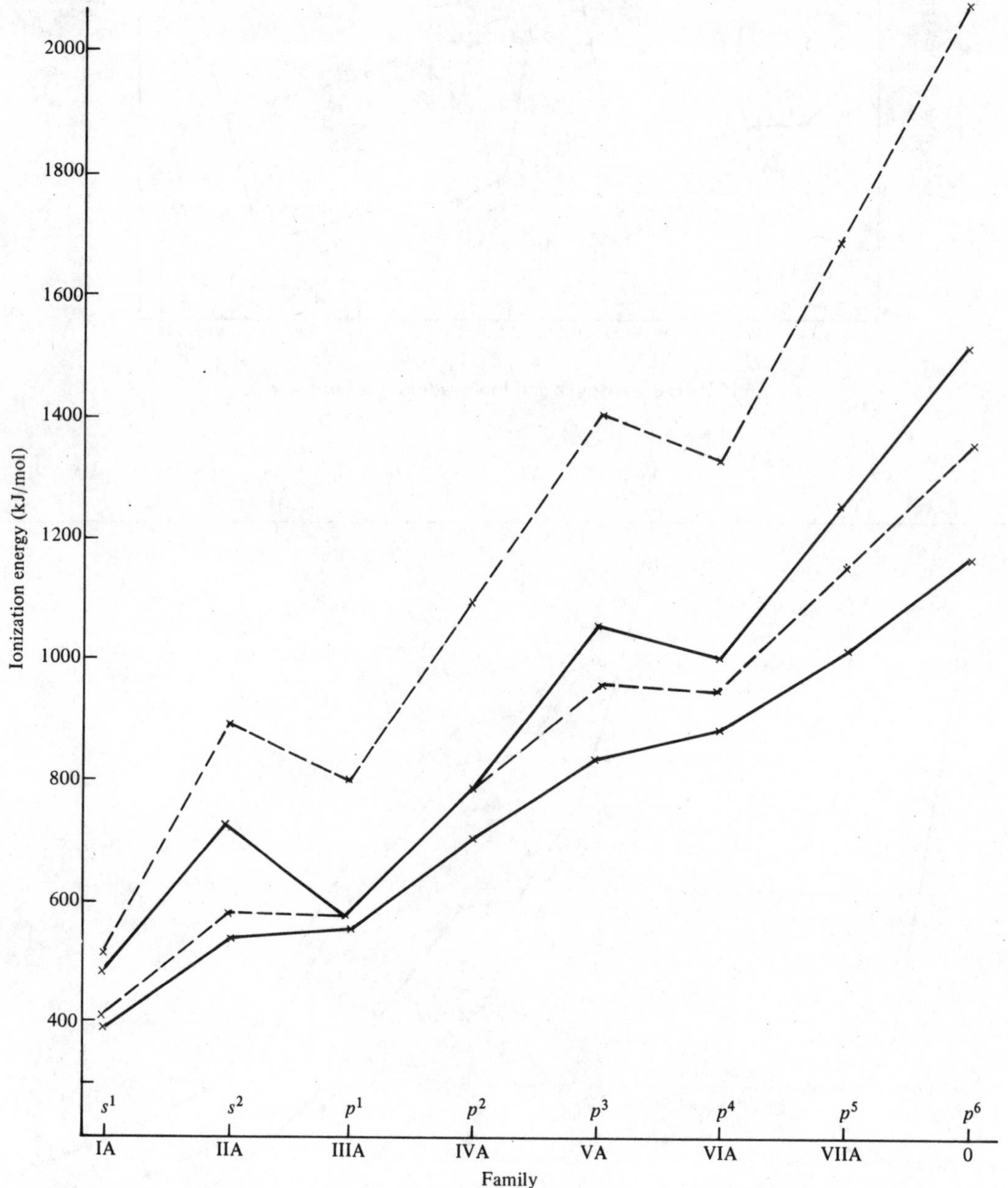

FIGURE 8-6 Ionization energies (kJ/mol) of the representative elements.

2. Ionization energy increases gradually but irregularly across a representative period (Figure 8-6). As the atomic size decreases, it becomes harder to remove an electron from the s^2 and p^3 configurations, and it is easier than expected to remove an electron from the p^1 and p^4 configurations. Half-full and full subshells are unusually stable.

3. Ionization energy gradually but irregularly increases across a transition period. Again, as atomic size decreases, removing the outer electron is harder (see Figure 8-7).

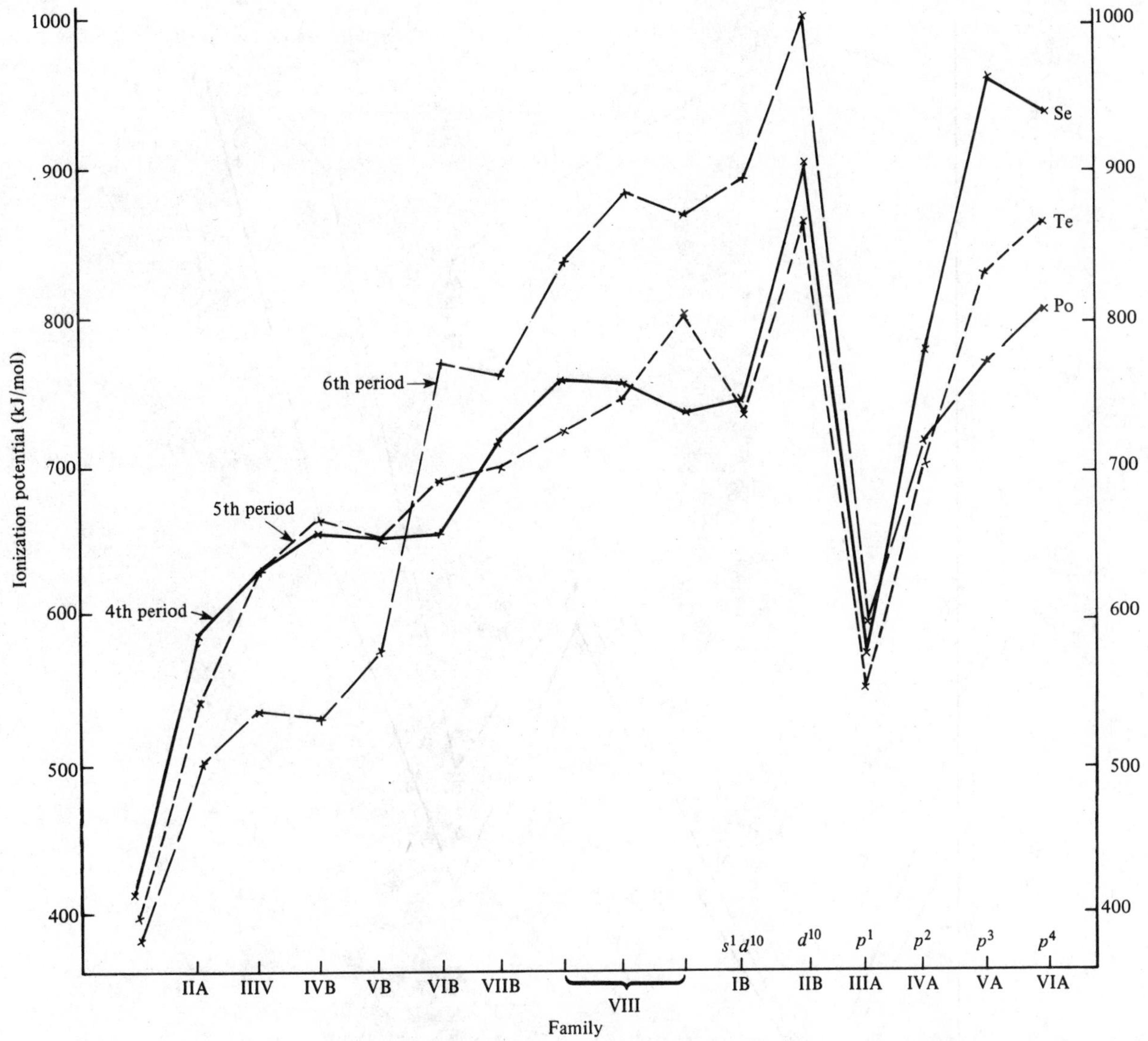

FIGURE 8-7 Ionization potentials for the elements of the fourth, fifth, and sixth periods.

4. There is no noticeable trend in the ionization potentials of the lanthanides.

5. *Electron affinity* is the energy required by the process $X(g) + e^-(g) \rightarrow X^-(g)$. This is an indication of how nonmetallic the element is. Two trends are evident in Figure 8-8: electron affinity increases down a group and decreases gradually but irregularly across a period.

6. *Electronegativity* is an attempt to combine ionization energy and electron affinity to obtain one number which will measure how strongly an electron attracts electrons. Again, two trends are evident: electronegativity increases across a period and decreases down a family.

★ **8. Relate an atom or ion's magnetic properties to its electron configuration.**

An ion's electron configuration is determined from that of its atom. The electrons removed to form a cation are those of highest principal quantum number. The resulting ion also obeys Hund's rule. When all electrons in the atom or ion are paired, the atom or ion is repelled by a magnetic field and is diamagnetic. If there are unpaired electrons, the atom or ion is paramagnetic and is attracted into a magnetic field. The amount of attraction depends on the number of unpaired electrons in each atom or ion.

★ **9. Use periodic relationships to predict physical and chemical properties of the elements and their simple compounds.**

If a property is plotted against atomic number, a periodic trend will be evident. For example, the boiling points of a number of hydrides follow.

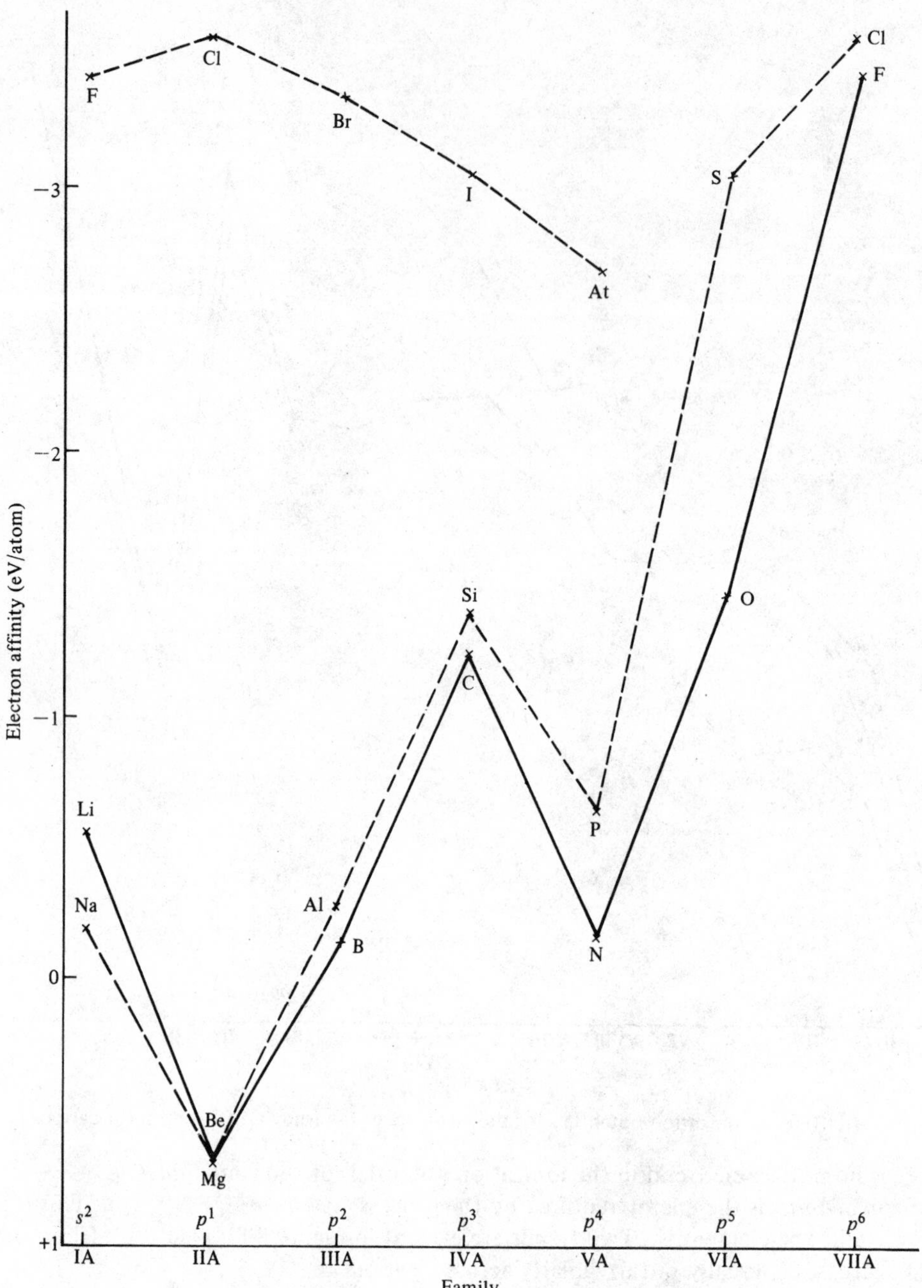

FIGURE 8-8 Electron affinities: $X(g) + e^- \rightarrow X^-(g)$.

Hydride formula:	PH_3	GeH_4	H_2Se	SbH_3
Boiling point, °C:	−87.7	−88.5	−41.5	−17.1
Central atom:	$Z = 15$	$Z = 32$	$Z = 34$	$Z = 51$

Suppose we wish to determine the boiling point of AsH_3. We can plot within a period (Figure 8-9) or within a family (Figure 8-10). Figure 8-9 gives a prediction of −64°C and Figure 8-10 a prediction of −52°C. The second is a better estimate of the true value of −55°C.

★ **10. Use the periodic table to help in writing chemical formulas and equations and naming compounds.**

Binary ionic compounds generally contain a cation with a charge equal to the family number of the metal. The anion has a charge equal to the nonmetal's family number minus eight. Series of compounds which

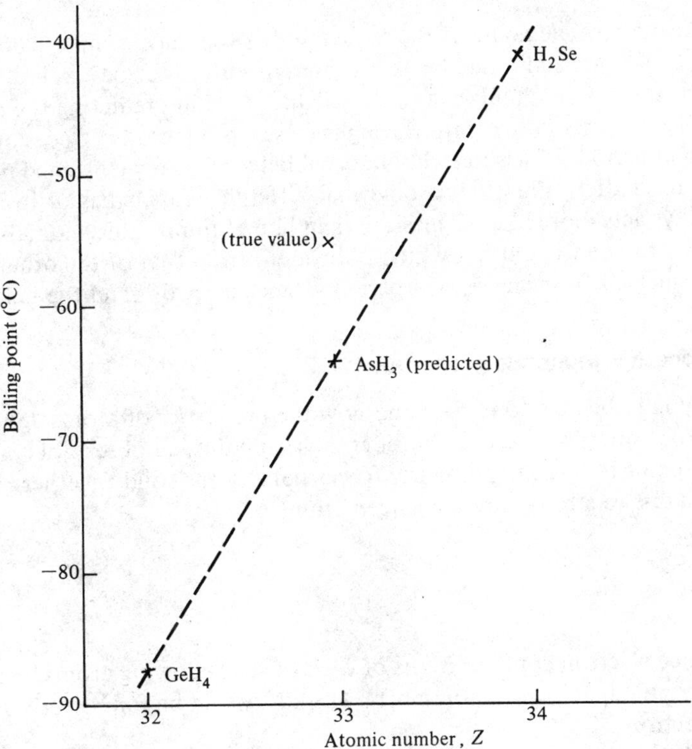

FIGURE 8-9 Boiling point vs. atomic number for GeH_4, AsH_3, and H_2Se.

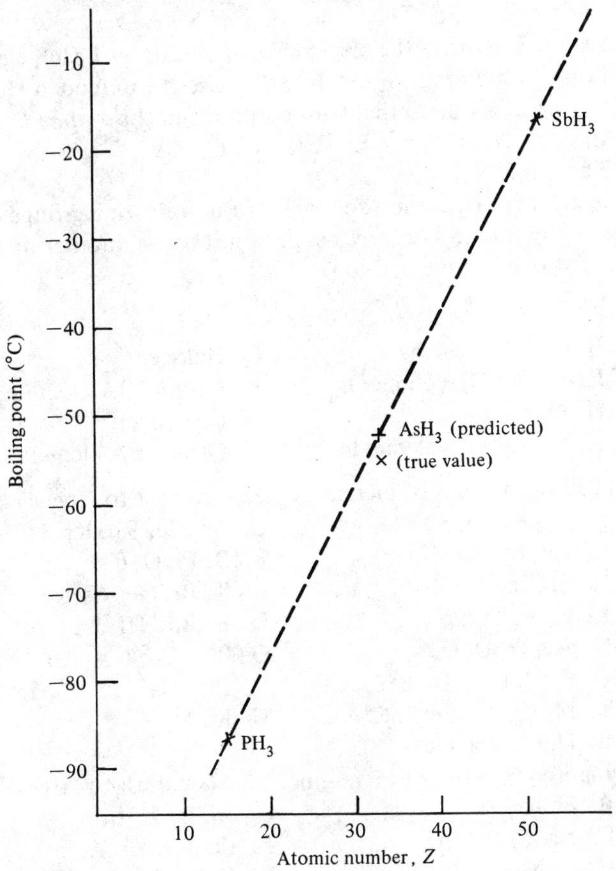

FIGURE 8-10 Boiling point vs. atomic number for PH_3, AsH_3, and SbH_3.

differ only in the substitution of elements of the same family often have similar names or formulas. Thus $NaClO_2$, $NaBrO_2$, and $NaIO_2$ are sodium chlorite, sodium bromite, and sodium iodite. ($NaFO_2$ has not been prepared.) In fact, the periodic table is a fairly reliable guide in predicting the names, formulas, and chemical relations of the elements in the third through the seventh periods. Occasionally the elements and compounds of the second period show somewhat unusual behavior. As mentioned *in the text*, the reactions of oxygen are difficult to predict. Fluorine is somewhat different in its behavior from the other halogens. And lithium in some ways acts more like magnesium than like sodium. This anomaly of the second period is due to helium's s^2 electron configuration, which is different from that of the other noble gases. Thus the nucleus is not well shielded from the second period valence electrons and the behavior of the element is somewhat unusual.

11. Relate physical properties to atomic properties.

This objective expects you to be able to understand how the properties of atoms determine the observable properties of matter. For example, when we consider melting point, an observable property, we should realize that the melting point is determined by the forces holding the solid together. Hence we believe a high melting point to be due to strong forces between atoms.

DRILL PROBLEMS

3. & 4. (1) Determine the valence electron configurations of each of the following atoms by referring only to the periodic table. Omit the principal quantum number. Thus, N would be s^2p^3. Also omit the d electrons. They are not valence electrons.

A. P　B. Si　C. Ne　D. Bi　E. Rb　F. Se
G. In　H. I　I. Cs　J. Xe　K. Ba　L. Ga
M. Po　N. Pb　O. Cl　P. Be

(2) Refer only to the periodic table, and write the electron configuration of each element which follows. Use the abbreviated *spdf* notation in which Mn is [Ar] $4s^2 3d^5$. Use the extended Hund's rule where necessary. Check your predictions against the actual configurations in the *Appendix in the text.*

A. Cu　B. Mo　C. Au　D. Eu　E. La　F. Os
G. Fe　H. V　I. Nb　J. Y

(3) Give the general valence electron configuration for each of the following groups of elements, using n to designate the principal quantum number. Use x as a superscript if the number of electrons in a subshell can have different values. The first one is done for you.

Inner transition elements: $ns^2(n-1)d^1(n-2)f^x$

A. Transition elements　B. Alkaline earths　C. Halogens
D. Group IVA elements　E. Group IIIA elements　F. Group VIA elements
G. Alkali metals　H. Noble gases　I. Chalcogens
J. Group IIIB elements　K. Group IVB elements　L. Group VA elements

6. Rewrite each of the lists which follow in order of increasing size (smallest to largest) of the species.

A. Ca, Sr, Mg, Be　B. Te, Po, O, S　C. Ar, He, Rn, Kr
D. Sn, Ge, Si, Pb　E. Ga, In, B, Al　F. B, Li, O, C
G. Bi, Cs, Tl, Ba　H. Sn, In, Te, Rb　I. K, Br, Ge, As
J. Mg, Al, Cl, P　K. K, V, Ti, Fe　L. Ba, Os, Hf, La
M. Ce^{3+}, W^{3+}, Tm^{3+}, Eu^{3+}　N. Ac, W, U, Os　O. P^{3-}, Ca^{2+}, Ar, Si^{4-}
P. O^{2-}, Na^+, C^{4-}, Ne　Q. Sc^{3+}, Cl^-, K^+, S^{2-}　R. Br^-, Ga^{5-}, Sr^{2+}, Y^{3+}
S. Si, Ge, O, Ne　T. Mg^{2+}, F^-, Be^{2+}, C^{4-}　U. K, Al, Na, N
V. N, Na^+, Li, Ne　W. Tl, Ga, Ba, Ge

7. (1) Rewrite each of the following lists in order of increasing value (smallest to largest) of ionization energy.

A. Rb, K, Na, Cs　B. N, As, Sb, P　C. Al, B, Tl, In
D. Be, Sr, Mg, Ca　E. Na, Cl, Al, Ar　F. Ca, Ge, Kr, As
G. Rb, Te, In, I　H. N, Ne, Li, B　I. F, Se, Ba, Ga
J. Sr, P, Sb, Ne　K. Cs, Cl, As, Sn　L. Al, In, Rb, F

(2) Rewrite each of the following lists in order of increasing value (smalles or most negative to largest) of electron affinity.

A. Br, Cl, F, I　B. N, P, Bi, Sb　C. Na, Rb, Li, K
D. K, Se, Ge, Br　E. I, Sb, In, Rb　F. F, P, In, Cs
G. Sb, Se, Cl, Tl

(3) Rewrite each of the following lists in order of increasing value of electronegativity.

A. N, F, O, C　B. K, Br, As, Ca　C. F, Cl, I, Br
D. Rb, Cs, K, Li　E. Rb, In, Ru, Se　F. Li, Na, F, B
G. Cs, F, Cl, As

8. Rewrite each of the following lists of atoms and ions in order of increasing value of the paramagnetism of each atom or ion. When two species have the same value, write them together in parentheses, such as (He, Ne).

A. Ce^{3+}, K^+, C, P　B. He, Cs^+, Sc, S　C. B, Si, P, S
D. K, Ca, Sc, Ti　E. V, Cr, Mn, Cu　F. Zn, Ca, As, Ti
G. Na, Na^+, S, S^-　H. Li, Be, B, C

9. (1) Referring to a periodic table and using the data given below, predict the values omitted from the tables which follow. Check your answers with data from a chemical handbook. How good are your predictions? (All temperatures are °C.)

Element	*Melting point*	*Boiling point*	*Critical temperature*	*Color*
F_2	−223	−188	A. _____	light yellow
Cl_2	−102	− 34.1	144	B. _____
Br_2	− 7.2	58.2	302	red-brown
I_2	114	185	553	deep violet
At_2	C. _____	D. _____	E. _____	F. _____

Substance	$\Delta\bar{H}_{vap}$, kJ/mol	*Boiling point*	*Melting point*
CH_4	8.9	−164	−182.48
SiH_4	12.5	−111.8	G. _____
GeH_4	H. _____	− 88.5	−165
SnH_4	18.8	I. _____	−150

Substance	*Boiling point*	*Melting point*
H_2O	J. _____	K. _____
H_2S	−60.8	−85.5
H_2Se	−41.5	−60.4
H_2Te	− 1.8	−48.9

	Substance					
	He	*Ne*	*Ar*	*Kr*	*Xe*	*Rn*
Melting point	−272.2	−248.6	−189.4	L. _____	−111.5	−71
Boiling point	−268.92	−246.02	−185.86	M. _____	−107.1	−65

(2) Using the data below, predict the melting point (°C), boiling point (°C), density of the element (g/cm³), and density of the oxide (g/cm³) for cesium.

	Element							
	K	*Ca*	*Sc*	*Rb*	*Sr*	*Y*	*Ba*	*La*
Melting point	64	839	1539	39	769	1523	725	920
Boiling point	774	1484	2832	688	1384	3337	1640	3454
Density	0.86	1.54	2.99	1.53	2.6	4.34	3.51	6.19
Oxide density	2.32	3.38	3.86	3.72	4.7	5.01	5.72	6.51

For cesium,

A. melting point _____ °C　B. boiling point _____ °C
C. density _____ g/cm³　D. oxide density _____ g/cm³

10. (1) Write the chemical formulas and give the correct names for all of the sulfides and fluorides of the elements in the third period of the periodic table (Na, Mg, Al, Si, P, S, Cl). Which of the fluorides are principally ionic and which ones are principally covalent? Which oxides would you expect to form an acidic solution in water and which ones would you expect to form a basic solution?

A. Na　B. Mg　C. Al　D. Si　E. P　F. S　G. Cl

(2) Write a balanced chemical equation for the combination reaction which occurs between each of the following pairs of elements and name each product.

A. $K + Se$ B. $Mg + N_2$ C. $Ca + C$ D. $H_2 + F_2$ E. $H_2 + N_2$
F. $B + O_2$ G. $Be + I_2$ H. $Al + S$ I. $Sr + P$ J. $In + Cl_2$

(3) The formula and name of each compound in the list below is followed by the symbol for an element, which is to replace the underlined element in the formula. Write the formula and give the name of the analogous compound.

Example: $H_2\underline{S}O_4$, sulfuric acid; Se: H_2SeO_4, selenic acid

A. $H_3\underline{P}O_3$, phosphorous acid, As
B. $Na\underline{Cl}O$, sodium hypochlorite, I
C. $H_3\underline{B}O_3$, boric acid, Al
D. $Na\underline{Al}O_2$, sodium aluminate, Ga
E. $Ag_2\underline{S}O_3$, silver sulfite, Te
F. $K_2\underline{Cr}O_4$, potassium chromate, Mo
G. $Ni\underline{S}O_4$, nickel(II)sulfate, Se
H. $K\underline{Mn}O_4$, potassium permanganate, Re

QUIZZES (20 minutes each)

Choose the best answer for each question.

Quiz A

1. The electrons lost when $Fe \rightarrow Fe^{2+}$ are (a) $4f$; (b) $3d$; (c) $4s$; (d) $3p$; (e) none of these.
2. A metalloid in the same periodic group as P is (a) N; (b) S; (c) Al; (d) As; (e) none of these.
3. An atom has the general ground-state electron *valence* configuration of ns^2np^5, where n is the principal quantum number. The element is (a) an alkali metal; (b) an alkaline earth metal; (c) an inert (noble) gas; (d) a halogen; (e) none of these.
4. If an element has some properties which are metallic and others which are nonmetallic, it is said to be (a) inert; (b) isoelectronic; (c) a metalloid; (d) an alloy; (e) none of these.
5. From left to right in a period of the periodic table, electronegativity (a) decreases; (b) increases; (c) remains the same; (d) shows irregular changes; (e) none of these.
6. In which of the following is there a consistent *decrease* in atomic radius as the atomic number increases? (a) halogens; (b) representative elements; (c) transition elements; (d) lanthanoids; (e) none of these.
7. Of the following, the element having the smallest ionization potential is (a) Mg; (b) Na; (c) K; (d) Ca; (e) Cs.
8. An atom having an atomic radius greater than that of S is (a) O; (b) Cl; (c) Ca; (d) Li; (e) none of these.

Quiz B

1. The number of $3d$ electrons in a Co^{3+} ion is (a) 2; (b) 4; (c) 6; (d) 7; (e) none of these.
2. A nonmetal in Group VA is (a) Sb; (b) As; (c) N; (d) Bi; (e) none of these.
3. Which of these ions is the smallest? (a) O^{2-}; (b) F^-; (c) Na^+; (d) Mg^{2+}; (e) Al^{3+}.
4. The transition elements are all metallic because of their (a) s electrons; (b) lack of s electrons; (c) atomic size; (d) d electrons; (e) none of these.
5. Of the following elements, which possesses the lowest (most negative) electron affinity? (a) As; (b) O; (c) S; (d) Se; (e) Te.
6. Atoms in which either s or p electrons are being added are called (a) lanthanides; (b) metalloids; (c) representative elements; (d) transition elements; (e) none of these.
7. Going across a representative period from left to right, the radii of atoms (a) decrease; (b) increase; (c) remain constant; (d) show irregular patterns; (e) none of these.
8. The more metallic an element, the lower is its (a) ionization potential; (b) number of electrons; (c) electron affinity; (d) penetration of electrons; (e) none of these.

Quiz C

1. The atom with an electronegativity greater than that of O is (a) H; (b) N; (c) S; (d) Rb; (e) none of these.

2. An atom having an atomic radius greater than that of Cs is (a) Ba; (b) Rb; (c) Sr; (d) Br; (e) none of these.
3. An element which is said to be an example of a metalloid is (a) S; (b) Zn; (c) Ge; (d) Re; (e) none of these.
4. The most common ion of an atom with the electronic configuration $1s^2\ 2s^2\ 2p^5$ would have the charge (a) +1; (b) −1; (c) +2; (d) 0; (e) none of these.
5. In the periodic table the vertical (up and down) columns are called (a) periods; (b) transitions; (c) families; (d) metalloids; (e) none of these.
6. A series of atoms or ions that have the same electronic configurations are said to be (a) degenerate; (b) isoelectronic; (c) amphoteric; (d) isotopic; (e) none of these.
7. A nonmetal will have a smaller ___ when compared to a metal of the same period. (a) atomic radius; (b) electronegativity; (c) ionization potential; (d) atomic weight; (e) none of these.
8. In the periodic table, in general, the electron affinity *increases* (a) top → bottom and right → left; (b) bottom → top and right → left; (c) top → bottom and left → right; (d) bottom → top and left → right; (e) none of these.

Quiz D

1. The species having a radius less than that of Ne is (a) Mg^{2+}; (b) F^-; (c) O^{2-}; (d) K^+; (e) none of these.
2. The representative elements are those which (a) are in the B groups; (b) fill *s* and *p* orbitals only; (c) fill *d* orbitals; (d) are metallic only; (e) none of these.
3. Which of the following elements would *not* be considered to be a metalloid? (a) Si; (b) As; (c) Ge; (d) Br; (e) Sb.
4. In general, the ionization potentials of elements *decrease* as one proceeds in the periodic table (a) bottom → top and right → left; (b) top → bottom and right → left; (c) bottom → top and left → right; (d) top → bottom and left → right; (e) none of these.
5. A metal will have a larger ___ when compared to a nonmetal of the same period. (a) ionization potential; (b) electron affinity; (c) number of valence electrons; (d) electronegativity; (e) none of these.
6. The electron lost when ionization occurs is the one with the (a) highest principal quantum number; (b) lowest principal quantum number; (c) outer electron with highest orbital quantum number; (d) highest orbital quantum number; (e) none of these.
7. An element which has a large radius and a small ionization potential is likely to be a(n) (a) nonmetal; (b) metalloid; (c) metal; (d) inert gas; (e) none of these.
8. Of the following, which element possesses the largest ionization potential? (a) Mg; (b) Ca; (c) Sr; (d) Ba; (e) Ra.

SAMPLE TEST (15 minutes)

			13	Al	27.4	14	Si	28
			$AlCl_3$		2.7	$SiCl_4$		2.3
			Al_2O_3		0.22	SiO_2		0.16
			118 pm		none	111 pm		none
30	Zn	65.2	*Z*	Ga	At wt	32	Ge	70
$SnCl_2$		7.1	Chloride		Density	$GeCl_4$		5.3
ZnO		0.092	Oxide		Specific heat	GeO_2		0.073
131 pm		none	Radius		Other oxide	122 pm		GeO
48	Cd	112	49	In	114	50	Sn	118
$CdCl_2$		8.7	$InCl_3$		7.3	$SnCl_4$		7.3
CdO		0.055	In_2O_3		0.057	SnO_2		0.054
148 pm		none	144 pm		In_2O	141 pm		SnO

Put yourself in the place of Mendeleev for a moment. Use the information in the partial periodic table above and anything which you have learned, and predict the following properties for gallium.

1. Atomic number
2. Atomic weight
3. Formula of chloride
4. Density
5. Specific heat
6. Radius
7. If there were another oxide of gallium, what would be its formula?

Chemical Bonding I: Basic Concepts

REVIEW OF OBJECTIVES

1. State the basic assumptions of Lewis theory.

Lewis theory assumes that an atom attempts to reach the electron configuration of the nearest noble gas. This is known as the *octet rule* since all noble gases except helium have eight valence electrons. An octet may be reached by losing or gaining electrons, or by sharing electrons. When electrons are lost, a cation is formed. When they are gained, an anion is formed. Anions and cations combine to form ionic compounds. When electrons are shared, a covalent bond is formed.

★ **2. Relate the Lewis symbol for an element to its position in the periodic table.**

The valence electron configurations of all elements in a representative family are identical except for the principal quantum number. The Lewis symbol is the element's symbol surrounded by dots—one dot for each valence electron. See Table 9-1 where X is used for the symbol of the element. Notice the following points about Lewis symbols.

1. There are four "sides" (top, bottom, left, and right) to a symbol. Each side can represent one valence orbital (s, p_x, p_y, p_z).
2. No given "side" represents any particular orbital. Thus, for oxygen the following are correct Lewis symbols.

   ·Ö·   :Ö·   ·Ö: :Ȯ: :Ȯ·   ·Ȯ:

3. Frequently pairs of electrons are represented by a line or a dash rather than two dots. Thus either Ba: or Ba| can represent barium.

TABLE 9-1
Lewis symbols for representative elements

Family	Electron configuration	Lewis structures General				Ions
		General	Examples			
IA	s^1	X·	Na·			X^+
IIA	s^2	X: *or* ·X·	Ba:	·Be·		X^{2+}
IIIA	s^2p^1	:X· *or* ·Ẋ·	·B:	·Ȧl·		X^{3+}
IVA	s^2p^2	:Ẋ· *or* ·X·	·C·	·Si·		$[\vert\overline{X}\vert]^{4-}$ or X^{4+}
VA	s^2p^3	:X·	·P·	·N·	·As:	$[\vert\overline{X}\vert]^{3-}$
VIA	s^2p^4	:X:	:Se·	·O·	·S·	$[\vert\overline{X}\vert]^{2-}$
VIIA	s^2p^5	:X:	:Cl·	$\vert\overline{F}\cdot$	:I·	$[\vert\overline{X}\vert]^{-}$
0	s^2p^6	:X:	:Ar:	$\vert\overline{Xe}\vert$		

★ **3. Draw Lewis structures for simple ionic compounds and distinguish these from covalent structures.**

When electrons are gained or lost, the cations and anions shown in the last column of Table 9-1 are formed. Notice that anion Lewis symbols are surrounded by square brackets to separate the electron dots from the ionic charge. Square brackets also are used around the Lewis structures of polyatomic ions for clarity.

★ **4. Propose a plausible skeleton structure for a molecule and draw the molecule's Lewis structure using the basic "rules" of Lewis theory.**

Too often students believe that they *must* start with the Lewis symbols for the elements in order to draw Lewis structures. The guidelines which follow avoid that difficulty.

1. Count the total number of valence electrons in the species, remembering to add electrons for anions and subtract them for cations. The number of valence electrons of each atom equals its family number.
2. Express the total number of valence electrons as the number of electron pairs by dividing the total by two.
3. Arrange the atoms in the correct molecular skeleton. In some instances this will be given to you. If it is not, the central atom often is written first. You may have to choose among several skeletons; use the octet rule and the formal charge on each atom.
4. Place the pairs around the atoms so that each atom, except H, has an octet if possible. Start by placing one bond between all adjacent atoms.
5. If an atom lacks an octet of electrons, consider double and triple bonds between that atom and an adjacent atom. But remember that the halogens (F, Cl, Br, and I) rarely form double bonds and H never does.
6. The central atom may have an expanded octet (see objective 9-9), but only if it is from the third period or higher.
7. As a first guess, try the following number of bonds around the atoms. One bond: H, F, Cl, Br, I. Two bonds: O, S, Se, Te, Be. Three bonds: N, P, As, B. Four bonds: C, Si, Ge.

EXAMPLE 9-1 Draw the Lewis structure of HClO.

(1) There are 1(H) + 7(Cl) + 6(O) = 14 valence electrons
(2) *or* 14 ÷ 2 = 7 pairs.
(3) Possible skeletons: H—Cl—O, H—O—Cl, O—H—Cl
(4) $\mathrm{H{-}\overline{\underline{Cl}}{-}\overline{\underline{O}}|}$ $\quad \mathrm{H{-}\overline{\underline{O}}{-}\overline{\underline{Cl}}|}$ $\quad \mathrm{|\overline{\underline{O}}{-}H{-}\overline{\underline{Cl}}|}$

The third structure shows that we cannot have H as a central atom. H can only have one pair of electrons, not two.

Based on guideline 7, $\mathrm{H{-}\overline{\underline{O}}{-}\overline{\underline{Cl}}|}$ is correct. We shall see later that the formal charge gives the same prediction.

EXAMPLE 9-2 Draw the Lewis structure of N_2O.

(1 & 2) 5(N) + 5(N) + 6(O) = 16 valence electrons = 8 pairs.
(3) Two possible skeletons: N—N—O and N—O—N.
(4) $\mathrm{|\overline{\underline{N}}{-}N{-}\overline{\underline{O}}|}$ and $\mathrm{|\overline{\underline{N}}{-}O{-}\overline{\underline{N}}|}$ are wrong, since the central atom has no octet.
(5) There are many possibilities.

N as central atom: $\mathrm{\overline{\underline{N}}{=}N{=}\overline{\underline{O}}|}$, $\mathrm{|N{\equiv}N{-}\overline{\underline{O}}|}$, $\mathrm{|\overline{\underline{N}}{-}N{\equiv}O|}$

O as central atom: $\mathrm{\overline{\underline{N}}{=}O{=}\overline{\underline{N}}}$, $\mathrm{|N{\equiv}O{-}\overline{\underline{N}}|}$

Based on guideline 7, none of these structures is correct. We need another criterion to decide between them (see Example 9-4).

★ **5. Compute the formal charge on each atom in a Lewis structure.**

★ **6. Use the formal charge to determine which of several Lewis structures is the "best."**

To determine the formal charge (f.c.) on an atom one uses equation [1] or equation [2].

f.c. = (group number) − (number of unshared electrons) − (number of shared electrons ÷ 2) [1]

Unshared electron pairs are called lone pairs (l.p.) and shared electron pairs are called bond pairs (b.p.) Thus,

f.c. = (group number) − (2 × number of lone pairs) − (number of bond pairs) [2]

The best structure is the one in which the formal charges are minimized, or the one in which the sum of the absolute values of the formal charges is the smallest. If there are formal charges remaining in the species, the positive formal charges should be on the least electronegative atoms, and the negative formal charges should be on the most electronegative atoms. Of course, there will always be some formal charge in an ion. Examples 9-3 and 9-4 illustrate the selection of the best Lewis structure using formal charge.

EXAMPLE 9-3 Which of the structures in Example 9-1 is the best? The calculations (according to equation [2]) are shown below the symbol of each atom.

Lewis structure	H	$\underline{\overline{\mathrm{Cl}}}$	$\underline{\overline{\mathrm{O}}}\vert$	H	$\underline{\overline{\mathrm{O}}}$	$\underline{\overline{\mathrm{Cl}}}\vert$
group number	1	7	6	1	6	7
−2 × lone pairs	−0	−4	−6	−0	−4	−6
−bond pairs	−1	−2	−1	−1	−2	−1
formal charge	0	+1	−1	0	0	0

(Structures: H — Cl — O| and H — O — Cl|)

Thus, the formal charge gives the same prediction as does guideline (7) of objective 9–4.

EXAMPLE 9-4 Which of the structures in Example 9-2 is the best?

Lewis structure	$\underline{\overline{\mathrm{N}}}$	= N =	$\underline{\overline{\mathrm{O}}}$	|N	≡ N —	$\underline{\overline{\mathrm{O}}}\vert$	$\vert\underline{\overline{\mathrm{N}}}$	— N ≡	O|
group number	5	5	6	5	5	6	5	5	6
−2 × lone pairs	−4	−0	−4	−2	−0	−6	−6	−0	−2
−bond pairs	−2	−4	−2	−3	−4	−1	−1	−4	−3
formal charge	−1	+1	0	0	+1	−1	−2	+1	+1

Lewis structure	$\underline{\overline{\mathrm{N}}}$	= O =	$\underline{\overline{\mathrm{N}}}$	|N	≡ O —	$\underline{\overline{\mathrm{N}}}\vert$
group number	5	6	5	5	6	5
−2 × lone pairs	−4	−0	−4	−2	−0	−6
−bond pairs	−2	−4	−2	−3	−4	−1
formal charge	+1	−2	+1	0	+2	−2

$\underline{\overline{\mathrm{N}}}$=N=$\underline{\overline{\mathrm{O}}}$ and |N≡N—$\underline{\overline{\mathrm{O}}}$| have the minimal formal charges. Of these two, |N≡N—$\underline{\overline{\mathrm{O}}}$| is the best, as it puts the negative formal charge on the most electronegative atom, oxygen.

★ **7. Draw reasonable resonance structures and recognize when they are necessary.**

Some compounds cannot be represented with a single Lewis structure. We write several equivalent structures called resonance structures. For example, ozone (O_3) has 18 valence electrons or 9 pairs. Two structures can be written: |$\underline{\overline{\mathrm{O}}}$—$\overline{\mathrm{O}}$=$\underline{\overline{\mathrm{O}}}$ and $\underline{\overline{\mathrm{O}}}$=$\overline{\mathrm{O}}$—$\underline{\overline{\mathrm{O}}}$|. These two resonance structures have the following features which are true of *all* resonance structures.

1. The total number of single, double, and triple bonds is the same in each resonance structure.
2. The molecular skeleton is the same in each structure.
3. The formal charge distribution is the same in each structure. Here, the central oxygen has a formal charge of +1, one terminal oxygen has a formal charge of 0 (the double-bonded one), and the other oxygen has a formal charge of −1.

All that is involved in going from one resonance structure to another is shifting a few pairs of electrons. Many students have the mistaken impression that the resonance hybrid (the molecule) "hops back and forth" between its various resonance forms. Instead, the difficulty is with Lewis theory itself;

a single structure is inadequate. In a similar fashion, one photograph does not comoletely describe a three-dimensional object such as a coffee cup; several photographs from different angles are needed. The coffee cup obviously does not hop back and forth between the various photographs. So also a resonance hybrid is a blending of the various resonance structures.

★ **8. Draw Lewis structures for odd-electron and electron-deficient species.**

When the total number of valence electrons is odd, there is no way to pair all of the electrons.

EXAMPLE 9-5 Draw the Lewis structure for ClO_2 where Cl is the central atom.

7 (Cl) + 2 X 6(O) = 19 valence electrons *or* 9½ pairs

Possible structures and formal charge calculations follow.

Lewis structure	$|\overline{\underline{O}}$	— $\dot{\overline{Cl}}$ —	$\overline{\underline{O}}|$	$|\dot{\underline{O}}$	— $\overline{\underline{Cl}}$ —	$\overline{\underline{O}}|$
group number	6	7	6	6	7	6
−2 X lone pairs	−6	−3	−6	−5	−4	−6
−bond pairs	−1	−2	−1	−1	−2	−1
−formal charge	−1	+2	−1	0	+1	−1

Thus, the resonance hybrid $|\dot{\underline{O}}—\overline{\underline{Cl}}—\overline{\underline{O}}| \leftrightarrow |\overline{\underline{O}}—\overline{\underline{Cl}}—\dot{\underline{O}}|$ is the best choice, based on formal charge. The unpaired electron is rarely considered to be a bonding electron.

Electron-deficient compounds occur when an atom other than hydrogen is surrounded by fewer than eight electrons. The atom is said to have an incomplete octet.

EXAMPLE 9-6 Draw the Lewis structure of BF_3.

3(B) + 3 X 7 (F) = 24 valence electrons *or* 12 pairs

```
|F̅—B—F̅|  or  |F̅—B=F̅ ↔ |F̅—B—F̅| ↔ F̅=B—F̅|
    |              |          ||         |
   |F|            |F|        |F|        |F|
```

The structure at left is electron deficient in that B is surrounded by only six electrons. Note that the formal charge on each atom in this structure is zero. There is no electron deficiency and the octet rule is obeyed in the resonance hybrid. But boron has a formal charge of −1 and the double-bonded fluorine has a formal charge of +1. The true structure is probably a resonance hybrid of all four structures.

★ **9. Know which elements can have expanded octets and be able to draw Lewis structures with expanded octets.**

For elements of the first and second periods, it is very difficult to place more than an octet around the central atom mainly because it costs too much energy (see Figure 7-6 for the relative energy spacing between the 2*p* and 3*s* orbitals), but also because the central atom is quite small (see Figure 8-2). This is not the case for elements of the third and higher periods, and these elements can have expanded octets in Lewis structures.

EXAMPLE 9-7 Draw the Lewis structure of ICl_3 where I is the central atom.

7 (I) + 3 X 7(Cl) = 28 valence electrons *or* 14 pairs

```
|C̅l—Ī—C̅l|
     |
   |Cl|
```

	I	each Cl
group number	7	7
−2 X lone pairs	−4	−6
−bond pairs	−3	−1
formal charge	0	0

★ **10. Predict the electron-pair geometry and the molecular shape of a molecule using VSEPR theory. Realize that multiple bonds act similarly to single bonds in determining molecular shape.**

Lewis theory says nothing about molecular shape. The valence-shell electron-pair repulsion (VSEPR) theory accounts for molecular shape. The basis of the theory is that pairs of electrons in the valence shell of an atom try to get as far apart as they can and still remain attached to the atom.

VSEPR theory uses the following terms. $AX_m E_n$: The formula of a molecule or an ion. A represents the *central atom.* X represents each of the *ligands*: atoms or groups of atoms bound to the central atom. E represents each of the *lone pairs*: unshared pairs of electrons on the central atom. m is the number of ligands or the number of *bonding pairs.* A double bond or a triple bond is counted as one bonding pair. n is the number of lone pairs. A lone electron, such as that of N in $\overline{O}{=}\dot{N}{-}\overline{O}|$, is counted as a lone pair. $m + n$ is the total number of electron pairs. This total determine the electron-pair geometry of the molecule or ion, as given in Table 9-2. The dashed lines in each sketch represent electron pairs pointing back, away from you, and the wedges represent electron pairs pointing forward, toward you. You may well have trouble seeing these electron-pair geometries. Most beginning students will find a set of models helpful.

TABLE 9-2
Electron-pair geometries

	Number of electron pairs				
	2	3	4	5	6
Electron-pair geometry	linear	equilateral triangle	tetrahedron	trigonal bipyramid	octahedron
Sketch	—A—	[sketch]	[sketch]	[sketch]	[sketch]
Bond angles	180°	120°	109.5°	120° (equatorial) 90° (axial)	90°

Although the total number of electron pairs determines the electron-pair geometry, we can only see the ligands. We only see the *effect* of the lone pairs. The possible VSEPR structures are given in Table 9-3. AX_4E is an irregular tetrahedron rather than a trigonal pyramid because of the differences in repulsions between types of electron pairs. They repel in the order given below.

lone pair > lone electron > triple bond > double bond > single bond [4]

TABLE 9-3
Summary of VSEPR possibilities

Formula	Example	Lone pairs	Bonding pairs	Molecular shape	Electron-pair geometry
AX_2	$BeCl_2$	0	2	linear	linear
AX_3	BF_3	0	3	triangular	triangular
AX_2E	$SnCl_2$	1	2	bent	triangular
AX_4	CF_4	0	4	tetrahedron	tetrahedron
AX_3E	NF_3	1	3	trigonal pyramid	tetrahedron
AX_2E_2	OF_2	2	2	bent	tetrahedron
AX_5	PCl_5	0	5	trigonal bipyramid	trigonal bipyramid
AX_4E	SF_4	1	4	irregular tetrahedron	trigonal bipyramid
AX_3E_2	ClF_3	2	3	T-shaped	trigonal bipyramid
AX_2E_3	XeF_2	3	2	linear	trigonal bipyramid
AX_6	SF_6	0	6	octahedron	octahedron
AX_5E	BrF_5	1	5	square pyramid	octahedron
AX_4E_2	XeF_4	2	4	square planar	octahedron

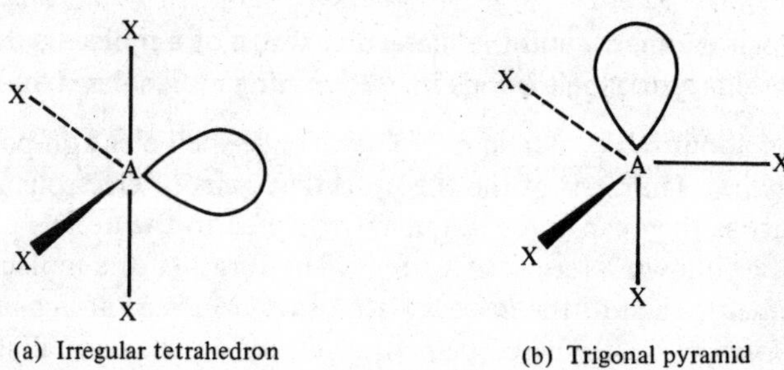

FIGURE 9-1 Possible shapes of AX_4E species.

Since there is more room around the equator of a trigonal bipyramid than at its axes, the lone pair occupies the equatorial position as shown in Figure 9-1(a). The shapes of all the species given in Table 9-3 are shown in Figure 9-2. You should make a model of each one so that you can see the shapes for yourself.

The application of VSEPR theory requires that you first draw the Lewis structure of the molecule or ion. Then, for each central atom, count the number of ligands and the number of lone pairs. From this and Table 9-3, which you should know well, name the molecular shape and draw a picture of the molecule. The correct shape of a molecule is predicted even if you have not drawn the best Lewis structure. Consider

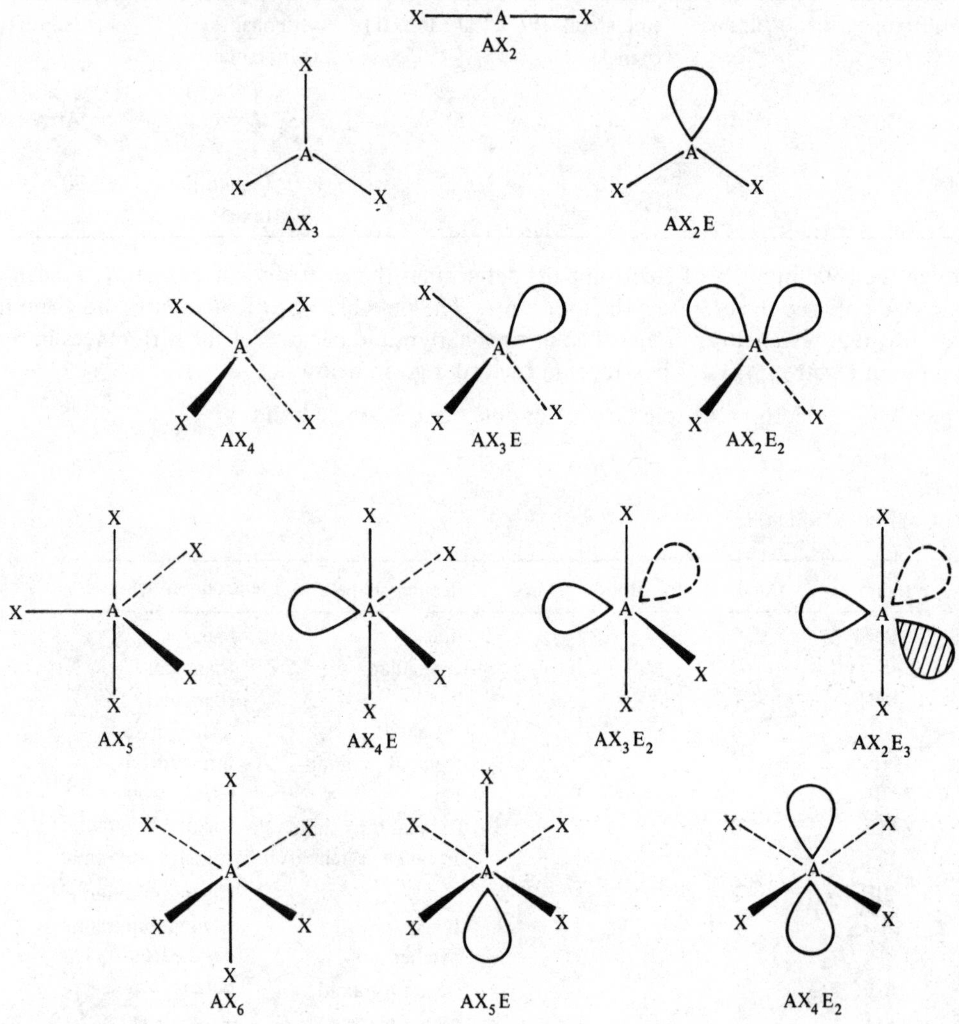

FIGURE 9-2 Shapes of the formulas of Table 9-3.

the three possibilities for NO_2 of Example 9-4. All three have two ligands and no lone pairs on nitrogen and predict a linear structure.

★ **11. Use bond distances to help in writing Lewis structures and bond energies to compute a reaction's enthalpy change; use a general knowledge of relative bond strengths to predict whether a reaction will be exothermic or endothermic.**

Bond order (single, double, triple) predicts relative bond length and strength.

bond strength: single < double < triple
bond length: single > double > triple [5]

We can use this information in helping us decide between various Lewis structures. In Example 9-6, we indicated the B—F bond to have some double-bond character. The bond length in BF_3 is somewhat shorter than an average B—F single bond.

Bond energies can be used to calculate an approximate $\Delta\bar{H}$ for a reaction involving products and reactants which are all gases. A fairly complete set of bond energies is given in Table 9-4.

TABLE 9-4
Bond energies (kJ/mol of bonds broken) and bond lengths (pm; in parentheses)

Bond	I	Br	Cl	S	P	Si	F	O	N	C	H
H	291 (170)	364 (151)	431 (136)	339 (133)	318 (142)	293 (148)	565 (101)	464 (97)	389 (100)	414 (110)	435 (74)
C	238 (213)	276 (193)	330 (177)	259 (181)	264 (187)	289 (187)	490 (135)	360 (143)	305 (148)	347 (154)	
N	176	243 (214)	201 (197)	205 (166)	209 (160)	326 (174)	264 (137)	201 (119)	163 (145)		
O	201 (183)	218 (165)	205 (147)	268 (140)	360 (161)	368 (161)	184 (142)	138 (148)			
F	268	251 (176)	255 (163)	285 (159)	490 (154)	540 (156)	155 (128)				
Si	213 (243)	289 (217)	360 (201)	226 (214)	213	176 (233)					
P	213	272 (213)	318 (204)	230 (186)	172 (223)						
S	180	213 (227)	276 (199)	264 (204)							
Cl	209 (232)	218 (218)	243 (199)								
Br	180	192 (228)									
I	151 (266)										

Bond	Energy (length)
P≡P	490
B—B	226 (177)
B—H	331 (116)

≡	C	N
N		946 (109)
C	837 (120)	891 (116)

=	C	O	N	S
S				427
N			418 (123)	485
O		498 (121)	607 (119)	331 (143)
C	611 (134)	707 (123)	615 (128)	531 (171)

EXAMPLE 9-8 Calculate the approximate enthalpy change for the uncatalyzed combustion of ammonia.

$$4\ NH_3(g) + 3\ O_2(g) \rightarrow 2\ N_2(g) + 6\ H_2O(g)$$

First we draw the Lewis structures of all species.

$$4\ \mathrm{H{-}\overline{N}{-}H}\ (\text{with H below N}) + 3\ \mathrm{\overline{\underline{O}}{=}\overline{\underline{O}}} \rightarrow 2\ \mathrm{N{\equiv}N} + 6\ \mathrm{H{-}\overline{\underline{O}}{-}H}$$

Then we determine how many bonds of each type are broken or formed and the energy required to break the bonds and produced by forming them.

Bonds broken	*Bonds formed*
12 N—H = 12 × 398 = 4668 kJ/mol	2 N≡N = 2 × 946 = 1892 kJ/mol
3 O=O = 3 × 498 = 1494 kJ/mol	12 O—H = 12 × 464 = 5568 kJ/mol
Total energy required = 6162 kJ/mol	Total energy produced = 7460 kJ/mol

Energy released has a negative sign and energy required has a positive sign.

$$\Delta \overline{H}^\circ = \text{Net energy} = +6162 \text{ kJ/mol} - 7460 \text{ kJ/mol} = -1298 \text{ kJ/mol}$$

This value of $\Delta \overline{H}^\circ$ is approximate. The actual value, computed from $\Delta \overline{H}^\circ_f$ s is − 1266.25 kJ/mol. Because $\Delta \overline{H}^\circ$s computed in this way normally have an error of up to 10%, they can be used only for approximations.

★ **12. Use electronegativities to determine if a bond is polar and use bond polarities and molecular shape to predict whether a molecule has a dipole moment.**

In a pure covalent bond, the bonding pair of electrons is equally shared by the two atoms. In a polar bond, the bonding pair is not shared equally but shifted toward the more electronegative atom. Thus, CO_2 and H_2O both possess polar bonds. Bond dipoles are drawn as an arrow with a cross on the base. The dipole points away from the more electropositive atom as shown in Figure 9-3. VSEPR theory predicts that CO_2 is linear and H_2O is bent. Since the two bond dipoles in CO_2 are equal and point in opposite directions, they cancel. CO_2 has no net dipole moment. But in H_2O the bond dipoles do not point in opposite directions and therefore they do not cancel. H_2O has a dipole moment.

FIGURE 9-3 Bond dipoles for CO_2 and H_2O

★ **13. Know how the ionic resonance energy affects bond energies and that it can be approximated using electronegativities.**

In many instances, it is possible to write both a covalent and an ionic Lewis structure for a molecule or an ion. The hydrogen halides (HF, HCl, HBr, and HI) are common examples. Some others are given in Figure 9-4. The larger the electronegativity difference is between the atoms which are broken apart, the greater will be the contribution of the ionic resonance structure. Resonance hybrids are more stable than the structure based on one resonance form would indicate. Hence, ionic resonance adds to the strength of the bond and makes it more difficult to break than a pure covalent bond.

$[NH_4]^+$ (H—N—H with H above and below) H—O—H Cl—N=O

NH_3 + H^+ [H—O|]$^-$ + H^+ [|Cl|]$^-$ + [|N≡O|]$^+$

FIGURE 9-4 Some ionic-covalent resonance forms.

★ **14. Know and be able to apply the conventions used in determining oxidation states.**

Because oxidation state is a formal rather than an experimental concept, it is possible to devise a rigid set of rules which work in nearly all circumstances. One set of rules, slightly different from that *of the text*, is given in Table 9-5.

TABLE 9-5
Determination of oxidation states

Method of applying the rules
1. Apply the rules from the top to the bottom of the list.
2. Search the list to find a rule which fits. Apply it.
3. Then start at the top again to find the next rule which fits.
Oxidation state rules
1. The O.S. (oxidation state) of all uncombined elements = 0.
2. The sum of the O.S. in a compound = 0.
3. The sum of the O.S. in an ion = ionic charge.
4. Alkali metals (IA) have O.S. = ±1.
5. Alkaline earths (IIA) have O.S. = +2.
6. H has O.S. = +1.
7. O has O.S. = −2.
8. F, Cl, Br, I (in order) have O.S. = −1.
9. S, Se, Te (in order) have O.S. = −2.
10. N, P (in order) have O.S. = −3.
11. Others have O.S. = group number or O.S. = group number − 8, with the more electronegative having the negative oxidation state.

In Example 9-9, the oxidation states are determined in the specified order and the number of the applicable rule is given in parentheses after the oxidation state.

EXAMPLE 9-9 Determine the oxidation state of each element in F_2, O_2^{2-}, Na_2S, CaC_2, HCl, HFO, ClF_3, CS_2, FeN, SiC, SO_3^{2-}.

F_2	F = 0 (1)		
O_2^{2-}	O = −1 (3)		
Na_2S	Na = +1 (4)	S = −2 (2)	
CaC_2	Ca = +2 (5)	C = −1 (2)	
HCl	H = +1 (6)	Cl = −1 (2)	
HFO	H = +1 (6)	O = −2 (7)	F = +1 (2)
ClF_3	F = −1 (8)	Cl = +3 (2)	
CS_2	S = −2 (9)	C = +4 (2)	
FeN	N = −3 (10)	Fe = +3 (2)	
SiC	C = −4 (11)	Si = +4 (2)	
SO_3^{2-}	O = −2 (7)	S = +4 (3)	

★ **15. Use oxidation states to name chemical substances.**

Oxidation states are helpful in balancing some chemical equations, (see objective 19–1a) and in naming compounds, particularly those compounds which contain oxyanions. Oxyanions are anions in which the central atom is surrounded by oxygen atoms. Their general formula is XO_n^{m-} where X is the central atom, n the number of oxygen atoms, and $m-$ the charge on the anion. For a given representative element X, the oxidation state of X varies between oxyanions in steps of 2, as is shown in Table 9-6 for chlorine oxyanions.

All other oxyanions of the same family with the same oxidation state have similar names. Thus $KBrO_3$ is sodium bromate and HFO is hypofluorous acid. Another generality for the representative elements is that the *-ate* anion and *-ic* acid endings are used when the oxidation state of the central atom equals the family number. The only exceptions to this occur in the halogens where the *-ate* and *-ic* endings correspond

TABLE 9-6
Salts and acids of chlorine oxyanions

Oxidation state	Salt	Example	Acid	Example
+1	hypo- -ite	$NaClO$ sodium hypochlorite	hypo- -ous	$HClO$ hypochlorous acid
+3	-ite	$NaClO_2$ sodium chlorite	-ous	HCl_2 chlorous acid
+5	-ate	$NaClO_3$ sodium chlorate	-ic	$HClO_3$ chloric acid
+7	per- -ate	$NaClO_4$ sodium perchlorate	per- -ic	$HClO_4$ perchloric acid

to a +5 oxidation state and in the noble gases where they correspond to +6. Thus, H_2SO_4 is sulfuric acid, since sulfur is in family VIA and has an oxidation state of +6 in this compound. Likewise, $Na_2B_4O_7$ has boron in an oxidation state of +3 and is sodium borate. Notice that the formulas of the compounds do not matter, only the oxidation state of the central atom.

DRILL PROBLEMS

2. Draw the Lewis symbol for each of the following atoms. You may use a periodic table for assistance.
A. He B. Li C. Ne D. In E. I F. Sb
G. Sn H. Sr I. S J. F K. C L. Ca
M. K N. Al O. P P. Se

3. Draw the Lewis structure of each of the following species.
A. LiH B. Na_2S C. $CaBr_2$ D. SrO E. Mg_3N_2 F. Sc_2S_3
G. NaF H. TiO_2 I. MgS J. $LaCl_3$ K. K_2Se L. Mg_2C
M. $CeCl_4$ N. AlN O. Cs_2Te P. Rb_3P

4. Draw the Lewis structure of each covalent species below.
A. CH_4 B. H_2CO C. CH_3OH D. N_2H_4 E. OF_2
F. NF_3 G. SiO_4^{4-} H. NOCl I. $GeCl_4$ J. C_2H_4
K. $SiCl_4$ L. Cl_2CO M. $HClO_2$ N. HOCN O. HFO
P. HNO_2 Q. H_2O_2 R. C_2H_2 S. AsF_3 T. BrO_4^-
U. PO_4^{3-} V. $SeBr_2$ W. PO_3^{3-} X. BF_4^- Y. OF^-
Z. ClO_3^- AA. HO_2^- AB. CN^- AC. HI AD. CCl_2H_2
AE. H_2CO_2 AF. C_2H_6 AG. O_2^{2-}

5. & 6. Draw at least two Lewis structures for each of the following species, evaluate the formal charge on each atom of each structure, and predict which structure is best.
A. HOCN B. HCN C. $HClO_3$ D. CO E. ONCl
F. CNS^- G. HCNS H. BCl_3 I. HCN J. $BeCl_2$
K. $OSeF_2$ L. CN_2^{2-} M. HNO_2 N. $POCl_3$ O. ClCN
P. HN_3 Q. H_2CN_2 R. NO_2Cl

7. Draw at least two resonance structures for each of the following resonance hybrids.
A. HCO_2^- B. NO_2^- C. N_3^- D. SO_2 E. CO_3^{2-}
F. BO_3^{3-} G. NO_3^- H. PO_3^- I. C_2O_3 J. SO_3
K. $C_2O_4^{2-}$ L. C_4H_4

8. Draw the most likely Lewis structure for each of the following species.
A. NO B. NO_2 C. $SnBr_2$ D. ClO_2 E. PbI_2
F. $BeCl_2$ G. PO_3 H. BeH_2 I. NCN^- J. BN
K. BI_3 L. CH_3 M. SO_2^+ N. BCl_3 O. O_2^-

9. Draw the most likely Lewis structure for each of the following species.
A. BrF_3 B. $SbCl_5^{2-}$ C. BrO_3^- D. I_3^- E. PF_3Cl_2
F. $PbCl_2$ G. H_2SO_3 H. $SbCl_5$ I. ICl_4^- J. $SnCl_6^{2-}$

K. IF_5 L. SO_3^{2-} M. XeF_4 N. SeF_6 O. ArF_2
P. SCl_4 Q. ClF_3 R. PO_4^{3-} S. IS_2^- T. XeF_2
U. XeO_3

10. Give the electron-pair geometry and the molecular shape and a perspective sketch (using solid, dashed, and wedged lines) of each of the following species.
A. BF_3 B. $GeCl_4$ C. HO_2^- D. BrF_3 E. $SbCl_5$
F. $PbBr_2$ G. H_2CO H. $BeCl_2$ I. KrF_4 J. ArF_2
K. SCl_4 L. NO_2^- M. NF_3 N. ClF_3 O. IF_5
P. PF_5 Q. ClO_4^- R. AsF_3 S. XeF_4 T. BCl_3
U. H_2S V. $POCl_3$ W. SF_4 X. CO_3^{2-} Y. NO_3^-
Z. N_2O AA. BF_4^-

11. Using the bond energies given in Table 9-4 predict the value of $\Delta \bar{H}°$ in each of the following reactions.
A. $CS_2(g) + 3\,O_2(g) \rightarrow CO_2(g) + 2\,SO_2(g)$
B. $CH_4(g) + 2\,O_2(g) \rightarrow CO_2(g) + 2\,H_2O(g)$
C. $H_2CO(g) + O_2(g) \rightarrow CO_2(g) + H_2O(g)$
D. $PCl_3(g) + F_2(g) \rightarrow PF_2Cl_3(g)$
E. $I_2(g) + 3\,Cl_2(g) \rightarrow 2\,ICl_3(g)$
F. $N_2(g) + 3\,H_2(g) \rightarrow 2\,NH_3(g)$
G. $2\,N_2H_2(g) + O_2(g) \rightarrow 2\,N_2(g) + 2\,H_2O(g)$
H. $4\,HCN(g) + 5\,O_2(g) \rightarrow 2\,H_2O(g) + 2\,N_2(g) + 4\,CO_2(g)$
I. $CO_2(g) + 2\,Cl_2(g) \rightarrow Cl_2CO(g) + Cl_2O(g)$
J. $SiH_4(g) + 4\,F_2(g) \rightarrow SiF_4(g) + 4\,HF(g)$
K. $CO_2(g) + 2\,H_2(g) \rightarrow CH_4O_2(g)$
L. $C_2H_6O(g) + 3\,O_2(g) \rightarrow 2\,CO_2(g) + 3\,H_2O(g)$
M. $PCl_5(g) + 4\,H_2O(g) \rightarrow H_3PO_4(g) + 5\,HCl(g)$ (Assume P = O is 710 kJ/mol)
N. $PCl_5(g) + H_2O(g) \rightarrow POCl_3(g) + 2\,HCl(g)$
O. $HCNS(g) + H_2O(g) \rightarrow HCNO(g) + H_2S(g)$
P. $C_3H_8(g) + 5\,O_2(g) \rightarrow 3\,CO_2(g) + 4\,H_2O(g)$

12. Which of the *molecules* in the question for objective 9–10 have a net dipole moment and which way does each one point?

14. & 15. For the compounds below, supply the correct name or formula and give the oxidation state of each element in the compound.
A. $NaClO_4$ B. selenic acid C. $(NH_4)_2S$
D. $CuIO_3$ E. H_2CO_3 F. phosphoric acid
G. sodium borate H. $NaNO_3$ I. $LiClO$
J. hyposulfurous acid K. $AlPO_4$ L. boric acid
M. $HClO_4$ N. nitrous acid O. magnesium chlorite
P. $ScAlO_3$ Q. Mg_2GeO_4 R. NH_4NO_3
S. HFO T. hyponitrous acid

QUIZZES (20 minutes each)

Choose the best answer to each question.

Quiz A

1. The oxidation state of N in HNO_2 is (a) +1; (b) +3; (c) +5; (d) −1; (e) none of these.
2. Potassium perbromate has a formula of (a) KBr; (b) K_2BrO_4; (c) $KBrO_4$; (d) $KBrO_2$; (e) none of these.
3. Which of the following should be paramagnetic? (a) HCl; (b) CO_2; (c) PCl_3; (d) ClO_2; (e) none of these.
4. In which compound do two ions composed of nonmetal atoms combine to from an ionic compound? (a) NH_4NO_3; (b) $Al_2(SO_4)_3$; (c) Na_2SO_3; (d) $AlCl_3$; (e) none of these.

5. Which of the following molecules does *not* obey the octet rule? (a) HCN; (b) PF_3; (c) CS_2; (d) NO; (e) none of these.
6. Which molecule has no polar bonds? (a) H_2CO; (b) CCl_4; (c) OF_2; (d) N_2O; (e) none of these.
7. Which of the following Lewis structures is *not* correct? (a) $\overline{O}=C=\overline{O}$; (b) $H_2B\text{—}H$ (B bonded to three H); (c) $|C=\overline{O}$; (d) $H\text{—}\overline{\underline{O}}\text{—}\overline{\underline{Cl}}|$; (e) none of these.
8. Of the following molecules, which contains the shortest bond distance? (a) Cl_2; (b) N_2; (c) O_2; (d) NH_3; (e) CO_2.
9. Which of the following compounds would be expected to have tetrahedral geometry? (a) AsF_3; (b) SF_4; (c) $SiCl_4$; (d) XeF_4; (e) none of these.
10. According to VSEPR theory the shape of ICl_4^- ion is (a) pyramidal. (b) linear; (c) tetrahedral; (d) square planar; (e) none of these.
11. Given the bond enthalpies I—Cl (209), H—H (435), H—I (297), H—Cl (431) in kJ/mol compute $\Delta \bar{H}^\circ$ in kJ/mol for $ICl_3(g) + 2\,H_2(g) \rightarrow HI(g) + 3\,HCl(g)$. (a) −93; (b) +264; (c) −523; (d) −84; (e) none of these within 2%.

Quiz B

1. In which compound does Mn have an oxidation state of +4? (a) $MnCl_2$; (b) MnO_2; (c) $MnSO_4$; (d) $KMnO_4$; (e) none of these.
2. Sodium chlorate has a formula of (a) $NaClO_4$; (b) $NaClO_3$; (c) $NaClO_2$; (d) NaClO; (e) none of these.
3. Which species below should be paramagnetic? (a) NO^-; (b) NO; (c) N_2O; (d) NO_2^-; (e) none of these.
4. Which of the following exhibits ionic bonding? (a) BF_3; (b) AsH_3; (c) SO_3; (d) BaO; (e) none of these.
5. When a molecule can be represented by more than one electronic structure , it is best described in terms of (a) VSEPR theory; (b) hybridization; (c) resonance; (d) multiple covalent bond; (e) none of these.
6. Which molecule has polar bonds but is itself not polar? (a) CH_3Cl; (b) H_2O; (c) SCl_2; (d) Cl_2; (e) none of these.
7. The incorrect Lewis structure below is (a) $|C\equiv O|$; (b) $\overline{\underline{S}}=\overline{\underline{O}}$; (c) $H\text{—}\overline{\underline{O}}\text{—}\overline{\underline{O}}\text{—}H$; (d) $|\overline{\underline{O}}\text{—}\overline{N}=\overline{\underline{O}}$; (e) none of these.
8. Which of the following rarely forms multiple bonds? (a) S; (b) C; (c) Cl; (d) O; (e) none of these.
9. Which of the following species would be expected to be trigonal planar? (a) $H_2C=O$; (b) H_3O^+; (c) NH_3; (d) $:CH_3$; (e) none of these.
10. The electron-pair geometry of H_2O is (a) tetrahedral; (b) trigonal planar; (c) bent; (d) linear; (e) none of these.
11. Given the bond enthalpies C=O (707), O=O (498), H—O (464), C—H (414) in kJ/mol, compute $\Delta \bar{H}^\circ$ in kJ/mol for $CH_4(g) + 2\,O_2(g) \rightarrow CO_2(g) + 2\,H_2O(g)$. (a) +618; (b) −519; (c) −618; (d) +259; (e) none of these within 2%.

Quiz C

1. In which compound does I have an oxidation state of +7? (a) HIO; (b) $NaIO_2$; (c) $Mg(IO_3)_2$; (d) $Al(IO_4)_3$; (e) none of these.
2. Which compound's name ends with "ite"? (a) $NaHCO_3$; (b) HNO_2; (c) $NaNO_3$; (d) $AlPO_3$; (e) none of these.
3. Which of the following is *not* paramagnetic? (a) NO; (b) CO; (c) NO_2; (d) BC; (e) none of these.
4. Which of the following exhibits covalent bonding? (a) NaF; (b) ICl; (c) K_2O; (d) SrI_2; (e) none of these.
5. Which of the following molecules is adequately represented by a single Lewis structure? (a) O_3; (b) NOCl; (c) SO_2; (d) N_2O; (e) none of these.

6. Which of the following does *not* have a molecular dipole moment? (a) HCl; (b) CO; (c) NCl_3; (d). BCl_3; (e) none of these.
7. As indicated by the Lewis structures which of the following species would probably not exist as a stable molecule? (a) CH_3O; (b) CH_2O; (c) CH_2O_2; (d) C_2H_2; (e) none of these.
8. Which atom below is often present in compounds which are electron deficient? (a) F; (b) O; (c) H; (d) B; (e) none of these.
9. The electron-pair geometry of NO_2^+ is (a) triangular; (b) bent; (c) tetrahedral; (d) octahedral; (e) none of these.
10. The molecular shape of PF_5 is (a) octahedron; (b) trigonal bipyramid; (c) irregular tetrahedron; (d) square pyramid; (e) none of these.
11. Given the bond enthalpies C—H (414), H—Cl (431), C—Cl (331), Cl—Cl (243) in kJ/mol, compute $\Delta\bar{H}°$ in kJ/mol for $CH_4(g) + 4\ Cl_2(g) \rightarrow CCl_4(g) + 4\ HCl(g)$. (a) +904; (b) +418; (c) −252; (d) −105; (e) none of these within 2%.

Quiz D

1. The oxidation state of Mn in $MgMnO_4$ is (a) +2; (b) +7; (c) +6; (d) +4; (e) none of these.
2. Which compound's name ends in "-ate"? (a) HIO_4; (b) Na_4SiO_3; (c) $KClO_2$; (d) HFO; (e) none of these.
3. Which of the following molecules is not paramagnetic? (a) NCl; (b) NO_2; (c) BrCl; (d) O_2; (e) none of these.
4. The greater the electronegativity difference between the two atoms in a bond, the greater the ___ of the bond, and the ___ it is. (a) covalent character; more stable; (b) ionic character; more stable; (c) ionic character; less stable; (d) covalent character; less stable; (e) none of these.
5. The most likely arrangement of atoms in S_2Cl_2 is (a) S—S—Cl—Cl; (b) S—Cl—S—Cl; (c) S—Cl—Cl—S; (d) Cl—S—S—Cl; (e) none of these.
6. Of the following, which has the largest dipole moment? (a) CH_4; (b) CH_3Cl; (c) BCl_3; (d) CO_2; (e) Cl_2.
7. As indicated by the Lewis structures which of the following species could probably not exist as a stable molecule? (a) NH_3; (b) N_2H_2; (c) N_2H_4; (d) N_2H_6; (e) none of these.
8. Which of the following contains the bond of largest energy? (a) H_2; (b) Cl_2; (c) CO_2; (d) N_2; (e) H_2O.
9. According to VSEPR theory the molecular shape of the I_3^- ion is (a) trigonal planar; (b) linear; (c) trigonal bipyramid; (d) bent; (e) none of these.
10. Which of the following electron pairs exhibits the largest amount of repulsion? (a) lone pair–lone pair; (b) bond pair–bond pair; (c) bond pair–lone pair; (d) lone pair–unpaired.
11. Given the bond enthalpies H—O (464), Cl—Cl (243), Cl—O (205), H—Cl (431) in kJ/mol compute $\Delta\bar{H}°$ in kJ/mol for $H_2O(g) + Cl_2(g) \rightarrow HOCl(g) + HCl(g)$. (a) −1100; (b) +393; (c) −393; (d) +71; (e) none of these within 2%.

SAMPLE TEST (30 minutes)

1. Draw the best Lewis structure of each of the following species and indicate the formal charge of each atom of the structure. If the species is a resonance hybrid, be sure to draw all of the resonance forms.

   a. PO_3^- b. NO_2^+ c. CH_3Cl d. IF_3

2. For each of the following Lewis structures give the names of the electron-pair geometry and the molecular shape. Sketch the molecule and indicate on the sketch the direction of the molecule's dipole moment, if any. For sketches use the "wedge and dash" convention.

   a. 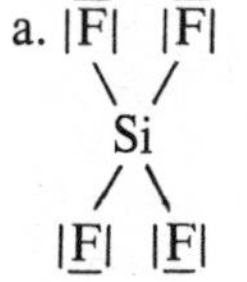

   b. 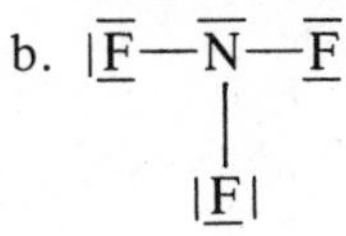

   c. 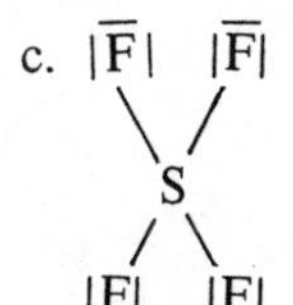

   d. 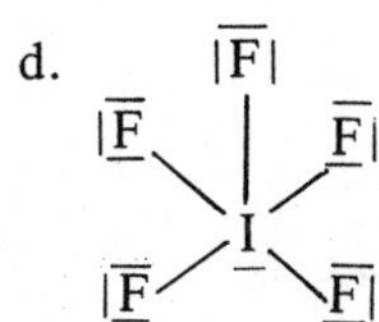

3. Give the name or formula, as appropriate, of each compound and the oxidation state of each atom.

   a. copper(II) sulfate
   b. $Na_2S_2O_3$
   c. magnesium chlorite
   d. Na_3BO_4
   e. ammonium oxide
   f. NI_3
   g. Ca_2XeO_4
   h. barium peroxide

Chemical Bonding II: Additional Aspects

REVIEW OF OBJECTIVES

1. Understand the basis of valence bond theory.

Valence bond theory states that a bond forms when two atomic orbitals overlap. Each such bond may contain two electrons with their spins paired. A large amount of overlap means a strong bond is created. Atomic orbitals with directional character (those which "point" in a certain direction) overlap better than those with no directional character. For example, *p* orbitals overlap better than do *s* orbitals. We say they overlap more efficiently or there is a greater amount (or degree) of overlap.

1a. Explain why pure atomic orbitals are not used to describe bonding in molecules and why hybrid orbitals are used instead.

An attempt to explain the bonding in the CH_4 molecule provides the clearest example of the need for hybridization. The promoted configuration of C, given in expression [1], permits the formation of four C—H bonds.

[He] [1] (2*s*) [1|1|1] (2*p*) [1]

Each bond results from the overlap of a half-filled orbital on carbon (2*s* or 2*p*) with a half-filled orbital on hydrogen (1*s*). These bonds disagree in two ways with the experimental results for CH_4. Although the four bonds in CH_4 are the same, *these* bonds differ from each other (three 1*s*–2*p* bonds and one 1*s*–2*s* bond). Also the predicted bond angles are 90°, compared to actual bond angles of 109.5°. We can combine the four half-filled pure atomic orbitals on the carbon in [1] to produce four equivalent hybrid orbitals.

C: [He] [1|1|1|1] (sp^3) [2]

Note that hybridization is used after we know the bond angles, which VSEPR theory can predict.

★ **2. Write hybridization schemes for the formation of sp, sp^2, sp^3, sp^3d, and sp^3d^2 hybrid orbitals.**

3. Predict the geometrical shapes of molecules in terms of the pure and hybrid orbitals involved in bonding.

The Lewis structures and central atom electron configurations of the CH_4, BCl_3, and BeF_2 molecules are given in Figure 10-1. Hybridization is especially useful in describing the bonding when the central atom is C, N, or O. The Lewis structures and orbital diagrams of NH_3 and H_2O are drawn in Figure 10-2.

Note that the hybridization can be determined from the Lewis structure. There are as many hybrid orbitals as there are ligands and lone pairs on the central atom. The lone-pair hybrid orbitals are full. For atoms with zero formal charge, the ligand hybrid bonding orbitals have only one electron. Coordinate covalent bonds require either a full or an empty hybrid orbital. Notice also that the formula of the hybrid orbital is its recipe. For example, an sp^3 orbital is one of four hybrid orbitals formed by averaging one *s* orbital with three *p* orbitals.

The properties of hybrid orbitals thus depend on the properties of the atomic orbitals which were combined to produce them. Consider direction. A *p* orbital points along a line. Thus if an *s* orbital combines with a *p* orbital, the two *sp* hybrids formed will point along a line. In similar fashion, sp^2 hybrid

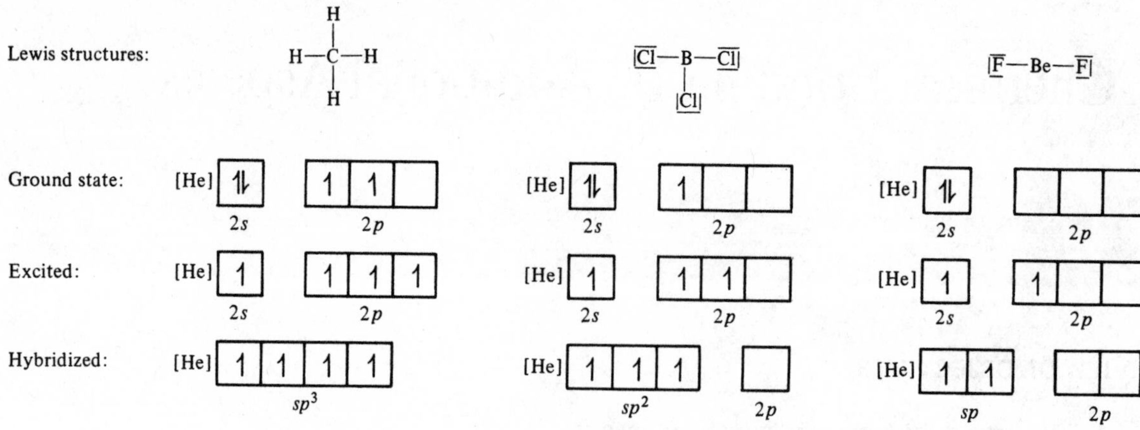

FIGURE 10-1 Bonding in CH_4, BCl_3, and BeF_2

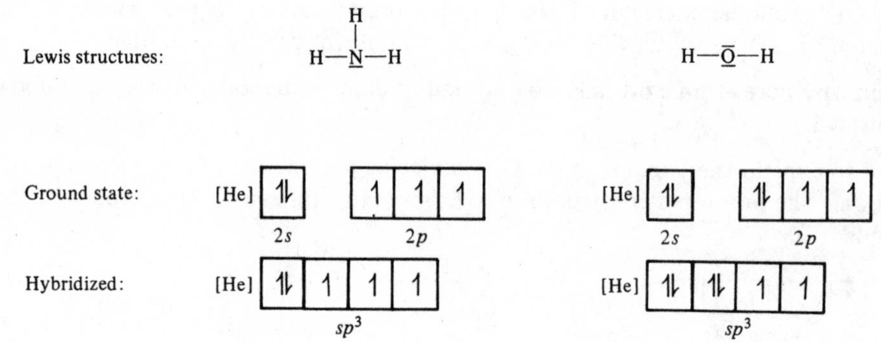

FIGURE 10-2 Bonding in NH_3 and H_2O.

orbitals are confined to a plane (they must be flat), since any two p orbitals lie in a plane. And four sp^3 orbitals fill all space. The results are summarized in Table 10-1.

TABLE 10-1
Geometry of hybrid orbitals

Number of ligands and lone pairs	Hybridization	Geometry of hybrid	Bond angles, degrees
2	sp	linear	180
3	sp^2	triangular	120
4	sp^3	tetrahedral	109.5
5	sp^3d	trigonal bipyramidal	120 (equatorial) 90 (axial)
6	sp^3d^2	octahedral	90

Sometimes the number of ligands and bond pairs totals five or six, meaning that five or six hydrid orbitals are necessary. Since there are only four s and p orbitals in a shell, d orbitals are included in the hybridization. The Lewis structures are orbital diagrams of SF_4, ClF_5 and XeF_4 molecules are drawn in Figure 10-3.

Notice that the technique is similar to that used in Figures 10-1 and 10-2, except that we have included d orbitals in the hybridization rather than just s and p orbitals. The geometries of all the hybrid orbitals which we have considered are given in Table 10-1.

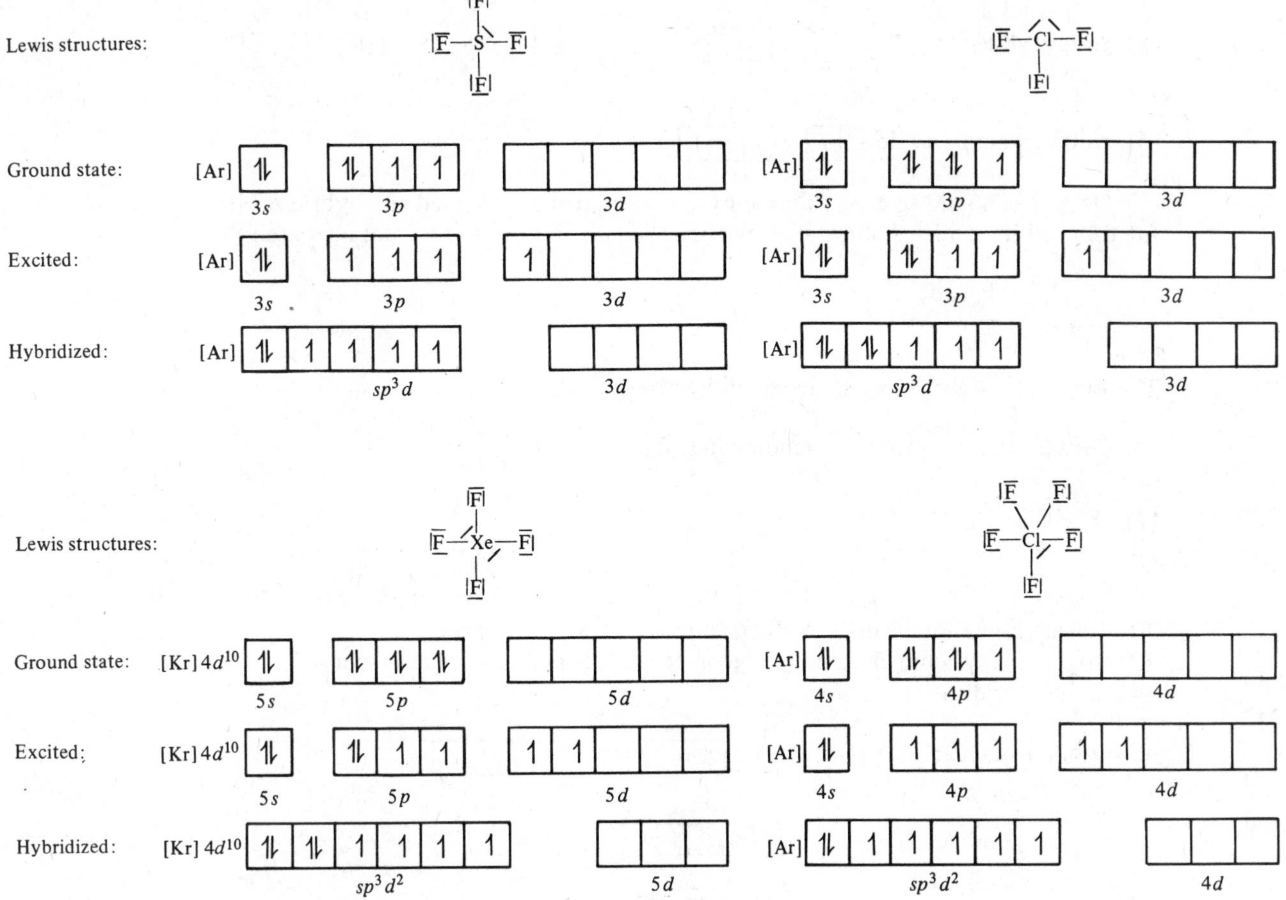

FIGURE 10-3 Bonding in SF_4, ClF_3, ClF_5, and XeF_4.

★ **4. Use the relationship between VSEPR theory and valence bond theory in predicting molecular shapes.**

Table 10-1 is very similar to Table 9-2, the electron-pair geometries of VSEPR theory. The bonding in single-bonded species is predicted in seven steps.

1. Draw the best Lewis structure for the species.
2. For each central atom, count the total number of ligands and lone pairs.
3. Using VSEPR theory, determine the electron-pair geometry and the molecular shape.
4. Using the information given in Table 10-1, determine the hybridization on the central atom.
5. Write the ground-state orbital diagram of the central atom (subtracting or adding electrons to account for the charge, if any, on the species) and the orbital diagram of the hybridization scheme found in step 4.
6. Write the ground-state orbital diagram of each ligand. The diagram may have to be modified if a coordinate covalent bond is formed. The ligands need not be hybridized unless they are also central atoms.
7. Overlap one half-filled ligand orbital with each half-filled hybrid orbital and describe the result. If the species has coordinate covalent bonds, you will overlap a full hybrid orbital with an empty ligand orbital (or an empty hybrid orbital with a full ligand orbital).

EXAMPLE 10-1 Describe the bonding in OF_2.

This is done by the steps outlined previously.

(1) |F̅—O̅—F̅| (2) 2 ligands + 2 lone pairs = 4 electron pairs. (3) tetrahedral electron-pair geometry; bent molecular shape. (4) sp^3 hybridization on O.

(5) ground state O: [He] 2s [⇅] 2p [⇅|1|1] hybridized O: [He] sp^3 [⇅|⇅|1|1]

(6) ground state F: [He] 2s [⇅] 2p [⇅|⇅|1]

(7) Oxygen is bound to each fluorine by the overlap of a half-filled sp^3 hybrid orbital on O with a half-filled $2p$ orbital on F. Abbreviated (writing the two fluorines as F_a and F_b to tell them apart):

$O(sp^3)^1—F_a(2p)^1$
$O(sp^3)^1—F_b(2p)^1$

The two lone pairs of oxygen are in sp^3 hybird orbitals.

EXAMPLE 10-2 Describe the bonding in ClF_3.

(1) |F̲—Cl—F̲|
         |
        |F̲|

(2) 3 ligands + 2 lone pairs = 5 electron pairs.
(3) trigonal bipyramid electron-pair geometry; T-shaped molecular geometry.
(4) sp^3d hybridization.

(5) ground stateCl: [Ne] 3s [⇅] 3p [⇅|⇅|1] [| | | |]

sp^3d-hybridized Cl: [Ne] sp^3d [⇅|⇅|1|1|1] 3d [| | |]

(6) ground state F: [He] 2s [⇅] 2p [⇅|⇅|1]

(7) Chlorine is bound to each fluorine by the overlap of a half-filled sp^3d hybrid orbital on Cl with a half-filled $2p$ orbital on F. Abbreviated:

$Cl(sp^3d)^1—F_a(2p)^1$
$Cl(sp^3d)^1—F_b(2p)^1$
$Cl(sp^3d)^1—F_c(2p)^1$

The two lone pairs of chlorine are in sp^3d hybrid orbitals.

★ **5. Describe multiple bonds between second period elements in terms of the overlap of *sp* and sp^2 (and pure 2*p*) orbitals to form σ bonds, and the sidewise overlap of *p* orbitals to form π bonds.**

A multiple bond consists of a σ bond and one or two π bonds. A π bond is formed by the side-to-side overlap of two *p* orbitals. σ bonds are formed by the following overlaps: *s–s, s–p, p–p* (end-to-end), hybrid–*p*, and hybrid–hybrid. *s* orbitals and hybrid orbitals do not overlap to form π bonds. A π bond is weaker than a σ bond because its overlap is not as efficient. σ bonds lie along the internuclear axis (the line joining the two atoms), whereas the two lobes of the π bond lie on either side of the axis. To account for π bonding, we add one more rule to the list first given in objective 10–4.

8. Overlap one half-filled *p* orbital on each ligand with one half-filled *p* orbital on the central atom to form each π bond.

EXAMPLE 10-3 Describe the bonding in ClNO.

(1) |C̅l̲—N̅=O̲ (2) 2 ligands + 1 lone pair = 3 electron pairs. (3) triangular electron-pair geometry; bent molecular geometry. (4) sp^2 hybridization.

		$2s$	$2p$			sp^2	$2p$
(5) ground state N:	[He]	[↑↓]	[↑ | ↑ | ↑]	sp^2-hybridized N:	[He]	[↑↓ | ↑ | ↑]	[↑]

		$3s$	$3p$			$2s$	$2p$
(6) ground state Cl:	[Ne]	[↑↓]	[↑↓ | ↑↓ | ↑]	ground state O:	[He]	[↑↓]	[↑↓ | ↑ | ↑]

(7) Sigma bonding:

$N(sp^2)^2$: lone pair
$N(sp^2)^1—Cl(3p)^1$
$N(sp^2)^1—O(2p_y)^1$

(8) Pi bonding:

$N(2p_z)^1—O(2p_z)^1$

The y and z subscripts on the $2p$ orbitals remind us not to use the same $2p$ orbital twice.

6. Propose plausible bonding schemes from experimental information about molecules (that is, bond lengths, bond angles, and so on).

To this point we have used theoretical models (Lewis theory and VSEPR) to predict the structures of molecules. However, when experimental information disagrees with theory, we discard the theoretical model

H_2S is an example of the conflict between theory and experiment. VSEPR theory predicts a tetrahedral electron-pair geometry.

$$H—\overline{\underline{S}}—H \qquad [3]$$

This leads to sp^3 hybridization and a predicted H—S—H bond angle of 109.5°. The actual bond angle is 92°. It is very unlikely that the two lone pairs of S exert such a strong influence that they "close down" the bond angle from 109.5° to 92°. It is much more likely that hybridization does not occur and that the bonding is between half-filled $3p$ orbitals on S and half-filled $1s$ orbitals on H.

7. Explain the fundamental basis of molecular orbital theory.

Molecular orbital theory puts the two atom centers in place and "pours" the electrons in around them. The electrons find the orbitals of lowest energy. These orbitals now extend over at least two atoms; they are not restricted to one atom as atomic orbitals were. Electrons in a bonding orbital spend most of their time between two nuclei and act rather like a "glue" holding the nuclei together. Electrons in an antibonding orbital spend most of their time outside the region between the two nuclei. The nuclei are not screened from each other by the negative charge of the electrons and hence they repel each other.

8. Know that two atomic orbitals combine to produce a bonding and an antibonding molecular orbital and sketch these molecular orbitals.

The bonding and antibonding molecular orbitals produced by the combination of two s atomic orbitals and of two p atomic orbitals are drawn in Figure 10-4.

The asterisk (*) superscript is used for an antibonding orbital and the b superscript (or sometimes no superscript) is used for a bonding orbital. The subscript (s or p) indicates the two atomic orbitals which combine to produce the molecular orbital.

★ **9. Predict electron configurations for molecules using molecular orbital diagrams.**

It is important to remember the energy order of the molecular orbitals formed between two elements in the second period. This order is shown in the molecular energy level diagram of Figure 10-5 where it is applied to CN^-, BeC, and NO. Notice that the molecular orbitals are filled with valence electrons from lowest energy to highest energy. Electrons are not paired until all orbitals of the same energy are half-filled.

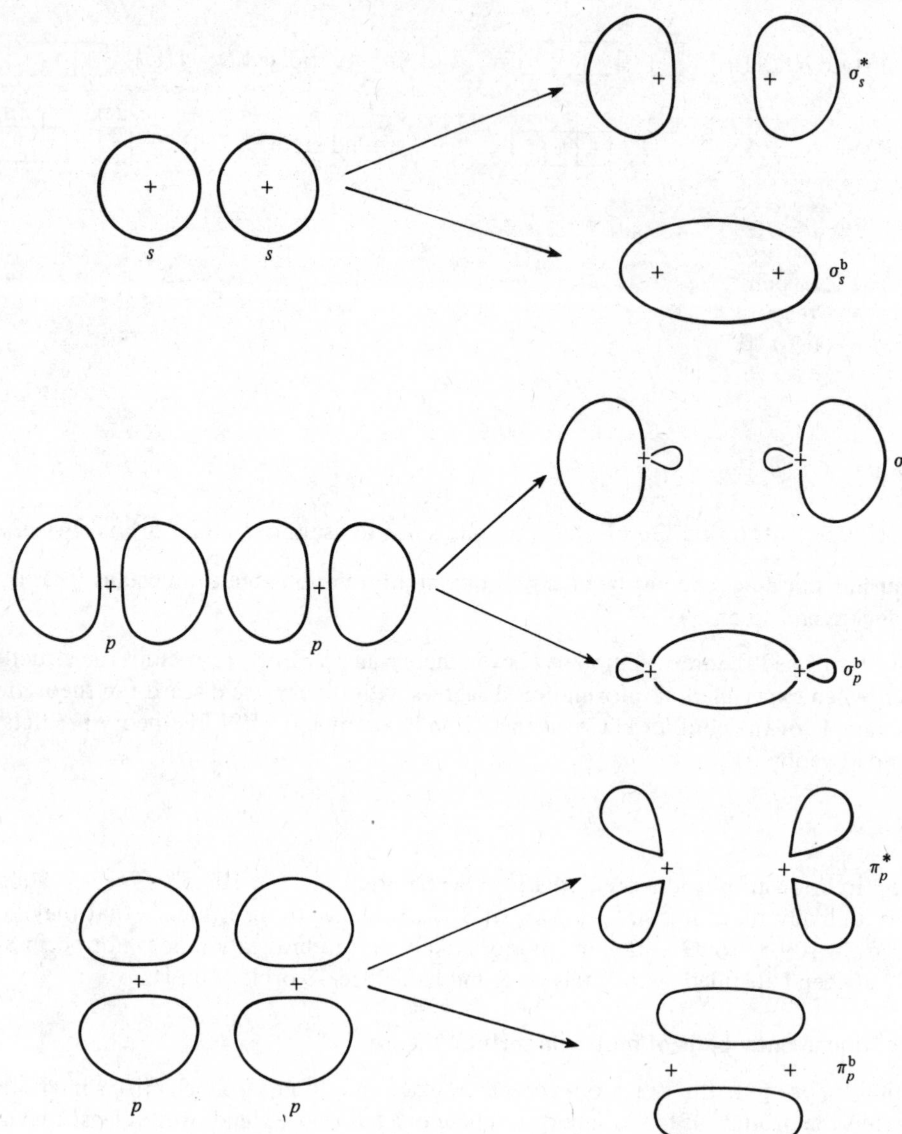

FIGURE 10-4 Molecular orbitals produced from *s* and *p* atomic orbitals.

9a. Use the electron configurations of molecules to determine the bond order of a molecule.

Molecular orbital theory defines bond order as follows.

$$\text{bond order} = \frac{\text{number of bonding electrons} - \text{number of antibonding electrons}}{2} \quad [4]$$

Lewis theory and valence bond theory concepts which are equivalent to bond orders of 1, 2, and 3 are given in Table 10-2.

TABLE 10-2
Concepts equivalent to bond order

Bond order	Lewis theory	Valence bond theory
1	single bond	one σ bond
2	double bond	one σ and one π bond
3	triple bond	one σ and two π bonds

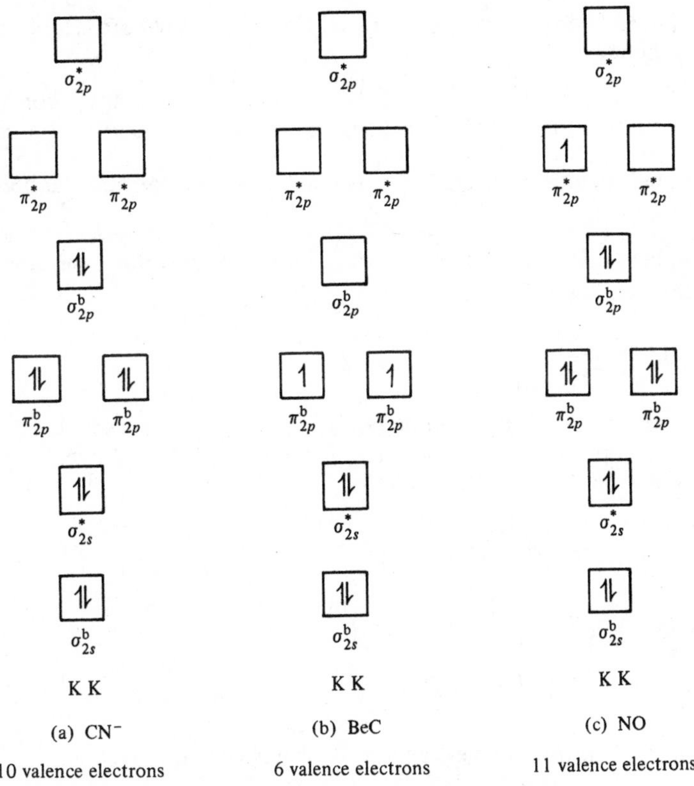

FIGURE 10-5 Molecular orbital energy level diagrams for CN^-, BeC, and NO.

> **EXAMPLE 10-5** What is the bond order of (a) CN^-, (b) BeC, and (c) NO?
> (a) CN^-: bond order = (8 − 2)/2 = 3
> (b) BeC: bond order = (4 − 2)/2 = 1
> (c) NO: bond order = (8 − 3)/2 = 2½

9b. Use the molecular orbital diagram to predict a molecule's magnetic properties.

A molecule with unpaired electrons is paramagnetic. Molecular orbital theory allows us to predict the number of unpaired electrons.

> **EXAMPLE 10-5** Predict the number of unpaired electrons and the magnetic properties of (a) CN^-, (b) BeC, and (c) NO.
> (a) CN^-: all electrons are paired, diamagnetic
> (b) BeC: two unpaired electrons, paramagnetic
> (c) NO: one unpaired electron, paramagnetic

9c. Write simplified molecular orbital diagrams.

Molecular orbital diagrams are more compact when all of the orbitals are written on the same line, as in Figure 10-6.

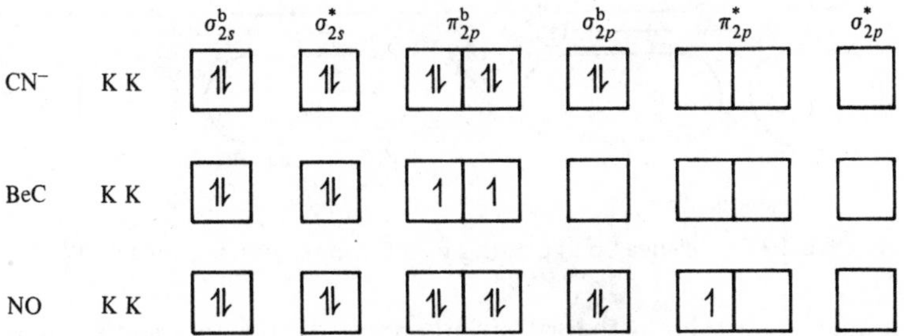

FIGURE 10-6 Compact molecular orbital diagrams for CN^-, BeC, and NO.

10. Describe bonding in the benzene molecule (C_6H_6) through Lewis structures, valence bond theory, and molecular orbital theory.

The benzene molecule is a specific example of a resonance hybrid, which we consider in general in objective 10–11. The delocalized π bond is probably best thought of as a six-electron, six-center delocalized orbital.

★ **11. Explain why a single valence bond structure is inadequate to describe the bonding in a resonance hybrid.**

Let us consider a simple species, the nitrite ion NO_2^-, by the steps outlined in objective 10–4. We indicate the two oxygens with O and Ø to distinguish them.

(1) [|O̲—N̄=Ø̲]$^-$ ↔ [O̲=N̄—Ø̲|]$^-$
resonance form *a* resonance form *b*

(2) 2 ligands + 1 lone pair = 3 electron pairs.

(3) triangular electron-pair geometry; bent (or angular) molecular shape.

(4) sp^2 hybridization on N.

(5) ground state N: [He] $2s$ [↑↓] $2p$ [↑↓|↑|↑] sp^2 hybridized N: [He] sp^2 [↑↓|↑↓|↑] $2p_y$ [↑]

(6) ground state O: [He] $2s$ [↑↓] $2p$ [↑↓|↑|↑]

modified O: [He] [↑↓] [↑↓|↑↓|] for coordinate covalent bond. The oxygen used depends on the resonance form; the single-bonded oxygen is coordinate covalent.

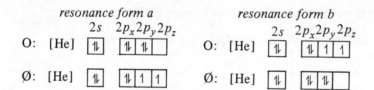

	resonance form a			*resonance form b*	
	$2s$	$2p_x 2p_y 2p_z$		$2s$	$2p_x 2p_y 2p_z$
O: [He]	[↑↓]	[↑↓|↑↓|]	O: [He]	[↑↓]	[↑↓|↑|↑]
Ø: [He]	[↑↓]	[↑↓|↑|↑]	Ø: [He]	[↑↓]	[↑↓|↑↓|]

(7) Sigma bonding descriptions

resonance form a	*resonance form b*
$N(sp^2)^2$—$O(2p_z)^0$	$N(sp^2)^1$—$O(2p_z)^1$
$N(sp^2)^1$—$Ø(2p_z)^1$	$N(sp^2)^2$—$Ø(2p_z)^0$

(8) Let us draw the p orbitals which are left, indicating the electrons in each with arrows. These are $2p_y$ orbitals. The two resonance forms are drawn in Figure 10-7. We see that in resonance form *a* the π bond forms between N and Ø, and in resonance form *b* the π bond forms between N and O.

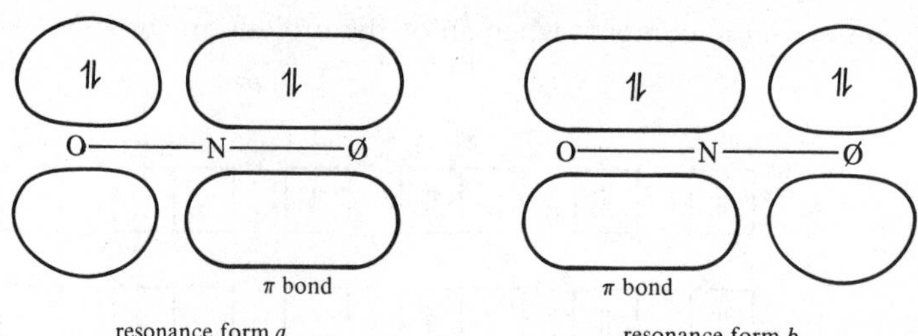

FIGURE 10-7 Valence bond pictures of the two resonance forms of NO_2^-.

Therefore we see that valence bond theory, strictly applied, still does not explain resonance structures. The problem is transferred from "lines between atoms" to pictures of p orbitals.

11a. Explain what is meant by a delocalized molecular orbital and how such orbitals are used to describe resonance hybrids.

Figure 10-7 does help us understand resonance hybrids. It reveals that the two resonance structures for NO_2^- differ by only one electron. Perhaps we should revise our concept of π bonding. Consider the following ideas.

1. The electron is not a classical particle but has properties that require us to speak only of a probability of finding it in a given region. How can we demand that an electron remain in the small region of a π bond?

2. The kinetic energy of a particle is K.E. $= mv^2/2 = p^2/2m$, where $p = mv$. The de Broglie wavelength of a particle is $\lambda = h/p$. Thus $p = h/\lambda$ and K.E. $= h^2/2m\lambda^2$. The longer the wavelength of a particle, the lower will be its kinetic energy. The longest wavelength of a particle is about the same size as the region in which it is confined. Thus, allowing electrons to move between more than two atoms should make the molecule more stable. This is precisely what we have observed: a resonance hybrid is more stable than expected based on one resonance structure.

The extra stability which a molecule has due to resonance is known as the resonance stabilization energy. It occurs because the electrons are not restricted to one region. The electrons are said to be delocalized. For the case of NO_2^- we would report one large π bond over the three atoms: a three-center, four-electron bond.

12. State the special physical properties of metals and describe how the electron sea and band theories account for them.

The special properties of metals are that they (1) conduct electricity, (2) conduct heat, (3) are malleable and ductile, and (4) have luster. A metal's ability to conduct electricity (its conductance) decreases when the metal is heated or when it contains impurities. Both the electron sea and the band theories account for the ability to conduct heat and electricity and the ease of deformation by thinking of the valence electrons being relatively free to move throughout the crystal. The electrons conduct electricity and their vibrations conduct heat. Bonds between the centers of metal atoms break and reform readily, accounting for the ease of deformation. The electron sea theory gives these valence electrons very little structure. The band theory requires that they be in molecular orbitals which extend over the entire crystal.

Luster is explained by electrons absorbing light and going to a higher energy orbital. The light is re-emitted when the electron drops back down to the lower orbital. Because there are so many very closely spaced orbitals, all wavelengths of light are absorbed and all are re-emitted.

Lower conductance at high temperatures is explained as being due to a disruption in the molecular orbitals because the atoms are vibrating (rather like walking across a stream on rocks during an earthquake). This also explains why small amounts of impurities lower the conductance of a metal (the rocks are at very different heights).

13. State how conductors, semiconductors and insulators differ and explain how the band theory explains these differences.

Conductors readily conduct an electric current. Insulators do not conduct an electric current unless a very high voltage is applied to them. And semiconductors conduct a current when only a moderate voltage is applied. The band theory explains these facts by noting that there is a wide energy gap (the band gap) between the full valence (or bonding) band and the empty conduction band. The band gap is smaller in a semiconductor and there is no band gap (or a very small one) for a conductor. A larger band gap means that electrons msut have a larger voltage applied to promote them into the conduction band.

13a. Understand the meaning of *n*-type and *p*-type semiconductors and the impurities used to form each.

Insulators can be turned into semiconductors by "doping" them with impurities. In one type, each impurity atom contains more electrons than do those of the insulator. Thus, there is a set of filled or partly filled orbitals due to the impurity within the band gap as shown in Figure 10-8a. A moderate voltage excites these impurity electrons into the conduction band where they conduct a current. Thus a negative particle, the electron, conducts the current in this *n*-type semiconductor.

In *p*-type semiconductors, the impurity atoms contain fewer valence electrons than do the atoms of the insulator. Thus empty impurity orbitals are present in the band gap. Moderate voltage excites electrons from the full valence band into these empty orbitals, leaving "holes" behind in the valence band. These holes move in the opposite direction to the current flow. It seems as if the positive holes carry the current. A *p*-type semiconductor is shown in Figure 10-8b.

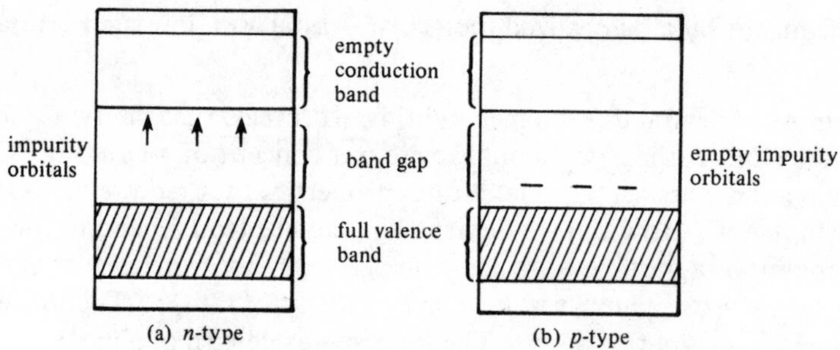

FIGURE 10-8 *n*-type and *p*-type semiconductors.

DRILL PROBLEMS

2. & 3. The central atom's orbitals are hybridized in each of the following species. Write the hybridization scheme for each species and give the electron-pair geometry and molecular shape of each one.

(1) Species with no *d* orbitals in the hybridization:

A. BeH_2 B. NH_4^+ C. $SnCl_2$ D. H_3O^+ E. PI_3
F. NH_2^- G. SI_2 H. OF_2 I. BCl_3 J. CCl_2
K. CF_2Cl_2 L. BF_4^- M. CH_3^- N. SiH_4 O. CH_3^+
P. PCl_2^-

(2) Species with an expanded octet:

A. SeF_2Cl_2 B. TeF_6 C. ClF_3 D. PCl_5 E. BrF_3
F. ArF_2 G. IF_5 H. ICl_2^- I. $SbCl_5$ J. I_3^-
K. PF_3Cl_2 L. BrF_5 M. KrF_4 N. $TeCl_4$ O. $SbCl_5^{2-}$
P. SF_4 Q. ICl_4^- R. ICl_3 S. SeF_6 T. XeF_4
U. $SnCl_6^{2-}$

4. Describe the bonding in each of the following species.

A. BeH_2 B. CH_3 C. KrF_4 D. BF_4^- E. $SnCl_2$
F. NH_4^+ G. ICl_4^- H. CH_3^+ I. SI_2 J. SeF_4
K. XeF_2 L. CCl_2 M. NH_2^- N. BrF_3 O. IF_5
P. ClO_2^- Q. BCl_3 R. $SbCl_5$ S. SeF_6 T. H_3O^+

5. Describe the bonding in each of the following species. The central atom of each species is underlined.

A. $N\underline{C}N^{2-}$ B. $H_2\underline{C}S$ C. $Cl_2\underline{CC}H_2$ D. $Cl_2\underline{C}S$ E. $S\underline{C}N^-$
F. $N\underline{N}O$ G. $\underline{C}O_2$ H. $H\underline{OC}N$ I. $H\underline{N}O$ J. $H\underline{C}N$
K. $H\underline{CC}H$ L. $\underline{N}O_2^+$ M. $\underline{C}OS$ N. $F\underline{P}O$ O. $H\underline{C}O\underline{O}H$

9. Write the simplified molecular orbital diagram of each of the species which follows. Based on that electron configuration determine the number of (1) bonding and (2) antibonding electrons, (3) the bond order, the number of (4) σ and (5) π electrons, and (6) the number of unpaired electrons.

A. NO^+ B. O_2^{2-} C. N_2^- D. CN^+ E. BeO
F. BN G. Be_2^+ H. CN I. NeF J. F_2^-
K. O_2^- L. NO^- M. LiB

11. Give a complete description of the σ and π bonding in each of the following species. The central atom is underlined in each case.

A. $\underline{N}O_2$ B. $\underline{S}O_3$ C. $\underline{B}Cl_3$ D. $\underline{O}_3$ E. $H\underline{C}O_2^-$
F. $O\underline{C}F^-$ G. $\underline{C}O_3^{2-}$ H. $\underline{B}F_3$

QUIZZES (20 minutes each)

Choose the best answer for each question.

Quiz A

1. The hybridization of N in NCl_2F is (a) *sp*; (b) sp^2; (c) sp^3; (d) not hybridized; (e) none of these.

2. The hybridization of P in PCl_5 is (a) not hybridized; (b) sp^3d^2 (c) sp^3d; (d) sp^3; (e) none of these.
3. Which of the following exhibits sp^2 hybridization? (a) $BeCl_2$; (b) BCl_3; (c) CCl_4; (d) NCl_3; (e) none of these.
4. The molecule of the following with the shortest C—O bond is (a) CO; (b) CO_2; (c) H_3COH; (d) H_2CO; (e) none of these.
5. A bond which has negligible electron density on the internuclear axis is a (a) single bond; (b) pi bond; (c) polar bond; (d) sigma bond; (e) none of these.
6. According to valence bond theory, bond strength is related to the degree of (a) orbital overlap; (b) covalent character; (c) resonance; (d) hybridization; (e) none of these.
7. A theory that can be used to explain why all bond distances and angles in a molecule such as methane are the same is (a) bond resonance; (b) delocalization of electrons; (c) bond polarities; (d) electronegativity; (e) bond hybridization.
8. Which of the following is predicted by molecular orbital theory to be paramagnetic? (a) CN^-; (b) CN^+; (c) NO^+; (d) LiB^{2+}; (e) none of these.

Quiz B

1. In the acetylene molecule C_2H_2 the hybridization of each C atom is (a) sp; (b) sp^2; (c) sp^3; (d) d^2sp^3; (e) none of these.
2. Which of the following molecules displays sp^2 hybridization? (a) OF_2; (b) $F_2C{=}O$; (c) BeH_2; (d) NH_3; (e) none of these.
3. The hybridization of S in SF_4 is (a) not hybridized; (b) sp^3d; (c) sp^3d^2; (d) sp^3; (e) none of these.
4. The orientation in space (geometry) of *sp*-hybridized orbitals is (a) perpendicular; (b) linear; (c) trigonal planar; (d) tetrahedral; (e) none of these.
5. If a double bond results from the sharing of four electrons, it consists of (a) 2σ bonds; (b) $1\sigma + 1\pi$ bond; (c) 2π bonds; (d) 1π bond; (e) none of these.
6. Of the following, the molecule that has the shortest bond is (a) H_2; (b) N_2; (c) O_2; (d) HCl; (e) CO_2.
7. According to simple molecular orbital theory, the peroxide ion, O_2^{2-}, has (a) no unpaired electrons; (b) a bond order of 3/2; (c) its highest energy electrons in σ^* orbitals; (d) no σ electrons; (e) none of these.
8. The double covalent bond in ethylene, C_2H_4, (a) includes a lone pair of electrons on one of the carbons; (b) is a sigma bond; (c) consists of one sigma and one pi bond; (d) is free to rotate because of delocalized electrons; (e) has a low electron density.

Quiz C

1. Which of the following molecules contains an sp^2-sp^2 sigma bond? (a) C_2H_4; (b) C_2H_6; (c) C_2H_2; (d) CH_4; (e) none of these.
2. The hybridization of the central N in N_2O is (a) not hybridized; (b) sp; (c) sp_2; (d) sp^3; (e) none of these.
3. The hybridization of Xe in XeF_4 is (a) not hybridized; (b) sp^3; (c) dsp^3; (d) sp^3d^2; (e) none of these.
4. If the wave functions describing the 2*s* and two of the 2*p* orbitals are combined, the identical orbitals derived form bond angles of (a) 90°; (b) 120°; (c) 180°; (d) 109.5°; (e) none of these.
5. A pi bond is (a) composed of two *s* orbitals; (b) composed of two *p* orbitals; (c) composed of an *s* and a *p* orbital; (d) stronger than a sigma bond; (e) none of these.
6. Generally, short bonds are (a) between electronegative atoms; (b) strong bonds; (c) polar bonds; (d) ionic bonds; (e) none of these.
7. The concept of an antibonding orbital is unique to the (a) valence bond theory; (b) theory of bond hybridization; (c) concept of resonance; (d) molecular orbital theory; (e) electron-pair repulsion theory.
8. A diatomic molecule has 15 electrons (including KK). Its bond order is (a) 2.5; (b) 2.0; (c) 1.5; (d) 1.0; (e) none of these.

Quiz D

1. Which of the following exhibits *sp* hybridization? (a) CO_2; (b) CCl_4; (c) H_2S; (d) NH_3; (e) none of these.
2. The hybridization of Cl in the perchlorate anion is (a) sp^3; (b) sp^2; (c) dsp^3; (d) not hybridized; (e) none of these.
3. The hybridization of Br in BrF_3 is (a) not hybridized; (b) sp^3d^2; (c) sp^3d; (d) sp^3; (e) none of these.
4. Which of the following does *not* use hybridized orbitals? (a) CH_4; (b) CO_2; (c) H_2O; (d) HCl; (e) none of these.
5. The σ bond (a) cannot be formed by two *p* orbitals; (b) is weaker than a π bond; (c) has high electron probability between atoms; (d) can only be formed by *s* orbitals; (e) none of these.
6. The shorter the internuclear distance between two bonded atoms, the (a) less stable the bond; (b) less multiple bonding character there is; (c) more energy is needed to break the bond; (d) more resonance there is; (e) none of these.
7. A pi bond is (a) stronger than a sigma bond; (b) concentrated along the bond axis; (c) a concept of bond hybridization theory only; (d) formed by the sidewise overlap of *p* orbitals; (e) none of these.
8. According to molecular orbital theory, NO has (not counting KK) (a) a bond order of 3/2; (b) 4 antibonding electrons; (c) 8 sigma electrons; (d) 3 pi electrons; (e) none of these.

SAMPLE TEST (25 minutes)

1. Consider a molecule with the Lewis structure given below. For the central atoms C^a, C^b, and O, list the following.

   $N{\equiv}C^a{-}C^b{-}\overline{\underline{O}}{-}H$, with $C^b{=}|S|$ (S double-bonded below C^b)

   a. Number of ligands
   b. Number of lone pairs
   c. Electron-pair geometry
   d. Molecular shape
   e. Orbitals in which the lone pairs (if any) are located
   f. Hybridization (if any)

   Now describe the bonding in the molecule by specifying which orbitals on each atom overlap to form the bonds in the molecule. Describe each bond separately.

   g. sigma bonds h. pi bonds

   What are the (ideal) values of the following bond angles?

   i. $N{-}C^a{-}C^b$ j. $C^a{-}C^b{-}S$
   k. $C^a{-}C^b{-}O$ l. $C^b{-}O{-}H$
2. Answer the following using the principles of molecular orbital theory.
   a. What is the bond order of NO?
   b. Which of the ions NO^+ or O_2^+ is more stable? Why?
   c. How many unpaired electrons are there in Ne_2^+, OF^+, CO?

Liquids, Solids, and Intermolecular Forces

REVIEW OF OBJECTIVES

1. Explain surface tension and describe several phenomena based on it.

Energy is released when atoms are attracted to each other. Forces of attraction exist between molecules and even between individual atoms. A molecule will have low energy if it is attracted to many other molecules. This molecule is more stable than a free molecule. The molecules in the body of a liquid are surrounded by and attracted to more molecules than those on the surface. The surface molecules are less stable. The liquid becomes as stable as possible by decreasing its surface area. Hence, it resists attempts to increase its surface area. When forces to the surface of another substance (adhesive forces) are stronger than forces within the liquid (cohesive forces), the liquid will wet that surface. Such a liquid will rise in a capillary tube.

★ 2. Describe vaporization, including its enthalpy, $\Delta\overline{H}_{vap}$, using the latter in calculations.

Adding energy to a liquid causes some of the molecules to leave the surface of the liquid or vaporize. The energy required to vaporize a mole of the liquid is known as the molar enthalpy of vaporization, $\Delta\overline{H}_{vap}$. Vaporization always is an endothermic process and thus $\Delta\overline{H}_{vap}$ is always positive.

EXAMPLE 11-1 The heats of vaporization of (a) H_2O, (b) CH_3OH, and (c) C_2H_5OH are 44.1, 37.4, and 42.3 kJ/mol, respectively. What mass, in *grams*, of each would have to vaporize in order to absorb 1.00 kJ of heat?

(a) $$1.00 \text{ kJ} \times \frac{\text{mol } H_2O}{44.1 \text{ kJ}} \times \frac{18.0 \text{ g } H_2O}{\text{mol}} = 0.408 \text{ g } H_2O$$

(b) $$1.00 \text{ kJ} \times \frac{\text{mol } CH_3OH}{37.4 \text{ kJ}} \times \frac{320 \text{ g } CH_3OH}{\text{mol}} = 0.856 \text{ g } CH_3OH$$

(c) $$1.00 \text{ kJ} \times \frac{\text{mol } C_2H_5OH}{42.3 \text{ kJ}} \times \frac{46.0 \text{ g } C_2H_5OH}{\text{mol}} = 1.087 \text{ g } C_2H_5OH$$

Heats of vaporization of some common compounds are given in Table 11-1.

2a. Explain what occurs whan a liquid vaporizes in a closed container: the dynamic equilibrium between a liquid and its vapor.

When a liquid is placed in an open container, eventually it all evaporates. If the container is closed, the vapor molecules are unable to escape. The concentration of molecules in the vapor increases. It becomes more likely that some of these molecules will condense. The vapor becomes saturated. Molecules condense from the vapor just as rapidly as they vaporize. From the ideal gas law ($PV = nRT$ or $P = RT \times n/V$) we see that this concentration (n/V) is proportional to a pressure. This pressure is the liquid's vapor pressure.

When the vapor is saturated, the two processes of vaporization and condensation occur at the same speed.

rate of vaporization = rate of condensation [1]

TABLE 11-1
Heat capacities and vaporization heats of some common compounds

Formula	Name	$\Delta\bar{H}_{vap}$, kJ/mol	Heat capacities, J mol^{-1} K^{-1} Liquid	Vapor	Normal boiling point, °C
NH_3	ammonia	31.2	76.1	44.4	− 33.35
SO_2	sulfur dioxide	26.8	85.2	39.9	− 10.0
HCN	hydrogen cyanide	30.7	70.7	36.0	26.0
$(C_2H_5)_2O$	diethyl ether	29.1	172	108	34.6
CS_2	carbon disulfide	28.4	76.1	45.6	46.3
$(CH_3)_2CO$	acetone	32.0	126	75.3	56.2
Br_2	bromine	33.9	75.7	36.1	58.78
$CHCl_3$	chloroform	31.4	115	65.7	61.2
CH_3OH	methanol	37.6	81.6	43.9	64.96
CCl_4	carbon tetrachloride	31.9	133	83.3	76.8
C_2H_5OH	ethanol	40.5	113	65.7	78.5
H_2O	water	44.1	75.3	36	100.0
HCOOH	formic acid	41.4	98.7	45.2	100.7
CH_3COOH	acetic acid	39.7	123	66.9	118.5

The rate of vaporization depends on four factors: temperature, forces between molecules, size of molecules, and surface area of the liquid. Increasing temperature causes liquid to vaporize more rapidly. Vaporization occurs more rapidly from a large surface area than from a small one. Increasing the forces between molecules or the size of the molecules slows down the rate of vaporization.

The rate of condensation depends on the pressure of the vapor and on the surface area. High pressures and large surface areas both increase the condensation rate. In the first case, there are more molecules present in the vapor which can condense. In the second case, the area which the molecules must hit in order to condense is larger.

3. Explain how vapor pressure and temperature are related and the meaning of boiling.

As the temperature increases, the vaporization rate increases and so does the vapor pressure. This increase in vapor pressure is tabulated or graphed against temperature. (Also see objective 11-5.)

When the vapor pressure of the liquid reaches atmospheric pressure, bubbles of vapor form within the liquid and the liquid boils. This occurs at the boiling point, or the normal boiling point if the external pressure is 1.00 atm.

★ **4. Determine vapor pressure experimentally, estimate values from tables and graphs, and predict whether vapor and/or liquid is present under given conditions.**

In the transpiration method, a known volume of an inert gas is bubbled through a weighed liquid. Both liquid and gas are at the same temperature. The gas which leaves the liquid is saturated. The liquid is reweighed. The difference in liquid masses divided by the mole weight of the liquid is the amount of liquid which has vaporized.

$$n_{\text{liquid}} = \frac{\text{liquid mass before bubbling} - \text{liquid mass after bubbling}}{\text{mole weight of liquid}} \qquad [2]$$

The final mixture is assumed to occupy the same volume as the inert gas does initially; only the pressure changes. Since both the temperature and the volume of the gas are known, the vapor pressure of the liquid (liq) can be determined from the ideal gas law.

$$P = n_{\text{liq}}RT/V \qquad [3]$$

Determining the amount of liquid and vapor present in a container of known volume and temperature involves applying the ideal gas law to determine the moles of vapor present. We use the vapor pressure as the pressure and the known values of volume and temperature. Thus we can determine the number of moles of vapor. Any substance left over must be liquid and is assumed to be of negligible volume.

★ **5. Use the Clausius-Clapeyron equation.**

The Clausius–Clapeyron equation [4] is important for two reasons. First it permits us to predict the vapor pressure of a liquid at many different temperatures. Second, it has the same form as two other important equations: the Arrhenius equation [5], which predicts the rate constant of a reaction at different temperatures (see objective 13-9), and the van't Hoff equation [6] (see objective 14-8), which predicts the equilibrium constant of a chemical reaction at different temperatures.

$$\ln \frac{P_2}{P_1} = \frac{-\Delta \bar{H}_{vap}}{R}\left(\frac{1}{T_2} - \frac{1}{T_1}\right) = 2.303 \log \frac{P_2}{P_1} \qquad [4]$$

$$\ln \frac{k_2}{k_1} = \frac{-E_a}{R}\left(\frac{1}{T_2} - \frac{1}{T_1}\right) \qquad [5]$$

$$\ln \frac{K_2}{K_1} = \frac{-\Delta \bar{H}_{rxn}}{R}\left(\frac{1}{T_2} - \frac{1}{T_1}\right) \qquad [6]$$

Thus, once we know how to use the Clausius–Clapeyron equation, we also will know how to use the other two. (Equations [5] and [6] are given just to show you the similarity of form. You do not have to learn them now.) There are five variables in the Clausius–Clapeyron equation: $\Delta \bar{H}_{vap}$, P_2, P_1, T_2, and T_1.

EXAMPLE 11-2 The vapor pressure of isopropyl alcohol is 100 mmHg at 39.5°C and 400 mmHg at 67.8°C. What is $\Delta \bar{H}_{vap}$ of isopropyl alcohol?

Remember that temperature *must* be in kelvins.

$P_1 = 100$ mmHg; $T_1 = 312.7$ K; $P_2 = 400$ mmHg; $T_2 = 341.0$ K

$$\ln \frac{P_2}{P_1} = \frac{-\Delta \bar{H}_{vap}}{R}\left(\frac{1}{T_2} - \frac{1}{T_1}\right)$$

$$\ln \frac{400 \text{ mmHg}}{100 \text{ mmHg}} = \frac{-\Delta \bar{H}_{vap}}{8.314 \text{ J mol}^{-1} \text{ K}^{-1}}\left(\frac{1}{341.0 \text{ K}} - \frac{1}{312.7 \text{ K}}\right)$$

$$\Delta \bar{H}_{vap} = 43{,}430 \text{ J/mol}$$

EXAMPLE 11-3 What is the normal boiling point of isopropyl alcohol?

$P_2 = 760$ mmHg; $T_2 = ?$; $P_1 = 100$ mmHg; $T_1 = 312.7$ K

$$\ln \frac{760 \text{ mmHg}}{100 \text{ mmHg}} = \frac{43{,}430 \text{ J/mol}}{8.314 \text{ J mol}^{-1} \text{ K}^{-1}}\left(\frac{1}{T_2} - \frac{1}{312.7 \text{ K}}\right)$$

$$T_2 = 355.9 \text{ K} = 82.7°\text{C}$$

6. Describe the significance of a substance's critical point.

Above the critical temperature a gas will not condense to a liquid no matter how much pressure is exerted on it. It will get denser and may become as dense as a liquid, but it will never show a meniscus. Similarly, above the critical pressure the familiar processes of condensation and boiling do not occur no matter how the temperature changes. The critical temperature represents a very high kinetic energy for the molecules. Their speeds are so large that short-range intermolecular forces are not strong enough to hold molecules together.

★ **6a. Understand terms which apply to the phase changes of solids.**

The melting point and freezing point are the same temperature. Melting also is called fusion and thus the heat absorbed is called the heat of fusion, $\Delta \bar{H}_{fus}$. The reverse of fusion, called solidification, has an associated heat of solidification, $\Delta \bar{H}_{sol}$.

$$\Delta \bar{H}_{fus} = -\Delta \bar{H}_{sol} \qquad [7]$$

$\Delta \bar{H}_{sol}$ is negative as solidification is exothermic.

When a solid vaporizes without first becoming a liquid, it sublimes. The process of sublimation is the reverse of deposition (gas to solid). The enthalpy of sublimation, $\Delta \bar{H}_{sub}$, is positive; that is, sublimation is endothermic.

$$\Delta \bar{H}_{dep} = -\Delta \bar{H}_{sub} \qquad [8]$$

Sublimation accomplishes the same change as melting and vaporization combined.

$$\Delta \bar{H}_{sub} = \Delta \bar{H}_{fus} + \Delta \bar{H}_{vap} \qquad [9]$$

$$\Delta \bar{H}_{dep} = \Delta \bar{H}_{cond} + \Delta \bar{H}_{sol} \qquad [10]$$

★ **7. Interpret the phase diagrams of simple substances and use phase diagrams to predict changes which occur as a substance is heated, cooled, or undergoes a change in pressure.**

A phase diagram summarizes the changes in phase of a given substance. The liquid–vapor curve is determined by the Clausius–Clapeyron equation. The points on the sublimation curve (the curve between solid and gas) also come from the Clausius–Clapeyron equation if $\Delta \bar{H}_{sub}$ is used in place of $\Delta \bar{H}_{vap}$. The slope of the fusion line is given by equation [11].

$$\frac{\Delta P}{\Delta T} = \frac{\Delta \bar{H}_{fus}}{T \Delta \bar{V}_{fus}} \qquad [11]$$

$\Delta \bar{V}_{fus}$ is the volume increase of one mole of solid on melting. (The line between solid and liquid is straight enough to draw with a ruler.) This line–the fusion curve–usually slopes upward and to the right (it has a positive slope) since $\Delta \bar{V}_{fus}$ is generally positive. In the case of water, however, $\Delta \bar{V}_{fus}$ is negative (ice floats on water) and the fusion curve slopes upward and to the left (it has a negative slope). The point at which the vapor pressure, sublimation, and fusion curves meet is the triple point where solid, liquid, and gas exist together. You should remember that pressure is plotted vertically and temperature horizontally by convention.

★ **8. Describe the difference between intra- and intermolecular forces, distinguish the different types of forces between molecules, and explain how they influence physical properties.**

Intermolecular forces are those which exist between molecules, whereas intramolecular forces hold a molecule together. Intermolecular forces are van der Waals forces and are of two types.

The first are dipole–dipole attractions. The negative end of one dipole is attracted by the positive end of another. Dipole–dipole forces are relatively weak, ranging from 0.01 to 0.2 kJ/mol.

The second type of force occurs between an instantaneous dipole in a normally nonpolar molecule and the dipole which this instantaneous dipole creates or induces in another nonpolar molecule. These forces are called London forces or exchange forces. Temporary dipoles are more easily created in large molecules, especially those having atoms of high atomic number. In these atoms the outer electrons are far from the nucleus and not held very firmly. Thus large atoms are said to be very polarizable. London forces are stronger for molecules with high atomic weight. They range from 0.4 to 10 kJ/mol.

9. State the factors which lead to hydrogen bond formation, explain how hydrogen bonds differ from other types of intermolecular forces, and describe the effects of hydrogen bonds on physical properties.

Hydrogen bonds are formed when a hydrogen atom is bound to a F, O, or N atom and attracted to another F, O, or N atom. A Cl or S atom may substitute for either F, O, or N atom but the resulting hydrogen bond is not as strong. One explanation is that the high electronegativity of the F, O, or N atom pulls so much of the bond pair of electrons toward it that the hydrogen nucleus is almost a bare proton. Thus a very intense dipole is created. It is doubtful that this is the full explanation, for the following reasons.

1. The hydrogen bond is a very strong intermolecular force, ranging from 15 to 40 kJ/mol. Strengths of other intermolecular forces rarely exceed 10 kJ/mol.
2. It is common to see a fixed limit on the number of hydrogen bonds formed. For example, two hydrogen bonds form to oxygen in water.
3. Hydrogen bonds have a reasonably well defined length, 2.74 Å between oxygens in ice. Dipole–dipole attractions normally show a range of lengths.

The required distance and number of hydrogen bonds makes the structure of ice more open than that of liquid water. Thus ice floats on water. The strength of the bond results in substances comprised of small molecules which have unusually high melting and boiling points and high heats of vaporization.

10. Describe aspects of network covalent bonding: the conditions which lead to it, the properties of solids in which it occurs, and some examples of its occurrence.

A network covalent solid is held together entirely by covalent bonds. In that respect a crystal of such a solid is a single molecule. Covalent bonds range from 150 to 900 kJ/mol. Network covalent solids are formed between the nonmetals and the metalloids of families IIIA, IVA, and VA. Metals are held together by metallic bonds, described in objective 10–12.

It is very difficult to break the strong covalent bonds which hold network covalent solids together. These solids have very high melting points (2000°C is not uncommon) and heats of fusion. They are very hard and thus make good abrasives. But they are brittle since once the bonds are broken they do not easily reform.

★ **11. & 12. Describe the features of ionic bonding: that lattice energy depends on ionic size and charge, that lattice energy effects the physical properties of ionic solids, and that lattice energy can be calculated by means of the Born–Haber cycle.**

The Born–Haber cycle divides the formation reaction [12] of an ionic solid into several steps, as shown in Figure 11-1 for $MgBr_2$.

$$Mg(s) + Br_2(l) \rightarrow MgBr_2(s) \quad \Delta\bar{H}_f^\circ = -517.6 \text{ kJ/mol} \qquad [12]$$

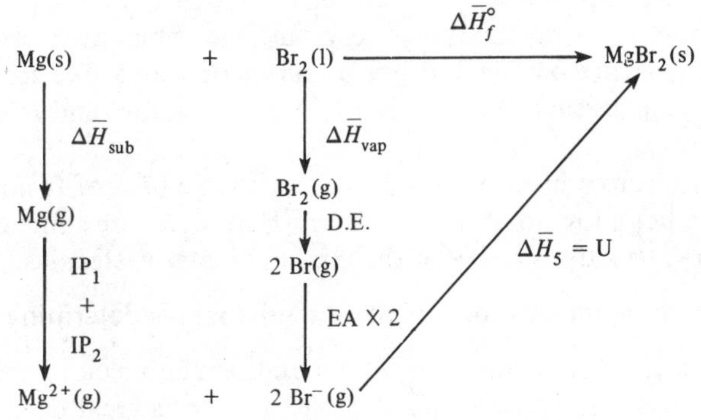

$Mg(s)$ + $Br_2(l)$ —$\Delta\bar{H}_f^\circ$→ $MgBr_2(s)$

$Mg(s)$ —$\Delta\bar{H}_{sub}$→ $Mg(g)$ —$IP_1 + IP_2$→ $Mg^{2+}(g)$

$Br_2(l)$ —$\Delta\bar{H}_{vap}$→ $Br_2(g)$ —D.E.→ $2\ Br(g)$ —EA X 2→ $2\ Br^-(g)$

$Mg^{2+}(g) + 2\ Br^-(g)$ —$\Delta\bar{H}_5 = U$→ $MgBr_2(s)$

FIGURE 11-1 Born–Haber cycle for $MgBr_2$.

The energy of each step is found as follows.

(1) The metallic solid is melted and then vaporized (or it is sublimed) and the heat of sublimation is measured: $\Delta\bar{H}_1 = \Delta\bar{H}_{sub}$.

$$Mg(s) \rightarrow Mg(g) \quad \Delta\bar{H}_1 = \Delta\bar{H}_{sub} = +150.2 \text{ kJ/mol}$$

(2) The metallic vapor is ionized to produce cations of the correct positive charge and the ionization potentials (IP) are measured: $\Delta H_2 = IP_1 + IP_2$ for Mg.

$$Mg(g) \rightarrow Mg^{2+}(g) + 2\,e^- \quad \Delta\bar{H}_2 = 2187.9 \text{ kJ/mol}$$

(3a) The nonmetal is vaporized if necessary and the heat of vaporization is measured: $\Delta\bar{H}_{3a} = \Delta\bar{H}_{vap}$ (or $\Delta\bar{H}_{sub}$ if the nonmetal is a solid).

$$Br_2(l) \rightarrow Br_2(g) \quad \Delta\bar{H}_{3a} = +30.7 \text{ kJ/mol}$$

(3) The nonmetal molecules are dissociated or broken apart into atoms, and the dissociation energy (D.E.) is measured: $\Delta\bar{H}_3 = \text{D.E.}$

$$Br_2(g) \rightarrow 2\,Br(g) \quad \Delta\bar{H}_3 = +193.9 \text{ kJ/mol}$$

(4) Electrons are added to the nonmetal atoms to produce anions of the correct negative charge and the electron affinity (EA) is measured: $\Delta\bar{H}_4$ = electron affinity × 2 (for 2 Br).

$$2\,Br(g) + 2\,e^-(g) \rightarrow 2\,Br(g)^- \quad \Delta\bar{H}_4 = -2710 \text{ kJ/mol}$$

(5) The gaseous ions are combined and the lattice energy is calculated: $\Delta\bar{H}_5 = U$ = lattice energy.

$$Mg^{2+}(g) + 2\,Br(g) \rightarrow MgBr_2(s) \quad \Delta\bar{H}_5 = ? \text{ kJ/mol}$$

We have created two pathways for making $MgBr_2$(s) from the elements: the formation reaction and steps (1) through (5). The energy required by each pathway must be the same. Hence

$$\begin{aligned}\Delta\bar{H}_f^\circ &= \Delta\bar{H}_1 + \Delta\bar{H}_2 + \Delta\bar{H}_{3a} + \Delta\bar{H}_3 + \Delta\bar{H}_4 + \Delta\bar{H}_5\\ &= \Delta\bar{H}_{sub} + (IP_1 + IP_2) + \Delta\bar{H}_{vap} + \text{D.E.} + 2 \times \text{EA} + U \qquad [13]\end{aligned}$$

$$-517.6 \text{ kJ/mol} = +150.2 \text{ kJ/mol} + (2187.9 \text{ kJ/mol}) + 30.7 \text{ kJ/mol} + 193.9 \text{ kJ/mol} - 2710 \text{ kJ/mol} + U$$

$$\text{or} \quad U = -367.9 \text{ kJ/mol}$$

Electron affinities are very imprecise because they are very hard to measure. If the lattice energy were precisely known, then the Born–Haber cycle could be used to determine the electron affinity.

The lattice energy of an ionic crystal can be calculated and the results agree well with those of the Born–Haber cycle. The only data needed are the type of crystal structure and the ionic charges and radii. All of these data come from the x-ray analysis of crystals. (see objectives 11–13 through 11–15). The calculations reveal that the lattice energy depends on terms that look like $z_a z_c/(r_a + r_c)$ where z_a and z_c are the anion and cation charges such as −1, −2, +1, and +3), and r_a and r_c are the anion and cation radii in picometers.

A large lattice energy means a high melting point and a large heat of fusion. We also would expect a large lattice energy to predict a low solubility in water. Here there are some exceptions because solubility also depends on the attractions between the ions and water molecules.

13. Describe the three packing models for spheres and how x rays determine crystal structures.

The three ways in which atoms are arranged in solid metals are cubic close packed (also known as *abc*), hexagonal close packed (*aba*), and body-centered cubic. It helps a great deal to make models to see these structures. You can use Styrofoam balls touching each other and held together with tooth picks. To see that the *abc* packing really is face-centered cubic, find three atoms on three different layers which touch each other and lie along a straight line. This is the diagonal of a face (corner, face center, corner). From this you should be able to see the rest of the face-centered cube. In Figure 11-2, the atoms of a face-centered cube are labeled with the letters of the layer (*a, b,* or *c*) each is in.

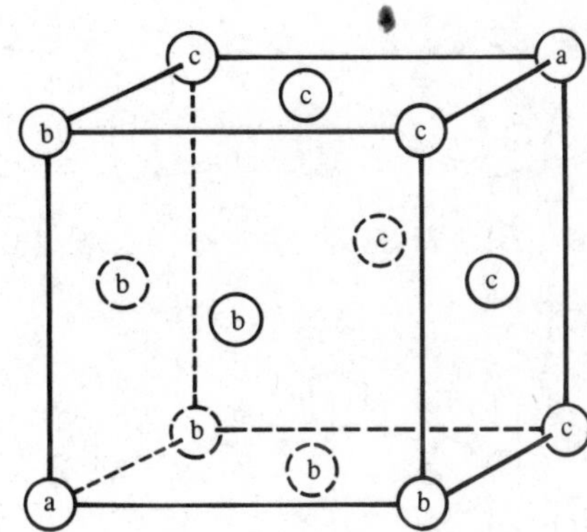

FIGURE 11-2 Close-packing face-centered cube.

The *text* explains in *Figure 11-30* how the spacing between layers of atoms (d) is related to the angle (θ) at which x rays strike the crystal. We see two types of layers in Figure 11-2, the b atom or c atom layers and the layers parallel to each face. Yet there are many other layers as well. This is hard to see in three dimensions unless you have a very good model. But you can see an arrangement of many rows in any orderly pattern: seat backs in a movie theater or tombstones in a military cemetary.

X rays bounce off planes of atoms somewhat like light is reflected from a mirror. A plane of atoms is a good "mirror" for x rays if it contains many electrons. Thus if there are many atoms in a plane or if the atoms have high atomic numbers, the reflected x-ray beam will be strong. The spacings between layers and the strengths of the reflected x-ray beams are used to find the structure of the crystal.

14. Explain what a unit cell is and how to use its dimensions in crystal structure calculations.

The smallest unit of a crystal which will produce the entire crystal by simple repetition is called the unit cell. You can see two-dimensional unit cells by looking at a wallpaper pattern (Figure 11-3). The dashed lines outline a "formula unit." Four of these formula units are needed in a unit cell since we cannot turn the formula units around in order to repeat the pattern. The solid lines outline a unit cell. Calculations involving unit cells are straightforward if you have a clear picture of which atoms are touching. In addition you should know how many unit cells "share" each atom on the outside. Those on a face are shared by two unit cells, for instance.

15. Calculate compound formulas by analysis of their unit cells and calculate sizes of ions from unit cell dimensions.

As was true in objective 11-14, this requires a clear mental picture of where the ions are in a unit cell. You also should know how many unit cells share each ion.

DRILL PROBLEMS

2. In each line below, the specified mass (m, g) of the indicated compound is heated from the initial temperature (t_i, °C) to the final temperature (t_f, °C) with the given amount of heat (q, kJ). Occasionally liquid and vapor are present together at the boiling point in which case the mass of the liquid is given (m_l, g). Please fill in the blanks in the table below. Data are given in Table 11-1. The first line is done as an example.

Compound	m, g	t_i,°C	t_f,°C	q, kJ	m_l, g
water	150	75.0	100.0	236.2	60
A. methanol	200	50.0	______	184.7	______
B. ethanol	204	20.2	100.0	______	0.00
C. sulfur dioxide	186	−51.0	− 10.0	______	46

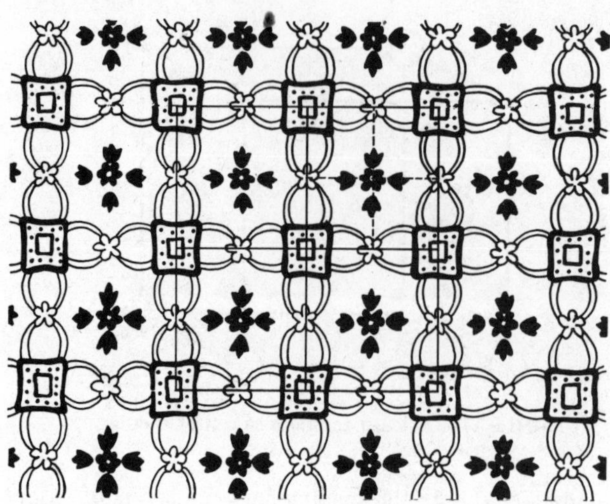

FIGURE 11-3 A wallpaper unit cell

Compound	m, g	t_i, °C	t_f, °C	q, kJ	m_l, g
D. hydrogen cyanide	______	−14.0	36.5	20.20	0.00
E. acetic acid	400	50.0	______	204	______
F. carbon disulfide	300	25.0	90	______	______
G. diethyl ether	55.0	25.0	______	1.43	______
H. carbon tetrachloride	______	25.0	76.8	16.4	14
I. chloroform	314	0.00	______	14.3	______
J. formic acid	87.0	41.0	126.0	______	0.00
K. acetone	435	8.2	56.2	______	100
L. bromine	124	20.40	______	______	24
M. ammonia	100	−52.6	______	8.17	______

4. (1) In each of the following transpiration experiments a given volume of noble gas (V) is passed through a liquid at temperature t. The liquid loses m grams of mass. Determine the vapor pressure in mmHg of each liquid.

Liquid	V, L	t, °C	m, g	*Liquid*	V, L	t, °C	m, g
A. acetone	214	−32.0	7.44	B. formic acid	86.7	20.0	7.64
C. diethyl ether	9.52	−10.0	4.94	D. chloroform	15.2	0.0	4.79
E. bromine	10.7	8.0	9.82	F. ethanol	83.1	− 5.0	1.83
G. methanol	98.3	−43.0	0.241				

(2) Use the data of *Figure 11-6 in the text* to help determine how much liquid and how much vapor of each substance is present in each container of volume V and at temperature T.

Substance	m, g	V, L	t, °C	*Substance*	m, g	V, L	t, °C
A. diethyl ether	25.0	10.0	20	B. benzene	10.0	5.2	40
C. water	2.14	11.6	80	D. aniline	5.79	8.2	120
E. toluene	14.2	7.3	100	F. benzene	12.0	4.9	60
G. diethyl ether	12.0	6.1	30				

5. (1) The vapor pressure of several liquids at two temperatures follow. Determine the heat of vaporization of each liquid and its normal boiling point.

Liquid	P_1, mmHg	t_1, °C	P_2, mmHg	t_2, °C
A. BrF_5	10.0	− 41.9	400	+ 25.7
B. $COCl_2$	40.0	− 50.3	100	− 35.6
C. H_2O_2	1.00	15.3	40.0	77.0
D. Si_2Cl_6	10.0	38.8	100	85.4
E. SO_2Cl_2	40.0	− 1.0	100	17.8
F. SiH_3F	10.0	−141.2	400	−106.8
G. Rb	1.00	297	400	620

(2) Use the data of Table 11-1 to determine the vapor pressure at the given temperature and the temperature needed to attain the given vapor pressure for each of the following liquids.

A. methanol, $t = 24.2°C$, $P = 15$ mmHg
B. bromine, $t = 75.8°C$, $P = 250$ mmHg
C. acetone, $t = 15.0°C$, $P = 30$ mmHg
D. $CHCl_3$, $t = 37.0°C$, $P = 300$ mmHg
E. SO_2, $t = -50.0°C$, $P = 500$ mmHg
F. HCOOH, $t = 25.0°C$, $P = 50$ mmHg
G. NH_3, $t = -50.0°C$, $P = 180$ mmHg
H. ethanol, $t = 50.0°C$, $P = 200$ mmHg

6a. Fill in the blanks in the table below. All enthalpies are in kJ/mol.

Substance	$\Delta \overline{H}_{fus}$	$\Delta \overline{H}_{vap}$	$\Delta \overline{H}_{sub}$	$\Delta \overline{H}_{sol}$	$\Delta \overline{H}_{cond}$	$\Delta \overline{H}_{dep}$
A. H_2O	6.01	44.1	______	______	______	______
B. In	______	______	______	______	−232.8	−243.5
C. LiI	______	176.9	______	______	______	−204.1
D. NaCl	______	181.8	229.0	______	______	______
E. LiBr	20.1	______	______	______	−158.6	______
F. HCOOH	______	41.4	60.4	______	______	______
G. BeO	______	______	725.1	−56.6	______	______

7. A. Given the following data for hydrogen, roughly sketch its phase diagram and label all regions. Solid vapor pressure at 10 K: 0.001 atm; normal melting point: 14.01 K; normal boiling point: 20.38 K; triple point: 13.95 K, 0.07 atm; critical point: 33.3 K, 12.8 atm.

B. Does H_2 freeze at 9.0 atm pressure? If so, what is the freezing point? If not, why not?
C. Does H_2 boil at 14.0 atm pressure? If so, what is the boiling point? If not, why not?
D. Does solid H_2 float on the liquid? Why or why not?
E. For hypothetical compound W, the vapor pressure of liquid and solid are as follows.

t, °C (solid)	−10	10	30	50	
P, atm (solid)	0.10	0.20	0.30	0.40	
t, °C (liquid)	50	150	200	250	300
P, atm (liquid)	0.40	0.64	0.76	0.88	1.00

The melting point of the solid varies with pressure as follows.

P, atm	0.40	1.00	1.60	2.20
t, °C	50	49.5	49.0	48.5

Above $t = 300°C$ liquid and vapor are indistinguishable. Sketch the phase diagram of compound W and label all points and regions.

F. Does compound W freeze at 0.90 atm pressure? If so, what is the freezing point? If not, why not?
G. Does compound W boil at 0.80 atm pressure? If so, estimate the boiling point. If not, why not?
H. Does compound solid W float on the liquid? Why or why not?

Refer to *Figures 11-12 and 11-13 in the text* and the two phase diagrams you have drawn to describe the phase changes which occur giving the approximate temperature and pressure for each change, under the following conditions.

I. H_2O $P_1 = 2$ mmHg to $P_2 = 100$ atm at $T = 273.155$ K (fixed)
J. H_2O $T_1 = 253$ K to $T_2 = 423$ K at $P = 3.00$ atm (fixed)
K. CO_2 $T_1 = 194.7$ K to $T_2 = 473.2$ K at $P = 2.00$ atm (fixed)
L. CO_2 $T_1 = 194.7$ K to $T_2 = 473.2$ K at $P = 6.40$ atm (fixed)
M. CO_2 $T_1 = 173.2$ K to $T_2 = 555.1$ K at $P = 80.0$ atm (fixed)
N. H_2 $T_1 = 5.0$ K to $T_2 = 40.1$ K at $P = 1.00$ atm (fixed)
O. H_2 $P_1 = 0.001$ atm to $P_2 = 10.0$ atm at $T = 14.0$ K (fixed)
P. W $P_1 = 0.10$ atm to $P_2 = 2.00$ atm at $T = 322.4$ K (fixed)
Q. W $T_1 = 273.0$ to $T_2 = 573.2$ at $P = 0.80$ atm (fixed)

8. For each of the following groups of molecules, state which has the largest and which has the smallest value of the indicated property.

A. Boiling point: Xe, HI, H_2Te

B. Heat of vaporization: PF_3, NCl_3 BCl_3
C. Vapor pressure at −25°C: HCl, HBr, HI
D. Vapor pressure at −10°C: CH_4, SiH_4, GeH_4
E. Boiling point: AlF_3, PF_3, ClF_3
F. Heat of vaporization: C_3H_8OH, CH_3OH, C_2H_5OH
G. Boiling point: H_2O, NH_3, HF
H. Heat of vaporization: Cl_2, I_2, Br_2
I. Vapor pressure at −10°C: CH_4, CF_4, CCl_4
J. Boiling point: CCl_3F, GeF_4, Br_2

11. For each of the following groups of compounds, state which has the largest and which the smallest value of the indicated property. (Remember that lattice energies are exothermic!)
A. Lattice energy: MgS, SrS, CaS
B. Melting point: NaH, NaBr, NaCl
C. Solubility (*M*): $CaCl_2$, CaI_2, SrI_2
D. Melting point: MgS, Na_2S, Na_3P
E. Solubility (*M*): CaF_2, CaO, $CaCl_2$
F. Lattice energy: $MgCO_3$, Na_2CO_3, $Al_2(CO_3)_2$
G. Melting point: LiF, LiI, LiCl
H. Lattice energy: K_2S, Na_2S, MgS
I. Solubility: $Pb(NO_3)_2$, $Mg(NO_3)_2$, $Ca(NO_3)_2$
J. Melting point: RbCl, $InCl_3$, $SrCl_2$

QUIZZES (20 minutes each)

Choose the best answer to each question.

Quiz A

1. The property of a liquid that does *not* depend on intermolecular forces is (a) surface tension; (b) boiling point; (c) vapor pressure; (d) heat of vaporization; (e) none of these.
2. 31.4 g of a solid requires 1.42 kJ of heat to melt. The solid has a mole weight of 154 g/mol. What is its heat of fusion in kJ/mol? (a) (1.42/154)(31.4); (b) (1.42/31.4)154; (c) (1.42/154)/31.4; (d) (1.42)(154)(31.4); (e) none of these.
3. In the phase diagram at right, point *A* is called the (a) triple point; (b) critical point; (c) melting point; (d) boiling point; (e) none of these.

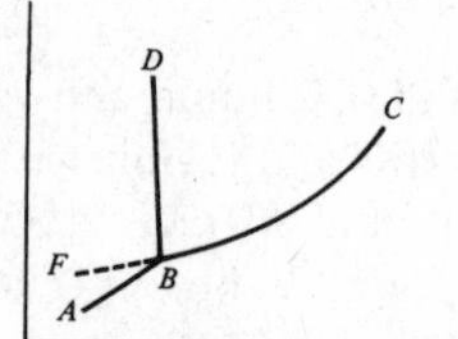

4. A liquid is in equilibrium with its vapor. If some of the vapor is allowed to escape, what is the *immediate* result? (a) vaporization rate decreases; (b) condensation rate decreases; (c) vaporization rate increases; (d) condensation rate increases; (e) none of these.
5. The process in which a solid is transformed into a vapor is called (a) vaporization; (b) sublimation; (c) gasification; (d) condensation; (e) none of these.
6. The vapor pressure of tetrachloroethene is given at four different temperatures. Which temperature is the normal boiling point? (a) 40.1°C = 40 torr; (b) 61.3°C = 100 torr; (c) 100.0°C = 400 torr; (d) 120.8°C = 760 torr; (e) none of these.
7. For anions of fixed size, which type of hole is the smallest? (a) tetrahedral; (b) octahedral; (c) hexagonal; (d) cubic; (e) cannot be determined.
8. 3.42 g of a liquid of mole weight 100.0 g/mole vaporizes when 42.0 L of inert gas at 300 K is bubbled through. The vapor pressure of the liquid in mmHg is (a) (3.42/100.0)(0.0821)(760); (b) (3.42/100.0)(8.314)(760)(300/42.0); (c) (3.42)(0.0821)(300/42.0); (d) insufficient information; (e) none of these.

Quiz B

1. A has a higher normal boiling point than B. This could be due to any of the factors below *except* the higher (a) mole weight of A; (b) vapor pressure of A; (c) intermolecular attractions of A; (d) vapor pressure of B; (e) none of these.
2. The liquid with the highest vapor pressure at $-50°C$ is which of the following? (a) Xe; (b) Ne; (c) Cl_2; (d) F_2; (e) CCl_4.
3. In the phase diagram at right, point H represents (a) the melting point; (b) the normal melting point; (c) the boiling point; (d) the normal boiling point; (e) none of these.

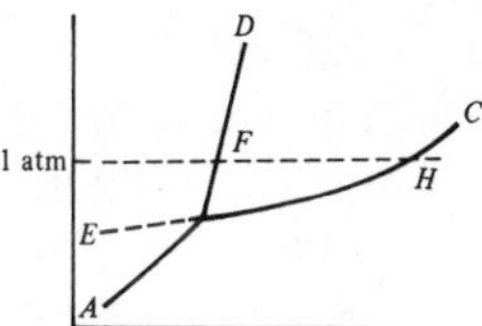

4. The process in which a gas is changed into a solid is called (a) vaporization; (b) condensation; (c) solidification; (d) deposition; (e) none of these.
5. A liquid is in equilibrium with its vapor. A thin layer of nonvolatile oil is poured on top of the liquid. What will now occur? (a) vaporization rate decreases; (b) condensation rate decreases; (c) vaporization rate increases; (d) condensation rate increases; (e) none of these.
6. The temperature at which a solid sublimes at 760 torr is called (a) the boiling point; (b) the normal boiling point; (c) the melting point; (d) the normal melting point; (e) none of these.
7. A face-centered cubic cell contains all or part of how many different atoms? (a) 2; (b) 6; (c) 8; (d) 14; (e) none of these.
8. 105 kJ of heat vaporizes what mass of a liquid if its mole weight is 86.0 g/mol and its molar heat of vaporization is 55.2 kJ/mol? (a) (105/55.2)/86.0; (b) (105/55.2) × 86.0; (c) (105/86.0) × 55.2; (d) (86.0/55.2)/105; (e) none of these.

Quiz C

1. The factor which has the largest effect on vapor pressure is (a) liquid surface area; (b) molecular dipole moment; (c) presence of hydrogen bonding; (d) liquid mole weight; (e) volume available for the vapor.
2. Which intermolecular force of the following is the strongest? (a) London; (b) hydrogen bonding; (c) dipole–dipole; (d) exchange; (e) all have the same strength.
3. In the phase diagram at right, point C is called (a) the critical point; (b) the triple point; (c) the melting point; (d) the boiling point; (e) none of these.

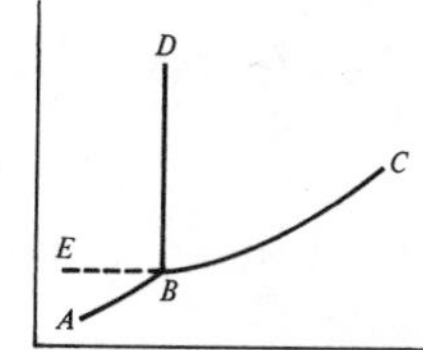

4. At the boiling point, the vapor pressure over a liquid is (a) 760 mmHg; (b) steadily decreasing; (c) constantly fluctuating; (d) atmospheric pressure; (e) none of these.
5. A liquid is in equilibrium with its vapor. Some vapor is allowed to escape. After equilibrium has been reestablished at the same temperature it is true that the (a) vaporization rate is greater. (b) vaporization rate is less; (c) condensation rate is greater; (d) condensation rate is less; (e) none of these.
6. The process in which a liquid is changed into gas is called (a) vaporization; (b) sublimation; (c) gasification; (d) condensation; (e) none of these.
7. 6.12 g of a solid with a mole weight of 79.0 g/mol is melted with 3.76 kJ of heat. The molar heat of fusion of the solid in kJ/mol is (a) (3.76/6.12) × 79.0; (b) (3.76/6.12)/79.0; (c) (3.76/79.0) × 6.12 (d) 3.76 × 6.12 × 79.0; (e) none of these.
8. The lowest melting solid of the following is (a) MgO; (b) NaCl; (c) CaS; (d) AlN; (e) Li_2O.

Quiz D

1. The mole weight of a compound directly affects all of the following *except* (a) vapor pressure of liquid; (b) vapor density; (c) solid density; (d) vapor pressure of solid; (e) none of these.

2. 4.25 kJ of heat is sufficient to melt 42 g of a solid of mole weight 210 g/mol. What is the heat of fusion of this solid in kJ/mol? (a) (4.25/210)(42); (b) (4.25/42)(210); (c) (4.25/210)/42; (d) (4.25)(210)(42); (e) none of these.
3. When the vapor pressure over a liquid equals atmospheric pressure, the temperature of the liquid equals (a) 100°C; (b) the boiling point; (c) the normal boiling point; (d) the vaporization point; (e) none of these.
4. Which of the following labels phases A, B, and C correctly in the phase diagram at right? (a) A = solid, B = gas, C = liquid; (b) B = liquid, A = gas, C = solid; (c) A = gas, B = solid, C = liquid; (d) C = gas, A = liquid, B = solid; (e) none of these.

A B C

5. The heat of sublimation equals the negative of the heat of (a) condensation; (b) vaporization; (c) solidification; (d) fusion; (e) none of these.
6. A liquid is in equilibrium with its vapor. Suddenly the pressure on the vapor is doubled. What will now occur? (a) vaporization rate increases; (b) condensation rate decreases; (c) condensation rate increases; (d) vaporization rate decreases; (e) none of these.
7. The highest melting solid of the following is (a) Mg_3N_2; (b) Ca_3P_2; (c) CaO; (d) NaCl; (e) $BaSO_4$.
8. The liquid with the highest vapor pressure at 232 K of the following is (a) H_2O; (b) NH_3; (c) CH_3OH; (d) CCl_3F; (e) CF_4.

SAMPLE TEST (20 minutes)

1. The normal boiling point of acetone is 56.2°C and the molar heat of vaporization is 32.0 kJ/mol. At what temperature will acetone boil under a pressure of 50.0 mmHg?
2. Sketch a face-centered cubic cell.
3. Describe the processes which lead to the formation of exchange forces within molecules.
4. You have the following ions available:

cations: Na^+, K^+, Ca^{2+}, Mg^{2+}
anions: F^-, Br^-, O^{2-}, S^{2-}

What cation and which anion would you expect to combine to form the highest melting compound? Carefully explain your choice.

Chapter 12

Mixtures

REVIEW OF OBJECTIVES

1. Explain how the relative forces between molecules predict whether an ideal solution, a nonideal solution, or a heterogeneous mixture will form.

1. An ideal solution is one in which the two components act as if each were still pure. The volume of the solution is the sum of the volumes of the two components. No heat is absorbed or given off when the solution is formed. When forces between like molecules (A ↔ A and B ↔ B) are about the same as the forces between unlike molecules (A ↔ B), the solution formed is ideal.

Often the "like" forces (A ↔ A and B ↔ B) are not the same as the unlike forces (A ↔ B).

2. When the "unlike" forces are stronger, molecules in solution are more strongly attracted than when pure. The two components will mix to form a solution and the extra energy is given off as heat; $\Delta \bar{H}_{soln} < 0$.

3. When the "unlike" forces are weaker than the "like" ones, the molecules in solution are less strongly attracted than when pure. Energy must be added during the solution process; $\Delta \bar{H}_{soln} > 0$.

4. When the difference between "like" and "unlike" forces is too large a solution does not form and a heterogeneous mixture is produced.

★ **2. Know and be able to use percent concentration units: % (vol/vol), % (mass/mass), and % (mass/vol).**

Many different ways of expressing concentration exist because of the many different ways in which solutions are used. Although chemists are usually concerned with moles of substance, others are often interested in weights or masses. Most concentration units express the quantity of solute in a certain quantity of solution. We can measure out solution and know how much of the solute we have.

All types of concentration calculations will be much easier if you use the following general technique:

(1) Write the definition of the concentration you are using. For example, the definition of % (mass/mass) is

$$\% (m/m) = \frac{\text{mass of solute}}{\text{mass of solution}} \times 100$$

(2) Determine the quantity of solute given in the statement of the problem and use this as the numerator.

(3) Determine the quantity of either solution or solvent as required by the definition, and use this as the denominator.

(4) Use the conversion factor method to separately change the units of numerator and denominator to agree with those given in the definition.

EXAMPLE 12-1 A solution of ethylene glycol in water contains 1.73 gal of ethylene glycol in 20.0 gal of solution. The solution has a density of 1.0119 g/cm^3. Ethylene glycol has a density of 1.1108 g/cm^3 and water has a density of 1.0000 g/cm^3. Ethylene glycol's mole weight is 62.07 g/mol and that of water is 18.02 g/mol. Compute the (a) % (vol/vol), (b) % (mass/vol), and (c) % (mass/mass) of this solution.

(a) $\dfrac{1.73 \text{ gal solute}}{20.0 \text{ gal solution}} \times 100 = 8.65\% \text{ (vol/vol)}$

(b) $\dfrac{1.73 \text{ gal solute} \times 4 \text{ qt/gal} \times 946 \text{ cm}^3\text{/qt} \times 1.1108 \text{ g/cm}^3}{20.0 \text{ gal solution} \times 4 \text{ qt/gal} \times 946 \text{ cm}^3\text{/qt}} \times 100 = 9.61\% \text{ (mass/vol)}$

(c) $\dfrac{1.73 \text{ gal solute} \times 4 \text{ qt/gal} \times 946 \text{ cm}^3\text{/qt} \times 1.1108 \text{ g/cm}^3}{20.0 \text{ gal solution} \times 4 \text{ qt/gal} \times 946 \text{ cm}^3\text{/qt} \times 1.0119 \text{ g/cm}^3} \times 100 = 9.50\% \text{ (mass/mass)}$

2a. Use the definitions of molarity and molality.

The two concentration units most frequently used by chemists are molarity and molality.

$$\text{molality } (m) = \frac{\text{mol solute}}{\text{kg solvent}} \qquad [1]$$

$$\text{molarity } (M) = \frac{\text{mol solute}}{\text{liter solution}} \qquad [2]$$

Molality is convenient for freezing-point depression and boiling-point elevation measurements as it does not change with temperature. Molarity is valuable when one wishes to mix two solutions together in order to react the solutes with each other. To obtain a certain amount of solute, in moles, one merely measures out a definite volume of solution.

EXAMPLE 12-2 What are (a) the molarity and (b) the molality of the ethylene glycol solution of Example 12-1?

(a) $$\text{Molarity} = \frac{1.73 \text{ gal solute} \times 4 \text{ qt/gal} \times 946 \text{ cm}^3\text{/qt} \times 1.1108 \text{ g/cm}^3 \times \text{mol}/62.07 \text{ g}}{20.0 \text{ gal solution} \times 4 \text{ qt/gal} \times 946 \text{ cm}^3\text{/qt} \times \text{L}/1000 \text{ cm}^3}$$

$$= \frac{117 \text{ mol solute}}{75.7 \text{ L solution}} = 1.55\ M$$

(b) To determine molality, we need the mass of the solvent.

$$\text{solution mass} = 75.7 \text{ L} \times \frac{1000 \text{ cm}^3}{\text{L}} \times \frac{1.0119 \text{ g}}{\text{cm}^3} \times \frac{\text{kg}}{1000 \text{ g}} = 76.6 \text{ kg soln}$$

$$= 75.7 \text{ L} \times \frac{1.0119 \text{ kg}}{\text{L}} = 76.6 \text{ kg soln}$$

$$\text{solute mass} = 117 \text{ mol solute} \times \frac{62.07 \text{ g}}{\text{mol}} \times \frac{\text{kg}}{1000 \text{ g}} = 7.27 \text{ kg solute}$$

$$\text{solvent mass} = \text{solution mass} - \text{solute mass} = 76.6 \text{ kg} - 7.27 \text{ kg} = 69.3 \text{ kg solvent}$$

$$\text{molality} = \frac{117 \text{ mol solute}}{69.3 \text{ kg solvent}} = 1.69\ m$$

Notice in part (a) that the units of solvent and solution volumes are not important, since both volumes are converted to cm^3. If the calculation is set up using the conversion factor method, unnecessary operations stand out.

Take care not to confuse concentration units, such as molarity, with amounts of material (moles).

2b. Use the definitions of mole fraction and mole percent.

Mole fraction is defined as the moles of solute divided by the total moles of solution. If n_A is the symbol for number of moles of substance A, then

$$\chi_A = \frac{n_A}{n_A + n_B + \cdots} = \text{mole fraction of A in solution} \qquad [3]$$

EXAMPLE 12-3 What is the mole fraction of ethylene glycol in the solution of Example 12-2?

$$n_{\text{EtGly}} = 117 \text{ mol}$$

$$n_{\text{H}_2\text{O}} = 69.3 \text{ kg} \times \frac{1000 \text{ g}}{\text{kg}} \times \frac{\text{mol H}_2\text{O}}{18.02 \text{ g H}_2\text{O}} = 3846 \text{ mol H}_2\text{O}$$

$$\chi_{\text{EtGly}} = \frac{n_{\text{EtGly}}}{n_{\text{EtGly}} + n_{\text{H}_2\text{O}}} = \frac{117 \text{ mol}}{117 \text{ mol} + 3846} = 0.0296$$

The mole percent is one hundred times the mole fraction.

$$\text{mol \% EtGly} = 2.96\%$$

3. Distinguish among unsaturated, saturated, and supersaturated solutions and describe how a solute may be purified by recrystallization.

An unsaturated solution can dissolve more solute. A saturated holds the maximum amount of the solute that it can at equilibrium. A supersaturated solution holds more than it can at equilibrium. If one adds solute to an unsaturated solution, some solute dissolves. If solute is added to a saturated solution, the amount of undissolved solute will not change. If solute is added to a supersaturated solution, the amount of *undissolved* solute will increase.

A solute may be purified by recrystallization. The temperature is lowered until solute precipitates. The crystalline solute then is redissolved in solvent to produce another saturated solution. This process is repeated as often as necessary.

4. Apply Henry's law to calculations of gas solubility as a function of pressure.

Henry's law states that the amount of gas which dissolves in solution increases as the gas pressure increases.

$$C = kP_{\text{gas}} \qquad [4]$$

There is no agreement about the units to be used for P_{gas} or for C, the concentration of gas in the solution. One must be very careful that units are used correctly when solving Henry's law problems. Henry's law data are given in Table 12-1.

TABLE 12-1
Gas solubilities in 100 cm^3 H_2O under 1.00 atm gas pressure

Gas	t, °C	Gas volume, cm^3 at STP	t, °C	Mass of gas dissolved, g
Ar	0	5.6	50	0.00536
H_2	0	2.14	50	0.000170
O_2	0	4.89	50	0.00351
O_3	0	49	0	0.105
N_2	0	2.33	40	0.00177
NO	0	7.34	60	0.00317
Kr	0	11.0	50	0.0175
CH_4	17	3.50	17	0.00250

EXAMPLE 12-4 At 0°C, 49 cm^2 of ozone measured at STP dissolves in 100 cm^3 of water under a pressure of 1.00 atm. What mass in grams of ozone (O_3) dissolves in 57.0 cm^3 of water under a pressure of 1750 mmHg?

We first compute the Henry's law constant.

$$\frac{49 \text{ cm}^3 \text{ at STP}}{100 \text{ cm}^3 \text{ H}_2\text{O}} \times \frac{\text{mol O}_3}{22414 \text{ cm}^3 \text{ at STP}} \times \frac{48.0 \text{ g O}_3}{100 \text{ cm}^3 \text{H}_2\text{O}} = k \times 1.00 \text{ atm}$$

$$k = \frac{0.105 \text{ g O}_3}{100 \text{ cm}^3 \text{ H}_2\text{O atm}}$$

Then we compute the concentration at 1750 mmHg.

$$C = \frac{0.105 \text{ g O}_3}{100 \text{ cm}^3 \text{ H}_2\text{O atm}} \times 1750 \text{ mmHg} \times \frac{1 \text{ atm}}{760 \text{ mmHg}} = \frac{0.242 \text{ g O}_3}{100 \text{ cm}^3 \text{ H}_2\text{O}}$$

Finally we compute the mass of O_3 in 57.0 cm^3 H_2O.

$$57.0 \text{ cm}^3 \text{ H}_2\text{O} \times \frac{0.242 \text{ g O}_3}{100 \text{ cm}^3 \text{ H}_2\text{O}} = 0.138 \text{ g O}_3$$

4a. Explain what a colligative property is and describe the properties of solutions which are colligative properties.

Colligative properties depend on the *number* of particles (molecules or ions) of solute in a given quantity of solution.

1. *Vapor pressure lowering* obeys Raoult's law.

$$P_A = \chi_A P_A^\circ \qquad [5]$$

P_A = the vapor pressure of substance A above a solution in which χ_A is the mole fraction of A in solution and P_A° is the vapor pressure of pure A.

2. *Boiling-point elevation.*

$$\Delta T_{bp} = K_B m \qquad [6]$$

m is the molality of the solution, ΔT_{bp} is the increase in the boiling point, and K_B is the boiling point elevation constant. K_B depends only on the solvent.

3. *Freezing-point depression.*

$$\Delta T_{fp} = K_F m \qquad [7]$$

m is the solution molality, ΔT_{fp} is the decrease in the freezing point, and K_F is the freezing-point depression constant. K_F depends only on the solvent.

4. *Osmotic pressure* obeys van't Hoff's law.

$$\pi = CRT \qquad [8]$$

C is the molarity of the solution, T is its absolute temperature, and R is the ideal gas constant.

★ **5. Apply Raoult's law. Describe the limitations and the applications of the law.**

Raoult's law, equation [5], is true only for ideal solutions. An ideal solution is described in objective 12-1 (type 1). For dilute real solutions, Raoult's law holds for the solvent but not for the solute. The two components of an ideal solution are often very similar chemically.

EXAMPLE 12-5 At 25°C, the vapor pressures of pure benzene and pure toluene are 95.1 and 28.4 mmHg, respectively. The total vapor pressure above a solution of these two liquids is 50.0 mmHg. What is the mole fraction of benzene in this solution?

The subscripts T and B stand for toluene and benzene. Then Raoult's law gives the vapor pressures.

$$P_T = \chi_T P_T^\circ = \chi_T \text{ (28.4 mmHg)} \qquad P_B = \chi_B P_B^\circ = \chi_B \text{ (95.1 mmHg)}$$

Dalton's law gives the total vapor pressure.

$$P = P_T + P_B = 50.0 \text{ mmHg}$$
$$= \chi_T(28.4 \text{ mmHg}) + \chi_B(95.1 \text{ mmHg})$$

Note that $\chi_T + \chi_B = 1$ or $\chi_T = 1 - \chi_B$.

$$P = 50.0 \text{ mmHg} = (1 - \chi_B)(28.4 \text{ mmHg}) + \chi_B(95.1 \text{ mmHg})$$
$$= 28.4 \text{ mmHg} - \chi_B(28.4 \text{ mmHg}) + \chi_B(95.1 \text{ mmHg})$$

The partial pressure of benzene is given by

$$P_B = \chi_B P_B^\circ = (0.324)(95.1 \text{ mmHg}) = 30.8 \text{ mmHg}$$

Then the mole fraction of benzene in the *vapor* is

$$\chi_{B,v} = \frac{30.8 \text{ mmHg}}{50.0 \text{ mmHg}} = 0.616$$

$\chi_B = 0.324$ is the mole fraction in the liquid and $\chi_{B,v} = 0.616$ is the mole fraction of benzene in the vapor. The plot of vapor pressure against mole fraction is called a vapor pressure diagram.

5a. Explain how liquid–vapor equilibrium in non-ideal solutions is different from that in ideal solutions.

A solution which is not ideal will not obey Raoult's law. This can occur in two ways. If the vapor pressure of the solution is *less* than Raoult's law predicts, we say the solution shows a negative deviation from Raoult's law. If the "unlike" forces are stronger than the "like" forces (see objective 12–1) the molecules are held in the liquid more strongly in the solution than in the pure liquid. The vapor pressure of such a solution is less than in an ideal solution. There is a negative deviation from Raoult's law.

If the solution's vapor pressure is *greater* than that predicted by Raoult's law, the solution is said to show a positive deviation from Raoult's law. In this case, the "unlike" forces are weaker than the "like" forces and the molecules are held in the solution liquid less well than they are in the pure liquids. There is a positive deviation from Raoult's law.

★ **6 & 7. Explain how vapor pressure lowering leads to boiling-point elevation and also to freezing-point depression. Use the equations for computing ΔT_{fp} and ΔT_{bp}.**

The vapor pressure of one component depends on its concentration. If the other component is nonvolatile, then the vapor pressure of the solution will decrease as the concentration of the nonvolatile substance increases. The presence of nonvolatile solute decreases the fraction of the surface occupied by volatile solvent molecules. Thus, the rate of vaporization is smaller, and the vapor pressure is less.

The liquid–vapor curve on a phase diagram, such as *Figure 12-9 in the text*, is lowered by the addition of a nonvolatile solute. In a similar fashion, if the solute does not freeze out with the solvent, the temperature at which the solution begins to freeze is lower than the freezing point of pure solvent. The constants K_B and K_F in equations [6] and [7] depend only on the solvent.

EXAMPLE 12-6 0.202 g of naphthalene (128 g/mol) lowers the freezing point of 10.453 g of cyclohexane by 3.08°C. 0.164 g of a solid of unknown mole weight depresses the freezing point of 12.011 g of cyclohexane by 1.28°C. What is the mole weight of the unknown?

We compute the molality of the naphthalene solution and then K_F.

$$\text{molality} = \frac{0.202 \text{ g naphthalene} \times 1 \text{ mol}/128 \text{ g}}{10.453 \text{ g cyclohexane} \times 1 \text{ kg}/100 \text{ g}} = 0.151\ m$$

$$\Delta T_{fp} = K_F m \quad or \quad K_F = \frac{\Delta T_{fp}}{m} = \frac{3.08°\text{C}}{0.151\ m} = 20.4°\text{C}/m$$

We compute the molality of the unknown solution.

$$m = \frac{\Delta T_{fp}}{K_F} = \frac{1.28°C}{20.4°C/m} = 0.0627\ m$$

From this we find the amount of solute and its mole weight

$$\text{moles solute} = 12.011 \text{ g solvent} \times \frac{\text{kg}}{1000 \text{ g}} \times \frac{0.0627 \text{ mol solute}}{\text{kg solvent}} = 7.54 \times 10^{-4} \text{ mol solute}$$

$$\text{mole weight} = \frac{0.164 \text{ g solute}}{7.54 \times 10^{-4} \text{ mol solute}} = 218 \text{ g/mol}$$

★ **8. Describe the process of osmosis and use van't Hoff's law of osmotic pressure, [8].**

Osmosis occurs when two solutions are separated by a semipermeable membrane. If the membrane were not present, the two solutions would mix and end up at some intermediate concentration. Since only the solvent can pass through the membrane, it flows from the dilute to the concentrated solution. The concentrated solution becomes more dilute. The osmotic pressure is exerted on the concentrated solution to keep the solvent from flowing across the membrane. *C* in equation [8] is the difference in concentrations and more correctly we have

$$\pi = (C_c - C_d)RT \qquad [9]$$

The subscripts stand for concentrated and dilute.

EXAMPLE 12-7 An isotonic solution has a concentration of 0.308 *M*. What osmotic pressure develops when a living cell (which basically contains such an isotonic solution) is placed in a 0.104 *M* sugar solution at 37°C?

$$\pi = (0.308 - 0.104)M \times 0.0821 \text{ L atm mol}^{-1} \text{ K}^{-1} (310 \text{ K}) = 5.19 \text{ atm } (= 76.3 \text{ lb/in.}^2)$$

★ **9. Describe how the theory of electrolytic dissociation explains the behavior of aqueous solutions of strong, weak, and nonelectrolytes including ionic concentrations and differences in values of colligative properties from the values computed by equations [6] through [9].**

Colligative property data indicate that equations [6] through [9] should be modified as shown in equations [10] through [13].

boiling-point elevation: $\Delta T_{bp} = iK_B m$ [10]

freezing-poing depression: $\Delta T_{fp} = iK_F m$ [11]

osmotic pressure: $\pi = iCRT$ [12]

$\pi = i(C_c - C_d)RT$ [13]

The value of *i*, the van't Hoff factor, depends on the type of solute and sometimes on its concentration, but not on which colligative property is measured. When the electrical conductance of aqueous solutions is measured, the solutes can be grouped into three types.

Nonelectrolytes produce aqueous solutions which have a conductance equal to that of pure water. The van't Hoff factor equals 1.

Weak electrolytes produce aqueous solutions with slightly greater conductance than that of pure water. Conductance increases as these solutions become more dilute. The van't Hoff factor is slightly larger than 1. The van't Hoff factor increases as the solution becomes more dilute, as does the molar conductance.

Strong electrolytes produce aqueous solutions with much greater conductance than that of pure water. The molar conductance of a strong electrolyte increases only very slightly as its solution becomes dilute. The van't Hoff factor of its aqueous solution is a bit less than 2, 3, 4, or some whole number larger than 1. The van't Hoff factor also increases slightly as the solution becomes dilute. The concentration trends in molar conductance and van't Hoff factor for a strong and a weak electrolyte are shown in Table 12-2.

By pointing out the similarity of the conductance trend to the van't Hoff factor trend, Svante Arrhenius showed that ions must be present in solutions of electrolytes at all times, even when they are not conducting a current.

TABLE 12-2
Variation of molar conductance (Λ)[a] and van't Hoff factor (i) with concentration for a weak electrolyte ($HC_2H_3O_2$) and a strong electrolyte (HCl)

Concentration,	HCl		$HC_2H_3O_2$	
mol/L	Λ	i	Λ	i
0.0001	425	2.00	128	1.33
0.0005	423	2.00	67.7	1.17
0.001	421	1.98	49.2	1.12
0.005	415	1.95	23.9	1.06
0.01	412	1.94	16.3	1.04
0.05	399	1.90	7.4	1.02
0.1	391	1.89	5.2	1.01

[a]The units of Λ are cm^2 mho/mol; i is unitless.

Dilute solutions have higher van't Hoff factors and molar conductances because more ions are present, according to Arrhenius. Arrhenius believed that the larger amount of water present in dilute solutions of electrolytes causes more solute to dissociate into ions.

Presently we believe that strong electrolytes dissociate *completely* into ions in aqueous solutions. All ionic compounds are strong electrolytes. A few covalent compounds also are strong electrolytes, namely HCl, HBr, HI, HNO_3, H_2SO_4, $HClO_4$, and a few others.

EXAMPLE 12-8 50.0 ml of 1.20 M NaCl is mixed with 30.0 ml of 0.800 M $CaCl_2$. What is the concentration of each ion in the final solution?

$$\text{final solution volume } (V_f) = 50.0 \text{ ml} + 30.0 \text{ ml} = 80.0 \text{ ml}$$

Compute the concentration of NaCl.

$$50.0 \text{ ml} \times \frac{1.20 \text{ mmol NaCl}}{\text{ml soln}} = 60.0 \text{ mmol NaCl}$$

$$[\text{NaCl}]_f = \frac{60.0 \text{ mmol NaCl}}{80.0 \text{ ml soln}} = 0.750\ M$$

We compute $[CaCl_2]_f$ in a different but equivalent way.

$$CaCl_2]_i\ V_i = [CaCl_2]_f\ V_f$$

$$(0.800\ M)(30.0 \text{ ml}) = [CaCl_2]_f(80.0 \text{ ml})$$

$$[CaCl_2]_f = \frac{(0.800\ M)(30.0 \text{ ml})}{80.0 \text{ ml}} = 0.300\ M$$

The only source of Ca^{2+} ions is $CaCl_2$. Thus $[Ca^{2+}] = [CaCl_2] = 0.300\ M$. likewise, the only source of Na^+ ions is NaCl and hence $[Na^+] = [NaCl] = 0.750\ N$.

But Cl^- ions are part of both solutes. Thus,

$$[Cl^-] = [Cl^- \text{ from } CaCl_2] + [Cl^- \text{ from } NaCl]$$

$$= 0.300\,M \times \frac{2 \text{ mol } Cl^-}{\text{mol } CaCl_2} + 0.750\,M \times \frac{1 \text{ mol } Cl^-}{\text{mol NaCl}} = 0.600\,M + 0.750\,M = 1.350\,M$$

10. Describe how interionic attractions in solution require modifications to Arrhenius's thoery.

We stated in objective 12–9 that all strong electrolytes dissociate into ions or ionize completely in aqueous solution. Why then are the van't Hoff factors not precisely equal to integers and why do the van't Hoff factors decrease as the solution becomes concentrated? The explanation given by Peter Debye and Erich Hŭckel is that positive and negative ions cluster around each other in aqueous solution. These clusters will be more likely to form in concentrated solutions because the ions are closer together on the average in a concentrated solution. In concentrated solutions there are more clusters, fewer particles, and the van't Hoff factor will be smaller than in dilute solutions.

11. Describe some of the properties of colloids, how colloids differ from solutions and heterogeneous mixtures, and classify colloidal mixtures.

Colloidal mixtures appear uniform to the naked eye but they are cloudy or foggy rather than clear as solutions are. Colloidal mixtures often can be coagulated by adding a solution of a strong electrolyte such as NaCl, NaOH, or HCl. This partly neutralizes the positive or negative charge which accumulates on the surface of each colloidal particle and which keeps them separated. The various types of colloids are given in *Table 12-4 in the text.* These eight types, their names, and one or two examples of each should be memorized.

DRILL PROBLEMS

2. The aqueous solution on each of the following lines is at 20°C. At 20°C the density of water (the solvent) is 0.99823 g/cm³ and the solutes all are liquids. Fill in the blanks in each line. The first line is done as an example.

Solute formula	*Volume, cm³*		*Mass, g*		*Density, g/cm³*		*Percent composition*		
	Soln	*Solute*	*Solvent*	*Soln*	*Soln*	*Solute*	*mass/mass*	*mass/mass*	*vol/vol*
CH_3COOH	88.39	12.01	77.40	90.00	1.0182	1.0491	14.00	14.26	13.59
A. CH_3COOH	____	____	____	31.16	1.0385	1.0491	30.00	____	____
B. CH_3COCH_3	50.444	3.16	47.50	____	____	0.7908	____	____	____
C. CH_3COCH_3	40.00	____	36.48	____	0.9967	0.7908	____	____	10.73
D. C_2H_5OH	134.51	____	____	____	0.8921	0.7893	____	53.53	____
E. C_2H_5OH	____	____	____	6.87	0.9820	0.7893	10.00	____	____
F. $(CH_2OH)_2$	59.441	4.87	54.60	____	____	1.1088	____	____	____
G. $(CH_2OH)_2$	120.00	____	115.64	____	1.0038	1.1088	____	____	3.63
H. HCOOH	137.994	____	____	____	1.0870	1.220	____	34.78	____
I. HCOOH	____	____	____	38.11	1.0587	1.220	24.00	____	____
J. $CHOH(CH_2OH)_2$	95.749	15.06	81.00	____	____	1.2613	____	____	____
K. $CHOH(CH_2OH)_2$	75.00	____	43.72	____	1.1209	1.2613	____	____	42.65
L. CH_3OH	83.673	____	____	____	0.8366	0.7914	____	70.27	____
M. CH_3OH	____	____	____	62.56	0.8762	0.7914	68.00	____	____

2a. Fill in the blanks on each line in the following table. All of these data are for actual aqueous solutions.

	Solute		*Solution*				
	Mol. wt. or Formula	*Number of moles*	*Volume, ml*	*Density, g/ml*	*Molarity, M*	*Molality, m*	*% by weight*
A.	$HC_2H_3O_2$	____	250.0	1.0250	3.414	____	____
B.	____	____	500.0	1.020	1.334	____	7.00
C.	$BaCl_2$	____	275.0	____	0.888	____	16.00
D.	HCl	1.270	400.0	1.0544	____	____	____
E.	____	1.245	____	1.056	2.490	____	10.00
F.	$Pb(NO_3)_2$	0.221	____	1.3059	1.104	____	____
G.	____	0.289	300.0	1.023	____	____	4.00
H.	$KHCO_3$	____	200.0	____	1.064	____	10.00
I.	KBr	____	750.0	1.107	____	____	14.00
J.	____	____	340.0	1.0402	0.907	____	6.50
K.	$NaHCO_3$	____	270.0	1.0408	____	____	6.00
L.	K_2CrO_4	0.200	____	1.172	1.207	____	____
M.	$NaNO_3$	____	750.0	____	5.043	____	34.00
N.	H_2SO_4	____	400.0	1.681	13.026	____	____
O.	NaOH	6.00	____	1.4299	____	____	40.00
P.	____	____	300.0	1.1972	5.326	____	26.00
Q.	H_3PO_4	2.047	____	1.2536	5.117	____	____
R.	CsCl	____	240.0	1.107	____	____	13.00

2b. Determine the mole fraction of the solute and the mole percent of the solvent for each solution in the table in objective 12–2a.

4. Use the data of Table 12-1 to determine the molality of each gas at each temperature under a pressure of 1.00 atm. The mass of 100 cm³ of water at each of the temperatures follows.

t, °C	0	17	40	50	60
m, kg	0.1000	0.0999	0.0992	0.0988	0.0983

Compute the pressure or the molality in solution of the gas.

A. Ar, $t = 0°C, P = 14.2$ atm
B. CH_4, $t = 17°C$, concn = 0.0120 *m*
C. O_2, $t = 50°C, P = 160$ mmHg
D. N_2, $t = 40°C$, concn = 0.000314 *m*
E. NO, $t = 60°C, P = 1000$ mmHg
F. O_3, $t = 0°C$, concn = 0.100 *m*
G. Kr, $t = 50°C, P = 1000$ mmHg
H. O_2, $t = 0°C$, concn = 0.0100 *m*
I. H_2, $t = 50°C, P = 100$ atm
J. H_2, $t = 50°C$, concn = 0.0100 *m*

5. In each of the following ideal solutions, two liquids, A and B, are mixed together. The vapor pressures of the pure liquids are P_A° and P_B° and their mole fractions in solution are χ_A and χ_B. The vapor pressure over the solution is *P*. Fill in the blanks in the table below.

	P_A, mmHg	χ_A	P_B, mmHg	χ_B	*P*, mmHg
A.	100	0.75	50	____	____
B.	180	____	60	____	125
C.	____	0.25	20	____	100
D.	140	0.30	____	____	220
E.	____	____	160	0.14	130
F.	190	____	270	0.35	____
G.	120	____	80	____	85
H.	220	____	70	____	100

7. In each line which follows, the given mass of solute (in grams) is dissolved in the mass of solvent specified. The solvent has the boiling-point elevation constant K_B and freezing-point depression constant K_F. Both constants have units of °C/molal. t_b and t_f are the boiling and freezing points of the pure solvent in °C. t'_b and t'_f are the boiling and freezing points of the solution in °C. m is the molality of the solution and MW is the mole weight of the solute in grams/mole. Fill in the blanks in the table which follows.

	Solvent					*Solute*		*Solution*		
	Mass, g	t_f, °C	t_b, °C	K_B, °C/*m*	K_F, °C/*m*	*Mass*, g	*MW*, g/mol	*m*	t'_b, °C	t'_f, °C
A.	800	16.62	117.9	3.07	3.90	17.2	____	0.201	118.52	____
B.	640	5.51	80.09	2.53	____	19.4	140	____	____	4.45
C.	750	5.68	210.81	5.24	____	____	126	0.244	____	3.97
D.	320	43.02	181.75	____	7.40	7.62	____	0.284	182.76	____
E.	500	0.00	100.00	0.512	1.86	12.7	78.2	____	____	−0.60
F.	600	6.55	80.74	2.79	19.6	____	64.1	____	81.77	____

8. In the table which follows, each line represents a solution with osmotic pressure π (mmHg), concentration C (mol/L), and temperature t (°C). V is the solution's volume (L), m the solute's mass (g), and MW is the solute's mole weight (g/mol). Fill in the blanks in each line.

	Solution				*Solute*	
	π, mmHg	C, mol/L	t,°C	V, L	*Mass*, g	*MW*, g/mol
A.	740	____	25	.250	____	75.2
B.	143	____	37	.375	1.42	____
C.	____	____	18	.800	3.14	146
D.	1476	____	20	.750	____	128
E.	476	____	23	.240	7.51	____
F.	____	____	15	.150	0.904	187
G.	1793	____	24	.400	____	207
H.	500	____	19	.500	1.37	____
I.	____	____	30	.650	3.27	209
J.	473	____	23	.450	____	150
K.	760	____	20.8	.120	0.816	____
L.	____	____	26.8	.350	2.06	314
M.	946	____	16.4	.100	____	200
N.	640	____	19.9	.175	0.943	____
O.	____	____	29.0	.180	0.0843	187

9. Solution A is mixed with Solution B. The volumes are additive. Compute the concentration of each ion in the final solution.

	Solution A			*Solution B*		
	Volume, cm^3	*Solute*	*Molarity*	*Volume*, cm^3	*Solute*	*Molarity*
A.	100	$LiNO_3$	0.241	240	$Ca(NO_3)_2$	0.618
B.	200	H_2SO_4	0.314	450	HCl	0.114
C.	400	$NaOH$	0.186	200	$Al(OH)_3$	0.916
D.	400	Na_3PO_4	0.126	150	$NaCl$	0.224
E.	620	HNO_3	1.07	180	$NaNO_3$	2.03
F.	250	$CaCl_2$	0.143	150	$MgCl_2$	0.321
G.	150	Na_2SO_4	0.187	350	$Al_2(SO_4)_3$	0.103
H.	100	Na_2SO_4	0.946	900	Na_3PO_4	0.204
I.	176	$NaBr$	0.700	224	$NaCl$	0.600
J.	894	$LiCl$	0.600	106	Li_2SO_4	0.800

QUIZZES (20 minutes each)

Choose the best answer to each question.

Quiz A

1. Moles of solute per mole of solvent is a definition of (a) mole fraction; (b) molarity; (c) molality; (d) solubility; (e) none of these.
2. A solution in which a relatively large amount of solute has been dissolved is called (a) unsaturated; (b) saturated; (c) supersaturated; (d) dilute; (e) none of these.
3. The concentration unit used in Raoult's law calculations is (a) mole fraction; (b) percent by weight; (c) molarity; (d) molality; (e) none of these.
4. 8.72 ml of a 14.0 *M* solution is diluted to 50.0 ml. What is the molarity of the resulting solution? (a) 14.0(8.72/50.0); (b) (14.0/8.72)/50.0; (c) 14.0(50.0/8.72); (d) 14.0(50.0)(8.72); (e) none of these.
5. 141 ml of 0.175 *M* solution of silver nitrate contains how many grams of solute? (a) (141/1000)(0.175)(277.8); (b) (141)(0.175)(153.9); (c) (141/169.9)(0.175); (d) (141/1000)(0.175)(169.9); (e) none of these.
6. Hexane's normal boiling point is 68.7°C. What is the mole fraction of nonvolatile solute in a hexane solution which has a vapor pressure of 600 mmHg at this temperature? (a) 68.7/600; (b) 600/760; (c) 160/600; (d) 160/760; (e) none of these.
7. 0.23 mol of solute depresses the freezing point of 267 g of solvent by 6.15°C. What is K_F for the solvent? (a) 6.15/(0.23/267); (b) 6.15/(0.23 × 0.267); (c) (6.15)(0.23/0.267); (d) (6.15)(0.23)(0.267); (e) none of these.
8. 8.40 g (0.20 mol) NaF dissolves in 153 g (8.50 mol) of water. What is the mole fraction of NaF in the solution? (a) 0.20/(8.50 + 0.20); (b) 0.20/(153/1000); (c) [8.40/(153 + 8.40)](100); (d) (8.40/153)(100); (e) none of these.

Quiz B

1. Moles of solute per liter of solution is a definition of (a) mole fraction; (b) molarity; (c) molality; (d) solubility; (e) none of these.
2. A solution which has the capacity to dissolve more solute is called (a) unsaturated; (b) saturated; (c) supersaturated; (d) concentrated; (e) none of these.
3. Which of the following can be most directly linked to the lowering of the vapor pressure by a nonvolatile solute? (a) osmotic pressure; (b) freezing-point depression; (c) boiling-point elevation; (d) solubility; (e) none of these.
4. 52.5 ml of a solution was diluted to a volume of 6.25 L and then had a concentration of 0.0316 *M*. What is the molarity of the concentrated solution? (a) 0.0316(52.5/6.25); (b) 0.0316(6.25/52.5); (c) 0.0316(52.5/6250); (d) 0.0316(52.5)(6.25); (e) none of these.
5. At 34.9°C ethanol has a vapor pressure of 100 mmHg. What is the mole fraction of *nonvolatile solute* in a solution with a vapor pressure of 92 mmHg at this temperature? (a) 34.9/100; (b) 92/34.9; (c) 100/92; (d) 92/100; (e) none of these.
6. 87.5 L of a 3.17 *M* solution of hydrochloric acid contains how many grams of solute? (a) (87.5/1000)(3.17)(36.5); (b) (87.5)(3.17)(52.5); (c) (87.5)(3.17)(36.5); (d) (87.5/1000)(3.17)(68.5); (e) none of these.
7. 17.4 L of a 0.623 *M* starch solution displays what osmotic pressure in atmospheres at 75°C? (a) (17.4)(0.623)(0.0821)(348); (b) (0.623)(0.0821)(75); (c) (17.4)(0.623)(75); (d) (17.4)(0.623/0.0821)(348); (e) none of these.
8. 23.4 g (0.40 mol) NaCl dissolves in 108 g (6.0 mol) of water. What is the molality of the solution? (a) 0.40/(0.40 + 6.0); (b) 0.40/(108/1000); (c) [23.4/(23.4 + 108)](100); (d) (23.4/108)(100); (e) none of these.

Quiz C

1. Moles of solute per liter of solvent is a definition of (a) mole fraction; (b) molality; (c) molarity; (d) solubility; (e) none of these.

2. The following always form solutions (if they do not react chemically) (a) a gas in a liquid; (b) a solid in a liquid; (c) two liquids; (d) two gases; (e) none of these.
3. Which of the following is not a colligative property? (a) freezing-point depression; (b) boiling-point elevation; (c) osmotic pressure; (d) solubility; (e) none of these.
4. How many ml of 6.25 M solution can be produced using 57.5 ml of 16.4 M solution? (a) (57.5)(6.25)(16.4); (b) 57.5(6.25/16.4); (c) 57.5(16.4/6.25); (d) 16.4(6.25/57.5); (e) none of these.
5. 81.2 g of cesium chloride (168.4 g/mol) is enough solute for how many ml of 4.00 M solution? (a) (81.2/168.4)/4.00; (b) (81.2/168.4)(4.00/1000); (c) (81.2/4.00)(168.4)(1000); (d) (81.2)(4.00)(168.4/1000); (e) none of these.
6. Acetic acid's normal boiling point is 118.1°C. What is the vapor pressure in mmHg of a solution in which there is 0.35 mol of nonvolatile solute to every mole of acetic acid at this temperature? (a) 760(0.35/1.35); (b) 760(0.35/1.00); (c) 118.1/760; (d) 760/118.1; (e) none of these.
7. 0.25 mol of a nonvolatile, nonionic solute dissolved in 300 g of water ($K_F = 1.86$) will lower the freezing point how many degrees? (a) (1.86)(0.25)(1000/300); (b) (1.86/0.25)(300/1000); (c) (1.86)(0.25)(300/1000); (d) (0.25/1.86)(1000/300); (e) none of these.
8. 23.4 g (0.30 mol) of calcium fluoride dissolves in 189 g (10.5 mol) of water. What is the weight percent of calcium fluoride in the solution? (a) 0.30(0.40 + 6.0); (b) 0.30(189/1000); (c) [23.4/(189 + 23.4)](100); (d) (23.4/189)(100); (e) none of these.

Quiz D

1. Moles of solute per mole of solution is a definition of (a) percent by weight; (b) mole fraction; (c) molality; (d) molarity; (e) none of these.
2. A homogeneous mixture is a definition of all (a) solvents; (b) solutes; (c) solutions; (d) fluids; (e) none of these.
3. Colligative properties are similar in that they all (a) were discovered in college laboratories; (b) are due to solvent molecules linked together; (c) have no harmful side effects; (d) depend on the number of particles in solution; (e) none of these.
4. What volume (in liters) of 0.0325 M solution can be produced from 41.6 ml of 0.742 M solution? (a) 41.6(0.742/0.0325); (b) 41.6(0.325/0.742); (c) (41.6/1000)(0.0325/0.742); (d) (1000/41.6)(0.742/0.0325); (e) none of these.
5. 864 ml of solution contains 143.9 g of sodium phosphate (164.0 g/mol). What is the molarity of the solution? (a) (164.0/143.9)(864/1000); (b) (143.9/164.0)(864/1000); (c) (143.9/164.0)(1000/864); (d) (164.0/143.9)(1000/864); (e) none of these.
6. 841 ml of a 0.625 M sugar solution displays what osmotic pressure in atmospheres at 100°C? (a) (0.625)(0.0821)(100); (b) (0.625)(0.841)(0.0821)(100); (c) (0.625)(0.841)(0.0821)(373); (d) (0.625)(0.0821)(373); (e) none of these.
7. 0.87 mol of solute depresses the freezing point of 742 g of solvent by 0.43 degrees. What is K_F for the solvent? (a) (0.43)(0.87/742); (b) (0.43)(0.87) (0.742); (c) 0.43/(0.87/742); (d) 0.43/(0.87/0.742); (e) none of these.
8. 15.9 g (0.15 mol) of sodium carbonate dissolves in 81 g (4.50 mol) of water. What is the weight percent of sodium carbonate in the solution? (a) [15.9/(15.9 + 81)](100); (b) (15.9/81)(100); (c) 0.15/(81/1000); (d) 0.15/(0.15 + 4.50); (e) none of these.

SAMPLE TEST (20 minutes)

1. A solution contains 750 g of ethanol (46.0 g/mol) and 85.0 g of sucrose (180.0 g/mol). The volume of the solution is 810.0 ml. Determine the values of
   a. the density of the solution
   b. the percent of sucrose in the solution
   c. the mole fraction of sucrose
   d. the molality of the solution
   e. the molarity of the solution
2. What volume of ethylene glycol ($C_2H_6O_2$, 62.0 g/mol, density = 1.12 g/cm^3) must be added to 20.0 L of water (H_2O, 18.0 g/mol, density = 1.00 g/cm^3) to produce a solution freezing at 14.0°F? The freezing-point depression constant of water is 1.86°C/m.

Chemical Kinetics

REVIEW OF OBJECTIVES

★ **1. Determine the exact rate of a chemical reaction by using a tangent line to the concentration vs. time curve for a chemical reaction.**

A tangent line is drawn to the concentration vs. time curve at the time for which one wishes to know the rate. This straight line should "follow" the curve as far as possible. The slope is then computed using two widely separated points.

$$\text{Slope} = \frac{\Delta\,[\text{graphed species}]}{\Delta t} = \frac{\text{concentration at time } t_1 - \text{concentration at time } t_2}{t_1 - t_2} \qquad [1]$$

2. Determine the initial rate of a chemical reaction, graphically or by calculation.

The graphical method of determining initial rates involves drawing a tangent line at the point where time, $t = 0$. One can also determine the initial rate by calculation. There are two data points: the initial concentration (that at $t = 0$) and the concentration a very short time later. One computes the rate as one does the slope of the tangent line.

2a. Know the meaning of reaction order and use the rate law to determine the order of a chemical reaction.

The law of mass action states that the rate of a chemical reaction depends on the concentrations of the reactants. The reaction rate of

$$C_2H_4Br_2 + 3\ KI \rightarrow C_2H_4 + 2\ KBr + KI_3$$

is given by

$$\text{rate} = -\frac{\Delta[C_2H_4Br_2]}{\Delta t} = k[C_2H_4Br_2]^m\,[KI]^n$$

where m and n are determined by experiment. In this case $m = 1$ and $n = 1$. Thus, this reaction is first order in $[C_2H_4Br_2]$ (since $m = 1$) and first order in [KI] (since $n = 1$). The reaction is said to be second order overall (since $m + n = 2$). We also say that this is a second-order reaction. The overall order is the sum of the orders of the various components.

★ **3. Apply the method of initial rates to determine the rate law for a reaction.**

We reviewed the determination of initial rates by two methods in objective 13–2. Another general method is the study of clock reactions which produce a color change after a short period of time. The time period can be varied by changing the concentrations of the reactants. Consider the general reaction [2].

$$a\,A + b\,B \rightarrow c\,C + d\,D \qquad [2]$$

One of the products reacts to produce a color change.

$$C + \text{indicator} \rightarrow \text{colored product} \qquad [3]$$

That same product, C, will react more rapidly with yet another substance.

$$C + E \rightarrow \text{other products} \quad [4]$$

Thus, C cannot produce a color until all of E is consumed.

A typical clock reaction uses I_2 as substance C. In the reaction whose rate is to be determined, [5], I_2 is produced.

$$2\,I^- + H_2O_2 + 2\,H^+ \rightarrow I_2 + 2\,H_2O \quad [5]$$

I_2 reacts with starch to produce a deep blue color.

$$I_2 + \text{starch} \rightarrow \text{dark blue color} \quad [6]$$

A small amount of $S_2O_3^{2-}$ is added. This reacts with the I_2, regenerating I^-, as shown in equation [7].

$$2\,S_2O_3^{2-} + I_2 \rightarrow 2\,I^- + S_4O_6^{2-} \quad [7]$$

Thus reaction [6] does not occur until $S_2O_3^{2-}$ is used up. Such a small concentration of $S_2O_3^{2-}$ is present compared to $[I^-]$ and $[H_2O_2]$ that the change in those two concentrations is negligible. Data from a typical series of experiments are given in Table 13-1 where the time is the period elapsed before the color appears.

TABLE 13-1
Initial rate data for the reaction $2\,I^- + H_2O_2 + 2\,H^+ \rightarrow I_2 + 2\,H_2O$

	Initial concentration, *M*			
	$[I^-]$	$[H_2O_2]$	Time, s	Rate, mol L^{-1} s^{-1}
1.	0.015	0.015	91	1.37×10^{-5}
2.	0.030	0.015	46	2.72×10^{-5}
3.	0.045	0.015	29	4.31×10^{-5}
4.	0.045	0.025	18	6.94×10^{-5}
5.	0.045	0.033	13	9.62×10^{-5}

$[S_2O_3^{2-}] = 0.0025\,M$ and $[H^+] = 1.7 \times 10^{-5}\,M$ throughout.

The rate of the reaction is given by

$$\text{rate} = -\frac{\Delta[H_2O_2]}{\Delta t} = \frac{\Delta[I^-]}{2\Delta t} = \frac{\Delta[H^+]}{2\Delta t}$$

The stoichiometry of reactions [5] and [7] shows that

$$\text{no. mol } I^- \text{ reacted} = \text{no. mol } S_2O_3^{2-} \text{ consumed}$$

Thus,

$$\text{rate} = \frac{\Delta[S_2O_3^{2-}]}{2\Delta t}$$

Since all the $S_2O_3^{2-}$ is used up, $\Delta[S_2O_3^{2-}] = 0.0025\,M$ and Δt is the elapsed time. These data can be used to determine the order of the chemical reaction.

EXAMPLE 13-1 Use the data of Table 13-1 to determine the order of reaction [5].
By the law of mass action, we write

$$\text{rate} = k[I^-]^x [H_2O_2]^y [H^+]^z$$

We cannot determine z since $[H^+]$ is constant throughout the reaction. The order of reaction with respect to a component cannot be determined unless the concentration of that component changes. Thus, we are dealing with the simplified rate law

$$\text{rate} = k'[I^-]^x [H_2O_2]^y \qquad [8]$$

The first three lines of data in Table 13-1 can be used to determine x. (They cannot be used to determine y because $[H_2O_2]$ is the same in all three cases.) Using the first two lines, we have, by substituting in equation [8],

$$1.37 \times 10^{-5} \text{ mol L}^{-1} \text{ s}^{-1} = k' (0.015\,M)^x \ (0.015\,M)^y$$
$$2.72 \times 10^{-5} \text{ mol L}^{-1} \text{ s}^{-1} = k' (0.030\,M)^x \ (0.015\,M)^y$$

Division of these two equations one by the other gives

$$0.504 = (0.500)^x$$

The other terms cancel. Taking the logarithm of both sides yields

$$\log 0.504 = x \log 0.500 \qquad or \qquad x = 0.298/0.301 = 0.990$$

In like fashion, we use lines 5 and 3 in Table 13-1 to find y.

$$9.62 \times 10^{-5} \text{ mol L}^{-1} \text{ s}^{-1} = k' (0.045\,M)^x (0.033\,M)^y$$
$$4.31 \times 10^{-5} \text{ mol L}^{-1} \text{ s}^{-1} = k' (0.045\,M)^x (0.015\,M)^y$$
$$2.23 = (2.20)^y \qquad or \qquad y = 1.017$$

This reaction is first order in each of $[I^-]$ and $[H_2O_2]$ and second order overall.

★ **4. Use the rate law and the concentrations of the reactants to determine the specific rate constant from the reactions rate or vice versa.**

In Example 13-1 we determined, for reaction [5],

$$\text{rate} = k' \ [I^-]^1 [H_2O_2]^1 \qquad [9]$$

EXAMPLE 13-2 What is the specific rate constant, k', for reaction [5]?
We use line 3 of Table 13-1.

$$4.31 \times 10^{-5} \text{ mol L}^{-1} \text{ s}^{1} = k' (0.045\,M)(0.015\,M)$$
$$k' = 0.0639 \text{ L mol}^{-1} \text{ s}^{-1}$$

$$\text{rate} = \frac{-\Delta[H_2O_2]}{\Delta t} = (0.0639 \text{ L mol}^{-1} \text{ s}^{-1}) \ [I^-]^1 [H_2O_2]^1 \qquad [10]$$

EXAMPLE 13-3 What is the rate of reaction [5] when $[I^-] = 0.020\,M$ and $[H_2O_2] = 0.080\,M$?

$$\text{rate} = (0.0639 \text{ L mol}^{-1} \text{ s}^{-1})(0.020\,M)(0.080\,M) = 10.2 \times 10^{-4} \text{ mol L}^{-1} \text{ s}^{-1}$$

★ **5. Use rate data, equations, and graphs to establish whether a reaction is zero order, first order, or second order.**

We shall consider the general reaction A → products for which rate $= -\Delta[A]/\Delta t$.

Zero order: The rate law is $-\Delta[A]/\Delta t = k$. The concentration of A at time t is given by

$$[A]_t = [A]_0 - kt$$

If we plot $[A]_t$ against time, the result is a straight line with a slope $= -k$.

First order: The rate law is $-\Delta[A]/\Delta t = k[A]$. The concentration of A at time t is given by

$$\log [A]_t - \log [A]_0 = \log ([A]_t/[A]_0) = -kt/2.303$$

or

$$[A]_t = [A]_0 \; 10^{-kt/2.303} = [A]_0 e^{-kt} \quad \text{where } e = 2.718$$

If we plot $\log [A]_t$ against time, the result is a straight line of slope $= -k/2.303$.

Second order: The rate law is $-\Delta[A]/\Delta t = k[A]^2$. The concentration of A at time t is given by

$$1/[A]_t = 1/[A]_0 + kt$$

If we plot $1/[A]_t$ against time, the result is a straight line of slope $= k$. Three sets of data are given in Table 13-2 and each set is plotted in various ways in Figure 13-1. Notice from Figure 13-1 that the reaction involving A is first order, that involving B is zero order, and the one involving C is second order.

TABLE 13-2
Concentration-time data for the reactions A → products, B → products, C → products

Time, s	[A]	log [A]	1/[A]	[B]	log[B]	1/[B]	[C]	log[C]	1/[C]
0	1.00	0.00	1.00	1.00	0.00	1.00	1.00	0.00	1.00
25	0.78	−0.108	1.28	0.75	−0.125	1.33	0.80	−0.097	1.25
50	0.61	−0.215	1.64	0.50	−0.301	2.00	0.67	−0.174	1.49
75	0.47	−0.328	2.13	0.25	−0.602	4.00	0.57	−0.244	1.75
100	0.37	−0.432	2.70	0.00	—	—	0.50	−0.301	2.00
150	0.22	−0.658	4.55				0.40	−0.398	2.50
200	0.14	−0.854	7.14				0.33	−0.481	3.03
250	0.08	−1.097	12.5				0.29	−0.538	3.45

★ **6. Use the concept of the half-life of a reaction for zero-order, first-order, and second-order reactions.**

The half-life of a reaction is the time needed for half of the reactant to be consumed. The expressions for the half-lives of various reaction orders are as follows.

Reaction order:	zero	first	second
Half-life:	$[A]_0/2k$	$0.693/k$	$1/k[A]_0$

7. Describe the factors which affect collision frequency and account for favorable collisions.

Collision theory states that all reactions are the result of collisions between reactant molecules. For a gaseous reaction, the number of collisions in a liter each second is called the collision number, denoted Z_{AB}.

$$Z_{AB} = \text{constant } [A]\;[B]\; k_{AB} \sqrt{T} \qquad [11]$$

k_{AB} is a constant which depends on the properties of the A and B molecules. The factors are not much different for reactions in aqueous solution.

Collision theory also requires that the collisions be good ones. The molecules must be oriented correctly in order to react. Thus, only a small fraction of collisions will lead to reactions.

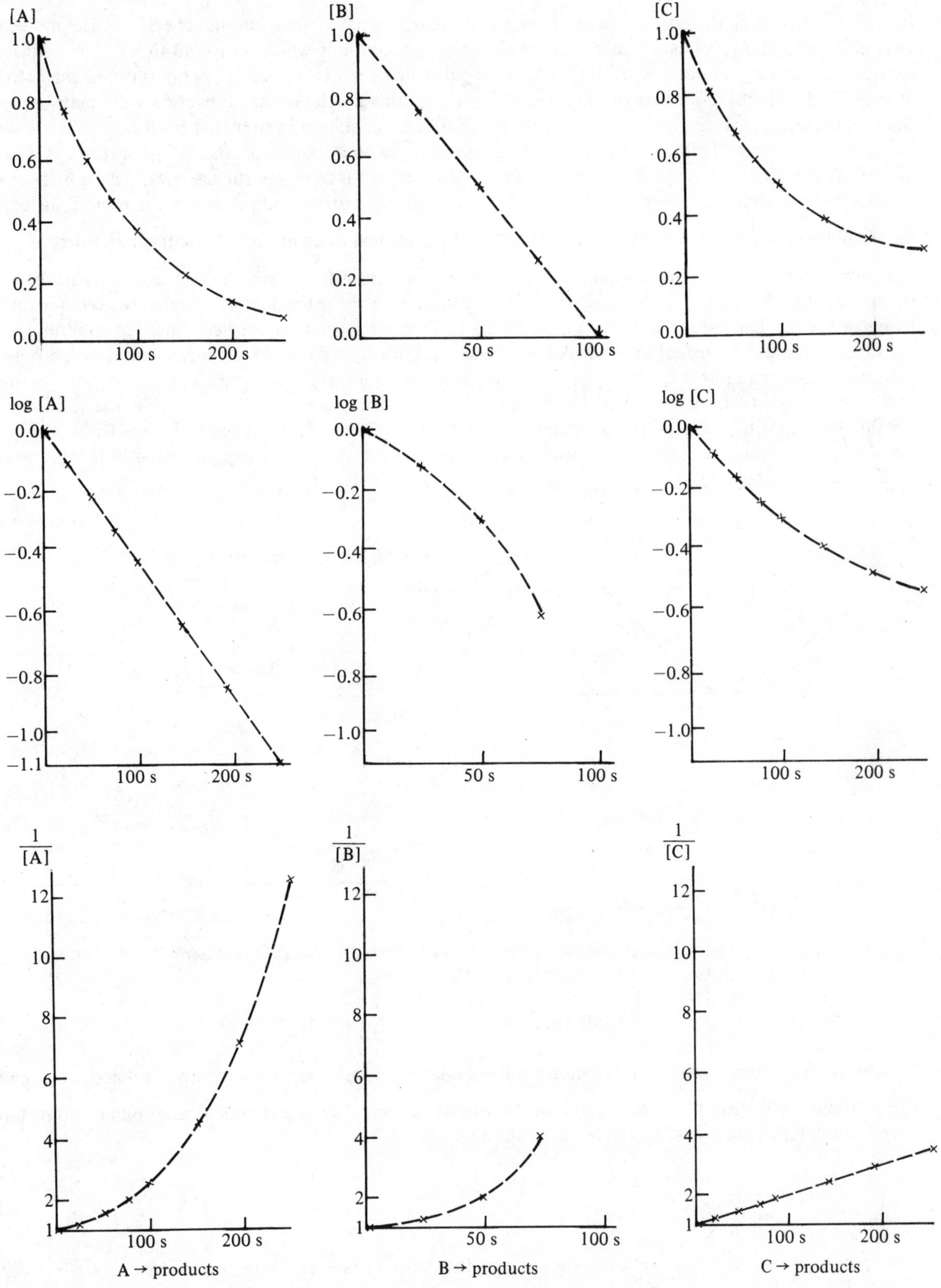

FIGURE 13-1 Graphs of the data of Table 13-2.

8. Explain the concept of activation energy.

In addition to having the correct orientation, each collision must possess enough energy for the molecules to react. Molecules repel each other because of the electron clouds which surround them. The collision energy must be large enough to overcome these repulsive forces. This needed energy is called the activation energy. If a correctly oriented collision possesses at least this much energy, a reaction will occur between the two molecules. Activation energy can be thought of as an energy barrier that must be overcome before a reaction can occur. Think for a moment of an automobile on a mountain road. The car can easily be driven off the road and down the mountainside. If a guard rail is in place, the car must have a high energy (similar to an activation energy) in order to break through the barrier and roll down the mountainside.

8a. Explain how transition-state theory extends the theoretical explanation of chemical kinetics.

Collision theory fails to explain many of the detalis of the rates of even simple reactions. Transition-state theory explains the rate of a chemical reaction by considering the intermediate or activated complex which forms as the reactants are transformed into products. Transition-state theory considers the bonding in the activated complex, the orientation of reactants necessary for it to form, the energy released when bonds are formed and required to break bonds, and the products which are produced. The theory depicts the path from reactants through activated complex to products using a reaction profile. The reaction profile for the decomposition of H_2O_2(aq), both catalyzed and uncatalyzed, is plotted in Figure 13-2. The reaction profile shows that for any exothermic reaction the reaction would occur instantly if there were no activation energy.

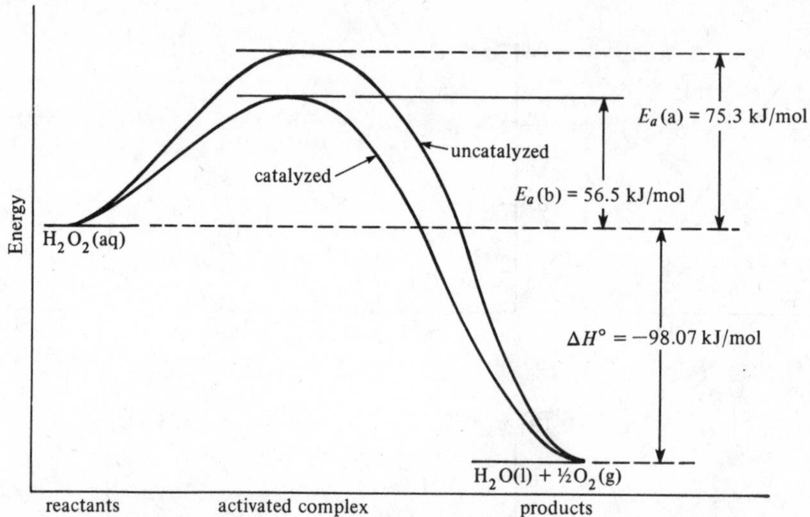

FIGURE 13-2 Reaction profiles of catalyzed and uncatalyzed reactions.
a. Uncatalyzed: $2\,H_2O_2(aq) \rightarrow 2\,H_2O(l) + O_2$
b. Catalyzed: $H_2O_2(aq) + I^-(aq) \rightarrow H_2O(l) + IO^-(aq)$
$IO^-(aq) + H_2O_2(aq) \rightarrow H_2O(l) + O_2(g) + I^-(aq)$

★ **9. Use the Arrhenius equation in calculations involving rate constants, temperatures, and activation energy.**

The Arrhenius equation [12] relates the rate constants (k_1 and k_2) of a chemical reaction at two different kelvin temperatures (T_1 and T_2) to the activation energy (E_a).

$$\ln \frac{k_1}{k_2} = 2.303 \log \frac{k_1}{k_2} = -\frac{E_a}{R}\left(\frac{1}{T_1} - \frac{1}{T_2}\right) \qquad [12]$$

The form of the Arrhenius equation is the same as that of the Clausius–Clapeyron equation (see objective 11-5). If you have forgotten how to use this type of equation, you should review the material which discusses the Clausius–Clapeyron equation.

10. Explain how a catalyst modifies the rate of a chemical reaction and how a homogenous catalyst differs from a heterogeneous one.

A *catalyst* is a substance which alters the rate of a chemical reaction while not being produced or consumed by the reaction. Some catalysts speed up reactions (positive catalysts or simply catalysts), and some slow reactions down (negative catalysts or more commonly *inhibitors*). Heterogeneous catalysts are in a different physical state of matter than is the reaction mixture (a solid catalyst in contact with a liquid or gas). All of the catalytic activity occurs on the surface of the solid (surface catalysis). Heterogeneous catalysts can be counteracted by poisons, which bond strongly to the surface. In some cases the catalyst determines the products of the reaction. An example is the reaction between $CO(g)$ and $H_2(g)$.

$$CO(g) + 3\,H_2(g) \xrightarrow{Ni} CH_4(g) + H_2O(g) \qquad [13]$$

$$CO(g) + 2\,H_2(g) \xrightarrow{ZnO/Cr_2O_3} CH_3OH(g) \qquad [14]$$

Homogeneous catalysts are in solution with the reaction mixture. For example, the decomposition of N_2O,

$$2\,N_2O(g) \xrightarrow{Cl_2} 2\,N_2(g) + O_2(g) \qquad [15]$$

is catalyzed by chlorine, as mechanism [16] shows.

$$\begin{array}{r} Cl_2(g) \rightarrow 2\,Cl(g) \\ 2 \times [N_2O(g) + Cl(g) \rightarrow N_2(g) + ClO(g)] \\ 2\,ClO(g) \rightarrow Cl_2(g) + O_2(g) \\ \hline \text{total:}\ 2\,N_2O(g) \rightarrow 2\,N_2(g) + O_2(g) \end{array} \qquad [16]$$

The decomposition of ozone is catalyzed by $N_2O_5(g)$.

$$\begin{array}{ll} \text{Mechanism:} & 2\,N_2O_5(g) \rightarrow 2\,N_2O_4(g) + O_2(g) \\ & 2 \times [O_3(g) + N_2O_4(g) \rightarrow O_2(g) + N_2O_5(g)] \\ \hline \text{Overall:} & 2\,O_3(g) \rightarrow 3\,O_2(g) \end{array}$$

Catalysts enhance the rate by lowering the activation energy of a reaction.

11. Explain the meaning of reaction mechanism, the difference between an elementary step and the overall reaction, and why a mechanism cannot be proved.

A reaction mechanism is a series of elementary steps which result in the overall reaction. For example, the catalyzed decomposition of N_2O [15] has the three reactions in [16] as its mechanism. The mechanism of a chemical reaction must meet several criteria. First, each of the elementary steps must involve at most three molecules as reactants. The steps may be unimolecular, bimolecular, or, rarely, termolecular. There is a very low chance that three molecules will collide at the same time. Second, the elementary steps must sum to the overall reaction. Finally, one must be able to derive the rate law from the mechanism. The chances that the mechanism is correct are greatly enhanced if one can detect some of the reactive intermediates of the mechanism. For example, mechanism [16] is more plausible if one can detect Cl and ClO in the reaction mixture.

★ **12. Derive the rate law from a simple mechanism using the concepts of steady-state condition and rate-determining step.**

An example of a reaction with two proposed mechanisms is equation [17].

$$2\,NO(g) + X_2(g) \rightarrow N_2O(g) + X_2O(g) \qquad [17]$$

$X_2(g)$ is $H_2(g)$, $O_2(g)$, $Cl_2(g)$, or $Br_2(g)$.
One mechanism is equations [18] using $X_2 = H_2$

$$\left.\begin{array}{ll} 2\,NO(g) \underset{k_2}{\overset{k_1}{\rightleftharpoons}} N_2O_2 & \text{(rapid)} \\ N_2O_2 + H_2 \xrightarrow{k_3} N_2O + H_2O & \text{(slow)} \end{array}\right\} \quad [18]$$

The rate of the reaction is found by using the slow step, the rate-determining step.

$$\text{rate} = \frac{\Delta[N_2O]}{\Delta t} = -\frac{\Delta[N_2O_2]}{\Delta t} = k_3[N_2O_2]\,[H_2]$$

Since N_2O_2 does not appear in the overall equation, we use the rapid equilibrium, assuming that it is proceeding as rapidly forward as reverse. This is known as the "steady-state condition."

forward rate = reverse rate

$$k_1[NO]^2 = k_2[N_2O_2] \quad \textit{or} \quad [N_2O_2] = k_1[NO]^2/k_2$$

$$\text{rate} = k_3\frac{k_1[NO]^2}{k_2}[H_2] = \frac{k_3k_1}{k_2}[NO]^2[H_2]$$

The other mechanism of reaction [17] is equations [19].

$$\left.\begin{array}{ll} NO + H_2 \underset{k_2}{\overset{k_1}{\rightleftharpoons}} NOH_2 & \text{(rapid)} \\ NOH_2 + NO \xrightarrow{k_3} N_2O + H_2O & \text{(slow)} \end{array}\right\} \quad [19]$$

This mechanism gives the same rate law as mechanism [18].

DRILL PROBLEMS

1. Concentration vs. time curves for reactions [20] and [21] are drawn in Figure 13-3.

$$C_2H_5Cl \rightarrow C_2H_4 + HCl \quad \text{at 700 K} \qquad [20]$$

$$2\,HI(g) \rightarrow H_2(g) + I_2(g) \quad \text{at 600 K} \qquad [21]$$

(1) Determine the exact rate of the indicated reaction at each of the following times.
For reaction [20]: A. 0 min B. 400 min C. 800 min D. 80 min E. 500 min F. 200 min G. 1000 min
For reaction [21]: H. 5 h I. 0 h J. 20 h K. 60 h L. 30 h M. 40 h N. 35 h

(2) Determine the time at which the indicated reactant has each of the following concentrations and determine the exact rate at this time.
For $[C_2H_5Cl]$ (reaction [20]): A. 0.90 *M* B. 0.45 *M* C. 0.30 *M* D. 0.18 *M*
For [HI] (reaction [21]): E. 3.60 *M* F. 1.80 *M* G. 0.90 *M* H. 1.20 *M*

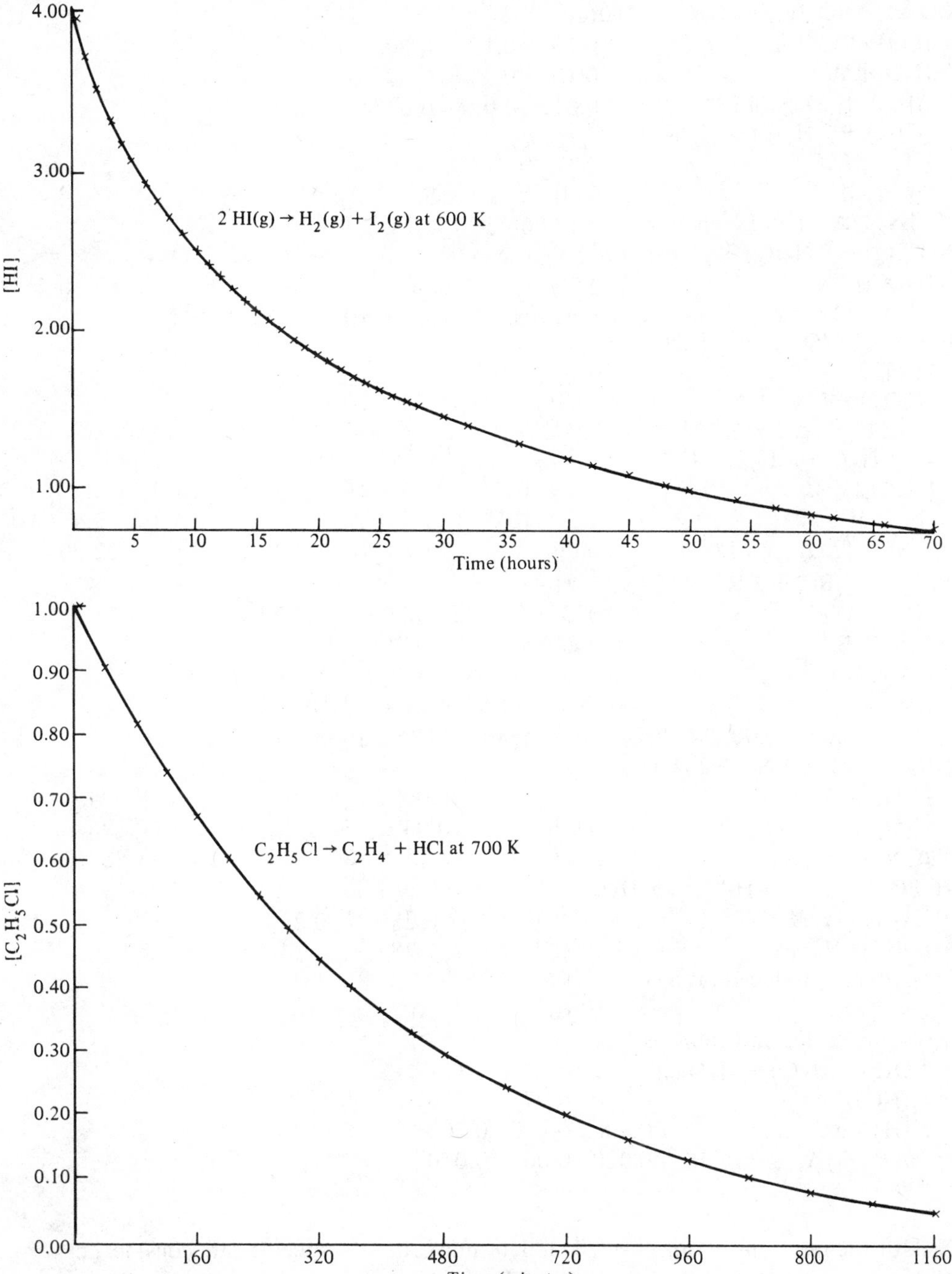

FIGURE 13-3 Data for objective 13-1 drill problems.

3. The initial rate of each of the following reactions at various concentrations of the reactant(s) is given on the following lines. Determine the rate law for each reaction (but do not determine a value for k) and state the overall order of the reaction.

A. $2\ N_2O_5(g) \rightarrow 4\ NO_2(g) + O_2(g)$

$[N_2O_5]$, M	0.170	0.340	0.680
$-\Delta[N_2O_5]/\Delta t$, mol L^{-1} h^{-1}	0.050	0.10	0.20

B. $CH_3CHO(g) \rightarrow CH_4(g) + CO(g)$

$[CH_3CHO]$, M	0.05	0.10	0.20
$-\Delta[CH_3CHO]/\Delta t$, mol L^{-1} s^{-1}	2.25×10^{-7}	9.00×10^{-7}	3.60×10^{-6}

C. $CO(g) + NO_2(g) \rightarrow CO_2(g) + NO(g)$

$[CO], M$	0.10	0.10	0.20
$[NO_2], M$	0.10	0.20	0.10
$\Delta[CO_2]/\Delta t$, mol L^{-1} s^{-1}	0.012	0.024	0.024

D. $2\ NO(g) + 2\ H_2(g) \rightarrow N_2(g) + 2\ H_2O(l)$

$[H_2], M$	0.37	0.37	0.74
$[NO], M$	0.60	1.20	1.20
$\Delta[N_2]/\Delta t$, mol L^{-1} h^{-1}	0.18	0.72	1.44

E. $NOCl(g) \rightarrow 2\ NO(g) + Cl_2(g)$ (at 27°C)

$[NOCl], M$	0.30	0.60	0.90
$\Delta[Cl_2]/\Delta t$, mol L^{-1} s^{-1}	3.60×10^{-9}	1.44×10^{-8}	3.24×10^{-8}

F. $F_2(g) + 2\ ClO_2(g) \rightarrow 2\ FClO_2(g)$

$[F_2], M$	0.10	0.10	0.20
$[ClO_2], M$	0.010	0.020	0.010
$\Delta[FClO_2]/\Delta t$, mol L^{-1} s^{-1}	0.0024	0.0048	0.0048

G. $F^- + CH_3Cl \rightarrow CH_3F + Cl^-$

$[CH_3Cl], M$	1.2×10^{-6}	2.4×10^{-6}	1.2×10^{-6}	2.4×10^{-6}
$[F^-], M$	1.2×10^{-6}	1.2×10^{-6}	2.4×10^{-6}	2.4×10^{-6}
$-\Delta[F^-]/\Delta t$, mol L^{-1} s^{-1}	0.69	1.38	1.38	2.76

H. $BrO_3^- + 5\ Br^- + 6\ H^+ \rightarrow 3\ Br_2 + 3\ H_2O$

$[BrO_3^-], M$	0.0333	0.0333	0.0667	0.0333
$[Br^-], M$	0.0667	0.133	0.0667	0.0667
$[H^+], M$	0.100	0.100	0.100	0.200
t, s	42.6	21.5	21.1	10.7

(t = time for 0.0020 M BrO_3^- to be consumed. Solution volume is 1 L.)

I. $NH_4^+ + NO_2^- \rightarrow N_2 + 2\ H_2O$

$[NH_4^+], M$	0.0092	0.0092	0.0488	0.0249
$[NO_2^-], M$	0.098	0.049	0.196	0.196
$\Delta[N_2]/\Delta t$, mol L^{-1} s^{-1}	3.49×10^{-7}	1.75×10^{-7}	3.70×10^{-6}	1.88×10^{-6}

J. $H_2PO_2^- + OH^- \rightarrow HPO_3^{2-} + H_2(g)$

$[H_2PO_2^-], M$	0.50	0.25	0.25
$[OH^-], M$	1.28	1.28	3.84
V_{H_2}, cm^3 produced (at STP)	19.5	25.0	135.0
t, s	10	50	30

(Assume solution volume is 1 L.)

K. $2\ NO(g) + H_2(g) \rightarrow N_2O(g) + H_2O(g)$ (at 1000 K)

$P_i(NO)$, atm	0.150	0.075	0.150
$P_i(H_2)$, atm	0.400	0.400	0.200
$-\Delta P_{total}/\Delta t$, atm/min	0.020	0.005	0.010

4. For each of the reactions in objective 13-3, determine first the specific rate constant, making sure to express it with the correct units and then the rates of the reaction when the concentrations are those given below.

A. $[N_2O_5] = 0.200\ M$; $[N_2O_5] = 1.00\ M$.
B. $[CH_3CHO] = 0.150\ M$; $[CH_3CHO] = 0.337\ M$.
C. $[CO] = 0.50\ M$ and $[NO_2] = 0.50\ M$; $[CO] = 1.20\ M$ and $[NO_2] = 0.60\ M$.
D. $[H_2] = 0.12\ M$ and $[NO] = 0.21\ M$; $[H_2] = 0.43\ M$ and $[NO] = 0.24\ M$.
E. $[NOCl] = 0.50\ M$; $[NOCl] = 0.23\ M$.
F. $[F_2] = 0.13\ M$ and $[ClO_2] = 0.27\ M$; $[F_2] = 0.29\ M$ and $[ClO_2] = 0.11\ M$.
G. $[CH_3Cl] = 9.4 \times 10^{-7}\ M$ and $[F^-] = 8.7 \times 10^{-7}\ M$; $[CH_3Cl] = 4.3 \times 10^{-7}\ M$ and $[F^-] = 10.2 \times 10^{-7}\ M$.
H. $[BrO_3^-] = 0.100\ M$, $[Br^-] = 0.243\ M$, and $[H^+] = 0.342\ M$;
$[BrO_3^-] = 0.076\ M$, $[Br^-] = 0.111\ M$, and $[H^+] = 0.114\ M$.
I. $[NH_4^+] = 0.0100\ M$ and $[NO_2^-] = 0.100\ M$; $[NH_4^+] = 0.0046\ M$ and $[NO_2^-] = 0.0043\ M$.
J. $[H_2PO_2^-] = 1.04\ M$ and $[OH^-] = 0.29\ M$; $[H_2PO_2^-] = 0.47\ M$ and $[OH^-] = 0.50\ M$.
K. $P_i(NO) = 0.147$ atm and $P_i(H_2) = 0.089$ atm; $P_i(NO) = 1.06$ atm, and $P_i(H_2) = 0.104$ atm.

5. Concentration–time data for various reactions are given below. Determine the order of each reaction for the component whose concentration varies and the value, with the correct units, of the specific rate constant.

A. $2\,NH_3(g) \rightarrow N_2(g) + 3\,H_2(g)$

$[NH_3]$, M	2.000	1.993	1.987
t, s	0	1.000	2.000

B. $CH_3COClN{-}C_6H_5\,(A) \rightarrow CH_3COHN{-}C_6H_4^+Cl^-$

[A], M	0.0245	0.0181	0.0133	0.0097	0.0071	0.0052
t, min	0	15	30	45	60	75

C. $2\,AsH_3(g) \rightarrow 2\,As(s) + 3\,H_2(g)$

$[AsH_3]$, M	0.0216	0.0164	0.0151	0.0137	0.0126	0.0115	0.0105
t, h	0	3.00	4.00	5.00	6.00	7.00	8.00

D. $NH_4CNO \rightarrow (NH_2)_2CO$

$[NH_4CNO]$, M	0.400	0.320	0.253	0.207	0.167
t, min	0	10.0	25.0	40.0	60.0

E. $2\,C_4H_6 \rightarrow C_8H_{12}$

$[C_4H_6]$, M	0.120	0.111	0.104	0.092
t, min	0	200	400	800

F. Cinnamylidene chloride(A) + $C_2H_5OH \rightarrow HCl + D$ (at 23°C)

[A], M	2.11×10^{-5}	1.98×10^{-5}	1.76×10^{-5}	1.33×10^{-5}	1.16×10^{-5}	9.56×10^{-6}	7.43×10^{-6}
t, min	0	10	31	67	100	133	178

Reaction run in C_2H_5OH

G. $(CH_3)_3CBr + H_2O \rightarrow (CH_3)_3COH + HBr$

$[(CH_3)_3CBr]$, M	0.1039	0.0896	0.0850	0.0776	0.0701	0.0639	0.0529	0.0380	0.0270	0.0207
t, min	0	3.15	4.10	6.20	8.20	10.0	13.5	18.3	26.0	30.8

H. $CH_3COOCH_3 + H_2O \rightarrow CH_3COOH + CH_3OH$

$[CH_3OH]$, M	0	0.02516	0.04960	0.07324	0.09621	0.1190	0.1404
t, min	0	15	30	45	60	75	90

($[CH_3COOCH_3] = 0.850\,M$ and $[H_2O] = 51.0\,M$ initially.)

I. $CH_3Br + I^- \rightarrow CH_3I + Br^-$

$[I^-]$, M	1.00	0.950	0.902	0.857
t, min	0	5	10	15

J. $BzOOPh + H_2O \rightarrow BzOOH + PhOH$ $\quad [H_2O] = 55.5\,M$

(BzOOPh = *p*-nitrophenyl ester of *N*-carbobenzoxylysine.)

[BzOOPh], M	3.388×10^{-5}	2.783×10^{-5}	2.290×10^{-5}	1.892×10^{-5}	1.538×10^{-5}
t, min	0	10	20	30	40

6. Determine the half time of each of the reactions in objective 13-5. Use the initial concentration of reactant, if necessary.

9. The rate constants or the rates at the same concentrations of various reactions at different temperatures are given in the following lines. Determine the activation energy in kJ/mol of each reaction and the rate or rate constant at the specified temperature.

A. $2\,NO_2(g) \rightarrow 2\,NO(g) + O_s(g)$ $\quad k = 0.775\ s^{-1}$ at 313 K
$\quad = 4.02\ s^{-1}$ at 378 K

E_a = ________ kJ/mol $\quad$ At 298 K, k = ________ s^{-1}

B. $CO + NO_2 \rightarrow CO_2 + NO$ $\quad k = 0.220\ M^{-1}\ s^{-1}$ at 650 K
$\quad = 23.0\ M^{-1}\ s^{-1}$ at 800 K

E_a = ________ kJ/mol $\quad$ At 300 K, k = ________ $M^{-1}\ s^{-1}$

C. $(CH_2COOH)_2CO \rightarrow (CH_3)_2C{=}O + 2\,CO_2$ $\quad k = 0.0548\ s^{-1}$ at 60°C
$\quad = 2.46 \times 10^{-5}\ s^{-1}$ at 0°C

E_a = ________ kJ/mol $\quad$ At 100 K, k = ________ s^{-1}

D. $(CH_2)_3 \rightarrow CH_2CHCH_3$

t, °C	470	485	500	510	519	530
k, s^{-1}	1.10×10^{-4}	2.61×10^{-4}	5.70×10^{-4}	10.21×10^{-4}	1.64×10^{-3}	2.86×10^{-3}

E_a = ________ kJ/mol $\quad$ At 1000°K, k = ________ s^{-1}

E. $CH_3I + C_2H_5ONa \rightarrow CH_3OC_2H_5 + NaI$

k, M^{-1} s^{-1}	5.60×10^{-5}	1.18×10^{-4}	2.45×10^{-4}	4.88×10^{-4}	1.00×10^{-3}
t, °C	0	6	12	18	24

E_a = ________ kJ/mol At 100°C, k = ________ M^{-1} s^{-1}

12. (1) For the reaction $CO + NO_2 \rightarrow CO_2 + NO$ the rate law under certain conditions is rate = $k[NO_2]^2$. Which of the following mechanisms is most plausible? Find the rate law for each one.

A. $CO + NO_2 \rightarrow CO_2 + NO$

B. $2\,NO_2 \rightarrow N_2 + 2\,O_2$ (slow)
$2\,CO + O_2 \rightarrow 2\,CO_2$ (fast)
$N_2 + O_2 \rightarrow 2\,NO$ (fast)

C. $2\,NO_2 \rightleftharpoons N_2O_4$ (fast)
$N_2O_4 + 2\,CO \rightarrow 2\,CO_2 + 2\,NO$ (slow)

D. $2\,NO_2 \rightarrow NO_3 + NO$ (slow)
$NO_3 + CO \rightarrow NO_2 + CO_2$ (fast)

(2) For the reaction $CO(g) + Cl_2(g) \rightarrow COCl_2(g)$ under certain conditions the rate law is rate = $k[CO][Cl_2]^{3/2}$. Which is the most plausible mechanism? Find the rate law for each one.

A. $\frac{1}{2}\,Cl_2 \rightleftharpoons Cl$ (fast)
$Cl + Cl_2 \rightleftharpoons Cl_3$ (fast)
$Cl_3 + CO \rightarrow COCl_2 + Cl$ (slow)
$Cl \rightleftharpoons \frac{1}{2}\,Cl_2$ (fast)

B. $Cl_2 + CO \rightarrow CCl_2 + O$ (slow)
$O + Cl_2 \rightarrow Cl_2O$ (fast)
$Cl_2O + CCl_2 \rightarrow COCl_2 + Cl_2$ (fast)

C. $\frac{1}{2}\,Cl_2 \rightleftharpoons Cl$ (fast)
$Cl + CO \rightleftharpoons COCl$ (fast)
$COCl + Cl_2 \rightarrow COCl_2 + Cl$. (slow)
$Cl \rightleftharpoons \frac{1}{2}\,Cl_2$ (fast)

D. $Cl_2 + CO \rightleftharpoons COCl + Cl$ (fast)
$COCl + Cl_2 \rightarrow COCl_2 + Cl$ (slow)
$Cl + Cl \rightarrow Cl_2$ (fast)

(3) For the reaction $H_2 + Br_2 \rightarrow 2\,HBr$ under certain conditions the rate law is rate = $k[H_2][Br_2]^{1/2}$. Which is the most plausible mechanism? Find the rate law for each one.

A. $H_2 + Br_2 \rightarrow 2\,HBr$

B. $H_2 \rightleftharpoons 2\,H$ (fast)
$H + Br_2 \rightarrow HBr + Br$ (slow)
$Br + H_2 \rightarrow HBr + H$ (fast)

C. $Br_2 \rightleftharpoons 2\,Br$ (fast)
$Br + H_2 \rightarrow HBr + H$ (slow)
$Br_2 + H \rightarrow HBr + Br$ (fast)

(4) Which mechanism is most plausible for $2\,NO + O_2 \rightarrow 2\,NO_2$ if the rate law is rate = $k[NO]^2[O_2]$? Find the rate law for each one.

A. $2\,NO + O_2 \rightarrow 2\,NO_2$

B. $2\,NO \rightleftharpoons N_2O_2$ (fast)
$N_2O_2 + O_2 \rightleftharpoons 2\,NO_2$ (slow)

C. $2\,NO \rightleftharpoons N_2 + O_2$ (fast)
$N_2 + 2\,O_2 \rightleftharpoons 2\,NO_2$ (slow)

(5) Which mechanism is most plausible for $C_4H_9Br + OH^- \rightarrow C_4H_9OH + Br^-$ if the rate law is rate = $k[C_4H_9Br]$? Find the rate law for each one.

A. $C_4H_9Br \rightarrow C_4H_9^+ + Br^-$ (slow)
$C_4H_9^+ + OH^- \rightarrow C_4H_9OH$ (fast)

B. $C_4H_9Br + OH^- \rightarrow C_4H_9OH + Br^-$

C. $C_4H_9Br + OH^- \rightarrow C_4H_8Br^- + H_2O$ (fast)
$C_4H_8Br^- \rightarrow C_4H_8 + Br^-$ (slow)
$C_4H_8 + H_2O \rightarrow C_4H_9OH$ (fast)

(6) Show that a plausible mechanism for $Cl_2 + CHCl_3 \rightarrow CCl_4 + HCl$ is

$Cl_2 \rightleftharpoons Cl$ (fast)
$Cl + CHCl_3 \rightarrow CCl_4 + H$ (slow)
$H + Cl \rightarrow HCl$ (fast)

and give the rate law which results.

(7) For the NO-catalyzed decomposition of O_3

$$2\,O_3(g) \xrightarrow{NO} 3\,O_2(g)$$

is the following mechanism plausible? What is the rate law?

$NO + O_3 \rightarrow NO_2 + O_2$ (slow)
$NO_2 + O_3 \rightarrow NO + 2\,O_2$ (fast)

QUIZZES (20 minutes each)

Choose the best answer to each question.

Quiz A

1. For $4\ OH + H_2S \rightarrow SO_2 + 2\ H_2O + H_2$ initial rate data are

[OH], M	13×10^{-12}	39×10^{-12}	39×10^{-12}
[H_2S], M	21×10^{-12}	21×10^{-12}	42×10^{-12}
Rate, $M\ s^{-1}$	1.4×10^{-6}	4.2×10^{-6}	8.4×10^{-6}

The rate law is rate $= k[OH]^x[H_2S]^y$ and (a) $x = 2, y = 2$; (b) $x = 2, y = 1$; (c) $x = 1, y = 2$; (d) $x = 1, y = 1$; (e) none of these.

2. The reaction $2\ NO_2Cl \rightarrow 2\ NO_2 + Cl_2$ is first order. The rate equation is thus: rate = (a) $k[Cl_2]$; (b) $k[NO_2]^2[Cl_2]/[NO_2Cl]^2$; (c) $k[NO_2Cl]^2$; (d) $k[NO_2Cl]$; (e) none of these.
3. For a given reaction a reactant with an initial concentration of 0.75 M is completely gone in 30 min. The reaction is thus ______ order with a rate constant of ______ . (a) first, 0.0462 min^{-1}; (b) zero, 0.025 $M\ min^{-1}$; (c) first, 0.025 min^{-1}; (d) zero, 0.050 $M\ min^{-1}$; (e) none of these.
4. What is the first-order rate constant for which the half-life is 57 seconds? (a) 0.018 s^{-1}; (b) 0.024 s^{-1}; (c) 0.009 s^{-1}; (d) 0.012 s^{-1}; (e) none of these.
5. For a given reaction rate $= k[A][B]^2$. Which of the following will change the value of k the most? (a) halving [B]; (b) doubling [A]; (c) removing product; (d) increasing both [A] and [B]; (e) none of these.
6. The rate of a chemical reaction is independent of the concentrations of the reactants. Thus the reaction is (a) first order; (b) second order; (c) exothermic; (d) catalyzed; (e) none of these.
7. For the reaction A → products time–concentration data are

Time, min	0	2	4	6	8
[A], M	1.00	0.80	0.60	0.40	0.20

This reaction is (a) catalyzed; (b) zero order; (c) first order; (d) second order; (e) none of these.

8. In the Haber process, nickel metal is used to increase the rate of the reaction $N_2(g) + 3\ H_2(g) \rightarrow 2\ NH_3(g)$. The nickel is called (a) an inhibitor; (b) a negative catalyst; (c) a homogeneous catalyst; (d) a heterogeneous catalyst; (e) none of these.

Quiz B

1. For the reaction $2\ HgCl_2 + C_2O_4^{2-} \rightarrow$ products data are

[$HgCl_2$], M	0.0836	0.0836	0.0418
[$C_2O_4^{2-}$], M	0.202	0.404	0.404
Init. rate, $M\ h^{-1}$	0.26	1.04	0.53

The rate law is rate $= [HgCl_2]^x[C_2O_4^{2-}]^y$. Thus (a) $x = 1, y = 1$; (b) $x = 2, y = 2$; (c) $x = 2, y = 1$; (d) $x = 1, y = 2$; (e) none of these.

2. For the reaction $2\ NO_2 + F_2 \rightarrow 2\ NO_2F$ the rate equation is rate $= k[NO_2][F_2]$. The order of the reaction is thus (a) zero; (b) third; (c) first; (d) second order in [NO_2]; (e) none of these.
3. A certain reaction is first order in [A], second order in [B]. When [A] = 3.0 M and [B] = 2.0 M, the rate is 0.144 $M\ s^{-1}$. What is this reaction's rate constant (in $M^{-2}\ s^{-1}$)? (a) 0.008; (b) 0.024; (c) 0.004; (d) 0.018; (e) none of these.
4. The rate constant for a first-order reaction is 0.0396 min^{-1}. Its half-life is (a) 175 min; (b) 17.5 min; (c) 25.3 min; (d) 35.0 min; (e) none of these.
5. Which of the following does *not* determine the rate of a reaction? (a) value of $\Delta H°$; (b) activation energy; (c) presence of catalyst; (d) temperature of reactants; (e) none of these.
6. The units of the specific rate constant for a zero-order reaction are (a) s^{-1}; (b) $M^{-1}\ s^{-1}$; (c) $M^{-2}\ s^{-1}$; (d) s; (e) none of these.
7. Which plot is typical of data for a first-order reaction?

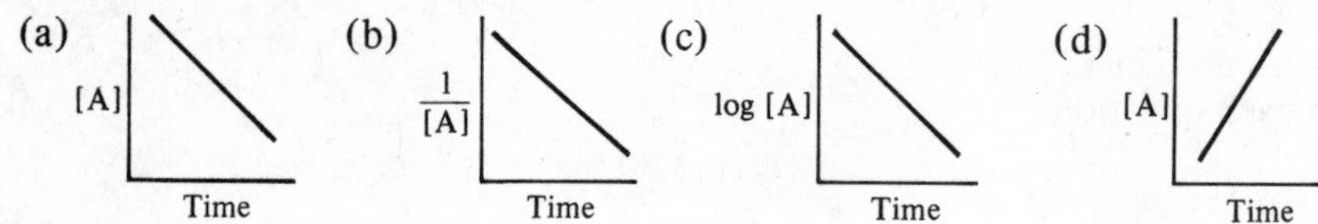

(e) none of these.

8. Which part of an elementary reaction must be exothermic? (a) reactants → products; (b) products → reactants; (c) reactants → activated complex; (d) products → activated complex; (e) activated complex → products.

Quiz C

1. For $2\ NO + O_2 \rightarrow 2\ NO_2$ initial rate data are

[NO], *M*	0.010	0.010	0.030
$[O_2]$, *M*	0.010	0.020	0.020
Rate, $M\ s^{-1}$	2.5×10^{-9}	5.0×10^{-9}	45.0×10^{-9}

The rate is rate $= k[NO]^x[O_2]^y$ and (a) $x = 1, y = 1$; (b) $x = 2, y = 1$; (c) $x = 1, y = 2$; (d) $x = 2, y = 2$; (e) none of these.

2. If the half-life of a reaction depends on the concentration of the reactant, then the reaction cannot be ______ order. (a) zero; (b) first; (c) second; (d) third; (e) none of these.
3. A reaction has the rate law rate $= k[A][B]^2$. Which will cause the rate to increase the most? (a) tripling [B]; (b) doubling [B]; (c) doubling [A]; (d) quadrupling [A]; (e) lowering temperature.
4. A reaction is first order. If its initial rate is 0.0200 $M\ s^{-1}$ and 25.0 days later its rate is $6.25 \times 10^{-4}\ M\ s^{-1}$, then its half-life is (a) 25.0 days; (b) 12.5 days; (c) 50.0 days; (d) 5.0 days; (e) none of these.
5. A combination of reactants that exists for an instant at the time of collision between reactants is called a(n) (a) catalyst; (b) activated complex; (c) reaction product; (d) rate-determining step; (e) none of these.
6. The correct units of the specific rate constant for a first-order reaction could be (a) $M^{-2}\ s^{-1}$; (b) s; (c) $M^{-1}\ s^{-1}$; (d) s^{-1}; (e) none of these.
7. For the reaction A → products time–concentration data are

Time, min	0	1	3	4
[A], *m*	1.00	0.50	0.25	0.20

This reaction is (a) zero order; (b) first order; (c) second order; (d) cannot be determined; (e) none of these.

8. Which of the following lowers the activation energy of a reaction? (a) adding reactants; (b) lowering the temperature; (c) removing products; (d) adding a catalyst; (e) none of these.

Quiz D

1. For $C_2H_4Br_2 + 3\ KI \rightarrow C_2H_4 + 2\ KBr + KI_3$ initial rate data are

$[C_2H_4Br_2]$, *M*	0.500	0.500	1.500
[KI], *M*	1.80	7.20	1.80
Rate, $M\ min^{-1}$	0.269	1.08	0.807

The rate law is rate $= k[C_2H_4Br_2]^x[KI]^y$ and (a) $x = 1, y = 2$; (b) $x = 2, y = 1$; (c) $x = 1, y = 1$; (d) $x = 0, y = 0$; (e) none of these.

2. The time required for the initial amount of material in a first-order reaction to decrease by a factor of two is known as the (a) reaction time; (b) activation time; (c) half-life; (d) reaction rate; (e) none of these.
3. If a reaction has a rate equation of rate $= k[A]^2[B]$, then it is (a) second order in [B]; (b) first order in [A]; (c) second order overall; (d) spontaneous; (e) none of these.
4. If a reaction is first order with a rate constant of $5.48 \times 10^{-2}\ s^{-1}$, how long is required for 3/4 of the initial concentration of reactant to be used up? (a) 18.2 s; (b) 36.5 s; (c) 25.3 s; (d) 6.3 s; (e) none of these.

5. The effect of a catalyst in a chemical reaction is to change the (a) heat evolved; (b) work done; (c) yield of product; (d) activation energy; (e) none of these.
6. The units of a first-order rate constant are (a) s^{-1}; (b) M^{-1}; (c) $M^{-1}\ s^{-1}$ (d) M s; (e) none of these.
7. Which plot is typical of data for a second-order reaction?

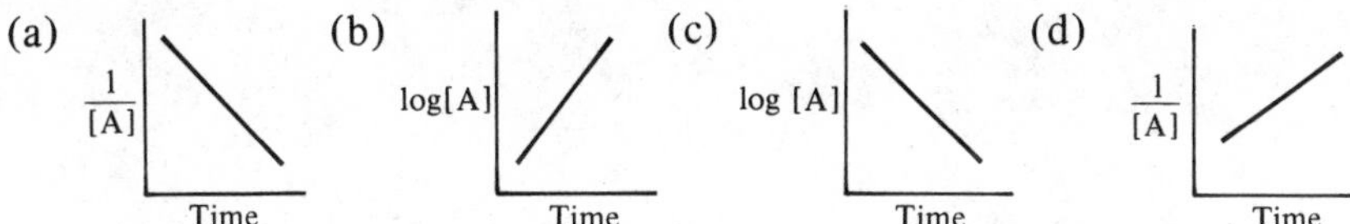

(e) none of these.

8. A reaction has rate = [A] [B]^2. Which of the following changes the rate constant, k, the least? (a) adding homogeneous catalyst; (b) adding inhibitor; (c) raising temperature 10°C; (d) raising temperature 20°C; (e) increasing [A].

SAMPLE TEST

1. A chemical reaction has a rate constant of $7.00 \times 10^{-9}\ h^{-1}$ at 400 K and $1.00 \times 10^{-4}\ h^{-1}$ at 500 K. What is the activation energy in kJ/mol for this reaction?
2. For the reaction $2\ HgCl_2(aq) + Na_2C_2O_4(aq) \rightarrow Hg_2Cl_2(s) + 2\ CO_2(g) + 2\ NaCl(aq)$ initial rate data are

Initial concentrations		*Initial rate*
$[HgCl_2]$, M	$[Na_2C_2O_4]$, M	$-\Delta[Na_2C_2O_4]/\Delta t$, $M\ h^{-1}$
0.0836	0.202	0.26
0.0836	0.404	1.04
0.0418	0.404	0.53

a. Write the rate equation for this reaction.
b. Determine the value of the rate constant for this reaction, being sure the units are correct.
c. What is the initial rate of this reaction when $[HgCl_2] = 0.200\ M$ and $[Na_2C_2O_4] = 0.100\ M$?

Principles of Chemical Equilibrium

REVIEW OF OBJECTIVES

1. Describe the condition of equilibrium in a reversible reaction.

Many reactions go to completion. This occurs if one of the products escapes from the reaction mixture as a gas or a precipitate or if a very stable product is formed (see objective 4–13b). Many other reactions end up at an equilibrium somewhere between reactants and products. The equilibrium condition is a common one, and not restricted to chemistry. For instance, although

man + woman → married couple [1]

looks like a one-way process, we know that it works both ways.

Equilibrium may be reached from many different starting posistions. Consider our "marriage" example, equation [1]. If everyone in a large city were to marry on January 1, we would expect some people to be single (through divorce or death, for example) within a year. Likewise, if all were single on January 1, we would expect some marriages during the year.

Reversible chemical reactions show similar behavior. We can start with either products or reactants and reach an equilibrium state. Consider reaction [2] at 352.6 K as an example.

$$2\ NO_2(g) \rightleftharpoons N_2O_4(g) \qquad [2]$$

The reaction is carried out in a 50.0 L container. The data for three experiments are given in Table 14-1.

TABLE 14-1
Equilibrium data for $2\ NO_2(g) \rightleftharpoons N_2O_4(g)$ at 352.6 K

		Amount, mol		Concentration, *M*	
Experiment	Substance	Initial	Final	Initial	Final
1	NO_2	1.000	0.8175	0.0200	0.01635
	N_2O_4	0.000	0.0912	0.000	0.00182
2	NO_2	0.000	0.4457	0.000	0.00891
	N_2O_4	0.250	0.0271	0.00500	0.000542
3	NO_2	0.160	0.210	0.00800	0.01050
	N_2O_4	0.040	0.0150	0.00200	0.000750

★ 1a. Describe how equilibrium concentrations are established experimentally.

Often an equilibrium mixture can be "frozen" by quickly cooling it or by adding an excess of a reagent that reacts completely with a reactant or a product. This is what is done with the mixture resulting from reaction [3], as described *in the text.*

$$2\ HI(g) \rightleftharpoons H_2(g) + I_2(g) \qquad [3]$$

Reaction [2] cannot be "frozen" readily because it is very rapid. Thus, reaction [2] must be studied under the conditions of equilibrium, 352.6 K and a 50.0 L vessel in this case.

NO_2 (g) is red-brown, whereas N_2O_4 (g) is colorless. It is possible to determine the intensity of color, and thus the concentration of NO_2 (g) visually or with a colorimeter. If we know the amounts of N_2O_4 (g) and NO_2 (g) placed in the container initially and the final concentration of NO_2 (g), we can readily determine the final amounts in moles and concentrations of both species.

EXAMPLE 14-1 0.160 mol NO_2 (g) and 0.040 mol N_2O_4 (g) are placed in a 20.0 L container and come to equilibrium at 352.6 K. At equilibrium for reaction [2], $[NO_2] = 0.01050\,M$. What are the equilibrium amounts and concentrations of all substances?

Since the container has a volume of 20.0 L, the final amount of NO_2 is

$$n_{NO_2} = 0.01050\,M \times 20.0\text{ L} = 0.210\text{ mol}$$

0.210 mol − 0.160 mol = 0.050 mol NO_2 is produced, and

$$n_{N_2O_4(\text{reacted})} = 0.050\text{ mol NO}_2 \times \frac{1\text{ mol N}_2\text{O}_4}{2\text{ mol NO}_2} = 0.025\text{ mol N}_2\text{O}_4\text{ reacted}$$

The final amount of N_2O_4 is

$$n_{N_2O_4} = n_{N_2O_4(\text{initial})} - n_{N_2O_4(\text{reacted})} = 0.040\text{ mol} - 0.025\text{ mol} = 0.015\text{ mol N}_2\text{O}_4$$

Finally, the equilibrium $[N_2O_4]$ is

$$[N_2O_4] = \frac{0.0150\text{ mol N}_2\text{O}_4}{20.0\text{ L}} = 0.000750\,M$$

All of this information can be concisely summarized below the equation for the reaction.

Reaction:	$2\,NO_2$ (g)	$\rightleftharpoons$	N_2O_4 (g)
Initial:	0.160 mol		0.040 mol
Change:	+0.050 mol		−0.025 mol
Equilibrium:	0.210 mol		0.015 mol

This is the source of the third set of data in Table 14-1.

★ **2. Write the equilibrium constant expression in terms of concentrations, K_c, for a reaction and use the value of K_c and the concentrations of all species but one to determine the equilibrium concentration of that species.**

The equilibrium constant can be written as the ratio of the concentrations–product concentrations over those of reactants–each raised to the power of its stoichiometric coefficient in the balanced equation. The equilibrium constant expressions for all reactions are written in much the same way (but see objectives 14-3 and 14-4). Finding one equilibrium concentration given all the others and the value of K_c is a matter of rearranging the expression to solve for the necessary concentration.

EXAMPLE 14-2 What is the equilibrium $[N_2O_4]$ if $[NO_2] = 0.100\,M$?

$$2\,NO_2(g) \rightleftharpoons N_2O_4(g) \qquad K_c = 6.81 \quad \text{at } 352.6\text{ K}$$

$$K_c = \frac{[N_2O_4]}{[NO_2]^2} \qquad or \qquad [N_2O_4] = K_c[NO_2]^2$$

Thus $\quad [N_2O_4] = (6.81)(0.100)^2 = 0.0681\,M$

★ **3. Determine K_c values for situations where chemical equations are reversed, multiplied through by constant coefficients, or added together.**

The reverse of reaction [2] is reaction [4].

$$N_2O_4(g) \rightleftharpoons 2\,NO_2(g) \qquad [4]$$

For reaction [4], $K_c = [NO_2]^2/[N_2O_4]$. K_c for reaction [2] is merely K_c for reaction [4] inverted. Thus, $K_{c[2]} = 1/K_{c[4]}$ and we determine $K_{c[4]} = 1/K_{c[5]} = 1/6.81 = 0.147$. In similar fashion, we can modify reaction [4] to obtain reaction [5].

$$\tfrac{1}{2}N_2O_4(g) \rightleftharpoons NO_2(g) \qquad [5]$$

For reaction [5]

$$K_{c[5]} = \frac{[NO_2]}{[N_2O_4]^{1/2}} = \sqrt{K_{c[4]}} = 0.383$$

And finally, reaction [4] can be followed by reaction [6].

$$2\,NO_2(g) \rightleftharpoons 2\,NO(g) + O_2(g) \qquad [6]$$

For reaction [6], $K_c = [NO]^2[O_2]/[NO_2]^2$. If reactions [4] and [6] are combined, reaction [7] results.

$$N_2O_4(g) \rightleftharpoons 2\,NO(g) + O_2(g) \qquad [7]$$

This reaction has

$$K_{c[7]} = \frac{[NO]^2[O_2]}{[N_2O_4]}$$

Notice that

$$K_{c[4]} \times K_{c[6]} = \frac{[NO_2]^2}{[N_2O_4]} \times \frac{[NO]^2[O_2]}{[NO_2]^2} = K_{c[7]}$$

★ **4. Write an expression for K_p and interconvert K_p and K_c when a reaction involves gases.**

K_p has the same form as does K_c except one uses partial pressures rather than concentrations. K_ps are used in reactions which involve mixtures of gases only. Although K_p and K_c may have different values, both of them are constant, as long as the temperature is fixed. K_c and K_p are related through the ideal gas equation $PV = nRT$ or $P = (n/V)RT$. Notice that (n/V) is a concentration. Thus, for reaction [2]

$$K_p = \frac{P_{N_2O_4}}{(P_{NO_2})^2} = \frac{[N_2O_4]RT}{([NO_2]RT)^2} = \frac{[N_2O_4]}{[NO_2]^2} \times \frac{1}{RT} = \frac{K_c}{RT}$$

(Note that a different expression for K_p results for another reaction, specifically one in which the stoichiometric coefficients of gases differ.) The value of R is 0.08206 L atm mol^{-1} K^{-1} and the pressure is in atmospheres.

EXAMPLE 14-3 What is K_p for the reaction

$$2\,NO_2(g) \rightleftharpoons N_2O_4(g) \qquad K_c = 6.81 \text{ at } 352.6\text{ K}$$

$$K_p = \frac{K_c}{RT} = \frac{6.81}{(0.08206)(352.6\text{ K})} = 0.235$$

Just as K_c has no units, neither does K_p. Conventionally, the partial pressures are always expressed in atmospheres. It is important to recognize that K_p and K_c are valid only at a fixed temperature. Merely multiplying or dividing by RT will not produce the value of the equilibrium constant at another temperature.

★ **4a. Know that the concentrations of pure liquids and solids are omitted from equilibrium constant expressions.**

Many experiments have investigated both the rates of chemical reactions and the position of equilibrium. In all of these, it has been found that the amount of pure liquid or pure solid present has no effect as long as *some* of the liquid or solid is present. Thus, the concentrations of pure liquids and solids are omitted from both rate laws and equilibrium constant expressions. Usually, this means that the solvent in a liquid solution also is omitted. But in concentrated solutions, when the solvent is a reactant or a product its concentration must be included. Consider reaction [8].

$$CH_3COOC_2H_5 + H_2O \rightleftharpoons CH_3COOH + C_2H_5OH \quad [8]$$

In dilute solution

$$K_c = \frac{[CH_3COOH]\,[C_2H_5OH]}{[CH_3COOC_2H_5]}$$

In concentrated solution

$$K_c = \frac{[CH_3COOH]\,[C_2H_5OH]}{[CH_3COOC_2H_5]\,[H_2O]}$$

In dilute solution H_2O acts almost as if it were pure.

★ **5. Calculate the numerical value of the equilibrium constant from equilibrium conditions.**

We now can determine the value of the equilibrium constant. Often it is helpful to write the concentrations of reactants and products beneath their formulas in the balanced chemical equation. It is quite useful to write three lines: initial concentrations, changes of concentrations, and equilibrium concentrations.

EXAMPLE 14-4 The reaction $H_2(g) + CO_2(g) \rightleftharpoons H_2O(g) + CO(g)$ reaches equilibrium at 500 K. Initially $[H_2] = 0.0420\,M$ and $[CO_2] = 0.0160\,M$. At equilibrium there is 0.194 mol CO_2 in the 14.0 L container. What is the value of K_c?

The equilibrium concentration of CO_2 is $[CO_2] = 0.194$ mol/14.0 L $= 0.0139\,M$. Thus, the concentration of CO_2 which has reacted is $[CO_2]_r = [CO_2]_i - [CO_2]_{eq} = 0.0160\,M - 0.0139\,M = 0.0021\,M$.

Reaction:	$H_2(g)$	+	$CO_2(g)$	$\rightleftharpoons$	$H_2O(g)$	+	$CO(g)$
Initial:	0.0420 M		0.0160 M		0.0000 M		0.0000 M
Change:			−0.0021 M				
Final:			0.0139 M				

Since one mole of $H_2(g)$ *reacts* for every mole of $CO_2(g)$ reacting and since one mole each of $H_2O(g)$ and CO_2 are *produced* for each mole of $CO_2(g)$ which reacts,

$$[H_2]_r = [CO_2]_r = 0.0021\,M \quad or \quad [H_2]_p = [CO_2]_p = -0.0021\,M$$

$$and\ [H_2O]_p = [CO]_p = [CO_2]_r = 0.0021\,M$$

	$H_2(g)$	+	$CO_2(g)$	$\rightleftharpoons$	$H_2O(g)$	+	$CO(g)$
Initial:	0.0420 M		0.0160 M		0.0000 M		0.0000 M
Change:	−0.0021 M		−0.0021 M		+0.0021 M		+0.0021 M
Equil:	0.0399 M		0.0139 M		0.0021 M		0.0021 M

Notice in every case $[\ ]_{eq} = [\ ]_i + [\ ]_c$. Finally notice that we can add and subtract concentrations *as long as the species involved are in the same container.*

$$K_c = \frac{[CO]\ [H_2O]}{[CO_2]\ [H_2]} = \frac{(0.0021)(0.0021)}{(0.0139)(0.0399)} = 8.0 \times 10^{-3}$$

★ **6. Predict the direction in which a reaction proceeds toward equilibrium by comparing the reaction quotient, Q_c or Q_p, with the equilibrium constant, K_c or K_p.**

The reaction quotient is written in the same way as the equilibrium constant expression. The difference is that the values of the concentrations and partial pressures are not necessarily those at equilibrium. The reaction quotient is valuable in predicting the direction in which the reaction will shift or move in reaching equilibrium. There are three possibilities.

$$\left.\begin{array}{l}\text{If } Q = K, \text{ the reaction is at equilibrium} \\ \text{If } Q < K, \text{ the reaction will shift right} \\ \text{If } Q > K, \text{ the reaction will shift left}\end{array}\right\} \qquad [9]$$

Shift right means that more products will be produced and reactants will be destroyed. This is the case in Experiment 1 of Table 14-1.

$$Q_{c,1} = \frac{[N_2O_4]_{1,i}}{[NO_2]^2_{1,i}} = \frac{0.000}{(0.0200)^2} = 0.00 < 6.81 = K_c$$

Shift left means that reactants are produced at the expense of products. This is the case for Experiment 2 of Table 14-1.

$$Q_{c,2} = \frac{[N_2O_4]_{2,i}}{[NO_2]^2_{2,i}} = \frac{(0.00500)}{(0.000)^2} = \infty > 6.81 = K_c$$

The same procedure is used in evaluating Q_p and comparing it with K_p, except partial pressures in atmospheres are used.

★ **6a. Use the ideal gas law and Dalton's law of partial pressures in working with partial pressure equilibrium constants.**

We also can add and subtract partial pressures. One advantage of working with partial pressures is that the total pressure is readily measured and Dalton's law of partial pressures can be used.

EXAMPLE 14-5 A container is filled with $CH_3OH(g)$ at 350 K and allowed to reach equilibrium. $CO(g) + 2\ H_2(g) \rightleftharpoons CH_3OH(g)$. At equilibrium the partial pressure of CH_3OH is 1.000 atm and the total pressure is 1.420 atm. What is the value of K_p?

Because of the stoichiometry of the reaction, $P_{H_2} = 2P_{CO}$ (twice as much H_2 is produced as CO when CH_3OH decomposes).

$$P_{total} = P_{CH_3OH} + P_{H_2} + P_{CO}$$

$$1.420 \text{ atm} = 1.000 \text{ atm} + 2P_{CO} + P_{CO} = 1.000 \text{ atm} + 3P_{CO} \quad \textit{or}$$

$$P_{CO} = (1.420 - 1.000)/3 = 0.140 \text{ atm}$$

Thus, $P_{H_2} = 2 \times 0.140 \text{ atm} = 0.280 \text{ atm}$ and

$$K_p = \frac{P_{CH_3OH}}{P_{CO}P_{H_2}^2} = \frac{1.000}{(0.140)(0.280)^2} = 91.1$$

★ **7. Calculate the equilibrium condition in a reversible reaction from a given set of initial conditions.**

Once the equilibrium constant is known, it can be used to predict the final concentrations of reactants and products. One of the easiest techniques to help keep track of the calculation is that used in objective 14–5. The equation for the reaction is written out. Below the formula of each species one writes the concentration or partial pressure which initially is present, which changes, and which is present at equilibrium. In this type of problem, one or several concentrations are not known. We need to express all the concentrations in terms of one unknown.

EXAMPLE 14-6 For $H_2(g) + CO_2(g) \rightleftharpoons H_2O(g) + CO(g)$, $K_c = 8.0 \times 10^{-3}$ at 500 K. What are the equilibrium conditions if initial conditions are $[H_2] = 0.0200\ M$, $[CO_2] = 0.0144\ M$, and $[CO] = 0.0100\ M$?

Some H_2O must be produced, otherwise $Q \leqslant 0$. Let $[H_2O]_{eq} = x$.

	$H_2(g)$	+	$CO_2(g)$	$\rightleftharpoons$	$H_2O(g)$	+	$CO(g)$
Initial:	$0.0200\ M$		$0.0144\ M$		$0.0000\ M$		$0.0100\ M$
Change:	$-x\ M$		$-x\ M$		$+x\ M$		$+x\ M$
Equil:	$(0.0200 - x)\ M$		$(0.0144 - x)\ M$		$x\ M$		$(0.0100 + x)\ M$

$$K_c = \frac{[H_2O]_{eq}[CO]_{eq}}{[H_2]_{eq}[CO_2]_{eq}} = \frac{(x)(0.0100 + x)}{(0.0200 - x)(0.0144 - x)} = 8.0 \times 10^{-3}$$

$$= \frac{0.0100\,x + x^2}{2.88 \times 10^{-4} - 0.0344x + x^2}$$

or $$0.992\,x^2 + 0.01028\,x - 2.304 \times 10^{-6} = 0$$

We use the quadratic equation to find the solution

$$x = \frac{-0.01028 \pm \sqrt{(0.01028)^2 - (4)(0.992)(-2.304 \times 10^{-6})}}{2(0.992)}$$

$$= -5.181 \times 10^{-3} \pm 5.401 \times 10^{-3} = 2.20 \times 10^{-4}\ M$$

We choose the positive root rather than the negative one because a negative concentration has no physical meaning. The equilibrium concentrations are

$$[H_2] = 0.0200 - x = 0.0200 - 0.00022 = 0.0198\ M$$
$$[CO_2] = 0.0144 - x = 0.0144 - 0.00022 = 0.0142\ M$$
$$[H_2O] = x = 0.00022\ M$$
$$[CO] = 0.0100 + x = 0.0100 + 0.00022 = 0.0102\ M$$

To check our results, we substitute into K_c.

$$K_c = \frac{[H_2O][CO]}{[H_2][CO_2]} = \frac{(0.00022)(0.0102)}{(0.0198)(0.0142)} = 8.0 \times 10^{-3}$$

EXAMPLE 14-7 For $Br_2(g) + Cl_2(g) \rightleftharpoons 2\,BrCl(g)$, $K_p = 7.21$ at 298 K. What is the equilibrium pressure of BrCl(g) if the initial pressure of $Br_2(g)$ is 1.000 atm and that of $Cl_2(g)$ is 2.000 atm?

Let x be the decrease in pressure of $Br_2(g)$. Then x is also the decrease in the pressure of $Cl_2(g)$ and $2x$ is the increase in the pressure of BrCl(g).

	$Br_2(g)$	+	$Cl_2(g)$	$\rightleftharpoons$	$2\,BrCl(g)$
Initial:	1.000 atm		2.000 atm		0.000 atm
Change:	$-x$ atm		$-x$ atm		$+2x$
Equil:	$(1.000 - x)$ atm		$(2.00 - x)$ atm		$(2x)$ atm

$$K_p = \frac{P^2_{\mathrm{BrCl}}}{P_{\mathrm{Br_2}}\,P_{\mathrm{Cl_2}}} = \frac{(2x)^2}{(1.000 - x)(2.000 - x)} = 7.21 \quad or \quad 3.21x^2 - 21.630x + 14.420 = 0$$

$$x = \frac{21.630 \pm \sqrt{(21.630)^2 = 4(3.21)(14.420)}}{2(3.21)} = 3.369 \pm 2.619 = 0.750 \text{ atm}$$

Thus,
$$P_{\mathrm{Br_2}} = 1.000 - x = 1.000 - 0.750 = 0.250 \text{ atm}$$
$$P_{\mathrm{Cl_2}} = 2.000 - x = 2.000 - 0.750 = 1.250 \text{ atm}$$
$$P_{\mathrm{BrCl}} = 2x = 2 \times 0.750 = 1.500 \text{ atm}$$

$$K_p = \frac{P^2_{\mathrm{BrCl}}}{P_{\mathrm{Br_2}}\,P_{\mathrm{Cl_2}}} = \frac{(1.500)^2}{(0.250)(1.250)} = 7.20$$

In this case, the positive root is not used because it would produce negative pressures of the reactants. Notice also that the line labeled "change" has x multiplied by the stoichiometric coefficients of each species.

★ **8. Use the van't Hoff equation to determine the value of the equilibrium constant at various temperatures.**

The van't Hoff equation [10]

$$\ln \frac{K_1}{K_2} = -\frac{\Delta \bar{H}^\circ}{R}\left(\frac{1}{T_1} - \frac{1}{T_2}\right) \qquad [10]$$

is similar in form to both the Clausius–Clapeyron equation (objective 11–5) and the Arrhenius equation (objective 13–9). The method used in solving these equations is discussed in objective 11–5. You should review the material if necessary.

★ **9. Use Le Châtelier's principle to qualitatively predict how a system at equilibrium will react in response to a stress.**

Because chemical equilibria are dynamic ones, they proceed toward products ("shift to the right") when something occurs which causes the forward reaction to go at a faster rate than the reverse reaction. If we increase the concentration of the reactants, the forward reaction will speed up. Also, if we decrease the concentration of the products, the reverse reaction will slow down. Of course, in each case, the system reaches a new equilibrium. In similar fashion, a stress which causes the reverse reaction's rate to be the faster makes the reaction proceed toward the reactants ("shift to the left").

In the special case of reactions in which some of the species are gases, concentrations can be changed by increasing or decreasing the pressure on the system. The pressure can be increased by squeezing the system into a smaller volume. If the pressure is increased on a system at equilibrium, the system tries to make its volume as small as possible. Thus it proceeds toward the side where the sum of the stoichiometric coefficients of gaseous species is the smaller.

Changing the temperature of a system at equilibrium causes the equilibrium to shift depending on whether the reaction is exothermic or endothermic. The easiest way to remember the direction of the shift is to think of heat as a product (in an exothermic reaction) or a reactant (in an endothermic reaction) of the reaction.

Exothermic: reactants → products + heat
Endothermic: reactants + heat → products [11]

Raising the temperature "increases the concentration of heat" and the exothermic reaction proceeds toward reactants. Of course, heat is not a substance but a form of energy and relations [11] are misleading. However, they do serve as a convenient memory aid. All of these "stresses" and their effects are summarized in Table 14-2.

TABLE 14-2
Effect of stresses on equilibrium systems

Type of stress	Type of reaction	Shift direction
Increase in reactant concentration	General	Right
Increase in product concentration	General	Left
Increase pressure *or* Decrease volume	$n_{g,P} > n_{g,R}$	Left
	$n_{g,P} < n_{g,R}$	Right
Decrease pressure *or* Increase volume	$n_{g,P} > n_{g,R}$	Right
	$n_{g,P} < n_{g,R}$	Left
Increase temperature	Exothermic	Left
	Endothermic	Right
Decrease temperature	Exothermic	Right
	Endothermic	Left

$n_{g,P}$ = sum of stoichiometric coefficients of gaseous products

$n_{g,R}$ = sum of stoichiometric coefficients of gaseous reactants

9a. Calculate the new concentrations or partial pressures after a stress has been exerted on an equilibrium system and it reaches a new equilibrium.

Changes in concentration and pressure cause no change in the equilibrium constant's value.

EXAMPLE 14-8 The volume of Experiment 2 in Table 14-1 is expanded form 20.0 to 50.0 L. In which direction will the reaction proceed and what will be the final concentrations once equilibrium is reestablished?

The "initial" concentrations after the expansion are determined by multiplying the 20.0 L concentrations by 20.0 L/50.0 L = 0.400. The decrease in pressure which occurs causes the reaction to proceed toward reactants.

	$2\,NO_2(g)$	$\rightleftharpoons$	$N_2O_4(g)$
Init. equil:	$0.01050\,M$		$0.000750\,M$
Volume to 50.0 L:	$0.00420\,M$		$0.000300\,M$
Change:	$+2x\,M$		$-x\,M$
Final equil:	$(0.00420 + 2x)M$		$(0.000300 - x)M$

The line labeled "Volume to 50.0 L" gives the concentrations at the instant that the volume is increased to 50.0 L, but before the final equilibrium.

$$K_c = \frac{[N_2O_4]}{[NO_2]^2} = \frac{(0.000300 - x)}{(0.00420 + 2x)^2} = 6.81$$

The quadratic equation gives

$$x = -0.02046 \pm 0.02062 = 0.00016\,M$$

The positive root is chosen since the negative root gives $x = -0.04104\,M$. This produces $[NO_2] = -0.07788\,M$. This root is discarded because negative concentrations have no physical meaning. Thus, $[NO_2] = 0.00452\,M$ and $[N_2O_4] = 0.000140\,M$. Notice that $[NO_2]$ has increased and $[N_2O_4]$ has decreased, as predicted. But have we decided the outcome of the calculation by *assuming* that $[NO_2]$ increased? Suppose we had assumed that $[NO_2]$ decreased by $2x$ and $[N_2O_4]$ increased by x.

$$[NO_2]_{eq} = 0.00420 - 2x \quad \text{and} \quad [N_2O_4]_{eq} = 0.000300 + x$$

$$K_c = \frac{[N_2O_4]}{[NO_2]^2} = \frac{(0.000300 + x)}{(0.00420 - 2x)^2} = 6.81 \quad \text{or} \quad x = -0.00016\,M$$

(The positive root gives the physically meaningless result of a negative $[NO_2]$.) We obtain the same result as before.

$$[NO_2]_{eq} = 0.00420 - 2(-0.00016) = 0.00452\,M$$
$$[N_2O_4]_{eq} = 0.000300 + (-0.00016) = 0.00014\,M$$

When a temperature change occurs, the value of the equilibrium constant changes, as given by the van't Hoff equation [10].

EXAMPLE 14-9 Consider the decomposition of PCl_5 (g).

$$PCl_5\,(g) \rightleftharpoons PCl_3\,(g) + Cl_2\,(g) \qquad [12]$$

At 500 K, equilibrium partial pressures are PCl_5 (g) = 1.285 atm, PCl_3 (g) = 0.715 atm, and Cl_2 (g) = 1.215 atm; $\Delta\bar{H}° = 92.59$ kJ/mol. If the temperature is raised to 550 K, what is the partial pressure of each species present?

The first step is to compute the equilibrium constant at 550 K, using the van't Hoff equation.

$$\ln\frac{K_1}{K_2}\left(= 2.303 \log \frac{K_1}{K_2}\right) = -\frac{\Delta\bar{H}°}{R}\left(\frac{1}{T_1} - \frac{1}{T_2}\right) = -\frac{92{,}590 \text{ J/mol}}{8.314 \text{ J mol}^{-1}\text{ K}^{-1}}\left(\frac{1}{500} - \frac{1}{550}\right) = -2.0248$$

$$\text{Thus} \quad \frac{K_1}{K_2} = e^{-2.0248}\ (= 10^{-2.0248/2.303}) = 0.13201 \qquad (e = 2.718)$$

$$\text{Now} \quad K_1 = \frac{P_{PCl_3}P_{Cl_2}}{P_{PCl_5}} = \frac{(0.715)(1.215)}{1.285} = 0.676$$

$$\text{And} \quad \frac{K_1}{K_2} = \frac{0.676}{K_2} = 0.13201 \quad \text{or} \quad K_2 = \frac{0.676}{0.13201} = 5.12$$

The setup:	PCl_5 (g)	$\rightleftharpoons$	PCl_3 (g)	+	Cl_2 (g)
Initial:	1.285 atm		0.715 atm		1.215 atm
Change:	$-x$ atm		$+x$ atm		$+x$ atm
Equil:	$(1.285 - x)$ atm		$(0.715 + x)$ atm		$(1.215 + x)$ atm

$$K_p = \frac{(0.715 + x)(1.215 + x)}{1.285 - x} = 5.12x$$

$$x = -3.525 \pm 4.259 \text{ atm} = 0.734 \text{ atm}$$

Partial pressures: PCl_5 (g) = 0.551 atm, PCl_3 (g) = 1.449 atm, Cl_2 (g) = 1.949 atm.

10. Appreciate that the equilibrium constant for a reaction is related to the rate laws of the forward and reverse reactions but that one must have detailed knowledge of the mechanism to establish this relationship.

For quite some time it was thought that the rate law for a chemical reaction could easily be obtained from the balanced chemical equation. The belief was that reaction orders and stoichiometric coefficients are equal, which is not necessarily true. However, one can obtain equilibrium constant expressions from mechanisms. This is one of the steps which can be used to establish the plausibility of a mechanism.

DRILL PROBLEMS ON OBJECTIVES

1a. The initial amount of each substance in each of the following reactions is given below the chemical formula of that substance. The volume of the container also is given along with the equilibrium amount of one substance. Determine the equilibrium concentrations of all substances.

	CH_4(g) +	CCl_4(g) ⇌	2 CH_2Cl_2(g) at 298 K	
A.	0.100 mol	0.640 mol	0.200 mol	$n_{CH_4} = 0.1502$ mol, $V = 5.000$ L
B.	0.200 mol	0.200 mol	0.320 mol	$n_{CCl_4} = 0.3118$ mol, $V = 8.00$ L
C.	0.560 mol	0.320 mol	0.320 mol	$n_{CH_2Cl_2} = 0.1569$ mol, $V = 4.00$ L
D.	0.3400 mol	0.3400 mol	0.5100 mol	$n_{CH_2Cl_2} = 0.1593$ mol, $V = 8.50$ L

	PCl_5(g) ⇌	PCl_3(g) +	Cl_2(g) at 600 *K*	
E.	0.100 mol	0.100 mol	0.100 mol	$n_{Cl_2} = 0.1848$ mol, $V = 4.00$ L
F.	0.300 mol	0.204 mol	0.153 mol	$n_{PCl_5} = 0.0897$ mol, $V = 3.00$ L
G.	0.144 mol	0.276 mol	0.072 mol	$n_{PCl_3} = 0.408$ mol, $V = 12.0$ L

	HCHO(g) ⇌	H_2(g) +	CO(g) at 773 K	
H.	2.50 mol	0.00 mol	0.00 mol	$n_{H_2} = 1.00$ mol, $V = 2.50$ L
I.	0.00 mol	4.10 mol	2.00 mol	$n_{CO} = 0.500$ mol, $V = 2.00$ L
J.	0.900 mol	0.000 mol	0.600 mol	$n_{HCHO} = 0.500$ mol, $V = 3.00$ L

	2 NO(g) +	Br_2(g) ⇌	2 NOBr(g) at 350 K	
K.	0.000 mol	0.400 mol	1.000 mol	$n_{NO} = 0.200$ mol, $V = 0.200$ L
L.	1.50 mol	4.60 mol	0.00 mol	$n_{NOBr} = 1.20$ mol, $V = 1.60$ L
M.	0.00 mol	8.75 mol	2.00 mol	$n_{NO} = 0.500$ mol, $V = 6.40$ L

	3 H_2(g) +	N_2(g) ⇌	2 NH_3 at 473 K	
N.	0.5800 mol	0.1930 mol	0.0000 mol	$n_{N_2} = 0.0097$ mol, $V = 0.525$ L
O.	0.0000 mol	0.0117 mol	0.5134 mol	$n_{H_2} = 0.0200$ mol, $V = 0.287$ L

2. (1) Write the equilibrium constant expression in terms of concentrations for each of the following reactions. Some numerical values of K_c are given for future problems.

A. $2\,NOBr(g) \rightleftharpoons 2\,NO(g) + Br_2(g)$
B. $4\,HCl(g) + O_2(g) \rightleftharpoons 2\,H_2O(g) + Cl_2(g)$ $K_c = 1.49 \times 10^3$ at 320 K
C. $N_2(g) + O_2(g) \rightleftharpoons 2\,NO(g)$ $K_c = 6.37 \times 10^{-16}$ at 298 K
D. $CH_4(g) + CCl_4(g) \rightleftharpoons 2\,CH_2Cl_2(g)$
E. $PCl_5(g) \rightleftharpoons PCl_3(g) + Cl_2(g)$
F. $HCHO(g) \rightleftharpoons H_2(g) + CO(g)$
G. $N_2(g) + 3\,H_2(g) \rightleftharpoons 2\,NH_3(g)$
H. $2\,H_2S(g) + 3\,O_2(g) \rightleftharpoons 2\,H_2O(g) + 2\,SO_2(g)$ $K_c = 1.74 \times 10^{45}$ at 1000 K
I. $2\,NH_3(g) + 6\,F_2(g) \rightleftharpoons 2\,NF_3(g) + 6\,HF(g)$

(2) For each of the following reactions, the value of K_c and the concentrations of all reactants but one are given. Determine the value of the omitted concentration.

	CH_3ONO(g) +	HCl(g) ⇌	CH_3OH(g) +	NOCl(g)	$K_c = 0.242$ at 323 K
A.	0.500 *M*	0.274 *M*	1.26 *M*	____ *M*	
B.	____ *M*	4.96 *M*	1.14 *M*	1.49 *M*	

	CH_4(g) +	CCl_4(g) ⇌	2 CH_2Cl_2(g)	$K_c = 0.0956$ at 298 K
C.	1.124 *M*	1.124 *M*	____ *M*	
D.	0.104 *M*	____ *M*	0.256 *M*	

	2 NOBr(g) ⇌	2 NO(g) +	Br_2(g)	$K_c = 0.1563$ at 350 K
E.	0.275 *M*	0.124 *M*	____ *M*	
F.	____ *M*	0.173 *M*	0.822 *M*	

	$N_2(g)$ +	$3\ H_2(g)$ ⇌	$2\ NH_3(g)$	$K_c = 1.40 \times 10^5$ at 473 K
G.	____ M	0.163 M	0.970 M	
H.	0.00100 M	0.0220 M	____ M	

	$Br_2(g)$ +	$Cl_2(g)$ ⇌	$2\ BrCl(g)$	$K_c = 6.30$ at 350 K
I.	0.146 M	____ M	0.227 M	
J.	0.082 M	0.077 M	____ M	

	$PCl_3(g)$ +	$Cl_2(g)$ ⇌	$PCl_5(g)$	$K_c = 1.784$ at 600 K
K.	0.149 M	____ M	0.206 M	
L.	0.200 M	0.111 M	____ M	

3. Based on your answers to, and the data of, the drill problems in objectives 14–1a and 14–2, write the equilibrium constant expression and determine its value for each of the following equations.

A. $H_2(g) + CO(g) \rightleftharpoons HCHO(g)$
B. $PCl_3(g) + Cl_2(g) \rightleftharpoons PCl_5(g)$
C. $2\ NH_3(g) \rightleftharpoons N_2(g) + 3\ H_2(g)$
D. $2\ BrCl(g) \rightleftharpoons Br_2(g) + Cl_2(g)$
E. $2\ CH_2Cl_2(g) \rightleftharpoons CH_4 + CCl_4(g)$
F. $CH_2Cl_2(g) \rightleftharpoons \frac{1}{2}\ CH_4(g) + \frac{1}{2}\ CCl_4(g)$
G. $NO(g) + \frac{1}{2}\ Br_2(g) \rightleftharpoons NOBr(g)$
H. $\frac{1}{2}\ N_2(g) + \frac{3}{2}\ H_2(g) \rightleftharpoons NH_3(g)$
I. $\frac{1}{2}\ Br_2(g) + \frac{1}{2}\ Cl_2(g) \rightleftharpoons BrCl(g)$
J. $NO(g) \rightleftharpoons \frac{1}{2}\ N_2(g) + \frac{1}{2}\ O_2(g)$
K. $H_2O(g) + Cl_2(g) \rightleftharpoons 2\ HCl(g) + \frac{1}{2}\ O_2(g)$
L. $H_2S(g) + \frac{3}{2}\ O_2(g) \rightleftharpoons H_2O(g) + SO_2(g)$

4. The value of K_p or K_c is given for each of the following reactions. Write the K_p expression for each reaction and find the value of the one of K_p or K_c which is not given.

A. $PCl_3(g) + Cl_2(g) \rightleftharpoons PCl_5(g)$ — $K_c = 1.784$ at 600 K
B. $Br_2(g) + Cl_2(g) \rightleftharpoons 2\ BrCl(g)$ — $K_p = 6.30$ at 350 K
C. $2\ H_2S(g) + 3\ O_2(g) \rightleftharpoons 2\ H_2O(g) + 2\ SO_2(g)$ — $K_c = 1.74 \times 10^{45}$ at 1000 K
D. $N_2(g) + 3\ H_2(g) \rightleftharpoons 2\ NH_3(g)$ — $K_c = 1.40 \times 10^5$ at 473 K
E. $N_2O_4(g) \rightleftharpoons 2\ NO_2(g)$ — $K_p = 0.113$ at 298 K
F. $2\ NOBr(g) \rightleftharpoons 2\ NO(g) + Br_2(g)$ — $K_c = 0.1563$ at 350 K
G. $CO(g) + 2\ H_2(g) \rightleftharpoons CH_3OH(g)$ — $K_p = 2.05 \times 10^4$ at 298 K
H. $CH_4(g) + CCl_4(g) \rightleftharpoons 2\ CH_2Cl_2(g)$ — $K_c = 0.0956$ at 298 K
I. $2\ NOCl(g) \rightleftharpoons 2\ NO(g) + Cl_2(g)$ — $K_p = 0.0658$ at 298 K
J. $4\ HCl(g) + O_2(g) \rightleftharpoons 2\ H_2O(g) + Cl_2(g)$ — $K_c = 1.49 \times 10^3$ at 320 K
K. $2\ H_2S(g) \rightleftharpoons 2\ H_2(g) + S_2(g)$ — $K_p = 3.16 \times 10^{-3}$ at 830 K
L. $N_2(g) + O_2(g) \rightleftharpoons 2\ NO(g)$ — $K_c = 6.37 \times 10^{-16}$ at 298 K

4a. Write the equilibrium constant expression in terms of concentrations, K_c, for each of the following equations.

A. $CO_2(g) + 2\ NH_3(g) \rightleftharpoons CO(NH_2)_2(l) + H_2O(l)$
B. $S(s) + 2\ CO(g) \rightleftharpoons SO_2(g) + 2\ C(s)$
C. $NH_4Cl(s) \rightleftharpoons NH_3(g) + HCl(g)$
D. $NH_3(g) + CH_3COOH(l) \rightleftharpoons NH_2CH_2COOH(s) + H_2(g)$
E. $SO_2Cl_2(l) \rightleftharpoons SO_2(g) + Cl_2(g)$
F. hydrogen(g) + oxygen(g) ⇌ water(l)
G. ammonium nitrate(s) ⇌ dinitrogen oxide(g) + water(g)
H. hydrogen sulfide(aq) + sodium hydroxide(aq) ⇌ sodium bisulfide(aq) + water(l)
I. phosphorous trichloride(g) + water(l) ⇌ phosphorous acid(aq) + hydrochloric acid(aq)
J. $4\ HNO_3(aq) + 3\ Ag(s) \rightleftharpoons 3\ AgNO_3(aq) + NO(g) + 2\ H_2O(l)$
K. $S(s) + 6\ HNO_3(aq) \rightleftharpoons H_2SO_4(aq) + 2\ H_2O(l) + 6\ NO_2(g)$
L. calcium carbonate(s) ⇌ calcium oxide(s) + carbon dioxide(g)
M. $Mg_3N_2(s) + 6\ H_2O(l) \rightleftharpoons Mg(OH)_2(s) + 2\ NH_3(g)$

5. Use the data from the drill problems of objective 14–1a to determine the value of the equilibrium constant, K_c, for each of the following reactions.

A. $CH_4(g) + CCl_4(g) \rightleftharpoons 2\ CH_2Cl_2(g)$ at 298 K
B. $PCl_5(g) \rightleftharpoons PCl_3(g) + Cl_2(g)$ at 600 K
C. $HCHO(g) \rightleftharpoons H_2(g) + CO(g)$ at 773 K
D. $2\ NO(g) + Br_2(g) \rightleftharpoons 2\ NOBr(g)$ at 350 K
E. $3\ H_2(g) + N_2(g) \rightleftharpoons 2\ NH_3(g)$ at 473 K

(2) The equilibrium pressure of each species is written below its formula in the following equations. Evaluate K_p in each case.

A. $2\,HI(g) \rightleftharpoons H_2(g) + I_2(g)$ at 298 K
0.400 atm, 0.0136 atm, 0.0136 atm

B. $CO(g) + 2\,H_2(g) \rightleftharpoons CH_3OH(g)$ at 298 K
0.300 atm, 0.300 atm, 554 atm

C. $SO_2Cl_2(l) \rightleftharpoons SO_2(g) + Cl_2(g)$ at 298 K
0.00442 atm, 0.00442 atm

D. $H_2(g) + CO_2(g) \rightleftharpoons H_2O(g) + CO(g)$ at 350 K
1.00 atm, 1.00 atm, 0.0110 atm, 0.0110 atm

6. The initial condition of pressure or concentration is given below the formula of each species in each of the following equations. Evaluate Q_c or Q_p for each reaction, compare the value with that given for K_c or K_p, and predict if the reaction will shift left or right or if it is at equilibrium.

$4\,HCl(g) + O_2(g) \rightleftharpoons 2\,H_2O(g) + Cl_2(g)$ $K_c = 1.49 \times 10^3$ at 320 K
A. 0.100 *M*, 0.0200 *M*, 0.122 *M*, 0.200 *M*
B. 0.100 *M*, 0.103 *M*, 0.409 *M*, 0.010 *M*

$CH_3ONO(g) + HCl(g) \rightleftharpoons CH_3OH(g) + NOCl(g)$ $K_c = 0.242$ at 323 K
C. 0.104 *M*, 0.246 *M*, 0.115 *M*, 0.0941 *M*
D. 0.346 *M*, 0.102 *M*, 0.212 *M*, 0.198 *M*

$CH_4(g) + CCl_4(g) \rightleftharpoons 2\,CH_2Cl_2(g)$ $K_c = 0.0956$ at 298 K
E. 0.1060 *M*, 0.02075 *M*, 0.01450 *M*
F. 0.207 *M*, 0.0156 *M*, 0.0142 *M*

$2\,NOBr(g) \rightleftharpoons 2\,NO(g) + Br_2(g)$ $K_c = 0.1563$ at 350 K
G. 0.396 *M*, 0.214 *M*, 0.289 *M*
H. 0.204 *M*, 0.311 *M*, 0.149 *M*

$N_2(g) + 3\,H_2(g) \rightleftharpoons 2\,NH_3(g)$ $K_c = 1.40 \times 10^5$ at 473 K
I. 0.214 *M*, 0.0163 *M*, 0.270 *M*
J. 0.0214 *M*, 0.163 *M*, 0.0270 *M*

$PCl_3(g) + Cl_2(g) \rightleftharpoons PCl_5(g)$ $K_c = 1.784$ at 600 K
K. 0.100 *M*, 0.100 *M*, 0.173 *M*
L. 0.204 *M*, 0.306 *M*, 0.104 *M*

$N_2O_4(g) \rightleftharpoons 2\,NO_2(g)$ $K_p = 0.113$ at 298 K
M. 0.260 atm, 0.152 atm
N. 0.115 atm, 0.214 atm

$Br_2(g) + Cl_2(g) \rightleftharpoons 2\,BrCl(g)$ $K_p = 6.30$ at 350 K
O. 0.216 atm, 0.216 atm, 0.304 atm
P. 0.143 atm, 0.157 atm, 0.424 atm

$PCl_5(g) \rightleftharpoons PCl_3(g) + Cl_2(g)$ $K_p = 0.675$ at 500 K
Q. 0.165 atm, 0.243 atm, 0.114 atm
R. 0.0464 atm, 0.302 atm, 0.147 atm

$H_2(g) + CO_2(g) \rightleftharpoons H_2O(g) + CO(g)$ $K_p = 8.31 \times 10^{-3}$ at 500 K
S. 0.206 atm, 0.206 atm, 0.114 atm, 0.114 atm
T. 0.814 atm, 0.514 atm, 0.0621 atm, 0.0214 atm

$SO_2Cl_2(l) \rightleftharpoons SO_2(g) + Cl_2(g)$ $K_p = 2.69$ at 360 K
U. 1.76 atm, 0.423 atm
V. 1.70 atm, 1.70 atm

6a. Evaluate K_p for each of the following reactions. The equilibrium pressure of each species is written below its formula and P is the total equilibrium pressure.

A. $N_2O_4(g) \rightleftharpoons 2\,NO_2(g)$ at 298 K
158 atm; $P = 2.00$ atm

B. $2\,HI(g) \rightleftharpoons H_2(g) + I_2(g)$ at 320 K
0.464 atm; $P = 1.000$ atm and $P_{H_2} = P_{I_2}$

C. $CO(g) + 2\,H_2(g) \rightleftharpoons CH_3OH(g)$ at 350 K
0.254 atm, 0.254 atm; $P = 2.000$ atm

D. $Br_2(g) + Cl_2(g) \rightleftharpoons 2\,BrCl(g)$ at 298 K
$P_{Br_2} = P_{Cl_2}$ 0.543 atm $P = 2.00$ atm
E. $SO_2Cl_2(l) \rightleftharpoons SO_2(g) + Cl_2(g)$ at 360 K
0.277 atm $P = 10.00$ atm
F. $H_2(g) + CO_2(g) \rightleftharpoons H_2O(g) + CO(g)$ at 500 K
0.916 atm 0.916 atm $P_{H_2O} = P_{CO}$ $P = 2.000$ atm
G. $PCl_5(g) \rightleftharpoons PCl_3(g) + Cl_2(g)$ at 500 K
0.551 atm 0.551 atm $P = 1.552$ atm

7. Use the data from the problems of objective 14-6. Determine the equilibrium concentrations or partial pressures for each part except A, B, G, H, I, and J. Additional problems follow in which the initial concentration is given below the formula of each species.

	$HCHO(g)$	$\rightleftharpoons$ $H_2(g)$	+ $CO(g)$	$K_c = 0.267$ at 773 K
W.	0.200 *M*	0.100 *M*	0.100 *M*	
X.	0.400 *M*	0.000 *M*	0.000 *M*	

8. The value of $\Delta\bar{H}°$ and/or the equilibrium constant at two different temperatures is given or requested for each of the following equations. Fill in each blank.
A. $CO(g) + 2\,H_2(g) \rightleftharpoons CH_3OH(g)$ $\Delta\bar{H}° =$ ______ kJ/mol $K_p = 91.4$ at 350 K $K_p = 2.05 \times 10^{-4}$ at 298 K
B. $HCHO(g) \rightleftharpoons H_2(g) + CO(g)$ $\Delta H° = 5.36$ kJ/mol $K_c =$ ______ at 450 K $K_c = 0.267$ at 773 K
C. $4\,HCl(g) + O_2(g) \rightleftharpoons 2\,H_2O(g) + Cl_2(g)$ $\Delta\bar{H}° = -114.47$ kJ/mol $K_c =$ ______ at 298 K $K_c = 1.49 \times 10^3$ at 320 K
D. $2\,P\,(white) + 3\,H_2(g) \rightleftharpoons 2\,PH_3(g)$ $\Delta\bar{H}° =$ ______ kJ/mol $K_p = 3.10 \times 10^6$ at 270 K $K_p = 7.62 \times 10^5$ at 330 K
E. $SO_2Cl_2(l) \rightleftharpoons SO_2(g) + Cl_2(g)$ $\Delta\bar{H}° =$ ______ kJ/mol $K_p = 2.69$ at 360 K $K_p = 4.05 \times 10^{-4}$ at 280 K
F. $Br_2(g) + Cl_2(g) \rightleftharpoons 2\,BrCl(g)$ $\Delta\bar{H}° = 29.37$ kJ/mol $K_p = 6.30$ at 350 K $K_p =$ ______ at 400 K $K_p = 1.03$ at ______ K
G. $PCl_5(g) \rightleftharpoons PCl_3(g) + Cl_2(g)$ $\Delta\bar{H}° = 92.59$ kJ/mol $K_p = 0.675$ at 500 K $K_p =$ ______ at 60 K $K_p = 1.000$ at ______ K

9. Each of the following reaction systems initially is at equilibrium. The indicated changes are made. Predict whether the system will shift right (R), shift left (L), or be unchanged (U) in regaining equilibrium by writing the appropriate letter in each blank.

$HCHO(g) \rightleftharpoons CO(g) + H_2(g)$ $\Delta\bar{H}° = +5.36$ kJ/mol
A. increase temperature ______ B. add 1.00 mol $CO(g)$ ______
C. remove 0.50 mol $H_2(g)$ ______ D. decrease volume ______

$NH_3(g) + CH_3COOH(l) \rightleftharpoons NH_2CH_2COOH(s) + H_2(g)$ $\Delta\bar{H}° = -6.90$ kJ/mol
E. add 1.00 mol $CH_3COOH(l)$ ______ F. increase pressure ______
G. increase pressure ______ H. remove 0.010 mol $H_2(g)$ ______

$2\,NOCl(g) \rightleftharpoons 2\,NO(g) + Cl_2(g)$ $\Delta\bar{H}° = +71.38$ kJ/mol
I. increase temperature ______ J. add 1.00 mol $Cl_2(g)$ ______
K. increase volume ______ L. increase pressure ______

$S(s) + 2\,CO(g) \rightleftharpoons SO_2(g) + 2\,C(s)$ $\Delta\bar{H}° = -75.81$ kJ/mol
M. increase pressure ______ N. decrease temperature ______
O. remove 0.0024 mol S(s) ______ P. add 0.0024 mol $SO_2(g)$ ______

QUIZZES (15 minutes each)

Answer the first question; then choose the best answer for each subsequent question.

Quiz A

1. Write the equilibrium constant expression K_c for the reaction sodium sulfite(aq) + chloric acid(aq) $\rightleftharpoons$ sodium chlorate(aq) + sulfur dioxide(g) + water(l).

2. For the reaction $PCl_3(g) + ICl(g) \rightleftharpoons PCl_4I(g)$, initially there are 1.20 mol PCl_3, 0.48 mol ICl, and 1.26 mol PCl_4I. If there are 1.06 mol PCl_3 present at equilibrium, how many moles of PCl_4 are then present? (a) 1.33; (b) 1.54; (c) 1.68; (d) 1.44; (e) none of these.
3. For $I_2(s) + Cl_2(g) \rightleftharpoons 2\ ICl(g)$, $K_c = [ICl]^2/[Cl_2]$. At equilibrium there are 0.300 mol Cl_2, 0.100 mol I_2, and 2.0 mol ICl in a 5.0 L container. What is K_c? (a) 0.075; (b) 2.7; (c) 0.0075; (d) 133; (e) none of these.
4. $CH_4(g) + 4\ Cl_2(g) \rightleftharpoons CCl_4(l) + 4\ HCl(g)$ $\Delta \bar{H}° = -397$ kJ/mol
The equilibrium above is displaced to the *right* if (a) the temperature is raised; (b) the pressure is lowered; (c) some carbon tetrachloride is removed; (d) some hydrogen chloride is added; (e) none of these.
5. $N_2(g) + O_2(g) \rightleftharpoons 2\ NO(g)$ $\Delta \bar{H}° = +21$ kJ/mol
The equilibrium above is displaced to the *right* if (a) the temperature is raised; (b) the pressure is lowered; (c) some nitrogen is removed; (d) some nitrogen monoxide is added; (e) none of these.
6. Which factor influences the value of the equilibrium constant for a reversible reaction? (a) addition of catalyst; (b) raising the temperature; (c) removing product; (d) removing reactant; (e) raising the pressure.
7. For the reaction $SbCl_5(g) \rightleftharpoons SbCl_3(g) + Cl_2(g)$, K_c equals (a) K_p; (b) RT/K_p; (c) $K_p(RT)$; (d) K_p/RT; (e) none of these.

Quiz B

1. Write the equilibrium constant expression K_p for the reaction $SCl_4(liq) + O_2(g) \rightleftharpoons SO_2(g) + 2\ Cl_2(g)$.
2. 10.0 mol NO and 26.0 mol O_2 are placed in an empty container. At equilibrium for $2\ NO + O_2 \rightleftharpoons 2\ NO_2$ there is 8.8 mol NO_2 present. How many moles of O_2 are present at equilibrium? (a) 17.2; (b) 8.4; (c) 21.6; (d) 4.4; (e) none of these.
3. For $CO_2(g) + H_2(g) \rightleftharpoons CO(g) + H_2O(g)$, $K_c = [CO][H_2O]/[CO_2][H_2]$. If there are 1.43 mol each of CO and H_2O, 0.572 mol H_2, and 4.572 mol CO_2 in a 4.0 L container at equilibrium, what is K_c? (a) 0.547; (b) 1.27; (c) 0.782; (d) 0.137; (e) none of these.
4. $N_2H_6CO_2(s) \rightleftharpoons 2\ NH_3(g) + CO_2(g)$ $\Delta \bar{H}° = +33$ kJ/mol
The equilibrium above is displaced to the left if (a) the pressure is lowered; (b) the temperature is lowered; (c) some $N_2H_6CO_2$ is removed; (d) some ammonia is removed; (e) none of these.
5. In the equilibrium $2\ O_3(g) \rightleftharpoons 3\ O_2(g)$, $\Delta \bar{H}° = -285$ kJ/mol. One can conclude that (a) high temperature favors ozone (O_3) formation; (b) low pressure favors ozone formation; (c) pressure does not affect the equilibrium; (d) ozone decomposes rapidly into oxygen; (e) none of these.
6. All of the following may shift the position of a reversible reaction at equilibrium *except* (a) concentration change; (b) pressure change; (c) temperature increase; (d) temperature decrease; (e) addition of heterogeneous catalyst
7. For the reaction $CS_2(l) + 3\ O_2(g) \rightleftharpoons CO_2(g) + 2\ SO_2(g)$, K_c equals (a) K_p; (b) RT/K_p; (c) $K_p(RT)$; (d) K_p/RT; (e) none of these.

Quiz C

1. Write the equilibrium constant expression K_c for the reaction $3\ Cu(s) + 8\ HNO_3(aq) \rightleftharpoons 3\ Cu(NO_3)_2(aq) + 2\ NO(g) + 4\ H_2O(l)$.
2. 0.300 mol NO, 0.200 mol Cl_2, and 0.500 mol ClNO were placed in a 25.0 L vessel. At equilibrium for $2\ NO(g) + Cl_2(g) \rightleftharpoons 2\ ClNO(g)$, there is 0.600 mol ClNO present. How many moles of Cl_2 are present at equilibrium? (a) 0.200; (b) 0.050; (c) 0.100; (d) 0.150; (e) none of these.
3. For the formation of NO_2, $K_c = [NO_2]^2/[NO]^2[O_2]$. At equilibrium in a 2.5 L container, there are 3.0 mol NO, 4.0 mol O_2, and 22.0 mol NO_2. K_c equals (a) 13.4; (b) 33.6; (c) 5.38; (d) 0.0116; (e) none of these.
4. $CO_2(g) + 2\ HCl(g) \rightleftharpoons Cl_2CO(g) + H_2O(g)$. The equilibrium of this exothermic reaction shifts to the *left* if (a) catalyst is removed; (b) pressure is increased; (c) carbon dioxide is removed; (d) temperature is lowered; (e) none of these.
5. All of the following may shift the position of a reaction at equilibrium *except* (a) concentration; (b) pressure; (c) temperature increase; (d) temperature decrease; (e) homogeneous catalyst.

6. In a reaction at equilibrium involving only gases, a pressure change shifts the position of equilibrium only when (a) heat is absorbed by the reaction proceeding to the right; (b) the gases are impure; (c) the collision rate increases; (d) the reaction is exothermic as written; (e) none of these.
7. For the reaction $2\ NO(g) \rightleftharpoons N_2O_4(g)$, K_p equals (a) K_c; (b) RT/K_c; (c) $K_c(RT)$; (d) K_c/RT; (e) none of these.

Quiz D

1. Write the equilibrium constant, K_p, for the reaction $CaCO_3(s) + SO_2(g) \rightleftharpoons CaSO_3(s) + CO_2(g)$.
2. In the reaction $2\ N_2O(g) + N_2H_4(g) \rightleftharpoons 3\ N_2(g) + 2\ H_2O(g)$ one starts with 0.10 mol N_2O and 0.25 mol N_2H_4 in a 10.0 L container. If there is 0.06 mol N_2O at equilibrium, how many moles of N_2 are then present? (a) 0.09; (b) 0.04; (c) 0.06; (d) 0.02; (e) none of these.
3. For the reaction of $PBr_3(g)$ with $Br_2(g)$, $K_c = [PBr_5]/[PBr_3][Br_2]$. At equilibrium in an 8.0 L vessel there are 1.60 mol PBr_3, 0.80 mol Br_2 and 3.20 mol PBr_5. What is K_c? (a) 2.50; (b) 20.0; (c) 0.313; (d) 0.400; (e) none of these.
4. Consider the endothermic reaction $N_2(g) + O_2(g) \rightleftharpoons 2\ NO(g)$ $\Delta\bar{H}° = +192$ kJ/mol. At 2000 K the equilibrium constant is 5.0×10^{-4}. At 2500 K the value of the equilibrium constant (a) is greater than 5.0×10^{-4}; (b) is less than 5.0×10^{-4}; (c) is 5.0×10^{-4}; (d) depends on [NO]; (e) depends on the concentration of oxygen.
5. $S_2Cl_2(l) + CCl_4(l) \rightleftharpoons CS_2(g) + 3\ Cl_2(g)$ $\Delta\bar{H}° = +84.31$ kJ/mol
The equilibrium above is displaced to the *right* if (a) some carbon tetrachloride is added; (b) the temperature is lowered; (c) the pressure is raised; (d) some carbon disulfide is removed; (e) none of these.
6. For the reaction $2\ N_2O(g) + N_2H_4(g) \rightleftharpoons 3\ N_2(g) + 2\ H_2O(g)$, K_p equals (a) K_c; (b) RT/K_c; (c) $K_c(RT)^2$; (d) K_c/RT; (e) none of these.
7. The system $2\ H_2O(g) \rightleftharpoons 2\ H_2(g) + O_2(g)$ is at equilibrium when (a) $[H_2]/[O_2] = 2/1$; (b) $[H_2O]$ decreases by 50% from its initial value; (c) $[H_2O]/([H_2] + [O_2]) = 2/3$; (d) H_2O molecules no longer decompose; (e) the total pressure remains constant.

SAMPLE TEST (20 minutes)

1. At 85°, $K_p = 1.19$ for $PCl_5(g) \rightleftharpoons PCl_3 + Cl_2$. What is the partial pressure of $PCl_5(g)$ at equilibrium if the initial pressures are 2.00 atm PCl_3, 1.00 atm Cl_2; and 0.00 atm PCl_5?
2. What is $\Delta\bar{H}°$ for a reaction if $K_p = 1.456$ at 273 K, and $K_p = 14.2$ at 298 K?
3. Predict whether each of the following actions will cause the equilibrium to shift left, shift right, or remain unchanged.

$AgCl(s) \rightleftharpoons Ag^+(aq) + Cl^-(aq)$

a. Add solid $AgNO_3$
b. Add solid AgCl

$2\ NO(g) + O_2(g) \rightleftharpoons 2\ NO_2(g)$ $\Delta\bar{H}°_{1000} = -116.9$ kJ/mol

c. Increase $[O_2]$
d. Add NO(g)
e. Increase total pressure by compression
f. Raise temperature

$CaCO_3(s) \rightleftharpoons CaO(s) + CO_2(g)$ (endothermic)

g. Remove $CO_2(g)$
h. Decrease total pressure by expansion
i. Add CaO(s)
J. Add catalyst

Thermodynamics, Spontaneous Change, and Equilibrium

REVIEW OF OBJECTIVES

1. Explain the meaning of the term *spontaneous change* as it applies to chemical reactions.

A reaction which eventually will occur when left to itself is a spontaneous reaction. One which will not eventually occur is called a nonspontaneous reaction. The distinction between spontaneity and speed is important. Simply because a reaction is spontaneous does not mean that it occurs rapidly. Silver tarnishes spontaneously but it does not do so rapidly.

2. Explain why entropy is important and how entropy is related to the disorder of the system.

We wish to find a property whose value or change in value indicates reaction spontaneity. We first consider heat. Many spontaneous reactions are exothermic, but not all of them are. Vaporizing water is an example of a spontaneous endothermic reaction.

Let's think about everyday changes: diving into a pool, spilling milk, and an automobile collision. All of these are spontaneous, and the reverse changes are nonspontaneous. In the reverse of an automobile collision, the scattered car parts fly off the roadway and reassemble into two undamaged cars which back away from each other. Nonspontaneous changes "look funny" because in them energy is not dissipated but is assembled. When an automobile part strikes the earth after a crash, its energy of motion is scattered: some causes the ground to shake, some produces sound, and some moves soil and pebbles. Reassembling all of this energy is very unlikely.

Thus, nonspontaneous changes do not occur because in the reverse change, the spontaneous one, energy has been scattered. Another way to say this is that entropy has increased. The second law of thermodynamics states that entropy increases in a spontaneous process. Entropy is related to the amount of disorder present. The more disorder present the higher the entropy is.

★ **3. Predict whether entropy increases or decreases for certain processes.**

If we think of entropy as a measure of disorder, determining the change of entropy is easier. When a solid melts, its orderly crystalline structure is broken apart and the resulting liquid is more disordered. Likewise, a gas is more disordered than the liquid because the gas molecules are not confined to the small volume of the liquid.

The physical process of mixing two substances also causes entropy to increase since the molecules or atoms are now mixed together. When a solid solute produces a liquid solution there is a large entropy increase because the very regular crystal structure of the solid is broken up and the solid molecules or ions are scattered throughout the solution. This entropy effect is great enough to cause ionic solids to dissolve even when a great deal of energy must be supplied. On the other hand, entropy *decreases* when a gas dissolves to form a liquid solution. Gases are very disordered and putting them in a liquid solution increases their order. Whenever the balanced chemical equation shows more moles of gaseous products than of gaseous reactants, there will be an entropy increase. Thus when $\Delta n_g > 0$, $\Delta S > 0$.

3a. Explain why entropy alone is not used to predict a spontaneous change and why free energy is needed.

It seems very easy to determine whether the entropy of a system increases (ΔS is positive) or decreases (ΔS is negative). However, it is the *total* entropy change, that of the system plus that of the surroundings, which determines whether or not a reaction is spontaneous. Only if this total entropy change, the entropy change of the universe, is positive is the reaction spontaneous. For a spontaneous change,

$$\Delta S_{univ} = \Delta S_{syst} + \Delta S_{surr} > 0 \quad [1]$$

ΔS_{surr} is often hard to compute. In addition, other measured properties (ΔH, T, P, volume, density, and so on) are properties of the *system*. We want the criterion of spontaneous change also to be a property of the system.

The free energy change is defined by

$$\Delta G = \Delta H - T\Delta S \quad [2]$$

Free energy is *negative* for a spontaneous change: $\Delta G < 0$. In fact we can show that $\Delta G = -T\Delta S_{univ}$ by starting with equation [1] and recognizing that $\Delta S = q/T$, where q is the heat absorbed at temperature T.

$$\Delta S_{univ} = \Delta S_{syst} - q_{surr}/T > 0 \quad [3]$$

Now the heat absorbed (positive sign) by the surroundings is the heat given off (negative sign) by the system.

$$\Delta S_{univ} = \Delta S_{syst} - q_{syst}/T > 0 \quad [4]$$

If the process occurs at constant pressure, then $q_{syst} = \Delta H_{syst}$, producing

$$\Delta S_{univ} = \Delta S_{syst} - \Delta H_{syst}/T > 0 \quad [5]$$

Multiplying through by $-T$ gives ΔG_{syst}

$$\Delta G_{syst} = -T\Delta S_{univ} = -T\Delta S_{syst} + \Delta H_{syst} < 0 \quad [6]$$

All of the above require that the process occur at constant temperature and pressure.

4. Write the equations which define free energy and free energy change and know that free energy decreases ($\Delta G < 0$) for a spontaneous change.

The defining equations are [7] and [2]

$$G = H - TS \quad [7]$$
$$\Delta G = \Delta H - T\Delta S \quad [2]$$

Equation [2] is produced from equation [7] only when temperature is constant or when the initial and final temperatures of a process are the same. Recall that ΔG decreases whenever ΔS_{univ} increases. Another view of equation [2] is as a balance between two trends. First, the system tries to become disordered, making ΔS positive and thus $-T\Delta S$ negative. The second trend is that the system tries to reach the lowest possible energy, making ΔH negative.

★ **4a. Qualitatively predict whether reactions are spontaneous or nonspontaneous.**

There are four possibilities in applying equation [2].

1. An exothermic reaction ($\Delta H < 0$) which decreases the order of the system ($\Delta S > 0$ or $-T\Delta S < 0$) must be spontaneous.
2. An exothermic reaction ($\Delta H < 0$) which increases the order of the system ($\Delta S < 0$ or $-T\Delta S > 0$) is spontaneous at low temperatures where the $-T\Delta S$ term is small and ΔH determines the sign of ΔG. As the temperature rises, $-T\Delta S$ gets larger and the reaction becomes nonspontaneous. Such a process is the condensation of a gas to form a liquid.
3. An endothermic reaction ($\Delta H > 0$) which decreases the order of the system ($\Delta S > 0$ or $-T\Delta S < 0$) is nonspontaneous at low temperatures where the $-T\Delta S$ term is small. At high temperatures, the $T\Delta S$ term increases and eventually the reaction becomes spontaneous. The dissolving of most ionic salts and dissociation of any substance into atoms both fall into this category.

4. An endothermic reaction ($\Delta H > 0$) which increases the order of the system ($\Delta S < 0$ or $-T\Delta S > 0$) is nonspontaneous at all temperatures.

★ **4b. Determine $\Delta\bar{G}°$ from tabulated data, both tables of $\Delta\bar{G}_f°$ and those of $\Delta\bar{H}_f°$ and $\bar{S}°$.**

$\Delta\bar{G}°$ is the standard molar free energy change of a reaction. If $\Delta\bar{G}°$ is negative, the reaction is spontaneous, and the products in their standard states will be produced from the reactants in their standard states. Thus, for reaction [8], the free energy change is -69.71 kJ.

$$2\ NO(g) + O_2(g) \rightarrow 2\ NO_2(g) \qquad \Delta\bar{G}° = -69.71\ kJ/mol \qquad [8]$$

This much free energy is produced when 2 mol $NO_2(g)$ at a total pressure of 1.000 atm is produced from 2 mol NO(g) and 1 mol $O_2(g)$, with each reactant having a partial pressure of 1.000 atm.

$\Delta\bar{G}_f°$ is the standard molar free energy of formation. $\Delta\bar{G}_f°$ is thus $\Delta\bar{G}°$ of a reaction which makes but one mole of product and in which the reactants are elements in their most stable forms. Products and reactants are in their standard states, as the superscript ° indicates. For example, equation [9] is the formation reaction for $NO_2(g)$.

$$\tfrac{1}{2}\ N_2(g) + O_2(g) \rightarrow NO_2(g) \qquad \Delta\bar{G}_f° = 33.85\ kJ/mol \qquad [9]$$

$\Delta\bar{G}°$ is determined from $\Delta\bar{G}_f°$ data in the same way that $\Delta\bar{H}°$ is determined from values of $\Delta\bar{H}_f°$ (see objective 6–12).

$$\Delta\bar{G}°_{rxn} = \sum_{prod} \nu_{reac}\,\Delta\bar{G}°_{f,\,prod} - \sum_{reac} \nu_{reac}\,\Delta\bar{G}°_{f,\,reac} \qquad [10]$$

where the ν's are the stoichiometric coefficients in the balanced chemical equation.

$$4\ NH_3(g) + 5\ O_2(g) \rightarrow 4\ NO(g) + 6\ H_2O(l) \qquad [11]$$

$\Delta\bar{G}°$ is computed

$$\Delta\bar{G}° = 4\Delta\bar{G}°_{f,\,NO(g)} + 6\Delta\bar{G}°_{f,\,H_2O(l)} - 4\Delta\bar{G}°_{f,\,NH_3(g)} - 5\Delta\bar{G}°_{f,\,O_2(g)} \qquad [12]$$
$$= (4 \times 86.69) + (6 \times -237.19) - (4 \times -16.64) - (5 \times 0.00) = -1009.82\ kJ/mol$$

Tabulated values of $\Delta\bar{G}_f°$ are valid for only one temperature, normally 298 K.

$\Delta\bar{G}°$ is also found using the Gibbs–Helmholtz equation.

$$\Delta\bar{G}° = \Delta\bar{H}° - T\Delta\bar{S}° \qquad [13]$$

$\Delta\bar{H}°$ is computed from $\Delta\bar{H}_f°$ data (as described in objective 6–12). $\Delta\bar{S}°$ is computed from $\bar{S}°$ data.

$$\Delta\bar{S}°_{rxn} = \sum_{prod} \nu_{prod}\,\bar{S}°_{prod} - \sum_{reac} \nu_{reac} - \bar{S}°_{reac} \qquad [14]$$

For reaction [11], $\Delta\bar{S}°$ is computed as follows.

$$\Delta\bar{S}° = 4\bar{S}°_{NO(g)} + 6\bar{S}°_{H_2O(l)} - 4\bar{S}°_{NH_3(g)} - 5\bar{S}°_{O_2(g)}$$
$$= (4 \times 210.62) + (6 \times 69.96) - (4 \times 192.51) - (5 \times 205.03) = -532.97\ J\ mol^{-1}\ K^{-1}$$

We computed $\Delta\bar{H}°$ for this reaction in Chapter 6 and obtained $\Delta\bar{H}° = -1168.86$ kJ/mol. Thus, using the Gibbs–Helmholtz equation at $T = 298.15$ K,

$$\Delta\bar{G}° = -1168.86\ kJ/mol - 298.15\ K \times (-532.97\ J\ mol^{-1}\ K^{-1}) \times kJ/1000\ J$$
$$= -1168.86\ kJ/mol + 158.91\ kJ/mol = -1009.95\ kJ/mol$$

★ **5. Use $\Delta\overline{G}° = \Delta\overline{H}° - T\Delta\overline{S}°$, the Gibbs-Helmholtz equation, at various temperatures.**

In objective 15–4b, we learned to determine $\Delta\overline{G}°$ from values of $\Delta\overline{G}_f°$ and from the Gibbs–Helmholtz equation [2]. The Gibbs–Helmholtz equation can be used with $\Delta\overline{H}°$ and $\Delta\overline{S}°$ data at 298 K only when $\Delta\overline{H}°$ and $\Delta\overline{S}°$ do not change with temperature, which is a good assumption over small temperature ranges (of one hundred degrees or less).

EXAMPLE 15-1 For the reaction

$$4\,NH_3(g) + 5\,O_2(g) \rightleftharpoons 4\,NO(g) + 6\,H_2O(l)$$

$\Delta\overline{H}° = -1168.86$ kJ/mol and $\Delta\overline{S}° = -532.97$ J mol^{-1} K^{-1}. Determine the value of $\Delta\overline{G}°$ at 350 K.

$$\Delta\overline{G}° = -1168.86 \text{ kJ/mol} - (350 \text{ K})(-532.97 \text{ J mol}^{-1} \text{ K}^{-1})(\text{kJ}/1000 \text{ J}) = -982.32 \text{ kJ/mol}$$

★ **6. Know that $\Delta\overline{G} = 0$ at equilibrium. For phase changes, use $\Delta\overline{S}_{tr} = \Delta\overline{H}_{tr}/T_{tr}$ = the molar entropy of transition.**

$\Delta\overline{G} = 0$ at equilibrium, the point where the reaction changes from being spontaneous in the forward direction to being spontaneous in the reverse direction. We can reach equilibrium by varying temperature, which we consider here, or by varying concentration.

Recall the Gibbs–Helmholtz equation,

$$\Delta\overline{G} = \Delta\overline{H} - T\Delta\overline{S} \qquad [2]$$

If $\Delta\overline{H}$ and $\Delta\overline{S}$ have the same sign (either both positive or both negative), then temperature can be varied so that $\Delta\overline{G}$ changes sign. At the temperature where the sign change occurs, $\Delta\overline{G} = 0$. For a phase change such as freezing or boiling, this temperature is the freezing point or the boiling point. For a general transition, it is the transition temperature, T_{tr}. At the normal transition point (where the external pressure is 1.000 atm)

$$\Delta\overline{G}_{tr}° = 0 = \Delta\overline{H}_{tr}° - T_{tr}\,\Delta\overline{S}_{tr}° \qquad [15]$$
$$\Delta\overline{S}_{tr}° = \Delta H_{tr}°/T_{tr} \qquad [16]$$

This provides a convenient way of determining $\Delta\overline{S}_{tr}°$, since $\Delta\overline{H}_{tr}°$ can be measured readily.

EXAMPLE 15-2 Determine the transition temperature for the change S(monoclinic) → S(rhombic) given the data

S(monoclinic):	$\Delta\overline{H}_f° = 0.297$ kJ/mol	$\overline{S}° = 32.55$ J mol^{-1} K^{-1}
S(rhombic):	$\Delta\overline{H}_f° = 0.00$ kJ/mol	$\overline{S}° = 31.88$ J mol^{-1} K^{-1}

For the transition reaction,

$$\Delta\overline{H}_{tr}° = \Delta\overline{H}_{f,S(rh)}° - \Delta\overline{H}_{f,S(mono)}° = 0.000 - 0.297 \text{ kJ/mol} = -0.297 \text{ kJ/mol}$$
$$\Delta\overline{S}° = \overline{S}_{S(rh)}° - \overline{S}_{S(mono)}° = 31.88 - 32.55 \text{ J mol}^{-1} \text{ K}^{-1} = -0.67 \text{ J mol}^{-1} \text{ K}^{-1}$$

Using equation [16]

$$-0.67 \text{ J mol}^{-1} \text{ K}^{-1} = \frac{-0.297 \text{ kJ/mol} \times 1000 \text{ J/kJ}}{T_{tr}} \quad or \quad T_{tr} = (0.297 \times 1000/0.67) \text{ K} = 433 \text{ K}$$

★ **7. Write thermodynamic equilibrium constant expressions K_{eq} for chemical reactions and relate these to K_p and K_c.**

★ **8. Compute values of K_{eq} from tabulated data and $\Delta\bar{G}^\circ = -RT \ln K_{eq}$.**

$\Delta\bar{G}$ and $\Delta\bar{G}^\circ$ are related by

$$\Delta\bar{G} = \Delta\bar{G}^\circ + RT \ln Q \qquad [17]$$

where Q is the reaction quotient, but is somewhat more restricted than shown in objective 14-6. If the reactants or products are gases, we *must* use partial pressures, *not* concentrations.

$$2\,NO(g) + O_2(g) \rightleftharpoons 2\,NO_2(g) \qquad [8]$$

$$Q = \frac{P^2_{NO_2(g)}}{P^2_{NO(g)}\,P_{O_2(g)}} \qquad [18]$$

This is because Q expresses a change from standard conditions.

Standard conditions:

Gases: Ideal gas at 1.000 atm pressure
Liquids: Pure liquid under 1.000 atm total pressure
Solids: Pure solid under 1.000 atm total pressure
Solute: Ideal solution at 1.000 M concentration

The free energy of pure liquids and solids does not change very much in the normal range of pressures which we can produce in the laboratory (0–5 atm). Pure liquids and solids are not included in the reaction quotient. The free energy of a gas does depend on pressure, and we use the partial pressure (never the concentration) in the reaction quotient. The free energy of solutes depends on their concentrations, which are used in the reaction quotient.

Equation [17] is quite important at equilibrium.

$$\Delta\bar{G} = 0 = \Delta\bar{G}^\circ + RT \ln Q_{eq} \quad or \quad -RT \ln Q_{eq} = \Delta\bar{G}^\circ = -RT \ln K_{eq} \qquad [20]$$

We use K_{eq}, the thermodynamic equilibrium constant, to replace Q_{eq}. K_{eq} has the same restrictions as Q_{eq}. For example, the partial pressures of gases must be used. For equilibrium [21], K_{eq} is given in [22].

$$CO_2(aq) \rightleftharpoons CO_2(g) \qquad [21]$$

$$K_{eq} = \frac{P_{CO_2(g)}}{[CO_2(aq)]} \qquad [22]$$

EXAMPLE 15-3 At 298 K, standard molar free energies are $CO_2(g) = -394.38$ kJ/mol and $CO_2(aq) = -386.23$ kJ/mol. What is $[CO_2]$ in a solution if $P_{CO_2} = 2.000$ atm above the solution?

$$\Delta\bar{G}^\circ = \Delta\bar{G}^\circ_{f,\,CO_2(g)} - \Delta\bar{G}^\circ_{f,\,CO_2(aq)} = -394.38 - (-386.23)\ \text{kJ/mol} = -8.15\ \text{kJ/mol}$$

$$-8150\ \text{J/mol} = -(8.314\ \text{J mol}^{-1}\ \text{K}^{-1})(298\ \text{K}) \ln K$$

$$\ln K = 3.290 \quad or \quad K = 26.8$$

$$26.8 = \frac{P_{CO_2(g)}}{[CO_2(aq)]} = \frac{2.000\ \text{atm}}{[CO_2(aq)]} \quad or \quad [CO_2(aq)] = 0.0745\ M$$

Note that there are two ways of computing the equilibrium constant at two temperatures. The first uses the van't Hoff equation [23].

$$\ln \frac{K_2}{K_1} = \frac{-\Delta \overline{H}^\circ}{R} \left(\frac{1}{T_2} - \frac{1}{T_1}\right) \qquad [23]$$

This was introduced in objective 14–8. The second uses the Gibbs–Helmholtz equation

$$\Delta \overline{G}^\circ = \Delta \overline{H}^\circ - T\Delta \overline{S}^\circ \qquad [2]$$

followed by equation [20]

$$\Delta \overline{G}^\circ = -RT \ln K_{eq} \qquad [20]$$

In both cases $\Delta \overline{H}^\circ$ and $\Delta \overline{S}^\circ$ do not vary with temperature.

9. Explain how absolute entropies of substances can be determined using the third law of thermodynamics.

The third law states that the entropy of a pure perfect crystalline solid is zero at 0 K. All that is necessary to determine $\overline{S}^\circ$ at 298 K is to find the entropy change in heating from 0 to 298 K. This has been done for several hundred substances. Using equation [14], we can determine $\overline{S}^\circ$ for one substance in a reaction if we know $\Delta \overline{S}^\circ_{rxn}$ and have values of $\overline{S}^\circ$ for all the other reactants and products. In this way we know the absolute entropies of most substances. We have no such absolute value of enthalpy (or of free energy either). All enthalpies and free energies are expressed relative to the stable elements rather than as absolute values.

10. Describe how a heat engine functions and the factors which limit its efficiency.

A heat engine takes a quantity of heat, q_h, from a high temperature (T_h) reservoir. Some of this heat is converted into work (w) and the rest of the heat, q_l, is emitted at a low temperature T_l. The fraction of the heat absorbed which is turned into work is called the efficiency of the engine.

$$\text{efficiency} = \frac{w}{q_h} = \frac{T_h - T_l}{T_h} \qquad [24]$$

(Recall from objective 6–4 that w has a positive sign when work is done by the system and q has a positive sign when the heat is absorbed by the system.) Air conditioners and heat pumps operate on the same principles as heat engines except they do it "backwards." The efficiency of a heat pump also is given by equation [24]. Thus if the temperature of the outside air is −10°C (14°F) and the temperature of a house is to be 20°C (68°F), the efficiency of the heat pump is

$$\text{efficiency} = \frac{T_h - T_l}{T_h} - \frac{293\text{ K} - 263\text{ K}}{293\text{ K}} = 0.102$$

Thus, the work needed to "pump" 400 kJ of heat into the house is given by

$$\text{efficiency} = \frac{w}{q_h} = \frac{w}{400\text{ kJ}} = 0.102 \quad \textit{or} \quad w = 40.8\text{ kJ}$$

Notice that a large temperature difference means that a great deal of work must be used to "pump" heat into the house. However, you also should notice that by using a heat pump more heat can be delivered into the house than if the energy used to run the pump (usually electricity) were converted directly into heat.

DRILL PROBLEMS

3. Predict whether ΔS is positive or negative for each of the following processes. (Do not *calculate* a value of ΔS.) In which case(s) is a prediction unclear?

A. $NH_3(g) + HCl(g) \rightarrow NH_4Cl(s)$
B. $BaCO_3(s) \rightarrow BaCO_3(aq)$
C. $AgNO_3(aq) + NaCl(aq) \rightarrow NaNO_3(aq) + AgCl(s)$
D. $N_2O_4(g) \rightarrow 2\ NO_2(g)$
E. $CaCO_3(s) \rightarrow CaO(s) + CO_2(g)$
F. $CaCO_3(s) + SO_3(g) \rightarrow CaSO_4(s) + CO_2(g)$
G. $PCl_3(g) + Cl_2(g) \rightarrow PCl_5(g)$
H. $2\ SO_2(g) + O_2(g) \rightarrow 2\ SO_3(g)$
I. $Br_2(g) + Cl_2(g) \rightarrow 2\ BrCl(g)$
J. $2\ H_2S(g) + 3\ O_2(g) \rightarrow 2\ H_2O(l) + 2\ SO_2(g)$
K. $N_2(g) + 3\ H_2(g) \rightarrow 2\ NH_3(g)$
L. $CO(g) + 2\ H_2(g) \rightarrow CH_3OH(g)$
M. $CH_4(g) + CCl_4(g) \rightarrow 2\ CH_2Cl_2(g)$
N. $2\ NOCl(g) \rightarrow 2\ NO(g) + Cl_2(g)$
O. $N_2(g) + O_2(g) \rightarrow 2\ NO(g)$
P. $CO_2(g) + 2\ NH_3(g) \rightarrow CO(NH_2)_2(l) + H_2O(l)$
Q. $S(s) + 2\ CO(g) \rightarrow SO_2(g) + 2\ C(gr)$
R. $SO_2Cl_2(l) \rightarrow SO_2(g) + Cl_2(g)$
S. $CO_2(g) \rightarrow CO_2(aq)$
T. $2\ O_3(g) \rightarrow 3\ O_2(g)$
U. $4\ HCl(g) + O_2(g) \rightarrow 2\ H_2O(g) + 2\ Cl_2(g)$
V. $H_2(g) + CO_2(g) \rightarrow H_2O(g) + CO(g)$
W. $2\ HI(g) \rightarrow H_2(g) + I_2(g)$
X. $HCHO(g) \rightarrow H_2(g) + CO(g)$

4a. & 4b. For each of the reactions in the drill problems of objective 15-3 compute $\Delta \bar{G}^\circ$, $\Delta \bar{H}^\circ$, and $\Delta \bar{S}^\circ$, using the data of Table 15-1. State whether each reaction is spontaneous (S) or nonspontaneous (N) and to which one of the categories (1, 2, 3, or 4) described in objective 15-4a it belongs.

TABLE 15-1
Thermodynamic Properties of Selected Substances

Substance	$\Delta \bar{H}_f^\circ$, kJ/mol	$\Delta \bar{G}_f^\circ$, kJ/mol	$\bar{S}^\circ$, J mol^{-1} K^{-1}	Substance	$\Delta \bar{H}_f^\circ$, kJ/mol	$\Delta \bar{G}_f^\circ$, kJ/mol	$\bar{S}^\circ$, J mol^{-1} K^{-1}
$NH_3(g)$	− 46.19	− 16.64	192.5	$I_2(g)$	62.26	19.37	260.6
$NH_4Cl(s)$	− 315.38	− 203.89	94.6	$HI(g)$	25.9	1.3	206.3
$NH_4HCO_3(s)$	− 852.3	− 660.1	120.9	$Li_2CO_3(s)$	−1215.6	−1132.4	90.37
$BaCO_3(s)$	−1218.8	−1138.9	112.1	$LiCl(s)$	− 408.8	− 243	213.4
$BaCO_3(aq)$	−1214.62	−1088.7	− 41.8	$LiOH(s)$	− 487.23	− 443.9	50
$Br_2(g)$	30.7	3.14	245.3	$Li_2O(s)$	− 595.8	− 560.49	37.9
$BrCl(g)$	14.7	− 0.88	239.9	$LiNO_3(s)$	− 482.33	− 390	105
$CaCO_3(s)$	−1206.87	−1128.76	92.9	$N_2(g)$	0.00	0.00	191.5
$CaCl_2(s)$	− 795.0	− 750.2	114	$NO(g)$	90.37	86.69	210.6
$Ca(OH)_2(s)$	− 986.59	− 896.76	76.1	$NO_2(g)$	33.85	51.84	240.5
$CaO(s)$	− 635.5	− 478.6	40	N_2O_4	9.67	98.28	304.3
$CaSO_4(s)$	−1432.7	−1320.3	106.7	$NOCl(g)$	52.59	66.36	264
$C(gr)$	0.00	0.00	5.69	$HNO_3(l)$	− 173.2	− 79.91	155.6
$CO(g)$	− 110.5	− 137.3	197.9	$O_2(g)$	0.00	0.00	205.03
$CO_2(g)$	− 393.5	− 394.4	213.6	$O_3(g)$	142	163.4	238
$CO_2(aq)$	− 412.9	− 386.2	121.3	$PCl_3(g)$	− 306.4	− 286.3	311.6
$CH_4(g)$	− 74.848	− 50.794	186.2	$PCl_5(g)$	− 398.9	− 324.6	353
$CH_3OH(g)$	− 201.2	− 161.9	238	$AgCl(s)$	− 127.03	109.70	96.11
$CH_2Cl_2(g)$	− 82.0	− 58.6	234.2	$AgNO_3(aq)$	− 100.67	− 33.4	220.4
$CCl_4(g)$	− 106.7	− 64.0	309.4	$NaCl(aq)$	− 407.11	− 393.0	115.5
$HCHO(g)$	− 115.9	− 110.0	218.7	$NaNO_3(aq)$	− 446.22	− 372.4	206.7
$CO(NH_2)_2(s)$	− 333.19	− 197.15	104.6	$S(s, rh)$	0.00	0.00	31.9
$Cl_2(g)$	0.00	0.00	223.0	$H_2S(g)$	− 20.15	− 33.02	205.6
$HCl(g)$	− 92.30	− 95.27	186.7	$SO_2(g)$	− 296.9	− 300.4	248.5
$H_2(g)$	0.00	0.00	130.6	$SO_3(g)$	− 395.2	− 370.4	256.2
$H_2O(g)$	− 241.8	− 228.6	188.7	$SO_2Cl_2(l)$	− 389	− 314	207
$H_2O(l)$	− 285.9	− 237.2	69.96				

5. Determine the value of $\Delta \bar{G}^\circ$ and K for each of the reactions in the drill problems of objective 15-3 at 200 and 400 K assuming no phase changes occur.

6. Fill in the blanks in the following table. All values of $\Delta\bar{H}_f^\circ$ and $\Delta\bar{H}_{tr}^\circ$ are in kJ/mol, all values of $\bar{S}^\circ$ and $\Delta\bar{S}_{tr}^\circ$ are in J mol^{-1} K^{-1}, all temperatures are in kelvins. Each line represents one transition, from substance A to substance B.

	Substance A	$\Delta\bar{H}_f^\circ$	$\bar{S}^\circ$	*Substance B*	$\Delta\bar{H}_f^\circ$	$\bar{S}^\circ$	$\Delta\bar{H}_{tr}^\circ$	$\Delta\bar{S}_{tr}^\circ$	T_{tr}
A.	$SbCl_3$ (g)	− 315	338	$SbCl_3$ (s)	− 382.2	186	______	______	______
B.	AsF_3 (g)	− 314	327	AsF_3 (l)	− 336	______	______	______	228
C.	BeO(c)	− 610.9	14.1	BeO(g)	49.4	197.4	______	______	______
D.	BCl_3 (l)	− 418.4	209	BCl_3 (g)	− 395	289.9	______	______	______
E.	Br_2 (g)	______	245.3	Br_2 (l)	0.00	152	______	______	266
F.	$Ca_3(PO_4)_2$ (α)	−4126	241	$Ca_3(PO_4)_2$ (β)	−4138	236	______	______	______
G.	I_2 (g)	62.25	260.6	I_2 (s)	0.00	116.7	______	______	______
H.	Mn(α)	0.00	31.8	Mn(γ)	1.55	32.3	______	______	______
I.	HgO(red)	− 90.71	______	HgO(yellow)	− 90.21	73.2	______	______	400

8. (1) For each of the reactions in the drill problems of objective 15–3, write the expression for the thermodynamic equilibrium constant, and evaluate the constant at 298 K. (2) Determine the value of $\Delta\bar{G}^\circ$ which (2) Determine the value of $\Delta\bar{G}^\circ$ which corresponds to each of the following sets of values of equilibrium constant (K) and temperature (T).

A. $K = 1, T = 298$ K
B. $K = 1, T = 500$ K
C. $K = 10^{-3}, T = 298$ K
D. $K = 10^{-3}, T = 200$ K
E. $K = 10^{-3}, T = 500$ K
F. $K = 10^{3}, T = 200$ K
G. $K = 10^{3}, T = 298$ K
H. $K = 10^{3}, T = 500$ K

QUIZZES (20 minutes each)

Choose the best answer for each question. Accept a numerical answer if it is within 5% of the correct value.

Quiz A

1.

	NH_3(g) +	½ O_2(g) →	N_2(g) +	H_2O(g)
$\bar{S}^\circ$, J mol^{-1} deg^{-1}	192.5	205.0	191.5	188.7

What is $\Delta\bar{S}^\circ$ for the above reaction in J mol^{-1} deg^{-1}? (a) +65.1; (b) −65.1; (c) −17.3; (d) +17.3; (e) none of these.

2.

	B_2H_6(g) +	3 Cl_2(g) →	2 BCl_3(g) +	6 HCl(g)
$\Delta\bar{G}_f^\circ$, kJ/mol	86.6	0.00	−388.7	22.8

$\Delta\bar{G}^\circ$ for this reaction in kJ/mol is (a) −291.6; (b) −279.3; (c) −727.2; (d) −452.5; (e) none of these.

3. For the reaction $SO_3(g) \rightarrow SO_2(g) + \frac{1}{2} O_2(g)$, $\Delta\bar{H}^\circ = 93.8$ kJ/mol and $\Delta\bar{S}^\circ = 326$ J mol^{-1} deg^{-1}. $\Delta\bar{G}^\circ$ for this reaction at 27°C in kJ/mol equals (a) 89.5; (b) 196; (c) 0.42; (d) 107.1; (e) none of these.

4. For $Cl_2(g) + F_2(g) \rightarrow 2\ ClF(g)$, $\Delta\bar{H}^\circ = -11.3$ kJ/mol, $\Delta\bar{S}^\circ = 9.25$ J mol^{-1} deg^{-1}. As temperature decreases for this reaction, (a) it eventually becomes nonspontaneous; (b) $\Delta\bar{G}^\circ$ decreases; (c) it reaches equilibrium; (d) it shifts left; (e) none of these.

5. The change in free energy of a reaction (a) $= \Delta H + T\Delta S$; (b) = work; (c) predicts speed; (d) depends on the standard state chose; (e) none of these.

6. An endothermic reaction is one for which (a) $\Delta H < 0$; (b) $\Delta H > 0$; (c) $\Delta G > 0$; (d) $G < 0$; (e) none of these.

7. Which of the following phrases is *not* used in the definition of standard enthalpy of formation? (a) most stable form; (b) heat evolved at constant pressure; (c) elements in standard states; (d) work at constant volume; (e) none of these.

8. Which of the following best expresses the increased degree of randomness associated with melting and sublimation, respectively? (a) $\Delta\bar{S}_{fus} = 4$ J mol^{-1} K^{-1}. $\Delta\bar{S}_{sub} = 120$ J mol^{-1} K^{-1}; (b) $\Delta\bar{S}_{fus} = 120$ J mol^{-1} K^{-1}; $\Delta\bar{S}_{sub} = 4$ J mol^{-1} K^{-1}; (c) $\Delta\bar{S}_{fus} = \Delta\bar{S}_{sub} = 0$; (d) $\Delta\bar{S}_{fus} = 4$ J mol^{-1} K^{-1}; $\Delta\bar{S}_{sub} = -120$ J mol^{-1} K^{-1}; (e) $\Delta\bar{S}_{fus} - \Delta\bar{S}_{sub} = 0$.

Quiz B

1. $C(gr) + 2H_2(g) \rightarrow CH_4(g)$

   $\bar{S}°$, J mol^{-1} deg^{-1} 5.69 130.58 186.19

   What is $\Delta\bar{S}°$ for the above reaction in J mol^{-1} deg^{-1}? (a) 80.67; (b) 49.92; (c) −49.92; (d) 115.23; (e) none of these.

2. $Cl_2O(g) + \frac{3}{2}O_2(g) \rightarrow 2ClO(g)$

   $\Delta\bar{G}_f°$, kJ/mol 97.9 0.00 123.4

   $\Delta\bar{G}°$ for this reaction in kJ/mol is (a) 25.5; (b) 148.9; (c) 221.3; (c) −25.5; (e) none of these.

3. For $Cl_2O(g) + \frac{3}{2}O_2(g) \rightarrow 2ClO_2$, $\Delta\bar{H}° = +126.4$ kJ/mol, $\Delta\bar{S}° = -74.9$ J mol^{-1} deg^{-1}. At 377°C, $\Delta\bar{G}°$ in kJ/mol equals (a) 98.3; (b) 77.8; (c) 175.1; (d) 51.5; (e) none of these.
4. For $ICl_3(s) \rightarrow ICl(g) + Cl_2(g)$, $\Delta\bar{H}° = 105.9$ kJ/mol, $\Delta\bar{S}° = 298.4$ J mol^{-1} deg^{-1}. As temperature decreases for this reaction, (a) it becomes spontaneous; (b) $\Delta\bar{G}°$ decreases; (c) it shifts right; (d) equilibrium is eventually reached; (e) none of these.
5. In a spontaneous process the entropy of the universe increases is a statement of the (a) zeroth law; (b) third law; (c) first law; (d) second law; (e) none of these.
6. The free energy change for a particular process is 136 kJ. Thus the process is (a) exothermic; (b) endothermic; (c) nonspontaneous; (d) spontaneous; (e) none of these.
7. Which of the following is *not* a state property? (a) heat; (b) enthalpy; (c) entropy; (d) free energy; (e) none of these.
8. The enthalpy of a reaction could be determined, at least approximately, from complete tables for each of the following kinds of data *except* (a) bond enthalpies; (b) heats of combustion; (c) ionization energies; (d) heats of formation; (e) none of these.

Quiz C

1. $CO_2(g) + 2HCl(g) \rightarrow COCl_2(g) + H_2O(g)$

   $\Delta\bar{G}_f°$, kJ/mol −394.4 −95.3 −210.5 −228.6

   For this reaction $\Delta\bar{G}°$ in kJ/mol equals (a) −145.8; (b) −439.1; (c) 50.6; (d) 146.0; (e) none of these.

2. $C_3H_4(g) + 2H_2(g) \rightarrow C_3H_8(g)$

   $\bar{S}°$, J mol^{-1} deg^{-1} 266.9 130.6 269.9

   For this reaction, what is $\Delta\bar{S}°$ in J mol^{-1} deg^{-1}? (a) −127.6; (b) −258.2; (c) 3.0; (d) +127.0; (e) none of these.

3. For $B_2H_6(g) + 3Cl_2(g) \rightarrow 2BCl_3(g) + 6HCl(g)$, $\Delta\bar{H}° = -1396.9$ kJ/mol, $\Delta\bar{S}° = 800.0$ J mol^{-1} deg^{-1}. $\Delta G°$ at 227°C in kJ/mol equals (a) −996.8; (b) −2196.9; (c) −400.0; (d) −1578.5; (e) none of these.
4. For $2NO(g) + Cl_2(g) \rightarrow 2NOCl(g)$, $\Delta\bar{H}° = -37.78$ kJ/mol, $\Delta\bar{S}° = -117.03$ J mol^{-1} deg^{-1}. As temperature increases for this reaction; (a) $\Delta\bar{G}°$ increases; (b) it becomes more spontaneous; (c) shifts right; (d) $\Delta\bar{S}°$ increases; (e) none of these.
5. If $\Delta G < 0$ for a reaction, then the reaction is said to be (a) spontaneous; (b) reversible; (c) endothermic; (d) exothermic; (e) none of these.
6. Thermodynamics *cannot* predict for a reaction the (a) speed; (b) position of equilibrium; (c) maximum amount of work available; (d) feasibility of the reaction; (e) none of these.
7. $C(graphite) + O_2(g) \rightarrow CO_2(g)$ $\Delta\bar{H}° = -393.5$ kJ/mol is *not* a (a) combustion reaction; (b) bond enthalpy; (c) formation reaction; (d) thermochemical equation; (e) none of these.
8. The energy available for useful work is (a) constant; (b) the free energy; (c) the entropy; (d) the internal energy; (e) the enthalpy.

Quiz D

1. $2KClO_4(s) \rightarrow 2KClO_3(s) + O_2(g)$

   $\bar{S}°$, J mol^{-1} deg^{-1} 151.0 143.0 205.0

   What is $\Delta\bar{S}°$ for the above reaction in J mol^{-1} deg^{-1}? (a) 196.9; (b) −196.9; (c) 188.9; (d) −188.9; (e) none of these.

2.

	$4\ NH_3(g)$ +	$7\ O_2(g)$ →	$4\ NO_2(g)$ +	$6\ H_2O(l)$
$\Delta\bar{G}_f^\circ$, kJ/mol	16.65	0.00	51.84	−237.19

$\Delta\bar{G}^\circ$ for this reaction in kJ/mol is (a) −1282.40; (b) 168.70; (c) −168.70; (d) −210.97; (e) none of these.

3. For the reaction $NH_3(g) + HCl(g) \rightarrow NH_4Cl(s)$, $\Delta\bar{H}^\circ = -176.90$ kJ/mol and $\Delta\bar{S}^\circ = -284.6$ J mol^{-1} deg^{-1}. What is $\Delta\bar{G}^\circ$ for this reaction at 400 K in kJ/mol? (a) 63.05; (b) −368.4; (c) 290.7; (d) −63.05; (e) none of these.
4. For $CaCO_3(s) \rightarrow CaO(s) + CO_2(g)$ $\Delta\bar{H}^\circ = 178$ kJ/mol, $\Delta\bar{S}^\circ = 160.5$ J mol^{-1} K^{-1}. As temperature increases for this reaction (a) it eventually becomes spontaneous; (b) $\Delta\bar{G}^\circ$ increases; (c) $\Delta\bar{S}^\circ$ increases; (d) the reaction becomes nonspontaneous; (e) nothing happens.
5. Which material has the largest entropy? (a) salt; (b) powdered sugar; (c) pure water; (d) salt water; (e) cannot be determined.
6. A reaction is spontaneous if (a) $\Delta H < 0$; (b) $\Delta S < 0$; (c) $\Delta G < 0$; (d) $\Delta S > 0$; (e) none of these.
7. The state function most closely associated with the second law is (a) enthalpy; (b) entropy; (c) internal energy; (d) temperature; (e) none of these.
8. What must be true of an isothermal system? (a) constant temperature; (b) no heat exchanged; (c) no work done; (d) closed to mass transfer; (e) none of these.

SAMPLE TEST (20 minutes)

1. Write the thermodynamic equilibrium constant expression for each of the following reactions.
   A. $Mg_3N_2(s) + 6\ H_2O(l) \rightarrow 3\ Mg(OH)_2(aq) + 2\ NH_3(aq)$
   B. $SO_2(g) + Cl_2(g) \rightarrow SO_2Cl_2(g)$
   C. $CO(g) + 2\ H_2(g) \rightarrow CH_3OH(l)$
   D. $Ag_2O(s) + H_2SO_4(aq) \rightarrow H_2O_{10} + Ag_2SO_4(s)$
2. Consider the reaction $PCl_5(g) \rightleftharpoons PCl_3(g) + Cl_2(g)$. At 298 K, $K_{eq} = 1.87 \times 10^{-7}$, $\Delta\bar{S}^\circ = 181.92$ J mol^{-1} K^{-1}.
   a. Is this reaction spontaneous at 298 K? Explain why or why not.
   b. Compute $\Delta\bar{H}^\circ$ for this reaction.
   c. Without performing any calculations, predict whether K_{eq} will increase or decrease when the temperature changes from 298 to 200 K. Explain your predition.
   d. Compute $\Delta\bar{G}^\circ$ for this reaction at 47°C. Carefully state the assumptions which you make during this calculation.
3. Consider the following four compounds.

Compound	$CaO(s)$	$CO(g)$	$CO_2(g)$	$COCl_2(g)$
$\bar{S}^\circ$, J mol^{-1} K^{-1}	40	198	214	289

Explain the increase in standard molar entropies in terms of disorder.

Solubility Equilibria in Aqueous Solutions

REVIEW OF OBJECTIVES

★ **1. Write the solubility product constant expression, K_{sp}, for a slightly soluble ionic compound.**

The K_{sp} expression is written in the same way as an equilibrium constant expression. The solubility equilibrium equation has a solid ionic compound as reactant and its ions in solution as products. The concentration of solid does not appear in the equilibrium constant expression. Thus, the K_{sp} expression simply is a product of two ionic concentrations, raised to appropriate powers. (Sometimes the solubility product constant is called the ion product constant.) There are twelve different types of ionic compounds (objective 3–6, Table 3-1). These produce six different forms of solubility product constants, as given in Table 16-1.

TABLE 16-1
Types of solubility equilibria

Salt formula	Solubility equilibrium	Solubility constant expression: General	Solubility constant expression: In terms of s
MX	$MX(s) \rightleftharpoons M^{+}(aq) + X^{-}(aq)$	$[M^{+}]\,[X^{-}]$	
	or $M^{2+}(aq) + X^{2-}(aq)$	$[M^{2+}]\,[X^{2-}]$	s^2
	or $M^{3+}(aq) + X^{3-}(aq)$	$[M^{3+}]\,[X^{3-}]$	
MX_2	$MX_2(s) \rightleftharpoons M^{2+}(aq) + 2\,X^{-}(aq)$	$[M^{2+}]\,[X^{-}]^2$	
	or $M^{4+}(aq) + 2\,X^{2-}(aq)$	$[M^{4+}]\,[X^{2-}]^2$	$4\,s^3$
M_2X	$M_2X(s) \rightleftharpoons 2\,M^{+}(aq) + X^{2-}(aq)$	$[M^{+}]^2\,[X^{2-}]$	
MX_3	$MX_3(s) \rightleftharpoons M^{3+}(aq) + 3\,X^{-}(aq)$	$[M^{3+}]\,[X^{-}]^2$	$27\,s^4$
M_3X	$M_3X(s) \rightleftharpoons 3\,M^{+}(aq) + X^{3-}(aq)$	$[M^{+}]^3\,[X^{3-}]$	
M_2X_3	$M_2X_3(s) \rightleftharpoons 2\,M^{3+}(aq) + 3\,X^{2-}(aq)$	$[M^{3+}]^2\,[X^{2-}]^3$	$108\,s^5$
M_3X_2	$M_3X_2(s) \rightleftharpoons 3\,M^{2+}(aq) + 2\,X^{3-}(aq)$	$[M^{2+}]^3\,[X^{3-}]^2$	
MX_4	$MX_4(s) \rightleftharpoons M^{4+}(aq) + 4\,X^{-}(aq)$	$[M^{4+}]\,[X^{-}]^4$	$256\,s^5$
M_3X_4	$M_3X_4(s) \rightleftharpoons 3\,M^{4+}(aq) + 4\,X^{3-}(aq)$	$[M^{4+}]^3\,[X^{3-}]^4$	$6912\,s^7$

K_{sp} values are not easy to determine because they are based on a very small weight of a salt in solution. Even a small error in this weight is magnified when the concentration is squared or cubed. For example, for AgCl the solubility is 1.9 mg/L. This gives $K_{sp} = 1.8 \times 10^{-10}$. If the solubility were misdetermined as 1.8 mg/L then $K_{sp} = 1.6 \times 10^{-10}$. This difficulty is reflected by the various values of K_{sp} cited by different sources. For AgCl five sources give 1.56×10^{-10}, 1.7×10^{-10}, 1.78×10^{-10}, 1.79×10^{-10}, and 1.8×10^{-10}.

★ **2. Calculate K_{sp} from an ionic compound's solubility or solubility from the value of K_{sp}.**

The right-hand column of Table 16-1 gives the expression for the solubility product constant of an ionic compound. In each expression, s is the compound's solubility in moles per liter of solution. These expressions can be used when the salt is the only source of its ions in solution. They cannot be used when one of the ions of the salt already is present in solution, that is, in common ion problems.

EXAMPLE 16-1 What is the molar solubility of aluminum hydroxide?

From *Table 16-1 in the text,* $K_{sp} = 1.3 \times 10^{-33}$ for $Al(OH)_3$. The solubility equilibrium is

$$Al(OH)_3(s) \rightleftharpoons Al^{3+}(aq) + 3\ OH^-(aq) \qquad [1]$$

The solubility product constant expression for $Al(OH)_3$ is then

$$K_{sp} = [Al^{3+}]\ [OH^-]^3 \qquad [2]$$

Let s be the molar solubility of $Al(OH)_3$. Then the $[Al^{3+}]$ and $[OH^-]$ in a saturated solution are

$$s\ \frac{\text{mol Al(OH)}_3}{\text{L soln}} \times \frac{\text{mol Al}^{3+}}{\text{mol Al(OH)}_3} = s\ \frac{\text{mol Al}^{3+}}{\text{L}}$$

$$s\ \frac{\text{mol Al(OH)}_3}{\text{L soln}} \times \frac{\text{3 mol OH}^-}{\text{mol Al(OH)}_3} = 3\,s\ \frac{\text{mol OH}^-}{\text{L}}$$

$$[Al^{3+}] = s \quad \textit{and} \quad [OH^-] = 3\,s \qquad [3]$$

Substitution produces equation [4].

$$K_{sp} = (s)\,(3s)^3 = 27s^4 \qquad [4]$$

Notice that the forms of the solubility equilibrium [1] and of the solubility product expression ([2] and [4]) are the same as are given in Table 16-1 for a salt with the general formula MX_3.

$$K_{sp} = 1.3 \times 10^{-33} = 27s^4 \quad \textit{or} \quad s^4 = (1.3 \times 10^{-33})/27$$

This gives $s = 2.6 \times 10^{-9}$ *M.*

EXAMPLE 16-2 The solubility of $Ca_3(PO_4)_2$ is 0.002 g/100 cm³ of solution at 25°C. What is the K_{sp} for $Ca_3(PO_4)_2$ at this temperature?

The solubility equilibrium for $Ca_3(PO_4)_2$ is

$$Ca_3(PO_4)_2(s) \rightleftharpoons 3\ Ca^{2+}(aq) + 2\ PO_4{}^{3-}(aq) \qquad [5]$$

The K_{sp} expression is

$$K_{sp} = [Ca^{2+}]^3\ [PO_4{}^{3-}]^2 \qquad [6]$$

Let s be the molar solubility of $Ca_3(PO_4)_2$.

$$[Ca^{2+}] = s\ \frac{\text{mol Ca}_3(\text{PO}_4)_2}{\text{L soln}} \times \frac{\text{3 mol Ca}^{2+}}{\text{mol Ca}_3(\text{PO}_4)_2} = 3s \qquad [7a]$$

$$[PO_4{}^{3-}] = s\ \frac{\text{mol Ca}_3(\text{PO}_4)_2}{\text{L soln}} \times \frac{\text{2 mol PO}_4{}^{3-}}{\text{mol Ca}_3(\text{PO}_4)_2} = 2\,s \qquad [7b]$$

Substituion produces equation [8].

$$K_{sp} = (3s)^3(2s)^2 = 27s^3 4s^2 = 108s^5 \qquad [8]$$

Notice that equations [5], and [6], and [8] have the same form as is given for a salt of general formula M_3X_2 in Table 16-1. The molar solubility of $Ca_3(PO_4)_2$ is

$$s = \frac{0.002 \text{ g } Ca_3(PO_4)_2}{100 \text{ cm}^3 \text{ soln}} \times \frac{1000 \text{ cm}^3}{\text{L soln}} \times \frac{\text{mol } Ca_3(PO_4)_2}{310.3 \text{ g}}$$

$$= 6.4 \times 10^{-5}\ M = 6 \times 10^{-5}\ M \quad \text{(significant figures)}$$

Using this value of s in equation [8] yields a value for K_{sp}.

$$K_{sp} = 108(6.4 \times 10^{-5})^5 = 1 \times 10^{-19}$$

(We used two significant figures throughout the calculation and then rounded back to one in the final result. This is an acceptable and generally followed practice.)

Notice that we used the term *salt* to mean ionic compound. Strictly, a chemist would consider only a soluble ionic compound to be a salt. However, chemists freely use the phrase "sparingly soluble salt."

★ **3. Calculate the effect of common ions on the aqueous solubilities of sparingly soluble salts.**

Objective 16–2 deals with the solubility of a salt in solutions in which it is the only solute. Both ions come from the salt. If an ion in solution is the same as one of the ions of the salt then less salt will dissolve than in pure water. Because the solution and the salt have one ion in common, this lower solubility is called the common ion effect. It can be explained using Le Châtelier's principle. Since some of the product (one of the ions) of the solubility equilibrium is present in solution, the equilibrium will lie to the left (toward undissolved solute) compared to where it would lie if no common ion were present. The expressions in the right-hand column of Table 16-1 *cannot* be used in common ion problems.

EXAMPLE 16-3 What is the molar solubility of $Al(OH)_3$ in a solution in which $[Al(NO_3)_3] = 0.0200\ M$? The solubility equilibrium follows, with the equilibrium concentration written below each ion. s is the solubility of $Al(OH)_3$.

	$Al(OH)_3(s) \rightleftharpoons$	$Al^{3+}(aq)$	+	$3\ OH^-(aq)$
Initial:		$0.0200\ M$		
Change:		$+s$		$+3s$
Equil:		$0.0200\ M + s$		$3s$

$$K_{sp} = [Al^{3+}]\,[OH^-]^3 = (0.0200\ M + s)(3s)^3 = 1.3 \times 10^{-33}$$

Let us assume that s is small compared to $0.0200\ M$. Then we have

$$(0.0200\ M)(3s)^3 = 1.3 \times 10^{-33}$$
$$s = 1.3 \times 10^{-11}\ M$$

s *is* small with respect to $0.0200\ M$. The common ion, Al^{3+}, greatly reduced the solubility of $Al(OH)_3$ from $2.6 \times 10^{-9}\ M$ (Example 16-1) to $1.3 \times 10^{-11}\ M$.

4. Describe how the presence of "uncommon" ions in solution or the formation of ion pairs in concentrated solutions increases the solubility of a sparingly soluble salt.

In a dilute solution each ion is completely surrounded by water molecules and does not feel the presence of the other ions because they are too far away. When the solution becomes more concentrated, the ions are closer together. Ions of opposite charge attract and those of like charge repel. Hence the ions clump into ion pairs. An ion pair acts more like a molecule than like two ions. Therefore more of the solute dissolves because more ions can be present in solution. The effective concentration or the activity becomes less than the formal concentration, the amount of solute which dissolves.

One indication of this difference between activity (a) and formal concentration (c) is that the activity coefficient (γ) becomes steadily smaller as the solution becomes more concentrated.

$$\gamma = a/c \qquad [9]$$

Another indication of the difference is the decrease in the van't Hoff factor as the solution becomes concentrated, as shown by the data in Table 12-2 (objective 12–9). The charge, not the identity, of ions influences the activity coefficient. Hence, a sodium ion (Na^+) and a silver ion (Ag^+) have the same effect.

★ **5. Determine whether a salt will precipitate from solution based on the concentrations of its ions.**

The ion product expression has the same form as the solubility product expression but the concentrations are not necessarily equilibrium concentrations. The ion product, Q, is related to the solubility product constant, K_{sp}, as shown in expression [10] (recall objective 14–6).

If $Q < K_{sp}$, the solute dissolves.
If $Q > K_{sp}$, the solute precipitates. [10]
If $Q = K_{sp}$, the solution is saturated.

EXAMPLE 16-4 150 ml solution with $[Ca^{2+}] = 1.2 \times 10^{-3}\ M$ is mixed with 100 ml solution with $[PO_4^{3-}] = 4.0 \times 10^{-3}\ M$. $K_{sp} = 13 \times 10^{-32}$ for $Ca_3(PO_4)_2$. Should $Ca_3(PO_4)_2$ precipitate when the solutions are mixed?

We first find the final concentration of each ion.

$$\text{Amount of } Ca^{2+} = 150 \text{ ml} \times \frac{\text{L}}{1000 \text{ ml}} \times 1.2 \times 10^{-3}\ M = 1.8 \times 10^{-4} \text{ mol } Ca^{2+}$$

$$\text{Amount of } PO_4^{3-} = 100 \text{ ml} \times \frac{\text{L}}{1000 \text{ ml}} \times 4.0 \times 10^{-3}\ M = 4.0 \times 10^{-4} \text{ mol } PO_4^{3-}$$

$$\text{Solution volume} = 150 \text{ ml} + 100 \text{ ml} = 250 \text{ ml} = 0.250 \text{ L}$$

$$[Ca^{2+}] = \frac{1.8 \times 10^{-4} \text{ mol}}{0.250 \text{ L}} = 7.2 \times 10^{-4}\ M$$

$$[PO_4^{3-}] = \frac{4.0 \times 10^{-4} \text{ mol}}{0.250 \text{ L}} = 1.6 \times 10^{-3}\ M$$

Q then is computed and compared to K_{sp}.

$$Q = [7.2 \times 10^{-4}]^3\ [1.6 \times 10^{-3}]^2 = 9.56 \times 10^{-16} > 1.3 \times 10^{-32} = K_{sp}$$

Thus precipitation should occur.

★ **6. Determine the concentration of ions remaining in solution after precipitation and predict whether precipitation is complete.**

Determining whether precipitation is complete when the concentration of one ion remains constant involves using the constant concentration in the solubility product constant expression. This gives the maximum possible concentration of the other ion.

EXAMPLE 16-5 A solution has $[I^-] = 1.3 \times 10^{-3}\ M$. If $[Pb^{2+}]$ is kept equal to $2.0 \times 10^{-2}\ M$, will precipitation of I^- be complete? For PbI_2, $K_{sp} = 7.1 \times 10^{-9}$.

The maximum $[I^-]$ which can exist in this solution is obtained first.

$$K_{sp} = [Pb^{2+}]\ [I^-]^2 = (2.0 \times 10^{-2})\ [I^-]^2 = 7.1 \times 10^{-9}$$
$$[I^-] = \sqrt{35.5 \times 10^{-10}} = 5.9 \times 10^{-5}\ M$$

This is 4.5% of the original $[I^-]$.

Most chemists agree that 99.9% of the original amount of an ion present in solution must precipitate in order for precipitation to be considered complete. Precipitation is complete if

$$C_{final} \leqslant 0.001\ C_{initial} \qquad [11]$$

C is the molar concentration of the ion being considered. Since less than that amount (only 95.5%) precipitates in this case, precipitation is not complete.

When the concentrations of both ions decrease, the calculation is somewhat more difficult. The easiest method is to assume that solute precipitates until all of one ion is consumed and then solve a common ion problem.

EXAMPLE 16-6 What will be the final concentration of each ion in the solution described in Example 16-4?

	$Ca_3(PO_4)_2(s)$ $\rightleftharpoons$	$3\ Ca^{2+}(aq)$ +	$2\ PO_4^{3-}$
Initial:		$7.2 \times 10^{-4}\ M$	$1.6 \times 10^{-3}\ M$
Max pptn:		$0\ M$	$(1.6 \times 10^{-3} - 4.8 \times 10^{-4})\ M$
Change:		$+3s$	$+2s$
Equil:		$3s$	$1.12 \times 10^{-3}\ M + 2s$

The $4.8 \times 10^{-4}\ M$ decrease in $[PO_4^{3-}]$ was computed as follows.

$$[PO_4^{3-}] = 7.2 \times 10^{-4}\ \frac{\text{mol } Ca^{2+}}{\text{L}} \times \frac{2 \text{ mol } PO_4^{3-}}{3 \text{ mol } Ca^{2+}} = 4.8 \times 10^{-4}\ M$$

Then the equilibrium expressions for ionic concentrations are substituted in the K_{sp} expression. Remember, $K_{sp} = 1.3 \times 10^{-32}$ for $Ca_3(PO_4)_2$.

$$[Ca^{2+}]^3\ [PO_4^{3-}]^2 = (3s)^3(1.12 \times 10^{-3} + 2s)^2 = 1.3 \times 10^{-32}$$

Let us assume $2s \ll 1.12 \times 10^{-3}\ M$.

$$(3s)^3(1.12 \times 10^{-3})^2 = 1.3 \times 10^{-32} = (27s^3)(1.25 \times 10^{-6}) \quad or \quad s = 7.3 \times 10^{-10}\ M$$

We now need to evaluate our assumption that $2s \ll 1.12 \times 10^{-3}\ M$. Is the following equation valid?

$$(3s)^3(1.12 \times 10^{-3})^2 = (3s)^3(1.12 \times 10^{-3} + 2s)^2$$

Substituting $s = 7.3 \times 10^{-10}$ and evaluating both sides, we find

$$(3 \times 7.3 \times 10^{-10})^3(1.12 \times 10^{-3})^2 = (3 \times 7.3 \times 10^{-10})^3(1.12 \times 10^{-3} + 2 \times 7.3 \times 10^{-10})^2$$
$$1.3 \times 10^{-32} = 1.3 \times 10^{-32}$$

Thus, the assumption is valid.

An easier way to evaluate the assumption is to see if the omitted quantity ($2s$ in this case) is more than 5% of the value to which it is added ($1.12 \times 10^{-3}\ M$). In this problem $2s = 1.5 \times 10^{-9}\ M = 0.00013\%$ of $1.12 \times 10^{-3}\ M$ and thus the assumption is valid.

The final concentrations are now computed.

$$[PO_4^{3-}] = 1.12 \times 10^{-3}\ M$$
$$[Ca^{2+}] = 3s = 2.19 \times 10^{-9}\ M$$

Notice that the concentration of calcium ion has decreased to less than 0.1% of its original value. Hence its precipitation is complete.

★ **7. Explain how fractional precipitation works and when it can be used.**

Fractional precipitation is the technique of separating one or more ions from solution in a precipitate while leaving other ions behind in solution. To separate two cations, an anion is added to the solution. As the concentration of anion increases, eventually the value of the ion product, Q, for one of the salts exceeds the value of its solubility product constant, K_{sp}. The anion concentration is increased until the first cation has completely precipitated (99.9% of the original amount of cation has precipitated). It is hoped that other cations will not have begun to precipitate at this point. If they have, fractional precipitation is not possible, at least not using this anion as a precipitating agent.

EXAMPLE 16-7 A solution has $[Ba(NO_3)_2] = 0.50\,M$, $[AgNO_3] = 3.0 \times 10^{-5}\,M$ and $[Zn(NO_3)_2] = 2.0 \times 10^{-5}\,M$. Solid sodium oxalate is added gradually. What is the $[C_2O_4^{2-}]$ when each cation (Ba^{2+}, Ag^+, and Zn^{2+}): (a) just begins to precipitate? (b) is completely precipitated? Which of the ions is completely separated from the others by fractional precipitation and which is not? Values of K_{sp} at 25°C are

Salt:	BaC_2O_4	ZnC_2O_4	$Ag_2C_2O_4$
K_{sp}:	1.5×10^{-8}	1.35×10^{-9}	1.1×10^{-11}

We first compute the $[C_2O_4^{2-}]$ needed to just start precipitation of each cation. At this point $Q = K_{sp}$.
BaC_2O_4: $K_{sp} = [Ba^{2+}][C_2O_4^{2-}]$

$$1.5 \times 10^{-8} = (5.0 \times 10^{-1})[C_2O_4^{2-}] \quad or \quad [C_2O_4^{2-}] = 3.0 \times 10^{-8}\,M$$

ZnC_2O_4: $K_{sp} = [Zn^{2+}][C_2O_4^{2-}]$

$$1.35 \times 10^{-9} = (2.0 \times 10^{-5})[C_2O_4^{2-}] \quad or \quad [C_2O_4^{2-}] = 6.8 \times 10^{-5}\,M$$

$Ag_2C_2O_4$: $K_{sp} = [Ag^+]^2[C_2O_4^{2-}]$

$$1.1 \times 10^{-11} = (3.0 \times 10^{-5}\,M)^2[C_2O_4^{2-}] \quad or \quad [C_2O_4^{2-}] = 1.2 \times 10^{-2}\,M$$

Next we determine the $[C_2O_4^{2-}]$ when each of the ions has completely precipitated, using 0.001 of each original cation concentration.

$$BaC_2O_4:\ 1.5 \times 10^{-8} = 5.0 \times 10^{-4}[C_2O_4^{2-}] \quad or \quad [C_2O_4^{2-}] = 3.0 \times 10^{-5}\,M$$
$$ZnC_2O_4:\ 1.35 \times 10^{-9} = 2.0 \times 10^{-8}[C_2O_4^{2-}] \quad or \quad [C_2O_4^{2-}] = 6.8 \times 10^{-2}\,M$$
$$Ag_2C_2O_4:\ 1.1 \times 10^{-11} = (3.0 \times 10^{-8})^2[C_2O_4^{2-}] \quad or \quad [C_2O_4^{2-}] = 1.2 \times 10^{4}\,M$$

Thus, the first ion to precipitate is Ba^{2+} at $[C_2O_4^{2-}] = 3.0 \times 10^{-8}\,M$. The precipitation of Ba^{2+} is complete when $[C_2O_4^{2-}] = 3.0 \times 10^{-5}\,M$. When the $[C_2O_4^{2-}]$ rises to $6.8 \times 10^{-5}\,M$, Zn^{2+} begins to precipitate. Thus Ba^{2+} is completely separated. When $[C_2O_4^{2-}] = 6.8 \times 10^{-2}\,M$, Zn^{2+} is com-plately precipitated, but Ag^+ begins to precipitate before this when $[C_2O_4^{2-}] = 1.2 \times 10^{-2}\,M$. Thus Zn^{2+} and Ag^+ are not separated by fractional precipitation. In addition, it is impossible to completely precipitate Ag^+ since $[C_2O_4^{2-}] = 1.2 \times 10^4\,M$ is an impossible concentration to reach.

8. State the general rules for the water solubilities of ionic compounds given in *Table 16-2 of the text.*

This is a memorization project that is easier if you use 3 X 5 cards. The table principally is organized by anions (nitrates, sulfates, hydroxides, and so on). Write the name and formula of each anion on the front of the card and the solubility rules for each type of cation on the back. Shuffle the cards and make sure you can recall the rules correctly. To make absolutely sure, make up a set of solubility rules arranged by groups of cations (all group IA cations, and so forth). Learn these as you did the anion cards.

★ **9. Write net ionic equations for precipitation reactions based on the solubility rules.**

Net ionic equations are best understood by considering an example. If a solution of $AgNO_3(aq)$ is mixed with a solution of NaCl(aq), a white precipitate of AgCl(s) forms.

$$NaCl(aq) + AgNO_3(aq) \rightarrow AgCl(s) + NaNO_3(aq) \qquad [12]$$

If a solution of $AgClO_3(aq)$ is mixed with a solution of $NH_4Cl(aq)$, $AgCl(s)$ also precipitates.

$$NH_4Cl(aq) + AgClO_3(aq) \rightarrow AgCl(s) + NH_4ClO_3(aq) \qquad [13]$$

Equations [12] and [13] can be rewritten to emphasize that ionic compounds dissociate completely into ions in aqueous solution.

$$Na^+(aq) + Cl^-(aq) + Ag^+(aq) + NO_3^-(aq) \rightarrow AgCl(s) + Na^+(aq) + NO_3^-(aq) \qquad [14]$$
$$NH_4^+(aq) + Cl^-(aq) + Ag^+(aq) + ClO_3^-(aq) \rightarrow AgCl(s) + NH_4^+(aq) + ClO_3^-(aq) \qquad [15]$$

Notice in equation [14] that $Na^+(aq)$ undergoes no change from reactants to products. Such an ion which undergoes no change in a reaction is called a *spectator ion*. A spectator ion does not affect the outcome of a reaction. $NO_3^-(aq)$, $NH_4^+(aq)$, and $ClO_3^-(aq)$ are also spectator ions. If we eliminate the spectator ions from equations [14] and [15], we obtain one equation.

$$Ag^+(aq) + Cl^-(aq) \rightarrow AgCl(s) \qquad [16]$$

Equation [16] is a net ionic equation. It states that when $Ag^+(aq)$ and $Cl^-(aq)$ ions combine in solution a precipitate of $AgCl(s)$ will form regardless of what spectator ions are present.

10. Describe how precipitation reactions are used in qualitative analysis.

Chemists use qualitative analysis when they wish to identify the elements, ions, or compounds present in an unknown substance. In general chemistry, however, qualitative analysis usually means identifying those cations and anions present in an unknown substance, which often is a mixture of ionic compounds. Although this mixture often is supplied as a mixture of solids, it is dissolved in water before being analyzed. The analysis then proceeds by fractional precipitation. The ions are precipitated in groups of five to six ions. The solid is separated from the solution. The precipitate then is treated to dissolve some of the compounds and leave others behind. The process of precipitation, separation, redissolving if necessary, and precipitation is repeated until each precipitate and solution contains only one cation. Each precipitate or solution then is treated with a reagent which produces a reaction characteristic of the ion present.

DRILL PROBLEMS

1. Write the solubility equilibrium equation and the solubility product expression for each of the following salts. The first is done as an example.
   Ag_2SO_4: $Ag_2SO_4(s) \rightleftharpoons 2\,Ag^+(aq) + SO_4^{2-}(aq)$ $\quad K_{sp} = [Ag^+]^2\,[SO_4^{2-}]$

A. $AgCN$	B. SrF_2	C. $TlBr$	D. $Zn_3(AsO_4)_2$
E. Hg_2Br_2	F. Ag_3AsO_4	G. Li_2CO_3	H. PbC_2O_4
I. $La(IO_3)_3$	J. $Ce_2(C_2O_4)_3$	K. $CdCO_3$	L. $AlPO_4$
M. Al_2S_3	N. $Ca(IO_3)_2$	O. CoS	P. $FeAsO_4$

2. Fill in the blanks in each of the following lines. The first is done as an example.

Compound	K_{sp}	*Molar solubility of cation, M*	*Molar solubility of anion, M*	*Compound solubility, g/100 ml soln*
Ag_2SO_4	1.4×10^{-5}	0.030	0.015	0.47
A. AgCNS	_____	1.08×10^{-6}	_____	_____
B. $SrCrO_4$	_____	_____	4.7×10^{-3}	_____
C. $TlIO_3$	_____	_____	_____	6.7
D. Hg_2CrO_4	2.0×10^{-9}	_____	_____	_____
E. $AlPO_4$	_____	7.9×10^{-10}	_____	_____
F. $Ba(BrO_3)_2$	_____	_____	1.9×10^{-2}	_____
G. $Be(OH)_2$	_____	_____	_____	1.5×10^{-5}
H. $Ca(IO_3)_2$	7.1×10^{-7}	_____	_____	_____

I. Cu_2S	______	1.7×10^{-16}	______	______
J. Tl_2CrO_4	______	______	6.3×10^{-5}	______
K. $Ag_2C_2O_4$	______	______	______	0.62
L. BiI_3	8.1×10^{-19}	______	______	______
M. Ag_3PO_4	______	1.4×10^{-4}	______	______
N. $La(IO_3)_3$	______	______	2.1×10^{-3}	______
O. $Ca_3(PO_4)_2$	______	______	______	2.2×10^{-3}
P. Al_2S_3	2.0×10^{-7}	______	______	______

3. Use the data of *Table 16-1 in the text* to predict the molar solubility of each of the following salts in a solution which contains the given concentration of one of its ions.

A. $BaSO_4$; $[SO_4^{2-}] = 4.3 \times 10^{-5}$ *M* B. AgI; $[I^-] = 7.2 \times 10^{-6}$ *M*
C. SnS; $[S^{2-}] = 3.1 \times 10^{-2}$ *M* D. $MgCO_3$; $[Mg^{2+}] = 1.7 \times 10^{-4}$ *M*
E. Ag_2CrO_4; $[Ag^{2+}] = 1.3 \times 10^{-3}$ *M* F. Hg_2Cl_2; $[Hg_2^{2+}] = 0.85$ *M*
G. $Fe(OH)_3$; $[Fe^{3+}] = 1.6 \times 10^{-2}$ *M* H. PbI_2; $[I^-] = 3.4$ *M*
I. Li_3PO_4; $[PO_4^{3-}] = 0.29$ *M* J. $Mg_3(PO_4^{3-}] = 0.87$ *M*

5. (1) in each part determine the concentration of the second compound which is just large enough to cause precipitation from a solution of the given concentration. Use the data of *Table 16-1 in the text.*

A. $[Cu(NO_3)_2] = 1.45 \times 10^{-13}$ *M*; $[Na_2S]$ B. $[AgNO_3] = 1.2 \times 10^{-6}$ *M*; [NaBr]
C. $[Sr(NO_3)_2] = 1.4 \times 10^{-3}$ *M*; $[Na_2CO_3]$ D. $[NiSO_4] = 4.7 \times 10^{-16}$ *M*; $[Na_2S]$
E. $[Pb(NO_3)_2] = 8.9 \times 10^{-3}$ *M*; $[MgSO_4]$ F. $[MgCl_2] = 3.4 \times 10^{-5}$ *M*; [NaF]
G. $[AgNO_3] = 5.0 \times 10^{-3}$ *M*; $[Na_2SO_4]$ H. $[Pb(NO_3)_2] = 1.6 \times 10^{-3}$ *M*; $[MgI_2]$
I. $[Al(NO_3)_3] = 1.7 \times 10^{-14}$ *M*; [NaOH] J. $[MgSO_4] = 2.4 \times 10^{-8}$ *M*; $[Na_3PO_4]$

(2) Determine if precipitation will occur in each of the following solutions. Use the data of *Table 16-1 in the text.*

A. $[Co^{2+}] = 3.2 \times 10^{-5}$ *M*; $[S^{2-}] = 1.6 \times 10^{-12}$ *M* B. $[Pb^{2+}] = 4.7 \times 10^{-3}$ *M*; $[SO_4^{2-}] = 7.0 \times 10^{-6}$ *M*
C. $[Ag^+] = 1.2 \times 10^{-5}$ *M*; $[I^-] = 9.2 \times 10^{-8}$ *M* D. $[Ba^{2+}] = 6.4 \times 10^{-2}$ *M*; $[SO_4^{2-}] = 1.6 \times 10^{-5}$ *M*
E. $[Sr^{2+}] = 3.2 \times 10^{-5}$ *M*; $[CO_3^{2-}] = 7.17 \times 10^{-7}$ *M* F. $[Pb^{2+}] = 8.6 \times 10^{-6}$ *M*; $[CrO_4^{2-}] = 1.7 \times 10^{-3}$ *M*
G. $[Ag^+] = 1.7 \times 10^{-2}$ *M*; $[CrO_4^{2-}] = 4.6 \times 10^{-5}$ *M* H. $[Mg^{2+}] = 3.7 \times 10^{-6}$ *M*; $[F^-] = 8.8 \times 10^{-3}$ *M*
I. $[Li^+] = 1.6$ *M*; $[PO_4^{3-}] = 4.2 \times 10^{-3}$ *M* J. $[Mg^{2+}] = 1.4 \times 10^{-5}$ *M*; $[PO_4^{3-}] = 7.9 \times 10^{-6}$ *M*

6. (1) For each of the salts which precipitates in the group (2) problems of objective 16–5, determine the final concentration of each ion after precipitation and then determine if precipitation of either anion or cation is complete.

(2) Do the same for each of the following solutions. (In each of these cases, precipitation *does* occur.)

A. $[Zn^{2+}] = 1.1 \times 10^{-5}$ *M*; $[S^{2-}] = 9.5 \times 10^{-10}$ *M* B. $[Hg_2^{2+}] = 3.4 \times 10^{-14}$ *M*; $[Cl^-] = 1.2 \times 10^{-7}$ *M*
C. $[Al^{3+}] = 1.6 \times 10^{-12}$ *M*; $[OH^-] = 2.7 \times 10^{-4}$ *M* D. $[Pb^{2+}] = 1.0$ *M*; $[Cl^-] = 1.5 \times 10^{-2}$ *M*
E. $[Ag^+] = 1.7 \times 10^{-6}$ *M*; $[Br^-] = 3.3 \times 10^{-3}$ *M* F. $[Bi^{2+}] = 2.7 \times 10^{-6}$ *M*; $[S^{2-}] = 4.6 \times 10^{-15}$ *M*

7. Use the data of *Table 16-1 in the text* to determine what anion or cation will produce a precipitate with each member of the following pairs of ions. Determine the concentration of precipitating agent which must be present to just cause precipitation of each ion and the concentration needed to completely precipitate each ion. Then determine if the two ions can be separated by fractional precipitation or not.

A. $[Cl^-] = 1.2 \times 10^{-6}$ *M*; $[Br^-] = 8.9 \times 10^{-4}$ *M*
B. $[Ba^{2+}] = 1.6 \times 10^{-5}$ *M*; $[Pb^{2+}] = 1.3 \times 10^{-5}$ *M*
C. $[Pb^{2+}] = 3.9 \times 10^{-4}$ *M*; $[Hg_2^{2+}] = 3.9 \times 10^{-4}$ *M*
D. $[Sr^{2+}] = 1.6 \times 10^{-8}$ *M*; $[Pb^{2+}] = 3.4 \times 10^{-5}$ *M* (use SO_4^{2-})
E. $[OH^-] = 9.6 \times 10^{-4}$ *M*; $[F^-] = 1.3 \times 10^{-1}$ *M* (use Mg^{2+})
F. $[Ag^+] = 4.6 \times 10^{-3}$ *M*; $[Pb^{2+}] = 2.3 \times 10^{-2}$ *M* (use CrO_4^{2-})
G. $[Zn^{2+}] = 7.9 \times 10^{-14}$ *M*; $[Sn^{2+}] = 2.9 \times 10^{-12}$ *M*
H. $[Li^+] = 6.0 \times 10^{-1}$ *M*; $[Mg^{2+}] = 7.4 \times 10^{-4}$ *M*

9. Write the balanced net ionic equation for each of the following equations in which a precipitate forms. If there is no precipitate, write "no rxn" for no reaction.

A. $H_2SO_4 + BaCl_2 \rightarrow$ B. $AgNO_3 + NaClO_3 \rightarrow$
C. $NaNO_3 + MgSO_4 \rightarrow$ D. $HgSO_4 + (NH_4)_2S \rightarrow$

E. $KBr + Pb(NO_3)_2 \rightarrow$
F. $(NH_4)_2CO_3 + FeCl_3 \rightarrow$
G. $NaOH + FeCl_3 \rightarrow$
H. $BaCl_2 + Na_2CO_3 \rightarrow$
I. $ZnCl_2 + H_2S \rightarrow$
J. $FeCl_3 + NaNO_3 \rightarrow$
K. $NH_4Cl + NaOH \rightarrow$
L. $Sr(NO_3)_2 + H_2SO_4 \rightarrow$
M. $Pb(NO_3)_2 + HCl \rightarrow$

QUIZZES (20 minutes each)

Choose the best answer for each question.

Quiz A

1. A saturated solution of copper(I) bromide has a concentration of 7.0×10^{-5} *M*. What is the K_{sp} of this compound? (a) 4.9×10^{-9}; (b) 4.9×10^{-10}; (c) 7.0×10^{-5}; (d) 14.0×10^{-5}; (e) none of these.
2. The solubility product of strontium fluoride is 2.8×10^{-9}. What is the molar solubility of this compound? (a) 2.8×10^{-9}; (b) $\sqrt{28} \times 10^{-5}$; (c) $\sqrt[3]{2.8} \times 10^{-3}$; (d) $\sqrt[3]{2.8/4} \times 10^{-3}$; (e) none of these.
3. The solubility product constant of $Mg(OH)_2$ is 9.0×10^{-12}. If a solution is 0.010 *M* with respect to Mg^{2+} ion, $[OH^-]$ required to start the precipitation of $Mg(OH)_2$ is (a) 9.0×10^{-10} *M*; (b) 1.5×10^{-7} *M*; (c) 3.0×10^{-7} *M*; (d) 1.5×10^{-5} *M*; (e) 3.0×10^{-5} *M*.
4. The K_{sp} of AgCl is 1.10×10^{-10}. AgCl will precipitate whenever (a) the $[Ag^+]$ exceeds 1.10×10^{-10}; (b) a solution containing Ag^+ is added to a solution containing Cl^-; (c) $[Ag^+] + [Cl^-]$ exceeds 1.10×10^{-1}; (d) $[Ag^+][Cl^-]$ exceeds 1.10×10^{-10}; (e) $[Ag^+][Cl^-]$ exceeds $\sqrt{1.10 \times 10^{-10}}$.
5. Which of the following has the largest molar solubility? (a) CuS ($K_{sp} = 8 \times 10^{-37}$); (b) Bi_2S_3 ($K_{sp} = 1 \times 10^{-70}$); (c) Ag_2S ($K_{sp} = 6 \times 10^{-51}$); (d) MnS ($K_{sp} = 7 \times 10^{-16}$).
6. Saturated solutions of cesium iodide, mercury(I) acetate, and calcium chlorate are mixed together. The precipitate which forms is (a) calcium acetate; (b) mercury(I) chlorate; (c) mercury(I) iodide; (d) cesium acetate; (e) nothing precipitates.
7. Which of the following techniques is *not* commonly used in qualitative analysis? (a) precipitation; (b) centrifugation; (c) redissolving; (d) confirmation; (e) all of these are used.

Quiz B

1. A saturated solution of lithium carbonate has a concentration of 1.62×10^{-2} *M*. What is the K_{sp} of this compound? (a) $4(1.62 \times 10^{-2})^3$; (b) $(1.62 \times 10^{-2})^3$; (c) $(1.62 \times 10^{-2})^2$; (d) 1.62×10^{-2}; (e) none of these.
2. The solubility product of copper(II) sulfide is 9.0×10^{-36}. What is the molar solubility of this compound? (a) $\sqrt{3} \times 10^{-18}$; (b) $\sqrt{9/4} \times 10^{-12}$; (c) $\sqrt{3/2} \times 10^{-18}$; (d) $\sqrt{9} \times 10^{-11}$; (e) none of these.
3. Saturated solutions of sodium sulfate, ammonium carbonate, and nickel(II) nitrate are mixed together. The precipitate which forms is (a) nickel(II) carbonate; (b) sodium carbonate; (c) nickel(II) sulfate; (d) ammonium sulfate; (e) nothing precipitates.
4. Which of the following has the largest molar solubility? (a) $BaSO_4$ ($K_{sp} = 1.1 \times 10^{-10}$); (b) AgCl ($K_{sp} = 1.6 \times 10^{-10}$); (c) $Mg(OH)_2$ ($K_{sp} = 2 \times 10^{-11}$); (d) $Cr(OH)_3$ ($K_{sp} = 6.3 \times 10^{-11}$).
5. The K_{sp} of AgCl is 1.6×10^{-10}. What is the maximum $[MnCl_2]$ that can exist in solution before precipitation occurs if the solution has $[AgNO_3] = 3.4 \times 10^{-4}$ *M*? (a) 4.7×10^{-5} *M*; (b) 2.4×10^{-5} *M*; (c) 4.7×10^{-7} *M*; (d) 2.4×10^{-7} *M*; (e) none of these.
6. A substance is said to be completely precipitated when it (a) has a concentration of 0.00 *M*; (b) has 0.1% of its original concentration; (c) cannot be precipitated by any known method; (d) has a concentration of less than $1/(6.023 \times 10^{23})$ *M*; (e) none of these.
7. A net ionic equation does *not* include the formula of the (a) cation; (b) anion; (c) solvent; (d) precipitate; (e) it includes all of these.

Quiz C

1. A saturated solution of barium chromate has a concentration of 1.55×10^{-5} *M*. What is the K_{sp} of this compound? (a) 1.55×10^{-5}; (b) $(2 \times 1.55 \times 10^{-5})2$; (c) $2(1.55 \times 10^{-5})$; (d) $1.55^2 \times 10^{-10}$; (e) none of these.
2. The solubility product of silver carbonate is 8.2×10^{-12}. What is the molar solubility of this compound? (a) $\sqrt{8.2} \times 10^{-6}$; (b) $\sqrt{8.2/4} \times 10^{-4}$; (c) 8.2×10^{-12}; (d) $\sqrt{82} \times 10^{-7}$; (e) none of these.
3. Saturated solutions of sodium phosphate, copper(II) chloride, and ammonium acetate are mixed together. the precipitate is (a) copper(II) acetate; (b) copper(II) phosphate; (c) sodium chloride; (d) ammonium phosphate; (e) nothing precipitates.
4. Which of the following has the largest molar solubility? (a) MgF_2 ($K_{sp} = 3.7 \times 10^{-8}$); (b) $MgCO_3$ ($K_{sp} = 3.5 \times 10^{-8}$); (c) $Mg_3(PO_4)_2$ ($K_{sp} = 1 \times 10^{-25}$); (d) Li_3PO_4 ($K_{sp} = 3.2 \times 10^{-9}$).
5. A solution has $[F^-] = 1.4 \times 10^{-3}$. What is the maximum $[Ca^{2+}]$ that can be present before CaF_2 ($K_{sp} = 2.7 \times 10^{-11}$) will precipitate? (a) 1.4×10^{-5}; (b) 7.0×10^{-6}; (c) 3.5×10^{-6}; (d) 5.6×10^{-5}; (e) none of these.
6. In which solution will $AgNO_3$ be the most soluble? (a) 0.01 *M* HCl; (b) pure water; (c) 0.01 *M* HNO_3 (d) cannot be determined; (e) equally soluble in two of the solutions.
7. Qualitative analysis *cannot* be used to determine (a) a compound's formula; (b) the presence of Na^+ in solution; (c) a compound's mole weight; (d) if a solid is $FeCO_3$ or $FeSO_4$; (e) it is used to determine all of these.

Quiz D

1. A saturated solution of magnesium fluoride has a concentration of 1.17×10^{-3} *M*. What is the K_{sp} of this compound? (a) 1.17×10^{-3}; (b) $(1.17 \times 10^{-3})^2$; (c) $4(1.17 \times 10^{-3})^3$; (d) $(1.17 \times 10^{-3})^3$; (e) none of these.
2. The solubility product of silver chloride is 1.7×10^{-10}. What is the molar solubility of this compound? (a) $\sqrt[3]{1.7/4} \times 10^{-4}$; (b) $\sqrt{1.7/2} \times 10^{-5}$; (c) $\sqrt{1.7} \times 10^{-5}$; (d) 1.7×10^{-10}; (e) none of these.
3. Which of the following has the largest molar solubility? (a) $Al(OH)_3$ ($K_{sp} = 1.3 \times 10^{-33}$); (b) CoS ($K_{sp} = 4.0 \times 10^{-21}$); (c) CuS ($K_{sp} = 6.3 \times 10^{-36}$); (d) Ag_2S ($K_{sp} = 6.3 \times 10^{-50}$).
4. Saturated solutions of barium chloride, calcium nitrate, and cobalt(III) iodide are mixed together. The precipitate is (a) calcium iodide; (b) calcium chloride; (c) barium iodide; (d) cobalt(III) chloride; (e) none of these.
5. In which solution will $BaSO_4$ be the most soluble? (a) $BaSO_4$ is insoluble in everything; (b) pure water; (c) 0.010 *M* $NaNO_3$; (d) 0.010 *M* $Ba(NO_3)_2$; (e) cannot be determined.
6. A solution has $[Ag^+] = 1.3 \times 10^{-4}$ *M*. What is the maximum $[CO_3^{2-}]$ that can be present before Ag_2CO_3 ($K_{sp} = 8.1 \times 10^{-12}$) will precipitate? (a) 1.2×10^{-4} *M*; (b) 9.6×10^{-4} *M*; (c) 4.8×10^{-4} *M*; (d) 3.1×10^{-8} *M*; (e) none of these.
7. Cl^- and SO_4^{2-} are added to a solution and a white precipitate forms. Which of the following ions *may* be present in the solution? (a) Cu^{2+}; (b) Ba^{2+}; (c) Mg^{2+}; (d) Hg^{2+}; (e) none of these.

SAMPLE TEST (20 minutes)

1. A holding pond has $[PO_4^{3-}] = 8.06 \times 10^{-4}$ *M*. It measures 100 m × 200 m × 8 m. What mass, in tons, of $Ca(NO_3)_2$ must be added to this holding pond to reduce $[PO_4^{3-}]$ to 1.00×10^{-12} *M*? For $Ca_3(PO_4)_2$, $K_{sp} = 1.30 \times 10^{-32}$.
2. An aqueous solution has $[CrO_4^{2-}] = 2.0 \times 10^{-3}$ *M* and $[Cl^-] = 1.0 \times 10^{-5}$ *M*. Concentrated $AgNO_3$ solution is added. Will AgCl ($K_{sp} = 1.6 \times 10^{-10}$) or Ag_2CrO_4 ($K_{sp} = 2.4 \times 10^{-12}$) precipitate first? Eventually $[Ag^+]$ should increase enough to cause precipitation of the second compound. What is the remaining concentration of the first ion which precipitates when the second just begins to precipitate?

Acids and Bases

REVIEW OF OBJECTIVES

1. Describe the similarities and differences among the Arrhenius, Brønsted-Lowry, and Lewis theories of acids and bases.

The Arrhenius acid-base theory defines an acid as a substance which produces hydrogen ions when it ionizes in water. A base produces hydroxide ions. The ionization of a typical acid is shown in equation [1], a base in equation [2].

$$HCl \rightarrow H^+(aq) + Cl^-(aq) \qquad [1]$$

$$NaOH \rightarrow Na^+(aq) + OH^-(aq) \qquad [2]$$

All *strong* acids and bases (see objective 17-5) follow the Arrhenius definition.

The Arrhenius theory does not explain the behavior of some common weak bases in aqueous solution or reactions which seem quite like aqueous acid-base reactions but which occur in other solvents. The Brønsted-Lowry theory explains these systems. In terms of this theory, an acid is a *proton donor* and a base is a *proton acceptor*. Typical reactions are shown in equations [3] and [4].

$$H_2O(l) + HCN(aq) \rightarrow CN^-(aq) + H_3O^+(aq) \qquad [3]$$

$$NH_3(aq) + H_2O(l) \rightarrow OH^-(aq) + NH_4^+(aq) \qquad [4]$$

In each equation, the base (proton acceptor) appears first on each side, and the acid (proton donor) appears second. The term "conjugate" is used to describe species which differ by a hydrogen ion only. Consider equation [3]. $CN^-(aq)$ is the conjugate base of the acid HCN(aq), *or* HCN(aq) is the conjugate acid of the base $CN^-(aq)$, *or* HCN(aq) and $CN^-(aq)$ are a conjugate acid-base pair. (The term "conjugate" is used in a similar fashion to the word "twin": Tom is Jim's twin, *or* Jim is Tom's twin, *or* Tom and Jim are twins.) All Arrhenius acids also are Brønsted-Lowry acids.

There remain some acid-base reactions which do not involve proton transfer. For example, equation [5] is an acid-base reaction.

$$Ca(OH)_2(aq) + H_2SO_4(aq) \rightarrow CaSO_4(aq) + 2H_2O(l) \qquad [5]$$

The reaction between the two anhydrides CaO(s) and $SO_3(g)$, equation [6], also an acid-base reaction.

$$CaO(s) + SO_3(g) \rightarrow CaSO_4(s) \qquad [6]$$

Yet equation [6] does not correspond to either the Arrhenius or the Brønsted-Lowry theory. (Anhydride literally means "no water." SO_3 is the anhydride of H_2SO_4 because H_2SO_4 can be made by adding H_2O to SO_3. Note that "hydroxide" means "hydrated oxide.")

The Lewis acid-base theory defines an acid as an electron pair acceptor ($SO_3(g)$ in equation [6]) and a base as an electron pair donor (the oxide ion of CaO(s) in equation [6]). The acid-base reaction is more easily seen once we draw Lewis structures.

$$[|\overline{\underline{O}}|]^{2-} + |\overline{\underline{O}}-\underset{\underset{|O|}{\|}}{S}-\overline{\underline{O}}| \rightarrow \left[\begin{array}{c} |\overline{O}| \\ | \\ |\overline{\underline{O}}-S-\overline{\underline{O}}| \\ | \\ |\underline{O}| \end{array}\right]^{2-} \qquad [7]$$

Lewis acid–base reactions result in a covalent bond being formed between the acid and the base. The donated and accepted pair of electrons form the bond—a coordinate covalent bond.

★ **2. Identify Brønsted-Lowry conjugate acids and bases and write equations of acid-base reactions.**

There are always four species in a Brønsted–Lowry equation, an acid and a base as reactants and the conjugate base and acid as products. Equation [4] is typical.

$$NH_3(aq) + H_2O(l) \rightleftharpoons OH^-(aq) + NH_4^+(aq) \qquad [4]$$

$NH_3(aq)$ is a base because it accepts a proton to become $NH_4^+(aq)$. $H_2O(l)$ is an acid; it donates a proton to $NH_3(aq)$. If the reverse reaction is considered, then $OH^-(aq)$ is a base as it accepts a proton to become $H_2O(l)$. $H_2O(l)$ and $OH^-(aq)$ are a conjugate acid–base pair. In like fashion, $NH_4^+(aq)$ is an acid as it donates a proton to $OH^-(aq)$ and becomes $NH_3(aq)$. $NH_4^+(aq)$ and $NH_3(aq)$ are the other conjugate acid–base pair in this reaction.

★ **3. Identify Lewis acids and bases and write equations for acid-base reactions which involve them.**

To be able to identify Lewis acids and bases you must be able to draw Lewis structures. (Review objectives 9-3 through 9-9 if necessary.) A Lewis base *must* have at least one lone pair of electrons; this pair will be donated. A Lewis acid either will be an electron-deficient species or one which can have an "expanded octet." When dealing with an ionic compound (such as CaO in equation [6]), consider each ion separately. In the case of CaO, O^{2-} is the Lewis base. (Sometimes O^{2-} is called the *primary* Lewis base and CaO is called the *secondary* Lewis base.)

4. Explain what self-ionization means and describe the nature of the proton in aqueous solution.

Self-ionization, or autoionization, is a reaction in which a compound which normally is thought of as covalent produces cations and anions. Many covalent compounds autoionize.

$$2\,NH_3 \rightleftharpoons NH_4^+ + NH_2^- \qquad [8]$$
$$2\,SO_2 \rightleftharpoons SO^{2+} + SO_3^{2-} \qquad [9]$$
$$2\,HC_2H_3O_2 \rightleftharpoons H_2C_2H_3O_2^+ + C_2H_3O_2^- \qquad [10]$$
$$N_2O_4 \rightleftharpoons NO_2 + NO_3^- \qquad [11]$$
$$COCl_2 \rightleftharpoons COCl^+ + Cl^- \qquad [12]$$
$$2\,H_2O \rightleftharpoons H_3O^+(aq) + OH^-(aq) \qquad [13]$$

The equilibrium constant for reaction [13] is given the symbol K_w and termed the *ion product* of water.

$$K_w = [H_3O^+]\,[OH^-] = 1.00 \times 10^{-14} \text{ at } 25°C \qquad [14]$$

A free proton cannot exist in aqueous solution. It is associated strongly with one water molecule (H_3O^+) and weakly with three others ($H_3O^+ \cdot 3\,H_2O$ *or* $H_9O_4^+$). The hydroxide ion (OH^-) is similarly associated with three water molecules ($OH^- \cdot 3\,H_2O$ or $H_7O_4^-$). Most chemists write the aqueous hydrogen ion as H_3O^+, often called the hydronium ion, and the aqueous hydroxide ion as OH^-.

5. Name the common strong acids and bases.

Strong acids and bases break apart totally into ions when they dissolve in water—they are completely ionized. Weak acids and bases, on the other hand, are only partly ionized. It is crucial that you firmly memorize the common strong acids and bases given in Table 17-1. The periodic table can help. The strong bases are the hydroxides of the Group IA and IIA elements with the exception of LiOH, $Be(OH)_2$, and $Mg(OH)_2$. Three of the strong acids are the hydrides of the halogens. HF is a weak acid.

TABLE 17-1
Some common strong acids and bases

Acids	Bases
HCl	NaOH
HBr	KOH
HI	RbOH
$HClO_4$	CsOH
HNO_3	$Ca(OH)_2$
H_2SO_4	$Sr(OH)_2$
	$Ba(OH)_2$

★ **6. Calculate ionic concentrations in aqueous solutions of strong electrolytes and relate $[H_3O^+]$ and $[OH^-]$ through K_w.**

Strong electrolytes completely ionize when dissolved in water. This includes strong acids and bases and all salts. When 0.0200 mol NaCl dissolves to form a liter of aqueous solution, that solution contains sodium ions and chloride ions with $[Na^+] = 0.0200\ M$ and $[Cl^-] = 0.0200\ M$. Likewise, when 1.5×10^{-4} mol $CaCl_2$ forms a liter of aqueous solution, $[Ca^{2+}] = 1.50 \times 10^{-4}\ M$ and $[Cl^-] = 3.00 \times 10^{-4}\ M$.

In similar fashion, a 0.0200 M solution of NaOH has $[Na^+] = 0.0200\ M$ and $[OH^-] = 0.0200\ M$. Furthermore, equation [14] relates $[OH^-]$ and $[H_3O^+]$.

$$K_w = [H_3O^+]\ [OH^-] = 1.00 \times 10^{-14} \quad \text{at } 25°C \qquad [14]$$

Since we know $[OH^-] = 0.0200\ M$, we can compute $[H_3O^+]$.

$$[H_3O^+]\ (0.0200\ M) = 1.00 \times 10^{-14} \quad \text{or} \quad [H_3O^+] = 5.00 \times 10^{-11}\ M$$

EXAMPLE 17-1 What is $[H_3O^+]$ in a $1.50 \times 10^{-4}\ M$ $Ca(OH)_2$ solution?

$$1.50 \times 10^{-4}\ M\ Ca(OH)_2 \times \frac{2 \text{ mol } OH^-}{1 \text{ mol } Ca(OH)_2} = 3.00 \times 10^{-4}\ M = [OH^-]$$

$$[H_3O^+]\ [OH^-] = [H_3O^+]\ 3.00 \times 10^{-4}\ M = 1.00 \times 10^{-14} \quad \text{or} \quad [H_3O^+] = 3.33 \times 10^{-9}\ M$$

★ **7. Given a value of any one of $[H_3O^+]$, $[OH^-]$, pH, and pOH, be able to compute values of the other three.**

Equation [14] relates $[H_3O^+]$ and $[OH^-]$. The definitions of pH and pOH are

$$pH = -\log\ [H_3O^+] \qquad [15]$$
$$pOH = -\log\ [OH^-] \qquad [16]$$

One other relationship is that between pH and pOH at 25°C

$$pH + p\ OH = 14.00 \qquad [17]$$

These expressions can be used to express a solution's acidity as pH, pOH, $[H_3O^+]$, or $[OH^-]$.

EXAMPLE 17-2 A solution with $[OH^-] = 2.50 \times 10^{-5}\ M$ has what pH, pOH, and $[H_3O^+]$?
pOH is most readily determined.

$$pOH = -\log\ [OH^-] = -\log(2.50 \times 10^{-5}) = 4.602$$

Then we determine pH.

$$pH + pOH = 14.00 = pH + 4.602 \quad or \quad pH = 9.40$$

Finally, we can find $[H_3O^+]$ in two ways.

$$[H_3O^+] = 10^{-pH} = 10^{-9.40} = 4.0 \times 10^{-10}\ M$$

or $$[H_3O^+]\ [OH^-] = 1.00 \times 10^{-14} = [H_3O^+]\ (2.50 \times 10^{-5})$$

$$[H_3O^+] = 4.00 \times 10^{-10}\ M$$

★ **8. Identify a weak acid or base, write the chemical equation for its ionization, and set up its ionization constant expression.**

An acid or base which is not strong (Table 17-1) must be weak. It's as simple as that. The ionization equations for all weak acids in water involve the acid donating a proton to a water molecule, producing H_3O^+ and the anion of the acid.

$$HCN(aq) + H_2O(l) \rightleftharpoons H_3O^+(aq) + CN^-(aq) \qquad [18]$$

$$HF(aq) + H_2O(l) \rightleftharpoons H_3O^+(aq) + F^-(aq) \qquad [19]$$

The ionization constant expression is written in the same way that *all* equilibrium constant expressions are written. Concentrations of products are in the numerator and those of reactants in the denominator.

$$K_a = \frac{[H_3O^+]\ [CN^-]}{[HCN]} \qquad K_a = \frac{[H_3O^+]\ [F^-]}{[HF]} \qquad [20]$$

The ionization equations for weak bases in water involve the base accepting a proton from a water molecule, producing OH^- and the cation of the base.

$$NH_3(aq) + H_2O(l) \rightleftharpoons NH_4^+(aq) + OH^-(aq) \qquad [21]$$

$$N_2H_4(aq) + H_2O(l) \rightleftharpoons N_2H_5^+(aq) + OH^-(aq) \qquad [22]$$

The ionization constant expressions are written in the usual fashion.

$$K_b = \frac{[NH_4^+]\ [OH^-]}{[NH_3]} \qquad K_b = \frac{[N_2H_5^+]\ [OH^-]}{[N_2H_4]} \qquad [23]$$

★ **9. Determine one of K_a, $[H_3O^+]$, or the molarity of a weak acid, given the other two (and perform similar calculations for a weak base). Know how to simplify these calculations by making suitable assumptions.**

$$HA(aq) + H_2{=}(l) \rightleftharpoons H_3O^+(aq) + A^-(aq) \qquad [24]$$

For equation [24] the ionization constant expression is

$$K_a = \frac{[H_3O^+]\ [A^-]}{[HA]} \qquad [25]$$

If HA is the only solute, then it is the only source of $A^-(aq)$ ions.

$$[H_3O^+] = [A^-] \qquad [26]$$

We use these expressions in three types of problems.

(1) *Determining* K_a *from* $[H^+]$ *and* $[HA]$. A common way to determine K_a experimentally is to measure the pH of a solution of known initial acid concentration. The initial concentration of acid (or base) also is known as the *formality*, that is, based on the *formulation* of the solution.

EXAMPLE 17-3 A 0.10 *M* solution of HN_3 has pH = 2.860. What is K_a for this acid?
We first write the equation and ionization constant expression.

$$HN_3(aq) + H_2O(l) \rightleftharpoons H_3O^+(aq) + N_3^-(aq)$$

$$K_a = \frac{[H_3O^+]\,[NH_3^-]}{[HN_3]}$$

Then we determine $[H_3O^+] = 10^{-pH} = 1.38 \times 10^{-3}\ M$. Next, we write the concentration of each species below its formula: that before ionization (I = initially), the change to reach equilibrium (C), and that at equilibrium (Eq).

	$HN_3(aq)$	+	$H_2O(l)$	$\rightleftharpoons$	$H_2O^+(aq)$	+	$N_3^-(aq)$
I:	0.101 *M*						
C:	−0.00138 *M*				+0.00138 *M*		+0.00138 *M*
Eq:	0.100 *M*				0.00138 *M*		0.00138 *M*

We then use the equilibrium concentrations to compute K_a.

$$K_a = \frac{[H_3O^+]\,[NH_3^-]}{[HN_3]} = \frac{(0.00138)\,(0.00138)}{0.100} = 1.90 \times 10^{-5}$$

(2) *Determining* $[H_3O^+]$ *from* K_a *and* $[HA]$. K_a and the initial acid concentration are given and $[H_3O^+]$ is computed. The setup is like that of Example 17-3, with $[H_3O^+] = x$.

EXAMPLE 17-4 What is $[H_3O^+]$ in a solution with $[HF] = 0.500\ M$? $K_a = 6.7 \times 10^{-4}$ for HF.
The setup is based on the ionization equation.

	$HF(aq)$	+	$H_2O(l)$	$\rightleftharpoons$	$H_3O^+(aq)$	+	$F^-(aq)$
I:	0.500 *M*						
C:	$-x$ *M*				$+x$ *M*		$+x$ *M*
Eq:	$(0.500 - x)$ *M*				x *M*		x *M*

Then substitute into the K_a expression.

$$K_a = \frac{[H_3O^+]\,[F^-]}{[HF]} = 6.7 \times 10^{-4} = \frac{(x)\,(x)}{0.500 - x}$$

There are two ways to solve this equation. The first uses the quadratic equation (objective 14-7). The second uses an approximation. With a small equilibrium constant, we expect very little product. Thus we assume $x \ll 0.500$ *or* $0.500 - x \simeq 0.500$. This gives

$$6.7 \times 10^{-4} \simeq \frac{x^2}{0.500} \quad or \quad x = 1.8 \times 10^{-2}\ M = 0.018\ M$$

It does not look as though 0.018 *M* is small compared to 0.500 *M*. Let us substitute into the original expression for K_a.

$$K_a = \frac{(0.018)\,(0.018)}{0.500 - 0.018} = 6.7 \times 10^{-4}$$

We see that $[H_3O^+] = 0.018\ M$ does satisfy the original equation.

A convenient rule of thumb is that x is small compared to the original acid concentration, [HA], if x is less than 5% of [HA]. Of course, you can only be sure that x is small enough by substituting into the original equation. This approximation is worth trying if the acid concentration is at least 1000 times larger than K_a. This is a cautious guideline and can be ignored, as Example 17-5 shows.

EXAMPLE 17-5 What is $[H_3O^+]$ in a 1.00 *M* $HClO_2$ solution?
From *Table 17-2 in the text,* $K_a = 1.2 \times 10^{-2}$ for $HClO_2$.

	$HClO_2(aq)$	$H_2O(l)$	$H_3O^+(aq)$	$ClO_2^-(aq)$
I:	1.00 *M*			
C:	$-x$ *M*		$+x$ *M*	$+x$ *M*
Eq:	$(1.00 - x)$ *M*		x *M*	x *M*

$$K_a = \frac{[H_3O^+]\,[ClO_2^-]}{HClO_2]} = \frac{(x)(x)}{1.00 - x} = 1.2 \times 10^{-2} \simeq \frac{x^2}{1.00}$$

We have disregarded the guideline cited above and assumed $x \ll 1.00$.

$$x^2 = (1.2 \times 10^{-2})(1.00) \quad or \quad x = 0.110\ M$$

Obviously 0.110 *M* is not small compared to 1.00 *M*. However, we can use it as a first guess.

$$\frac{(x)(x)}{1.00 - 0.110} = \frac{x^2}{0.89} \simeq 1.2 \times 10^{-2} \quad or \quad x = 0.103\ M$$

The two results (0.11 *M* and 0.103 *M*) differ by very little as one more substitution shows.

$$\frac{(x)(x)}{1.00 - 0.103} = \frac{x^2}{0.897} \simeq 1.2 \times 10^{-2} \quad or \quad x = 0.104\ M$$

These last two values (0.103 *M* and 0.104 *M*) give a two-significant-figure answer of $[H_3O^+] = 0.10\ M$.

This technique is known as the method of successive approximations. It is quite time saving and much easier than solving the quadratic equation, especially with an electronic calculator. Note that when two successive approximations agree to three significant figures you should stop, and use the last value.

(3) *Determining* [HA] *from* K_a *and* $[H^+]$. The last type of calculation determines the concentration of a given weak acid to produce a solution of a certain pH.

EXAMPLE 17-6 What $[HNO_2]$ is needed to produce a solution with pH = 2.200?
$K_a = 5.13 \times 10^{-4}$ for HNO_2.
We first find $[H_3O^+] = 10^{-pH} = 10^{-2.200} = 6.31 \times 10^{-3}\ M$.

Setup:	$HNO_2(aq)$ + $H_2O(l)$ $\rightleftharpoons$	$H_3O^+(aq)$ +	NO_2^-
I:	x *M*		
C:	-0.00631 *M*	$+0.00631$ *M*	$+0.00631$ *M*
Eq:	$(x - 0.00631)$ *M*	0.00631 *M*	0.00631 *M*

$$K_a = \frac{(0.00631)^2}{x - 0.00631} = 5.13 \times 10^{-4} \quad or \quad x = 0.0839\ M = [HNO_2]$$

Often students can solve problems for weak acids but not for weak bases. Weak base problems are easier if you remember that $[OH^-]$ is as important for bases as $[H_3O^+]$ is for acids.

EXAMPLE 17-7 What is the pH of a 0.750 M $C_2H_5NH_2$ solution? $K_b = 4.3 \times 10^{-4}$ for $C_2H_5NH_2$

Setup:	$C_2H_5NH_2(aq) + H_2O(l)$	$\rightleftharpoons$	$C_2H_5NH_3^+(aq)$	+ $OH^-(aq)$
I:	0.750 M			
C:	$-x$ M		$+x$ M	$+x$ M
Eq:	$(0.750 - x)$ M		x M	x M

$$K_b = \frac{[C_2H_5NH_3^+]\,[OH^-]}{[C_2H_5NH_2]} = 4.3 \times 10^{-4} = \frac{(x)(x)}{0.750 - x} \simeq \frac{x^2}{0.750}$$

We have assumed $x \ll 0.750\,M$. Then $x = 1.8 \times 10^{-2}\,M$. By substituting,

$$\frac{x^2}{0.750 - x} = \frac{(0.018)^2}{0.750 - 0.018} = 4.4 \times 10^{-4}$$

This agrees with the value of K_a. Thus $x = 1.8 \times 10^{-2}\,M = [OH^-]$.

$$\text{pOH} = -\log(1.8 \times 10^{-2}) = 1.74 \quad \textit{and} \quad \text{pH} = 14.00 - \text{pOH} = 14.00 - 1.74 = 12.26$$

★ **10. Describe the ionization of a polyprotic acid in aqueous solution and determine the concentrations of the various species in solution.**

Polyprotic acids ionize in several steps, one step for each ionizable hydrogen in the acid.

$$H_2C_2O_4(aq) + H_2O(l) \rightleftharpoons H_3O^+(aq) + HC_2O_4^-(aq) \qquad K_{a_1} = 5.4 \times 10^{-2}$$
$$HC_2O_4^-(aq) + H_2O(l) \rightleftharpoons H_3O^+(aq) + C_2O_4^{2-}(aq) \qquad K_{a_2} = 5.4 \times 10^{-5}$$

EXAMPLE 17-8 What is the concentration of each species present in a 1.00 M oxalic acid solution? We solve the first ionization.

Setup:	$H_2C_2O_4(aq) + H_2O(l)$	$\rightleftharpoons$ $H_3O^+(aq)$	+ $HC_2O_4^-(aq)$
I:	1.00 M		
C:	$-x$ M	$+x$ M	$+x$ M
Eq:	$(1.00 - x)$ M	x M	x M

$$K_{a_1} = \frac{[H_3O^+]\,[HC_2O_4^-]}{H_2C_2O_4]} = 5.4 \times 10^{-2} = \frac{(x)(x)}{1.00 - x} \simeq \frac{x^2}{1.00}$$

We have assumed $x \ll 1.00$. Thus $x = 0.232\,M$. We use successive approximations to find a final answer.

$x^2/(1.00 - 0.232) = 5.4 \times 10^{-2}$ *or* $x = 0.204\,M$
$x^2/(1.00 - 0.204) = 5.4 \times 10^{-2}$ *or* $x = 0.207\,M$
$x^2/(1.00 - 0.207) = 5.4 \times 10^{-2}$ *or* $x = 0.207\,M$

Then the second ionization is solved.

Setup:	$HC_2O_4^-(aq) + H_2O(l)$	$\rightleftharpoons$ $H_3O^+(aq)$	+ $C_2O_4^{2-}$
I:	0.207 M	0.207 M	
C:	$-x$ M	$+x$ M	$+x$ M
Eq:	$(0.207 - x)$ M	$(0.207 + x)$ M	x M

$$K_{a_2} = \frac{[H_3O^+]\,[C_2O_4^{2-}]}{[HC_2O_4^{2-}]} = 5.4 \times 10^{-5} = \frac{(x)(0.207 + x)}{0.207 - x} \simeq \frac{x(0.207)}{0.207}$$

We have assumed $x \ll 0.207$. This produces $x = 5.4 \times 10^{-5}\,M = [C_2O_4^{2-}]$. Clearly, our assumption is valid. Notice that $[H_3O^+]$ produced in the second ionization does not change the $[H_3O^+]$ produced in the first step.

$[C_2O_4^{2-}] = 5.4 \times 10^{-5}\ M$ $[H_3O^+] = [HC_2O_4^-] = 0.207\ M$ $[H_2C_2O_4] = 0.793\ M$

★ **11. Predict which ions hydrolyze and whether salt solutions are acidic, basic, or neutral.**

All salts ionize completely when they dissolve in water (objective 17-6). The anion of a strong acid does not react with water.

$$NO_3^-(aq) + H_2O(l) \rightarrow \text{no reaction} \qquad [27]$$

However, the anion of a weak acid accepts a proton from a water molecule to produce an acid molecule and a hydroxide ion.

$$NO_2^-(aq) + H_2O(l) \rightleftharpoons HNO_2(aq) + OH^-(aq) \qquad [28]$$

This process is known as *hydrolysis*. Notice that NO_2^-, the anion of the weak acid, is a base—a proton acceptor. In fact, there is little difference in overall form between equations [28] and [29];

$$NH_3(aq) + H_2O(l) \rightleftharpoons NH_4^+(aq) + OH^-(aq) \qquad [29]$$

Cations of strong bases do not react with water.

$$Na^+(aq) + H_2O(l) \rightarrow \text{no reaction} \qquad [30]$$

Yet, the cation of a weak base hydrolyzes, forming the base and H_3O^+.

$$CH_3NH_3^+(aq) + H_2O(l) \rightarrow CH_3NH_2(aq) + H_3O^+(aq) \qquad [31]$$

Thus, weak base cations are proton donors, or bases.

Salts can be of four types, as follows.

1. *Cation of strong base and anion of strong acid.* Hydrolysis occurs in neither case (see reactions [27] and [30]), and the resulting solution is neutral.
2. *Cation of strong base and anion of weak acid.* The cation does not hydrolyse ([30]), but the anion does (as in [28]). The OH^- thus formed produces a basic solution.
3. *Cation of weak base and anion of strong acid.* The anion does not hydrolyze ([27]), but the cation does (as in [31]). The resulting solution is acidic.
4. *Cation of weak base and anion of weak acid.* Both the cation and the anion hydrolyze. The one which does so most extensively determines the acidity of the solution.

The relative strengths of the acid which supplied the anion and of the base which supplied the cation determine the acidity of the salt solution. If the base is stronger, the salt solution is basic. If the acid is stronger, the salt solution is acidic.

★ **12. Write ionic equations representing hydrolysis and compute the pH of salt solutions.**

Hydrolysis problems are set up in the same way as were weak acid and weak base problems in objective 17-9. The sole difference is that the ionization constant, (called a hydrolysis constant, K_h), normally is not tabulated but must be computed. For the anion of a weak acid,

$$K_w = K_a K_h \quad \text{or} \quad K_h = K_w/K_a \qquad [32]$$

For the cation of a weak base,

$$K_w = K_b K_h \quad \text{or} \quad K_h = K_w/K_b \qquad [33]$$

EXAMPLE 17-9 What is the pH of a 0.125 *M* sodium benzoate solution? $K_a = 6.3 \times 10^{-5}$ for benzoic acid.

$$NaC_7H_5O_2 \rightarrow Na^+(aq) + C_7H_5O_2^-(aq)$$

Na^+ does not hydrolyze, but the anion does.

Setup:	$C_7H_5O_2^-(aq)$ + $H_2O(l)$ ⇌	$HC_7H_5O_2(aq)$ +	$OH^-(aq)$
I:	0.125 *M*		
C:	$-x$ *M*	$+x$ *M*	$+x$ *M*
Eq:	$(0.125 - x)$ *M*	x *M*	x *M*

$$K_h = \frac{[HC_7H_5O_2]\,[OH^-]}{[C_7H_5O_2^-]} = \frac{(x)(x)}{0.125 - x} = \frac{K_w}{K_a} = \frac{1.00 \times 10^{-14}}{6.3 \times 10^{-5}} = 1.59 \times 10^{-10} \simeq \frac{x^2}{0.125}$$

or $x = 4.5 \times 10^{-6}\ M = [OH^-]$

We have assumed $x \ll 0.125\ M$. $4.5 \times 10^{-6}\ M$ clearly is much smaller than 0.125 *M*. We obtain pOH = 5.35 *or* pH = 14.00 − pOH = 8.65.

Notice the very strong similarity between this calculation and Example 17-7.

★ **13. Use the relative strengths of Brønsted-Lowry acids and bases to predict the direction of acid-base reactions.**

The products of the reaction of an acid with a base are the conjugate base and the conjugate acid.

$$HC_2H_3O_2 + CH_3NH_2 \rightleftharpoons CH_3NH_3^+ + C_2H_3O_2^- \qquad [34]$$

Do products or reactants predominate in this mixture? Remember that the better acid is the better proton donor. Yet if an acid is a very good proton donor, there will be very little of it present in solution. Instead, mainly its conjugate base will be present. Since $HC_2H_3O_2$ ($K_a = 1.74 \times 10^{-5}$) is a stronger acid than $CH_3NH_3^+$ ($K_a = K_h = 2 \times 10^{-9}$), reaction [34] lies to the right. Notice also that CH_3NH_2 ($K_b = 5 \times 10^{-4}$) is a stronger base than $C_2H_3O_2^-$ ($K_b = K_h = 5.75 \times 10^{-10}$). Hence, the equilibrium lies to the side of the weaker acid and the weaker base.

★ **14. Define what an oxyacid is and predict the relative strengths of oxyacids based on their molecular structures.**

An oxyacid is one in which the ionizable proton is bound to oxygen, as in structure [35].

rest of molecule—E—O—H [35]

When the O—H bond breaks readily, the oxyacid is a strong one. The O—H bond will break readily if atom E is highly electronegative. Thus, for the hypohalous acids HOCl > HOBr > HOI. However, the electronegativities of elements can be altered by the atoms bonded to E. In general, the following factors increase the electronegativity of E (and increase the oxyacid strength).

1. Strongly electronegative elements bound to E (FCOOH > ClCOOH > HCOOH).
2. High positive oxidation state and formal charge of E. Thus, for the chlorine oxyacids $HClO_4 > HClO_3 > HClO_2 > HClO$, which is the same trend in which chlorine's oxidation state decreases. Highly electronegative atoms bound to atoms next to E also increase the strength of an acid ($CH_2FCOOH > CH_2ClCOOH > CH_3COOH$), although their effect is less than that of atoms directly bound to E.

DRILL PROBLEMS

2. (1) Label the Brønsted–Lowry acids and bases in each of the following equations. Make sure to label both conjugate pairs.

A. $H_2S + CO_3^{2-} \rightleftharpoons HCO_3^- + HS^-$
B. $H_3O^+ + HS^- \rightleftharpoons H_2S + H_2O$
C. $HS^- + OH^- \rightleftharpoons H_2O + S^{2-}$
D. $H_2O + NH_2^- \rightleftharpoons NH_3 + OH^-$
E. $HCO_3^- + OH^- \rightleftharpoons H_2O + CO_3^{2-}$
F. $HCN + OH^- \rightleftharpoons H_2O + CN^-$
G. $NH_4^+ + OH^- \rightleftharpoons NH_3 + H_2O$
H. $HSO_4^- + C_2H_3O_2^- \rightleftharpoons HC_2H_3O_2 + SO_4^{2-}$
I. $H_3PO_4 + CN^- \rightleftharpoons HCN + H_2PO_4^-$
J. $HSO_4^- + CN^- \rightleftharpoons HCN + SO_4^{2-}$

(2) Complete each of the following equations. The acid is given first in each case. Label each conjugate acid–base pair.

A. $HCl + NH_3 \rightleftharpoons$
B. $H_3O^+ + H_2PO_4^- \rightleftharpoons$
C. $HC_2H_3O_2 + HS^- \rightleftharpoons$
D. $HN_3 + CH_3NH_2 \rightleftharpoons$
E. $CH_3NH_3^+ + OH^- \rightleftharpoons$
F. $HNO_2 + N_3^- \rightleftharpoons$

3. Draw the Lewis structure for each reactant in the following reactions and indicate which is the acid and which is the base.

A. $H_2O + SO_2 \rightarrow H_2SO_3$
B. $BeF_2 + 2\,F^- \rightarrow BeF_4^{2-}$
C. $NH_3 + HCl \rightarrow NH_4Cl$
D. $CO_2 + OH^- \rightarrow HCO_3^-$
E. $Ag^+ + 2\,NH_3 \rightarrow Ag(NH_3)_2^+$
F. $O^{2-} + H_2O \rightarrow 2\,OH^-$
G. $BF_3 + F^- \rightarrow BF_4^-$
H. $HCl + H_2O \rightleftharpoons H_3O^+ + Cl^-$
I. $H_2O + BF_3 \rightarrow H_2OBF_3$
J. $S^{2-} + SO_3 \rightarrow S_2O_3^{2-}$
K. $H^+ + CO_3^{2-} \rightarrow HCO_3^-$
L. $H_2O + CO_2 \rightarrow H_2CO_3$
M. $BF_3 + CH_3OH \rightarrow CH_3OH{\cdot}BF_3$

6. & 7. Fill in the blanks in the table below. The first line is an example.

Solute formula	*Concentration* M	*Concentration* g/L	*Acidity* $[H^+]$	*Acidity* $[OH^-]$	*Acidity* pH	*Acidity* pOH
HCl	0.020	0.73	0.020	5.0×10^{-13}	1.70	12.30
A. NaOH	0.040					
B. H_2SO_4			0.00125			
C. $Ca(OH)_2$				0.0333		
D. RbOH				0.0375		
E. $HClO_4$		3.84				
F. $Ba(OH)_2$		0.513				
G. HNO_3	0.0125					
H. KOH				0.045		
I. $Sr(OH)_2$					9.13	
J. CsOH						4.65
K. HBr					3.15	
L. HI						12.75

8. For each weak acid or weak base below write the equation for ionization in water and the ionization constant expression.

A. HOBr
B. $(CH_3)_2NH$
C. $HC_6H_7O_2$
D. N_2H_4
E. $HC_3H_5O_3$
F. $(CH_3)_3N$
G. $HC_3H_5O_2$
H. $HC_2HCl_2O_2$
I. H_3BO_3
J. $HC_2Cl_3O_2$

9. (1) The initial concentration (or formality) of each acid or base is given below, along with an indication of the solution's acidity. Compute the ionization constant of the acid or base in each case.

A. HOBr, 0.250 M, pH = 4.640
B. $(CH_3)_2NH$, 0.400 M, $[OH^-] = 0.0165\ M$
C. $HC_6H_7O_2$, 0.300 M, pOH = 11.687
D. N_2H_4, 0.0100 M, pH = 9.996
E. $HC_3H_5O_3$, 1.20 M. $[H^+] = 0.0313\ M$
F. $(CH_3)_3N$, 0.140 M, pH = 11.503
G. $HC_3H_5O_2$, 0.0200 M, pH = 3.282
H. $HC_2HCl_2O_2$, 2.20 M, $[H^+] = 0.254$
I. H_3BO_3, 0.0400 M, pOH = 8.683
J. $HC_2Cl_3O_2$, 1.50 M, $[H^+] = 0.466\ M$

(2) Determine the pH of each of the following solutions, using the data of *Table 17-2 in the text.*

A. 0.250 M $HC_2H_3O_2$
B. 1.20 M $HC_7H_5O_2$
C. 0.820 M $HCHO_2$
D. 0.400 M HNO_2
E. 0.230 M HF
F. 1.00 M $HClO_2$
G. 1.20 M NH_3
H. 2.60 M CH_3NH_2
I. 5.10 M $C_2H_5NH_2$
J. 0.510 M HN_3 ($K_a = 1.90 \times 10^{-5}$ for HN_3)
K. 0.510 M $HONH_2$
L. 0.150 M $C_6H_5NH_2$

10. Determine the pH, final acid concentration, and concentration of all anions in the following solutions, using the data of *Table 17-3 in the text.*
A. 0.00460 M H_2CO_3 B. 0.0100 M H_2S C. 1.20 M $H_2C_2O_4$
D. 0.750 M H_3PO_4 E. 0.900 M H_3PO_3 F. 1.00 M H_2SO_3

11. For each of the following salts, write the reaction for the salt dissolving in water. Based on the ions present predict whether the solution is acidic, basic, or neutral. Finally, write any hydrolysis reactions which occur.
A. NaCl B. NH_4Cl C. N_2H_5Br D. KNO_3 E. $CsC_2H_3O_2$
E. Na_2CO_3 G. $C_6H_5NH_3I$ H. $Ca(ClO)_2$ I. $RbClO_2$ J. $(HONH_3)_2SO_4$
K. SrF_2 L. $C_2H_5NH_3NO_3$ M. NH_4CN N. $CH_3NH_3ClO_2$ O. $HONH_3F$

12. (1) 1.00 mol of each of the salts in parts A through L of the problems of objective 17-11 is used to form 1.00 L of aqueous solution. Determine the pH of each of these solutions.
(2) Determine the pH of each of the following solutions.
A. 3.00 mmol sodium acetate in 15.0 ml solution
B. 5.00 mmol calcium benzoate in 50.0 ml solution
C. 12.5 mmol potassium formate in 12.5 ml solution
D. 3.20 mmol barium nitrite in 16.0 ml solution
E. 1.79 mmol rubidium fluoride in 20.0 ml solution
F. 12.1 mmol cesium chlorite in 10.0 ml solution
G. 6.10 mmol ammonium sulfate in 25.0 ml solution
H. 5.37 mmol methylammonium sulfate in 20.0 ml solution
I. 26.4 mmol ethylammonium nitrate in 60.0 ml solution
J. 177.44 mmol hydrazine chloride (N_2H_5Cl) in 180.0 ml solution ($K_b = 9.8 \times 10^{-7}$)
K. 2.28 mmol aniline bromide in 250.0 ml solution
L. 11.0 mmol ammonium iodide in 80.0 ml solution

13. Equilibrium in each reaction in the two groups of problems in objective 17-2 lies to the right. Rank all the conjugate acid-base pairs in order of decreasing acid strength (strongest to weakest). Use the data of *Table 17-2 in the text* if necessary. Then complete the following equations and use your ranking to predict whether each equilibrium lies to the left or to the right.
A. $H_2O + N_3^- \rightleftharpoons$ B. $HNO_2 + OH^- \rightleftharpoons$ C. $H_3O^+ + CN^- \rightleftharpoons$
D. $NH_3 + CN^- \rightleftharpoons$ E. $HCN + H_2PO_4^- \rightleftharpoons$ F. $H_3PO_4 + NH_2^- \rightleftharpoons$
G. $H_3PO_4 + OH^- \rightleftharpoons$ H. $H_3O^+ + NH_2^- \rightleftharpoons$ I. $HCO_3^- + C_2H_3O_2^- \rightleftharpoons$
J. $HSO_4^- + HS^- \rightleftharpoons$ K. $H_2S + OH^- \rightleftharpoons$ L. $H_2O + C_2H_3O_2^- \rightleftharpoons$
M. $HCO_3^- + SO_4^{2-} \rightleftharpoons$ N. $HSO_4^- + OH^- \rightleftharpoons$

14. Predict which acid of each of the following pairs is the stronger and briefly explain why.
A. H_3BO_3 *or* H_2CO_3 B. H_2SO_4 *or* H_2SO_3 C. H_3PO_4 *or* H_3AsO_4
D. $HClO_3$ *or* $HClO_4$ E. HBrO *or* HClO F. HNO_2 *or* HNO_3
G. H_2SO_4 *or* H_2SeO_4 H. FC_6H_4OH *or* ClC_6H_4OH I. CF_3OH *or* CH_3OH
J. $HBrO_3$ *or* H_2SeO_3 K. H_3PO_4 *or* $HClO_4$ L. H_2CO_3 *or* H_4SiO_4

QUIZZES (20 minutes each)

Choose the best answer for each question.

Quiz A

1. In the reaction $BF_3 + NH_3 \rightarrow F_3B{:}NH_3$, BF_3 accepts an electron pair and acts as (a) an Arrhenius base; (b) a Brønsted acid; (c) a Lewis acid; (d) a Lewis base; (e) none of these.
2. Which one of the following five statements about Brønsted-Lowry acids and bases is true? (a) An acid and its conjugate base react to form a salt and water. (b) The acid H_2O is its own conjugate base. (c) The conjugate base of a strong acid is a strong base. (d) The conjugate base of a weak acid is a strong base. (e) A base and its conjugate acid react to form a neutral solution.
3. Nitrous acid, HNO_2, is 0.37% ionized in 3.0 M solution. What is K_a for this acid? (a) $(3.0)(0.37)^2/(99.63)$; (b) $(3.0)(0.0037)^2/(0.9963)$; (c) $(0.0037)^2/(0.9963)$; (d) $[0.9963/(0.0037)^2]/(3.0)$; (e) none of these.

4. A 2.4 *M* solution of a weak base has $[OH^-] = 0.0034\,M$. What is K_b for the base? (a) 0.0034; (b) 0.0034/2.4; (c) $(2.4)^2/0.0034$; (d) $(0.0034/2.4)^2$ (e) none of these.
5. 7200 ml of solution contains 0.216 mmol of potassium hydroxide. What is the pH of this solution? (a) 10.143; (b) 4.523; (c) 3.857; (d) 9.477; (e) none of these.
6. pOH = 3.14 is equivalent to (a) pH = 11.86; (b) $[H^+] = 1.38 \times 10^{-10}$; (c) $[OH^-] = 7.25 \times 10^{-4}$; (d) acidic solution; (e) none of these.
7. $CO_2(g)$ acts as an acid in the reaction $CaO(s) + CO_2(g) \rightarrow CaCO_3(s)$ because it (a) turns blue litmus red; (b) reacts with a metal; (c) is a proton donor; (d) is an electron-pair acceptor; (e) none of these.
8. In order of decreasing strength: $OH^- > ClO^- > NO_2^-$. Which of the following equilibria lies to the right? (a) $NO_2^- + HClO \rightleftharpoons HNO_2 + ClO^-$; (b) $H_2O + HClO \rightleftharpoons H_3O^+ + ClO^-$ (c) $OH^- + HNO_2 \rightleftharpoons H_2O + NO_2^-$; (d) $H_2O + ClO^- \rightleftharpoons OH^- + HClO$; (e) none of these.
9. Which of the following is the strongest acid? (a) H_2SO_4; (b) H_2SO_3; (c) H_2SeO_4; (d) $HONH_2$; (e) NaOH.

Quiz B

1. In the reversible reaction $HCO_3^-(aq) + OH^-(aq) \rightleftharpoons CO_3^{2-}(aq) + H_2O$ the Brønsted acids are (a) HCO_3^- and CO_3^{2-}; (b) HCO_3^- and H_2O; (c) OH^- and H_2O; (d) OH^- and CO_3^{2-}; (e) none of these.
2. *Proton donor* is an abbreviated definition of a (a) Brønsted–Lowry acid; (b) Brønsted–Lowry base; (c) Lewis acid; (d) Lewis base; (e) none of these.
3. Propionic acid, $HC_3H_5O_2$, is 0.42% ionized in 0.80 *M* solution. What is K_a for this acid? (a) $0.80(0.0042)^2/(0.9958)$; (b) $(0.80)(0.42)^2/(99.58)$; (c) $(0.0042)^2/(0.9958)$; (d) $(0.9958/0.80)/(0.0042)^2$; (e) none of these.
4. In a 2.00 *M* solution of HNO_2, $[H^+] = 0.030\,M$. What is K_a for this acid? (a) 2.0/0.030; (b) 0.030/2.0; (c) $(0.030)^2/(2.00)$; (d) $2.00/(0.030)^2$; (e) none of these.
5. 250 ml of solution contains 0.132 mmol of perchloric acid. What is the pH of this solution? (a) 3.880; (b) 2.398; (c) 10.120; (d) 3.277; (e) none of these.
6. $[OH^-] = 3.0 \times 10^{-10}\,M$ is equivalent to (a) pH = 4.522; (b) pOH = 10.478; (c) $3.33 \times 10^{-4}\,M = [H^+]$; (d) acidic solution; (e) none of these.
7. The following are all polyprotic acids *except* (a) H_2SO_4 (b) H_3BO_3; (c) $HClO_4$; (d) H_3PO_3; (e) none of these.
8. In order of decreasing strength $HF > HC_2H_3O_2 > HCN$. Which of the following equilibria lies to the right? (a) $HCN + C_2H_3O_2^- \rightleftharpoons CN^- + HC_2H_3O_2$; (b) $HF + CN^- \rightleftharpoons HCN + F^-$; (c) $HCN + H_2O \rightleftharpoons H_3O^+ + CN^-$; (d) $HC_2H_3O_2 + F^- \rightleftharpoons C_2H_3O_2^- + HF$; (e) none of these.
9. Which of the following is the strongest acid? (a) $HC_2H_3O_2$; (b) $HC_2HF_2O_2$; (c) H_2O; (d) NH_3; (e) $HC_2H_2FO_2$.

Quiz C

1. In the reaction $HCl(g) + NaOH(s) \rightarrow NaCl(s) + H_2O(g)$, HCl(g) acts as an acid because it (a) turns blue litmus red; (b) reacts with a metal; (c) is an electron-pair acceptor; (d) is a proton donor; (e) none of these.
2. A Lewis base is defined as (a) a proton donor; (b) a proton acceptor; (c) hydrogen ion donor; (d) a hydrogen ion acceptor; (e) none of these.
3. Acetic acid, $HC_2H_3O_2$, is 0.11% ionized in 1.5 *M* solution. What is K_a for this acid? (a) $(0.11)^2/(99.89)$; (b) $(0.0011)^2/(0.9989)$; (c) $(99.89)/(0.11)^2$; (d) $(0.9989/1.5)/(0.0011)^2$; (e) none of these.
4. A 0.30 *M* weak acid solution has $[H^+] = 6.8 \times 10^{-5}$. K_a of the acid is (a) 1.5×10^{-8}; (b) 6.8×10^{-5}; (c) 4.6×10^{-9}; (d) 2.3×10^{-4}; (e) none of these.
5. 500 ml of solution contains 1.50 mmol of nitric acid. What is the pH of this solution? (a) 2.824; (b) 2.699; (c) 2.523; (d) 11.477; (e) none of these.

6. pH = 4.25 is equivalent to (a) pOH = 9.75; (b) $[H^+] = 5.61 \times 10^{-4}$ *M*; (c) $[OH^-] = 5.61 \times 10^{-5}$ *M*; (d) a basic solution; (e) none of these.
7. Which pair does *not* represent an acid and its anhydride? (a) H_3PO_4, P_4O_{10}; (b) H_2CO_3, CO_2; (c) $HClO_2$, Cl_2O; (d) HNO_3, N_2O_5; (e) H_3BO_3, B_2O_3.
8. The equilibria $HClO + CN^- \rightleftharpoons ClO^- + HCN$ *and* $HC_2H_3O_2 + ClO^- \rightleftharpoons HClO + C_2H_3O_2^-$ lie to the right. Which list in order of decreasing strength is correct? (a) $C_2H_3O_2^- > ClO^- > CN^-$; (b) $C_2H_3O_2^- > CN^- > ClO^-$; (c) $HC_2H_3O_2 > HCN > HClO$; (d) $HCN > HClO > HC_2H_3O_2$; (e) none of these.
9. Which of the following is the strongest acid? (a) HBrO; (b) HIO_2; (c) $HBrO_2$; (d) $HClO_2$; (e) $HClO_3$.

Quiz D

1. The conjugate acid of HPO_4^{2-} is (a) PO_4^{3-}; (b) $H_2PO_4^-$; (c) H_3PO_4; (d) H_3O^+; (e) P_2O_5.
2. *Proton acceptor* is an abbreviated definition of (a) Brønsted–Lowry base; (b) Brønsted–Lowry acid; (c) Lewis base; (d) Lewis acid; (e) none of these.
3. Formic acid, HCH_2O, is 0.915% ionized in 2.5 *M* solution. What is K_a for this acid? (a) $(0.99085/2.5)/(0.00915)^2$ (b) $(0.00915)^2/(0.99085)$; (c) $(2.5)(0.00915)^2/(0.99085)$; (d) $(2.5)(0.915)^2/(99.085)$; (e) none of these.
4. In a 2.00 *M* solution of weak base BOH, $[OH^-] = 0.04$ *M*. What is K_b? (a) 0.02; (b) 8×10^{-4}; (c) 4×10^{-4}; (d) 1.6×10^{-3}; (e) none of these.
5. 1200 ml of solution contains 0.0720 mmol of sulfuric acid. What is the pH of this solution? (a) 3.921; (b) 4.301; (c) 9.699; (d) 1.143; (e) none of these.
6. $[H^+] = 2.5 \times 10^{-4}$ *M* is equivalent to (a) pH = 4.40; (b) pOH = 11.60; (c) $[OH^-] = 4.0 \times 10^{10}$ *M*; (d) acidic solution; (e) none of these.
7. P_4O_6 is the anhydride of (a) HPO_3; (b) $H_4P_2O_7$; (c) H_3PO_4; (d) H_3PO_3; (e) none of these.
8. The equilibria $OH^- + HClO \rightleftharpoons H_2O + ClO^-$ *and* $ClO^- + HNO_2 \rightleftharpoons HClO + NO_2^-$ lie to the right. Which list in order of decreasing strength is correct? (a) $HClO > HNO_2 > H_2O$; (b) $ClO^- > NO_2^- > OH^-$ (c) $NO_2^- > ClO^- > OH^-$ (d) $HNO_2 > HClO > H_2O$.
9. Which of the following is the strongest acid? (a) H_3AlO_3; (b) H_2SiO_3; (c) H_3PO_3; (d) H_2SO_3; (e) $HClO_3$.

SAMPLE TEST (30 minutes)

1. Benzoic acid (C_6H_5COOH, 122.0 g/mol) has $K_a = 6.3 \times 10^{-5}$. What is the pH of a solution formulated by dissolving 3.050 g of acid in enough water to make 0.250 L of solution?
2. Classify the following acid–base reactions in terms of the acid–base concept which they represent. Specify the most elementary concept which is applicable; in order of increasing complexity, the acid concepts are Arrhenius, Brønsted–Lowry, and Lewis. Indicate which substance(s) is(are) acids and which is(are) bases.
   a. $HF + N_2H_4 \rightleftharpoons F^- + N_2H_5^+$
   b. $O^{2-} + H_2O \rightleftharpoons 2\ OH^-$
   c. $SOI_2 + BaSO_3 \rightleftharpoons Ba^{2+} + 2\ I^- + 2\ SO_2$
   d. $HgCl_3^- + Cl^- \rightleftharpoons HgCl_4^{2-}$
3. All four of the equilibria below lie toward the right.

   $H_2SO_3 + F^- \rightleftharpoons HSO_3^- + HF$
   $CH_3NH_3^+ + OH^- \rightleftharpoons CH_3NH_2 + H_2O$
   $N_2H_5^+ + CH_3NH_2 \rightleftharpoons N_2H_4 + CH_3NH_3^+$
   $HF + N_2H_4 \rightleftharpoons F^- + N_2H_5^+$

   a. Rank all of the acids involved in order of decreasing acid strength.
   b. Rank all of the bases involved in order of decreasing base strength.
   c. State whether the two equilibria below will lie primarily toward the right or toward the left.
      (i) $HF + OH^- \rightleftharpoons F^- + H_2O$
      (ii) $CH_3NH_3^+ + HSO_3^- \rightleftharpoons CH_3NH_2 + H_2SO_3$
4. 3.00 mol of calcium chlorite is dissolved in enough water to produce 2.50 L of solution. $K_a = 2.95 \times 10^{-8}$ for HClO and $K_a = 1.2 \times 10^{-2}$ for $HClO_2$. Compute the pH of the solution produced.

Additional Aspects of Equilibria in Aqueous Solutions

REVIEW OF OBJECTIVES

★ **1. Describe the effect of a common ion on weak-acid or weak-base ionization and compute the concentrations of all species present in solutions of weak acids or bases and their common ions.**

The ionization of a weak acid or a weak base is an equilibrium, governed by Le Châtelier's principle. If we increase the concentration of one of the products, the equilibrium will shift left. Consider the ionization of a weak acid. We use the techniques of Chapter 17 to compute the $[H_3O^+]$ or $[F^-]$ in an aqueous solution of HF.

EXAMPLE 18-1 What are $[F^-]$ and $[H_3O^+]$ in 0.500 M HF? From *Table 17-2 in the text*, $K_a = 6.7 \times 10^{-4}$.

Setup:	HF(aq)	+	H_2O	⇌	$H_3O^+(aq)$	+	$F^-(aq)$	[1]
I:	0.500 M							
C:	$-x\ M$				$+x\ M$		$+x\ M$	
Eq:	$(0.500-x)M$				$x\ M$		$x\ M$	

$$K_a = \frac{[H_3O^+][F^-]}{[HF]} = 6.7 \times 10^{-4} = \frac{(x)(x)}{0.500-x} = \frac{x^2}{0.500}$$

We assumed $x \ll 0.500\ M$. Then, $x = 0.018\ M = [H_3O^+] = [F^-]$. x is small (less than 5%) compared to 0.500 M. The percent ionization of HF then is computed.

$$\%\ \text{ionization} = \frac{0.018\ M}{0.500\ M} \times 100 = 3.6\%$$

If we add H_3O^+ or F^- to the solution, the equilibrium will shift to the left, and the percent ionization of HF will decrease. Example 18-2 shows what occurs if we add 0.100 mol H_3O^+ to the solution of Example 18-1.

EXAMPLE 18-2 What are $[H_3O^+]$ and $[F^-]$ in 0.500 M HF to which 0.100 mol H_3O^+ is added to each liter?

Setup:	HF(aq)	+	H_2O	⇌	$H_3O^+(aq)$	+	$F^-(aq)$
I:	0.500 M				0.100 M		
C:	$-x\ M$				$+x\ M$		$+x\ M$
Eq:	$(0.500-x)M$				$(0.100+x)M$		$x\ M$

$$K_a = \frac{[H_3O^+][F^-]}{[HF]} = 6.7 \times 10^{-4} = \frac{(0.100+x)x}{0.500-x} \simeq \frac{0.100\ x}{0.500}$$

We have assumed $x \ll 0.100\ M$. This gives $x = (0.500)(6.7 \times 10^{-4})/0.100 = 3.4 \times 10^{-3}\ M = [F^-]$. Thus x is small (less than 5%, actually 3.4%) compared to 0.100 M.

$$\%\ \text{ionization} = \frac{0.0034\ M}{0.500\ M} \times 100 = 0.68\% \quad ([H_3O^+] = 0.103\ M)$$

This is less than the 3.6% of Example 18-1, as we predicted. The presence of one of the product ions has suppressed the ionization of the weak acid, as predicted by Le Châtelier's principle. This effect on a reaction which has ions as products is known as the *common ion effect.* Adding either one of the product ions to the solution suppresses ionization.

Let us see what effect the addition of fluoride ion will have. We will add less F^- ion than we did H_3O^+ ion in Example 18-2 and thus we expect the suppression of the ionization to be less. Thus the percent ionization we obtain should be larger than that of Example 18-2 but less than that of Example 18-1.

EXAMPLE 18-3 What is $[H_3O^+]$ and $[F^-]$ in 0.500 *M* HF to which 0.0400 mol F^- is added to each liter?

Setup:	HF(aq)	+ H_2O ⇌	H_3O^+(aq)	+ F^-(aq)
I:	0.500 *M*			0.0400 *M*
C:	$-x$ *M*		$+x$ *M*	$+x$ *M*
Eq:	$(0.500 - x)$ *M*		x *M*	$(0.0400 + x)$ *M*

$$K_a = \frac{[H_3O^+][F^-]}{[HF]} = 6.7 \times 10^{-4} = \frac{(0.0400 + x)(x)}{0.500 - x} \simeq \frac{(0.0400)\,x}{0.500}$$

We assumed $x \ll 0.0400\ M$. This gives $x = 8.38 \times 10^{-3}\ M$, which is *not* small compared to 0.0400 *M*. We use the technique of successive approximations (see Objective 17-9, Example 17-5).

$$\frac{(0.0400 + x)(x)}{0.500 - x} \simeq \frac{(0.0400 + 0.0083)(x)}{0.500 - 0.0083} = \frac{0.0483\,x}{0.492} \simeq 6.7 \times 10^{-4}$$

Then $x = (6.7 \times 10^{-4})(0.492)/0.0483 = 0.00682\ M$. We use another cycle of approximation.

$$\frac{(0.0400 + x)x}{0.500 - x} \simeq \frac{(0.0400 + 0.0068)x}{0.500 - 0.0068} = \frac{0.0468\,x}{0.494} = 6.7 \times 10^{-4}$$

Then $x = (6.7 \times 10^{-4})(0.494)/0.0468 = 7.07 \times 10^{-3}\ M$ *or* 0.00707 *M*. These two values are in fair agreement. The quadratic equation gives 0.0070 *M*, as does one more cycle of successive approximation. Thus, we have $[H_3O] = 0.0070\ M$ and $[F^-] = 0.0400 + 0.0070 = 0.0470\ M$.

$$\%\ \text{ionization} = \frac{0.0070\ M}{0.500\ M} \times 100 = 1.4\%$$

This is more than the 0.68% of Example 18-2, as we predicted. But it is still less than the 3.6% of Example 18-1 where HF was the only solute.

We now work the same types of problems for a solution of weak base (trimethylamine, $(CH_3)_3N$, for which $K_b = 7.4 \times 10^{-5}$).

EXAMPLE 18-4 What are $[OH^-]$, $[(CH_3)_3NH^+]$, and the percent ionization in solutions with the following concentrations before ionization? (a) $[(CH_3)_3N] = 0.400\ M$; (b) $[(CH_3)_3N] = 0.400\ M$ and $[OH^-] = 0.0900\ M$; (c) $[(CH_3)_3N] = 0.400\ M$ and $[(CH_3)_3NH^+] = 0.0500\ M$.

(a) Setup:	$(CH_3)_3N$(aq)	+ H_2O ⇌	$(CH_3)_3NH^+$(aq)	+ OH^-(aq)
I:	0.400 *M*			
C:	$-x$ *M*		$+x$ *M*	$+x$ *M*
Eq:	$(0.400 - x)$ *M*		x *M*	x *M*

$$K_b = \frac{[(CH_3)_3NH^+][OH^-]}{[(CH_3)_3N]} = \frac{(x)(x)}{(0.400 - x)} = 7.4 \times 10^{-5} \simeq \frac{x^2}{0.400}$$

We assumed $x \ll 0.40\ M$. Then $x = 5.4 \times 10^{-3}\ M = [OH^-] = [(CH_3)_3NH^+] \ll 0.400\ M$.

$$\%\ \text{ionization} = \frac{5.4 \times 10^{-3}}{0.400} \times 100 = 1.4\%$$

(b) Setup: $(CH_3)_3N(aq) + H_2O \rightleftharpoons (CH_3)_3NH^+(aq) + OH^-(aq)$

	$(CH_3)_3N(aq)$	$(CH_3)_3NH^+(aq)$	$OH^-(aq)$
I:	$0.400\ M$		$0.0900\ M$
C:	$-x\ M$	$+x\ M$	$+x\ M$
Eq:	$(0.400 - x)\ M$	$x\ M$	$(0.0900 + x)\ M$

$$K_b = \frac{(x)(0.0900 + x)}{0.400 - x} = 7.4 \times 10^{-5} \simeq \frac{x(0.0900)}{0.400}$$

We assumed $x \ll 0.0900\ M$. This gives $x = 3.3 \times 10^{-4}\ M = [(CH_3)_3NH^+] \ll 0.0900\ M$ and $[OH^-] = 0.0900 + 0.003 = 0.0903\ M$.

$$\%\ \text{ionization} = \frac{3.3 \times 10^{-4}}{0.400} \times 100 = 0.083\%$$

(c) Setup: $(CH_3)_3N(aq) + H_2O \rightleftharpoons (CH_3)_3NH^+(aq) + OH^-(aq)$

	$(CH_3)_3N(aq)$	$(CH_3)_3NH^+(aq)$	$OH^-(aq)$
I:	$0.400\ M$	$0.0500\ M$	
C:	$-x\ M$	$+x\ M$	$+x\ M$
Eq:	$(0.400 - x)\ M$	$(0.0500 + x)\ M$	$x\ M$

$$K_b = \frac{(0.0500 + x)(x)}{0.400 - x} = 7.4 \times 10^{-5} \simeq \frac{x(0.0500)}{0.400}$$

We assumed $x \ll 0.0500\ M$. This gives $x = 5.9 \times 10^{-4}\ M = [OH^-] \ll 0.0500\ M$, and $[(CH_3)_3NH^+] = 0.0500 + 0.0006 = 0.0506\ M$.

$$\%\ \text{ionization} = \frac{5.9 \times 10^{-4}}{0.400} \times 100 = 0.15\%$$

You should be aware of the source of the common ion. H_3O^+ or OH^- comes from a strong acid or a strong base (see Table 17-1 in objective 17-5). The anion of a weak acid comes from a salt in which the cation is that of a strong base. NaF will add F^- ion to a solution. The cation of a weak base comes from a salt in which the anion is that of a strong acid. $(CH_3)_3NHCl$ will add $(CH_3)_3NH^+$ ion to a solution.

2. Explain why the pH of water changes markedly when a small amount of H_3O^+ or OH^- is added and why the pH of a buffer does not change very much with a similar addition.

A buffer can be either (a) a solution of a weak acid and about the same amount of the weak acid's anion *or* (b) a solution of a weak base and about the same amount of the weak base's cation.

The solution of Example 18-4(c) is a buffer. It contains a weak base, $0.400\ M\ (CH_3)_3N$, and its cation, $0.0500\ M\ (CH_3)_3NH^+$. We might think the solution of Example 18-3 to be a buffer. It contains a weak acid, $0.500\ M$ HF, and its anion, $0.0400\ M\ F^-$. Most chemists would not think of this as a buffer because the concentrations should differ by less than a factor of 10. That is, for the buffer of a weak acid,

$$0.10 \leqslant \frac{[\text{acid's anion}]}{[\text{acid}]} \leqslant 10.0 \qquad [2]$$

and for the buffer of a weak base,

$$0.10 \leqslant \frac{[\text{base's cation}]}{[\text{base}]} \leqslant 10.0 \qquad [3]$$

In Example 18-3 $[F^-]//[HF] = 0.0400/0.500 = 0.08$. This we would not think of this as a buffer.

A buffer keeps the pH of a solution constant by reacting with small amounts of added H_3O^+ and OH^- to remove them from solution. Consider first the buffer of a weak acid, a solution with $[HF] = 1.00\ M$ and $[F^-] = 0.500\ M$.

$$HF(aq) + H_2O(l) \rightleftharpoons H_3O^+(aq) + F^-(aq) \qquad [4]$$

Addition of a small amount of H_3O^+ consumes the weak acid's anion and produces the weak acid.

$$H_3O^+(aq) + F^-(aq) \rightleftharpoons H_2O + HF(aq) \qquad [5]$$

Addition of a small amount of OH^- consumes the weak acid and produces its anion.

$$OH^-(aq) + HF(aq) \rightarrow H_2O + F^-(aq) \qquad [6]$$

Notice in both reactions [5] and [6] one of the fluorine-containing substances, either anion or acid, is consumed and the other is produced. The only effect of adding H_3O^+ or OH^- is to produce H_2O and change the $[F^-]/[HF]$ ratio.

A weak base buffer operates somewhat differently. Consider a buffer of 0.400 *M* CH_3NH_2 and 1.00 *M* $CH_3NH_3^+$.

$$CH_3NH_2(aq) + H_2O \rightleftharpoons CH_3NH_3^+(aq) + OH^-(aq) \qquad [7]$$

Addition of a small amount of H_3O^+ consumes weak base.

$$H_3O^+(aq) + CH_3NH_2(aq) \rightarrow CH_3NH_3^+(aq) + H_2O \qquad [8]$$

Addition of a small amount of OH^- consumes weak base cation.

$$OH^-(aq) + CH_3NH_3^+(aq) \rightarrow CH_3NH_2(aq) + H_2O \qquad [9]$$

The sole effect of adding H_3O^+ or OH^- is to produce H_2O and change the $[CH_3NH_3^+]/[CH_3NH_2]$ ratio.

2a. Describe how buffer solutions can be prepared.

There are three ways of making a buffer which contains a weak acid.

1. Place nearly equal quantities of a weak acid and its salt in solution. For instance, 0.600 mol $HC_2H_3O_2$ plus 0.400 mol $KC_2H_3O_2$ in solution is an acetic acid–acetate ion buffer.
2. Partly neutralize the weak acid with a strong base. Thus 1.000 mol $HC_2H_3O_2$ plus 0.400 mol KOH yields the same acetic acid–acetate ion buffer.

	$HC_2H_3O_2$	+	KOH	→	$C_2H_3O_2^-(aq)$	+	$K^+(aq)$	+	H_2O
before rxn:	1.000 mol		0.400 mol						
after rxn:	0.600 mol		0 mol		0.400 mol		0.400 mol		

3. Partly neutralize the salt of the weak acid's anion with strong acid. 1.000 mol $KC_2H_3O_2$ plus 0.600 mol HCl also produces a buffer.

	$K^+(aq)$	+	$C_2H_3O_2^-(aq)$	+	$H_3O^+(aq)$	+	$Cl^-(aq)$	→
before rxn:	1.000 mol		1.000 mol		0.600 mol		0.600 mol	
after rxn:	0.400 mol		0.400 mol		0 mol		0 mol	

	$HC_2H_3O_2(aq)$	+	H_2O	+	$K^+(aq)$	+	$Cl^-(aq)$
after rxn:	0.600 mol				0.600 mol		0.600 mol

This last buffer has more $K^+(aq)$ and $Cl^-(aq)$ present than did the previous two. However, these two ions are spectator ions.

A weak base buffer also can be made in three ways.

1. The weak base and about the same amount of its salt (0.700 mol NH_3 + 0.300 mol NH_4Cl).
2. A weak base partly titrated with a strong acid (1.000 mol NH_3 + 0.300 mol HCl).
3. A salt of the weak base's cation partly titrated with a strong base (1.000 mol NH_4Cl + 0.700 mol NaOH).

3. Know the limitations of the basic equations which are used to determine the pH of buffer solutions by understanding their derivations.

Let us determine the $[H_3O^+]$ and pH of the HF–F^- buffer of objective 18-2.

EXAMPLE 18-5 What are the $[H_3O^+]$ and pH of a solution with initial concentrations of $[HF] = 1.00\ M$ and $[F^-] = 0.500\ M$.

Setup:	HF(aq)	+	H_2O	⇌	H_3O^+(aq)	+	F^-(aq)
I:	1.00 *M*						0.500 *M*
C:	$-x\ M$				$+x\ M$		$+x\ M$
Eq:	$(1.00 - x)\ M$				$x\ M$		$(0.500 + x) M$

$$K_a = \frac{[H_3O^+][F^-]}{[HF]} = \frac{(x)(0.500 + x)}{1.00 - x} = 6.7 \times 10^{-4} \simeq \frac{x(0.500)}{1.00}$$

We assumed $x \ll 0.500\ M$. This gives $x = 1.4 \times 10^{-3}\ M = [H_3O^+] \ll 0.500\ M$. Then pH = 2.85.

The approximation produces the following expression.

$$K_a = \frac{x([F^-]_i)}{[HF]_i} \qquad [10]$$

The concentrations are initial ones before dissociation occurs. Equation [10] is easier to solve than the exact expression.

$$K_a = \frac{x([F^-]_i + x)}{([HF]_i - x)} \qquad [11]$$

Equation [10] can be used if $[F^-]_i$ and $[HF]_i$ differ by less than a factor of 10. This is the same condition which we imposed on a buffer, expression [2]. Recognizing that $x = [H_3O^+]$, we obtain

$$pK_a = pH - \log \frac{[F^-]_i}{[HF]_i} \quad or \quad pH = pK_a + \log \frac{[F^-]_i}{[HF]_i} \qquad [12]$$

If expression [2] is true, then for any weak acid buffer (where HA = weak acid and A^- = its anion),

$$pH = pK_a + \log \frac{[A^-]_i}{[HA]_i} \qquad [13]$$

If expression [2] is true, then for any weak base (B) the expression is (BH^+ = the weak base's cation),

$$pOH = pK_b + \log \frac{[BH^+]_i}{[B]_i} \qquad [14]$$

★ **4. Compute a buffer's pH given the concentrations of the buffer components and the value of K_a or K_b.**

This illustrates application of equations [13] and [14].

EXAMPLE 18-6 What is the pH of a solution in which $[HCOOH] = 0.800\ M$ and $[Ca(HCOO)_2] = 0.230\ M$?

We first need to compute $[HCOO^-]$.

$$\frac{0.230 \text{ mol } Ca(HCOO)_2}{L} \times \frac{2 \text{ mol } HCOO^-}{\text{mol } Ca(HCOO)_2} = 0.460\ M = [HCOO^-]$$

The ratio $[HCOO^-]/[HCOOH]$ equals $(0.460\ M/0.800\ M) = 0.575$ and satisfies expression [2]. From *Table 17-2 in the text* for formic acid $K_a = 1.8 \times 10^{-4}$ and $pK_a = 3.74$.

$$pH = pK_a + \log\frac{[A^-]_i}{[HA]_i} = 3.74 + \log 0.575 = 3.50$$

EXAMPLE 18-7 What is the pH of a solution in which $[C_2H_5NH_2] = 0.750\ M$ and $[C_2H_5NH_3NO_3] = 0.250\ M$? The ratio $[C_2H_5NH_3^+]/[C_2H_5NH_2]$ is $(0.250\ M/0.750\ M) = 0.333$ and satisfies expression [3]. From *Table 17-2 in the text* for ethylamine, $K_b = 4.3 \times 10^{-4}$ and $pK_b = 3.37$.

$$pOH = pK_b + \log\frac{[BH^+]_i}{[B]_i} = 3.37 + \log 0.333$$

$$pH = 14.00 - pOH = 14.00 - 2.89 = 11.11$$

★ **5. Determine the change in the pH of a buffer caused by the addition of a small amount of strong acid or strong base.**

When a small amount of H_3O^+ is added to a weak acid buffer, some of the weak acid's anion is consumed.

$$A^-(aq) + H_3O^+(aq) \rightarrow H_2O + HA(aq) \qquad [5a]$$

When a small amount of OH^- is added to a weak acid buffer, some of the weak acid is consumed.

$$HA(aq) + OH^-(aq) \rightarrow H_2O + A^-(aq) \qquad [6a]$$

When a small amount of H_3O^+ is added to a weak base buffer, some of the weak base is consumed.

$$B(aq) + H_3O^+(aq) \rightarrow H_2O + BH^+(aq) \qquad [8a]$$

When a small amount of OH^- is added to a weak base buffer, some of the weak base's cation is consumed.

$$BH^+(aq) + OH^-(aq) \rightarrow H_2O + B(aq) \qquad [9a]$$

The effect of this small addition is to change the ratio $[A^-]/[HA]$ for an acid buffer or the ratio $[BH^+]/[B]$ for a base buffer.

Thus the procedure when strong acid or strong base is added is to compute the amounts of the two components of the buffer present after the appropriate reaction [5a], [6a], [8a], or [9a] occurs. Then we compute the ratio $[A^-]/[HA]$ or $[BH^+]/[B]$, make sure it obeys expression [2] or [3], and determine the pH or pOH using equation [13] or [14].

EXAMPLE 18-8 0.050 mol of NaOH is added to 1 L of the buffer of Example 18-7. What is the pH?

Setup:	$C_2H_5NH_2(aq)$	+	H_2O	$\rightleftharpoons$	$C_2H_5NH_3^+(aq)$	+	$OH^-(aq)$
I:	0.750 *M*				0.250 *M*		0.050 *M*
after rxn [9a]:	0.800 *M*				0.200 *M*		

$[C_2H_5NH_3^+]/[C_2H_5NH_2] = (0.200\ M)/0.800\ M) = 0.250$, which satisfies expression [3]. Using equation [14], we find

$$pOH = pK_b + \log\frac{[C_2H_5NH_3^+]}{[C_2H_5NH_2]} = 3.37 + \log 0.250 = 2.77$$

$$pH = 14.00 - 2.77 = 11.23$$

This is an increase of 0.12 pH unit. If the NaOH had been added to water, the pH would have gone from pH = 7.00 to pH = 12.70, an increase of 5.70 pH units.

★ **6. Define and compute values for buffer range and buffer capacity.**

Buffer range is the range of pH values over which a buffer satisfies expression [2] or [3]. Thus we have

$$\text{pH range of acid buffer} = pK_a \pm 1.00$$
$$\text{pOH range of base buffer} = pK_b \pm 1.00 \qquad [15]$$

The capacity of a buffer is the moles of strong acid (H_3O^+) or strong base (OH^-) which the buffer can absorb before expression [2] or expression [3] becomes invalid. The capaicty of a buffer for OH^- may differ from its capacity for H_3O^+. Buffer capacity depends also on the total volume of buffer solution. 10 L of buffer solution has five times the buffer capacity of 2.0 L. Another factor is the concentrations of the two components of the buffer. A buffer with [HF] = 1.00 *M* and [F^-] = 0.500 *M* has twice the capacity of one with [HF] = 0.500 *M* and [F^-] = 0.250 *M*.

EXAMPLE 18-9 What is the capacity toward (a) strong acid and (b) strong base of 2.00 L of buffer with [HF] = 0.400 *M* and [F^-] = 0.700 *M*? (Note that [HF] + [F^-] = 1.100 *M* throughout this problem since no fluorine-containing species is added.)
(a) The buffer reacts with all of the added strong acid.

Setup:	F^- (aq)	+	H_3O^+(aq)	⇌	HF(aq)	+	H_2O
I:	0.700 *M*		*x M*		0.400 *M*		
C:	−*x M*		−*x M*		+*x M*		
final:	(0.700 − *x*)*M*				(0.400 + *x*)*M*		

The buffer is exhausted when enough acid is added so that [F^-]/[HF] = 0.100 = (0.700 − *x*)/(0.400 + *x*). This gives *x* = 0.600 *M*. Thus the buffer capacity toward H_3O^+ is

$$\frac{0.600 \text{ mol } H_3O^+}{\text{L}} \times 2.00 \text{ L solution} = 1.20 \text{ mol } H_3O^+$$

(b) The buffer reacts with all of the added strong base.

Setup:	HF(aq)	+	OH^-(aq)	→	F^-(aq)	+	H_2O
I:	0.400 *M*		*x M*		0.700 *M*		
C:	−*x M*		−*x M*		+*x M*		
final:	(0.400 − *x*)*M*				(0.700 + *x*)*M*		

The buffer is exhausted when enough base is added so that [F^-]/[HF] = 10.0 = (0.700 + *x*)/(0.400 − *x*). This gives *x* = 0.300 *M*. Thus the buffer capacity toward strong base is

$$\frac{0.300 \text{ mol } OH^-}{\text{L}} \times 2.00 \text{ L soln} = 0.600 \text{ mol } OH^-$$

7. Explain how the blood buffer system works.

Blood contains at least three buffers, the most important one being a H_2CO_3–HCO_3^- buffer. The equilibrium reaction is

$$H_2CO_3(aq) + H_2O \rightleftharpoons H_3O^+(aq) + HCO_3^-(aq) \qquad [16]$$

The ratio [HCO_3^-]/[H_2CO_3] = 20 to maintain pH = 7.4. Thus, there is a large amount of HCO_3^- present to absorb excess acidity. Excess base reacts with H_2CO_3 which is replenished from CO_2 in the lungs.

$$CO_2(g) + H_2O \rightleftharpoons H_2CO_3(aq) \qquad [17]$$

8. Explain how an acid-base indicator works to detect the equivalence point in a titration.

An indicator is a weak acid in which the undissociated acid, HIn, has a different color than the anion, In^-. The pH color change range of an indicator spans two pH units, from one unit below to one unit above pK_{In} of the indicator. In the titration procedure, the material to be titrated is placed in a flask, indicator is added, and titrant of known concentration is added from a buret until the indicator changes color—at the endpoint. The equivalence point occurs when chemically equivalent amounts of acid and base are present in solution. If the indicator has been chosen correctly (see objective 18–10), the endpoint will be the same as the equivalence point.

★ **9. Calculate the pH values necessary to plot a titration curve of a strong acid with a strong base.**

The common features of plotting titration curves are most easily seen in the titration of a strong acid by a strong base where the complications of a small ionization constant are absent. Consider the titration of 25.00 ml of 0.112 *M* NaOH with 0.100 *M* HCl solution. We use strong acid as titrant to provide an example which is different from that of the text book. We have divided the procedure into seven steps.

(1) Write the titration reaction as a net ionic equation.

$$NaOH(aq) + HCl(aq) \rightarrow NaCl(aq) + H_2O(l) \qquad [18]$$

$$OH^-(aq) + H_3O^+(aq) \rightarrow 2\,H_2O(l) \qquad [19]$$

(2) Determine the amount of substance being titrated.

$$25.00 \text{ ml NaOH soln} \times \frac{0.112 \text{ mmol NaOH}}{\text{mol soln}} = 2.80 \text{ mmol NaOH}$$

(3) Find the volume of titrant to reach the equivalence point.

$$2.80 \text{ mmol NaOH} \times \frac{1 \text{ mmol HCl}}{1 \text{ mmol NaOH}} \times \frac{1.00 \text{ ml HCl soln}}{0.100 \text{ mmol HCl}} = 28.0 \text{ ml HCl soln}$$

This volume is known also as the 100% titration point. Now consider that you want to draw a curve like Figure 18-1 by calculating as few points as possible. A good titration curve can be drawn from the pH at 0%, 10%, 50%, 90%, 100%, and 110% titration. For each point (except 0%), you need (a) the volume of titrant added V_t, (b) the total volume of the solution V_s, (c) the amount (in moles) of each species in solution, and (d) the concentration of each species.

(4) Determine the pH at 0% titration.

$$[OH^-] = \frac{2.80 \text{ mmol}}{25.00 \text{ ml}} = 0.112\,M = [Na^+]$$

$$pOH = -\log(0.112) = 0.951 \quad \textit{or} \quad pH = 13.049$$

(5) Determine the pH at 100% titration (V_t = 28.00 ml and V_s = 53.00 ml). We find the number of moles of each species.

	OH^- (aq) +	H_3O^+(aq) →	$2\,H_2O(l)$
before rxn:	2.80 mmol	2.80 mmol	
after rxn:	0 mmol	0 mmol	

Thus, the solution is neutral, and pH = 7.000. At the equivalence point of a *strong* acid–*strong* base titration, pH = 7.

(6) Determine the pH at 110% titration (V_t = 30.8 ml and V_s = 55.80 ml).

	OH^- (aq) +	H_3O^+(aq) → $2\ H_2O$
before rxn:	2.80 mmol	3.08 mmol
after rxn:	0 mmol	0.28 mmol

Since neither Cl^- nor Na^+ hydrolyzes, they do not affect the solution's pH and we need not calculate their concentrations. Thus

$$[H_3O^+] = \frac{0.28 \text{ mmol}}{55.8 \text{ ml}} = 5.0 \times 10^{-3}\ M \quad or \quad pH = 2.30$$

The pH after the equivalence point is based upon the total volume of the solution and the excess amount (in mol or mmol) of titrant added. This is true of *every* titration in which the titrant is a strong acid or a strong base.

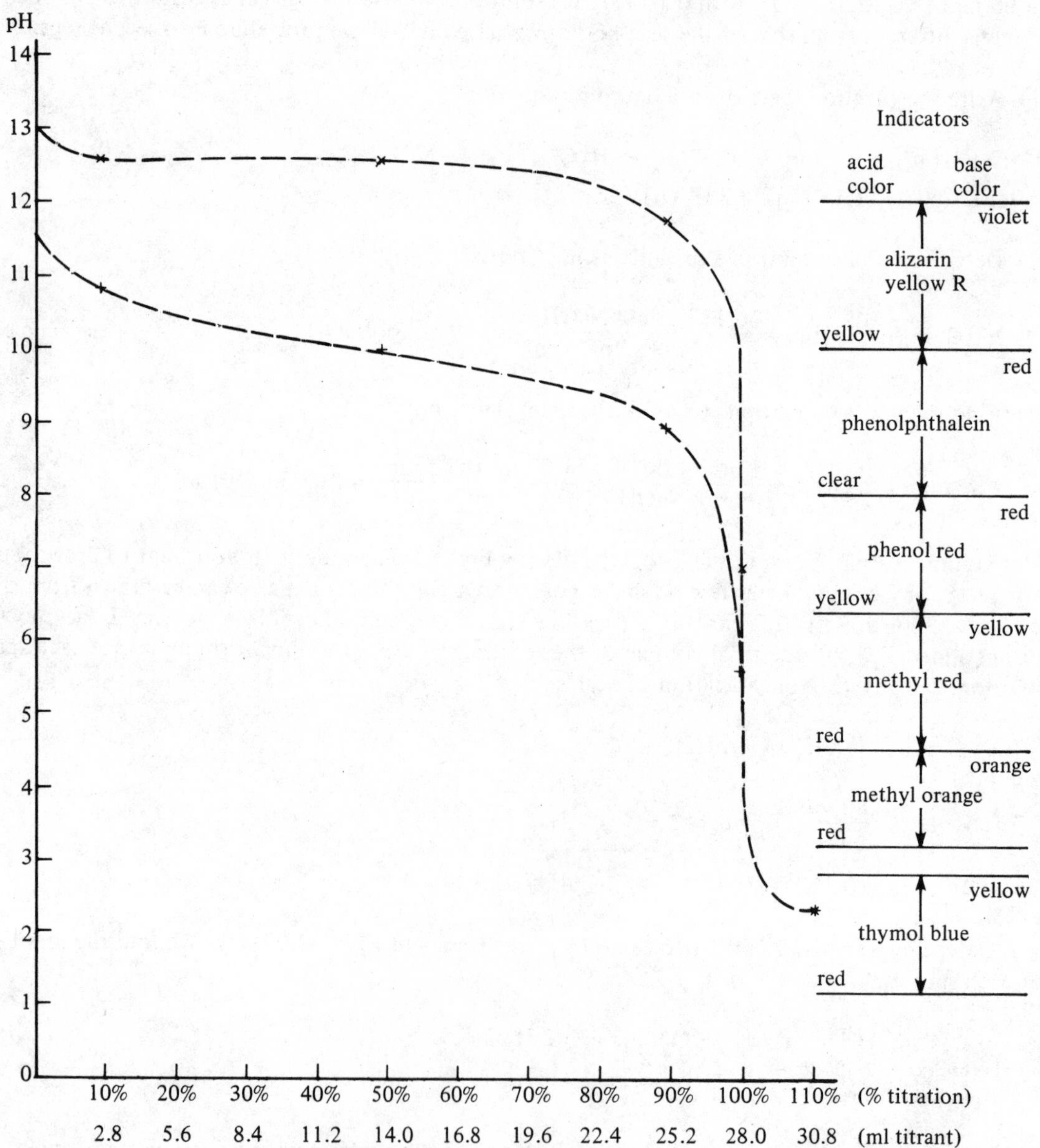

FIGURE 18-1 Titration curves for titrating 25.00 ml of 0.112 M NaOH (×) or $(CH_3)_3N$ (+) with 0.100 M HCl.

(7) Compute the pH between 0% and 100% titration.

50% titration (V_t = 14.00 ml and V_s = 39.00 ml)

	OH^- (aq) +	H_3O^+(aq) →	$2\ H_2O$
before rxn:	2.80 mmol	1.40 mmol	
after rxn:	1.40 mmol	0 mmol	

$$[OH^-] = \frac{1.40 \text{ mmol}}{39.0 \text{ ml}} = 3.59 \times 10^{-2}\ M$$

pOH = 1.444 *and* pH = 12.556

10% titration (V_t = 2.80 ml and V_s = 27.80 ml)

	OH^- (aq) +	H_3O^+(aq) →	$2\ H_2O$
before rxn:	2.80 mmol	0.28 mmol	
after rxn:	2.52 mmol	0 mmol	

$$[OH^-] = \frac{2.52 \text{ mmol}}{27.8 \text{ ml}} = 9.06 \times 10^{-2}\ M$$

pOH = 1.043 *and* pH = 12.597

90% titration (V_t = 25.20 ml and V_s = 50.20 ml)

	OH^- (aq) +	H_3O^+(aq) →	$2\ H_2O$
before rxn:	2.80 mmol	2.52 mmol	
after rxn:	0.28 mmol	0 mmol	

$$[OH^-] = \frac{0.28 \text{ mmol}}{50.2 \text{ ml}} = 5.58 \times 10^{-3}\ M$$

pOH = 2.253 *and* pH = 11.747

★ **9a. Determine the pH values during the course of the titration of a weak acid with a strong base or of a weak base with a strong acid.**

We titrate 25.00 ml of 0.112 *M* $(CH_3)_3N$ (K_b = 7.4 × 10^{-5}) with 0.100 *M* HCl. The concentrations of acid and base and the volume of base to be titrated are the same as we used in objective 18–9. We follow the same procedure as in objective 18–9.

(1) The titration reaction:

$$(CH_3)_3N(aq) + HCl(aq) \rightarrow (CH_3)_3NHCl(aq)$$
$$(CH_3)_3N(aq) + H_3O^+(aq) \rightarrow (CH_3)_3NH^+(aq) + H_2O$$

(2) The amount of $(CH_3)_3NH$ being titrated:

$$25.00 \text{ ml } (CH_3)_3N \text{ soln} \times \frac{0.112 \text{ mmol } (CH_3)_3N}{\text{ml soln}} = 2.80 \text{ mmol } (CH_3)_3N$$

(3) The volume of titrant needed:

$$2.80 \text{ mmol } (CH_3)_3N \times \frac{\text{mmol HCl}}{\text{mmol } (CH_3)_3N} \times \frac{1.00 \text{ ml HCl soln}}{0.100 \text{ mmol HCl}} = 28.0 \text{ ml HCl soln}$$

(4) pH at 0% titration: Now we solve a weak base problem (see objective 17-9 if necessary).

	$(CH_3)_3N(aq)$ + H_2O ⇌	$(CH_3)_3NH^+(aq)$ +	OH^-
I:	0.112 M		
C:	$-x$ M	$+x$ M	$+x$ M
Eq:	$(0.112 - x)$ M	x M	x M

$$K_b = \frac{[(CH_3)_3NH^+][OH^-]}{[(CH_3)_3N]} = \frac{(x)(x)}{0.112 - x} = 7.4 \times 10^{-5} \simeq \frac{x^2}{0.112} \quad \text{(assuming } x \ll 0.112\text{)}$$

$x = 2.9 \times 10^{-3}$ M = $[OH^-] \ll 0.112$ M pOH = 2.54 *and* pH = 11.46

(5) pH at 100% titration (V_t = 28.0 ml and V_s = 53.0 ml)

	$(CH_3)_3N(aq)$ +	$H_3O^+(aq)$ →	$(CH_3)_3NH^+(aq)$ + H_2O
before rxn:	2.80 mmol	2.80 mmol	
after rxn:	0 mmol	0 mmol	2.80 mmol

Now we have the hydrolysis of a weak base's cation (see objective 17-12).

$[(CH_3)_3NH^+]_i$ = 2.80 mmol/53.0 ml = 0.0528 M

	$(CH_3)_3NH^+(aq)$ + H_2O ⇌	$(CH_3)_3N(aq)$ +	$H_3O^+(aq)$
I:	0.0528 M		
C:	$-x$ M	$+x$ M	$+x$ M
Eq:	$(0.0528 - x)$ M	x M	x M

$$K_h = \frac{[(CH_3)_3N][H_3O^+]}{[(CH_3)_3NH^+]} = \frac{1.00 \times 10^{-14}}{7.4 \times 10^{-5}} = 1.35 \times 10^{-10} = \frac{(x)(x)}{0.0528 - x} \simeq \frac{x^2}{0.0528} \quad \text{(assuming } x \ll 0.0528\text{)}$$

$x = 2.7 \times 10^{-6}$ M = $[H_3O^+] \ll 0.0528$ and pH = 5.57

The pH is 7.00 at the equivalence point *only* for a strong acid-strong base titration.
(6) pH at 110% titration: This is the same calculation with the same result as step (6) of objective 18-19: pH = 2.30.
(7) pH at points between 0% and 100% titration:
50% titration (V_t = 14.00 ml and V_s = 39.00 ml)

	$(CH_3)_3N(aq)$ +	$H_3O^+(aq)$ ⇌	$(CH_3)_3NH^+(aq)$ + H_2O
before rxn:	2.80 mmol	1.40 mmol	
after rxn:	1.40 mmol	0 mmol	1.40 mmol

$[(CH_3)_3N]$ = 1.40 mmol/39.00 ml = $[(CH_3)_3NH^+]$

This is a buffer solution, and we can use equation [14].

$$\text{pOH} = \text{p}K_b + \log \frac{[(CH_3)_3NH^+]_i}{[(CH_3)_3N]_i} = 4.13 + \log \frac{1.40 \text{ mmol}/39.0 \text{ ml}}{1.40 \text{ mmol}/39.0 \text{ ml}}$$

Notice that the two volumes are the same. Hence they cancel. This is particularly helpful in titration calculations. Note also that the number of millimoles of each species is the same at the 50% point.

pOH = pK_b + log 1 = pK_b = 4.13 *and* pH = 9.87

The 50% titration point is the *half-equivalence point.* When a weak acid is titrated with a strong base, pH = pK_a at this point.

10% titration (V_t = 2.80 ml and V_s = 27.80 ml)

	$(CH_3)_3N(aq)$	+ $H_3O^+(aq)$	→ $(CH_3)_3NH^+(aq)$	+ H_2O
before rxn:	2.80 mmol	0.28 mmol		
after rxn:	2.52 mmol	0 mmol	0.28 mmol	

Again we have a buffer and thus we use equation [14].

$$\text{pOH} = 4.13 + \log \frac{0.28 \text{ mmol}}{2.52 \text{ mmol}} = 4.13 - 0.95 = 3.18 \quad \textit{and} \quad \text{pH} = 10.82$$

We used the mmol of weak base and its cation in the ratio, since they are in the same volume. A further simplification is possible. Consider that 10% titration means that the fraction titrated = 0.10 and the fraction untitrated = 0.90. Notice that in this case 0.28 mmol = (0.10) (2.80 mmol) and 2.52 mmol = 90.90) (2.80 mmol). Thus,

$$\text{pOH} = 4.13 + \log \frac{(0.10)(2.80 \text{ mmol})}{(0.90)(2.80 \text{ mmol})} = 4.13 + \log \frac{(0.10)}{(0.90)}$$

In general, for the titration of a weak base by a strong acid,

$$\text{pOH} = pK_b + \log \frac{\text{fraction of base titrated}}{\text{fraction of base untitrated}} \qquad [20]$$

For the titration of a weak acid by a strong base,

$$\text{pH} = pK_a + \log \frac{\text{fraction of acid titrated}}{\text{fraction of acid untitrated}} \qquad [21]$$

Equations [20] and [21] are based on equations [14] and [13].

$$\text{pOH} = pK_b + \log \frac{[BH^+]_i}{[B]_i} \quad [14] \qquad \text{pH} = pK_a + \log \frac{[A^-]_i}{[HA]_i} \quad [13]$$

These two equations depend on conditions [3] and [2].

$$0.10 \leqslant \frac{[BH^+]_i}{[B]_i} \leqslant 10.0 \quad [3] \qquad 0.10 \leqslant \frac{[A^-]_i}{[HA]_i} \leqslant 10.0 \quad [2]$$

This restricts the use of equations [20] and [21] to the region from 9% titrated to 91% titrated, which is called the buffer region.

90% titration: We can use equation [20] directly.

$$\text{pOH} = pK_b + \log \frac{0.90}{0.10} = 4.13 + 0.95 = 5.08 \quad \textit{and} \quad \text{pH} = 8.92$$

★ **10. Plot titration curves and use those curves to determine the initial pH, buffer region, and the pH of the equivalence point and to select an appropriate indicator.**

The data of objectives 18-9 and 18-9a are plotted in Figure 18-1, with the NaOH data as x's and the $(CH_3)_3N$ data as +'s. The abscissa (the horizontal axis) can be labeled either percent titration or volume of titration or volume of titrant. Notice the gradual change in pH for the weak base in the buffer region.

TABLE 18-1
Titration of a strong and a weak base with a strong acid
(results of objectives 18-9 and 18-9a)

Percent titration	Volume of titrant, ml	pH for the titration of NaOH	pH for the titration of $(CH_3)_3N$
0	0.00	13.049	11.46
10	2.80	12.597	10.82
50	14.00	12.556	9.87
90	25.20	11.747	8.92
100	28.00	7.000	5.57
110	30.80	2.30	2.30

To choose an indicator we consider the equivalence point. For the NaOH–HCl titration we could choose phenolphthalein, which is red at pH = 10 and clear at pH = 8, but the color change from red to just clear is a bit hard to see. A better indicator is phenol red: red at pH = 8 and yellow at pH = 6.4.

Phenol red would not work for the $(CH_3)_3N$–HCl titration because it would be starting to change color at about 96% titration. A better indicator would be methyl red: yellow at pH = 6.2 and red at pH = 4.5. It might seem that this would be suitable for the NaOH–HCl titration. But we prefer that the equivalence point of the titration fall within the pH color change range of the indicator.

★ **11. Describe, through chemical equations and calculations, the effect of pH on the precipitation and solubilities of certain slightly soluble substances.**

Many metal hydroxides are insoluble (*see Table 16-2 in the text*). $Fe(OH)_3$ is an example.

$$Fe(OH)_3\,(s) \rightleftharpoons Fe^{3+}(aq) + 3\ OH^-(aq) \qquad K_{sp} = 4.0 \times 10^{-38} \qquad [22]$$

If we add strong acid to a saturated solution of $Fe(OH)_3\,(s)$, $H_3O^+(aq)$ from the acid reacts with OH^- (aq) from the $Fe(OH)_3$. The equilibrium of equation [22] shifts right. $Fe(OH)_3$ is soluble in a strongly acidic solution. This is an acid–base neutralization.

$$Fe(OH)_3\,(s) + 3\ HCl\ (aq) \rightleftharpoons Fe^{3+}(aq) + 3\ Cl^-\ (aq) + 3\ H_2O \qquad [23]$$

All acids will enhance the $Fe(OH)_3$ solubility, *including* a weak base's cation

$$Fe(OH)_3\,(s) + 3\ NH_4^+\,(aq) \rightleftharpoons Fe^{3+}(aq) + 3\ NH_3\,(aq) + 3\ H_2O \qquad [24]$$

An insoluble hydroxide can precipitate from a neutral solution because of the hydrolysis of the cation.

$$FeCl_3\,(aq) + 6\ H_2O = Fe^{3+}(aq) + 3\ Cl^-\ (aq) + 6\ H_2O \rightleftharpoons Fe(OH)_3\,(s) + 3\ Cl^-\ (aq) + 3\ H_3O^+(aq) \quad [25]$$

EXAMPLE 18-10 What is the solubility of $Fe(OH)_3\,(s)$ ($K_{sp} = 4.0 \times 10^{-38}$) in (a) pure water and (b) a solution maintained at pH = 2.00?

(a) $K_{sp} = [Fe^{3+}][OH^-]^3 = (s)(3s)^3 = 4.0 \times 10^{-38}$ *or* $s = 2 \times 10^{-10}\ M$
(b) pH = 2.00 is pOH = 12.00; thus $[OH^-] = 1.0 \times 10^{-12}\ M$.

$$4.0 \times 10^{-38} = [Fe^{3+}](1.0 \times 10^{-12})^3 \quad or \quad [Fe^{3+}] = 4.0 \times 10^{-2}\ M$$

Another group of compounds whose solutbilities are affected by pH are those in which the anion is the anion of a weak acid.

$$SrF_2\,(s) \rightleftharpoons Sr^{2+}(aq) + 2\ F^-\ (aq) \qquad [26]$$

The addition of H_3O^+ (aq) removes F^- (aq) from solution, which shifts equation [26] to the right.

$$H_3O^+ (aq) + F^- (aq) \rightleftharpoons HF (aq) + H_2O \qquad [27]$$

12. Determine $[H_3O^+]$ or $[S^{2-}]$ in H_2S (aq) solutions using a combined equilibrium constant, $K_{a_1} \times K_{a_2}$.

For a diprotic acid, H_2A, $[A^{2-}] = K_{a_2}$ (objective 17-10). There are two assumptions: the two ionization constants must differ by more than a factor of 1000, and *all* of the A^{2-} and H_3O^+ must come from the diprotic acid. When a common ion is present, we can relate $[H_3O^+]$ and $[A^{2-}]$ through a combined equilibrium constant, $K_{a_1} \times K_{a_2}$. For H_2S

$$H_2S(aq) + H_2O \rightleftharpoons H_3O^+ (aq) + HS^- (aq) \qquad K_{a_1} = 1.1 \times 10^{-7}$$
$$HS^-(aq) + H_2O \rightleftharpoons H_3O^+ (aq) + S^{2-} (aq) \qquad K_{a_2} = 1.0 \times 10^{-14}$$
$$H_2S(aq) + 2\, H_2O \rightleftharpoons 2\, H_3O^+ (aq) + S^{2-}(aq) \qquad K = K_{a_1} K_{a_2} = 1.1 \times 10^{-21} \qquad [28]$$

$$K = \frac{[H_3O^+]^2 [S^{2-}]}{[H_2S]} = 1.1 \times 10^{-21} \qquad [29]$$

H_2S is considered because very often we wish to precipitate metal ions as their sulfides. Precipitation is normally done by saturating the solution with H_2S. At 25°C, the concentration of a saturated solution is $[H_2S] = 0.10\, M$. Thus [29] becomes

$$K = [H_3O^+]^2 [S^{2-}] = 1.1 \times 10^{-22} \quad \text{(in a saturated } H_2S \text{ solution)} \qquad [30]$$

★ **13. Predict whether metal sulfides will precipitate from saturated H_2S (aq) solutions of known pH.**

Equation [30] can be used to find the $[S^{2-}]$ in a solution of known pH. This $[S^{2-}]$ then can be used in the solubility product constant expression for a metal sulfide.

EXAMPLE 18-10 A solution is maintained at pH = 4.75 by an $HC_2H_3O_2$–$NaC_2H_3O_2$ buffer. The solution contains Pb^{2+} and Mn^{2+}, each at a concentration of 0.100 *M*. The solution is saturated with H_2S. Will either of the metal sulfides precipitate? $K_{sp}(PbS) = 8.0 \times 10^{-28}$ and $K_{sp}(MnS) = 2.5 \times 10^{-13}$.

pH = 4.75 means $[H_3O^+] = 1.78 \times 10^{-5}$. Using equation [30]

$$[H_3O^+]^2 [S^{2-}] = (1.78 \times 10^{-5})^2 [S^{2-}] = 1.1 \times 10^{-22} \quad or \quad [S^{2-}] = 3.5 \times 10^{-13}\, M$$

From this, we compute the maximum concentration of each ion which can be present in solution based on the value of K_{sp}.

$$[Pb^{2+}][S^{2-}] = [Pb^{2+}](3.5 \times 10^{-13}) = 8.0 \times 10^{-28} \quad or \quad [Pb^{2+}] = 2.3 \times 10^{-15}\, M$$
$$[Mn^{2+}][S^{2-}] = [Mn^{2+}](3.5 \times 10^{-13}) = 2.5 \times 10^{-13} \quad or \quad [Mn^{2+}] = 7.1 \times 10^{2}\, M$$

PbS will precipitate, while MnS will not. Of course, 710 mol Mn^{2+} will not dissolve in a liter of solution; no manganese(II) compound is *that* soluble.

14. Define and compute values for equivalent weight, equivalent, and solution normality.

An equivalent of an acid or base in the quantity of the acid or base which produces or consumes one mole of hydrogen ions. It is convenient to define *n* as follows.

$$n = \frac{\text{number of equivalents}}{\text{mole of acid or base}} \qquad [31]$$

n will always be a positive whole number ($n = 1, 2, 3$, and so forth). For many acids, n equals the number of hydrogens in the acid's formula. This is the case for simple acids such as HF, HCl, HBr, HI, $HClO_4$, HNO_3, and HCN. For organic acids, n is the number of —COOH groups in the acid's formula. Thus $n = 1$ for HCOOH (formic acid) and CH_3COOH (acetic acid).

For many bases, n is the number of OH groups in the formula of the base. Thus $n = 1$ for NaOH, TlOH, and CsOH; $n = 2$ for $Mg(OH)_2$, $Fe(OH)_2$, and $Ba(OH)_2$; $n = 3$ for bases such as $Al(OH)_3$. For organic bases, n is the number of $—NH_2$ groups in the base's formula. Thus $n = 1$ for CH_3NH_2 (methylamine) and $C_2H_5NH_2$ (ethylamine) as well as for NH_3 (ammonia). For polyprotic acids, the maximum value of n, n_{max}, is the number of hydrogens (or —COOH groups) in the formula. Thus $n_{max} = 2$ for H_2SO_4, H_2SO_3, and $(COOH)_2$ (oxalic acid, an organic acid), and $n_{max} = 3$ for H_3PO_4. For polyprotic acids, the value of n may be different for the acid in different reactions.

The value of n is the number of equivalents per mole.

$$\text{equivalent weight}\left(\frac{\text{g}}{\text{eq}}\right) = \frac{\text{mole weight (g/mol)}}{n\text{ (eq/mol)}} \qquad [32]$$

$$\text{normality} = \frac{\text{eq solute}}{\text{L solution}} = \text{molarity}\left(\frac{\text{mol solute}}{\text{L soln}}\right) \times n\left(\frac{\text{eq solute}}{\text{mol solute}}\right) \qquad [33]$$

EXAMPLE 18-11 What is the equivalent weight of $Ba(OH)_2$, and what is the normality of a 0.102 M $Ba(OH)_2$ solution?

Since there are two hydroxide groups in the formula $Ba(OH)_2$, $n = 2$.

$$\text{equivalent weight} = \frac{171.35\text{g Ba(OH)}_2\text{/mol}}{2\text{ eq/mol}} = \frac{85.67\text{g Ba(OH)}_2}{\text{eq}}$$

$$\text{normality} = 0.102\,\frac{\text{mol Ba(OH)}_2}{\text{L}} \times \frac{2\text{ eq Ba(OH)}_2}{\text{mol}} = 0.204\,N$$

★ **14a. Explain why a substance may have more than one equivalent weight and why one equivalent of acid always reacts with one equivalent of base.**

Consider reactions [34] and [35] between NaOH and H_2SO_4.

$$NaOH + H_2SO_4 \rightarrow NaHSO_4 + H_2O \qquad [34]$$

$$2\,NaOH + H_2SO_4 \rightarrow Na_2SO_4 + 2\,H_2O \qquad [35]$$

In equation [34] one mole of NaOH reacts with each mole of H_2SO_4, and in equation [35] two moles of NaOH react with each mole of H_2SO_4. Yet in both equations one equivalent of NaOH reacts with one equivalent of H_2SO_4! In equation [34] one mole of H_2SO_4 produces one mole of hydrogen ions. Thus one mole of H_2SO_4 equals one equivalent in equation [34] or $n = 1$. The equivalent weight of sulfuric acid is 98 g/mol ÷ 1 eq/mol = 98 g/eq. In equation [35], on the other hand, $n = 2$ and thus H_2SO_4's equivalent weight is 98 g/mol ÷ 2 eq/mol = 49 g/eq.

★ **14b. Apply the concepts of equivalent weight and normality to solve solution stoichiometry problems.**

Volume of acid × normality of acid = volume of base × normality of base.

$$V_A \times N_A = V_B \times N_B \qquad [36]$$

EXAMPLE 18-12 17.4 ml of 0.1000 N NaOH titrates 12.3 ml of sulfuric acid solution. What is the normality of the acid?

$$12.3\text{ ml} \times N_A = 17.4\text{ ml} \times 0.1000\,N \quad \textit{or} \quad N_A = 0.141\,N$$

Thus, we label the acid "0.141 N H_2SO_4."

This can cause problems. Notice the difference if the normality is defined according to equation [34] or according to equation [35]. According to equation [34] the mass of H_2SO_4 per liter of solution is

$$1.00 \text{ L} \times \frac{0.141 \text{ eq } H_2SO_4}{\text{L}} \times \frac{98 \text{ g } H_2SO_4}{\text{eq}} = 14 \text{ g } H_2SO_4$$

According to equation [35], the mass of H_2SO_4 per liter is

$$1.00 \text{ L} \times \frac{0.141 \text{ eq } H_2SO_4}{\text{L}} \times \frac{49 \text{ g } H_2SO_4}{\text{eq}} = 6.9 \text{ g } H_2SO_4$$

We have no way of knowing which is correct unless we know which reaction occurred during the titration.

DRILL PROBLEMS

1. Determine the pH of each of the following solutions, first, when only the weak acid or weak base is present and then when both substances are present. Initial concentrations are given in each case.
A. $[HC_2H_3O_2] = 0.250\,M$, $[NaC_2H_3O_2] = 0.120\,M$
B. $[HC_2H_3O_2] = 0.250\,M$, $[HCl] = 0.140\,M$
C. $[HC_7H_5O_2] = 1.20\,M$, $[Ca(C_7H_5O_2)_2] = 0.130\,M$
D. $[HCHO_2] = 0.820\,M$, $[HNO_3] = 0.240\,M$
E. $[HNO_2] = 0.400\,M$, $[Ba(NO_2)_2] = 0.0480\,M$
F. $[HCHO_2] = 0.620\,M$, $[KCHO_2] = 0.340\,M$
G. $[HClO_2] = 1.00\,M$, $[CsClO_2] = 0.138\,M$
H. $[NH_3] = 1.20\,M$, $[KOH] = 0.320\,M$
I. $[CH_3NH_2] = 0.260\,M$, $[CH_3NH_3Cl] = 0.130\,M$
J. $[C_2H_5NH_2] = 0.150\,M$, $NaOH] = 0.216\,M$
K. $[(CH_3)_3N] = 0.460\,M$, $[(CH_3)_3NH] = 0.819\,M$ ($K_b = 7.4 \times 10^{-5}$)
L. $[NH_3] = 0.510\,M$, $[(NH_4)_2SO_4] = 0.774\,M$
M. $[CH_3NH_2] = 0.104\,M$, $[Ca(OH)_2] = 0.0102\,M$
N. $[C_2H_5NH_2] = 0.630\,M$, $[C_2H_5NH_3NO_3] = 1.89\,M$

4. The buffer solutions on the following lines are made up as described in objective 18–2a. Determine the initial concentrations of the weak acid and its anion, or of the weak base and its cation. Use these concentrations to determine the pH of each buffer. (The concentrations given are formalities, that is, how the solution was made up, not the concentrations at equilibrium.)
A. $[HC_2H_3O_2] = 1.450\,M$, $[NaC_2H_3O_2] = 0.270\,M$
B. $[HC_7H_5O_2] = 1.300\,M$, $[KOH] = 0.640\,M$
C. $[NaCHO_2] = 0.815\,M$, $[HBr] = 0.105\,M$
D. $[NH_3] = 0.750\,M$, $[NH_4I] = 0.250\,M$
E. $[C_2H_5NH_2] = 2.31\,M$, $[HNO_3] = 1.02\,M$
F. $[CH_3NH_3Cl] = 0.555\,M$, $[CsOH] = 0.114\,M$
G. $[HF] = 1.296\,M$, $[NaF] = 1.045\,M$
H. $[HC_2H_2ClO_2] = 2.93\,M$, $[Mg(OH)_2] = 1.07\,M$
I. $[Ca(NO_2)_2] = 0.926\,M$, $[HClO_4] = 1.302\,M$
J. $[CH_3NH_2] = 0.990\,M$, $[CH_3NH_3ClO_4] = 0.443\,M$
K. $[(CH_3)_3N] = 1.236\,M$, $[HI] = 0.341\,M$ ($K_b = 7.4 \times 10^{-5}$)
L. $[(NH_4)_2SO_4] = 0.1140\,M$, $[KOH] = 0.0731\,M$
M. $[HCHO_2] = 1.946\,M$, $[Mg(CHO_2)_2] = 0.104\,M$
N. $[HC_2H_3O_2] = 0.0561\,M$, $[Ca(OH)_2] = 0.0112\,M$
O. $[NaC_7H_5O_2] = 0.743\,M$, $[H_2SO_4] = 0.256\,M$
P. $[(CH_3)_3NHBr] = 0.831\,M$, $[KOH] = 0.218\,M$ ($K_b = 7.4 \times 10^{-5}$)
Q. $[CH_3NH_2] = 1.214\,M$, $[CH_3NH_3NO_3] = 0.885\,M$
R. $[C_2H_5NH_2] = 1.149\,M$, $[HClO_4] = 1.001\,M$

5. The amount of strong acid or of strong base given on each line below is added to the given volume of the corresponding buffer in the problems of objective 18–4. Determine the final pH in both cases (addition of strong acid, or addition of strong base) for each solution.
A. 0.0520 mol to 0.750 L
B. 0.0130 mol to 0.800 L
C. 0.00780 mol to 1.00 L
D. 0.0110 mol to 121 ml
E. 0.544 mol to 2.04 L
F. 0.123 mol to 5.91 L
G. 0.247 mol to 1.20 L
H. 1.32 mol to 11.4 L
I. 0.963 mol to 8.71 L

J. 0.0231 mol to 0.604 L   K. 0.150 mol to 0.890 L   L. 1.09 mol to 75.9 L
M. 0.0231 mol to 0.561 L   N. 0.196 mol to 103 L   O. 0.0931 mol to 1.52 L
P. 0.161 mol to 3.75 L   Q. 7.14 mol to 10.5 L   R. 0.100 mol to 1.00 L

6. For each of the buffers in the problems of objective 18-4, determine the buffer range. Then, using the volume of each buffer given in the problems of objective 18-5, determine the capacity of each buffer for both strong acid and strong base. Express each capacity in moles of strong acid or strong base.

9. & 9a. Determine the pH at 0%, 10%, 50%, 90%, 100%, and 110% titration for each of the following titrations. (Objective 9: A through G; objective 9a: H through N.)

	Substance being titrated			*Titrant*	
	Volume, ml	*Formula*	*Molarity*	*Formula*	*Molarity*
A.	25.00	HCl	0.245	KOH	0.200
B.	15.00	NaOH	0.250	HNO_3	0.100
C.	30.00	CaOH	2.50	HI	1.00
D.	10.00	$HClO_4$	0.120	RbOH	0.100
E.	20.00	HBr	0.250	KOH	0.100
F.	16.00	NaOH	0.624	H_2SO_4	0.100
G.	40.00	$Ca(OH)_2$	0.0100	HCl	0.0250
H.	25.00	HNO_2	0.245	KOH	0.200
I.	15.00	CH_3NH_2	0.250	HNO_3	0.100
J.	30.00	$C_2H_5NH_2$	2.50	HI	1.00
K.	10.00	HF	0.120	RbOH	0.100
L.	20.00	$HCHO_2$	0.250	KOH	0.100
M.	16.00	CH_3NH_2	0.624	H_2SO_4	0.100
N.	40.00	C_5H_5N	0.0200	HCl	0.0250

10. For each of the titrations in the problems of objectives 18-9 and 18-9a, plot the titration curve. Indicate the equivalence point and, for the titration of a weak acid or base, the buffer region. Finally, choose a suitable indicator from those given in Figure 18-1.

11. Determine the solubility of each of the following compounds in a solution maintained at pH = 2.00, 7.00, and 10.00, using the data of *Table 16-1 in the text* where needed.
A. $Al(OH)_3$ B. $Cr(OH)_3$ C. $Mg(OH)_2$ D. $Be(OH)_2$ ($K_{sp} = 1.6 \times 10^{-22}$)
E. $Ba(OH)_2$ F. $Fe(OH)_3$ G. $Ca(OH)_2$ H. AgOH ($K_{sp} = 2.0 \times 10^{-8}$)

13. Use the data of *Table 16-1 in the text* and determine the pH at which precipitation of each metal sulfide will just begin to occur if the metal ion concentration is as given below and the solution is saturated with H_2S.
A. $Co^{2+} = 1.40\ M$ B. $Fe^{2+} = 0.140\ M$ C. $Ni^{2+} = 0.210\ M$
D. $Bi^{3+} = 3.0 \times 10^{-20}\ M$ E. $Cu^{2+} = 3.0 \times 10^{-20}\ M$ F. $Hg^{2+} = 1.0 \times 10^{-10}\ M$
G. $Ag^{+} = 5.0 \times 10^{-5}\ M$

14a. Compute the equivalent weight and the normality of each reactant in the equations which follow. The molarity of each reactant is given in parenthesis after its formula.
A. $2\ HCl\ (0.104\ M) + Ca(OH)_2 (0.0521\ M) \rightarrow CaCl_2 + 2\ H_2O$
B. $H_2SO_4 (0.704\ M) + KOH (0.197\ M) \rightarrow KHSO_4 + H_2O$
C. $HNO_3 (0.146\ M) + LiOH (0.412\ M) \rightarrow LiNO_3 + H_2O$
D. $3\ HBr (0.904\ M) + Al(OH)_3 (0.222\ M) \rightarrow AlBr_3 + 3\ H_2O$
E. $H_2SO_4 (0.818\ M) + Ca(OH)_2 (0.525\ M) \rightarrow CaSO_4 + 2\ H_2O$
F. $H_3PO_4 (0.200\ M) + Al(OH)_3 (0.332\ M) \rightarrow AlPO_4 + 3\ H_2O$
G. $H_3PO_4 (0.165\ M) + Sr(OH)_2 (0.227\ M) \rightarrow SrHPO_4 + 2\ H_2O$
H. $H_2C_2O_4 (0.774\ M) + NaOH (0.146 M) \rightarrow NaHC_2O_4 + H_2O$

14b. Fill in the blanks in the table which follows assuming that the two solutions react completely with each other in a titration.

	Acid solution		*Base solution*	
	Volume, ml	*Normality*	*Volume, ml*	*Normality*
A.	______	0.2431	27.46	0.1000
B.	25.00	______	19.46	0.1000
C.	7.265	0.8417	______	0.1746
D.	27.84	0.2500	20.00	______

E. ______	0.2000	21.04	0.1946
F. 40.00	______	37.43	0.1000
G. 33.14	0.7142	______	0.2000
H. 49.24	0.1500	30.00	______

QUIZZES (20 minutes each)

Choose the best answer for each question.

Quiz A

1. What volume in ml of 2.0 M H_2SO_4 is needed to neutralize 7.8 g of $Al(OH)_3$ (78.0 g/mol)? $Al_2(SO_4)_3$ and water are the titration products. (a) 150; (b) 75; (c) 300; (d) 500; (e) none of these.
2. A weak base BOH has $K_b = 4.0 \times 10^{-5}$. If $[OH^-] = 2.0 \times 10^{-5}$, what must $[B^+]/[BOH]$ equal? (a) 1.0; (b) 0.5; (c) 1.5; (d) 8.0; (e) none of these.
3. The following substances may be added to 1 L of water to prepare a buffer: (a) 1 mol $HC_2H_3O_2$ and 1 mol HCl; (b) 1 mol NH_3(aq) and 1 mol NaOH (c) 1 mol NH_4Cl and 1 mol HCl; (d) 1 mol $HC_2H_3O_2$ and 0.5 mol NaOH; (e) none of these.
4. 20.0 ml of 0.200 M NaOH is added to 50.0 ml of 0.100 M $HC_2H_3O_2$ ($K_a = 1.74 \times 10^{-5}$). What is the pH of this solution? (a) 4.23; (b) 9.77; (c) 5.35; (d) 9.26; (e) 3.00.
5. The solution which s added from the buret during a titration is the (a) buffer; (b) titrant; (c) indicator; (d) base; (e) none of these.
6. A weak acid and the sodium salt of its anion in water in equimolar amounts has (a) pH > 7; (b) pH < 7; (c) pH = 7; (d) depends only on concentration; (e) none of these.
7. An indicator, HIn, is purple, and its anion In is yellow. The indicator changes color at pH 8–10. This indicator will be yellow in which of the following? (a) 0.010 M HCl(aq); (b) 0.10 M $NaC_2H_3O_2$ ($K_a = 1.8 \times 10^{-5}$ for $HC_2H_3O_2$); (c) pure H_2O; (d) 0.010 M NaOH; (e) none of these.

Quiz B

1. What volume in ml of 1.50 M NaOH is needed to neutralize 45.0 ml of 0.500 M acetic acid? (a) 15.0; (b) 22.5; (c) 33.8; (d) 135; (e) none of these.
2. A weak acid has $K_a = 4.2 \times 10^{-3}$ M. If $[A^-] = 2.0$ what must [HA] be so that $[H^+] = 2.1 \times 10^{-3}$ M? (a) 0.5 M; (b) 2.0 M; (c) 1.0 M; (d) 1.5 M; (e) none of these.
3. The addition of NH_4Cl to a solution of NH_3 would (a) decrease the total $[NH_4^+]$; (b) decrease the $[NH_3]$; (c) decrease the K_i of NH_3; (d) increase the $[OH^-]$ of the solution; (e) decrease the pH of the solution.
4. A strong base and the chlorine salt of its cation in water (a) has pH > 7; (b) has pH < 7; (c) has pH = 7; (d) depends on $[Cl^-]$; (e) none of these.
5. Phenolphthalein (color change range of pH 8–10) may be used as an indicator for the titration of (a) a weak acid with a weak base; (b) a weak base with a strong acid; (c) a weak acid with a strong base; (d) any acid with any base; (e) any base with any acid.
6. 10.0 ml of 0.100 M NH_3 ($K_b = 1.74 \times 10^{-5}$) is mixed with 5.00 ml of 0.200 M NH_4Cl. The resulting solution has (a) pH = 4.76; (b) $[NH_4^+]$ larger than in 0.100 M NH_3; (c) $[OH^-] = 3.6 \times 10^{-5}$ M; (d) $[H^+]$ of about 10^{-3} M; (e) none of these.
7. In the neutralization of 50.0 ml of 0.100 M BOH (a weak base with $K_b = 1.6 \times 10^{-7}$) with 0.100 M H_2SO_4, the most correct description of the solution at the midpoint of titration, i.e., half-neutralized, is a solution (a) whose volume is 75.0 ml and which contains some undissociated BOH molecules and some B^+, OH^-, and HSO_4^- ions; (b) whose volume is 62.5 ml and which contains the same species listed in (a); (c) in which $[B^+]$ is about the same as [BOH]; (d) in which $[B^+]$ is about 4×10^{-4} M; (e) none of these.

Quiz C

1. What volume in ml of 1.7 M H_2SO_4 is needed to neturalize 68 ml of 2.5 M NaOH? Na_2SO_4 and water are the titration products. (a) 100; (b) 200; (c) 50; (d) 46; (e) none of these.

2. A weak acid has $K_a = 1.00 \times 10^{-3}$. If [HA] = 1.00 M what must be $[A^-]$ for the pH to be 2.7? (a) 2.7 M; (b) 2.0 M; (c) 0.50 M; (d) 0.37 M; (e) none of these.
3. Which one of the following would *not* be a good buffer pair? (a) potassium carbonate and potassium bicarbonate; (b) ammonium chloride and ammonia; (c) boric acid and sodium borate; (d) sodium chloride and sodium hydroxide; (e) all would be good.
4. A substance which displays little change of pH when small amounts of acid or base are added is called a(n) (a) buffer; (b) indicator; (c) salt; (d) titrant; (e) none of these.
5. Which condition characterizes the equivalence point of the titration of a weak acid with a strong base? (a) a slight excess of titrant is present; (b) pH = 7.00; (c) the indicator must change color; (d) pH = pK_a; (e) none of these.
6. Which factor governs the selection of an indicator? (a) volume of titrant; (b) pH at the equivalence point; (c) concentration of the titrant; (d) final solution volume; (e) none of these.
7. 25.0 ml of 0.200 M NaOH is added to 50.0 ml of 0.100 M $HC_2H_3O_2$ ($K_a = 1.74 \times 10^{-5}$). What is the pH of the final solution? (a) 4.74; (b) 9.26; (c) 9.74; (d) 12.78; (e) none of these.

Quiz D

1. What volume in ml of 2.50 M H_3PO_4 is needed to neutralize 150.0 ml of 0.500 M KOH? The titration products are potassium phosphate and water. (a) 30.0 ml; (b) 10.0 ml; (c) 90.0 ml; (d) 750 ml; (e) none of these.
2. A weak acid HA has $K_a = 1.4 \times 10^{-3}$. In order to produce a solution with $[H^+] = 5.6 \times 10^{-3}$ the ratio $[A^-]/[HA]$ must equal (a) 4.0; (b) 0.25; (c) 2.00; (d) 1.00; (e) none of these.
3. $HC_2H_3O_2$ will be ionized to the greatest degree in which of the following solutions? (a) 0.010 M $HC_2H_3O_2$ and 0.10 M HCl; (b) 0.010 M $HC_2H_3O_2$ and 0.10 M $KC_2H_3O_2$; (c) 0.0010 M $HC_2H_3O_2$ and 0.10 M $NaC_2H_3O_2$; (d) 0.010 M $HC_2H_3O_2$; (e) 0.0010 M $HC_2H_3O_2$.
4. The region of pH over which an indicator changes color is (a) the buffer region; (b) the equivalence region; (c) the overtitration region; (d) the pH color change range; (e) none of these.
5. At the equivalence point of a titration (a) the indicator must change color; (b) pH = pK_a; (c) pH = 7.00; (d) equivalents of acid = equivalents of base; (e) none of these.
6. The indicator HIn is yellow and its anion In^- is green. The indicator changes color from pH = 5.1 to pH = 7.1. This indicator will be yellow in which of the following? (a) 0.01 M HCl(aq); (b) 0.10 M NH_4Cl ($K_b = 1.8 \times 10^{-5}$ for NH_3); (c) pure H_2O; (d) 0.10 M NaOH; (e) none of these.
7. 50.0 ml of 0.100 M NH_3, 10.0 ml of 0.100 M NH_4Cl, and 40.0 ml of 0.050 M HCl are mixed. The resulting solution (a) contains 5.0 mmol NH_3, 2.0 mmol HCl, and 0.1 mmol NH_4Cl; (b) is a buffer with pH = pK_b for ammonia; (c) has $[Cl^-] \simeq 0.30\ M$; (d) has $[NH_3] \simeq 0.30\ M$; (e) none of these.

SAMPLE TEST (20 minutes)

1. 7.500 g of weak acid HA is added to sufficient distilled water to produce 500.0 ml of solution with pH = 2.716. This solution is titrated with NaOH(aq) solution. At the half-equivalence point, pH = 4.602. What is the equivalent weight of the acid?
2. The titration curve at right was obtained in general chemistry laboratory using a pH meter. The titrant was either 0.100 M NaOH or 0.100 M HCl. The unknown being titrated weighed 0.400 g.
   a. Was the unknown a weak acid or a weak base?
   b. What is the mol weight of the unknown?
   c. What is the unknown's ionization constant?
   d. What would be the pH color change range of a suitable indicator for this titration? Choose a suitable indicator from those given in Figure 18-1.

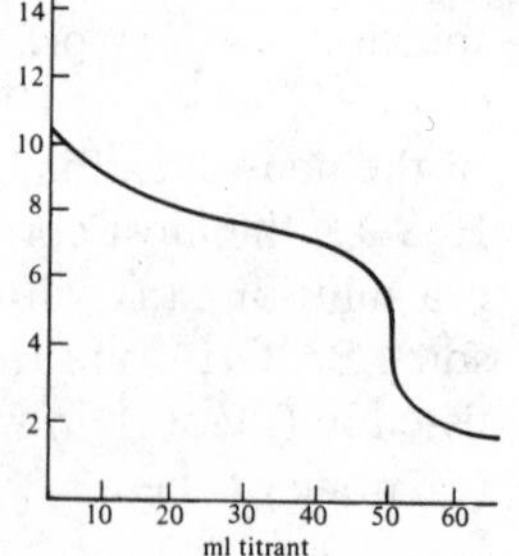

3. A solution has $[ZnCl_2] = 0.0500\ M$, $[NaC_2H_3O_2] = 2.00\ M$, and $[HC_2H_3O_2] = 1.00\ M$. What is $[Zn^{2+}]$ after the solution is saturated with H_2S? A saturated solution has $[H_2S] = 0.100\ M$. For H_2S, $K_1 = 1.0 \times 10^{-7}$ and $K_2 = 1.1 \times 10^{-14}$. For ZnS, $K_{sp} = 1.0 \times 10^{-21}$; for $HC_2H_3O_2$, $K_a = 1.74 \times 10^{-5}$.

Oxidation–Reduction and Electrochemistry

REVIEW OF OBJECTIVES

1. Identify an oxidation-reduction reaction based on changes in oxidation state.

We learned how to assign oxidation states to atoms in objective 9–14. When some of the atoms change oxidation state in going from reactants to products, we say that an oxidation–reduction reaction or a *redox* reaction has occurred. An atom is oxidized when its oxidation state increases. An atom is reduced when its oxidation state decreases (or is reduced). Oxidation always accompanies reduction in a chemical reaction. They never occur separately.

★ 1a. Balance oxidation-reduction reactions by the oxidation-state change method.

The oxidation-state change method is the quicker method of balancing redox reactions (see objective 10–2). Its steps are as follows.

$$Cu(s) + HNO_3(aq) \rightarrow Cu(NO_3)_2(aq) + NO(g) + H_2O(l)$$

1. Write the oxidation state of each element below its symbol.

$$\underset{0}{Cu} + \underset{+1\;\; +5\;\; -2}{HNO_3} \rightarrow \underset{+2\;\; +5\;\; -2}{Cu(NO_3)_2} + \underset{+2\;\; -2}{NO} + \underset{+1\;\; -2}{H_2O}$$

2. Determine which element is oxidized and connect its reactant and product forms with an arrow above the equation. Write the change in oxidation state above the arrow. Similarly identify the reduced element.

$$\overbrace{\underset{0}{Cu} + \underset{+1\;\; +5\;\; -2}{HNO_3} \rightarrow \underset{+2\;\; +5\;\; -2}{Cu}}^{+2}(NO_3)_2 + \underset{+2\;\; -2}{NO} + \underset{+1\;\; -2}{H_2O}$$

(Cu: 0 → +2, change +2; N in HNO_3 +5 → N in NO +2, change −3)

3. Multiply the oxidation-state increase and the oxidation-state decrease by whole numbers so that they are the same magnitude. The whole number multipliers are used as coefficients for the compound (or element) at each end of the arrow.

$$3\,\underset{0}{Cu} + 2\,\underset{+1\;\; +5\;\; -2}{HNO_3} \rightarrow 3\,\underset{+2\;\; +5\;\; -2}{Cu(NO_3)_2} + 2\,\underset{+2\;\; -2}{NO} + \underset{+1\;\; -2}{H_2O}$$

(Cu → Cu: 3(+2); N in HNO_3 → N in NO: 2(−3))

4. Balance the rest of the equation by inspection. Do not change the coefficients you have already determined unless the atoms in that compound appear on the other side of the equation with two oxidation states. The coefficients of Cu, $Cu(NO_3)_2$, and NO are not changed. But HNO_3 contains the nitrogen atom which appears on the product side with two oxidation states (+5 in $CU(NO_3)_2$ and +2 in NO). Since there are 8 N atoms on the right-hand side, 8 is the coefficient of HNO_3.

$$3\ Cu(s) + 8\ HNO_3(aq) \rightarrow 3\ Cu(NO_3)_2(aq) + 2\ NO(g) + 4\ H_2O(l)$$

★ **2. Use the ion-electron method to balance oxidation-reduction equations. This includes being able to write balanced half-equations.**

Although the ion-electron method is more time consuming than the oxidation-state change method, it produces two balanced half-equations which can be used to determine the standard cell voltage of the reaction (see objective 19-6). The emphasis is on the actual substances oxidized and reduced rather than on individual atoms. We illustrate the method in balancing the following redox reaction.

$$HCl(aq) + MnO_2(s) \rightarrow Cl_2(g) + H_2O(l) + MnCl_2(aq)$$

1. Identify the substances which are oxidized or reduced, separate them into ions if that is how they exist in the reaction mixture, and write two *couples*. A couple consists of the oxidized and the reduced species of an element separated by an arrow with the reactant written first. Here chlorine changes oxidation state from being combined in HCl(aq) to being uncombined in $Cl_2(g)$. Manganese changes oxidation state from $MnO_2(s)$ to $MnCl_2(aq)$. Chlorine is present as $Cl^-(aq)$ ions in HCl(aq) and manganese as $Mn^{2+}(aq)$ ions in $MnCl_2(aq)$. Because $MnO_2(s)$ is a solid, it is not separated into its ions.

$Cl^-(aq) \rightarrow Cl_2(g)$ *or* $Cl^-(aq)/Cl_2(g)$

$MnO_2(s) \rightarrow Mn^{2+}(aq)$ *or* $MnO_2(s)/Mn^{2+}(aq)$

2. Balance all atoms except H and O.

$$2\ Cl^-(aq) \rightarrow Cl_2(g)$$

3. In acid solution, use H_2O and $H^+(aq)$ to balance H and O atoms. (We consider basic solution later.) First add one $H_2O(l)$ for each O atom needed. Then add one $H^+(aq)$ for each H atom needed.

$$MnO_2(s) \rightarrow Mn^{2+}(aq) + 2\ H_2O(l)$$
$$MnO_2(s) + 4\ H^+(aq) \rightarrow Mn^{2+}(aq) + 2\ H_2O(l)$$

4. Balance charge by adding electrons.

$$2\ Cl^-(aq) \rightarrow Cl_2(g) + 2\ e^- \qquad [1]$$
$$2\ e^- + MnO_2(s) + 4\ H^+(aq) \rightarrow Mn^{2+}(aq) + 2\ H_2O(l) \qquad [2]$$

These are two balanced half-equations. Equation [1] is an oxidation; chloride is oxidized to chlorine, and electrons are produced. Equation [2] is a reduction; manganese(IV) is reduced to manganese(II), and electrons are consumed.

5. Multiply the two half-equations by whole numbers so that the total number of electrons produced equals the total number consumed. Add the resulting (multiplied) half-equations and eliminate substances which appear on both sides.

$$2\ Cl^-(aq) + MnO_2(s) + 4\ H^+(aq) \rightarrow Cl_2(g) + Mn^{2+}(aq) + 2\ H_2O(l)$$

6. Add spectator ions as needed to produce the original substances. In this case, we add 2 $Cl^-(aq)$ to each side.

$MnO_2(s) + 4\ HCl(aq) \rightarrow Cl_2(g) + MnCl_2(aq) + 2\ H_2O(l)$ [3]

In basic solution only step 3 changes.

$KMnO_4(aq) + H_2S(g) \rightarrow MnO_2(s) + H_2S(s) + KOH(aq) + H_2O(l)$

1. and 2. Write half-equations and balance all atoms except H and O.

$MnO_4^-(aq) \rightarrow MnO_2(s)$ [4]
$H_2S(g) \rightarrow S(s)$ [5]

3. For each O that is deficient, add 2 $OH^-(aq)$ to that side of the equation and 1 $H_2O(l)$ to the other side. For each H that is deficient, add 1 $H_2O(l)$ to that side and 1 $OH^-(aq)$ to the other side. Equation [4] is 2 O deficient on the product side.

$MnO_4^-(aq) + 2\ H_2O(l) \rightarrow MnO_2(s) + 4\ OH^-(aq)$

Equation [5] is 2 H deficient on the product side.

$H_2S(g) + 2\ OH^-(aq) \rightarrow S(s) + 2\ H_2O(l)$

4. Balance charge and produce balanced half-equations.

$3\ e^- + MnO_4^-(aq) + 2\ H_2O(l) \rightarrow MnO_2(s) + 4\ OH^-(aq)$ [6]
$H_2S(g) + 2\ OH^-(aq) \rightarrow S(s) + 2\ H_2O(l) + 2\ e^-$ [7]

5. Equation [6] is multiplied by 2, equation [7] by 3.

$2\ MnO_4^-(aq) + 4\ H_2O(l) + 3\ H_2S(g) + 6\ OH^-(aq) \rightarrow 2\ MnO_2(s) + 8\ OH^-(aq) + 3\ S(s) + 6\ H_2O(l)$

Eliminating species which appear on both sides produces

$2\ MnO_4^-(aq) + 3\ H_2S(g) \rightarrow 2\ MnO_2(s) + 2\ OH^-(aq) + 3(s) + 2\ H_2O(l)$

6. 2 $K^+(aq)$ are added to each side.

$2\ KMnO_4(aq) + 3\ H_2S(g) \rightarrow 2\ MnO_2(s) + 2\ KOH(aq) + 3\ S(s) + 2\ H_2O(l)$ [8]

A guideline to use is that all substances in aqueous solution are separated into their ions, but solids, liquids, and gases are not. This guideline is not hard and fast.

★ **3. Identify oxidizing and reducing agents.**

An oxidizing agent (or oxidant) accepts electrons from the substance which is being oxidized. A reducing agent (or reductant) gives electrons to the substance which is being reduced. Thus the oxidizing agent itself is reduced and the reducing agent is oxidized. The compound or the ion is the oxidizing or reducing agent, not the atom which changes oxidation state. In equation [3] $MnO_2(s)$ is the oxidizing agent, and $HCl(aq)$ or $Cl^-(aq)$ is the reducing agent.

★ **4. Describe how a voltaic cell operates, using the concepts of electrodes, salt bridge, half-cell reactions, net cell reaction, and cell diagram.**

An oxidation–reduction reaction can be run in an electrochemical cell. If the reaction is spontaneous a chemical change produces electricity. This is a *galvanic* or a *voltaic* cell. If the reaction is not spontaneous, electricity produces a chemical change. This is an *electrolytic* cell (see objective 19–11).

Consider a spontaneous reaction.

$$CuSO_4(aq) + Fe(s) \rightarrow Cu(s) + FeSO_4(aq)$$

This reaction produces two half-equations.

$$Cu^{2+}(aq) + 2\,e^- \rightarrow Cu(s) \quad [9]$$
$$Fe(s) \rightarrow Fe^{2+}(aq) + 2\,e^- \quad [10]$$

If we physically separate these half-reactions, the electrons from Fe(s) have to travel to combine with Cu^{2+}(aq) ions. This flow of electrons is an electrical current.

The first step in physically separating the half-reactions is to create two half-cells: (1) an iron bar immersed in a 1.00 *M* solution of $FeSO_4$(aq) and (2) a copper bar immersed in a 1.00 *M* solution of $CuSO_4$(aq). If we connect the two electrodes (the iron bar and the copper bar) with a wire, as in Figure 19-1(a), no current flows. This is because when electrons come from the iron bar, Fe^{2+} ions go into solution. Thus the $FeSO_4$ solution becomes positively charged. This charge prevents the current from flowing.

One way to make sure that the solutions are uncharged is to allow them to mix together. But then the Cu^{2+} ions will move into the iron half-cell and react directly with the iron bar. If we put another solution between the $CuSO_4$(aq) and $FeSO_4$(aq) solutions (Figure 19-1b), the ions can move through that solution. Yet the Cu^{2+} ions will not reach the iron nail. The solution in the middle is called a salt bridge. It is an aqueous solution of a strong electrolyte.

The electrode is the solid metal bar which is placed in the solution, although sometimes the entire half-cell is called the electrode. Oxidation occurs at the anode. Reduction occurs at the cathode. (To help you remember, note that both anode and oxidation begin with a vowel and cathode and reduction begin with a consonant. Note also that anions move toward the anode and cations move toward the cathode.) The electrolyte is either (1) the solution containing ions or (2) the solute of this solution. For instance, either 1.00 *M* $CuSO_4$(aq), or $CuSO_4$ is the electrolyte.

A cell diagram is a more compact way of representing an electrochemical cell. In cell diagrams, the anode is always on the left, the cathode on the right. The electrolytes are at the center of the diagram and the electrodes are on the edges. The boundary between each phase is a solid line. The cell diagram for Figure 19-1(b) is $Fe|FeSO_4(1.00\,M)||CuSO_4(1.00\,M)|Cu$. The double line represents the salt bridge. Spectator ions often are not included: $(Fe|Fe^{2+}(1.00\,M)||Cu^{2+}(1.00\,M)|Cu)$. Perhaps the easiest way to think of cell diagrams is to trace the path of the charge from the anode to the cathode through the solution. Simply write down every species you encounter.

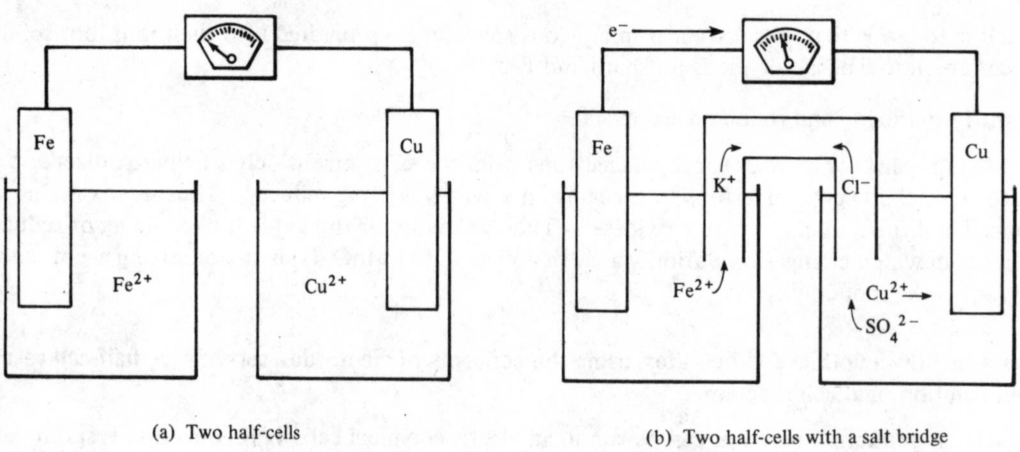

FIGURE 19-1 Construction of a galvanic or voltaic cell.

Sometimes neither the oxidized nor reduced form of one half-cell can be made into a metal bar. For the reaction

$$Zn(s) + Cl_2(g) \rightarrow ZnCl_2(aq)$$

the half-equations are

anode: $Zn(s) \rightarrow Zn^{2+}(aq) + 2\,e^-$

cathode: $Cl_2(g) + 2\,e^- \rightarrow 2\,Cl^-(aq)$

The best way to make the cathode is to pass a stream of chlorine gas over a surface of finely divided platinum, called platinum black. The cell diagram is $Zn|Zn^{2+}(aq)||Cl^-(aq)|Cl_2(g)|Pt$.

5. Describe the standard hydrogen electrode and explain how other standard electrode potentials are related to it.

The standard hydrogen electrode (S.H.E.) is similar to the chlorine electrode described above. A platinum black electrode is immersed in a solution with $[H^+] = 1.00\ M$ and $H_2(g)$ under a pressure of 1.00 atm is bubbled past the electrode. The potential of this electrode (or half-cell) is set equal to 0.000 V. The potential of any other electrode is the voltage of a cell in which the other electrode is paired with the S.H.E. The sign of the potential is positive if the S.H.E. is the anode and negative if the S.H.E. is the cathode.

★ **6. Use the tabulated standard potentials, $E°$, to determine $E°_{cell}$ for an oxidation–reduction reaction and predict whether the reaction is spontaneous.**

An oxidation–reduction equation produces two half-equations. The potentials of both reactions are given in a table of standard reduction potentials such as *Table 19-2 in the text.*

$$5\,H_2O_2(aq) + 2\,KMnO_4(aq) + 6\,HCl(aq) \rightarrow 2\,MnCl_2(aq) + 8\,H_2O(l) + 5\,O_2(g) \qquad [11]$$

The two reduction half-equations for equation [11] are

$$MnO_4^-(aq) + 8\,H^+(aq) + 5\,e^- \rightarrow Mn^{2+}(aq) + 4\,H_2O \qquad E° = +1.51\ V \qquad [12]$$

$$O_2(g) + 2\,H^+(ag) + 2\,e^- \rightarrow H_2O_2(aq) \qquad E° = +0.682\ V \qquad [13]$$

The balanced net ionic equation for equation [11] is twice half-equation [12] minus five times half-equation [13]. The half-cell potentials are added in the same way as the half-equations *except* that the potentials are *not* multiplied by integers.

$$E° = +1.51 - 0.682 = +0.83\ V$$

When the resulting potential of the cell is positive, as it is for reaction [11], the reaction is spontaneous. A negative cell potential indicates a nonspontaneous reaction.

★ **7. Quantitatively and qualitatively predict the effect of varying conditions (concentrations and gas pressures) on values of E_{cell}.**

The Nernst equation [14] describes how the potential of a cell depends on concentration and gas pressure.

$$E_{cell} = E°_{cell} - \frac{RT}{n\mathcal{F}} \ln Q = E°_{cell} - \frac{0.05915}{n} \log Q \quad \text{at } 25°C \qquad [14]$$

Q is the reaction quotient. For reaction [11],

$$Q = \frac{P^5_{O_2}\,[MnCl_2]^2}{[H_2O_2]^5\,[KMnO_4]^2\,[HCl]^6}$$

Increasing the concentration or pressure of the products decreases the cell voltage, making the reaction less spontaneous. Increasing the concentration or pressure of reactants increases the cell voltage. n is the number of electrons transferred in the balanced oxidation– reduction equation.

EXAMPLE 19-1 If $[AgNO_3] = 0.100\,M$ and $[Cu(NO_3)_2] = 2.00\,M$, what is the potential of the cell $Cu|Cu(NO_3)_2(aq)||AgNO_3(aq)|Ag$?

$$\begin{array}{ll} Ag^+(aq) + e^- \rightarrow Ag(s) & E^\circ = +0.799\text{ V} \\ Cu(s) \rightarrow Cu^{2+}(aq) + 2\,e^- & E^\circ = -0.337\text{ V} \\ \hline 2\,Ag^+(aq) + Cu(s) \rightarrow Cu^{2+}(aq) + 2\,Ag(s) & E^\circ = +0.462\text{ V} \end{array}$$

$n = 2$ for this reaction. The Nernst equation gives

$$E = +0.462\text{ V} - \frac{0.05915}{2}\log\frac{[Cu^{2+}]}{[Ag^+]^2}$$

$$= 0.462\text{ V} - \frac{0.05915}{2}\log\frac{(2.00)}{(0.100)^2} = 0.462\text{ V} - 0.068\text{ V} = 0.394\text{ V}$$

★ **8. Know and be able to use the relationships that exist between ΔG°, E°_{cell}, and K.**

A negative $\Delta\bar{G}$ and a positive E_{cell} indicate a spontaneous reaction. However $\Delta\bar{G}$ is an extensive property, whereas E is intensive. If E is multiplied by the number of moles of electrons transferred, the product is extensive.

$$\Delta\bar{G} = -n\mathcal{F}E \qquad [15]$$

$\mathcal{F}$ is the number of coulombs of charge per mole of electrons, $\mathcal{F} = 96{,}500$ C/mol = Faraday's constant. If reactants and products are in their standard state

$$\Delta\bar{G}^\circ = -n\mathcal{F}E^\circ \qquad [16]$$

$$= -RT\ln K_{eq}$$

$$n\mathcal{F}E^\circ = RT\ln K_{eq} \qquad [17]$$

We can compute a reaction's equilibrium constant from its value of E°.

EXAMPLE 19-2 What is $\Delta\bar{G}^\circ$ and K_{eq} for $2\,AgNO_3(aq) + Cu(s) \rightarrow Cu(NO_3)_2(aq) + 2\,Ag(s)$? From Example 19-1, $E^\circ = 0.462$ V.

$$\Delta\bar{G}^\circ = -n\mathcal{F}E^\circ = -(2\text{ mol e}^-)(96{,}500\text{ C/mol e}^-)(0.462\text{ V}) = -89.2 \times 10^3\text{ J/mol}$$

Note that 1 joule = 1 volt-coulomb.

$$\Delta\bar{G}^\circ = -RT\ln K_{eq}$$

$$-89.2 \times 10^3\text{ J/mol} = -(8.314\text{ J/mol}^{-1}\text{ K}^{-1})(298\text{K})\ln K_{eq}$$

$$\ln K_{eq} = 36.0 \quad \textit{or} \quad K_{eq} = 4.3 \times 10^{15}$$

EXAMPLE 19-3 What is $\Delta\bar{G}$ for $2\,AgNO_3(aq) + Cu(s) \rightarrow Cu(NO_3)_2(aq) + 2\,Ag(s)$ when $[AgNO_3] = 0.100\,M$ and $[Cu(NO_3)_2] = 2.00\,M$?

In Example 19-1 we found $E = 0.394$ V under these conditions.

$$\Delta\bar{G} = -n\mathcal{F}E = -(2\text{ mol e}^-)(96{,}500\text{ C/mol e}^-)(0.394\text{ V}) = -76.0 \times 10^3\text{ J/mol}$$

9. Describe some common voltaic cells: the flashlight or dry cell, the lead storage battery, and the fuel cell.

A battery is a device in which several cells are linked together. For the dry cell and the cells of the lead storage battery you should know the answers to the following questions.

(1) What are the anode material and the cathode material?
(2) What are the cell reaction and the anode and cathode half-reactions?
(3) What does the cell look like? Sketch the cell.
(4) What is the cell diagram?
(5) What are the standard potentials of each half-cell and of the full cell?

Fuel cells often are based on combustion reactions.

10. Explain the corrosion of metals in electrochemical terms.

The corrosion of a metal is simply its oxidation in the presence of oxygen. Metals are often protected from corrosion by coating: either with another metal like zinc or chromium or with paint. Another means of protection is a sacrifical anode. An active metal, such as magnesium, is connected to the metal to be protected. The active metal oxidizes first and only when it is consumed will the protected metal corrode. Some metals protect themselves from corrosion with an insoluble and firmly bound compound on the surface. Aluminum forms Al_2O_3 which gives the metal a dull appearance and copper forms a blue-green mixture of $CuCO_3$ and $Cu(OH)_2$. If the insoluble compound is removed, the fresh surface soon corrodes.

11. Describe an electrolytic cell and how it differs from a voltaic cell.

In electrolytic cells electricity causes a chemical change. The cell reaction often is a deomposition. (Electrolytic means breaking with electricity.) The cell reaction usually is nonspontaneous and electricity overcomes the nonspontaneity. The principal problem is keeping the products from reacting. For example, an important industrial process is the electrolysis of brine (NaCl) solutions.

$$2\ NaCl(aq) + 2\ H_2O(l) \rightarrow 2\ NaOH(aq) + Cl_2(g) + H_2(g) \qquad [18]$$

$H_2(g)$ and $Cl_2(g)$ explode when mixed. Thus, the electrolysis cell is designed to keep these gases separate. Reaction [18] is nonspontaneous.

$$2\ Cl^-(aq) \rightarrow Cl_2(g) + 2\ e^- \qquad E° = -1.360\ V$$
$$2\ H_2O + 2\ e^- \rightarrow H_2(g) + 2\ OH^-(aq) \qquad E° = -0.828\ V$$

$$2\ H_2O + 2\ Cl^-(aq) \rightarrow Cl_2(g) + H^2(g) + H_2(g) + 2\ OH(aq) \qquad E° = -2.188\ V$$

The applied voltage has to be positive and larger than +2.188 V to cause reaction [18] to proceed.

★ **12. Identify the possible half-reactions which might occur in an electrolysis and choose which pair will occur based on the highest (least negative) cell potential.**

First write all the half-reactions which might occur, along with their standard potentials by referring to a table of standard electrode potentials like *Table 19-2 in the text.* Then select one oxidation and one reduction, chosen so that the sum of their potentials is the largest (least negative).

EXAMPLE 19-4 A solution with $[Cu(NO_3)_2] = 0.500\ M$, $[ZnCl_2] = 0.500\ M$, and $[FeBr_2] = 0.500\ M$ is electrolyzed between inert electrodes. What are the initial products at the anode and at the cathode, and what minimum voltage must be used?

The possible half-equations are

$$Cu^{2+}(aq) + 2\ e^- \rightarrow Cu(s) \qquad E° = +0.337\ V$$
$$Zn^{2+}(aq) + 2\ e^- \rightarrow Zn(s) \qquad E° = -0.763\ V$$
$$Fe^{2+}(aq) + 2\ e^- \rightarrow Fe(s) \qquad E° = -0.440\ V$$

$NO_3^-(aq) + 4\,H^+ + 3\,e^- \rightarrow NO(g) + 2\,H_2O \quad E° = +0.96$ V
$2\,Br^- \rightarrow Br_2 + 2\,e^- \quad E° = -1.065$ V
$2\,Cl^- \rightarrow Cl_2 + 2\,e^- \quad E° = -1.360$ V

Water also can electrolyze.

$2\,H_2O \rightarrow O_2(g) + 4\,H^+(aq) + 4\,e^- \quad E° = -1.229$ V
$2\,H^+(aq) + 2\,e^- \rightarrow H_2(g) \quad E° = 0.000$ V

We are tempted to pick the NO_3^- reduction until we realize that anions move away from the cathode where reduction occurs. The cation with the highest half-cell potential is $Cu^{2+}(aq)$. The oxidation of $Br^-(aq)$ has the highest potential.

$Cu^{2+} + 2\,e^- \rightarrow Cu(s) \quad E° = +0.337$ V
$2\,Br^-(aq) \rightarrow Br_2(l) + 2\,e^- \quad E° = -1.065$ V

$Cu^{2+}(aq) + 2\,Br^-(aq) \rightarrow Cu(s) + Br_2(l) \quad E° = -0.728$ V

The Nernst equation is now used

$$E = E° - \frac{0.05915}{n} \log \frac{1}{[Cu^{2+}][Br^-]^2}$$

$$= -0.728 \text{ V} - \frac{0.05915}{2} \log \frac{1}{(0.500)(1.00)^2} = -0.737 \text{ V}$$

★ **13. Use Faraday's laws to relate the quantity of chemical change produced by a given amount of change.**

Voltage is the driving force of electrochemical change. The quantity of chemical change is measured by the quantity of charge produced or consumed. The rate of chemical change is measured by the current. If current and voltage seem similar, an analogy with water may help. Voltage is similar to water pressure and current is similar to rate of flow (perhaps measured in gallons/minute).

Current is measured in amperes.

ampere = coulomb/second [19]

Charge is measured in coulombs (C) or Faradays ($\mathcal{F}$).

1 Faraday = 96,500 = 1 mol e^- [20]

The conversion factor method uses these relationships.

EXAMPLE 19-5 A 20.0 A current is used to plate copper out of a $CuSO_4(aq)$ solution. How long must the current be applied in order to plate out 1.00 lb of Cu?

The half-equation is that of the reduction of $Cu^{2+}(aq)$.

$Cu^{2+}(aq) + 2\,e^- \rightarrow Cu(s)$

Then we determine the time required.

$$1.00 \text{ lb Cu} \times \frac{454 \text{ g Cu}}{1 \text{ lb Cu}} \times \frac{\text{mol Cu}}{63.5 \text{ g Cu}} \times \frac{2 \text{ mol e}^-}{\text{mol Cu}} \times \frac{96{,}500 \text{ C}}{\text{mol}} \times \frac{\text{s}}{20.0 \text{ C}} \times \frac{\text{hr}}{3600 \text{ s}} = 19.2 \text{ h}$$

The concentration of $CuSO_4$ changes during this process.

EXAMPLE 19-6 A 12.4 A current is used to electrolyze 5.20 L of a 3.00 *M* $AgNO_3$(aq) solution. What is [Ag^+] after 1.50 h?

We first compute the amount of Ag plated out.

$$1.50 \text{ hr} \times \frac{3600 \text{ s}}{\text{hr}} \times \frac{12.4 \text{ C}}{\text{s}} \times \frac{\text{mol } e^-}{96{,}500 \text{ C}} \times \frac{\text{mol } Ag^+}{\text{mol}} = 0.694 \text{ mol } Ag^+$$

The amount of Ag^+ originally present is found.

$$5.250 \text{ L} \times \frac{3.000 \text{ mol } AgNO_3}{\text{L soln}} \times \frac{\text{mol } Ag^+}{\text{mol } AgNO_3} = 15.750 \text{ mol } Ag^+$$

Then we find the amount of Ag^+ left.

$$15.750 \text{ mol } Ag^+ - 0.694 \text{ mol } Ag^+ = 15.056 \text{ mol } Ag^+$$

Finally we compute the final [Ag^+].

$$[Ag^+] = 15.056 \text{ mol } Ag^+/5.250 \text{ L} = 2.868\ M.$$

★ **14. Use the concepts of equivalent weight and normality to perform stoichiometric calculations based on oxidation–reduction reactions.**

In an oxidation–reduction reaction, one equivalent is the amount of oxidizing or reducing agent which produces or consumes one mole of electrons. In equation [1], 2 mol Cl^-(aq) produces 2 mol electrons. One mol Cl^-(aq) is one equivalent (1 eq). In equation [2], 1 mol MnO_2(s) consumes 2 mol e^- and equals 2 eq. The equivalent weight is the mole weight divided by the number of equivalents per mole.

EXAMPLE 19-7 What is the equivalent weight of $KMnO_4$ in equation [8]?

According to equation [6] 1 mol MnO_4^- or 1 mol $KMnO_4$ consumes 3 mol e^- and equals 3 eq.

$$\frac{158.0 \text{ g } KMnO_4}{\text{mol } KMnO_4} \times \frac{\text{mol } KMnO_4}{3 \text{ eq } KMnO_4} = 52.67 \frac{\text{g } KMnO_4}{\text{eq}}$$

One equivalent of oxidizing agent reacts with one equivalent of reducing agent. Thus, in equation [8] one equivalent of $KMnO_4$ reacts completely with one equivalent of H_2S. Normality is defined as the equivalents of solute per liter of solution. The normality of a solution is its molarity multiplied by the number of equivalents per mole.

EXAMPLE 19-8 0.0250 eq H_2S react completely with 74.2 ml of $KMnO_4$ solution. What is the normality of the solution?

Since 1 eq H_2S = 1 eq $KMnO_4$.

$$N = \frac{0.0250 \text{ eq } H_2S}{74.2 \text{ ml soln}} \times \frac{1 \text{ eq } KMnO_4}{1 \text{ eq } H_2S} \times \frac{1000 \text{ ml}}{\text{L}} = 0.337\ N$$

The molarity of this solution is

$$\frac{0.337 \text{ eq } KMnO_4}{\text{L soln}} \times \frac{\text{mol } KMnO_4}{3 \text{ eq } KMnO_4} = 0.112\ M$$

DRILL PROBLEMS

1a. Balance each of the following reactions by the oxidation state change method.

A. $Ag(s) + HNO_3(aq) \rightarrow AgNO_3(aq) + H_2O(l) + NO(g)$
B. $HCl(aq) + PbO_2(s) \rightarrow H_2O(l) + Cl_2(g) + PbCl_2(aq)$
C. $Al(s) + HBr(aq) \rightarrow AlBr_3(aq) + H_2(g)$
D. $BaSO_4(s) + C(s) \rightarrow BaS(s) + CO(g)$
E. $Br_2(l) + H_2O(l) + SO_2(g) \rightarrow HBr(aq) + H_2SO_4(aq)$
F. $Br_2(l) + KOH(aq) \rightarrow KBr(aq) + KBrO_3(aq) + H_2O(l)$
G. $C(s) + HNO_3(aq) \rightarrow CO_2(g) + H_2O(l) + NO_2(g)$
H. $Ca(PO_3)_2 + C \rightarrow Ca_3(PO_4)_2 + CO + P_4$
I. $ClO_2(g) + H_2O_2(aq) + KOH(aq) \rightarrow H_2O(l) + KClO_2(aq) + O_2(g)$
J. $Cu(s) + HNO_3(aq) \rightarrow Cu(NO_3)_2(aq) + NO_2(g) + H_2O(l)$
K. $HClO_3(aq) \rightarrow HClO_4(aq) + ClO_2(g) + H_2O(l)$
L. $H_3AsO_3(aq) + H_2O(l) + I_2(s) \rightarrow HI(aq) + H_3AsO_4(aq)$
M. $Cr(OH)_3(aq) + Na_2O_2(aq) \rightarrow Na_2CrO_4(aq) + NaOH(aq) + H_2O(l)$
N. $FeI_2(aq) + H_2SO_4(aq) \rightarrow Fe_2(SO_4)_3(aq) + I_2(s) + SO_2(g) + H_2O(l)$
O. $FeS(s) + HNO_3(aq) \rightarrow Fe(NO_3)_3(aq) + S(s) + NO_2(g) + H_2O(l)$

2. Write the two half-equations for each of the following equations and use these to balance each equation by the ion-electron method.

A. $CuSO_4(aq) + H_2O_2(aq) \rightarrow Cu(s) + O_2(g) + H_2SO_4(aq)$
B. $Mg(s) + AgNO_3(aq) \rightarrow Ag(s) + Mg(NO_3)_2(aq)$
C. $Al(s) + H_2SO_4(aq) \rightarrow H_2(g) + Al_2(SO_4)_3(aq)$
D. $Fe_2(SO_4)_3(aq) + Pb(s) \rightarrow PbSO_4(aq) + Fe(s)$
E. $NaI(aq) + F_2(g) \rightarrow NaF(aq) + I_2(s)$
F. $H_2(g) + KClO(aq) \rightarrow KCl(aq) + H_2O(l)$, in basic solution
G. $MnO_2(s) + HCl(aq) \rightarrow MnCl_2(aq) + H_2O(l) + Cl_2(g)$
H. $I_2(s) + H_2O(l) + Br_2(l) \rightarrow HBr(aq) + HIO_3(aq)$
I. $Ag(s) + HNO_3(aq) \rightarrow AgNO_3(aq) + NO(g) + H_2O(l)$
J. $S(s) + H_2O(l) + Pb(NO_3)_2(aq) \rightarrow Pb(s) + H_2SO_3(aq) + HNO_3(aq)$
K. $O_2(g) + H_2O(l) \rightarrow O_3(g) + H_2O_2(aq)$
L. $H_2S(g) + Br_2(l) \rightarrow S(s) + HBr(aq)$
M. $SnSO_4(aq) + FeSO_4(aq) \rightarrow Sn(s) + Fe_2(SO_4)_3(aq)$
N. $H_2SO_4(aq) + S(s) + H_2O(l) \rightarrow H_2SO_3(aq)$
O. $I_2(s) + H_2O(l) \rightarrow HI(aq) + HIO_3(aq)$

3. What are the oxidizing agent and the reducing agent in each equation in the problems of objective 19-2?

4. Draw the voltaic cells for A through J in the problems of objective 19-2. Label the anode and the cathode. Indicate the direction of movement of all ions, including those of the salt bridge, $K^+(aq)$ and $Cl^-(aq)$. Draw the cell diagram. You may use either platinum or graphite as an inert electrode.

6. For each reaction in the problems of objective 19-2, use the data of *Table 19-2 in the text* to determine E°_{cell} and state whether the reaction is spontaneous or nonspontaneous.

7. Determine the potential of the first ten cells in the problems of objective 19-2, if all concentrations are 1.00 M and all gas pressures are 1.00 atm, except the following.

A. $[CuSO_4] = 4.00\,M$, $P_{O_2} = 0.210$ atm
B. $[AgNO_3] = 0.150\,M$, $[Mg(NO_3)_2] = 2.75\,M$
C. $[H_2SO_4] = 6.00\,M$, $P_{H_2} = 0.100$ atm
D. $[PbSO_4] = 1.30 \times 10^{-5}\,M$
E. $[NaF] = 2.50\,M$, $[NaI] = 0.400\,M$
F. $P_{H_2} = 6.40$ atm, $[KCl] = 1.50\,M$
G. $[HCl] = 6.00\,M$, $P_{Cl_2} = 0.0120$ atm
H. $[HBr] = 0.100\,M$, $[HIO_3] = 0.100\,M$
I. $[HNO_3] = 3.00\,M$, $P_{NO} = 4.00$ atm
J. $[HNO_3] = 4.00\,M$, $H_2SO_3 = 0.250\,M$

8. Determine ΔG° and K_{eq} for the first ten cells in the problems of objective 19-2. Determine ΔG for each of the cells in the problems of objective 19-7.

12. For each of the following solutions, use the data of *Table 19-2 in the text* to predict the products of electrolysis at the anode and at the cathode. Write the net ionic equation for the electrolysis reaction. Then use the Nernst equation to predict the minimum voltage which must be imposed for electrolysis to occur. Assume any products are in their standard state.

A. $[Na_2SO_4] = 1.00\ M$, $[MgCl_2] = 1.50\ M$
B. $[CuCl_2] = 1.00\ M$, $[NaNO_3] = 0.500\ M$
C. $[HCl] = 6.20\ M$, $[AlBr_3] = 2.00\ M$
D. $[KOH] = 1.25\ M$, $[NaNO_3] = 2.00\ M$
E. $[CuNO_3] = 0.130\ M$, $[SnCl_2] = 3.15\ M$
F. $[FeSO_4] = 1.25\ M$, $[AlI_3] = 0.0240\ M$

13. A. A constant current of 10 A is passed through an electrolytic cell for 1 h and 30 min. How many Faradays are passed?
B. A solution of $Sn(NO_3)_2$ is electrolyzed by passing 85.0 A of current for 72.0 min. How many grams of tin plate out?
C. Two cells containing solutions of $AgNO_3$ and $CuSO_4$ are connected in series and electrolyzed. The cathode in the $AgNO_3$ cell gains 1.078 g. How much has the cathode in the other cell gained?
D. A solution of $Cu_3(PO_4)_2$ is electrolyzed by passing 17.2 A of current for 145 min. How many grams of Cu plate out?
E. A solution of $Hg_2(NO_3)_2$ is electrolyzed by passing 108 A of current for 95.0 min. How many grams of mercury plate out?
F. A solution of copper(II) sulfate is electrolyzed. Assuming no gas evolution at the cathode, for how long must a current of 1.93 A flow to deposit 64.0 g of copper?
G. A solution of $Au_2(SO_4)_3$ is electrolyzed by passing 104 A of current for 165 min. What mass of gold plates out?
H. What volume of oxygen (at STP) can be liberated during the passage of 5.00 $\mathscr{F}$ of electricity?
I. A solution of $Al(NO_3)_3$ is electrolyed by passing 144 A of current for 102 min. What mass of aluminum plates out?
J. A solution of $Cr(NO_3)_3$ is electrolyzed with a current of 15.0 A for 36.2 min. What mass of chromium plates out?
K. A solution of $AuCl_3$ is electrolyzed by passing 85.0 A of current for 17.6 min. What mass of gold plates out?
L. What mass of silver can be deposited by the passage of a constant current of 5.00 A for 2.00 h through a $AgNO_3$ solution?

14. Determine the equivalent weight of the oxidizing agent and the reducing agent in each equation in the problems of objective 19-2. Then use each of the following sets of titration data to determine the normality of the titrant.
A. 25.00 ml $CuSO_4(aq)$ titrates 16.00 ml 0.250 M H_2O_2
B. 14.70 ml $AgNO_3(aq)$ titrates 27.2 mg Mg(s)
C. 52.15 ml $H_2SO_4(aq)$ titrates 19.2 mg Al(s)
D. 85.17 ml $Fe_2(SO_4)_3(aq)$ titrates 41.7 mg Pb(s)
E. 24.25 ml NaI(aq) titrates 17.4 mg $F_2(g)$
F. 19.71 ml KClO(aq) titrates 1.25 mg $H_2(g)$
G. 25.41 ml HCl(aq) titrates 57.6 mg $MnO_2(g)$
I. 19.75 ml $HNO_3(aq)$ titrates 174 mg Ag(s)
M. 27.21 ml $SnSO_4(aq)$ titrates 19.25 ml 0.250 M $FeSO_4(aq)$

QUIZZES (20 minutes each)

Choose the best answer for each question.

Quiz A

1. When the equation $HClO_3 + H_2O + I_2 \rightarrow HIO_3 + HCl$ is balanced with the smallest integer coefficients, the coefficient of chloric acid is (a) 10; (b) 12; (c) 6; (d) 8; (e) none of these.
2. ____$Cr_2O_7^{2-}$ + ____I^- + ____$H^+ \rightarrow$ ____Cr^{3+} + ____I_2 + ____H_2O
The correct coefficient for I^- in the balanced equation is (a) 2; (b) 3; (c) 6; (d) 14; (e) none of these.
3. When the equation $Br_2 + KOH + MnBr_2 \rightarrow MnO_2 + KBr + H_2O$ is balanced with the smallest integer coefficients, the coefficient of H_2O is (a) 3; (b) 4; (c) 1; (d) 2; (e) none of these.
4. In the reaction $Br_2 + 2\ H_2O + SO_2 \rightarrow 2\ HBr + H_2SO_4$ the equivalent weight of SO_2 is (a) 64.1 g; (b) 128.2 g; (c) 21.4 g; (d) 32.1 g; (e) none of these.

5. The cell reaction and $E°$ of the spontaneous cell made from the Zn/Zn^{2+} (0.76 V) and $2\ Br^-/Br_2$ (−1.07 V) half-cells are (a) $Zn^{2+} + 2\ Br^- \rightarrow Br_2 + Zn$, +1.83 V; (b) $Br_2 + Zn° \rightarrow Zn^{2+} + 2\ Br^-$, +1.83 V; (c) $Br_2 + Zn° \rightarrow Zn^{2+} + 2\ Br^-$, +0.31 V; (d) $Zn^{2+} + 2\ Br^- \rightarrow Br_2 + Zn$, +1.30 V; (e) none of these.
6. Consider the half-cell of Pb metal in contact with 1 M $PB(NO_3)_2$ connected to the half-cell of Ag metal in contact with 1.0 M $AgNO_3$ in a complete circuit connected with an exterior wire (standard reduction potentials: Pb −0.13, Ag +0.80 V). If NaCl is added to the half-cell containing $AgNO_3$, and AgCl precipitates, (a) the voltage of the cell would become more positive; (b) the voltage of the cell would become less positive; (c) the voltage of the cell would not change; (d) the equilibrium constant of the cell reaction would change; (e) the ΔG of the cell would remain the same.
7. The law which relates the amount of material oxidized or reduced to the amount of charge passed is due to (a) Volta; (b) Faraday; (c) Nernst; (d) Mendeleev; (e) Avogadro.
8. In the cell $Zn|Zn^{2+}||Ni^{2+}|Ni$ the zinc is called the (a) electrolyte; (b) cathode; (c) anode; (d) oxidizing agent; (e) none of these.
9. What volume of H_2 (measured at(STP)is produced by the electrolysis of a 2.0 M H_2SO_4 solution? A current of 0.50 A is passed for 30 min. (a) 418 ml; (b) 52 ml; (c) 209 ml; (d) 104 ml; (e) none of these.
10. Suppose that the cell $Sn^{2+} + Zn° \rightarrow Sn° + Zn^{2+}$, $E° = 0.537$ V will run until one of the reactants is completely gone. If the cell is made of 30 ml of 0.50 M Sn^{2+}, 30 ml of 0.50 M Zn^{2+}, 10 g Zn, and 18.2 g Sn, which one will run out first? (a) Sn^{2+} solution; (b) Zn^{2+} solution; (c) Sn strip; (d) Zn strip; (e) none of these, two reactants will run out simultaneously.

Quiz B

1. When the half-equation $NO_3^- + H_2O \rightarrow NO + OH^-$ is balanced with the smallest integer coefficients, the coefficient of OH^- is (a) 3; (b) 2; (c) 4; (d) 1; (e) none of these.
2. When the equation $KMnO_4 + KNO_2 + H_2O \rightarrow MnO_2 + KNO_3 + KOH$ is balanced with the smallest integer coefficients, the coefficient of KNO_3 is (a) 1; (b) 2; (c) 3; (d) 4; (e) none of these.
3. When the equation $HI + HNO_2 \rightarrow H_2O + NO + I_2$ is balanced with the smallest integer coefficients, the sum of all coefficients is (a) 5; (b) 7; (c) 6; (d) 8; (e) none of these.
4. In the reaction $2\ H_2O + 3\ KCN + 2\ KMnO_4 \rightarrow 3\ KCNO + 2\ MnO_2 + 2\ KOH$ here the equivalent weight of $KMnO_4$ is (a) 158 g; (b) 52.7 g; (c) 79.0 g; (d) 316 g; (e) none of these.
5. The cell reaction and $E°$ of the spontaneous cell made from the Ag/Ag^+ (−0.80 V) and Cl^-/Cl_2 (−1.36 V) half-cells are (a) $Cl_2 + 2\ Ag \rightarrow 2\ Ag^+ + 2\ Cl^-$, 0.56 V; (b) $Cl_2 + 2\ Ag \rightarrow 2\ Ag^+ + 2\ Cl^-$, 1.12 V; (c) $Cl_2 + 2\ Ag \rightarrow 2\ Ag^+ + 2\ Cl^-$, 2.16 V; (d) $2\ Ag^+ + 2\ Cl^- \rightarrow Cl_2 + 2\ Ag$, 1.08 V; (e) none of these.
6. In the cell $Fe^{2+}|Fe^{3+}||Cu^{2+}|Cu$, which will increase the cell voltage the *most?* (a) halve $[Cu^{2+}]$; (b) halve $[Fe^{2+}]$; (c) double $[Cu^{2+}]$; (d) double $[Fe^{2+}]$; (e) cut Cu electrode in half.
7. If the voltage of an electrochemical cell is negative then the cell reaction is (a) nonspontaneous; (b) slow; (c) exothermic; (d) spontaneous; (e) none of these.
8. The equation which relates ion concentrations and gas pressures to cell voltages is called (a) Raoult's law; (b) Le Châtelier's principle; (c) Volta's theory; (d) Faraday's law; (e) none of these.
9. What mass of copper (at wt = 63.54) can be deposited by the passage of 9650 C of electricity through a $CuSO_4$ solution? (a) 12.7 g; (b) 6.35 g; (c) 3.18 g; (d) 7.98 g; (e) none of these.
10. A copper electrode weighed 35.42 g before the electrolysis of a copper(II) sulfate solution and 36.69 g after the electrolysis had run for 20 s. The equivalent weight of copper for this electrolysis is 31.77 g. Compute the amperage of the current which was used. (a) 3860 A; (b) 157 A; (c) 193 A; (d) 259 A; (e) none of these.

Quiz C

1. When the half-reaction $ClO_3^- + H^+ \rightarrow Cl^- + H_2O$ is balanced with the smallest integer coefficients, the coefficient of H_2O is (a) 6; (b) 5; (c) 2; (d) 3; (e) none of these.
2. When the equation $Cs_2MnO_4 + H_2O \rightarrow CsMnO_4 + CsOH + MnO_2$ is balanced with the smallest integer coefficients, the coefficient of MnO_2 is (a) 1; (b) 2; (c) 3; (d) 4; (e) none of these.

3. When the equation $HCl + H_2C_2O_4 + MnO_2 \rightarrow MnCl_2 + CO_2 + H_2O$ is balanced with all integer coefficients, the coefficient of CO_2 is (a) 1; (b) 2; (c) 3; (d) 4; (e) none of these.
4. In the reaction $8\ HMnO_4 + 5\ AsH_3 + 8\ H_2SO_4 \rightarrow 5\ H_3AsO_4 + 8\ MnSO_4 + 12\ H_2O$ the equivalent weight of AsH_3 is (a) 77.9 g; (b) 26.0 g; (c) 15.6 g; (d) 9.74 g; (e) none of these.
5. The cell reaction and $E°$ of the spontaneous cell made from the Fe/Fe^{2+}(0.44 V) and Sn/Sn^{2+} (0.14 V) half-cells are (a) $Fe^{2+} + Sn \rightarrow Sn^{2+} + Fe$, −0.30 V; (b) $Fe^{2+} + Sn \rightarrow Sn^{2+} + Fe$, +0.30 V; (c) $Fe° + Sn^{2+} \rightarrow Sn + Fe^{2+}$, −0.30 V; (d) $Fe° + Sn^{2+} \rightarrow Sn + Fe^{2+}$, +0.58 V; (e) none of these.
6. For the cell $Cu|Cu^+||Al^{3+}|Al$, which will increase the cell voltage the most? (a) double $[Al^{3+}]$; (b) halve $[Cu^+]$; (c) double $[Cu^+]$; (d) halve $[Al^{3+}]$; (e) cut the Al electrode in half.
7. One mole of electrons has a charge of (a) 96,500 A; (b) 1.60×10^{-19} C; (c) 6.02×10^{23} A; (d) 96,500 C; (e) none of these.
8. In a galvanic cell, oxidation occurs at the (a) anode; (b) cathode; (c) salt bridge; (d) electrolyte; (e) none of these.
9. 1.00 L of a 1.500 *M* $Al_2(SO_4)_3$ solution is electrolyzed between platinum electrodes for 1.20 h using a current of 62.0 A. What is $[Al^{3+}]$ at the end of the electrolysis? (a) 0.57 *M*; (b) 0.93 *M*; (c) 2.07 *M*; (d) not enough Al present; (e) none of these.
10. A solution of CuBr is electrolyzed by passing 35.0 A of current for 17.0 min. What mass in grams of Cu (63.5 g/mol) plates out? (a) 26.5; (b) 53.1; (c) 11.8; (d) 23.5; (e) none of these.

Quiz D

1. After balancing the ionic equation $MnO_4^- + Cl^- + H^+ \rightarrow Mn^{2+} + Cl_2 + H_2O$, the sum of the simplest set of integral coefficients of the six substances would be (a) 21; (b) 24; (c) 38; (d) 43; (e) 51.
2. When the equation $ClO_2 + H_2O_2 + KOH \rightarrow H_2O + KClO_2 + O_2$ is balanced with the smallest integer coefficients, the coefficient of H_2O is (a) 3; (b) 5; (c) 2; (d) 4; (e) none of these.
3. When the equation $HNO_2 \rightarrow HNO_3 + NO + H_2O$ is balanced with the smallest integer coefficients, the sum of all coefficients is (a) 7; (b) 6; (c) 9; (d) 10; (e) none of these.
4. In the reaction $2\ Bi(OH)_3 + 3\ Na_2SnO_2 \rightarrow 2\ Bi + 3\ H_2O + 3\ Na_2SnO_3$ the equivalent weight of $Bi(OH)_3$ is (a) 86.7 g; (b) 260 g; (c) 130 g; (d) 173 g; (e) none of these.
5. The cell reaction and $E°$ of the spontaneous cell made from the Sn^{2+}/Sn^{4+} (−0.15 V) and $H_2S/S°$ (−0.14 V) half-cells are (a) $Sn^{4+} + H_2S \rightarrow 2\ H^+ + S° + Sn^{2+}$, 0.29 V; (b) $Sn^{2+} + 2\ H^+ + S° \rightarrow Sn^{4+} + H_2S$, −0.29 V; (c) $Sn^{4+} + H_2S \rightarrow 2\ H^+ + S° + Sn^{2+}$, +0.01 V; (d) $2\ H^+ + S° + Sn^{2+} \rightarrow Sn^{4+} + H_2S$, −0.01 V; (e) none of these.
6. For the cell $Ag|Ag^+||Br^-|Br_2$, which will increase the cell voltage the *most*? (a) double $[Ag^+]$; (b) triple $[Br^-]$; (c) cut the Ag electrode in half; (d) remove half of the Br_2; (e) halve $[Ag^+]$.
7. Consider the half-cell of Pb metal in contact with 1.00 *M* $Pb(NO_3)_2$ connected to the half-cell of Ag metal in contact with 1.00 *M* $AgNO_3$ in a complete circuit connected with an exterior wire (standard reduction potentials: Pb = −0.13 V, Ag = +0.80 V). (a) The Pb electrode increases in mass. (b) Electrons flow from the Pb electrode to the Ag electrode. (c) The Ag electrode is the anode of the cell. (d) NO_3^- ions migrate from the lead half-cell to the silver half-cell. (e) The Ag electrode dissolves slowly.
8. A solution of $CuCl_2$ is electrolyzed by passing 35.0 A for 17.0 min. What mass in grams of Cu (63.5 g/mol) plates out? (a) 24.9; (b) 49.8; (c) 47.0; (d) 23.5; (e) none of these.
9. The amount of substance which produces a mole of electrons is known as (a) a Lewis base; (b) an equivalent; (c) a reducing agent; (d) an oxidizer; (e) none of these.
10. How many hours must a current of 14.0 A flow to produce 5.02 g Al (27.0 g/mol) from a solution of $Al(NO_3)_3$ (213 g/mol)? (a) 1.07; (b) 0.135; (c) 0.356; (d) 0.405; (e) none of these.

SAMPLE TEST (20 minutes)

1. The reaction $3\ Pb(NO_3)_2 + 2\ Al \rightarrow 2\ Al(NO_3)_3 + 3\ Pb$ is used in a galvanic cell.
   a. Write the cell diagram, using a KCl salt bridge.

b. From the list of reduction couples determine $E°$ of the cell.
Pb^{2+}/Pb, $E° = -0.126$ V; Al^{3+}/Al, $E° = -1.66$ V; Pb^{4+}/Pb^{2+}, $E° = 1.455$ V; NO_3^-/NO, $E° = 0.96$ V.

c. Determine E when $[Pb(NO_3)_2] = 4.00\ M$ and $[Al(NO_3)_3] = 0.0200\ M$.

2. 50.0 ml of 0.100 M $CuSO_4(aq)$ is electrolyzed with a 0.965 A current for 1.00 min. When electrolysis ends what is
   a. $[Cu^{2+}]$? b. pH, assuming pH = 7.00 initially?
3. Balance the following oxidation–reduction reactions.
   a. $KMnO_4(aq) + H_2S(g) \rightarrow MnO_2(s) + S + KOH(aq) + H_2O(l)$
   b. $NiS(s) + KClO_3(aq) + HCl(aq) \rightarrow NiCl_2(aq) + KCl(aq) + S(s) + H_2O(l)$

The Chemistry of Selected Representative Elements

REVIEW OF OBJECTIVES

★ **1. Explain physical properties in terms of their atomic properties and their positions in the periodic table.**

You should know the trends of physical and atomic properties summarized in Table 20-1 and be able to predict relative values for different elements.

TABLE 20-1
Periodic trends of physical and atomic properties of elements

Property	Behavior down a group	Behavior across a period
ionization potential	decrease	increase
atomic or cationic radius	increase	decrease
hydration energy of cation	decrease	increase
standard reduction potential	decrease	increase
density of solid	increase	increase
electrical conductivity for metals	decrease	increase
melting points of metals	decrease	increase
melting points of nonmetals	increase	decrease

2. Describe how the free elements of groups IA, IIA, and VIIA and phosphorus are produced from naturally occurring compounds.

Elements of groups IA and IIA are very commonly found as the halides in nature. The elements cannot be isolated from aqueous solution because of their very negative reduction potentials. Thus, the metals are produced by electrolysis of their molten (fused) salts. Chloride salts are abundant.

$$2\ NaCl(l) \xrightarrow{\sim\sim} 2\ Na(l) + Cl_2(g)$$

Often a flux is added to the salt to lower its melting point ($CaCO_3$ is added to NaCl).

The halogens often are produced by the electrolysis of molten salts. This is the only method possible for $F_2(g)$ because of its large positive reduction potential. Electrolysis of aqueous halide solutions produces the other halogens.

Na(s) and $Cl_2(g)$ produce the heavier members of each family by displacement.

$$Cl_2 + 2\ Br^- \rightarrow Br_2 + 2\ Cl^- \quad \text{(in aqueous solution)}$$
$$Na + K^+ \rightarrow K + Na^+ \quad \text{(in the melt)}$$

Phosphorus is prepared by reduction of P_4O_{10} with carbon.

$$P_4O_{10} + 5\ C \xrightarrow{\Delta} P_4 + 5\ CO_2$$

P_4O_{10} is produced from phosphate rock by reaction with sand (SiO_2) at high temperature.

$$2\ Ca_3(PO_4)_3 + 6\ SiO_2 \rightarrow 6\ CaSiO_3 + P_4O_{10}$$

S, N_2, and O_2 are "mined": S from extensive underground deposits, and $N_2(g)$ and $O_2(g)$ from air. These processes are described *in the text*.

★ **3. Describe important uses of the more common representative elements and their compounds.**

This is a 3 X 5 card project. Use the summaries in Table 20-2.

TABLE 20-2
Uses of representative elements and their compounds

Substance	*Important or unique uses*
	Group IA
Li metal	electrical batteries; future fusion fuel (objective 23-12)
Li_2CO_3	medication for gout and mental illness
$LiAlH_4$	reducing agent for organic reactions
Na metal	reducing agent in chemical manufacture; in sodium vapor lamps; future coolant in fusion reactors
NaOH	(caustic soda or soda lye) paper manufacture, aluminum ore purification; chemical manufacturing, petroleum refining; soap production
Na_2CO_3	(soda) glass; water softener in detergents
Na_2SO_4	glass, soap, and paper pulp manufacture; dyeing textiles
Na_4SiO_4	(water glass) soap and water softener; glue and sizing material
$Na_6P_6O_{18}$	water softener in detergents
NaCl	chemical manufacture; refrigeration; household use
$NaNO_3$	manufacture of fertilizers, KNO_3, and HNO_3
$NaHCO_3$	(bicarbonate of soda) stomach antacid; baking soda
NaCN	photographic process; in metal electroplating baths; rat poison
KOH	manufacture of soft soap
K_2CO_3	(potash, which gave the element its name) hard glass ingredient
KCl	fertilizer production (K^+ is a plant nutrient)
KNO_3	oxidizing agent in gun powder; dye production
$KMnO_4$	common laboratory and industrial oxidizing agent
Rb	metal and compounds have no important uses
Cs metal	photoelectric cells
	Group IIA
Be metal	windows in x-ray tubes; in copper alloys which must be flexible and conduct electricity; in alloys for nonsparking safety tools; in aircraft alloys for lightness and strength
Mg metal	lightweight, strong alloys often with Al. flashbulbs
MgO	furnace liner as it is very high melting; antacid
$MgSO_4$	in sizing paper, cotton, and leather; epsom salts
Ca metal	to remove oxygen from molten alloys
CaO	(lime) in plaster and mortar; in agriculture; as a cheap base in the chemical industry, furnace lining
$CaCO_3$	(limestone, marble, chalk) glass manufacture; building material; flux to remove SiO_2 in metallurgy $CaCO_3 + SiO_2 \rightarrow CaSiO_3 + CO_2(g)$ paper whitener
$CaCl_2$	by-product of Na_2CO_3 manufacture; to melt ice on roads; to absorb water to settle the dust on roads
$CaSO_4 \cdot 2\ H_2O$	(gypsum) reversibly dehydrates to plaster of Paris
$Ca(NO_3)_2 \cdot 4\ H_2O$	fertilizer
Sr	compounds used in flares and fire works for the red color
$BaSO_4$	white pigment for paint and paper (lithopone ($BaSO_4 + ZnS$) is a white pigment)
	Group IIIA
B	to harden steel; control rods for nuclear reactors
B_4C_3	industrial abrasive
Borax	($Na_2B_4O_7 \cdot 10\ H_2O$) weak base; water softener
B_2O_3	ingredient with SiO_2 of borosilicate glass (Pyrex)
H_3BO_3	antiseptic; for fireproofing fabric
Al	structural metal often alloyed with Cu, Mn, Si, Zn, and Fe; "silver" paint pigment; electric transmission lines; foil; in the thermite process $Fe_2O_3 + 2Al \rightarrow Al_2O_3 + 2Fe$ for welding and incendiary bombs

TABLE 20-2 *(continued)*

Substance	*Important or unique uses*
Al_2O_3	refractory (high temperature resistant) furnace liner; industrial abrasive; synthetic jewels
$Al_2(SO_4)_3$	for sizing paper
Alum	$(KAl(SO_4)_2 \cdot 12\ H_2O)$ mordant to fix dye to cloth; to clarify water, size paper, and fireproof fabric
	Group IVA
Si	semiconductor for computing microcircuitry
SiO_2	glass; Portland cement; sandpaper
Silicones	lubricants and rubbers
Na_4SiO_4	(water glass) fabric and paper sizing; industrial glue; laundry detergent water softener (partly replacing $Na_6P_6O_{18}$)
Silicates	water-softening equipment
SiC	industrial abrasive
	Group VA
N_2	inert atmosphere for air-sensitive reactions and working active metals
NH_3	refrigerant, fertilizer
N_2O	(laughing gas) inhalation anesthetic
HNO_3	to make nitrate salts for fertilizers, plastics, dyes, and explosives
$NaNO_3$	meat preservative
KNO_3	gunpowder ingredient
$AgNO_3$	photography
NH_4NO_3	fertilizer; explosive (amatol is a mixture of NH_4NO_3 and TNT, trinitrotoluene)
NH_4Cl	as a flux to clean oxides from metal surfaces in galvanizing and soldering
P	red form in the striking strip of safety matches; smoke bombs; tracer bullets; burned in air to make P_4O_{10}
P_4S_3	in the tip of kitchen matches
P_4O_{10}	laboratory drying agent; with H_2O it forms H_3PO_4
$Ca(H_2PO_4)_2$	(triple superphosphate) fertilizer
H_3PO_4	fertilizer manufacture; in soft drinks, in dyeing
	Group VIA
O_2	steel refining; high temperature torches
O_3	industrial oxidant; water purification
Na_2O_2	paper and fabric bleach
H_2O_2	germicide; bleach
S	manufacture of H_2SO_4; vulcanization of rubber; in fireworks, gunpowder, and matches
H_2SO_4	principal product of the chemical industry; make fertilizers and plastics; clean steel; produce alum
SO_2	refrigerant, bleach, food preservative
Sulfites	(as Na_2SO_3) bleaches for natural fabrics and paper
$Na_2S_2O_3$	("hypo") photography; to remove excess Cl_2 used to bleach fabric and paper
	Group VIIA
F_2	manufacture of fluorocarbons as lubricants and nonstick coatings (Teflon)
HF	etching glass ($SiO_2 + 4\ HF \rightarrow SiF_4 + 2\ H_2O$)
NaF	insecticide; rat poison; very low concentrations used in drinking water to prevent tooth decay
Cl_2	water purification; plastic manufacture; solvent production; pulp and paper bleach; poison gas (bertholite) in World War I
HCl	cleaning metals and masonary walls; removing boiler scale; refining some ores
$KClO_3$	oxidant used in fireworks; weed killer
Ca (OCl) Cl	(bleaching powder) produces $Cl_2(g)$ when wet
Br_2	to manufacture fire retardants
Bromates	as oxidants in small-scale reactions
$C_2H_4Br_2$	in "leaded" gasoline to remove lead from the engine
I_2	antiseptic; in medications of the thyroid gland

★ **4. Write equations for the reactions between the group IA and IIA metals and the halogens, oxygen, nitrogen, hydrogen, acids, and water.**

This is a 3 X 5 card project. Use the reactions in Table 20-3. Be sure to memorize the conditions for each reaction.

TABLE 20-3
Some reactions of the group IA and IIA metals

	Group IA	Group IIA
X_2:	$2\ M(s) + X_2(g) \rightarrow 2\ MX(s)$	$M(s) + X_2(g) \rightarrow MX_2(s)$
O_2:	$4\ Li(s) + O_2(g) \rightarrow 2\ Li_2O(s)$	$2\ M(s) + O_2(g) \rightarrow 2\ MO(s)$
	$2\ Na(s) + O_2(g) \rightarrow Na_2O_2(s)$	Ba forms BaO_2 above 500°C
	$M'(s) + O_2(g) \rightarrow MO_2(s)$	
	M′ = K, Rb, Cs	
N_2:	$6\ Li(s) + N_2(g) \rightarrow 2\ Li_3N(s)$	$3\ M(s) + N_2(g) \rightarrow M_3N_2(s)$
H_2:	$2\ M(s) + H_2(g) \rightarrow 2\ MH(s)$	$M'(s) + H_2(g) \rightarrow M'H_2(s)$
		M′ = Ca, Sr, Ba
H^+:	$2\ M(s) + 2\ H^+ \rightarrow 2\ M^+ + H_2(g)$	$M(s) + 2\ H^+ \rightarrow M^{2+} + H_2(g)$
H_2O:	$2\ M(s) + 2\ H_2O \rightarrow 2\ M^+ + 2\ OH^- + H_2(g)$	$M'(s) + 2\ H_2O \rightarrow M^{2+} + 2\ OH^- + H_2(g)$
		M′ = Ca, Sr, Ba
		$Mg(s) + H_2O \xrightarrow{\Delta} MgO(s) + H_2(g)$

★ **5. Write oxidation-reduction equations, involving the halogens, nitrogen compounds, sulfur compounds, O_2, O_3, and H_2O_2.**

This is a 3 X 5 card project. Use the reactions in *Table 20-4 in the text.* Also, lighter halogens displace heavier ones from salts.

$$Cl_2(g) + 2\ I^- \rightarrow I_2(s) + 2\ Cl^-$$

When oxygen is used as an oxidizing agent, it forms water or an oxide salt (except for the peroxides and superoxides of groups IA and IIA). Ozone forms oxygen in addition to water or an oxide salt.

$$2\ e^- + 2\ H^+ + O_3 \rightarrow O_2 + H_2O \qquad E° = +2.07\ V$$

Hydrogen peroxide can be oxidized to O_2 (H_2O_2/O_2) or reduced to OH^-(H_2O_2/OH^-) or an oxide (H_2O_2/H_2O). The couple (see objective 20-6) for each reaction is written in parentheses. The electrode potential diagrams for oxygen are given in Figure 20-1.

Acid Solution

$$O_2 \xrightarrow{0.68\ V} H_2O_2 \xrightarrow{1.77\ V} H_2O$$

Basic Solution

$$O_2 \xrightarrow{-0.6\ V} O_2^- \xrightarrow{0.4\ V} HO_2^- \xrightarrow{0.87\ V} OH^-$$

$$O_2 \xrightarrow{-0.08\ V} HO_2^-$$

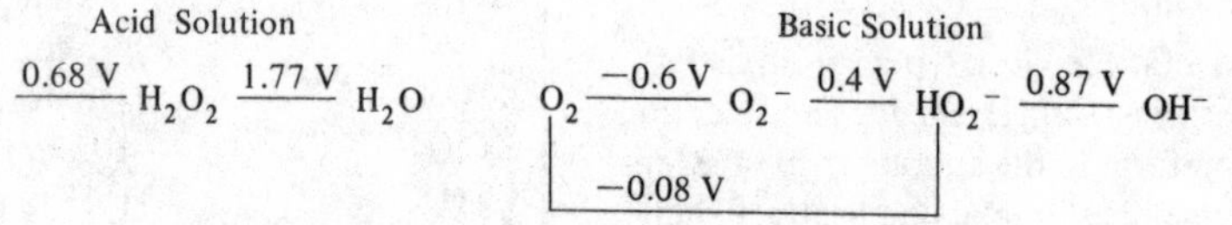

FIGURE 20-1 Electrode potential diagrams for oxygen.

Sulfurous acid and sulfites can be either reducing agents (H_2SO_3/SO_4^{2-}) or oxidizing agents (H_2SO_3/S). But sulfides can only be oxidized (H_2S/S). Sulfuric acid is an oxidizing agent when hot and concentrated (SO_4^{2-}/SO_2). Thiosulfate ion, in which sulfur has a +4 oxidation state, is a reducing agent ($S_2O_3^{2-}/S_4O_6^{2-}$). The electrode potential diagrams for sulfur are given in Figure 20-2.

Ammonia is oxidized to NO(g) by oxygen in the present of a Pt catalyst.

$$4\ NH_3(g) + 5\ O_2(g) \xrightarrow{Pt} 4\ NO(g) + 6\ H_2O(g)$$

Nitric acid always is an oxidizing agent (NO_3^-/N_2O, NO_3^-/NO, or NO_3^-/NO_2). Nitrite ion or nitrous acid can be either a reducing agent (HNO_2/NO_3^-) or an oxidizing agent (HNO_2/NO). The electrode potential diagrams for nitrogen are given in *Figure 20-12 in the text.*

Acid Solution	Basic Solution
$S_2O_8^{2-} \xrightarrow{2.01\ V} SO_4^{2-} \xrightarrow{0.17\ V} H_2SO_3 \xrightarrow{0.45\ V} S \xrightarrow{0.141\ V} H_2S$	$SO_4^{2-} \xrightarrow{-0.91\ V} SO_3^{2-} \xrightarrow{-0.61\ V} S \xrightarrow{-0.48\ V} S^{2-}$

FIGURE 20-2 Electrode potential diagrams for sulfur.

★ **6. Use electrode potential diagrams to predict standard oxidation potentials.**

In electrode potential diagrams the reduced and oxidized forms of an element are connected with a line. The standard reduction potential is written above each line. The two forms of the element are called a couple. Thus SO_4^{2-}/SO_3^{2-} is a couple. The couple can be expanded into a complete half-equation in the same way we balanced half-equations (see objective 19-2).

in base: $SO_4^{2-} + H_2O + 2e^- \rightarrow SO_3^{2-} + 2\,OH^- \quad E° = -0.91\ V$

We cannot add potentials as we did to obtain full cell equations, since the result is a half-equation, but we *can* add values of $\Delta \bar{G}° = -n\mathcal{F}E°$.

$$SO_4^{2-} + H_2O + 2\,e^- \rightarrow SO_3^{2-} + 2\,OH^- \quad E_1° = -0.91\ V; \quad \Delta\bar{G}° = 2(0.91)\mathcal{F}$$

$$SO_3^{2-} + 3\,H_2O + 4\,e^- \rightarrow S + 6\,OH^- \quad E_2° = -0.61\ V; \quad \Delta\bar{G}° = 4(0.61)\mathcal{F}$$

$$SO_4^{2-} + 4\,H_2O + 6\,e^- \rightarrow S + 8\,OH^- \quad \Delta\bar{G}° = 2(0.91)\mathcal{F} + 4(0.61)\mathcal{F} = -6\mathcal{F}E_3°$$

Thus $-6E_3° = 4.26$ *or* $E_3° = -4.26/6 = -0.71\ V$

7. Explain the role of ozone in the atmosphere.

Ozone is formed in the upper atmosphere when ultraviolet light (with a wavelength of 260 nm) is absorbed by oxygen. The ozone molecule absorbs ultraviolet light (210–290 nm). It acts as a sunscreen, preventing this high energy (410–570 kJ/mol) radiation from reaching the earth's surface. When the radiation is absorbed, the O_3 molecule dissociates, turning the energy into kinetic energy of the fragments.

★ **8. Distinguish among normal oxides, peroxides, and superoxides and among acidic, basic, and amphoteric oxides.**

In normal oxides, oxygen has an oxidation state of −2. In peroxides the anion is O_2^{2-} with oxygen in a −1 oxidation state. Many ionic peroxides have a large cation. Covalent peroxides contain an oxygen–oxygen single bond as is the case in hydrogen peroxide, H—O—O—H. Larger cations require a still larger anion, the superoxide ion, O_2^-, with oxygen in a −1/2 oxidation state.

Acidic oxides form an acidic solution when they are dissolved in water. Basic oxides form a basic solution. Solutions of amphoteric oxides are basic or acidic, depending on whether they are reacted with a strong acid or a strong base.

Acidic oxides are those of the nonmetals: Cl, Br, I, S, Se, N, P, As, C, Si, and B. Basic oxides are those of the metals: Li, Na, K, Rb, Cs, Mg, Ca, Sr, Ba, Tl, and Bi. Amphoteric oxides are those of the metalloids: Be, Al, Ga, Ge, Sn, Pb, and Sb. For transition elements, acidic oxides have the element in a high oxidation state (+6 or larger). The common amphoteric oxides of transition metals are ZnO, CdO, and Cr_2O_3.

9. Describe the different molecular and/or physical forms of oxygen, sulfur and phosphorus.

Oxygen, O_2, and ozone, O_3, are the two allotropes of oxygen. Ozone has a sharp, pungent odor and is an excellent oxidizing agent.

The two solid allotropes of sulfur are rhombic and monoclinic. Rhombic crystals are somewhat squat, although we normally see this form as a powder, often called flowers of sulfur. Monoclinic crystals are long and needle shaped, but the monoclinic form is unstable at room temperature. There are several forms of liquid sulfur. Melting solid sulfur allows S_8 ring molecules to move freely. Higher temperatures produce S_8 chains which entangle and the liquid becomes more viscous. Still higher temperatures break the chains apart, making the liquid less viscous.

Phosphorus has the form of tetrahedral P_4 molecules in white phosphorus, in the liquid, and in the vapor below 800°C. White phosphorus, or yellow phosphorus, is a highly reactive waxy solid melting at 44.1°C. It burns spontaneously in air and is poisonous, very volatile, and soluble in CS_2 (l). Red phosphorus is made by heating white phosphorus at 400°C for several hours. Red phosphorus is very much less reactive and less volatile than white phosphorus, and it is insoluble in CS_2 (l) and nonpoisonous. Black phosphorus is formed when heat and pressure are applied to red or white phosphorus (200°C, 4000 atm *or* 25°C, 11,500 atm), or when phosphorus is heated in the presence of a catalyst. It is very unreactive, does not ignite in air below 400°C, conducts electricity, and has a high density (2.65 g/cm^3 compared to 1.83 g/cm^3 for white and 2.34 g/cm^3 for red phosphorus). The structure consists of pleated sheets of phosphorus atoms and is somewhat flaky like graphite.

10. Describe a number of thio compounds by name, formula, and structure.

The common thio ions are shown in Figure 20-3. The bond angles are approximately tetrahedral in all of these structures. Both dithionite and thiosulfate are good reducing agents. Sodium dithionite is used as a bleach for dyes.

$$S_2O_4^{2-} + 4\,OH^- \rightarrow 2\,SO_3^{2-} + 2\,H_2O + 2\,e^- \qquad E° = +1.12\text{ V}$$

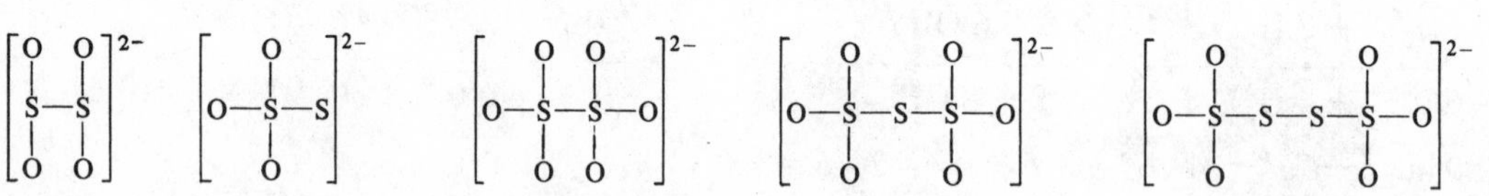

dithionite thiosulfate dithionate trithionate tetrathionate

FIGURE 20-3 Common thio anions.

★ 11. Predict whether a metal sulfide will dissolve in water, acids, bases, in HNO_3 (aq), or aqua regia.

This is a 3 X 5 card project. Use *Table 20-7 in the text.* Write the conditions on one side and the sulfides which dissolve on the other. Note that the water-soluble sulfides also are soluble in 0.3 *M* HCl, 3 *M* HNO_3, and aqua regia. Those soluble in 0.3 *M* HCl also are soluble in 3 *M* HNO_3 and aqua regia, but not in water. Those soluble in 3 *M* HNO_3 also are soluble in aqua regia, but not in water or 0.3 *M* HCl. Those soluble in bases or in a basic sulfide ion solution generally are not soluble in acids.

★ 12. Name oxyacids and their salts according to a scheme based on H_2O molecule loss–ortho, meta, and pyro.

1. Starting with the element E in oxidation state $n+$, form the hydroxy compound $E(OH)_n$.
2. If $E(OH)_n$ (more correctly written H_nEO_n) or its anion exists, it is the ortho acid. Thus H_4SiO_4 is orthosilicic acid. If not, loss of one water molecule yields the ortho acid, with formula $H_{n-2}EO_{n-1}$. Thus, since H_5PO_5 does not exist, H_3PO_4 is orthophosphoric acid.
3. The meta acid is formed by the loss of one water molecule from one molecule of the ortho acid. Thus H_2SiO_3 is metasilicic acid, and HPO_3 is metaphosphoric acid.
4. The pyro acid is formed by the loss of one water molecule from *two* molecules of the ortho acid. Thus $H_4P_2O_7$ is pyrophosphoric acid, and $H_2S_2O_7$ is pyrosulfuric acid.

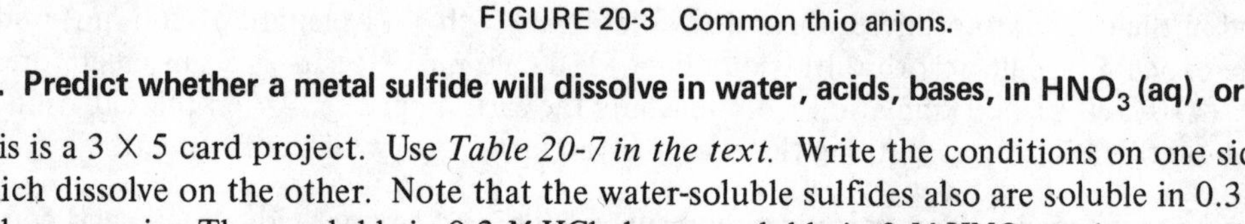

$$\text{H—O—}\underset{\text{O}}{\overset{\text{O}}{\underset{\|}{\overset{\|}{\text{S}}}}}\text{—O—H} + \text{H—O—}\underset{\text{O}}{\overset{\text{O}}{\underset{\|}{\overset{\|}{\text{S}}}}}\text{—O—H} \rightleftharpoons \text{H—O—}\underset{\text{O}}{\overset{\text{O}}{\underset{\|}{\overset{\|}{\text{S}}}}}\text{—O—}\underset{\text{O}}{\overset{\text{O}}{\underset{\|}{\overset{\|}{\text{S}}}}}\text{—O—H} + H_2O \qquad [1]$$

orthosulfuric acid pyrosulfuric acid

5. Sometimes, as in the case of H_4SiO_4, the acid itself does not exist. Nonetheless, compounds containing the anion of that acid, SiO_4^{4-}, are called orthosilicates.

In order to use these rules, you need to know the ortho acids given in Table 20-4. Very few of these acids actually exist. However, their anions all exist. H_2CO_3, HNO_3, H_2SO_4, and H_2SO_3 are rarely named as ortho acids.

TABLE 20-4
Common ortho acids

-ic acids					
Representative elements				Transition elements	-ous acids
H_3BO_3	H_2CO_3	HNO_3		H_3VO_4	H_2SO_3
H_3AlO_3	H_4SiO_4	H_3PO_4	H_2SO_4	H_3WO_4	H_3PO_3
	H_4GeO_4	H_3AsO_4	H_2SeO_4	H_4ZrO_4	H_3AsO_3
	H_4SnO_4	H_3SbO_4	H_6TeO_6	H_4TlO_4	
		H_3BiO_4		H_3NbO_4	

13. Describe the arrangement of Si and O atoms in the principal forms of silicate minerals.

Silicate minerals contain SiO_4 tetrahedra, linked together in different ways. (1) Distinct $SiO_4{}^{4-}$ anions exist in the crystal. Many of these, like Na_4SiO_4, are soluble in water. Insoluble ones often contain a divalent cation: Be_2SiO_4, Zn_2SiO_4, Mg_2SiO_4, Fe_2SiO_4, and Mn_2SiO_4. (2) $SiO_4{}^{4-}$ions are joined into short chains. This is the case with pyrosilicates, containing the $Si_2O_7{}^{6-}$ anion, as $Sc_2Si_2O_7$ and $Zn_4(OH)_2Si_2O_7$. (3) Rings are formed with either three or six silicon atoms: $Si_3O_9{}^{6-}$ or $Si_6O_{18}{}^{12-}$ (Figure 20-4). These occur in $BeTiSi_3O_9$, $Ca_2BaSi_3O_9$, and $Be_3Al_2Si_6O_{18}$, beryl. (4) The anions link up to form single-stranded infinite chains, the amphiboles. The pyroxene anion, $(SiO_3{}^{2-})_n$, occurs in $MgSiO_3$, $CaMg(SiO_3)_2$, and $LiAl(SiO_3)_2$. The amphibole anion, $(Si_4O_{11}{}^{6-})_n$, occurs in $Ca_2Mg_5(Si_4O_{11})_2(OH)_2$. The chains run parallel through the crystal with the cations lying between them and

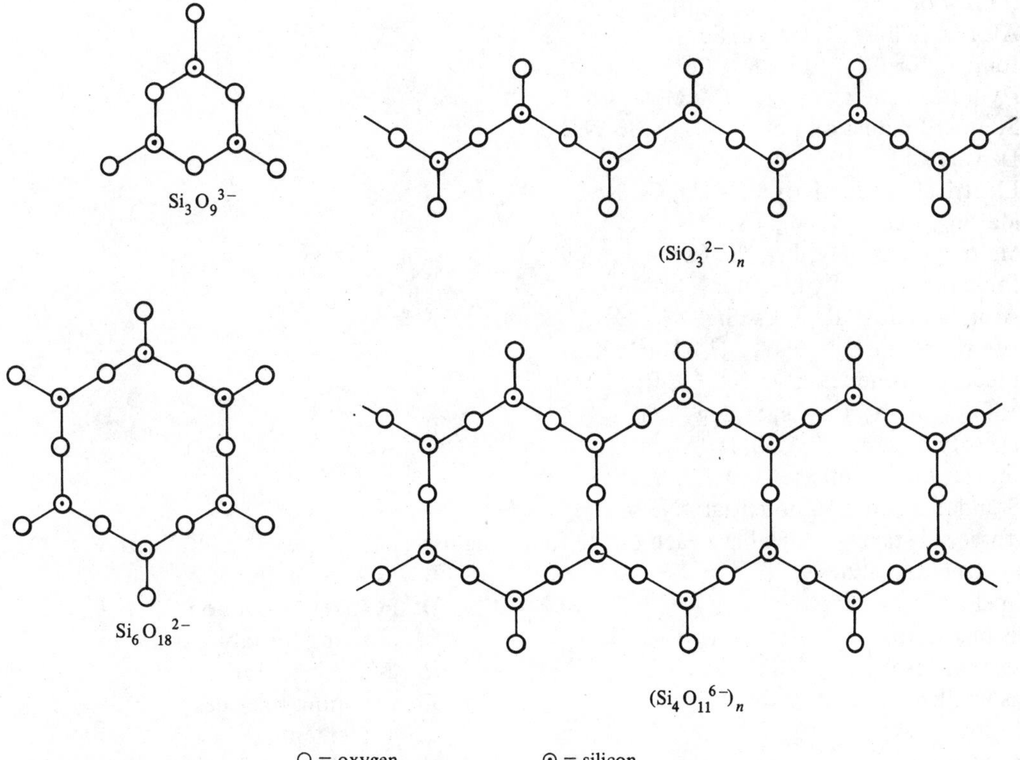

FIGURE 20-4 Polysilicate ions

holding them together. Asbestos is an amphibole. (5) Infinite sheets are formed with formula $(Si_2O_5{}^{2-})_n$. The cations are located between the sheets and the crystals cleave readily into sheets. Such a substance is mica (*Figure 20-15b in the text*). (6) The tetrahedra link into a three-dimensional network of formula $(SiO_2)_n$. Quartz is such a material.

14. Write formulas and names for some organosilicon compounds and equations for their reactions.

When a proxene chain has organic groups such as $-CH_3$ substituted for the side oxygens, the resulting compound is a silicone. Silicones are produced by a condensation reaction of $(CH_3)_2Si(OH)_2$.

$$HO-\underset{CH_3}{\overset{CH_3}{Si}}-OH + n\,HO-\underset{CH_3}{\overset{CH_3}{Si}}-OH \xrightarrow[\text{(many times)}]{-H_2O} HO-\underset{CH_3}{\overset{CH_3}{Si}}-O\left(\underset{CH_3}{\overset{CH_3}{Si}}-O\right)_{n-1}\underset{CH_3}{\overset{CH_3}{Si}}-OH \qquad [2]$$

Few individual silicones are named because the condensation reaction is difficult to stop at a precise point. The mixture is an oil or a grease depending on the chain length. When chains are crosslinked, that is, when there are chemical bonds between chains, the product is a rubber-like material. Silicones flow freely and remain pliable at low temperatures. They resist chemical attack and are not broken down at high temperature as are hydrocarbon molecules.

DRILL PROBLEMS

1. Rewrite each of the following groups of species in order of increasing (smallest to largest) value of the given property. Base your predictions on what you have learned thus far.

A. Ionization potential: Ca, Mg, Ba, C
B. Atomic radius: K, Br, Ca, Se
C. Ionic radius: Cs^+, Li^+, K^+, Be^{2+}
D. Hydration energy: Cs^+, Al^{3+}, Mg^{2+}, Ca^{2+}
E. Standard reduction potential: Ca, K, Na, Li
F. Density of solid: S, Mg, Na, I
G. Electrical conductivity: Ca, Al, Cs, Rb
H. Melting point: Al, Mg, Cs, Ca
I. Melting point: Mg, Rb, Na, Cs
J. Ionic radius: Al^{3+}, Li^+, Mg^{2+}, Si^{4+}
K. Atomic radius: Br, I, Cs, Sr
L. Hydration energy: Na^+, Al^{3+}, Mg^{2+}, K^+
M. Electrical conductivity: Na, Cs, Rb, Li
N. Melting point: Ca, Cs, Sr, Mg
O. Density of solid: P, C, S, I
P. Ionization potential: Cs, Al, F, Sr
Q. Standard reduction potential: Na, Al, Mg

3. List three substances which have each of the following uses.

A. in structural alloys
B. as water softeners
C. in electrical devices
D. in soap production
E. as medications
F. as sizing for fabric or paper
G. as explosives
H. as a refrigerant
I. as fertilizers
J. for lining furnaces
K. in fire works
L. as pigments
M. as reducing agents
N. in water ourification
O. as oxidizing agents
P. as poisons

Q. to produce or use dyes
R. to fire retard or resist
S. in paper manufacture
T. in plaster, cement, or mortar
U. in glass
V. as abrasives
W. What does "sizing" mean?

4. & 5. Complete and balance the following equations. ("No reaction" may be a correct answer.)
A. potassium + oxygen →
B. aluminum + fluorine →
C. strontium + water →
D. strontium + iodine →
E. calcium oxide + water →
F. sodium + oxygen →
G. cesium + water →
H. magnesium + hydrochloric acid →
I. magnesium + hot water →
J. sodium + nitrogen →
K. barium + oxygen →
L. $NaBr(aq) + I_2(s) \rightarrow$
M. $H_2(g) + F_2(g) \rightarrow$
N. $HI(aq) + O_2(g) \rightarrow$
O. $Mg(s) + H_2(g) \rightarrow$
P. $Li(s) + N_2(g) \rightarrow$
Q. $Cl_2(g) + S_8(s) \rightarrow$
R. $Li(s) + O_2(g) \rightarrow$
S. $Be(s) + H_2(g) \rightarrow$
T. $Cl_2(g) + H_2S(g) \rightarrow$
U. $Br_2(l) + NH_3(g) \rightarrow$
V. $Na(s) + Cl_2(g) \rightarrow$
W. $Li(s) + H_2(g) \rightarrow$
X. $Cl_2(g) + H_2O(l) \rightarrow$
Y. $F_2(g) + H_2O(l) \rightarrow$

6. Write the balanced half-reaction and determine the standard reduction potential for each of the following couples. Use the data of *Figures 20-6 and 20-12 in the text* and Figures 20-1 and 20-2 in this book.
A. O_2/H_2O (acidic)
B. O_2/OH^- (basic)
C. O_2^-/OH^- (basic)
D. $HClO/Cl^-$ (acidic)
E. ClO_4^-/Cl_2 (acidic)
F. ClO_4^-/Cl^- (acidic)
G. $HClO_2/Cl^-$ (acidic)
H. ClO_3^-/Cl_2 (basic)
I. ClO_4^-/Cl_2 (basic)
J. ClO_2^-/Cl^- (basic)
K. NO_3^-/NO (acidic)
L. NO_3^-/NO (basic)
M. NO_3^-/HNO_2 (acidic)
N. NO_3^-/NO_2^- (basic)
O. NO_3^-/NH_4^+ (acidic)
P. HNO_2/N_2 (acidic)
Q. SO_4^{2-}/S (acidic)
R. SO_4^{2-}/S^{2-} (basic)

8. (1) Classify each of the following as acidic, basic, or amphoteric oxides.
A. CaO
B. CO_2
C. PbO
D. SiO_2
E. SO_2
F. ClO_2
G. BeO
H. NO_2
I. SnO
J. BaO
K. Al_2O_3
L. Tl_2O
M. Na_2O
N. P_2O_5
O. MgO

(2) Complete and balance each of the following reactions. ("No reaction" may be the correct answer.)
A. $CaO + SiO_2 \rightarrow$
B. $Al_2O_3 + SO_2 \rightarrow$
C. $NO + CO_2 \rightarrow$
D. $NaO + CaO \rightarrow$
E. $BaO + SO_2 \rightarrow$
F. $PbO + P_2O_5 \rightarrow$
G. $Na_2O + Al_2O_3 \rightarrow$

11. Complete and balance each of the following equations. ("No reaction" may be correct answer.)
A. CuS + aqua regia →
B. $SnS + H_2O \rightarrow$
C. $Na_2S + H_2O \rightarrow$
D. $MnS + H_2O \rightarrow$
E. $PbS + HCl(aq) \rightarrow$
F. $CdS + HNO_3(aq) \rightarrow$
G. $As_2S_3 + (NH_4)_2S(aq) \rightarrow$
H. $CuS + HCl(aq) \rightarrow$
I. ZnS + aqua regia →
J. $CaS + HNO_3(aq) \rightarrow$
K. $CoS + HNO_3(aq) \rightarrow$
L. $CuS + KOH(aq) \rightarrow$
M. $Na_2S + KOH(aq) \rightarrow$

12. Give the correct name or formula of each of the following compounds.
A. Na_2SiO_3
B. $H_4As_2O_7$
C. $Ca_2B_2O_5$
D. $MgSnO_3$
E. pyrosilicic acid
F. sodium metaluminate
G. calcium pyrophosphate
H. iron(III) metaborate
I. barium orthocarbonate
J. magnesium orthobismuthate

QUIZZES (15–20 minutes each)

Choose the best answer for each question.

Quiz A

1. Silicate minerals have all of the following types of silicon–oxygen anions *except* (a) SiO_4^{4-} tetrahedra;

(b) short chains of tetrahedra; (c) rings of 3, 4, 5, and 6 tetrahedra; (d) infinite chains of tetrahedra; (e) infinite sheets of tetrahedra.

2. Calcium pyrosilicate has the formula (a) Ca_2SiO_4; (b) $CaSiO_3$; (c) CaH_2SiO_4; (d) $Ca_3Si_2O_7$; (e) none of these.
3. Which has the highest electrical conductivity? (a) Al; (b) Na; (c) Cs; (d) Ba; (e) Ca.
4. Which has the largest atomic radius? (a) Rb; (b) Sr; (c) Mg: (d) Al; (e) Li.
5. Which is *not* produced using electricity? (a) Na; (b) Cl_2; (c) Al; (d) Mg; (e) P_4.
6. Which is used as an antiseptic? (a) sodium chloride; (b) calcium carbonate; (c) boric acid; (d) ammonium nitrate; (e) dinitrogen oxide.
7. Which is *not* used to clean metals? (a) hydrochloric acid; (b) ammonium chloride; (c) potassium chlorate; (d) sulfuric acid; (e) none of these.
8. Which will form an acidic aqueous solution? (a) aluminum oxide; (b) boron oxide; (c) sodium oxide; (d) calcium oxide; (e) lead(II) oxide.

Quiz B

1. Sodium metasilicate is (a) $NaHSiO_3$; (b) Na_4SiO_4; (c) Na_2SiO_3; (d) $Na_6Si_2O_7$; (e) none of these.
2. Which has the smallest density? (a) Li; (b) Cs; (c) Ba; (d) Mg; (e) Na.
3. Which has the greatest ionization potential? (a) Al; (b) Cs; (c) Ca; (d) Na; (e) Ba.
4. In quartz, SiO_4 tetrahedra are joined in (a) chains; (b) rings; (c) infinite sheets; (d) a three-dimensional lattice; (e) none of these.
5. Which is *not* found free in nature? (a) N_2; (b) O_2; (c) P_4; (d) S_8; (e) none of these.
6. Which is *not* used as an abrasive? (a) calcium oxide; (b) boron carbide; (c) aluminum oxide; (d) silicon dioxide; (e) silicon carbide.
7. Which is used in food? (a) phosphoric acid; (b) calcium chloride; (c) hydrogen peroxide; (d) potassium chlorate; (e) silver nitrate.
8. Which is an amphoteric oxide? (a) zinc oxide; (b) lithium oxide; (c) selenium trioxide; (d) carbon dioxide; (e) none of these.

Quiz C

1. Which has the lowest melting point? (a) Al; (b) Cs; (c) Li; (d) Mg; (e) Ba.
2. Which has the largest radius? (a) Ba; (b) Mg; (c) Be; (d) Li; (e) Al.
3. Cesium orthophosphate has the formula (a) Cs_3PO_4; (b) CsH_2PO_4; (c) $CsPO_3$; (d) $Cs_4P_2O_7$; (e) none of these.
4. In asbestos fibers, SiO_4 tetrahedra are joined in (a) a three-dimensional lattice; (b) infinite sheets; (c) infinite chains; (d) rings; (e) none of these.
5. Which element *must* be produced by electrolysis? (a) Cl_2; (b) Na; (c) F_2; (d) K; (e) none of these.
6. Which is used in the walls of houses? (a) calcium sulfate dihydrate; (b) calcium chloride; (c) aluminum oxide; (d) barium nitrate; (e) sodium silicate.
7. Which is *not* used in glass? (a) sodium carbonate; (b) boron trioxide; (c) potassium nitrate; (d) silicon dioxide; (e) none of these.
8. Which will ignite spontaneously in air? (a) sodium; (b) black phosphorus; (c) fluorine; (d) monoclinic sulfur; (e) none of these.

Quiz D

1. Which has the highest standard reduction potential? (a) Ca; (b) Ba; (c) Mg; (d) Sr; (e) Li.
2. Which of the following melts at the highest temperature? (a) Cl_2; (b) F_2; (c) I_2; (d) O_2; (e) Br_2.
3. The name of $Mg_2As_2O_5$ is (a) magnesium arsenite; (b) magnesium orthoarsenate; (c) magnesium pyroarsenate; (d) magnesium metaarsenite; (e) none of these.
4. In mica, SiO_4 tetrahedra are joined (a) not at all; (b) in long chains; (c) in rings; (d) in short chains; (e) none of these.
5. Carbon is used in the production of (a) K; (b) Ca; (c) Na; (d) Cl_2; (e) P_4.

6. Which is used as a water softener? (a) lithium carbonate; (b) sodium nitrate; (c) sodium carbonate; (d) potassium chloride; (e) hydrochloric acid.
7. Which is *not* used as a pigment? (a) barium sulfate; (b) aluminum; (c) calcium carbonate; (d) magnesium oxide; (e) none of these.
8. Which is *not* composed of small (less than ten atoms) molecules? (a) white phosphorus; (b) ozone; (c) monoclinic sulfur; (d) red phosphorous; (e) rhombic sulfur.

SYNTHESES

Rather than sample tests, this chapter concludes with twenty syntheses. You should give the reaction or series of reactions which will produce the desired end product from the list of reagents given. The product must be pure unless it is an aqueous solution. If the product is a solid, you must indicate how the solid is recovered from solution (evaporation, precipitation, or some other means). You may make any intermediates or by-products which you wish, but you must indicate how the by-products are separated from the desired end product. Money is no object. Use large-scale industrial processes if necessary. You also may use heat, light, and electricity as you need. You do not need to use all of the reagents listed.

1. $BaO(s)$ from $Ba(s)$, $O_2(g)$, and $H_2O(l)$
2. $NaCl(s)$ from $Na(s)$, $H_2O(l)$, and $HCl(aq)$
3. $Li_2CO_3(s)$ from $Li(s)$, $H_2O(l)$, and $CO_2(g)$
4. $SrSO_4(s)$ from $Sr(s)$, $Cl_2(g)$, $H_2O(l)$, and $H_2SO_4(aq)$
5. $Al_2(SO_4)_3$ from $Al(s)$, $H_2SO_4(aq)$, and $O_2(g)$
6. $H_2(g)$ from $Mg(s)$, $NH_3(g)$, and $H_2O(l)$
7. $Na_2CO_3(s)$ from $Na_2O(s)$ and $Li_2CO_3(s)$
8. $Ca(OH)_2(s)$ from $CaCO_3(s)$, $H_2O(l)$, $H_2(g)$, and $O_2(g)$
9. $BaCO_3(s)$ from $Ba(s)$, $O_2(g)$, and $C(s)$
10. $BaSO_3(s)$ from $Ba(s)$, $O_2(g)$, $H_2O(l)$, and $S(s)$
11. $HBr(g)$ from $Na(s)$, $Br_2(l)$, and any strong acid (specify which one) except HBr
12. H_3PO_4 from any elements; use no compounds
13. $NH_3(g)$ from $Li(s)$, $N_2(g)$, and $H_2O(l)$
14. $H_2(g)$ from $Al(s)$, $Ca(s)$, $NH_3(g)$, and $H_2O(l)$
15. $CaCO_3(s)$ from $Ca(s)$, $O_2(g)$, $H_2O(l)$, and $C(s)$
16. $CuCO_3(s)$ from $HNO_3(aq)$, $H_2O(l)$, and any elements
17. $LiNO_3(s)$ from $HNO_3(aq)$ and any elements
18. $H_2Se(g)$ from $Ca(s)$, $Se(s)$, and a strong acid
19. $HI(g)$ from Mg, I_2, and any strong acid
20. $H_3PO_3(aq)$ from any elements

Chapter 21

The Chemistry of Transition Elements

REVIEW OF OBJECTIVES

★ **1. State ways in which the transition elements differ from representative elements and know the trends in their properties.**

Transition elements usually mean those of families IIIB through IIB. Often the zinc group (IIB), sometimes the copper group (IB), and occasionally the scandium group (IIIB) are excluded from the transition elements. All of the transition metals except those of group IIB (Zn, Cd, and Hg) have high melting and boiling points, and high heats of fusion and of vaporization. Most are good conductors of heat and electricity especially those of group IB (Cu, Ag, and Au). They are denser than representative elements. Many transition metal compounds are highly colored and paramagnetic owing to the partly filled underlying *d* orbitals.

Except for those of groups IIIB (Sc, Y, Li) and IIB (Zn, Cd), the transition elements exhibit more than one oxidation state. Higher oxidation states are common in combination with highly electronegative nonmetals: oxygen, fluorine, and chlorine. An increase in highest oxidation state across each period peaks in family VII and declines thereafter. Higher oxidation states are more important for heavier members of each family. Thus, Fe(II) and Fe(III) are most important for iron; Os(IV), OS(VI), and Os(VIII) for osmium. Higher oxidation states of a given element form more acidic oxides. Thus CrO is basic, Cr_2O_3 is amphoteric, and CrO_3 is acidic.

One notes the following trends. A general but not constant decrease in atomic radius occurs across a period with the smallest radii in group VIII, group VIII elements being the most dense. The elements are denser but softer toward the bottom of each group. Across each period the electronegativity increases, the reduction potential becomes more positive, and the first ionization potential increases.

2. Describe the lanthanoid contraction and explain how it affects the properties of the transition elements.

The lanthanoid contraction is the gradual decrease in atomic and ionic radii that occurs from La to Lu (Figure 8-4, objective 8-6). Because of the lanthanoid contraction, the atoms and ions of each group of the second and third transition series are almost of the same size (Figure 8-3). Because they have the same valence electron configurations, their properties are virtually the same. This similarity is closest at the beginning of the transition series, as shown by the data in Table 21-1.

TABLE 21-1
Periodic Properties of Niobium, Tantalum, Silver, and Gold

	Nb	Ta	Ag	Au
ionic radius, pm	70	73	126	137 (+1)
ionization potential, kJ/mol	653	577	732	891
oxidation states	+5	+5	+1	+3, +1
heat of fusion, kJ/mol	27	28	11.3	12.7
electrical conductance, mho	0.080	0.081	0.616	0.42

★ **3. Describe sources and uses of the elements of the first transition series.**

This is a 3 X 5 card project.

Scandium is produced by electrolysis of a molten mixture of $ScCl_3$, LiCl, and KCl. It is too rare ($150 or more per gram) for important uses.

Titanium ores are rutile (TiO_2), perovskite ($CaTiO_3$), ilmenite ($FeTiO_3$), and titanite ($TiSiO_4$ and Ca_2SiO_4). Treatment with HCl or Cl_2 produces $TiCl_4$. Reduction with Mg yields Ti ($TiCl_4 + 2\ Mg \rightarrow 2\ MgCl_2 + Ti$). Titanium alloys are strong, lightweight, and heat and corrosion resistant. They are used for aircraft, jet engines, and pipes in chemical plants.

Vanadium is found as V_2O_3, $Pb(VO_4)Cl$, $Pb(VO_3)_2$, and $BiVO_4$. The ores are treated with strong HCl and NH_4Cl is added to produce $(NH_4)_3VO_5$. Roasting of $(NH_4)_3VO_5$ produces V_2O_5. Reduction of V_2O_5 with Ca or Mg produces the metal. Vanadium steel is used for automotive springs and axles because of its toughness. Alloyed with Ti it is both strong and heat resistant and is used in rockets.

Chromium's principal ore is chromite, $FeCr_2O_4$. Reduction with carbon produces ferrochrome: $FeCr_2O_4 + 4\ C \rightarrow Fe + 2\ Cr + 4\ CO(g)$. Chromium compounds are produced by roasting with Na_2CO_3 in air: $4\ FeCr_2O_3 + 8\ Na_2CO_3 + 7\ O_2 \rightarrow 2\ Fe_2O_3 + 8\ Na_2CrO_4 + 8\ CO_2$. Chrome steel is hard and tough. Stainless steel is 14% Cr. Nichrome (80% Ni and 20% Cr) is used for electrical resistance heaters. Chrome plating of steel protects against corrosion.

Manganese's principal ore is MnO_2. Reduction with Al produces the metal: $3\ MnO_2 + 4\ Al \rightarrow 4\ Al_2O_3 + 3\ Mn$. Reduction with C also works. A steel alloy containing 12% Mn is used for armor plate and earth-moving equipment. Manganese also improves the ease of working molten steel.

Iron is found as Fe_2O_3, Fe_3O_4, and $FeCO_3$. Iron is reduced with carbon and carbon monoxide (produced from coal): $Fe_2O_3(s) + C(s) \rightarrow 2\ Fe(l) + 3\ CO(g)$; $Fe_2O_3(s) + 3\ CO(g) \rightarrow 2\ Fe(l) + 3\ CO_2(g)$. Limestone is also added; it removes SiO_2 impurities from the iron: $CaCO_3(s) \xrightarrow{\Delta} CaO(s) + CO_2(g)$; $CaO(s) + SiO_2(l) \rightarrow CaSiO_3(l)$. The $CaSiO_3$ slag is solidified and used to make cement. The iron–carbon mixture solidifies into steel (0.5–2.0% C) whose properties depend on the carbon content.

Cobalt's common ores are $CoAs_2$, CoAsS, and Co_3S_4. An involved series of reactions produces Co_2O_3 which is reduced by C or $H_2(g)$ at high temperature. Cobalt is alloyed with Fe and other metals to produce heat-resistant metal-cutting tools and surgical instruments. Some other alloys are magnetic.

Nickel occurs with Cu and Fe as NiS. After being roasted to the oxide, the ore is reduced with carbon to a mixture of Ni, Cu, and Fe: $2\ NiS + 3\ O_2 \rightarrow 2\ NiO + 2\ SO_2$; $2\ NiO + C \rightarrow 2\ Ni + CO_2(g)$. Nickel is separated by CO(g) at 60°C in the Monel process: $Ni(s) + 4\ CO(g) \rightleftharpoons Ni(CO)_4(g)$. Above 200°C, $Ni(CO)_4$ decomposes, releasing free Ni(s). The mixture of Ni, Cu, and Fe from the ore is Monel, very resistant to chemical attack. Nickel plate makes iron corrosion resistant.

Copper is found as Cu_2O, $CuFeS_2$, and Cu_3FeS_3, often mixed together. Roasting in air liberates free copper: $2\ CuFeS_2(s) + 4\ O_2(g) \rightarrow Cu_2S(l) + 2\ FeO(s) + 3\ SO_2(g)$; $Cu_2S(l) + O_2(g) \rightarrow 2\ Cu(l) + SO_2(g)$. Silica ($SiO_2$) in the ore traps FeO as slag. $FeO(s) + SiO_2(l) \xrightarrow{\Delta} FeSiO_3(l)$. The copper is refined electrolytically and used for electrical wiring. The unrefined copper is used for plumbing and limited structural uses (rain gutters, roof flashing).

Zinc ores are $ZnCO_3$, ZnS, Zn_2SiO_4, and ZnO. It is reduced from the ore by carbon at high temperatures. The metal vaporizes at these temperatures and is condensed outside the furnace. Zinc is used to galvanize iron, produce alloys such as brass and solder, and make dry cells for flashlights.

★ **4. Know the important compounds of the stable oxidation states of the elements of the first transition series.**

This is a 3 X 5 card project. Use Table 21-2.

★ **5. Write equations for some important oxidation-reduction reactions of permanganate ion and of dichromate ion.**

MnO_4^- is somewhat the stronger oxidizing agent.

$$MnO_4^- + 8\ H^+ + 5\ e^- \rightarrow Mn^{2+} + 4\ H_2O \qquad E° = +1.51\ V \qquad [1]$$

$$Cr_2O_7^{2-} + 14\ H^+ + 6\ e^- \rightarrow 2\ Cr^{3+} + 7\ H_2O \qquad E° = +1.33\ V \qquad [2]$$

Both ions are much better oxidants in acid than in base.

$$MnO_4^- + 2\ H_2O + 3\ e^- \rightarrow MnO_2 + 4\ OH^- \qquad E° = +0.59\ V \qquad [3]$$

$$CrO_4^{2-} + 4\ H_2O + 3\ e^- \rightarrow Cr(OH)_3(s) + 5\ OH^- \qquad E° = -0.13\ V \qquad [4]$$

Table 21-2
First transition series compounds

Sc	no important compounds
TiO_2	high quality white pigment for paper, plastics, and ceramics
$TiCl_4$	smoke screens as it produces dense clouds of TiO_2 with H_2O
TiC	edges for cutting tools
$BaTiO_3$	high performance capacitors as a dielectric
V_2O_5	catalyst for H_2SO_4 production
$PbCrO_4$	yellow paint pigment
Cr_2O_3	green pigment for paints, glass, and ceramics
Chrome alum	($KCr(SO_4)_2 \cdot 12\,H_2O$) dye mordant
Na_2CrO_4	prevents corrosion in boilers and radiators; cleaning solution with H_2SO_4
$FeCr_2O_4$	lining open-hearth furnaces for steel production
$Na_2Cr_2O_7$	tanning leather; photography; oxidizing agent
MnO_2	decolorizing glass; drier for paints; in dry cells
$KMnO_4$	versatile laboratory oxidizing agent
$FeCl_3$	water clarification
$FeSO_4$	fertilizer; pigment in ink, dye, and paint; wood preservative
$Fe_4[Fe(CN)_6]_3$	ink and paint pigment; blueprints
Fe_2O_3	paint and cosmetic pigment; abrasive
CoO	blue glass and ceramic pigment
Ni_2O_3	Edison storage battery (nickel–cadmium battery)
$CuSO_4$	to kill algae in drinking water; calico dyes
$Cu_3(AsO_4)_2$	fungicide and insecticide
Cu_2O	ruby glass pigment; fungicide for seeds
CuO	blue–green glass and ceramic pigment
CuCl	insecticide; absorbent for CO
$ZnCrO_4$	yellow pigment in paint to resist corrosion
ZnO	white pigment in automobile tires mainly; in burn ointments
ZnS	part (with $BaSO_4$) of lithopone, a white pigment; fluorescent screens for television
$ZnCl_2$	fireproofing agents
$ZnHPO_4$	dental cement

6. Discuss the chromate (CrO_4^{2-})-dichromate ($Cr_2O_7^{2-}$) equilibrium and the effect of pH on the concentrations of these ions in aqueous solution.

$Cr_2O_7^{2-}$ is a good oxidizing agent (see equation [2]) and a poor precipitating agent (nearly all dichromates are soluble). CrO_4^{2-} is a poor oxidizing agent (see equation [4]) but a good precipitating agent. The two ions are in equilibrium in aqueous solution.

$$2\,CrO_4^{2-} + 2\,H^+ \rightleftharpoons Cr_2O_7^{2-} + H_2O \qquad K_c = 3.2 \times 10^{14} \qquad [5]$$

$$[Cr_2O_7^{2-}]/[CrO_4^{2-}]^2 = 3.2 \times 10^{14}[H^+]^2 \qquad [6]$$

If we know the total chromium(VI) concentration and the pH of a solution, we can determine $[CrO_4^{2-}]$ and $[Cr_2O_7^{2-}]$.

EXAMPLE 21-1 0.200 mol $K_2Cr_2O_7$ is added to 1.00 L of a pH = 5.000 buffer. Determine $[CrO_4^{2-}]$ in the final solution.

$[H^+] = 1.00 \times 10^{-5} M$. In the final solution $[Cr_2O_7^{2-}] + 0.5[CrO_4^{2-}] = 0.200\,M$.

Setup:	$2\,CrO_4^{2-}$ +	$2\,H^+$	$\rightleftharpoons$	$Cr_2O_7^{2-}$	$+ H_2O$
I:		$1.00 \times 10^{-5}\ M$		$0.200\ M$	
C:	$+2x\ M$			$-x\ M$	
Eq:	$2x\ M$	$1.00 \times 10^{-5}\ M$		$(0.200 - x)\ M$	

$$\frac{[Cr_2O_7^{2-}]}{[CrO_4^{2-}]^2} = \frac{0.200 - x}{(2x)^2} = 3.2 \times 10^{14}(1.00 \times 10^{-5})^2 = 3.2 \times 10^4$$

Assuming $x \ll 0.200$, then $0.200/4x^2 = 3.2 \times 10^4$ *or* $x = 1.25 \times 10^{-3}$ *M*. Thus, $[CrO_4^{2-}] = 2.50 \times 10^{-3}$ *M* and $[Cr_2O_7^{2-}] = 0.198$ *M*.

Using the same method as Example 21-1, $[Cr_2O_7^{2-}] = 2.0 \times 10^{-3}$ *M* and $[CrO_4^{2-}] = 0.396$ *M* in a solution buffered at pH = 9.000.

7. Write chemical equations showing the amphoteric properties of Zn and Cr(III) oxides and hydroxides.

You should memorize the following equations.

$$Cr(OH)_3 + 3\,H^+ \rightarrow Cr^{3+} + 3\,H_2O$$
$$Cr(OH)_3 + OH^- \rightarrow CrO_2^- + 2\,H_2O$$
$$Zn(OH)_2 + 2\,H^+ \rightarrow Zn^{2+} + 2\,H_2O$$
$$Zn(OH)_2 + 2\,OH^- \rightarrow ZnO_2^{2-} + 2\,H_2O$$

The analogous equations for Al_2O_3 are

$$Al(OH)_3 + 3\,H^+ \rightarrow Al^{3+} + 3\,H_2O$$
$$Al(OH)_3 + OH^- \rightarrow AlO_2^- + 2\,H_2O$$

8. Describe ferromagnetism and the features of atomic structure which lead to it.

Ferromagnetism is the ability of a substance to become strongly and relatively permanently magnetic. For ferromagnetism to be important, the substance must already possess magnetic domains, areas in which the magnetic moments are all aligned. If the atoms are small, they will get close enough to pair up ($\uparrow\downarrow$) and no domains will form. (You can see this pairing with two small magnets. Place one free on a table and slide the other up to it: side to side and north pole to north pole. When the moving magnet gets close, the free magnet will suddenly swing around.) If the atoms are too large, they will not feel each other's paramagnetism.

In the influence of a strong magnetic field, the domains line up in the same direction. The magnetism of the material is destroyed by heat or vibration.

9. Describe the formation of metal carbonyls.

Only $Fe(CO)_5$ and $Ni(CO)_4$ are formed by direct union of the metal with CO(g). $Fe(CO)_5$ is formed only at high temperature and pressure. Other methods of formation follow.

$$2\,CoCO_3 + 2\,H_2 + 8\,CO \rightarrow Co_2(CO)_8 + 2\,CO_2 + 2\,H_2O \qquad [7]$$

$$VCl_3 + CO + Na\,(excess) \xrightarrow[120^\circ C,\ 300\ atm]{diglyme} [Na(diglyme)_2][V(CO)_6] \qquad [8]$$

$$[Na(diglyme)_2][V(CO)_6] \xrightarrow[sublime\ at\ 50^\circ C]{H_3PO_4} V(CO)_6 \qquad [9]$$

From Mn on, the metal carbonyl attempts to attain the Kr electron configuration [$V(CO)_6$ is octahedral].

10. Describe qualitative tests for detecting Fe^{2+} and Fe^{3+}.

The necessary tests are summarized in *Table 21-5 in the text.* You should commit them to memory.

11. Discuss the separations and tests for ions in the ammonium sulfide group of the qualitative analysis scheme.

The tests are outlined in *Figure 21-5 in the text* and described in the accompanying paragraphs and marginal notes. You should be able to reproduce the essential features of *Figure 21-5* from memory. In addition, you should be able to write chemical reactions for each step and explain the observations (formation of a precipitate, development of a color, and so forth). Examples of these reactions are given below. The numbers in parentheses are those of the steps in *Figure 21-5.*

(1) Treat with NH_3-NH_4Cl buffer and $(NH_4)_2S$.

$Fe^{3+} + 3\ NH_3 + 3\ H_2O \rightarrow Fe(OH)_3 + 3\ NH_4^+$ [10]
$Fe^{2+} + (NH_4)_2S \rightarrow FeS(s) + 2\ NH_4^+$ [11]

(2) Treat precipitate with aqua regia, HCl–HNO_3.

$Fe(OH)_3(s) + 3\ H^+ \rightarrow Fe^{3+} + 3\ H_2O$ [12]
$NiS(s) + 2\ NO_3^- + 8\ H^+ \rightarrow 3\ Ni^{2+} + 2\ NO(g) + 3\ S(s) + 4\ H_2O$ [13]
$MnS(s) + 2\ H^+ \rightarrow Mn^{2+} + H_2S(g)$ [14]

(3) Treat solution with NaOH(aq).

$Mn^{2+} + 2\ OH^- \rightarrow Mn(OH)_2(s)$ [15]
$Fe^{3+} + 3\ OH^- \rightarrow Fe(OH)_3(s)$ [16]
$Al^{3+} + 4\ OH^- \rightarrow Al(OH)_4^-$ [17]
$Zn^{2+} + 4\ OH^- \rightarrow Zn(OH)_4^{2-}$ [18]

Then treat with H_2O_2, which forms HO_2^- in base.

$Mn(OH)_2(s) + HO_2^- \rightarrow MnO_2(s) + OH^- + H_2O$ [19]
$2\ Co(OH)_2(s) + HO_2^- + H_2O \rightarrow 2\ Co(OH)_3(s) + OH^-$ [20]
$2\ Cr(OH)_4^- + 3\ HO_2^- \rightarrow 2\ CrO_4^{2-} + OH^- + 5\ H_2O$ [21]

(4) Treat precipitate from step (3) with HCl(aq), then NH_3(aq).

$Fe(OH)_3(s) + 3\ H^+ \rightarrow Fe^{3+} + 3\ H_2O$ [22]
$Fe^{3+} + 3\ NH_3 + 3\ H_2O \rightarrow Fe(OH)_3(s) + 4\ NH_4^+$ [23]
$MnO_2(s) + 4\ H^+ + 2\ Cl^- \rightarrow Mn^{2+} + Cl_2(g) + 2\ H_2O$ [24]
$Ni(OH)_2(s) + 2\ H^+ \rightarrow Ni^{2+} + 2\ H_2O$ [25]
$Ni^{2+} + 6\ NH_3 \rightarrow [Ni(NH_3)_6]^{2+}$ [26]
$Co^{3+} + 6\ NH_3 \rightarrow [Co(NH_3)_6]^{3+}$ [27]

(5) Treat the precipitate from step (4) with HCl(aq).

$Fe(OH)_3(s) + 3\ H^+ \rightarrow Fe^{3+} + 3\ H_2O$ [28]

Then test the solution, with KSCN(aq) for example.

$Fe^{3+} + SCN^- + 5\ H_2O \rightarrow [Fe(H_2O)_5NCS]^{2+}$ (wine red) [29]

(6) Treat the solution from step (4) with $(NH_4)_2S$.

$2\ Co(NH_3)_6^{3+} + 3\ (NH_4)_2S \rightarrow 2\ CoS(s) + S(s) + 6\ NH_4^+ + 12\ NH_3$ [30]
$Ni(NH_3)_6^{2+} + (NH_4)_2S \rightarrow NiS(s) + 2\ NH_4^+ + 6\ NH_3$ [31]
$Mn^{2+} + (NH_4)_2S \rightarrow MnS(s) + 2\ NH_4^+$ [32]

Treatment with HCl dissolves MnS(s).

$MnS(s) + 2\ H^+ \rightarrow Mn^{2+} + H_2S(g)$ [33]

(7) Treat the CoS(s) and NiS(s) with aqua regia, then NH_3(aq).

$NiS(s) + 2\,NO_3^- + 8\,H^+ \rightarrow 3\,Ni^{2+} + 2\,NO(g) + 3\,S(s) + 4\,H_2O$ [34]
$CoS(s) + NO_3^- + 4\,H^+ \rightarrow CO^{3+} + NO(g) + S(s) + 2\,H_2O$ [35]
$Ni^{2+} + 6\,NH_3 \rightarrow [Ni(NH_3)_6]^{2+}$ [36]
$Co^{3+} + 6\,NH_3 \rightarrow [Co(NH_3)_6]^{3+}$ [37]

Treat half with dimethylglyoxime (DMG).

$[Ni(NH_3)_6]^{2+} + 2\,DMG^- \rightarrow Ni(DMG)_2$ (scarlet, s) $+ 6\,NH_3$ [38]

Treat the other half with H_2SO_4, NaF, and NH_4SCN.

$[Co(NH_3)_6]^{3+} + 3\,H_2SO_4 \rightarrow Co^{3+} + 6\,NH_4^+ + 3\,SO_4^{2-}$ [39]
$Co^{3+} + 2\,Cl^- \rightarrow Co^{2+} + Cl_2(g)$ (Cl^- from aqua regia) [40]
$Co^{2+} + 4\,SCN^- \rightarrow [Co(SCN)_4]^{2-}$ (blue) [41]

★ **12. Based on the results of laboratory tests, state which ions are present or absent in a qualitative analysis unknown.**

The precipitates and solution colors which appear in the course of a qualitative analysis tell you which ions are present in your unknown. The absence of a precipitate or a color often indicates which ions are not present. This uses the data of *Figure 21-5 in the text.*

DRILL PROBLEMS

1. Rewrite each of the following lists in order of increasing value (smallest to largest) of the indicated property.
A. atomic radius: Mn, Sc, Fe, Ti
B. density: Cr, Sc, Os, Fe
C. highest oxidation state: Cr, Sc, V, Mn
D. acidity: MnO, Mn_2O_7, MnO_3, MnO_2
E. first ionization potential: Zn, Sc, Mn, Fe
F. number of unpaired electrons: Fe, V, Sc, Mn
G. density: Ti, Pd, Nb, Pt
H. acidity: VO, V_2O_3, V_2O_5, VO_2
I. highest oxidation state: V, Ti, Mn, Y
J. number of unpaired electrons: Cu^+, Fe^{3+}, V^{3+}, Ni^{2+}
K. atomic radius: Ti, Cr, Fe, Ca

3. Give the chemical symbol of the transition element or elements with the following properties, source, or uses.
A. Mg is used to produce this metal
B. metal produced by electrolysis
C. metal refined by electrolysis
D. used in electrical wires
E. never used in structural alloys
F. many ores are sulfides
G. metal vaporizes during reduction from ores
H. used to coat iron to protect it from corrosion
I. present in all steels
J. forms heat-resistant alloys
K. found in many magnets

4. Give the chemical formula of the transition metal compound or compounds with the following uses.
A. pigment for paper
B. fluorescent screens
C. glass pigment
D. paint pigment
E. insecticide
F. ingredient of burn ointments
G. used in H_2SO_4 manufacture
H. oxidizing agent
I. used in dyeing
J. corrosion preventative
K. used in water treatment
L. used in electrical batteries

5. Complete and balance the following equations in aqueous solution.
A. $KMnO_4 + Na_2C_2O_4 + H_2SO_4 \rightarrow CO_2(aq) +$
B. $K_2Cr_2O_7 + KBr + H_2SO_4 \rightarrow Br_2(l) +$
C. $H_2S + KMnO_4 \rightarrow KOH + SO_2(g) +$
D. $K_2Cr_2O_7 + SnSO_4 + H_2SO_4 \rightarrow Sn(SO_4)_2 +$
E. $KMnO_4 + K_2O_2 \rightarrow KOH + O_2(g) +$
F. $Cd + KMnO_4 + H_2SO_4 \rightarrow CdSO_4 +$
G. $K_2Cr_2O_7 + HNO_2 \rightarrow KNO_3 +$
H. $NaMnO_4 + NaI \rightarrow I_2(s)$
I. $Na_2CrO_4 + SnCl_2 + HCl \rightarrow SnCl_4 +$
J. $HMnO_4 + AsH_3 + H_2SO_4 \rightarrow H_3AsO_4 +$

K. $KMnO_4 + FeSO_4 + H_2SO_4 \rightarrow Fe_2(SO_4)_3 +$ L. $Cr(OH)_3 + Na_2O_2 \rightarrow NaOH +$

12. Each of the following paragraphs gives the results of the qualitative analysis for a different unknown. Use these results to state which ions are definitely present and absent and which are uncertain. All unknowns contain ions from qualitative analysis groups 3–5. (See *Figure 16-3 in the text*). (Flame tests are summarized in Table 7-2 of objective 7–3.)

A. An unknown was treated with NH_4Cl–NH_3 buffer producing no precipitate. Further treatment with $(NH_4)_2S$ produced a light precipitate which was separated from the solution. When the solution was treated with $(NH_4)_2CO_3$ a white precipitate formed. The remaining solution gave an orange-yellow color to a flame. The white precipitate dissolved in HCl and gave a brick red color to a flame. The light precipitate dissolved completely in HCl and did not reform when NaOH was added.

B. An unknown was treated with NH_4Cl–NH_3 buffer and produced a brownish red precipitate. Addition of $(NH_4)_2S$ produced no further precipitate. The solution remaining gave no precipitate with $(NH_4)_2CO_3$ but gave a violet color to a flame. The brownish red precipitate dissolved in HCl(aq) but reformed when the solution was made basic. Treatment of this precipitate with HCl(aq) followed by addition of KSCN(aq) produced a dark red color in solution.

C. An unknown gave no precipitate on treatment with NH_4Cl–NH_3 buffer but a black precipitate when $(NH_4)_2S$ was added. The resulting solution gave a white precipitate on treatment with $(NH_4)_2CO_3$. The solution above the white precipitate gave no positive flame tests. However, when the white precipitate dissolved in HCl(aq) the solution gave a yellow-green color to a flame. The black precipitate did not dissolve in HCl(aq) but did in aqua regia. Addition of NH_3(aq) produced a faint blue solution, which turned red on the addition of dimethylglyoxime.

QUIZZES (20 minutes each)

Choose the best answer for each question.

Quiz A

1. Which displays ferromagnetism? (a) Co; (b) Cu; (c) Ti; (d) Cr; (e) none of these.
2. Which has the greatest density? (a) Mn; (b) Ti; (c) Cr; (d) V; (e) Fe.
3. Which is the best oxidizing agent? (a) MnO_4^- in acid; (b) MnO_4^- in base; (c) CrO_4^{2-} in base; (d) $Cr_2O_7^{2-}$ in acid; (e) CrO_4^{2-} in acid.
4. MnO_4^- produces what manganese-containing species when used as an oxidant in base? (a) MnO_4^{2-}; (b) Mn; (c) Mn^{2+}; (d) Mn_2O_3; (e) none of these.
5. Which is most basic? (a) Cr_2O_3; (b) CrO_3; (c) CrO; (d) CO_2; (e) ClO_2.
6. Which has a tetrahedral shape? (a) $Fe(CO)_5$; (b) $Ni(CO)_4$; (c) $Co_2(CO)_8$; (d) $Mn_2(CO)_{10}$; (e) none of these.
7. The paramagnetism of transition element compounds is due to (a) paired electrons spinning in opposite directions; (b) unpaired electrons in *d* or *f* orbitals; (c) shared valence electrons; (d) unshared valence electron pairs; (e) unpaired electrons in *s* or *p* orbitals.

Quiz B

1. Which gives high-temperature strength to steel? (a) Sc; (b) Zn; (c) Cu; (d) Co; (e) none of these.
2. Which has the lowest first ionization potential? (a) Fe; (b) Ni; (c) Co: (d) Mn; (e) Ti.
3. Which is a green pigment? (a) Cr_2O_3; (b) $PbCrO_4$; (c) ZnO; (d) CoO; (e) none of these.
4. $Cr_2O_7^{2-}$ produces what species when used as an oxidant in base? (a) CrO_3^{2-}; (b) CrO_3; (c) Cr^{3+}; (d) $Cr(OH)_3$; (e) none of these.
5. Which is most acidic? (a) Mn_2O_7; (b) MnO_2; (c) MnO; (d) MgO; (e) Mn_2O_3.
6. Which can be formed by warming the metal in CO(g)? (a) $V(CO)_6$; (b) $Co_2(CO)_8$; (c) $Ni(CO)_4$; (d) $Mn_2(CO)_{10}$; (e) none of these.
7. A property common to transition metals and representative metals is that type of metal (a) is found in many different oxidation states; (b) produces colored compounds; (c) has high electronegativities; (d) exhibits one oxidation state equal to the group number; (e) reacts with water to produce hydrogen gas.

Quiz C

1. Which is very resistant to chemical attack? (a) Fe; (b) Ni; (c) Cu; (d) Zn; (e) none of these.
2. Which has the largest radius? (a) Ti; (b) Fe? (c) Co; (d) Ni; (e) Cr.
3. Which is *not* used in dyeing? (a) $CuSO_4$; (b) ZnO; (c) $FeSO_4$; (d) $KCr(SO_4) \cdot 12\ H_2O$; (e) all are used.
4. Which will most enhance the oxidizing strength of MnO_4^-? (a) double $[H^+]$; (b) double $[MnO_4^-]$; (c) halve $[H^+]$; (d) halve $[Mn^{2+}]$; (e) halve $[MnO_4^-]$.
5. Which will *not* dissolve in acid solution? (a) Al_2O_3; (b) P_2O_5; (c) MgO; (d) Sc_2O_3; (e) all will dissolve.
6. Which is a common test for Fe^{2+}? (a) brownish red oxide; (b) red color with KSCN(aq); (c) white precipitate with NaCl(aq); (d) red color with NH_3(aq); (e) none of these.
7. The last step in the production of copper metal used for electrical conduction is (a) smelting; (b) crushing; (c) roasting; (d) reduction; (e) electrolytic refining.

Quiz D

1. Which is produced in the smallest amounts industrially? (a) Fe; (b) Cr; (c) Mn; (d) Cu; (e) Sc.
2. Which has the highest oxidation state in some of its compounds? (a) Mn; (b) Sc; (c) Cu; (d) Zn; (e) V.
3. Which is *not* used to control insects, fungi, or algae? (a) $CuSO_4$; (b) $ZnCl_2$; (c) CuCl; (d) $Cu_3(AsO_4)_2$; (e) Cu_2O.
4. Under which conditions is Hg^{2+}(aq) most likely to be formed in a 0.100 *M* K_2CrO_4, 0.100 *M* $Hg_2(NO_3)_2$ solution? (a) high temperature; (b) low pH; (c) addition of KOH; (d) none of these will work.
5. Which will dissolve in basic solution? (a) $Ni(OH)_2$; (b) MgO; (c) ZnO; (d) Fe_2O_3; (e) none will dissolve.
6. Which is a common test for Fe^{3+}? (a) green precipitate with NaOH; (b) reddish brown color with $K_3[Fe(CN)_6]$; (c) blue color with $K_4[Fe(CN)_6]$; (d) white precipitate with NaCl(aq); (e) none of these.
7. The transition elements are *not* characterized by (a) tendency to form complex ions; (b) ability to have several different oxidation states; (c) greater reactivity from left to right of each period; (d) form colored compounds; (e) none of these.

SAMPLE TEST (20 minutes)

1. An alloy is suspected of containing Fe, Ni, and Cu. Describe how you would qualitatively analyze this alloy for these three elements, including dissolving the alloy. Write the chemical equation for each reaction which occurs during the analysis.
2. a. Write equations which demonstrate the production of aluminum chloride and sodium aluminate from the oxide.
   b. What mass of oxide is needed to produce 100.0 g of each of the two products, using the reactions written in part a?
3. Use the couples MnO_4^-/Mn^{2+}, +1.51 V, and $MnO_2(s)/Mn^{2+}$, 1.23 V, to draw an electrode potential diagram for manganese and determine $E°$ of $MnO_4^-/MnO_2(s)$.

Complex Ions and Coordination Compounds

REVIEW OF OBJECTIVES

★ **1. Identify the central atom and the ligands of a complex ion. Determine the coordination number and oxidation state of the central atom and the net charge on the complex ion.**

The formula of a coordination compound has the *complex ion* enclosed in brackets, [ ]. Thus the complex ion of $[Fe(NH_3)_5(NO_3)](NO_3)_2$ is $[Fe(NH_3)_5(NO_3)]^{2+}$, that of $[Cr(NH_3)_6]Cl_3 \cdot H_2O$ is $[Cr(NH_3)_6]^{3+}$, and that of $K_2[Zn(CN)_4]$ is $[Zn(CN)_4]^{2-}$. The *net charge* on the complex ion is that needed to balance the total charge of the simple cations and/or anions in the compound. The *central atom* or ion is the metal atom in the complex: Fe^{3+} in $[Fe(NH_3)_5(NO_3)]^{2+}$, Cr^{3+} in $[Cr(NH_3)_6]^{3+}$, and Zn^{2+} in $[Zn(CN)_4]^{2-}$. The *ligands* are the groups attached to the central ion: NH_3 and NO_3^- in $[Fe(NH_3)_5(NO_3)]^{2+}$, NH_3 in $[Cr(NH_3)_6]^{3+}$, and CN^- in $[Zn(CN)_4]^{2-}$. The ligands are fairly common ions and simple molecules (see Table 22-2). The *oxidation state* of the central ion is determined by the charge on the complex and the total charges of the ligands.

$$\text{complex ion charge} = \text{total charge on ligands} + \text{complex ion oxidation state} \qquad [1]$$

The *coordination number* is the number of places where ligands are bonded to the central ion. If all the ligands are monodentate, the coordination number equals the number of ligands.

★ **2. Know the coordination numbers of some common metal ions and the names and formulas of common unidentate and multidentate ligands.**

The coordination numbers of common metal ions given in Table 22-1 should be committed to memory. The names, formulas, and charges of the various ligands in Table 22-2 also should be memorized.

TABLE 22-1
Coordination numbers of common metal ions

Coordination number(s)	Ion
2 only	Ag^+
2 or 4	Cu^+, Au^+
4 only	Zn^{2+}, Au^{3+}, Cd^{2+}, Pt^{2+}
4 or 6	Co^{2+}, Ni^{2+}, Cu^{2+}, Al^{3+}
6 only	Ca^{2+}, Fe^{2+}, Sc^{3+}, Cr^{3+}, Fe^{3+}, Co^{3+}, Pt^{4+}

★ **3. Write the unique names for complex ions and coordination compounds based on formulas and unique formulas based on names.**

The following rules are a restatement of those *in the text.*

1. Name the cation first, the anion second.
2. Each complex ion is named in the order: anion ligands, netural ligands, central ion. (To help remember this order, note that it is one of increasing charge.) Multiatom ligands are written before single atom ligands (cyano before iodo, for instance). In writing formulas, this order is reversed.
3. Ligand names are those given in Table 22-2.

TABLE 22-2
Formulas and names of common ligands

Unidentate ligands–anions					
OH^-	hydroxo	NH_2^-	amido	SO_3^{2-}	sulfito
H^-	hydro	NO_3^-	nitrato	SO_4^{2-}	sulfato
F^-	fluoro	$—NO_2^-$	nitro	$S_2O_3^{2-}$	thiosulfato
Cl^-	chloro	$—ONO^-$	nitrito	O^{2-}	oxo
Br^-	bromo	$—CN^-$	cyano	O_2^{2-}	peroxo
I^-	iodo	$—NC^-$	isocyano	CO_3^{2-}	carbonato
ClO_2^-	chlorito	$—NCS^-$	thiocyanato	Ac^-	acetato ($C_2H_3O_2^-$)
ClO_3^-	chlorato	$—SCN^-$	isothiocyanato	$—SCN^-$	
Unidentate ligands-molecules					
NH_3	ammine	H_2O	aquo	CH_3NH_2	methylamine
NO	nitrosyl	CO	carbonyl	C_6H_5N	pyridine
N_2	nitrogeno				
Multidentate ligands[a]					
$C_2O_4^{2-}$	oxalato (2) (*or* ox)	en	ethylenediamine (2)		
o-phen	*o*-phenanthroline (2)	dien	diethylenetriamine (3)		
EDTA	ethylenediaminetetraacetato (6)	trien	triethylenetetramine (4)		

[a]Numbers in parentheses are the number of unidentate ligands which each multidentate ligand replaces. This is the denticity of the multidentate ligand.

4. The number of ligands of a given type is indicated by the prefixes mono- (1, used for emphasis only), di- (2), tri- (3), tetra- (4), penta- (5), and hexa- (6), for unidentate ligands, and bis- (2), tris- (3), and tetrakis- (4) for multidentate ligands.
5. The oxidation state of the central metal atom is given as a Roman numeral in parentheses, after the name of the atom.
6. Complex *anion* names always end with -ate, followed by the appropriate Roman numeral. If the name of the metal ends with -um, -ium, or -enum, the ending is replaced with -ate in anion complexes.

   Al aluminate   Cr chromate   Mo molybdate

   The following metal names are used in anion complexes.

Co	cobaltate	As	arsenate	W	tungstate
Mn	manganate	Sb	antimonate	Zn	zincate
Cu	cuprate	Ni	niccolate	Sn	stannate
Ag	argentate	Fe	ferrate	Pb	plumbate
Au	aurate				

Some examples follow.

$[Ag(NH_3)_2]Cl$	diamminesilver(I) chloride
$[Co(NH_3)_3Cl_3]$	trichlorotriamminecobalt(III)
$K_4[Fe(CN)_6]$	potassium hexacyanoferrate(II)
$[Ni(CO)_4]$	tetracarbonylnickel(IV)
$[Cu(en)_2]SO_4$	bisethylenediaminecopper(II)
$[Pt(NH_3)_4][PtCl_6]$	tetraammineplatinum(II) hexachloroplatinate(IV)

★ **4. Draw reasonable structures for complex ions based on their names and formulas.**

The coordination number (C.N.) of the metal ion in a complex is a guide to the geometry of the ligands around that ion. C.N. = 2 has a linear geometry, and that of C.N. = 6 is octahedral. C.N. = 4 can be either square planar, as it is for Ni^{2+}, Cu^{2+}, and Pt^{2+}; or tetrahedral, as it is for Ni^{2+}, Co^{2+}, Zn^{2+}, Cd^{2+}, and Al^{3+} The square planar geometry is shown by the less active metals which have C.N. = 4, but Ni^{2+} shows both geometries. The structures of four complexes are in Figure 22-1.

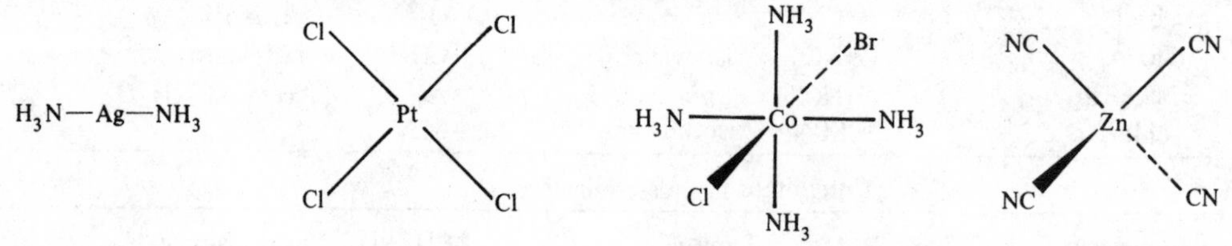

$H_3N—Ag—NH_3$

$[Ag(NH_3)_2]^+$

diamminesilver

$[PtCl_4]^{2-}$

tetrachloroplatinate(II)

$[Co(NH_3)_4ClBr]^+$

chlorobromotetraamminecobalt(III)

$[Zn(CN)_4]^{2-}$

tetracyanozincate

FIGURE 22-1 Structures of four complex ions.

★ **5. Describe the different types of isomerism possible in complex ions and identify by name, formula, and structure the various isomers of specific complexes.**

Isomers are compounds with the same formulas but different structures and thus different chemical or physical properties. Coordination compounds show four types of isomerism. (1) Ionization isomers have different ions as ligands. For example, $[Co(NH_3)_5SO_4]Br$ is red and gives a positive test for Br^-ion when in solution, but $[Co(NH_3)_5Br]SO_4$ is green and gives a positive sulfate test. (2) Linkage isomerism occurs when the ligand attaches to the central atom in different ways. For example, nitropentaamminecobalt(III) chloride, $[Co(NH_3)_5(CO_2)]Cl_2$, is yellow, while nitritopentaamminecobalt(III) chloride, $[Co(NH_3)_5(ONO)]Cl_2$, is red. The other possible linkage isomer ligands are CN^-, SCN^-, and CO. (3) Coordination isomerism occurs when a given ligand is bonded to the cation on one isomer and to the anion in the other. The complexes $[Co(NH_3)_4(NO_2)_2]$ and $[Co(NH_3)_2(NO_2)_4]$ are one example. (4) Geometric isomers differ in the arrangement of the ligands around the central metal atom. This is most easily seen in square planar complexes, such as $[Pt(NH_3)_2Cl_2]$.

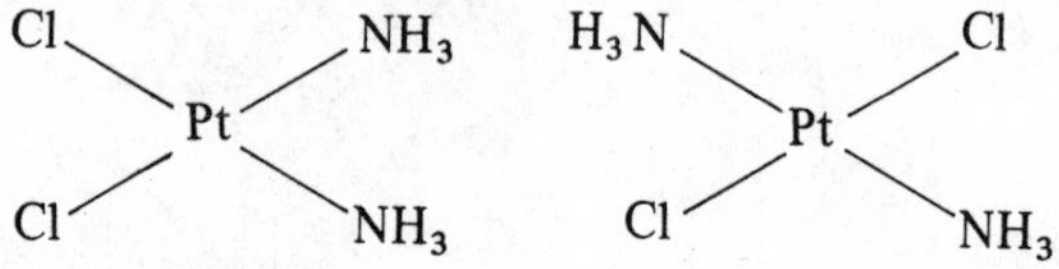

cis isomer

trans isomer

dichlorodiammineplatinum(II)

In the *trans* isomer the ammines are across the Pt from each other, on opposite sides. In the *cis* isomer they are next to each other. Geometric isomers also occur in octahedral complexes.

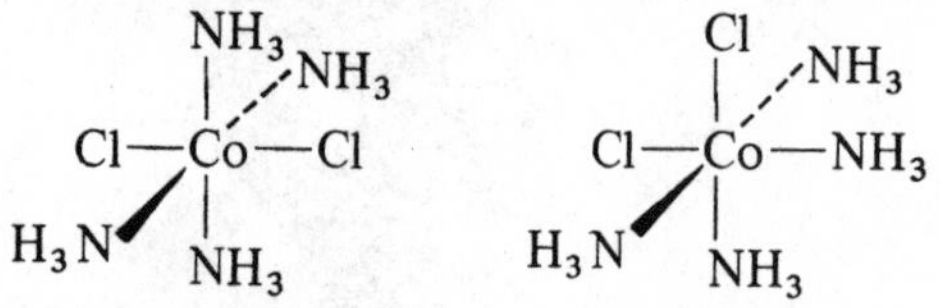

trans isomer

cis isomer

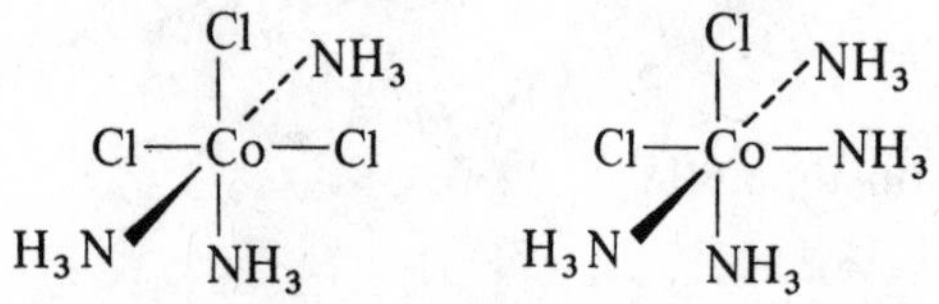

trans isomer

cis isomer

6. Use valence bond theory to describe the structure and bonding of complex ions.

In valence bond theory a complex is held together by coordinate covalent bonds. The geometry about the central atom corresponds to its hybridization, *sp* for linear, sp^3 for tetrahedral, dsp^2 for square planar, and d^2sp^3 for octahedral. The *s* and *p* orbitals are those of the valence shell of the metal atom. Thus, for the metals Ca through Ge the 4*s* and 4*p* orbitals are used for bonding. Strong bonding ligands use the inner *d* orbitals, 3*d* orbitals for Ca through Ge. These are inner orbital complexes. Weak bonding ligands use the outer *d* orbitals, 4*d* for Ca through Ge. These are called outer orbital complexes. The electron configurations of various complexes, the number of unpaired electrons (encircled) for each, and whether the complex is an inner or outer orbital complex are shown in Figure 22-2.

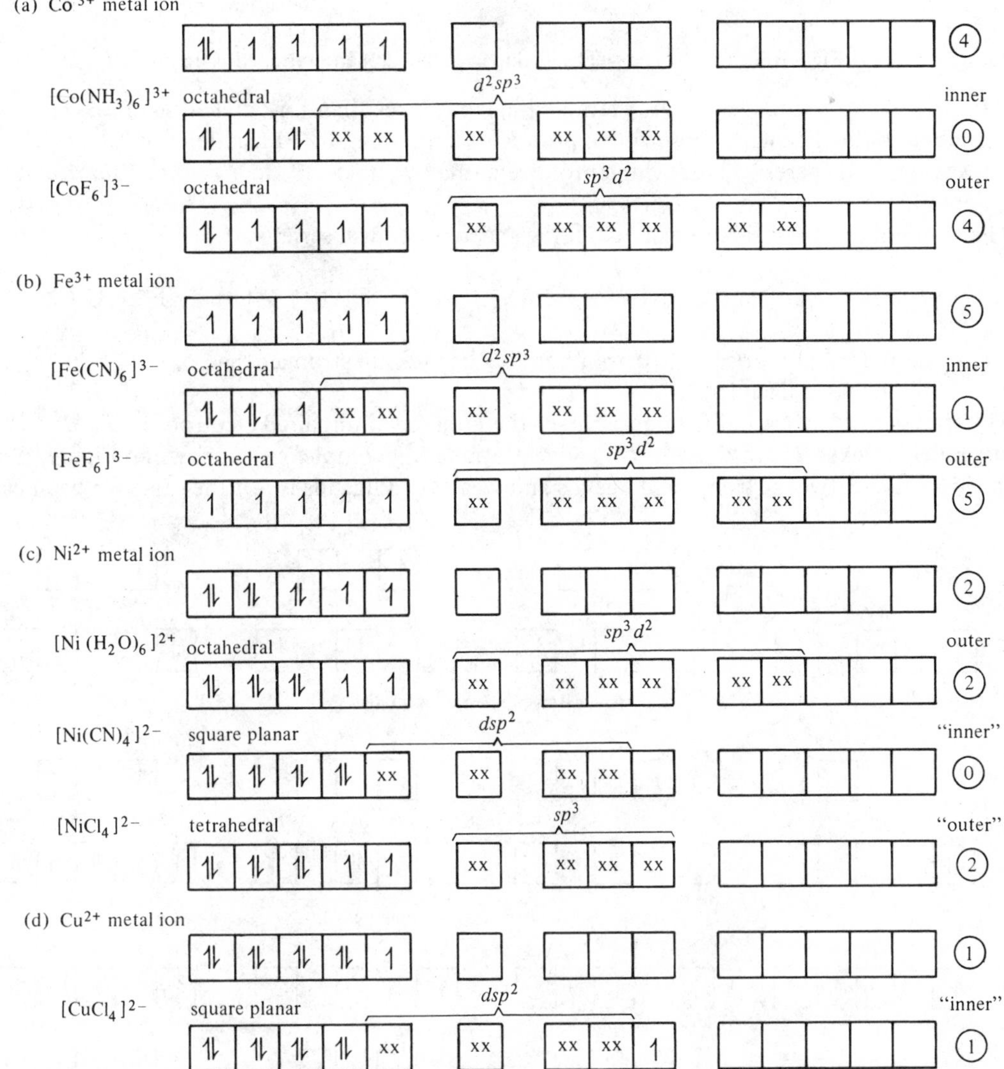

FIGURE 22-2 Orbital diagrams for some inner and outer orbital complexes

7. Explain the crystal field theory of bonding in complex ions.

★ **8. Use the spectrochemical series to make predictions about *d* level splitting and the number of unpaired electrons in complex ions.**

In crystal field theory the ligand electrons repel the valence shell electrons of the central metal atom. This makes the five *d* orbitals, which are the same energy in the isolated atom, of different energies in the complex. The difference in energies which occurs is known as the *crystal field splitting*. It is shown for octahedral and tetrahedral geometries in Figure 22-3. The crystal field splitting energy is symbolized by

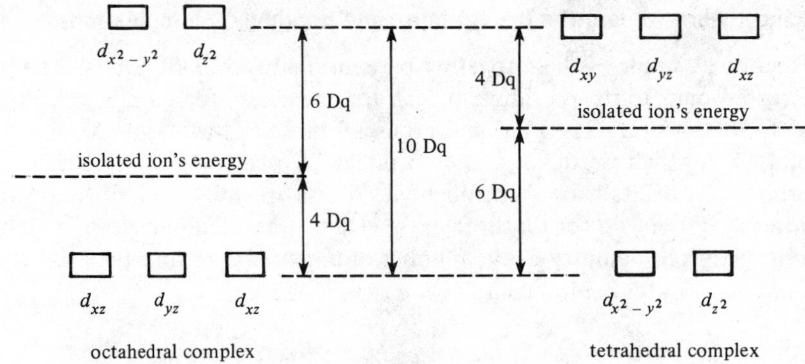

FIGURE 22-3 Ligand field splitting in octahedral and tetrahedral complexes.

$\Delta = 10$ Dq. 10 Dq is much smaller for tetrahedral complexes than for octahedral ones. The size of 10 Dq is determined by the ligands. Those which produce a large value of 10 Dq are called *strong field ligands* and are strong Lewis bases. Those which produce a small value of 10 Dq are *weak field ligands* and are weak Lewis bases.

The strength of ligands is summarized in the spectrochemical series.

$$CN^- > -NO_2^- > en > py \simeq -NH_3 > -NCS^- > H_2O \simeq C_2O_4^{2-} > OH^- > F^- > Cl^- > Br^- > I^- \quad [2]$$

This series should be memorized. Nitrogen bonding ligands are stronger than oxygen-bonding ones. The halides are the weakest ligands.

The strength of the crystal field determines the number of unpaired electrons in d^4, d^5, d^6, and d^7 octahedral complexes and in d^3, d^4, d^5, and d^6 tetrahedral complexes, as shown in Figure 22-4. The dividing line between strong field ligands and weak field ligands is not the same for each cation.

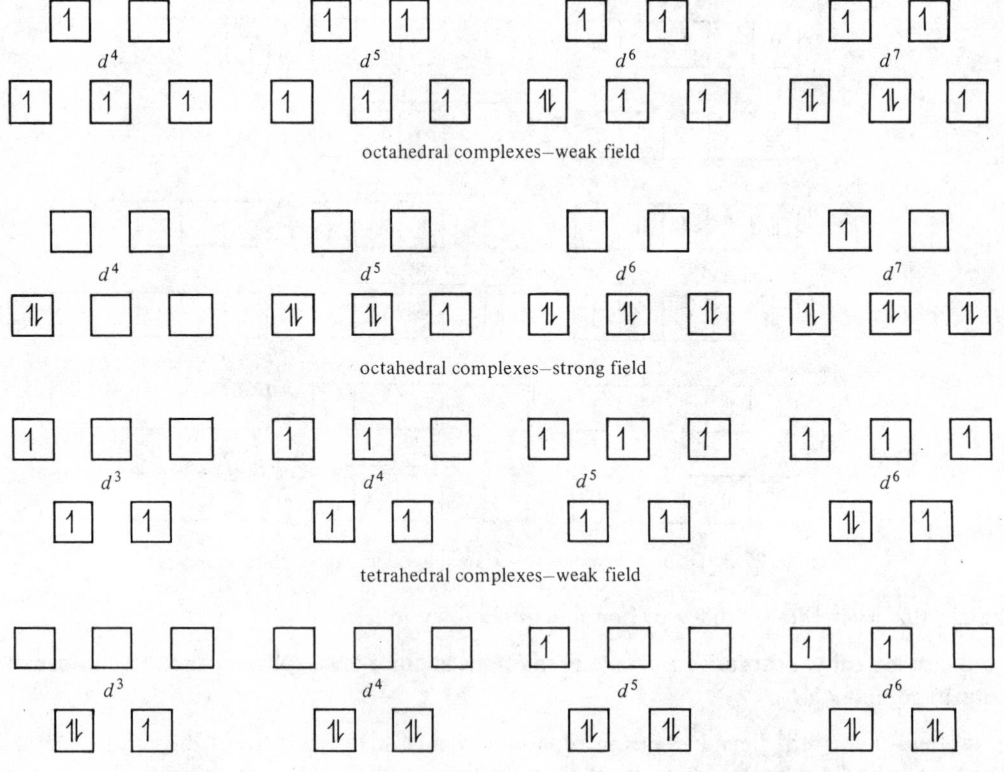

FIGURE 22-4 Strong and weak field configurations in octahedral and tetrahedral complexes.

9. Explain the origin of color in aqueous solutions of complex ions.

The size of 10 Dq determines the color which a complex shows. When white light strikes a complex ion, electrons in the low energy set of *d* orbitals absorb light of energy 10 Dq and we see the remaining light, that which is not absorbed. Values of 10 Dq and the resulting colors are given in Table 22-3.

TABLE 22-3
Colors of complex ions with different values of 10 Dq

10 Dq = Δ (approx.)		λ (approx),	Color	Complementary
J/molecule	kJ/mol	nm	absorbed	color seen
3.06×10^{-19}	185	650	red	green
3.31×10^{-19}	200	600	orange	blue
3.43×10^{-19}	206	580	yellow	violet
3.82×10^{-19}	230	520	green	red
4.23×10^{-19}	255	470	blue	orange
4.85×10^{-19}	292	410	violet	yellow

★ **10. Write equations showing the effect of complex-ion formation on other equilibrium processes such as solubility equilibria.**

In the precipitation of the ammonium sulfide group Fe^{3+} is precipitated as the hydroxide.

$$Fe(OH)_3(s) \rightleftharpoons Fe^{3+} + 3\ OH^- \qquad K_{sp} = 4 \times 10^{-38} \qquad [3]$$

If NaCN(aq) is added, free Fe^{3+} forms a complex.

$$Fe^{3+} + 6\ CN^- \rightleftharpoons [Fe(CN)_6]^{3-} \qquad K_f = 1 \times 10^{12} \qquad [4]$$

Equation [3] is displaced to the left, and some $Fe(OH)_3(s)$ dissolves.

★ **11. Use complex ion formation constants, K_f, to compute the concentrations of free ion, ligands and complex ions in solution.**

Although Pb^{2+} will precipitate as $PbCl_2(s)$, the addition of excess Cl^- will redissolve the solid because of the formation of $[PbCl_3]^-(aq)$.

$$Pb^{2+} + 3\ Cl^- \rightleftharpoons [PbCl_3]^- \qquad K_f = 2.4 \times 10^1 \qquad [5]$$

EXAMPLE 22-1 What is the equilibrium $[Pb^{2+}]$ if a 0.0100 *M* Pb^{2+} solution is made 0.400 *M* in Cl^-? Line R is the concentrations when all the $Pb^{2+}(aq)$ reacts.

Setup:	Pb^{2+}	+	$3\ Cl^-$	⇌	$[PbCl_3]^-$
I:	0.0100 *M*		0.400 *M*		
R:	0 *M*		0.370 *M*		0.0100 *M*
C:	$+x\ M$		$+3x\ M$		$-x\ M$
Eq:	$x\ M$		$(0.370 + 3x)M$		$(0.0100 - x)\ M$

$$K_f = \frac{0.0100 - x}{x(0.370 + 3x)^3} \simeq \frac{0.0100 - x}{x(0.370)^3} = 24 \quad or \quad x = 0.00451$$

We have assumed $3x \ll 0.370\ M$. This is not quite the case, so we go through two cycles of approximation to find $x = 0.0026\ M$. $[Pb^{2+}] = 0.00425\ M$, the concentration of free Pb^{2+}.

We used the method of successive approximations (objective 17-9, Example 17-5). This method is essential here since the exact equation is fourth order and has no simple solution.

★ **12. Use K_f values along with K_{sp} values to determine the solubilities of slightly soluble solutes in the presence of complexing reagents.**

The presence of a complexing reagent reduces the concentration of the free metal ion. This reduction may be enough that no precipitate forms even in the presence of a precipitating agent. For example, CdS will precipitate when Cd^{2+} and S^{2-} are present even at low concentrations.

$$CdS(s) \rightleftharpoons Cd^{2+} + S^{2-} \qquad K_{sp} = 8.0 \times 10^{-27} \qquad [6]$$

The addition of CN^- ion to the solution lowers $[Cd^{2+}]$.

$$Cd^{2+} + 4\,CN^- \rightleftharpoons [Cd(CN)_4]^{2-} \qquad K_f = [Cd(CN)_4{}^{2-}]/[Cd^{2+}][CN^-]^4 \qquad [7]$$

EXAMPLE 22-2 One liter of solution has $[S^{2-}] = 3.2 \times 10^{-8}\,M$. (a) What is the maximum amount of $Cd(NO_3)_2$ that may be added without a precipitate forming? (b) If the solution also has $[CN^-] = 0.100\,M$, what is the maximum amount of $Cd(NO_3)_2$ that may be added?

(a) Substitution into the K_{sp} expression for reaction [6] produces the maximum $[Cd^{2+}]$.

$$[Cd^{2+}][S^{2-}] = [Cd^{2+}][3.2 \times 10^{-8}] = 8.0 \times 10^{-27}$$
$$[Cd^{2+}] = 2.5 \times 10^{-19}\,M$$

Thus, we could add only 2.5×10^{-19} mol $Cd(NO_3)_2$.

(b) We know $[Cd^{2+}] = 2.5 \times 10^{-19}\,M$ at equilibrium.

Setup:	Cd^{2+}	+	$4\,CN^-$	$\rightleftharpoons$	$[Cd(CN)_4]^{2-}$
I:			$0.100\,M$		
C:	$+2.5 \times 10^{-19}\,M$		$-4x\,M$		$+x\,M$
Eq:	$2.5 \times 10^{-19}\,M$		$(0.100 - 4x)M$		$x\,M$

$$K_f = \frac{x}{(2.5 \times 10^{-19})(0.100 - 4x)^4} = 7.1 \times 10^{18} \simeq \frac{x}{(2.5 \times 10^{-19})(0.100)^4}$$

We assume $4x \ll 0.100\,M$. This gives the result $x = 1.78 \times 10^{-4}\,M = [Cd(CN)_4{}^{2-}]$. Practically all of the cadmium is present in the complex, and thus we can add 1.78×10^{-4} mol $Cd(NO_3)_2$ to 1 L of solution (7.12×10^{14} times more than in part (a)).

13. Explain amphoterism from the viewpoint of complex-ion equilibria.

Consider $[Al(H_2O)_6]^{3+}$ as a Brønsted–Lowry acid.

$$[Al(H_2O)_6]^{3+} + 3\,OH^- \rightarrow [Al(H_2O)_3](s) + 3\,H_2O$$
$$[Al(H_2O)_3(OH)_3] + OH^- \rightarrow [Al(H_2O)_2(OH)_4]^- + H_2O$$

We can replace the protons with a strong acid.

$$[Al(H_2O)_2(OH)_4]^- + H_3O^+ \rightarrow [Al(H_2O)_3(OH)_3](s) + H_2O$$
$$[Al(H_2O)_3(OH)_3](s) + 3\,H_3O^+ \rightarrow [Al(H_2O)_6]^{3+} + 3\,H_2O$$

14. Describe ways in which complex-ion equilibria are used in qualitative analysis.

Complex ion equilibria are used to separate one ion or a group of ions from a larger group of ions or to confirm the presence of an ion with a distinctive color. Some separations are

1. Often Ag^+ is separated from the mixed precipitate of qualitative analysis group 1 by adding $NH_3(aq)$. Neither $Hg_2{}^{2+}$ nor Pb^{2+} forms a very stable ammine complex, but Ag^+ does.

$$AgCl(s) + 2\,NH_3(aq) \rightleftharpoons [Ag(NH_3)_2]^+ + Cl^-$$

2. Al^{3+}, Cr^{3+}, and Zn^{2+} are kept in solution by adding OH^-, while $Mn(OH)_2$, $Co(OH)_2$, $Ni(OH)_2$, and $Fe(OH)_3$ precipitate in the ammonium sulfide group.
3. $NH_3(aq)$ keeps $[Ni(NH_3)_6]^{2+}$ and $[Co(NH_3)_6]^{3+}$ in solution, while $Fe(OH)_3(s)$ precipitates.

Some confirmations are

1. The formation of $[Fe(H_2O)_5CNS]^{2+}$ confirms Fe^{3+}.

$$Fe^{3+} + SCN^- + 5\ H_2O \rightarrow [Fe(H_2O)_5CNS]^{2+}$$

2. The formation of $Ni(DMG)_2$ confirms Ni^{2+}.

$$Ni[(NH_3)_6]^{2+} + 2\ DMG^- \rightarrow Ni(DMG)_2 + 6\ NH_3$$

3. $Pb(C_2H_3O_2)_2$ formation begins the confirmation of Pb.

$$PbSO_4(s) + 2\ C_2H_3O_2^- \rightarrow Pb(C_2H_3O_2)_2(aq) + SO_4^{2-}$$

15. Describe how complex-ion chemistry is used in photograph development, electroplating, metallurgy. and water treatment.

Review the last section of *Chapter 22 in the text* where these processes are described. Write down your description of each process, including all chemical reactions which occur.

DRILL PROBLEMS

1. For each of the following complex ions, give the central atom and its oxidation state, the coordination number, and the formulas of the ligands.

A. $[Ag(S_2O_3)_2]^{3-}$ B. $[AlH_4]^-$ C. $[Co(H_2O)_2(CN)_4]^-$
D. $[Pt(NH_3)_2Cl_4]$ E. $[Ni(NH_3)_4]^{2+}$ F. $[Cr(NH_3)_2(SCN)_4]^-$
G. $[Fe(en)_3]^{3+}$ H. $[Pt(NO_2)_4]^{2-}$ I. $[Co(NH_3)_5Cl]^{2+}$
J. $[Al(H_2O)_5OH]^{2+}$ K. $[Pt(NH_3)_3Cl_3]^+$ L. $[Fe(CO)_4]$
M. $[Mn(NO)(CN)_5]^{3-}$ N. $[AuF_4]^-$ O. $[Co(NH_3)_4(NH_2)_2]^+$
P. $[SbCl_5]^{2-}$ Q. $[NiCl_2(en)_2]$ R. $[Fe(CN)_6]^{4-}$
S. $[Ni(NH_3)_2Br_2]$ T. $[Fe(H_2O)_4(OH)_2]^+$ U. $[Ni(H_2O)_2(NH_3)_4]^{2+}$

2. (1) List all the ions for each coordination number.

A. two (2) B. six (6) C. four (4) or six (6)

(2) Give the coordination number(s) of the following ions.

A. Cu^{2+} B. Fe^{2+} C. Fe^{3+} D. Ca^{2+} E. Co^{2+}
F. Au^+ G. Al^{3+} H. Co^{3+} I. Ag^+

(3) Give the name or formula, as appropriate, and the denticity (1 for unidentate, 2 for bidentate, and so forth) of the following ligands. The first is done as an example.

Cl^- chloro (1)

A. $—NO_3^-$ B. EDTA C. triethylenetetraamine
D. ammine E. hydroxo F. carbonyl
G. $—NO_2^-$ H. thiocyano I. NO
J. N_2 K. fluoro L. sulfato
M. cyano N. $—ONO^-$

3. (1) Name all the ions listed in the problems of objective 22-1. (2) Then give the correct name or formula, as appropriate, for each of the following.

A. $Na_3[Au(CN)_4]$ B. sodium dithiosulfatoargentate
C. $K_3[Co(NO_2)_6]$ D. dibromodiammineplatinum(II)
E. $[Co(NH_3)_4Cl_2]Br$ F. dichlorotetraaquochromium(III) bromide

G. tetrachlorodiaquoplatinum(IV)
H. $K_2[PtCl_6]$
I. diamminesilver chloride
J. hexaamminenickel(II) sulfate
K. $Na[Cr(en)_2(SO_4)_2]$
L. $[Al(H_2O)_6][Co(CN)_6]$
M. $Ca[Cr(NH_3)_2(SCN)_4]_2$
N. $[Co(NH_3)_6]ClSO_4$
O. sodium trisoxalatochromate(III)
P. bisethylenediaminecopper(II) chloride

4. Draw a reasonable structure for each of the complexes given in the problems of objective 22-1.

5. Use these ten coordination compounds in answering the questions below.

1. $Li[Al(CN)_4]$
2. $[Co(NH_3)_6]ClSO_4$
3. $[Co(H_2O)_4(CN)_2]Cl$
4. $[Cu(en)_2(NH_3)_2]SO_4$
5. $[Al(H_2O)_6][Co(CN)_6]$
6. $[Pt(H_2O)_2(NO_2)_2]$
7. $[Cr(H_2O)_4Cl_2]Br$
8. $[Pt(H_2O)_4][PtCl_6]$
9. $[Co(NH_3)_5Cl]SO_4$
10. $[Mn(NO)_3(CN)_3]$

A. Identify all of the compounds which have ionization isomers and give the names and formulas of two ionization isomers of each compound.
B. Identify all of the compounds which have linkage isomers and give the names of two linkage isomers of each compound.
C. Identify all of the compounds which have coordination isomers and give the formulas of two coordination isomers of each compound.
D. Identify all of the complex ions which have geometric isomerism. Draw the structures and designate each geometric isomer as *cis* or *trans.*

8. Predict whether each of the following complex ions will have a strong field or a weak field and predict the number of unpaired electrons in each complex.

A. $[Co(NH_3)_6]^{3+}$
B. $[Cr(en)_3]^{3+}$
C. $[PtCl_6]^{2-}$
D. $[Cu(ox)_3]^{4-}$
E. $[Fe(CN)_6]^{4-}$
F. $[CoCl_4]^{2-}$
G. $[CoI_6]^{3-}$
H. $[Ni(C_2O_4)_3]^{4-}$
I. $[Sc(H_2O)_3Cl_3]$
J. $[Co(NH_3)_4]^{2+}$

10. Write equations for the equilibrium reactions which occur in aqueous solutions of the following species. Does formation of a complex increase or decrease the amount of precipitate?

A. Ag^+, $S_2O_3^{2-}$, Cl^-, Na^+
B. Hg^{2+}, I^-, Ag^+, NO_3^-
C. Zn^{2+}, CN^-, S^{2-}, Na^+
D. Fe^{2+}, CN^-, OH^-, K^+
E. Al^{3+}, F^-, Ca^{2+}, Li^+
F. Cu^+, CN^-, Ag^+, Cl^-
G. Al^{3+}, F^-, OH^-, Na^+
H. Co^{3+}, S^{2-}, NH_3, Cl^-
I. Cu^{2+}, NH_3, OH^-, Na^+

11. Determine the concentrations of free metal ion and complex ion each solution in which the initial metal ion and ligand concentrations are as given below. Neglect the acid and base reactions of the ligands and cations. Use the data of *Table 22-5 in the text* as needed.

A. $[F^-] = 0.100\,M$, $[Al^{3+}] = 0.002\,M$
B. $[Cl^-] = 1.00\,M$, $[Pb^{2+}] = 8.2 \times 10^{-5}\,M$
C. $[S_2O_3^{2-}] = 0.310\,M$, $[Ag^+] = 6.7 \times 10^{-3}\,M$
D. $[CN^-] = 0.850\,M$, $[Zn^{2+}] = 5.0 \times 10^{-4}\,M$
E. $[CN^-] = 0.850\,M$, $[Cu^{2+}] = 5.0 \times 10^{-4}\,M$
F. $[CN^-] = 0.850\,M$, $[Fe^{2+}] = 5.0 \times 10^{-4}\,M$
G. $[CN^-] = 0.850\,M$, $[Fe^{3+}] = 5.0 \times 10^{-4}\,M$
H. $[NH_3] = 1.52\,M$, $[Co^{3+}] = 1.4 \times 10^{-5}\,M$
I. $[NH_3] = 0.200\,M$, $[Ag^+] = 1.3 \times 10^{-4}\,M$
J. $[I^-] = 1.00\,M$, $[Hg^{2+}] = 2.4 \times 10^{-6}\,M$
K. $[Cl^-] = 1.00\,M$, $[Hg^{2+}] = 2.4 \times 10^{-6}\,M$

12. Determine the concentration of free metal ion (after a complex forms but before precipitation occurs) and state whether a precipitate will form or not. The initial concentration of each species is given. You may neglect the acid and base reactions between water and the ligand and the cation.

A. $[Ag^+] = 0.0100\,M$, $[I^-] = 0.0100\,M$, $[NH_3] = 5.00\,M$
B. $[Ag^+] = 0.0100\,M$, $[Cl^-] = 0.0100\,M$, $[NH_3] = 5.00\,M$
C. $[Zn^{2+}] = 0.0100\,M$, $[S^{2-}] = 0.0100\,M$, $[EDTA^{4-}] = 0.100\,M$ ($K_f = 3.9 \times 10^{16}$ for $[Zn(EDTA)]^{2-}$)
D. $[Ag^+] = 0.0200\,M$, $[Br^-] = 0.0100\,M$, $[S_2O_3^{2-}] = 0.250\,M$
E. $[Hg^{2+}] = 0.0100\,M$, $[SO_4^{2-}] = 0.0200\,M$, $[I^-] = 0.400\,M$ ($K_{sp} = 7.4 \times 10^{-7}$ for $HgSO_4$)
F. $[Cu^{2+}] = 0.0400\,M$, $[S^{2-}] = 0.0200\,M$, $[NH_3] = 2.00\,M$
G. $[Ag^{2+}] = 0.0100\,M$, $[S^{2-}] = 0.00500\,M$, $[CN^-] = 1.00\,M$

QUIZZES (20 minutes each)

Choose the best answer or fill in the blank.

Quiz A

1. $[Fe(C_2O_4)_3]^{3-}$ has a coordination number of (a) 2; (b) 3; (c) 4; (d) 6; (e) none of these.

2. Au^{3+} shows a coordination number of (a) 2 only; (b) 2 or 4; (c) 4 only; (d) 4 or 6; (e) 6 only.
3. The nitrito ligand has the formula (a) $—NO_2^-$; (b) $—NO_3^-$; (c) $—ONO^-$; (d) NO; (e) none of these.
4. The name of $[Au(NH_3)_2Cl_2]Br$ is ______________________.
5. The formula of trisethylenediaminecobalt(III) acetate is ______________________.
6. $[Fe(CN)_6]^{4-}$ has how many unpaired electrons? (a) 2; (b) 0; (c) 4; (d) 3; (e) none of these.
7. Coordination isomerism could be shown by (a) $Li[AlH_4]$; (b) $[Ag(NH_3)_2][CuCl_2]$; (c) $[Co(NH_3)_4Cl_2]Br$; (d) $[Pt(H_2O)_4Cl_2]$; (e) none of these.
8. The formation constant for the complex $Zn(NH_3)_4^{2+}$ is the equilibrium constant for the reaction represented by (a) $Zn^{2+}(aq) + 4\,NH_3(aq) \rightleftharpoons [Zn(NH_3)_4]^{2+}(aq)$;
(b) $[Zn(NH_3)_3(H_2O)]^{2+}(aq) + NH_3(aq) \rightleftharpoons [Zn(NH_3)_4]^{2+} + H_2O$;
(c) $Zn(s) + 4\,NH_3(aq) \rightleftharpoons [Zn(NH_3)_4]^{2+} + 2\,e^-$;
(d) $[Zn(H_2O)_4]^{2+}(aq) + 4\,NH_3(aq) \rightleftharpoons [Zn(NH_3)_4]^{2+}(aq) + 4\,H_2O$.

Quiz B

1. $[Co(en)_2Cl_2]^+$ has a coordination number of (a) 2; (b) 4; (c) 6; (d) 3; (e) none of these.
2. Cu^{2+} shows a coordination number of (a) 2 only; (b) 2 or 4; (c) 4 only; (d) 4 or 6; (e) 6 only.
3. The carbonyl ligand has the formula (a) CO; (b) CO_3^{2-}; (d) CN^-; (e) none of these.
4. The name of $Ca[CuCl_4]$ is ______________________.
5. The formula of potassium pentachloroantimonate(III) is ______________________.
6. $[CoCl_6]^{4-}$ has how many unpaired electrons? (a) 6; (b) 3; (c) 1; (d) 0; (e) none of these.
7. Ionization isomerism could be shown by (a) $[Co(en)_2Cl_2]$; (b) $Na[Ag(CN)_2]$; (c) $[Cr(NH_3)_5Cl]I_2$; (d) $[PtCl_4][Pt(NH_3)_4Cl_2]$; (e) none of these.
8. The $[Fe(CN)_6]^{3-}$ complex ion (a) exhibits square planar geometry; (b) is diamagnetic; (c) involves d^2sp^3 hybridization of Fe(III); (d) has two unpaired electrons; (e) none of these.

Quiz C

1. $[Zn(en)Cl_2]$ has a coordination number of (a) 2; (b) 3; (c) 4; (d) 6; (e) none of these.
2. Au^+ shows a coordination number of (a) 2 only; (b) 2 or 4; (c) 4 only; (d) 4 or 6; (e) 6 only.
3. The oxalato ligand has the formula (a) $C_2O_4^{2-}$; (b) O^{2-}; (c) O_2^-; (d) CO_3^{2-}; (e) none of these.
4. The name of $K_2[Pt(NH_3)_2Cl_4]$ is ______________________.
5. The formula of calcium tetrachlorodiamminechromate(III) is ______________________.
6. $[Pt(NH_3)_6]^{4+}$ has how many unpaired electrons? (a) 0; (b) 3; (c) 2; (d) 1; (e) none of these.
7. Linkage isomerism can be shown by (a) $[Pt(H_2O)_4Cl_2]$; (b) $[Co(NH_3)_4Cl_2]Br$; (c) $[Zn(H_2O)_4][CdCl_4]$; (d) $K[Ag(CN)_2]$; (e) none of these.
8. Which of the following is a chelating ligand? (a) H_2O; (b) $H_2NCH_2CH_2NH_2$; (c) HCl; (d) NH_3; (e) $S_2O_3^{2-}$.

Quiz D

1. $[Cr(en)(NH_3)(H_2O)_2]^{3+}$ has a coordination number of (a) 3; (b) 4; (c) 5; (d) 6; (e) none of these.
2. Al^{3+} shows a coordination number of (a) 2 only; (b) 2 or 4; (c) 4 only; (d) 4 or 6; (e) 6 only.
3. The hydroxo ligand has the formula (a) OH^-; (b) H_2O; (c) O^{2-}; (d) $C_2O_4^{2-}$; (e) none of these.
4. The name of $Na_2[Co(NO)_2Cl_4]$ is ______________________.
5. The formula of potassium tetracyanodimethylamineferrate(II) is ______________________.
6. A $[Co(H_2O)_4(OH)_2]^+$ ion has how many unpaired electrons? (a) 0; (b) 4; (c) 1; (d) 3; (e) none of these.
7. Geometric isomerism can be shown by (a) $[Ag(NH_3)(CN)]$; (b) $Na_2[Cd(NO_2)_4]$; (c) $[PtCl_4I_2]$; (d) $[Au(CN)_4][Pt(NH_3)_3Cl]$; (e) none of these.
8. One mole of a compound with empirical formula $CoCl_3 \cdot 4\,NH_3$ yields one mol AgCl on treatment with excess $AgNO_3$. Ammonia is not removed by treatment with concentrated H_2SO_4. The formula

of this compound is (a) $Co(NH_3)_4Cl_3$; (b) $[Co(NH_3)_4]Cl_3$; (c) $[Co(NH_3)_3Cl_3]NH_3$; (d) $[Co(NH_3)_4Cl_2]Cl$.

SAMPLE TEST (20 minutes)

1. For each of the following complexes draw the *d* orbital splitting diagram and predict how many unpaired electrons are in the complex.
   a. $[Co(CN)_4]^{2-}$ b. $W(CO)_6$ c. $[MnI_4]^{2-}$ d. $[Fe(CN)_6]^{3-}$
2. A compound contains 24.8% Na, 34.2% Cu, and 41.0% F. A 0.010 *M* solution has an osmotic pressure at 298 K of 559 mmHg. What is the formula and the name of this compound?
3. 350.0 ml of 0.200 *M* $AgNO_3$ (aq) is added to 250.0 ml of 0.240 *M* Na_2SO_4 (aq) and Ag_2SO_4 ($K_{sp} = 1.4 \times 10^{-5}$) precipitates. 400.0 ml of 0.500 *M* $Na_2S_2O_3$ (aq) is added to this mixture. What mass of Ag_2SO_4(s) remains? $K_f = 1.7 \times 10^{13}$ for $[Ag(S_2O_3)_2]^{3-}$.

Chapter 23

Nuclear Chemistry

REVIEW OF OBJECTIVES

1. Name the different types of radioactive decay processes and describe the characteristics of their radiation.

Alpha (α) *decay* involves nuclides with an atomic number larger than 83 ($Z > 83$) and a mass number larger than 200 ($A > 200$). It often leaves the nucleus in an excited state. The alpha particle is a ^4He nucleus, $^4He^{2+}$. Thus, the atomic number decreases by two and the mass number by four units. The alpha particle has large ionizing power but low penetrating power; it can be stopped by a sheet of paper.

Beta (β) *decay* occurs when electrons are emitted. The nuclide's mass number is unchanged, but its atomic number increases by one. β particles are less ionizing and more penetrating than α particles. They are stopped by about 0.5 mm of Al, whereas an α particle is stopped by 0.015 mm of Al.

Gamma (γ) *decay* is the emission of high-energy photons. This is how the nucleus gets rid of excess energy. It occurs within one nanosecond of some other decay process. If the high-energy (excited) nucleus survives for more than a nanosecond, it is called an "isomer" and its gamma decay is called an *isomeric transition* (IT). Gamma rays have relatively low ionizing power but a high penetrating power. They are stopped by 5 to 11 mm of Al.

Positron (β^+) *emission* occurs only in artificial nuclides. A positron is a positively charged electron. Positron emission leaves the mass number unchanged and decreases the atomic number by one. Positrons have almost no penetrating power.

Electron capture (EC) occurs when the nucleus captures or absorbs one of its atoms, usually one in the *K* or *L* shell. An "isomer" is formed which emits x rays or γ rays to get rid of its excess energy.

★ **2. Complete nuclear equations for radioactive decay processes.**

Make sure that the sum of the mass numbers and the sum of the atomic numbers are the same on each side of the equation. Remember that the nass number is the preceding superscript of the atomic symbol and the atomic number is the preceding subscript. A decay process has one nuclide on the left side (the "parent" nucleus) and another on the right side (the "daughter" nucleus) along with the emitted particle: alpha (^4_2He), beta ($^{0}_{-1}e$), or positron ($^{0}_{+1}e$).

parent nucleus → daughter nucleus + emitted particle [1]

EXAMPLE 23-1 Alpha decay of ^{210}Po yields what nuclide?

$$^{210}_{84}Po \rightarrow ? + ^4_2He$$

The daughter has an atomic number of 82 ($84 = 82 + 2$) and a mass number of 206 ($210 = 206 + 4$). An atomic number of 82 corresponds to Pb. Thus, the product is $^{206}_{82}Pb$.

3. Describe the three natural radioactive decay series, using the uranium series as an example; and give some examples of where these series are found in the environment.

$^{238}_{72}U$, $^{232}_{90}Th$, and $^{235}_{92}U$ are the naturally occurring parents of three decay series: the uranium series, the thorium series, and the actinium series, respectively. These three series are shown in Figure 23-1. Note that the atomic numbers (on the horizontal axis) are offset so that the series are not plotted on top of each other.

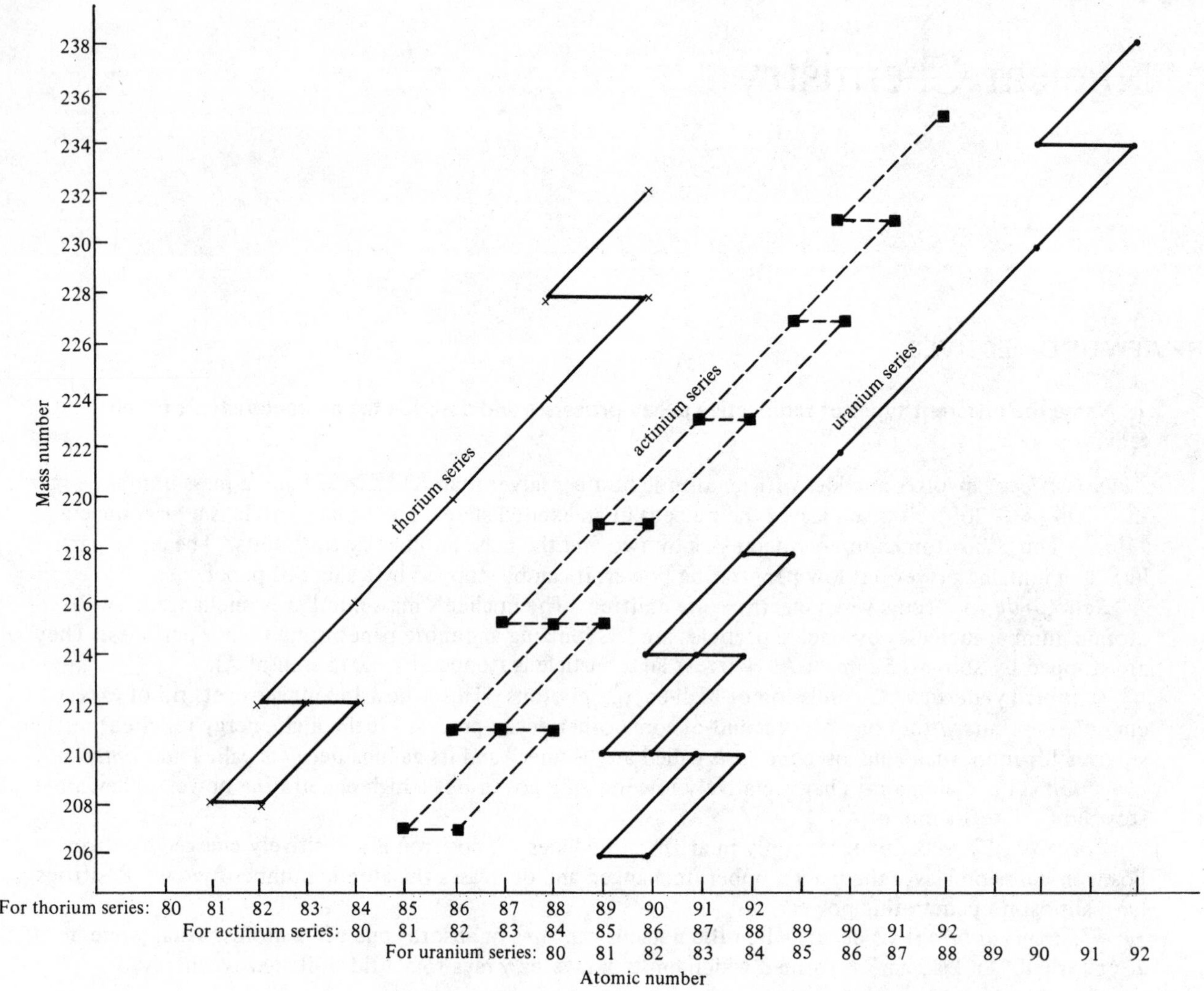

FIGURE 23-1 The thorium (X), actinium (■), and uranium (●) decay series.

The thorium series is the $4n$ series (the mass numbers of its nuclides are multiples of 4). The uranium series is the $4n + 2$ series, and the actinium series is the $4n + 3$ series. Half-lives and isotope masses of the nuclides in these three series are given in Table 23-1.

The isotopes of these series are spread throughout the environment. Starting with the rock (such as granite) in which uranium and thorium are commonly found, the parents and the daughters are spread by weathering processes. Certain plants concentrate these elements and thus are a source of the isotopes. Mining activities speed up the dispersion of these elements by bringing rocks to the surface where they are exposed to the weather and erode faster.

★ **4. Write equations for the artificial production of nuclides.**

Many of these equations look like equation [2].

target nucleus + bombarding particle → emitted particle + product nucleus [2]

Occasionally more than one particle and/or product nucleus results. A shorthand notation is given in equation [3].

target nucleus (bombarding particle, emitted particle) product nucleus [3]

Thus, the bombardment of ^{242}Cm by alpha particles is

$$^{242}_{96}Cm + ^{4}_{2}He \rightarrow ^{245}_{98}Cf + ^{1}_{0}n, \quad [4]$$

$$^{242}_{96}Cm(\alpha, n)^{245}_{98}Cf \quad [5]$$

Abbreviated symbols (Table 23-2) of the particles are used. Predicting the products is not expected. But by balancing mass numbers and atomic numbers, you can predict one of the four species in equation 2], given the other three.

TABLE 23-1
Half-lives and isotope masses of nuclides in the three naturally occurring radioactive series

Uranium series			Actinium series			Thorium series		
Nuclide	Half-life	Isotope mass	Nuclide	Half-life	Isotope mass	Nuclide	Half-life	Isotope mass
^{235}U	4.51×10^9 y	238.0508	^{238}U	7.13×10^8 y	235.0439	^{232}Th	1.41×10^{10} y	232.0381
^{234}Th	24.1 d	234.0458	^{231}Th	25.5 h	231.0363	^{228}Ra	6.7 y	228.0311
^{234}Pa	6.75 h	234.0433	^{231}Pa	3.25×10^4 y	231.0359	^{228}Ac	6.13 h	228.0311
^{234}U	2.47×10^5 y	234.0409	^{227}Ac	21.6 y	227.0278	^{228}Th	1.91 y	228.0287
^{230}Th	8.0×10^4 y	230.0331	^{227}Th	18.17 d	227.0278	^{224}Ra	3.64 d	224.0202
^{226}Ra	1602 y	226.0254	^{223}Fr	22 min	233.0198	^{220}Rn	53.3 s	220.0114
^{222}Rn	3.82 d	222.0175	^{223}Ra	11.4 d	223.0186	^{216}Po	145 ms	216.0019
^{218}Po	3.05 min	218.0089	^{219}At	54 s	219.0113	^{212}Pb	10.64 h	211.9919
^{218}At	2.0 s	218.0086	^{219}Rn	4.0 s	219.0095	^{212}Bi	60.6 min	211.9913
^{214}Pb	26.8 min	213.9998	^{215}Bi	8 min	215.0018	^{212}Po	0.30 μs	211.9889
^{214}Bi	19.7 min	213.9987	^{215}Po	1.8 ms	214.9995	^{208}Tl	3.10 min	207.9820
^{214}Po	150 μs	213.9952	^{215}Pt	100 μs	214.9987	^{208}Pb	stable	207.9766
^{210}Tl	1.32 min	209.9901	^{211}Pb	36.1 min	210.9887			
^{210}Pb	20.4 y	209.9842	^{211}Bi	2.15 min	210.9873			
^{210}Bi	5.0 d	209.9842	^{211}Po	0.52 s	210.9866			
^{210}Po	138 d	209.9829	^{207}Tl	4.78 min	206.9775			
^{206}Tl	4.19 min	205.9761	^{207}Pb	stable	206.9757			
^{206}Pb	stable	205.9745						

TABLE 23-2
Abbreviated symbols for some particles involved in nuclear reactions

Name	Complete symbol	Abbreviated symbol	Mass, amu
alpha particle	$^{4}_{2}He^{2+}$	α	4.001507
beta particle	$^{0}_{-1}e$	β	0.000548
or electron		*or* β^-	
neutron	$^{1}_{0}n$	n	1.008665
proton	$^{1}_{1}H^+$	p	1.007277
deuteron	$^{2}_{1}H^+$	d	2.013554
helium atom	$^{4}_{2}He^0$		4.002603
positron	$^{0}_{1}e$	β^+	
hydrogen atom	$^{1}_{1}H^0$		1.007825
deuterium atom	$^{2}_{1}H^0$		2.014102

5. Name some of the transuranium elements and describe how they are made.

The transuranium elements are those with atomic number larger than 92 and are made by bombarding lighter nuclei with other particles. The equations for their production are given in Table 23-3. The names and discoverers of elements 104 and 105 have yet to be decided. Neptunium, plutonium, americium, curium, berkelium, and californium are available commercially in kilogram quantities. Where two reactions are given, the first is the reaction of discovery. The second reaction is that of commercial preparation. You should memorize the commercial preparations for neptunium through californium.

TABLE 23-3
Production of transuranium elements

Element	Equation	Discovers and date
neptunium	$^{238}_{92}U(n, \beta)\,^{239}_{93}Np$	McMillan and Abelson Berkeley, CA (1940)
	or $^{235}_{92}U(n, \gamma)\,^{236}_{92}U(n, \gamma)\,^{237}_{92}U \xrightarrow{\beta^-} {}^{237}_{93}Np$	In nuclear reactors.
plutonium	$^{238}_{92}U(d, 2n)\,^{238}_{93}Np \xrightarrow{\beta^-} {}^{238}_{94}Pu$	Seaborg, McMillan, Kennedy, Wahl Berkeley, CA (1940)
	or $^{238}_{92}U(n, \gamma)\,^{239}_{92}U \xrightarrow{\beta^-} {}^{239}_{93}Np \xrightarrow{\beta^-} {}^{239}_{94}Pu$	In nuclear reactors
americium	$^{239}_{94}Pu(n, \gamma)\,^{240}_{90}Pu(n, \gamma)\,^{241}_{94}Pu \xrightarrow{\beta^-} {}^{241}_{95}Am$	Seaborg, James, Morgan, Ghiorso Chicago, IL (1944)
curium	$^{239}_{94}Pu(\alpha, n)\,^{242}_{96}Cm$	Seaborg, James, Ghiorso Berkeley, CA (1944)
	or $^{241}_{95}Am(n, \gamma)\,^{242\,m}_{95}Am \xrightarrow{\beta^-} {}^{242}_{96}Cm$	In nuclear reactors
berkelium	$^{241}_{95}Am(\alpha, 2n)\,^{243}_{97}Bk$	Thompson, Ghiorso, Seaborg Berkeley, CA (Dec 1949)
californium	$^{242}_{96}Cm(\alpha, n)\,^{245}_{98}Cf$	Thompson, Street, Ghiorso, Seaborg Berkeley, CA (1950)
	or $^{249}_{97}Bk(n, \gamma)\,^{250}_{97}Bk \xrightarrow{\beta^-} {}^{250}_{98}Cf$	In nuclear reactors
einsteinium	$^{238}_{92}U + 15\,^{1}_{0}n \longrightarrow {}^{253}_{99}Es + 7\,^{0}_{-1}e$ products of first hydrogen bomb	Ghiorso and colleagues Berkeley, CA (Dec 1952)
fermium	$^{238}_{92}U + {}^{16}_{8}O \longrightarrow {}^{250}_{100}Fm + 4\,^{1}_{0}n$ products of first hydrogen bomb	Ghiorso and colleagues Berkeley, CA (Dec 1952)
mendelevium	$^{253}_{99}Es(\alpha, n)\,^{256}_{101}Md$	Ghiorso, Harvey, Choppin, Thompson, Seaborg Berkeley, CA (1955)
nobelium	$^{246}_{96}Cm(^{12}_{6}C, 4n)\,^{254}_{102}No$	Ghiorso, Sikkeland, Walton, Seaborg Berkeley, CA (Apr 1958)
lawrencium	$^{252}_{98}Cf(^{11}_{5}B, 5n)\,^{258}_{103}Lw$	Ghiorso, Sikkeland, Larsh, Latimer Berkeley, CA (Mar 1961)
element 104 (kurchatovium)	$^{242}_{94}Pu + {}^{22}_{10}Ne \longrightarrow {}^{260}_{104}Ku + 4\,^{1}_{0}n$	Workers at Joint Nuclear Research Institute, Dubna, USSR (1964)
(rutherfordium)	$^{249}_{98}Cf + {}^{12}_{6}C \longrightarrow {}^{257}_{104}Ru + 4\,^{1}_{0}n$	Ghiorso and colleagues Berkeley, CA (1969)
element 105 (hahnium)	$^{249}_{98}Cf + {}^{15}_{7}N \longrightarrow {}^{260}_{105}Ha + 4\,^{1}_{0}n$	Ghiorso and colleagues Berkeley, CA (Mar 1970)
(no name proposed)	$^{243}_{95}Am + {}^{22}_{10}Ne \longrightarrow {}^{260}_{105}105 + 5\,^{1}_{0}n$	Flerov and colleagues Dubna, USSR (1967)

6. Describe how a charged-particle accelerator operates.

A charged-particle accelerator produces beams of charged particles having very high energies per particle. Often these high-energy particles are atomic nuclei and thus are positively charged. Charged particles are accelerated by an electrical field which exerts a force on them. In a circular accelerator the polarity of the electrical field (whether it is positive or negative) in each half of the accelerator alternates as the particles move in a nearly circular path. The field alternates so that it always accelerates the particles. Such circular accelerators also are called cyclotrons.

In a synchrontron, the beam of charged particles travels through a donut-shaped tube. Magnetic fields are used to keep the beam in the center of the tube (focusing magnets) and to bend the beam into a circular path (deflection magnets). The particles are accelerated by many electrical fields spaced around the ring (or donut). The voltage of each field varies so that the particles are accelerated as they pass. As the particles move around the ring more rapidly, the field must vary more rapidly. (Think of a steel ball traveling around the outer track which surrounds a roulette whell. If you want to speed the ball up by hitting it each time it passes by, you have to hit it more often as it goes faster.) The strength of the deflection magnets also must increase to keep the particles in a circular path.

Linear accelerators also use electrical fields of increasing strength to accelerate particles. However, particles go around a synchrotron many times, being accelerated constantly. Thus a synchrotron can accelerate a particle to a much higher speed than can a linear accelerator.

★ **7. Given two of the quantities: rate of radioactive decay, half-life, and number of atoms in a sample of a radioactive nuclide, calculate the third.**

These three quantities are related.

$$t_{1/2} = 0.693/\lambda \qquad [6]$$

$$\text{decay rate} = \lambda N \qquad [7]$$

In these equations $t_{1/2}$ is the half-life of the nuclide, λ the decay constant of the nuclide, and N the number of atoms in the sample. Decay rate also is known as activity.

EXAMPLE 23-2 A 1.00×10^{-6} g sample of a nuclide with an atomic weight of 231 g/mol decays at a rate of 1.00×10^{-5} atom/min. What are the half-life and identity of the nuclide (Table 23-1)?

$$N = 1.00 \times 10^{-6}\ \text{g} \times \frac{\text{mol}}{231\ \text{g}} \times \frac{6.023 \times 10^{23}\ \text{atoms}}{\text{mol}} = 2.61 \times 10^{14}\ \text{atoms}$$

Now we determine the decay constant and the half-life.

$$1.00 \times 10^{-5}\ \text{atom/min} = \lambda(2.61 \times 10^{14}\ \text{atoms}) \quad or \quad \lambda = 3.83 \times 10^{-20}/\text{min}$$

$$t_{1/2} = \frac{0.693}{3.83 \times 10^{-20}/\text{min}} = 1.81 \times 10^{19}\ \text{min}$$

$$t_{1/2} = 1.81 \times 10^{19}\ \text{min} \times \frac{\text{h}}{60\ \text{min}} \times \frac{\text{d}}{24\ \text{h}} \times \frac{\text{y}}{365\ \text{d}} = 3.44 \times 10^{3}\ \text{y}$$

This is quite close to the half-life of ^{231}Pa.

★ **8. Determine the ages of rocks from the measured ratio of a stable nuclide to a radioactive one and the ages of carbon-containing materials from the decay rate of ^{14}C.**

The age of a rock can be found from the relative amounts of the parent and the final stable product of one of the three decay series.

$$\log(N_t/N_0) = \log N_t - \log N_0 = -\lambda t/2.303 \qquad [8]$$

N_t is the number of atoms of parent nuclide present now and N_0 is the number of atoms of parent present when the rock was formed.

EXAMPLE 23-3 A rock has 18.05 g of ^{235}U for every 1.00 g of ^{207}Pb. Assume that all the ^{207}Pb was produced by the decay of ^{235}U and estimate the age of the rock.

The half-life of ^{235}U is 7.13×10^8 y, and thus

$$\lambda = \frac{0.693}{t_{1/2}} = \frac{0.693}{7.13 \times 10^8 \text{ y}} = 9.72 \times 10^{-10}/\text{y}$$

N_t is found from the mass of ^{235}U.

$$18.05 \text{ g } ^{235}\text{U} \times \frac{\text{mol } ^{235}\text{U}}{235 \text{ g}} \times \frac{6.023 \times 10^{23} \text{ atoms}}{\text{mol}} = 4.63 \times 10^{22} \text{ atoms of } ^{235}\text{U}$$

We also determine the number of ^{207}Pb atoms.

$$1.00 \text{ g } ^{207}\text{Pb} \times \frac{\text{mol } ^{207}\text{Pb}}{207 \text{ g}} \times \frac{6.023 \times 10^{23} \text{ atoms}}{\text{mol}} = 0.291 \times 10^{22} \text{ atoms of } ^{207}\text{Pb}$$

Each atom of ^{235}U produces an atom of ^{207}Pb (Figure 23-1). The overall equation is

$$^{235}_{92}\text{U} \rightarrow {}^{207}_{82}\text{Pb} + 7\,{}^{4}_{2}\text{He} + 4\,{}^{0}_{-1}\beta$$

$$\begin{aligned} \text{Thus,}\quad N_0 &= N_t + \text{number of } ^{207}\text{Pb atoms present now} \\ &= 4.63 \times 10^{22} + 0.291 \times 10^{22} \text{ atoms} \\ &= 4.92 \times 10^{22} \text{ atoms of } ^{235}\text{U} \end{aligned}$$

$$\log \frac{N_t}{N_0} = \log \frac{4.63 \times 10^{22}}{4.92 \times 10^{22}} = -0.0264$$

$$= -\frac{\lambda t}{2.303} = -\frac{(9.72 \times 10^{-10}/\text{y})t}{2.303} \qquad \textit{or} \qquad t = 6.25 \times 10^7 \text{ y}$$

Equation [8] also can be used when only the decay rate (λN) is known at two different times.

EXAMPLE 23-4 A sample of radioactive nuclide has a decay rate of 1.000×10^6 β emissions/min. 100 min later, the decay rate is 14.7% of the initial rate. What is the half-life of the nuclide? Use the data of Table 23-1 and Figure 23-1 to identify it.

$$\text{rate at 100 min} = (1.000 \times 10^6/\text{min})(0.147) = 0.147 \times 10^6/\text{min}$$

$$\log \frac{N_t}{N_0} = \log \frac{0.147 \times 10^6/\text{min}}{1.000 \times 10^6/\text{min}} = -0.833 = -\frac{\lambda(100 \text{ min})}{2.303} \qquad \textit{or} \qquad \lambda = 0.0192/\text{min}$$

$$t_{1/2} = \frac{0.693}{\lambda} = \frac{0.693}{0.0192/\text{min}} = 36.1 \text{ min}$$

^{211}Pb is the only nuclide in Table 23-1 which has a 36.1 min half-life, and ^{211}Pb is a β emitter (Figure 23-1).

★ **9. Calculate the energies associated with nuclear reactions.**

In spontaneous nuclear reactions, the products have less mass than the reactants. This mass difference appears as energy and is determined by equation [9].

$$E = mc^2 \qquad (c = 3.00 \times 10^8 \text{ m/s, the speed of light}) \qquad [9]$$

EXAMPLE 23-5 How much energy in MeV is produced by the alpha decay of each $^{235}_{92}U$ atom?

Reaction:	$^{235}_{92}U$	$\rightarrow$	$^{231}_{90}Th$	+	$^{4}_{2}He$
Nuclide masses:	235.0439		231.0363		4.0026

Mass difference = 235.0439 − (231.0363 + 4.0026) = 0.0050 amu

$$E = mc^2 = 0.0050 \text{ amu} \times \frac{1.660 \times 10^{-27} \text{ kg}}{\text{amu}} \times (3.00 \times 10^8 \text{ m/s})^2$$

$$= 7.47 \times 10^{-13} \text{ J} \times \frac{1 \text{ MeV}}{1.602 \times 10^{-13} \text{ J}} = 4.7 \text{ MeV}$$

Note that

6.023×10^{23} amu = 1.000 g *or* 1.660×10^{-24} g = 1.000 amu
96,500 C = 6.023×10^{23} electrons = 1.000 $\mathcal{F}$ *or* 1 electron = 1.602×10^{-19} C

Also, be sure that the masses of the electrons are taken into account. Although ^{235}U emits an alpha particle ($^{4}_{2}He^{2+}$), the calculation is performed as if it has emitted a helium-4 atom ($^{4}_{2}He^{0}$).

★ **10. Determine the average nuclear binding energy per nucleon for a nuclide.**

A nuclide always weighs less than the sum of the masses of its particles. For example, a ^{12}C atom has a mass of 12.00000 amu.

total particle mass = (6 × electron mass) + (6 × neutron mass) + (6 × proton mass)
= (6 × 0.000548 amu) + (6 × 1.008665 amu) + (6 × 1.007277 amu)
= 12.09894 amu

The mass defect is the difference between the total particle mass and the mass of the nuclide, and binding energy is the mass defect expressed in units of energy, J or MeV.

mass defect = 12.09894 amu − 12.00000 amu = 0.09894 amu

$$\text{binding energy} = 0.09894 \text{ amu} \times \frac{1.000 \times 10^{-3} \text{ kg}}{6.023 \times 10^{23} \text{ amu}} \times (3.00 \times 10^8 \text{ m/s})^2$$

$$= 1.478 \times 10^{-11} \text{ J} \times \frac{1 \text{ eV}}{1.602 \times 10^{-19} \text{ J}} \times \frac{\text{MeV}}{10^6 \text{ eV}} = 92.29 \text{ MeV}$$

Often binding energy is expressed as energy per nucleon.

$$\frac{\text{binding energy}}{\text{nucleon}} = \frac{92.29 \text{ MeV}}{12 \text{ nucleons}} = 7.690 \frac{\text{MeV}}{\text{nucleon}}$$

The higher the binding energy per nucleon is the more stable the nucleus is. Two light nuclei of low stability can fuse to produce a more stable heavy nucleus. Also, a heavy nucleus of low stability can break apart or fission to produce more stable light nuclei.

★ **11. Describe the factors which determine nuclear stability, tell whether a nuclide is likely to be stable or radioactive, and predict the type of decay process expected for a radioactive nuclide.**

Nuclei tend to be stable if they have a magic number of protons or neutrons, as given in Table 23-4. Nuclei also tend to be stable if they have an even number of neutrons and/or an even number of protons. All nuclei with $Z > 83$ are unstable.

The unstable nuclei decay by α, β, or β^+ emission, or electron capture. We can predict the type of decay: α decay if in the belt of stability with $Z > 83$, β decay if above and to the left of the belt of stability, and β^+ decay or electron capture if below and to the right of the belt of stability.

TABLE 23-4
Magic numbers of protons (Z) and neutrons (N)

Z	2	8	20	28	50	82	114		
N	2	8	20	28	50	82	126	184	196

12. Describe nuclear fission and nuclear fusion including the problems with using them as sources of energy.

Nuclear fission is the splitting apart of large nuclei into more stable smaller ones, often initiated by neutrons. The fission reaction of ^{235}U is not a simple process. Two possibilities are

$$^{235}_{92}U + ^{1}_{0}n \rightarrow ^{144}_{54}Xe + ^{90}_{38}Sr + 2\,^{1}_{0}n \qquad [10]$$

$$^{235}_{92}U + ^{1}_{0}n \rightarrow ^{140}_{56}Ba + ^{193}_{36}Kr + 3\,^{1}_{0}n \qquad [11]$$

These reactions also occur in the atomic bomb. About 3.20×10^{-11} J or 200 MeV is produced by each ^{235}U fission. Once started by a stray neutron, the reaction continues because more neutrons are produced than are consumed. The neutrons given off are moving too fast to split ^{235}U nuclei. They are slowed down by a graphite moderator in the reactor. The ^{1}H nuclei of the reactor's cooling water also serve as moderators. Boron control rods absorb neutrons to stop the reaction.

$$^{10}_{5}B + ^{1}_{0}n \rightarrow ^{7}_{3}Li + ^{4}_{2}He \qquad [12]$$

The ^{1}H nuclei of the cooling water also absorb neutrons. Because of this, ^{235}U fuel is enriched to 1–4% from a natural 0.7%.

If heavy water is used as cooling water, the fuel need not be enriched. $^{1}_{1}H$ nuclei absorb neutrons 600 times better than do the $^{2}_{1}H$ nuclei of heavy water. The CANDU reactor of Canada uses heavy water as a coolant. The savings are considerable; enriched fuel is about five times as expensive to produce as the fuel used by the CANDU reactor.

In breeder reactors, ^{239}Pu is produced from ^{238}U (natural abundance = 99.3%). See Table 23-3 for the reactions. Plutonium has the benefits of an abundant raw material, ^{238}U, and no need for moderation since fast neutrons are more efficient than slow ones. Two disadvantages are plutonium's toxicity and its use in nuclear weapons.

In a fusion reaction, light nuclei bind together to form heavier, more stable ones. The overall reaction in the sun is

$$4\,^{1}_{1}H \rightarrow ^{4}_{2}He + 2\,^{0}_{+1}e^- + 26.7 \text{ MeV} \qquad [13]$$

Two fusion reactions are being considered for commercial use.

$$^{6}_{3}Li + ^{2}_{1}H \rightarrow 2\,^{4}_{2}He + 22.4 \text{ MeV} \qquad [14]$$

$$5\,^{2}_{1}H \rightarrow ^{4}_{2}He + ^{3}_{2}He + ^{1}_{1}H + 2\,^{1}_{0}n + 24.9 \text{ MeV} \qquad [16]$$

Although the products of reactions [14] and [15] are nonradioactive, high gamma and neutron radiation cause the coolant and the reactor vessel to become radioactive.

All nuclear reactors have the advantage of producing large quantities of energy from small amounts of fuel. On the other hand, the reactors produce nuclear radiation while they are operating and leave the reactor radioactive.

13. Explain the effect of ionizing radiation on matter and describe several radiation-detection devices based on this effect.

When ionizing radiation passes through matter, it leaves a trail of ions in its path. It does this by knocking electrons off the atoms and molecules which it encounters. In the cloud chamber and the bubble chamber, the ions promote the formation of droplets of liquid and of vapor, respectively. In a Geiger–Müller counter ions create a pathway for an electric spark.

Because of their lack of charge, neutrons penetrate as well as gamma rays. They damage matter by combining with stable nuclei to produce new ones which often are radioactive, a process known as transmutation.

14. Know the units used to measure radiation dosages, discuss some of the biological hazards of ionizing radiation, and list sources of radiation to which the general public is exposed.

The units of radiation dosage are in *Table 23-5 in the text.* Rem abbreviates "radiation equivalent–man" and depends on the amount of biological damage. Radiation can kill directly and quickly by ionizing molecules to stop an organism from functioning. Radiation can disrupt individual cells, causing some of them to reproduce without limit. Cancer is one result of such uncontrolled growth. Radiation can change genetic material, causing mutations in the offspring. Radiation also can destroy only part of an organism as a serious burn from chemicals or fire will destroy tissue.

There are many sources of radiation in the environment. Natural sources are discussed in objective 23–3. They produce an annual background of 130 mrem annually per person. X rays for dentistry and medicine also are a source of radiation, as are nuclear power plants.

15. Discuss some of the practical, beneficial uses of radioisotopes.

Radioisotopes are widely used in medicine to deliver radiation to the cancer cells to be destroyed without irradiating many normal cells. This is done by injecting the radioisotope or by using natural body processes. (Iodine will concentrate in the thyroid gland.) Radioisotopes are used as tracers, to detect the fate of certain substances during plant and animal growth, and in industrial processes and chemical reactions. Certain radioisotopes concentrate in specific organs of the body. The organ then can be readily seen by a radiation-detecting camera, allowing us to see abnormalities. Radiosotopes also are used industrially in quality control, as in the production of aluminum foil or plastic film. The isotope is placed below the moving sheet and a detector above. The radiation reaching the detector depends on the thickness of the aluminum or plastic.

TABLE 23-5
Decay modes, half-lives, and isotope masses of some nuclides

			Isotope mass, amu	
Nuclide	Decay mode	Half-life	Parent	Daughter
^{3}H	β^-	12.26 y	3.016050	3.016030
^{6}He	β^-	0.81 s	6.018893	6.015125
^{7}Be	EC	53.37 d	7.016929	7.016004
^{8}Be	α	2×10^{-16} s	8.0053	4.002603
^{12}B	β^-	0.02 s	12.0143	8.022487
^{13}N	β^+	9.96 m	13.005738	13.003354
^{37}Ar	EC	35 d	36.966772	36.965898
^{61}Co	β^-	1.65 h	60.932440	60.931056
^{90}Sr	β^-	28 y	89.907747	89.907163
^{98}Tc	β^-	1.5×10^{6} y	97.907110	97.905289
^{109}In	β^+	4.3 h	108.907096	108.904928
^{161}Tm	EC	30 m	160.933730	160.929950
^{194}Au	β^+	39.5 h	193.965418	193.962725

DRILL PROBLEMS

2. (1) Complete each of the following equations.

A. $^{210}Pb \rightarrow$ ______ $+ \, ^{210}Bi$
B. $^{8}Be \rightarrow \, ^{4}He +$ ______
C. $^{205}Pb +$ ______ $\rightarrow \, ^{205}Tl$
D. $^{227}Pa \rightarrow$ ______ $+ \, ^{223}Ac$
E. ______ $\rightarrow \, ^{4}He + \, ^{228}Th$
F. $^{194}Hg +$ ______ $\rightarrow \, ^{194}Au$
G. ______ $\rightarrow \, ^{0}_{-1}e + \, ^{200}Hg$
H. $^{6}He \rightarrow \, ^{0}_{-1}e +$ ______
I. $^{191}Os \rightarrow$ ______ $+ \, ^{191}Ir$
J. ______ $\rightarrow \, ^{0}_{+1}e + \, ^{17}O$
K. $^{199}Pb \rightarrow$ ______ $+ \, ^{199}Tl$
L. ______ $+ \, ^{0}_{-1}e \rightarrow \, ^{37}Cl$
M. $^{210}Pb \rightarrow \, ^{4}He +$ ______
N. $^{191}Hg \rightarrow \, ^{0}_{+1}e +$ ______
O. ______ $\rightarrow \, ^{4}He + \, ^{218}Po$

(2) Write a nuclear equation for the reaction which occurs when each nuclide below decays in the manner indicated.
A. ^{7}Be (EC) B. ^{191}Hg (β^+) C. ^{177}Pt (α) D. ^{3}H (β^-) E. ^{177}W (EC)
F. ^{109}In (β^+) G. ^{186}Re (β^-) H. ^{235}U (α) I. ^{12}B (α) J. ^{161}Tm (EC)
K. ^{98}Tc (β^-)

4. (1) Write full and shorthand equations for each of the following reactions.
A. $^{59}Co(p, n)$_______ B. ^{9}Be (^{6}Li,_______)^{14}N C. $^{14}N(n,$ _______$)^{9}Be$
D. _______$(p, \alpha)^{12}C$ E. _______$(p, d)^{4}He$ F. _______$(d, \alpha)^{21}Ne$
G. $^{7}Li(\alpha,$ _______$)^{10}B$ H. $^{9}Be(\alpha, n)$_______ I. $^{35}Cl(n, p)$_______
J. _______$(p, n)^{44}Sc$ K. $^{27}Al(d, \alpha)$_______ L. _______$(\alpha, p)^{28}Al$
(2) Expand each of the abbreviated equations given in Table 23-3.
A. neptunium discovery B. neptunium in reactors C. plutonium discovery
D. americium E. curium discovery F. curium in reactors
G. berkelium H. californium I. mendelevium
J. nobelium K. lawrencium

7. (1) Find $t_{1/2}$ and λ of each nuclide and the activity of the given mass. Use the data of Tables 23-1 and 23-5 as needed.
A. ^{223}Fr, 1.00 μg B. ^{61}Co, 4.00 pg C. ^{98}Tc, 7.00 g
D. ^{3}H, 1.31 mg E. ^{194}Au, 1.00 g F. ^{228}Ra, 1.32 g
(2) Find $t_{1/2}$ and λ of each nuclide and the mass needed to produce the given activity.
A. ^{6}He, 3.3×10^{15}/s B. ^{7}Be, 5.1×10^{15}/d C. ^{194}Au, 19.4×10^{16}/s
D. ^{3}H, 187×10^{20}/m E. ^{90}Sr, 8.46×10^{13}/m F. ^{212}Bi, 34.5×10^{15}/s
(3) Find $t_{1/2}$ and λ of each nuclide based on mass number, mass, and activity.
A. $A = 214$, 45.3 μg, 3.3×10^{15}/s B. $A = 109$, 7.56 pg, 1.87×10^{9}/s
C. $A = 212$, 0.165 g, 8.46×10^{15}/s D. $A = 37$, 4.20 μg, 9.41×10^{11}/m
E. $A = 215$, 25.2 g, 1.02×10^{20}/s F. $A = 210$, 37.2 μg, 145×10^{10}/m

8. (1) Given the initial decay rate, the elapsed time, and the final decay rate (in that order), determine the half-life of each nuclide.
A. 1.43×10^{8}/s, 20.4 d, 6.73×10^{7}/s B. 1.94×10^{7}/m, 12.1 h, 8.43×10^{5}/m
C. 7.93×10^{12}/s, 1.41 m, 5.73×10^{11}/s D. 3.14×10^{5}/s, 8.75 m, 1.72×10^{5}/s
E. 1.77×10^{12}/m, 7.63 d, 1.82×10^{11}/m F. 9.32×10^{6}/s, 1.32 d, 4.14×10^{5}/s
G. 4.17×10^{10}/m, 4.00 d, 1.00×10^{10}/m H. 8.00×10^{12}/s, 10.0 d, 9.00×10^{10}/s
(2) In each part below, the weight ratio of two isotopes (radioactive/stable) in a sample is followed by the half-life of the first isotope. A_1 is the mass number of the radioactive nuclide, and A_2 is the mass number of the stable isotope. Assume none of the stable isotope was present when the sample formed and determine the age of the sample.
A. $A_1 = 231, A_2 = 227$, 8.00/0.625, 3.4×10^{4} y B. $A_1 = 209, A_2 = 205$, 6.50/1.25, 103 y
C. $A_1 = 233, A_2 = 209$, 0.265/1.00, 1.6×10^{5} y D. $A_1 = 210, A_2 = 210$, 1.13/0.132, 19.4 y
E. $A_1 = 41, A_2 = 41$, 7.30/1.00, 8.0×10^{4} y F. $A_1 = 14, A_2 = 14$, 1.26/5.00, 5700 y
(3) In each part below, the initial rate of decay of a sample is followed by the rate of decay at some later time and the half-life of the nuclide which is decaying. Determine the age of each sample.
A. 3.12×10^{4}/s, 164/s, 7.20 y B. 6.64×10^{9}/m, 7.30×10^{5}/m, 5.70×10^{3} y
C. 1.72×10^{5} d, 4.44×10^{4}/d, 8.00×10^{4} y D. 8.52×10^{6}/h, 1.66×10^{4}/h, 5.27 y
E. 1.96×10^{4}/h, 127/d, 16.0 y F. 8.95×10^{6}/h, 47.5/s, 2.60 y

9. Use the data of Tables 23-2 and 23-5 to determine the energy associated with the decay of each of the following nuclides. Determine each energy both in MeV/atom and in kJ/mol.
A. ^{3}H B. ^{6}He C. ^{7}Be D. ^{8}Be E. ^{12}B
F. ^{13}N G. ^{37}Ar H. ^{61}Co I. ^{90}Sr J. ^{98}Tc
K. ^{109}In L. ^{161}Tm M. ^{194}Au

10. The isotope mass in amu of the most abundant stable nuclide of an element is given in each part below. Compute the average nuclear binding energy per nucleon for each nuclide in MeV. Then plot the energies you compute against atomic number.

A. ^{1}H, 1.007825
B. ^{56}Fe, 55.934936
C. ^{4}He, 4.002603
D. ^{58}Ni, 57.935342
E. ^{9}Be, 9.012186
F. ^{64}Zn, 63.929146
G. ^{12}C, 12.000000
H. ^{80}Se, 79.916527
I. ^{16}O, 15.994915
J. ^{84}Kr, 83.911503
K. ^{20}Ne, 19.992440
L. ^{90}Zr, 89.904700
M. ^{24}Mg, 23.985042
N. ^{102}Ru, 101.904348
O. ^{28}Si, 27.976928
P. ^{114}Cd, 113.903360
Q. ^{32}S, 31.972074
R. ^{130}Te, 129.906238
S. ^{40}Ar, 39.962384
T. ^{138}Ba, 137.905000
U. ^{40}Ca, 39.962589
V. ^{142}Nd, 141.907663
W. ^{48}Ti, 47.947960
X. ^{158}Gd, 157.924178
Y. ^{52}Cr, 51.940513
Z. ^{166}Er, 165.932060

11. Predict whether each of the following nuclides is likely to be stable or radioactive. If radioactive, predict the type of decay process which will occur.

A. ^{8}B
B. ^{234}U
C. ^{19}F
D. ^{119}Cd
E. ^{50}Sc
F. ^{212}Po
G. ^{88}Sr
H. ^{17}F
I. ^{226}Ra
J. ^{50}Mn
K. ^{106}In
L. ^{197}Au
M. ^{63}Co

QUIZZES (20 minutes each)

Choose the best answer for each question.

Quiz A

1. The alpha decay of ^{226}Ra produces (a) ^{3}He; (b) ^{4}Li; (c) ^{224}Rn; (d) ^{224}Po; (e) none of these.
2. Which of the following could be a member of the thorium series which begins with ^{232}Th? (a) ^{223}Fr; (b) ^{216}Po; (c) ^{221}Rn; (d) ^{214}Pb; (e) none of these.
3. Neutron bombardment of ^{23}Na produces an isotope which is a beta emitter. After beta emission, the final product is (a) ^{24}Na; (b) ^{24}Mg; (c) ^{23}Ar; (d) ^{24}Ar; (e) none of these.
4. A nuclide has a decay rate of 2.00×10^{10}/s. 25.0 days later its decay rate is 6.25×10^{8}/s. What is the nuclide's half-life? (a) 25.0 d. (b) 12.5 d. (c) 50.0 d; (d) 5.00 d; (e) none of these.
5. A nuclide has a half-life of 35.0 h. What is the value of its decay constant? (a) 0.0285; (b) 0.0198; (c) 24.3; (d) 0.0412. (e) none of these.
6. The binding energy per nucleon is largest for (a) ^{3}He; (b) ^{59}Co; (c) ^{235}U; (d) ^{98}Tc; (e) ^{31}P.
7. The most massive particle is (a) alpha; (b) beta; (c) gamma; (d) positron; (e) neutron.
8. Based on magic numbers, which nuclide is the most stable? (a) ^{3}He; (b) ^{16}O; (c) ^{15}N; (d) ^{119}Sn; (e) ^{206}Pb.

Quiz B

1. The electron capture of ^{41}Ca produces (a) ^{41}K; (b) ^{40}Ca; (c) ^{42}Ca; (d) ^{41}Sc; (e) none of these.
2. Which could be a member of the actinium series which begins with ^{235}U? (a) ^{223}Ra; (b) ^{221}Ra; (c) ^{214}Bi; (d) ^{216}Po; (e) none of these.
3. Proton bombardment of ^{230}Th followed by emission of two alpha particles produces (a) ^{222}Rn; (b) ^{223}Fr; (c) ^{223}Ra; (d) ^{222}Fr; (e) none of these.
4. A nuclide has a half-life of 1.91 y. Its decay constant has a numerical value of (a) 1.32; (b) 2.76; (c) 0.363. (d) 0.524. (e) none of these.
5. The activity of a radioactive sample declines to 1.00% of its original value in 300 days. What is the half-life of the nuclide in the sample? (a) 3.35×10^{-5} d; (b) 0.0154 d; (c) 0.00667 d; (d) 3.00 d; (e) none of these.
6. The binding energy per nucleon is smallest for (a) ^{13}C; (b) ^{3}He; (c) ^{52}Cr; (d) ^{56}Fe; (e) none of these.
7. The most highly charged particle of the following is (a) alpha; (b) beta; (c) gamma; (d) positron; (e) neutron.
8. Based on magic numbers, which nuclide is the least stable? (a) ^{96}Nb; (b) ^{119}Sn; (c) ^{40}K; (d) ^{15}O; (e) ^{40}Ca.

Quiz C

1. The beta decay of ^{90}Sr produces (a) ^{90}Sr; (b) ^{91}Sr; (c) ^{89}Sr; (d) ^{89}Rb; (e) none of these.
2. Which could be a member of the uranium series which begins with ^{238}U? (a) ^{215}Po; (b) ^{213}Po; (c) ^{210}Po; (d) $^{212}Po^-$ (e) none of these.
3. Alpha particle bombardment of ^{27}Al followed by neutron emission produces (a) ^{30}P; (b) ^{30}Si; (c) ^{31}Si; (d) ^{29}P; (e) none of these.
4. A nuclide's activity decreases 75% in 4.00 days. Its half-life is (a) 2.00 d; (b) 1.00 d; (c) 4.00 d; (d) 0.347 d; (e) none of these.
5. A nuclide is a beta emitter with a 28 y half-life. The ratio of its mass to the mass of its stable product in a sample is 1.00/8.25. If none of the stable product was present initially, what is the age of the sample? (a) 89.9 y; (b) 85.3 y; (c) 231 y; (d) 259 y; (e) none of these.
6. The binding energy per nucleon is largest for isotopes of (a) U; (b) Co; (c) Cs; (d) He; (e) Hg.
7. The most ionizing radiation is of what type? (a) alpha; (b) beta; (c) gamma; (d) positron; (e) neutron.
8. Based on magic numbers, which nuclide is the most stable? (a) ^{91}Nb; (b) ^{91}Zr; (c) ^{58}Co; (d) ^{13}C; (e) ^{20}Ne.

Quiz D

1. The beta decay of ^{45}Ca produces (a) ^{45}K; (b) ^{45}Sc; (c) ^{44}K; (d) ^{44}Ca; (e) none of these.
2. Which could be a member of the uranium series which begins with ^{238}U? (a) ^{236}U; (b) ^{217}At; (c) ^{216}Po; (d) ^{219}At; (e) none of these.
3. Deuteron (^2_1H) bombardment of ^{96}Mo followed by neutron emission produces (a) ^{98}Tc; (b) ^{97}Tc; (c) ^{97}Nb; (d) ^{98}Mo; (e) none of these.
4. A nuclide has a decay constant of 4.28×10^{-4}/h. If the activity of a sample is 3.14×10^5/s, how many atoms of the nuclide are present in the sample? (a) 2.64×10^{12}; (b) 7.34×10^8; (c) 2.04×10^6; (d) 4.40×10^{10}; (e) none of these.
5. The activity of a nuclide declines to 10% of its original value in 145 d. What is the decay constant of the nuclide? (a) 0.0159/d; (b) 63.0/d; (c) 0.00690/d; (d) .00478/d; (e) none of these.
6. The binding energy per nucleon is smallest for isotopes of (a) Li; (b) Co; (c) Ge; (d) Sc; (e) S.
7. The least penetrating radiation is of what type? (a) alpha; (b) beta; (c) gamma. (d) positron; (e) neutron.
8. Based on magic numbers, which nuclide is the least stable? (a) ^{59}Ni; (b) ^{51}V; (c) ^{122}Sb; (d) ^{16}O; (e) ^{12}C.

SAMPLE TEST (30 minutes)

1. If there were no nuclear explosions, would the ratio of ^{12}C to ^{14}C in living material increase, decrease, or remain the same? Briefly explain why.
2. An atom of ^{253}Es decays to one of ^{237}Np. What kinds of particles are given off during this process, and how many of each are given off?
3. Write or complete, as appropriate, and balance each of the following nuclear equations.
   a. alpha emission by ^{243}Cm
   b. positron emission by ^{18}F
   c. electron capture by ^{88}Zr
   d. $^{10}B(\alpha, n)$
   e. $^{45}Sc(\alpha, p)$
   F. ______ $+ {}^2H \rightarrow 2\,{}^1n + {}^{51}Cr$
4. ^{11}Be decays via the reaction $^{11}Be \rightarrow {}^{0}_{-1}e + {}^{11}B + \gamma$. What is the maximum energy of the gamma ray produced if atomic masses are $^{11}B = 11.00931$ amu, $^{11}Be = 11.0216$ amu, ${}^{0}_{-1}e = 0.00055$ amu (1.00 amu = 932.8 MeV)?
5. How many ^{238}U atoms would decay in a mole of ^{238}U during 995 million years? The half-life of ^{238}U is 4.51×10^9 y.

Organic Chemistry

REVIEW OF OBJECTIVES

1. Give examples of alkane, alkene, alkyne, and aromatic hydrocarbon.

Hydrocarbons contain only carbon and hydrogen. Alkanes have only single bonds; alkenes have at least one double bond, and alkynes have at least one triple bond. Aromatic hydrocarbons have a benzene ring.

★ **2. Draw structural formulas and condensed formulas for hydrocarbon molecules given systematic (IUPAC) names.**

★ **3. Name hydrocarbon molecules, given structural or condensed formulas.**

TABLE 24-1
The first ten alkanes

Chain length	Formula	Name
1	CH_4	methane
2	CH_3CH_3	ethane
3	$CH_3CH_2CH_3$	propane
4	$CH_3(CH_2)_2CH_3$	butane
5	$CH_3(CH_2)_3CH_3$	pentane
6	$CH_3(CH_2)_4CH_3$	hexane
7	$CH_3(CH_2)_5CH_3$	heptane
8	$CH_3(CH_2)_6CH_3$	octane
9	$CH_3(CH_2)_7CH_3$	nonane
10	$CH_3(CH_2)_8CH_3$	decane

For *noncyclic hydrocarbons* the IUPAC rules are

1. The longest hydrocarbon chain determines the base name (see Table 24-1).
2. The longest chain must contain any double or triple bond.
3. The base name ends in -ane if no multiple bonds are present, -ene for a double bond, and -yne for a triple bond.
4. The multiple bond's position is shown by a number which precedes the base name and is separated from it by a hyphen. This number must be as small as possible. There are always two ways to number the longest carbon chain depending on where you start.
5. *Alkyl groups* (side chains or branches) are named by changing their alkane names from -ane to -yl. Their positions on the chain are indicated by the number of the carbon to which they are attached.

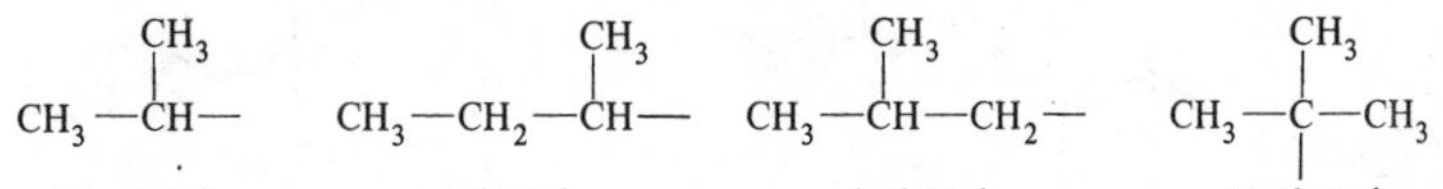

CH$_3$—CH(CH$_3$)— isopropyl; CH$_3$—CH$_2$—CH(CH$_3$)— *sec*-butyl; CH$_3$—CH(CH$_3$)—CH$_2$— isobutyl; CH$_3$—C(CH$_3$)(—)—CH$_3$ *tert*-butyl

FIGURE 24-1 Names and structures of some alkyl groups.

This number is separated from the alkyl group name by a hyphen. The alkyl group numbers must be as small as possible.

6. There must be a number prefix for *each* side chain even if the same number is repeated. The number of alkyl groups of one type is given as a prefix (di-, tri-, tetra-, penta-, hexa-, hepta-, and so on) to the alkyl group name.
7. The side chains are named in alphabetical order.
8. Numbers are separated from each other by commas and from letters by hyphens. There are no spaces in a name.

For *cyclic hydrocarbons* the rules are

9. The number of carbons in the ring determines the base name, which always begins with cyclo- for nonaromatic hydrocarbons.
10. A double or triple bond in the ring is assumed to be between carbons 1 and 2. Numbering proceeds around the ring so that the side chains have the lowest numbers possible.
11. Cyclic hydrocarbon names follow rules 5, 6, 7, and 8.

Aromatic hydrocarbons are named as benzene derivatives.

12. The side-chain positions are designated by numbers which are as small as possible. The largest side chain is on carbon 1.
13. For two groups on the ring, the position of the second group can be named. Positions 2 and 6 are ortho (*o*-), 3 and 5 are meta (*m*-), and 4 is para (*p*-).
14. If aromatic hydrocarbons are named as derivatives of toluene, the methyl group is on carbon 1.
15. Aromatic hydrocarbon names follow rules 5, 6, 7, and 8.

★ **4. Determine all the possible skeletal isomers of a hydrocarbon of a given formula.**

An abbreviated way of drawing hydrocarbon molecules is to draw only the bonds. All bonds are shown except those to hydrogen atoms.

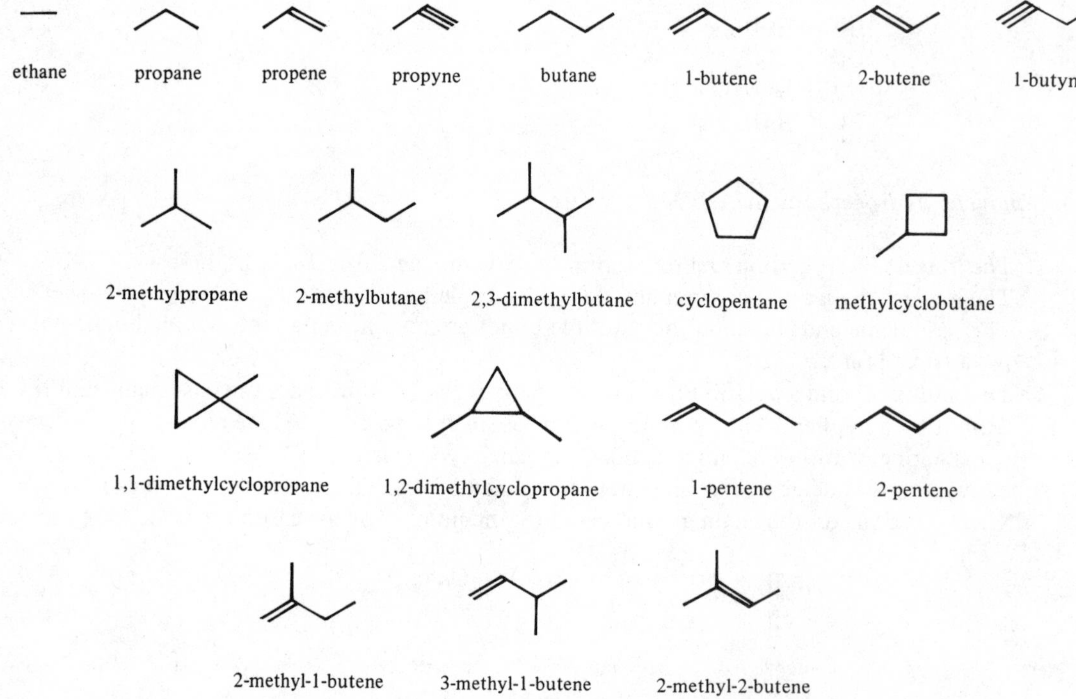

FIGURE 24-2 Abbreviated skeletons of some hydrocarbons.

TABLE 24-2
Physical properties of hydrocarbons

Effect of molecular weight–straight-chain alkanes

Name	Formula	MW, g/mol	m.p., °C	b.p., °C	$\Delta\bar{H}_{fus}$, kJ/mol	$\Delta\bar{H}_{vap}$, kJ/mol
methane	CH_4	16.04	−182.5	−164	0.937	8.908
ehtane	C_2H_6	30.1	−183.3	− 88.6	2.862	15.648
propane	C_3H_8	44.1	−181.7	− 42.1	3.527	20.133
butane	C_4H_{10}	58.1	−138.3	− 0.5	4.661	24.271
pentane	C_5H_{12}	72.2	−129.7	36.1	8.427	27.593
hexane	C_6H_{14}	86.2	− 95.3	69.0	13.079	31.911
heptane	C_7H_{16}	100.2	− 90.6	98.4	14.163	35.187
octane	C_8H_{18}	114.23	− 56.8	125.7	20.652	38.581

Effect of branching–heptanes

Name	Structure	m.p., °C	b.p., °C	$\Delta\bar{H}_{fus}$, kJ/mol	$\Delta\bar{H}_{vap}$, kJ/mol
n-heptane		− 90.6	98.4	14.163	35.187
2-methylhexane	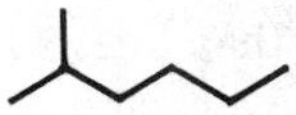	−118.2	90.0	8.870	35.727
2,2-dimethylpentane	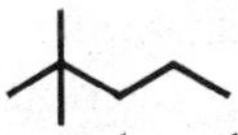	−123.8	79.2	5.862	33.920
2,4-dimethylpentane		−119.9	89.8	6.686	34.171
3,3-dimethylpentane	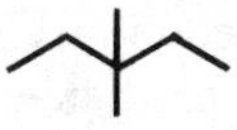	−134.9	80.5	7.067	34.079
3-ethylpentane	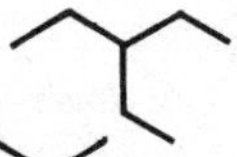	−118.6	93.5	9.552	36.162
2,2,3-trimethylbutane	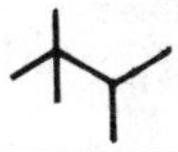	− 25.0	80.9	2.201	32.497

Effect of π bonding

Name	Structure	MW, g/mol	m.p., °C	b.p., °C	$\Delta\bar{H}_{fus}$, kJ/mol	$\Delta\bar{H}_{vap}$, kJ/mol
n-pentane		72.2	−129.7	36.1	8.427	27.593
1-pentene		70.4	−166.2	30.0	5.837	28.999
2-pentene		70.4	−140.2	36.4	8.389	n.a.[a]
1,3-pentadiene		68.1	−148.8	42.0	6.142	30.598
cyclohexane	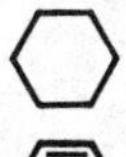	84.16	6.6	80.7	2.632	32.765
cyclohexene	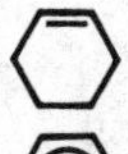	82.15	−103.5	82.9	3.293	n.a.[a]
benzene		78.12	5.53	80.1	9.954	42.903

[a]n.a. indicates data are not available.

EXAMPLE 24-1 Use this abbreviated notation to draw and name all of the isomers with formula C_5H_{10}.

These isomers are the last nine in Figure 24-2

5. Describe the conformations of molecules, specifically the eclipsed and staggered forms of ethane and the boat and chair forms of cyclohexane.

Two conformations of a molecule differ only in rotations of bonds within the molecule. You can see different conformations by building a model of the molecule and rotating the groups around each C—single bond. The Newman projections of the conformations of ethane are shown in *Figure 24-3 in the text.* In a Newman projection you are looking at a carbon–carbon bond head on.

Stable conformations have atoms as far apart as possible. In the boat and chair conformations of cyclohexane (*Figure 24-4 in the text*), the hydrogen atoms are eclipsed on the sides of the boat and those on the "bow" and "stern" are very close to each other. It is not necessary to break any bonds in going from boat to chair. One merely rotates about the single bonds, as you can prove with a model. You should also know the difference between equatorial positions and axial positions. Because there is more room available (more freedom) at equatoria positions, this is where large groups such as *t*-butyl (—$C(CH_3)_3$) tend to be.

★ **6. Discuss the physical properties of aliphatic and aromatic hydrocarbons in relation to their bonding, structures, and molecular weights.**

Within a series of hydrocarbons, such as the alkanes, boiling point increases with molecular weight. London forces between larger molecules are stronger, and it is more difficult to disrupt the intermolecular attractions. The melting points and the molar heats of fusion and of vaporization increase with mole weight for the same reason. A branched molecule boils at a lower temperature than does a straight-chain one with the same number of carbons. The branched molecule has less surface area and hence less area over which intermolecular forces can act. The melting points and the molar heats of fusion and vaporization also decrease as branching increases. Finally we notice that the number of π electrons in a molecule increases the intermolecular forces. For molecules with the same number of carbons those with more π electrons have larger molar heats of fusion and vaporization, although there is no clear trend in melting and boiling points. Data illustrating these predictions are given in Table 24-2. Predictions based on molecular weight are the best ones. Boiling points and molar heats of vaporization are predicted better than are melting points and molar heats of fusion.

★ **7. Identify compounds in which *cis-trans* isomerism occurs.**

Cis-trans isomers have two structural features.

1. A carbon–carbon bond is not free to rotate.
2. If either carbon of the bond has two identical groups bound to it, *cis-trans* isomers *cannot* exist.

If a compound has either a double bond or a ring, you should consider *cis-trans* isomerism. You then should look for two different groups bound to each carbon atom. In 2-butene, the double bond creates *cis-trans* isomerism (Figure 24-3). However, in propene there cannot be *cis-trans* isomerism because one of

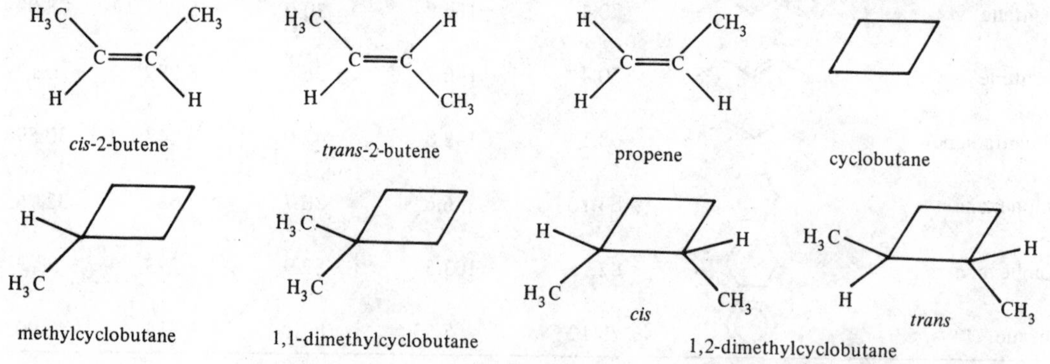

H_3C CH_3 C=C H H
cis-2-butene

H_3C H C=C H CH_3
trans-2-butene

H CH_3 C=C H H
propene

cyclobutane

H H_3C
methylcyclobutane

H_3C H_3C
1,1-dimethylcyclobutane

H H_3C H CH_3
cis

H_3C H H CH_3
trans

1,2-dimethylcyclobutane

FIGURE 24-3 Geometric isomerism in butene, propene, and derivatives of cyclobutane.

the two carbons has two identical groups attached. Likewise, cyclobutane, methylcyclobutane, and 1,1-dimethylcyclobutane do not display *cis-trans* isomerism. However, 1,2-dimethylcyclobutane does display *cis-trans* isomerism. *Cis-trans* isomers are also called geometric isomers or stereoisomers.

★ **8. Write equations for several reactions used to prepare alkanes, alkenes, and alkynes.**

These equations are summarized below and should be memorized. R represents any alkyl group.

(a) Hydrogenation of multiple bonds.

$$\gt C{=}C\lt + H_2 \xrightarrow[\text{heat/pressure}]{\text{Pt or Pd}} -\overset{H}{\underset{|}{\overset{|}{C}}}-\overset{H}{\underset{|}{\overset{|}{C}}}- \qquad [1]$$

$$-C{\equiv}C- + 2\,H_2 \xrightarrow[\text{heat/pressure}]{\text{Pt or Pd}} -\underset{H}{\overset{H}{C}}-\underset{H}{\overset{H}{C}}- \qquad [2]$$

(b) Wurtz reaction: chain length is doubled.

$$R{-}Br + 2\,Na \rightarrow 2\,NaBr + R{-}R \qquad [3]$$

(c) Alkali carboxylates fused with alkali hydroxides.

$$R{-}\overset{O}{\overset{\|}{C}}{-}ONa + NaOH \xrightarrow{\text{heat}} Na_2CO_3 + R{-}H \qquad [4]$$

(d) Dehydration of an alcohol.

$$-\underset{H}{\overset{|}{C}}-\underset{OH}{\overset{|}{C}}- \xrightarrow[\text{heat}]{H_2SO_4} \gt C{=}C\lt + H_2O \qquad [5]$$

(e) Dehydrohalogenation of an alkyl halide.

$$-\underset{H}{\overset{|}{C}}-\underset{Cl}{\overset{|}{C}}- \xrightarrow[\text{alcohol (solvent)}]{\text{KOH in}} \gt C{=}C\lt + KCl + H_2O \qquad [6]$$

(f) Extension of alkyne chain length using sodium amide.

$$H{-}C{\equiv}C{-}H + NaNH_2 \rightarrow NH_3 + H{-}C{\equiv}C^-\ Na^+$$
$$H{-}C{\equiv}C{-}Na^+ + R{-}CH_2Br \rightarrow H{-}C{\equiv}C{-}CH_2R + NaBr \qquad [7]$$

(g) Double dehydrohalogenation of an alkyl dihalide.

$$-\underset{Cl}{\overset{H}{C}}-\underset{Cl}{\overset{H}{C}}- \xrightarrow[\text{alcohol (solvent)}]{\text{KOH in}} -\overset{H}{C}{=}\overset{Cl}{C}- \xrightarrow[\text{alcohol (solvent)}]{\text{KOH in}} -C{\equiv}C- \qquad [8]$$

9. Explain why alkanes and aromatic hydrocarbons react by substitution and alkenes and alkynes react by addition.

For alkanes, substitution is the only possible type of reaction, as carbon is capable of forming only four bonds. For alkenes and alkynes, addition reactions produce more energy than do substitution reactions. Consider hydrogenation of a double bond.

$$>C{=}C< \;+ H{-}H \rightarrow -\overset{H}{\underset{|}{\overset{|}{C}}}-\overset{H}{\underset{|}{\overset{|}{C}}}- \qquad [9]$$

The net result is that a C=C bond (611 kJ/mol) and a H—H bond (435 kJ/mol) are broken and a C—C bond (347 kJ/mol) and two C—H bonds (414 kJ/mol) are formed. Thus, the enthalpy change for hydrogenation of a double bond is −127 kJ/mol.

Aromatic hydrocarbons are considerably more stable than we might expect based on the number of single and double bonds present (see objectives 10–11 and 10–11a). This extra stability is the resonance stabilization energy. If an aromatic hydrocarbon participates in an addition reaction, the resonance stabilization energy is lost.

10. Write equations for the reactions of alkanes with halogens and with oxygen, emphasizing the radical chain nature of the alkane-halogen reaction.

When an alkane reacts with a halogen (F_2, Cl_2, Br_2, or I_2, symbolized as X_2), halogen atoms substitute for some of the hydrogens, producing the halogenated hydrocarbon and HX. The reaction proceeds by a free-radical chain mechanism consisting of initiation, propagation, and termination steps. A free radical is one of the species produced when a bond breaks and the two electrons in the bond are split between the two fragments, one going with each. This is homolytic cleavage of the bond. Free-radical halogenation of an alkane follows these steps.

Initiation: $X{-}X \xrightarrow[\text{light}]{\text{heat or}} 2\,X\cdot$ [10]

Propagation: $R{-}H + X\cdot \rightarrow R\cdot + H{-}X$ [11]

$R\cdot + X{-}X \rightarrow R{-}X + X\cdot$

Termination: $X\cdot + \cdot X \rightarrow X{-}X$ *and* $R\cdot + \cdot X \rightarrow R{-}X$ *and* $R\cdot + \cdot R \rightarrow R{-}R$ [12]

The relative strengths of the R—X and H—X bonds compared to R—H and X—X determine the energy and speed of the reaction. In general, reactions of F_2 are faster and more energetic than those of Cl_2, Br_2, or I_2. Any number of hydrogens may be substituted producing a mixture of products. All hydrocarbons react with oxygen to produce carbon dioxide and water.

★ **11. Use Markovnikov's rule to predict the products of an addition reaction at a multiple bond.**

Markovnikov's rule states that the more positive fragment (usually a hydrogen atom) of an unsymmetrical addition reagent attaches to the carbon atom of the multiple bond which has the largest number of hydrogen atoms. For alkynes with the triple bond at the end of the molecule, the last carbon has the most hydrogen atoms (one). For alkenes, there are three possibilities. They are shown in Figure 24-4. The carbon to which the positive fragment would add is shown by an arrow. R is some group other than hydrogen.

$$R{-}C{\equiv}\underset{\uparrow}{C}{-}H \qquad R{-}\overset{H}{\overset{|}{C}}{=}\underset{\uparrow}{\overset{H}{\overset{|}{C}}}{-}H \qquad R{-}\overset{R}{\overset{|}{C}}{=}\underset{\uparrow}{\overset{H}{\overset{|}{C}}}{-}H \qquad R{-}\overset{R}{\overset{|}{C}}{=}\underset{\uparrow}{\overset{R}{\overset{|}{C}}}{-}H$$

FIGURE 24-4 Markonikov addition sites for positive fragments.

12. Describe the free-radical polymerization of an alkene, as in the preparation of polyethylene from ethylene.

This reaction consists of initiation, propagation, and termination steps. There are two differences from alkane halogenation. First, there is very little initiator present. In halogenation, there are about equal amounts of halogen and alkane, while here the reaction mixture is principally alkene. Second, propagation consists of one reaction not two. The propagating free radical is an ever-lengthening molecule. Organic peroxides form free radicals easily.

Initiation: $RO{-}OR \rightarrow 2\,RO\cdot$ [13]

Propagation depends on the alkene monomer.

Polyethylene initiation and propagation (ethylene, $CH_2{=}CH_2$, monomer.)

$$RO\cdot + CH_2{=}CH_2 \rightarrow ROCH_2CH_2\cdot$$
$$ROCH_2CH_2\cdot + CH_2{=}CH_2 \rightarrow RO(CH_2)_3CH_2\cdot \qquad [14]$$
$$RO(CH_2)_3CH_2\cdot + CH_2{=}CH_2 \rightarrow RO(CH_2)_5CH_2\cdot$$
and so forth

Polyvinyl chloride initiation and propagation (vinyl chloride, $CH_2{=}CHCl$, monomer)

$$RO\cdot + CH_2{=}CHCl \rightarrow ROCH_2CHCl\cdot$$
$$ROCH_2CHCl\cdot + CH_2{=}CHCl \rightarrow ROCH_2CHClCH_2CHCl\cdot \qquad [15]$$
$$ROCH_2CHClCH_2CHCl\cdot + CH_2{=}CHCl \rightarrow RO(CH_2CHCl)CH_2CHCl\cdot$$

Polystyrene initiation and propagation (styrene, $CH_2{=}CH\phi$, monomer; $\phi = C_6H_5$, a phenyl group)

$$RO\cdot + CH_2{=}CH\phi \rightarrow ROCH_2CH\phi\cdot$$
$$ROCH_2CH\phi\cdot + CH{=}CH\phi \rightarrow ROCH_2CH\phi CH_2CH\phi \qquad [16]$$
$$ROCH_2CH\phi CH_2CH\phi + CH_2{=}CH\phi \rightarrow RO(CH_2CH\phi)CH_2CH\phi\cdot$$

Termination occurs when any two free radicals combine.

13. Name the common functional groups and give examples of compounds containing them.

While the descriptive chemistry of inorganic compounds is based on the periodic table, organic chemistry is based on functional groups. Organic compounds with the same functional group react in similar ways. Some of the common classes of organic compounds are given in Table 24-3. R is any alkyl group.

TABLE 24-3
Some common classes of organic compounds

Class of compound	General formula	Examples and names		
alkane	$R{-}H$	CH_3CH_3 ethane	$CH_3CH(CH_3)CH_3$ 2-methylpropane	cyclohexane
alkene	$R_2C{=}CR_2$	$H_2C{=}CHCH_3$ 1-propene	$(CH_3)_2C{=}C(CH_3)_2$ 2,3-dimethyl-2-butene	cyclopentene

Table 20-4 (*continued*)

Class of compound	General formula	Example and names		
alkyne	R—C≡C—R	$CH_3C{\equiv}CCH_3$ 2-butyne	$CH_3CH(CH_3)C{\equiv}CCH_2CH_3$ 2-methyl-3-hexyne	
arene (aromatic hydrocarbon)	C_6H_5—H *or* Ar—H	C_6H_5—H benzene	C_6H_5—CH_3 methylbenzene *or* toluene	C_6H_5—$CH(CH_3)CH_3$ isopropylbenzene
alkyl halide	R—X	CH_3CH_2Br bromoethane	$CH_3CF_2CH_2CH_3$ 2,2-difluorobutane	I—C_6H_{10}—I 1,4-diiodocyclohexane
alcohol	R—OH	$CH_3CH_2CH(OH)CH_2CH_3$ 3-pentanol	CH_3—$C(CH_3)(OH)$—CH_2CH_3 2-methyl-2-butanol	C_4H_7—OH cyclobutanol
ether	R—O—R	CH_3—O—CH_3 dimethyl ether		C_4H_7—O—$CH(CH_3)_2$ cyclobutyl isopropyl ether
aldehyde	R—C(=O)—H	$CH_3C(=O)$—H ethanal *or* acetaldehyde		$CH_3CH_2CH_2C(=O)$—H butanal *or* butyraldehyde
ketone	R—C(=O)—R′	$CH_3C(=O)CH_3$ propanone *or* acetone	$CH_3CH(CH_3)CH_2C(=O)CH_3$ 4-methyl-2-pentanone	C_6H_{10}=O cyclohexanone
acid	R—C(=O)—OH	$CH_3C(=O)$—OH ethanoic acid *or* acetic acid		$CH_3CH(CH_3)CH_2C(=O)$—OH 3-methylbutanoic acid
ester	R—C(=O)—O—R′	$CH_3C(=O)$—OCH_3 methyl ethanoate *or* methyl acetate		$CH_3CH(CH_3)CH_2C(=O)$—OCH_2CH_3 ethyl 3-methylbutanoate
amine	R—NH_2	$CH_3CH_2NH_2$ ethylamine	$CH_3CH_2CH(CH_3)NH_2$ 2-aminobutane	C_6H_{11}—NH_2 cyclohexylamine

TABLE 24-4
Characteristics of common classes of organic compounds

Class of compounds	Structural group present
alkane	only C—H and C—C single bonds
alkene	a C=C double bond
alkyne	a C≡C triple bond
arene	an aromatic ring, (benzene ring)—
alkyl halide	an alkyl group bonded to a F, Cl, Br, or I atom
alcohol	an —OH group bonded to a C atom
ether	two alkyl groups bonded to an O atom
aldehyde	a —C(=O)—H group bonded to an alkyl group
ketone	two alkyl groups bonded to a —C(=O)— group
acid	an alkyl group bonded to a —C(=O)—OH group
ester	two alkyl groups bonded to each end of a —C(=O)—O— group
amine	an alkyl group bonded to an —NH_2 group

★ **14. Write structural formulas, identify possible isomers, and name organic compounds containing functional groups.**

You should memorize the structural formulas in Table 24-3. The summary in Table 24-4 may help in writing structural formulas. Different structural isomers are found by drawing all the possible carbon skeletons and then placing the functional group in all possible positions. Nomenclature depends on the class of compound. Alcohols, alkyl halides, ketones, and amines have names obtained from the corresponding alkane, with the position of the group on the chain indicated with the smallest possible number. This number precedes the base name and is separated from it by a dash. The -ane ending of the base name is replaced by the ending given in Table 24-5. In both aldehydes and carboxylic acids the function group is at the end of the longest chain and the group's carbon is numbered 1.

TABLE 24-5
Endings for classes of organic compounds

Class of compounds	Ending
alkyl halide	-yl halide (as -yl iodide)
alcohol	-ol
ether	-yl ether
aldehyde	-anal
ketone	-one
acid	-anoic acid
ester	-anoate
amine	-yl amine

Esters are derived from acids by replacing the H atom in the —C(=O)—OH group with an alkyl group. The alkyl group name precedes that of the acid and the -oic acid ending is replaced by -oate. In ethers the two alkyl group names are followed by "ether." Alkyl groups in ethers have the oxygen-bonded carbons numbered 1.

15. Describe methods of preparing alcohols, ethers, aldehydes, ketones, acids, and amines; and write equations for some typical reactions of these classes of organic compounds.

Methods of preparation are summarized below.

a. Alcohols

Hydration of alkenes:

$$>C{=}C< + H_2O \xrightarrow{H_2SO_4} -\overset{|}{\underset{H}{\underset{|}{C}}}-\overset{|}{\underset{OH}{\underset{|}{C}}}- \qquad [17]$$

Hydrolysis of alkyl halides:

$$-\overset{|}{\underset{|}{C}}-\overset{|}{\underset{X}{\underset{|}{C}}}- + OH^- \rightarrow -\overset{|}{\underset{|}{C}}-\overset{|}{\underset{OH}{\underset{|}{C}}}- + X^- \qquad [18]$$

Production of methanol:

$$CO(g) + 2\ H_2(g) \xrightarrow[\substack{200\text{ atm} \\ ZnO,\ Cr_2O_3}]{350°C} CH_3OH(g) \qquad [19]$$

b. Ethers

Elimination of water between two alcohol molecules:

$$R{-}OH + HO{-}R' \xrightarrow{\text{conc } H_2SO_4} R{-}O{-}R' + H_2O \qquad [20]$$

c. Aldehydes and ketones. Oxidation of alcohols.

Primary alcohols to aldehydes:

$$RCH_2OH \xrightarrow[H^+]{Cr_2O_7{}^{2-}} R{-}\overset{\overset{O}{\|}}{C}{-}H \xrightarrow[H^+]{Cr_2O_7{}^{2-}} R{-}\overset{\overset{O}{\|}}{C}{-}OH \qquad [21]$$

$$RCH_2OH \xrightarrow[200\text{–}300°C]{Cu} R{-}\overset{\overset{O}{\|}}{C}{-}H \qquad [22]$$

Secondary alcohols to ketones:

$$R{-}CH{-}R' \xrightarrow[\textit{or}\ Cu,\ 200\text{–}300°C]{KMnO_4\ \textit{or}\ K_2Cr_2O_7} R{-}\overset{\overset{O}{\|}}{C}{-}R' \qquad [23]$$

d. Carboxylic acids

Oxidation of a primary alcohol:

$$RCH_2OH \xrightarrow[\textit{or}\ Cr_2O_7{}^{2-},\ H^+]{KMnO_4,\ OH^-} R\overset{\overset{O}{\|}}{C}{-}OH \qquad [24]$$

Oxidation of an aldehyde:

$$R\overset{\overset{O}{\|}}{C}{-}H \xrightarrow[\textit{or}\ Cr_2O_7{}^{2-},\ H^+]{KMnO_4,\ OH^-} R\overset{\overset{O}{\|}}{C}{-}OH \qquad [25]$$

e. Amines

$$R{-}NO_2 \xrightarrow[HCl]{Fe} R{-}NH_3^+Cl^- \xrightarrow{NaOH} R{-}NH_2 \qquad [26]$$

Reactions of these classes of compounds are summarized in the following general equations.

f. Alcohols

1. Dehydration (see equation [5]).
2. Reactions with an acid halide.

$$R{-}OH + R'\overset{\overset{O}{\|}}{C}{-}X \rightarrow R'{-}\overset{\overset{O}{\|}}{C}{-}O{-}R + HX \qquad [27]$$

3. Reactions with carboxylic acids.

$$R{-}OH + R'{-}\overset{\overset{O}{\|}}{C}{-}OH \overset{H^+}{\rightleftharpoons} R'{-}\overset{\overset{O}{\|}}{C}{-}OR + H_2O \qquad [28]$$

4. Reactions with nitric acid.

$$R{-}OH + HONO_2 \rightarrow R{-}ONO_2 + H_2O \qquad [29]$$

5. Reactions with alkali hydroxides.

$$R{-}OH + NaOH \rightleftharpoons R{-}O^- + Na^+ + H_2O \qquad [30]$$

6. Reaction with sodium.

$$Na^0 + R{-}OH \rightarrow R{-}O^-Na^+ + \tfrac{1}{2}\,H_2(g) \qquad [31]$$

g. Ethers

1. Stable when attacked by most oxidizing and reducing agents and dilute acids and alkalis.
2. Cleavage by strong acids.

$$R{-}O{-}R' + 2\,HCl \rightarrow R{-}Cl + R'{-}Cl + H\,O \qquad [32]$$

h. Aldehydes

1. Oxidation to acids (see equation [21]).
2. Reduction with hydrogen.

$$R{-}\overset{\overset{O}{\|}}{C}{-}H \xrightarrow{H_2,\,Ni} RCH_2OH \qquad [33]$$

i. Ketones

Reduction by hydrogen.

$$R{-}\overset{\overset{O}{\|}}{C}{-}R' \xrightarrow{H_2,\,Ni} RCHOHR' \qquad [34]$$

j. Acids

1. Reaction with ammonia followed by heating.

$$R-\overset{\overset{\displaystyle O}{\|}}{C}-OH + NH_3 \rightarrow R-\overset{\overset{\displaystyle O}{\|}}{C}-O^-NH_4^+ + \xrightarrow[P_2O_5]{\Delta} R-C{\equiv}N + 2H_2O \qquad [35]$$

2. Reaction with an alcohol to give an ester (see equation [28]).
3. Elimination of water between two acid molecules.

$$R-\overset{\overset{\displaystyle O}{\|}}{C}-OH \xrightarrow[\text{heat}]{P_2O_5} R-\overset{\overset{\displaystyle O}{\|}}{C}-O-\overset{\overset{\displaystyle O}{\|}}{C}-R \qquad [36]$$

k. Amines

Reaction with an alkyl halide.

$$RNH_2 + R'X \rightarrow R-\underset{\underset{\displaystyle R'}{|}}{NH} \qquad [37]$$

These reactions should be memorized.

★ **16. Propose schemes for synthesizing some common organic compounds.**

You should be able to put together the reactions given in equations [1] through [12] and [17] through [37] to synthesize simple organic compounds.

EXAMPLE 24-2 Produce propyl butanoate from simple alcohols.

$$CH_3CH_2CH_2CH_2OH \xrightarrow{KMnO_4} CH_3CH_2\overset{\overset{\displaystyle O}{\|}}{C}-OH$$

$$CH_3CH_2CH_2\overset{\overset{\displaystyle O}{\|}}{C}-OH + HOCH_2CH_2CH_3 \xrightarrow{H^+} CH_3CH_2CH_2\overset{\overset{\displaystyle O}{\|}}{C}-OCH_2CH_2CH_3 + H_2O$$

Often it is easier to work backward, determining what reactants are needed to produce the desired compound and then figuring out how to make those reactants in the same way, always keeping in mind what the starting materials are.

DRILL PROBLEMS

2. Draw structural formulas for each of the following compounds. (You may draw either the *cis* or the *trans* isomer for those compounds which exhibit isomerism.)

A. 3-methyl-3-hexene
B. 2-pentene
C. 2-methylbutane
D. 2,2,4-trimethylpentane
E. 2-butyne
F. 2-methylethylbenzene
G. toluene
H. *m*-xylene
I. 3-ethylcyclopentene
J. 2,3,4-trimethylpentane
K. 2,3-dimethylbutane
L. 2,4-dimethyl-4-ethylheptane
M. 2,3-dimethyl-2-butene
N. 3-methyl-4-ethyl-3-hexene
O. 2-pentyne
P. 1,3-dimethylcyclohexane
Q. 3,5-dimethylcyclopentene
R. 3-methylcyclopentene
S. cyclohexylcyclohexane
T. 1,1-dimethyl-4-ethylcyclopentane

U. 1-methylcyclopentene

V. 1,2,3,4-tetramethylcyclobutene

W. 1,3,5-trimethylbenzene

3. Give the systematic (IUPAC) name of each of the following compounds.

A. $CH_3CH_2CHCH_3$ (with CH_3 on the CH)

B. $H_2C{=}CH(CH_2CH_3)$ (H, H on one carbon; H and CH_2CH_3 on the other)

C. $(CH_3)_2C{=}C(CH_2CH_3)_2$

D. $CH_3CHCHCH_2CH_3$ (with CH_3 above the first CH and CH_3 below the second CH)

E. $CH_2-CH-CH_2CH_3$ (ring: CH_2 and CH joined through CH_2)

F. Cyclohexane ring with CH_3 and CH_3 on adjacent carbons

G. Benzene ring with CH_3 and CH_2 on adjacent carbons

H. Cyclohexane ring with $CH_2CH_2CH_3$

I. Benzene ring with $-C(CH_3)_2-CH_3$ (CH_3 above, $-CH_3$, CH_3 below)

J. $CH_3CH_2CH_2CHCH_2CH_2CH_3$ (with CH_3 on the CH)

K. $CH_3CH_2C{\equiv}CH$

L. $CH_3CH{=}CHCH_3$

M. $CH_3CH_2CH_2CH{=}CH_2$

N. $CH{\equiv}CCH_3$

O. C_3H_8

P. CH_3CHCH_3 (with CH_3 on the CH)

Q. $CH_3-C-CH-CH_3$ (with CH_3 above and CH_3 below the C; CH_3 above the CH)

R. $CH_3CH-C-CH_2CH_2CH_3$ (with CH_3 above the CH; CH_2CH_3 above and CH_2CH_3 below the C)

S. $CH_3CH-CHCH_2CH_3$ (with CH_3 above the first CH and CH_2CH_3 above the second CH)

T. $CH_3CHCH_2CH_2CH_3$ (with CH_3 on the CH)

U. $CH_3CH_2CH-CCH_3$ (with CH_3 above the CH; CH_3 above and CH_3 below the C)

V. $CH_3CH_2CH_2CH_2CCH_2CH_2CH_3$ (with CH_3 above and CH_3 below the C)

W. Cyclohexene ring with $-CH_3$

4. Draw all the possible skeletal isomers of each of the following hydrocarbons. Then name each isomer.
A. aromatic compounds of formula C_9H_{12}
B. C_4H_8
C. cyclic compounds of formula C_6H_{10}
D. C_6H_{14}
E. C_4H_{10}
F. C_5H_{10}
G. hydrocarbons of molecular weight 86

6. Predict which compound in each group below has the highest value of the listed property and which one has the lowest value.

Melting point
A. cyclohexane; hexane; benzene
B. ethyne; ethane; ethene
C. pentane; 2,2-dimethylpropane; 2-methylbutane
D. benzene; 1,4-dimethylbenzene; toluene

Boiling point
E. butane; propane; hexane
F. cyclohexane; benzene; cyclohexene
G. butane; cyclobutane; methylcyclopropane
H. 3,3-dimethylpentane; 2-methylhexane; *n*-heptane

Molar heat of fusion
I. methane; ethane; ethene
J. ethyne; propyne; butyne
K. *n*-hexane; 2,2-dimethylbutane; 3-methylpentane
L. cyclohexane; hexane; benzene

Molar heat of vaporization
M. xylene; benzene; toluene
N. 3,3-dimethylpentane; 2-methylhexane; *n*-heptane
O. cyclohexane; hexane; benzene
P. butane; pentane; propane

7. (1) Which of the following compounds show *cis-trans* isomerism? Draw both isomers and indicate which is *cis* and which is *trans*, or indicate "none."
A. 1-butene
B. 2-butene
C. 1,1-dichloroethene
D. 1,2-dichloroethene
E. 2-methyl-2-butene
F. 1-pentene
G. 1,1-dimethylcyclobutane
H. 1,2-dimethylcyclobutane
I. 2-pentene
J. 3-hexene

(2) Which of the compounds in the drill problems for objective 24–2 display *cis-trans* isomerism? Draw the *cis* isomer in each case.

8. Write the complete equation for each of the following reactions.
A. 1-bromohexane with KOH in alcohol
B. 1-propanol → propylene
C. ethanol with H_2SO_4 and heat
D. chloroethane → butane
E. 1,1-dichloropropane → propyne
F. 2-chloropropane → propylene
G. 3-bromo-2,3-dimethylpentane with KOH in alcohol
H. 1-butene → butane
I. 2-chlorobutane → NaCl

11. Predict the product of each of the following reactions.
A. 2-methyl-2-pentene + HCl →
B. 3-methyl-2-pentene + $H_2O \xrightarrow{H_2SO_4}$
C. 1-butene + HI →
D. 2-methyl-2-butene + HBr →
E. 1-butene + $H_2O \xrightarrow[HgSO_4]{H_2SO_4}$
F. 2-methylcyclohexene + HCl →

14. (1) Give the name of each compound.
A. $CH_3CH_2CHBrCH_2$
B. $(CH_3)_2CH_2CHOHC(CH_3)_3$
C. $CH_3CH_2CH_2COCH_2CH_3$
D. $CH_3CH_2CH_2CH_2COOH$
E. $(CH_3)_3CCHO$
F. $CH_3OCH_2CH_2CH_3$
G. $CH_3CH_2CH_2CH_2CH_2NH_2$
H. HCOOH
I. $CH_3CH_2COOCH_2CH_3$

J. $(CH_3)_3COH$ K. $(CH_3)_3COCH_2CH_3$ L. $CH_3CCl_2CHClCH_2CH_3$
M. $CH_3CH_3COCH_2CH_3$ N. $CH_3CH_2COOCH_2CH_2CH_3$ O. $CH_3CH_2CH_2CH_2CHO$

(2) Give the condensed structural formula of each compound.
A. butanone B. 2-methylbutanal C. 2-methylpentanoic acid
D. 3-bromopentane E. methyl butanoate F. propyl isopropyl ether.
G. 3-methylpentanal H. 2,2-dichloropropane I. 2-amino-3-methylpentane
J. 3-hexanol K. 2-propanol L. 3-aminopentane
M. 2-methylpropanoic acid N. 1-iodo-2-methylbutane O. 2-pentanone

16. Detail all the steps in synthesizing the following compounds from the given starting material.
A. propyne from ethyne B. ethene from ethanal C. propene from propane
D. 2-butene from ethane E. propanone from propane F. diethyl ether from ethane
G. propanal from propane H. ethyl butanoate from ethane I. cyclohexane from hexane

QUIZZES (20 minutes each)

Choose the best answer for each question.

Quiz A

1. The IUPAC name of $(CH_3)_2CHCH_2CH_3$ is (a) isopentane; (b) *sec*-pentane; (c) 3-methylbutane; (d) 2-methylbutane; (e) none of these.
2. The formula of 2-methyl-1-butanol is (a) $CH_3CH_2COH(CH_3)_2$; (b) $CH_3CH_2CH(CH_3)CH_3OH$; (c) $CH_3CH(CH_3)CH_2OH$; (d) $CH_3COH(CH_3)_2$; (e) none of these.
3. C_4H_8 has how many skeletal isomers, including geometric isomers? (a) 2; (b) 3; (c) 4; (d) 5; (e) none of these.
4. Which compound is the lowest boiling? (a) methane; (b) ethene; (c) ethane; (d) cyclopropane; (e) ethyne.
5. Which compound displays *cis-trans* isomerism? (a) cyclopropane; (b) 1-chloro-1-methylcyclopropane; (c) 1,1-dichlorocyclopropane; (d) 2-chloro-1-methylcyclopropane; (e) none of these.
6. What reactant could *not* be used to produce an alkene in fewer than three steps? (a) bromoethane; (b) bromobutane; (c) methane; (d) propyne; (e) none of these.
7. Which class of compounds is least reactive? (a) ethers. (b) alcohols; (c) ketones; (d) alkyl halides; (e) aldehydes.
8. To produce an organic ester one uses a carboxylic acid and an (a) alkyl halide; (b) alkane; (c) alcohol; (d) aldehyde; (e) none of these.

Quiz B

1. The IUPAC name of $H_2C{=}C(CH_3)CH(Cl)CH_3$ is (a) 4-chloro-2-methylbutene; (b) 2-chloro-2-methyl-4-butene; (c) 4-chloro-2-methylpentene; (d) 2-chloro-4-methyl-4-butene; (e) none of these.
2. The formula of 2-methylbutanal is (a) $CH_3CH_2CH(CH_3)CHOH$; (b) $CH_3CH(CH_3)CHOH$; (c) $CH_3CH_2CH(CH_3)CHO$; (d) $CH_3CH(CH_3)CHO$; (e) none of these.
3. C_5H_{12} has how many skeletal isomers? (a) 2; (b) 3; (c) 4; (d) 5; (e) none of these.
4. Which compound has the lowest molar heat of vaporization? (a) hexane; (b) cyclohexane; (c) benzene; (d) heptane; (e) 2-heptene.
5. Which compound does *not* display *cis–trans* isomerism? (a) 2-butene; (b) 2-methyl-1-cyclopentanol; (c) 1,2-dichloroethene; (d) 1,1-dichlorocyclopropane; (e) none of these.
6. What colıld be used to produce an alkane in one step? (a) an alkene; (b) an alcohol; (c) an acid; (d) an alkali metal carboxylate; (e) none of these.
7. A free-radical chain reaction is used to prepare (a) methanol; (b) methanal; (c) methyl chloride; (d) dimethyl ether; (e) none of these.
8. To produce an alcohol from a ketone one uses (a) Cu, heat; (b) HCl; (c) H_2, Ni; (d) NH_3; (e) none of these.

Quiz C

1. The formula of 2-chloro-1-butene is (a) $CH_2{=}CClCH_2CH_3$; (b) $CH_3CCl{=}CHCH_3$; (c) $CH_2{=}CClCH_3$; (d) $CH_3CCl{=}CH_2$; (e) none of these.
2. The name of $CH_3CH_2COCH_2CH_3$ is (a) diethyl ether; (b) ethyl propyl ether; (c) butanone; (d) 3-pentanone; (e) none of these.
3. C_4H_9Cl has how many skeletal isomers? (a) 1; (b) 2; (c) 3; (d) 4; (e) none of these.
4. Which compound is the highest melting? (a) propane; (b) propene; (c) cyclopropane; (d) propyne; (e) methylpropane.
5. Which of the following is the most stable conformation? (a) boat cyclohexane; (b) eclipsed ethane; (c) eclipsed hydrogens in the central bond of *n*-butane; (d) eclipsed propane; (e) chair methylcyclohexane with the methyl equatorial.
6. To add to a double bond, which group of reactants is *not* used? (a) HCl; (b) H_2,Pt; (c) Na; (d) H_2O, H_2SO_4; (e) none of these.
7. A free-radical chain reaction is *not* used to produce (a) bromoethane; (b) polystyrene; (c) polyethylene; (d) ethanol; (e) none of these.
8. To produce an ether from methanol, one uses (a) heat; (b) concentrated H_2SO_4; (c) KOH in alcohol; (d) Cu, heat; (e) none of these.

Quiz D

1. The name of $CH_3CCl{=}CBr_2$ is (a) 1,1-dibromo-2-chloropropane; (b) 3,3-dibromo-2-chloroethane; (c) 1,1-dibromo-2-chloropropene; (d) 3,3-dibromo-2-chloropropene; (e) none of these.
2. The formula of 2-methylbutanal is (a) $CH_3CH_2CH(CH_3)CHO$; (b) $(CH_3)_2CHCH_2CHO$; (c) $(CH_3)_2CHCHO$; (d) $CH_3CH(CH_3)CHO$; (e) none of these.
3. C_3H_8O has how many skeletal isomers? (a) 1; (b) 2; (c) 3; (d) 4; (e) none of these.
4. Which compound has the highest molar heat of fusion? (a) butane; (b) 2-butene; (c) cyclobutane; (d) methylcyclopropane; (e) methylcyclobutane.
5. In which molecule can the hydrogen–hydrogen nonbonded distance be the *shortest*? (a) boat form of *cis*-1,4-dimethylcyclohexane; (b) eclipsed ethane; (c) staggered ethane; (d) eclipsed butane; (e) chair form of *cis*-1,4-dimethylcyclohexane.
6. Which could produce an alkene in one step? (a) an amine; (b) an alkyl halide; (c) an alkyl dihalide; (d) an alkane; (e) all of these could be used.
7. Which class of compounds is the most oxidized? (a) alkanes; (b) alcohols; (c) acids; (d) aldehydes; (e) ketones.
8. To produce an aldehyde from 2-butanol, what reactant is used? (a) MnO_4^-; (b) Cu, heat; (c) $Cr_2O_7^{2-}$; (d) H_2SO_4: (e) impossible.

SAMPLE TEST (20 minutes)

1. Draw all of the ethers of formula $C_4H_{10}O$. Name each compound.
2. Explain why propanol is soluble in water but hexanol is not.
3. Consider the dehydrohalogenation of 2-bromobutane in the presence of KOH. Draw the structures of all the products and name them.
4. Give the names and structures of compounds A, B, C, and D formed in the following sequence of reactions.

$$\text{2-methylpropanal} \xrightarrow[\text{Pt}]{H_2} \text{A} \xrightarrow[200^\circ\text{C}]{H_2SO_4} \text{B} \xrightarrow{\text{HBr}} \text{C} \xrightarrow[\text{alcohol}]{\text{KOH}} \text{D}$$

5. Draw the various conformations of 1-propanol as Newman projections around the Cl–C2 bond. Which is the most stable and which the least stable?

Chapter 25,

Chemistry of the Living State

REVIEW OF OBJECTIVES

1. List the four principal types of substances found in cells—lipids, polysaccharides, proteins, and nucleic acids—and describe the chemical composition of each.

Lipids readily dissolve in nonpolar solvents. They are nonpolar or of very low polarity. Lipids are subdivided into triglycerides (fats and oils), phosphatides or phospholipids, and waxes. See objectives 25-2, 25-3, and 25-4.

Polysaccharides are carbohydrates composed of more than ten monosaccharide units. A monosaccharide is either an aldehyde or a ketone with hydroxy groups (—OH) on all other carbons. Aldehyde monosaccharides are aldoses; ketone ones are ketoses. See objectives 25-5 and 25-7.

Proteins are polymers of amino acids. An α-amino acid is a carboxylic acid with an amino group (—NH_2 attached to the α-carbon, the carbon bonded to the carboxylic group (—COOH). These acids have the general formula shown in Figure 25-1. R groups of common amino acids are given in *Table 25-4 in the text.* See objectives 25-9 and 25-10.

Nucleic acids are composed of phosphoric acid, pentose sugars (ribose and 2-deoxyribose) and the purine and pyrimidine bases shown in *Figure 25-20 in the text.* See objective 25-14.

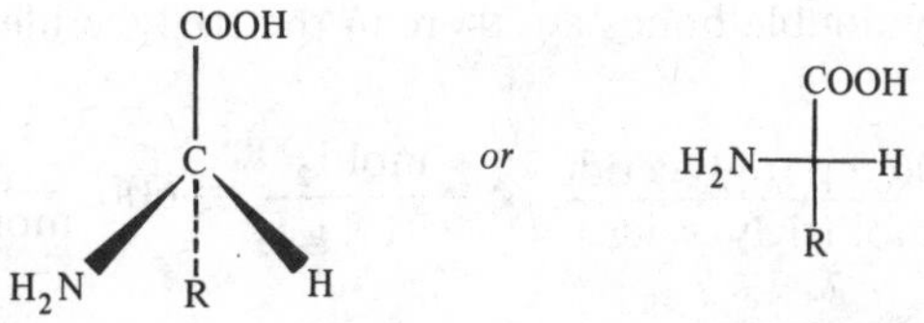

COOH, C, H_2N, R, H *or* COOH, H_2N—C—H, R

FIGURE 25-1 General formula for amino acids.

2. Write structural formulas and names of triglycerides and indicate whether their constituent fatty acids are saturated or unsaturated.

Triglycerides are esters of glycerol and carboxylic acids with long hydrocarbon chains (Figure 25-2). When the caroxylic acids are saturated, meaning they contain no double (C=C) bonds, the triglyceride is a saturated fat. Saturated fats are waxy solids, such as lard. When the R groups are unsaturated, containing one or more double bonds, the triglyceride is an unsaturated fat. Unsaturated fats are liquids commonly called oils. Because of the reactive double bonds, oils react with oxygen in the air to become rancid.

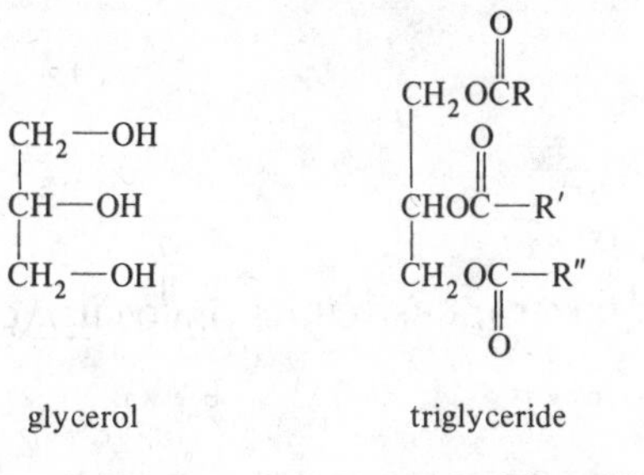

glycerol	triglyceride
CH_2—OH	$CH_2OC(=O)R$
CH—OH	$CHOC(=O)$—R′
CH_2—OH	$CH_2OC(=O)$—R″

FIGURE 25-2 General formula of triglycerides.

Fats are named beginning with "glyceryl," followed by the names of the fatty acid anions. (The anion of stearic acid, $C_{17}H_{35}COOH$, is the stearate anion, $C_{17}H_{35}COO^-$.) A prefix indicates the number of anions of a given type. In a mixed triglyceride in which the fatty acids all are different, they are named in alphabetical order and the *-ate* endings of the first two are changed to *-o*. All three names are written together with no spaces. The names of common fatty acids are given in *Table 25-2 in the text.*

3. Relate the structures, saponification values, and iodine numbers of triglycerides.

The sponification value is the mass in milligrams of KOH which reacts with one gram of the triglyceride. We know 3 mol KOH reacts with 1 mol of triglyceride.

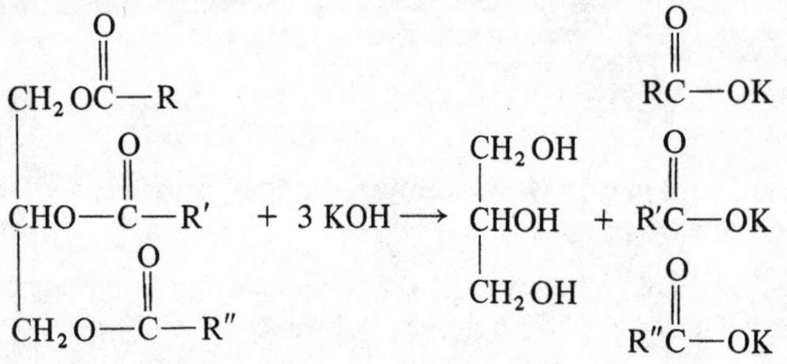

$$\begin{array}{l} CH_2OC(=O)-R \\ | \\ CHO-C(=O)-R' \\ | \\ CH_2O-C(=O)-R'' \end{array} + 3\,KOH \longrightarrow \begin{array}{l} CH_2OH \\ | \\ CHOH \\ | \\ CH_2OH \end{array} + \begin{array}{l} RC(=O)-OK \\ R'C(=O)-OK \\ R''C(=O)-OK \end{array} \qquad [1]$$

The saponification value is used to determine the mole weight of a triglyceride.

EXAMPLE 25-1 What is the mole weight of a triglyceride with a saponification value of 185.7?

$$185.7 \text{ mg KOH} \times \frac{1.00 \text{ g}}{1000 \text{ mg}} \times \frac{\text{mol KOH}}{56.1 \text{ g}} \times \frac{\text{mol triglyceride}}{3 \text{ mol KOH}} = 1.103 \times 10^{-3} \text{ mol}$$

$$MW = 1.00 \text{ g}/1.103 \times 10^{-3} \text{ mol} = 906.3 \text{ g/mol}$$

The iodine number is the mass in grams of I_2 which reacts with 100 g of triglyceride by addition of I_2 across the double bonds.

EXAMPLE 25-2 How many double bonds are there in the triglyceride of Example 25-1 if its iodine number is 168 g of I_2?

$$\frac{168 \text{ g } I_2}{100 \text{ g triglyceride}} \times \frac{906.3 \text{ g triglyceride}}{\text{mol triglyceride}} \times \frac{\text{mol } I_2}{253.8 \text{ g } I_2} = 600 \frac{\text{mol } I_2}{\text{mol triglyceride}}$$

There are six double bonds in the triglyceride molecule.

4. Explain how phosphatides and waxes, which also are lipids, differ from triglycerides.

Phosphatides (or phospholipids) are esters of glycerol with two fatty acids and a derivative of phosphoric acid (Figure 25-3). There are two major classes: lecithins, in which $-A$ is $-CH_2CH_2\overset{+}{N}(CH_3)_3$, and cephalins, in which $-A$ is $-CH_2CH_2\overset{+}{N}H_3$. A wax is an ester of a long-chain *mono*hydric alcohol (an alcohol with *one* OH group) with a fatty acid.

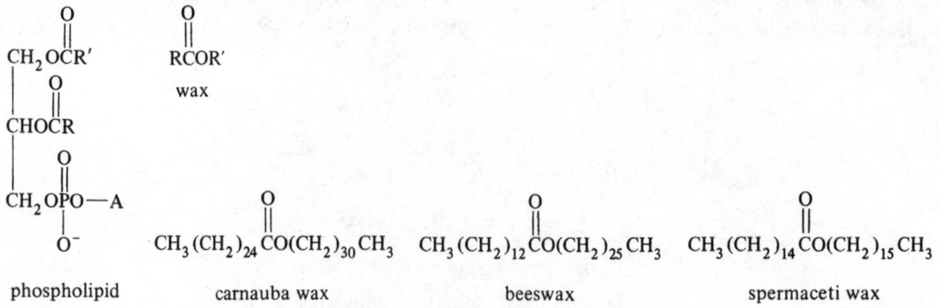

$$\begin{array}{l} CH_2OC(=O)R' \\ | \\ CHOC(=O)R \\ | \\ CH_2OP(=O)(O^-)O-A \end{array}$$

phospholipid

$RC(=O)OR'$

wax

$CH_3(CH_2)_{24}C(=O)O(CH_2)_{30}CH_3$

carnauba wax

$CH_3(CH_2)_{12}C(=O)O(CH_2)_{25}CH_3$

beeswax

$CH_3(CH_2)_{14}C(=O)O(CH_2)_{15}CH_3$

spermaceti wax

FIGURE 25-3 Structures of phospholipids and waxes.

5. Classify carbohydrates as monosaccharides, oligosaccharides, and polysaccharides, and give example of each.

The general formula for a monosaccharide is $(CH_2O)_n$ where $n = 3, 4, 5, 6$, etc. The total number of carbon atoms in the molecule determines the name: triose ($n = 3$), tetrose ($n = 4$), pentose ($n = 5$), hexose ($n = 6$), and so on. Whether the monosaccharide is an aldose or a ketose is indicated by a prefix, aldo- or keto-. In addition the position of the C=O in a ketose is indicated by a number (Figure 25-4). With the exception of ketotriose, there are several optical isomers of each monosaccharide (see objective 25-6); the number of optical isomers is given in parentheses in the figure.

				CHO
		CHO	CH_2OH	CHOH
CHO	CH_2OH	CHOH	C=O	CHOH
CHOH	C=O	CHOH	CHOH	CHOH
CH_2OH	CH_2OH	CH_2OH	CH_2OH	CH_2OH
aldotriose (2)	ketotriose (1)	aldotetrose (4)	ketotetrose (2)	aldopentose (8)

		CHO	CH_2OH	CH_2OH
CH_2OH	CH_2OH	CHOH	C=O	CHOH
C=O	CHOH	CHOH	CHOH	C=O
CHOH	C=O	CHOH	CHOH	CHOH
CHOH	CHOH	CHOH	CHOH	CHOH
CH_2OH	CH_2OH	CH_2OH	CH_2OH	CH_2OH
2-ketopentose (4)	3-ketopentose (3)	aldohexose (16)	2-ketohexose (8)	3-ketohexose (8)

FIGURE 25-4 Names of monosaccharides.

Oligosaccharides are composed of from two to ten monosaccharide units. The number of saccharide units is given by a numerical prefix: disaccharide, trisaccharide, tetrasaccharide, and so on. Polysaccharides contain more than ten monosaccharide units. Common disaccharides are maltose, lactose, cellobiose, and sucrose (see *Figure 25-7 in the text*). Common polysaccharides are starch, cellulose (both shown in *Figure 25-8 in the text*), glycogen, and amylopectin. All of these are polymers of D-glucose.

★ **6. Describe the phenomenon of optical activity and the structural features of a molecule that produce it.**

An optically active molecule is one which rotates the plane of polarized light passing through it. Light is accompanied by both an electric field and a magnetic field, which vibrate at right angles to the direction of travel. If we could see this vibration, light traveling at us would look like Figure 25-5a. When light is plane polarized, the electric or magnetic field vibrates in one plane (Figure 25-5b). Light can be polarized in two ways: by passing it through a polarizing prism or by reflecting it off a flat surface. You probably have seen light polarized by a flat surface. It looks like shimmering water (a mirage) at a distance and often is seen on the highway on bright days.

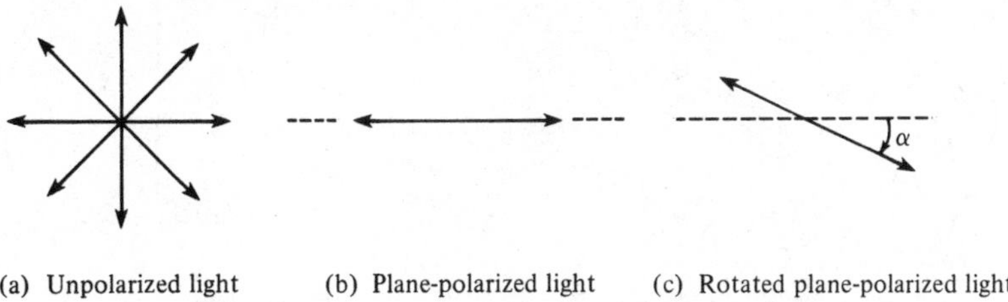

(a) Unpolarized light (b) Plane-polarized light (c) Rotated plane-polarized light

FIGURE 25-5 The polarization of light.

Optically active molecules rotate the plane of polarized light, as shown in Figure 25-5c, where the plane is rotated by an angle α. A molecule is optically active if it cannot be superimposed on its mirror image. If there are four different groups bonded to a carbon atom in a molecule, that carbon atom is termed a chiral carbon or a chiral center. (A chiral carbon formerly was referred to as an asymmetric carbon.) A chiral carbon often is present in an optically active molecule. A molecule with only one chiral carbon must be optically active. The easiest way to see optical activity is to build a model of the molecule and of its mirror image and see if they can be superimposed. After some practice with models you can use sketches. There are two types of sketches which you can draw: wedge and dash sketches, and Fischer projections, both shown in Figure 25-6 for CHFClBr. In Fischer projections the groups above and below the chiral carbon are assumed to point away from you and the groups on either side point toward you. Two compounds which differ only in their optical activity are called enantiomers.

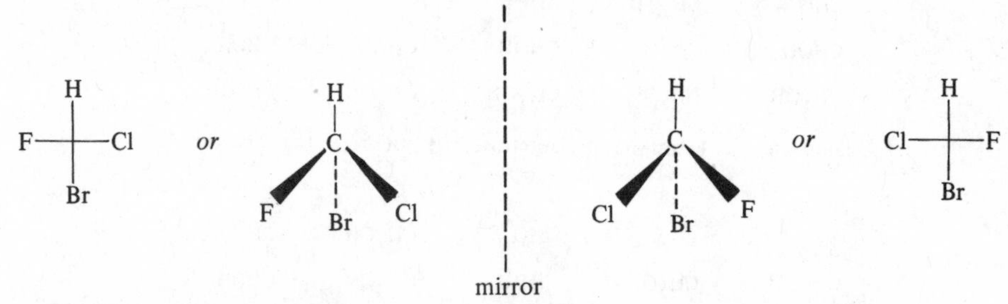

H, F—+—Cl, Br or H, C, F, Br, Cl | mirror | H, C, Cl, Br, F or H, Cl—+—F, Br

FIGURE 25-6 Wedge and dash sketches (in center) and Fischer projections (on outside) of the two enantiomers of CHFClBr.

The presence of a chiral carbon atom does not guarantee optical activity. A molecule may *lack* a chiral carbon and yet *be* optically active, that is, possess a nonsuperimposable mirror image (for example, 1-bromo-1-chloro-2-fluoro-1,2-propadiene, shown in Figure 25-7). Or a molecule may possess two or more

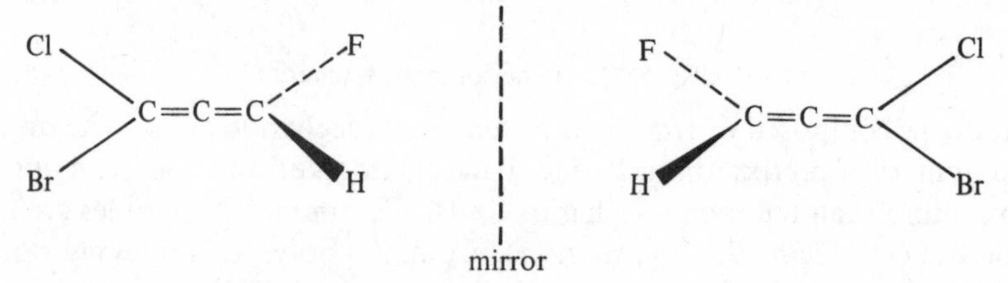

Cl, Br >C=C=C< F, H | mirror | F, H >C=C=C< Cl, Br

FIGURE 25-7 Wedge and dash drawings of the two enantiomers of 1-bromo-1-chloro-2-fluoro-1,2-propadiene.

chiral carbons and yet the mirror image *is* superimposable (for example, 2,3-dichlorobutane, shown in Figure 25-8).

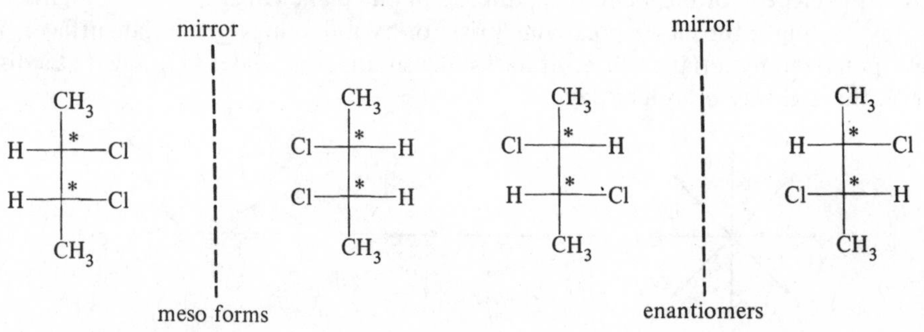

mirror: CH_3; H—*—Cl; H—*—Cl; CH_3 | CH_3; Cl—*—H; Cl—*—H; CH_3 — meso forms

mirror: CH_3; Cl—*—H; H—*—Cl; CH_3 | CH_3; H—*—Cl; Cl—*—H; CH_3 — enantiomers

FIGURE 25-8 Fischer projections of the meso forms and enantiomers of 2,3-dichlorobutane (* designates a chiral carbon).

7. Describe the conversion of a straight-chain monosaccharide into its cyclic form, and the joining of monosaccharide units into polysaccharides.

The aldohexoses do not exist in the straight-chain form shown in Figure 25-4 but rather as six-membered rings. The principal evidence for the ring is that two forms of D-glucose exist: α-D-glucose and β-D-glucose. Whereas the straight-chain form of glucose has four chiral carbons (numbered 2–5 in Figure 25-9), the ring form has five (1–5 in Figure 25-9). α-D-Glucose and β-D-glucose also are known as pyranoses. The ring opens and closes readily in aqueous solution and thus the α and β forms of D-glucose interconvert. At 25°C, the equilibrium mixture contains about two molecules of β-D-glucose for every α-D-glucose molecule. The chair conformations of α-D-glucose and β-D-glucose in Figure 25-9 show that the —OH on carbon 1 is axial in α-D-glucose and equatorial in β-D-glucose. The equatorial position is favored for a large group (objective 24–5), and β-D-glucose is more stable.

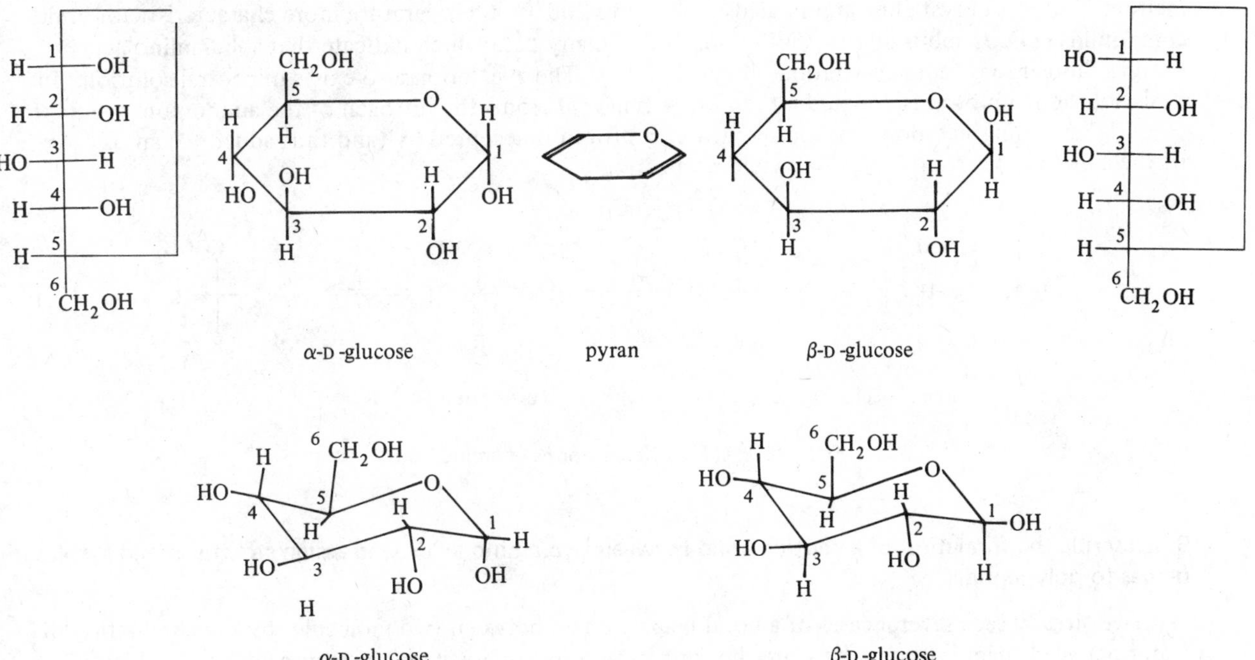

FIGURE 25-9 α- and β-D-glucose.

Monosaccharides join together to form disaccharides, other oligosaccharides, and polysaccharides with the loss of one water molecule for each bond that is formed. The linkage reaction is given in equation [2]. Note that is is the —OH groups on two molecules which react.

$$\text{>C(OH)H} + \text{HO-C<} \rightleftharpoons \text{>C(H)-O-C<} + H_2O \qquad [2]$$

Hexoses can join between carbon 1 on one molecule and carbon 4 on the other, a (1→4) linkage, or they can join by a (1→6) linkage. These linkages may be α or β (axial or equatorial from carbon 1). The monomers or subunits and the linkages for common disaccharides and polysaccharides are given in Table 25-1.

8. Show how the form adopted by an amino acid in solution varies with the pH.

Two groups on an amino acid change form depending on acidity: the amino group (—NH_2) and the carboxylic acid group (—COOH). We have shown both these groups as uncharged (Figure 25-1). Since

TABLE 25-1
Joining of monosaccharides

Carbohydrate name	Name of subunit(s)	Linkage(s)
maltose	glucose	(1→4)
lactose	galactose, glucose	(1→4)
cellobiose	glucose	(1→4)
α-amylose (starch)	glucose	(1→4)
amylopectin (also a component of starch)	glucose	(1→4) backbone, α(1→6) branches to side chains
glycogen (abundant in liver and muscle)	glucose	Same as amylopectin but more highly branched
cellulose	glucose	β(1→4)

the forces between uncharged molecules are relatively low, we would expect solid amino acids to be low melting. Yet most crystalline amino acids melt above 200°C, a temperature more characteristic of ionic compounds ($LiNO_3$ melts at 264°C). This is one of many data which indicate that solid amino acids exist as dipolar ions called zwitterions (Figure 25-10). The zwitterion also exists in neutral solution. In basic solution, a proton is donated by (and thus removed from) the nitrogen of the ammonium group ($—NH_3^+$) yielding an anion. In acidic solution, a proton is accepted by (and thus added to) an oxygen of the carboxylate group ($—COO^-$) yielding a cation.

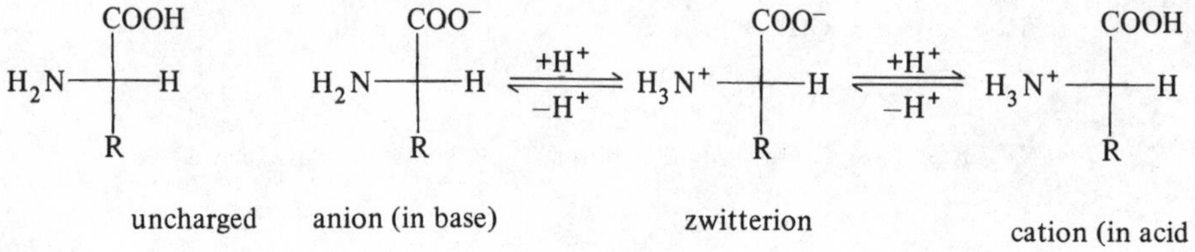

$$\underset{\text{uncharged}}{H_2N—\overset{COOH}{\underset{R}{C}}—H} \qquad \underset{\text{anion (in base)}}{H_2N—\overset{COO^-}{\underset{R}{C}}—H} \underset{-H^+}{\overset{+H^+}{\rightleftharpoons}} \underset{\text{zwitterion}}{H_3N^+—\overset{COO^-}{\underset{R}{C}}—H} \underset{-H^+}{\overset{+H^+}{\rightleftharpoons}} \underset{\text{cation (in acid}}{H_3N^+—\overset{COOH}{\underset{R}{C}}—H}$$

FIGURE 25-10 Different forms of amino acids.

9. Describe the formation of a peptide bond between two amino acids, and assign structures and systematic names to polypeptides.

We have already seen several cases of a bond being formed between two molecules by the elimination of water between them. Among these are the formation of pyrophosphates and pyrosulfates in objective 20-12 and the formation of ethers and esters in equations [20] and [27] of objective 24-15. An analogous reaction occurs between two amino acids.

$$\begin{matrix}H\\H\end{matrix}\!\!>N—\overset{R}{\underset{H}{C}}—C\!\!<\!\!\begin{matrix}OH\\O\end{matrix} + \begin{matrix}H\\H\end{matrix}\!\!>N—\overset{R}{\underset{H}{C}}—C\!\!<\!\!\begin{matrix}OH\\O\end{matrix} \longrightarrow \begin{matrix}H\\H\end{matrix}\!\!>N—\overset{R}{\underset{H}{C}}—\overset{O}{\overset{\|}{C}}—\underset{N}{N}—\overset{R}{\underset{H}{C}}—C\!\!<\!\!\begin{matrix}OH\\O\end{matrix} + H_2O$$

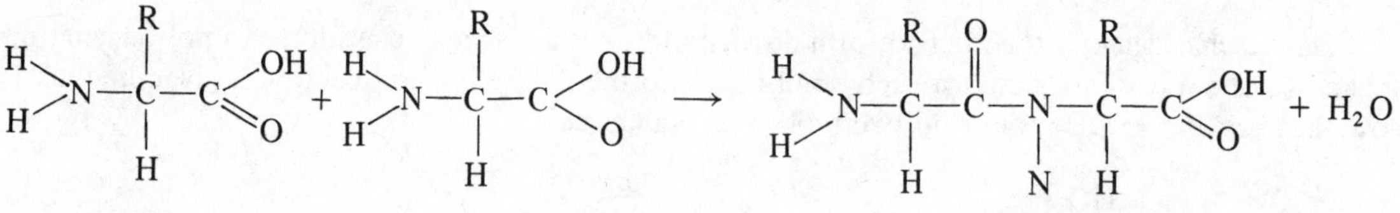

A polypeptide is named by naming the amino acids in order starting at the N-terminal end. Except for the last amino acid (the one at the C-terminal end) the -an or -ine ending of each amino acid is changed to -yl. For large polypeptides, more than ten amino acids, only the peptide sequence is given. This starts at the N-terminal end and used the symbols given in *Table 25-4 in the text.* The symbols, names, and structures should be memorized.

★ **10. Determine the sequence of amino acids in a polypeptide chain from information acquired in the hydrolysis of the polypeptide.**

Degradation means that we break the molecule apart, identify the fragments, and then deduce the structure. In determining the structure of a polypeptide, a large "marker" group is attached to the N-terminal end (the amino group, $—NH_2$). The polypeptide is gently hydrolyzed by heating gently in a mildly acidic or alkaline solution. (A more precise method of hydrolysis is treatment with selective enzymes. Some of these enzymes are so specific that they only hydrolyze the peptide bond joining two distinct amino acids as, for example, an alanine–glycine bond.) Hydrolysis is the reverse of peptide bond formation. The N-terminal marker then is placed on each fragment. The process of gentle hydrolysis followed by marking the N-terminal group is repeated until the chain has been degraded to di-, tri-, and tetrapeptides. The identities of these small molecules are determined by conventional means: melting point, solubility, spectral analysis, and so forth. Putting together the sequence of the polypeptide is a matter of piecing together these fragments.

11. Explain the meaning of primary, secondary, tertiary, and quaternary structure of a protein.

The *primary* structure of a protein is the sequence of amino acids in the molecule, starting at the N-terminal end.

The *secondary* structure refers to how the backbone of the polypeptide chain is arranged in space. Most often the polypeptide chain has the form of an α-helix. Hydrogen bonds are formed between the carboxyl oxygen atoms of one amino acid and the amide nitrogen of the amino acid four positions down the chain. These hydrogen bonds are shown as dashed lines in *Figure 25-12 in the text.*

The *tertiary* structure describes how different parts of the α-helix are held together. The R groups of the amino acids point outward from the helix and therefore can attract each other. Thus the helix will bend into a three-dimensional coil rather like a twisted worm. The forces which hold the tertiary structure together form between the atoms of the R groups. They are of four types (Figure 25-11).

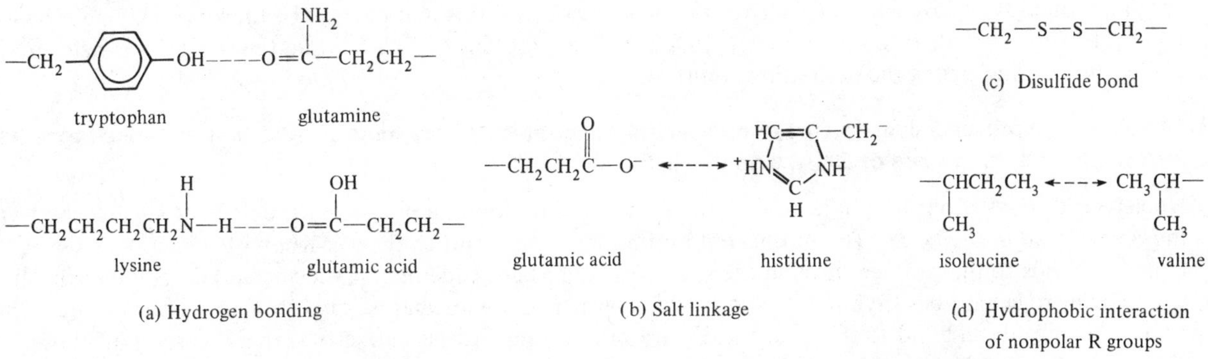

$-CH_2-C_6H_4-OH\cdots O{=}C(NH_2)-CH_2CH_2-$

tryptophan glutamine

$-CH_2CH_2CH_2CH_2N(H)-H\cdots O{=}C(OH)-CH_2CH_2-$

lysine glutamic acid

(a) Hydrogen bonding

$-CH_2CH_2C(=O)-O^- \leftarrow\cdots\rightarrow {}^+HN$ (imidazole ring: $HC{=}C-CH_2-$, NH, C–H)

glutamic acid histidine

(b) Salt linkage

$-CH_2-S-S-CH_2-$

(c) Disulfide bond

$-CH(CH_3)CH_2CH_3 \leftarrow\cdots\rightarrow CH_3CH(CH_3)-$

isoleucine valine

(d) Hydrophobic interaction of nonpolar R groups

FIGURE 25-11 Interactions which influence tertiary structure.

(a) *Hydrogen bonds* link $-NH_2$ or $-OH$ groups of one amino acid's R group and $>C{=}O$ groups of another's. The amino acids with $-NH_2$ groups are asparagine, glutamine, tryptophan, lysine, arginine and histidine. Those with $-OH$ groups are serine, 4-hydroxyproline, threonine, and tyrosine. Those with $>C{=}O$ groups are asparagine, glutamine, aspartic acid, and glutamic acid.
(b) *Salt linkages* occur between acidic and basic R groups. Acidic amino acids are aspartic acid and glutamic acid. Basic ones are lysine, arginine, and histidine.
(c) Disulfide bonds join the two "halves" of cystine.
(d) Nonpolar R groups, such as those in glycine, alanine, valine, leucine, isoleucine, phenylalanine, and proline, tend to point inward in the molecule, away from the polar solvent.

In addition to these attractions between R groups, the protein may be wrapped around and bound to another type of molecule. Thus in hemoglobin the proteins (called globins) are bound to a heme molecule.

The *quaternary* structure of a protein is how two or more individual polypeptide chains are packed together to form the final protein. Many proteins possess only one polypeptide chain and thus have no quaternary structure. But in hemoglobin, for example, four globin chains and four heme molecules combine to produce the final protein.

12. In general terms, explain how lipids, polysaccharides, and proteins are metabolized in the human body and how the energy released by metabolism is stored.

The body breaks down lipids, polysaccharides, and proteins by hydrolysis of the bond between the parts. Thus lipids break down into glycerol and fatty acids, polysaccharides into monosaccharides, and proteins into amino acids.

Lipids, polysaccharides, and proteins are not rapidly hydrolyzed. The human body uses protein catalysts, called enzymes, to speed up these reactions. Both the fatty acids and the monosaccharides are further broken down within the body, resulting ultimately in carbon dioxide and water. Some are stored as fat deposits in the body and as carbohydrate deposits, principally glycogen in liver and muscle tissue. Amino acids can be further metabolized to provide energy but they also are used as raw materials for protein synthesis.

13. Explain enzyme action in terms of the "lock-and-key" model.

Enzymes are protein catalysts. Each enzyme speeds up a certain type of chemical reaction. For example, hydrolases speed up hydrolysis reactions. Other enzymes control the rate of peptide bond formation, disulfide bond formation or breakage, and so forth. Enzymes can be quite specific. There are enzymes for triglyceride hydrolysis which will not affect the rate of polysaccharide hydrolysis. Enzymes also are stereospecific. An enzyme may catalyze a reaction involving α-D-glucose but not affect a reaction involving α-L-glucose.

The molecule on which the enzyme acts is known as the substrate. The involved structure of an enzyme and its high specificity are strong evidence that the substrate fits almost perfectly into a pocket in the enzyme, called the active site. The active site often is only a very small portion of the large enzyme molecule. The substrate fits into the active site much as a key does into a lock. While the substrate is held in place, the enzyme causes the desired reaction.

14. Name the principal constituents of nucleic acids and indicate how these constituents are linked together into chains and, in the case of DNA, a double helix.

Nucleic acids consist of phosphate groups, the purine and pyrimidine bases, and the pentose sugars (shown in *Figure 25-20 in the text*). The purine and pyrimidine bases bond to the 1′ carbon of the pentose sugar. Guanine bonds to the pentose through the same nitrogen as does adenine. Cytosine and uracil bond through the same nitrogen as does thymine. A *nucleotide* consists of a phosphate group bound to a nucleoside. The phosphate group can bond to the 5′ or the 3′ carbon of both pentoses and also to the 2′ carbon of ribose. However, all naturally occurring nucleotides have the phosphate group bound to the 5′ carbon.

Nucleotides form chains by a bond between the phosphate group on one nucleotide and the 3′ carbon on the next nucleotide. This is known as a 3′–5′ linkage. A portion of a nucleic acid chain is shown in *Figure 25-21 in the text.*

The single-stranded DNA forms a double-stranded helix by the formation of hydrogen bonds. A purine (the larger molecules: adenine and guanine) always is hydrogen-bonded to a pyrimidine (the smaller molecules: thymine and cytosine). This base pairing holds the two strands of the chain together. The base pairing and a model of the double helix are shown in *Figure 25-22 in the text.*

15. Explain how DNA replicates itself during cell division; and outline the process of protein synthesis indicating the roles of DNA, mRNA, and tRNA.

In the replication of DNA, the molecule unwinds gradually. As it does so, nucleotides in the cell attach to the exposed base pairs of each of the unwinding chains. The phosphate–pentose bonds are formed through the action of enzymes. The exact details are complicated and have not been completely worked out.

In one-celled organisms protein synthesis begins with transcription, the production of an RNA copy of part of a DNA strand. This close copy is messenger RNA or mRNA and is similar to a copy of a master blueprint. The mRNA molecule, which is single stranded, leaves the nucleus for the cytoplasm of the cell, where it attaches to one or more ribosomes. This grouping of an mRNA molecule and several ribosomes is a polysome. Ribosomes are made of protein and ribosomal RNA or rRNA. Molecules of transfer RNA or tRNA are attracted to the polysomes. There a portion of the tRNA molecule, called an anticodon, matches up with a codon on mRNA. Each codon specifies a particular amino acid.

An amino acid is bound to the end of the tRNA molecule away from the anticodon and has been carried along to the polysome with the tRNA. An enzyme in the cell then forms the peptide bond between adjacent amino acids.

DRILL PROBLEMS

2. (1) Name the following triglycerides.

A. $CH_2OOC(CH_2)_7CH{=}CH(CH_2)_7CH_3$
$|$
$CHOOC(CH_2)_7CH{=}CH(CH_2)_7CH_3$
$|$
$CH_2OOC(CH_2)_7CH{=}CH(CH_2)_7CH_3$

B. $CH_2OOC(CH_2)_8CH_3$
$|$
$CHOOC(CH_2)_8CH_3$
$|$
$CH_2OOC(CH_2)_8CH_3$

C. $CH_2OOC(CH_2)_{10}CH_3$
$|$
$CHOOC(CH_2)_7CH{=}CHCH_2CH_3$
$|$
$CH_2OOC(CH_2)_8CH_3$

D. $CH_2OOC(CH_2)_7(CH{=}CH)_3(CH_2)_3CH_3$
$|$
$CHOOC(CH_2)_7(CH{=}CH)_3(CH_2)_3CH_3$
$|$
$CH_2OOC(CH_2)_7(CH{=}CH)_3(CH_2)_3CH_3$

(2) Draw the condensed formula of the following triglycerides.
A. glyceryl dipalmitoleate
B. glyceryl lauromyristopalmitate
C. glyceryl dilaurolinoleate
D. glyceryl linolenate
E. glyceryl ricinoleate
F. glyceryl dioleolaurate

3. (1) Determine the average mole weights and the average number of double bonds per molecule for each of the following oils by using the given average values of the saponification value and the iodine number (in that order).
A. butter (220, 27)
B. coconut oil (256, 8.8)
C. soybean oil (192, 132)
D. safflower oil (191, 148)
(2) Determine the saponification value and the iodine number of each of the following triglycerides.
A. glyceryl oleate
B. glyceryl eleosterate
C. glyceryl stearate
D. glyceryl dilaurolinoleate

6. Draw the enantimoers in Fischer projection for each of the following molecules which is optically active.
A. 2-chloropentane
B. 3-chloro-1-pentene
C. $CH_3CH(NH_2)COOH$
D. $CH_3CH_2CHOHCH_3$
E. 2-chlorobutane
F. 1-chloro-3-methylpentane
G. 1,2-dichlorobutane
H. 1,4-dichlorobutane
I. 1,2-dichloropentane
J. 2-chloropentanol
K. 1,3-dibromopentane
L. 1-bromo-3-chloro-1-butene
M. 3-chloro-4-methyl-1-pentane

10. (1) Based on the fragments which follow, determine the sequence of each polypeptide starting with the N-terminal end. Each fragment starts at the N-terminal end.
A. Lys-Asp-Gly, Glu-Ser-Gly, Ala-Ala-Glu, Asp-Gly-Ala, Ala-Glu-Ser
B. Lys-Phe-Ile, Arg-Glu-Lys, Ala-Ala-His, Glu-Lys-Phe, Ala-His-Arg-Glu
C. Cys-Lys-Ala, Tyr-Cys-Lys, Arg-Arg-Gly, Ala-Arg-Arg
D. Phe-Ala, Ser-Ala-Gly, Glu-Ser-Ala, Ala-Glu
E. Val-Ala-Lys-Glu, Met-Gly-Gly-Phe, Val-Met-Tyr-Cys, Glu-Glu-Phe-Val, Tyr-Cys-Glu, Glu-Phe-Val, Glu-Trp-Met, Gly-Gly-Phe
(2) Name the results of A through D above.

QUIZZES (15–20 minutes each)

Choose the best answer for each question.

Quiz A

1. Which function is not regulated by a hormone? (a) pregnancy; (b) vision; (c) metabolism; (d) growth; (e) reproduction.

2. The mole weight of a triglyceride can be determined from its (a) iodine number; (b) oxygen content; (c) unsaturation; (d) saponification value; (e) none of these.
3. All lipids contain (a) nitrogen atoms; (b) long-chain alcohols; (c) glycerol; (d) a phosphate group; (e) none of these.
4. Which of the following is not a monosaccharide? (a) glucose; (b) ribose; (c) glyceraldehyde; (d) sucrose; (e) fructose.
5. Which molecule is not optically active? (a) 1,2-dichlorobutane; (b) 1,4-dichlorobutane; (c) 1,3-dichlorobutane; (d) 1,2-dichloropropane; (e) none of these.
6. What symbol does not specify how a compound rotates polarized light? (a) d; (b) +; (c) *dl;* (d) D; (e) none of these.
7. Amino acids are joined together in proteins by (a) a 3′–5′ linkage; (b) a $\beta(1 \rightarrow 4)$ linkage; (c) DNA; (d) an ester; (e) none of these.
8. The R group $NH_2CH_2CH_2$— is that of which amino acid? (a) alanine; (b) serine; (c) threonine; (d) arginine; (e) none of these.
9. Glycine is (a) a sugar; (b) an amino acid; (c) a nucleoside; (d) a lipid; (e) none of these.

Quiz B

1. Which of the following is not present in DNA? (a) purine; (b) pentose; (c) phosphate; (d) heme; (e) pyrimidine.
2. The number of double bonds in a triglyceride molecule can be determined from its (a) mole weight; (b) saponification value; (c) iodine number; (d) oxygen content; (e) none of these.
3. Lipids always contain (a) glycerol; (b) phosphate groups; (c) double bonds; (d) fatty acids; (e) none of these.
4. Which of the following is a monosaccharide? (a) sucrose; (b) glycogen; (c) starch; (d) cellulose; (e) none of these.
5. Which molecule is optically active? (a) 1,2-dichlorobutane; (b) 1,4-dichlorobutane; (c) *cis*-1,2-dichlorocyclobutane; (d) *cis*-2-butene; (e) none of these.
6. D refers to (a) rotation of plane polarized light; (b) a meso form; (c) configuration of sugars; (d) racemic mixtures; (e) none of these.
7. What is present in all amino acid molecules? (a) a chiral carbon; (b) two nitrogen atoms; (c) a peptide bond; (d) a —COOH or —COO^- group; (e) none of these.
8. Glycine has what —R group? (a) —CH_3; (b) —H; (c) —CH_2CH_2COOH; (d) —CH_2SH.
9. 2′-Deoxyribose is (a) a nucleoside; (b) a sugar; (c) a wax; (d) a nucleotide; (e) a purine.

Quiz C

1. All of the following are major components of every cell except (a) triglycerides; (b) carbohydrates; (c) proteins; (d) nucleic acids; (e) hormones.
2. Which of the following fatty acids is unsaturated? (a) palmitic acid; (b) oleic acid; (c) lauric acid; (d) stearic acid; (e) none of these.
3. Biological waxes are (a) the same as triglycerides; (b) the same as lecithins; (c) soluble in water; (d) esters of long-chain alcohols; (e) none of these.
4. Which of the following does *not* contain six carbon atoms? (a) deoxyribose; (b) glucose; (c) aldohexose; (d) methylcyclopentane; (e) benzene;
5. Which molecule is optically active? (a) 2-chlorobutane; (b) 1-chlorobutane; (c) *trans*-propene; (d) *cis*-propene; (e) none of these.
6. Which of the following is optically active? (a) racemate; (b) *dl*; (c) an enantiomer; (d) *DL*; (e) none of these.
7. In basic solution, an amino acid has what charges? (a) + and −; (b) − only; (c) + only; (d) no charge; (e) none of these.
8. The R— group of serine is (a) —CH_2OH; (b) —CH_2COOH; (c) —$CH_2CH_2CH_3$; (d) —$CH_2CH_2CH_2CH_2NH_2$; (e) none of these.
9. Cytosine is (a) an amino acid; (b) a nucleoside; (c) a purine; (d) a sugar; (e) none of these.

Quiz D

1. All of the following contain both carbon and nitrogen atoms except (a) nucleosides; (b) nucleotides; (c) pyrimidines; (d) purines; (e) glucose.
2. A fatty acid usually has (a) many branched chains; (b) many double bonds; (c) no double bonds; (d) an odd number of carbon atoms; (e) none of these.
3. Which of the following is *false* about lipids? (a) some are triglycerides; (b) they are soluble in water; (c) they are soluble in hexane; (d) some are lecithins; (e) all are true.
4. Which of the following is *not* a monosaccharide? (a) ribose; (b) fructose; (c) glucose; (d) glycogen; (e) pentose.
5. Enantiomers *always* (a) have an asymmetric carbon; (b) have different physical properties; (c) change the color of light; (d) rotate polarized light; (e) none of these.
6. Which of the following is *not* broken by hydrolysis with dilute acid? (a) DNA; (b) peptide bonds; (c) polysaccharides; (d) ring forms of hexoses; (e) triglycerides.
7. At the isoelectric point an amino acid has what charges? (a) + and −; (b) none; (c) + only; (d) − only; (e) none of these.
8. $—CH_2—C_6H_4—OH$ is the R group of (a) tryptophan; (b) tyrosine; (c) serine; (d) phenylalanine; (e) none of these.
9. Which of the following is a pyrimidine? (a) adenine; (b) glycine; (c) phenylalanine; (d) thymine; (e) none of these.

SAMPLE TEST (20 minutes)

1. Draw the cyclic forms of threose, $OHC(CHOH)_2CH_2OH$, remembering that five- or six-membered rings are more stable than larger or smaller ones.
2. Describe three structural features of proteins which influence their tertiary structure. Give an example of each feature.
3. On gentle hydrolysis a protein gives the following polypeptides, with the N-terminal end first in each case. Give the amino acid sequence of the protein.
   Gly-His-Leu, Phe-Val-Asp, Cys-Gly-Ser-His, His-Leu-Cys-Gly, Asp-Gly-His, Gly-Ser-His, Phe-Val

Chapter 26

Natural Resources, the Environment, and Synthetic Materials

REVIEW OF OBJECTIVES

★ **1. Name a number of key chemicals of commerce, describe how they are manufactured, and list some of their uses.**

The top 50 chemicals produced in the United States are given in *Table 26-12 in the text*, along with the method of manufacture and the uses of the top 20. You should be familiar with the production and uses of all inorganic substances in the list of 50 and also of the 10 most important organic substances. A brief summary of each of these follows. The ranking of the substance in parentheses follows its formula.

Sulfuric acid, H_2SO_4 (1). *Uses:* Manufacture of fertilizers such as $(NH_4)_2SO_4$ and of sulfate-containing chemicals such as Na_2SO_4 and $Al_2(SO_4)_3$; as a general strong acid in the manufacture of other chemicals such as HCl and H_3PO_4; in cleaning metal surfaces; and in refining petroleum. *Production:* By the contact process (*Section 26-8 in the text*) using pure sulfur mined by the Frausch process (*Section 26-8 in the text*); or by the lead chamber process (*Section 26-8 in the text*) using sulfur recovered from metal and petroleum refining.

Lime, CaO (2). *Uses:* As a base in the manufacture of chemicals; raw material for Na_2CO_3; as a flux in steel production; removal of pollutants from industrial wastes and sewage. *Production:* Thermal decomposition of limestone.

$$CaCO_3(s) \xrightarrow{\Delta} CaO(s) + CO_2(g) \qquad [1]$$

Ammonia, NH_3 (3). *Uses:* Fertilizers; industrial refrigerant; as a raw material in the production of nitrates in fertilizers, plastics, and explosives. *Production:* From $N_2(g)$ and $H_2(g)$ by the Haber process (*Section 14-8 in the text*).

Oxygen, O_2 (4). *Uses:* Steel making (removal of carbon by oxidation); welding; in medicine. *Production:* Distillation of liquid air (*Section 26-2 in the text*).

Nitrogen, N_2 (5). *Uses:* Production of NH_3 by the Haber process; as a liquid for refrigeration; inert atmosphere when welding active metals; as a packing gas for foods. *Production:* Distillation of liquid air (*Section 26-2 in the text*).

Ethylene, $H_2C{=}CH_6$ (6). *Uses:* As a raw material for ethylene glycol (antifreeze), polyethylene, ethanol (solvent), and styrene and vinyl chloride (both used to make polymers). *Production:* Cracking of petroleum gases, ethane, and propane. (*Section 26-9 in the text*).

Sodium hydroxide, NaOH (7). *Uses:* Aluminum refining; petroleum refining to remove HNO_3 and H_2SO_4; soap and detergent production; as a strong base in pulp and paper production and the manufacture of many chemicals; treatment of industrial wastes. *Production:* Electrolysis of NaCl(aq) (*Section 19-9 in the text*).

Chlorine, Cl_2 (8). *Uses:* Purification of drinking water; production of plastics (as polyvinyl chloride) and solvents (as carbon tetrachloride); as a bleach for paper and fabrics. *Production:* Electrolysis of NaCl(aq) (*Section 19-9 in the text*).

Phosphoric acid, H_3PO_4 (9). *Uses:* In the production of fertilizers, detergents, and food additives; to rustproof metals before painting. *Production:* Reaction of phosphate rock with sulfuric acid. There are extensive deposits of phosphate rock in Florida, Tennessee, and the western United States.

$$Ca_3(PO_4)_2 + 3\,H_2SO_4 + 6\,H_2O \rightarrow 2\,H_3PO_4(aq) + 3\,CaSO_4 \cdot 2\,H_2O(s) \qquad [2]$$

Nitric acid, HNO_3 (10). *Uses:* As a nitrating agent in the manufacture of plastics, dyes, explosives, and lacquers; in the production of fertilizers. *Production:* By catalytic oxidation of NH_3 in the Ostwald process (objective 13–9; *Section 20-7 in the text*).

Sodium carbonate, Na_2CO_3 (11). *Uses:* Raw material for glass and soap; general cleaner (washing soda); as a water softener. *Production:* Mined as trona ores in the western United States; produced from NaCl and $CaCO_3$ in the Solvay process (objective 4–14).

Ammonium nitrate, NH_4NO_3 (12). *Uses:* As a fertilizer and as an explosive. *Production:* Direct reaction of ammonia and nitric acid.

$$NH_3(g) + HNO_3(aq) \rightarrow NH_4NO_3(aq) \quad [3]$$

The water is evaporated and NH_4NO_3 is shipped as a solid, which is much more efficient than shipping ammonia gas or nitric acid solutions.

Propylene, $CH_3CH{=}CH_2$ (13). *Uses:* As a raw material for solvents, polymers, detergents, and rubbers; in the manufacture of propylene glycol (antifreeze). *Production:* Cracking of petroleum gases (*Section 26-9 in the text*).

Urea, $O{=}C(NH_2)_2$ (14). *Uses:* High nitrogen fertilizers; protein supplement feeds for livestock; production of plastics and adhesives. *Production:* Direct reaction of $CO_2(g)$ and $NH_3(g)$ at high pressure (225 atm) and temperature (180°C) to produce ammonium carbamate, $NH_4CO_2NH_2(aq)$, equation [4]. This is followed by decomposition to urea at lower pressures (20 atm), equation [5].

$$CO_2(g) + 2\,NH_3(g) \xrightleftharpoons{H_2O} NH_4CO_2NH_2(aq) \quad [4]$$
$$NH_4CO_2NH_2(aq) \rightleftharpoons O{=}C(NH_2)_2(aq) + H_2O \quad [5]$$

Benzene, C_6H_6 or ϕ—H (15). *Uses:* Production of polymers as rubbers, plastics, and nylons; production of and use as solvent. *Production:* Separation from petroleum and coal tar by distillation; reforming of cyclohexanes and cyclopentanes (*Section 26-9 in the text*).

Toluene, $C_6H_5CH_3$ or ϕ—CH_3 (16). *Uses:* Production of benzene, solvents and coatings, explosives; motor fuel and aviation gasoline; in polyurethane foams. *Production:* Same methods as benzene.

Ethylene dichloride, CH_2ClCH_2Cl (17). *Uses:* Production of vinyl chloride and ethylene diamine; solvent. *Production:* Addition of Cl_2 to ethylene in the presence of ethylene dibromide at 50°C.

$$CH_2{=}CH_2(g) + Cl(g) \xrightarrow{C_2H_4Br_2} CH_2ClCH_2Cl \quad [6]$$

Ethyl benzene, $C_6H_5CH_2CH_3$ or ϕ—CH_2CH_3 (18). *Uses:* Raw material for styrene and solvent. *Production:* Reaction of benzene and ethylene.

$$\phi\text{—}H + CH_2{=}CH_2 \xrightarrow{H_3PO_4} \phi\text{—}CH_2CH_3 \quad [7]$$

Vinyl chloride, $CH_2{=}CHCl$ (19). *Uses:* Production of vinyl plastics including polyvinyl chloride (objective 24–12, equation [15]). *Production:* Elimination of HCl from ethylene dichloride (objective 24–8, Equation [6]).

$$CH_2ClCH_2Cl \xrightarrow[\text{KOH (alcohol)}]{500^\circ C \text{ or}} CH_2{=}CHCl + HCl$$

Styrene, $C_6H_5CH{=}CH_2$ or ϕ—$CH{=}CH_2$ (20). *Uses:* styrene plastics such as polystyrene and synthetic rubber. *Production:* Dehydrogenation of ethylbenzene.

$$\phi\text{—}CH_2CH_3 \xrightarrow[AlCl_3]{600^\circ C} \phi\text{—}CH{=}CH_2 + H_2(g) \quad [8]$$

Methanol, CH_3OH (21). *Uses:* Production of formaldehyde and polymers; solvent. *Production:* Catalytic combination of carbon monoxide and hydrogen at high temperatures (300°C) and pressures (250–275 atm) (*Section 24-5 in the text*).

$$CO(g) + H_2(g) \xrightarrow{Cu} CH_3OH(l) \quad [9]$$

Carbon dioxide, CO_2 (23). *Uses:* Food and industrial refrigeration (Dry Ice); carbonated beverages; fire extinguishers; production of Na_2CO_3. *Production:* Burning of carbon containing materials; by-product of fermentation and of calcining limestone (equation [1]).

Hydrochloric acid, HCl (26). *Uses:* Cleaning metal surfaces, removal of boiler scale; refining tin ores; food processing. *Production:* From sodium chloride with sulfuric acid.

$$2\ NaCl + H_2SO_4 \rightarrow Na_2SO_4 + 2\ HCl \qquad [10]$$

As a by-product of chlorinating hydrocarbons, for example,

$$C_6H_6 + Cl_2 \rightarrow C_6H_5Cl + HCl \qquad [11]$$

By direct union of the elements.

$$H_2(g) + Cl_2(g) \rightarrow 2\ HCl(g). \qquad [12]$$

(Both $H_2(g)$ and $Cl_2(g)$ are produced during the electrolysis of NaCl(aq) solutions.)

Ammonium sulfate, $(NH_4)_2SO_4$ (31). *Uses:* Fertilizer; fireproofing fabric; tanning leather. *Production:* Scrubbing by-product ammonia from coke oven gas with H_2SO_4.

$$2\ NH_3 + H_2SO_4 \rightarrow (NH_4)_2SO_4 \qquad [13]$$

Coke, used as a fuel in steel manufacture, is produced by heating coal in the absence of air.

Carbon black, C (34). *Uses:* Pigment and toughener in automobile tires and other rubber products; pigment in plastics, inks, and paints. *Production:* Partial oxidation of hydrocarbons, the same process which produces soot.

Aluminum sulfate, $Al_2(SO_4)_3$ (37). *Uses:* Clarifying water; sizing paper; as a mordant for dyes. *Production:* Reaction of bauxite (principally Al_2O_3) with H_2SO_4.

$$Al_2O_3 + 3\ H_2SO_4 \rightarrow Al_2(SO_4)_3 + 3\ H_2O \qquad [14]$$

Sodium sulfate, Na_2SO_4 (39). *Uses:* Manufacture of kraft paper for digesting pulpwood; detergent production; production of glass, dyes, and textiles. *Production:* By-product of the production of HCl from NaCl and H_2SO_4, equation [10].

Calcium chloride, $CaCl_2$ (41). *Uses:* Melting ice and snow on roadways; solutions used to lay dust on the highways and in low-temperature refrigeration. *Production:* By-product of the production of Na_2CO_3 by the Solvay process (objective 4–14).

Sodium silicates: many forms, from sodium metasilicate (Na_2SiO_2) to sodium sesquisilicate ($Na_4SiO_4 \cdot Na_2SiO_3 \cdot 11H_2O$) to sodium orthosilicate (Na_4SiO_4) (46). *Uses:* Production of soaps and detergents, pigments, and adhesives; cleaning metals; water and paper treatment. Adhesives are used for cardboard, plywood, and flooring. *Production:* Reaction of sodium carbonate with sand at 1400°C.

$$Na_2CO_3 + n\ SiO_2 \rightarrow Na_2O(SiO_2)_n + CO_2 \qquad [15]$$

Sodium tripolyphosphate, $Na_5P_3O_{10}$ (47). *Uses:* Water softeners as sequestering agents (see objective 22–15). *Production:* From sodium carbonate and phosphoric acid.

$$2\ Na_2CO_3 + 3\ H_3PO_4 \rightarrow 2\ NaH_2PO_4 + Na_2HPO_4 + 2\ CO_2 + 2\ H_2O \qquad [16]$$

$$NaH_2PO_4 + 2\ Na_2HPO_4 \xrightarrow{\Delta} Na_5P_3O_{10} + 2\ H_2O \qquad [17]$$

Titanium dioxide, TiO_2 (49). *Use:* White pigment for paint, paper, and plastics. *Production:* Ilmenite ($FeTiO_3$) is dissolved in concentrated H_2SO_4. The $FeSO_4$ is precipitated out. The resulting $TiOSO_4$ solution is concentrated and boiled with seeds of TiO_2. TiO_2 then precipitates.

2. Describe how air is liquefied and how O_2, N_2, and Ar are obtained from liquid air.

Air is liquefied by first compressing it to a pressure of 5–6 atm. On expansion it cools to less than 75 K and liquefies. The liquid air is separated by fractional distillation by the boiling points of the components: 77.40 K for N_2 (78.1%), 90.19 K for O_2 (20.9%), and 87.27 K for Ar (0.9%).

3. Outline the natural processes by which atmospheric nitrogen is fixed and then returned to the atmosphere —the nitrogen cycle.

Lightning forms nitrogen oxides from nitrogen and oxygen.

$$N_2 + O_2 \rightarrow NO_x$$

Nitrogen oxides react further with water to form nitrates. Bacteria in the root nodules of legumes such as peas and beans also produce nitrates in the soil. Plants absorb the soil nitrates and form proteins and amino acids. Dead plants and animals decay with the help of bacteria to form ammonia. Bacteria turn ammonia into nitrites and then into nitrates which can be absorbed by plants. Other bacteria change nitrates into elemental nitrogen which returns to the atmosphere. This cycle is summarized in *Figure 26-2 in the text.*

★ **4. Outline the steps required to produce pure Zn, Cu, Fe, Al, Mg, and Ti from their naturally occurring forms and write equations for the key reactions involved.**

Zinc ores are roasted in oxygen.

$$2\ ZnS(s) + 3\ O_2(g) \xrightarrow{\Delta} 2\ ZnO(s) + 2\ SO_2(g) \qquad [18]$$

The ZnO(s) is reduced with carbon.

$$ZnO(s) + C(s) \xrightarrow{\Delta} Zn(g) + CO(g) \qquad [19]$$

The zinc can be refined by distillation or ZnO(s) can be dissolved in H_2SO_4 and then electrolyzed after purifying the solution.

$$ZnO(s) + H_2SO_4 \rightarrow ZnSO_4(aq) + H_2O \qquad [20]$$
$$ZnSO_4(aq) + H_2O \rightarrow Zn(s) + H_2SO_4(aq) + \tfrac{1}{2}\ O_2(g) \qquad [21]$$

Copper ores are concentrated by flotation. They are roasted at temperatures below 800°C to produce FeO from the FeS in the ore.

$$2\ FeS(s) + 3\ O_2(g) \rightarrow 2\ FeO(s) + 2\ SO_2(g) \qquad [22]$$

The resulting mixture is heated to 1400°C in the presence of sand, SiO_2, forming silicate slag.

$$FeO(s) + SiO_2(s) \rightarrow FeSiO_3(l) \qquad [23]$$

The Cu_2S which remains has air blown through it.

$$Cu_2(S)(l) + 3\ O_2(g) \rightarrow 2\ Cu_2O + 2\ SO_2(g) \qquad [24]$$
$$2\ Cu_2O + Cu_2S(l) \rightarrow 6\ Cu(l) + SO_2(g) \qquad [25]$$

The copper is poured into molds. As it solidifies, bubbles of SO_2 freeze giving the appearance of blisters and the name of *blister copper.* Blister copper is used for copper pipe, rain gutters, and other structural purposes. Much copper is used to conduct electricity. For this use, it is refined electrolytically (*Section 19-9 in the text*) with blister copper as the anode.

Iron is produced from oxide ores such as Fe_2O_3 and Fe_3O_4. The oxides are reduced by CO(g) and H_2(g).

$Fe_2O_3 + 3\ CO \rightarrow 2\ Fe + 3\ CO_2$ [26]
$Fe_2O_3 + 3\ H_2 \rightarrow 2\ Fe + 3\ H_2O$ [27]

H_2 and CO are produced from coke (see $(NH_4)_2SO_4$ production in objective 26–1), oxygen, and water.

$2\ C + O_2 \rightarrow 2\ CO$ *and* $C + CO_2 \rightarrow 2\ CO$ *and* $C + H_2O \rightarrow CO + H_2$ [28]

Many impurities are removed in a slag formed using $CaCO_3$.

$CaCO_3 \rightarrow CaO + CO_2$
$CaO + SiO_2 \rightarrow CaSiO_3$ [29]
$3\ CaO + P_2O_5 \rightarrow Ca_3(PO_4)_2$

The final product is called pig iron and contains 3–4% C.

Aluminum is produced by the Hall–Heroult process. Bauxite ores are treated with concentrated NaOH(aq) which dissolves the Al_2O_3 but not other metal oxides. Dilution of the sodium aluminate solution precipitates $Al(OH)_3$, which is heated to 1000°C to form alumina.

Al_2O_3 (in bauxite) $+ 6\ NaOH \rightarrow 2\ Na_3AlO_3 + 3\ H_2O$ [30]
$Na_3AlO_3 + 3\ H_2O \rightarrow Al(OH)_3 + 3\ NaOH$ [31]
$2\ Al(OH)_3 \xrightarrow{\Delta} Al_2O_3 + 3\ H_2O$ [32]

The alumina is dissolved in cryolite, Na_3AlF_6, and electrolyzed between carbon electrodes.

$3\ C(s) + 4\ Al^{3+} + 6\ O^{2-} \rightarrow 4\ Al(l) + 3\ CO_2(g)$ [33]

Magnesium is obtained from seawater, using quicklime produced from the $CaCO_3$ in seashells.

$CaCO_3(s) \xrightarrow{\Delta} CaO(s) + CO_2(g)$ [34]
$CaO(s) + H_2O(l) \xrightarrow{\Delta} Ca(OH)_2(aq)$ [35]
$Ca(OH)_2(aq) + Mg^{2+}(aq) \rightarrow Mg(OH)_2(s) + Ca^{2+}(aq)$ [36]

After the $Mg(OH)_2(s)$ is filtered and washed, it is treated with HCl(aq) to produce $MgCl_2(aq)$.

$Mg(OH)_2(s) + 2\ HCl(aq) \rightarrow MgCl_2(aq) + 2\ H_2O(l)$ [37]

The $MgCl_2(aq)$ is evaporated to dryness, then melted and electrolyzed in a steel vessel with a carbon anode.

$MgCl_2(l) \rightarrow Mg(l) + Cl_2(g)$ [38]

Titanium is produced from rutile ore, TiO_2. The oxide is converted to the chloride.

$TiO_2(s) + 2\ Cl_2(g) + 2\ C(s) \rightarrow TiCl_4(g) + 2\ CO(g)$ [39]

The chloride is reduced by magnesium metal at high temperatures (800°C) under an inert atmosphere (He gas).

$TiCl_4(g) + 2\ Mg(l) \rightarrow Ti(s) + 2\ MgCl_2(l)$ [40]

5. Describe the processes that are used to increase the yield of gasoline from petroleum and improve its performance in internal combustion engines.

Gasoline consists of hydrocarbons with six to nine carbon atoms per molecule. Most of the hydrocarbons in petroleum are quite a bit larger. When heated with a catalyst, these long-chain hydrocarbons break down–a process known as cracking. Other catalysts form double bonds and rearrange straight chains into branched ones–reforming. Very short two- to four-carbon chains combine together to form branched hydrocarbon chains–alkylation. Finally, toluene and other aromatic hydrocarbons are added.

6. Illustrate the principal methods of polymer formation–free-radical addition and condensation–through structural formulas of monomers and polymers.

Free-radical addition polyerization was described in objective 24–12. Condensation polymerization occurs when a small molecule such as water is eliminated between two parts of the growing molecule. Examples of condensation polymerization are the growth of polysaccharides (objective 25–7), polypeptides (objective 25–9), and polynucleotides (objective 25–14) and the formation of polyphosphates and polysilicates (objective 20–12).

7. Distinguish between natural and synthetic polymers and among elastomers, fibers, and plastics.

In addition to polysaccharides, proteins, and polynucleotides, rubber also is a natural polymer. Rubber is composed of isoprene monomers as shown in Figure 26-1. Synthetic polymers include polyethylene, polystyrene, polyvinyl chloride, dacron, nylon, neoprene, teflon, and lucite. These are classified and summarized in *Table 26-11 in the text.* Elastomers are polymers which can deform or stretch under stress. Fibers are long single- or double-stranded chains. Plastics are crosslinked chains that form a somewhat rigid two- or three-dimensional structure. Thus they can be formed into films such as mylar or solids as polyvinyl chloride.

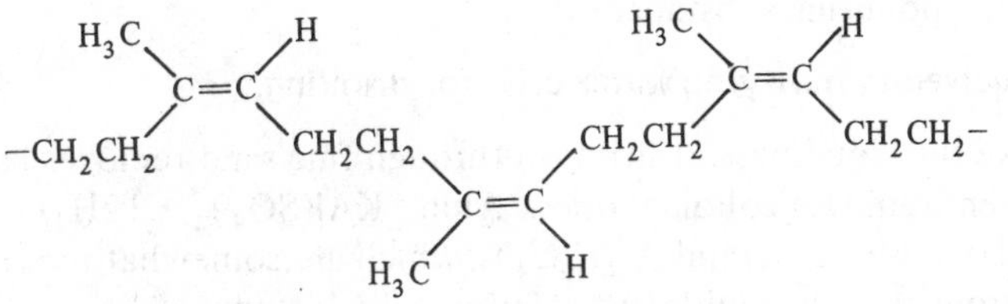

H_3C H H_3C H
C=C C=C
$-CH_2CH_2$ CH_2CH_2 CH_2CH_2 CH_2CH_2-
C=C
H_3C H

FIGURE 26-1 Rubber–polyisoprene.

★ **8. Explain how temporary and permanent hardness arises in water and describe several methods of softening water.**

Water hardness is caused by Mg^{2+}, Ca^{2+}, and Fe^{2+} cations and multiply charged anions. Temporary hardness is due to the bicarbonate ion, HCO_3^-. Boiling will make such water soft.

$$2\,HCO_3^- \xrightarrow{\Delta} CO_3^{2-} + H_2O + CO_2\,(g) \qquad [41]$$

The carbonate ion precipitates the divalent cations as carbonates–$MgCO_3$, $CaCO_3$, $FeCO_3$–commonly called boiler scale. Other methods of softening hard water involve either sequestering the divalent metal ions with chelating agents (see objective 22–15) or removing them by ion exchange (see objective 26–10). A final method of softening temporary hard water is by adding a strong base.

$$OH^- + HCO_3^- \rightarrow H_2O + CO_3^{2-} \qquad [42]$$
$$M^{2+} + CO_3^{2-} \rightarrow MCO_3\,(s)$$

Lime (CaO) is used in treating municipal water supplies.

$$CaO\,(s) + H_2O\,(l) \rightarrow Ca(OH)_2\,(aq) \qquad [43]$$

Permanent hard water is due to multiply charged anions other than carbonate, such as sulfate. It cannot be softened by boiling, but Na_2CO_3 can be added to precipitate $MgCO_3$, $CaCO_3$, and $FeCO_3$.

9. Describe the cleaning action of soaps and detergents.

Soaps and detergents are sodium or potassium salts of long-chain fatty acids. Soaps are carboxylate fatty acids; they have a terminal —COO^- group. Detergents are sulfonate fatty acids–with a terminal —OSO_3^- group. Often the R group of a detergent is aromatic. The principal advantage of detergents is that their calcium and magnesium salts are soluble. Calcium and magnesium salts of soaps form a precipitate known as soap scum (bathtub ring). Soaps and detergents clean by keeping small droplets of oil suspended in solution. The nonpolar R group dissolves in the oil droplet, while the polar carboxylate or sulfonate group extends into the water of the solution. Because all the polar groups are negatively charged, the droplets repel each other and do not condense and separate out of solution.

10. Explain how an ion-exchange process works.

The action of zeolites as water softeners is one example of ion exchange. In the use of zeolites, Ca^{2+}, Mg^{2+}, and Fe^{2+} ions in water are replaced by Na^+ ions. When the solution containing the divalent cations passes through the channels in the zeolite, the dipositive cations are attracted to its silicate structure and held there. The Na^+ ions go into solution. Thus temporary hard water becomes a solution of $NaHCO_3$ (baking soda) on passage through a zeolite. The zeolite is "recharged" by passing a concentrated NaCl solution through it. The very high $[Na^+]$ forces the dipositive cations out of the zeolite, replacing them with Na^+ ions.

11. Discuss how the BOD and COD tests relate to water pollution.

Impurities in polluted water often use oxygen as they decompose. Fish and other aquatic animals need this dissolved oxygen to live. The biochemical oxygen demand (BOD) measures the amount of oxygen needed by microorganisms as they consume the polluting substances. Chemical reactions also can consume oxygen. Thus the chemical oxygen demand (COD) measures the amount of strong oxidizing agent needed to oxidize all of the polluting substances.

12. Outline the steps involved in purifying water used for drinking.

The first step is to remove the cloudiness. Filtration through fine sand removes large particles. Treatment with a clarifying agent removes colloidal ones. Alum, $KAl(SO_4)_2 \cdot 12H_2O$, is a common clarifying agent, but it is being replaced by $FeCl_3$ and $Al_2(SO_4)_3$ which are somewhat more economical to produce. All of these substances produce an insoluble but gelatinous hydroxide.

$$Al^{3+} + 3\,OH^- \rightarrow Al(OH)_3\,(s)$$
$$Fe^{3+} + 3\,OH^- \rightarrow Fe(OH)_3\,(s) \qquad [44]$$

As the hydroxide settles, it takes the small colloidal particles with it. The water then may be treated with an inexpensive softener such as $Ca(OH)_2$ or Na_2CO_3. Aeration removes unwanted dissolved gases such as H_2S, SO_2, and NH_3 and dissolves N_2 and O_2. Water with no dissolved gases tastes "flat." Aeration also kills some bacteria. The final step is treatment with a germicide. Although chlorine gas commonly is used in the United States, it has the disadvantage of transforming some organic chemicals into harmful compounds and giving the water a disagreeable taste. Ozone is being used more frequently.

13. List some common air pollutants and describe their sources and methods used to control them.

The internal combustion engine produces four major air pollutants: carbon monoxide, hydrocarbons, lead, and nitrogen oxides. Recent redesign of automobile engines has reduced the amounts of these pollutants Nitrogen oxides are produced when nitrogen and oxygen are heated at high pressures. Lowering the operating pressure of the internal combustion engine (reducing the compression ratio) has reduced the quantity of nitrogen oxides. Carbon monoxide and hydrocarbon emissions have been reduced in two ways. First, more air is mixed with the fuel (the engine runs "leaner"), giving more complete combustion. Second, a catalytic converter has been added to encourage complete oxidation. The catalyst in the converter is poisoned by lead. Lead is produced from tetraethyllead, $Pb(CH_2CH_3)_4$, which is added to gasoline to increase its octane number. Catalytic converters prohibit the use of tetraethyllead, removing a major source of lead pollution.

Sulfur oxides are produced in industrial operations, such as the roasting of metal sulfide ores and in burning high sulfur coal. This problem is being attacked at two points. Methods are being developed to remove sulfur from coal before it is burned. Or SO_2 is removed as it is produced. The fluidized bed method burns coal in the presence of limestone which absorbs the SO_2 to yield gypsum, $CaSO_4$. Air is continually passed through the combustion bed of finely ground coal and limestone to promote contact between the reactants. The air makes the bed look like a fluid; hence the name. The final method of removing SO_2 (g) is to bubble it through a basic solution such as slaked lime, $Ca(OH)_2$. This process is known as scrubbing. Its principal disadvantage is the resulting large volume of wet $CaSO_3$ which must be disposed of.

Carbon dioxide results from the combustion of fossil fuels. Some does enter the atmosphere from the burning of wood, but this amounts to recycling CO_2 which was recently removed during the growth of the tree. An increased concentration of CO_2 poses the danger that the temperature of the earth may rise, because of the greenhosue effect. This occurs because CO_2 (g) allows ultraviolet light to pass through but not infrared light. The temperature rises in much the same way as it does in an automobile on a bright winter day and for the same reason.

14. Discuss the factors involved in the formation of photochemical smog, the eutrophication of a lake, and environmental mercury poisoning.

Smog formation often is due to a temperature inversion in which a layer of warm air sits above the cooler air at the surface of the earth. This prevents the surface air from mixing with the rest of the atmosphere. Pollutants reach high concentrations near the surface. Industrial smog consists mainly of particulate matter and sulfur oxides. Photochemical smog is distinguished by its high ozone levels. O_3 is produced photochemically from mitrogen oxides and oxygen. Because ozone is an effective oxidizing agent, it readily combines with unburned hydrocarbons to produce irritating organic compounds.

Eutrophication refers to the process where a clear body of water turns into a cloudy one, fish die, the water becomes more cloudy, and eventually a swamp develops. This is a natural process, but the addition of nutrients to the water speeds it up. With a lot of food, microscopic plants called algae thrive and many more grow than can be supported by dissolved oxygen in the water. They die and sink to the bottom where their decay also consumes oxygen. Fish cannot live when the water has little dissolved oxygen and thus they disappear. The lake "dies," meaning that all aquatic life is gone. Both phosphates and nitrates added to water increase the rate of eutrophication.

Mercury compounds have long been known to be poisonous. Hatters formerly used hot mercury(II) nitrate to soften felt. They often developed chronic mercury poisoning or "hatter's disease." The phrase "mad as a hatter" and the Mad Hatter in *Alice in Wonderland* are based on this occupational disease. Elemental mercury was thought to be inert, but recent work has shown that some bacteria consume it. The mercury then passes up the food chain and concentrates in fish.

DRILL PROBLEMS

1. List at least two key chemicals which fit each of the following descriptions.

A. strong acid
B. strong base
C. fertilizer
D. produced from NH_3
E. produced using H_2SO_4
F. used for water treatment
G. used in metal fabrication and/or production
H. refrigerant
I. produced by electrolysis
J. used as a solvent
K. has no important uses other than polymer production
L. pigment
M. in detergents

4. Write the equation for each of the following processes.

A. reducing copper ore to metallic copper
B. roasting zinc ore
C. generating the reducing agent from iron ore
D. producing metallic magnesium
E. purifying aluminum ore
F. initial treatment of titanium ore
G. separation of $Mg(OH)_2$ from solution
H. producing metallic aluminum
I. formation of silicate slag in iron metallurgy

8. Write one or several chemical equation to describe each of the following processes.

A. softening temporary hard water by boiling
B. softening hard water by adding $Ca(OH)_2$
C. softening hard water by adding Na_2CO_3
D. formation of soap scum
E. use of a zeolite to soften hard water
F. sequestering with sodium tripolyphosphate

QUIZZES (20 minutes each)

Choose the best answer to each question.

Quiz A

1. Which of the following is *not* one of the top 50 chemicals? (a) H_2SO_4; (b) N_2; (c) O_2; (d) NaCl; (d) CH_3OH.
2. Which of the following is mined and used directly? (a) Na_2CO_3; (b) $Al_2(SO_4)_3$; (c) CaO; (d) TiO_2; (e) none of these.
3. Which pollutant is due to the internal combustion engine? (a) SO_2; (b) particles; (c) CO; (d) CO_2; (e) none of these.
4. Electrostatic precipitators are used to remove what pollutant? (a) PO_4^{3-} from water; (b) SO_2 from air; (c) H_2S and SO_2 from water; (d) dust from air; (e) none of these.
5. Which metal is produced from sulfide ores? (a) Mg; (b) Cu; (c) Ti; (d) Mg; (e) none of these.
6. During the natural cycle, nitrogen does *not* appear in which form? (a) N_2; (b) NH_3; NO_3^-; (d) NO_2^-; (e) it appears in all of these forms.

Quiz B

1. The top ten chemicals are almost all (a) acids; (b) inorganic; (c) organic; (d) metals; (e) elements.
2. Which of the following is *not* used in water treatment? (a) $Na_5P_3O_{10}$; (b) CaO; (c) Na_2CO_3; (d) $Al_2(SO_4)_3$; (e) all are used.
3. Which pollutant causes streams and lakes to eutrophy? (a) PO_4^{3-}; (b) lead; (c) SO_2; (d) CO; (e) none of these.
4. The fluidized bed method burns coal with (a) water; (b) liquid oxygen; (c) gasoline; (d) Na_2CO_3; (e) none of these.
5. Which metal is electrolyzed as the chloride? (a) Cu; (b) Al; (c) Ti; (d) Fe; (e) none of these.
6. Mercury is a hazard in the form of (a) the element; (b) insoluble compounds; (c) water-soluble compounds; (d) all compounds; (e) all forms.

Quiz C

1. Which element is *not* one of the top 50 chemicals? (a) N_2; (b) O_2; (c) C; (d) H_2; (e) none of these.
2. Which of the following is used as a fuel? (a) O_2; (b) toluene; (c) CH_2ClCH_2Cl; (d) benzene; (e) none of these.
3. Which pollutant is important in industrial smog? (a) NO; (b) SO_2; (c) CO; (d) CO_2; (e) particulates.
4. Catalytic converters remove or reduce all pollutants *except* (a) CO; (b) hydrocarbons; (c) lead; (d) nitrogen oxides; (e) none of these.
5. Which metal is *not* produced or refined by electrolysis? (a) Cu; (b) Ti; (c) Al; (d) Mg; (e) none of these.
6. Water hardness affects the action of (a) detergents; (b) soaps; (c) aeration; (d) eutrophication; (e) none of these.

Quiz D

1. Which acid is *not* one of the top 50 chemicals? (a) H_2SO_4; (b) HCl; (c) $HC_2H_3O_2$; (d) HNO_3; (e) $HClO_4$.
2. Which of the following is used as a fertilizer? (a) $Na_5P_3O_{10}$; (b) H_3PO_4; (c) H_2SO_4; (d) $(NH_4)_2SO_4$; (e) none of these.
3. Which pollutant is removed by "scrubbing"? (a) CO_2; (b) particulates; (c) SO_2; (d) CO: (e) lead.
4. What water treatment step kills bacteria? (a) filtration; (b) softening; (c) treatment with $Al_2(SO_4)_3$; (d) aeration; (e) none of these.
5. Which metal may be refined by distillation? (a) Zn; (b) Cu; (c) Mg; (d) Ti; (e) none of these.
6. Permanent hardness is *not* removed by (a) ion exchange; (b) Na_2CO_3; (c) $Na_5P_3O_{10}$; (d) aeration; (e) none of these.

SAMPLE TEST (20 minutes)

1. Why are alkali metals and alkaline earths recovered from seawater, while copper, lead, zinc, and iron are mined as sulfide and oxide ores?
2. What compounds are produced using H_2SO_4 in the production process, either as a reactant or to provide an acidic medium for reaction?
3. Name two air pollutants produced principally by the internal combustion engine and explain how they are controlled.

Appendix I

Answers and Solutions

CHAPTER 1

Drill Problems

8. A. 0°C B. 37.8°C C. 209°F D. −3.9°C E. 212°F F. 39°F G. −26°C H. 260°C I. −76°F J. −459.57°F

9. & 11. (a) A. 88 in. B. 205 fl oz C. 7.244 mi D. 2.346 lb E. 165.4 mm F. 3.74×10^4 μm G. 0.146 L H. 0.03754 m^3 I. 2.72×10^7 mg J. 0.454 lb K. 8.46 fl oz L. 2.23 m M. 0.355 L N. 85.0 kg O. 22 cm P. 3.78 L Q. 236 cm^3 R. 14.2 g S. 57.7 kg T. 5.92 gal U. 0.998 oz V. 3.38 fl oz W. 16.4 yd

(2) A. 0.765 m^3 B. 1.31 yd^3 C. 1728 $in.^3$ D. 6.45 cm^3 E. 929 cm^2 F. 202 gal G. 7.35 ft^3 H. 4.10 L

10. A. 5.00 g, 0.176 oz B. 96.5 g, 3.40 oz C. 56.7 g, 2.00 oz D. 197 g E. 250 g F. 4.41 cm^3 G. 5.60 cm^3 H. 57.7 cm^3 I. 23.5 cm^3 J. 836 cm^3 K. 208 lb L. 746 g M. 17.6 $in.^3$ N. 7.17 $in.^3$

10a. A. 2.86 g B. 0.13 ton Al, 87 L Fe C. 3.7×10^5 L N_2, 3.2×10^3 L air D. 71.4 lb solder E. 20 lb bleach, 2.3 gal bleach F. 0.306 gal whiskey G. 1.99 L vinegar H. 2.27×10^3 g sulfuric acid I. \$0.50, 2.0×10^2 pennies J. \$33.60, 3.72 g silver nitrate

12. & 13. (a) A. 4 B. 6 C. 4 D. 4 E. 2 F. 4–6 G. 3 H. 4 I. 8 J. 5 K. 6 L. 7 M. 6 N. 4 O. 5 P. 5 Q. 2–4 R. 1–5 S. 4 T. 6 U. 6 V. 3 W. 1–4 X. 3

(2) A. 6.168 B. 213.2 C. 1.200×10^3 D. 3136 E. 6.196 F. 14.16 G. 0.002246 H. 152.0 I. 0.001987 J. 3.024×10^5 K. 14.16 L. 3.141×10^4

(3) A. 0.592 B. 1.701×10^{-23} C. 56 D. 2×10^4 or 1.7×10^4 or 1.75×10^4 E. 8.9×10^2 F. 3.0×10^1 G. 13.6 H. 0.21 or 0.208 or 0.2078 I. 15.3 J. 3.60×10^7

(4) A. 122 B. 87.6 C. −91 D. 108.8 E. 4.362 F. 696 G. 1033.7 H. 75.9

(5) A. 1.4×10^3 B. 412 C. −1.33 D. 3.8 E. 1.98

13a. A. 3.74×10^{-3} B. 1.2×10^3 C. 4.06389×10^3 D. 1.751×10^5 E. 6.4604×10^{10} F. 6.627×10^{-27} G. 9.475×10^{-3} H. 3.74×10^4 I. 1.42×10^{-4} J. 1.7645×10^4 K. 2.12×10^8 L. 2.66×10^{-3} M. 8.43×10^{17} N. 9.400×10^7 O. 4.963×10^{-8} P. 8.43214×10^{-1} Q. 2.12×10^8 R. 8.39×10^{-1} S. 8.9413×10^2 T. 8.314×10^{-7} U. 4.90006×10^5 V. 9.204×10^8 W. 8.7012×10^{27} X. 1.413×10^{-7} Y. 1.7645×10^{-11} Z. 2.66 AA. 8.134×10^{-5}

Quizzes

A: 1. (d) 2. (a) 3. (e) 4. (e) 5. (d) 6. (d) 7. (b) 8. (b) 9. (a) 10. (e) 90°F 11. (c) 12. (d)

B: 1. (a) 2. (a) 3. (a) 4. (e) 5. (a) 6. (d) 7. (c) 8. (c) 9. (e) 10. (a) 11. (a) 12. (d)

C: 1. (c) 2. (b) 3. (c) 4. (d) 5. (a) 6. (c) 7. (e) 8. (c) 9. (e) 10. (e) 11. (e) 12. (b)

D: 1. (b) 2. (d) 3. (b) 4. (b) 5. (d) 6. (a) 7. (c) 8. (b) 9. (a) 10. (c) 11. (c) 12. (b)

Sample Test

1. $10.72\ \text{g} \times \dfrac{0.417\ \text{g Au}}{\text{g ring}} \times \dfrac{\text{lb}}{454\ \text{g}} \times \dfrac{16\ \text{oz}}{\text{lb}} \times \dfrac{\$652.50}{\text{oz}} = \$103$

2. a. physical—no change of substance, only of physical state b. physical—separation of a mixture c. chemical—two new substances are produced d. chemical—a compound is produced from elements e. physical—separation of a mixture air, a mixture (later separated physically); pressure, temperature (not forms of matter); natural gas, possibly a mixture, more likely a compound since it is used in a reaction; steam, carbon dioxide, compounds; hydrogen, one of the elements; ammonia gas, a compound.

3. a. $12.5 \dfrac{\text{lb}}{\text{in.}^2} \times 16\ \text{oz} \times \left(\dfrac{\text{in.}}{2.54\ \text{cm}}\right)^2 = 31.0\ \text{oz/cm}^2$

$31.0 \dfrac{\text{oz}}{\text{cm}^2} \times \dfrac{\text{lb}}{16\ \text{oz}} \times \dfrac{\text{kg}}{2.20\ \text{lb}} \times \left(\dfrac{100\ \text{cm}}{\text{m}}\right)^2 = 8.81 \times 10^3\ \text{kg/m}^2$

b. $(77.4°\text{F} - 32.0)\dfrac{5}{9} = 25.2°\text{C}$ c. $5.2\ \text{m}^3 \times \dfrac{1000\ \text{L}}{\text{m}^3} = 5.2 \times 10^3\ \text{L} \times \dfrac{\text{qt}}{.946\ \text{L}} = 5.5 \times 10^3\ \text{qt}$

CHAPTER 2

Drill Problems

1. (1) A. 8.21 g products, 1.80 g water B. 8.15 g water, 6.35 g Cu, 79.8% Cu C. 10.8 g water, 60.0% water D. 2.23 g Fe, 69.9% Fe, 0.592 g carbon dioxide, 0.592 ton carbon dioxide E. 14.36 g products, 7.96 g copper(II) oxide F. 10.8 g water, 19.2 g oxygen, 4.27 lb. oxygen
(2) A. 28.6 g S, 28.5 g oxygen B. 27.3 g C, 72.7 g oxygen C. 8.32 g hydrogen, 66.7 g oxygen D. 21.1 g oxygen, 53.0 g Ca E. 23.1 g table salt, 9.1 g Na F. 182 g ammonia, 150 g nitrogen
(3) Mass ratios are given in the same order as the compounds are listed, followed by whole number ratios.
A. g K/g O = 4.88:2.45:1.63 or 1.99:1.50:1.00 or about 6:3:2 B. g C/g H = 12.0:3.00:4.00:5.99 or about 12:3:4:6 C. g Cl/g O = 4.43:2.22:0.634 or 6.99:3.50:1.00 or about 14:7:2 D. g Cl/g S = 1.11:2.22:4.43 or 1.00:2.00:3.99 or about 1:2:4 E. g N/g H = = 4.68:7.00:42.5:13.9 or 1:00:1.50:9.08:2.97 or about 2:3:18:6 F. g P/g H = 10.2:10.2:10.4 or about 1:1:1; g O/g P = 2.07:1.54:1.03 or 2.01:1.50:1.00 or about 4:3:2 G. g S/g H = 16:16:16 or 1:1:1; g O/g S = 1.50:1.99:2.49 or about 3:4:5

8. A. $^{81}Br^-$, −1, 46 n B. $^{59}Co^{3+}$, $Z = 27$, 24 e^- C. +2, $A = 43$, $Z = 20$, 18 e^-, 23 n D. $^{15}N^{3-}$, $A = 15$, 10 e^- E. ^{20}Ne, 10 e^-, 10 n F. $^{127}I^-$, −1, 74 n G. $^{23}Na^+$, $Z = 11$, 10 e^- H. 4+, $A = 192$, $Z = 76$, 72 e^-, 116 n I. impossible since $A < A - Z$ J. $^{52}Cr^{2+}$, 22 e^-, 28 n K. $^{60}Co^{2+}$, +2, 33 n L. $^{17}F^-$, $Z = 9$, 10 e^- M. −2, $A = 80$, $Z = 34$, 36 e^-, 46 n N. $^{14}C^{4-}$, $Z = 6$, 10 e^- O. $^{118}Sn^{4+}$, 46 e^-, 68 n

9. A. 246.5314 B. 1.11435 C. 5.06364 D. 3.62797 E. 162.219 F. 254.293 G. 249.140 H. 159.868 I. 10.6212 J. 41.6073 K. 54.2572 L. 0.383873

10. A. Li, 6.941, 92.58% B. 10.81, 20.0%, 80.0% C. C, 13.0, 1.11% D. Ne, 20.18, 9.6% E. Cu, 69.5%, 30.5% F. 35.453, 36.947, 24.47% G. K, 41, 6.9% H. Ga, 69.7, 39.6% I. 79.904, 50.7%, 49.3% J. 85.47, 86.91, 27.85%

Quizzes

A: 1. (a) 2. (c) 3. (a) 4. (b) 5. (c) 6. (c) 7. (c) 8. (c)
B: 1. (c) 2. (b) 3. (c) 4. (a) 5. (e) 6. (b) 7. (a) 8. (a)
C: 1. (a) 2. (e) 3. (b) 4. (d) 5. (d) 6. (d) 7. (b) 8. (d)
D: 1. (e) 2. (a) 3. (e) 4. (b) 5. (b) 6. (d) 7. (e) 8. (e)

Sample Test

1. $\frac{16.00 \text{ g O}}{\text{mol O}} \times \frac{\text{mol O}}{\text{mol X}} \times \frac{46.7 \text{ g X}}{53.5 \text{ g O}} = 14.0 \frac{\text{g X}}{\text{mol}}$

2. a. isotope b. radioactivity c. atomic number d. Dalton e. cathode tube emission f. Millikan g. Rutherford h. fundamental particle I. Thomson

3. [10.013 + (11.009 × 4)/5 = 10.810 amu (boron)

CHAPTER 3

Drill Problems

1. A. 1.01, 0.416 g, 2.48 × 10^{23} atoms B. S, 2.72 mol, 1.64 × 10^{24} atoms C. 16.0, 25.4 g, 9.58 × 10^{23} atoms D. 12.0, 6.02 g, 0.501 mol E. Cl, 1.52 g, 2.57 × 10^{22} atoms F. N, 0.153 mol, 9.21 × 10^{22} atoms G. 24.3, 4.08 mol, 2.46 × 10^{24} atoms H. P, 155 g, 5.00 mol I. 79.9, 4.89 × 10^{-3} g, 3.69 × 10^{19} atoms J. 39.1, 5.64 × 10^{-3} g, 1.44 × 10^{-4} mol K. 9.01, 4.52 × 10^{11} g, 3.02 × 10^{34} atoms L. F, 1.59 × 10^{-5} mol, 9.57 × 10^{18} atoms

3. A. 472.2 g/mol B. 58.5 g/mol C. 260.7 g/mol D. 106.3 g/mol E. 84.0 g/mol F. 213.0 g/mol G. 208.3 g/mol H. 34.0 g/mol I. 27.0 g/mol J. 301.2 g/mol K. 152.0 g/mol L. 27.6 g/mol

3a. A. 152.0 g/mol, 1.14 mol B. 93.9 g/mol, 232 g C. 58.5 g/mol, 3.98 mol D. 159.4 g/mol, 11.1 g E. 162.3 g/mol, 0.346 mol F. 34.0 g/mol, 66.7 mol G. 40.0 g/mol, 58.8 g H. 76.3 g/mol, 0.638 g I. 324.6 g/mol, 0.0127 mol J. 99.0 g/mol, 789 g K. 85.0 g/mol, 7.64 mol L. 144.9 g/mol, 316 g

5. & 6. A. sodium chloride B. aluminum sulfate C. strontium chloride D. chromium(II) hydrogen phosphate E. sodium thiosulfate F. copper(I) chloride G. iron(III) phosphate H. lithium sulfite I. potassium hydrogen sulfate N. chromium(III) cyanide O. barium sulfate P. $KMnO_4$ Q. $NaC_2H_3O_2$ R. $FeCl_3$ S. $Sr(NO_3)_2$ T. $AgClO_3$ U. Cu_2O V. $Hg_2(NO_3)_2$ W. $Fe(NO_2)_3$ X. $Sr(HCO_3)_2$ Y. $Zn(H_2PO_4)_2$ Z. K_2CrO_4 AA. $Mg(CN)_2$ BB. Al_2O_3 CC. NaOH DD. $Ca(OCl)_2$
BB. Al_2O_3 CC. NaOH DD. $Ca(OCl)_2$

5. A. water B. hydrogen sulfide C. carbon dioxide D. dinitrogen trioxide E. diphosphorus pentoxide F. iodine pentachloride G. nitrogen trichloride H. sulfur tetrachloride I. chlorine dioxide J. sulfur trioxide K. NO L. P_2O_5 M. NH_3 N. HF O. SiF_4 P. XeF_6 Q. PBr_3 R. SiS_2 S. CH_4 T. BCl_3

7. A. 1.05 × 10^{23} C atoms B. 4.01 × 10^{-3} g NH_3 C. 19.8 kg $CsIO_3$ D. 1.57 × 10^{24} O atoms E. 2.70 × 10^{24} HCl molecules F. 5.83 × 10^{24} atoms G. 1.21 Mg H_2SO_4 H. 6.88 kg $(NH_4)_2Cr_2O_7$ I. 2.82 × 10^{24} atoms J. 0.0266 g $BaCl_2$ K. 2.06 × 10^{25} O atoms L. 7.36 mol C M. 0.500 mol H N. 111 mol C O. 2.70 mol Al

8. & 9. A. H_2SO_3, 82.06 g/mol, 58.54% O B. 40.0 g/mol, 57.5% Na, 40.0% O, 2.5% H C. $MgCO_3$, 84.3 g/mol, 28.9% Mg D. 213.0 g/mol, 12.7% Al, 19.7% N, 67.6% O E. $LiClO_4$, 106.4 g/mol, 33.3% Cl F. 153.4 g/mol, 42.6% Zn, 15.6% C, 41.7% O G. K_2MnO_4, 197.1 g/mol, 32.5% O H. 76.3 g/mol, 31.8% Mg, 31.4% C, 36.7% N I. $CuCO_3$, 123.5 g/mol, 9.7% C J. 98.0 g/mol, 3.1% H, 31.6% P, 65.3% O K. $Hg(BrO_3)_2$, 456.4 g/mol, 44.0% Hg

10. A. 0.406 g C, 0.102 g H, 0.812 g O; $C_2H_6O_3$ B. 61.72 g C, 12.87 g H, 0 g O; C_2H_5 C. 3.05 g C, 1.03 g H, 4.06 g O; CH_4O D. 0.0140 g C, 0.00118 g H, 0 g O, CH E. 0.658 g C, 0.110 g H, 0.175 g O; $C_5H_{10}O$

F. 6.11 g C, 1.53 g H, 4.06 g O; C_2H_6O G. 7.77 g C, 1.30 g H, 10.33 g O; CH_2O H. 3.23 g C, 0.6501 g H, 3.44 g O; $C_5H_{12}O_4$ I. 0.00665 g C, 0.00112 g H, 0.0177 g O; CH_2O_2 J. 0.106 g C, 0.0178 g H, 0.432 g O; CH_2O_3 K. 60.6 g C, 5.04 g H, 80.4 g O; CHO L. 86.62 g C, 5.82 g H, 0 g O; C_5H_4
11. A. 67.49% Ba B. 10.92% Mg C. 73.20% Pb D. 0.668% Ca E. 29.42% Al F. 24.7% Cr G. 4.27% Li H. 52.20% F I. 15.44% S J. 95.45% C
12. A. 58.71 g/mol B. 55.87 g/mol C. 15.6 g/mol D. 23.00 g/mol E. 140.1 g/mol F. 26.97 g/mol G. 39.11 g/mol H. 144.2 g/mol

Quizzes

A: 1. (d) 2. (d) 3. (b) 4. (c) 5. (e) 6. (b) 7. (c) 8. (d) 9. (d) 10. (b) 11. IF_5
B: 1. (a) 2. (a) 3. (c) 4. (e) 5. (d) 6. (b) 7. (b) 8. (d) 9. (b) 10. N_2O_3 11. sulfur trioxide
C: 1. (d) 2. (d) 3. (d) 4. (b) 5. (c) 6. (c) 7. (a) 8. (c) 9. (a) 10. dichlorine heptoxide 11. SiF_4
D: 1. (a) 2. (a) 3. (b) 4. (e) 5. (d) 6. (e) 7. (b) 8. (a) 9. (d) 10. P_2O_3 11. sulfur tetrachloride

Sample Test

1. $16.88 \text{ g } CO_2 \times \frac{12.01 \text{ g C}}{44.01 \text{ g } CO_2} = 4.606 \text{ g C} \times \frac{\text{mol C}}{12.01 \text{ g}}$ $= 0.3835$ mol C

$9.21 \text{ g } H_2O \times \frac{2.016 \text{ g H}}{18.01 \text{ g } H_2O} = 1.03 \text{ g H} \times \frac{\text{mol H}}{1.008 \text{ g H}}$

$= 1.023$ mol H

mass O = 9.72 g − 4.606 g C − 1.030 g H = 4.08 g O

$\times \frac{\text{mol O}}{16.0 \text{ g O}} = 0.255$ mol O

0.384 mol C/.255 = 1.51 mol C 1.023 mol H/.255 = 4.01 mol H 0.255 mol O/.255 = 1.00 mol O $C_3H_8O_2$

2.

$$\frac{2.9 \text{ g Fe} \times \text{mol Fe}/55.8 \text{ g Fe} \times 6.023 \times 10^{23} \text{ Fe atoms/mol Fe}}{2.6 \times 10^{13} \text{ red blood cells}}$$

$= 1.2 \times 10^9$ Fe atoms/red blood cell

3. a. NH_4CN b. magnesium phosphate c. $Fe(C_2H_3O_2)_2$ d. lead(II) sulfide e. $HgCl_2$ f. potassium bromite

CHAPTER 4

Drill Problems

2. A. $2 Al + 3 MgO \rightarrow 3 Mg + Al_2O_3$ B. $AlCl_3 + 3 NH_4OH \rightarrow Al(OH)_3 + 3 NH_4Cl$ C. $3 AgNO_3 + Na_3PO_4 \rightarrow Ag_3PO_4 + 3 NaNO_3$ D. $Cl_2 + 2 KI \rightarrow 2 KCl + I_2$ E. $Fe_2(SO_4)_3 + 3 Ca(OH)_2 \rightarrow 2 Fe(OH)_3 + 3 CaSO_4$ F. $Ba(NO_3)_2 + (NH_4)_2CO_3 \rightarrow BaCO_3 + 2 NH_4NO_3$ G. $2 KOH + H_2SO_4 \rightarrow K_2SO_4 + 2 H_2O$ H. $Fe(OH)_2 + 2 HCl \rightarrow FeCl_2 + 2 H_2O$ I. $CuSO_4 + H_2S \rightarrow CuS + H_2SO_4$ J. $2 AgNO_3 + K_2CrO_4 \rightarrow Ag_2CrO_4 + 2 KNO_3$

2a. (1) A. potassium dichromate B. silver bromate C. magnesium bisulfite D. potassium hypoiodite E. sodium perchlorate F. potassium thiocyanate G. lead(IV) carbonate H. copper(II) oxalate I. potassium oxide J. thallium(I) sulfide K. tin(IV) Manganate or tin(II) permanganate L. Manganese(II) iodate M. nickel(II) cyanide N. manganese(II) cyanate O. cadmium sulfate P. manganese(II) sulfite Q. ammonium dichromate R. cobalt(II) manganate S. silver thiocyanate T. lithium peroxide U. mercury(I) acetate V. thallium(III) sulfide W. silver dichromate X. gold(III) sulfate Y. magnesium iodate Z. cadmium bisulfite
(2) A. SrO_2 B. $MnSO_3$ C. PbC_2O_4 D. $RbBrO_3$ E. $Mg(CNO)_2$ F. NaHS G. $Ca(IO)_2$ H. FeO_2 I. Ag_2S J. $Ba(IO_3)_2$ K. $CdSO_3$ L. K_2MnO_4 M. $AsCl_3$ N. $Cr(BrO_2)_2$ O. $Sn(CO_3)_2$ P. As_2S_3 Q. $Mn(HCO_3)_2$ R. $Pb(CO_3)_2$ S. $Au_2Cr_2O_7$ T. $K_2C_2O_4$ U. MnS_2O_3 V. H_2O_2 W. $Au(IO_3)_3$ X. NaCN Y. $Cu(CNO)_2$ Z. SnF_2

2b. A. sulfuric acid B. HNO_3 C. H_2SO_4 D. acetic acid E. $HC_2H_3O_2$ F. hydrochloric acid G. phosphoric acid H. sulfurous acid I. iodic acid J. HF K. HNO_2 L. hypofluorous acid M. oxalic acid N. HIO_4 O. manganic acid P. HBrO Q. HCN R. hypoiodous acid S. H_2CO_3 T. $HMnO_4$ U. $HClO_4$ V. chlorous acid

3. A. $4 P + 5 O_2 \rightarrow 2 P_2O_5$ B. $2 Na + O_2 \rightarrow Na_2O_2$ C. $2 Al + 6 HCl \rightarrow 2 AlCl_3 + 3 H_2$ D. $Ca + 2 H_2O \rightarrow Ca(OH)_2 + H_2$ E. $2 FeCl_3 + 3 Ca(OH)_2 \rightarrow 2 Fe(OH)_3 + 3 CaCl_2$ F. $2 Al + N_2 \rightarrow 2 AlN$ G. $6 HCl + Fe_2O_3 \rightarrow 3 H_2O + 2 FeCl_3$ H. $3 Cl_2 + 3 H_2O \rightarrow 5 HCl + HClO_2$ I. $CaSO_3 + H_2SO_4 \rightarrow CaSO_4 + H_2O + SO_2$ J. $Al(OH)_3 + 3 HCl \rightarrow AlCl_3 + 3 H_2O$ K. $2 NaCl + H_2SO_4 \rightarrow Na_2SO_4 + 2 HCl$ L. $2 Pb(NO_3)_2 \rightarrow 2 PbO + 4 NO + 3 O_2$ M. $3 HNO_2 \rightarrow HNO_3 + 2 NO + H_2O$ N. $3 Ca(OH)_2 + 2 H_3PO_4 \rightarrow Ca_3(PO_4)_2 + 6 H_2O$ O. $SiF_4 + 2 H_2O \rightarrow 4 HF + SiO_2$

3a. A. $Cu + 2 Fe^{3+} \rightarrow Cu^{2+} + 2 Fe^{2+}$ B. $Zn + 2 H^+ \rightarrow Zn^{2+} + H_2$ C. $2 H^+ + S^{2-} \rightarrow H_2S(g)$ D. $Pb^{2+} + 2 Hg^{2+} \rightarrow Pb^{4+} + Hg_2{}^{2+}$ E. $2 Fe^{3+} + 3 Sn^{2+} \rightarrow 2 Fe + 3 Sn^{4+}$ F. $3 H^+ + N^{3-} \rightarrow NH_3(g)$ G. $6 CN^- + Fe^{2+} \rightarrow Fe(CN)_6{}^{4-}$ H. $2 Bi^{3+} + 3 S^{2-} \rightarrow Bi_2S_3(s)$
(2) A. $2 Cl^- + Pb^{2+} \rightarrow PbCl_2(s)$ B. $3 Ca^{2+} + 2 PO_4{}^{3-} \rightarrow Ca_3(PO_4)_2(s)$ C. $Ba^{2+} + CO_3{}^{2-} \rightarrow BaCO_3(s)$ D. $Cl^- + H^+ \rightarrow HCl(g)$ E. $OH^- + H^+ \rightarrow H_2O(l)$ F. $S^{2-} + 2 H^+ \rightarrow H_2S(g)$ G. $2 Ag^+ + CrO_4{}^{2-} \rightarrow Ag_2CrO_4(s)$ H. $Ba^{2+} + SO_4{}^{2-} \rightarrow BaSO_4(s)$ I. $Cd^{2+} + S^{2-} \rightarrow CdS(s)$ J. $Fe^{3+} + 3 OH^- \rightarrow Fe(OH)_3(s)$

4. C = combination, De = decomposition, Di = displacement, M = metathesis
A. C: $2 Al + 3 Br_2 \rightarrow 2 AlBr_3$ B. Di: $2 Al + Fe_2O_3 \rightarrow 2 Fe + Al_2O_3$ C. M: $AlCl_3 + 3 KOH \rightarrow 3 KCl + Al(OH)_3$ D. M: $BaCl_2 + Na_2CO_3 \rightarrow BaCO_3 + 2 NaCl$ E. M: $BaCl_2 + 2 AgNO_3 \rightarrow Ba(NO_3)_2 + 2 AgCl$ F. C: $BaO + SO_3 \rightarrow$

$BaSO_4$ G. M: $Ba(OH)_2 + H_2CO_3 \rightarrow BaCO_3 + 2\,H_2O$
H. C: $Br_2 + H_2 \rightarrow 2\,HBr$ I. M: $Cd(NO_3)_2 + (NH_4)_2S \rightarrow CdS + 2\,NH_4NO_3$ J. Di: $Ca + 2\,H_2O \rightarrow Ca(OH)_2 + H_2$
K. Di: $6\,HCl + 2\,Al \rightarrow 2\,AlCl_3 + 3\,H_2$ L. C: $H_2O + Li_2O \rightarrow 2\,LiOH$ M. M: $3\,Ba(OH)_2 + 2\,H_3PO_4 \rightarrow Ba_3(PO_4)_2 + 6\,H_2O$ N. C: $BaO + H_2O \rightarrow Ba(OH)_2$
O. M: $CaO + 2\,HCl \rightarrow CaCl_2 + H_2O$ P. C: $CaO + CO_2 \rightarrow CaCO_3$ Q. M: $Ca(OH)_2 + 2\,HNO_3 \rightarrow Ca(NO_3)_2 + 2\,H_2O$
R. M: $CaO + 2\,HNO_3 \rightarrow Ca(NO_3)_2 + H_2O$
S. C: $NH_3(g) + HCl(g) \rightarrow NH_4Cl(s)$ T. C: $2\,SO_2 + O_2 \rightarrow 2\,SO_3$ U. Di: $2\,AgNO_3 + Cu \rightarrow Cu(NO_3)_2 + 2\,Ag$
V. C: $Cl_2 + 2\,FeCl_2 \rightarrow 2\,FeCl_3$ W. Di: $Cl_2 + 2\,KI \rightarrow 2\,KCl + I_2$ X. C: $N_2 + 3\,H_2 \rightarrow 2\,NH_3$
Y. M: $2\,Al(OH)_3 + 3\,H_2SO_4 \rightarrow 6\,H_2O + Al_2(SO_4)_3$

5. A. $2\,CH_3OH + 3\,O_2 \rightarrow 2\,CO_2 + 4\,H_2O$ B. $2\,C_6H_6 + 15\,O_2 \rightarrow 12\,CO_2 + 6\,H_2O$ C. $C_5H_{12} + 8\,O_2 \rightarrow 5\,CO_2 + 6\,H_2O$ D. $C_{12}H_{22}O_{11} + 12\,O_2 \rightarrow 12\,CO_2 + 11\,H_2O$
E. $2\,CO + O_2 \rightarrow 2\,CO_2$ F. $HC_2H_3O_2 + 2\,O_2 \rightarrow 2\,CO_2 + 2\,H_2O$ G. $2\,C_7H_6O_2 + 15\,O_2 \rightarrow 14\,CO_2 + 6\,H_2O$
H. $2\,C_9H_6O_4 + 17\,O_2 \rightarrow 18\,CO_2 + 6\,H_2O$ I. $C_{10}H_8 + 12\,O_2 \rightarrow 10\,CO_2 + 4\,H_2O$ J. $C_{19}H_{28}O_2 + 25\,O_2 \rightarrow 19\,CO_2 + 14\,H_2O$

6. & 7. A. 35.4 g HCl, 52.4 g $FeCl_3$, 17.4 cm^3 H_2O
B. 40.5 g $Fe(OH)_3$, 20.5 g H_2O C. 17.8 g $Fe(OH)_3$, 27.0 g $FeCl_3$ D. 50.8 g O_2, 43.7 g CO_2' 21.5 cm^3 H_2O
E. 10.4 g C_5H_{12}, 15.6 g H_2O F. 0.410 g C_5H_{12}, 0.640 L CO_2, 0.616 cm^3 H_2O G. 0.314 g H_2, 1.77 g NH
H. 11.0 g N_2, 2.37 g H_2 I. 90.1 g N_2, 175 L NH_3
J. 10.6 g HNO_3, 6.05 g H_2O, 3.76 L NO   K. 13.3 g HNO_3, 6.34 g NO, 22.5 g HCl   L. 12.2 L HCl, 6.56 g H_2O, 4.08 L NO   M. 8.30 g HNO_3, 0.988 g NO
N. 9.20 g Cu, 27.1 g $Cu(NO_3)_2$ O. 460 g HNO_3, 513 g $Cu(NO_3)_2$, 40.8 L NO   P. 0.802 cm^3 Cu, 1.69 L NO, 2.71 g H_2O

8. & 9. (1) A. 51.26 g, 0.8535 mol   B. 46.30 g, 3.175 *M*
C. 73.2 g, 200 ml (.200 L)   D. 50.9 g, 0.244 mol
E. 0.244 mol, 167 ml   F. 0.492 mol, 2.83 *M*   G. 21.30 g, 0.2128 mol   H. 0.1155 mol, 0.3301 *M*   I. 781 g, 2.06 L (2.06×10^3 ml)   J. 33.7 g, 166 ml   K. 511.0 g, 5.210 mol   L. 0.223 mol, 0.745 *M*
(2) A. $[KNO_3] = 0.0526\,M$, 570 ml   B. 240 ml HCl soln, 360 ml H_2O C. 64.8 ml water, 152 ml total
D. $[NaCl] = 0.271\,M$, 620 ml total   E. 31.3 ml $MgSO_4$ soln, 269 ml water   F. 840 ml total, 700 ml water   G. $[K^+] = 0.117\,M$, 720 ml total
H. 44.4 ml $Al(NO_3)_3$ soln, 356 ml water   I. $[Na^+] = 0.228\,M$, 300 ml total   J. 135 ml total, 85.0 ml KCl soln
K. $[Na^+] = 0.456\,M$, 300 ml total   L. 305 ml $MgSO_4$ soln, 195 ml Na_2SO_4 soln   M. 300 ml KCl soln, $[KCl] = 1.90\,M$
N. $[NO_3^-] = 3.00\,M$, 500 ml total

10. A. 4.19 g Ag_3PO_4, $[NaNO_3] = 0.300\,M$
B. 31.5 ml Na_3PO_4 soln, $[NaNO_3] = 0.473\,M$
C. 131 ml $AgNO_3$ soln, 36.6 g Ag_3PO_4
D. 0.178 M Na_3PO_4 soln, 32.0 ml $NaNO_3$ soln
E. 9.48 g HCN, 176 ml $MgSO_4$ soln   F. 13.4 g $Mg(CN)_2$, 29.2 ml H_2SO_4 soln   G. 45.9 g $Mg(CN)_2$, 32.5 g HCN, $[MgSO_4] = 3.50\,M$ H. 26.7 g $Mg(CN)_2$, 18.9 g HCN
I. 11.3 ml H_2SO_4 soln, 1.22 g H_2O J. 55.4 g Al_2O_3, 29.3 g H_2O K. $[Al_2(SO_4)_3] = 0.333\,M$, 3.53 g H_2O
L. 14.0 g Al_2O_3, 412 ml H_2SO_4 soln   M. $[KOH] = 7.06\,M$, 42.5 g CO_2, $[K_2CO_3] = 3.53\,M$ N. 4.27 g CO_2, 194 ml K_2CO_3 soln, 1.75 g H_2O O. $[KOH] = 0.429\,M$, 0.548 g H_2O P. 3.81 g CO_2, 1.56 g H_2O Q. $[H_2SO_4] = 1.82\,M$, 121 ml K_2SO_3 soln, 3.28 g H_2O R. 217 ml KOH soln, 5.15 g H_2O S. 88.3 ml H_2SO_3 soln, 124 ml K_2SO_3 soln

11. A. 0.0750 *M*   B. 0.165 *M*   C. 1.25 *M*   D. 1.18 *M*
E. 0.0510 *M*   F. 3.10 *M*   G. 0.0388 *M*   H. 19.4%
I. 0.0697 *M*   J. 0.384 *M*   K. 0.0919 *M*   L. 41.3%
M. 4.44%   N. 62.5%   O. 0.142 *M*

12. A. 64.8 g Ag_3PO_4 produced, 23.1 g $AgNO_3$ left
B. 22.1 g H_2O produced, 23.0 g H_2SO_4 left
C. 6.79 g CO produced, 9.7 g C left   D. 0.220 g H_2 produced, 6.2 g HCl left   E. 34.1 g MgS produced, 6.6 g Mg left   F. 68.8 g CuCl produced, 6.7 g HCl left   G. 32.8 g H_2O produced, 29.5 g SiO_2 left   H. 46.6 g H_2O produced, 175 g $Al(OH)_3$ left   I. 57.8 g H_2SO_4 produced, 121 g HNO_3 left   J. 212 g $FeCl_3$ produced, 100 g Fe_2O_3 left   K. 70.3 g H_2O produced, 64.1 g H_2S left   L. 92.0 g NaCl produced, 5.8 g HCl left, 116 g Na_2TeO_3 left   M. 219 g $ZnCl_2$ produced, 137 g H_3AsO_4 left, 11 g HCl left   N. 42.0 g K_2SO_4 produced, 7 g H_2SO_4 left, 48 g Hg left   O. 19.9 g Cl_2 produced, 48.2 g C_2H_3OCl left, 45 g H_2SO_4 left

13. A. 5.03 g NaCl, 172 ml NaCl soln   B. 8.45 g CO_2, 2.70×10^3 ml HCl soln   C. 61.6 g CO_2, 110.6 g solid
D. 1.23 L KOH soln, 13.8 g H_2O E. 0.563 g H_2, 2.79 L HCl soln   F. 33.4 g H_2O, 535 ml H_2SO_4 soln   G. 20.4 g $NaNO_3$, 41.9 solid

13a. A. 19.9 g H_2SO_4 B. 17.9 g O_2 C. 153 g NaCl
D. 152 ml H_2SO_4 soln   E. 15.3 g Cu   F. 255 g HNO_3
G. 1.03 g H_2 H. 21.6 g $CaCl_2$ I. 25.1 g NH_3 J. 120 g $CaCO_3$ K. 301 g AgCl   L. 283 ml HNO_3 soln
M. 1.97 g P, 6.78 g Cl_2

14. $CuS + 2\,O_2 + H_2O \rightarrow CuO + H_2SO_4$
$6\,NaCl + 3\,H_2SO_4 + 2\,Fe + 3\,CuO \rightarrow 3\,Na_2SO_4 + 2\,FeCl_3 + 3\,Cu + 3\,H_2O$
$6\,N_2 + 18\,H_2 + 21\,O_2 \rightarrow 14\,H_2O + 8\,HNO_3 + 4\,NO$
$CaCO_3 + 2\,NH_4Cl \rightarrow CO_2 + CaCl_2 + 2\,NH_3 + H_2O$
$2\,P + 3\,Cl_2 + 6\,H_2O + 6\,AgNO_3 \rightarrow 2\,H_3PO_3 + 6\,AgCl + 6\,HNO_3$

15. A. 91.6%   B. 63.6 g PCl_3 C. 29.0 g P   D. 79.7%
E. 59.4 g CaO   F. 98.1 g $CaCO_3$ G. 94.4%   H. 249 g O_2
I. 20.8 g H_2O J. 64.0%   K. 330 g Fe   L. 2.01 g H_2
M. 89.8%   N. 5.93 g H_2O O. 3.29 g H_2S

Quizzes

A: 1. sodium nitrite   2. H_2SO_4 3. (d)   4. (e) (sum = 9)
5. (a)   6. (b)   7. $Na_2S + 2\,HCl \rightarrow 2\,NaCl + \underline{H_2S(g)}$
8. (b)   9. (d)   10. (a)

B: 1. magnesium chlorate   2. NaFO   3. (b)   4. (b)
5. (b)   6. (d)   7. $Al_2O_3 + 3\,H_2SO_4 \rightarrow Al_2(SO_4)_3 + 3\,\underline{H_2O}$
8. (c)   9. (e)   10. (c)

C: 1. rubidium perbromate   2. HNO_3 3. (c)   4. (c)
5. (b)   6. (b)   7. $2\,NaOH + H_2SO_4 \rightarrow Na_2SO_4 + 2\,\underline{H_2O}$
8. (d)   9. (a)   10. (b)

D: 1. sulfuric acid   2. $NaHCO_3$ 3. (c)   4. (e) (sum = 9)
5. (c)   6. (b)   7. $CaCO_3 + 2\,HCl \rightarrow CaCl_2 + \underline{H_2O} + \underline{CO_2}$
8. (d)   9. (b)   10. (a)

Sample Test

1. a. lead(II) thiocyanate b. $Pb(S_2O_3)_2$ C. As_2S_3 d. manganese(II) hypobromite e. nitrous acid f. NH_4HCO_3 g. HIO_4 h. SnS
2. 200.0 ml × 0.240 *M* × 2 mmol K^+/mmol K_2SO_4 = 96.0 mmol K^+. Let *V* be volume of KNO_3 solution added, in ml

$$0.400\,M = \frac{96.0 \text{ mmol} + (0.160\,M \times V)}{200.0 + V} \quad or \quad V = 66.7 \text{ ml}$$

3. a. $BaCl_2 + 2\,AgNO_3 \rightarrow Ba(NO_3)_2 + 2\,AgCl$
b. $Ca(OH)_2 \xrightarrow{\Delta} CaO + H_2O$
c. $NH_3 + HCl \rightarrow NH_4Cl$ d. $Zn + CuSO_4 \rightarrow ZnSO_4 + Cu$
e. $2\,C_2H_6O_2 + 5\,O_2 \rightarrow 4\,CO_2 + 6\,H_2O$

$$4.\ 55.2 \text{ g CuO} \times \frac{\text{mol CuO}}{79.5 \text{ g CuO}} \times \frac{1 \text{ mol } H_2O}{1 \text{ mol CuO}} = 0.694 \text{ mol } H_2O$$

$$158 \text{ ml} \times \frac{\text{L}}{1000 \text{ ml}} \times \frac{2.70 \text{ mol HCl}}{\text{L}} \times \frac{1 \text{ mol } H_2O}{2 \text{ mol HCl}} =$$

0.213 mol H_2O

0.213 mol H_2O × 18.0 g H_2O/mol = 3.84 g H_2O

$$5.\ 26.4 \text{ g} \times \frac{0.400 \text{ g CaO}}{\text{g mixture}} \times \frac{\text{mol CaO}}{56.1 \text{ g CaO}} \times \frac{\text{mol } CaCl_2}{\text{mol CaO}} \times$$

$$\frac{111.1 \text{ g } CaCl_2}{\text{mol } CaCl_2} = 20.9 \text{ g } CaCl_2$$

$$26.4 \text{ g} \times \frac{0.600 \text{ g NaOH}}{\text{g mixture}} \times \frac{\text{mol NaOH}}{40.0 \text{ g NaOH}} \times \frac{\text{mol NaCl}}{\text{mol NaOH}} \times$$

$$\frac{58.5 \text{ g NaCl}}{\text{mol NaCl}} = 23.2 \text{ g NaCl}$$

Total mass of solid = 20.9 g $CaCl_2$ + 23.2 g NaCl = 44.1 g

CHAPTER 5

Drill Problems

0. A. 441 lb/in.^{2} = 3.04 × 10^3 kPa B. 2.75 lb/in.^{2} = 1.89 × 10^4 Pa C. 16.5 atm = 1.67 × 10^3 kPa D. 3.80 × 10^5 torr = 5.07 × 10^7 Pa E. 0.658 atm = 6.67 × 10^4 Pa F. 4.93 × 10^{-3} atm = 3.75 torr G. 34.0 atm = 3.45 × 10^6 atm H. 0.511 lb/in.^{2} = 2.64 mmHg
2. A. 6.13 L B. 39.5 atm C. 1.16 × 10^{-4} L D. 23.0 atm E. 12.6 L F. 0.334 atm G. 1.51 × 10^3 ft^3 H. 257 kPa I. 187 L J. 756 mmHg
3. A. 8.73 L B. 1.59 × 10^3 K C. 170 L D. −24.5°C E. 24.5 L F. 1.22 × 10^3 K G. 13.6 L H. −214°C
7. A. 49.7 L B. 187 K C. 0.277 mol D. 22.4 atm E. 31.9 qt F. −72.0°C G. 19.9 mol H. 6.57 L I. 112 torr J. 8.50 L K. 24.3 g H_2O L. 0.337 lb/in.^{2} M. 284°F N. 0.418 L O. 7.22 g CH_4 P. 44.5 torr
7a. (1) A. 215 K B. 21.9 L C. 2.65 atm D. 1.30 × 10^3 K E. 1.32 L F. 0.342 atm G. 559 K H. 143 L I. 0.688 atm J. 715 K K. 7.27 L L. 12.1 atm
(2) A. 10.7 mol B. 25.1 atm C. 0.634 mol D. 685°C E. 2.90 mol F. 67.8 L
8. A. 2.03 mol, 15.4 g/mol, 31.3 g B. 3.02 L, 32.3 g/mol, 24.8 g/L C. 19.4 g/mol, 307 K, 0.474 g/L D. 0.511 atm, 14.5 g, 0.418 g/L E. 1.11 × 10^3 K, 42.0 g, 4.04 g/L F. 422 mol, 33.4 kg, 249 g/L G. 13.2 L, 181 g, 13.7 g/L H. 15.5 L, 40.0 g/mol, 4.92 g/L I. 24.2 L, 5.15 mol, 17.2 g/L J. 95.9 L, 1.08 atm, 205 g K. 333 L, 0.0853 atm, 82.5 g/mol L. 95.2 L, 2.72 atm, 9.00 mol M. 0.0881 L, 0.0116 mol, 409 g/mol N. 0.546 mol, 24.5 g/mol, 13.4 g O. 99.7 g/mol, 203 K, 542 g P. 0.770 mol, 204 K, 649 g
8a. A. 0.459 mol, 42.1 g/mol, C_3H_6 B. 0.788 mol, 128 g/mol, $C_4H_4F_4$ C. 0.394 mol, 186 g/mol, C_6F_6 D. 0.0548 mol, 32.0 g/mol, N_2H_4 E. 0.109 mol, 84.4 g/mol, C_6H_{12} F. 3.50 mol, 48.0 g/mol, O_3 G. 0.0244 mol, 52.1 g/mol, C_4H_4 H. 21.5 mol, 46.0 g/mol, NO_2 I. 0.237 mol, 40.0 g/mol, C_2H_2N J. 2.72 mol, 58.0 g/mol, $C_2H_2O_2$ K. 0.723 mol, 60.0 g/mol, $C_2H_4O_2$ L. 0.570 mol, 30.0 g/mol, CH_2O_2
9. (1) A. 59.3 L O_2, 37.1 L CO_2 B. 141 L O_2, 105 L H_2O C. C_5H_{12} limiting; 33.8 L CO_2, 40.5 L H_2O D. 81.6 L H_2, 54.4 L NH_3 E. H_2 limiting; 16.8 L NH_3 F. 10.7 L N_2, 32.1 L H_2 G. 6.09 L H_2O, 3.05 L NO H. 3.26 L HCl, 1.09 L NO, 1.63 L Cl_2 I. 0.973 L H_2O, 0.487 L NO J. 4.61 L NO, 6.92 L H_2O K. O_2 limiting; 33.7 L NO, 50.5 L H_2O L. 3.43 L O_2, 4.11 L H_2O M. 38.4 L NH_3, 28.8 L O_2 N. O_2 limiting; 12.4 L N_2, 37.2 L H_2O O. 9.73 L NH_3, 7.30 L O_2, 4.87 L N_2
(2) A. 12.9 L CO_2 B. O_2 limiting, 22.6 L H_2O C. 101 L O_2, 67.1 L CO_2 D. 7.15 L O_2, 4.29 L CO_2 E. 2.82 g O_2, 1.59 g H_2O, 8.16 L CO_2 F. C_6H_6 limiting, 3.07 L H_2O G. CH_4 limiting, 12.3 L CO_2 H. $C_2H_6O_2$ limiting, 2.07 L CO_2 I. 8.96 L CO_2 J. 14.8 L CO_2, 12.2 g H_2O
10. A. 48.2 L B. 2.53 atm C. 308 K D. 584 atm E. 139 K F. 7.41 atm G. 15.5 L H. 6.13 atm I. 160 K
14. & 15. A. He 1356 m/s, Ne 608.8 m/s, H_2 1927 m/s, N_2 516.8 m/s, O_2 483.6 m/s, CO_2 412.3 m/s, Ar 432.8 m/s, H_2O 644.5 m/s, NH_3 662.8 m/s, CH_4 682.9 m/s B. He 14.4 K, Ne 72.8 K, H_2 7.3 K, N_2 101.1 K, O_2 115.5 K, CO_2 158.8 K, Ar 144.1 K, CH_4 57.9 K, NH_3 61.5 K, H_2O 65.0 K C. 2.65 times faster D. 1.069 times faster E. 25.3 hr F. 536 hr

Quizzes

A. 1. (b) 2. (a) 3. (d) 4. (b) 5. (a) 6. (c) 7. (c) 8. (e) 9. (c) 10. (c)
B: 1. (c) 2. (d) 3. (b) 4. (d) 5. (a) 6. (a) 7. (c) 8. (a) 9. (b) 10. (c)
C: 1. (d) 2. (a) 3. (e) 4. (a) 5. (b) 6. (b) 7. (e) 8. (c) 9. (b) 10. (d)
D: 1. (b) 2. (a) 3. (d) 4. (b) 5. (d) 6. (b) 7. (a) 8. (a) 9. (e) 10. (e)

Sample Test

1. a. 1.80 atm, 182 kPa b. 0.0566 m^3, 56.6 L c. 33.3°C, 306.5 K
2. $n = PV/RT$ = (1.80 atm)(56.6 L)/(0.08206 L atm mol^{-1} K^{-1}(306.5 K) = 4.05 mol (MW) = (1.305 lb X 453.5 g/lb)/4.05 mol = 146 g/mol
3. (0.08206 L atm mol^{-1} K^{-1})(1000 ml/L)(760 mmHg/atm) (mol/1000 mmol) = 62.37 ml mmHg mol^{-1} K^{-1}
4. $n_A = PV/RT$ = (1.067 atm)(14.20 L)/ (0.08206 L atm mol^{-1} K^{-1})(303.1 K) = 0.6092 mol n_B = (26.42 atm)(1.251 L)/(0.08206 L atm mol^{-1} K^{-1}) (327.5 K) = 1.230 mol n_{total} = 1.839 mol a. $P = nRT/V$ = (1.839 mol)(0.08206 L atm mol^{-1} K^{-1}) (291.0 K)/(5.000 L) = 8.78 atm b. $P_A = (n_A/n_{total})P$ = (0.6092 mol/1.839 mol)(8.78 atm) = 2.91 atm c. $V_B = (n_B/n_{total})V$ = (1.230 mol/1.839 mol)(5.000 L) = 3.34 L
5. a. Ne b. He c. He d. equal pressures

CHAPTER 6

Drill Problems

2. (1) A. 30.5°C B. 441 J C. 0.62 J g^{-1} °C^{-1} D. 117 g E. 29.9°C F. 1.18 kJ G. 0.862 J g^{-1} °C^{-1} H. 157 g I. 21.2°C J. 1.5 mol K. 24.2 J mol^{-1} deg^{-1} L. 0.27 kJ M. 20.0°C (2) A. 1.8 J mol^{-1} deg^{-1} B. 20.4°C C. 153.5°C D. 522 g E. 6.53 g F. 0.208 J g^{-1} °C^{-1} G. 73.7°C H. 46.0°C I. 22.3°C
5. In order, the values are q, w, and ΔE. A. −196 J, +123 J, −319 J B. −189 J, −247 J, + 58 J C. +647 J, +92.4 J, +555 J D. +1362 J, +321 J, −1041 J E. −142 J, −254 J, +112 J F. +802 J, −897 J, + 1699 J G. −1432 J, −937 J, −495 J H. −972 J, +432 J, −1404 J
7. A. 0.47 kJ/°C B. 40.7 kJ/g C. 21.3°C D. 0.79 g E. 0.716 kJ/°C F. 48 kJ/g G. 1.09 g H. 63.2°F
8. $\Delta \bar{E}$ is given first, followed by $\Delta \bar{H}$ (all in kJ/mol). A. −2667, −2672 B. −3061, −3063 C. −96.91, −91.83 D. −547.0, −563.5 E. −72.47, −72.47 F. −8981.2, −9015.9 G. −333.2, −338.1 H. + 177.20, + 184.73
9. A. +39.7 kJ/mol B. 21.8°C C. 244 g H_2O D. +24.6 kJ/mol E. 40.3°C F. 18.4°C G. + 25.1 kJ/mol
10. All values are in kJ/mol. A. +107.6 B. −406.8 C. −112.3 D. −411.0 E. −167.4 F. −217.5 G. +406 H. −529 I. −25.5 J. +226.8 K. −155.2

10a. 2 C (graphite) + 3 $H_2(g)$ + ½ $O_2(g) \rightarrow C_2H_5OH(l)$ B. $N_2(g)$ + 4 $H_2(g)$ + Sb(c, III) + 5/2 $Cl_2 \rightarrow (NH_4)_2SbCl_5(s)$ C. 2 Hg(l) + $Cl_2(g) \rightarrow Hg_2Cl_2(s)$ D. 3/2 $H_2(g)$ + P(s, white) + 2 $O_2(g) \rightarrow H_3PO_4(s)$ E. Na(s) + ½ $I_2(s)$ + 3/2 $O_2(g) \rightarrow NaIO_3(s)$ F. Sn(s, white) + $F_2(g) \rightarrow SnF_2(s)$ G. Xe(g) + 3/2 $O_2(g) \rightarrow XeO_3(g)$ H. ½ $H_2(g)$ + ½ $N_2(g)$ + 3/2 $O_2(g) \rightarrow HNO_3(l)$ I. K(s) + ½ $Br_2(l)$+ 3/2 $O_2(g) \rightarrow KBrO_3(s)$ J. ½ $I_2(s)$ + 3/2 $Cl_2(g) \rightarrow ICl(g)$

12. All values are in kJ/mol. A. +177.9 B. −176.9 C. −126.7 D. −260.8 E. + 226.3 F. −92.8 G. −1530.6 H. −1169.2 I. −113.04 J. −71.7 K. −308.4 L. −323.2 M. −115.2 N. +873.1 O. −65.2

Quizzes

A: 1. (a) 2. (c) 3. (d) 4. (d) 5. (e) 6. (b) 7. (e) (−103 kJ/mol) 8. (b)
B: 1. (c) 2. (b) 3. (c) 4. (a) 5. (c) 6. (c) 7. (e) (−108.8 kJ/mol) 8. (d)
C: 1. (b) 2. (b) 3. (a) 4. (c) 5. (b) 6. (c) 7. (a) 8. (e) (−1125.6 kJ/mol)
D: 1. (d) 2. (d) 3. (e) (+24.8 J) 4. (b) 5. (e) 6. (d) 7. (d) 8. (b)

Sample Test

1. a. Sn(s, white) + 2 $Cl_2(g) \rightarrow SnCl_4(g)$ b. 7 C (graphite) + 3 $H_2(g)$ + $O_2(g) \rightarrow C_6H_5COOH(s)$ c. C (graphite) + ½ $O_2(g)$ + $Cl_2(g) \rightarrow COCl_2(g)$
2. a. −185 kJ/mol B. −807 kJ/mol
3. $5.00\ g \times \frac{mol\ LiCl}{42.4\ g} \times \frac{37.2\ kJ}{mol} = 4.39\ kJ \times \frac{1000\ J}{kJ} \times \frac{g\ °C}{4.00\ J} = 1097\ g°C$

Δt = 1097 g °C/115.0 g = 9.54°C. Thus t_f = 29.5°C.

CHAPTER 7

Drill Problems

1. & 2. 1.1 X 10^3 nm, i.r. B. 1.9 X 10^{18} Hz, γ ray C. 12 m, TV D. 200 kHz, radio E. 1.71 X 10^{-5} nm, γ ray F. 4.13 X 10^{10} Hz, microwave G. 5.83 km, radio H. 242 MHz, radar I. 4.04 X 10^{-8} cm, x ray J. 5.95 X 10^{11} kHz, visible K. 95.2 nm, uv L. 2.410 X 10^7 Hz, TV M. 3.55 X 10^{-15} m, x ray N. 2.21 X 10^5 MHz, microwave O. 5.98 X 10^3 Å, visible P. 3.64 X 10^9 MHz, uv Q. 2.05 X 10^{-5} km, microwave R. 2.27 X 10^{21} Hz, x ray S. 0.355 cm, microwave T. 7.43 X 10^{19} MHz, x ray
4. A. 2, Balmer, visible B. 3, Lyman, uv C. 379.9 nm, Balmer, visible D. 1875 nm, Paschen, ir E. 2, Balmer, visible F. 5, Balmer, visible G. 1945 nm, Brackett, ir H. 12372 nm, Humphreys, ir I. 5, Pfund, ir J. 2, Lyman, uv K. 389.0 nm, Balmer, visible L. 92.3 nm, Lyman, uv
5. A. 1.95 X 10^{18} Hz, 1.29 X 10^{-8} erg, 7.78 X 10^5 kJ/mol B. 6.94 X 10^{-12} erg, 1.05 X 10^{15} Hz, 286 nm C. 2.86 m, 6.96 X 10^{-19} erg, 4.19 X 10^{-5} kJ/mol D. 0.0644 kJ/mol, 1.61 X 10^{11} Hz, 1.85 X 10^6 nm E. 5.69 X 10^{14} Hz, 3.77 X 10^{-12} erg, 227 kJ/mol F. 4.73 X 10^{-13} Hz,

7.14×10^{13} Hz, 4.20×10^{-4} cm G. 4.90×10^{4} nm, 4.06×10^{-14} erg, 2.44 kJ/mol H. 4.90×10^{-6} kJ/mol, 1.23×10^{7} Hz, 24.5 m I. 2.24×10^{5} Hz, 1.48×10^{-21} erg, 8.94×10^{-8} kJ/mol J. 8.73×10^{-15} erg, 1.32×10^{12} Hz, 0.0228 cm K. 0.586 km, 3.39×10^{-21} erg, 2.04×10^{-7} kJ/mol L. 1.89×10^{4} kJ/mol, 4.74×10^{16} Hz, 6.33×10^{-3} pm M. 4.88×10^{9} Hz, 3.23×10^{-17} erg, 1.95×10^{-3} kJ/mol N. 1.20×10^{-14} erg, 1.82×10^{12} Hz, 0.165 mm O. 8.77 nm, 2.27×10^{-10} erg, 1.37×10^{4} kJ/mol P. 7.47×10^{7} kJ/mol, 1.87×10^{20} Hz, 1.60 pm

10. (1) A. $m_l = 0$ B. $3p_x, 3p_y, 3p_z; m_l = -1, 0, +1$ C. $4d_{xy}, 4d_{yz}, 4d_{xz}, 4d_{x^2-y^2}, 4d_{z^2}; m_l = -2, -1, 0, +1, +2$ D. $m_l = 0$ E. $m_l = -3, -2, -1, 0, +1, +2, +3$ F. $4p_x, 4p_y, 4p_z; m_l = -1, 0, +1$ G. $m_l = 0$ H. $2p_x, 2p_y, 2p_z; m_l = 1, 0, +1$ I. $5d_{xy}, 5d_{yz}, 5d_{xz}, 5d_{x^2-y^2}, 5d_{z^2}$; $m_l = -2, -1, 0, +1, +2$ J. $3d_{xy}, 3d_{yz}, 3d_{xz}, 3d_{x^2-y^2}, 3d_{z^2}; m_l = -2, -1, 0, +1, +2$

(2) A. $1s$; 2 electrons B. $3s, 3p, 3d$; 18 electrons C. $2s, 2p$; 8 electrons D. $4s, 4p, 4d, 4f$; 32 electrons E. $5s, 5p, 5d, 5f, 5g$; 50 electrons

11. See Fig. A-1.

13. A. (3); $1s^2 2s^2 2p_x^1 2p_y^1 2p_z^1$ B. (5); $1s^2 2s^2 2p^6 3s^2 3p^1$ C. (5); $1s^2 2s^2 2p^1$ D. (5); $1s^2 2s^2 2p^6 3s^2 3p^3$ E. (4); $[Ar] 4s^1 3d^{10}$ F. (5); $1s^2 2s^2$ G. (2); [Ne] ↑↓ H. (1); $1s^2 2s^2 2p_x^1 2p_y^1$ I. (1); $1s^2 2s^2 2p^6 3s^2 3p^6 4s^2 3d^3$ J. (3); $[Ne] 3s^2 3p_x^2 3p_y^1 3p_z^1$ K. (4); $[Ar] 4s^2 3d^5$ L. (5); $1s^2 2s^2 2p^3$ M. (4); $[Kr] 5s^1 4d^{10}$ N. (5); $1s^2 2s^2 2p^6 3s^1$ O. (3); $[Kr] 5s^2 4d_{xy}^2 4d_{xz}^2 4d_{yz}^1 4d_{z^2}^1 4d_{x^2-y^2}^1$ P. (1); $[Ne] 3s^2 3p^6 4s^2 3d^1$ Q. (5); $1s^2 2s^2 2p^6 3s^2 3p^5$ R. (3); $1s^2 2s^2 2p_x^1 2p_y^1$ S. (5); [Ne] ↑↓ ↑↓ ↑↓ ↑↓ T. (1); $1s^2 2s^2 2p_x^1$

U. When two subshells are very close in energy, an electron can move from one to the other if that move results in the increase in the number of empty, half-filled, or full electron shells. Cr is $[Ar] 4s^1 3d^5$; Ag is $[Kr] 5s^1 4d^{10}$.

V. Each orbital of a subshell must contain one electron before electrons are paired in the subshells of that orbital. N is $1s^2 2s^2 2p_x^1 2p_y^1 2p_z^1$; Si is $[Ne] 3s^2 3p_x^1 3p_y^1$.

W. Electrons fill orbitals in the order given in expression [15], Fig. 7-4, and Fig. 7-5. K is $1s^2 2s^2 2p^6 3s^2 3p^6 4s^1$; Fr is $1s^2 2s^2 2p^6 3s^2 3p^6 4s^2 3d^{10} 4p^6 5s^2 4d^{10} 5p^6 6s^2 4f^{14} 5d^{10} 6p^6 7s^1$

X. No two electrons may have the same set of four quantun numbers. C is $1s^2 2s^2$ ↑ ↑ _, *not* $1s^2 2s^2$ ↑↑ _ _ and *not* $1s^3 2s^3$.

14. (1) A. Sc $[Ar] 4s^2 3d^1$ B. C $1s^2 2s^2 2p_x^1 2p_y^1$ C. F $1s^2 2s^2 2p_x^2 2p_y^2 2p_z^1$ D. Ti $[Ar] 4s^2 3d^2$ E. Al $[Ne] 3s^2 3p^1$ F. Cl $1s^2 2s^2 2p^6 3s^2 3p^5$ G. Cr $[Ar] 4s^1 3d^5$ H. Y $[Ar] 4s^2 3d^{10} 4p^6 5s^2 4d^1$ I. Sc $1s^2 2s^2 2p^6 3s^2 3p^6 4s^2 3d^1$ J. B $1s^2 2s^2 2p^1$ K. N $1s^2 2s^2 2p_x^1 2p_y^1 2p_z^1$

(2) A. S B. Sc C. Zr D. Tl E. Ce F. Mo, Tc G. V H. Se I. Sr

(3) A. $[He] 2s^2 2p_x^1 2p_y^1 2p_z^1$; [He] ↑↓ (2s) ↑ ↑ ↑ (2p)
B. $[Ne] 3s^2 3p_x^2 3p_y^1 3p_z^1$; [Ne] ↑↓ (3s) ↑↓ ↑ ↑ (3p)
C. $[Ne] 3s^2 3p_x^2 3p_y^2 3p_z^1$; [Ne] ↑↓ (3s) ↑↓ ↑↓ ↑ (3p)
D. $[Ne] 3s^2 3p_x^1 3p_y^1$; [Ne] ↑↓ (3s) ↑ ↑ _ (3p)
E. $[Ar] 4s^1 3d^{10}$; [Ar] ↑ (4s) ↑↓ ↑↓ ↑↓ ↑↓ ↑↓ (3d)
F. $[Ne] 3s^1$; [Ne] ↑ (3s)
G. $[Xe] 6s^1$; [Xe] ↑ (6s)
H. $[Xe] 6s^2 5d^1 4f^1$; [Xe] ↑ (6s) ↑ _ _ _ _ (5d) ↑ _ _ _ _ _ _ (4f)
I. $[Ar] 4s^2 3d^1$; [Ar] ↑↓ (4s) ↑ _ _ _ _ (3d)
J. $[He] 2s^2 2p_x^2 2p_y^1 2p_z^1$; [He] ↑ (2s) ↑↓ ↑ ↑ (2p)
K. $[Ar] 4s^2 3d^6$; [Ar] ↑↓ (4s) ↑↓ ↑ ↑ ↑ ↑ (3d)
L. $[Kr] 5s^2$; [Kr] ↑↓ (5s)

(4) A. K $[Ar] 4s^1$ B. C $[He] 2s^2 2p^2$ C. Mn $[Ar] 4s^2 3d^5$ D. Sc $[Ar] 4s^2 3d^1$ E. Cr $[Ar] 4s^1 3d^5$ F. Au $[Xe] 6s^1 5f^{14} 3d^{10}$ G. Si $[Ne] 3s^2 3p^2$ H. Zn $[Ar] 4s_2 3d^{10}$ I. Mg $[Ne] 3s^2$ J. F $[He] 2s^2 2p^5$ K. P $[Ne] 3s^2 3p^3$ L. Fe $[Ar] 4s^2 3d^6$ M. U $[Rn] 7s^2 6d^1 5f^3$ N. Ne $[He] 2s^2 2p^6$ O. Pr $[Xe] 6s^2 5d^1 4f^2$ actually $[Xe] 6s^2 5d^0 4f^3$ P. Ag $[Kr] 5s^1 4d^{10}$ Q. Al $[Ne] 3s^2 3p^1$ R. Sn $[Kr] 5s^2 4d^{10} 5p^2$ S. Ge $[Ar] 4s^2 3d^{10} 4p^2$ T. Mo $[Kr] 5s^1 4d^5$ U. Ga $[Ar] 4s^2 3d^{10} 4p^1$ V. Ca $[Ar] 4s^2$ W. I $[Kr] 5s^1 4d^{10} 5p^5$ X. W $[Xe] 6s^1 4f^{14} 5d^5$ actually $[Xe] 6s^2 4f^{14} 5d^4$ Y. B $[He] 2s^2 2p^1$ Z. Cu $[Ar] 4s^1 3d^{10}$

Quizzes

A: 1. (a) 2. (c) 3. (b) 4. (a) 5. (c) 6. (d) 7. (c) 8. (a) 9. (a) 10. (b) 11. (c) 12. (e) (Sc)
B: 1. (c) 2. (d) 3. (e) 4. (d) 5. (c) 6. (d) 7. (b) 8. (c) 9. (c) 10. (d) 11. (b) 12. (d)
C: 1. (d) 2. (c) 3. (d) 4. (c) 5. (b) 6. (e) 7. (c) 8. (d) 9. (b) 10. (c) 11. (b) 12. (a)
D: 1. (b) 2. (b) 3. (a) 4. (b) 5. (d) 6. (b) 7. (c) 8. (a) 9. (d) 10. (d) 11. (c) 12. (b)

Sample Test

1. $E = \dfrac{hc}{\lambda} = \dfrac{6.627 \times 10^{-34}\text{ J-s} \times 3.00 \times 10^{8}\text{ m/s}}{3.28\text{ m}} =$ 6.06×10^{-26} J/photon

$\overline{E} = 6.06 \times 10^{-26}$ J/photon $\times 6.023 \times 10^{23}$ photon/mol $\times$ kJ/1000 J $= 3.65 \times 10^{-5}$ kJ/mol

2. See Figs. 7-2 and 7-3.

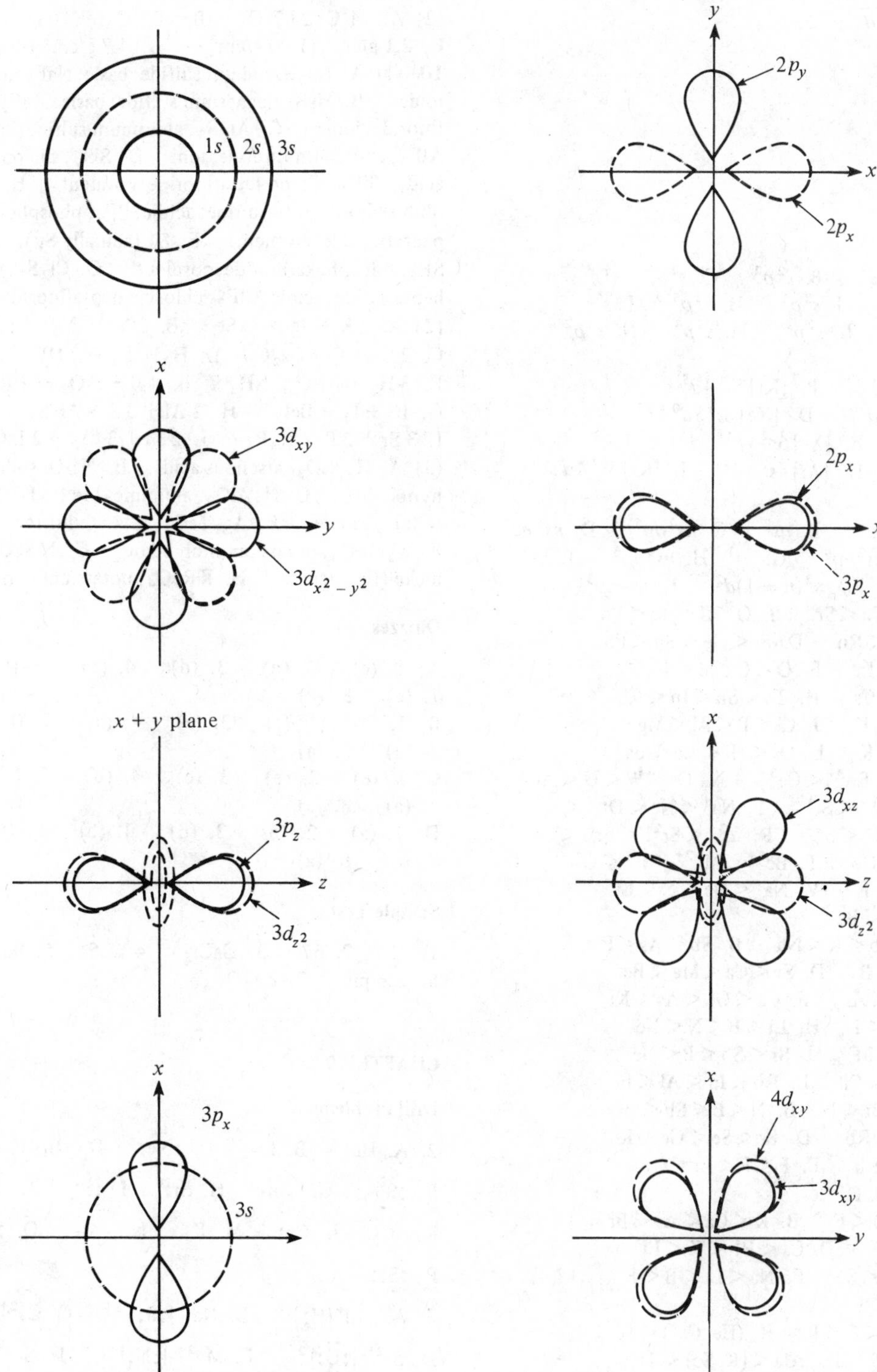

FIGURE A-1 Answers to objective 7-11 drill problems.

3. a. $1s^2 2s^2 2p^6 3s^2 3p_x^1 3p_y^1 3p_z^1$
b. $1s^2 2s^2 2p^6 3s^2 3p^6 4s^2 3d^5$
c. $1s^2 2s^2 2p^6 3s^2 3p_x^1 3p_y^1$
4. a. [Ar] $\underset{4s}{\underline{\uparrow\downarrow}}\ \underset{3d}{\underline{\uparrow\downarrow}\ \underline{\uparrow}\ \underline{\uparrow}\ \underline{\uparrow}}$
b. [Ne] $\underset{3s}{\underline{\uparrow\downarrow}}\ \underset{3p}{\underline{\uparrow}\ \underline{\ \ }\ \underline{\ \ }}$
c. [He] $\underset{2s}{\underline{\uparrow\downarrow}}\ \underset{2p}{\underline{\uparrow\downarrow}\ \underline{\uparrow}\ \underline{\uparrow}}$

CHAPTER 8

Drill Problems

3. & 4. (1) A. s^2p^3 B. s^2p^2 C. s^2p^6 D. s^2p^3
E. s^1 F. s^2p^4 G. s^2p^1 H. s^2p^5 I. s^1
J. s^2p^6 K. s^2 L. s^2p^1 M. s^2p^4 N. s^2p^2
O. s^2p^5 P. s^2
(2) A. $[Ar]4s^1 3d^{10}$ B. $[Kr]5s^1 4d^5$
C. $[Xe]6s^1 4f^{14} 5d^{10}$ D. $[Xe]6s^2 5d^0 4f^7$
E. $[Xe]6s^2 5d^1$ F. $[Xe]6s^2 4f^{14} 5d^6$
G. $[Ar]4s^2 3d^6$ H. $[Ar]4s^2 3d^3$ I. $[Kr]5s^2 4d^3$
J. $[Kr]5s^2 4d^1$
(3) A. $ns^2(n-1)d^x$ B. ns^2 C. ns^2np^5 D. ns^2np^2
E. ns^2np^1 F. ns^2np^4 G. ns^1 H. ns^2np^6 I. ns^2np^4
J. $ns^2(n-1)d^1$ K. $ns^2(n-1)d^2$ L. ns^2np^3
6. A. Be < Mg < Ca < Sr B. O < S < Te < Po
C. He < Ar < Kr < Rn D. Si < Ge < Sn < Pb
E. B < Al < Ga < In F. O < C < B < Li
G. Bi < Tl < Ba < Cs H. Te < Sn < In < Rb
I. Br < As < Ge < K J. Cl < P < Al < Mg
K. Fe < V < Ti < K L. Os < Hf < La < Ba
M. $W^{3+} < Tm^{3+} < Eu^{3+} < Ce^{3+}$ N. Os < W < U < Ac
O. $Ca^{2+} < Ar < P^{3-} < Si^{4-}$ P. $Na^+ < Ne < O^{2-} < C^{4-}$
Q. $Sc^{3+} < K^+ < Cl^- < S^{2-}$ R. $Y^{3+} < Sr^{2+} < Br^- < Ga^{5-}$
S. Ne < O < Si < Ge T. $Be^{2+} < Mg^{2+} < F^- < C^{4-}$
U. N < Al < Na < K V. $Na^+ < Ne < N < Li$
W. Ge < Ga < Tl < Ba
7. (1) A. Cs < Rb < K < Na B. Sb < As < P < N
C. Tl < In < Al < B D. Sr < Ca < Mg < Be
E. Na < Al < Cl < Ar F. Ca < Ge < As < Kr
G. Rb < In < Te < I H. Li < B < N < Ne
I. Ba < Ga < Se < F J. Sr < Sb < P < Ne
K. Cs < Sn < As < Cl L. Rb < In < Al < F
(2) A. F < Cl < Br < I B. N < P < Sb < Bi
C. Li < Na < K < Rb D. Br < Se < Ge < K
E. I < Sb < In < Rb F. F < P < In < Cs
G. Cl < Se < Sb < Tl
(3) A. C < N < O < F B. K < Ca < As < Br
C. I < Br < Cl < F D. Cs < Rb < K < Li
E. Rb < Ru < In < Se F. Na < Li < B < F
G. Cs < As < Cl < F
8. A. $K^+ < Ce^{3+} < C < P$ B. $(He, Cs^+) < Sc < S$
C. B < (Si, S) < P D. Ca < (K, Sc) < Ti
E. Cu < V < Mn < Cr F. (Zn, Ca) < Ti < As
G. $Na^+ < (Na, S^-) < S$ H. Be < (Li, B) < C
9. The predicted value is given first, followed by the actual value in parentheses.
(1) A. 74°C (−129°C) B. yellow-green (same)
C. 330°C (302°C) D. 411°C (337°C) E. 1000°C (unknown) F. black (unknown) G. −170°C (−185°C)
H. 15.6 kJ/mol (15.1 kJ/mol) I. −64°C (−52°C)
J. −70°C (100°C) K. −97°C (0°C)
L. −150.5°C (−157.3°C) M. −146.5°C (−152°C)
(2) A. 14°C (28.7°C) B. 602°C (690°C)
C. 2.1 g/cm³ (1.90 g/cm³) D. 4.7 g/cm³ (4.25 g/cm³)
10. (1) A. Na_2S, sodium sulfide; basic, NaF, sodium fluoride; ionic B. MgS, magnesium sulfide; basic; MgF_2, magnesium fluoride; ionic C. Al_2S_3, aluminum sulfide; amphoteric; AlF_3, aluminum fluoride; ionic D, SiS_2, silicon sulfide; acidic; SiF_4, silicon tetrafluoride; covalent E. P_2S_5, diphosphorus pentasulfide; acidic; PF_5, phosphorus pentafluoride; covalent F. S_4 (actually S_8), sulfur; acidic; SF_6, sulfur hexafluoride; covalent G. Cl_2S_7, dichlorine heptasulfide; acidic; ClF_7, chlorine heptafluoride; covalent
(2) A. $2\,K + Se \rightarrow K_2Se$ B. $3\,Mg + N_2 \rightarrow Mg_3N_2$
C. $2\,Ca + C \rightarrow Ca_2C$ D. $H_2 + F_2 \rightarrow 2\,HF$
E. $3\,H_2 + N_2 \rightarrow 2\,NH_3$ F. $4\,B + 3\,O_2 \rightarrow 2\,B_2O_3$
G. $Be + I_2 \rightarrow BeI_2$ H. $2\,Al + 3\,S \rightarrow Al_2S_3$
I. $3\,Sr + 2\,P \rightarrow Sr_3P_2$ J. $2\,In + 3\,Cl_2 \rightarrow 2\,InCl_3$
(3) A. H_3AsO_3, arsenous acid B. NaIO, sodium hypoiodite C. H_3AlO_3, aluminic acid D. $NaGeO_2$, sodium gallate E. Ag_2TeO_3, silver tellurite
F. K_2MoO_4, potassium molybdate G. $NiSeO_4$, nickel(II) selenate H. $KReO_4$, potassium perrhenate

Quizzes

A: 1. (c) 2. (d) 3. (d) 4. (c) 5. (b) 6. (b)
7. (e) 8. (c)
B: 1. (c) 2. (c) 3. (e) 4. (a) 5. (b) 6. (c)
7. (a) 8. (a)
C: 1. (e) 2. (e) 3. (c) 4. (b) 5. (c) 6. (b)
7. (a) 8. (a)
D: 1. (a) 2. (b) 3. (d) 4. (b) 5. (b) 6. (a)
7. (c) 8. (a)

Sample Test

1. 31 2. 67 3. $GaCl_3$ 4. 5.5 5. 0.090
6. 126 pm 7. Ga_2O

CHAPTER 9

Drill Problems

2. A. He: B. Li· C. $:\overset{\cdot\cdot}{\underset{\cdot\cdot}{Ne}}:$ D. $\cdot\overset{\cdot}{In}\cdot$ E. $:\overset{\cdot\cdot}{\underset{\cdot\cdot}{I}}\cdot$
F. $:\overset{\cdot}{\underset{\cdot}{Sb}}\cdot$ G. $\cdot\overset{\cdot}{\underset{\cdot}{Sn}}\cdot$ H. Sr: I. $:\overset{\cdot}{\underset{\cdot}{S}}:$ J. $:\overset{\cdot\cdot}{\underset{\cdot\circ}{F}}\cdot$
K. $\cdot\overset{\cdot}{\underset{\cdot}{C}}\cdot$ L. Ca: M. K· N. $\cdot\overset{\cdot}{Al}\cdot$ O. $:\overset{\cdot}{P}\cdot$
P. $:\overset{\cdot}{\underset{\cdot}{Se}}:$
3. A. $Li^+[H:]^-$ B. $Na^+\ [:\overset{\cdot\cdot}{\underset{\cdot\cdot}{S}}:]^{2-}$ C. $Ca^{2+}\ [:\overset{\cdot\cdot}{\underset{\cdot\cdot}{Br}}:]^-$
D. $Sr^{2+}\ [:\overset{\cdot\cdot}{\underset{\cdot\cdot}{O}}:]^{2-}$ E. $Mg^{2+}\ [:\overset{\cdot\cdot}{\underset{\cdot\cdot}{N}}:]^{3-}$ F. $Sc^{3+}\ [:\overset{\cdot\cdot}{\underset{\cdot\cdot}{S}}:]^{2-}$
G. $Na^+\ [:\overset{\cdot\cdot}{\underset{\cdot\cdot}{F}}:]^-$ H. $Ti^{4+}\ [:\overset{\cdot\cdot}{\underset{\cdot\cdot}{O}}:]^{2-}$ I. $Mg^{2+}\ [:\overset{\cdot\cdot}{\underset{\cdot\cdot}{S}}:]^{2-}$
J. $La^{3+}\ [:\overset{\cdot\cdot}{\underset{\cdot\cdot}{Cl}}:]^-$ K. $K^+\ [:\overset{\cdot\cdot}{\underset{\cdot\cdot}{Se}}:]^{2-}$ L. $Mg^{2+}\ [:\overset{\cdot\cdot}{\underset{\cdot\cdot}{C}}:]^{4-}$
M. $Ce^{4+}\ [:\overset{\cdot\cdot}{\underset{\cdot\cdot}{Cl}}:]^-$ N. $Al^{3+}\ [:\overset{\cdot\cdot}{\underset{\cdot\cdot}{N}}{\circ}]^{3-}$ O. $Cs^+\ [:\overset{\cdot\cdot}{\underset{\cdot\cdot}{Te}}:]^{2-}$
P. $Rb^+\ [:\overset{\cdot\cdot}{\underset{\cdot\cdot}{P}}:]^{3-}$

4. A. H—C(H)(H)—H B. (H)(H)C=O C. H—C(H)(H)—O—H

D. H—N(H)—N(H)—H E. |F—O—F| F. |F—N(|F|)—F|

G. $[Si(|O|)_4]^{4-}$ H. O=N—Cl| I. |Cl—Ge(|Cl|)(|Cl|)—Cl|

J. H—C(H)=C(H)—H K. |Cl—Si(|Cl|)(|Cl|)—Cl| L. (|Cl)(|Cl)C—O

M. H—O—Cl—O| N. H—O—C≡N O. H—O—F|

P. H—O—N=O Q. H—O—O—H R. H—C≡C—H

S. |F—As(|F|)—F| T. $[|O—Br(|O|)(|O|)—O|]^{-}$ U. $[|O—P(|O|)(|O|)—O|]^{3-}$

V. |Br—Se—Br| W. $[|O—P(|O|)—O|]^{3-}$ X. $[|F—B(|F|)(|F|)—F|]^{-}$

Y. $[|O—F|]^{-}$ Z. $[|O—Cl(|O|)—O|]^{-}$ AA. $[H—O—O|]^{-}$

AB. $[|C≡N|]^{-}$ AC. H—I| AD. |Cl—C(H)(H)—Cl|

AE. H(H—O)C=O AF. H—C(H)(H)—C(H)(H)—H AG. $[|O—O|]^{2-}$

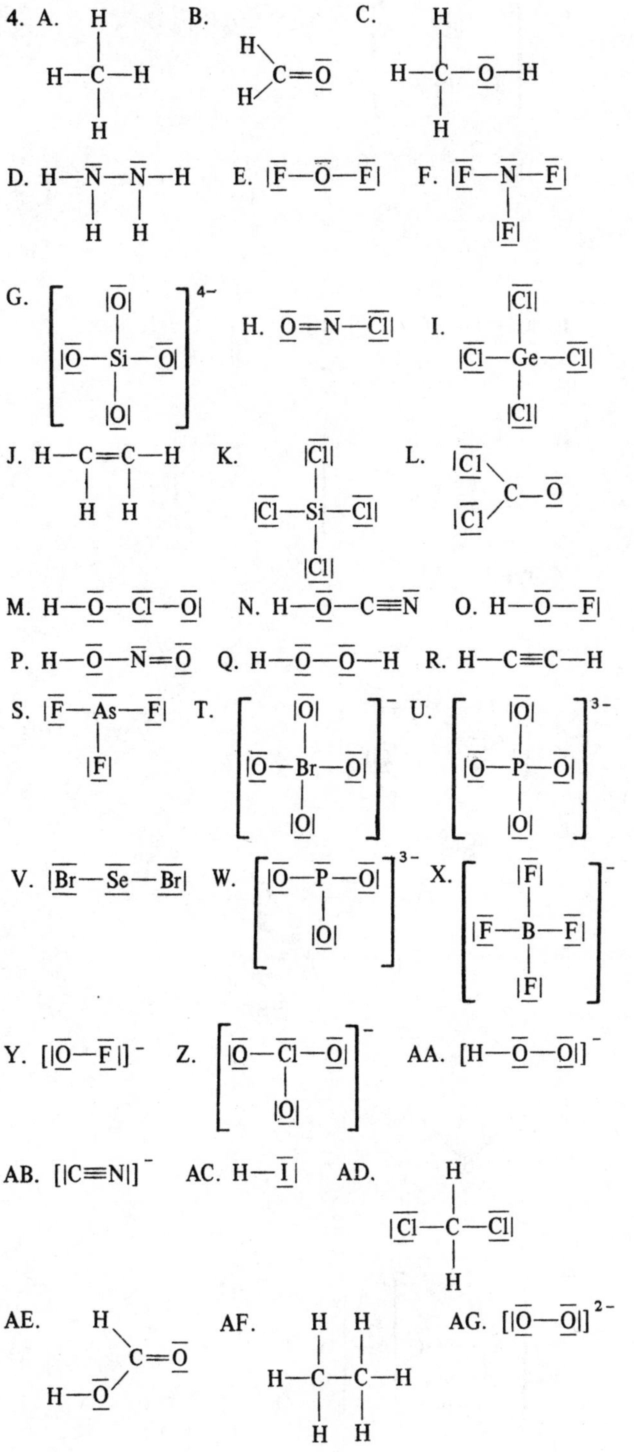

5. & 6. Formal charges are given in parentheses after each structure when different from zero. The "best" structure is drawn first in each case.

A. H—O—C≡N|; H—O—N≡C| (N, +1; C, −1)

B. H—C≡N|; H—N≡C| (N, +1; C, −1)

C. H—O—Cl(|O|)—O| (Cl, +2; O, −1); H—Cl(|O|)(|O|)—O| (Cl, +3; O, −1)

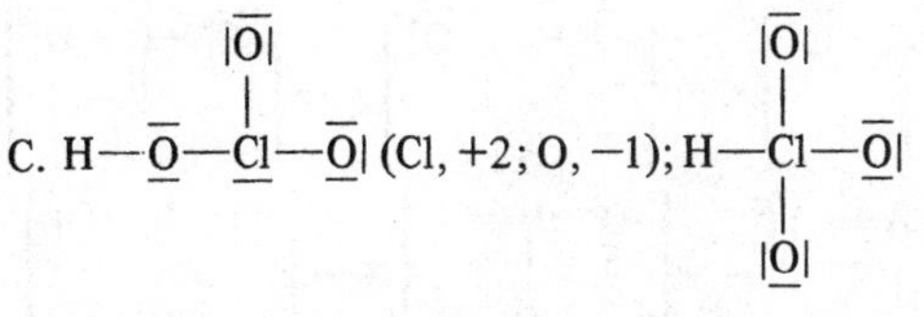

D. |C≡O| (C, −1; O, +1); |C=O (C, −2; O, +2)

E. O=N—Cl|; N=O—Cl| (N, −1; O, +1)

F. $[N=C=S]^{-}$ (N, −1); $[C=N=S]^{-}$ (C, −2; N, +1)

G. H—N=C=S; H—C=N=S (C, −1; N, +1)

H. |Cl—B(|Cl|)—Cl|; Cl=B(|Cl|)—Cl| (=Cl, +1; B, −1)

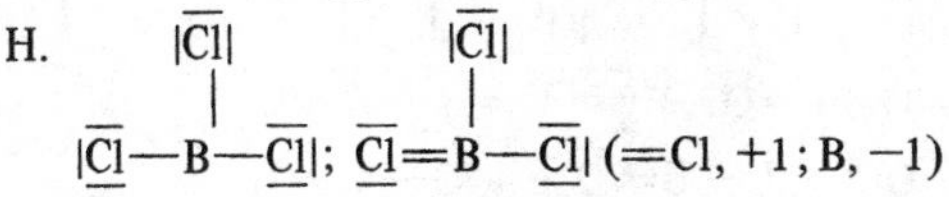

I. H—C≡N|; H—N≡C| (N, +1; C, −1)

J. |Cl—Be—Cl|; Cl=Be—Cl| (=Cl, +1; Be, −1)

K. |F—O—Se—F|; O—Se(|F|)—F| (O, −1; Se, +1); |Se—O(|F|)—F| (Se, −1; O, +1)

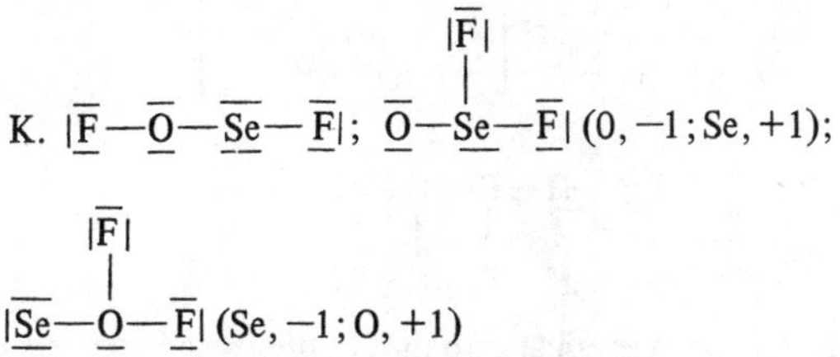

L. $[|N=C=N|]^{2-}$ (both N, −1); $[|C=N=N|]^{2-}$ (C, −2; N, +1; N, −1)

M. H—O—N=O; H—N(|O|)=O (N, +1; —O, −1)

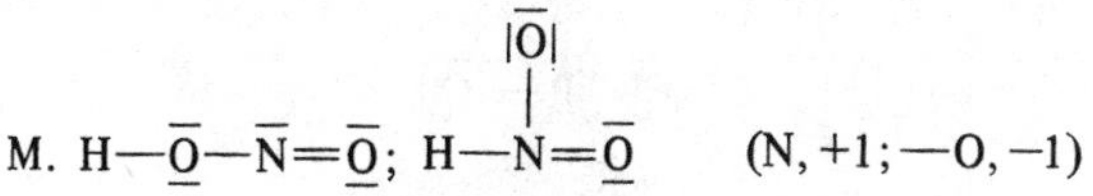

N. O=P(|Cl|)(|Cl|)—Cl|; |Cl—O—P(|Cl|)(|Cl|)|

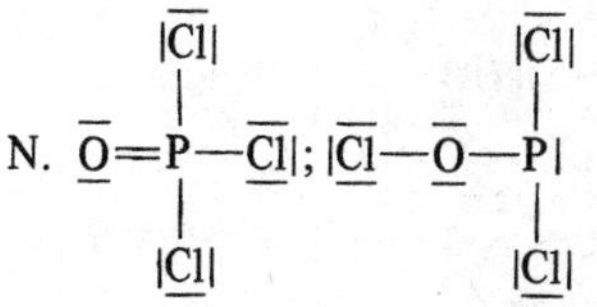

O. |Cl—C≡N|; |Cl—N≡C| (N, +1, ≡C, −1)

P. H—N≡N=N (=N, +1; =N, −1); H—N≡N—N| (N, +1; N, +1; N, −2)

Q. (H)(H)C=N=N (N, +1; N, −1); (H)(H)N=C=N (N, +1; N, −1)

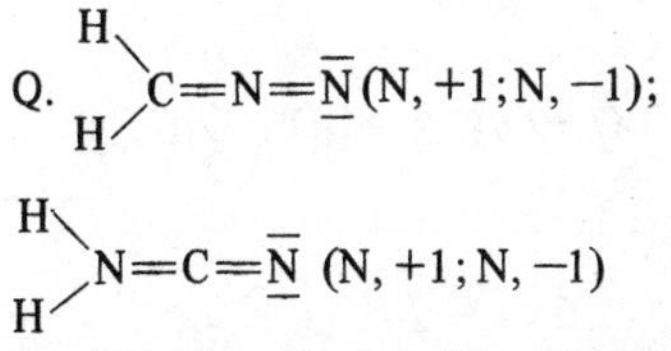

R. |Cl—O—N=O; |Cl—O—O=N (O, −1; N, +1)

7. A. $[H—C(|O|)=O|]^{-}$ ⟷ $[H—C(=|O|)—O|]^{-}$

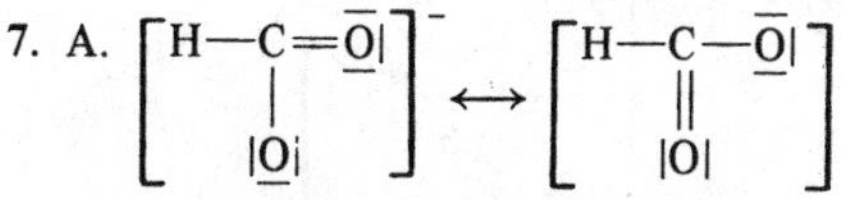

B. $[O=N—O|]^{-}$ ⟷ $[|O—N=O]^{-}$

C. $[N=N=N]^{-}$ ⟷ $[|N≡N—N|]^{-}$ ⟷ $[|N—N≡N|]^{-}$

D. O=S—O| ⟷ |O—S=O

E. 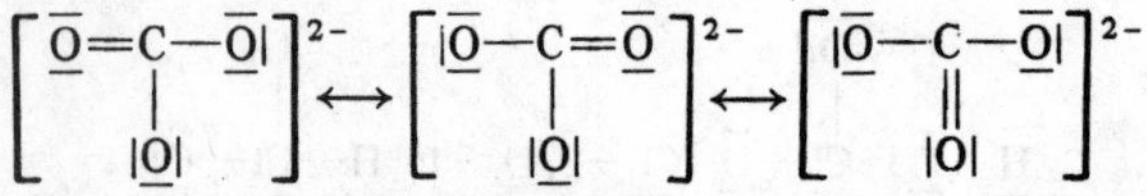

F. 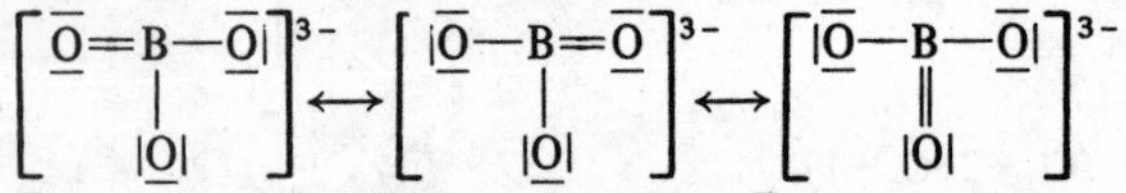

G. 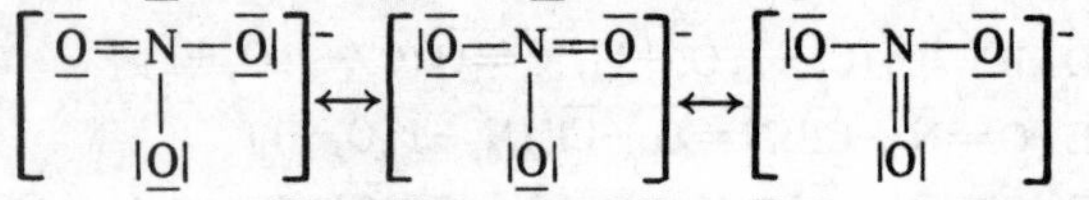

H. 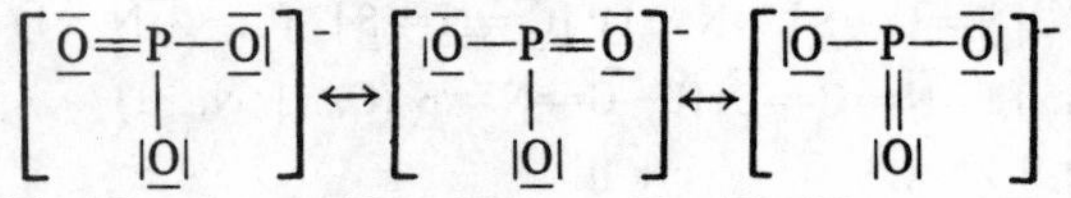

I. O=C—O=C=O ↔ O=C=O—C=O

J. 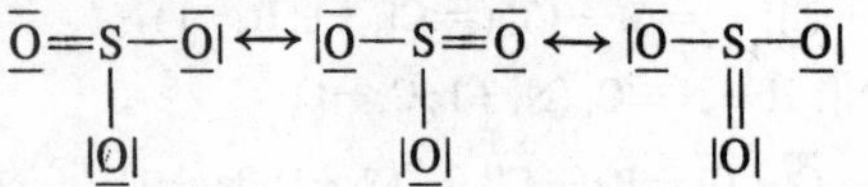

K. 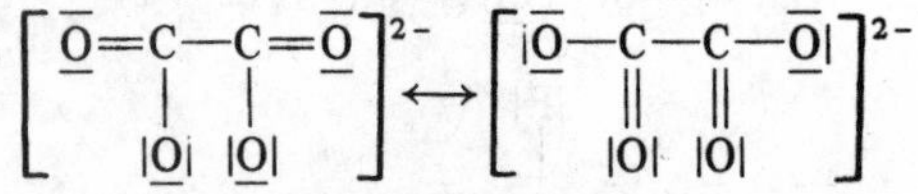

L. 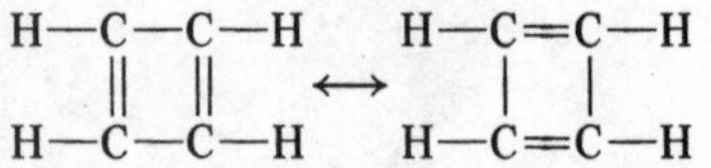

8. All formal charges equal zero unless otherwise indicated.

A. Ṅ=O B. |O—Ṅ=O ↔ O—Ṅ=O| (—O, −1; N, +1)

C. |Br—Sn—Br| D. O=Ċl—O| ↔ |O—Ċl=O

(Cl, +1; —O, −1)

E. |I—Pb—I| F. |Cl—Be—Cl|

G. 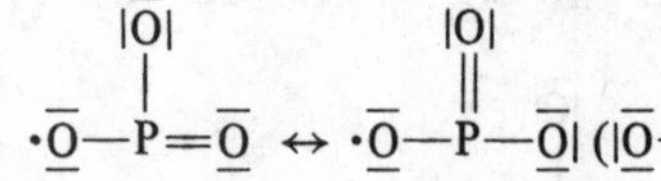 (|O—, −1; P, +1)

and four other resonance forms

H. H—Be—H I. [|N≡C—N·]⁻ ↔ [·N—C≡N|]⁻

(—N, −1) J. B≡N| K. 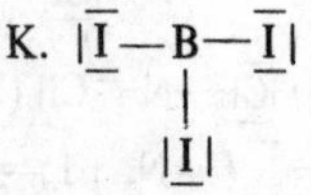

L. 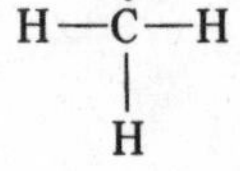 M. [O=S—O·]⁺ ↔ [·O—S=O]⁺ (S, +1)

N. 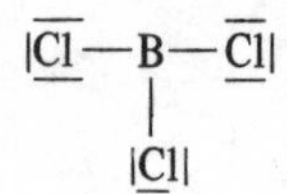 O. [|O—O|]⁻ ↔ [|O—O|]⁻ (|O—, −1)

9. All formal charges equal zero unless otherwise indicated.

A. 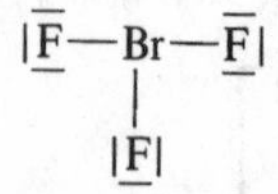 B. 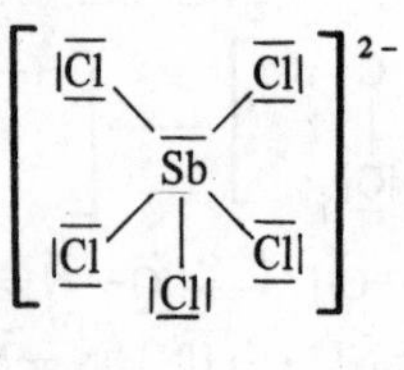 (Sb, −2)

C. 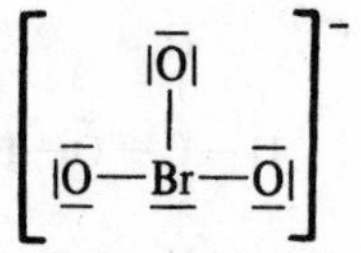 (all O, −1; Br, +2)

D. [|I—I—I|]⁻ (central I, −1) E. 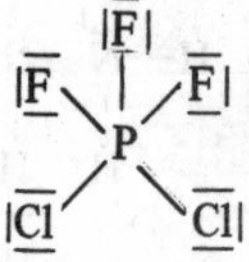

F. |Cl—Pb—Cl| G. 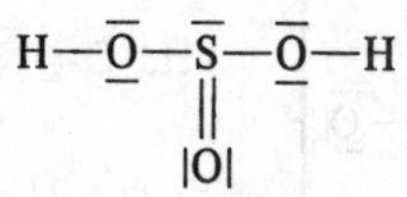

H. 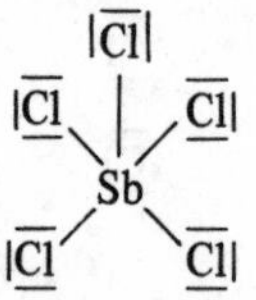 I. 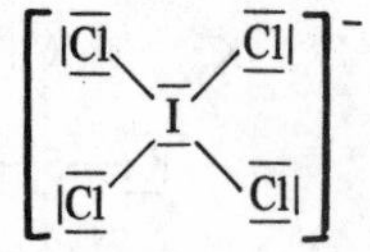 (I, −1)

J. 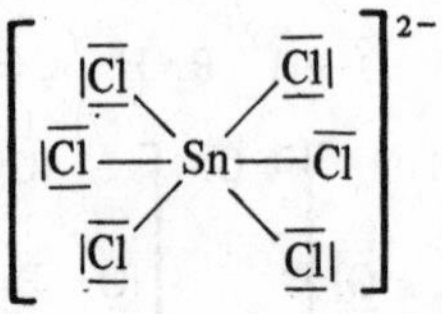 (Sn, −2) K. 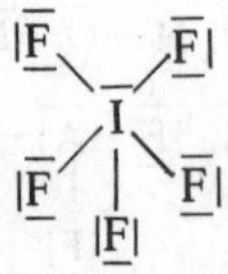

L. 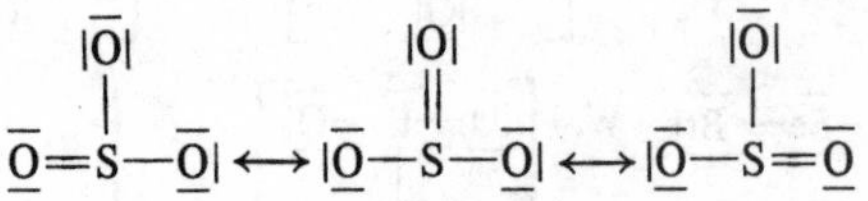 (—O, −1)

M. 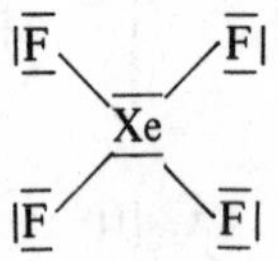 N. 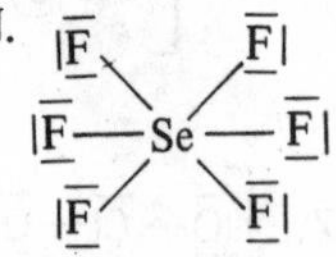 O. |F—Ar—F|

P. 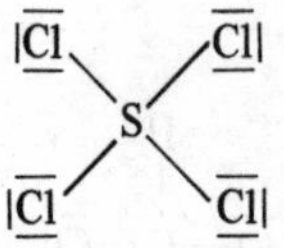 Q. 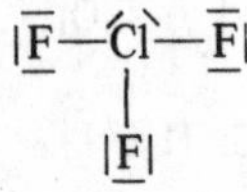

R. 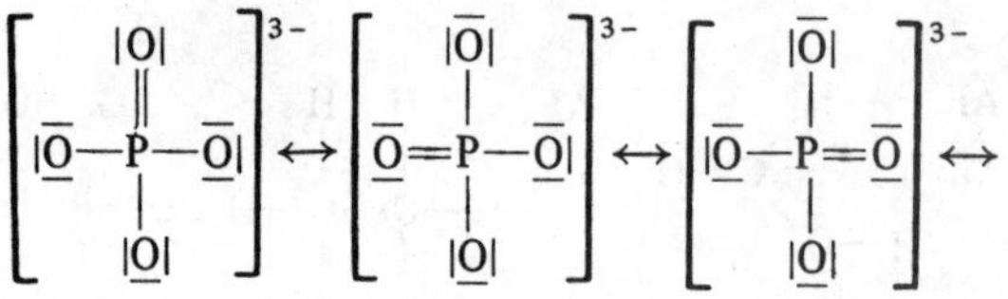

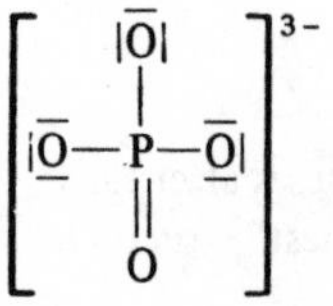 (—O, −1) S. [|S—I—S|]⁻ (S, −1; I, +1)

T. |F—Xe—F| U. 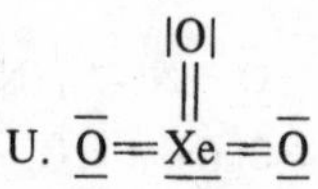

10. Electron pair geometry is given first, and molecular shape is given second, abbreviated as follows: lin, linear; tripl, trigonal planar; tet, tetrahedron; tripyr, trigonal pyramid; tbp, trigonal bipyramid; irtet, irregular tetrahedron; T, T-shaped; oct, octahedron; sqpyr, square pyramid; sqpl, square planar.

A. tripl, tripl B. tet, tet 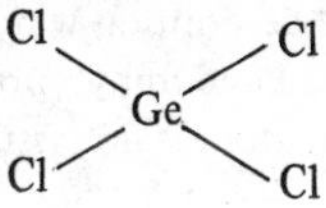 C. tet, bent

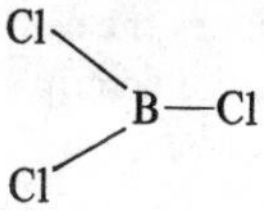

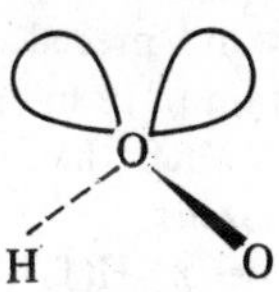

D. tbp, T 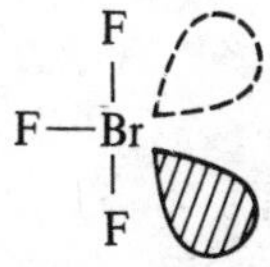 E. tbp, tbp 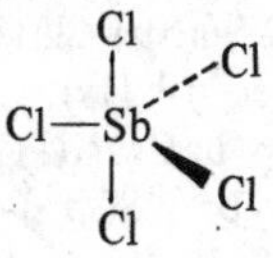 F. tripl, bent

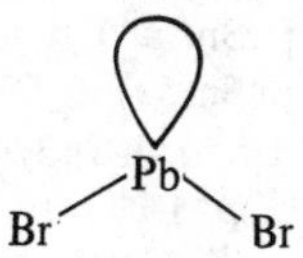

G. tripl, tripl 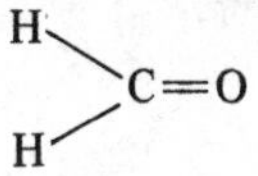 H. lin, lin I. oct, lin

Cl—Be—Cl

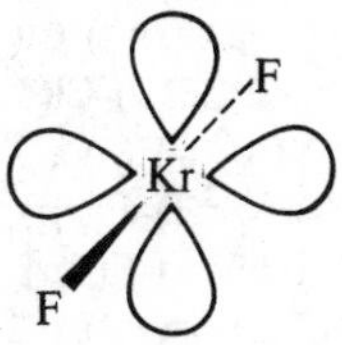

J. tbp, lin 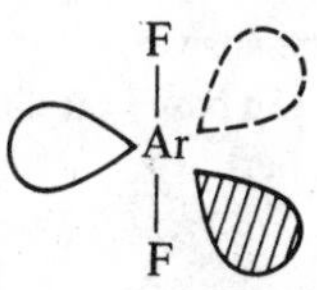 K. tbp, irtet 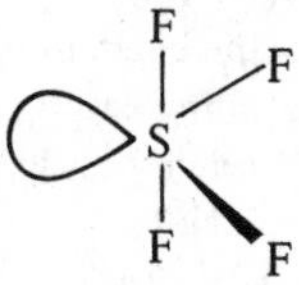 L. tripl, bent

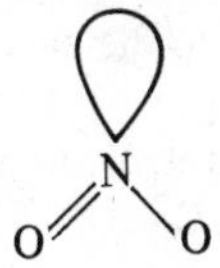

M. tet, tripyr 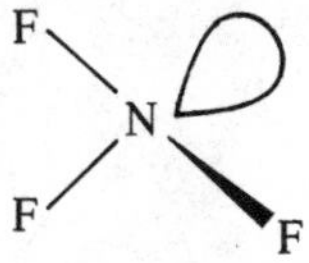 N. tbp, T 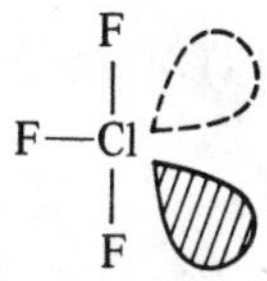 O. oct, sqpyr

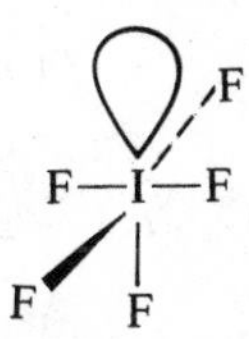

P. tbp, tpb 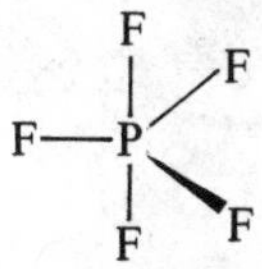 Q. tet, tet 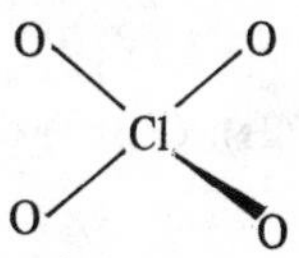 R. tet, tripyr

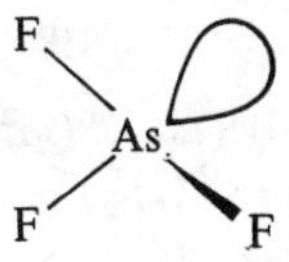

S. oct, sqpl 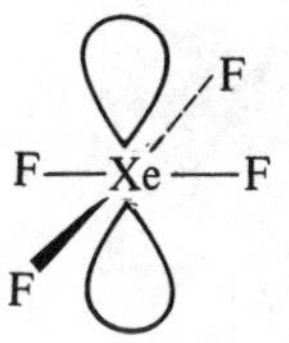 T. tripl, tripl 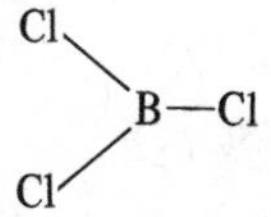 U. tet, bent

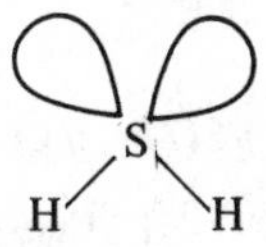

V. tet, tet 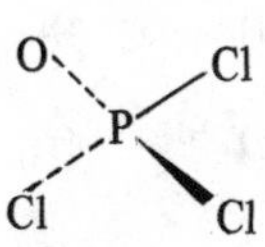 W. tbp, irtet 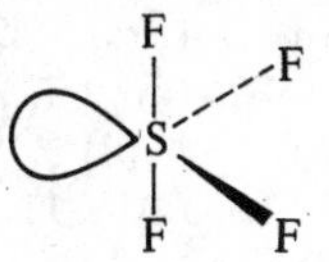 X. tripl, tripl

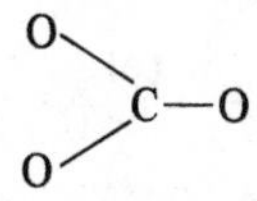

Y. tripl, tripl 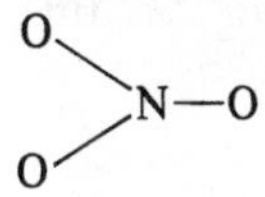 Z. lin, lin AA. tet, tet

N—N—O

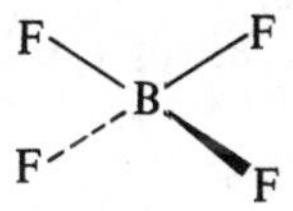

11. All values are in kJ/mol.
A. −56 B. −618 C. −309 D. −821
E. −374 F. −83 G. +88 H. −638
I. +121 J. −2628 K. −158 L. −814
M. −35 N. −8 O. +24 P. −1458

12. D. F. 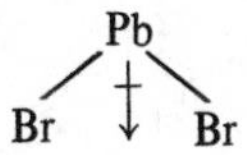 G.

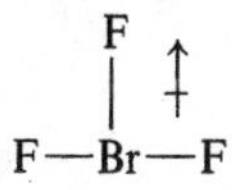

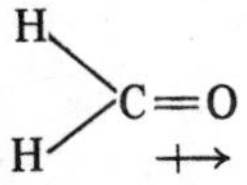

K. 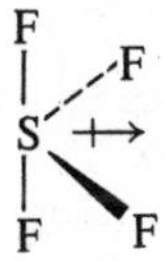 L.  M.

N. 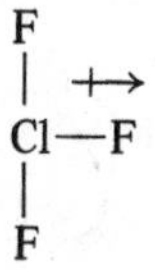 O. 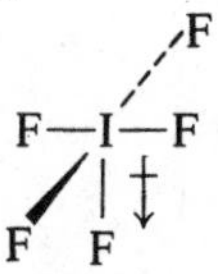 R.

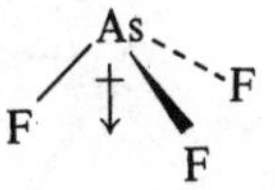

U. 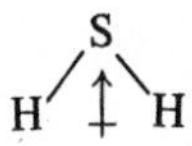 V 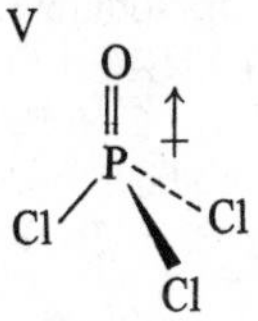 W. 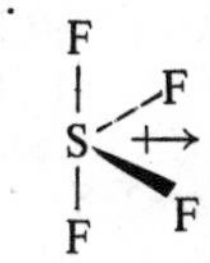 Z.

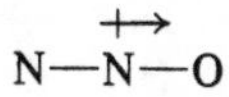

N—N—O

14. & 15. A. sodium perchlorate: Na +1, Cl +7, O −2 B. H_2SeO_4: H +1, Se +6, O −2 C. ammonium sulfide: H + 1, N −3, S−2 D. copper(I) iodate: Cu + 1, I +5, O −2 E. carbonic acid: H + 1, C + 4, O −2 F. H_3PO_4: H +1, P +5, O −2 G. Na_3BO_3: Na +1, B +3, O−2 H. sodium nitrate: Na +1, N +5, O −2 I. lithium hypochlorite: Li +1, Cl +1, O −2 J. H_2SO_2: H +1, S +2, O −2 K. aluminum phosphate: Al +3, P +5, O −2 L. H_3BO_3: H +1, B +3, O −2 M. perchloric acid: H +1, Cl +7, O −2 N. HNO_2: H +1, N+3, O −2 O. $Mg(ClO_3)_2$: Mg +2, Cl +5, O −2 P. scandium aluminate: Sc +3, Al +3, O −2 Q. magnesium germinate: Mg +2, Ge +4, O −2 R. ammonium nitrate: N −3, H +1, N +5, O −2 S. hypofluorous acid: H +1, F +1, O −2 T. HNO: H +1, N +1, O −2

Quizzes

A: 1. (b) 2. (c) 3. (d) 4. (a) 5. (d) 6. (e) 7. (c) 8. (b) 9. (c) 10. (d) 11. (a)
B: 1. (b) 2. (b) 3. (b) 4. (d) 5. (c) 6. (e) 7. (d) 8. (c) 9. (a) 10. (a) 11. (c)
C: 1. (d) 2. (d) 3. (b) 4. (b) 5. (b) 6. (d) 7. (a) 8. (d) 9. (e) (linear) 10. (b) 11. (e) (−420)
D: 1. (c) 2. (e) 3. (c) 4. (c) 5. (d) 6. (b) 7. (d) 8. (d) 9. (b) 10. (a) 11. (d)

Sample Test

1. Formal charge is given only when not zero.

a.

$[\,|\overline{\underline{O}}-P(=\overline{O}|)-\overline{\underline{O}}|\,]^- \longleftrightarrow [\,\overline{\underline{O}}=P(-|\overline{\underline{O}}|)-\overline{\underline{O}}|\,]^- \longleftrightarrow [\,|\overline{\underline{O}}-P(-|\overline{\underline{O}}|)=\overline{\underline{O}}\,]^-$

(—O, −1; P, +1)

b. $[\overline{O}=N=\overline{O}]^+$ (N, + 1) c. H, H, H and $|\overline{\underline{Cl}}|$ bonded to C

d. $|\overline{\underline{F}}|$ bonded to I; $|\overline{\underline{F}}-\overline{I}-\overline{\underline{F}}|$

2. Electron pair geometry is given first, followed by molecular shape, abbreviated as in answers for objective 9-10.
a. tet, tet b. tet, tripyr c. tb, irtet d. oct, sqpl

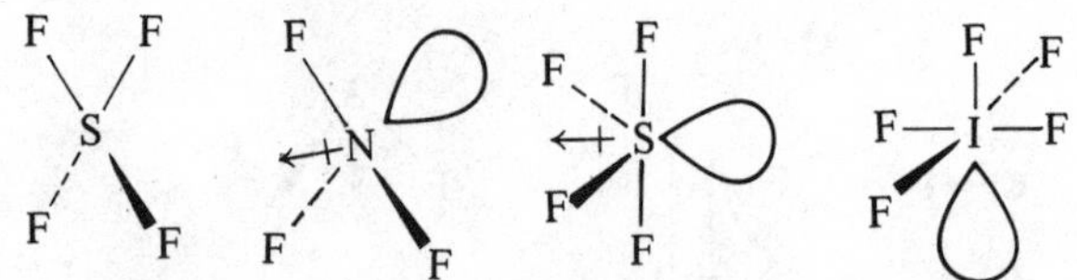

3. a. $CuSO_4$: Cu +2, S +6, O −2 b. sodium thiosulfate: Na +1, S +2, O −2 C. $Mg(ClO_2)_2$: Mg +2, Cl +3, O −2 D. sodium perborate: Na +1, B +5, O −2 E. $(NH_4)_2O$: N −3, H +1, O −2 F. nitrogen triiodide: N +3, I −1 g. calcium xenate: Ca +2, Xe +6, O −2 H. BaO_2: Ba +2, O −1

CHAPTER 10

Drill Problems

Abbreviations are same as used in answers for objective 9–10.

2. & 3. (1) A. *sp*, lin, lin B. sp^3, tet, tet C. sp^2, tripl, bent D. sp^3, tet, tripyr E. sp^3, tet, tripyr F. sp^3, tet, bent G. sp^3, tet, bent H. sp^3, tet, bent I. sp^2, tripl, tripl J. sp^2, tripl, bent K. sp^3, tet, tet L. sp^3, tet, tet M. sp^3, tet, tripyr N. sp^3, tet, tet O. sp^2, tripl, tripl P. sp^3, tet, bent
(2) A. sp^3d, tbp, irtet B. sp^3d^2, oct, oct C. sp^3d, tbp, T D. sp^3d, tbp, tbp E. sp^3d, tbp, T F. sp^3d, tbp, lin G. sp^3d^2, oct, sqpyr H. sp^3d, tbp, lin I. sp^3d, tbp, tbp J. sp^3d, tbp, lin K. sp^3d, tbp, tbp L. sp^3d^2, oct, sqpyr M. sp^3d^2, oct, sqpl N. sp^3d, tbp, irtet O. sp^3d^2, oct, sqpyr P. sp^3d, tbp, irtet Q. sp^3d^2, oct, sqpl R. sp^3d, tbp, T S. sp^3d^2, oct, oct T. sp^3d^2, oct, sqpl U. sp^3d^2, oct, oct

4. All bonds are σ bonds unless specified as π bonds. The number of bonds of a given type is given before the abbreviated description of the bond. l.p. means lone pair; l.e. means lone or unpaired electron. Only the central atom's lone pairs and lone electrons are indicated. In the cases where there is some doubt, hyb precedes the description which assumes the central atom to be hybridized and unhyb precedes the description in which the central atom is not assumed to be hybridized.
A. 2 Be(*sp*)-H(1*s*) B. 3 C(sp^3)-H(1*s*), l.e. in C(sp^3)
C. 4 Kr(d^2sp^3)-F(2*p*), 1 l.p. in Kr(d^2sp^3)
D. 4 B(sp^3)-F(2*p*) E. hyb: 2 Sn(sp^2)-Cl(3*p*), 1 l.p. in Sn(sp^2); unhyb: 2 Sn(5*p*)-Cl(3*p*), 1 l.p. in Sn(5*s*) F. 4 N(sp^3)-H(1*s*)
G. 4 I(sp^3d^2)-Cl(3*p*), 2 l.p. in I(sp^3d^2)
H. 3 C(sp^2)-H(1*s*) I. hyb: 2 S(sp^3)-I (5*p*), 2 l.p. in S(sp^3); unhyb: 2 S(3*p*)-I(5*p*), l.p. in S(3*p*), l.p. in S(3*s*) J. 4 Se(sp^3d)-F(2*p*), l.p. in Se(sp^3d)
K. 2 Xe(sp^3d)-F(2*p*), 3 l.p. in Xe(sp^3d)
L. hyb: 2 C(sp^2)-Cl(3*p*), l.p. in C(sp^2); unhyb: 2 C(2*p*)-Cl(3*p*), l.p. in C(2*s*)
M. 2 N(sp^3)-H(1*s*), 2 l.p. in N(sp^3)
N. 3 Br(sp^3d)-F(2*p*), l.p. in Br(sp^3d)
O. 5 I(sp^3d^2)-F(2*p*), 1 l.p. in I(sp^3d^2)
P. 2 Cl(sp^3)-O(2*p*), 2 l.p. in Cl(sp^3) Q. 3 B(sp^2)-Cl(3*p*)
R. Sb(sp^3d)-Cl(3*p*) S. 6 Se(sp^3d^2)-F(2*p*)
T. 3 O(sp^3)-H(1*s*), l.p. in O(sp^3)

5. Refer to the paragraph at the beginning of the answers for objective 10–4. These bonding descriptions are based on the Lewis structure which is drawn first in each part.
A. $[\overline{N}^a=C=\overline{N}^b]^{2-}$, 2 C(*sp*)-N(2*p*), π C($2p_y$)-N^a($2p_y$), π C($2p_z$)-N^b($2p_z$)

B. H^a and H^b bonded to C; $C=\overline{\underline{S}}$ C(sp^2)-H^a(1*s*), C(sp^2)-H^b(1*s*), C(sp^2)-S($3p_y$), π($2p_z$)-S($3p_z$)

C. $|\overline{\underline{Cl}}^a$ and $|\overline{\underline{Cl}}^b$ bonded to C^a; C=C; H^a and H^b bonded to C^b C^a(sp^2)-Cl^a(3*p*), C^a(sp^2)-Cl^b(3*p*), C^b(sp^2)-H^a(1*s*), C^b(sp^2)-H^b(1*s*), C^a(sp^2)-C^b(sp^2), π C^a($2p_z$)-C^b($2p_z$)

D. $|\overline{\underline{Cl}}^a$ and $|\overline{\underline{Cl}}^b$ bonded to C; $C=\overline{\underline{S}}$ Cl^a(3*p*)-C(sp^2), Cl^b(3*p*)-C(sp^2), C(sp^2)-S(3*p*), π C($2p_z$)-S($3p_z$)

E. $[\overline{S}=C=\overline{N}]^-$, C(*sp*)-S($3p_y$), C(*sp*)-N($2p_z$), π C($2p_y$)-N($2p_y$), π C($2p_z$)-S($3p_z$)

F. $|N^a\equiv N^b-\overline{\underline{O}}|$, N^a($2p_x$)-N^b(*sp*), N^b(*sp*)-O($2p_z$), π N^a($2p_y$)-N^b($2p_y$), π N^a($2p_z$)-N^b($2p_z$)

G. $\overline{O}^a{=}C{=}\overline{O}^b$, $O^a(2p_y)$-C(sp), $O^b(2p_z)$-C(sp), π $O^a(2p_z)$-$C(2p_z)$, π $O^b(2p_y)$-$C(2p_y)$

H. $H{-}\overline{O}{-}C{\equiv}N|$, H(1$s$)-O($sp^3$), O($sp^3$)-C($sp$), C($sp$)-$N(2p_x)$, 2 l.p. in O($sp^3$), π $C(2p_y)$-$N(2p_y)$, π $C(2p_z)$-$N(2p_z)$

I. $H{-}\overline{N}{=}\overline{O}$, H(1$s$)-N($sp^2$), N($sp^2$)-$O(2p_y)$, l.p. in N($sp^2$), π $N(2p_z)$-$O(2p_z)$

J. $H{-}C{\equiv}N|$, H(1s)-C(sp), C(sp)-$N(2p_x)$, π $N(2p_y)$-$C(2p_y)$, π $N(2p_z)$-$C(2p_z)$

K. $H^a{-}C^a{\equiv}C^b{-}H^b$, $H^a(1s)$-$C^a(sp)$, $H^b(1s)$-$C^b(sp)$, $C^a(sp)$-$C^b(sp)$, π $C^a(2p_y)$-$C^b(2p_y)$, π $C^a(2p_z)$-$C^b(2p_z)$

L. $[\overline{O}^a{=}N{=}\overline{O}^b]^+$, $O^a(2p_y)$-N(sp), N(sp)-$O^b(2p_z)$, π $O^a(2p_z)$-$N(2p_z)$, π $N(2p_y)$-$O^b(2p_y)$

M. $\overline{O}{=}C{=}\overline{S}$, $O(2p_y)$-C(sp), C(sp)-$S(3p_z)$, π $O(2p_z)$-$C(2p_z)$, π $C(2p_y)$-$S(3p_y)$

N. $|\overline{F}{-}\overline{P}{=}\overline{O}$, $F(2p_z)$-P(sp^2), P(sp^2)-$O(2p_y)$, l.p. in P(sp^2), π $P(3p_z)$-$O(2p_z)$

O. $H^a{-}C({=}\overline{O}^a){-}\overline{O}^b{-}H^b$

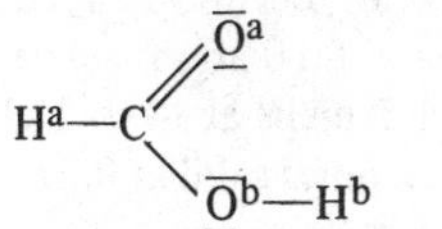

$H^a(1s)$-C(sp^2), C(sp^2)-$O(2p_y)$, C(sp^2)-$O^b(sp^3)$, $O^b(sp^3)$-$H^b(1s)$, 2 l.p. in $O^b(sp^3)$, π $C(2p_z)$-$O^a(2p_z)$

8. Simplified molecular orbital diagram is given first (in the order $\sigma^b_{2s}, \sigma^*_{2s}, \pi^b_{2p}, \sigma^b_{2p}, \pi^*_{2p}, \sigma^*_{2p}$) followed by answers (1)-(6).

A. KK ↑↓ ↑↓ ↑↓ ↑↓ ↑↓ __ __ __ ; 8, 2, 3, 6, 4, 0

B. KK ↑↓ ↑↓ ↑↓ ↑↓ ↑↓ ↑↓ ↑↓ __ ; 8, 6, 1, 6, 8, 0

C. KK ↑↓ ↑↓ ↑↓ ↑↓ ↑↓ ↑ ↑↓ __ ; 8, 3, 5/2, 6, 5, 1

D. KK ↑↓ ↑↓ ↑↓ ↑↓ __ __ __ __ ; 6, 2, 2, 4, 4, 0

E. KK ↑↓ ↑↓ ↑↓ ↑↓ __ __ __ __ ; 6, 2, 2, 4, 4, 0

F. KK ↑↓ ↑↓ ↑↓ ↑↓ __ __ __ __ ; 6, 2, 2, 4, 4, 0

G. KK ↑↓ ↑ __ __ __ __ __ __ ; 2, 1, 1/2, 3, 0, 1

H. KK ↑↓ ↑↓ ↑↓ ↑↓ ↑ __ __ __ ; 7, 2, 5/2, 5, 4, 1

I. KK ↑↓ ↑↓ ↑↓ ↑↓ ↑↓ ↑↓ ↑↓ ↑ ; 8, 7, 1/2, 7, 8, 1

J. KK ↑↓ ↑↓ ↑↓ ↑↓ ↑↓ ↑↓ ↑↓ ↑ ; 8, 7, 1/2, 7, 8, 1

K. KK ↑↓ ↑↓ ↑↓ ↑↓ ↑↓ ↑↓ ↑ __ ; 8, 5, 3/2, 6, 7, 1

L. KK ↑↓ ↑↓ ↑↓ ↑↓ ↑↓ ↑ ↑ __ ; 8, 4, 2, 6, 6, 2

M. KK ↑↓ ↑↓ __ __ __ __ __ __ ; 2, 2, 0, 4, 0, 0

9. Refer to the paragraph at the beginning of the solutions for objective 10-4. These descriptions are based on the resonance structure drawn first in each part.

A. $\overline{O}^a{=}\dot{N}{-}\overline{O}^b| \leftrightarrow |\overline{O}{-}\dot{N}{=}\overline{O}$; $O^a(2p_y)$-N(sp^2), l.p. in N(sp^2), π $O^a(2p_z)$-$O^b(2p_z)$ (3-electron, 3-center π bond)

B. $\overline{O}^a{=}\overline{S}{-}\overline{O}^c|$ (with $|\overline{O}^b|$ on S) $\leftrightarrow$ $|\overline{O}{-}\overline{S}{=}\overline{O}$ (with $|\overline{O}|$ on S) $\leftrightarrow$ $|\overline{O}{-}\overline{S}{-}\overline{O}|$ (with $|\overline{O}|$ double-bonded to S);

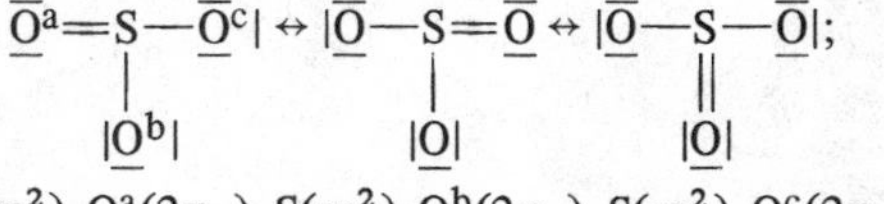

S(sp^2)-$O^a(2p_y)$, S(sp^2)-$O^b(2p_y)$, S(sp^2)-$O^c(2p_y)$, π $S(3p_z)$-$O^a(2p_z)$-$O^b(2p_z)$-$O^c(2p_z)$ (6-electron, 4-center π bond)

C. $|\overline{Cl}^a{-}B(|\overline{Cl}^c|){=}\overline{Cl}^b \leftrightarrow \overline{Cl}{=}B(|\overline{Cl}|){-}\overline{Cl}| \leftrightarrow |\overline{Cl}{-}B({=}|Cl|){-}\overline{Cl}|$;

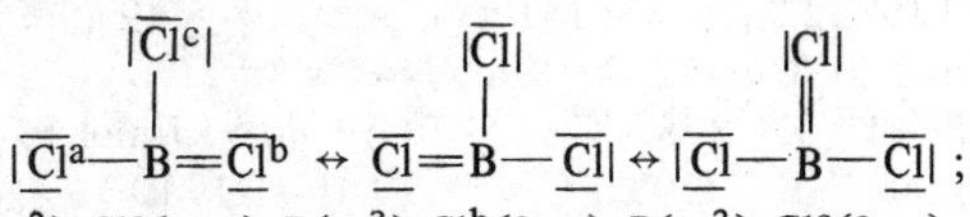

B(sp^2)-$Cl^a(3p_y)$, B(sp^3)-$Cl^b(3p_y)$, B(sp^2)-$Cl^c(3p_y)$, π $B(2p_z)$-$Cl^a(3p_z)$-$Cl^b(3p_z)$-$Cl^c(3p_z)$ (6-electron, 4-center π bond)

D. $\overline{O}^a{=}\overline{O}^b{-}\overline{O}^c| \leftrightarrow |\overline{O}{-}\overline{O}{=}\overline{O}$; $O^a(2p_y)$-$O^b(sp^2)$, $O^c(2p_y)$-$O^b(sp^2)$, l.p. in $O^b(sp^2)$, π $O^a(2p_z)$-$O^b(2p_z)$-$O^c(2p_z)$ (4-electron, 3-center π bond)

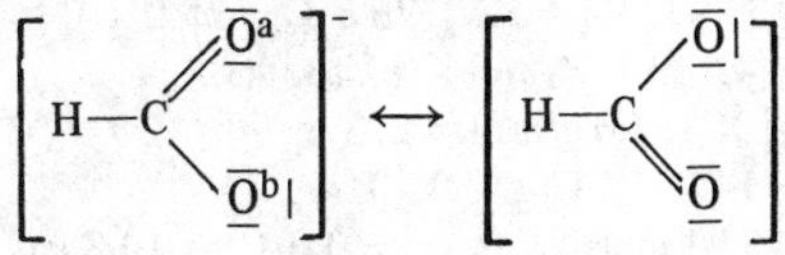

E. $[H{-}C({=}\overline{O}^a){-}\overline{O}^b|]^- \leftrightarrow [H{-}C({-}\overline{O}|){=}\overline{O}]^-$

H(1s)-C(sp^2), C(sp^2)-$O^a(2p_y)$, C(sp^2)-$O^b(2p_y)$, π $C(2p_z)$-$O^a(2p_z)$-$O^b(2p_z)$ (4-electron, 3-center π bond)

F. $\overline{O}{=}\overline{C}{-}\overline{F}| \leftrightarrow |\overline{O}{-}\overline{C}{=}\overline{F}$; $O(2p_y)$-C(sp^2)-$F(2p_y)$, l.p. in C(sp^2), π $O(2p_z)$-$C(2p_z)$-$F(2p_z)$ (4-electron, 3-center π bond)

G. $[|\overline{O}^a{-}C({=}|\overline{O}^b){-}\overline{O}^c|]^{2-} \leftrightarrow [|\overline{O}{-}C({-}|\overline{O}|){=}\overline{O}]^{2-} \leftrightarrow [\overline{O}{=}C({-}|\overline{O}|){-}\overline{O}|]^{2-}$

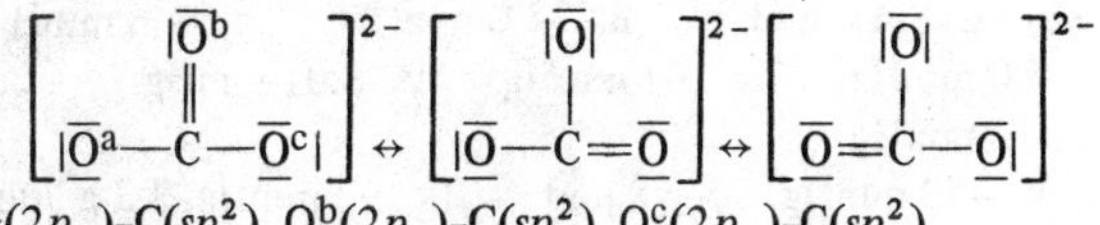

$O^a(2p_y)$-C(sp^2), $O^b(2p_y)$-C(sp^2), $O^c(2p_y)$-C(sp^2), π $O^a(2p_z)$-$O^b(2p_z)$-$C(2p_z)$ (4-center, 6-electron π bond)

H. Same as BCl^3 except 2p orbitals used on ligands.

Quizzes

A: 1. (c) 2. (c) 3. (b) 4. (a) 5. (b) 6. (a) 7. (c) 8. (e)

B: 1. (a) 2. (b) 3. (b) 4. (b) 5. (b) 6. (b) 7. (a) 8. (c)

C: 1. (a) 2. (b) 3. (d) 4. (b) 5. (b) 6. (b) 7. (d) 8. (a)

D: 1. (a) 2. (a) 3. (c) 4. (d) 5. (c) 6. (c) 7. (d) 8. (c)

Sample Test

1. a. 2, 3, 2 b. 0, 0, 2 c. linear, triangular planar, tetrahedral d. linear, triangular planar, bent e. none, none, sp^3 f. sp, sp^2, sp^3 g. $N(2p_x)$-$C^a(sp)$, $C^a(sp)$-$C^b(sp^2)$, $C^b(sp^2)$-$S(3p_x)$, $C^b(sp^2)$-O(sp^3), O(sp^3)-H(1s) H. $N(2p_y)$-$C^a(2p_y)$, $N(2p_z)$-$C^a(2p_z)$, $C^b(2p_z)$-$S(3p_y)$ I. 180° J. 120° K. 120° L. 109.5°

2. a. 5/2 b. NO^+ as it has a bond order of 3 compared to 5/2 for O_2^+ C. 1, 2, 0

CHAPTER 11

Drill Problems

2. Ex. 236.2 kJ = 150 g × mol/18.0 g × 0.0753 kJ mol^{-1} K^{-1} (100.0°C − 75.0°C) + 90 g × mol/18.0 g × 44.1 kJ/mol.

A. 200 g × mol/32.0 g × 0.0816 kJ mol^{-1} K^{-1} × (64.96°C − 50.0°C) = 7.6 kJ; (184.7 kJ − 7.6 kJ) × mol/37.6 kJ × 32.0 g/mol = 151 g vaporize; m_L = 49 g; t_f = 64.96°C   B. q = 204 g × mol/46.0 g × [0.113 kJ mol^{-1} K^{-1} (78.5°C − 20.2°C) + 40.5 kJ/mol + 0.0657 kJ mol^{-1} K^{-1} (100.0°C − 78.5°C)] = 215 kJ C. Same method as example; 68.7 kJ   D. 20.2 kJ = m × mol/27.0 g [0.0707 kJ mol^{-1} K^{-1} (26.0°C + 14.0°C) + 30.7 kJ/mol + 0.0360 kJ mol^{-1} K^{-1} (36.5°C − 26.0°C)]; m = 16.1 g   E. Same method as A; t_f = 118.5°C, m_L = 177 g   F. Same method as B; q = 126 kJ.   G. Same method as A; t_f = 34.6°C, m_L = 54.5 g   H. q = 14.0 g × mol/154.0 g × [39.1 kJ/mol + 0.133 kJ mol^{-1} K^{-1} (76.8°C − 25.0°C)] = 4.18 kJ; (16.4 kJ − 4.18 kJ) × mol-K/[0.133 kJ × (76.8°C − 25.0°C)] × 154.0 g/mol = 273 g; total mass = 273 + 14.0 = 287 g   I. 314 g × mol/119.5 g × 0.115 kJ mol^{-1} K^{-1} (t_f − 0.0°C) = 14.3 kJ; t_f = 47.3°C   J. Same method as B; 92.1 kJ K. Same method as example; 230 kJ L. t_f = 58.78°C; q = 124 g × mol/159.8 g × 0.0757 kJ mol^{-1} K^{-1} (58.78°C − 20.40°C) + 100 g × mol/159.8 g × 33.9 kJ/mol = 23.5 kJ M. Same method as I; t_f = −34.35°C

4. (1) A. 8.43 mmHg   B. 35.0 mmHg   C. 94.6 mmHg D. 45.0 mmHg   E. 101 mmHg   F. 8.01 mmHg G. 1.10 mmHg

(2) A. 450 mmHg, 6.8 g liquid   B. 190 mmHg, 2.3 g liquid C. 370 mmHg, no liquid   D. 110 mmHg, 2.4 g liquid E. 570 mmHg, no liquid   F. 400 mmHg, 4.6 g liquid G. 650 mmHg, no liquid

5. (1) A. 31.4 kJ/mol, 41.7°C   B. 27.4 kJ/mol, 5.0°C C. 50.2 kJ/mol, 149°C   D. 46.0 kJ/mol, 139.7°C E. 32.1 kJ/mol, 70.3°C   F. 19.6 kJ/mol, −98.9°C G. 78.5 kJ/mol, 678°C

(2) A. 14.3 mmHg, 47.0°C   B. 1020 mmHg, 45.8°C C. 1.06 mmHg, 34.6°C   D. 30.2 mmHg, 53.9°C E. 84.6 mmHg, −19°C   F. 0.240 mmHg, 71.2°C G. 237 mmHg, −53.56°C   H. 25.2 mmHg, 66.8°C

6a. In order the enthalpies (in kJ/mol) are $\Delta\bar{H}^\circ_{fus}$, $\Delta\bar{H}^\circ_{vap}$, $\Delta\bar{H}^\circ_{sub}$, $\Delta\bar{H}^\circ_{sol}$, $\Delta\bar{H}^\circ_{cond}$, and $\Delta\bar{H}^\circ_{dep}$.
A. 6.01, 44.1, 50.1, −6.01, −44.1, −50.1   B. 10.7, 232.8, 243.5, −10.7, −232.8, −243.5   C. 27.2, 176.9, 204.1, −27.2, −176.9, −204.1   D. 47.2, 181.8, 229.0, −47.2, −181.8, −229.0   E. 20.1, 158.6, 178.7, −20.1, −158.6, −178.7   F. 19.0, 41.4, 60.4, −19.0, −41.4, −60.4 G. 56.6, 668.5, 725.1, −56.6, −668.5, −725.1

7. A.

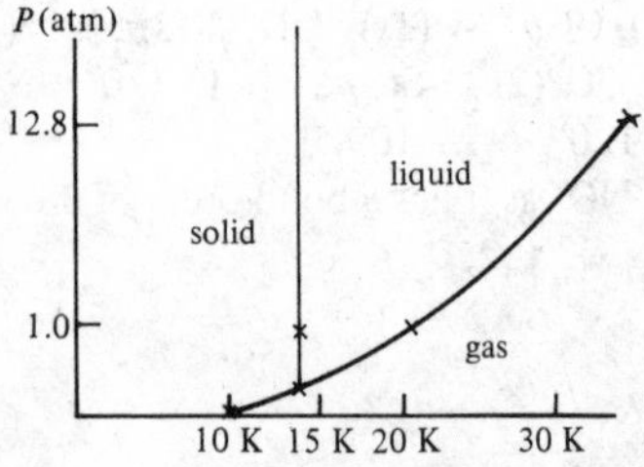

B. Yes, at about 14.00 K   C. No; the critical pressure is 12.8 atm.   D. No; the solid-liquid line slopes upward to the right.

E.

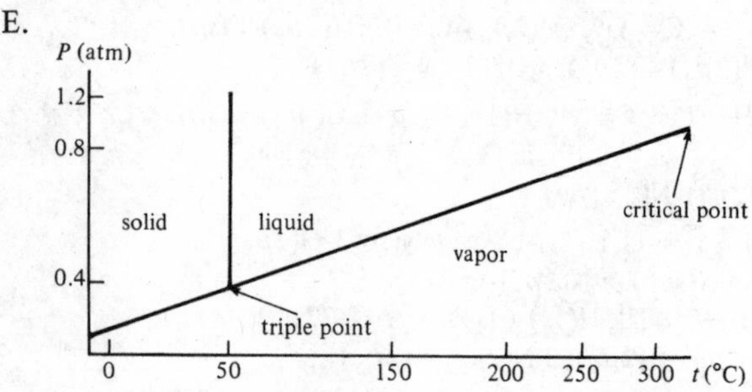

F. Yes, about 49.6°C   G. Yes, about 218°C
H. Yes; the solid-liquid line slopes upward to the left.
I. Begins as a vapor; turns solid at about 5 mmHg, turns liquid between 300 and 400 mmHg and remains liquid.   J. Begins as a solid; turns liquid at about 273.13 K; vaporizes at 131°C (from Clausius–Clapeyron equation).   K. Begins as a solid; sublimes at about −70°C.   L. Begins as a solid; melts at about −56.7°C; vaporizes at perhaps 0°C.   M. Begins as a solid; melts at about −55°C; never vaporizes as 80.0 atm is above the critical pressure.   N. Begins as a solid; melts at 14.01 K; boils at 20.38 K.   O. Starts as a vapor; becomes solid at 0.07 atm; turns liquid at about 0.8 atm and remains so.
P. Begins as a vapor; becomes a solid at 0.40 atm; turns liquid at about 1.40 atms and remains so.   Q. Begins as a solid; melts at about 49.6°C; vaporizes at about 225°C.

8. A. HI, Xe   B. PF_3, BCl_3 C. HBr, HCl D. CH_4, GeH_4 E. PF_3, AlF_3 F. CH_3OH_5, C_3H_8OH. G. H_2O, HF   H. I_2, Cl_2 I. CH_4, CCl_4 J. CCl_3F, Br_2

11. A. SrS, MgS   B. NaH, NaBr   C. SrI_2, $CaCl_2$ D. MgS, Na_2S E. $CaCl_2$, CaO   F. $Al_2(CO_3)_2$, Na_2CO_3 G. LiF, LiI   H. MgS, K_2S I. $Pb(NO_3)_2$, $Mg(NO_3)_2$ J. RbCl, $INCl_3$

Quizzes

A: 1. (e)   2. (b)   3. (e)   4. (b)   5. (b)   6. (d) 7. (a)   8. (e)
B: 1. (b)   2. (e)   3. (d)   4. (d)   5. (a)   6. (e) 7. (c)   5. (b)
C: 1. (c)   2. (b)   3. (a)   4. (d)   5. (e)   6. (a) 7. (a)   8. (b)
D: 1. (c)   2. (b)   3. (b)   4. (e)   5. (e)   6. (c) 7. (d)   8. (e)

Sample Test

1. $-8.314 \frac{J}{\text{mol-K}} \ln \frac{50.0}{760.0} = 32.0 \times 10^3 \left(\frac{1}{T} - \frac{1}{329.4}\right)$; T = −6.0°C
2. See Fig. 11-2.
3. Review objective 11-8.
4. MgO. The lattice energy depends on $Z_A Z_c/(r_a + r_c)$. To obtain the largest lattice energy we need the most highly charged ions of the smallest radii.

CHAPTER 12

Drill Problems

2. A. 30.00 cm^3, 8.91 cm^3, 21.80 g, 31.16%, 29.70% B. 50.00 g, 0.9912 g/cm^3, 5.00%, 4.96%, C. 4.29 cm^3, 40.13 g, 9.11%, 9.13% D. 91.22 cm^3, 48.00 g, 120.00 g, 60.00%, 67.81% E. 6.995 cm^3, 0.870 cm^3, 6.18 g, 9.81%, 12.43% F. 60.00 g, 1.0094 g/cm^3, 9.00%, 9.08%, 8.19% G. 4.35 cm^3, 120.46 g, 4.00%, 4.02% H. 39.34 cm^3, 102.00 g, 150.00 g, 32.00%, 28.51% I. 36.00 cm^3, 7.50 cm^3, 28.96 g, 25.41%, 20.83% J. 100.00 g, 1.044 g/cm^3, 19.00%, 19.84%, 15.73% K. 31.99 cm^3, 84.07 g, 48.00%, 53.80% L. 74.30 cm^3, 11.20 g, 70.00 g, 84.00%, 88.80% M. 71.40 cm^3, 53.75 cm^3, 20.02 g, 59.58%, 75.29%

2a. A. 0.8535 mol, 4.163 m, 19.99% B. 53.5 g/mol, 0.667 mol, 1.406 *m* C. 0.224 mol, 1.156 g/ml, 0.9391 *m* D. 3.175 *M*, 3.383 *m*, 10.98% E. 42.40 g/mol, 500.0 ml, 2.620 *m* F. 200 ml, 1.17 *m*, 28.0% G. 42.5 g/mol, 0.963 *M*, 0.981 *m* H. 0.2128 mol, 1.065 g/ml, 1.110 *m* I. 0.9768 mol, 1.302 *M*, 1.368 *m* J. 74.54 g/mol, 0.3084 mol, 0.9326 *m* K. 0.2007 mol, 0.7434 *M*, 0.7598 *m* L. 165.7 ml, 1.29 *m*, 20.0% M. 3.782 mol, 1.261 g/ml, 6.060 *m* N. 5.210 mol, 32.31 *m*, 76.06% O. 420 ml, 14.3 *M*, 16.7 *m* P. 58.44 g/mol, 6.012 *m*, 1.598 mol Q. 400.0 ml, 6.803 *m*, 40.00% R. 0.205 mol, 0.8548 *M*, 0.8873 *m*

2b. A. 0.06977, 93.023% B. 0.0247, 97.53% C. 0.0166, 98.34% D. 0.05744, 94.256% E. 0.04507, 95.493% F. 0.0208, 97.92% G. 0.0172, 98.28% H. 0.01959, 98.041% I. 0.02404, 97.596% J. 0.0165, 98.35% K. 0.0135, 98.65% L. 0.225, 77.5% M. 0.09846, 90.154% N. 0.3677, 63.23% O. 0.231, 76.9% P. 0.09769, 90.231% Q. 0.1092, 89.08% R. 0.01573, 98.427%

4. A. 0.0355 *m* B. 7.67 atm C. 0.000234 *m* D. 0.493 atm E. 0.0144 *m* F. 0.457 atm G. 0.00278 *m* H. 4.58 atm I. 0.0854 *m* J. 1.17 atm

5. A. $\chi_B = 0.25, P = 87.5$ B. $\chi_A = 0.542, \chi_B = 0.458$ C. $P_A = 340, \chi_B = 0.75$ D. $P_B = 254, \chi_B = 0.70$ E. $P_A = 125, \chi_A = 0.86$ F. $\chi_A = 0.65, P = 218$ G. $\chi_A = 0.125, \chi_B = 0.875$ H. $\chi_A = 0.200, \chi_B = 0.800$

7. A. 106 g/mol, 15.83°C B. 4.88°C/*m*, 0.217 *m*, 80.64°C C. 7.00°C/*m*, 23.1 g, 212.09°C D. 3.56°C/*m*, 83.8 g/mol, 40.91°C E. 0.325 *m*, 100.17°C F. 14.2 g, 0.369 *m*, −0.69°C

8. A. 0.0398 *M*, 0.749 g B. 0.00740 *M*, 512 g/mol C. 488 mmHg, 0.0269 *M* D. 0.0808 *M*, 7.75 g E. 0.0258 *M*, 1214 g/mol F. 579 mmHg, 0.0322 *M* G. 0.0968 *M*, 8.02 g H. 0.0275 *M*, 99.8 g/mol I. 455 mmHg, 0.0241 *M* J. 0.0256 *M*, 1.73 g K. 0.0414 *M*, 164 g/mol L. 351 mmHg, 0.0187 *M* M. 0.0524 *M*, 1.04 g N. 0.0350 *M*, 154 g/mol O. 47.2 mmHg, 0.00250 *M*

9. A. $[Li^+] = 0.0709\ M$, $[Ca^{2+}] = 0.436\ M$, $[NO_3^-] = 0.943\ M$ B. $[Cl^-] = 0.0788\ M$, $[SO_4^{2-}] = 0.0966\ M$, $[H^+] = 0.2720\ M$ C. $[Na^+] = 0.124\ M$, $[Al^{3+}] = 0.305\ M$, $[OH^-] = 1.040\ M$ D. $[Cl^-] = 0.0611\ M$, $[PO_4^{3-}] = 0.0916\ M$, $[Na^+] = 0.3360\ M$ E. $[H^+] = 0.829\ M$, $[Na^+] = 0.457\ M$, $[NO_3^-] = 1.286\ M$ F. $[Ca^{2+}] = 0.0894\ M$, $[Mg^{2+}] = 0.120\ M$, $[Cl^-] = 0.420\ M$ G. $[Na^+] = 0.112\ M$, $[Al^{3+}] = 0.144\ M$, $[SO_4^{2-}] = 0.272\ M$ H. $[SO_4^{2-}] = 0.0946\ M$, $[PO_4^{3-}] = 0.184\ M$, $[Na^+] = 0.741\ M$ I. $[Br^-] = 0.308\ M$, $[Cl^-] = 0.336\ M$, $[Na^+] = 0.644\ M$ J. $[Cl^-] = 0.536\ M$, $[SO_4^{2-}] = 0.0848\ M$, $[Li^+] = 0.706\ M$

Quizzes

A: 1. (e) 2. (e) (concentrated) 3. (a) 4. (a) 5. (d) 6. (d) 7. (e) 8. (a)
B: 1. (b) 2. (a) 3. (c) 4. (e) 5. (e) (8/100) 6. (c) 7. (e) 8. (b)
C: 1. (e) 2. (d) 3. (d) 4. (c) 5. (e) 6. (e) 7. (a) 8. (c)
D: 1. (b) 2. (c) 3. (d) 4. (e) 5. (c) 6. (d) 7. (d) 8. (a)

Sample Test

1. A. (750 g + 85 g)/810 ml = 1.03 g/ml

b. [85 g/(750 g + 85 g)] X 100% = 10.2%

c. $$\frac{85.0\text{ g} \times \text{mol}/180.0\text{ g}}{(85.0\text{ g} \times \text{mol}/180.0\text{ g}) + (750\text{ g} \times \text{mol}/46.0\text{ g})} = 0.0281 = \chi_{\text{sucrose}}$$

d. $$\frac{85.0\text{ g} \times \text{mol}/180.0\text{ g}}{750\text{ g} \times \text{kg}/1000\text{ g}} = 0.630\ m$$

e. $$\frac{85.0\text{ g} \times \text{mol}/180.0\text{ g}}{810\text{ ml} \times \text{L}/1000\text{ ml}} = 0.583\ M$$

2. $(14.0°\text{F} - 32)(5/9) = -10°\text{C}; \Delta t_f = 10.0°\text{C} = K_f m$; $m = 10.0°\text{C}/(1.86°\text{C}/m) = 5.38\ m$
mols of solute = 20.0 L H_2O X (kg/L)(5.38 *m*) = 108 mol

$$108\text{ mol} \times \frac{62.0\text{ g}}{\text{mol}} \times \frac{\text{cm}^3}{1.12\text{ g}} \times \frac{\text{L}}{1000\text{ cm}^3}$$

= 5.95 L ethylene glycol

CHAPTER 13

Drill Problems

1. (1) A. 2.9×10^{-3} mol L^{-1} min^{-1} B. 9.3×10^{-4} mol L^{-1} min^{-1} C. 3.4×10^{-4} mol L^{-1} min^{-1} D. 2.1×10^{-3} mol L^{-1} min^{-1} E. 7.0×10^{-4} mol L^{-1} min^{-1} F. 1.4×10^{-3} mol L^{-1} min^{-1} G. 2.2×10^{-4} mol L^{-1} min^{-1} H. 0.14 mol L^{-1} hr^{-1} I. 0.23 mol L^{-1} hr^{-1} J. 0.051 mol L^{-1} hr^{-1} K. 0.010 mol L^{-1} hr^{-1} L. 0.031 mol L^{-1} hr^{-1} M. 0.018 mol L^{-1} hr^{-1} N. 0.028 mol L^{-1} hr^{-1}
(2) A. 44 min, 2.3×10^{-3} mol L^{-1} min^{-1} B. 320 min, 1.1×10^{-3} mol L^{-1} min^{-1} C. 484 min, 7.6×10^{-4} mol L^{-1} min^{-1} D. 688 min, 5.1×10^{-4} mol L^{-1} min^{-1} E. 1.6 hr, 0.28 mol L^{-1} hr^{-1} F. 21.2 hr, 0.044 mol L^{-1} hr^{-1} G. 60.6 hr, 0.010 mol L^{-1} hr^{-1} H. 40.7 hr, 0.018 mol L^{-1} hr^{-1}

3. A. $k[N_2O_5]$, first B. $k[CH_3CHO]^2$, second C. $k[CO][NO_2]$, second D. $k[NO]^2[H_2]$, third E. $k[NOCl]^2$, second F. $k[F_2][ClO_2]$, second G. $k[CH_3Cl][F^-]$, second H. $k[BrO_3^-][Br^-][H^+]^2$, fourth I. $k[NH_4^+][NO_2^-]$, second J. $k[H_2PO_2^-][OH^-]^2$, third K. $k[NO]^2[H_2]$, third
4. A. 0.294/hr, 0.0588 mol L^{-1} hr^{-1}, 0.294 mol L^{-1} hr^{-1} B. 9.00×10^{-5} L mol^{-1} hr^{-1}, 2.03×10^{-6} mol L^{-1} s^{-1}, 1.02×10^{-5} mol L^{-1} s^{-1} C. 1.2 L mol^{-1} s^{-1}, 0.30 mol L^{-1} s^{-1}, 0.86 mol L^{-1} s^{-1} D. 1.35 L^2 mol^{-2} h^{-1}, 7.15×10^{-3} mol L^{-1} h^{-1}, 0.0335 mol L^{-1} s^{-1} E. 4.0×10^{-8} L mol^{-1} s^{-1}, 1.0×10^{-8} mol L^{-1} s^{-1}, 2.1×10^{-9} mol^{-1} s^{-1} F. 2.4 L^2 mol^{-2} s^{-1}, 0.084 mol L^{-1} s^{-1}, 0.077 mol L^{-1} s^{-1} G. 4.8×10^{11} L mol^{-1} s^{-1}, 0.39 mol L^{-1}, s^{-1}, 0.21 mol L^{-1} s^{-1} H. 2.11 L^3 mol^{-3} s^{-1}, 0.00601 mol L^{-1} s^{-1}, 2.32×10^{-4} mol L^{-1} s^{-1} I. 3.9×10^{-4} L mol^{-1} s^{-1}, 3.9×10^{-7} mol L^{-1} s^{-1}, 7.7×10^{-9} mol L^{-1} s^{-1} J. 5.3×10^{-5} L^2 mol^{-2} s^{-1}, 4.6×10^{-6} mol L^{-1} s^{-1}, 6.2×10^{-6} mol L^{-1} s^{-1} K. 2.2 atm^{-2} min^{-1}, 4.3×10^{-3} atm/min, 0.260 atm/min
5. A. second, 1.7×10^{-3} mol L^{-1} s^{-1} B. first, 0.0207/min C. first, 0.0902/hr D. second, 0.0581 L mol^{-1} min^{-1} E. second, 3.17×10^{-3} L mol^{-1} min^{-1} F. first, 5.86×10^{-3}/min G. first, 0.0523/min H. first, 2.01×10^{-3}/min I. first, 0.0103/min J. first, 1.974×10^{-2}/min
6. A. 2.9×10^2 s B. 33.5 min C. 7.68 hr D. 43.0 min E. 2.63×10^3 min F. 118 hr G. 13.3 min H. 345 min I. 67.3 min J. 35.11 min
9. A. 24.91 kJ/mol, 0.479/s B. 134.01 kJ/mol, 6.0×10^{-14}/s C. 97.10 kJ/mol, 4.9×10^{-39}/s D. 269.36 kJ/mol, 8.09/s E. 80.96 kJ/mol, 0.797 L mol^{-1} s^{-1}
12. (1) A. rate = $k[CO][NO_2]$ B. rate = $k[NO_2]_2$ C. rate = $k[NO_2]^2[CO]^2$ D. rate = $k[NO_2]^2$ Since B involves an unlikely fast termolecular step, D is more plausible. They both give the same total reaction.
(2) A. rate = $k[Cl_2]^{3/2}[CO]$ B. rate = $k[Cl_2][CO]$ C. rate = $k[Cl_2]^{3/2}[CO]$ D. rate = $k[Cl_2]^{3/2}[CO]$ A, C, and D all sum to the total reaction and give the correct rate law, but D does so in an unlikely way, and A contains Cl_3, a very unlikely intermediate. Thus C seems the most plausible.
(3) A. rate = $k[H_2][Br_2]$ B. rate = $k[Br_2][H_2]^{1/2}$ C. rate = $k[H_2][Br_2]^{1/2}$ If the first step in B and C is disregarded as occurring to a very small extent, all three sum to the overall reaction. Only C gives the correct rate law, and it is the most plausible.
(4) A. rate = $k[NO]^2[O_2]$ B. rate = $k[NO]^2[O_2]$ C. rate = $k[NO]^2[O_2]$ All sum to the overall reaction and give the correct rate law. However, both A and C have unlikely termolecular steps. Thus B is most plausible.
(5) A. rate = $k[C_4H_9Br]$ B. rate = $k[C_4H_9Br][OH^-]$ C. rate = $k[C_4H_9Br][OH^-]/[H_2O]$ All sum to the overall reaction, but only B gives the correct rate law.
(6) Sums to the overall reaction if the first step is disregarded as proceeding only to a minor extent. No termolecular collisions. rate = $k[CH_3Cl][Cl_2]^{1/2}$
(7) Sums to the overall reaction and contains no termolecular collisions. rate = $k[O_3][NO]$

Quizzes

A: 1. (d) 2. (d) 3. (b) 4. (d) 5. (e) (all change the *rate*) 6. (e) (zero order) 7. (b) 8. (d)
B: 1. (d) 2. (e) 3. (e) (0.012) 4. (b) 5. (a) 6. (e) (L mol^{-1} s^{-1}) 7. (c) 8. (e)
C: 1. (b) 2. (b) 3. (a) 4. (d) 5. (b) 6. (d) 7. (c) 8. (d)
D: 1. (c) 2. (c) 3. (e) 4. (c) 5. (d) 6. (a) 7. (d) 8. (e) (changes the *rate*)

Sample Test

1. -8.314 J mol^{-1} K^{-1} ln $(7.00 \times 10^{-9})/(1.00 \times 10^{-4}) = E_a(1/400 - 1/500)$; $E_a = 159.1$ kJ/mol
2. a. rate = $k[HgCl_2][Na_2C_2O_4]^2$ b. 76.2 L^2 mol^{-2} hr^{-1} c. 0.152 mol L^{-1} hr^{-1}

CHAPTER 14

Drill Problems

1a. A. $[CH_4] = 0.0300\,M$, $[CCl_4] = 0.138\,M$, $[CH_2Cl_2] = 0.0199\,M$ B. $[CH_4] = [CCl_4] = 0.0390\,M$, $[CH_2Cl_2] = 0.0121\,M$ C. $[CH_4] = 0.1604\,M$, $[CCl_4] = 0.1004\,M$, $[CH_2Cl_2] = 0.0392\,M$ D. $[CH_4] = [CCl_4] = 0.5154\,M$, $[CH_2Cl_2] = 0.01874\,M$ E. $[PCl_5] = 0.0038\,M$, $[PCl_3] = [Cl_2] = 0.0462\,M$ F. $[PCl_5] = 0.0299\,M$, $[PCl_3] = 0.1381\,M$, $[Cl_2] = 0.1211$ G. $[PCl_5] = 0.00100\,M$, $[PCl_3] = 0.0340\,M$, $[Cl_2] = 0.0170\,M$ H. $[HCHO] = 0.600\,M$, $[H_2] = [CO] = 0.400\,M$ I. $[HCHO] = 0.750\,M$, $[H_2] = 1.300\,M$, $[CO] = 0.250\,M$ J. $[HCHO] = 0.167\,M$, $[H_2] = 0.133\,M$, $[CO] = 0.333\,M$ K. $[NO] = 1.00\,M$, $[Br_2] = 2.50\,M$, $NOBr] = 4.00\,M$ L. $[NO] = 0.188\,M$, $[Br_2] = 2.50\,M$, $[NOBr] = 0.750\,M$ M. $[NO] = 0.0781\,M$, $[Br_2] = 1.41\,M$, $[NOBr] = 0.234\,M$ N. $[H_2] = 2.152\,M$, $[N_2] = 0.0185\,M$, $[NH_3] = 0.698\,M$ O. $[H_2] = 0.0697\,M$, $[N_2] = 0.0697\,M$, $[N_2] = 0.0640\,M$, $[NH_3] = 1.742\,M$
2. (1) A. $[NO]^2[Br_2]/[NOBr]^2$ B. $[H_2O]^2[Cl_2]/[HCl]_4[O_2]$ C. $[NO]^2/[N_2][O_2]$ D. $[CH_2Cl_2]^2/[CH_4][CCl_4]$ E. $[PCl_3][Cl_2]/[PCl_5]$ F. $[H_2][CO]/[HCHO]$ G. $[NH_3]^2/[N_2][H_2]^3$ H. $[H_2O]^2[SO_2]^2/[H_2S]^2[O_2]^3$ I. $[NF_3]^2[HF]^6/[NH_3]^2[F_2]^6$
(2) A. 0.0263 *M* B. 1.42 *M* C. 0.348 *M* D. 6.59 *M* E. 0.769 *M* F. 0.157 *M* G. 0.00155 *M* H. 0.0386 *M* I. 0.0560 *M* J. 0.199 *M* K. 0.775 *M* L. 0.0396 *M*
3. A. $[HCHO]/[H_2][CO] = 3.75$ B. $[PCl_5]/[PCl_3][Cl_2] = 1.784$ C. $[N_2][H_2]^3/[NH_3]^2 = 7.14 \times 10^{-6}$ D. $[Br_2][Cl_2]/[BrCl]^2 = 0.159$ E. $[CH_4][CCl_4]/[CH_2Cl_2]^2 = 10.48$ F. $\sqrt{[CH_4][CCl_4]}/[CH_2Cl_2] = 3.23$ G. $[NOBr]/[NO]\sqrt{[Br_2]} = 2.529$ H. $[NH_3]/[N_2]^{1/2}[H_2]^{3/2} = 374$ I. $[BrCl]\sqrt{[Br_2][Cl_2]} = 2.51$

J. $\sqrt{[N_2][O_2]}/[NO] = 3.96 \times 10^7$
K. $[HCl]^2\sqrt{[O_2]}/[H_2O]\sqrt{[Cl_2]} = 0.0259$
L. $[H_2O][SO_2]/[H_2S][O_2]^{3/2} = 4.17 \times 10^{22}$
4. A. $P_{PCl_5}/P_{PCl_3}P_{Cl_2}$, $K_p = 0.0362$ B. $P^2_{BrCl}/P_{Br_2}P_{Cl_2}$, $K_c = 6.30$ C. $P^2_{H_2O}P^2_{SO_2}/P^3_{H_2S}P^2_{SO_2}$, $K_p = 2.12 \times 10^{43}$
D. $P^2_{NH_3}/P^3_{H_2}P_{N_2}$, $K_p = 92.9$ E. $P^2_{NO_2}/P_{N_2O_4}$, $K_c = 4.62 \times 10^{-3}$ F. $P^2_{NO}P_{Br_2}/P^2_{NOBr}$, $K_p = 4.489$ G. $P_{CH_3OH}/P^2_{H_2}P_{CO}$, $K_c = 1.23 \times 10^7$
H. $P^2{}_{CH_2Cl_2}/P_{CH_4}P_{CCl_4}$, $K_p = 0.0956$
I. $P^2{}_{NO}P_{Cl_2}/P^2_{NOCl}$, $K_c = 2.69 \times 10^{-3}$
J. $P^2_{H_2O}P_{Cl_2}/P^4_{HCl}P_{O_2}$, $K_p = 0.0956$
K. $P^2_{H_2}P_{S_2}/P^2_{H_2S}$, $K_c = 4.64 \times 10^{-5}$
L. $P^2_{NO}/P_{N_2}P_{O_2}$, $K_p = 6.37 \times 10^{-16}$
4a. A. $1/[CO_2][NH_3]^2$ B. $[SO_2]/[CO]^2$
C. $[NH_3][HCl]$ D. $[H_2]/[NH_3]$ E. $[SO_2][Cl_2]$
F. $1/[H_2]^2[O_2]$ G. $[N_2O][H_2O]^2$
H. $[NaHS]/[H_2S][NaOH]$ I. $[H_3PO_3][HCl]^3/[PCl_3]$
J. $[AgNO_3]_3[NO]/[HNO_3]^4$
K. $[H_2SO_4][NO_2]^6/[HNO_3]^6$ L. $[CO_2]$ M. $[NH_3]^2$
5. (1) A. 0.0954 B. 0.562 C. 0.267 D. 6.4
E. 1.40×10^5
(2) A. 1.16×10^{-3} B. 2.05×10^4 C. 1.95×10^{-5}
D. 1.21×10^{-4}
6. A. $Q_c = 1.49 \times 10^3 = K_c$, equilibrium
B. $Q_c = 162 < K_c$, right C. $Q_c = 0.423 > K_c$, left
D. $Q_c = 1.189 > K_c$, left E. $Q_c = 0.0956 = K_c$, equilibrium
F. $Q_c = 0.0624 < K_c$, right G. $Q_c = 0.0844 < K_c$, right
H. $Q_c = 0.346 > K_c$, left I. $Q_c = 7.87 \times 10^4 > K_c$, right
J. $Q_c = 7.87 < K_c$, right K. $Q_c = 17.3 > K_c$, left
L. $Q_c = 1.67 < K_c$, right M. $Q_p = 0.0889 < K_p$, right
N. $Q_p = 0.398 > K_p$, left O. $Q_p = 1.98 < K_p$, right
P. $Q_p = 8.01 > K_p$, left Q. $Q_p = 0.168 < K_p$, right
R. $Q_p = 0.957 > K_p$, left S. $Q_p = 0.306 > K_p$, left
T. $Q_p = 3.18 \times 10^{-3} < K_p$, right
U. $Q_p = 0.744 < K_p$, right V. $Q_p = 2.89 > K_p$, left
6a. A. $K_p = 0.112$ B. $K_p = 0.334$ C. $K_p = 91.0$
D. $K_p = 0.556$ E. $K_p = 2.69$ F. $K_p = 8.4 \times 10^{-3}$
G. $K_p = 0.675$
7. C. $[CH_3ONO] = 0.1203\,M$, $[HCl] = 0.2623\,M$, $[CH_3OH] = 0.0987\,M$, $[NOCl] = 0.0778\,M$
D. $[CH_3ONO] = 0.418\,M$, $[HCl] = 0.174\,M$, $[CH_3OH] = 0.140\,M$, $[NOCl] = 0.126\,M$ E. is at equilibrium F. $[CH_4] = 0.2057\,M$, $[CCl_4] = 0.0143\,M$, $[CH_2Cl_2] = 0.0168\,M$ K. $[PCl_3] = [Cl_2] = 0.201\,M$, $[PCl_5] = 0.0720\,M$ L. $[PCl_5] = 0.1079\,M$, $[PCl_3] = 0.2001\,M$, $[Cl_2] = 0.3021\,M$
M. $P_{N_2O_4} = 0.245$ atm, $P_{NO_2} = 0.167$ atm
N. $P_{N_2O_4} = 0.185$ atm, $P_{NO_2} = 0.144$ atm
O. $P_{Br_2} = P_{Cl_2} = 0.163$ atm, $P_{BrCl} = 0.410$ atm
P. $P_{Br_2} = 0.157$ atm, $P_{Cl_2} = 0.171$ atm, $P_{BrCl} = 0.410$ atm
Q. $P_{PCl_5} = 0.089$ atm, $P_{PCl_3} = 0.319$ atm, $P_{Cl_2} = 0.190$ atm
R. $P_{PCl_5} = 0.058$ atm, $P_{PCl_3} = 0.290$ atm, $P_{Cl_2} = 0.135$ atm
S. $P_{H_2} = P_{CO_2} = 0.293$ atm, $P_{H_2O} = P_{CO} = 0.027$ atm
T. $P_{H_2} = 0.795$ atm, $P_{CO_2} = 0.495$ atm, $P_{H_2O} = 0.081$ atm, $P_{CO} = 0.040$ atm U. $P_{SO_2} = 2.44$ atm, $P_{Cl_2} = 1.10$ atm
V. $P_{SO_2} = P_{Cl_2} = 1.64$ atm W. $P_{HCHO} = 0.121$ atm, $P_{H_2} = P_{CO} = 0.179$ atm X. $P_{HCHO} = 0.180$ atm, $P_{H_2} = P_{CO} = 0.220$ atm
8. A. 216.9 kJ/mol B. 0.147, 355 K C. 3.57×10^4, 385 K D. −17.32 kJ/mol E. 92.2 kJ/mol F. 22.2, 297 K G. 7.81×10^{-72}, 509 K
9. A. R B. L C. R D. L E. U F. U G. R
H. R I. R J. L K. R L. L M. R N. R
O. U P. L

Quizzes

A: 1. $[NaClO_3]^2[SO_2]/[Na_2SO_3][HClO_3]^2$ 2. (e) (1.40)
3. (b) 4. (e) 5. (a) 6. (b) 7. (d)
B: 1. $P_{SO_2}P^2_{Cl_2}/P_{O_2}$ 2. (c) 3. (c) 4. (b) 5. (a)
6. (e) 7. (a)
C: 1. $[Cu(NO_3)_2]^3[NO]_2/[HNO_3]^8$ 2. (d) 3. (b)
4. (c) 5. (e) 6. (e) 7. (d)
D: 1. P_{CO_2}/P_{SO_2} 2. (c) 3. (b) 4. (a) 5. (d)
6. (c) 7. (e)

Sample Test

1. $PCl_5 \rightleftharpoons PCl_3 + Cl_2$

	2.00	1.00
x	$-x$	$-x$
x	$2.00 - x$	$1.00 - x$

$1.19 = (2.00 - x)(1.00 - x)/x$
$x = (4.19 \pm \sqrt{17.56 - 8.00})/2 = 0.549 \text{ atm} = P_{PCl_5}$
2. $\ln(1.456/14.2) = -\Delta H°/8.314 \text{ J mol}^{-1}\text{ K}^{-1} \times (1/273 - 1/298)$; $\Delta \bar{H}° = +61.6$ kJ/mol
3. a. left b. no effect c. right d. right
e. right f. left g. right h. right i. no effect
j. no effect

CHAPTER 15

Drill Problems

3. + for $\Delta S > 0$, − for $\Delta S < 0$, u for unclear.
A. − B. + C. − D. + E. + F. u
G. − H. − I. u J. − K. − L. −
M. u N. + O. u P. − Q. − R. +
S. − T. + U. − V. u W. u X. +
4a. & 4b. In order, numbers are $\Delta \bar{G}°$ (in kJ/mol), $\Delta \bar{H}°$ (in kJ/mol), and $\Delta \bar{S}°$ (in J mol^{-1} K^{-1}).
A. −91.98, −176.89, −284.6; S, (2) B. +50.2, +4.2, −153.9; N (4) C. +163.7, −65.47, −33.1; N, (2)
D. +5.40, +58.03, +176.7; N, (3) E. + 255.8, +177.9, +160.7; N, (3) F. −215.5, −224.1, −28.8; S, (2) G. −38.3, −92.5, −182; S, (2)
H. −140.0, −196.6, −189.6; S, (2) I. −4.90, −1.3, +11.5; S, (1) J. −1009.2, −1125.3, −389.4, S, (2) K. −33.28, −92.38, −198.3; S, (2) L. −24.6, −90.7, −221; S, (2) M. −2.4, +17.5, −27.2; S, (4)
N. +75.56, +75.36, +116, N, (3) O. +173.38, +180.74, +24.7; N, (3) P. −6.7, −133.2, −424.0; S, (2) Q. −25.8, −75.9, −167.8; S, (2) R. +14, +92, +265; N, (3) S. +8.2, −19.4, −92.3; N, (2)

T. −326.8, −284, +139; S, (1) U. −76.1, −114.4, −128.4; S, (2) V. +41.2, +28.5, +42.4; S, (3) W. +16.8, +10.5, −21.4; N, (4) X. −27.3, +5.4, +109.8; S, (3)

5. Value for $\Delta\bar{G}^\circ$ is given first, followed by K_{eq}.
A. −119.97, 2.2×10^{31} (200 K); −63.05, 1.7×10^{8} (400 K)
B. +34.98, 7.3×10^{-10} (200 K); 65.76, 2.6×10^{-9} (400 K)
C. −58.85, 2.3×10^{15} (200 K); −52.23, 6.6×10^{6} (400 K)
D. +22.69, 1.2×10^{-6} (200 K); −12.65, 44.9 (400 K)
E. +145.8, 8.5×10^{-39} (200 K), 113.62, 1.5×10^{-15} (400 K)
F. −218.3, 1.1×10^{57} (200 K); −212.5, 5.8×10^{27} (400 K)
G. −56.1, 4.5×10^{14} (200 K), −19.7, 374 (400 K)
H. −158.7, 2.8×10^{41} (200 K); −120.8, 5.9×10^{15} (400 K)
I. −3.6, 8.71 (200 K); −5.9, 5.9 (400 K)
J. −1047.42, 10^{274} (200 K); −969.54, 3.9×10^{126} (400 K)
K. −52.72, 5.9×10^{13} (200 K); −13.06, 50.8 (400 K)
L. −46.5, 1.4×10^{12} (200 K); −2.3, 2.00 (400 K)
M. +22.9, 1.0×10^{-6} (200 K); 28.4, 1.97×10^{-4} (400 K)
N. 52.16, 2.4×10^{-14} (200 K); 29.86, 1.7×10^{-4} (400 K)
O. 175.8, 1.2×10^{-46} (200 K); 170.86, 4.9×10^{-23} (400 K)
P. −48.4, 4.4×10^{12} (200 K); +36.4, 1.8×10^{-5} (400 K)
Q. −42.3, 1.1×10^{11} (200 K); −8.78, 14 (400 K)
R. +39, 6.5×10^{-11} (200 K); −14, 67 (400 K)
S. −0.94, 1.76 (200 K); 17.5, 5.15×10^{-3} (400 K)
T. −312, 2.7×10^{81} (200 K); −340, 2.2×10^{44} (400 K)
U. −88.7, 1.5×10^{23} (200 K); −63.0, 1.7×10^{8} (400 K)
V. +20.0, 5.9×10^{-6} (200 K); +11.5, 0.031 (400 K)
W. 14.8, 1.4×10^{-4} (200 K); 19.1, 3.2×10^{-3} (400 K)
X. −16.6, 2.1×10^{4} (200 K); −38.5, 1.1×10^{5} (400 K)

6. Transitions all are from the first to the second substance. Values given are $\Delta\bar{H}^\circ_{tr}$ (in kJ/mol), $\Delta\bar{S}^\circ_{tr}$ (in J mol^{-1} K^{-1}), and T_{tr} in order unless otherwise indicated.
A. −67.2, −152, 442 K B. −22, −96, +231 J mol^{-1} K^{-1} = $\bar{S}^\circ$ of AsF_3(l) C. +660.3, + 183.3, 3602 K D. +23.4, +80.9, 289 K E. −24.8, −93.3, 24.8 kJ/mol = $\Delta\bar{H}^\circ_f$ of Br_2(g) F. −12, −5, 2400 K G. −62.25, −143.9, 432.6 K H. 1.55, 0.5, 3100 K I. 0.50, 1.25, 71.95 J mol^{-1} K^{-1} = $\bar{S}^\circ$ for HgO (yellow)

8. (1) Expression for K_{eq} is followed by value of K_{eq} at 298 K.
A. $1/P_{NH_3}P_{HCl}$; 1.3×10^{16} B. $[BaCO_3]$; 1.6×10^{-9}
C. $[NaNO_3]/[AgNO_3][NaCl]$; 2.0×10^{-29}
D. $P^2_{NO_2}/P_{N_2O_4}$; 0.113 E. P_{CO_2}; 1.4×10^{-45}
F. P_{CO_2}/P_{SO_3}; 6.0×10^{37} G. $P_{PCl_5}/P_{PCl_3}P_{Cl_2}$; 5.2×10^{6} H. $P^2_{SO_3}/P^2_{SO_2}P_{O_2}$; 3.5×10^{24}
I. $P^2_{BrCl}/P_{Br_2}P_{Cl_2}$; 7.23 J. $P^2_{SO_2}/P^2_{H_2S}P^3_{O_2}$; 7×10^{176}
K. $P^2_{NH_3}/P^3_{H_2}P_{N_2}$; 6.8×10^{5} L. $P_{CH_3OH}/P_{CO}P^2_{H_2}$; 2.1×10^{4} M. $P^2_{CH_2Cl_2}/P_{CH_4}P_{CCl_4}$; 2.63
N. $P^2_{NO}P_{Cl_2}/P^2_{NOCl}$; 5.7×10^{-14} O. $P^2_{NO}/P_{N_2}P_{O_2}$; 4.1×10^{-31} P. $1/P_{CO_2}P^2_{NH_3}$; 15 Q. P_{SO_2}/P^2_{CO}; 3.3×10^{4} R. $P_{SO_2}P_{Cl_2}$; 3.5×10^{-3} S. $[CO_2]/P_{CO_2}$; 3.7×10^{-2} T. $P^3_{O_2}/P^2_{O_3}$; 1.9×10^{57}
U. $P^2_{H_2O}P^2_{Cl_2}/P^4_{HCl}P_{O_2}$; 2.2×10^{13}
V. $P_{H_2O}P_{CO}/P_{H_2}P_{CO_2}$; 6.0×10^{-8} W. $P_{H_2}P_{I_2}/P^2_{HI}$; 1.1×10^{-3} X. $P_{H_2}P_{CO}/P_{HCHO}$; 6.1×10^{4}

(2) Values of $\Delta\bar{G}^\circ$ (in kJ/mol): A. 0.00 B. 0.00 C. 17.1 D. 11.5 E. 28.7 F. −11.5 G. −17.1 H. −28.7

Quizzes

A: 1. (a) 2. (c) 3. (e) (−4.0) 4. (d) 5. (a) 6. (b) 7. (d) 8. (a)
B: 1. (e) (−80.66) 2. (b) 3. (c) 4. (e) 5. (d) 6. (c) 7. (a) 8. (c)
C: 1. (d) 2. (b) 3. (e) (−1796.9) 4. (a) 5. (a) 6. (a) 7. (b) 8. (b)
D: 1. (c) 2. (a) 3. (d) 4. (a) 5. (d) 7. (b) 8. (a)

Sample Test

1. a. $P^2_{NH_3}[Mg(OH)_2]^3$ b. $P_{SO_2Cl_2}/P_{SO_2}P_{Cl_2}$ c. $1/P_{CO}P^2_{H_2}$ d. $1/[H_2SO_4]$
2. a. $\Delta\bar{G}^\circ = -RT \ln K_{eq} = -(8.314 \text{ J mol}^{-1} \text{ K}^{-1})(298 \text{ K}) \ln (1.87 \times 10^{-7}) = 38.38$ kJ/mol. The reaction is non-spontaneous as $\Delta\bar{G}^\circ > 0$ and $K_{eq} < 1$.
b. $\Delta\bar{G}^\circ = \Delta\bar{H}^\circ - T\Delta S^\circ$; 38.38 kJ/mol = $\Delta\bar{H}^\circ -$ 298 K (0.18192 kJ mol^{-1} K^{-1}) *or* $\Delta\bar{H}^\circ = 92.60$ kJ/mol
c. As temperature decreases, the $-T\Delta S$ factor becomes less negative. Thus $\Delta\bar{G}^\circ$ becomes more positive, making K_{eq} smaller. Let's check.
$\Delta G^\circ = 92.60 \text{ kJ/mol} - 200(0.18192 \text{ kJ mol}^{-1} \text{ K}^{-1}) = 56.211 \text{ kJ/mol} = RT \ln K_{eq}$ *or* $K_{eq} = 2.08 \times 10^{-15}$
This is in accord with Le Chatelier's principle. Lowering the temperature of an endothermic reaction shifts the equilibrium left.
d. $\Delta\bar{G}^\circ = \Delta\bar{H}^\circ - T\Delta\bar{S}^\circ = 92.60 \text{ kJ/mol} - 320 \text{ K}(0.18192 \text{ kJ mol}^{-1} \text{ K}^{-1}) = 34.39$ kJ/mol. We assumed that $\Delta\bar{H}^\circ$ and $\Delta\bar{S}^\circ$ remain constant with temperature.
3. CaO(s) is a solid and thus more ordered than any gas. The remaining gases have more and more atoms. There are increasingly more ways in which the molecules can bend and stretch, and thus they are more disordered.

CHAPTER 16

Drill Problems

1. A. $AgCN(s) \rightarrow Ag^+(aq) + CN^-(aq)$; $K_{sp} = [Ag^+][CN^-]$
B. $SrF_2(s) \rightarrow Sr^{2+}(aq) + 2\ F^-(aq)$; $K_{sp} = [Sr^{2+}][F^-]^2$
C. $TlBr(s) \rightarrow Tl^+(aq) + Br^-(aq)$; $K_{sp} = [Tl^+][Br^-]$
D. $Zn_3(AsO_4)_2 \rightarrow 3\ Zn^{2+}(aq) + 2\ AsO_4{}^{3-}(aq)$; $K_{sp} = [Zn^{2+}]^3[AsO_4{}^{3-}]^2$
E. $Hg_2Br_2 \rightarrow Hg_2{}^{2+}(aq) + 2\ Br^-(aq)$; $K_{sp} = [Hg_2{}^+][Br^-]^2$
F. $Ag_3AsO_4 \rightarrow 3\ Ag^+(aq) + AsO_4{}^{3-}(aq)$; $K_{sp} = [Ag^+]^3[AsO_4{}^{3-}]$
G. $Li_2CO_3 \rightarrow 2\ Li^+(aq) + CO_3{}^{2-}(aq)$; $K_{sp} = [Li^+]^2[CO_3{}^{2-}]$
H. $PbC_2O_4 \rightarrow Pb^{2+}(aq) + C_2O_4{}^{2-}(aq)$; $K_{sp} = [Pb^{2+}][C_2O_4{}^{2-}]$
I. $La(IO_3)_3 \rightarrow La^{3+}(aq) + 3\ IO_3{}^-(aq)$; $K_{sp} = [La^{3+}][IO_3{}^-]^3$
J. $Ce_2(C_2O_4)_3 \rightarrow 2\ Ce^{3+}(aq) + 3\ C_2O_4{}^{2-}(aq)$; $K_{sp} = [Ce^{3+}]^2[C_2O_4{}^{2-}]^3$
K. $CdCO_3 \rightarrow Cd^{2+}(aq) + CO_3{}^{2-}(aq)$; $K_{sp} = [Cd^{2+}][CO_3{}^{2-}]$
L. $AlPO_4 \rightarrow Al^{3+}(aq) + PO_4{}^{3-}(aq)$; $K_{sp} = [Al^{3+}][PO_4{}^{3-}]$

M. $Al_2S_3 \rightarrow 2\ Al^{3+}(aq) + 3\ S^{2-}(aq); K_{sp} = [Al^{3+}]^2 [S^{2-}]^3$
N. $Ca(IO_3)_2 \rightarrow Ca^{2+}(aq) + 2\ IO_3^-(aq); K_{sp} = [Ca^{2+}][IO_3^-]^2$
O. $CoS \rightarrow Co^{2+}(aq) + S^{2-}(aq); K_{sp} = [Co^{2+}][S^{2-}]$
P. $FeAsO_4 \rightarrow Fe^{3+}(aq) + AsO_4^{3-}(aq); K_{sp} = [Fe^{3+}][AsO_4^{3-}]$
2. A. 1.16×10^{-12}, 1.08×10^{-6} *M*, 1.79×10^{-5} g
B. 2.2×10^{-5}, 4.7×10^{-3} *M*, 9.5×10^{-2} g C. 3.1×10^{-2}, 0.18 *M*, 0.18 *M* D. 4.5×10^{-5} *M*, 4.5×10^{-5} *M*, 2.3×10^{-3} g
E. 6.3×10^{-19}, 7.9×10^{-10} *M*, 9.7×10^{-7} g F. 3.2×10^{-6}, 9.3×10^{-3} *M*, 0.37 g G. 1.6×10^{-16}, 3.4×10^{-6} *M*, 6.8×10^{-6} *M* H. 5.6×10^{-3} *M*, 1.1×10^{-2} *M*, 0.22 g
I. 2.5×10^{-48}, 8.5×10^{-17} *M*, 1.4×10^{-15} g
J. 1.0×10^{-12}, 1.3×10^{-4} *M*, 3.3×10^{-3} g
K. 3.4×10^{-8}, 4.1×10^{-3} *M*, 2.0×10^{-3} *M*
L. 1.3×10^{-5} *M*, 3.9×10^{-5} *M*, 7.8×10^{-4} g
M. 1.3×10^{-16}, 4.8×10^{-5} *M*, 2.0×10^{-3} g
N. 6.5×10^{-12}, 6.9×10^{-4} *M*, 4.6×10^{-2} g
O. 1.9×10^{-19}, 2.1×10^{-4} *M*, 1.4×10^{-6} *M*
P. 3.6×10^{-2} *M*, 5.4×10^{-2} *M*, 0.27 g
3. A. 2.6×10^{-6} *M* B. 1.2×10^{-11} *M*
C. 3.2×10^{-24} *M* D. 2.1×10^{-4} *M* E. 1.4×10^{-6} *M*
F. 6.2×10^{-10} *M* G. 4.5×10^{-13} *M*
H. 6.1×10^{-10} *M* I. 7.4×10^{-4} *M* J. 1.7×10^{-9} *M*
5. (1) A. 4.3×10^{-23} *M* B. 4.2×10^{-7} *M*
C. 7.9×10^{-8} *M* D. 6.8×10^{-4} *M* E. 1.8×10^{-6} *M*
F. 3.3×10^{-2} *M* G. 0.56 *M* H. 1.1×10^{-3} *M*
I. 4.2×10^{-7} *M* J. 1.3×10^{-3} *M*
(2) Values of Q are given, followed by *yes* if precipitation should occur.
A. 5.12×10^{-17}, yes B. 3.3×10^{-8}, yes
C. 1.10×10^{-12}, yes D. 1.0×10^{-6}, yes
E. 2.5×10^{-11}, no F. 1.5×10^{-8}, yes
G. 1.3×10^{-8}, yes H. 2.9×10^{-10}, no
I. 1.7×10^{-2}, yes J. 1.7×10^{-25}, no
6. The concentrations of the two ions are followed by the formula(s) of the ion(s) for which precipitation is complete (or by neither).
(1) A. $[Co^{2+}] = 3.2 \times 10^{-5}$ *M*, $[S^{2-}] = 1.3 \times 10^{-16}$ *M*, S^{2-} B. $[Pb^{2+}] = 4.6 \times 10^{-3}$ *M*, $[SO_4^{2-}] = 3.5 \times 10^{-6}$ *M*, neither C. $[Ag^+] = 1.2 \times 10^{-5}$ *M*, $[I^-] = 7.1 \times 10^{-12}$ *M*, I^- D. $[Ba^{2+}] = 6.4 \times 10^{-2}$ *M*, $[SO_4^{2-}] = 1.7 \times 10^{-9}$ *M*, SO_4^{2-} F. $[Pb^{2+}] = 1.7 \times 10^{-10}$ *M*, $[CrO_4^{2-}] = 1.7 \times 10^{-3}$ *M*, Pb^{2+}
G. $[Ag^+] = 1.7 \times 10^{-2}$ *M*, $[CrO_4^{2-}] = 8.4 \times 10^{-9}$ *M*, CrO_4^{2-} I. $[Li^+] = 1.6$ *M*, $[PO_4^{3-}] = 3.2 \times 10^{-9}$ *M*, PO_4^{3-}
(2) A. $[Zn^{2+}] = 1.1 \times 10^{-5}$ *M*, $[S^{2-}] = 9.1 \times 10^{-17}$ *M*, S^{2-} B. $[Hg_2^{2+}] = 3.4 \times 10^{-4}$ *M*, $[Cl^-] = 6.2 \times 10^{-8}$ *M*, neither C. $[Al^{3+}] = 6.6 \times 10^{-23}$ *M*, $[OH^-] = 2.7 \times 10^{-4}$ *M*, Al^{3+} D. $[Pb^{2+}] = 1.0$ *M*, $[Cl^-] = 4.0 \times 10^{-3}$ *M*, neither E. $[Ag^+] = 1.5 \times 10^{-10}$ *M*, $[Br^-] = 3.3 \times 10^{-3}$ *M*, Ag^+ F. $[Bi^{2+}] = 2.7 \times 10^{-6}$ *M*, $[S^{2-}] = 2.4 \times 10^{-29}$ *M*, S^{2-}
7. The formula of the precipitating ion is given first, followed by its concentrations needed to just cause precipitation and for complete precipitation of each ion; "yes" means that the two ions can be separated by fractional precipitation.
A. Ag^+: Cl^- 1.3×10^{-4} *M*, 0.13 *M*; Br^- 5.6×10^{-10} *M*, 5.6×10^{-7} *M*; yes B. SO_4^{2-}: Ba^{2+} 6.9×10^{-6} *M*, 6.9×10^{-3} *M*; Pb^{2+} 1.2×10^{-3} *M*, 1.2 *M*; no (barely)
C. S^{2-}: Pb^{2+} 2.1×10^{-24} *M*, 2.1×10^{-21} *M*; Hg_2^{2+} 4.1×10^{-49} *M*, 4.1×10^{-46} *M*; yes (Cl^- also can be used as a precipitating ion.) D. SO_4^{2-}: Sr^{2+} 20 *M*, 2.0×10^4 *M*; Pb^{2+} 4.7×10^{-4} *M*, 0.47 *M*; yes
E. Mg^{2+}: OH^- 2.3×10^{-5} *M*, 23 *M*; F^- 2.2×10^{-6} *M*, 2.2 *M*; no F. CrO_4^{2-}: Ag^+ 1.1×10^{-7} *M*, 0.11 *M*; Pb^{2+} 1.2×10^{-11} *M*, 1.2×10^{-8} *M*; yes G. S^{2-}: Zn^{2+} 1.3×10^{-8} *M*, 1.3×10^{-5} *M*; Sn^{2+} 3.4×10^{-14} *M*, 3.4×10^{-11} *M*; yes H. PO_4^{3-}: Li^+ 1.6×10^{-8} *M*, 11 *M*; Mg^{2+} 1.6×10^{-8} *M*, 5.0×10^{-4} *M*; no
9. $SO_4^{2-}(aq) + Ba^{2+}(aq) \rightarrow BaSO_4(s)$ B. no rxn
C. no rxn D. $Hg^{2+}(aq) + S^{2-}(aq) \rightarrow HgS(s)$
E. $2\ Br^-(aq) + Pb^{2+}(aq) \rightarrow PbBr_2(s)$
F. $3\ CO_3^{2-}(aq) + 2\ Fe^{3+}(aq) \rightarrow Fe_2CO_3(s)$
G. $3\ OH^-(aq) + Fe^{3+}(aq) \rightarrow Fe(OH)_3(s)$
H. $Ba^{2+}(aq) + CO_3^{2-}(aq) \rightarrow BaCO_3(s)$
I. $Zn^{2+}(aq) + S^{2-}(aq) \rightarrow ZnS(s)$ J. no rxn K. no rxn
L. $Sr^{2+}(aq) + SO_4^{2-}(aq) \rightarrow SrSO_4(s)$
M. $Pb^{2+}(aq) + 2\ Cl^-(aq) \rightarrow PbCl_2(s)$

Quizzes

A: 1. (a) 2. (d) 3. (e) 4. (d) 5. (d) 6. (c) 7. (e)
B: 1. (a) 2. (e) 3. (a) 4. (d) 5. (d) 6. (b) 7. (c)
C: 1. (d) 2. (b) 3. (b) 4. (d) 5. (a) 6. (c) 7. (c)
D: 1. (c) 2. (c) 3. (a) 4. (e) 5. (c) 6. (c) 7. (b)

Sample Test

1. The concentration of PO_4^{3-} removed is
$\Delta[PO_4^{3-}] = 8.06 \times 10^{-4}\ M - 1.00 \times 10^{-12}\ M = 8.06 \times 10^{-4}\ M$
The volume of the pond is $100\ m \times 200\ m \times 8.00\ m \times 1000\ L/m^3 = 1.60 \times 10^8\ L$
The $[Ca^{2+}]$ which must be present in solution when precipitation is complete is given by $[Ca^{2+}]^3[PO_4^{3-}]^2 = [Ca^{2+}]^3(1.00 \times 10^{-12})^2 = 1.30 \times 10^{-32}$ *or* $[Ca^{2+}] = 2.35 \times 10^{-6}\ M$
The $Ca(NO_3)_2$ is needed both (1) to form precipitate and (2) to maintain the needed $[Ca^{2+}]$.
(1) $1.60 \times 10^8\ L \times 1.5 \times 8.06 \times 10^{-4}\ M = 1.93 \times 10^5$ mol $Ca(NO_3)_2$
(2) $1.60 \times 10^8\ L \times 2.35 \times 10^{-3}\ M = 3.76 \times 10^5$ mol $Ca(NO_3)_2$
total $= 5.69 \times 10^5$ mol

5.69×10^5 mol $Ca(NO_3)_2 \times 164.1$ g/mol $\times$ lb/453.5 g $\times$ ton/2000 lb = 103 tons
2. $[Ag^+]^2(2.0 \times 10^{-3}\ M) = 2.4 \times 10^{-12}$ *or* $[Ag^+] = 3.5 \times 10^{-5}\ M$ for CrO_4^{2-} pptn
$[Ag^+](1.0 \times 10^{-5}\ M) = 1.6 \times 10^{-10}$ *or* $[Ag^+] = 1.6 \times 10^{-5}\ M$ for Cl^- pptn
AgCl precipitates first. When Ag_2CrO_4 begins to precipitate $(3.5 \times 10^{-5}\ M)[Cl^-] = 1.6 \times 10^{-10}$ *or* $[Cl^-] = 4.6 \times 10^{-6}\ M$, 46% of its initial value.

CHAPTER 17

Drill Problems

2. (a) All species appear in the order acid, base, acid, base in the given equations.
(2) The products are followed by one of the conjugate pairs in parenthese, conjugate base written first.
A. $Cl^- + NH_4^+$ (NH_3, NH_4^+) B. $H_2O + H_3PO_4$ (H_2O, H_3O^+) C. $C_2H_3O_2^- + H_2S$ (HS^-, H_2S)
D. $N_3^- + CH_3NH_3^+$ (N_3^-, HN_3) E. $CH_3NH_2 + H_2O$ (OH^-, H_2O) F. $NO_2^- + HN_3$ (NO_2^-, HNO_2)
3. The base is drawn first in each case.
A. H—O—H, O=S—O| ↔ |O—S=O
B. [|F|]⁻, |F—Be—F|
C. H—N(—H)—H, H⁺ from H—Cl|
D. [H—O|]⁻, O=C=O E. H—N(—H)—H, Ag⁺
F. [|O|]²⁻, H⁺ from H—O—H G. [|F|]⁻, |F—B(—F)—F|
H. H—O—H, H⁺ from H—Cl|
I. H—O—H, |F—B(—|F|)—F|
J. [S]²⁻, O=S(—|O|)—O| ↔ |O—S(—|O|)=O ↔ |O—S(=|O|)—O|
K. [O=C(—|O|)—O|]²⁻ ↔ [|O—C(—|O|)=O]²⁻ ↔ [|O—C(=|O|)—O|]²⁻, H⁺
L. H—O—H, O=C=O
M. H—O—C(—H)(—H)—H, |F—B(—|F|)—F|

6. & 7. A. 1.6 g/l, 2.5×10^{-13} M, 0.040 M, 12.60, 1.40
B. 6.25×10^{-4} M, 0.0613 g/L, 8.00×10^{-12} M, 2.903, 11.097 C. 1.67×10^{-2} M, 1.23 g/L, 3.00×10^{-13} M, 12.522, 1.478 D. 0.0375 M, 3.84 g/L, 2.67×10^{-13} M, 12.574, 1.426 E. 0.0382 M, 0.0382 M, 2.62×10^{-13} M, 1.418, 12.582 F. 2.995×10^{-3} M, 1.67×10^{-12} M, 5.99×10^{-3} M, 11.777, 2.223
G. 0.788 g/L, 0.0125 M, 8.00×10^{-13} M, 1.903, 12.097
H. 0.045 M, 2.5 g/L, 2.2×10^{-13} M, 12.65, 1.35
I. 6.7×10^{-6} M, 8.2×10^{-4} g/L, 7.4×10^{-10} M, 1.3×10^{-5} M, 4.87 J. 2.2×10^{-5} M, 3.4×10^{-3} g/L, 4.5×10^{-10} M, 2.2×10^{-5} M, 9.35 K. 7.1×10^{-4} M, 0.057 g/L, 7.1×10^{-4} M, 1.4×10^{-11} M, 10.85
L. 0.056 M, 7.2 g/L, 0.056 M, 1.8×10^{-13} M, 1.25

8. A. $HOBr + H_2O \rightleftharpoons H_3O^+ + OBr^-$; $K_a = [H_3O^+][OBr^-]/[HOBr]$ B. $(CH_3)_2NH + H_2O \rightleftharpoons (CH_3)_2NH_2^+ + OH^-$; $K_b = [(CH_3)_2NH_2^+][OH^-]/[(CH_3)_2NH]$ C. $HC_6H_7O_2 + H_2O \rightleftharpoons C_6H_7O_2^- + H_3O^+$; $K_a = [C_6H_7O_2^-][H_3O^+]/[HC_6H_7O_2]$ D. $N_2H_4 + H_2O \rightleftharpoons N_2H_5^+ + OH^-$; $K_b = [N_2H_5^+][OH^-]/[N_2H_4]$
E. $HC_3H_5O_3 + H_2O \rightleftharpoons C_3H_5O_3^- + H_3O^+$; $K_a = [H_3O^+][C_3H_5O_3^-]/[HC_3H_5O_3]$ F. $(CH_3)_3N + H_2O \rightleftharpoons (CH_3)_3NH^+ + OH^-$; $K_b = [(CH_3)_3NH^+][OH^-]/[(CH_3)_3N]$ G. $HC_3H_5O_2 + H_2O \rightarrow C_3H_5O_2^- + H_3O^+$; $K_a = [H_3O^+][C_3H_5O_2^-]/[HC_3H_5O_2]$ H. $HC_2HCl_2O_2 + H_2O \rightleftharpoons C_2HCl_2O_2^- + H_3O^+$; $K_a = [H_3O^+][C_2HCl_2O_2^-]/[HC_2HCl_2O_2]$ I. $H_3BO_3 + H_2O \rightleftharpoons H_2BO_3^- + H_3O^+$; $K_a = [H_3O^+][H_2BO_3^-]/[H_3BO_3]$ J. $HC_2Cl_3O_2 + H_2O \rightleftharpoons C_2Cl_3O_2^- + H_3O^+$; $K_a = [H_3O^+][C_2Cl_3O_2^-]/[HC_2Cl_3O_2]$

9. (1) A. 2.10×10^{-9} B. 7.10×10^{-4} C. 8.02×10^{-5} D. 9.92×10^{-7} E. 8.38×10^{-4} F. 7.41×10^{-5} G. 1.40×10^{-5} H. 3.32×10^{-2} I. 5.81×10^{-10} J. 0.210
(2) A. 2.68 B. 2.06 C. 1.92 D. 1.84 E. 1.92 F. 0.98 G. 11.66 H. 12.56 I. 12.67 J. 2.03 K. 9.83 L. 8.90

10. A. pH = 4.36, $[H_2CO_3] = 4.6 \times 10^{-3}$ M, $[HCO_3^-] = 4.4 \times 10^{-5}$ M, $[CO_3^{2-}] = 5.6 \times 10^{-11}$ M B. pH = 4.48, $[H_2S] = 1.00 \times 10^{-2}$ M, $[HS^-] = 3.3 \times 10^{-5}$ M, $[S^2] = 1.0 \times 10^{-14}$ M C. pH = 0.64, $[H_2C_2O_4] = 0.97$ M, $[HC_2O_4^-] = 0.23$ M, $[C_2O_4^{2-}] = 5.4 \times 10^{-5}$ M
D. pH = 1.20, $[H_3PO_4] = 0.686$ M, $[H_2PO_4^-] = 0.064$ M, $[HPO_4^{2-}] = 6.2 \times 10^{-8}$ M, $[PO_4^{3-}] = 4.7 \times 10^{-19}$ M
E. pH = 0.72, $[H_3PO_3] = 0.711$ M, $[H_2PO_3^-] = 0.189$ M, $[HPO_3^-] = 2.5 \times 10^{-7}$ M pH = 0.97, $[H_2SO_3] = 0.89$ M, $[HSO_3^-] = 0.11$ M, $[SO_3^{2-}] = 6.3 \times 10^{-8}$ M

11. Only the products of the dissolving reactions are written.
A. $Na^+(aq) + Cl^-(aq)$; neutral; no hydrolysis
B. $NH_4^+(aq) + Cl^-(aq)$; acidic; $NH_4^+ + H_2O \rightleftharpoons NH_3(aq) + H_3O^+$ C. $N_2H_5^+(aq) + Br^-(aq)$; acidic; $N_2H_5^+ + H_2O \rightleftharpoons N_2H_4(aq) + H_3O^+$ D. $K^+(aq) + NO_3^-(aq)$; neutral; no hydrolysis E. $Cs^+(aq) + C_2H_3O_2^-(aq)$; basic; $C_2H_3O_2^- + H_2O \rightleftharpoons HC_2H_3O_2(aq) + OH^-$ F. $2\ Na^+(aq) + CO_3^{2-}(aq)$; basic; $CO_3^{2-} + H_2O \rightleftharpoons HCO_3^- + OH^-$
G. $C_6H_5NH_3^+(aq) + I^-(aq)$; basic; $C_6H_5NH_3^+ + H_2O \rightleftharpoons C_6H_5NH_2(aq) + H_3O^+$
H. $Ca^{2+}(aq) + 2\ ClO^-(aq)$; basic; $ClO^- + H_2O \rightleftharpoons HClO(aq) + OH^-$ I. $Rb^+(aq) + ClO_2^-(aq)$; basic; $ClO_2^- + H_2O \rightleftharpoons HClO_2(aq) + OH^-$ J. $2\ HONH_3^+(aq) + SO_4^{2-}(aq)$; acidic; $HONH_3^+ + H_2O \rightleftharpoons HONH_2(aq) + H_3O^+$
K. $Sr^{2+}(aq) + 2\ F^-(aq)$; basic; $F^- + H_2O \rightleftharpoons HF(aq) + OH^-$
L. $C_2H_5NH_3^+(aq) + NO_3^-(aq)$; acidic; $C_2H_5NH_3^+ + H_2O \rightleftharpoons C_2H_5NH_2(aq) + H_3O^+$ M. $NH_4^+(aq) + CN^-(aq)$; basic; $NH_4^+ + H_2O \rightleftharpoons NH_3(aq) + H_3O^+$; $CN^- + H_2O \rightleftharpoons HCN(aq) + OH^-$ N. $CH_3NH_3^+(aq) + ClO_2^-(aq)$; acidic; $CH_3NH_3^+ + H_2O \rightleftharpoons CH_3NH_2(aq) + H_3O^+$; $ClO_2^- + H_2O \rightleftharpoons HClO_2(aq) + OH^-$ O. $HONH_3^+(aq) + F^-(aq)$; acidic; $HONH_3^+ + H_2O \rightleftharpoons HONH_2(aq) + H_3O^+$; $F^-(aq) + H_2O \rightleftharpoons HF(aq) + OH^-$

12. (1) A. 7.00 B. 4.62 C. 4.00 D. 7.00 E. 9.38 F. 10.19 G. 2.32 H. 10.92 I. 7.96 J. 2.83 K. 8.74 L. 5.32
(2) A. 9.03 B. 8.75 C. 8.87 D. 8.45 E. 8.06 F. 8.00 G. 4.76 H. 5.48 I. 5.50 J. 4.00 K. 3.348 L. 5.051

13. Acids: $HCl > H_3O^+ > HSO_4^- > H_2S > H_3PO_4 > HNO_2 > HN_3 > HC_2H_3O_2 > H_2S > NH_4^+ > HCN > HCO_3^- > CH_3NH_3^+ > H_2O \sim HS^-$
$S^{2-} \sim OH^- > CH_3NH_2 > CO_3^{2-} > CN^- > NH_3 > HS^- > C_2H_3O_2^- > N_3^- > NO_2^- > H_2PO_4^- > HS^- > SO_4^{2-} > H_2O > Cl^-$
The products of each reaction follow, acid first.
A. $HN_3 + OH^-$, left B. $H_2O + NO_2^-$, left C. $HCN + H_2O$, right D. $HCN + NH_2^-$, left E. $H_3PO_4 + CN^-$, left F. $NH_3 + H_2PO_4^-$, right G. $H_2O + H_2PO_4^-$, right H. $NH_3 + H_2O$, right I. $HC_2H_3O_2 + CO_3^{2-}$, left J. $H_2S + SO_4^{2-}$, right *or* $H_2SO_4 + S^{2-}$, left K. $H_2O + HS^-$, right L. $HC_2H_3O_2 + OH^-$, left M. $HSO_4^- + CO_3^{2-}$, left N. $H_2O + SO_4^{2-}$, right

14. A. H_2CO_3 more electronegative central atom B. H_2SO_4 higher oxidation state of sulfur C. H_3PO_4 more electronegative central atom D. $HClO_4$ higher oxidation state of chlorine E. HClO more electronegativ central atom F. HNO_3 higher oxidation state of nitroge
G. H_2SO_4 more electronegative central atom
H. FC_6H_4OH greater inductive effect by F than Cl
I. CF_3OH greater inductive effect by F than H
J. $HBrO_3$ more double-bonded oxygens on central atom
K. $HClO_4$ more double-bonded oxygens on central atom
L. H_2CO_3 more electronegative central atom

Quizzes

A: 1. (c) 2. (d) 3. (b) 4. (e) 5. (d) 6. (c) 7. (d) 8. (c) 9. (a)
B: 1. (b) 2. (a) 3. (a) 4. (c) 5. (d) 6. (d) 7. (c) 8. (b) 9. (b)
C: 1. (d) 2. (e) 3. (e) 4. (a) 5. (c) 6. (a) 7. (c) 8. (e) 9. (e)
D: 1. (b) 2. (a) 3. (c) 4. (b) 5. (a) 6. (d) 7. (d) 8. (d) 9. (e)

Sample Test

1. $[HA] = \frac{3.050 \text{ g}}{0.250 \text{ L}} \times \frac{\text{mol}}{122.0 \text{ g}} = 0.100\,M$ *or* $[H_3O^+] = 2.5 \times 10^{-3}\,M$ and pH = 2.60
2. a. Brønsted-Lowry; acids: HF, $N_2H_5^+$; bases: N_2H_4, F^- b. Brønsted-Lowry; acids: H_2O, OH^-; bases: O^{2-}, OH^- c. Lewis; acid: SOI_2; base: $BaSO_3$ d. Lewis; acid: $HgCl_3^-$; base: Cl^-
3. a. $H_2SO_3 > HF > N_2H_5^+ > CH_3NH_3^+ > H_2O$
b. $OH^- > CH_3NH_2 > N_2H_2 > F^- > HSO_3^-$
c. (i) to the right; (ii) to the left
4. $[ClO_2^-] = 2 \times 3.00$ mol/2.50 L $= 2.40\,M$; $K_h = 1.00 \times 10^{-14}/1.2 \times 10^{-2} = 8.3 \times 10^{-13}$; $[OH^-] = 1.4 \times 10^{-6}\,M$ *or* pH = 8.15

CHAPTER 18

Drill Problems

1. A. 2.68, 4.44 B. 2.68, 0.85 C. 2.06, 3.54 D. 1.92, 0.62 E. 1.84, 2.67 F. 1.98, 3.48 G. 0.98, 1.20 H. 11.66, 13.51 I. 12.06, 11.00 J. 11.89, 13.33 K. 11.77, 9.62 L. 11.47, 8.76 M. 11.84, 12.31 N. 12.22, 10.16

4. A. pH = 4.03 B. $[HC_7H_5O_2] = 0.660\,M$, $[C_7H_5O_2^-] = 0.640\,M$, pH = 4.19 C. $[HCHO_2] = 0.105\,M$, $[CHO_2^-] = 0.710\,M$, pH = 4.57 D. pH = 9.72 E. $[C_2H_5NH_2] = 1.29\,M$, $[C_2H_5NH_3^+] = 1.02\,M$, pH = 10.74 F. $[CH_3NH_2] = 0.111\,M$, $[CH_3NH_3^+] = 0.441\,M$, pH = 10.10 G. pH = 3.08 H. $[HC_2H_2ClO_2] = 0.79\,M$, $[C_2H_2ClO_2^-] = 2.14\,M$, pH = 3.30 I. $[HNO_2] = 1.302\,M$, $[NO_2^-] = 0.550\,M$, pH = 2.916 J. pH = 11.05 K. $[(CH_3)_3N] = 0.922\,M$, $[(CH_3)_3NH^+] = 0.314\,M$, pH = 10.34 L. $[NH_3] = 0.0731\,M$, $[NH_4^+] = 0.1549\,M$, pH = 8.915 M. $[CHO_2^-] = 0.208\,M$, pH = 2.77 N. $[HC_2H_3O_2] = 0.0337\,M$, $[C_2H_3O_2^-] = 0.0224\,M$, pH = 4.58 O. $[HC_7H_5O_2] = 0.512\,M$, $[C_7H_5O_2] = 0.231\,M$, pH = 3.86 P. $[(CH_3)_3N] = 0.218\,M$, $[(CH_3)_3NH^+] = 0.613\,M$, pH = 9.42 Q. pH = 10.84 R. $[C_2H_5NH_2] = 0.148\,M$, $[C_2H_5NH_3^+] = 1.001\,M$, pH = 9.80

5. The pH after acid addition precedes the pH after base addition.
A. 3.88, 4.15 B. 4.17, 4.21 C. 4.54, 4.61 D. 9.52, 9.96 E. 10.53, 10.95 F. 9.99, 10.20 G. 2.91, 3.23 H. 3.22, 3.39 I. 2.783, 3.034 J. 11.00, 11.10 K. 10.06, 10.74 I. 8.781, 9.035 M. 2.67, 2.86 N. 4.52, 4.64 O. 3.60, 4.01 P. 9.30, 9.53 Q. 10.23, 11.66 R. 9.27, 10.07

6. Answers are given in the order buffer range, acid capacity (mol H^+), base capacity (mol OH^-).
A. 3.76-5.76, 0.0852, 0.970 B. 3.20-5.20, 0.417, 0.433 C. 2.75-4.75, 0.636, 0.0309 D. 8.24-10.24, 0.0798, 0.0193 E. 9.63-11.63, 2.20, 1.65 F. 9.70-11.70, 0.376, 2.31 G. 2.17-4.17, 0.999, 1.30 H. 1.87-3.87, 21.4, 5.97, I. 2.29-4.29, 3.32, 9.87 J. 9.70-11.70, 0.519, 0.189 K. 8.87-10.87, 0.721, 0.179 L. 8.24-10.24, 3.98, 106 M. 2.75-4.75, 0.00683, 0.982 N. 3.76-5.76, 1.78, 2.95 O. 3.20-5.20, 0.248, 0.676 P. 8.87-10.87, 0.534, 2.02 Q. 9.70-11.70, 10.7, 7.29 R. 9.63-11.63, 0.0435, 0.897

9. & 9a. Given in the order pH at 0%, 10%, 50%, 90%, 100%, and 110% titration.
A. 0.61, 0.71, 1.12, 1.93, 7.00, 12.02 B. 13.40, 13.26, 12.74, 11.89, 7.00, 2.18 C. 14.40, 14.26, 13.74, 12.89, 7.00, 1.18 D. 0.92, 1.02, 1.43, 2.24, 7.00, 11.71 E. 0.60, 0.74, 1.25, 2.11, 7.00, 11.82 F. 13.80, 13.63, 13.08, 12.21, 7.00, 1.85 G. 12.30, 12.24, 11.85, 11.07, 7.00, 2.97 H. 1.95, 2.34, 3.29, 4.24, 8.17, 12.02 I. 12.05, 11.65, 10.70, 9.75, 5.92, 2.18 J. 12.52, 11.58, 10.63, 9.68, 5.39, 1.18 K. 2.06, 2.22, 3.17, 4.12, 7.96, 11.71 L. 2.17, 2.80, 3.75, 4.70, 8.30, 11.82 M. 12.25, 11.65, 10.70, 9.75, 5.75, 1.85 N. 8.80, 6.25, 5.30, 4.35, 3.63, 2.97

10. Suitable indicators: A. through G. phenol red for all seven titrations H. phenolphthalein I. methyl red J. methyl red K. phenolphthalein L. phenolphthalein M. methyl red N. indistinct equivalence point; no indicator possible.
11. Concentrations are given at pH = 2, pH = 7, and pH = 10 in that order.
A. 2.6×10^{-9} *M*, 1.3×10^{-12} *M*, 1.3×10^{-21} *M*
B. 1.2×10^{-3} *M*, 1.2×10^{-3} *M*, 1.2×10^{-3} *M*
C. 1.7×10^{-4} *M*, 1.7×10^{-4} *M*, 1.4×10^{-4} *M*
D. 3.4×10^{-8} *M*, 1.1×10^{-8} *M*, 1.6×10^{-14} *M*
E. 0.108 *M*, 0.108 *M*, 0.108 *M* F. 2×10^{-10} *M*, 4×10^{-17} *M*, 4×10^{-26} *M* G. 0.011 *M*, 0.011 *M*, 0.011 *M*
H. 1.4×10^{-4} *M*, 1.4×10^{-4} *M*, 1.0×10^{-4} *M*
13. A. 0.71 B. 2.81 C. 2.07 D. 1.32
E. 3.14 F. −9.92 G. −9.31 (The last two sulfides cannot be dissolved in the solutions described by adding acid.)
14a. A. HCl: 36.5 g/eq, 0.104 *N*; $Ca(OH)_2$: 37.1 g/eq, 0.104 *N* B. H_2SO_4: 98.1 g/eq, 0.704 *N*; KOH: 56.1 g/eq, 0.197 *N* C. HNO_3: 63.0 g/eq, 0.146 *N*; LiOH: 23.9 g/eq, 0.412 *N* D. HBr: 80.9 g/eq, 0.904 *N*; $Al(OH)_3$: 26.0 g/eq, 0.666 *N* E. H_2SO_4: 49.1 g/eq, 1.64 *N*; $Ca(OH)_2$: 37.1 g/eq, 1.05 *N*
F. H_3PO_4: 32.7 g/eq, 0.600 *N*; $Al(OH)_3$: 26.0 g/eq, 0.996 *N* G. H_3PO_4: 49.0 g/eq, 0.330 *N*; $Sr(OH)_2$: 60.8 g/eq, 0.454 *N* H. $H_2C_2O_4$: 90.0 g/eq, 0.774 *N*; NaOH: 40.0 g/eq, 0.146 *N*
14b. 11.30 ml B. 0.07784 *N* C. 35.03 ml
D. 0.3480 *N* E. 20.47 ml F. 0.09358 *N*
G. 118.3 ml H. 0.2462 *N*

Quizzes

A: 1. (b) 2. (e) (2.0) 3. (d) 4. (c) 5. (b)
6. (e) (pH = pK_a) 7. (d)
B. 1. (a) 2. (c) 3. (e) 4. (a) 5. (b) 6. (b)
7. (c) (no OH^- present)
C: 1. (c) 2. (c) 3. (d) 4. (a) 5. (e) [(c) = endpoint]
6. (b) 7. (e) (8.79)
D: 1. (b) 2. (b) 3. (e) 4. (d) 5. (d) 6. (a)
7. (e) (pOH = pK_b)

Sample Test

1. pK_a = 4.602 is $K_a = 2.50 \times 10^{-5}$; pH = 2.716 is $[H^+] = 1.92 \times 10^{-3}$ *M*. $(1.92 \times 10^{-3})^2/[HA] = 2.50 \times 10^{-5}$ *or* [HA] = 0.148 *M*. Thus $[HA]_i = [HA] + [H^+] =$ 0.150 *M*.
0.500 L × 0.150 *M* = 0.0750 mol HA = 7.500 g *and* MW = 7.500 g/0.0750 mol = 100 g/mol
2. a. weak base
b. 50 ml HCl × L/1000 ml × 0.100 mol = 5.0×10^{-3} mol HCl
MW = 0.400 g/5.0×10^{-3} mol = 80 g/mol
c. pH = 8.0 at midpoint *or* pOH = 6.0 = pK_b. Thus $K_b = 1 \times 10^{-6}$.
d. pH = 5 to pH = 3, methyl orange
3. First compute $[H^+]$.
pH = pK_a + log $[A^-]/[HA]$ = 4.74 + log(2.00/1.00) = 5.04 *or* $[H^+] = 9.1 \times 10^{-6}$ *M*
Then compute $[S^{2-}]$.
$1.1 \times 10^{-22} = [H^+]^2[S^{2-}] = (9.1 \times 10^{-6})^2[S^{2-}]$ *or* $[S^{2-}] = 1.3 \times 10^{-12}$ *M*
Finally, $[Zn^{2+}]$ is found.
$1.0 \times 10^{-21} = [Zn^{2+}][S^{2-}] = [Zn^{2+}](1.3 \times 10^{-12})$ *or* $[Zn^{2+}] = 7.5 \times 10^{-10}$ *M*.

CHAPTER 19

Drill Problems

1a. A. $3\,Ag + 4\,HNO_3 \rightarrow 3\,AgNO_3 + 2\,H_2O + NO$
B. $4\,HCl + PbO_2 \rightarrow 2\,H_2O + Cl_2 + PbCl_2$
C. $2\,Al + 6\,HBr \rightarrow 2\,AlBr_3 + 3\,H_2$ D. $BaSO_4 + 4\,C \rightarrow BaS + 4\,CO$ E. $Br_2 + 2\,H_2O + SO_2 \rightarrow 2\,HBr + H_2SO_4$ F. $3\,Br_2 + 6\,KOH \rightarrow 5\,KBr + KBrO_3 + 3\,H_2O$ G. $C + 4\,HNO_3 \rightarrow CO_2 + 2\,H_2O + 4\,NO_2$
H. $3\,Ca(PO_3)_2 + 10\,C \rightarrow Ca_3(PO_4)_2 + 10\,CO + P_4$
I. $2\,ClO_2 + H_2O_2 + 2\,KOH \rightarrow 2\,H_2O + 2\,KClO_2 + O_2$
J. $Cu + 4\,HNO_3 \rightarrow Cu(NO_3)_2 + 2\,NO_2 + 2\,H_2O$
K. $3\,HClO_3 \rightarrow HClO_4 + 2\,ClO_2 + H_2O$ L. $H_3AsO_3 + H_2O + I_2 \rightarrow 2\,HI + H_3AsO_4$ M. $2\,Cr(OH)_3 + 3\,Na_2O_2 \rightarrow 2\,Na_2CrO_4 + 2\,NaOH + 2\,H_2O$ N. $2\,FeI_2 + 6\,H_2SO_4 \rightarrow Fe_2(SO_4)_3 + 2\,I_2 + 3\,SO_2 + 6\,H_2O$
O. $FeS + 6\,HNO_3 \rightarrow Fe(NO_3)_3 + S + 3\,NO_2 + 3\,H_2O$
2. A. $H_2O_2 \rightarrow 2\,H^+ + O_2 + 2\,e^-$; $Cu^{2+} + 2\,e^- \rightarrow Cu$; $CuSO_4 + H_2O_2 \rightarrow Cu + O_2 + H_2SO_4$ B. $Mg \rightarrow Mg^{2+} + 2\,e^-$; $Ag^+ + e^- \rightarrow Ag$; $Mg + 2\,AgNO_3 \rightarrow Ag + Mg(NO_3)_2$
C. $Al \rightarrow Al^{3+} + 3\,e^-$; $2\,H^+ + 2\,e^- \rightarrow H_2$; $2\,Al + 3\,H_2SO_4 \rightarrow Al_2(SO_4)_3 + 3\,H_2$ D. $Pb \rightarrow Pb^{2+} + 2\,e^-$; $Fe^{3+} + 3\,e^- \rightarrow Fe$ ($E° = -0.036$ V); $Fe_2(SO_4)_3 + 3\,Pb \rightarrow 3\,PbSO_4 + 2\,Fe$
E. $2\,I^- \rightarrow I_2 + 2\,e^-$; $F_2 + 2\,e^- \rightarrow 2\,F\cdot$; $2\,NaI + F_2 \rightarrow 2\,NaF + I_2$ F. $H_2 + 2\,OH^- \rightarrow 2\,H_2O + 2\,e^-$; $ClO^- + H_2O + 2\,e^- \rightarrow Cl^- + 2\,OH^-$; $H_2 + KClO \rightarrow KCl + H_2O$ G. $2\,Cl^- \rightarrow Cl_2 + 2\,e^-$; $MnO_2 + 4\,H^+ + 2\,e^- \rightarrow Mn^{2+} + 2\,H_2O$; $MnO_2 + 4\,HCl \rightarrow MnCl_2 + Cl_2 + 2\,H_2O$ H. $I_2 + 6\,H_2O \rightarrow 2\,IO_3^- + 12\,H^+ + 10\,e^-$; $Br_2 + 2\,e^- \rightarrow 2\,Br^-$; $I_2 + 6\,H_2O + 5\,Br_2 \rightarrow 10\,HBr + 2\,HIO_3$ I. $Ag \rightarrow Ag^+ + e^-$; $NO_3^- + 4\,H^+ + 3\,e^- \rightarrow NO + 2\,H_2O$; $3\,Ag + 4\,HNO_3 \rightarrow 3\,AgNO_3 + NO + 2\,H_2O$ J. $S + 3\,H_2O \rightarrow SO_3^{2-} + 6\,H^+ + 4\,e^-$; $Pb^{2+} + 2\,e^- \rightarrow Pb$; $S + 3\,H_2O + 2\,Pb(NO_3)_2 \rightarrow 2\,Pb + H_2SO_3 + 4\,HNO_3$ K. $O_2 + H_2O \rightarrow O_3 + 2\,H^+ + 2\,e^-$; $O_2 + 2\,H^+ + 2\,e^- \rightarrow H_2O_2$; $H_2O + 2\,O_2 \rightarrow O_3 + H_2O_2$ L. $H_2S \rightarrow S + 2\,H^+ + 2\,e^-$; $Br_2 + 2\,e^- \rightarrow 2\,Br^-$; $H_2S + Br_2 \rightarrow 2\,HBr + S$ M. $Fe^{2+} \rightarrow Fe^{3+} + e^-$; $Sn^{2+} + 2\,e^- \rightarrow Sn$; $SnSO_4 + 2\,FeSO_4 \rightarrow Sn + Fe_2(SO_4)_3$
N. $S + 3\,H_2O \rightarrow H_2SO_3 + 4\,H^+ + 4\,e^-$; $SO_4^{2-} + 4\,H^+ + 2\,e^- \rightarrow H_2SO_3 + H_2O$; $S + 2\,H_2SO_4 + H_2O \rightarrow 3\,H_2SO_3$
O. $I_2 + 6\,H_2O \rightarrow 2\,IO_3^- + 12\,H^+ + 10\,e^-$; $I_2 + 2\,e^- \rightarrow 2\,I^-$; $3\,I_2 + 3\,H_2O \rightarrow HIO_3 + 5\,HI$
3. Oxidizing agent given first, followed by reducing agent.
A. Cu^{2+} or $CuSO_4$, H_2O_2 B. Ag^+ or $AgNO_3$, Mg
C. H^+ or H_2SO_4, Al D. Fe^{3+} or $Fe_2(SO_4)_3$, Pb
E. F_2, I^- or NaI F. ClO^- or KClO, H_2 G. MnO_2, Cl^- or HCl H. Br_2, I_2 I. NO_3^- or HNO_3, Ag
J. Pb^{2+} or $Pb(NO_3)_2$, S K. O_2, H_2O L. Br_2, H_2S
M. Sn^{2+} or $SnSO_4$, Fe^{2+} or $FeSO_4$ N. SO_4^{2-} or H_2SO_4, S O. I_2, I_2

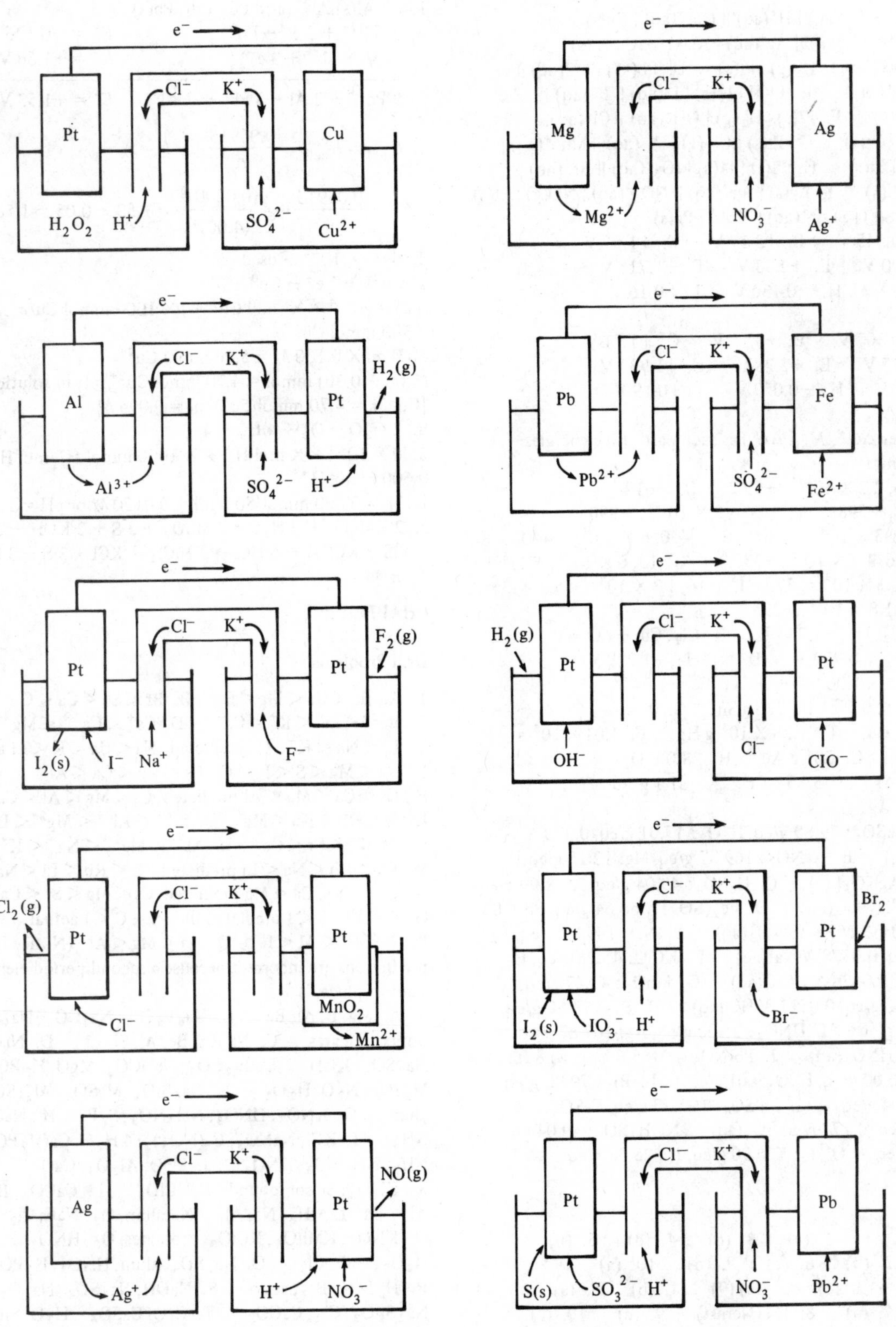

FIGURE A-2 Answers to objective 19-4 drill problems.

4. Sketches of the cells are in Fig. A-2. The anode is the left half-cell of each sketch. Cell diagrams follow.
A. Pt(s) | H_2O_2(aq) | H^+(aq) || Cu^{2+}(aq) | Cu(s)
B. Mg(s) | Mg^{2+}(aq) || Ag^+(aq) | Ag(s) C. Al(s) | Al^{3+}(aq) || H^+(aq) | H_2(g) | Pt(s) D. Pb(s) | Pb^{2+}(aq) || Fe^{3+}(aq) | Fe(s) E. Pt(s) | I_2(s) | I^-(aq) || F^-(aq) | F_2(g) | Pt(s) F. Pt(s) | H_2(g) | OH^-(aq) || Cl^-(aq), ClO^-(aq) | Pt(s) G. Pt(s) | Cl_2(g) | Cl^-(aq) || Mn^{2+}(aq) | MnO_2(s) | Pt(s) H. Pt(s) | I_2(s) | IO_3^-(aq) || Br^-(aq) | Br_2(l) | Pt(s) I. Ag(s) | Ag^+(aq) || NO_3^-(aq) | NO(g) | Pt(s)
J. Pt(s) | S(s) | SO_3^{2-}(aq) || Pb^{2+} | Pb(s)
6. A. −0.345 V B. +3.17 V C. +1.66 V
D. +0.090 V E. +2.33 V F. +1.718 V
G. −0.13 V H. −0.130 V I. +0.16 V
J. −0.58 V
7. A. −0.307 V B. +3.11 V C. +1.71 V
D. +0.235 V E. +2.28 V F. +1.737 V
G. +0.02 V H. −0.059 V I. +0.19 V
J. −0.61 V
8. In order $\Delta\bar{G}°$, K_{eq}, $\Delta\bar{G}$ for each part. Free energies are in kJ/mol.
A. +66.6, 2.2×10^{-12}, +59.2 B. −612, 1×10^{107}, −598 C. −961, 2×10^{168}, −990
D. −52, 1.3×10^{9}, −136 E. −450, 6×10^{78}, −440
F. −331.6, 1.3×10^{58}, −335.2 G. 13, 6×10^{-3}, −2
H. 125, 1.1×10^{-22}, 57 I. −46, 1.3×10^{8}, −55
J. −224, 1.8×10^{39}, −235
12. A. Cl_2, H_2, −1.746 V B. Cl_2, Cu, +1.064 V
C. Cl_2, H_2, −0.972 V D. O_2, H_2, −1.229 V
E. Cl_2, Cu, −1.002 V F. I_2, Fe, −1.04 V
13. A. 0.560 $\mathscr{F}$ B. 226 g Sn C. 0.3174 g Cu
D. 49.3 g Cu E. 1.28×10^3 g Hg F. 1.01×10^5 s = 28.0 hr G. 701 g Au H. 28.0 L O_2
I. 82.1 g Al J. 5.85 g Cr K. 61.1 g Au
L. 40.2 g Ag
14. A. $CuSO_4$: 79.80 g/eq, H_2O_2: 17.01 g/eq, 0.320 N $CuSO_4$(aq) B. $AgNO_3$: 169.87 g/eq, Mg: 12.15 g/eq, 0.152 N $AgNO_3$(aq) C. H_2SO_4: 49.04 g/eq, Al: 8.99 g/eq, 0.0410 N H_2SO_4(aq) D. $Fe_2(SO_4)_3$: 66.64 g/eq, Pb: 103.6 g/eq, 0.00473 N $Fe_2(SO_4)_3$(aq) E. NaI: 149.89 g/eq, F_2: 19.00 g/eq, 0.0378 N NaI(aq) F. KClO: 45.28 g/eq, H_2: 1.01 g/eq, 0.0628 N KClO(aq) G. MnO_2: 43.47 g/eq, HCl: 36.46 g/eq, 0.0521 N HCl(aq) H. Br_2: 79.90 g/eq, I_2: 25.38 g/eq I. HNO_3: 21.00 g/eq, Ag: 107.87 g/eq, 0.0817 N HNO_3(aq) J. $Pb(NO_3)_2$: 165.6 g/eq, S: 8.02 g/eq K. O_2: 16.00 g/eq, H_2O: 9.01 g/eq L. Br_2: 79.90 g/eq, H_2S: 17.04 g/eq M. Sn SO_4: 107.37 g/eq, $FeSO_4$: 151.90 g/eq, 0.177 N $SnSO_4$(aq) N. H_2SO_4: 49.04 g/eq, S: 8.02 g/eq O. I_2: 126.90 g/eq, I_2: 25.38 g/eq

Quizzes

A: 1. (e) (5) 2. (c) 3. (d) 4. (d) 5. (b)
6. (a) 7. (b) 8. (c) 9. (d) 10. (a)
B: 1. (c) 2. (c) 3. (e) (9) 4. (b) 5. (a)
6. (d) 7. (a) 8. (e) (Nernst) 9. (c) 10. (c)
C: 1. (d) 2. (a) 3. (b) 4. (d) 5. (e) 6. (b)
7. (d) 8. (a) 9. (e) (1.04 M) 10. (d)
D: 1. (d) 2. (c) 3. (a) 4. (a) 5. (c) 6. (e)
7. (b) 8. (e) (11.7) 9. (b) 10. (a)

Sample Test

1. a. Al(s)|Al^{3+}(aq)||Pb^{2+}(aq)|Pb(s)
b.

$$\begin{array}{ll} 3\,(Pb^{2+} + 2\,e^- \rightarrow Pb^0) & E° = -0.126\text{ V} \\ 2(Al \rightarrow Al^{3+} + 3\,e^-) & E° = +1.66\text{ V} \\ \hline 3\,Pb^{2+} + 2\,Al \rightarrow 3\,Pb^0 + 2\,Al^{3+} & E° = +1.53\text{ V} \end{array}$$

c. $E_{cell} = E°_{cell} - \dfrac{0.05915}{n}\log Q =$

$$1.53 - \frac{0.05915}{6}\log\frac{(0.0200)^2}{(4.00)^3} = 1.53 + 0.05 = 1.58\text{ V}$$

2. 6.00×10^{-4} $\mathscr{F}$ used.
a. $Cu^{2+} + 2\,e^- \rightarrow Cu^0$
$6.00 \times 10^{-4}\,\mathscr{F} \times$ (mol Cu/$\mathscr{F}$) $\times$ 1000 mmol Cu/mol Cu = 0.300 mmol Cu
50.0 ml $\times$ 0.100 M = 5.00 mmol Cu^{2+}
(5.00 − 0.30) mmol = 4.70 mmol Cu^{2+} left in solution
[Cu^{2+}] = 4.70 mmol/50.0 ml = 0.094 M
b. $2\,H_2O \rightarrow O_2 + 4\,H^+ + 4\,e^-$
$6.00 \times 10^{-4}\,\mathscr{F} \times$ mol H^+/$\mathscr{F}$ $\times$ 1000 mmol H^+/mol H^+ = 0.600 mmol H^+
[H^+] = 0.600 mmol/50.0 ml = 0.0120 M or pH = 1.921
c. $2\,KMnO_4 + 3\,H_2S \rightarrow 2\,MnO_2 + 3\,S + 2\,KOH + 2\,H_2O$
$3\,NiS + KClO_3 + 6\,HCl \rightarrow 3\,NiCl_2 + KCl + 3\,S + 3\,H_2O$

CHAPTER 20

Drill Problems

1. A. Ba < Ca < Mg < C B. Br < Se < Ca < C
C. $Be^{2+} < Li^+ < K^+ < Cs^+$ D. $Cs^+ < Ca^{2+} < Mg^{2+} < Al^{3+}$
E. Li < Na < K < Ca predicted, Na < Ca < K < Li actual
F. Na < Mg < S < I G. Cs < Rb < Ca < Al
H. Cs < Ca < Mg < Al predicted, Cs < Mg < Al < Ca actual
I. Cs < Rb < Na < Mg J. $Si^{4+} < Al^{3+} < Mg^{2+} < Li^+$
K. Br < I < Sr < Cs L. $Al^{3+} < Mg^{2+} < Na^+ < K^+$
M. Cs < Rb < Na < Li predicted, Cs < Rb < Li < Na actual
N. Cs < Sr < Ca < Mg predicted, Cs < Mg < Sr < Ca actual
O. C < P < S < I predicted, P < S < C < I actual
P. Cs < Sr < Al < F Q. Na < Mg < Al (Notice how often predictions are incorrect because a second period element is "out of place.")
3. A. Mg, B, Al, Be B. $Na_6P_6O_{18}$, Na_2CO_3, Na_4SiO_4, borax, silicates C. Na, Cs, Be, Al, Si, Li D. NaOH, Na_2SO_4, KOH E. Li_2CO_3, $NaHCO_3$, MgO, H_3BO_3, I_2, $MgSO_4$, N_2O, H_2O_2 F. Na_4SiO_4, $MgSO_4$, $Al_2(SO_4)_3$, alum G. KNO_3, HNO_3, NH_4NO_3, S, P H. NaCl, SO_2, NH_3 I. KCl, $NaNO_3$, $Ca(NO_3)_2 \cdot 4\,H_2O$, $Ca(H_2PO_4)_2$, NH_3, NH_4NO_3, HNO_3 J. MgO, Al_2O_3, CaO
K. KNO_3, Sr compounds, S, $KClO_3$ L. $CaCO_3$, $BaSO_4$, Al M. $LiAlH_4$, Na, Al N. alum, O_3, NaF; Cl_2
O. KNO_3, $KMnO_4$, $KClO_3$, bromates, O_3, HNO_3 P. NaCN, H_2O_2, NaF, Cl_2 Q. Na_2SO_4, alum, HNO_3, H_3PO_4, KNO_3
R. H_3BO_3, Br_2, alum S. NaOH, Na_2SO_4, Na_2O_2, sulfates, $Na_2S_2O_3$, Cl_2, $CaCO_3$ T. CaO, $CaSO_4 \cdot 2H_2O$, SiO_2
U. Na_2CO_3, Na_2SO_4, K_2CO_3, B_2O_3, SiO_2, $CaCO_3$
V. B_4C_3, Al_2O_3, SiO_2, SiC W. Sizing is a material used to fill in the pores of surfaces of paper, textiles, or leather. A synonym is glazing.

4. & 5. A. $K(s) + O_2(g) \rightarrow KO_2(s)$ B. $2\ Al(s) + 3\ F_2(g) \rightarrow 2\ AlF_3(s)$ C. $Sr(s) + 2\ H_2O(l) \rightarrow Sr(OH)_2(aq) + H_2(g)$ D. $Sr(s) + I_2(s) \rightarrow SrI_2(s)$ E. $CaO(s) + H_2O(l) \rightarrow Ca(OH)_2$(aq *or* s) F. $2\ Na(s) + O_2(g) \rightarrow Na_2O_2(s)$ G. $2\ Cs(s) + 2\ H_2O(l) \rightarrow 2\ CsOH(aq) + H_2(g)$ H. $Mg(s) + 2\ HCl(aq) \rightarrow MgCl_2(aq) + H_2(g)$ I. $Mg(s) + H_2O(l) \xrightarrow{\Delta} MgO(s) + H_2(g)$ J. $Na(s) + N_2(g) \rightarrow$ no reaction K. $Ba(s) + O_2(g) \rightarrow BaO_2(s)$ L. $NaBr(aq) + I_2(s) \rightarrow$ no reaction M. $H_2(g) + F_2(g) \rightarrow 2\ HF(g)$ N. $HI(aq) + O_2(g) \rightarrow$ no reaction O. $Mg(s) + H_2(g) \rightarrow$ no reaction P. $6\ Li(s) + N_2(g) \rightarrow 2\ Li_3N(s)$ Q. $4\ Cl_2(g) + S_8(s) \rightarrow 4\ S_2Cl_2(g)$ R. $4\ Li(s) + O_2(g) \rightarrow 2\ Li_2O(s)$ S. $Be(s) + H_2(g) \rightarrow$ no reaction T. $8\ Cl_2(g) + 8\ H_2S(g) \rightarrow 16\ HCl + S_8$ U. $3\ Br_2(l) + 8\ NH_3(g) \rightarrow 6\ NH_4Br + N_2$ V. $2\ Na(s) + Cl_2(g) \rightarrow 2\ NaCl$ W. $Li(s) + H_2(g) \rightarrow$ no reaction X. $Cl_2(g) + H_2O(l) \rightarrow HCl(aq) + HOCl(aq)$ Y. $2\ F_2(g) + 2\ H_2O(l) \rightarrow 4\ HF(aq) + O_2(g)$

6. A. $O_2 + 4\ H^+ + 4\ e^- \rightarrow 2\ H_2O$, +1.23 V B. $O_2 + 2\ H_2O + 4\ e^- \rightarrow 4\ OH^-$, +0.40 V C. $O_2^- + 2\ H_2O + 3\ e^- \rightarrow 4\ OH^-$, +0.71 V D. $HClO + H^+ + 2\ e^- \rightarrow Cl^- + H_2O$, +1.49 V E. $2\ ClO_4^- + 16\ H^+ + 14\ e^- \rightarrow Cl_2 + 8\ H_2O$, +1.39 V F. $ClO_4^- + 8\ H^+ + 8\ e^- \rightarrow Cl^- + 4\ H_2O$, +1.39 V G. $HClO_2 + 3\ H^+ + 4\ e^- \rightarrow Cl^- + 2\ H_2O$, +1.56 V H. $2\ ClO_3^- + 6\ H_2O + 10\ e^- \rightarrow Cl_2 + 12\ OH^-$, +0.48 V I. $2\ ClO_4^- + 8\ H_2O + 14\ e^- \rightarrow Cl_2 + 16\ OH^-$, +0.45 V J. $ClO_2^- + 2\ H_2O + 4\ e^- \rightarrow Cl^- + 4\ OH^-$, +0.77 V K. $NO_3^- + 4\ H^+ + 3\ e^- \rightarrow NO + 2\ H_2O$, +0.96 V L. $NO_3^- + 2\ H_2O + 3\ e^- \rightarrow NO + 4\ OH^-$, −0.14 V M. $NO_3^- + 3\ H^+ + 2\ e^- \rightarrow HNO_2 + H_2O$, +0.94 V N. $NO_3^- + H_2O + 2\ e^- \rightarrow NO_2^- + 2\ OH^-$, +0.02 V O. $NO_3^- + 10\ H^+ + 8\ e^- \rightarrow NH_4^+ + 3\ H_2O + 8\ e^-$, +0.88 V P. $2\ HNO_2 + 6\ H^+ + 6\ e^- \rightarrow N_2 + 4\ H_2O$, +1.45 V Q. $SO_4^{2-} + 8\ H^+ + 6\ e^- \rightarrow S + 4\ H_2O$, +0.36 V R. $SO_4^{2-} + 4\ H_2O + 8\ e^- \rightarrow S^{2-} + 8\ OH^-$, −0.65 V

8. (1) A. basic B. acidic C. amphoteric D. acidic E. acidic F. acidic G. amphoteric H. acidic I. amphoteric J. basic K. amphoteric L. amphoteric M. basic N. acidic O. basic (2) A. $CaO + SiO_2 \rightarrow CaSiO_3$ B. $Al_2O_3 + 3\ SO_2 \rightarrow Al_2(SO_3)_3$ C. no reaction D. no reaction E. $BaO + SO_2 \rightarrow BaSO_3$ F. $3\ PbO + P_2O_5 \rightarrow Pb_3(PO_4)_2$ G. $3\ Na_2O + Al_2O_3 \rightarrow 2\ Na_3AlO_3$

11. A. $3\ CuS + 8\ HNO_3 \rightarrow 3\ Cu(NO_3)_2 + 3\ S + 2\ NO + 4\ H_2O$ B. no reaction C. $Na_2S + H_2O \rightarrow 2\ Na^+(aq) + HS^-(aq) + OH^-(aq)$ D. no reaction E. no reaction F. $3\ CdS + 8\ HNO_3 \rightarrow 3\ Cu(NO_3)_2 + 3\ S + 2\ NO + 4\ H_2O$ G. $As_2S_3 + (NH_4)_2S \rightarrow 2\ AsS_2^- + 2\ NH_4^+$ H. no reaction I. $ZnS + H^+(aq) \rightarrow Zn^{2+}(aq) + HS^-(aq)$ J. $CaS + H_2O \rightarrow Ca^{2+}(aq) + HS^-(aq) + OH^-(aq)$ K. $CoS + H^+(aq) \rightarrow Co^{2+}(aq) + HS^-(aq)$ L. no reaction M. no reaction

12. A. sodium metasilicate B. pyroarsenic acid C. calcium pyroborate D. magnesium metastannate E. $H_6Si_2O_7$ F. $NaAlO_2$ G. $Ca_2P_2O_7$ H. $Fe(BO_2)_3$ I. $BaCO_3$ J. $Mg_3(BiO_4)_2$

Quizzes

A: 1. (c) (3 & 6 only, not 4 or 5) 2. (d) 3. (a) 4. (a) 5. (e) 6. (c) 7. (c) 8. (b)
B: 1. (c) 2. (a) 3. (a) 4. (d) 5. (c) 6. (a) 7. (a) 8. (a)
C: 1. (b) 2. (a) 3. (a) 4. (c) 5. (c) 6. (a) 7. (c) 8. (e)
D: 1. (c) 2. (c) 3. (e) 4. (e) (sheets) 5. (e) 6. (c) 7. (d) 8. (d)

Syntheses

ESTD = evaporate solution to dryness
1. $Ba(s) + 2\ H_2O(l) \rightarrow Ba(OH)_2(aq) + H_2(g)$ ESTD; $Ba(OH)_2 \xrightarrow{\Delta} BaO(s) + H_2O(g)$. *Or* $2\ Ba(s) + O_2(g) \rightarrow 2\ BaO(s)$ at low temperatures
2. $2\ Na(s) + 2\ H_2O(l) \rightarrow 2\ NaOH(aq) + H_2(g)$; $NaOH(aq) + HCl(aq) \rightarrow NaCl(aq) + H_2O(l)$ ESTD. *Or* $2\ Na(s) + 2\ HCl(aq) \rightarrow 2\ NaCl(aq) + H_2(g)$, but this would be a very violent reaction: *Or* $2\ HCl(aq) \xrightarrow{\sim\sim} H_2(g) + Cl_2(g)$; gases separate naturally, Cl_2 at anode, H_2 at cathode; then $2\ Na(s) + Cl_2(g) \rightarrow 2\ NaCl(s)$ (pretty violent)
3. $2\ Li(s) + 2\ H_2O(l) \rightarrow 2\ LiOH(aq) + H_2(g)$ ESTD carefully; $2\ LiOH(s) \rightarrow Li_2O(s) + H_2O(g)$; $Li_2O(s) + CO_2(g) \rightarrow Li_2CO_3(s)$ 4. $Sr(s) + 2\ H_2O(l) \rightarrow Sr(OH)_2(aq) + H_2(g)$; $Sr(OH)_2(aq) + H_2SO_4(aq) \rightarrow SrSO_4(aq) + 2\ H_2O(l)$ ESTD
5. $2\ Al(s) + 3\ H_2SO_4(l) \rightarrow Al_2(SO_4)_3(aq) + 3\ H_2(g)$ ESTD
6. $Mg(s) + H_2O(l) \xrightarrow{\Delta} MgO(s) + H_2(g)$ 7. $Li_2CO_3(s) \xrightarrow{\Delta} Li_2O_2(s) + CO_2(g)$; $Na_2O(s) + CO_2(g) \rightarrow Na_2CO_3(g)$
8. $CaCO_3(s) \xrightarrow{\Delta} CaO(s) + CO_2(g)$; $CaO(s) + H_2O(l) \rightarrow Ca(OH)_2(aq)$ ESTD carefully 9. $2\ Ba(s) + O_2(g) \rightarrow 2\ BaO(s)$ at low temperatures; $C(s) + O_2(g) \rightarrow CO_2(g)$; $BaO(s) + CO_2(g) \rightarrow BaCO_3(s)$ 10. $2\ Ba(s) + O_2(g) \rightarrow 2\ BaO(s)$ at low temperatures; $S(s) + O_2(g) \rightarrow SO_2(g)$; $BaO(s) + SO_2(g) \rightarrow BaSO_3(s)$ 11. $2\ Na(s) + Br_2(l) \rightarrow 2\ NaBr(s)$; $3\ NaBr(s) + H_3PO_4(aq) \rightarrow Na_3PO_4(aq) + 3\ HBr(g)$. Use $H_3PO_4(aq)$ as the strong acid, since HCl(aq) is too volatile, and $H_2SO_4(aq)$ and $HNO_3(aq)$ will oxidize some of the Br^- to $Br_2(l)$. 12. $2\ H_2(g) + O_2(g) \rightarrow 2\ H_2O(l)$; $P_4(s) + 5\ O_2(g) \rightarrow P_4O_{10}(s)$; $P_4O_{10}(s) + 6\ H_2O(l) \rightarrow 4\ H_3PO_4$ 13. $6\ Li(s) + N_2(g) \rightarrow 2\ Li_3N(s)$; $Li_3N(s) + 3\ H_2O(l) \rightarrow 3\ LiOH(aq) + NH_3(g)$
14. $Ca(s) + 2\ H_2O(l) \rightarrow Ca(OH)_2(aq) + H_2(g)$
15. $Ca(s) + 2\ H_2O(l) \rightarrow Ca(OH)_2(aq) + H_2(g)$ ESTD; $Ca(OH)_2(s) \xrightarrow{\Delta} CaO(s) + H_2O(g)$; $C(s) + O_2(g) \rightarrow CO_2(g)$; $CaO(s) + CO_2(g) \rightarrow CaCO_3(s)$ 16. $2\ Cu(s) + 8\ HNO_3(aq) \rightarrow 3\ Cu(NO_3)_2(aq) + 2\ NO(g) + 4\ H_2O(l)$; heat strongly to boil off NO(g). $C(s) + O_2(g) \rightarrow CO_2(g)$; $2\ Mg(s) + O_2(g) \rightarrow 2\ MgO(s)$; $MgO(s) + CO_2(g) \rightarrow MgCO_3$; $MgCO_3(s) + Cu(NO_3)_2(aq) \rightarrow CuCO_3(s) + Mg(NO_3)_2(aq)$; filter mixture and dry solid. 17. $2\ H_2(g) + O_2(g) \rightarrow 2\ H_2O(l)$; $2\ Li(s) + 2\ H_2O(l) \rightarrow 2\ LiOH(aq) + H_2(g)$; $LiOH(aq) + HNO_3(aq) \rightarrow LiNO_3(aq) + H_2O(l)$ ESTD
18. $Ca(s) + Se(s) \rightarrow CaSe(s)$; $CaSe(s) + 2\ HCl(aq) \rightarrow CaCl_2(aq) + H_2Se(g)$ 19. $Mg(s) + I_2(s) \rightarrow MgI_2(s)$; $3\ MgI_2(s) + 2\ H_3PO_4(aq) \rightarrow Mg_3(PO_4)_2(aq) + 6\ HI(g)$.

Use H_3PO_4 for the same reasons as in synthesis 11.
20. $P_4(s) + 6\ Br_2(l) \rightarrow 4\ PBr_3(l); 2\ H_2(g) + O_2(g) \rightarrow$
$2\ H_2O(l); PBr_3(l) + 3\ H_2O(l) \rightarrow H_3PO_3(aq) + 3\ HBr(g)$.
Use water sparingly.

CHAPTER 21

Drill Problems

1. A. $Fe < Mn < Ti < Sc$ B. $Sc < Cr < Fe < Os$
C. $Sc < Ti < Cr < Fe$ D. $MnO < MnO_2 < MnO_3 < Mn_2O_7$
E. $Sc < Mn < Fe < Zn$ F. $Sc < V < Fe < Mn$
G. $Ti < Nb < Pd < Pt$ H. $VO < V_2O_3 < VO_2 < V_2O_5$
I. $Y < Ti < V < Mn$ J. $Cu^+ < V^{3+} < Ni^{2+} < Fe^{3+}$
K. $Fe < Cr < Ti < Ca$
3. A. Ti, V B. Sc C. Cu D. Cu E. Sc
F. Cu, Co, Ni G. Zn H. Zn, Ni, Cr I. Fe
J. Ti, V K. Fe, Co, Ni
4. A. TiO_2 B. ZnS C. CoO, Cu_2O, CuO, Cr_2O_3
D. Cr_2O_3, $PbCrO_4$, $FeSO_4$, $Fe_4[Fe(CN)_6]_3$, Fe_2O_3, $ZnCrO_4$ E. CuCl, $Cu_3(AsO_4)_2$ F. ZnO
G. V_2O_5 H. $KMnO_4$, $Na_2Cr_2O_7$
I. $KCr(SO_4)_2 \cdot 12\ H_2O$, $FeSO_4$, $CuSO_4$
J. Na_2CrO_4, $ZnCrO_4$ K. $FeCl_3$, $CuSO_4$
L. MnO_2, Ni_2O_3
5. A. $2\ KMnO_4 + 5\ Na_2C_2O_4 + 8\ H_2SO_4 \rightarrow$
$2\ MnSO_4 + 10\ CO_2 + 5\ Na_2SO_4 + K_2SO_4 + 8\ H_2O$
B. $K_2Cr_2O_7 + 6\ KBr + 7\ H_2SO_4 \rightarrow 3\ Br_2 +$
$4\ K_2SO_4 + Cr_2(SO_4)_3 + 7\ H_2O$
C. $H_2S + 2\ KMnO_4 \rightarrow 2\ KOH + SO_2 + 2\ MnO_2$
D. $K_2Cr_2O_7 + 3\ SnSO_4 + 7\ H_2SO_4 \rightarrow$
$3\ Sn(SO_4)_2 + K_2SO_4 + Cr_2(SO_4)_3 + 7\ H_2O$
E. $2\ KMnO_4 + 3\ H_2O_2 \rightarrow 3\ O_2 + 2\ MnO_2 +$
$2\ H_2O + 2\ KOH$
F. $5\ Cd + 2\ KMnO_4 + 8\ H_2SO_4 \rightarrow 5\ CdSO_4 +$
$2\ MnSO_4 + K_2SO_4 + 8\ H_2O$
G. $K_2Cr_2O_7 + 3\ HNO_2 + 5\ HCl \rightarrow 2\ KNO_3 +$
$4\ H_2O + CrCl_3 + CrCl_2NO_3$
H. $2\ NaMnO_4 + 6\ NaI + 4\ H_2O \rightarrow 3\ I_2(s) +$
$2\ MnO_2 + 8\ NaOH$
I. $2\ Na_2CrO_4 + 3\ SnCl_2 + 16\ HCl \rightarrow 3\ SnCl_4 +$
$2\ CrCl_3 + 4\ NaCl + 8\ H_2O$
J. $8\ HMnO_4 + 5\ AsH_3 + 8\ H_2SO_4 \rightarrow 5\ H_3AsO_4 +$
$8\ MnSO_4 + 12\ H_2O$
K. $2\ KMnO_4 + 10\ FeSO_4 + 8\ H_2SO_4 \rightarrow$
$5\ Fe_2(SO_4)_3 + 2\ MnSO_4 + K_2SO_4 + 8\ H_2O$
L. $2\ Cr(OH)_3 + 3\ Na_2O_2 \rightarrow 2\ Na_2CrO_4 +$
$2\ NaOH + 2\ H_2O$
12. Ions which are present: A. Na^+, Sr^{2+}, Zn^{2+}
B. K^+, Fe^{3+} C. Ba^{2+}, Ni^{2+}

Quizzes

A: a. (a) 2. (e) 3. (a) 4. (e) (MnO_2) 5. (c)
6. (b) 7. (b)
B: 1. (d) 2. (e) 3. (a) 4. (d) 5. (a) 6. (c)
7. (d)
C: 1. (b) 2. (a) 3. (b) 4. (a) 5. (b) 6. (e)
7. (e)
D: 1. (e) 2. (a) 3. (b) 4. (b) 5. (c) 6. (c)
7. (c)

Sample Test

1. *a.* Dissolve in nitric acid.
$Fe(s) + 2\ H^+(aq) \rightarrow Fe^{2+}(aq) + H_2(g)$
$Ni(s) + 2\ H^+(aq) \rightarrow Ni^{2+}(aq) + H_2(g)$
$3\ Cu(s) + 2\ NO_3^-(aq) + 8\ H^+(aq) \rightarrow$
$3\ Cu^{2+}(aq) + 2\ NO + 4\ H_2O$
b. Treat with NH_3-NH_4Cl, $(NH_4)_2S$.
$Cu^{2+}(aq) + 4\ NH_3 \rightarrow Cu(NH_3)_4^{2+}(aq)$
$Fe^{2+}(aq) + (NH_4)_2S \rightarrow FeS(s) + 2\ NH_4^+(aq)$
$Ni^{2+}(aq) + (NH_4)_2S \rightarrow NiS(s) + 2\ NH_4^+(aq)$
c. Treat remaining solution with Zn(s).
$Zn(s) + [Cu(NH_3)_4]^{2+}(aq) \rightarrow$
$[Zn(NH_3)_4]^{2+}(aq) + Cu(s)$
d. Treat precipitate from step *b.* with aqua regia.
$FeS(s) + NO_3^- + 4\ H^+ \rightarrow Fe^{3+} + NO(g) +$
$S(s) + 2\ H_2O$
$NiS(s) + 2\ NO_3^- + 8\ H^+ \rightarrow 3\ Ni^{2+} + 2\ NO(g) +$
$3\ S(s) + 4\ H_2O$
e. Treat solution with NH_3(aq).
$Fe^{3+}(aq) + 3\ NH_3 + 3\ H_2O \rightarrow Fe(OH)_3(s) + 4\ NH_4^+$
$Ni^{2+}(aq) + 6\ NH_3 \rightarrow [Ni(NH_3)_6]^{2+}$
f. Test solution from *e.* with dimethylglyoxime.
$[Ni(NH_3)_6]^{2+} + 2\ DMG^- \rightarrow Ni(DMG)_2$ (scarlet, s) +
$6\ NH_3$
g. Dissolve solid from *e.* with HCl then test with KSCN(aq).
$Fe(OH)_3(s) + 3\ H^+ \rightarrow Fe^{3+} + 3\ H_2O$
$Fe^{3+} + SCN^- + 5\ H_2O \rightarrow [Fe(H_2O)_5NCS]^{2+}$ (wine red)

2. a. $Al_2O_3(s) + 6\ HCl(aq) \rightarrow 3\ H_2O + 2\ AlCl_3(aq)$
$Al_2O_3(s) + 6\ NaOH(aq) \rightarrow 2\ Na_3AlO_3(aq) + 3\ H_2O$

b. $100.0\ g\ AlCl_3 \times \frac{mol\ AlCl_3}{133.5\ g} \times \frac{mol\ Al_2O_3}{2\ mol\ AlCl_3} \times \frac{102.0\ g}{mol\ Al_2O_3} =$
$38.20\ g\ Al_2O_3$

$100.0\ g\ Na_3AlO_3 \times \frac{mol\ Na_3AlO_3}{144.0\ g} \times \frac{mol\ Al_2O_3}{2\ mol\ Na_3AlO_3} \times$
$\frac{102.0\ g}{mol\ Al_2O_3} = 35.42\ g\ Al_2O_3$

3. $MnO_4^- \xrightarrow{1.70\ V} MnO_2 \xrightarrow{1.23\ V} Mn^{2+}$; $MnO_4^- \rightarrow Mn^{2+}$: 1.51 V

CHAPTER 22

Drill Problems

1. A. Ag, +1, 2, $S_2O_3^{2-}$ B. Al, +3, 4, H^-
C. Co, +3, 6, H_2O & CN^- D. Pt, +4, 6, NH_3 & Cl^-
E. Ni, +2, 4, NH_3 F. Cr, +3, 6, NH_3 & SCN^-
G. Fe, +3, 6, en H. Pt, +2, 4, NO_2^-
I. Co, +3, 6, NH_3 & Cl^- J. Al, + 3, 6, H_2O & OH^-
K. Pt, +4, 6, NH_3 & Cl^- L. Fe, 0, 4, CO
M. Mn, +2, 6, NO & CN^- N. Au, +3, 4, F^-
O. Co, +3, 6, NH_3 & NH_2^- P. Sb, +3, 5, Cl^-
Q. Ni, +2, 6, Cl^- & en R. Fe, +2, 6, CN^-
S. Ni, +2, 4, NH_3 & Br^- T. Fe, +3, 6, H_2O & OH^-
U. Ni, +2, 6, H_2O & NH_3

2. (1) A. Ag^+ B. Ca^{2+}, Fe^{2+}, Sc^{3+}, Cr^{3+}, Fe^{3+}, Co^{3+}, Pt^{4+} C. Co^{2+}, Ni^{2+}, Cu^{2+}, Al^{3+}
(2) A. 4,6 B. 6 C. 6 D. 6 E. 4,6 F. 2,4 G. 4,6 H. 6 I. 2
(3) A. nitrato (1) B. ethylenediaminetetraacetato (6) C. trien (4) D. NH_3(1) E. OH^- (1) F. CO(1) G. nitro (1) H. —NCS^- (1) I. nitrosyl (1) J. nitrogeno (1) K. F^-(1) L. SO_4^{2-} (1) M. CN^- (1) N. nitrito (1)
3. (1) A. dithiosulfatoargentate(I) ion B. tetrahydroaluminate(III) ion C. tetracyanodiaquocobaltate(III) ion D. tetrachlorodiammineplatinum(IV) E. tetramminenickel(II) ion F. tetrathiocyanatodiamminechromate(III) ion G. trisethylenediamineiron(III) ion H. tetranitroplatinate(II) ion I. chloropentaamminecobalt(III) ion J. hydroxopentaaquoaluminum(III) ion K. trichlorotriammineplatinum(IV) ion L. tetracarbonyliron(0) M. pentacyanonitrosylmanganate(II) ion N. tetrafluoroaurate(III) ion O. diamidotetraamminecobalt(III) ion P. pentachloroantimonate(III) ion Q. bisethylenediaminedichloronickel(II) R. hexacyanoferrate(II) ion S. dibromodiamminenickel(II) T. dihydroxotetraaquoiron(III) ion U. tetraamminediaquonickel(II) ion
(2) A. sodium tetracyanoaurate(I) B. $Na_3[Ag(S_2O_3)_2]$ C. potassium hexanitrocobaltate(III) D. $[Pt(NH_3)_2Br_2]$ E. dichlorotetraamminecobalt(III) bromide F. $[Cr(H_2O)_4Cl_2]Br$ G. $[Pt(H_2O)_2]Cl_4$ H. potassium hexachloroplatinate(IV) I. $[Ag(NH_3)_2]Cl$ J. $[Ni(NH_3)_6]SO_4$ K. sodium disulfatobisethylenediaminecuprate(II) L. hexaaquoaluminum hexacyanocobaltate(III) M. calcium tetraisothiocyanatodiamminechromate(III) N. hexaaminecobalt(III) chloride sulfate O. $Na_3[Cr(C_2O_4)_3]$ P. $[Cu(en)_2]Cl_2$
4. A. $[S_2O_3—Ag—S_2O_3]^-$

B. [H, H, Al, H, H]$^-$
C. [H_2O, CN, H_2O—Co—OH_2, NC, H_2O]$^-$
D. Cl, NH_3, Cl—Pt—Cl, H_3N, Cl
E. [H_3N, NH_3, Ni, H_3N, NH_3]$^{2+}$
F. [NH_3, SCN, NCS—Cr—SCN, NCS, NH_3]$^-$
G. [en, Fe, en, en]$^{3+}$
H. [O_2N, NO_2, Pt, O_2N, NO_2]$^{2-}$
I. [NH_3, NH_3, Cl—Co—NH_3, NH_3, NH_3]$^{2+}$
J. [OH_2, OH_2, H_2O—Al—OH_2, HO, OH_2]$^{2+}$
K. [NH_3, Cl, Cl—Pt—NH_3, Cl, NH_3]$^+$
L. OC, CO, Fe, OC, CO
M. [CN, NO, NC—Mn—CN, NC, CN]$^{3-}$
N. [F, F, Au, F, F]$^-$
O. [NH_3, NH_2, H_3N—Co—NH_3, H_2N, NH_3]$^{2+}$
P. [Cl, Cl, Cl—Sb—Cl, Cl]$^{2-}$
Q. Cl, en, Ni, en, Cl
R. [CN, CN, NC—Fe—CN, NC, CN]$^{4-}$
S. Br, NH_3, Ni, Br, NH_3
T. [H_2O, OH, H_2O—Fe—OH_2, HO, H_2O]$^-$
U. [H_2O, NH_3, Ni, H_2O, NH_3]$^{2-}$

5. A. 3: $[Co(H_2O)_4(CN)_2]Cl$, dicyanotetraaquocobalt(III) chloride
$[Co(H_2O)_4(CN)Cl]CN$, chlorocyanotetraaquocobalt(III) cyanide
7: $[Cr(H_2O)_4Cl_2]Br$, dichlorotetraaquochromium(III) bromide
$[Cr(H_2O)_4ClBr]Cl$, bromochlorotetraaquochromium(III) chloride
9: $[Co(NH_3)_5Cl]SO_4$, chloropentaamminecobalt(III) chloride
$[Co(NH_3)_5SO_4]Cl$, sulfatopentaamminecobalt(III) sulfate
B. 1: lithium tetracyanoaluminate, lithium tetraisocyanoaluminate
3: dicyanotetraaquocobalt(III) chloride, diisocyanotetraaquocobalt(III) chloride

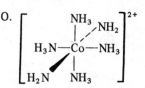

5: hexaaquoaluminum hexacyanocobaltate(III), hexaaquoaluminum hexaisocyanocobaltate(III)
6: dinitrodiaquoplatinum(II), dinitritodiaquoplatinum(II)
10: tricyanotrinitrosylmanganese(III), triisocyanotrinitrosylmanganese(III)
C. 5: $[Al(H_2O)_6][Co(CN)_6]$, $[Co(H_2O)_6][Al(CN)_6]$
8: $[Pt(H_2O)_4Cl_2][PtCl_4]$
D. 3:

OH₂ / CN / H₂O—Co—OH₂ / NC / OH₂ — *trans*

OH₂ / OH₂ / H₂O—Co—OH₂ / NC / CN — *cis*

4:

en / NH₃ / Co / H₃N / en — *trans*

en / NH₃ / Co—NH₃ / en — *cis*

6:

H₂O, NO₂ / Pt / O₂N, OH₂ — *trans*

H₂O, NO₂ / Pt / H₂O, NO₂ — *cis*

7:

H₂O / OH₂ / Cl—Cr—Cl / H₂O / H₂O — *trans*

H₂O / Cl / H₂O—Cr—Cl / H₂O / H₂O — *cis*

10:

NO / CN / NC—Mn—NO / NC / NO — *trans*

NO / NO / NC—Mn—NO / NC / CN — *cis*

8. A. strong, 0 B. strong, 3 C. weak, 4
D. weak, 1 E. strong, 0 F. weak, 3 G. weak, 4
H. weak, 2 I. weak, 0 J. strong, 3

10. A. $Ag^+ + 2\,S_2O_3^{2-} \rightleftharpoons Ag(S_2O_3)_2^{3-}$
$S_2O_3^{2-} + H_2O \rightleftharpoons HS_2O_3^- + OH^-$
$Ag^+ + Cl^- \rightleftharpoons AgCl(s)$ decreases precipitate
B. $Ag^+ + I^- \rightleftharpoons AgI(s)$
$Hg^{2+} + 4\,I^- \rightleftharpoons HgI_4^{2-}$
$AgI(s) + I^- \rightleftharpoons AgI_2^-$ decreases precipitate
C. $Zn^{2+} + S^{2-} \rightleftharpoons ZnS(s)$
$Zn^{2+} + 4\,CN^- \rightleftharpoons [Zn(CN)_4]^{2-}$
$CN^- + H_2O \rightleftharpoons HCN(aq) + OH^-$ decreases precipitate
D. $Fe^{2+} + 2\,OH^- \rightleftharpoons Fe(OH)_2(s)$
$Fe^{2+} + 6\,CN^- \rightleftharpoons [Fe(CN)_6]^{4-}$
$CN^- + H_2O \rightleftharpoons HCN + OH^-$ decreases precipitate
E. $Al^{3+} + 3\,F^- \rightleftharpoons AlF_3(s)$
$Ca^{2+} + 2\,F^- \rightleftharpoons CaF_2(s)$
$AlF_3(s) + 3\,F^- \rightleftharpoons AlF_6^{3-}$
$F^- + H_2O \rightleftharpoons HF + OH^-$ decreases precipitate
F. $Cu^+ + Cl^- \rightleftharpoons CuCl(s)$
$Ag^+ + Cl^- \rightleftharpoons AgCl(s)$
$Cu^+ + 2\,CN^- \rightleftharpoons [Cu(CN)_2]^-$
$Ag^+ + 2\,CN^- \rightleftharpoons [Ag(CN)_2]^-$
$CN^- + H_2O \rightleftharpoons HCN + OH^-$ decreases precipitate
G. $Al^{3+} + 3\,OH^- \rightleftharpoons Al(OH)_3(s)$
$Al^{3+} + 6\,F^- \rightleftharpoons AlF_6^{3-}$
$F^- + H_2O \rightleftharpoons HF + OH^-$ decreases precipitate
H. $2\,Co^{3+} + 3\,S^{2-} \rightleftharpoons Co_2S_3(s)$
$Co^{3+} + 3\,OH^- \rightleftharpoons Co(OH)_3(s)$
$Co^{3+} + 6\,NH_3 \rightleftharpoons [Co(NH_3)]^{6+}$
$S^{2-} + H_2O \rightleftharpoons HS^- + OH^-$
$NH_3 + H_2O \rightleftharpoons NH_4^+ + OH^-$ decreases precipitate
I. $Cu^{2+} + 2\,OH^- \rightleftharpoons Cu(OH)_2(s)$
$Cu^{2+} + 4\,NH_3 \rightleftharpoons Cu(NH_3)_4^{2+}$
$NH_3 + H_2O \rightleftharpoons NH_4^+ + OH^-$ decreases precipitate

11. Free ion concentration is given first, followed by that of complex ion.
A. $6.4 \times 10^{-17}\,M$, $0.002\,M$ B. $3.3 \times 10^{-6}\,M$, $7.9 \times 10^{-5}\,M$ C. $4.5 \times 10^{-15}\,M$, $0.0067\,M$
D. $9.7 \times 10^{-22}\,M$, $5.0 \times 10^{-4}\,M$ E. $4.6 \times 10^{-31}\,M$, $5.0 \times 10^{-4}\,M$ F. $1.4 \times 10^{-40}\,M$, $5.0 \times 10^{-4}\,M$
G. $1.4 \times 10^{-45}\,M$, $5.0 \times 10^{-4}\,M$ H. $2.5 \times 10^{-40}\,M$, $1.4 \times 10^{-5}\,M$ I. $2.0 \times 10^{-10}\,M$, $1.3 \times 10^{-4}\,M$
J. $1.3 \times 10^{-36}\,M$, $2.4 \times 10^{-6}\,M$ K. $2.0 \times 10^{-21}\,M$, $2.4 \times 10^{-6}\,M$

12. A. $[Ag^+] = 2.5 \times 10^{-11}\,M$, $Q = 2.5 \times 10^{-13}$, precipitate forms B. $[Ag^+] = 2.5 \times 10^{-11}\,M$, $Q = 2.5 \times 10^{-13}$, no precipitate C. $[Zn^{2+}] = 2.6 \times 10^{-18}\,M$, $Q = 2.6 \times 10^{-20}$, precipitate forms
D. $[Ag^+] = 2.7 \times 10^{-14}\,M$, $Q = 2.7 \times 10^{-16}$, no precipitate E. $[Hg^{2+}] = 3.1 \times 10^{-31}\,M$, $Q = 6.3 \times 10^{-33}$, no precipitate F. $[Cu^{2+}] = 1.7 \times 10^{-17}\,M$, $Q = 3.3 \times 10^{-19}$, precipitate forms
G. $[Ag^+] = 1.9 \times 10^{-21}\,M$, $Q = 9.3 \times 10^{-24}$, precipitate forms

Quizzes

A: 1. (d) 2. (c) 3. (c) 4. dichlorodiamminegold(III) bromide 5. $[Co(en)_3](C_2H_3O_2)_3$ 6. (b) 7. (b) 8. (a)

B: 1. (c) 2. (d) 3. (a) 4. calcium tetrachlorocuprate(II) 5. $K_2[SbCl_5]$ 6. (b) 7. (c) 8. (c)

C: 1. (c) 2. (b) 3. (a) 4. potassium dichlorodiammineplatinate(II) 5. $Ca[Cr(NH_3)_2Cl_4]_2$ 6. (a) 7. (d) 8. (b)

D: 1. (c) 2. (d) 3. (a) 4. sodium tetrachlorodinitrosylcobaltate(II) 5. $K_2[Fe(CH_3NH_2)_2(CN)_4]$ 6. (b) 7. (c) 8. (d)

Sample Test

1. Number of unpaired electrons is given in parentheses.

a.	b.	c.	d.
↑ ↑ ↑	↑ _	↑ ↑ ↑	_ _
⇅ ⇅	↑ ↑ ↑	↑ ↑	⇅ ⇅ ↑
strong (3)	weak (4)	weak (5)	strong (1)

2. 24.8 g Na × mol/23.0 g = 1.08 mol Na
34.2 g Cu × mol/63.5 g = 0.539 mol Cu
41.0 g F × mol/19.0 g = 2.16 mol F
559 mmHg × atm/760 mmHg =
$i(0.010\ M)(0.0821\ \text{L atm mol}^{-1}\ \text{K}^{-1})(298\ \text{K})$
$i = 3.00$ Thus $Na_2[CuF_4]$, sodium tetrafluorocuprate(II)
3. Initially: $[Ag^+] = 0.0700\ M$, $[SO_4^{2-}] = 0.0600\ M$, $[S_2O_3^{2-}] = 0.200\ M$

$$\frac{[Ag(S_2O_3)_2^{3-}]}{[Ag^+][S_2O_3^{2-}]^2} = \frac{0.0700 - x}{x(0.0600 + 2x)^2} = 1.7 \times 10^{13}$$

or $x = 1.1 \times 10^{-12}\ M = [Ag^+]$
$Q = [Ag^+]^2[SO_4^{2-}] = 7.8 \times 10^{-26} < 1.4 \times 10^{-5} = K_{sp}$.
It all dissolves.

CHAPTER 23

Drill Problems

2. (1) A. ${}^{0}_{-1}e$ B. ${}^{4}_{2}He$ C. ${}^{0}_{-1}e$ D. ${}^{4}_{2}He$ E. ${}^{232}_{92}U$
F. ${}^{0}_{-1}e$ G. ${}^{200}_{79}Au$ H. ${}^{6}_{3}Li$ I. ${}^{0}_{-1}e$ J. ${}^{17}_{9}F$
K. ${}^{0}_{+1}e$ L. ${}^{37}_{18}Ar$ M. ${}^{206}_{80}Hg$ N. ${}^{191}_{79}Au$ O. ${}^{222}_{86}Rn$
(2) A. ${}^{7}_{4}Be + {}^{0}_{-1}e \to {}^{7}_{3}Li$ B. ${}^{191}_{80}Hg \to {}^{0}_{+1}e + {}^{191}_{79}Au$
C. ${}^{177}_{78}Pt \to {}^{4}_{2}He + {}^{173}_{76}Os$ D. ${}^{3}_{1}H \to {}^{0}_{-1}e + {}^{3}_{2}He$
E. ${}^{177}_{74}W + {}^{0}_{-1}e \to {}^{177}_{73}Ta$ F. ${}^{109}_{49}In \to {}^{0}_{+1}e + {}^{109}_{48}Cd$
G. ${}^{186}_{75}Re \to {}^{0}_{-1}e + {}^{186}_{76}Os$ H. ${}^{235}_{92}U \to {}^{4}_{2}He + {}^{231}_{90}Th$
I. ${}^{12}_{5}B \to {}^{4}_{2}He + {}^{8}_{3}Li$ J. ${}^{161}_{69}Tm + {}^{0}_{-1}e \to {}^{161}_{68}Er$
K. ${}^{98}_{43}Tc \to {}^{0}_{-1}e + {}^{98}_{44}Ru$
4. (1) A. ${}^{59}_{27}Co + {}^{1}_{1}H \to {}^{1}_{0}n + {}^{59}_{28}Ni$; ${}^{59}Co(p, n){}^{59}Ni$
B. ${}^{9}_{4}Be + {}^{6}_{3}Li \to {}^{14}_{7}N + {}^{1}_{0}n$; ${}^{9}Be({}^{6}Li, n){}^{14}N$
C. ${}^{14}_{7}N + {}^{1}_{0}n \to {}^{9}_{4}Be + {}^{6}_{3}Li$; ${}^{14}N(n, {}^{6}Li){}^{9}Be$
D. ${}^{15}_{7}N + {}^{1}_{1}H \to {}^{4}_{2}He + {}^{12}_{6}C$; ${}^{15}N(p, \alpha){}^{12}C$
E. ${}^{5}_{2}He + {}^{1}_{1}H \to {}^{2}_{1}H + {}^{4}_{2}He$; ${}^{5}He(p, d){}^{4}He$
F. ${}^{23}_{11}Na + {}^{2}_{1}H \to {}^{4}_{2}He + {}^{21}_{10}Ne$; ${}^{23}Na(d, \alpha){}^{21}Ne$
G. ${}^{7}_{3}Li + {}^{4}_{2}He \to {}^{10}_{5}B + {}^{1}_{0}n$; ${}^{7}Li(\alpha, n){}^{10}B$
H. ${}^{9}_{4}Be + {}^{4}_{2}He \to {}^{1}_{0}n + {}^{12}_{6}C$; ${}^{9}Be(\alpha, n){}^{12}C$
I. ${}^{35}_{17}Cl + {}^{1}_{0}n \to {}^{1}_{1}H + {}^{35}_{16}S$; ${}^{35}Cl(n, p){}^{35}S$
J. ${}^{44}_{20}Ca + {}^{1}_{1}H \to {}^{1}_{0}n + {}^{44}_{21}Sc$; ${}^{44}Ca(p, n){}^{44}Sc$
K. ${}^{27}_{13}Al + {}^{2}_{1}H \to {}^{4}_{2}He + {}^{25}_{12}Mg$; ${}^{27}Al(d, \alpha){}^{25}Mg$
L. ${}^{25}_{12}Mg + {}^{4}_{2}He \to {}^{1}_{1}H + {}^{28}_{13}Al$; ${}^{25}Mg(\alpha, p){}^{28}Al$
(2) A. ${}^{238}_{92}U + {}^{1}_{0}n \to {}^{0}_{-1}e + {}^{239}_{93}Np$
B. ${}^{235}_{92}U + {}^{1}_{0}n \to {}^{236}_{92}U + \gamma$; ${}^{236}_{92}U + {}^{1}_{0}n \to {}^{237}_{92}U + \gamma$;
${}^{237}_{92}U \to {}^{237}_{93}Np + {}^{0}_{-1}e$
C. ${}^{238}_{92}U + {}^{2}_{1}H \to {}^{238}_{93}Np + 2\,{}^{1}_{0}n$; ${}^{238}_{93}Np \to {}^{238}_{94}Pu + {}^{0}_{-1}e$
D. ${}^{239}_{94}Pu + {}^{1}_{0}n \to {}^{240}_{94}Pu + \gamma$; ${}^{240}_{94}Pu + {}^{1}_{0}n \to {}^{241}_{94}Pu + \gamma$;
${}^{241}_{94}Pu \to {}^{241}_{95}Am + {}^{0}_{-1}e$
E. ${}^{239}_{94}Pu + {}^{4}_{2}He \to {}^{242}_{96}Cm + {}^{1}_{0}n$
F. ${}^{241}_{95}Am + {}^{1}_{0}n \to {}^{242}_{95}Am + \gamma$; ${}^{242}_{95}Am \to {}^{242}_{96}Cm + {}^{0}_{-1}e$
G. ${}^{241}_{95}Am + {}^{4}_{2}He \to {}^{243}_{97}Bk + 2\,{}^{1}_{0}n$
H. ${}^{242}_{96}Cm + {}^{4}_{2}He \to {}^{245}_{98}Cf + {}^{1}_{0}n$
I. ${}^{253}_{99}Es + {}^{4}_{2}He \to {}^{256}_{101}Md + {}^{1}_{0}n$
J. ${}^{256}_{96}Cm + {}^{12}_{6}C \to {}^{254}_{102}No + 4\,{}^{1}_{0}n$
K. ${}^{252}_{98}Cf + {}^{11}_{5}B \to {}^{258}_{103}Lw + 5\,{}^{1}_{0}n$

7. (1) Given in the order $t_{1/2}$, λ, activity.
A. 22 min, 0.0315/min, 8.5×10^{13}/min B. 1.65 h, 0.42/h, 1.7×10^{10}/h C. 1.5×10^{6} y, 4.6×10^{-7}/y, 2.0×10^{16}/y D. 12.26 y, 0.05653/y, 1.49×10^{19}/y
E. 39.5 h, 0.0175/h, 5.45×10^{19}/h F. 6.7 y, 0.10/y, 3.6×10^{20}/y
(2) Given in the order $t_{1/2}$, λ, mass.
A. 0.81 s, 0.86/s, 38 ng B. 53.37 d, 0.01298/d, 4.6 μg
C. 39.5 h, 0.0175/h, 12.9 g D. 12.26 y, 0.05653/y, 866 kg
E. 28 y, 0.025/y, 268 mg F. 60.6 min, 0.0114/min, 63.9 mg
(3) Given in the order half-life, decay constant.
A. 27 s, 0.026/s B. 15.5 s, 0.045/s C. 10.7 h, 1.81×10^{-5}/s D. 14.0 h, 1.38×10^{-6}/s
E. 8.00 m, 1.44×10.3/s F. 14.2 h, 1.36×10^{-5}/s
8. (1) A. 18.8 d B. 2.67 h C. 0.372 min
D. 10.1 min E. 2.32 d F. 0.293 d G. 1.94 d
H. 1.54 d
(2) A. 3.8×10^{3} y B. 26.6 y C. 3.81×10^{5} y
D. 3.09 y E. 1.5×10^{4} y F. 1.32×10^{4} y
(3) A. 54.5 y B. 7.50×10^{4} y C. 1.56×10^{5} y
D. 12.4 y E. 19.0 y F. 14.9 y
9. A. 2.0×10^{-5} amu, 1.8×10^{9} kJ/mol, 0.019 MeV
B. 0.003768 amu, 3.162×10^{11} kJ/mol, 3.514 MeF
C. 0.000377 amu, 3.16×10^{10} kJ/mol, 0.352 MeV
D. 0.000094 amu, 7.9×10^{9} kJ/mol, 0.088 MeV
E. 0.0143 amu, 1.20×10^{12} kJ/mol, 13.3 MeV
F. 0.001288 amu, 1.081×10^{11} kJ/mol, 1.201 MeV
G. 0.000326 amu, 2.74×10^{10} kJ/mol, 0.304 MeV
H. 0.001384 amu, 1.161×10^{11} kJ/mol, 1.291 MeV
I. 0.000548 amu, 4.90×10^{10} kJ/mol, 0.545 MeV
J. 0.001821 amu, 1.528×10^{11} kJ/mol, 1.698 MeV
K. 0.001072 amu, 8.996×10^{10} kJ/mol, 0.9997 MeV
L. 0.003232 amu, 2.712×10^{11} kJ/mol, 3.014 MeV
M. 0.001597 amu, 1.340×10^{11} kJ/mol, 1.489 MeV
10. Binding energy per nucleon is given first, then atomic number.
A. 0.000 MeV, 1 B. 8.801 MeV, 26 C. 7.082 MeV, 2
D. 8.742 MeV, 28 E. 6.470 MeV, 4 F. 8.746 MeV, 30
G. 7.689 Me V, 6 H. 8.721 MeV, 34 I. 7.985 MeV, 8
J. 8.728 MeV, 36 K. 8.042 MeV, 10 L. 8.720 MeV, 40
M. 8.270 MeV, 12 N. 8.617 MeV, 44 O. 8.458 MeV, 14
P. 8.542 MeV, 48 Q. 8.503 MeV, 16 R. 8.440 MeV, 52
S. 8.605 MeV, 18 T. 8.405 MeV, 56 U. 8.561 MeV, 20
V. 8.356 MeV, 60 W. 8.733 MeV, 22 X. 8.211 MeV, 64
Y. 8.786 MeV, 24 Z. 8.142 MeV, 68 Results are plotted in Fig. A-3.
11. A. ${}^{8}_{5}B \to {}^{8}_{4}Be + {}^{0}_{+1}e$ B. ${}^{238}_{92}U \to {}^{234}_{90}Th + {}^{4}_{2}He$ C. ${}^{19}_{9}F$ stable
D. ${}^{119}_{48}Cd \to {}^{119}_{49}In + {}^{0}_{-1}e$ E. ${}^{50}_{21}Sc \to {}^{50}_{22}Ti + {}^{0}_{-1}e$
F. ${}^{212}_{84}Po \to {}^{208}_{82}Pb + {}^{4}_{2}He$ G. ${}^{88}_{38}Sr$ stable
H. ${}^{17}_{9}F \to {}^{17}_{8}O + {}^{0}_{+1}e$ I. ${}^{226}_{88}Ra \to {}^{222}_{86}Rn + {}^{4}_{2}He$
J. ${}^{50}_{25}Mn \to {}^{50}_{24}Cr + {}^{0}_{+1}e$ K. ${}^{106}_{49}In \to {}^{106}_{48}Cd + {}^{0}_{+1}e$
L. ${}^{197}_{79}Au$ stable M. ${}^{63}_{27}Co \to {}^{63}_{28}Ni + {}^{0}_{-1}e$

Quizzes

A: 1. (e) (${}^{222}Rn$) 2. (b) 3. (b) 4. (d) 5. (b)
6. (b) 7. (a) 8. (b)

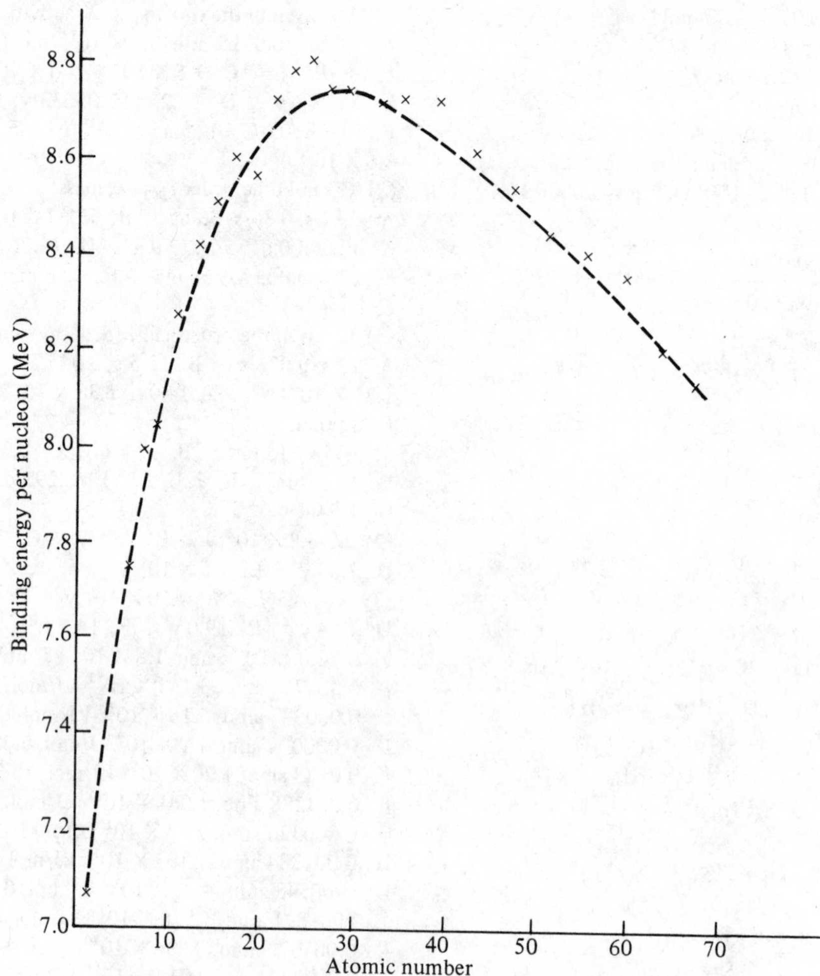

FIGURE A-3 Answers to objective 23-10 drill problems.

B: 1. (a) 2. (a) 3. (b) 4. (c) 5. (e) (45d) 6. (b) 7. (a) 8. (a)
C: 1. (e) (^{90}Y) 2. (c) 3. (a) 4. (a) 5. (a) 6. (b) 7. (a) 8. (e)
D: 1. (b) 2. (e) 3. (b) 4. (a) 5. (a) 6. (a) 7. (d) 8. (b)

Sample Test

1. Remain the same. ^{14}C is not produced by nuclear explosions but by cosmic rays in the upper atmosphere. $^{14}_{7}N + ^{1}_{0}n \rightarrow ^{14}_{6}C + ^{1}_{1}H$

2. Only α ($^{4}_{2}$He) and β ($^{0}_{-1}$e) particles are given off; $^{253}_{99}Es \rightarrow ^{237}_{93}Np + 4\,^{4}_{2}He + 2\,^{0}_{-1}e$. Thus four α particles and and two β particles are emitted.

3. a. $^{243}_{96}Cm \rightarrow ^{4}_{2}He + ^{239}_{94}Pu$ b. $^{18}_{9}F \rightarrow ^{0}_{+1}e + ^{18}_{8}O$ c. $^{88}_{40}Zr + ^{0}_{-1}e \rightarrow ^{88}_{39}Y$ D. $^{10}_{5}B + ^{4}_{2}He \rightarrow ^{1}_{0}n + ^{13}_{7}N$ e. $^{45}_{21}Sc + ^{4}_{2}He \rightarrow ^{1}_{1}H + ^{48}_{22}Ti$ f. $^{51}_{23}V + ^{2}_{1}H \rightarrow 2\,^{1}_{0}n + ^{51}_{24}Cr$

4. (11.0216 amu − 11.00931 amu) × 932.8 MeV/amu = 11.46 MeV

5. $\log(N_t/N_0) = -0.693t/2.303t_{1/2} = -0.693(995 \times 10^6)/(2.303 \times 4.51 \times 10^9) = -0.0664$
$N_t = 0.858N_0 = 0.858 \times 6.023 \times 10^{23}$ atoms
number decayed $= N_0 - N_t = (6.023 - 5.17) \times 10^{23} = 8.5 \times 10^{22}$ atoms

CHAPTER 24

Drill Problems

2. A. $CH_3CH_2C(CH_3){=}CHCH_2CH_3$ B. $CH_3CH{=}CHCH_2CH_3$

C. $CH_3CH(CH_3)CH_2CH_3$ D. $CH_3C(CH_3)_2CH_2CH(CH_3)CH_3$

E. $CH_3C{\equiv}C{-}CH_3$

F. 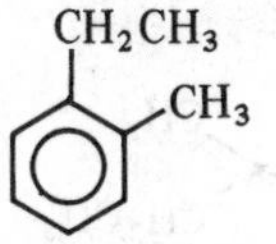 (benzene ring with CH_2CH_3 and CH_3)

G.  (benzene ring with CH_3)

H. 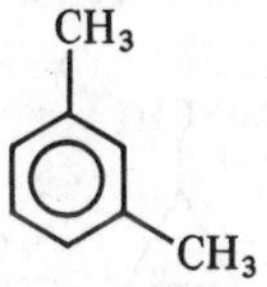 (benzene ring with CH_3 and CH_3)

I. 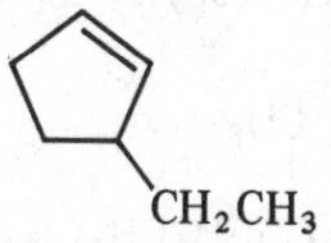 (cyclopentene ring with CH_2CH_3)

J. 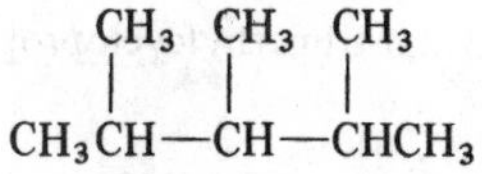 $CH_3CH(CH_3){-}CH(CH_3){-}CH(CH_3)CH_3$

K. 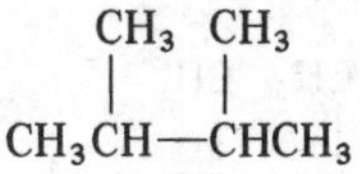 $CH_3CH(CH_3){-}CH(CH_3)CH_3$

L. 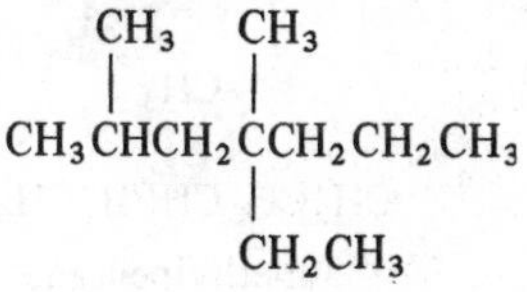 $CH_3CH(CH_3)CH_2C(CH_3)(CH_2CH_3)CH_2CH_2CH_3$

M. 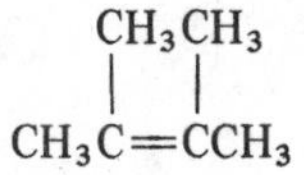 $CH_3C(CH_3){=}C(CH_3)CH_3$

N. 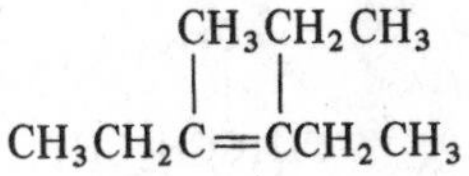 $CH_3CH_2C(CH_3){=}C(CH_2CH_3)CH_2CH_3$

O. $CH_3C{\equiv}CCH_2CH_3$

P. 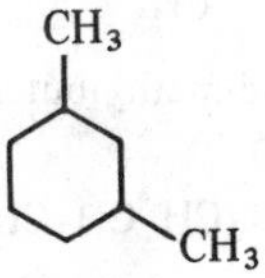 (cyclohexane ring with CH_3 and CH_3)

Q. 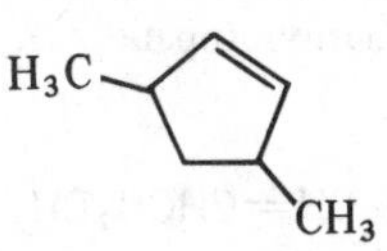 (cyclopentene ring with H_3C and CH_3)

R. 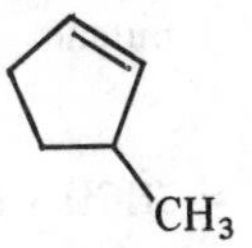 (cyclopentene ring with CH_3)

S. 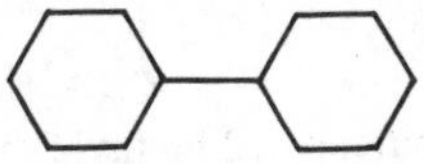 (two cyclohexane rings joined)

T. 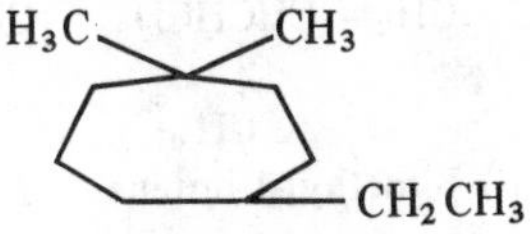 (cycloheptane ring with H_3C, CH_3 and CH_2CH_3)

U. 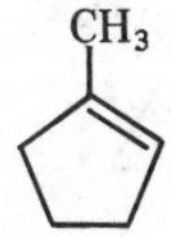 (cyclopentene ring with CH_3)

V. 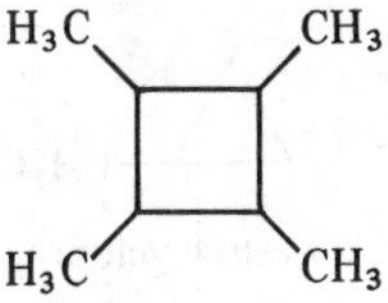 (cyclobutane ring with H_3C, CH_3, H_3C, CH_3)

W. 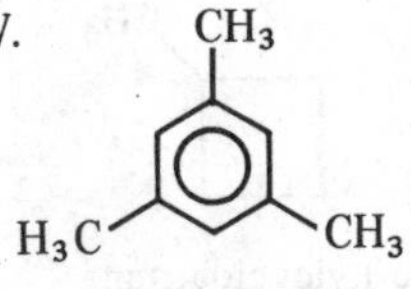 (benzene ring with CH_3, H_3C, CH_3)

3\. A. 2-methylbutane B. 1-butene
C. 3-ethyl-2-methyl-2-pentene D. 2,3-dimethylpentane
E. ethylcyclopropane F. 1,2-dimethylcyclohexane
G. 1-pentene H. 4-*n*-propylcyclohexene I. *t*-butylbenzene
J. 4-methylheptane K. 1-butyne L. 2-butene
M. 1-pentane N. 1-propyne *or* propyne O. propane
P. 2-methylpropane Q. 2,2,3-trimethylbutane
R. 3,3-diethyl-2-methylhexane S. 3-ethyl-2-methylpentane
T. 2-methylpentane U. 2,2,3-trimethylpentane
V. 4,4-dimethyloctane W. 4-methylcyclohexene

4\. A.

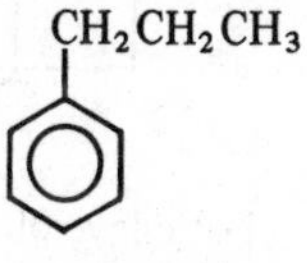

(benzene ring with $CH_2CH_2CH_3$) *n*-propylbenzene

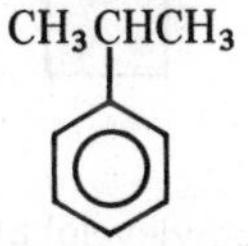

(benzene ring with CH_3CHCH_3) isopropylbenzene

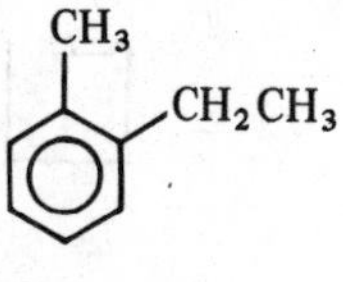

(benzene ring with CH_3 and CH_2CH_3) *o*-ethyltoluene

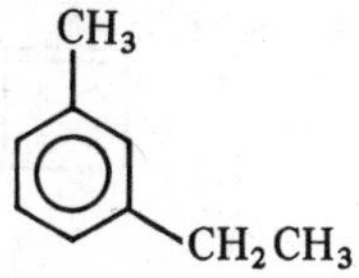

(benzene ring with CH_3 and CH_2CH_3) *m*-ethyltoluene

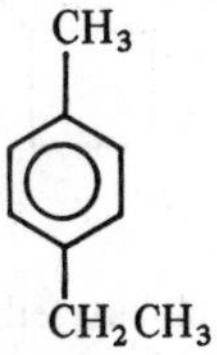

(benzene ring with CH_3 and CH_2CH_3) *p*-ethyltoluene

(benzene ring with CH_3, CH_3, CH_3) 1,2,3-trimethylbenzene

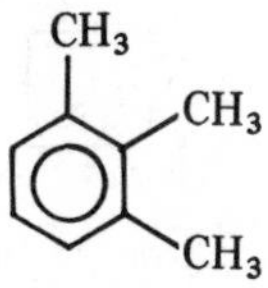

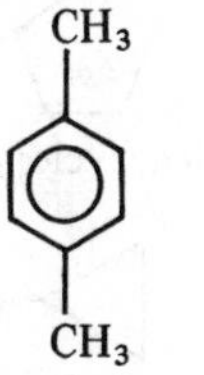

(benzene ring with CH_3, CH_3) 1,2,4-trimethylbenzene

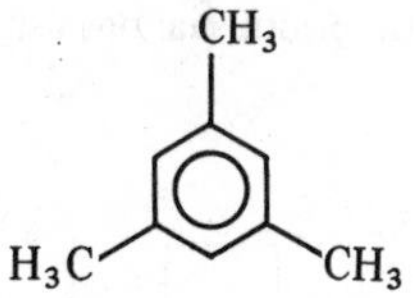

(benzene ring with CH_3, H_3C, CH_3) 1,3,5-trimethylbenzene

B. $H_2C{=}CHCH_2CH_3$ 1-butene

$CH_3CH{=}CHCH_3$ 2-butene

(square) cyclobutane

(triangle with CH_3) methylcyclopropane

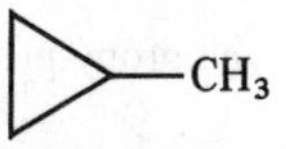

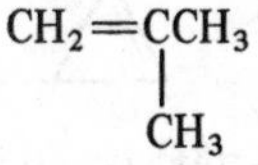

$CH_2{=}C(CH_3)CH_3$ 2-methyl-1-propene

(hexagon with double bond) cyclohexene

(cyclopentene ring with CH_3) 1-methylcyclopentene

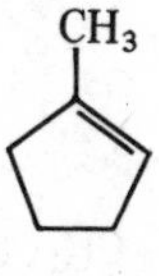

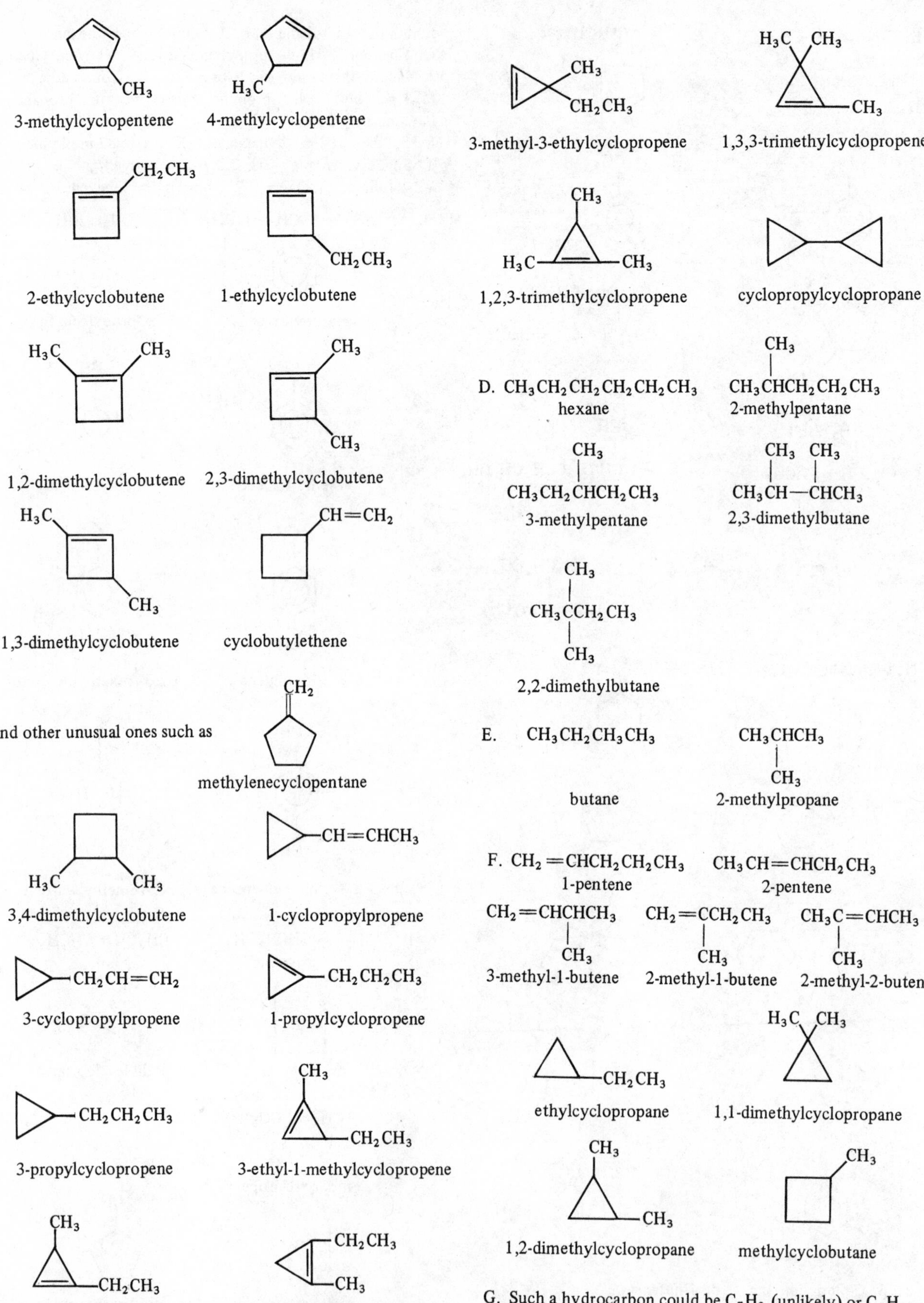

G. Such a hydrocarbon could be C_7H_2 (unlikely) or C_6H_{14}. Thus, the answers are the same as for D.

6. H for highest value; L for lowest value.

A. benzene H, hexane L B. ethyne H, ethane L C. pentane H, 2,2-dimethylpropane L D. 1,4-dimethylbenzene H, benzene L E. hexane H, butane L F. benzene H, cyclohexane L G. butane H, cyclobutane L H. *n*-heptane H, 3,3-dimethylpentane L I. ethene H, methane L J. butyne H, ethyne L K. *n*-hexane H, 2,2-dimethylbutane L L. benzene H, hexane L M. xylene H, benzene L N. *n*-heptane H, 3,3-dimethylpentane L O. hexane H, benzene L P. pentane H, propane L

7. (1) A. none

B. *cis*: H_3C(H)C=C(H)CH_3 (both CH_3 on the same side); *trans*: H_3C(H)C=C(CH_3)H (the CH_3 groups on opposite sides)

C. none

D. *cis*: Cl(H)C=C(H)Cl (both Cl on the same side); *trans*: Cl(H)C=C(Cl)H (the Cl atoms on opposite sides)

E., F., G. none

H. *cis*: cyclobutane ring with H_3C and CH_3 on adjacent carbons, same side; *trans*: cyclobutane ring with CH_3 and CH_3 on adjacent carbons, opposite sides

I. *cis*: CH_3(H)C=C(H)CH_2CH_3; *trans*: CH_3(H)C=C(CH_2CH_3)H

J. *cis*: CH_3CH_2(H)C=C(H)CH_2CH_3; *trans*: CH_3CH_2(H)C=C(CH_2CH_3)H

(2)

A. CH_3CH_2(H_3C)C=C(H)CH_2CH_3

B. H_3C(H)C=C(H)CH_2CH_3

P., Q., V.

```
        CH3        CH3
        |          |
----C---------C----
        |          |
        H          H
```

P., Q., and V. display *cis-trans* isomerism. In the *cis* isomer in each case, two methyl groups are above the plane of the ring (the dashed line above), and two hydrogens are below that plane. In the cyclobutene the two methyl groups considered are bonded to carbons 3 and 4 of the ring. Carbons 1 and 2 are connected by a double bond.

8. A. $BrCH_2CH_2CH_2CH_2CH_2CH_3 \xrightarrow[\text{alcohol}]{\text{KOH}} CH_2{=}CHCH_2CH_2CH_2CH_3 + KBr + H_2O$

B. $HOCH_2CH_2CH_3 \xrightarrow[\text{heat}]{H_2SO_4} CH_2{=}CHCH_3 + H_2O$

C. $HOCH_2CH_3 \xrightarrow[\text{heat}]{H_2SO_4} H_2C{=}CH_2 + H_2O$

D. $ClCH_2CH_3 + 2\,Na \rightarrow CH_3CH_2CH_2CH_3 + 2\,NaCl$

E. $Cl_2CHCH_2CH_3 \xrightarrow[\text{alcohol}]{\text{KOH}} HC{\equiv}CCH_3 + 2\,KCl + 2\,H_2O$

F. $CH_3CHClCH_3 \xrightarrow[\text{alcohol}]{\text{KOH}} CH_2{=}CHCH_3 + KCl + H_2O$

G. $CH_3CH(CH_3){-}CCl(CH_3)CH_2CH_3 \xrightarrow[\text{alcohol}]{\text{KOH}} CH_3C(CH_3){=}C(CH_3)CH_2CH_3 +$ $KCl + 2\,H_2O$ and some $CH_3CH(CH_3){-}C(CH_3){=}CHCH_3$

H. $CH_2{=}CHCH_2CH_3 \xrightarrow{H_2/Pt} CH_3CH_2CH_2CH_3$

I. $CH_3CHClCH_2CH_3 + 2\,Na \rightarrow CH_3CHCH_2CH_3 + 2\,NaCl$ (with $CH_3CHCH_2CH_3$ bonded below) 3,4-dimethylhexane)

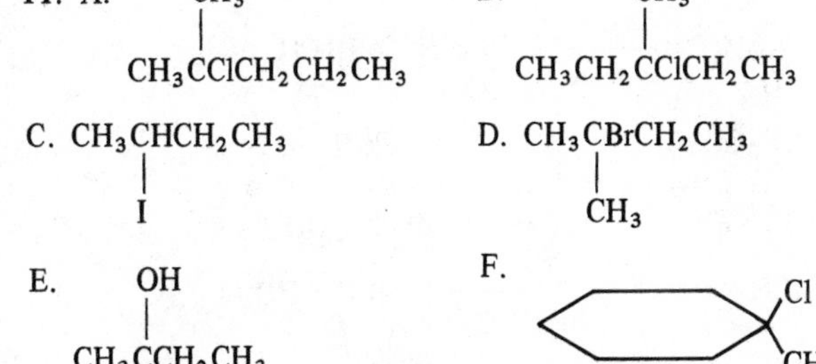

14. (1) A. 2-bromobutane B. 2,2,4-trimethyl-3-pentanol C. 3-hexanone D. pentanoic acid E. 2,2-dimethylpropanal F. methyl *n*-propyl ether G. *n*-pentylamine H. methanoic acid *or* formic acid I. ethyl propanoate J. 2,2-dimethylethanol K. ethyl 2,2-dimethylethyl ether L. 2,2,3-trichloropentane M. 3-pentanone N. *n*-propyl propanoate O. pentanal

(2) A. $CH_3OCH_2CH_3$ B. $CH_3CH_2CH(CH_3)CHO$ C. $CH_3CH_2CH_2CH(CH_3)COOH$ D. $CH_3CH_2CHBrCH_2CH_3$ E. $CH_3CH_2CH_2COOCH_3$ F. $CH_3CH_2CH_2OCH(CH_3)_2$ G. $CH_3CH_2CH(CH_3)CH_2CHO$ H. $CH_3CCl_2CH_3$ I. $CH_3CH(NH_2)CH(CH_3)CH_2CH_3$ J. $CH_3CH_2CHOHCH_2CH_2CH_3$ K. $CH_3CHOHCH$ L. $CH_3CH_2CH(NH_2)CH_2CH_3$ M. $CH_3CH(CH_3)COOH$ N. $CH_2ICH(CH_3)CH_2CH_3$ O. $CH_3COCH_2CH_2CH_3$

16. A. $CH{\equiv}CH + NaNH_2 \rightarrow NH_3 + HC{\equiv}C^- Na^+$
$HC{\equiv}C^- Na^+ + CH_3Br \rightarrow HC{\equiv}CCH_3 + NaBr$

B.
$$CH_3\overset{\overset{O}{\|}}{C}{-}H \xrightarrow[H_2SO_4]{H_2/Ni} CH_3CH_2OH$$
$$CH_3CH_2OH \xrightarrow[heat]{H_2SO_4} CH_2{=}CH_2$$

C. $CH_3CH_2CH_3 \xrightarrow{Cl_2} CH_3CH_2CH_2Cl + CH_3CHClCH_3$
$$\text{chloropropane (either one)} \xrightarrow[alcohol]{KOH} CH_3CH{=}CH_3 + KCl + H_2O$$

D. $CH_3CH_3 + Cl_2 \rightarrow CH_3CH_2Cl + HCl$
$2\,CH_3CH_2Cl + 2\,Na \rightarrow CH_3CH_2CH_2CH_3 + 2\,NaCl$
$CH_3CH_2CH_2CH_3 + Cl_2 \rightarrow CH_3CH_2CH_2CH_2Cl +$
$CH_3CH_2CHClCH_3 + HCl$
$$CH_3CH_2CHClCH_3 \xrightarrow[alcohol]{KOH} CH_3CH_2CH{=}CH_2 +$$
$CH_3CH{=}CHCH_3 + KCl + H_2O$

E. $CH_3CH_2CH_3 + Cl_2 \rightarrow CH_3CHClCH_3 +$
$CH_3CH_2CH_2Cl + HCl$
$$CH_3CHClCH_3 + OH^- \rightarrow CH_3\underset{\underset{OH}{|}}{C}HCH_3 + Cl^-$$
$$CH_3\underset{\underset{OH}{|}}{C}HCH_3 \xrightarrow{K_2Cr_2O_7} CH_3\underset{\underset{O}{\|}}{C}CH_3$$

F. $CH_3CH_3 + Cl_2 \rightarrow CH_3CH_2Cl + HCl$
$CH_3CH_2Cl + OH^- \rightarrow CH_3CH_2OH + Cl^-$
$$CH_3CH_2OH \xrightarrow[conc]{H_2SO_4} CH_3CH_2OCH_2CH_3$$

G. $CH_3CH_2CH_3 + Cl_2 \rightarrow CH_3CHClCH_3 +$
$CH_3CH_2CH_2Cl + HCl$
$CH_3CH_2CH_2Cl + OH^- \rightarrow CH_3CH_2CH_2OH + Cl^-$
$$CH_3CH_2CH_2OH \xrightarrow[200\text{–}300°C]{Cu} CH_3CH_2CHO$$

H. $CH_3CH_3 + Cl_2 \rightarrow CH_3CH_2Cl + HCl$
$CH_3CH_2Cl + OH^- \rightarrow CH_3CH_2OH + Cl^-$
$2\,CH_3CH_2Cl + 2\,Na \rightarrow CH_3CH_2CH_2CH_3 + 2\,NaCl$
$CH_3CH_2CH_2CH_3 + Cl_2 \rightarrow CH_3CH_2CHClCH_3 +$
$CH_3CH_2CH_2CH_2Cl + HCl$
$CH_3CH_2CH_2CH_2Cl + OH^- \rightarrow CH_3CH_2CH_2CH_2OH$
$$CH_3CH_2CH_2CH_2OH \xrightarrow{KMnO_4} CH_3CH_2CH_2COOH$$
$CH_3CH_2CH_2COOH + CH_3CH_2OH \rightarrow$
$$CH_3CH_2CH_2\overset{\overset{O}{\|}}{C}{-}OCH_2CH_3 + H_2O$$

I. $CH_3CH_2CH_2CH_2CH_2CH_3 + Cl_2 \rightarrow$ many isomers, including $ClCH_2CH_2CH_2CH_2CH_2CH_2Cl$

$ClCH_2CH_2CH_2CH_2CH_2CH_2Cl + 2\,Na \rightarrow$ (cyclohexane ring) $+ 2\,NaCl$

Quizzes

A: 1. (d) 2. (b) 3. (c) 4. (a) 5. (d) 6. (c) 7. (a) 8. (c)
B: 1. (e) 2. (a) 3. (b) 4. (a) 5. (d) 6. (a) 7. (c) 8. (c)
C: 1. (a) 2. (d) 3. (d) 4. (e) 5. (e) 6. (c) 7. (d) 8. (b)
D: 1. (c) 2. (a) 3. (c) 4. (e) 5. (a) 6. (b) 7. (c) 8. (b)

Sample Test

1. $CH_3CH_2OCH_2CH_3$ diethyl ether; $CH_3OCH_2CH_2CH_3$ methyl propyl ether; $CH_3O\underset{\underset{CH_3}{|}}{C}HCH_3$ methyl isopropyl ether

2. Propanol contains an —OH group in a three-carbon molecule. This —OH group bonds to water molecules. The forces between like molecules approximate those between unlike molecules. Thus a solution forms. In the case of hexanol, however, the long six-carbon chain forms weak bonds to water and the unlike forces from hexanol to water are much weaker than the "like" forces between water molecules.

3. $CH_2{=}CHCH_2CH_3$
1-butene

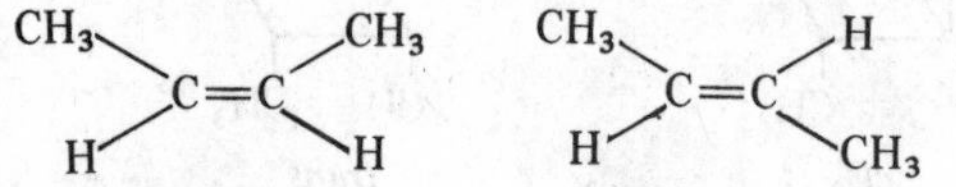

(CH₃ and CH₃ on same side of C=C, H and H on same side) *cis*-2-butene

(CH₃ and H on top, H and CH₃ on bottom of C=C) *trans*-2-butene

4.
$$CH_3\overset{\overset{CH_3}{|}}{C}H\underset{\underset{H}{|}}{C}{=}O \xrightarrow[Pt]{H_2} CH_3\overset{\overset{CH_3}{|}}{C}HCH_2OH \xrightarrow[200°C]{H_2SO_4}$$
2-methylpropanal 2-methylpropanol

$$CH_3\overset{\overset{CH_3}{|}}{C}{=}CH_2 \xrightarrow{HBr} CH_3\overset{\overset{CH_3}{|}}{\underset{\underset{Br}{|}}{C}}CH_3$$
2-methyl-2-propene 2-bromo-2-methylpropane

$$\xrightarrow[(alcohol)]{KOH} \text{2-methyl-2-propene}$$

5. (Newman projections) Left: front carbon CH₃ (top), H, H; back carbon H, H, OH (bottom). Right: front carbon CH₃ (top), H, OH; back carbon H, H, H (bottom).

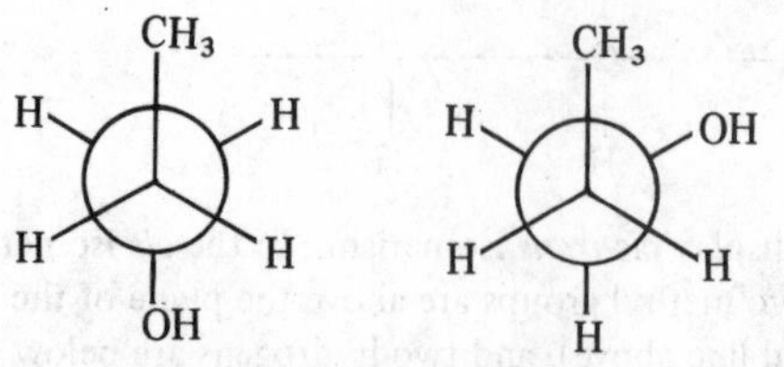

H CH_3 / H —H / H H / OH

HO CH_3 / H —H / H H / H

CHAPTER 25

Drill Problems

2. (1) A. glyceryl oleate B. glyceryl caprate C. glyceryl caprolaurolinolenate D. glyceryl eleostearate

(2) A. CH_2—$OOC(CH_2)_7CH{=}CH(CH_2)_5CH_3$
CH—$OOC(CH_2)_7CH{=}CH(CH_2)_5CH_3$
CH_2—$OOC(CH_2)_7CH{=}CH(CH_2)_5CH_3$

B. $CH_2OOC(CH_2)_{10}CH_3$
$CHOOC(CH_2)_{12}CH_3$
$CH_2OOC(CH_2)_{14}CH_3$

C. $CH_2OOC(CH_2)_{10}CH_3$
$CHOOC(CH_2)_{10}CH_3$
$CH_2OOC(CH_2)_7(CH{=}CHCH_2)_2(CH_2)_3CH_3$

D. $CH_2OOC(CH_2)_7(CH{=}CHCH_2)_3CH_3$
$CHOOC(CH_2)_7(CH{=}CHCH_2)_3CH_3$
$CH_2OOC(CH_2)_7(CH{=}CHCH_2)_3CH_3$

E. $CH_2OOC(CH_2)_7CH{=}CHCH_2CH(OH)(CH_2)_5CH_3$
$CHOOC(CH_2)_7CH{=}CHCH_2CH(OH)(CH_2)_5CH_3$
$CH_2OOC(CH_2)_7CH{=}CHCH_2CH(OH)(CH_2)_5CH_3$

F. $CH_2OOC(CH_2)_7CH{=}CH(CH_2)_7CH_3$
$CHOOC(CH_2)_7CH{=}CH(CH_2)_7CH_3$
$CH_2OOC(CH_2)_{10}CH_3$

3. (1) A. 765.0 g/mol; 0.81 double bond/trigylceride B. 657.4 g/mol; 0.23 double bond/trigylceride C. 876.6 g/mol; 4.56 double bonds/triglyceride D. 881.2 g/mol; 5.14 doble bonds/triglyceride

(2) A. 885.40 g/mol; SV = 190.08; 3 C=C/molecule; IN = 86.00 B. 873.31 g/mol; SV = 192.72; 9 C=C/molecule; IN = 261.56 C. 891.46 g/mol; SV = 188.79; 0 C=C/molecule; IN = 0.00 D. 719.11 g/mol; SV = 234.04; 2 C=C/molecule; IN = 70.59

6. A. CH_3 / H—Cl / $CH_2CH_2CH_3$ and CH_3 / Cl—H / $CH_2CH_2CH_3$

B. $CH{=}CH_2$ / H—Cl / CH_2CH_3 and $CH{=}CH_2$ / Cl—H / CH_2CH_3

C. COOH / H—NH_2 / CH_3 and COOH / H_2N—H / CH_3

D. CH_3 / H—OH / CH_2CH_3 and CH_3 / HO—H / CH_2CH_3

E. CH_3 / H—Cl / CH_2CH_3 and CH_3 / Cl—H / CH_2CH_3

F. CH_2CH_2Cl / H—CH_3 / CH_2CH_3 and CH_2CH_2Cl / H_3C—H / CH_2CH_3

G. CH_2Cl / H—Cl / CH_2CH_3 and CH_2Cl / Cl—H / CH_2CH_3

H., I., J. not optically active

K. CH_2CH_2Br / H—Br / CH_2CH_3 and CH_2CH_2Br / Br—H / CH_2CH_3

L. $CH{=}CHBr$ / H—Cl / CH_3 and $CH{=}CHBr$ / Cl—H / CH_3

M. $CH{=}CH_2$ / H—Cl / H_3C—CH—CH_3 and $CH{=}CH_2$ / Cl—H / H_3C—CH—CH_3

10. (1) A. Lys-Asp-Gly-Ala-Ala-Glu-Ser-Gly B. Ala-Ala-His-Arg-Glu-Lys-Phe-Ile C. Tyr-Cys-Lys-Ala-Arg-Arg-Gly D. Phe-Ala-Glu-Ser-Ala-Gly E. Val-Ala-Lys-Glu-Glu-Phe-Val-Met-Tyr-Cys-Glu-Trp-Met-Gly-Gly-Phe

(2) A. Lysylaspartylglycylalanylalanylglutylserylglycine
B. Alanylalanylhistidylarginylglutyllysylphenylalanylisoleucine
C. Tyrosylcysteyllysylalanylarginylarginylglycine
C. Phenylalanylglutylserylalanylglycine

Quizzes

A. 1. (b) 2. (d) 3. (c) 4. (d) 5. (b) 6. (d)
7. (e) 8. (e) 9. (b)
B. 1. (d) 2. (c) 3. (a) 4. (e) 5. (a) 6. (c)
7. (d) 8. (b) 9. (b)
C. 1. (e) 2. (b) 3. (d) 4. (a) 5. (a) 6. (c)
7. (b) 8. (a) 9. (e) (a pyrimidine)
D: 1. (e) 2. (e) 3. (b) 4. (d) 5. (d) 6. (d)
7. (a) 8. (b) 9. (d)

Sample Test

1. H—C=O / HO—C—H / H—C—OH / CH_2OH (Fischer projection); two furanose ring structures (ring O; H, H / OH, H / H, OH / H, OH and H, OH / OH, H / H, OH / H, OH)

2. Refer to objectives 25-11 and Fig. 25-1.
3. Phe-Val-Asp-Gly-His-Leu-Cys-Gly-Ser-His

CHAPTER 26

Drill Problems

1. A. H_2SO_4, HCl, H_3PO_4, HNO_3 B. CaO, NaOH
C. NH_3, NH_4NO_3, $(NH_4)_2SO_4$, $O{=}C(NH_2)_2$
D. NH_4NO_3, $(NH_4)_2SO_4$ E. $(NH_4)_2SO_4$, H_2SO_4, HCl, $Al_2(SO_4)_3$, Na_2SO_4 F. CaO, Cl_2, Na_2CO_3, $Al_2(SO_4)_3$, $Na_5P_3O_{10}$ G. sodium silicates, HCl, O_2, NaOH, H_3PO_4, H_2SO_4, CaO, N_2 H. NH_3, CO_2, N_2, $CaCl_2$
I. NaOH, Cl_2 H. CH_3OH, C_6H_6, $C_6H_5CH_3$, CH_2ClCH_2Cl K. styrene, vinyl chloride L. carbon black, TiO_2 M. Na_2CO_3, $Na_5P_3O_{10}$, sodium silicates

2. A. $Cu_2S(l) + 3\,O_2(g) \rightarrow 2\,Cu_2O(l) + SO_2(g)$
$2\,Cu_2O(l) + Cu_2S(l) \rightarrow 6\,Cu(l) + SO_2(g)$
B. $2\,ZnS(s) + 3\,O_2 \rightarrow 2\,ZnO(s) + 2\,SO_2(g)$
C. $2\,C(s) + O_2(g) \rightarrow 2\,CO(g)$ *and* $C(s) + CO_2(g) \rightarrow 2\,CO(g)$ *and* $C(s) + H_2O(g) \rightarrow CO(g) + H_2(g)$ (at different temperatures)
D. $MgCl(l) \rightleftharpoons Mg(l) + Cl_2(g)$ E. Al_2O_3 (in bauxite) + $6\,NaOH(aq) \rightarrow 2\,Na_3AlO_3(aq) + 3\,H_2O$
$Na_3AlO_3(aq) + 3\,H_2O \rightarrow Al(OH)_3(s) + 3\,NaOH(aq)$
$2\,Al(OH)_3(s) \rightarrow Al_2O_3(s) + 3\,H_2O$
F. $TiO_2(s) + 2\,Cl_2(g) + 2\,C(s) \rightarrow TiCl_4(g) + 2\,CO(g)$
G. $Mg^{2+}(aq) + 2\,OH^-$ (from $Ca(OH)_2$) $\rightarrow Mg(OH)_2(s)$
H. $3\,C(s) + 4\,Al^{3+} + 6\,O^{2-} \rightarrow 4\,Al(l) + 3\,CO_2(g)$
I. $CaO(s) + SiO_2(l) \rightarrow CaSiO_3(l)$
8. A. $2\,HCO_3^-(aq) \xrightarrow{\Delta} CO_3^{2-}(aq) + H_2O + CO_2(g)$
B. $OH^-(aq) + HCO_3^-(aq) \rightarrow H_2O + CO_3^{2-}(aq)$
C. $M^{2+}(aq) + CO_3^{2-}(aq) \rightarrow MCO_3(s)$ (M^{2+} is a hard water cation: Ca^{2+}, Mg^{2+}, Fe^{2+}) This also is the last step of parts A and B. D. $2\,RCOO^-(aq) + M^2+(aq) \rightarrow M(RCOO)_2$ ($RCOO^-$ is a long-chain fatty acid anion—the anion of soap).
E. Zeolite—Na_2 + $M^{2+}(aq) \rightarrow$ Zeolite—M + $2\,Na^+(aq)$
F. $M^{2+}(aq) + P_3O_{10}{}^{5-}(aq) \rightarrow$ soluble and stable complex

Quizzes

A: 1. (d) 2. (a) 3. (c) 4. (d) 5. (b) 6. (e)
B: 1. (b) 2. (e) 3. (a) 4. (e) ($CaCO_3$) 5. (e) (Mg)
6. (e)
C: 1. (d) 2. (b) 3. (b) 4. (d) 5. (b) 6. (b)
D: 1. (c) 2. (d) 3. (c) 4. (d) 5. (a) 6. (c)

Sample Test

1. Practically all alkali metal and alkaline earth compounds are soluble in water. Hence they dissolve in rainwater and are carried to the sea. Copper, lead, zinc, and iron oxides and sulfides are insoluble, however, and thus remain where they are formed.
2. See objective 26-1: sulfuric acid, phosphoric acid, hydrochloric acid, ammonium sulfate, aluminum sulfate, sodium sulfate.
3. See objective 26-13.

Appendix II

Selected Tables and Figures from Petrucci's *General Chemistry*

TABLE 3-1
Some simple ions

Name	Symbol	Name	Symbol
Positive ions (cations)		copper(II) or cupric	Cu^{2+}
lithium	Li^{+}	zinc	Zn^{2+}
sodium	Na^{+}	silver	Ag^{+}
potassium	K^{+}	mercury(I) or mercurous	Hg_2^{2+}
rubidium	Rb^{+}	mercury(II) or mercuric	Hg^{2+}
cesium	Cs^{+}	lead(II) or plumbous	Pb^{2+}
magnesium	Mg^{2+}		
calcium	Ca^{2+}	**Negative ions (anions)**	
strontium	Sr^{2+}	hydride[c]	H^{-}
barium	Ba^{2+}	nitride	N^{3-}
aluminum	Al^{3+}	oxide	O^{2-}
chromium(II) or chromous	Cr^{2+}	sulfide	S^{2-}
chromium(III) or chromic	Cr^{3+}	fluoride	F^{-}
iron(II) or ferrous	Fe^{2+}	chloride	Cl^{-}
iron(III) or ferric	Fe^{3+}	bromide	Br^{-}
copper(I) or cuprous	Cu^{+}	iodide	I^{-}

[a] The arrangement of ions in this table is similar to the arrangement of the elements in the periodic table (see Figure 3-4).

[b] Unlike other common ions, which are monatomic, the mercurous ion is *diatomic*. The ion is referred to as mercury(I) because two ions with *single* positive charges (Hg^{+}) are joined together to form the species Hg_2^{2+}. Formulas and names thus take the form: Hg_2Cl_2 = mercury(I) chloride and $HgCl_2$ = mercury(II) chloride.

[c] Hydrogen may also appear as a positive ion (H^{+}) in water solutions or other mixtures, but not in pure compounds.

TABLE 3-3
Some common polyatomic ions

Name	Formula	Typical compound
Cation		
ammonium	NH_4^{+}	NH_4Cl
Anions		
acetate	$C_2H_3O_2^{-}$	$NaC_2H_3O_2$
carbonate	CO_3^{2-}	Na_2CO_3
hydrogen carbonate (or bicarbonate)	HCO_3^{-}	$NaHCO_3$
hypochlorite	ClO^{-}	$NaClO$
chlorite	ClO_2^{-}	$NaClO_2$
chlorate	ClO_3^{-}	$NaClO_3$
perchlorate	ClO_4^{-}	$NaClO_4$
chromate	CrO_4^{2-}	Na_2CrO_4
cyanide	CN^{-}	$NaCN$
hydroxide	OH^{-}	$NaOH$
nitrite	NO_2^{-}	$NaNO_2$
nitrate	NO_3^{-}	$NaNO_3$
permanganate	MnO_4^{-}	$NaMnO_4$
phosphate	PO_4^{3-}	Na_3PO_4
hydrogen phosphate	HPO_4^{2-}	Na_2HPO_4
dihydrogen phosphate	$H_2PO_4^{-}$	NaH_2PO_4
sulfite	SO_3^{2-}	Na_2SO_3
sulfate	SO_4^{2-}	Na_2SO_4
hydrogen sulfate (or bisulfate)	HSO_4^{-}	$NaHSO_4$
thiosulfate	$S_2O_3^{2-}$	$Na_2S_2O_3$

TABLE 12-4
Some common types of colloids

Dispersed phase	Dispersion medium	Type	Examples
solid	liquid	sol	clay sols, colloidal gold
liquid	liquid	emulsion	oil in water, milk, mayonnaise
gas	liquid	foam	soap and detergent suds, whipped cream, meringues
solid	gas	aerosol	smoke, dust-laden air
liquid	gas	aerosol	fog, mist (as in aerosol products)
solid	solid	solid sol	ruby glass, certain natural and synthetic gems, blue rock salt, black diamond
liquid	solid	solid emulsion	opal, pearl
gas	solid	solid foam	pumice, lava, volcanic ash

[a] In water purification it is sometimes necessary to precipitate clay particles or other suspended colloidal materials. This is often done by treating the water with an aluminum compound, such as $Al_2(SO_4)_3$. The negatively charged clay particles are neutralized by Al^{3+} ions and coagulate or settle from solution. Clay sols are also suspected of adsorbing organic substances, such as pesticides, and distributing them in the environment.

[b] Smogs are complex materials that are at least partly colloidal. The suspended particles are both solid (smoke) and liquid (fog): smoke + fog = smog. Other constituents of smog are molecular, such as sulfur dioxide, carbon monoxide, nitric oxide, and ozone.

[c] The bluish haze of tobacco smoke and the brilliant sunsets in desert regions are both attributable to the scattering of light by colloidal particles suspended in air.

TABLE 16-1
Solubility product constants at 25°C

Solute	Solubility equilibrium	K_{sp}
aluminum hydroxide	$Al(OH)_3(s) \rightleftharpoons Al^{3+}(aq) + 3\,OH^-(aq)$	1.3×10^{-33}
barium carbonate	$BaCO_3(s) \rightleftharpoons Ba^{2+}(aq) + CO_3^{2-}(aq)$	5.1×10^{-9}
barium hydroxide	$Ba(OH)_2(s) \rightleftharpoons Ba^{2+}(aq) + 2\,OH^-(aq)$	5×10^{-3}
barium sulfate	$BaSO_4(s) \rightleftharpoons Ba^{2+}(aq) + SO_4^{2-}(aq)$	1.1×10^{-10}
bismuth(III) sulfide	$Bi_2S_3(s) \rightleftharpoons 2\,Bi^{3+}(aq) + 3\,S^{2-}(aq)$	1×10^{-97}
cadmium sulfide	$CdS(s) \rightleftharpoons Cd^{2+}(aq) + S^{2-}(aq)$	8.0×10^{-27}
calcium carbonate	$CaCO_3(s) \rightleftharpoons Ca^{2+}(aq) + CO_3^{2-}(aq)$	2.8×10^{-9}
calcium fluoride	$CaF_2(s) \rightleftharpoons Ca^{2+}(aq) + 2\,F^-(aq)$	2.7×10^{-11}
calcium hydroxide	$Ca(OH)_2(s) \rightleftharpoons Ca^{2+}(aq) + 2\,OH^-(aq)$	5.5×10^{-6}
calcium sulfate	$CaSO_4(s) \rightleftharpoons Ca^{2+}(aq) + SO_4^{2-}(aq)$	9.1×10^{-6}
chromium(III) hydroxide	$Cr(OH)_3(s) \rightleftharpoons Cr^{3+}(aq) + 3\,OH^-(aq)$	6.3×10^{-11}
cobalt(II) sulfide	$CoS(s) \rightleftharpoons Co^{2+}(aq) + S^{2-}(aq)$	4.0×10^{-21}
copper(II) sulfide	$CuS(s) \rightleftharpoons Cu^{2+}(aq) + S^{2-}(aq)$	6.3×10^{-36}
iron(II) sulfide	$FeS(s) \rightleftharpoons Fe^{2+}(aq) + S^{2-}(aq)$	6.3×10^{-18}
iron(III) hydroxide	$Fe(OH)_3(s) \rightleftharpoons Fe^{3+}(aq) + 3\,OH^-(aq)$	4×10^{-38}
lead(II) chloride	$PbCl_2(s) \rightleftharpoons Pb^{2+}(aq) + 2\,Cl^-(aq)$	1.6×10^{-5}
lead(II) chromate	$PbCrO_4(s) \rightleftharpoons Pb^{2+}(aq) + CrO_4^{2-}(aq)$	2.8×10^{-13}
lead(II) iodide	$PbI_2(s) \rightleftharpoons Pb^{2+}(aq) + 2\,I^-(aq)$	7.1×10^{-9}
lead(II) sulfate	$PbSO_4(s) \rightleftharpoons Pb^{2+}(aq) + SO_4^{2-}(aq)$	1.6×10^{-8}
lead(II) sulfide	$PbS(s) \rightleftharpoons Pb^{2+}(aq) + S^{2-}(aq)$	8.0×10^{-28}
lithium phosphate	$Li_3PO_4(s) \rightleftharpoons 3\,Li^+(aq) + PO_4^{3-}(aq)$	3.2×10^{-9}
magnesium carbonate	$MgCO_3(s) \rightleftharpoons Mg^{2+}(aq) + CO_3^{2-}(aq)$	3.5×10^{-8}
magnesium fluoride	$MgF_2(s) \rightleftharpoons Mg^{2+}(aq) + 2\,F^-(aq)$	3.7×10^{-8}
magnesium hydroxide	$Mg(OH)_2(s) \rightleftharpoons Mg^{2+}(aq) + 2\,OH^-(aq)$	2×10^{-11}
magnesium phosphate	$Mg_3(PO_4)_2(s) \rightleftharpoons 3\,Mg^{2+}(aq) + 2\,PO_4^{3-}(aq)$	1×10^{-25}
manganese(II) sulfide	$MnS(s) \rightleftharpoons Mn^{2+}(aq) + S^{2-}(aq)$	2.5×10^{-13}
mercury(I) chloride	$Hg_2Cl_2(s) \rightleftharpoons Hg_2^{2+}(aq) + 2\,Cl^-(aq)$	1.3×10^{-18}
mercury(II) sulfide	$HgS(s) \rightleftharpoons Hg^{2+}(aq) + S^{2-}(aq)$	1.6×10^{-52}
nickel(II) sulfide	$NiS(s) \rightleftharpoons Ni^{2+}(aq) + S^{2-}(aq)$	3.2×10^{-19}
silver bromide	$AgBr(s) \rightleftharpoons Ag^+(aq) + Br^-(aq)$	5.0×10^{-13}
silver carbonate	$Ag_2CO_3(s) \rightleftharpoons 2\,Ag^+(aq) + CO_3^{2-}(aq)$	8.1×10^{-12}
silver chloride	$AgCl(s) \rightleftharpoons Ag^+(aq) + Cl^-(aq)$	1.6×10^{-10}
silver chromate	$Ag_2CrO_4(s) \rightleftharpoons 2\,Ag^+(aq) + CrO_4^{2-}(aq)$	2.4×10^{-12}
silver iodide	$AgI(s) \rightleftharpoons Ag^+(aq) + I^-(aq)$	8.5×10^{-17}
silver sulfate	$Ag_2SO_4(s) \rightleftharpoons 2\,Ag^+(aq) + SO_4^{2-}(aq)$	1.4×10^{-5}
silver sulfide	$Ag_2S(s) \rightleftharpoons 2\,Ag^+(aq) + S^{2-}(aq)$	6.3×10^{-50}
strontium carbonate	$SrCO_3(s) \rightleftharpoons Sr^{2+}(aq) + CO_3^{2-}(aq)$	1.1×10^{-10}
strontium sulfate	$SrSO_4(s) \rightleftharpoons Sr^{2+}(aq) + SO_4^{2-}(aq)$	3.2×10^{-7}
tin(II) sulfide	$SnS(s) \rightleftharpoons Sn^{2+}(aq) + S^{2-}(aq)$	1.0×10^{-25}
zinc sulfide	$ZnS(s) \rightleftharpoons Zn^{2+}(aq) + S^{2-}(aq)$	1.0×10^{-21}

TABLE 16-2
Some general rules for the water solubilities of common ionic compounds

1. All common salts of the alkali (IA) metals—including ammonium (NH_4^+) salts—are **soluble.**
2. All nitrates (NO_3^-), chlorates (ClO_3^-), perchlorates (ClO_4^-), and acetates ($C_2H_3O_2^-$) are **soluble.** Silver acetate is only **moderately soluble.**
3. The chlorides (Cl^-), bromides (Br^-), and iodides (I^-) of most metals are **soluble.** The principal *exceptions* are those of Pb^{2+}, Ag^+, and Hg_2^{2+}.
4. All sulfates (SO_4^{2-}) are **soluble** *except* for those of Sr^{2+}, Ba^{2+}, Pb^{2+}, and Hg_2^{2+}. Sulfates of Ca^{2+} and Ag^+ are only **moderately soluble.**
5. All carbonates (CO_3^{2-}), chromates (CrO_4^{2-}), and phosphates (PO_4^{3-}) are **insoluble** *except* for those of the alkali metals (including ammonium).
6. The group IA metal hydroxides (OH^-) are **soluble.** The hydroxides of Ca^{2+}, Sr^{2+}, and Ba^{2+} are **moderately soluble.** The rest of the hydroxides are **insoluble.**
7. The sulfides of all metals are **insoluble** *except* for those of NH_4^+ and the IA and IIA metals.

[a] Generally speaking, if a saturated solution of an ionic solute is greater than about 0.10 *M*, the solute is said to be soluble; if less than about 0.01 *M*, insoluble; and if of an intermediate concentration (i.e., between about 0.01 *M* and 0.10 *M*), moderately soluble.

TABLE 17-2
Ionization constants for some weak acids and weak bases in water at 25°C

	Ionization equilibrium	Ionization constant, *K*
Acid		$K_a =$
acetic	$HC_2H_3O_2 + H_2O \rightleftharpoons H_3O^+ + C_2H_3O_2^-$	1.74×10^{-5}
benzoic	$HC_7H_5O_2 + H_2O \rightleftharpoons H_3O^+ + C_7H_5O_2^-$	6.3×10^{-5}
chlorous	$HClO_2 + H_2O \rightleftharpoons H_3O^+ + ClO_2^-$	1.2×10^{-2}
formic	$HCHO_2 + H_2O \rightleftharpoons H_3O^+ + CHO_2^-$	1.8×10^{-4}
hydrocyanic	$HCN + H_2O \rightleftharpoons H_3O^+ + CN^-$	4.0×10^{-10}
hydrofluoric	$HF + H_2O \rightleftharpoons H_3O^+ + F^-$	6.7×10^{-4}
hypochlorous	$HClO + H_2O \rightleftharpoons H_3O^+ + ClO^-$	2.95×10^{-8}
monochloroacetic	$HC_2H_2ClO_2 + H_2O \rightleftharpoons H_3O^+ + C_2H_2ClO_2^-$	1.35×10^{-3}
nitrous	$HNO_2 + H_2O \rightleftharpoons H_3O^+ + NO_2^-$	5.13×10^{-4}
phenol	$HOC_6H_5 + H_2O \rightleftharpoons H_3O^+ + C_6H_5O^-$	1.6×10^{-10}
Base		$K_b =$
ammonia	$NH_3 + H_2O \rightleftharpoons NH_4^+ + OH^-$	1.74×10^{-5}
aniline	$C_6H_5NH_2 + H_2O \rightleftharpoons C_6H_5NH_3^+ + OH^-$	4.30×10^{-10}
ethylamine	$C_2H_5NH_2 + H_2O \rightleftharpoons C_2H_5NH_3^4 + OH^-$	4.3×10^{-4}
hydroxylamine	$HONH_2 + H_2O \rightleftharpoons HONH_3^+ + OH^-$	9.1×10^{-9}
methylamine	$CH_3NH_2 + H_2O \rightleftharpoons CH_3NH_3^+ + OH^-$	5×10^{-4}
pyridine	$C_5H_5N + H_2O \rightleftharpoons C_5H_5NH^+ + OH^-$	2.0×10^{-9}

TABLE 17-3
Ionization constants of some common polyprotic acids

Acid	Ionization equilibria	Ionization constants, *K*
carbonic	$H_2CO_3 + H_2O \rightleftharpoons H_3O^+ + HCO_3^-$	$K_{a_1} = 4.2 \times 10^{-7}$
	$HCO_3^- + H_2O \rightleftharpoons H_3O^+ + CO_3^{2-}$	$K_{a_2} = 5.6 \times 10^{-11}$
hydrosulfuric	$H_2S + H_2O \rightleftharpoons H_3O^+ + HS^-$	$K_{a_1} = 1.1 \times 10^{-7}$
	$HS^- + H_2O \rightleftharpoons H_3O^+ + S^{2-}$	$K_{a_2} = 1.0 \times 10^{-14}$
oxalic	$H_2C_2O_4 + H_2O \rightleftharpoons H_3O^+ + HC_2O_4^-$	$K_{a_1} = 5.4 \times 10^{-2}$
	$HC_2O_4^- + H_2O \rightleftharpoons H_3O^+ + C_2O_4^{2-}$	$K_{a_2} = 5.4 \times 10^{-5}$
phosphoric	$H_3PO_4 + H_2O \rightleftharpoons H_3O^+ + H_2PO_4^-$	$K_{a_1} = 5.9 \times 10^{-3}$
	$H_2PO_4^- + H_2O \rightleftharpoons H_3O^+ + HPO_4^{2-}$	$K_{a_2} = 6.2 \times 10^{-8}$
	$HPO_4^{2-} + H_2O \rightleftharpoons H_3O^+ + PO_4^{3-}$	$K_{a_3} = 4.8 \times 10^{-13}$
phosphorous	$H_3PO_3 + H_2O \rightleftharpoons H_3O^+ + H_2PO_3^-$	$K_{a_1} = 5.0 \times 10^{-2}$
	$H_2PO_3^- + H_2O \rightleftharpoons H_3O^+ + HPO_3^{2-}$	$K_{a_2} = 2.5 \times 10^{-7}$
sulfurous	$H_2SO_3 + H_2O \rightleftharpoons H_3O^+ + HSO_3^-$	$K_{a_1} = 1.3 \times 10^{-2}$
	$HSO_3^- + H_2O \rightleftharpoons H_3O^+ + SO_3^{2-}$	$K_{a_2} = 6.3 \times 10^{-8}$

TABLE 19-2
Some selected standard electrode potentials

Reduction half-reaction	$E°$, V
Acidic solution	
$F_2(g) + 2\,e^- \longrightarrow 2\,F^-(aq)$	+2.87
$O_3(g) + 2\,H^+(aq) + 2\,e^- \longrightarrow O_2(g) + H_2O$	+2.07
$S_2O_8^{2-}(aq) + 2\,e^- \longrightarrow 2\,SO_4^{2-}(aq)$	+2.01
$H_2O_2(aq) + 2\,H^+(aq) + 2\,e^- \longrightarrow 2\,H_2O$	+1.77
$MnO_4^-(aq) + 8\,H^+(aq) + 5\,e^- \longrightarrow Mn^{2+}(aq) + 4\,H_2O$	+1.51
$PbO_2(s) + 4\,H^+(aq) + 2\,e^- \longrightarrow Pb^{2+}(aq) + 2\,H_2O$	+1.455
$Cl_2(g) + 2\,e^- \longrightarrow 2\,Cl^-(aq)$	+1.360
$Cr_2O_7^{2-}(aq) + 14\,H^+(aq) + 6\,e^- \longrightarrow 2\,Cr^{3+}(aq) + 7\,H_2O$	+1.33
$MnO_2(s) + 4\,H^+(aq) + 2\,e^- \longrightarrow Mn^{2+}(aq) + 2\,H_2O$	+1.23
$O_2(g) + 4\,H^+(aq) + 4\,e^- \longrightarrow 2\,H_2O$	+1.229
$2\,IO_3^-(aq) + 12\,H^+(aq) + 10\,e^- \longrightarrow I_2(s) + 6\,H_2O$	+1.195
$Br_2(l) + 2\,e^- \longrightarrow 2\,Br^-(aq)$	+1.065
$NO_3^-(aq) + 4\,H^+(aq) + 3\,e^- \longrightarrow NO(g) + 2\,H_2O$	+0.96
$Ag^+(aq) + e^- \longrightarrow Ag(s)$	+0.799
$Fe^{3+}(aq) + e^- \longrightarrow Fe^{2+}(aq)$	+0.771
$O_2(g) + 2\,H^+(aq) + 2\,e^- \longrightarrow H_2O_2(aq)$	+0.682
$I_2(s) + 2\,e^- \longrightarrow 2\,I^-(aq)$	+0.54
$Cu^+(aq) + e^- \longrightarrow Cu(s)$	+0.52
$H_2SO_3(aq) + 4\,H^+(aq) + 4\,e^- \longrightarrow S(s) + 3\,H_2O$	+0.45
$Cu^{2+}(aq) + 2\,e^- \longrightarrow Cu(s)$	+0.337
$SO_4^{2-}(aq) + 4\,H^+(aq) + 2\,e^- \longrightarrow H_2SO_3(aq) + H_2O$	+0.17
$Sn^{4+}(aq) + 2\,e^- \longrightarrow Sn^{2+}(aq)$	+0.15
$S(s) + 2\,H^+(aq) + 2\,e^- \longrightarrow H_2S(g)$	+0.141
$2\,H^+(aq) + 2\,e^- \longrightarrow H_2(g)$	0.0000
$Pb^{2+}(aq) + 2\,e^- \longrightarrow Pb(s)$	−0.126
$Sn^{2+}(aq) + 2\,e^- \longrightarrow Sn(s)$	−0.136
$Fe^{2+}(aq) + 2\,e^- \longrightarrow Fe(s)$	−0.440
$Zn^{2+}(aq) + 2\,e^- \longrightarrow Zn(s)$	−0.763
$Al^{3+}(aq) + 3\,e^- \longrightarrow Al(s)$	−1.66
$Mg^{2+}(aq) + 2\,e^- \longrightarrow Mg(s)$	−2.37
$Na^+(aq) + e^- \longrightarrow Na(s)$	−2.714
$Ca^{2+}(aq) + 2\,e^- \longrightarrow Ca(s)$	−2.89
$K^+(aq) + e^- \longrightarrow K(s)$	−2.925
$Li^+(aq) + e^- \longrightarrow Li(s)$	−3.045
Basic solution	
$O_3(g) + H_2O + 2\,e^- \longrightarrow O_2(g) + 2\,OH^-$	+1.24
$ClO^-(aq) + H_2O + 2\,e^- \longrightarrow Cl^- + 2\,OH^-$	+0.89
$O_2(g) + 2\,H_2O + 4\,e^- \longrightarrow 4\,OH^-(aq)$	+0.401
$CrO_4^{2-}(aq) + 4\,H_2O + 3\,e^- \longrightarrow Cr(OH)_3(s) + 5\,OH^-$	−0.13
$S(s) + 2\,e^- \longrightarrow S^{2-}(aq)$	−0.48
$2\,H_2O + 2\,e^- \longrightarrow H_2(g) + 2\,OH^-(aq)$	−0.828
$SO_4^{2-}(aq) + H_2O + 2\,e^- \longrightarrow SO_3^{2-}(aq) + 2\,OH^-(aq)$	−0.93

TABLE 20-4
Selected reactions of the halogen elements

Reaction with	Reaction equation	Remarks
alkali metals	$2\,M + X_2 \longrightarrow 2\,MX$	
alkaline earth metals	$M + X_2 \longrightarrow MX_2$	
other metals (e.g., Fe)	$2\,Fe + 3\,X_2 \longrightarrow 2\,FeX_3$	
hydrogen	$H_2 + X_2 \longrightarrow 2\,HX$	extremely rapid with F_2; rapid with Cl_2 when exposed to light; slow with Br_2 and I_2
sulfur	$4\,X_2 + S_8 \longrightarrow 4\,S_2X_2$	with Cl_2 and Br_2; F_2 forms SF_6
phosphorus	$6\,X_2 + P_4 \longrightarrow 4\,PX_3$	PX_5 also forms (except with I_2)
other halogens	$I_2 + Cl_2 \longrightarrow 2\,ICl$	other known interhalogen compounds include ClF, ClF_3, BrCl, BrF, BrF_3, BrF_5, IBr, ICl_3, IF_5, and IF_7
water	(1) $2\,X_2 + 2\,H_2O \longrightarrow 4\,H^+ + 4\,X^- + O_2(g)$	reverse reaction with I_2
	(2) $X_2 + H_2O \longrightarrow H^+ + X^- + XOH$	with F_2, reaction (1) only
hydrogen sulfide	$8\,X_2 + 8\,H_2S \longrightarrow 16\,H^+ + 16\,X^- + S_8$	
ammonia	$3\,X_2 + 8\,NH_3 \longrightarrow 6\,NH_4X + N_2$	I_2 forms $NI_3 \cdot NH_3$

TABLE 20-7
Solubilities of some metal sulfides

Soluble in				
H_2O	0.3 M HCl (K_{sp})	3 M HNO_3 (K_{sp})	Aqua regia (K_{sp})	KOH(aq) or $(NH_4)_2S_n$(aq) (K_{sp})
K_2S	MnS (2.5×10^{-13})	CdS (8.0×10^{-27})	HgS (1.6×10^{-52})	SnS (1.0×10^{-25})
Na_2S	FeS (6.3×10^{-18})	PbS (8×10^{-28})		As_2S_3
CaS	CoS (4.0×10^{-21})	CuS (6.3×10^{-36})		Sb_2S_3
	ZnS (1.0×10^{-21})			

TABLE 21-5
Some qualitative tests for iron(II) and iron(III)

Reagent	Iron(II)	Iron(III)
NaOH(aq)	green precipitate	red-brown precipitate
$K_4[Fe(CN)_6]$	white precipitate, turning blue rapidly	Prussian blue precipitate
$K_3[Fe(CN)_6]$	Turnbull's blue precipitate	red-brown coloration (no precipitate)
KSCN	no coloration	deep-red coloration

TABLE 25-2
Some common fatty acids

Common name	IUPAC name	Formula
	Saturated acids	
lauric acid	dodecanoic acid	$C_{11}H_{23}CO_2H$
myristic acid	tetradecanoic acid	$C_{13}H_{27}CO_2H$
palmitic acid	hexadecanoic acid	$C_{15}H_{31}CO_2H$
stearic acid	octadecanoic acid	$C_{17}H_{35}CO_2H$
	Unsaturated acids	
oleic acid	9-octadecenoic acid	$C_{17}H_{33}CO_2H$
linoleic acid	9,12-octadecadienoic acid	$C_{17}H_{31}CO_2H$
linolenic acid	9,12,15-octadecatrienoic acid	$C_{17}H_{29}CO_2H$
eleostearic acid	9,11,13-octadecatrienoic acid	$C_{17}H_{29}CO_2H$

TABLE 22-5
Formation constants for some complex ions

Complex ion	Equilibrium reaction	K_f
$[AlF_6]^{3-}$	$Al^{3+} + 6\,F^- \rightleftharpoons [AlF_6]^{3-}$	6.7×10^{19}
$[Cd(CN)_4]^{2-}$	$Cd^{2+} + 4\,CN^- \rightleftharpoons [Cd(CN)_4]^{2-}$	7.1×10^{18}
$[Co(NH_3)_6]^{3+}$	$Co^{3+} + 6\,NH_3 \rightleftharpoons [Co(NH_3)_6]^{3+}$	4.5×10^{33}
$[Cu(CN)_3]^{2-}$	$Cu^+ + 3\,CN^- \rightleftharpoons [Cu(CN)_3]^{2-}$	2×10^{27}
$[Cu(NH_3)_4]^{2+}$	$Cu^{2+} + 4\,NH_3 \rightleftharpoons [Cu(NH_3)_4]^{2+}$	2.1×10^{14}
$[Fe(CN)_6]^{4-}$	$Fe^{2+} + 6\,CN^- \rightleftharpoons [Fe(CN)_6]^{4-}$	1×10^{37}
$[Fe(CN)_6]^{3-}$	$Fe^{3+} + 6\,CN^- \rightleftharpoons [Fe(CN)_6]^{3-}$	1×10^{42}
$[PbCl_3]^-$	$Pb^{2+} + 3\,Cl^- \rightleftharpoons [PbCl_3]^-$	2.4×10^{1}
$[HgCl_4]^{2-}$	$Hg^{2+} + 4\,Cl^- \rightleftharpoons [HgCl_4]^{2-}$	1.2×10^{15}
$[HgI_4]^{2-}$	$Hg^{2+} + 4\,I^- \rightleftharpoons [HgI_4]^{2-}$	1.9×10^{30}
$[Ni(CN)_4]^{2-}$	$Ni^{2+} + 4\,CN^- \rightleftharpoons [Ni(CN)_4]^{2-}$	1×10^{22}
$[Ag(NH_3)_2]^+$	$Ag^+ + 2\,NH_3 \rightleftharpoons [Ag(NH_3)_2]^+$	1.6×10^{7}
$[Ag(CN)_2]^-$	$Ag^+ + 2\,CN^- \rightleftharpoons [Ag(CN)_2]^-$	5.6×10^{18}
$[Ag(S_2O_3)_2]^{3-}$	$Ag^+ + 2\,S_2O_3{}^{2-} \rightleftharpoons [Ag(S_2O_3)_2]^{3-}$	1.7×10^{13}
$[Zn(NH_3)_4]^{2+}$	$Zn^{2+} + 4\,NH_3 \rightleftharpoons [Zn(NH_3)_4]^{2+}$	2.9×10^{9}
$[Zn(CN)_4]^{2-}$	$Zn^{2+} + 4\,CN^- \rightleftharpoons [Zn(CN)_4]^{2-}$	1×10^{18}

TABLE 25-4
Some common amino acids

Name	Symbol	Formula	p*I*
		Neutral amino acids	
glycine	Gly	$HCH(NH_2)CO_2H$	5.97
alanine	Ala	$CH_3CH(NH_2)CO_2H$	6.00
valine	Val	$(CH_3)_2CHCH(NH_2)CO_2H$	5.96
leucine	Leu	$(CH_3)_2CHCH_2CH(NH_2)CO_2H$	6.02
isoleucine	Ileu or Ile	$CH_3CH_2CH(CH_3)CH(NH_2)CO_2H$	5.98
serine	Ser	$HOCH_2CH(NH_2)CO_2H$	5.68
threonine	Thr	$CH_3CHOHCH(NH_2)CO_2H$	5.6
phenylalanine	Phe	$C_6H_5CH_2CH(NH_2)CO_2H$	5.48
methionine	Met	$CH_3SCH_2CH_2CH(NH_2)CO_2H$	5.74
cysteine	Cys	$HSCH_2CH(NH_2)CO_2H$	5.05
cystine	$(Cys)_2$	$-[SCH_2CH(NH_2)CO_2H]_2$	4.8
tyrosine	Tyr	$4\text{-}HOC_6H_4CH_2CH(NH_2)CO_2H$	5.66
tryptophan	Trp	(indole ring, N–H) $-CH_2CH(NH_2)CO_2H$	5.89
proline	Pro	(pyrrolidine ring, N–H) $-CO_2H$	6.30
hydroxyproline	Hyp	HO (pyrrolidine ring, N–H) $-CO_2H$	
		Acidic amino acids	
aspartic acid	Asp	$HO_2CCH_2CH(NH_2)CO_2H$	2.77
glutamic acid	Glu	$HO_2CCH_2CH_2CH(NH_2)CO_2H$	3.22
		Basic amino acids	
lysine[a]	Lys	$H_2N(CH_2)_4CH(NH_2)CO_2H$	9.74
arginine	Arg	$H_2NCNHNH(CH_2)_3CH(NH_2)CO_2H$	10.76
histidine	His	(imidazole ring, N, N–H) $-CH_2CH(NH_2)CO_2H$	

TABLE 26-11
Some synthetic carbon-chain polymers

Name	Monomer(s)	Polymer	Uses
Elastomers			
neoprene [polychloroprene]	$H_2C{=}CH{-}C(Cl){=}CH_2$ (chloroprene)	$\left(\!-CH_2{-}CH{=}C(Cl){-}CH_2-\!\right)_x$	wire and cable insulators industrial hoses and belts, shoe soles and heels, gloves
GRS, SBR, Buna S [poly(butadiene-co-styrene)]	$H_2C{=}CHCH{=}CH_2$ (1,3-butadiene) + $C_6H_5CH{=}CH_2$ (styrene)	$\left(\!-CH_2CH{=}CHCH_2CH_2{-}CH(C_6H_5)-\!\right)_x$	tires, hoses, flooring, shoe soles and heels
Fibers			
Dacron, Terylene, Fortrel	$HOCH_2CH_2OH$ (ethylene glycol) + $HO_2C{-}C_6H_4{-}CO_2H$ (terephthalic acid)	$\left(\!-C({=}O){-}C_6H_4{-}C({=}O){-}O{-}CH_2CH_2{-}O-\!\right)_x$	fabrics, boat sails, tire cord
nylon 66	$HO_2C(CH_2)_4CO_2H$ (adipic acid) + $H_2N(CH_2)_6NH_2$ (1,6-hexanediamine)	$\left(\!-C({=}O){-}(CH_2)_4{-}C({=}O){-}NH{-}(CH_2)_6{-}NH-\!\right)_x$	fabrics, hosiery, rope
Plastics			
polyethylene	$H_2C{=}CH_2$ (ethylene)	$\left(\!-CH_2{-}CH_2-\!\right)_x$	household products, bottles, tubing
PVC, "vinyl" [poly(vinyl chloride)]	$H_2C{=}CHCl$ (vinyl chloride)	$\left(\!-CH_2{-}CH(Cl)-\!\right)_x$	bottles, records, floor tile, food wrap
Teflon [poly(tetrafluoroethylene)]	$F_2C{=}CF_2$ (tetrafluoroethylene)	$\left(\!-CF_2{-}CF_2-\!\right)_x$	insulation, gaskets, nonstick surfaces (ovenwear, frying pans)
Lucite, Plexiglas [poly(methyl methacrylate)]	$H_2C{=}C(CH_3){-}CO_2CH_3$ (methyl methacrylate)	$\left(\!-CH_2{-}C(CH_3)(CO_2CH_3)-\!\right)_x$	signs, display cabinets, combs, dentures, auto tail- and signal-light lenses, reflectors

TABLE 26-12
The top 50 chemicals produced in the United States (1979)

Rank	Millions of tons	Chemical	Formula	Method of manufacture	Principal uses	Page reference
1	42.0	sulfuric acid	H_2SO_4	catalytic oxidation of SO_2 to SO_3, followed by reaction with H_2O	manufacture of fertilizers, chemicals; oil refining	686
2	19.4	lime	CaO	thermal decomposition of $CaCO_3$	steelmaking; manufacture of chemicals; water treatment	684
3	18.1	ammonia	NH_3	Haber process from N_2 and H_2; coal tar by-product	manufacture of fertilizers, nitric acid, ammonium compounds, cleaning agents; refrigerant	362
4	17.7	oxygen	O_2	distillation of liquid air	steelmaking; welding; medical uses	662
5	15.0	nitrogen	N_2	distillation of liquid air	blanketing atmospheres; low temperatures	662
6	14.6	ethylene	$CH_2{=}CH_2$	catalytic cracking of petroleum	manufacture of polyethylene, ethylene oxide and glycol, vinyl chloride, styrene	694
7	12.4	sodium hydroxide	$NaOH$	electrolysis of NaCl(aq)	manufacture of chemicals, pulp and paper, aluminum, textiles, soaps and detergents	683
8	12.1	chlorine	Cl_2	electrolysis of NaCl(aq)	manufacture of chemicals, pulp and paper, plastics (PVC), solvents; water treatment	504
9	10.1	phosphoric acid	H_3PO_4	reaction of phosphate rock with H_2SO_4; P_4O_{10}, with water	manufacture of fertilizers and detergents	520
10	8.6	nitric acid	HNO_3	Ostwald process: oxidation of NH_3, followed by reaction with water	manufacture of explosives, fertilizers, plastics, dyes, and lacquers	517
11	8.3	sodium carbonate	Na_2CO_3	Solvay process from NaCl, NH_3, $CaCO_3$; natural ore deposits	manufacture of glass, chemicals, pulp and paper, detergents	684
12	7.8	ammonium nitrate	NH_4NO_3	reaction of NH_3 and HNO_3	manufacture of fertilizers, explosives	517
13	7.2	propylene	$CH_3CH{=}CH_2$	catalytic cracking of petroleum	manufacture of plastics, fibers, solvents	607
14	6.9	urea	$CO(NH_2)_2$	heating CO_2 and NH_3 under pressure	manufacture of fertilizers, plastics, pharmaceuticals	596
15	6.4	benzene		catalytic cracking and reforming of petroleum	manufacture of polystyrene, nylon, other polymers	691
16	5.9	toluene	CH_3	catalytic cracking and reforming of petroleum	manufacture of benzene and other organic chemicals	609
17	5.9	ethylene dichloride	CH_2ClCH_2Cl	chlorination of ethylene	manufacture of vinyl chloride	607
18	4.3	ethylbenzene	C_2H_5	catalytic cracking and reforming of petroleum.	manufacture of styrene	691
19	3.8	vinyl chloride	$CH_2{=}CHCl$	elimination of HCl from CH_2ClCH_2Cl	manufacture of vinyl plastics	694
20	3.7	styrene	$CH{=}CH_2$	dehydrogenation of ethylbenzene	manufacture of styrene plastics, synthetic rubber	693

21 methanol
22 terephthalic acid
23 carbon dioxide
24 xylene
25 formaldehyde
26 hydrochloric acid
27 ethylene oxide
28 ethylene glycol
29 *p*-xylene
30 cumene
31 ammonium sulfate
32 butadiene (1,3-)
33 acetic acid
34 carbon black
35 phenol
36 acetone
37 aluminum sulfate
38 cyclohexane
39 sodium sulfate
40 propylene oxide
41 calcium chloride
42 acrylonitrile
43 vinyl acetate
44 isopropyl alcohol
45 adipic acid
46 sodium silicate
47 sodium tripolyphosphate
48 acetic anhydride
49 titanium dioxide
50 ethanol

FIGURE 7-3
The electromagnetic spectrum.

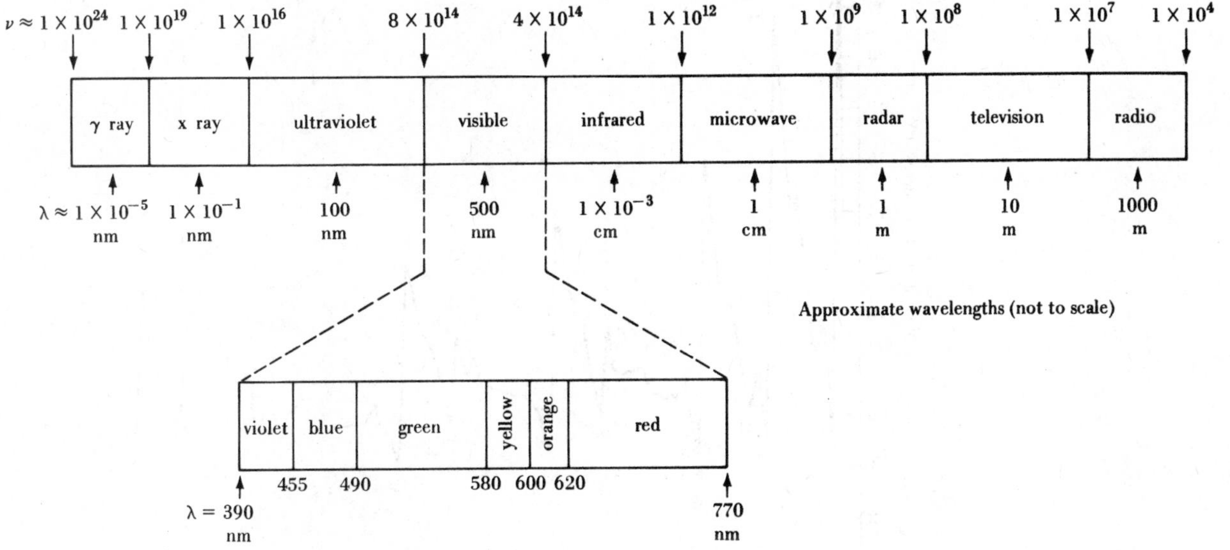

FIGURE 7-13
Energy-level diagram for the hydrogen atom.

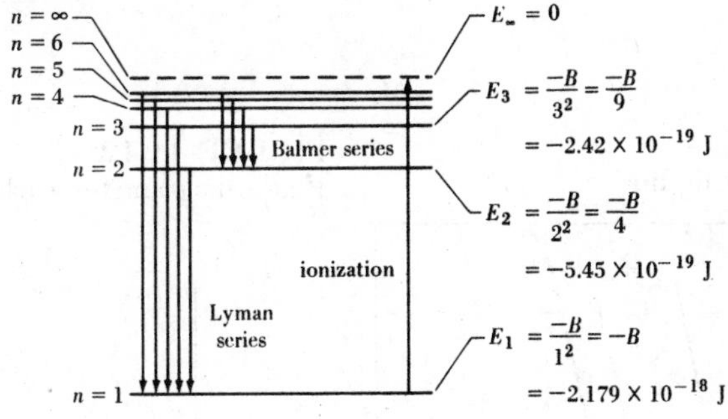

FIGURE 8-1
An illustration of the periodic law—atomic volume as a function of atomic number.

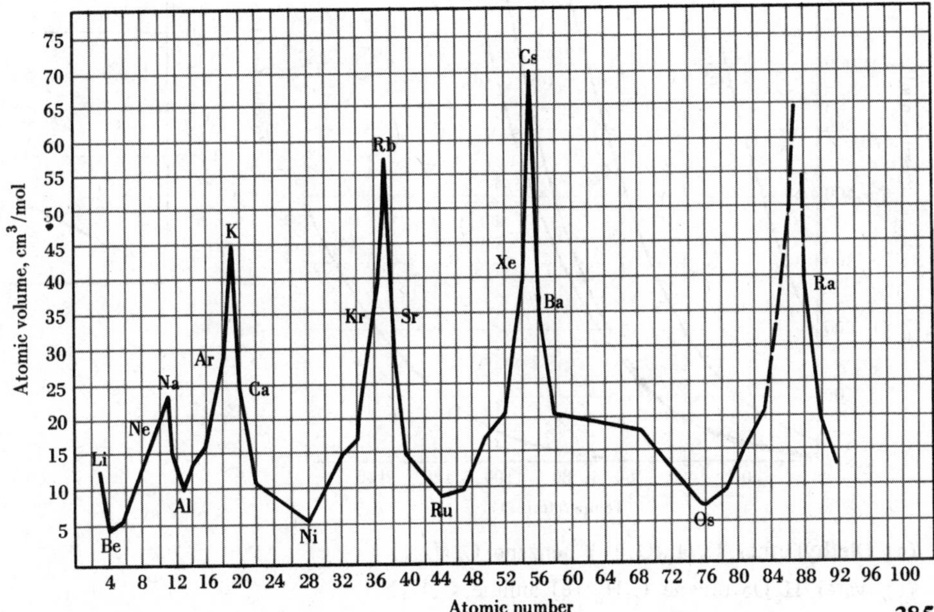

FIGURE 8-8
First ionization energies as a function of atomic number.

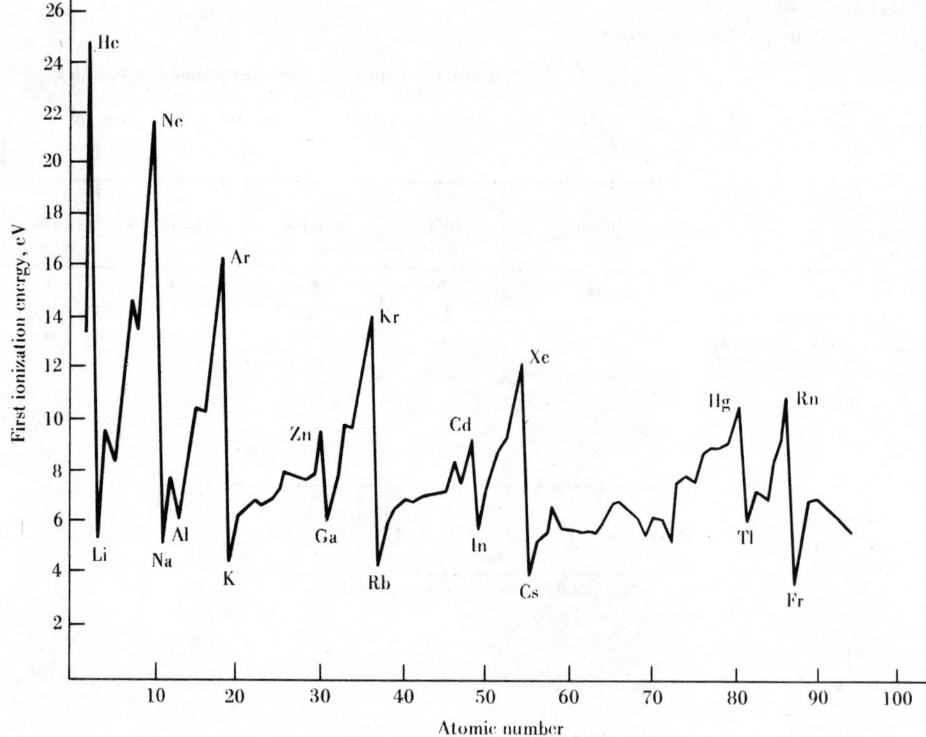

FIGURE 11-6
Vapor pressure curves of several liquids.

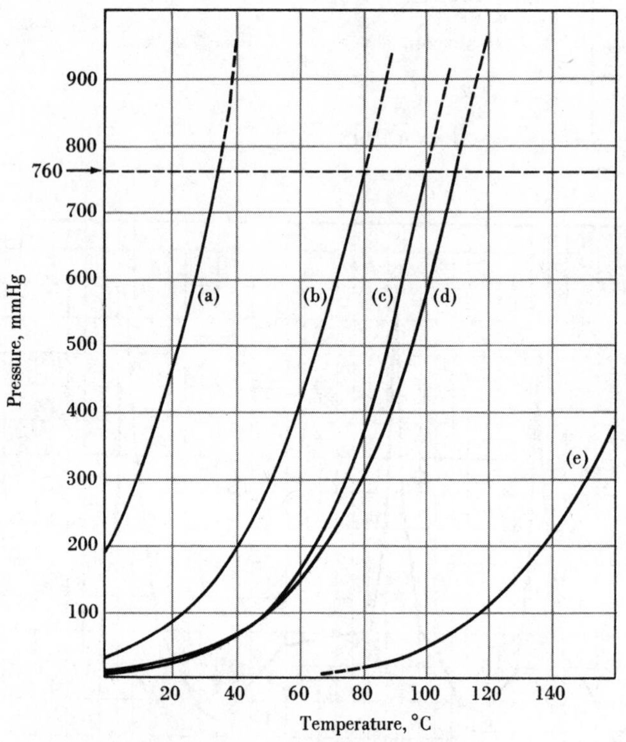

(a) Diethyl ether, $C_4H_{10}O$; (b) benzene, C_6H_6;
(c) water, H_2O; toluene, C_7H_8; (e) aniline, C_6H_7N.

FIGURE 11-12
Phase diagram for carbon dioxide.

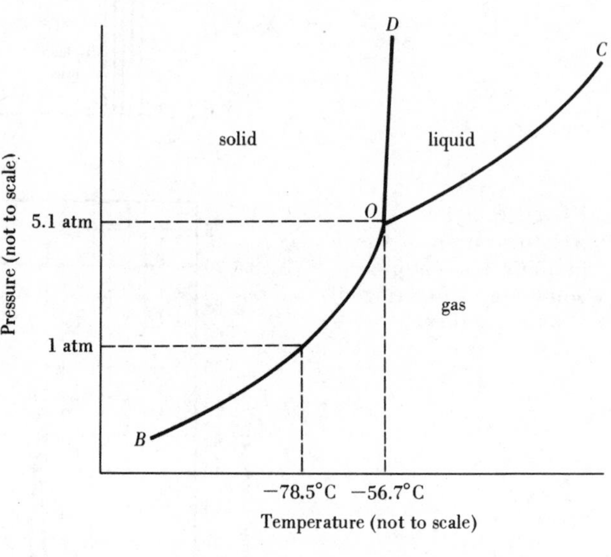

FIGURE 11-13
Phase diagram for water.

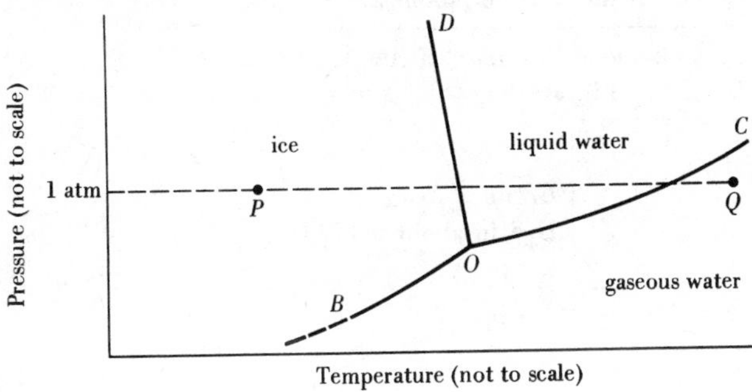

FIGURE 11-30
Determination of crystal structure by x-ray diffraction.

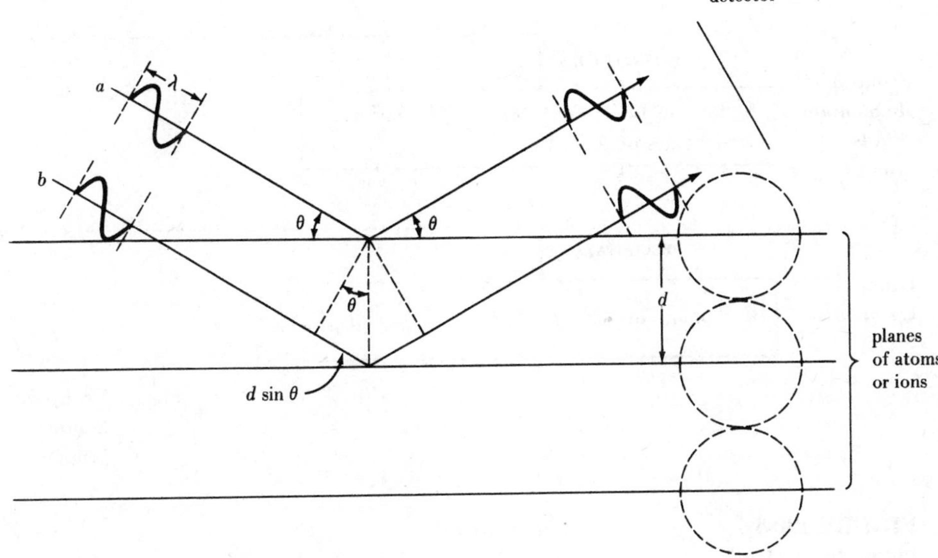

FIGURE 12-9
Vapor pressure lowering by a nonvolatile solute.

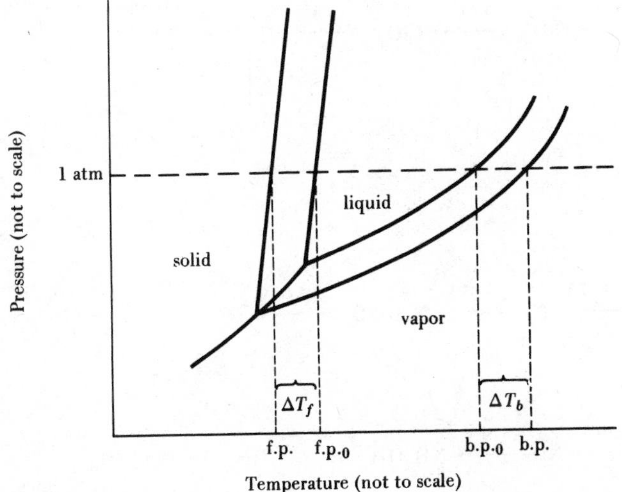

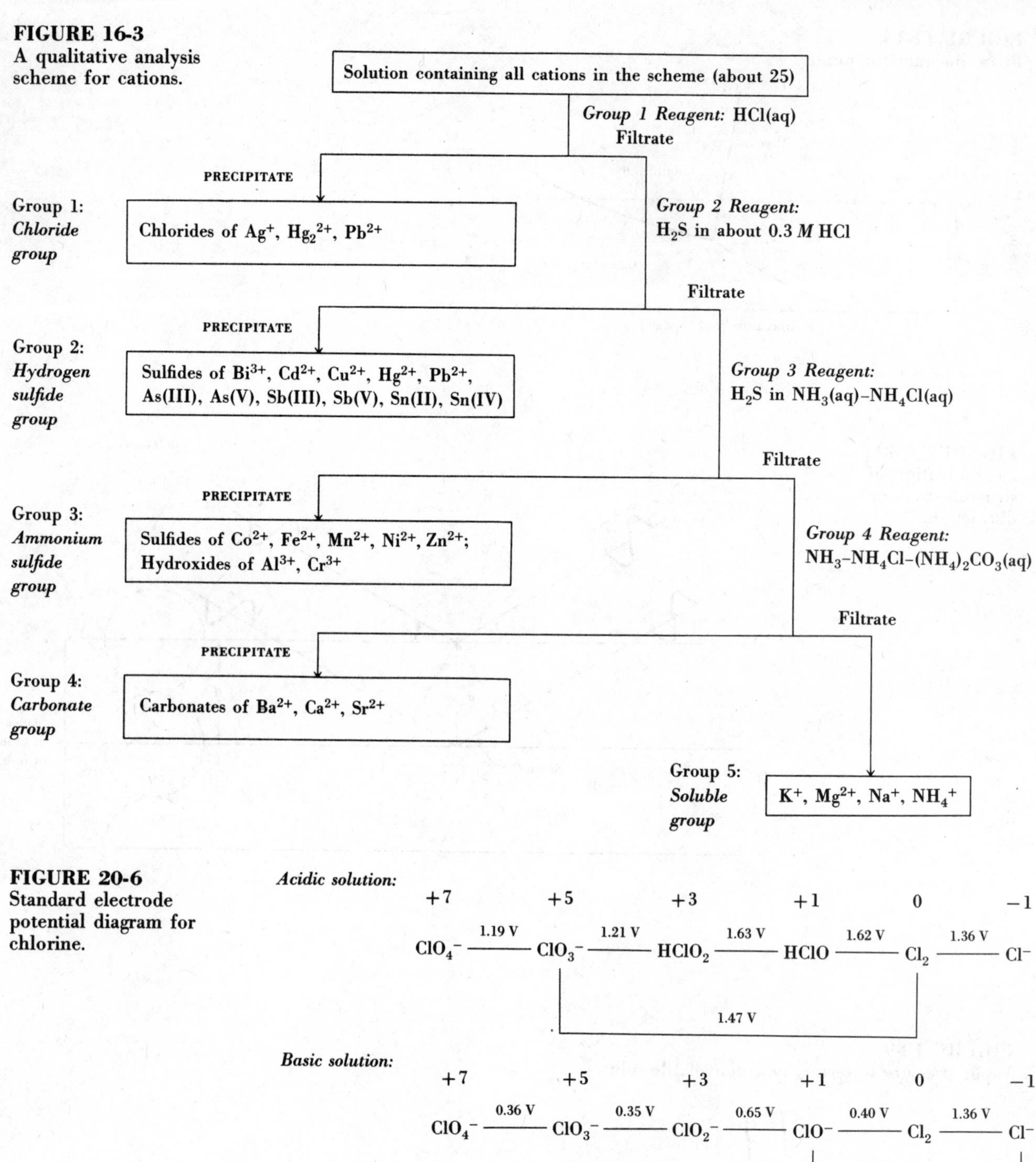

FIGURE 16-3
A qualitative analysis scheme for cations.

FIGURE 20-6
Standard electrode potential diagram for chlorine.

FIGURE 20-12
Electrode potential diagram for nitrogen.

Acidic solution:

$$NO_3^- \xrightarrow{+0.81\text{ V}} NO_2 \xrightarrow{+1.07\text{ V}} HNO_2 \xrightarrow{+0.99\text{ V}} NO \xrightarrow{+1.59\text{ V}} N_2O \xrightarrow{+1.77\text{ V}} N_2 \xrightarrow{-1.87\text{ V}} NH_3OH^+ \xrightarrow{+1.46\text{ V}} N_2H_5^+ \xrightarrow{+1.24\text{ V}} NH_4^+$$

Basic solution:

$$NO_3^- \xrightarrow{-0.85\text{ V}} NO_2 \xrightarrow{+0.88\text{ V}} NO_2^- \xrightarrow{-0.46\text{ V}} NO \xrightarrow{+0.76\text{ V}} N_2O \xrightarrow{+0.94\text{ V}} N_2 \xrightarrow{-3.04\text{ V}} NH_2OH \xrightarrow{+0.74\text{ V}} N_2H_4 \xrightarrow{+0.10\text{ V}} NH_3$$

FIGURE 20-15
Silicate anions.

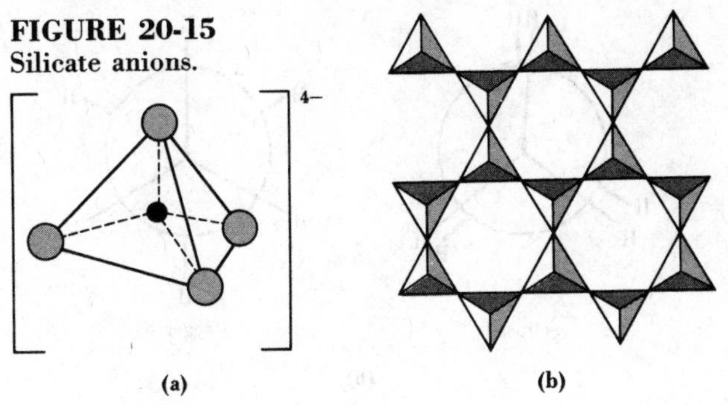

(a) The simple ion, SiO_4^{4-}. (b) A portion of the anion structure of mica.

FIGURE 21-5
Qualitative analysis of the ammonium sulfide group.

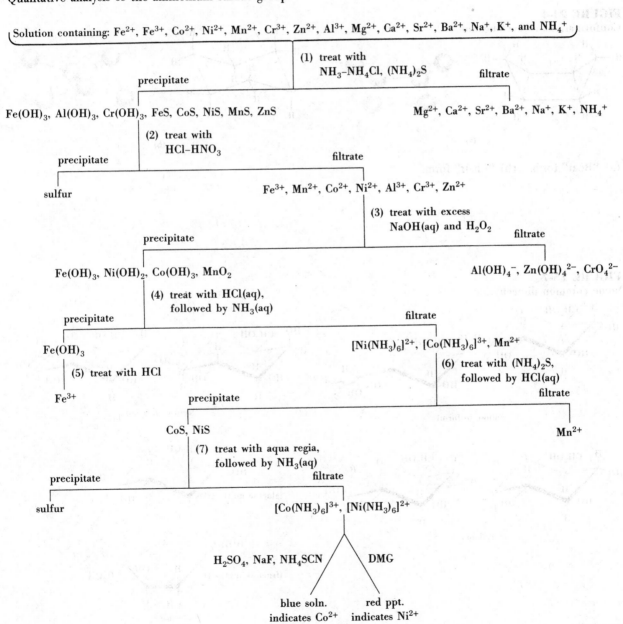

Solution containing: Fe^{2+}, Fe^{3+}, Co^{2+}, Ni^{2+}, Mn^{2+}, Cr^{3+}, Zn^{2+}, Al^{3+}, Mg^{2+}, Ca^{2+}, Sr^{2+}, Ba^{2+}, Na^+, K^+, and NH_4^+

(1) treat with NH_3–NH_4Cl, $(NH_4)_2S$

- precipitate: $Fe(OH)_3$, $Al(OH)_3$, $Cr(OH)_3$, FeS, CoS, NiS, MnS, ZnS
- filtrate: Mg^{2+}, Ca^{2+}, Sr^{2+}, Ba^{2+}, Na^+, K^+, NH_4^+

(2) treat with HCl–HNO_3

- precipitate: sulfur
- filtrate: Fe^{3+}, Mn^{2+}, Co^{2+}, Ni^{2+}, Al^{3+}, Cr^{3+}, Zn^{2+}

(3) treat with excess NaOH(aq) and H_2O_2

- precipitate: $Fe(OH)_3$, $Ni(OH)_2$, $Co(OH)_3$, MnO_2
- filtrate: $Al(OH)_4^-$, $Zn(OH)_4^{2-}$, CrO_4^{2-}

(4) treat with HCl(aq), followed by NH_3(aq)

- precipitate: $Fe(OH)_3$
- filtrate: $[Ni(NH_3)_6]^{2+}$, $[Co(NH_3)_6]^{3+}$, Mn^{2+}

(5) treat with HCl

- Fe^{3+}

(6) treat with $(NH_4)_2S$, followed by HCl(aq)

- precipitate: CoS, NiS
- filtrate: Mn^{2+}

(7) treat with aqua regia, followed by NH_3(aq)

- precipitate: sulfur
- filtrate: $[Co(NH_3)_6]^{3+}$, $[Ni(NH_3)_6]^{2+}$

H_2SO_4, NaF, NH_4SCN → blue soln. indicates Co^{2+}

DMG → red ppt. indicates Ni^{2+}

FIGURE 24-3
Rotation about the C—C bond in ethane.

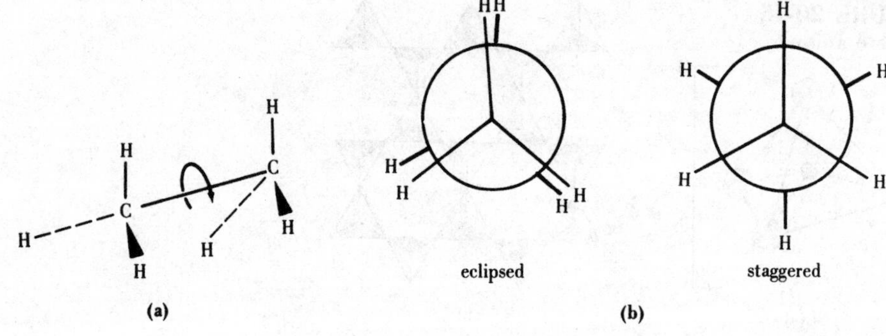

(a) Rotation about the C–C bond. (b) Newman projections of C_2H_6.

FIGURE 24-4
Conformations of cyclohexane.

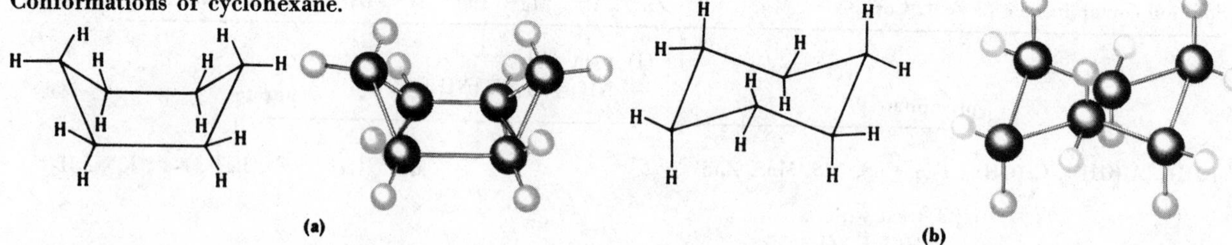

(a) "Boat" form. (b) "Chair" form.

FIGURE 25-7
Some common disaccharides.

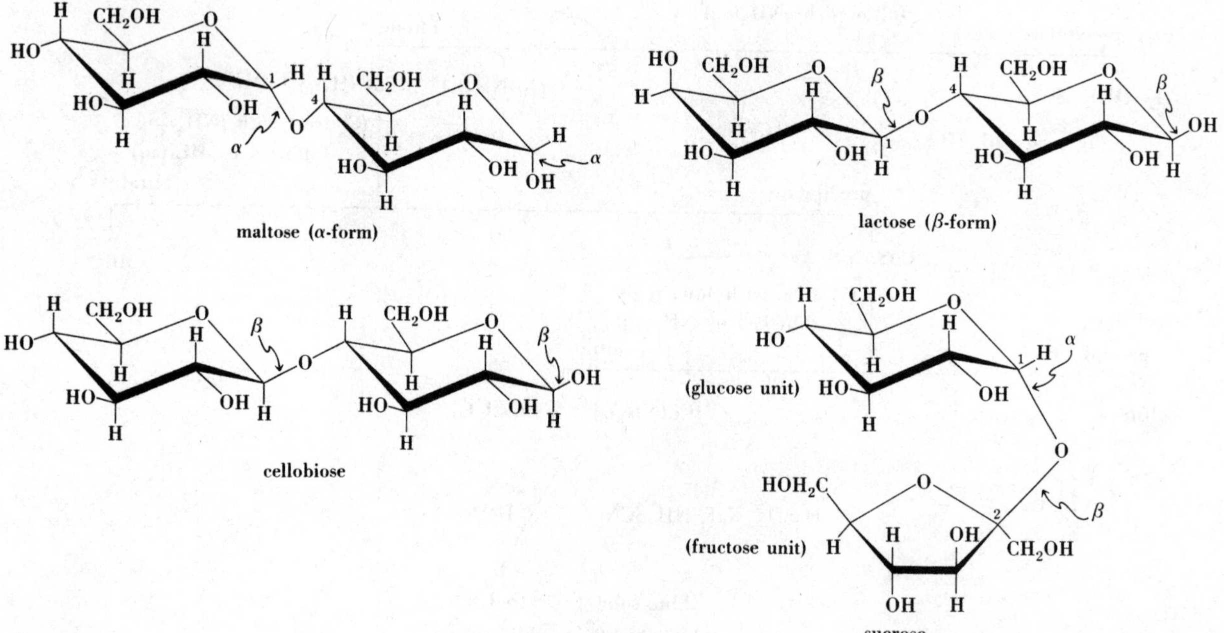

FIGURE 25-8
Two common polysaccharides.

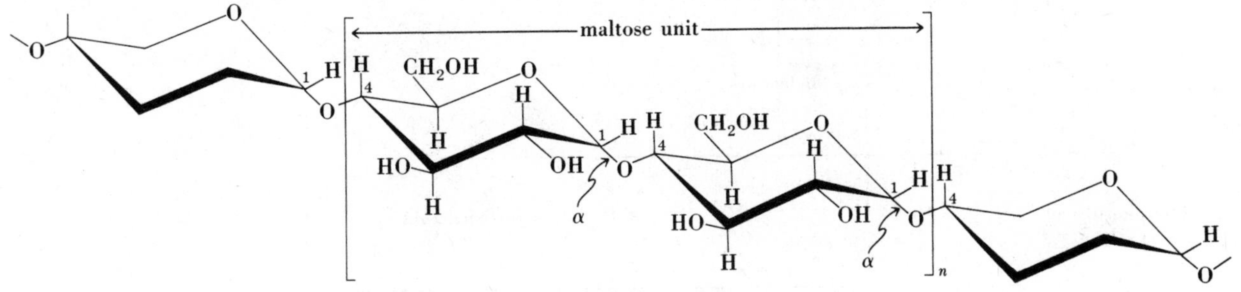

maltose unit
CH2OH
HO
OH
α
n

starch

cellobiose unit
CH2OH
HO
OH
β
n

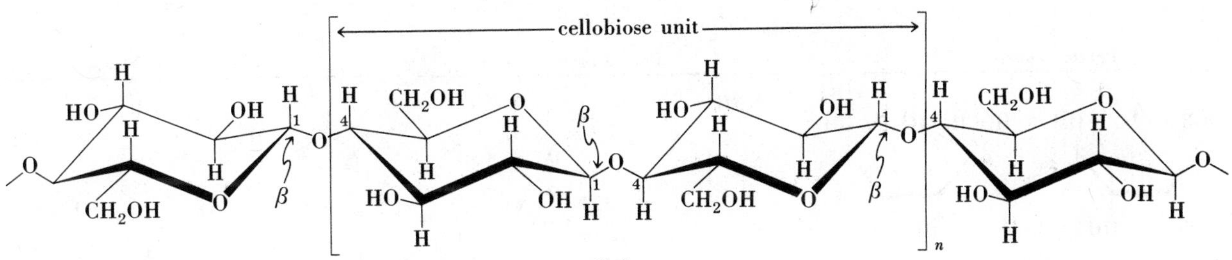

cellulose

FIGURE 25-12
An alpha helix—secondary structure of a protein.

R—C—H
C=O
N—H
N
H
O
C

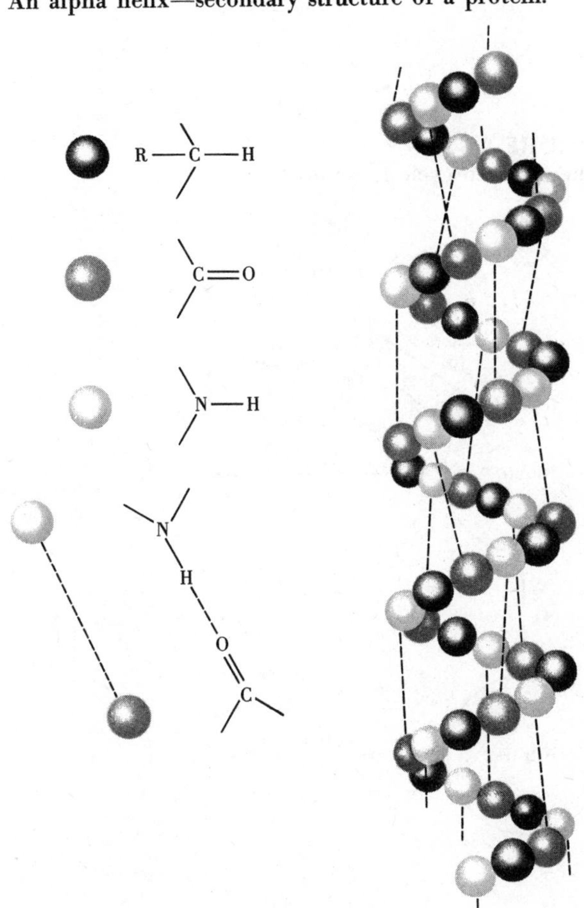

FIGURE 25-20
Hydrolysis products of nucleic acids.

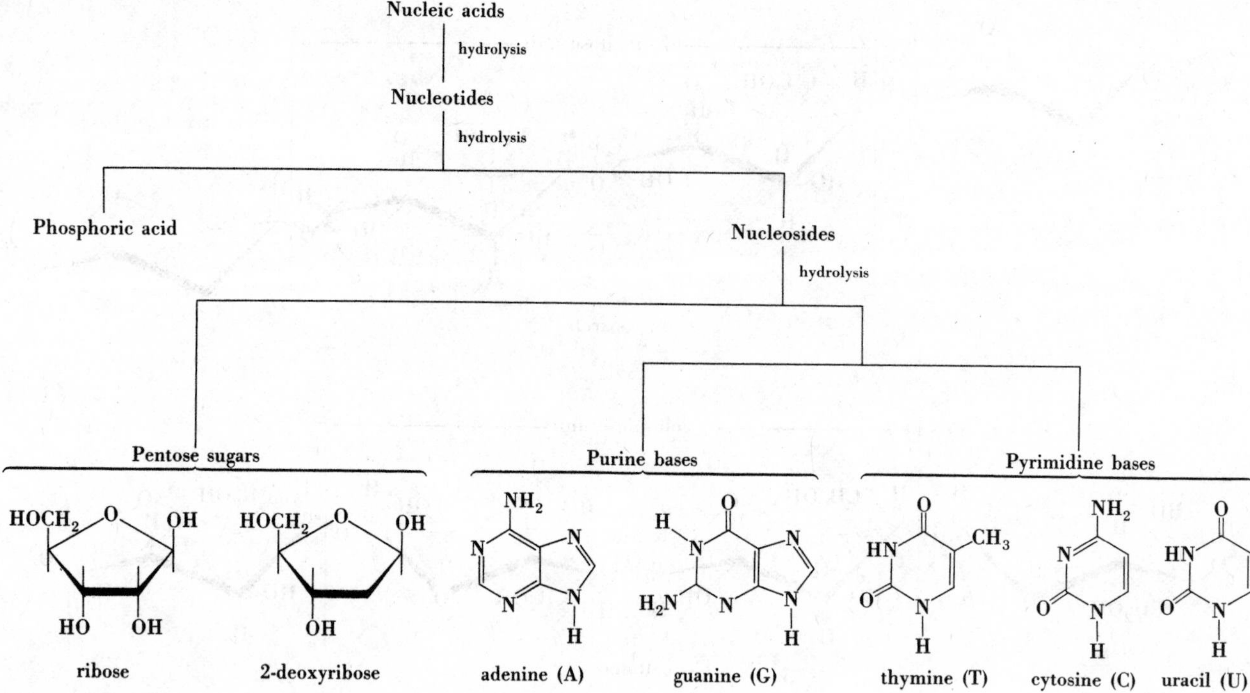

FIGURE 25-22
DNA model.

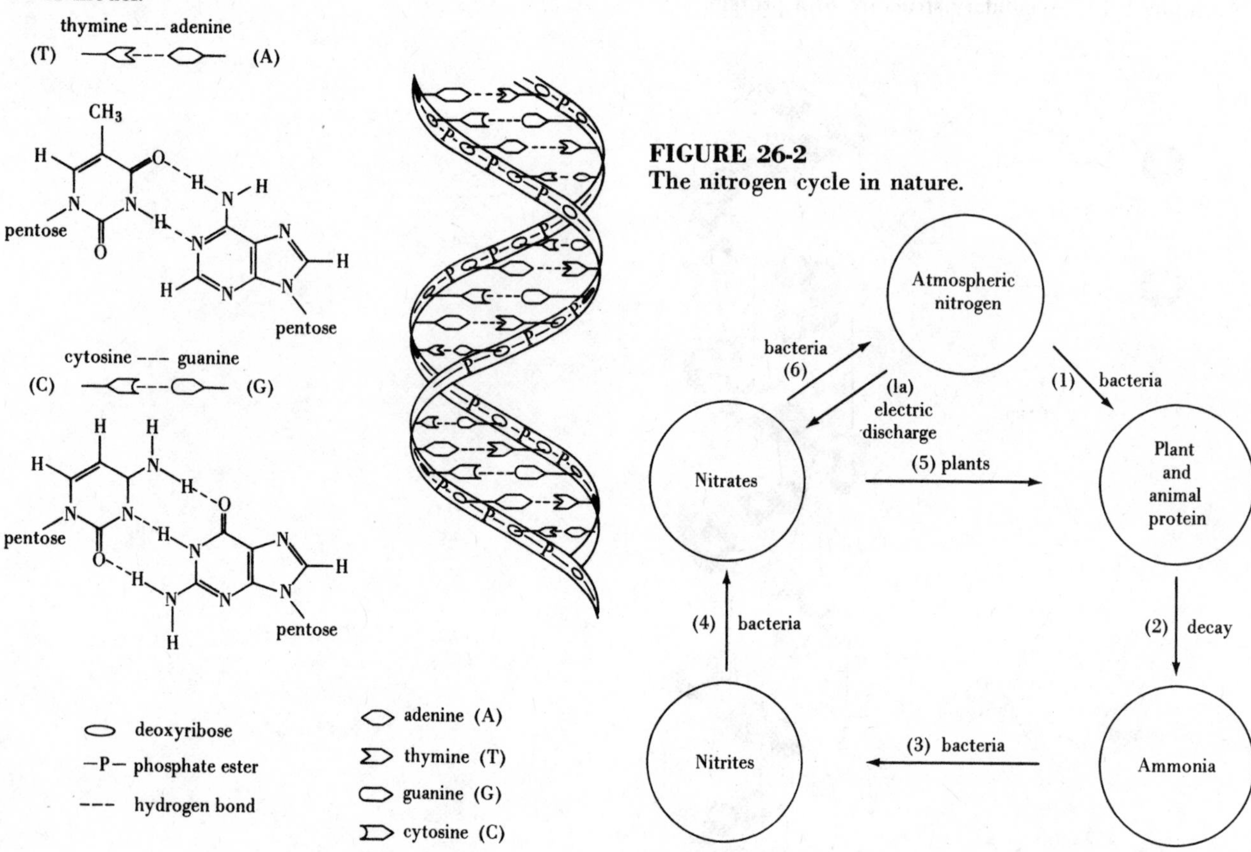

FIGURE 26-2
The nitrogen cycle in nature.

Index

B

C

D

E

F

G

H

I

J

K

L

P

Q

R

S

T